SACRED WRITINGS

JUDAISM

CHRISTIANITY

ISLAM

CONFUCIANISM

HINDUISM

&

BUDDHISM

EDITED BY
JAROSLAV PELIKAN

SACRED WRITINGS

VOLUME 5
HINDUISM:
THE RIG VEDA

SACRED WRITINGS

HINDUISM:
THE RIG VEDA

TRANSLATED BY
RALPH T. H. GRIFFITH

QUALITY PAPERBACK BOOK CLUB
NEW YORK

CONTENTS

INTRODUCTION

Title. The title Rig Veda has long since permanently established itself in English usage, whether scholarly or popular. From time to time there have been slight variations in transliteration and in the use of diacritical marks for the Sanskrit characters, including the rendering "Ṛgveda" employed by Griffith for the translation we are using. An early reference to the Rig Veda in English, dated 1776, identifies it as "the Reig Beid," but soon thereafter it was being called "the Rigvéda." The more complete official title is *Rig Veda Samhitā*. The Sanskrit word *veda* means "knowledge," especially sacred knowledge, and therefore might in some ways be rendered more appropriately with the English word "wisdom." In modern Slovak, my mother tongue, *veda* is still the word for "knowledge" and the Indo-European root is also reflected in *wissen*, the German verb "to know," as well as in the English word *wit*. "Veda" is used as the title not only for the Rig Veda, but for the other three primary books of revelation in Hinduism: Yajur Veda, Sāma Veda, and Atharva Veda (see "Canon" below). Among the four, the Rig Veda is, in the words of our translator, Ralph T. H. Griffith, "the oldest, the most important, and the most generally interesting." *Rig* is a transliteration, more or less accurate, of the Sanskrit word for "praise"; it appears to be a reflection of the central place occupied here by the element of praise and prayer, "Mantra," which together with its correlative of "Brahmana" ("critical reflection" or "rational contemplation") may be said to constitute the core of Vedic religion and philosophy, especially that of the Rig Veda: "The sages make their voices heard with hymns" (10:64.15).

Composition and Authorship. There are just over one thousand hymns in the Rig Veda, comprising a total of something more than ten thousand verses. Although some collections of the Rig Veda in the tradition of India have based their grouping of its verses on a distribution creating eight sections of roughly equal length, the principle followed here has sought to employ the historic origins of the material as the basis for the grouping, which has produced the ten books offered here. As the notes to the present edition indicate, the Hindu religious and literary tradition has identified some of the seers to whom it ascribes the composition, under the sway of divine inspiration, of various of the Vedic hymns. Thus there are in Book 1 sixteen such seers altogether, the first two hymns being attributed to "Madhucchandās Vaiśvāmitra, a son or descendant of the famous Viśvāmitra," the hymns from the twelfth to the twenty-third inclusive to "Medhātithi, son of Kanva," and so on. Sanskritists are largely in agreement, however, that many, perhaps most, of these hymns, like their counterparts in others of the traditions represented in these *Sacred Writings*, were both composed orally and transmitted orally long before being set down in written form; to the present day they are memorized and recited by devout Hindus as oral tradition. That oral emphasis is indicated by the very use of the general title "śruti" ("that which was heard") for the collection of the four Vedas, and it is reflected, for example, in such a formula as this: "O Indra, Lord of Hundred Powers, with all our songs we invoke Thy names" (3:37.3). The identification of the writers as "seers," moreover, emphasizes their passive role as instruments for the several deities whose praises the Rig Veda sings, which must significantly modify the use of a modern and secular term like "author" for them: "These holy songs he [Indra] taught the bard who praised him" (3:34.5). Because of the strict requirement that the hymns be recited with precise observance of every detail, and with the rituals attending the recitation being scrupulously followed (e.g., 8:31.1–2), the composition—or compilation—of the Rig Veda and its related materials must be understood in the light of the liturgical requirements of the older Vedic religion and of the Brahmanism and Hinduism that succeeded it.

Language and Text. The language of the Rig Veda is usually identified as a dialect of archaic Sanskrit, for which it and the other three Vedas form the principal corpus of literature. Because of its vital importance as the oldest Indo-European language for which a large body of literature has been preserved, Sanskrit (and the Vedic dialect in connection with it) is seen as fundamental to the history of all the Indo-European language families. As a consequence of its linguistic interest, therefore, the Rig Veda has been the object of intense attention not only from scholars of India or of Hindu religion and philosophy, but from scholars of Greek, Latin, Germanic, and Slavic comparative philology. Sanskrit grammars and lexicons, intended principally for students of linguistics, may often illumine the religious and liturgical significance of individual passages in the Rig Veda, as the editor's notes to many of the hymns (e.g., 7:97) make clear. There nevertheless remain many difficulties, linguistic as well as textual, for both Eastern and Western scholars (see, as one example among many, 8:52.1, with the translator's note).

In any consideration of the language and text of the Rig Veda, it is impossible not to speak about the work of one of the most widely celebrated of modern scholars and popularizers in the history of religions, Friedrich Max Müller. Max Müller is best known for editing the fifty-one volume *Sacred Books of the East*, published by the Clarendon Press between 1879 and 1910, a collection of, as he himself described them, "translations of all the most important works of the seven non-Christian religions [, which] have exercised a profound influence on the civilizations of the continent of Asia." Less well known to the general public was his work as editor of the Sanskrit text of the Rig Veda in six volumes, which came out between 1849 and 1874. Vedic scholars both in India and in the West have expressed their admiration for this edition, because he established the original text of the Rig Veda in accordance with the canons of critical philology. It was Max Müller's edition that served as the basis of the present translation by Ralph T. H. Griffith (see "Translations" below).

Canon and Authority. The Rig Veda is the oldest of the four Vedas that comprise the central "canon" of the older Vedic religion and of the Brahmanism and Hinduism that emerged from it, the other three being, as already mentioned above: Yajur Veda, Sāma Veda, and Atharva Veda. The four Vedas taken together, as Joseph Mitsuo Kitagawa has summarized their position, "constitute the revealed ('Śruti,' or 'that which was heard') literature, and they provide the basis of religious authority in Hindu orthodoxy." But it is in keeping with the genius of Hinduism, as Kitagawa immediately goes on to point out, that it "has never insisted on the acceptance of any one interpretation of its doctrines" and that therefore such a term as his phrase "religious authority in Hindu orthodoxy" must not be understood according to Western theological categories. Nevertheless, what makes the Rig Veda part of that "canon" and invests it with that "authority" is its very adaptability to the Hindu refusal to fix a creed or dogma. In a familiar formula from Book 1 of the Rig Veda, which has often been quoted by those who would interpret Hindu religion as implicitly monotheistic, "They call him Indra, Mitra, Varuna, Agni, and he is heavenly nobly-winged Garutmān. To what is One, sages give many a title: they call it Agni, Yama, Mātariśvan" (1:164.46). To understand the authority of the Rig Veda, it is also necessary to keep constantly in mind its location within the body of Sanskrit literature (see chapter 11 of *On Searching the Scriptures*); for not only does it, especially in its later books, contain elements that strike the outside reader as "secular"—a term that is at best anachronistic in this context—but the Rig Veda and the other Vedas occupy a place in the national culture that is analogous in some respects to that of the several epics in various other national literatures, including the Greek and the Nordic.

Traditional Interpretation. The distinction mentioned earlier, between Mantra as praise and prayer and Brahmana as critical reflection or rational contemplation, has also shaped the traditional interpretation of the Rig Veda. The Brahmanas are normative commentaries on the several Vedas, explaining in prose the imagery of the Vedic hymns and prescribing ritual, while Aranyakas, a title usually translated as "Forest Texts," present interpretations of the Mantras and of ritual that are sometimes characterized as "mystical." The most widely known of the commentaries, which are in fact compositions in their own right, are the Upanishads, in which the language of the Vedas serves as the basis for cosmological and philosophical ideas that are in some respects already anticipated here in the Rig Veda (see 3:54.8, and the translator's note there). The designation of the Vedas, Brahmanas, Aranyakas, and Upanishads as "śruti" forms of revelation has its counterpart in the body of Sanskrit literature called "śmriti," meaning "that which is remembered," of which the best known to Western readers is the Bhagavad Gita. As is the case with other Sacred Books, such as the Tanakh and the Qur'ān, the eminence of these books as monuments of the culture of India means that they form part of the education also of those who do not conform to the orthodox tradition. For example, when Mohandas K. Gandhi was growing up, as he says in his autobiography, he "read with interest Max Müller's book, *India—What Can It Teach Us?* and the translation of the *Upanishads* published by the Theosophical Society"; that reading, Mahatma Gandhi continues, "enhanced my regard for Hinduism, and its beauties began to grow upon me. It did not, however, prejudice me against other religions."

Translations and This Translation. Horace Hayman Wilson, professor of Sanskrit at Oxford and author of a *Sanskrit-English Dictionary* published in 1819, undertook a translation of large parts of the Rig Veda into English, which began to appear in 1850. But Friedrich Max Müller's work on the original Sanskrit text of the Rig Veda made it possible for Ralph T. H. Griffith to prepare a complete English translation, whose preface is dated 25 May 1889. He published an improved edition in 1896. So well established has Griffith's rendition of the Rig Veda become that it was taken as the basis for the modern Indian edition of the Rig Veda in English, published at Delhi in 1973 and again in 1976. For these reasons, and because it presents the complete Rig Veda rather than merely selections from it, the Griffith version is the one being presented here, but the reader should be aware that there are several renderings of such selections into English, among which the sprightly and erudite collection by Wendy Doniger O'Flaherty for Penguin Books is especially appealing.

Jaroslav Pelikan

SACRED WRITINGS

HINDUISM:
THE RIG VEDA

BOOK THE FIRST

HYMN I.   *Agni.*

1 I LAUD Agni, the chosen Priest, God,
   minister of sacrifice,
   The hotar, lavishest of wealth.

2 Worthy is Agni to be praised by living as
   by ancient seers.
   He shall bring hitherward the Gods.

3 Through Agni man obtaineth wealth, yea,
   plenty waxing day by day,
   Most rich in heroes, glorious.

4 Agni, the perfect sacrifice which thou
   encompassest about
   Verily goeth to the Gods.

5 May Agni, sapient-minded Priest, truthful, most gloriously great,
   The God, come hither with the Gods.

6 Whatever blessing, Agni, thou wilt grant
   unto thy worshipper,
   That, Angiras, is indeed thy truth.

7 To thee, dispeller of the night, O Agni,
   day by day with prayer
   Bringing thee reverence, we come ;

8 Ruler of sacrifices, guard of Law eternal,
   radiant One,
   Increasing in thine own abode.

9 Be to us easy of approach, even as a father
   to his son :
   Agni, be with us for our weal.

HYMN II.   *Vāyu.*

1 BEAUTIFUL Vāyu, come, for thee these Soma
   drops have been prepared :
   Drink of them, hearken to our call.

2 Knowing the days, with Soma juice poured
   forth, the singers glorify
   Thee, Vāyu, with their hymns of praise.

The first two hymns of this Book are ascribed to the Ṛṣi or seer Madhucchandas Vaiśvāmitra, a son or descendant of the famous Viśvāmitra. The deity to whom this hymn is addressed is Agni, the God of fire, the most prominent, next to Indra, of the deities of the Ṛgveda. Agni is the messenger and mediator between earth and heaven announcing to the Gods the hymns, and conveying to them the oblations of their worshippers, inviting them with the sound of his crackling flames and bringing them down to the place of sacrifice. As concentrating in himself the various sacrificial duties of different classes of human priests, Agni is called the *Purohita* or chosen priest, the *proepositus* or *proeses*. He is a *Ṛtvij*, a priest or minister who sacrifices at the proper seasons, and a *Hotar*, an invoking priest, a herald who calls the Gods to enjoy the offering. All riches are at his disposal, and he is the most bountiful rewarder, both directly and indirectly, of the pious whose oblations he carries to the Gods.

2 *Ancient seers* : said by Sāyaṇa to be Bhṛgu, Aṅgiras, and others. The expression indicates the existence of earlier hymns.

3 *Most rich in heroes* : the heroes here spoken of, who accompany the acquisition and increase of wealth, are brave sons and dependents.

4 *Perfect* : uninterrupted by Rākṣasas or fiends, who are unable to mar a sacrifice which Agni protects on all sides.

6 *Aṅgiras* : here a name of Agni. The Aṅgirases appear to have been regarded as a race of higher beings between Gods and men, the typical first sacrificers, whose ritual is the pattern which later priests must follow.

8 *Law eternal*. The word used to denote the conception of the order of the world is *ṛtá*. Everything in the universe which is conceived as showing regularity of action may be said to have the *ṛtá* for its principle. In its most general application the conception expressed by the word occupied to some extent the place of natural and moral law, fate, or the will of a supreme God. See Wallis, *The Cosmology of the Rgveda*, p. 92.

In thine own abode : své dáme, suá domo, in the sacrificial hall or chamber in which fire-worship is performed, and in which the fire (*Agni*) increases as the oblations of clarified butter are poured upon it by the priest.

1 *Vāyu* : God of the wind.

Soma drops : libations of the juice of the Soma, or Moon-plant, said to be the Acid Asclepias or Sarcostema Viminalis. The plant was gathered by moonlight on certain mountains, stripped of its leaves, and then carried to the place of sacrifice ; the stalks having been there crushed by the priests were sprinkled with water and placed on a sieve or stainer, whence, after further pressure, the acid juice trickled into a vessel called Droṇa ; after which it was mixed with flour etc., made to ferment, and then offered in libations to the Gods or drunk by the Brāhmans, by both of whom its exhilarating qualities were supposed to be highly prized. This famous plant has remained unidentified till recently (see Max Müller, Biographies of Words, Appendix III.) 'Dr. Aitchison has lately stated that Soma must be the *Ephedra pachyclade*, which in the Harirud valley is said to bear the name of *hum, huma,* and *yahma*. This supposition is confirmed by Dr. Joseph Bornmüller, a botanist long resident in Kerman, who identifies the Soma plant with some kind of Ephedrá, probably *Ephedra distachya*, but who remarks that different varieties of Ephedra are to be found from Siberia to the Iberia peninsula, so that we must give up the hope of determining the original home of the Aryas by means of the habitat of the Soma plant' (Quarterly Review, No. 354, October 1894, p. 455).

2 *Knowing the days* : knowing the proper days for sacrifices ; or perhaps, knowing or marking the time of daybreak, the exact time for the commencement of sacrificial rites.

3 Vāyu, thy penetrating stream goes forth
unto the worshipper,
Far-spreading for the Soma draught.

4 These, Indra-Vāyu, have been shed ; come
for our offered dainties' sake :
The drops are yearning for you both.

5 Well do ye mark libations, ye Vāyu and
Indra, rich in spoil !
So come ye swiftly hitherward.

6 Vāyu and Indra, come to what the Soma-
presser hath prepared :
Soon, Heroes, thus I make my prayer.

7 Mitra, of holy strength, I call, and foe-
destroying Varuṇa,
Who make the oil-fed rite complete.

8 Mitra and Varuṇa, through Law, lovers
and cherishers of Law,
Have ye obtained your mighty power.

9 Our Sages, Mitra-Varuṇa, of wide dominion, strong by birth,
Vouchsafe us strength that worketh well.

HYMN III.   *Aśvins*

1 YE Aśvins, rich in treasure, Lords of splendour, having nimble hands,
Accept the sacrificial food.

2 Ye Aśvins, rich in wondrous deeds, ye
heroes worthy of our praise,
Accept our songs with mighty thought.

3 Nāsatyas, wonder-workers, yours are these
libations with clipt grass :
Come ye whose paths are red with flame.

4 O Indra, marvellously bright, come, these
libations long for thee,
Thus by fine fingers purified.

5 Urged by the holy singer, sped by song,
come, Indra, to the pravers,
Of the libation-pouring priest.

6 Approach, O Indra, hasting thee, Lord of
Bay Horses, to the prayers.
In our libation take delight.

7 Ye Viśvedevas, who protect, reward, and
cherish men, approach
Your worshipper's drink-offering.

8 Ye Viśvedevas, swift at work, come hither
quickly to the draught,
As milch-kine hasten to their stalls.

9 The Viśvedevas, changing shape like serpents, fearless, void of guile,
Bearers, accept the sacred draught !

---

3 *Hymns of praise* : *ukthas*, lauds recited or spoken,
in opposition to verses that are chanted or sung.

4 Indra and Vāyu are here conjointly addressed in
a dual compound, Indravāyū. Indra was the favourite
national deity of the Āryan Indians in the Vedic Age,
and more hymns were dedicated to his honour than to the
praise of any other divinity. He is the God who reigns
over the intermediate region or atmosphere; he fights
against and conquers with his thunderbolt the demons
of drought and darkness, and is in general the type of
noble heroism.

7 According to Sāyaṇa, Mitra presides over the
day as Varuṇa over the night; hence the closest connexion subsists between these two deities who are more
frequently invoked together than Varuṇa is invoked
singly; together they uphold and rule the earth and
sky, together they guard the world, together they promote religious rites, avenge sin, and are the lords of
truth and light.

Oil-fed : performed with *ghṛtam* (the modern *ghī*),
and clarified butter, or butter which has been boiled
gently and then allowed to cool. The butter is then
used for culinary purposes and also offered in sacrifice
to the Gods. *Complete* : by granting the worshipper's
prayer.

8 *Through Law* : i.e. in accordance with *ṛtá*, the
eternal law or everlasting order of the universe. See I. 1. 8.

---

1 'The Aśvins seem to have been a puzzle even to
the oldest Indian Commentators. Yāska thus refers to
them in the Nirukta, XII. 1 :—'Next in order are the
deities whose sphere is the heaven; of these the Aśvins are
the first to arrive….Who then are these Aśvins ? 'Heaven
and Earth', say some; 'Day and Night', say others; 'The
Sun and Moon', say others; 'Two Kings, performers of
holy acts,' say the legendary writers'. Professor Roth
thus speaks of these Gods: 'The two Aśvins, though, like
the ancient interpreters of the Veda, we are by no means
agreed as to the conception of their character, hold
nevertheless, a perfectly distinct position in the entire
body of the Vedic deities of light. They are the earliest

bringers of light in the morning sky, who in their
chariots hasten onward before the dawn, and prepare the
way for her.'—J. Muir, *O. S. Texts*, V. 234.

Nimble hands : hands outstretched and quick to seize
the offerings.

2 *Rich in wondrous deeds* : some of these deeds for the
protection and benefit of those who craved the aid of the
Aśvins are mentioned in Hymns CXII., CXVI., and the
three following, of this Book.

3 *Nāsatyas*, derived by Indian Commentators from
na+asatya 'not untrue,' is a name of common occurrence
applied jointly to the two Aśvins. *Nāsatya* is said to be
specially the name of one of the A vins, the other being
then called Dasra, 'wonder-worker', or perhaps 'destroyer'
(of the wicked).

With clipt grass. The sacred *Kuśa* grass (Poa cyno-
suroides), after having the roots cut off, is spread on
the *vedi* or altar; and upon it the libation of Soma juice,
or oblation of clarified butter is poured out. It is also
spread over the sacrificial ground or floor to serve as a
seat for the Gods and the sacrificers.

4 *Thus by fine fingers purified* : carefully strained by
the priests.

6 *Lord of Bay Horses* : Harivān and Haryaśva,
'having bay or tawny horses', are frequently occurring
epithets of Indra.

7 *Ye Viśvedevas* : Viśve devāḥ may have originally
denoted 'all the Gods collectively,' though the introduc-
tion of the Viśvas under the name *viśvadevāḥ* or *viśvedevāḥ*
as a separate troop of deities seems to have taken place
at an early period. It is sometimes difficult to decide
whether the expression *viśvedevāḥ* refers to all the Gods
or the particular troop.

9 *Ehīmāyāsaḥ* appears to be another form of *ahīmā-
yāsaḥ* which is explained by Bohtlingk, and Roth as
'multiform or versatile like a snake, showing the same
variety of colour and shape.' Sāyaṇa explains it as 'those
who have obtained knowledge universally'. It is more
than probable, says Professor Wilson, that the origin
and import of the term were forgotten when Sāyaṇa
wrote.

10 Wealthy in spoil, enriched with hymns, may
      bright Sarsavatī desire,
   With eager love, our sacrifice.

11 Inciter of all pleasant songs, inspirer of
      all gracious thought,
   Sarasvatī accept our rite !

12 Sarasvatī, the mighty flood,—she with her
      light illuminates,
   She brightens every pious thought.

HYMN IV.   *Indra.*

1 As a good cow to him who milks, we call
      the doer of fair deeds,
   To our assistance day by day.

2 Come thou to our libations, drink of Soma,
      Soma-drinker thou !
   The rich One's rapture giveth kine.

Bearers, of riches, according to Sāyaṇa.

10 *Sarasvatī* 'is a goddess of some, though not of
very great importance in the Ṛgveda. As observed by
Yāska (Nirukta ii, 23) she is celebrated both as a river
and as a deity...She was, no doubt, primarily a river
deity, as her name, "the watery", clearly denotes, and
in this capacity she is celebrated in a few separate
passages. Allusion is made in the Hymns, as well as in
the Brāhmaṇas...to sacrifices being performed on the
banks of this river and of the adjoining Dṛ.advatī; and
the Sarasvatī in particular seems to have been associated
with the reputation for sanctity, which according to the
well-known passage in the Institutes of Manu, was ascribed
to the whole region, called Brahmāvartta, lying between
these two small streams, and situated immediately to the
westward of the Jumna. The Sarasvatī thus appears to
have been to the early Indians what the Ganges (which
is only twice named in the Ṛgveda) became to their
descendants...When once the river had acquired a divine
character, it was quite natural that she should be regarded
as the patroness of the ceremonies which were celebrated on the margin of her holy waters, and that
her direction and blessing should be invoked as
essential to their proper performance and success. The
connection into which she was thus brought with sacred
rites may have led to the further step of imagining her to
have an influence on the composition of the hymns which
formed so important a part of the proceedings, and of
identifying her with Vāc, the goddess of speech.'—J.
Muir, *O. S. Texts*, V. 338.

12 'Sāyaṇa explains : "the Sarasvatī by her act (of
flowing) displays a copious flood." Roth in his Illustrations of the Nirukta (xi. 26). p. 152, translates, "a
mighty stream is Sarasvatī; with her light she lightens,
illuminates, "all pious minds," He, however, regards
the commencing words as figurative, and not as referring
to the river. Benfey renders : "Sarasvatī, by her light,
causes the great sea to be known; she shines through all
thoughts." He understands the "great sea" as the
universe, or as life...The conceptions of Sarasvatī as a
river, and as the directness of ceremonies, may be blended
in the passage.'—Muir, *O. S. T.*, V. p. 339.

1 *The doer of fair deeds* : Indra.
2 Indra is especially the lord of Soma and its chief
drinker. The exhilaration produced by drinking the
fermented juice offered in libations stimulates his warlike
energies and disposes him to give out of his boundless
riches liberal rewards in the shape of cattle and other
wealth to those who worship him.

3 So may we be acquainted with thine inner-
      most benevolence :
   Neglect us not, come hitherward.

4 Go to the wise unconquered One, ask thou
      of Indra, skilled in song,
   Him who is better than thy friends.

5 Whether the men who mock us say, Depart
      unto another place,
   Ye who serve Indra and none else;

6 Or whether, God of wondrous deeds, all
      our true people call us blest,
   Still may we dwell in Indra's care.

7 Unto the swift One bring the swift, man-
      cheering, grace of sacrifice,
   That to the Friend gives wings and joy.

8 Thou, Śatakratu, drankest this and wast
      the Vṛtras' slayer ; thou
   Helpest the warrior in the fray.

9 We strengthen, Śatakratu, thee, yea, thee
      the powerful in fight,
   That, Indra, we may win us wealth.

10 To him the mighty stream of wealth,
      prompt friend of him who pours the juice,
   Yea, to this Indra sing your song.

HYMN V.   *Indra.*

1 O COME ye hither, sit ye down : to Indra
      sing ye forth, your song,
   Companions, bringing hymns of praise.

2 To him the richest of the rich, the Lord of
      treasures excellent,
   Indra, with Soma juice outpoured.

3 May he stand by us in our need and in
      abundance for our wealth :

6 The general meaning of this and the two preceding
verses seems to be : Indra is the best friend and protector,
and so long as we enjoy his friendship and protection we
care nothing for the revilings of the ungodly who mock
at our faithful worship.

7 *The swift One* : Indra. The Soma juice which
exhilarates men or heroes and accompanies or graces the
sacrifice is also called swift both because it flows quickly
and because it makes Indra hasten to the solemnity. *The
Friend,* is Indra whom the juice, exhilarates and sends
quickly to the sacrifice.

8 *Śatakratu,* a name of Indra, 'is explained by Sāyaṇa,
he who is connected with a hundred (many) acts, religious rites (*bahukarmayukta*), either as their performer or
their object : or it may be rendered 'endowed with great
wisdom;' *kratu* implying either *karma,* act, or *prajñā,*
knowledge.'—Wilson. *The Vṛtras,* the enemies, the
oppressors, or obstructors, are 'the hostile powers in the
atmosphere who malevolently shut up the watery
treasures in the clouds. These demons of drought, called
by a variety of names, as Vṛttra, Ahi, Suṣṇa, Namuci,
Pipru, Śambara, Uraṇa, etc., etc., armed on their side,
also, with every variety of celestial artillery, attempt,
but in vain, to resist the onset of the gods.'—Muir, *O.S.
Texts,* V. 95.

1 *Companions.* The call is addressed to the ministering
priests.

3 'Two separate cases appear to be meant: *yoge,*
where the God must recognize the necessity of his intervention, and *purandhyām,* where he may deem it superfluous'—Ludwig.

May he come nigh us with his strength.

4 Whose pair of tawny horses yoked in
 battles foemen challenge not :
 To him, to Indra sing your song.

5 Nigh to the Soma-drinker come, for his
 enjoyment, these pure drops,
 The Somas mingled with the curd.

6 Thou, grown at once to perfect strength,
 wast born to drink the Soma juice,
 Strong Indra, for preēminence.

7 O Indra, lover of the song, may these quick
 Somas enter thee :
 May they bring bliss to thee the Sage.

8 Our chants of praise have strengthened
 thee, O Śatakratu, and our lauds :
 So strengthen thee the songs we sing.

9 Indra, whose succour never fails, accept
 these viands thousandfold,
 Wherein all manly powers abide.

10 O Indra, thou who lovest song, let no man
 hurt our bodies, keep
 Slaughter far from us, for thou canst.

HYMN VI.   *Indra.*

1 THEY who stand round him as he moves
 harness the bright, the ruddy Steed :
 The lights are shining in the sky.

2 On both sides to the car they yoke the
 two bay coursers dear to him,
 Bold, tawny, bearers of the Chief.

3 Thou, making light where no light was,
 and form, O men : where form was not,
 Wast born together with the Dawns.

4 Thereafter they, as is their wont, threw
 off the state of babes unborn,
 Assuming sacrificial names.

4 At the sight of whose chariot and horses all enemies
flee.

9 *Wherein all manly powers abide.* The oblations of
worshippers, as well as their hymns of praise, stimulate
and strengthen the Gods for deeds of heroism.

1 *They who stand round* : lokatreyavartinaḥ prāṇinaḥ,
'the living beings of the three worles,' is Sāyaṇa's explanation. Probably the Maruts, Inɔra's constant companions are intended.

The bright, the ruddy Steed, (bradhnám aruṣám), is
probably the Sun, with whom Indra is frequently connected.

2 *On both sides* : vípakṣasā : harnessed on different
sides.

3 *Thou,* i.e. the Sun. *O men !* is perhaps merely an
exclamation expressive of admiration. If maryāḥ, men,
be taken to mean the Maruts, the words thou, making,
wast born, although in the singular number, may apply
to these Gods regarded as one host or company and born
at one birth.

4 *Threw off the state of babes unborn :* according to
Prof. M. Muller 'assumed again the form of new-born
babes.' 'The idea that the Maruts assumed the form
of a garbha, lit. of an embryo or a new-born child, is
only meant to express that the storms burst forth from

5 Thou, Indra, with the Tempest-Gods, the
 breakers down of what is firm,
 Foundest the kine even in the cave.

6 Worshipping even as they list, singers laud
 him who findeth wealth,
 The far-renowned, the mighty One.

7 Mayest thou verily be seen coming by fearless Indra's side :
 Both joyous, equal in your sheen.

8 With Indra's well beloved hosts, the blameless, hastening to heaven,
 The sacrificer cries aloud.

9 Come from this place, O Wanderer, or
 downward from the light of heaven:
 Our songs of praise all yearn for this.

10 Indra we seek to give us help, from here,
 from heaven above the earth,
 Or from the spacious firmament.

HYMN VII.   *Indra.*

1 INDRA the singers with high praise, Indra
 reciters with their lauds,
 Indra the choirs have glorified.

2 Indra hath ever close to him his two
 bay steeds and word-yoked car,
 Indra the golden, thunder-armed.

3 Indra hath raised the Sun on high in
 heaven, that he may see afar:
 He burst the mountain for the kine.

the womb of the sky as soon as Indra arises to do battle
against the demon of darkness. As assisting Indra in
this battle, the Maruts, whose name retained for a
long time its purely appellative meaning of storms, attained their rank as deities by the side of Indra, or as the
poet expresses it, they assumed their sacred name. This
seems to be the whole meaning of the later legend that
the Maruts, like the Ṛbhus were not originally gods,
but became deified for their works.' M. Muller. *Ṛgveda
Saṁhitā*, i. p. 25.

5 *The Tempest-Gods* : the Maruts, the friends and
helpers of Indra.
The kine : are streams of water and the beams of light
which follow their effusion. *The cave* is the thick dark
cloud which holds the imprisoned waters and which Indra
cleaves asunder with his thunderbolt or lightning.

7 *Thou* : the host of Maruts. According to Benfey,
the Sun.

8 *The sacrificer cries aloud.* This is the interpretation
proposed by Professor Max Müller, but it is only conjectural and not altogether satisfactory. Benfey translates : Mightdy shines the sacrifice; and Ludwig : The
warrior sings triumphantly.

9 *From this place* : from earth.
Wanderer : (parijman) here applied to Indra.
10 *The spacious firmament* : the expanse between earth
and heaven.

1 *The choirs* : (vāṇī) referring perhaps to both
singers and chanters.
2 *The golden* : i.e. richly decorated (sarvābharaṇa-
bhūṣitaḥ) according to Sāyaṇa.
3 *The mountain* : is the mountain-shaped mass of
thick cloud, and the *kine* are the waters as in I. 6, 5.
The words ádri and párvata mean both mountain and
cloud, these being constantly seen in close juxtaposition
and being often indistinguishable one from the other.

4 Help us, O Indra, in the frays, yea, frays,
   where thousand spoils are gained,
   With awful aids, O awful One.

5 In mighty battle we invoke Indra, Indra
   in lesser fight,
   The Friend who bends his bolt at fiends.

6 Unclose, our manly Hero, thou for ever
   bounteous, yonder cloud,
   For us, thou irresistible.

7 Still higher, at each strain of mine, thunder-
   armed Indra's praises rise:
   I find no laud worthy of him.

8 Even as the bull drives on the herds, he
   drives the people with his might,
   The Ruler irresistible :

9 Indra who rules with single sway men,
   riches, and the fivefold race
   Of those who dwell upon the earth.

10 For your sake from each side we call Indra
   away from other men :
   Ours, and none others', may he be.

HYMN VIII.   *Indra.*

1 INDRA, bring wealth that gives delight, the
   victor's ever-conquering wealth,
   Most excellent, to be our aid;

2 By means of which we may repel our foes
   in battle hand to hand,
   By thee assisted with the car.

3 Aided by thee, the thunder-armed, Indra,
   may we lift up the bolt,
   And conquer all our foes in fight.

4 With thee, O Indra, for ally with missile-
   darting heroes, may
   We conquer our embattled foes.

5 Mighty is Indra, yea supreme; greatness
   be his, the Thunderer :
   Wide as the heaven extends his power ;

6 Which aideth those to win them sons, who
   come as heroes to the fight,
   Or singers loving holy thoughts.

7 His belly, drinking deepest draughts of
   Soma, like an ocean swells,
   Like wide streams from the cope of heaven.

8 So also is his excellence, great, vigorous,
   rich in cattle, like
   A ripe branch to the worshipper.

9 For verily thy mighty powers, Indra, are
   saving helps at once
   Unto a worshipper like me.

10 So are his lovely gifts; let lauds and
   praises be to Indra sung,
   That he may drink the Soma juice.

HYMN IX.   *Indra.*

1 COME, Indra, and delight thee with the
   juice at all the Soma feasts,
   Protector, mighty in thy strength.

2 To Indra pour ye forth the juice, the active
   gladdening juice to him
   The gladdening, omnific God.

3 O Lord of all men, fair of cheek, rejoice
   thee in the gladdening lauds,
   Present at these drink-offerings.

4 Songs have outpoured themselves to thee,
   Indra, the strong, the guardian Lord,
   And raised themselves unsatisfied.

5 Send to us bounty manifold, O Indra,
   worthy of our wish,
   For power supreme is only thine.

6 O Indra, stimulate thereto us emulously
   fain for wealth,
   And glorious, O most splendid One.

7 Give, Indra, wide and lofty fame, wealthy
   in cattle and in strength,
   Lasting our life-time, failing not.

8 Grant us high fame, O Indra, grant riches
   bestowing thousands, those
   Fair fruits of earth borne home in wains.

9 Praising with songs the praise-worthy who
   cometh to our aid, we call
   Indra, the Treasure-Lord of wealth.

---

9 *The fivefold race* : Benfey explains this as 'the whole
inhabited world.' But the expression seems to mean the
Āryan settlements or tribes only, and not the indigenous
inhabitants of the country. The five tribes or settlements
were probably the confederation of the Turvaśas, Yadus,
Anus, Druhyus, and Purus. Sāyaṇa's explanation is
'those who are fit for habitations,' and the phrase is said
to imply the four castes and Niṣādas or indigenous barbarians. But there were no such distinctions of caste when
the hymn was composed.

---

2 *With the car* : *árvatā*, literally, with a horse, is explained by Sāyaṇa to mean fighting on horseback. But
horses seem to have been used in war as drawers of chariots
only, and *árvatā* here stands for *rathena*, with a car or
chariot.

3 *May we lift up the bolt.* The thunderbolt here spoken
of is sacrifice which, when employed against enemies, is
as powerful a weapon as the bolt of Indra.

---

10 *Let lauds and praises be to Indra sung* : more exactly,
'be lauds, spoken and sung, to Indra given; *uktha* being
properly the laud that is recited, and *stoma* the hymn of
praise that is sung.

---

4 *And raised themselves unsatisfied* : *ájoṣāḥ*, not contented, that is, with prayers ever new. Ludwig observes
that the Sāmaveda has preserved the correct reading
sajoṣāḥ, 'with one accord.'

8 *Those fair fruits of earth brought home in wains.* 'The
original of this hymn, as of many others, is so concise and
elliptical as to be unintelligible without the liberal ampli-
fication of the Scholiast. We have in the text simply
."those car-having viands," *tā rathinīr iṣaḥ*, meaning,
Sāyaṇa says, those articles of food which are conveyed in
cars, carts, or waggons, from the site of their production;
as rice, barley, and other kinds of grain.'—Wilson.

The meaning of *rathinīr* is not clear.

10 To lofty Indra, dweller by each libation, the pious man

Sings forth aloud a strengthening hymn.

HYMN X. *Indra.*

1 THE chanters hymn thee, they who say the word of praise magnify thee.

The priests have raised thee up on high, O Śatakratu, like a pole.

2 As up he clomb from ridge to ridge and looked upon the toilsome task,

Indra observes this wish of his, and the Ram hastens with his troop.

3 Harness thy pair of strong bay steeds, long-maned, whose bodies fill the girths,

And, Indra, Soma-drinker, come to listen to our songs of praise.

4 Come hither, answer thou the song, sing in approval, cry aloud.

Good Indra, make our prayer succeed, and prosper this our sacrifice.

5 To Indra must a laud be said, to strengthen him who freely gives,

That Śakra may take pleasure in our friendship and drink-offerings.

6 Him, him we seek for friendship, him for riches and heroic might.

For Indra, he is Śakra, he shall aid us while he gives us wealth.

7 Easy to turn and drive away, Indra, is spoil bestowed by thee.

Unclose the stable of the kine, and give us wealth O Thunder-armed

8 The heaven and earth contain thee not, together, in thy wrathful mood.

Win us the waters of the sky, and send us kine abundantly.

9 Hear, thou whose ear is quick, my call; take to thee readily my songs

O Indra, let this laud of mine come nearer even than thy friend.

10 We know thee mightiest of all, in battles hearer of our cry.

Of thee most mighty we invoke the aid that giveth thousandfold.

11 O Indra, Son of Kuśika, drink our libation with delight.

Prolong our life anew, and cause the seer to win a thousand gifts.

12 Lover of song, may these our songs on every side encompass thee :

Strengthening thee of lengthened life, may they be dear delights to thee.

HYMN XI. *Indra.*

1 ALL sacred songs have magnified Indra expansive as the sea,

The best of warriors borne on cars, the Lord, the very Lord of strength.

2 Strong in thy friendship, Indra, Lord of power and might, we have no fear.

We glorify with praises thee, the never-conquered conqueror.

3 The gifts of Indra from of old, his saving succours, never fail,

When to the praise-singers he gives the boon of substance rich in kine.

4 Crusher of forts, the young, the wise, of strength unmeasured, was he born

Sustainer of each sacred rite, Indra, the Thunderer, much-extolled.

5 Lord of the thunder, thou didst burst the cave of Vala rich in cows.

---

1 'The concluding phrase, *twā...ud vaṁśam iva yemire,* "they have raised thee, like a bamboo," is rather obscure. The Scholiast says, they have elevated Indra, as tumblers raise a bamboo—on the summit of which they balance themselves; a feat not uncommon in India: or, as *vaṁśa* means, also, a family, it may be rendered, as ambitious persons raise their family to consequence.'—Wilson.

2 The text has only, mounting from ridge to ridge, or from height to height, which the scholiast completes by observing that this is said of the Yajamāna, the person who institutes or performs a regular sacrifice and pays the expenses of it, who goes to the mountain to gather the Soma-plant, fuel, etc. Ludwig thinks that Indra is meant, rising higher and higher, and yet not delaying to come to the sacrifice.

The Ram, (*vṛṣṇíḥ*) is Indra, and his flock or troop are the Maruts.

Hastens : comes quickly to the sacrifice.

5 *Śakra,* a common name of Indra, used in the next stanza as an epithet='the powerful', from *śak,* to be able.

7 *Easy to turn :* The Booty spoken of in the Ṛgveda consists chiefly of cattle, which with Indra's assistance are easily turned and driven away from the enemy who possesses them.

Unclose the stable of the kine : Open the thick cloud that holds the water imprisoned, and fertilize our fields with rain.

9 *Thy friend :* probably the *vájra* or thunderbolt which is Indra's inseparable associate and ally.

11 *Son of Kuśika :* Kuśika was the father or the grandfather of Viśvāmitra who was the father of the poet or seer of this hymn. This epithet Kauśika, son of Kuśika, is here applied to Indra as being the chief or special God of the seer's family.

12 *Of lengthened life*=immortal.

---

1 This hymn is ascribed to Jetar the son of Madhucchandas the seer of the preceding hymn.

Expansive as the sea : cf. I. 8, 7. Or the expression may be, as Wilson says, 'a vague mode of indicating the universal diffusion of Indra as the firmament.

4 *Crusher of forts :* destroyer or breaker-down of the clouds that withhold the rain, which are regarded as the forts or strongholds of Vṛtra and the other hostile powers of the air.

5 *The cave of Vala :* Vala is the brother of Vṛtra, or Vṛtra himself under another name, who stole the cows of the Gods and hid them in a cave, that is, kept the light and waters imprisoned in dark clouds.

The Gods came pressing to thy side, and
free from terror aided thee.

6 I, Hero, through thy bounties am come to
the flood addressing thee.

Song-lover, here the singers stand and
testify to thee thereof.

7 The wily Śuṣṇa, Indra ! thou o'erthrewest with thy wondrous powers.

The wise beheld this deed of thine : now
go beyond their eulogies.

8 Our songs of praise have glorified Indra
who ruleth by his might,

Whose precious gifts in thousands come,
yea, even more abundantly.

HYMN XII.   *Agni.*

1 WE choose Agni the messenger, the herald,
master of all wealth,

Well skilled in this our sacrifice.

2 With callings ever they invoke Agni, Agni,
Lord of the House,

Oblation-bearer, much beloved.

3 Bring the Gods hither, Agni, born for him ·
who strews the sacred grass :

Thou art our herald, meet for praise.

4 Wake up the willing Gods, since thou,
Agni, performest embassage :

Sit on the sacred grass with Gods.

5 O Agni, radiant One, to whom the holy
oil is poured, burn up

Our enemies whom fiends protect.

6 By Agni Agni is inflamed, Lord of the
House, wise, young, who bears

The gift : the ladle is his mouth.

7 Praise Agni in the sacrifice, the Sage
whose ways are ever true,

The God who driveth grief away.

8 God, Agni, be his strong defence who,
lord of sacrificial gifts,

Worshippeth thee the messenger.

9 Whoso with sacred gift would fain call Agni
to the feast of Gods,

O Purifier, favour him.

10 Such, Agni, Purifier, bright, bring hither
to our sacrifice,

To our oblation bring the Gods.

11 So lauded by our newest song of praise
bring opulence to us,

And food, with heroes for our sons.

12 O Agni, by effulgent flame, by all invokings of the Gods,

Show pleasure in this laud of ours.

HYMN XIII.   *Agni.*

1 AGNI, well-kindled, bring the Gods for him
who offers holy gifts.

Worship them, Purifier, Priest.

2 Son of Thyself, present, O Sage, our
sacrifice to the Gods today.

Sweet to the taste, that they may feast.

3 Dear Narāśaṁsa, sweet of tongue, the giver
of oblations, I

Invoke to this our sacrifice.

4 Agni, on thy most easy car, glorified, hither
bring the Gods :

Manu appointed thee as Priest.

5 Strew, O ye wise, the sacred grass that
drips with oil, in order due,

Where the Immortal is beheld.

---

6 *To the flood* : i. e, to Indra, the river or sea of
bounty.

7 *The wily Śuṣṇa* : Śuṣṇa is described as a demon
slain by Indra. The word means drier up; *bhūtānāṅ
śoṣaṇahetu*, cause of the drying up of beings, the excessive
heat and drought before the Rains, which Indra puts an
end to.

Now go beyond their eulogies : i. e. do deeds worthy of
still higher praise. Or it may mean, make their eulogies
endure.

1 The Hymns from XII to XXIII inclusive are
ascribed to Medhātithi, son of Kaṇva.

The messenger : the mediator between men and Gods.
The herald : *devānām āhvātāram*, the inviter of the Gods, is
Sāyaṇa's explanation.

3 *Born* : newly produced by attrition for the man
who has prepared and spread the sacrificial grass as a seat
for the expected deities.

6 *By Agni Agni is inflamed* : The fire into which the
oblation is poured is lighted by the application of other
fire.

Young : as newly born each time the fire is produced.
The ladle : used for pouring the sacrificial butter into the
fire.

8 *Lord of sacrificial gifts* : the wealthy patron or
institutor of the sacrifice.

9 *O Purifier* : *pāvaka*, purifying is in later Sanskrit
a common word for fire.

This is one of the Āpri or propitiatory hymns, consisting of invocations to a series of deified objects, and said to
be introductory to the animal sacrifice. All the deified
objects addressed in this hymn are said by Sāyaṇa to be
forms of Agni.

1 *For him who offers holy gifts* : for the institutor of the
sacrifice.

2 *Son of Thyself*. Tanūnapāt, son or descendant of
oneself, is a frequently recurring name of Agni so called
because fire is sometimes self-generated, as in the lightning, or produced by attrition, and not necessarily derived
from other fire. Other fanciful derivations are given.

3 *Narāśaṁsa* : 'Praise of Men' is one of Agni's mystical
names.

4 *Manu* : is the man *par excellence*, or the representative man and father of the human race, regarded as the
first institutor of sacrifices and religious ceremonies.

5 *The immortal* : according to Sāyaṇa either the
clarified butter or Agni the God.

6 Thrown open be the Doors Divine, unfailing, that assist the rite,

For sacrifice this day and now.

7 I call the lovely Night and Dawn to seat
them on the holy grass

At this our solemn sacrifice.

8 The two Invokers I invite, the wise, divine
and sweet of tongue,

To celebrate this our sacrifice.

9 Iḷā, Sarasvatī, Mahī, three Goddesses who
bring delight,

Be seated, peaceful, on the grass.

10 Tvaṣṭar I call, the earliest born, the
wearer of all forms at will :

May he be ours and ours alone.

11 God, Sovran of the Wood, present this
our oblation to the Gods,

And let the giver be renowned.

12 With Svāhā pay the sacrifice to Indra in
the offerer's house :

Thither I call the Deities.

HYMN XIV. *Viśvedevas.*

1 To drink the Soma, Agni, come, to our
service and our songs.

With all these Gods; and worship them.

2 The Kaṇvas have invoked thee; they, O
Singer, sing thee songs of praise :

Agni, come hither with the Gods;

3 Indra, Vāyu, Bṛhaspati, Mitra, Agni,
Pūṣan, Bhaga,

Ādityas, and the Marut host.

4 For you these juices are poured forth that
gladden and exhilarate,

The meath-drops resting in the cup.

5 The sons of Kaṇva fain for help adore
thee, having strewn the grass,

With offerings and all things prepared.

6 Let the swift steeds who carry thee, thou-
ght-yoked and dropping holy oil,

Bring the Gods to the Soma draught.

7 Adored, the strengtheners of Law, unite
them, Agni, with their Dames :

Make them drink meath, O bright of tongue.

6 *The Doors Divine* : the doors of the chamber in
which the oblation is offered.

Unfailing : the signification of *asaścdtaḥ* in the text is
uncertain. Sāyaṇa explains the word variously in various
places.

8 *The two Invokers.* It seems uncertain who these
two invokers or priests (*hotārā*) are, whether Agni and
Āditya, or Agni and Varuṇa, or Varuṇa and Āditya See
M. Müller's *A. S. Literature*, p. 464.

9 *Iḷā* : the Goddess of sacred speech and action.

Sarasvatī : see I. 3. 10.

Mahī : 'the great' (Goddess), said to be identical
with Bhāratī, also a Goddess of speech.

10 *Tvaṣṭar*, is the Hephaistos, or Vulcan, of the Indian
pantheon, the ideal artist, the divine artisan, the most
skilful of workmen, versed in all wonderful and admirable
contrivances.

11 *God, Sovran of the Wood* : vanaspati, lord of the wood;
usually, a large tree; here said to be an Agni,—as if the
fuel and the burning of it were identified. Or the Sacrificial Post may be intended, which is enumerated among
the Āpri deities or deified objects.

12 *Svāhā* is the sacred word or exclamation (Hail !
Blessing !) used in pouring the oblation on the fire.
According to Sāyaṇa, Svāhā also may be identified with
Agni.

2 *The Kaṇvas* : sons or descendants of Kaṇva, men of
the same family as the seer of the hymn.

3 *Indra, Vāyu,* etc. The names of these Gods are in
the accusative case, governed by 'they (the Kaṇvas) have
invoked,' or 'worship them,' understood.

Bṛhaspati, 'alternating with Brahmaṇaspati is the name
of a deity in whom the action of the worshipper upon the
Gods is personified. He is the suppliant, the priest who
intercedes with the Gods for men, and protects them
against the wicked. Hence he appears as the prototype
of the priests and the priestly order, and is also designated
as the Purohita of the divine community. The essential
difference between the original idea represented in this
God and those expressed in most of the other and older
deities of the Veda consists in the fact that the latter are
personifications of various departments of nature, or of
physical forces, while the former is the product of moral
ideas and an impersonation of the power of devotion.'
Muir, *O. S. Texts*, V. 272.

Pūṣan is a God who protects and multiplies cattle
and human possessions generally. In character he is a
solar deity, beholds the entire universe, and is a guide on
roads and journeys.

Bhaga, the gracious Lord and protector, is regarded as
the bestower of wealth.

Ādityas. 'There (in the highest heaven) dwell and
reign those Gods who bear in common the name of
Ādityas. We must, however, if we would discover their
earliest character, abandon the conceptions which in a
later age, and even in that of the heroic poems, were
entertained regarding these deities. According to this
conception they were twelve Sun-gods, bearing evident
reference to the twelve months. But for the most ancient
period we must hold fast the primary signification of their
name. They are the inviolable, imperishable, eternal
beings. Aditi, eternity or the eternal, is the element
which sustains them and is sustained by them…The eternal
and inviolable element in which the Ādityās dwell, and
which forms their essence, is the celestial light…The
Ādityas, the Gods of this light, do not therefore by any
means coincide with any of the forms in which light is
manifested in the universe. They are neither sun, nor
moon, nor stars, nor dawn, but the eternal sustainers of
this luminous life, which exists, as it were, behind all these
phenomena'. Roth, quoted by Muir, *O.S. Texts*, V. p.56.

The Marut host : the Maruts are the Gods of the winds
and storms, the companions and friends of Indra. They
are said in the Veda to be the sons of Rudra and Pṛśni,
the latter being explained by Sāyaṇa as 'the many-coloured earth,' but regarded by Professor Roth as a personification of the speckled clouds.

7 *Unite them with their Dames* : *pdtnīvatas kṛdhi* : make
them (come) with their consorts.

8 Let them, O Agni, who deserve worship
   and praise drink with thy tongue
   The meath in solemn sacrifice.

9 Away, from the Sun's realm of light, the
   wise invoking Priest shall bring
   All Gods awaking with the dawn.

10 With all the Gods, with Indra, with Vāyu,
   and Mitra's splendours, drink,
   Agni, the pleasant Soma juice.

11 Ordained by Manu as our Priest, thou
   sittest, Agni, at each rite :
   Hallow thou this our sacrifice.

12 Harness the Red Mares to thy car, the
   Bays, O God, the flaming ones :
   With those bring hitherward the Gods.

HYMN XV.   *Rtu.*

1 O INDRA drink the Soma juice with Rtu;
   let the cheering drops
   Sink deep within, which settle there.

2 Drink from the Purifier's cup, Maruts,
   with Rtu; sanctify
   The rite, for ye give precious gifts.

3 O Neṣṭar, with thy Dame accept our
   sacrifice; with Rtu drink,
   For thou art he who giveth wealth.

4 Bring the Gods, Agni; in the three appointed places set them down :
   Surround them, and with Rtu drink.

5 Drink Soma after the Rtus, from the
   Brāhmaṇa's bounty : undissolved,
   O Indra, is thy friendship's bond.

6 Mitra, Varuṇa, ye whose ways are firm—a
   Power that none deceives—,
   With Rtu ye have reached the rite.

7 The Soma-pressers, fain for wealth, praise
   the Wealth-giver in the rite,

In sacrifices praise the God.

8 May the Wealth-giver grant to us riches
   that shall be far renowned.
   These things we gain among the Gods.

9 He with the Rtus fain would drink,
   Wealth-giver, from the Neṣṭar's bowl.
   Haste, give your offering, and depart.

10 As we this fourth time, Wealth-giver,
   honour thee with the Rtus, be
   A Giver bountiful to us.

11 Drink ye the meath, O Aśvins bright with
   flames, whose acts are pure. who with
   Rtus accept the sacrifice.

12 With Rtu, through the house-fire, thou,
   kind Giver, guidest sacrifice :
   Worship the Gods for the pious man.

HYMN XVI.   *Indra.*

1 LET thy Bay Steeds bring thee, the Strong,
   hither to drink the Soma draught—
   Those, Indra, who are bright as suns.

2 Here are the grains bedewed with oil :
   hither let the Bay Coursers bring
   Indra upon his easiest car.

3 Indra at early morn we call, Indra in
   course of sacrifice,
   Indra to drink the Soma juice.

4 Come hither, with thy long-maned Steeds,
   O Indra, to the draught we pour :
   We call thee when the juice is shed.

5 Come thou to this our song of praise, to
   the libation poured for thee :
   Drink of it like a stag athirst.

---

9   *The wise invoking Priest* : Agni, who calls the Gods.
10 *All the Gods* : or Viśvedevas; see I.3.7.
11 *Manu* : see I.13.4.

———

1   *Rtu* : meaning generally a season, a sixth part
of the Indian year, is here personified and addressed as a
deity.
2   *The Purifier's cup* : the sacrificial vessel of the Potar,
or Purifier, who pours into the fire the libation for the
Maruts.
3   *O Neṣṭar* : the Neṣṭar is one of the chief officiating priests, who leads forward the wife of the institutor
of the sacrifice. In this place Neṣṭar is said to be another
name for the God Tvaṣṭar from his having on some
occasion assumed the function of a Neṣṭar priest.
4   *The three appointed places* : by the three sacrificial
fires.
5   *The Brāhmaṇa's bounty.* The Brāhmaṇa here is
said to be the Brāhmaṇācchaṁsī, one of the sixteen
priests employed in sacrifices; and perhaps his office may
have been to hold some ladle or vase in which the
offering is presented.
7   *The Soma-pressers* : *grāvahastāsaḥ,* men having
stones in their hands with which to bruise the Soma plant.
The Wealth giver is Agni.

In the rite, In sacrifices : 'in the *adhvara* and in the
yajñas, the first is said to be the primary or essential ceremony, such as the Agniṣṭoma; the second, the modified
ceremonies, such as the Ukthya which is elsewhere termed
an offering with Soma juice.' Wilson.

10 *As we this fourth time* : Agni, as Draviṇodās or
Wealth-giver, has now been celebrated in four stanzas
instead of the usual *trca* or triad; or we may translate
with Ludwig, 'As we in fourth place,' Agni being fourth
in the invocation (Indra, Maruts, Tvaṣṭar, Agni).

12 *Through the house-fire.* The *gārhapatya* is the sacred
fire perpetually maintained by the householder; the fire
from which fires for sacrificial purposes are lighted.

———

1   *Bright as suns* : *sūracakṣasaḥ.* Sāyaṇa understands
this to refer to the priests, and Wilson renders accordingly:
may (the priests), radiant as the sun (make thee manifest).
2   *Easiest car*; *sukhátame ráthe* : that is, most easily
moving, swiftest.
3   *Indra at early morn we call.* Although not more
particularly named, the specification implies the morning,
mid-day, and evening worship.
5   *Like a stag athirst* : like a *gaura* (Bos Gaurus) a
kind of buffalo.
'Drink like a thirsty buffalo,' would perhaps be a more
strictly accurate rendering.

6 Here are the drops of Soma juice expressed on sacred grass : thereof
Drink, Indra, to increase thy might.

7 Welcome to thee be this our hymn, reaching thy heart, most excellent :
Then drink the Soma juice expressed.

8 To every draught of pressed-out juice Indra, the Vṛtra-slayer, comes,
To drink the Soma for delight.

9 Fulfil, O Śatakratu, all our wish with horses and with kine :
With holy thoughts we sing thy praise.

HYMN XVII. *Indra-Varuṇa.*

1 I CRAVE help from the Imperial Lords, from Indra-Varuṇa; may they
Both favour one of us like me.

2 Guardians of men, ye ever come with ready succour at the call
Of every singer such as I.

3 Sate you, according to your wish, O Indra-Varuṇa, with wealth :
Fain would we have you nearest us.

4 May we be sharers of the powers, sharers of the benevolence
Of you who give strength bounteously.

5 Indra and Varuṇa, among givers of thousands, meet for praise,
Are Powers who merit highest laud.

6 Through their protection may we gain great store of wealth, and heap it up :
Enough and still to spare, be ours.

7 O Indra-Varuṇa, on you for wealth in many a form I call :
Still keep ye us victorious.

8 O Indra-Varuṇa, through our songs that seek to win you to ourselves,
Give us at once your sheltering help.

9 O Indra-Varuṇa, to you may fair praise which I offer come,
Joint eulogy which ye dignify.

1 Indra the Hero and Varuṇa the King are addressed conjointly as a dual deity, Indrāvaruṇa. The most prominent of the other dual deities are Agni-Soma, Indra-Vāyu, Indra-Agni, Indra-Bṛhaspati, Indra-Soma, Mitra-Varuṇa, Indra-Pūṣan, Indra-Vṣṇu, Dyaus-Pṛthivī and Soma-Rudra.

Brahmaṇaspati. See I. 14, 3. Professor Wilson says : 'The Scholiast furnishes us with no account of the station or functions of this divinity. The etymology will justify Dr. Roth's definition of him as the deity of sacred prayer, or rather, perhaps, of the text of the Veda; but whether he is to be considered as a distinct personification or as a modified form of one of those already recognized, and especially of Agni, is doubtful, His giving wealth, healing disease, and promoting nourishment, are properties not peculiar to him; and his being associated with Indra and Soma, while it makes him distinct from them, leaves

HYMN XVIII. *Brahmaṇaspati.*

1 O BRAHMAṆAPSATI, make him who presses Soma glorious,
Even Kakṣīvān Auśija.

2 The rich, the healer of disease, who giveth wealth, increaseth store,
The prompt,—may he be with us still.

3 Let not the foeman's curse, let not a mortal's onslaught fall on us :
Preserve us, Brahmaṇaspati.

4 Ne'er is the mortal hero harmed whom Indra, Brahmaṇaspati,
And Soma graciously inspire.

5 Do, thou, O Brahmaṇaspati, and Indra, Soma, Dakṣiṇā,
Preserve that mortal from distress.

6 To the Assembly's wondrous Lord, to Indra's lovely Friend who gives
Wisdom, have I drawn near in prayer.

7 He without whom no sacrifice, e'en of the wise man, prospers; he
Stirs up the series of thoughts.

8 He makes the oblation prosper, he promotes the course of sacrifice :
Our voice of praise goes to the Gods.

him Agni as his prototype. His being, in an especial manner, connected with prayer appears more fully in a subsequent passage, Hymn XL. Agni is, in an especial degree, the deity of the Brahman ; and, according to some statements, the Ṛgveda is supposed to proceed from him; a notion, however, which according to Medhā-tithi, the commentator on Manu, was suggested by its opening with the hymn to Agni, *Agnim iḷe.'*

Kakṣīvān, called Auśija, or son of Uśij, was a renowned Ṛṣi or seer, of the family of Pajra, and the author of several of the hymns of the Ṛgveda.

2 *The rich, the healer of disease* : Brahmaṇaspati.

4 *Soma* : the God who represents and animates the juice of the Soma plant. He was in former times the Indian Dionysus or Bacchus. 'The simple minded Aryan people,' says Professor Whitney, 'whose whole religion was a worship of the wonderful powers and phenomena of nature, had no sooner perceived that this liquid (Soma juice) had power to elevate the spirits, and produce a temporary frenzy, under the influence of which the individual was prompted to, and ca able of, deeds beyond his natural powers, than they found in it something divine : it was to their apprehension a God, endowing those into whom it entered with godlike powers; the plant which afforded it became to them the king of plants; the process of preparing it became a holy sacrifice. The high antiquity of this cultus is attested by the references to it found occurring in the Persian Avesta.' See Muir, *O. S. Texts,* V. 258.

5 *Dakiṣṇā* : properly the present made to the priests at the conclusion of a sacrifice, here personified as a Goddess.

6 *The Assembly's wondrous Lord* : Sadasaspati, the master or protector of the assembly of priests, is here a title of Agni.

9 I have seen Narāśaṁsa, him most resolute,
  most widely famed,
  As 'twere the Household Priest of heaven.

HYMN XIX.   *Agni, Maruts.*

1 To this fair sacrifice to drink the milky
  draught thou art invoked :
  O Agni, with the Maruts come.

2 No mortal man, no God exceeds thy mental power, O Mighty one :
  O Agni, with the Maruts come.

3 All Gods devoid of guile, who know the
  mighty region of mid-air :
  O Agni, with those Maruts come.

4 The terrible, who sing their song, not to
  be overcome by might :
  O Agni, with those Maruts come.

5 Brilliant, and awful in their form, mighty,
  devourers of their foes :
  O Agni, with those Maruts come.

6 Who sit as Deities in heaven, above the
  sky-vault's luminous sphere :
  O Agni, with those Maruts come.

7 Who scatter clouds about the sky, away
  over the billowy sea :
  O Agni, with those Maruts come.

8 Who with their bright beams spread
  them forth over the ocean in their might :
  O Agni, with those Maruts come.

9 For thee, to be thine early draught, I pour
  the Soma-mingled meath :
  O Agni, with the Maruts come.

HYMN XX.   *Ṛbhus.*

1 For the Celestial Race this song of praise
  which gives wealth lavishly
  Was made by singers with their lips.

2 They who for Indra, with their mind,
  formed horses harnessed by a word,
  Attained by works to sacrifice.

---

9 *Household Priest* : *sádmamakhasam* ; according to
Sāyaṇa, 'radiant as heaven,' according to Ludwig, 'as
one who fought to win heaven's seat.'

Narāśaṁsa has already occurred as a name of Agni
(I. 13. 3.) The meaning appears to be : through my
invocation and praise I have reached the Gods, and with
the eye of the spirit have looked on Agni in heaven.

---

1 *For the Celestial Race* : *devāya janmane*, the divine
class or race of the Ṛbhus, the three sons of Sudhanvan
who is said to have been a descendant of Aṅgiras. They
were named severally Ṛbhu, Vibhvan, and Vāja and
styled collectively Ṛbhus from the name of the eldest.
Through their assiduous performance of good works they
obtained divinity and became entitled to receive praise
and adoration. They are supposed to dwell in the solar
sphere, and there is an indistinct identification of them
with the rays of the sun; but, whether typical or not,
they prove the admission, at an early date of the doctrine
that men might become divinities.' Wilson.

---

3 They for the two Nāsatyas wrought a light
  car moving every way :
  They formed a nectar-yielding cow.

4 The Ṛbhus with effectual prayers, honest,
  with constant labour, made
  Their Sire and Mother young again.

5 Together came your gladdening drops
  with Indra by the Maruts girt,
  With the Adityas, with the Kings.

6 The sacrificial ladle, wrought newly by
  the God Tvaṣṭar's hand—
  Four ladles have ye made thereof.

7 Vouchsafe us wealth, to him who pours
  thrice seven libations, yea, to each
  Give wealth, pleased with our eulogies.

8 As ministering Priests they held, by pious
  acts they won themselves,
  A share in sacrifice with Gods.

HYMN XXI.   *Indra-Agni.*

1 Indra and Agni I invoke ; fain are we
  for their song of praise :
  Chief Soma-drinkers are they both.

2 Praise ye, O men, and glorify Indra-Agni
  in the holy rites :
  Sing praise to them in sacred songs.

3 Indra and Agni we invite, the Soma-drinkers, for the fame
  Of Mitra, to the Soma-draught.

4 Strong Gods, we bid them come to this
  libation that stands ready here :

---

3 *The two Nāsatyas* : the Aśvins. See I. 3. 3. The
Ṛbhus may have been the first to attempt the bodily
representation of the horses of Indra and the chariot of
the Aśvins.

4 *Sire and Mother* : Heaven and Earth, which they,
as deities of the seasons, refresh and restore to youth.

5 'According to Aśvalāyana, as quoted by Sāyaṇa,
the libations offered at the third daily (or evening) sacrifice are presented to Indra along with the Adityas, together with Ṛbhu, Vibhvan, and Vāja, with Bṛhaspati
and the Viśvadevas.' Wilson.

6 'Tvaṣṭar, in the Paurāṇik mythology, is the carpenter or artisan of the Gods; so Sāyaṇa says of him, he
is a divinity whose duty, with relation to the Gods, is
carpentry...Sāyaṇa also calls the Ṛbhus the disciples of
Tvaṣṭar.....The act ascribed to them in the text, of
making one ladle four, has, probably, rather reference
to some innovation in the objects of libation than to
the mere multiplication of the wooden spoons used to
pour out the Soma juice. The *Nīti-Mañjarī* says that
Agni, coming to a sacrifice which the Ṛbhus celebrated,
became as one of them, and, therefore, they made the
ladle fourfold, that each might have his share.' Wilson.

7 Or the 'thrice seven' may refer to *rdināni*, grant
thrice seven rich treasures.

---

1 *Indra and Agni* : addressed conjointly as a dual
deity, Indrāgni, that is, Indra-Agni, See. I. 17. 1.

3 *For the fame of Mitra* : the meaning is not clear.
Mitra appears to be regarded as the guardian of the world.
Sāyaṇa takes Mitra in the sense of friend, and refers it
to the institutor of the sacrifice.

Indra and Agni, come to us.

5 Indra and Agni, mighty Lords of our assembly, crush the fiends :
Childless be the devouring ones.

6 Watch ye, through this your truthfulness, there in the place of spacious view :
Indra and Agni, send us bliss.

HYMN XXII. *Aśvins and Others*

1 WAKEN the Aśvin Pair who yoke their car at early morn : may they
Approach to drink this Soma juice.

2 We call the Aśvins Twain, the Gods borne in a noble car, the best
Of charioteers, who reach the heavens.

3 Dropping with honey is your whip, Aśvins, and full of pleasantness :
Sprinkle therewith the sacrifice.

4 As ye go thither in your car, not far, O Aśvins, is the home
Of him who offers Soma juice.

5 For my protection I invoke the golden-handed Savitar :
He knoweth, as a God, the place.

6 That he may send us succour, praise the Waters' Offspring Savitar :
Fain are we for his holy ways.

7 We call on him, distributer of wondrous bounty and of wealth,
On Savitar who looks on men.

8 Come hither, friends, and seat yourselves ;
Savitar, to be praised by us,
Giving good gifts, is beautiful.

9 O Agni, hither bring to us the willing Spouses of the Gods,
And Tvaṣṭar, to the Soma draught.

10 Most youthful Agni, hither bring their Spouses, Hotrā, Bhāratī,
Varūtrī, Dhiṣaṇā, for aid.

11 Spouses of Heroes, Goddesses, with whole wings may they come to us
With great protection and with aid.

12 Indrāṇī, Varuṇānī, and Agnāyī hither I invite,
For weal, to drink the Soma juice.

13 May Heaven and Earth, the Mighty Pair, bedew for us our sacrifice,
And feed us full with nourishments.

14 Their water rich with fatness, there in the Gandharva's steadfast place,
The singers taste through sacred songs.

15 Thornless be thou, O Earth, spread wide before us for a dwelling-place :
Vouchsafe us shelter broad and sure.

16 The Gods be gracious unto us even from the place whence Viṣṇu strode
Through the seven regions of the earth !

10 *Hotrā* is called the wife of Agni, or the personified invocation; *Bhāratī* is Holy Speech or Prayer; *Varūtrī* is explained as 'she who is' to be chosen, the excellent; and *Dhiṣaṇā* is said to be a synonym of Vāk or Vāgdevī, the Goddess of Speech.

11 *With whole wings* : literally, with unclipped wings; that is, swift as birds whose wings have not been cut.

12 *Indrāṇī, Varuṇānī, and Agnāyī* : are respectively the consorts of Indra, Varuṇa, and Agni.

14 *Their water rich in fatness* : the fertilizing rain sent by Heaven and Earth. The meaning appears to be : the holy singers enjoy, as guerdon for their hymns, the kindly rain and other good gifts which are sent down from the reigons above by the great parents Heaven and Earth.

The Gandharva's steadfast place : Though in later times the Gandharvas are regarded as a class, in the Ṛgveda more than one is seldom mentioned. He is commonly designated as 'the heavenly Gandharva,' whose habitation is the sky, and whose especial duty is to guard the heavenly Soma, which the Gods obtain through his permission.

16 *Viṣṇu* : This God, 'the all-pervading or encompassing,' is not placed in the Veda in the foremost rank of deities, and, though frequently invoked with Indra, Varuṇa, the Maruts, Rudra, Vāyu and the Ādityas, his superiority to them is never stated, and he is even described in one place as celebrating the praise of Indra and deriving his power from that God. The point which distinguishes him from the other Vedic deities is chiefly his striding over the heavens, which he is said to do in three paces, explained as denoting the threefold manifestation of light in the form of fire, lightning and the sun, or as designating the three daily stations of the sun, in his rising, culminating and setting.

The meaning of the stanza is obscure : Wilson, after Sāyaṇa, translates : 'May the Gods preserve us (from that portion) of the earth whence Viṣṇu, (aided) by the seven metres, stepped,' and notes : 'According to the Taittirīyas, as cited by the scholiast, the Gods with Viṣṇu at their head subdued the invincible earth, using the seven metres of the Veda as their instruments. Sāyaṇa conceives the text to allude to the *Trivikrama Avatāra*, in which Viṣṇu traversed the three worlds in three steps.

5 *Crush the fiends* : the Rākṣasas, demons who go about at night, ensnaring and even devouring human beings, disturbing sacrifices and devout men, and generally hostile to the Āryan race.

6 *In the place of spacious view* : Sāyaṇa explains 'in the station which preëminently makes known the experience of results (of actions) that is in heaven (*Svarga*).' In the place where what is hidden will be made known.

3 *Your whip* : the *madhukaṣā* or Honey-whip of the Aśvins is perhaps the stimulating morning breeze. See Atharva-veda IX. 1, the whole of which hymn is a glorification of this wondrous whip.

5 *Savitar* : the generator or vivifier, is a name of the Sun, in the Veda sometimes identified with and sometimes distinguished from Sūrya.

6 *The Waters' Offspring Savitar* : son or offspring of the Waters, *apām nápāt*, is an epithet more frequently applied to Agni. Sāyaṇa explains it otherwise as 'one who does not cherish (na pālakam) the water, but dries it up with his heat.'

17 Through all this world strode Viṣṇu;
    thrice his foot he planted, and the
    whole
    Was gathered in his footstep's dust.

18 Viṣṇu, the Guardian, he whom none
    deceiveth, made three steps ; thence-
    forth
    Establishing his high decrees.

19 Look ye on Viṣṇu's works, whereby the
    Friend of Indra, close-allied,
    Hath let his holy ways be seen.

20 The princes evermore behold that loftiest
    place where Viṣṇu is,
    Laid as it were an eye in heaven.

21 This, Viṣṇu's station most sublime, the
    singers, ever vigilant,
    Lovers of holy song, light up.

HYMN XXIII. *Vāyu and Others.*

1 STRONG are the Somas ; come thou nigh;
    these juices have been mixt with
    milk :
    Drink, Vāyu, the presented draughts.

2 Both Deities who touch the heaven, Indra
    and Vāyu we invoke
    To drink of this our soma juice.

3 The singers, for their aid, invoke Indra
    and Vāyu, swift as mind,
    The thousand-eyed, the Lords of thought.

4 Mitra and Varuṇa, renowned as Gods of
    consecrated might,
    We call to drink the Soma juice.

5 Those who by Law uphold the Law,
    Lords of the shining light of Law,
    Mitra I call, and Varuṇa.

6 Let Varuṇa be our chief defence, let
    Mitra guard us with all aids :
    Both make us rich exceedingly.

7 Indra, by Maruts girt, we call to drink
    the Soma juice : may he
    Sate him in union with his troop.

8 Gods, Marut hosts whom Indra leads,
    distributers of Pūṣan's gifts,

    Hearken ye all unto my cry.

9 With conquering Indra for ally, strike
    Vṛtra down, ye bounteous Gods :
    Let not the wicked master us.

10 We call the Universal Gods, and Maruts
    to the Soma draught,
    For passing strong are Pṛśni's Sons.

11 Fierce comes the Maruts' thundering voice,
    like that of conquerors, when ye go
    Forward to victory, O Men.

12 Born of the laughing lightning. may the
    Maruts guard us everywhere :
    May they be gracious unto us.

13 Like some lost animal, drive to us, bright
    Pūṣan, him who bears up heaven,
    Resting on many-coloured grass.

14 Pūṣan the Bright has found the King,
    concealed and hidden in a cave,
    Who rests on grass of many hues.

15 And may he duly bring to me the six
    bound closely, through these drops,
    As one who ploughs with steers brings
    corn.

16 Along their paths the Mothers go, Sisters
    of priestly ministrants,
    Mingling their sweetness with the milk.

17 May Waters gathered near the Sun, and
    those wherewith the Sun is joined,
    Speed forth this sacrifice of ours.

18 I call the Waters, Goddesses, wherein our
    cattle quench their thirst ;
    Oblations to the Streams be given.

19 Amrit is in the Waters ; in the Waters
    there is healing balm :
    Be swift, ye Gods, to give them praise.

20 Within the Waters—Soma thus hath told
    me—dwell all balms that heal,

The phrase "preserve us from the earth" implies according to the commentary, the hindrance of the sin of those inhabiting the earth.'

17 *The whole was gathered in his footstep's dust* : This is the meaning according to Sāyaṇa. Viṣṇu was so mighty that the dust raised by his footstep enveloped the whole world, or the earth was formed from the dust of his strides.

20 *The Princes* : the Sūris, the wealthy patrons of sacrifice.

21 *Light up* : glorify with their praises.
This hymn is addressed to Vāyu, Indra, Mitra, Varuṇa, the Viśve Devas, Pūṣan, the Waters, Agni.

3 *Lords of thought* : dhī, thought, means especially in the Veda holy thought, devotion, prayer, a religious rite, a sacrifice.

8 *Pūṣan* is the guardian of flocks and herds and of property in general.

10 *Pṛśnimātaraḥ* : Pṛśni's sons, those who have for their mother Pṛśni, the many-coloured earth or the speckled cloud; the Maruts.

11 *O Men* : O heroic Maruts.

13 *Him who bears up heaven* : Soma, the juice which prompts the world-sustaining deeds of the Gods.

14 *The King* : Soma.
Concealed and hidden in a cave : in a place difficult of access; the reference is to the flight of Agni. See III. 9. 4.

15 *The six* : the six seasons, spring, summer, the rains, autumn, winter, the dews. *Through these drops* : May this libation induce him to bring etc.

16 *The Mothers* : the Waters, regarded as the close allies of the priests, as they are mingled with the ingredients of the Soma libation.

19 *Amrit* : nectar, the drink that confers immortality; the Greek Ambrosia.

20 *Soma thus hath told me* : Soma is especially lord of medicinal plants.

And Agni, he who blesseth all. The
Waters hold all medicines.

21 O Waters, teem with medicine to keep my
body safe from harm,

So that I long may see the Sun.

22 Whatever sin is found in me, whatever
evil I have wrought.

If I have lied or falsely sworn, Waters,
remove it far from me.

23 The Waters I this day have sought, and
to their moisture have we come :

O Agni, rich in milk, come thou, and
with thy splendour cover me.

24 Fill me with splendour, Agni ; give offspring and length of days ; the Gods

Shall know me even as I am, and Indra
with the Ṛṣis, know.

HYMN XXIV. *Varuṇa and Others.*

1 WHO now is he, what God among Immortals, of whose auspicious name we may
bethink us ?

Who shall to mighty Aditi restore us, that
I may see my Father and my Mother ?

24 *Indra with the Ṛṣis* : Perhaps the seven great Ṛṣis
are intended,—Marīci, Atri, Aṅgiras, Pulastya, Pulaha,
Kratu, and Vasiṣṭha.

—————

This hymn, addressed to Varuṇa, Prajāpati, Agni,
Savitar, and Bhaga, is the first of a series attributed to
Sunaḥśepa, the son of Ajigarta. The legend is told in
full detail in the *Aitareya Brāhmaṇa.* A king, named
Hariścandra, worships Varuṇa in order to obtain a
son, promising to sacrifice to him his first-born. A son
is born, named Rohita; but the king delays the sacrifice
until Rohita grows up, when his father communicates to
him his intended fate. Rohita refuses submission, and
spends several years in the forest away from home. There,
at last, he meets with Ajīgarta, a Ṛṣi in great distress,
and persuades him to part with his second son Sunaḥśepa
to be offered, as a substitute to Varuṇa. Sunaḥśepa is
about to be sacrificed, when, by the advice of Vi.vā-
mitra, one of the officiating priests, he appeals to the
Gods, and is liberated. See Wilson, *Ṛgveda,* i. p.
60., Muir, *O. S. Texts,* i. 355, 407, 413, and M. Müller,
A. S. Literature, p. 408.

1 *Mighty Aditi* : Professor Müller (*Trans. of the
Ṛgveda,* 1. 230) says that 'Aditi, an ancient god or
goddess, is in reality the earliest name invented to express the Infinite; not the Infinite as the result of a long
process of abstract reasoning, but the visible Infinite, the
endless expanse beyond the earth, beyond the clouds,
beyond the sky.'

'These words (Who shall to mighty Aditi restore us ?)
may be understood as spoken by some one in danger of
death...who prayed to be permitted again to behold the
face of nature...If we should understand the father and
mother whom the suppliant is anxious to behold, as
meaning heaven and earth, it would become still more
probable that Aditi is to be understood as meaning
nature.' Muir, *O. S. Texts,* v. 45.

Sāyaṇa explains Aditi in the text as Earth; Roth, as
freedom or security; Benfey, as sinlessness.

2 Agni the God the first among the Immortals,—of his auspicious name let us
bethink us.

He shall to mighty Aditi restore us, that
I may see my Father and my Mother.

3 To thee, O Savitar, the Lord of precious
things, who helpest us

Continually, for our share we come—

4 Wealth, highly lauded ere reproach hath
fallen on it, which is laid,

Free from all hatred, in thy hands.

5 Through thy protection may we come to
even the height of affluence

Which Bhaga hath dealt out to us.

6 Ne'er have those birds that fly through air
attained to thy high dominion or thy
might or spirit ;

Nor these the waters that flow on for
ever, nor hills, abaters of the wind's
wild fury.

7 Varuṇa, King, of hallowed might, sustaineth erect the Tree's stem in the baseless region.

Its rays, whose root is high above, stream
downward. Deep may they sink within
us, and be hidden.

8 King Varuṇa hath made a spacious pathway, a pathway for the Sun wherein to
travel.

Where no way was he made him set his
footstep, and warned afar whate'er afflicts
the spirit.

9 A hundred balms are thine, O King, a
thousand ; deep and wide-reaching also
be thy favours.

Far from us, far away drive thou Destruction. Put from us e'en the sin we have
committed.

10 Whither by day depart the constellations
that shine at night, set high in heaven
above us ?

5 *Which Bhaga hath dealt out to us* : the riches which
the distributer of wealth, Bhaga, Fate or Fortune, has
allotted to us.

7 *Vánasya stúpam* in the text appears to mean 'the
stem of the tree,' and Sāyaṇa's explanation 'the mass or
pile of light' seems forced and unnatural. The phrase
is not clear, but perhaps the ancient myth of the world-
tree, the source of life, may be alluded to.

9 *Ni ṛti* is Decay or Destruction personified, the
Goddess of death and corruption. Sāyaṇa calls her
pāpadevatā, the deity of sin.

10 *Varuṇa's holy laws* : Varuṇa is the chief of the lords
of natural order. His activity displays itself preëminently
in the control of the most regular phenomena of nature.
See Wallis, *Cosmology of the Ṛgveda,* p. 97 f. The connexion
appears to be: Fear not: the laws of Varuṇa are inviolable,
and the constellations will duly reappear.

Varuṇa's holy laws remain unweakened, and through the night the Moon moves on in splendour.

11 I ask this of thee with my prayer adoring; thy worshipper craves this with his oblation.

Varuṇa, stay thou here and be not angry ; steal not our life from us, O thou Wide-Ruler.

12 Nightly and daily this one thing they tell me, this too the thought of mine own heart repeateth.

May he to whom prayed fettered Śunaḥ-śepa, may he the Sovran Varuṇa release us.

13 Bound to three pillars captured Śunaḥśepa thus to the Āditya made his supplication.

Him may the Sovran Varuṇa deliver, wise, ne'er deceived, loosen the bonds that bind him.

14 With bending down, oblations, sacrifices, O Varuṇa, we deprecate thine anger :

Wise Asura, thou King of wide dominion, loosen the bonds of sins by us committed.

15 Loosen the bonds, O Varuṇa, that hold me, loosen the bonds above, between, and under.

So in thy holy law may we made sinless belong to Aditi, O thou Āditya.

HYMN XXV.   *Varuṇa.*

1 WHATEVER law of thine, O God, O Varuṇa, as we are men, Day after day we violate.

2 Give us not as a prey to death, to be destroyed by thee in wrath, To thy fierce anger when displeased.

3 To gain thy mercy, Varuṇa, with hymns we bind thy heart, as binds The charioteer his tethered horse.

4 They flee from me dispirited, bent only on obtaining wealth, As to their nests the birds of air.

5 When shall we bring, to be appeased, the Hero, Lord of warrior might, Him, the far-seeing Varuṇa ?

6 This, this with joy they both accept in common : never do they fail The ever-faithful worshipper.

7 He knows the path of birds that fly through heaven, and, Sovran of the sea, He knows the ships that are thereon.

8 True to his holy law, he knows the twelve moons with their progeny: He knows the moon of later birth.

9 He knows the pathway of the wind, the spreading, high, and mighty wind : He knows the Gods who dwell above.

10 Varuṇa, true to holy law, sits down among his people ; he, Most wise, sits there to govern all.

11 From thence perceiving he beholds all wondrous things, both what hath been, And what hereafter will be done.

12 May that Āditya, very wise, make fair paths for us all our days : May he prolong our lives for us.

13 Varuṇa, wearing golden mail, hath clad him in a shining robe : His spies are seated round about.

14 The God whom enemies threaten not, nor those who tyrannize o'er men, Nor those whose minds are bent on wrong.

15 He who gives glory to mankind, not glory that is incomplete, To our own bodies giving it.

16 Yearning for the wide-seeing One, my thoughts move onward unto him, As kine unto their pastures move.

---

13 *Three pillars*, or trees, apparently the sacrificial post, a sort of tripod.

The Āditya is Varuṇa, one of the sons of Aditi. See I. 14. 3.

14 *Asura* : an incorporeal, spiritual, divine being; the Zend Ahura.

15 *The bonds* : according to Sāyaṇa, the ligatures fastening the head, the waist and the feet. But the bonds of sin are here intended.

May we belong to Aditi: May we be restored to freedom and the enjoyment of nature.

4 *They flee* : apparently, my enemies; but the passage is very obscure.

6 *Both* : Varuṇa and Mitra. Why Mitra is thus suddenly introduced is not clear. The stanza breaks the connexion between stanzas 5 and 7; and is probably an interpolation.

7 Varuṇa is King of the air and of the sea, the latter being often regarded as identical with the former.

8 *The twelve moons with their progeny* the twelve months with the days which are their offspring.

The moon of later birth : the thirteenth, the supplementary or intercalary month of the luni-solar year.

13 *His spies* : Varuṇa's spies, messengers or angels, are probably the rest of the Ādityas. See M. Müller, *A. S. Literature*, p. 536.

17 Once more together let us speak, because
my meath is brought: priest-like
Thou eatest what is dear to thee.

18 Now saw I him whom all may see, I saw
his car above the earth :
He hath accepted these my songs.

19 Varuṇa, hear this call of mine : be gracious unto us this day
Longing for help I cried to thee.

20 Thou, O wise God, art Lord of all, thou
art the King of earth and heaven :
Hear, as thou goest on thy way.

21 Release us from the upper bond, untie
the bond between, and loose
The bonds below, that I may live.

HYMN XXVI. *Agni.*

1 O WORTHY of oblation, Lord of prospering
powers, assume thy robes,
And offer this our sacrifice.

2 Sit ever to be chosen, as our Priest, most
youthful, through our hymns,
O Agni, through our heavenly word.

3 For here a Father for his son, Kinsman
for kinsman worshippeth,
And Friend, choice-worthy, for his friend.

4 Here let the foe-destroyers sit, Varuṇa,
Mitra, Aryaman,
Like men, upon our sacred grass.

5 O ancient Herald, be thou glad in this
our rite and fellowship :
Hearken thou well to these our songs.

6 Whate'er in this perpetual course we
sacrifice to God and God,
That gift is offered up in thee

7 May he be our dear household Lord,
Priest, pleasant and. choice-worthy :
may
We, with bright fires, be dear to him.

8 The Gods, adored with brilliant fires,
have granted precious wealth to us :
So, with bright fires, we pray to thee.

9 And, O Immortal One, so may the eulogies
of mortal men
Belong to us and thee alike.

10 With all thy fires, O Agni, find pleasure
in this our sacrifice,
And this our speech, O Son of Strength.

HYMN XXVII. *Agni.*

1 WITH worship will I glorify thee, Agni,
like a long-tailed steed,
Imperial Lord of sacred rites.

2 May the far-striding Son of Strength,
bringer of great felicity,
Who pours his gifts like rain, be ours.

3 Lord of all life, from near; from far, do
thou, O Agni evermore
Protect us from the sinful man.

4 O Agni, graciously announce this our
oblation to the Gods,
And this our newest song of praise.

5 Give us a share of strength most high, a
share of strength that is below,
A share of strength that is between.

6 Thou dealest gifts, resplendent One; nigh,
as with waves of Sindhu, thou
Swift streamest to the worshipper.

7 That man is lord of endless strength
whom thou protectest in the fight,
Agni, or urgest to the fray.

8 Him, whosoever he may be, no man may
vanquish, mighty One :
Nay, very glorious power is his.

9 May he who dwells with all mankind
bear us with war-steeds through the
fight,
And with the singers win the spoil.

10 Help, thou who knowest lauds, this work,
this eulogy to Rudra, him

---

17 *My meath* : or honey (*mádhu*), the libation of
Soma juice.

18 *Now saw I him* : I saw Varuṇa, visible to the mental
eye of his worshippers.

21 *Release us from the upper bond* : see I.24. 15.

---

1 *Assume thy robes* : clothe thyself in thy vesture of
flames.

2 *Most youthful* : continually renewed for sacrifice,
either from the household fire or by repeated attrition.

3 *For here a Father for his son* : Agni, who stands in
the place of father, kinsman, and friend to his worshipper.

4 *Aryaman* : the name of an Āditya commonly invoked together with Varuṇa and Mitra. He is said to
preside over twilight.

Like men : or, according to Sāyaṇa, as they sate
at the sacrifice of Manus, who is the same as Manu.

---

10 *Son of Strength* : the appellation is of frequent occurrence, and is sometimes applied to Indra also as a
specially mighty God. The expression, applied to Agni,
alludes to the strength employed in rubbing together the
two pieces of wood to generate fire.

1 *Like a long-tailed steed* : Agni, or Fire, is likened to
a horse, probably, on account of his impetuosity ; and
his long flames, curled and driven by the wind, are compared to the horse's flowing tail. Sāyaṇa explains :
scattering our foes with thy flames as a horse brushes
away the flies that trouble him.

6 *Sindhu* : the Indus; or the word may stand for
any river, and the expression mean, with great
abundance.

9 *With the singers* : the priests who sing hymns of
praise at the sacrifice.

10 *Thou who knowest lauds* : (*jarābodha* seems to refer
to the Ṛṣi or poet of the hymn, not to Agni.
Rudra : the Roarer, or Howler, is here a name of
Agni, on account of the loud crackling or roaring of his
flames. Or the word may signify red, bright. See Pischel,
Vedische Studien, 1, pp. 55 sqq.

Adorable in every house.

11 May this our God, great, limitless, smoke-
banbered, excellently bright,
Urge us to strength and holy thought.

12 Like some rich Lord of men may he, Agni,
the banner of the Gods,
Refulgent, hear us through our lauds.

13 Glory to Gods, the mighty and the lesser,
glory to Gods the younger and the elder !
Let us, if we have power, pay the Gods
worship : no better prayer than this, ye
Gods, acknowledge.

HYMN XXVIII.   *Indra, Etc.*

1 THERE where the broad-based stone is
raised on high to press the juices out,
O Indra, drink with eager thirst the
droppings which the mortar sheds.

2 Where, like broad hips, to hold the juice,
the platters of the press are laid,
O Indra, drink with eager thirst the
droppings which the mortar sheds.

3 There where the woman marks and learns
the pestle's constant rise and fall,
O Indra, drink with eager thirst the
droppings which the mortar sheds.

4 Where, as with reins to guide a horse, they
bind the churning-staff with cords,
O Indra, drink with eager thirst the droppings which the mortar sheds.

5 If of a truth in every house, O Mortar,
thou art set for work,
Here give thou forth thy clearest sound,
loud as the drum of conquerors.

---

12   *The banner of the Gods* : who like a banner brings
the Gods together ; or it may be rendered 'the herald of
the Gods,' he who notifies to them, as Sāyaṇa explains it.

13.   These distinctions of greater and lesser, older
and younger Gods, or as we should say, angels, are nowhere further explained. Śunaḥśepa, it is said, by the
advice of Agni, worships the Viśvedevas or the Universal
Gods. The Viśvedevas, as a separate troop or class of
Gods, are ten in number, especially worshipped at funeral
obsequies, and moreover, according to the laws of Manu,
entitled to daily offerings.

This hymn—a song sung during the preparation of
the Soma juice—is said to be addressed to Indra, and
to the pestle and mortar and other utensils used in the
work.

2   *Platters* : two shallow plates, one being used as a
receiver and the other as a cover.

4   *They bind the churning-staff with cords* : the churning stick is moved by a rope passed round its handle
and round a post used as a pivot.

5   *O Mortar* : according to Sāyaṇa the divinities
presiding over the mortar and pestle, and not the implements themselves, are addressed.

---

6 O Sovran of the Forest, as the wind
blows soft in front of thee,
Mortar, for Indra press thou forth the
Soma juice that he may drink.

7 Best strength-givers, ye stretch wide jaws,
O Sacrificial Implements,
Like two bay horses champing herbs.

8 Ye Sovrans of the Forest, both swift, with
swift pressers press to-day
Sweet Soma juice for Indra's drink.

9 Take up in beakers what remains : the
Soma on the filter pour,
And on the ox-hide set the dregs.

HYMN XXIX.   *Indra.*

1 O SOMA DRINKER, ever true, utterly hopeless though we be,
Do thou, O Indra, give us hope of beauteous horses and of kine,
In thousands, O most wealthy One.

2 O Lord of Strength, whose jaws are
strong, great deeds are thine, the
powerful :
Do thou, O Indra, give us hope of beauteous horses and of kine,
In thousands, O most wealthy One.

3 Lull thou asleep, to wake no more, the
pair who on each other look :
Do thou, O Indra, give us hope of beauteous horses and of kine,
In thousands, O most wealthy One.

4 Hero, let hostile spirits sleep, and every
gentler genius wake :
Do thou, O Indra, give us hope of beauteous horses and of kine,
In thousands, O most wealthy One.

5 Destroy this ass, O Indra, who in tones
discordant brays to thee :

---

6   *O Sovran of the Forest* : (*vanaspati*) a large tree;
used in this place, by metonymy, for the mortar, and
in verse 8, in the dual number, for the mortar and pestle.

7   *Strength-givers* : explained by Sāyaṇa as especially
givers of food. The two platters mentioned above are
probably meant. When the upper platter is raised to
receive the juice of the Soma stalks the aperture between
the two is like a horse's mouth when he chews succulent
grass.

9   This verse is addressed to the ministering priest.
What remains : after the libation. *The filter* or sieve was
used to purify the juice before it was poured into the
receptacle. *Ox-hide* : laid under the mortar.

---

3   *The pair who on each other look* : 'The text is very
elliptical and obscure, It is, literally : Put to sleep the
two reciprocally looking: let them sleep, not being
awakened. The Scholiast calls them the two female
messengers of Yama (the God of the Dead).' Wilson.

5   *This ass* : our adversary, says the Scholiast, 'Therefore is he called an ass, as braying, or uttering harsh
sounds intolerable to hear.'

Do thou, O Indra, give us hope of beauteous horses and of kine,
In thousands, O most wealthy One.

6 Far distant on the forest fall the tempest
in a circling course !
Do thou, O Indra, give us hope of beauteous horses and of kine,
In thousands, O most wealthy One.

7 Slay each reviler, and destroy him who
in secret injures us :
Do thou, O Indra, give us hope of beauteous horses and of kine
In thousands, O most wealthy One.

HYMN XXX.   *Indra.*

1 WE seeking strength with Soma-drops fill
full your Indra like a well,
Most liberal, Lord of Hundred Powers,

2 Who lets a hundred of the pure, a thousand of the milk-blent draughts
Flow, even as down a depth, to him;

3 When for the strong, the rapturous joy he
in this manner hath made room
Within his belly, like the sea.

4 This is thine own. Thou drawest near,
as turns a pigeon to his mate :
Thou carest too for this our prayer.

5 O Hero, Lord of Bounties, praised in
hymns, may power and joyfulness
Be his who sings the laud to thee.

6 Lord of a Hundred Powers, stand up to
lend us succour in this fight :
In others too let us agree.

7 In every need, in every fray we call as
friends to succour us
Indra the mightiest of all.

8 If he will hear us let him come with
succour of a thousand kinds,
And all that strengthens, to our call.

9 I call him mighty to resist, the Hero of
our ancient home,
Thee whom my sire invoked of old.

10 We pray to thee, O much-invoked, rich in
all precious gifts, O Friend,
Kind God to those who sing thy praise.

11 O Soma-drinker, Thunder-armed, Friend
of our lovely-featured dames
And of our Soma-drinking friends.

12 Thus, Soma-drinker, may it be ; thus,
Friend, who wieldest thunder, act
To aid each wish as we desire.

13 With Indra splendid feasts be ours, rich
in all strengthening things wherewith,
Wealthy in food, we may rejoice.

14 Like thee, thyself, the singers' Friend,
thou movest, as it were, besought,
Bold One, the axle of the car.

15 That, Śatakratu, thou to grace and please
thy praisers, as it were,
Stirrest the axle with thy strength.

16 With champing, neighing loudly-snorting
horses Indra hath ever won himself
great treasures.
A car of gold hath he whose deeds are
wondrous received from us, and let us
too receive it.

17 Come, Aśvins, with enduring strength
wealthy in horses and in kine,
And gold, O ye of wondrous deeds.

18 Your chariot yoked for both alike, immortal, ye of mighty acts,
Travels, O Aśvins, in the sea.

19 High on the forehead of the Bull one
chariot wheel ye ever keep,
The other round the sky revolves.

---

6 *Far distant on the forest* : may the cyclone or tempest
expend its fury on the wood, and not come nigh us.
The word *kuṇḍṛṇācī*, which I have rendered in accordance with Sāyaṇa, means elsewhere a certain kind of
animal, a lizard according to Sāyaṇa. This passage
may perhaps mean, 'may the wind fall on the forest with
the *kuṇḍṛṇācī*, whatever that may be.

---

1 *Lord of Hundred Powers* : Śatakratu.

3 *The strong, the rapturous joy* : the exhilarating Soma
juice.

4 *This is thine own* : this Soma libation is for thee
alone.

6 *In this fight* : the hymn is a prayer for aid in a
coming battle.

9 *The Hero of our ancient home* : the tutelary God of
our family.

11 *Friend of our lovely-featured dames* : the meaning of
śipriṇīnām in the text is very doubtful. Wilson, following
Sāyaṇa, paraphrases : (bestow upon) us, thy friends,
(abundance of cows) with projecting jaws. Benfey takes
the word to mean beautiful women. Ludwig suggests
helmeted, from a possible form *śipriṇi*, agreeing with
viśām, of men, understood. Roth considers the reading
to be faulty, and suggests, *śipriṇīvan*, in the vocative case,
agreeing with Soma-drinker.

14 The lines in this and the following stanza referring
to the axle and the chariot or wain are somewhat obscure
and have been variously interpreted. Ludwig's explanation, which I follow, appears to be the simplest and
the best. The expression, movest, or stirrest, the axle,
which is the firmest and strongest part of the car, is
intended to signify Indra's great strength exerted at his
worshippers' prayer.

16 The hymn really ends with the preceding stanza.
The *car of gold* given to Indra is the hymn. The car of
gold prayed for is abundant wealth.

18 *The sea* : the ocean of air.

19 *The Bull* : apparently the Sun. The car of the
Aśvins stands at his head or in front of him, and the
Aśvins precede him in his course round heaven. But the
meaning is not very clear.

20 What mortal, O immortal Dawn, enjoyeth
 thee ? Where lovest thou ?
 To whom, O radiant, dost thou go ?

21 For we have had thee in our thoughts
 whether anear or far away,
 Red-hued and like a dappled mare.

22 Hither, O Daughter of the Sky, come
 thou with these thy strengthenings,
 And send thou riches down to us.

HYMN XXXI.   *Agni.*

1 THOU, Agni, wast the earliest Aṅgiras, a
 Seer; thou wast, a God thyself, the
 Gods' auspicious Friend.

 After thy holy ordinance the Maruts, sage,
 active through wisdom, with their glittering spears, were born.

2 O Agni, thou, the best and earliest Aṅgiras,
 fulfillest as a Sage the holy law of Gods.

 Sprung from two mothers, wise, through
 all existence spread, resting in many a
 place for sake of living man.

3 To Mātariśvan first thou, Agni, wast disclosed, and to Vivasvān through thy
 noble inward power.

 Heaven and Earth, Vasu ! shook at the
 choosing of the Priest : the burthen thou
 didst bear, didst worship mighty Gods.

4 Agni thou madest heaven to thunder for
 mankind; thou, yet more pious, for pious
 Purūravas.

When thou art rapidly freed from thy
 parents, first eastward they bear thee
 round, and, after, to the west.

5 Thou, Agni, art a Bull who makes our
 store increase, to be invoked by him
 who lifts the ladle up.

 Well knowing the oblation with the hallowing word, uniting all who live, thou
 lightenest first our folk

6 Agni, thou savest in the synod when pursued e'en him, farseeing One ! who walks
 in evil ways.

 Thou, when the heroes fight for spoil
 which men rush round, slayest in war
 the many by the hands of few.

7 For glory, Agni, day by day, thou liftest
 up the mortal man to highest immortality,

 Even thou who yearning for both races
 givest them great bliss, and to the prince
 grantest abundant food.

8 O Agni, highly lauded, make our singer
 famous that he may win us store of riches:

 May we improve the rite with new performance. O Earth and Heaven, with
 all the Gods, protect us.

9 O blameless Agni lying in thy Parents'
 lap, a God among the Gods, be watchful for our good.

 Former of bodies, be the singer's Providence : all good things hast thou sown for
 him, auspicious One !

10 Agni, thou art our Providence, our Father
 thou : we are thy brethren and thou
 art our spring of life.

 In thee, rich in good heroes, guard of high
 decrees, meet hundred, thousand treasures, O infallible !

11 Thee, Agni, have the Gods made the first
 living One for living man, Lord of the
 house of Nahuṣa.

---

20 We are reminded of the old Grecian myth of
Eos and Tithonus. Uṣas, Dawn, or Morning, is the
daughter of personified Heaven, Dyaus, or Dyu.

This hymn, and the four following, are ascribed to
Hiraṇyastūpa, son of Aṅgiras.

 1 *Thou, Agni, wast the earliest Aṅgiras* : the Aṅgirases
are the most important priestly family mentioned in the
Veda. See I. 1. 6.

 With their glittering spears : the spears of the Maruts or
Storm-Gods are lightning flashes.

 2 *The holy law of Gods* : sacrifice to the Gods, which
Agni performs.

 Sprung from two mothers : from the two pieces of wood
used to produce fire.

 3 *Mātariśvan* : the name of a divine being described
in I.60.1 as bringing the hidden Agni to Bhṛgu, and
identified by Sāyaṇa with Vāyu the God of wind.

 Vivasvān : 'the brilliant'; he appears to be the God of
daylight and the morning sun, the personification of all
manifestations of light. He is said to be the father of
Yama, and the Gods are called his offsprings.

 Vasu : (good) often used as a name or epithet of
Agni. The Vasus as a class of Gods, eight in number,
were at first personifications of natural phenomena.

 4 *Purūravas* : son of Budha. He is said to have
instituted the three sacrificial fires. Agni, to reward him,
sent thunder the forerunner of rain.

Freed from thy parents : produced and separated from
the fire-sticks.

 Eastward they bear thee : the fire is first applied to light
the Āhavanīya fire and then the Gārhapatya.

 5 *A Bull* : exceedingly strong.

 With the hallowing word : the exclamation *Vaṣaṭ*: may
he (Agni) bear it (to the Gods), used at the moment of
pouring the sacrificial oil or clarified butter on the fire.

 6 *Agni, thou savest in the synod* : the *viddtha*, synod or
sacrificial assembly, seems to have been regarded as an
inviolable asylum.

 7 *Both races* : Gods and men.

 The prince : the Sūri, the noble or eminent man who
institutes and pays the charges of the sacrifice.

 9 *Thy Parents* : here said to mean Heaven and Earth.

 Former of bodies : giver of children

 11 *Nahuṣa* : one of the great progenitors of the human
race.

 Iḷā : the personification of prayer, and the first teacher
of the rules of sacrifice.

 What time a Son was born : this Son is Agni himself.

 Hiraṇyastūpa, the Ṛṣi of the hymn, is the son or

Ilā they made the teacher of the sons of men, what time a Son was born to the father of my race.

12 Worthy to be revered, O Agni, God, preserve our wealthy patrons with thy succours, and ourselves.

Guard of our seed art thou, aiding our cows to bear, incessantly protecting in thy holy way.

13 Agni, thou art a guard close to the pious man; kindled art thou, four-eyed ! for him who is unarmed.

With fond heart thou acceptest e'en the poor man's prayer, when he hath brought his gift to gain security.

14 Thou, Agni gainest for the loudly-praising priest the highest wealth, the object of a man's desire.

Thou art called Father, caring even for the weak, and wisest, to the simple one thou teachest lore.

15 Agni, the man who giveth guerdon to the priests, like well-sewn armour thou guardest on every side.

He who with grateful food shows kindness in his house, an offerer to the living, is the type of heaven.

16 Pardon, we pray, this sin of ours, O Agni,— the path which we have trodden, widely straying,

Dear Friend and Father, caring for the pious, who speedest nigh and who inspirest mortals.

17 As erst to Manus, to Yayāti, Aṅgiras, so Aṅgiras ! pure Agni ! come thou to our hall.

Bring hither the celestial host and seat them here upon the sacred grass, and offer what they love.

18 By this our prayer be thou, O Agni, strengthened, prayer made by us after our power and knowledge.

Lead thou us, therefore, to increasing riches; endow us with thy strength-bestowing favour.

HYMN XXXII. *Inrda.*

1 I WILL declare the manly deeds of Indra, the first that he achieved, the Thunder-wielder.

He slew the Dragon, then disclosed the waters, and cleft the channels of the mountain torrents.

2 He slew the Dragon lying on the mountain : his heavenly bolt of thunder Tvaṣṭar fashioned.

Like lowing kine in rapid flow descending the waters glided downward to the ocean.

3 Impetuous as a bull, he chose the Soma, and in three sacred beakers drank the juices.

Maghavan grasped the thunder for his weapon, and smote to death this firstborn of the dragons.

4 When, Indra, thou hadst slain the dragon's firstborn, and overcome the charms of the enchanters,

Then, giving life to Sun and Dawn and Heaven, thou foundest not one foe to stand against thee.

5 Indra with his own great and deadly thunder smote into pieces Vṛtra, worst of Vṛtras.

As trunks of trees, what time the axe hath felled them, low on the earth so lies the prostrate Dragon.

6 He, like a mad weak warrior, challenged Indra, the great impetuous many-slaying Hero.

He, brooking not the clashing of the weapons, crushed—Indra's foe—the shattered forts in falling.

descendant of Aṅgiras, who, as one of the first introducers of the sacrificial fire and the rites of worship, is regarded as the generator or father of Agni. The meaning of the verse is that Agni was appointed priest, and *Ilā* teacher of the rules of divine worship in the earliest time when Agni was first born on earth as sacrificial fire.

13 *Four-eyed* : illuminating the four cardinal points, or looking in all directions.

15 *An offerer to the living* : probably, one who offers food and hospitality to a human being, the *nṛyajña*, worship of man, of Manu. Or it may mean as Ludwig suggests, one who offers a sacrifice that transports the sacrificer at once, living, to heaven.

16 *Yayāti* : a celebrated king, one of the sons of Nahuṣa.

1 'In this and subsequent Sūktas we have an ample elucidation of the original purport of the legend of Indra's slaying Vṛtra, converted by the Paurāṇik writers into a literal contest between Indra and an Asura, or chief o the Asuras, from what in the Vedas is merely an allegorical narrative of the production of rain. Vṛtra, sometimes also named Ahi, is nothing more than the accumulation of vapour condensed or figuratively shut up in, or obstructed by, a cloud. Indra, with his thunderbolt, or atmospheric or electrical influence, divides the aggregated mass, and vent is given to the rain which then descends upon the earth.' Wilson.

2 *The Dragon* : Ahi, literally a serpent. *Tvaṣṭar* is the artist of the Gods.

3 *Maghavan* : the wealthy and liberal; Lord Bountiful.

In three sacred beakers : t̤kadrukeṣu : according to Sāyaṇa, on the Ṭikadrukas, the first three days of the Abhiplava ceremony.

4 *The charms of the enchanters* : magical or supernatural powers ascribed to Vṛtra and his allies.

7 Footless and handless still he challenged Indra, who smote him with his bolt between the shoulders.
Emasculate yet claiming manly vigour, thus Vṛtra lay with scattered limbs dissevered.

8 There as he lies like a bank-bursting river, the waters taking courage flow above him.
The Dragon lies beneath the feet of torrents which Vṛtra with his greatness had encompassed.

9 Then humbled was the strength of Vṛtra's mother : Indra hath cast his deadly bolt against her.
The mother was above, the son was under, and like a cow beside her calf lay Dānu.

10 Rolled in the midst of never-ceasing currents flowing without a rest for ever onward.
The waters bear off Vṛtra's nameless body : the foe of Indra sank to during darkness.

11 Guarded by Ahi stood the thralls of Dāsas,. the waters stayed like kine held by the robber.
But he, when he had smitten Vṛtra, opened the cave wherein the floods had been imprisoned.

12 A horse's tail wast thou when he, O Indra, smote on thy bolt; thou, God without a second,
Thou hast won back the kine, hast won the Soma; thou hast let loose to flow the Seven Rivers.

13 Nothing availed him lightning, nothing thunder, hailstorm or mist which had spread around him:
When Indra and the Dragon strove in battle, Maghavan gained the victory for ever.

14 Whom sawest thou to avenge the Dragon, Indra, that fear possessed thy heart when thou hadst slain him;
That, like a hawk affrighted through the regions, thou crossedst nine-and-ninety flowing rivers ?

15 Indra is King of all that moves and moves not, of creatures tame and horned, the Thunder-wielder.
Over all living men he rules as Sovran, containing all as spokes within the felly.

HYMN XXXIII.   *Indra.*

1 COME, fain for booty let us seek to Indra : yet more shall he increase his care that guides us.
Will not the Indestructible endow us with perfect knowledge of this wealth, of cattle ?

2 I fly to him invisible Wealth-giver as flies the falcon to his cherished eyrie,
With fairest hymns of praise adoring Indra, whom those who laud him must invoke in battle.

3 Mid all his host, he bindeth on the quiver : he driveth cattle from what foe he pleaseth :
Gathering up great store of riches, Indra. be thou no trafficker with us, most mighty.

4 Thou slewest with thy bolt the wealthy Dasyu, alone, yet going with thy helpers, Indra !
Far from the floor of heaven in all directions, the ancient riteless ones fled to destruction.

5 Fighting with pious worshippers, the riteless turned and fled, Indra ! with averted faces.

---

9 *Dānu* : according to Sāyaṇa, the mother of Vṛtra.
11 *Thralls of Dāsas* : in the power of Vṛtra and his allies. Dāsa is a general name applied in the Veda to certain evil beings or demons, hostile to Indra and to men ; it means, also, a savage, a barbarian, one of the non-Āryan inhabitants of India.

The robber : *paṇi* (literally, one who barters and traffics) means a miser, a niggard ; an impious man who gives little or nothing to the Gods. The word is used also as the name of a class of envious demons watching over treasures, and as an epithet of the fiends who steal cows and hide them in mountain caverns.

12 *A horse's tail wast thou* : destroying thy enemies as easily as a horse sweeps away flies with his tail. Cf. I. 27.1.
The Seven Rivers : according to Professor Max Müller, the Indus, the five rivers of the Panjab (Vitastā, Asiknī, Paruṣṇī, Vipāś, Śutudrī) and the Sarasvatī. Lassen and Ludwig put the Kubhā in the place of the last-named.

14 This flight of Indra is frequently alluded to. It is said that he fled thinking that he had committed a great sin in killing Vṛtra.
Nine-and-ninety : used indefinitely for a great number..

1 *Fain for booty* : *gavyāntaḥ*, literally seeking or eager for kine, that is, booty or wealth consisting chiefly of cattle.

3 *Be thou no trafficker with us* : Do not deal illiberally with us like a petty trader : do not give sparingly, nor demand too much in return.

4 *The wealthy Dasyu* : according to Sāyaṇa, 'Vṛtra the robber,' the withholder of the fertilizing rain. The Dasyus are also a class of demons, enemies of gods and men, and sometimes the word means a savage, a barbarian.

The ancient riteless ones : the followers of Vṛtra; here apparently identified with indigenous races who had not adopted, or were hostile to, the ritual of the Veda.
5 *The Stayer* : he who stands firm in battle. The word in the text *sthātar* appears to correspond exactly with the Latin Stator (Jupiter Stator). See Benfey, *Orient und Occident*, 1. 48.

When thou, fierce Lord of the Bay Steeds,
the Stayer, blewest from earth and
heaven and sky the godless.

6 They met in fight the army of the blameless : then the Navagvas put forth all
their power.
They, like emasculates with men contending, fled, conscious, by steep paths
from Indra, scattered.

7 Whether they weep or laugh, thou hast
o'erthrown them, O Indra, on the sky's
extremest limit.
The Dasyu thou hast burned from heaven,
and welcomed the prayer of him who
pours the juice and lauds thee.

8 Adorned with their array of gold and
jewels, they o'er the earth a covering
veil extended.
Although they hastened, they o'ercame not
Indra : their spies he compassed with
the Sun of morning.

9 As thou enjoyest heaven and earth, O
Indra, on every side surrounded with thy
greatness,
So thou with priests hast blown away the
Dasyu, and those who worship not with
those who worship.

10 They who pervaded earth's extremest limit
subdued not with their charms the
Wealth-bestower :
Indra, the Bull, made his ally the thunder, and with its light milked cows from
out the darkness.

11 The waters flowed according to their nature;
he mid the navigable streams waxed
mighty.
Then Indra, with his spirit concentrated,
smote him for ever with his strongest
weapon.

12 Indra broke through Ilībiśa's strong castles,
and Śuṣṇa with his horn he cut to
pieces :
Thou, Maghavan, for all his might and
swiftness, slewest thy fighting foeman
with thy thunder.

13 Fierce on his enemies fell Indra's weapon :
with his sharp bull he rent their forts
in pieces.
He with his thunderbolt dealt blows on
Vṛtra; and conquered, executing all
his purpose.

14 Indra, thou helpest Kutsa whom thou
lovedst, and guardedst brave Daśadyu
when he battled.
The dust of trampling horses rose to heaven, and Śvitrā's son stood up again
for conquest.

15 Śvitrā's mild steer, O Maghavan thou
helpest in combat for the land, mid
Tugra's houses.
Long stood they there before the task was
ended : thou wast the master of the
foemen's treasure.

HYMN XXXIV.   Aśvins.

1 Ye who observe this day be with us even
thrice : far-stretching is you bounty,
Aśvins and your course.
To you, as to a cloak in winter, we cleave
close : you are to be drawn nigh unto
us by the wise.

2 Three are the fellies in your honey-bearing
car, that travels after Soma's loved one,
as all know.
Three are the pillars set upon it for support:
thrice journey ye by night, O Aśvins,
thrice by day.

3 Thrice in the self-same day, ye Gods who
banish want, sprinkle ye thrice to-day our
sacrifice with meath ;

6 *The Navagvas* : the name of a mythological family
often associated with that of Aṅgiras, and described as
sharing in Indra's battles, regulating the worship of the
Gods, etc.
8 *With the Sun of morning* : 'We revert here to the
allegory. The followers of Vṛtra are here said to be
the shades of night which are dispersed by the rising of
the sun : according to the Brāhmaṇa "Verily the sun,
when he rises in the east, drives away the Rākṣasas."
                                                        Wilson
10 *Milked cows* : struck the cloud with his lightning,
and made the milky streams of fertilizing rain flow forth.
12 *Ilībiśa's strong castles* : Ilībiśa is said by Sāyaṇa to
be Vṛtra 'who sleeps in caverns of the earth.' Probably
one of the confederate demons is intended.
Śuṣṇa with his horn : the demon of drought, 'furnished',

says the Scholiast, 'with weapons like the horns of bulls
and buffaloes.' The meaning of 'horned' or 'with his
horn' is simply 'mighty', the horn being used, as in
Hebrew potery, as the emblem of strength.
13 *With his sharp bull* : the rushing thunderbolt.
14 *Kutsa* said to have been a Ṛṣi or seer, founder
of a religious family or school, and elsewhere spoken of
as the particular friend of Indra.
Daśadyu, is also said to have been a Ṛṣi, but nothing
is known of him. The same may be said of Śvaitreya or
Śvitrya, the son of a woman named Śvitrā.
15 The meaning of *tugryāsu* in the text is not clear.
Sāyaṇa explains it by 'in the waters;' Benfey translates
'among Tugra's daughters,' and the Petersburg Lexicon
takes it to mean 'among the families of the Tugryans.'
Mild steer : strong but gentle son.

1 *Be present with us even thrice* ; that is, at all the
three daily sacrifices.
2 *Soma* : is here the Moon. His darling is Jyotsnā
or Kaumudi Moonlight, identified with Sūryā, the light
borrowed from the Sun.

And thrice vouchsafe us store of food with plenteous strength, at evening, O ye Aśvins, and at break of day.

4 Thrice come ye to our home, thrice to the righteous folk, thrice triply aid the man who well deserves your help.

Thrice, O ye Aśvins, bring us what shall make us glad ; thrice send us store of food as nevermore to fail.

5 Thrice, O ye Aśvins, bring to us abundant wealth : thrice in the Gods' assembly, thrice assist our thoughts.

Thrice, grant ye us prosperity, thrice grant us fame ; for the Sun's daughter hath mounted your three-wheeled car.

6 Thrice, Aśvins, grant to us the heavenly medicines, thrice those of earth and thrice those that the waters hold.

Favour and health and strength bestow upon my son ; triple protection, Lords of Splendour, grant to him.

7 Thrice are ye to be worshipped day by day by us : thrice, O ye Aśvins, ye travel around the earth.

Car-borne from far away, O ye Nāsatyas, come, like vital air to bodies, come ye to the three.

8 Thrice, O ye Aśvins, with the Seven Mother Streams; three are the jars, the triple offering is prepared.

Three are the worlds, and moving on above the sky ye guard the firm-set vault of heaven through days and nights.

9 Where are the three wheels of your triple chariot, where are the three seats thereto firmly fastened ?

When will ye yoke the mighty ass that draws it, to bring you to our sacrifice. Nāsatyas ?

10 Nāsatyas, come : the sacred gift is offered up; drink the sweet juice with lips that know the sweetness well.

Savitar sends, before the dawn of day, your car, fraught with oil, various-coloured, to our sacrifice.

11 Come, O Nāsatyas, with the thrice-eleven Gods; come, O ye Aśvins, to the drinking of the meath.

Make long our days of life, and wipe out all our sins : ward off our enemies; be with us evermore.

12 Borne in your triple car, O Aśvins, bring us present prosperity with noble offspring.

I cry to you who hear me for protection : be ye our helpers where men win the booty.

HYMN XXXV.   *Savitar.*

1 AGNI I first invoke for our prosperity; I call on Mitra, Varuṇa, to aid us here.

I call on Night who gives rest to all moving life; I call on Savitar the God to lend us help.

2 Throughout the dusky firmament advancing, laying to rest the immortal and the mortal,

Borne in his golden chariot he cometh, Savitar, God who looks on every creature.

3 The God moves by the upward path, the downward; with two bright Bays, adorable, he journeys.

Savitar comes, the God from the far distance, and chases from us all distress and sorrow.

4 His chariot decked with pearl, of various colours, lofty, with golden pole, the God hath mounted,

The many-rayed One, Savitar the holy, bound, bearing power and might, for darksome regions.

5 Drawing the gold-yoked car his Bays, white-footed, have manifested light to all the peoples.

Held in the lap of Savitar, divine One, all men, all beings have their place for ever.

6 Three heavens there are ; two Savitar's, adjacent : in Yama's world is one, the home of heroes.

---

5 *For the Sun's daughter.* Sūryā who is called the consort of the Aśvins.

7 *Nāsatyas* ; a common appellation of the Aśvins See 1. 3. 3.

To the three : to the three daily sacrifices.

8 *The Seven Mother Streams* : see I. 32. 12
Three are the jars : three sorts of pitchers, used to contain and pour out the Soma juice at the three daily sacrifices.

Three worlds : earth, middle air, and heaven.

9 *The mighty ass* : according to the *Nighaṇṭu* 'two asses are the steeds of the Aśvins.'

10 *Savitar* : implying that the Aśvins are to be worshipped with this hymn at dawn. Savitar is the Sun.

---

11 *The thrice-eleven Gods* : 'This is authority for the usual Paurāṇik enumeration of thirty-three deities, avowedly resting on Vedic texts. The list is, there, made up of the eight Vasus; eleven Rudras; twelve Ādityas, Prajāpati, and Vaṣaṭkāra.' Wilson.

---

6 *Two Savitar's* : heaven and earth, or the heaven of day and the heaven of night. *As on a linch-pin*; the linch-pin is the emblem of stability, retaining its position unchanged by the revolution of the wheels. So the Gods remain unmoved, unaffected by death or change, unlike the mortals who depart to the realm of Yama. See J. Ehni, Der Mythus des Yama, p. 115.

As on a linch-pin, firm, rest things immortal : he who hath known it let him here declare it.

7 He, strong of wing, hath lightened up the regions, deep-quivering Asura, the gentle Leader.
Where now is Sūrya, where is one to tell us to what celestial sphere his ray hath wandered ?

8 The earth's eight points his brightness hath illumined, three desert regions and the Seven Rivers.
God Savitar the gold-eyed hath come hither, giving choice treasures unto him who worships.

9 The golden-handed Savitar, far-seeing, goes on his way between the earth and heaven,
Drives away sickness, bids the Sun approach us, and spreads the bright sky through the darksome region.

10 May he, gold-handed Asura, kind Leader, come hither to us with his help and favour.
Driving off Rākṣasas and Yātudhānas, the God is present, praised in hymns at evening.

11 O Savitar, thine ancient dustless pathways are well established in the air's mid-region :
O God, come by those paths so fair to travel, preserve thou us from harm this day, and bless us.

HYMN XXXVI. *Agni.*

1 WITH words sent forth in holy hymns, Agni we supplicate, the Lord
Of many families who duly serve the Gods, yea, him whom others also praise.

2 Men have won Agni, him who makes their strength abound : we, with oblations, worship thee.
Our gracious-minded Helper in our deeds of might, be thou, O Excellent, this day.

3 Thee for our messenger we choose, thee, the Omniscient, for our Priest.
The flames of thee the mighty are spread wide around : thy splendour reaches to the sky.

4 The Gods enkindle thee their ancient messenger,—Varuṇa, Mitra, Aryaman.
That mortal man, O Agni, gains through thee all wealth, who hath poured offerings unto thee.

5 Thou, Agni, art a cheering Priest, Lord of the House, men's messenger :
All constant high decrees established by the Gods, gathered together, meet in thee.

6 In thee, the auspicious One, O Agni, youthfullest, each sacred gift is offered up :
This day, and after, gracious, worship thou our Gods, that we may have heroic sons.

7 To him in his own splendour bright draw near in worship the devout.
Men kindle Agni with their sacrificial gifts, victorious o'er the enemies.

8 Vṛtra they smote and slew, and made the earth and heaven and firmament a wide abode.
The glorious Bull, invoked, hath stood at Kaṇva's side : loud neighed the Steed in frays for kine.

9 Seat thee, for thou art mighty ; shine, best entertainer of the Gods.
Worthy of sacred food, praised Agni ! loose the smoke, ruddy and beautiful to see.

10 Bearer of offerings, whom, best sacrificing Priest, the Gods for Manu's sake ordained ;
Whom Kaṇva, whom Medhyātithi made the source of wealth, and Vṛṣan and Upastuta.

11 Him, Agni, whom Medhyātithi, whom Kaṇva kindled for his rite,
Him these our songs of praise, him, Agni, we extol : his powers shine out preëminent.

7 *He, strong of wing :* (*suparṇáḥ*) an epithet or a name of the Sun, *Asura :* the immortal and divine One.
9 *Bids the Sun approach us :* Sāyaṇa says 'approaches the Sun', and observes that although Savitar and the Sun are the same as regards their divinity, yet they are two different forms, and therefore one may be said to go to the other.
10 *Yātudhānas :* a class of demons or evil spirits, much like Rākṣasas, but more particularly practisers of sorcery.

This Hymn and the twelve following are ascribed to Kaṇva, a very celebrated Ṛṣi who is called the son of Ghora and is said to belong to the family of Aṅgiras.

5 The preservation of the whole world rests, according to the Vedic view, on the sacrifices offered by men, as these give the Gods strength and enable them to perform their duties.
8 *The glorious Bull :* the mighty Agni, strong as a bull and impetuous as a war horse, has aided his favourite Kaṇva in battle.
10 *Medhyātithi :* Sāyaṇa takes this word to be an epithet of Kaṇva, 'entertainer of guests who are worthy of sacrificial food.' But it appears to be the name of a Ṛṣi of Kaṇva's family, the seer of twenty-eight hymns of Book VIII. and IX.
Vṛṣan and Upastuta : rendered by Wilson, after Sāyaṇa, 'Indra and some other worshipper,' are also apparently the names of two other Ṛṣis.

12 Make our wealth perfect thou, O Agni,
  Lord divine : for thou hast kinship with
  the Gods.
  Thou rulest as a King o'er widely-famous
  strength : be good to us, for thou art
  great.

13 Stand up erect to lend us aid, stand up
  like Savitar the God :
  Erect as strength-bestower we call aloud,
  with unguents and with priests, on thee.

14 Erect, preserve us from sore trouble; with
  thy flame burn thou each ravening
  demon dead.
  Raise thou us up that we may walk and
  live : so thou shalt find our worship
  mid the Gods.

15 Preserve us, Agni, from the fiend, preserve
  us from malicious wrong.
  Save us from him who fain would injure
  us or slay, Most Youthful, thou with
  lofty light.

16 Smite down as with a club, thou who
  hast fire for teeth, smite thou the wicked,
  right and left.
  Let not the man who plots against us in
  the night, nor any foe prevail o'er us.

17 Agni hath given heroic might to Kaṇva,
  and felicity :
  Agni hath helped our friends, hath helped
  Medhyātithi, hath helped Upastuta to
  win.

18 We call on Ugradeva, Yadu, Turvaśa,
  by means of Agni, from afar;
  Agni, bring Navavāstva and Bṛhadratha,
  Turvīti, to subdue the foe.

19 Manu hath stablished thee a light, Agni,
  for all the race of men :
  Sprung from the Law, oil-fed, for Kaṇva
  hast thou blazed, thou whom the people
  reverence.

20 The flames of Agni full of splendour and
  of might are fearful, not to be approached.
  Consume for ever all demons and sorcerers, consume thou each devouring fiend.

HYMN XXXVII.   *Maruts.*

1 SING forth, O Kaṇvas, to your band of
  Maruts unassailable,
  Sporting, resplendent on their car :

2 They who, self-luminous, were born together, with the spotted deer,
  Spears, swords, and glittering ornaments.

3 One hears, as though 'twere close at hand,
  the cracking of the whips they hold ;
  They gather glory on their way.

4 Now sing ye forth the God-given hymn
  to your exultant Marut host,
  The fiercely-vigorous, the strong.

5 Praise ye the Bull among the cows ; for
  'tis the Maruts' sportive band :
  It strengthened as it drank the rain.

6 Who is your mightiest, Heroes, when, O
  shakers of the earth and heaven,
  Ye shake them like a garment's hem ?

7 At your approach man holds him down
  before the fury of your wrath :
  The rugged-jointed mountain yields.

8 They at whose racings forth the earth,
  like an age-weakened lord of men,
  Trembles in terror on their ways.

9 Strong is their birth : vigour have they
  to issue from their Mother ; strength,
  Yea, even twice enough, is theirs.

10 And these, the Sons, the Singers, in their
  racings have enlarged the bounds,
  So that the kine must walk knee-deep.

11 Before them, on the ways they go, they
  drop this offspring of the cloud,
  Long, broad, and inexhaustible.

---

13 *Stand up erect* : Agni, as erect, is identified by
Sāyaṇa with the *yūpa* or sacrificial post to which the
victims, at an animal sacrifice, were bound. Accordingly
he takes *añjibhiḥ* to mean 'with unguents' wherewith the
post was anointed. This word may however refer to the
ornaments—another signification of the word—worn by
the ministering priests.

17 *Agni hath helped our friends* : Sāyaṇa takes *mitrā*
in the text as *mitrāṇi*, friends. Benfey and Ludwig consider it to mean, the former Mitra, and the latter the
two Mitras i.e. Mitra and Varuṇa ; and they translate
respectively 'Agni and Mitra protected.' and 'Agni, as
Mitra (and Varuṇa) hath favoured.'

18 Turvaśa and Yadu are frequently mentioned together as eponymi of tribes of those names. The poet
appears to pray for the return of Navavāstva, whoever
he may have been, to protect the heme attacked by the
Dasyus or robbers, and perhaps also to strengthen his
prayer by an appeal to the spirits of departed heroes.

20 *Demons and sorcerers* : Rākṣasas and evil spirits who
practise sorcery.

For an exhaustive explanation of this and other Hymns
to the Maruts, see M. Müller's Vedic Hymns, Part I.
(Sacred Books of the East, XXXII.)

5 *The Bull among the cows* : the band of Storm-Gods
preeminent among the clouds as a bull is among cows.

6 That is, where all are so mighty it would be superfluous to ask who is mightiest.
  Like a garment's hem : or, according to Sāyaṇa 'like
a tree's high top.

10 *The Singers* : the loud-voiced Maruts.
  The Maruts have spread themselves over the sky and
caused so much rain to fall that the cows in the pastures
are up to their knees in water. But see Ludwig, Ueber
die neuesten Arbeiten auf dem Gebiete der Ṛgveda-
rorachung. Prag. 1893.

12 O Maruts, as your strength is great, so
have ye cast men down on earth,
So have ye made the mountains fall.

13 The while the Maruts pass along, they talk
together on the way :
Doth any hear them as they speak ?

14 Come quick with swift steeds, for ye have
worshippers among Kaṇva's sons :
May you rejoice among them well.

15 All is prepared for your delight. We are
their servants evermore,
To live as long as life may last.

HYMN XXXVIII.   *Maruts.*

1 WHAT now ? When will ye take us by
both hands, as a dear sire his son,
Gods, for whom sacred grass is clipped ?

2 Now whither ? To what goal of yours
go ye in heaven, and not on earth ?
Where do your cows disport themselves ?

3 Where are your newest favours shown ?
Where, Maruts, your prosperity ?
Where all your high felicities ?

4 If, O ye Maruts, ye the Sons whom Pṛśni
bore, were mortal, and
Immortal he who sings your praise.

5 Then never were your praiser loathed
like a wild beast in pasture-land,
Nor should he go on Yama's path.

6 Let not destructive plague on plague hard
to be conquered, strike us down :
Let each, with drought, depart from us.

7 Truly, they the fierce and mighty Sons
of Rudra send their windless
Rain e'en on the desert places.

8 Like a cow the lightning lows and follows,
motherlike, her youngling,
When their rain-flood hath been loosened.

9 When they inundate the earth they spread
forth darkness e'en in day time,
With the water-laden rain-cloud.

10 O Maruts, at your voice's sound this
earthly habitation shakes,
And each man reels who dwells therein.

11 O Maruts, with your strong-hoofed steeds,
unhindered in their courses, haste
Along the bright embanked streams.

12 Firm be the fellies of your wheels, steady
your horses and your cars,
And may your reins be fashioned well.

13 Invite thou hither with this song, for
praise, Agni the Lord of Prayer,
Him who is fair as Mitra is.

14 Form in thy mouth the hymn of praise :
expand thee like a rainy cloud :
Sing forth the measured eulogy.

15 Sing glory to the Marut host, praiseworthy, tuneful, vigorous :
Here let the Strong Ones dwell with us.

HYMN XXXIX.   *Maruts.*

1 WHEN thus, like flame, from far away,
Maruts, ye cast your measure forth,
To whom go ye, to whom, O shakers of
the earth, moved by whose wisdom,
whose design ?

2 Strong let your weapons be to drive away
your foes, firm for resistance let them be.
Yea, passing glorious must be your warrior
might, not as a guileful mortal's strength.

3 When what is strong ye overthrow, and
whirl about each ponderous thing,
Heroes, your course is through the forest
trees of earth, and through the fissures
of the rocks.

---

2 *Where do your cows disport themselves ?* : perhaps, as
M. Müller suggests where tarry your herds ?' *viz.* the
clouds. Why do you remain in the sky, and not come
down to earth ? Or, according to Ludwig : 'Where
do the cows feed that are to supply milk and butter for
sacrifice to you ? Where is the place in which sacrifice
is to be offered to you ?'

5 *Like a wild beast* : or, unwelcome like a deer in the
home-pasture or meadow reserved for the cows.
Yama's path : the path that leads to Yama the God of
the Departed.

6 *Destructive plague* : nírṛtiḥ; sin. M. Müller.
Drought : greed. M. Müller.

7 *Sons of Rudra* : or 'dear to Rudra,' who is the
father of the Maruts.
Windless rain : steady rain, not blown away ; that
sinks into the ground; the wind generally ceasing as
soon as heavy rain begins to fall.

8 The thunder follows the lightning as a cow lowing
follows her calf.

13 *Agni, the Lord of Prayer* : 'Agni is frequently invoked together with the Maruts, and is even called marut-
sakhā, the friend of the Maruts, viii. 92.

14. It seems better, therefore, to refer brahmaṇaspatim
to Agni, than, with Sāyaṇa, to the host of the Maruts.
Brahmaṇaspati and Bṛhaspati are both varieties of Agni,
the priest and purohita of Gods and men, and as such
he is invoked together with the Maruts in other
passages, i. 40, 1. M. Müller.

14 *Expand thee* : addressed to the poet of the hymn.

15 *Tuneful* : so in I. 37. 10 'And these the Sons, the
Singers.' The song of the Maruts is the music or singing
of the winds.

---

1 *Maruts, ye cast your measure forth* : 'In this passage
we must take measure, not in the abstract sense, but as
a measuring line, which is cast forward to measure the
distance of an object, an image perfectly applicable to
the Maruts, who seem with their weapons to strike the
trees and mountains when they themselves are still far
off.' M. Müller.

4 Consumers of your foes, no enemy of
   yours is found in heaven or on the earth :
Ye Rudras, may the strength, held in this
   bond, be yours, to bid defiance even now.
5 They make the mountains rock and reel,
   they rend the forest-kings apart.
Onward, ye Maruts, drive, like creatures
   drunk with wine, ye Gods with all your
   company.
6 Ye to your chariot have yoked the spotted
   deer : a red deer, as a leader, draws.
Even the Earth herself listened as ye came
   near, and men were sorely terrified.
7 O Rudras, quickly we desire your succour
   for this work of ours.
Come to us with your aid as in the days
   of old, so now for frightened Kaṇva's
   sake.
8 Should any monstrous foe, O Maruts,
   sent by you or sent by mortals threaten
   us,
Tear ye him from us with your power and
   with your might, and with the succours
   that are yours.
9 For ye, the worshipful and wise, have guarded Kaṇva perfectly.
O Maruts, come to us with full protecting
   help, as lightning flashes seek the rain.
10 Whole strength have ye, O Bounteous
   Ones ; perfect, earth-shakers, is your
   might.
Maruts, against the poet's wrathful enemy
   send ye an enemy like a dart.

HYMN XL. *Brahmaṇaspati*

1 O BRAHMAṆASPATI, stand up : God-serving
   men, we pray to thee.
May they who give good gifts, the Maruts,
   come to us. Indra, most swift, be thou
   with them.
2 O Son of Strength, each mortal calls to
   thee for aid when spoil of battle waits
   for him.
O Maruts, may this man who loves you
   well obtain wealth of good steeds and
   hero might.

3 May Brahmanaspati draw nigh, may
   Sūnṛtā the Goddess come,
And Gods bring to this rite which gives
   the five-fold gift the Hero, lover of
   mankind.
4 He who bestows a noble guerdon on the
   priest wins fame that never shall decay.
For him we offer sacred hero-giving food,
   peerless and conquering easily.
5 Now Brahmaṇaspati speaks forth aloud the
   solemn hymn of praise,
Wherein Indra and Varuna, Mitra, Aryaman, the Gods, have made their dwelling
   place.
6 May we in holy synods, Gods ! recite
   that hymn, peerless, that brings felicity.
If you, O Heroes, graciously accept this
   word, may it obtain all bliss from you.
7 Who shall approach the pious ? who the
   man whose sacred grass is trimmed ?
The offerer with his folk advances more
   and more : he fills his house with precious
   things.
8 He amplifies his lordly might, with kings
   he slays : e'en mid alarms he dwells
   secure
In great or lesser fight none checks him,
   none subdues,—the wielder of the
   thunderbolt.

HYMN XLI.

Varuṇa, Mitra, Aryaman.

1 NE'ER is he injured whom the Gods
   Varuṇa, Mitra, Aryaman,
The excellently wise, protect.
2 He prospers ever, free from scathe, whom
   they, as with full hands, enrich,
Whom they preserve from every foe.

---

3 *May Sūnṛtā the Goddess come* : Sūnṛtā (Pleasantness) is, according to Sāyaṇa the Goddess of Speech
(Vāgdevatā) in the form of lover of truth.
   The fivefold gift : an offering of grain, gruel, curdled
milk, rice-cake, and curds.

4 *Sacred food* : *íḷā* or *íḍā*, sacrificial food, or a libation,
especially a holy libation coming between the Prayāja
and the Anuyāja the fore-sacrifice and the after-sacrifice;
the preliminary and the final offering.

5 *Now Brahmaṇaspati speaks forth* : 'Professor Roth
remarks : The thunder is his (Brahmaṇaspati's)
voice. The voice of thunder, again, as the voice of the
superintendent of prayer, is by a beautiful transference
brought into connection with the prayer which, spoken
on earth, finds, as it were, its echo in the heights of
heaven.' Muir *O. S. Texts*, V. p. 279. note.

8 *The wielder of the thunderbolt* : meaning, Sāyaṇa
says, Brahmaṇaspati, and so far identifying him with
Indra. Ludwig refers the expression to the pious sacrificer who is said to be armed, as it were, with Brahmaṇaspati's thunderbolt.

---

4 *Held in this bond* : together with your race. M.
Müller.

9 *As lightning-flashes seek the rain* : 'Lightning precedes the rain, and may therefore be represented as
looking about for the rain.' M. Müller.

---

1 *O Brahmaṇaspati* : Agni is sometimes called Brahmaṇaspati, or Lord of Prayer. See 1. 38. 13.

3 The Kings drive far away from him his
   troubles and his enemies,
   And lead him safely o'er distress.
4 Thornless, Ādityas, is the path, easy for
   him who seeks the Law:
   With him is naught to anger you.
5 What sacrifice, Ādityas, ye Heroes guide
   by the path direct,—
   May that come nigh unto your thought.
6 That mortal, ever unsubdued, gains wealth
   and every precious thing,
   And children also of his own.
7 How, my friends, shall we prepare
   Aryaman's and Mitra's laud,
   Glorious food of Varuṇa ?
8 I point not out to you a man who strikes
   the pious, or reviles :
   Only with hymns I call you nigh.
9 Let him not love to speak ill words : but
   fear the One who holds all four
   Within his hand, until they fall.

HYMN XLII.   *Puṣan.*

1 SHORTEN our ways, O Pūṣan, move aside
   obstruction in the path :
   Go close before us, cloud-born God.
2 Drive, Puṣan, from our road the wolf,
   the wicked inauspicious wolf,

3 *The Kings* : Varuṇa, Mitra, and Aryaman.
4 *Ādityas* : the three Gods named above, with others
See I. 14. 3.
9 *But fear the One who holds all four* : Wilson remarks :
'The text has *caturaś cid dadamānād vibhīyāṇ ā nidhātoḥ*,
he may fear from one holding four until the fall. The
meaning is supplied by the Scholiast with the assistance of
Yāska, *caturokṣān dhārayataḥ...kitavāt*, from a gambler
holding four dice...That is, where two men are playing
together, the man who has not the throw of the dice
is in anxious apprehension lest it should be against him.'
Benfey thinks that 'the holder of the four (dice)' is God
who holds in his hands and decides the destinies of man.
Ludwig maintains that there is no reference to dice,
either of gambling or destiny, and that 'the four' are
Varuṇa, Mitra, Bhaga, and Aryaman. The pious man
when he possesses these four as friends should fear to let
them go. Bergaigne (La Religion Vedique, III. 158)
is of opinion that the cords or nooses of Varuṇa, with
which he catches and punishes the wicked, are intended.

1 *Shorten our ways, O Pūṣan* : Pūṣan is usually a
synonym of the Sun; that is, he is one of the twelve
Ādityas. According to the tenour of this hymn, he is
the deity presiding especially over roads and journeyings.
Cloud-born : with reference, perhaps, to the close
connexion between nourishing the earth, which is one
of Puṣan's especial duties, and the cloud that gives the
necessary rain. But in Ṛgveda. VIII. 4. 15, 16, Pūṣan
is called *vimocana*, the deliverer, (from sin, according
to Sàyaṇa), and perhaps *vimuco napāt* may mean the
same thing. See Muir *O. S. Texts*, V. 175, where the
whole hymn is translated.
2 *The wolf* : *vṛka*=Swedish and Norwegian *varg*,
which signifies not only wolf, but also a wicked godless
man.

Who lies in wait to injure us.
3 Who lurks about the path we take, the
   robber with a guileful heart :
   Far from the road chase him away.
4 Tread with thy foot and trample out the
   firebrand of the wicked one,
   The double-tongued, whoe'er he be.
5 Wise Pūṣan, Wonder-Worker, we claim
   of thee now the aid wherewith
   Thou furtheredst our sires of old.
6 So, Lord of all prosperity, best wielder of
   the golden sword,
   Make riches easy to be won.
7 Past all pursuers lead us, make pleasant
   our path and fair to tread :
   O Pūṣan, find thou power for this.
8 Lead us to meadows rich in grass : send
   on our way no early heat :
   O Pūṣan, find thou power for this.
9 Be gracious to us, fill us full, give, feed
   us, and invigorate :
   O Pūṣan, find thou power for this.
10 No blame have we for Pūṣan; him we
   magnify with songs of praise:
   We seek the Mighty One for wealth.

HYMN XLIII.   *Rudra.*

1 WHAT shall we sing to Rudra, strong,
   most bounteous, excellently wise,
   That shall be dearest to his heart ?
2 That Aditi may grant the grace of Rudra
   to our folk, our kine,
   Our cattle and our progeny;
3 That Mitra and that Varuṇa, that Rudra
   may remember us,
   Yea, all the Gods with one accord.
4 To Rudra Lord of sacrifice, of hymns and
   balmy medicines,
   We pray for joy and health and strength.
5 He shines in splendour like the Sun, refulgent as bright gold is he,
   The good, the best among the Gods.
6 May he grant health into our steeds, well-
   being to our rams and ewes,
   To men, to women, and to kine.
7 O Soma, set thou upon us the glory of a
   hundred men,
   The great renown of mighty chiefs.

1 Rudra appears in this hymn as a gentle and beneficent deity, presiding especially over medicinal plants.
2 *That Aditi may grant the grace* : Aditi is said by
Sāyaṇa to mean here the earth, and is accordingly so
translated by Wilson. Benfey explains the word by
'Sinlessness,' and Ludwig takes it as a masculine deity
meaning Rudra himself.
6 *May he grant health* : here Rudra appears as *paśu-
pāti*, Lord and guardian of cattle.

8 Let not malignities, nor those who trouble
   Soma, hinder us.
   Indu, give us a share of strength.
9 Soma ! head, central point, love these ;
   Soma ! know these as serving thee,
   Children of thee Immortal, at the highest
   place of holy law.

HYMN XLIV.   *Agni.*

1 IMMORTAL Jātavedas, thou many-hued fulgent gift of Dawn,
   Agni, this day to him who pays oblations
   bring the Gods who waken with the
   morn.
2 For thou art offering-bearer and loved
   messenger, the charioteer of sacrifice :
   Accordant with the Aśvins and with Dawn
   grant us heroic strength and lofty fame.
3 As messenger we choose to-day Agni the
   good whom many love,
   Smoke-bannered spreader of the light, at
   break of day glory of sacrificial rites.
4 Him noblest and most youthful, richly-
   worshipped guest, dear to the men who
   offer gifts,
   Him, Agni Jātavedas, I beseech at dawn
   that he may bring the Gods to us.
5 Thee, Agni, will I glorify, deathless nourisher of the world,
   Immortal, offering-bearer, meet for sacred
   food, preserver, best at sacrifice.
6 Tell good things to thy praiser, O most
   youthful God, as richly worshipped,
   honey-tongued,
   And, granting to Praskaṇva lengthened
   days of life, show honour to the Heavenly Host.
7 For the men, Agni, kindle thee as all-
   possessor and as Priest ;

So Agni, much-invoked, bring hither with
   all speed the Gods, the excellently wise,
8 At dawn of day, at night, Uṣas and
   Savitar, the Aśvins, Bhaga, Agni's self :
   Skilled in fair rites, with Soma poured, the
   Kaṇvas light thee, the oblation-wafting
   God.
9 For, Agni, Lord of sacrifice and messenger
   of men art thou :
   Bring thou the Gods who wake at dawn,
   who see the light, this day to drink the
   Soma juice.
10 Thou shonest forth, O Agni, after former
   dawns, all visible, O rich in light.
   Thou art our help in battle-strife, the
   Friend of man, the great high priest in
   sacrifice.
11 Like Manu, we will stablish thee, Agni,
   performer of the rite,
   Invoker, ministering Priest, exceeding wise,
   the swift immortal messenger.
12 When as the Gods' High Priest, by
   many loved, thou dost their mission as
   their nearest Friend,
   Then, like the far-resounding billows of
   the flood, thy flames, O Agni, roar aloud.
13 Hear, Agni, who hast ears to hear, with
   all thy train of escort Gods ;
   Let Mitra, Aryaman, seeking betimes our
   rite, seat them upon the sacred grass.
14 Let those who strengthen Law, who
   bountifully give, the life-tongued Maruts,
   hear our praise.
   May Law-supporting Varuṇa with the
   Aśvins twain and Uṣas, drink the Soma
   juice.

HYMN XLV   *Agni.*

1 WORSHIP the Vasus, Agni ! here, the
   Rudras, the Ādityas, all
   Who spring from Manu, those who know
   fair rites, who pour their blessings down.

---

8 *Those who trouble Soma* : probably the people of the
hills who interfere with the gathering of the Soma plant
which has to be sought there.
Indu : literally 'drop;' from the same root as Indra,
the Rainer; a name of the Moon as rain-giver, and of
Soma which is identified with it.
9 *At the highest place of holy law* : at the place where
sacrifice is duly performed. 'The whole verse is difficult, possibly a later addition.' Max Müller.

This Hymn and the six following are ascribed to the
Ṛ i Praskaṇva, the son of Kaṇva who is the seer of the
preceding group.
1 *Immortal Jātavedas* : Jātavedas is a common epithet
of Agni, the meaning of which is explained in five ways;
1. 'knowing all created beings; 2. possessing all creatures; 3. known by created beings; 4. possessing riches;
5. possessing wisdom.'
2 *The Aśvins* : see I.3.1.
Dawn : the Goddess Uṣas ; Morning personified.

11 *Like Manu* : the representative man and father
of the human race and the first institutor of religious
ceremonies.
12 *Of the flood* : or of Sindhu; the word meaning
either that river (the Indus) in particular, or any river
or gathering of waters in general.
13 *Let Mitra, Aryaman* : and Varuṇa, understood.
14 *The fire-tongued Maruts* : who consume the
sacrifice by means of the tongue-like flames of Agni.

---

1 *Vasus, Rudras, Ādityas* : three classes of Gods
who make up almost the whole number of the thirty-
three deities spoken of in the next stanza.
Who spring from Manu : Manu appears here as
Prajāpati, the progenitor of Gods as well as of men.

2 Agni, the Gods who understand give ear
  unto the worshipper :
  Lord of Red Steeds, who lovest song,
  bring thou those Three-and-Thirty
  Gods.
3 O Jātavedas, great in act, hearken thou
  to Praskaṇva's call,
  As Priyamedha erst was heard, Atri,
  Virūpa, Aṅgiras.
4 The sons of Priyamedha skilled in lofty
  praise have called for help
  On Agni who with fulgent flame is Ruler
  of all holy rites.
5 Hear thou, invoked with holy oil, bountiful giver of rewards,
  These eulogies, whereby the sons of Kaṇva
  call thee to their aid.
6 O Agni, loved by many, thou of fame
  most wondrous, in their homes
  Men call on thee whose hair is flame, to
  be the bearer of their gifts.
7 Thee, Agni, best to find out wealth, most
  widely famous, quick to hear,
  Singers have stablished in their rites
  Herald and ministering Priest.
8 Singers with Soma pressed have made
  thee, Agni, hasten to the feast,
  Great light to mortal worshipper, what
  time they bring the sacred gift.
9 Good, bounteous, Son of Strength, this
  day seat here on sacred grass the Gods
  Who come at early morn, the host of
  heaven, to drink the Soma juice.
10 Bring with joint invocations thou, O Agni,
   the celestial host :
   Here stands the Soma, bounteous Gods :
   drink this expressed ere yesterday.

HYMN XLVI.   Aśvins.

1 Now Morning with her earliest light shines
  forth, dear Daughter of the Sky :
  High, Aśvins, I extol your praise,
2 Sons of the Sea, mighty to save discoverers of riches, ye

2 *Lord of Red Steeds* : Agni, whose horses are
flames of fire.
Three-and-Thirty Gods : see I. 34. 11.
3 Priyamedha, Atri, and Virūpa are famous
Ṛsis, the seers of many hymns of the Ṛgveda. Aṅgiras has already been mentioned. See I. 1. 6.
9 *Son of Strength* : made or generated by strong
friction; 'kindled through agitation to a flame'.
10 *Expressed ere yesterday* : prepared two days
before in order that the juice might ferment before
it was used.

1 *Morning* : Uṣas or Dawn, personified as a
Goddess.
Aśvins : see I. 3. 1.
2 *Sons of the Sea* : offspring of the celestial
ocean, the atmosphere.

Gods with deep thought who find out
wealth.
3 Your giant coursers hasten on over the
  region all in flames,
  When your car flies with winged steeds.
4 He, liberal, lover of the flood, Lord of the
  House, the vigilant,
  Chiefs ! with oblations feeds you full.
5 Ye have regard unto our hymns, Nāsatyas,
  thinking of our words :
  Drink boldly of the Soma juice.
6 Vouchsafe to us, O Aśvin Pair, such
  strength as, with attendant light,
  May through the darkness carry us.
7 Come in the ship of these our hymns to
  bear you to the hither shore :
  O Aśvins, harness ye the car.
8 The heaven's wide vessel is your own : on
  the flood's shore your chariot waits :
  Drops, with the hymn, have been prepared.
9 Kaṇvas, the drops are in the heaven; the
  wealth is at the waters' place :
  Where will ye manifest your form ?
10 Light came to lighten up the branch, the
   Sun appeared as it were gold :
   And with its tongue shone forth the dark.
11 The path of sacrifice was made to travel
   to the farther goal :

4 *He, liberal, lover of the flood* : evidently Agni
and not the Sun. Agni's connexion with water is
frequently alluded to, and he is often called the Lord
and Guardian of the house or family.
6 *The darkness* : in the shape of poverty or want
according to the Scholiast.
7 The poet appears to invite the Aśvins to yoke
their chariot for part of the journey and come to
meet his hymn which shall bear them as in a ship
through the sky. The middle air or atmosphere is the
sea between heaven and earth, and the earth is the
hither shore.
8 *Vessel* : (*aritram*). a vehicle in the shape of a
ship, says Sāyaṇa. You have already the ship of our
songs to bear you through the sky, and now your
chariot has reached the earth and the place where, together with this hymn, the Soma juice has been prepared for a libation to you.
9 The drops, or Soma libation, and the wealth
or treasure, and the sky and the place of rivers appear
here to be parallelisms, both pairs of expressions signifying the same thing. The oblation is said to have already 1 ached the heaven where the Aśvins will receive
it. Sāyaṇa's paraphrase which Wilson has followed, seems
forced and unnatural. 'Kaṇvas, (ask this of the
Aśvins): (How) do the rays (of the sun proceed)
from the sky ? : (How) does the dawn (rise) in the
region of the waters ?
10 *Light came to lighten up the branch* : the branch
is probably the sacrificial fire. Cf. 'The other fires are
verily thy branches' (I. 59. 1). The epithet 'dark'
may refer to the darkening of the fire by the sunlight
or by the smoke.
11 Sacrifice is the path which leads the Gods
from heaven to earth, and the way through heaven is
made visible by the sacrificial fire or by the daylight.

The road of heaven was manifest.

12 The singer of their praise awaits whatever
grace the Aśvins give,
Who save when Soma gladdens them.

13 Ye dwellers with Vivasvān come, auspicious, as to Manu erst;
Come to the Soma and our praise.

14 O circumambient Aśvins, Dawn follows the
brightness of your way :
Approve with beams our solemn rites.

15 Drink ye of our libations, grant protection,
O ye Aśvins Twain,
With aids which none may interrupt.

HYMN XLVII.   *Aśvins.*

1 Aśvins, for you who strengthen Law this
sweetest Soma hath been shed.
Drink this expressed ere yesterday and
give riches to him who offers it.

2 Come, O ye Aśvins, mounted on your
triple car three-seated, beautiful of
form
To you at sacrifice the Kaṇvas send the
prayer : graciously listen to their call.

3 O Aśvins, ye who strengthen Law, drink
ye this sweetest Soma juice.
Borne on your wealth-fraught car come
ye this day to him who offers, ye of
wondrous deeds.

4 Omniscient Aśvins, on the thrice-heaped
grass bedew with the sweet juice the
sacrifice.
The sons of Kaṇva, striving heavenward,
call on you with draughts of Soma juice
out-poured.

5 O Aśvins, with those aids wherewith ye
guarded Kaṇva carefully,
Keep us, O Lords of Splendour : drink
the Soma juice, ye strengtheners of holy
law.

6 O Mighty Ones, ye gave Sudās abundant
food, brought on your treasure-laden
car ;
So now vouchsafe to us the wealth which
many crave, either from heaven or from
the sea.

7 Nāsatyas, whether ye be far away or close
to Turvaśa,
Borne on your lightly-rolling chariot come
to us, together with the sunbeams come.

8 So let your coursers, ornaments of sacrifice,
bring you to our libations here.
Bestowing food on him who acts and gives
aright, sit, Chiefs, upon the sacred grass.

9 Come, O Nāsatyas, on your car decked
with a sunbright canopy,
Whereon ye ever bring wealth to the worshipper, to drink the Soma's pleasant
juice.

10 With lauds and songs of praise we call
them down to us, that they, most rich,
may succour us;
For ye have ever in the Kaṇvas' well-
loved house, O Aśvins, drunk the Soma
juice.

HYMN XLVIII.   *Dawn.*

1 DAWN on us with prosperity, O Uṣas,
Daughter of the Sky,
Dawn with great glory, Goddess, Lady of
the Light, dawn thou with riches,
Bounteous One.

2 They, bringing steeds and kine, boon-
givers of all wealth, have oft sped
forth to lighten us.
O Uṣas, waken up for me the sounds of
joy : send us the riches of the great.

3 Uṣas hath dawned, and now shall dawn,
the Goddess, driver forth of cars
Which, as she cometh nigh, have fixed
their thought on her, like glory-seekers
on the flood.

4 Here Kaṇva, chief of Kaṇva's race, sings
forth aloud the glories of the heroes'
names,—
The princes who, O Uṣas, as thou comest
near, direct their thoughts to liberal
gifts.

5 Like a good matron Uṣas comes carefully
tending everything :
Rousing all life she stirs all creatures that
have feet, and makes the birds of air
fly up.

6 She sends the busy forth, each man to his

---

10 *With lauds* : *ukthébhiḥ,* answering, according to
Sāyaṇa, to what in the Brāhmaṇa is called Śastram (to
be recited by the Hotar) while the Stoma (stotram)
song, is sung by the Sāma-priests.

1 *Uṣas* : Morning, Dawn, personified.

2 *They* : the Dawns of preceding days.

3 The approach of Dawn sets cars or wains in
motion in the same way as it causes ships or boats
that have anchored during the night to move out to the
open water.

4. *The princes* are the wealthy patrons or institutors of sacrifice, who bear all expenses and remunerate
the priests.

---

13 *Vivasvān* : the 'Brilliant,' a name of the morning heaven personified. He is regarded as the father
of Yama, Manu, and the Aśvins. See X. 17. 2 note.

---

6 *Sudās* : a king, the son of Pijavana. See VII.
18. 5-25.

7 *Nāsatyas* : Aśvins. See I. 3. 3.
Turvaśa : the tribe or family called after the chief
of this name, frequently mentioned in the Ṛgveda.
See I. 36. 18.

pursuit : delay she knows not as she springs.

O rich in opulence, after thy dawning birds that have flown forth no longer rest.

7 This Dawn hath yoked her steeds afar, beyond the rising of the Sun :

Borne on a hundred chariots she, auspicious Dawn, advances on her way to men.

8 To meet her glance all living creatures bend them down : Excellent One, she makes the light.

Uṣas, the Daughter of the Sky, the opulent, shines foes and enmities away.

9 Shine on us with thy radiant light, O Uṣas, Daughter of the Sky,

Bringing to us great store of high felicity, and beaming on our solemn rites.

10 For in thee is each living creature's breath and life, when, Excellent ! thou dawnest forth.

Borne on thy lofty car, O Lady of the Light, hear, thou of wondrous wealth, our call.

11 O Uṣas, win thyself the strength which among men is wonderful.

Bring thou thereby the pious unto holy rites, those who as priests sing praise to thee.

12 Bring from the firmament, O Uṣas, all the Gods, that they may drink our Soma juice,

And, being what thou art, vouchsafe us kine and steeds, strength meet for praise and hero might.

13 May Uṣas whose auspicious rays are seen resplendent round about,

Grant us great riches, fair in form, of all good things, wealth which light labour may attain.

14 Mighty One, whom the Ṛṣis of old time invoked for their protection and their help,

O Uṣas, graciously answer our songs of praise with bounty and with brilliant light.

15 Uṣas, as thou with light to day hast opened the twin doors of heaven,

So grant thou us a dwelling wide and free from foes. O Goddess, give us food with kine.

16 Bring us to wealth abundant, sent in every shape, to plentiful refreshing food,

To all-subduing splendour, Uṣas, Mighty One, to strength, thou rich in spoil and wealth.

HYMN XLIX.   *Dawn.*

1 E'EN from above the sky's bright realm come, Uṣas, by auspicious ways :

Let red steeds bear thee to the house of him who pours the Soma juice.

2 The chariot which thou mountest, fair of shape, O Uṣas light to move,—

Therewith, O Daughter of the Sky, aid men of noble fame today.

3 Bright Uṣas, when thy times return, all quadrupeds and bipeds stir,

And round about flock winged birds from all the boundaries of heaven.

4 Thou dawning with thy beams of light illumest all the radiant realm.

Thee, as thou art, the Kaṇvas, fain for wealth, have called with sacred songs.

HYMN L.   *Sūrya.*

1 His bright rays bear him up aloft, the God who knoweth all that lives,

Sūrya, that all may look on him.

2 The constellations pass away, like thieves, together with their beams,

Before the all-beholding Sun.

3 His herald rays are seen afar refulgent o'er the world of men,

Like flames of fire that burn and blaze.

4 Swift and all beautiful art thou, O Sūrya, maker of the light,

Illuming all the radiant realm.

5 Thou goest to the hosts of Gods, thou comest hither to mankind,

Hither all light to be beheld.

6 With that same eye of thine wherewith thou lookest, brilliant Varuṇa,

Upon the busy race of men,

7 Traversing sky and wide mid-air, thou metest with thy beams our days,

Sun, seeing all things that have birth.

8 Seven Bay Steeds harnessed to thy car bear thee, O thou farseeing One,

God, Sūrya, with the radiant hair.

9 Sūrya hath yoked the pure bright Seven, the daughters of the car ; with these,

His own dear team, he goeth forth.

---

1 *Let red steeds bear thee* : the Scholiast explains *aruṇḍpsavaḥ* as the purple cows, the vehicles of morning, that is, the dark red clouds that accompany the dawn.

1 *The God who knoweth all that live* : *jātavedasam,* here an epithet of Sūrya the Sun-God.

6 *Varuṇa* : the word is, as Sāyaṇa points out, used here as an appellative (the encompasser) and applied to Sūrya. Sāyaṇa explains it as *aniṣṭan vāraka,* averter of evil.

9 *Sūrya hath yoked the pure bright Seven* : the seven steeds that draw his car, and which, as intimately connected therewith, are called the daughters of the chariot. The number seven has reference to the seven days of the week.

10 Looking upon the loftier light above the darkness we have come
To Sūrya, God among the Gods, the light that is most excellent.

11 Rising this day, O rich in friends, ascending to the loftier heaven,
Sūrya, remove my heart's disease, take from me this my yellow hue.

12 To parrots and to starlings let us give away my yellowness,
Or this my yellowness let us transfer to Haritāla trees.

13 With all his conquering vigour this Āditya hath gone up on high,
Giving my foe into mine hand : let me not be my foeman's prey.

HYMN LI.   *Indra.*

1 MAKE glad with songs that Ram whom many men invoke, worthy of songs of praise, Indra, the sea of wealth;
Whose gracious deeds for men spread like the heavens abroad : sing praise to him· the Sage, most liberal for our good.

2 As aids the skilful Ṛbhus yearned to Indra strong to save, who fills mid-air, encompassed round with might,

Rushing in rapture; and ·o'er Śatakratu came the gladdening shout that urged him on to victory.

3 Thou hast disclosed the kine's stall for the Aṅgirases, and made a way for Atri by a hundred doors.
On Vimada thou hast bestowed both food and wealth, making thy bolt dance in the sacrificer's fight.

4 Thou hast unclosed the prisons of the waters; thou hast in the mountain seized the treasure rich in gifts.
When thou hadst slain with might the dragon Vṛtra, thou, Indra, didst raise the Sun in heaven for all to see.

5 With wondrous might thou blewest enchanter fiends away, with powers celestial those who called on thee in jest.
Thou, hero-hearted, hast broken down Pipru's forts, and helped Ṛjiśvan when the Dasyus were struck dead.

6 Thou savedst Kutsa when Śuṣṇa was smitten down; to Atithigva gavest Śambara for a prey.
E'en mighty Arbuda thou troddest under foot : thou from of old wast born to strike the Dasyus dead.

7 All power and might is closely gathered up in thee; thy bounteous spirit joys in drinking Soma juice.

---

11 'This verse and the two following constitute a *ṭṛca* or triplet, the repetition of which, with due formalities, is considered to be curative of disease,' Wilson.

12 The yellowness here spoken of is probably the colour of the skin in jaundice. The *hāridravā* of the text is said by Sāyaṇa to mean *haritāladruma*, a haritāla tree ; but there seems to be no tree of that name. *Haritāla*, means, usually, yellow orpiment, and *haridrava* a yellow vegetable powder. The word *hāridrava* is explained in the Petersburg Lexicon as a certain yellow bird.

To parrots and to starlings : similarly among the Romans, People with the jaundice were called 'icterici' according to Pliny (H.N. xxx. II), from the fanciful notion that the disease was cured by looking at the icterus, one of the many varieties of the sturnidae or starling family. The bird was said to die instead of the patient.

This hymn and the six following are attributed to the Ṛṣi Savya, who is called the son of Aṅgiras.

1 *That Ram* : that famous ram, Indra. See I. 10. 2. Here the reference is to a fighting-ram; or, according to Sāyaṇa, to a legend which says that Indra came in the form of a ram to Medhātithi's sacrifice, and drank the Soma juice.

2 *The skilful Ṛbhus* : see I. 20. 1. Sāyaṇa says that the Maruts are here intended, who encouraged Indra when all the Gods had deserted him.

Rushing in rapture : when exhilarated by. draughts of Soma.

'Here again,' says Professor Max Müller, 'the difficulty of rendering Vedic thought in English, or any other modern language, becomes apparent, for we have no poetical word to express·a high state of mental excitement produced by drinking the intoxicating juice

of the Soma or other plants, which has not something opprobrious mixed up with it, while in ancient times tha⁺ state of excitement was celebrated as a blessing of the gods, as not unworthy of the gods themselves, nay, as a state in which both the warrior and the poet would perform their highest achievements. The German *Rausch* is the nearest approach to the Sanskrit mada.'

In this version *mada* has generally been rendered by rapture, delight, transport, or wild joy.

Śatakratu : Indra. See I. 4. 8.

The kine's stall : the dark cloud that holds the waters imprisoned.

The Aṅgirases : an ancient priestly family. See I. I. 6.

Atri : a Ṛṣi usually enumerated with the Aṅgirases among the *prajāpatis* or progenitors of men. Indra freed him from captivity, showing him a hundred ways of escape. *Vimada* was also a Ṛṣi of ancient times.

4. *The mountain* : the cloud. *The treasure* is the fertilizing rain.

Didst raise the Sun : according to Sāyaṇa, didst free the Sun which had been hidden by Vṛtra.

5. *Those who called on thee in jest* : literally, called on thee or offered to thee above or over the shoulder, apparenⁱly an ancient proverbial expression applied to those who instead of sacrificing to the Gods put the intended oblation into their own mouths.

Pipru is one of the demons of the air; his *forts* are the clouds that withhold the rain; *Ṛjiśvan* is a pious worshipper oppressed by the Dasyus, robbers or barbarians.

6. *Śuṣṇa*, 'the Drier-up,' is the personification of the excessive heat before the rains ; a demon of drought. *Śambara* and *Arbuda* are similar demons of the atmosphere. *Atithigva* is another name of the liberal prince Divodāsa.

Known is the thunderbolt that lies within thine arms : rend off therewith all manly prowess of our foe.

8 Discern thou well Āryas and Dasyus; punishing the lawless give them up to him whose grass is strewn.

Be thou the sacrificer's strong encourager : all these thy deeds are my delight at festivals.

9 Indra gives up the lawless to the pious man, destroying by the Strong Ones those who have no strength.

Vamra when glorified destroyed the gathered piles of the still waxing great one who would reach the heaven.

10 The might which Uśanā hath formed for thee with might rends in its greatness and with strength both worlds apart.

O Hero-souled, the steeds of Vāta, yoked by thought, have carried thee to fame while thou art filled with power.

11 When Indra hath rejoiced with Kāvya Uśanā, he mounts his steeds who swerve wider and wider yet.

The Strong hath loosed his bolt with the swift rush of rain, and he hath rent in pieces Śuṣṇa's firm-built forts.

12 Thou mountest on thy car amid strong Soma draughts : Śāryāta brought thee those in which thou hast delight.

Indra, when thou art pleased with men whose Soma flows thou risest to unchallenged glory in the sky.

13 To old Kakṣivān, Soma-presser, skilled in song, O Indra, thou didst give the youthful Vṛcayā.

Thou, very wise, wast Menā, Vrsanaśva's child : those deeds of thine must all be told at Soma feasts.

14 The good man's refuge in his need is Indra, firm as a doorpost, praised among the Pajras.

Indra alone is Lord of wealth, the Giver, lover of riches, chariots, kine, and horses.

15 To him the Mighty One, the self-resplendent, verily strong and great, this praise is uttered.

May we and all the heroes, with the princes, be, in this fray, O Indra, in thy keeping.

HYMN LII. *Indra.*

1 I GLORIFY that Ram who finds the light of heaven, whose hundred nobly-natured ones go forth with him.

With hymns may I turn hither Indra to mine aid,—the Car which like a strong steed hasteth to the call.

2 Like as a mountain on firm basis, unremoved, he, thousandfold protector, waxed in mighty strength,

When Indra, joying in the draughts of Soma juice, forced the clouds, slaying Vṛtra stayer of their flow.

3 For he stays e'en the stayers, spread o'er laden cloud, rooted in light, strengthened in rapture by the wise.

---

8 The Āryas are, first, the people who speak the language of the Veda, and the Dasyus are the original and hostile peoples of India. Later, the former and the true and loyal people, faithful to Indra and the Gods, and the latter are the wicked and godless.

Whose grass is strewn : the faithful worshipper, the priest who has trimmed and strewn the sacred grass for the Gods.

9 *Vamra* : the second half of the stanza is unintelligible. Wilson remarks : 'The text is obscure, *Vamro vi jaghāna sandihaḥ*; Vamra destroyed the collection. The Scholiast says that a Ṛṣi named Vamra took advantage of Indra's absence from sacrifice, to carry away the accumulated heap of offerings.

10 The Ṛṣi Uśanā, called also Kāvya or Kavi's son, appears in the Veda as the especial friend of Indra. In I. 121, 12. he is said to have given Indra, his thunderbolt: 'The bolt which Kāvya Uśanā erst gave thee.' Here, also, 'the might' means the conquering thunderbolt, although in other places its fabrication is attributed to Tvaṣṭar.

The steeds of Vāta : horses of the Wind-God, horses swift as wind.

11 *When Indra hath rejoiced*: drunk the exhilarating Soma.

12 *Śāryāta* : a Rājarṣi or royal Ṛṣi of the family of Bhṛgu.

Brought thee those : draughts of Soma juice.

Thou risest to unchallenged glory : when thou hast exhilarated thyself with the Soma offered by thy worshippers thou performest thy most glorious deeds.

13 *Kakṣivān* : a Ṛṣi, son of Uśij. See I. 18. 1. *Vṛcayā*, the damsel who was given to him, is not mentioned elsewhere.

Menā : according to a later legend, Indra became, himself, the daughter of Vṛsanaśva.

14 *Among the Pajras* : an ancient priestly family said to be identical with the Aṅgirases.

15 *In this fray* : the hymn appears to have been addressed to Indra for aid in a coming battle.

1 *That Ram* : that famous warrior. See I. 51. 1. *Whose hundred nobly-natured ones* : see verse 4.

3 *For he stays e'en the stayers* : the words of the text *sá hi dvaro dvariṣu vavrá ūdhani*, are very difficult. Sāyaṇa's paraphrase, adopted by Wilson, is loose but seems to give the general sense of the passage. 'He who is victorious over his enemies, who is spread through the dewy (firmament)' 'The stayer among the stayers,' is probably the conqueror who checks the demons who obstruct the rain, and *ūdhan*, the udder (of the sky) means the rain-giving clouds, over which Indra, as God of the firmament, is extended as a covering.

Indra with thought, with skilled activity,
I call, most liberal giver, for he sates
him with the juice.

4 Whom those that flow in heaven on sacred grass, his own assistants, nobly-natured, fill full like the sea,—
Beside that Indra when he smote down Vrtra stood his helpers, straight in form, mighty, invincible.

5 To him, as in wild joy he fought with him who stayed the rain, his helpers sped like swift streams down a slope,
When Indra, thunder-armed, made bold by Soma draughts, as Trta cleaveth Vala's fences, cleft him through.

6 Splendour encompassed thee, forth shone thy warrior might : the rain-obstructer lay in mid-air's lowest deep,
What time, O Indra, thou didst cast thy thunder down upon the jaws of Vritra hard to be restrained.

7 The hymns which magnify thee, Indra, reach to thee even as water-brooks flow down and fill the lake.
Tvaṣṭar gave yet more force to thine appropriate strength, and forged thy thunderbolt of overpowering might.

8 When, Indra, thou whose power is linked with thy Bay Steeds hadst smitten Vrtra, causing floods to flow for man,
Thou heldst in thine arms the metal thunderbolt, and settest in the heaven the Sun for all to see.

9 In fear they raised the lofty self-resplendent hymn, praisegiving and effectual, leading up to heaven,
When Indra's helpers fighting for the good of men, the Maruts, faithful to mankind, joyed in the light.

10 Then Heaven himself, the mighty, at that Dragon's roar reeled back in terror when, Indra, thy thunderbolt
In the wild joy of Soma had struck off

with might the head of Vrtra, tyrant of the earth and heaven.

11 O Indra, were this earth extended forth tenfold, and men who dwell therein multiplied day by day,
Still here thy conquering might, Maghavan, would be famed : it hath waxed vast as heaven in majesty and power.

12 Thou, bold of heart, in thine own native might, for help, upon the limit of this mid-air and of heaven,
Hast made the earth to be the pattern of thy strength : embracing flood and light thou reachest to the sky.

13 Thou art the counterpart of earth, the Master of lofty heaven with all its mighty Heroes :
Thou hast filled all the region with thy greatness : yea, of a truth there is none other like thee.

14 Whose amplitude the heaven and earth have not attained, whose bounds the waters of mid-air have never reached,—
Not, when in joy he fights the stayer of the rain : thou, and none else, hast made all things in order due.

15 The Maruts sang thy praise in this encounter, and in thee all the Deities delighted,
What time thou, Indra, with thy spiky weapon, thy deadly bolt, smotest the face of Vrtra.

HYMN LIII. *Indra.*

1 WE will present fair praise unto the Mighty One, our hymns to Indra in Vivasvān's dwelling-place;
For he hath ne'er found wealth in those who seem to sleep : those who give wealth to men accept no paltry praise.

2 Giver of horses, Indra, giver, thou, of kine, giver of barley, thou art Lord and guard of wealth :
Man's helper from of old, not disappointing hope, Friend of our friends, to thee as such we sing this praise.

---

4 *His own assistants* : the inspiring Soma draughts.

5 *His helpers* : his constant allies, the Maruts.

As Trta cleaveth : Sāyaṇa refers to a legend which says that Trta fell into a well, and the Asuras heaped coverings over its mouth ; but he broke through them with ease. So Indra broke down the defences of the demon Vala. See Wilson's note on the passage.

But Trta appears to be Indra's associate Agni. See Macdonell, J.R.A.S. July, 1893.

6 *The rain-obstructer* : the demon Vrtra.

7 *Tvaṣṭar* : the Vulcan or Hephaestus of the Indian Gods.

8 *The metal thunderbolt* : *vájram áyasám*, usually translated 'iron thunderbolt'; but we do not know for certain what metal *áyas* (Latin aes) was.

9 *In fear they raised* : that is, Indra's worshippers in fear of Vrtra.

11 If the earth were ten times as large and populous as it is, thy fame would extend over the whole of it.

14 *The waters of mid-air* : the aerial ocean the firmament.

He fights : said of Indra. We should expect 'thou fightest;' but this and similar sudden changes of person are common in the Veda.

1 *Vivasvān's dwelling-place* : the seat of the sacrificer, the representative of the celestial Vivasvān.

Those who seem to sleep : Indra derives no advantage from those who are remiss in their religious duties.

3 Indra most splendid, powerful, rich in
   mighty deeds, this treasure spread around is known to be thine own.
   Gather therefrom, O Conqueror, and bring
   to us : fail not the hope of him who
   loves and sings to thee.

4 Well pleased with these bright flames and
   with these Soma drops, take thou away
   our poverty with seeds and kine.
   With Indra scattering the Dasyu through
   these drops, freed from their hate may
   we obtain abundant food.

5 Let us obtain, O Indra, plenteous wealth
   and food, with strength exceeding glorious, shining to the sky :
   May we obtain the Goddess Providence,
   the strength of heroes, special source
   of cattle, rich in steeds.

6 These our libations strength-inspiring,
   Soma draughts, gladdened thee in the
   fight with Vṛtra, Hero Lord,
   What time thou slewest for the singer
   with trimmed grass ten thousand Vṛtras,
   thou resistless in thy might.

7 Thou goest on from fight to fight intre-
   pidly, destroying castle after castle here
   with strength.
   Thou, Indra, with thy friend who
   makes the foe bow down, slewest from
   far away the guileful Namuci.

8 Thou hast struck down in death Karañja,
   Parṇaya, in Atithigva's very glorious
   going forth.
   Unyielding, when Ṛjiśvan compassed them
   with siege, thou hast destroyed the hundred forts of Vaṅgṛida.

9 With all-outstripping chariot-wheel, O
   Indra, thou far-famed, hast overthrown
   the twice ten Kings of men,
   With sixty thousand nine-and-ninety followers, who came in arms to fight with
   friendless Suśravas.

10 Thou hast protected Suśravas with succour,
   and Tūrvayāṇa with thine aid, O
   Indra.
   Thou madest Kutsa, Atithigva, Āyu, subject
   unto this King, the young, the mighty.

6 *Ten thousand Vṛtras* : countless demons like
Vṛtra.

7 *With thy friend* : the thunderbolt. Or *nāmyā*
may mean 'with Nami' as thy confederate.
Namuci : 'non-looser (of the heavenly waters)''
another demon of drought.

8 *Karañja*, *Parṇaya* and *Vaṅgṛda* are Asuras or
demons; *Atithigva* has been mentioned before, I. 51.
6, and Ṛjiśvan in verse 5 of the same hymn.

9 *Suśravas*, and *Tūrvayāṇa* in the next verse, are
said to be kings.

11 May we protected by the Gods hereafter
   remain thy very prosperous friends, O
   Indra.
   Thee we extol, enjoying through thy favour
   life long and joyful and with store of
   heroes.

HYMN LIV.   *Indra.*

1 URGE us not, Maghavan, to this distress-
   ful fight, for none may comprehend the
   limit of thy strength.
   Thou with fierce shout hast made the
   woods and rivers roar : did not men run
   in crowds together in their fear?

2 Sing hymns of praise to Śakra, Lord of
   power and might ; laud thou and magnify Indra who heareth thee,
   Who with his daring might, a Bull exceeding strong in strength, maketh him
   master of the heaven and earth.

3 Sing forth to lofty Dyaus a strength-bestowing song, the Bold, whose resolute
   mind hath independent sway.
   High glory hath the Asura, compact of
   strength, drawn on by two Bay Steeds :
   a Bull, a Car is he.

4 The ridges of the lofty heaven thou madest
   shake ; thou, daring, of thyself smotest
   through Śambara,
   When bold with gladdening juice, thou
   warredst with thy bolt, sharp and two-
   edged, against the banded sorcerers.

10 *Kutsa* has been mentioned (I. 33. 14.) as a
favourite of Indra, but is here represented, together
with Atithigva and Āyu, as chastised by him.
   This King : Suśravas, or Turvayāṇa these names
perhaps denote the same individual.

—

1 *Urge us not, Maghavan* : the verb, urge, which
is not in the text, is supplied by Sāyaṇa. The meaning appears to be, Do not, O Indra, force us into any
conflict in which we may have thee for our opponent.

2 *Śakra* : 'the Mighty,' a name of Indra.

3 *Sing forth to lofty Dyaus* : Heaven. The God
who is represented in the Veda as the consort of Earth
and the progenitor of the Gods is called Dyaus or
Dyauṣpitar, names identical in origin with Zeus, or
Zeus, pater, and Jupiter, or Diespiter, the appellations
given to the supreme God of the Greeks and Romans.
In this place Sāyaṇa identifies Dyaus with Indra, who
seems, in later times, to have succeeded to the functions
assigned to the former God. See Muir, *Original Sanskrit Texts*, v. 33.
   The Asura : the divine One, Indra as the supreme
Dyaus.

4 *Śambara* : a demon. See I. 51. 6.
   The banded sorcerers : the fiends of the atmosphere
who use enchantments or supernatural powers in their
conflicts with Indra.

5 When with a roar that fills the woods,
thou forcest down on wind's head the
stores which Śuṣṇa kept confined,
Who shall have power to stay thee firm
and eager-souled from doing still this
day what thou of old hast done?

6 Thou helpest Narya, Turvaśa, and Yadu,
and Vayya's son Turvīti, Śatakratu !
Thou helpest horse and car in final battle ;
thou breakest down the nine-and-ninety
castles.

7 A hero-lord is he, King of a mighty folk,
who offers free oblations and promotes
the Law,
Who with a bounteous guerdon welcomes
hymns of praise : for him flows down
the abundant stream below the sky.

8 His power is matchless, matchless is his
wisdom; chief, through their work, be
some who drink the Soma,
Those, Indra, who increase the lordly
power, the firm heroic strength of thee
the Giver.

9 Therefore for thee are these abundant
beakers Indra's drink, stone-pressed juices
held in ladles.
Quaff them and satisfy therewith thy
longing; then fix thy mind upon bestowing treasure.

10 There darkness stood, the vault that stayed
the waters' flow: in Vṛtra's hollow side
the rain-cloud lay concealed.
But Indra smote the rivers which the obstructer stayed, flood following after
flood, down steep declivities.

11 So give us, Indra, bliss-increasing glory ;
give us great sway and strength that
conquers people.
Preserve our wealthy patrons, save our
princes ; vouchsafe us wealth and food
with noble offspring.

HYMN LV.   *Indra.*

1 Though e'en this heaven's wide space and
earth have spread them out, nor heaven
nor earth may be in greatness Indra's
match.
Awful and very mighty, causing woe to

men, he whets his thunderbolt for sharp-
ness, as a bull.

2 Like as the watery ocean, so doth he receive the rivers spread on all sides in their
ample width.
He bears him like a bull to drink of Soma
juice, and will, as Warrior from of old,
be praised for might.

3 Thou swayest, Indra, all kinds of great
manly power, so as to bend, as't were,
even that famed mountain down.
Foremost among the Gods is he through
hero might, set in the van, the Strong
One, for each arduous deed.

4 He only in the wood is praised by worshippers, when he shows forth to men
his own fair Indra-power.
A friendly Bull is he, a Bull to be desired
when Maghavan auspiciously sends forth
his voice.

5 Yet verily the Warrior in his vigorous
strength stirreth up with his might great
battles for mankind ;
And men have faith in Indra, the resplendent One, what time he hurleth down
his bolt, his dart of death.

6 Though, fain for glory, and with strength
increased on earth, he with great might
destroys the dwellings made with art,
He makes the lights of heaven shine forth
secure, he bids, exceeding wise, the
floods flow for his worshipper.

7 Drinker of Soma, let thy heart incline to
give ; bring thy Bays hitherward, O
thou who hearest praise.
Those charioteers of thine, best skilled to
draw the rein, the rapid sunbeams,
Indra, lead thee not astray.

8 Thou bearest in both hands treasure that
never fails ; the famed One in his body
holds unvanquished might.

---

5 *Śuṣṇa* : a demon of drought.

6 *Thou helpest Narya* : some chief or Ṛṣi so named
or the word may be an adjective, manly, qualifying
Turvaśa.

Turvaśa, Yadu, Turvīti have been mentioned before.
See I. 36. 18.

—

1 *As a bull* : as a bull sharpens his horns.
Causing woe to men : as the punisher of the wicked.

4 *A friendly Bull is he* : Maghavan, the mighty
Indra, is here represented in his gracious mood, strong
yet gentle. But *vṛṣā*, the male, the bull, the strong,
may also mean the strong Soma; *maghávā* means also
the rich institutor of a sacrifice, a worshipper; and *dhenā*
means cow as well as voice. Accordingly Professor
Max Müller translates the passage : 'The strong Soma
is pleasing, the strong Soma is delicious, when the
sacrificer safely brings the cow', in order that the Soma
may be mixed with milk. See *Vedic Hymns*, Part I., p.
148.

In the wood, in the first line of the verse seems to
be an allusion to the forest life of Brāhmans.

5 In this verse Indra is represented as a terrible
God, and in the following verse as sometimes sending
affliction' but generally blessing men with light and
with kindly rain.

O Indra, in thy members many powers abide, like wells surrounded by the ministering priests.

HYMN LVI. *Indra.*

1 For this man's full libations held in ladles, he hath roused him, eager, as a horse to meet the mare.
He stays his golden car, yoked with Bay Horses, swift, and drinks the Soma juice which strengthens for great deeds.

2 To him the guidance-following songs of praise flow full, as those who seek gain go in company to the flood.
To him the Lord of power, the holy synod's might, as to a hill, with speed, ascend the loving ones.

3 Victorious, great is he ; in manly battle shines, unstained with dust, his might, as shines a mountain peak ;
Wherewith the iron one, fierce e'en against the strong, in rapture, fettered wily Śushṇa fast in bonds.

4 When Strength the Goddess, made more strong for help by thee, waits upon Indra as the Sun attends the Dawn,
Then he who with his might unflinching kills the gloom stirs up the dust aloft, with joy and triumphing.

5 When thou with might, upon the framework of the heaven, didst fix, across, air's region firmly, unremoved,
In the light-winning war, Indra, in rapturous joy, thou smotest Vṛtra dead and broughtest floods of rain.

6 Thou with thy might didst grasp the holder-up of heaven, thou who art mighty also in the seats of earth.
Thou, gladdened by the juice, hast set the waters free, and broken Vṛtra's stony fences through and through.

1. *This man* : the institutor of the sacrifice. *He* : Indra.
2. *The flood ·* (*samudrá*) any large gathering of waters not necessarily the sea or ocean.
The holy synod : an assembly for worship of the Gods.
The loving ones : the songs of loving praise. I find the stanza unintelligible; and the version (based chiefly on Grassmann's) which I offer is merely a temporary makeshift.
3. *The iron one* : the thunderbolt, made o *áyas*, iron or other metal.
4. *By thee* : by Soma.
5. *In the light-winning war* : waged with the demons of the air for rain and the light which follows the dispersion of the clouds.
6. *The holder-up of heaven* : perhaps the thunderbolt, with which Indra maintains order.

HYMN LVII. *Indra.*

1 To him most liberal, lofty Lord of lofty wealth, verily powerful and strong, I bring my hymn,—
Whose checkless bounty, as of waters down a slope, is spread abroad for all that live, to give them strength.

2 Now all this world, for worship, shall come after thee—the offerer's libations like floods to the depth,
When the well-loved one seems to rest upon the hill, the thunderbolt of Indra, shatterer wrought of gold.

3 To him the terrible, most meet for lofty praise, like bright Dawn, now bring gifts with reverence in this rite,
Whose being, for renown, yea, Indra-power and light, have been created, like bay steeds, to move with speed.

4 Thine, Indra, praised by many, excellently rich ! are we who trusting in thy help draw near to thee.
Lover of praise, none else but thou receives our laud : as earth loves all her creatures, love thou this our hymn.

5 Great is thy power, O Indra, we are thine. Fulfil, O Maghavan, the wish of this thy worshipper.
After thee lofty heaven hath measured out its strength : to thee and to thy power this earth hath bowed itself.

6 Thou, who hast thunder for thy weapon, with thy bolt hast shattered into pieces this broad massive cloud.
Thou hast sent down the obstructed floods that they may flow : thou hast, thine own for ever, all victorious might.

HYMN LVIII. *Agni.*

1 Ne'er waxeth faint the Immortal, Son of Strength, since he, the Herald, hath become Vivasvān's messenger.
On paths most excellent he measured out

2. *When the well-loved one* : when the lightning-laden cloud is resting on the mountain, men pray to Indra in order that he may discharge his celestial artillery and bring down the rain.
5. *After thee* : the heaven has taken thy might as a pattern for its own might.

———

This Hymn and the five following are ascribed to Nodhas, the son of Gotama.
1. *Vivasvān's messenger* : Vivasvān is the morning heaven and personification of the sacrificer of the Gods.
He measured out mid-air : this act is ascribed to Indra in I. 56. 5.

mid-air: he with oblation calls to service of the Gods.

2 Never decaying, seizing his appropriate food, rapidly, eagerly through the dry wood he spreads.

His back, as he is sprinkled, glistens like a horse : loud hath he roared and shouted like the heights of heaven?

3 Set high in place o'er all that Vasus, Rudras do, immortal, Lord of riches, seated as High Priest ;

Hastening like a car to men, to those who live, the God without delay gives boons to be desired.

4 Urged by the wind he spreads through dry wood as he lists, armed with his tongues for sickles, with a mighty roar.

Black is thy path, Agni, changeless, with glittering waves ! when like a bull thou rushest eager to the trees.

5 With teeth of flame, wind-driven, through the wood he speeds, triumphant like a bull among the herd of cows,

With bright strength roaming to the ever-lasting air : things fixed, things moving quake before him as he flies.

6 The Bhṛgus established thee among man-kind for men, like as a treasure, beau-teous, easy to invoke;

Thee, Agni, as a herald and choice-worthy guest, as an auspicious Friend to the Celestial Race.

7 Agni, the seven tongues' deftest Sacrificer, him whom the priests elect at solemn worship,

The Herald, messenger of all the Vasus, I serve with dainty food, I ask for riches.

8 Grant, Son of Strength, thou rich in friends, a refuge without a flaw this day to us thy praisers.

O Agni, Son of Strength, with forts of iron preserve thou from distress the man who lauds thee.

9 Be thou a refuge, Bright One, to the singer, a shelter, Bounteous Lord, to those who worship.

Preserve the singer from distress, O Agni. May he, enriched with prayer, come soon and early.

HYMN LIX.   Agni.

1 THE other fires are, verily, thy branches; the Immortals all rejoice in thee, O Agni.

Centre art thou, Vaiśvānara, of the people, sustaining men like a deep-founded pillar.

2 The forehead of the sky, earth's centre, Agni became the messenger of earth and heaven.

Vaiśvānara, the Deities produced thee, a God, to be a light unto the Ārya.

3 As in the Sun firm rays are set for ever, treasures are in Vaiśvānara, in Agni.

Of all the riches in the hills, the waters, the herbs, among mankind, thou art the Sovran.

4 As are the great World-halves, so are their Son's praises ; skilled, as a man, to act, is he the Herald.

Vaiśvānara, celestial, truly mighty, most manly One, hath many a youthful con-sort.

5 Even the lofty heaven, O Jātavedas Vaiśvānara, hath not attained thy great-ness.

Thou art the King of lands where men are settled, thou hast brought comfort to the Gods in battle.

6 Now will I tell the greatness of the Hero whom Pūru's sons follow as Vṛtra's slayer:

Agni Vaiśvānara struck down the Dasyu, cleave Śambara through and shattered down his fences.

---

2 *As he is sprinkled* : with clarified butter.

3 *Vasus, Rudras* : two classes of Gods. See I. 34. 11.

4 The description of Agni in this verse and the next applies, not to the sacrificial fire, but to the fire that clears the jungle as the new settlers advance into the country.

6 *The Bhṛgus* : one of the most eminent priestly families of more ancient times.

Friend to the Celestial Race : as bearing to the Gods the oblations of their worshippers.

7 *Agni, the seven tongues' deftest Sacrificer* : the seven tongues appear to be the tongue-like flames which Agni employs to consume the oblations.

1 *Thy branches* : merely offshoots of thee.

Vaiśvānara : a name of Agni; common to, dwell-ing with, and benefiting all Ārya men.

4 Vast as heaven and earth, which constitute the world, are the praises offered to Agni their son.

Skilled, as a man, to act : duties of the heavenly Hotar, invoking priest, or herald, being regarded as similar to those of the earthly functionary.

Many a youthful consort : the flames.

6 *Pūru's sons* : men in general ; Pūru being regarded as their progenitor.

Struck down the Dasyu : the demon who stayed the rain. The deeds usually ascribed to Indra are here attributed to Agni, that is, Agni is identified with Indra.

7 Vaiśvānara, dwelling by his might with all men, far-shining, holy mid the Bharadvājas,
Is lauded, excellent, with hundred praises by Purūṇītha, son of Śatavani.

HYMN LX. *Agni.*

1 As 'twere some goodly treasure Mātariśvan brought, as a gift, the glorious Priest to Bhṛgu,
Banner of sacrifice, the good Protector, child of two births, the swiftly moving envoy.

2 Both Gods and men obey this Ruler's order, Gods who are worshipped, men who yearn and worship.
As Priest he takes his seat ere break of morning, House-Lord, adorable with men, Ordainer.

3 May our fair praise, heart-born, most recent, reach him whose tongue, e'en at his birth, is sweet as honey ;
Whom mortal priests, men, with their strong endeavour, supplied with dainty viands, have created.

4 Good to mankind, the yearning Purifier hath among men been placed as Priest choice-worthy.
May Agni be our Friend, Lord of the Household, protector of the riches in the dwelling.

5 As such we Gotamas with hymns extol thee, O Agni, as the guardian Lord of riches,
Decking thee like a horse, the swift prize-winner. May he, enriched with prayer, come soon and early.

7 *The Bharadvājas* : the descendants of the Ṛṣi Bharadvāja.
Purūṇītha : a king of that name, says Sāyaṇa; probably the institutor of the sacrifice. The name does not occur again, and nothing is known regarding him.

---

1 *Mātariśvan* : a divine or semi-divine being, who as the messenger of Vivasvān brings down from heaven Agni who had hitherto been concealed. The explanation of Mātariśvan as Vāyu, the God of wind, does not appear to be justified by Ṛgveda texts. See Muir, *O. S. Texts*, v. 204.
The glorious Priest : Agni. *Bhṛgu* : the chief of the ancient priestly family who bear that name. *Banner of sacrifice* : announcer of sacrifice by his crackling flames. *Child of two births* : born of heaven and earth and again from the two fire-sticks, when he is consecrated. *Swiftly moving envoy* : messenger between Gods and men. See I.1. 1 note.
3 *Sweet as honey* : with tasting the sweet libations. *Have created* : by rapid agitation of the fire-stick.
5 *We Gotamas* : descendants of Gotama, men of the family to which the Ṛṣi of the hymn belongs.
Decking thee : trimming thee, to make thee shine as men groom a race-horse in the morning.

HYMN LXI *Indra.*

1 EVEN to him, swift, strong, and high-exalted, I bring my song of praise as dainty viands,
My thought to him resistless, praise-deserving, prayers offered most especially to Indra.

2 Praise, like oblation, I present, and utter aloud my song, my fair hymn to the Victor.
For Indra, who is Lord of old, the singers have decked their lauds with heart and mind and spirit.

3 To him then with my lips mine adoration, winning heaven's light, most excellent, I offer,
To magnify with songs of invocation and with fair hymns the Lord, most bounteous Giver.

4 Even for him I frame a laud, as fashions the wright a chariot for the man who needs it,—
Praises to him who gladly hears our praises, a hymn well-formed, all-moving, to wise Indra.

5 So with my tongue I deck, to please that Indra, my hymn, as 'twere a horse, through love of glory,
To reverence the Hero, bounteous Giver, famed far and wide, destroyer of the castles.

6 Even for him hath Tvaṣṭar forged the thunder, most deftly wrought, celestial, for the battle,
Wherewith he reached the vital parts of Vṛtra, striking—the vast, the mighty—with the striker.

7 As soon as, at libations of his mother, great Viṣṇu had drunk up the draught, he plundered.
The dainty cates, the cooked mess; but

---

4 *For the man who needs it* : and orders it to be made. *Tátsináya* is a difficult word. Wilson renders it, after Sāyaṇa, (that the driver) may, thence, (obtain) food.

5 *The castles* : the strongholds of the atmospheric demons of drought, the castles of rain-imprisoning cloud.

6 *The striker* : the thunderbolt or lightning.

7 *His mother* Indra's mother Aditi who gave him Soma to drink as soon as he was born. See III. 32. 9, 10; 48. 2. 3; VII. 98. 3. *Dainty cates* : the demon's store of rain. *One stronger* : the mightier Indra. *The wild boar* : the fierce demon Vṛtra. Cf. VIII. 66. 10. *The mountain* : the massive cloud in which Vṛtra was enveloped. For my corrected version of this stanza I am indebted to Prof. A.A. Macdonell's article on Mythological Studies in the Ṛgveda, Royal Asiatic Society Journal, January, 1895.

One stronger transfixed the wild boar, shooting through the mountain.

8 To him, to Indra, when he slew the Dragon, the Dames, too, Consorts of the Gods, wove praises.

The mighty heaven and earth hath he encompassed : thy greatness heaven and earth, combined, exceed not.

9 Yea, of a truth, his magnitude surpasseth the magnitude of earth, mid-air, and heaven.

Indra, approved by all men, self-resplendent, waxed in his home, loud-voiced and strong for battle.

10 Through his own strength Indra with bolt of thunder cut piece-meal Vṛtra, drier up of waters.

He let the floods go free, like cows imprisoned, for glory, with a heart inclined to bounty.

11 The rivers played, through his impetuous splendour, since with his bolt he compassed them on all sides.

Using his might and favouring him who worshipped, he made a ford, victorious, for Turvīti.

12 Vast, with thine ample power, with eager movement, against this Vṛtra cast thy bolt of thunder.

Rend thou his joints, as of an ox, dissevered, with bolt oblique, that floods of rain may follow.

13 Sing with new lauds his exploits wrought aforetime, the deeds of him, yea, him who moveth swiftly,

When, hurling forth his weapons in the battle, he with impetuous wrath lays low the foemen.

14 When he, yea, he, comes forth the firmset mountains and the whole heaven and earth, tremble for terror.

May Nodhas, ever praising the protection of that dear Friend, gain quickly strength heroic.

15 Now unto him of these things hath been given what he who rules alone o'er much, electeth.

Indra hath helped Etaśa, Soma-presser, contending in the race of steeds with Sūrya.

16 Thus to thee, Indra, yoker of Bay Coursers, the Gotamas have brought their prayers to please thee.

Bestow upon them thought, decked with all beauty. May he, enriched with prayer, come soon and early.

HYMN LXII.   *Indra.*

1. LIKE Aṅgiras a gladdening laud we ponder to him who loveth song, exceeding mighty.

Let us sing glory to the far-famed Hero who must be praised with fair hymns by the singer.

2 Unto the great bring ye great adoration, a chant with praise to him exceeding mighty,

Through whom our sires, Aṅgirases, singing praises and knowing well the places, found the cattle.

3 When Indra and the Aṅgirases desired it, Saramā found provision for her offspring.

Bṛhaspati cleft the mountain, found the cattle : the heroes shouted with the kine in triumph.

4 Mid shout, loud shout, and roar, with the

16 The hymn ends with the refrain that concludes also Hymns I. 58 and 60.

---

1 *Like Aṅgiras* : after the manner of Aṅgiras, one of the first institutors of religious ceremonies.

2 *Found the cattle* : the rain-clouds, or the rays of light which follow the effusion of rain.

3 *Saramā found provision for her offspring* : Saramā, the hound of Indra and mother of the two dogs called after their mother Sārameyas who are the watchdogs of Yama the God of the Dead, is said to have pursued and recovered the cows stolen by the Paṇis; which has been supposed to mean that Saramā is the Dawn who recovers the rays of the Sun that have been carried away by night. The legend says that Saramā agreed to go in search of the stolen cattle on condition that the milk of the cows should be given to her young ones. Ludwig is of opinion that the word 'offspring' in the text refers not to Saramā's young ones, but to the decandants of the Aṅgirases Cf. I. 72. 8.

Bṛhaspati cleft the mountain : Bṛhaspati or Brahamanaspati is the Lord of prayer. 'It is, therefore,' as Professor Roth observes, 'brahma, prayer, with which the God breaks open the hiding-place of the enemy. Prayer pierces through to the object of its desire, and attains it.'

4 The *seven singers* are probably the Aṅgirases themselves : the *Navagvas* and *Daśagvas* are also the Aṅgirases or their priestly allies. They are called *speeder* as hastily following the track of the stolen cows. *Vala* is the fiend who keeps the cows imprisoned.

8 *The Dames, the Consorts of the Gods* : according to Sāyaṇa these are the personified Gāyatrī and other metres of the Veda. The Celestial Waters are probably intended.

11. *Turvīti* : Sāyaṇa says that this Ṛṣi had been immersed in water, and that Indra brought him to dry land.

14 *Nodhas* : the Ṛṣi or seer of the hymn.

15 Praises and sacrifice have been offered to Indra. He himself possesses everything else. Such praises and sacrifice led Indra to help Etaśa, his worshipper, in his rivalry of Sūrya and his horses. See II. 19. 5, note.

Navagvas, seven singers, hast thou,
heavenly, rent the mountain;
Thou hast, with speeders, with Daśagvas,
Indra, Śakra, with thunder rent obstructive Vala.

5 Praised by Aṅgirases, thou, foe-destroyer,
hast, with the Dawn, Sun, rays, dispelled the darkness.
Thou Indra, hast spread out the earth's
high ridges, and firmly fixed the region
under heaven.

6 This is the deed most worthy of all honour,
the fairest marvel of the Wonder-Worker,
That, nigh where heaven bends down, he
made four rivers flow full with waves
that carry down sweet water.

7 Unwearied, won with lauding hymns, he
parted of old the ancient Pair, united
ever.
In highest sky, like Bhaga, he the doer of
marvels set both Dames and earth and
heaven.

8 Still born afresh, young Dames, each in
her manner, unlike in hue, the Pair in
alternation
Round heaven and earth from ancient
time have travelled, Night with her
dark limbs, Dawn with limbs of splendour.

9 Rich in good actions, skilled in operation,
the Son with might maintains his perfect
friendship.
Thou in the raw cows, black of hue or
ruddy, storest the ripe milk glossy white
in colour.

10 Their paths, of old connected, rest uninjured; they with great might preserve the
immortal statutes.

6 *Nigh where heaven bends down* : flowing away to
the distant horizon. The *four rivers* are not specified
by Sāyaṇa, who merely says they are the Ganges and
others.

7 *The ancient Pair* : Heaven and Earth. *Bhaga* is
here the Supreme God. *Both Dames* : Night and
Morning.

9 *The Son with might* : Sāyaṇa takes *śdvasā*, 'with
might,' in the sense of the genitive *śdvasaḥ*, and explains : the Son of Might, that is the exceedingly strong
one. But this seems forced. *The son* is Indra.
Thou in the raw cows : the cows are called raw, as
contrasted with the warm milk matured or cooked in
their udders. The colour of the milk is also contrasted
with that of the cows, as in the German child's ditty
quoted by Zimmer: 'O sage mir, wie geht es zu, gibt
weisse Milch die rothe Kuh.'

10 *Their paths* : the courses of Night and Morning.
The Sisters : a frequently occurring appellation of
the fingers as employed in acts of worship. *The haughty
Lord* : Indra.

For many thousand holy works the Sisters
wait on the haughty Lord like wives
and matrons.

11 Thoughts ancient, seeking wealth, with
adoration, with newest lauds have sped
to thee, O Mighty.
As yearning wives cleave to their yearning
husband, so cleave our hymns to thee,
O Lord most potent.

12 Strong God, the riches which thy hands
have holden from days of old have perished not nor wasted.
Splendid art thou, O Indra, wise, unbending : strengthen us with might, O Lord
of Power.

13 O mighty Indra, Gotama's son Nodhas
hath fashioned this new prayer to thee
Eternal,
Sure leader, yoker of the Tawny Coursers.
May he, enriched with prayer, come
soon and early.

HYMN LXIII.   *Indra.*

1. Thou art the Mighty One ; when born, O
Indra, with power thou terrifiedst earth
and heaven;
When, in their fear of thee, all firm-set
mountains and monstrous creatures shook
like dust before thee.

2 When thy two wandering Bays thou dravest hither, thy praiser laid within thine
arms the thunder,
Wherewith, O Much-invoked, in will resistless, thou smitest foemen down and
many a castle.

3 Faithful art thou, these thou defiest, Indra;
thou art the Ṛbhus' Lord, heroic, victor.
Thou, by his side, for young and glorious
Kutsa, with steed and car in battle
slewest Śuṣṇa,

4 That, as a friend, thou furtheredst, O Indra,
when, Thunderer, strong in act, thou
crushedst Vṛtra ;
When, Hero, thou, great-souled, with easy
conquest didst rend the Dasyus in their
distant dwelling.

2 *Thy praiser* : the praises of the worshipper strengthen Indra, and urge him to the performance of glorious
exploits.

3 *The Ṛbhus' Lord* : Chief over the three semi-
divine beings who by their good works raised themselves
to immortality and godhead. See I. 20. *Kutsa* : has
been mentioned before as protected by Indra. See I.
33. 14; 51. 6.

4 *Dasyus* : hostile demons, or perhaps savage
tribes.

5 This doest thou, and art not harmed, O
  Indra, e'en in the anger of the strongest
  mortal.
  Lay thou the race-course open for our
  horses : as with a club, slay, Thunder-
  armed ! our foemen.
6 Hence men invoke thee, Indra, in the
  tumult of battle, in the light-bestowing
  conflict.
  This aid of thine, O Godlike One, was
  ever to be implored in deeds of might
  in combat.
7 Warring for Purukutsa thou, O Indra,
  Thunder-armed ! breakest down the
  seven castles ;
  Easily, for Sudās, like grass didst rend them,
  and out of need, King, broughtest gain
  to Pūru.
8 O Indra, God who movest round about
  us, feed us with varied food plenteous as
  water—
  Food wherewithal, O Hero, thou bestowest
  vigour itself to flow to us for ever.
9 Prayers have been made by Gotamas, O
  Indra, addressed to thee, with laud for
  thy Bay Horses.
  Bring us in noble shape abundant riches.
  May he, enriched with prayer, come
  soon and early.

HYMN LXIV.   *Maruts.*

1. BRING for the manly host, wise and majes-
   tical, O Nodhas, for the Maruts bring
   thou a pure gift.
   I deck my songs as one deft-handed, wise
   in mind prepares the water that hath
   power in solemn rites.
2 They spring to birth, the lofty Ones, the
  Bulls of Heaven, divine, the youths of
  Rudra, free from spot and stain;
  The purifiers, shining brightly even as
  suns, awful of form like giants, scattering
  rain-drops down.

3 Young Rudras, demon-slayers, never growing old, they have waxed, even as mountains, irresistible.
  They make all beings tremble with their
  mighty strength, even the very strongest,
  both of earth and heaven.
4 With glittering ornaments they deck them
  forth for show ; for beauty on their
  breasts they bind their chains of gold.
  The lances on their shoulders pound to
  pieces ; they were born together, of
  themselves, the Men of Heaven.
5 Loud roarers, giving strength, devourers
  of the foe, they make the winds, they
  make the lightnings with their powers.
  The restless shakers drain the udders of
  the sky, and ever wandering round fill
  the earth full with milk.
6 The bounteous Maruts with the fatness-
  dropping milk fill full the waters which
  avail in solemn rites.
  They lead, as 'twere, the Strong Horse
  forth, that it may rain: they milk the
  thundering, the never-failing spring.
7 Mighty, with wondrous power and marvellously bright, selfstrong like mountains, ye glide swiftly on your way.
  Like the wild elephants ye eat the forests
  up when ye assume your strength among
  the bright red flames.
8 Exceeding wise they roar like lions mightily, they, all-possessing, are beauteous
  as antelopes ;
  Stirring the darkness with lances and
  spotted deer, combined as priests, with
  serpents' fury through their might.
9 Heroes who march in companies, befriend-
  ing man, with serpents' ire through
  strength, ye greet the earth and heaven.
  Upon the seats, O Maruts, of your chariots,
  upon the cars stands lightning visible
  as light.

7 *Purukutsa* : a favourite of Indra and of the
Aśvins. See I. 112. 7; 174. 2; IV. 42. 8, note. *Sudās*
(See I. 47. 6) and *Pūru* are kings or chiefs of clans.
8 *Who movest round about us*; *párijman*, circumambient, is an epithet applied to the Sun also and to the
chariot of the Aśvins.
9 *With laud for thy Bay Horses* : this is clearly the
sense of the words as they stand. Sāyaṇa explains
'with reverence to thee connected with thy baẏ horses.'

———

1 *O Nodhas* : the Ṛṣi or seer of the hymn
addresses this line to Nodhas.
2 *The Bulls of Heaven* : or of Dyu or Dyaus.

3 *Young Rudras* : the Maruts, or Storm-Gods, are
the sons of Rudra.
Demon-slayers : slayers of the clouds that give no
rain.
4 *The lances*, as well as their other bright ornaments, are the lightning flashes.
5 *The udders of the sky* : the full clouds. *The milk*,
is the sweet fertilizing rain.
6 *The Strong Horse* : is the rain cloud, which in
the same line is called a spring or well.
8 *Combined as priests* : the music of wind and
storm being regarded as the Maruts' song of praise. But
the meaning of the words thus rendered is not clear.
Sāyaṇa, Benfey, and Max Müller give other interpretations.

10 Lords of all riches, dwelling in the home
   of wealth, endowed with mighty vigour,
   singers loud of voice,
   Heroes, of powers infinite, armed with
   strong men's rings, the archers, they
   have laid the arrow on their arms.
11 They who with golden fellies make the
   rain increase drive forward the big
   clouds like wanderers on the way.
   Self-moving, brisk, unwearied, they o'erthrow the firm; the Maruts with bright
   lances make all things to reel.
12 The progeny of Rudra we invoke with
   prayer, the brisk, the bright, the
   worshipful, the active Ones
   To the strong band of Maruts cleave for
   happiness, the chasers of the sky,
   impetuous, vigorous.
13 Maruts, the man whom ye have guarded
   with your help, he verily in strength
   surpasseth all mankind.
   Spoil with his steeds he gaineth, treasure
   with his men; he winneth honourable
   strength and prospereth.
14 O Maruts, to the worshippers give glorious
   strength invincible in battle, brilliant,
   bringing wealth,
   Praiseworthy, known to all men. May
   we foster well, during a hundred winters,
   son and progeny.
15 Will ye then, O ye Maruts, grant us riches,
   durable, rich in men, defying onslaught.
   A hundred, thousandfold, ever increasing?
   May he, enriched with prayer, come
   soon and early.

HYMN LXV.*   *Agni.*

1. ONE-MINDED, wise, they tracked thee like
   a thief lurking in dark cave with a stolen
   cow ;

10 *Armed with strong men's rings*: the meaning of
vṛṣakhādayaḥ is uncertain; but the *khādi* seems to have
been a ring worn on the arm and foot. It may
also have been used as a weapon, as the sharp-edged
quoits are used by the Sikhs. *Vṛṣan*, as Professor Max
Müller observes, 'conveys the meaning of strong, though
possibly with the implied idea of rain-producing, fertilizing'.

12 *The worshipful*: the meaning of *vaninam* is
uncertain. Wilson, after Sāyaṇa, translates it by 'water
shedding,' *vana* being said to mean water. Ludwig
suggests 'dwelling in the woods,' instead of 'fighting'
which he gives in his translation. 'Worshipful' is
Professor Max Müller's suggestion, and I adopt it for the
present.

15 *Enriched with prayer*: either, generally, invoked
by many worshippers, or rich through the hymn just
recited. This last hemistich is the usual refrain of the
hymns ascribed to Nodhas.

I have generally followed Professor Max Müller in
his translation of this hymn. See his *Vedic Hymns,*
Part I.

Thee claiming worship, bearing it to Gods:
   there nigh to thee sate all the Holy
   Ones.
2 The Gods approached the ways of holy
   Law; there was a gathering vast as
   heaven itself.
   The waters feed with praise the growing
   Babe, born nobly in the womb, the seat
   of Law.
3 Like grateful food, like some wide dwelling-
   place, like a fruit-bearing hill, a wholesome stream.
   Like a steed urged to run in swift career,
   rushing like Sindhu, who may check his
   course ?
4 Kin as a brother to his sister floods, he
   eats the woods as a King eats the rich.
   When through the forest, urged by wind,
   he spreads, verily Agni shears the hair
   of earth.
5 Like a swan sitting in the floods he pants;
   wisest in mind mid men he wakes at
   morn.
   A Sage like Soma, sprung from Law, he
   grew like some young creature, mighty,
   shining far.

HYMN LXVI.   *Agni.*

1. LIKE the Sun's glance, like wealth of
   varied sort, like breath which is the life,
   like one's own son,
   Like a swift bird, a cow who yields her
   milk, pure and refulgent to the wood
   he speeds.
2 He offers safety like a pleasant home, like
   ripened corn, the Conqueror of men.

* This and the eight following hymns are ascribed
to the Ṛṣi Parāśara, son of Śakti the son of Vasiṣṭha.
They are generally difficult, and not seldom unintelligible.

1 *They tracked thee*: the Gods followed Agni who
had fled away, carrying with him the sacrifice as a thief
carries off a cow. The *dark cave* is the depth of the
waters in which Agni hid himself.

2 *The seat of Law*: the place of sacrifice, the
law ordained for ever.

3 *Sindhu*: the Indus, or any great river.

4 *As a King eats the rich* supports his state by levy-
ing contributions from the wealthy.
The hair of earth: grass and shrubs, which forest-
fires destroy.

5 *He pants*: after his rapid flight to the waters
in which he hid himself.
He wakes at morn: at the time of the early morn-
ing sacrifice.
A Sage like Soma: like the deified Soma. 'As
Soma creates or causes useful plants to grow, so Agni
creates, or extracts from them, their nutritive faculty,—
Wilson (from Sāyaṇa).

2 *Like a steed*: like a war-horse who helps to
win spoil in battle.

Like a Seer lauding, famed among the
folk ; like a steed friendly he vouch-
safes us power.

3 With flame insatiate, like eternal might;
caring for each one like a dame at
home ;
Bright when he shines forth, whitish mid
the folk, like a car, gold-decked, thundering to the fight.

4 He strikes with terror like a dart shot
forth, e'en like an archer's arrow tipped
with flame;
Master of present and of future life, the
maidens' lover and the matrons' Lord.

5 To him lead all your ways : may we
attain the kindled God as cows their
home at eve.
He drives the flames below as floods their
swell : the rays rise up to the fair
place of heaven.

HYMN LXVII.   *Agni.*

1. VICTORIOUS in the wood, Friend among
men, ever he claims obedience as a King.
Gracious like peace, blessing like mental
power, Priest was he, offering-bearer,
full of thought.

2 He, bearing in his hand all manly might,
crouched in the cavern, struck the Gods
with fear.
Men filled with understanding find him
there, when they have sung prayers formed within their heart.

3 He, like the Unborn, holds the broad
earth up; and with effective utterance
fixed the sky.
O Agni, guard the spots which cattle love:
thou, life of all, hast gone from lair to
lair.

4 Whoso hath known him dwelling in his
lair, and hath approached the stream of
holy Law,—
They who release him, paying sacred rites,
—truly to such doth he announce great
wealth.

5 He who grows mightily in herbs, within
each fruitful mother and each babe
she bears,
Wise, life of all men, in the waters'
home,—for him have sages built as
'twere a seat.

HYMN LXVIII.   *Agni.*

1. COMMINGLING, restless, he ascends the sky,
unveiling nights and all that stands or
moves,
As he the sole God is preëminent in greatness among all these other Gods.

2 All men are joyful in thy power, O God,
that living from the dry wood thou art
born.
All truly share thy Godhead while they
keep, in their accustomed ways, eternal
Law.

3 Strong is the thought of Law, the Law's
behest; all works have they performed;
he quickens all.
Whoso will bring oblation, gifts to thee,
to him, bethinking thee, vouchsafe thou
wealth.

4 Seated as Priest with Manu's progeny, of
all these treasures he alone is Lord.
Men yearn for children to prolong their
line, and are not disappointed in their
hope.

5 Eagerly they who hear his word fulfil his
wish as sons obey their sire's behest.

---

4 *The stream of holy Law* : or as Sāyaṇa explains,
the supporter of the truth or of ¡sacrifice, that is, Agni.
They who release him : free him, by attrition, from
the fire-sticks.

---

1 *Commingling* : Agni, devouring and fusing
together with his flames and smoke the elements of the
oblations which he bears to the Gods.
3 I can make nothing of the first hemistich.
Wilson, after Sāyaṇa, paraphrases : 'Praises are addressed
to him who has repaired (to the solemnity); oblations
are offered to him who has gone (to the sacrifice);
in him is all sustenance; (and to him) have all (devout
persons) performed (the customary) rites'.
4 *Manu's progeny* : all Āryan men.
Men yearn for children : men have children at their
desire, as the reward of their faithful worship of Agni.
5 *He, the House-Friend* : he Agni, who is the friend
and guardian of every house in his character of the
household fire, as the Sun, the Creator, the Supreme
God, made the heaven and adorned it with stars.

---

4 *The maidens' lover* : the offering to Agni being
an essential part of the marriage-service.
The matrons' Lord : children being especially the
gift of Agni, in whose worship the wife of the sacrificer
bears an important part. I have not attempted to
imitate the rhythm of the original, and have contented
myself with preserving the same number of syllables in
each line.

---

1 *Victorious in the wood* : subduing the fuel and
burning it to ashes.
2 *Crouched in the cavern* : concealed in the dark
depth of the waters. See I. 65. 1.
3 *The Unborn* : the Sun ; regarded as the Supreme God.
The spots which cattle love : as thou knowest by experience how pleasant it is to find a safe place of
refuge, do not burn up the places where the cattle find
refuge and food.

He, rich in food, unbars his wealth like doors : he, the House-Friend, hath decked heaven's vault with stars.

HYMN LXIX. *Agni.*

1. BRIGHT, splendid, like Dawn's lover, he hath filled the two joined worlds as with the light of heaven.
When born, with might thou hast encompassed them : Father of Gods, and yet their Son wast thou.

2 Agni, the Sage, the humble, who discerns like the cow's udder, the sweet taste of food,
Like a bliss-giver to be drawn to men, sits gracious in the middle of the house.

3 Born in the dwelling like a lovely son, pleased, like a strong steed, he bears on the folk.
What time the men and I, with heroes, call, may Agni then gain all through Godlike power.

4 None breaks these holy laws of thine when thou hast granted audience to these chieftains here.
This is thy boast, thou smotest with thy peers, and joined with heroes dravest off disgrace.

5 Like the Dawn's lover, spreading light, well-known as hued like morn, may he remember me.
They, bearing of themselves, unbar the doors : they all ascend to the fair place of heaven.

HYMN LXX. *Agni.*

1. MAY we, the pious, win much food by prayer, may Agni with fair light pervade each act,—

1 *Like Dawn's lover* : both the Sun and Agni are called the lovers of Uṣas or Dawn. Agni is so called from his making his appearance as sacrificial fire at the earliest break of day.
The two joined worlds : earth and heaven coupled into a single dual conception.

2 *Like the cow's udder* ; Agni discerns and selects the sweet savours of oblations in the same manner as the udder of a cow selects and assimilates the sweet juices of grass and herbs for the production of milk.

3 The meaning of the second hemistich is not clear. Wilson, after Sāyaṇa, renders it : 'Whatever (divine) beings I may, along with other men, invoke (to the ceremony) thou, Agni, assumest all (their) celestial natures.'

5 *They, bearing of themselves* ; either, his rays bearing up the oblation of their own accord, or the steeds who freely draw the chariot of Dawn.

1 *Pervade each act* ; be present and regulate all our acts of worship; or the meaning may be 'attain each gift,' receive every oblation that we offer.

He the observer of the heavenly laws of Gods, and of the race of mortal man.

2 He who is germ of waters, germ of woods, germ of all things that move not and that move,—
To him even in the rock and in the house: Immortal One, he cares for all mankind.

3 Agni is Lord of riches for the man who serves him readily with sacred songs.
Protect these beings thou with careful thought, knowing the races both of Gods and men.

4 Whom many dawns and nights, unlike, make strong, whom, born in Law, all things that move and stand,—
He hath been won, Herald who sits in light, making effectual all our holy works.

5 Thou settest value on our cows and woods: all shall bring tribute to us to the light.
Men have served thee in many and sundry spots, parting, as 'twere, an aged father's wealth.

6 Like a brave archer, like one skilled and bold, a fierce avenger, so he shines in fight.

HYMN LXXI. *Agni.*

1. LOVING the loving One, as wives their husband, the sisters of one home have urged him forward,
Bright-coloured, even as the cows love morning, dark, breaking forth to view, and redly beaming.

2 Our sires with lauds burst e'en the firm-set fortress, yea, the Aṅgirases, with roar, the mountain.
They made for us a way to reach high heaven, they found us day, light, day's sign, beams of morning.

3 They stablished order, made his service fruitful ; then parting them among the longing faithful,

2 *To him even in the rock* : I can make nothing out of this. Wilson, after Sāyaṇa, paraphrases : '(They offer oblations) on the mountain, or in the mansion, to that Agni ;' but this cannot be the meaning. Ludwig suggests an alteration of the text, so that the meaning would be, 'even within the stone is his dwelling.'

5 'Agni, confer excellence upon our valued cattle; and may all men bring us acceptable tribute.'—Wilson.

1 *The loving One,* : Agni. *The sisters of one home* ; the fingers that serve him by kindling the fire, etc. *The cows* : the clouds brightened by the approach of Dawn.

2 The priestly Aṅgirases, the earliest institutors of religious worship, caused by prayer and praise the mountain-like cloud, that held the rain imprisoned, to be opened.

3 *His service* : the worship of Agni.

Not thirsting after aught, they come, most active, while with sweet food the race of Gods they strengthen.

4 Since Mātariśvan, far-diffused, hath stirred him, and he in every house grown bright and noble,
He, Bhṛgu-like, hath gone as his companion, as on commission to a greater Sovran.

5 When man poured juice to Heaven, the mighty Father, he knew and freed himself from close embracement.
The archer boldly shot at him his arrow, and the God threw his splendour on his Daughter.

6 Whoso hath flames for thee within his dwelling, or brings the worship which thou lovest daily,
Do thou of double might increase his substance : may he whom thou incitest meet with riches.

7 All sacrificial viands wait on Agni as the Seven mighty Rivers seek the ocean.
Not by our brethren was our food discovered : find with the Gods care for us, thou who knowest.

8 When light hath filled the Lord of men for increase, straight from the heaven descends the limpid moisture.
Agni hath brought to light and filled with spirit the youthful host blameless and well providing.

9 He who like thought goes swiftly on his journey, the Sun, alone is ever Lord of riches.
The Kings with fair hands, Varuṇa and Mitra, protect the precious nectar in our cattle.

10 O Agni, break not our ancestral friendship, Sage as thou art, endowed with deepest knowledge.
Old age, like gathering cloud, impairs the body : before that evil be come nigh protect me.

---

4 *Mātariśvan* : the divine or semi-divine being who brought Agni to Bhṛgu.

5 This verse is very obscure. The meaning of the first hemistich seems to be that when oblations were offered to Dyaus or Heaven Agni shone forth freed from encompassing night. Who the archer is, whether Mātariśvan or Agni, is uncertain, nor is it clear at whom the arrow was shot. *The God* may be Dyaus, and *his Daughter* may be Uṣas or Dawn.

7 *The Seven mighty Rivers* : see I. 32 12.
Not by our brethren ; we do not look to our kinsmen for food, but depend upon Agni and the other Gods.

8 *The Lord of men* : according to Sāyaṇa, the sacrificer. Perhaps Indra is meant who comes attended by *the youthful host* of Maruts.

HYMN LXXII. *Agni.*

1. THOUGH holding many gifts for men, he humbleth the higher powers of each wise ordainer.
Agni is now the treasure-lord of treasures, for ever granting all immortal bounties.

2 The Gods infallible all searching found not him, the dear Babe who still is round about us.
Worn weary, following his track, devoted, they reached the lovely highest home of Agni.

3 Because with holy oil the pure Ones, Agni, served thee the very pure three autumn seasons,
Therefore they won them holy names for worship, and nobly born they dignified their bodies.

4 Making them known to spacious earth and heaven, the holy Ones revealed the powers of Rudra.
The mortal band, discerning in the distance, found Agni standing in the loftiest station.

5 Nigh they approached, one-minded, with their spouses, kneeling to him adorable paid worship.
Friend finding in his own friend's eye protection, they made their own the bodies which they chastened.

---

1 Wilson, after Sāyaṇa, translates : 'Agni...... appropriates the prayers addressed to the eternal creator.' The meaning appears to be that although Agni bestows many good gifts on men, his flames are at times terribly destructive.

2 The flight of Agni and his pursuit by the Gods have been mentioned before (I. 65. 1). The idea here is as Ludwig observes, that the Gods did not really find Agni—visible though he be in his earthly form—until they attained to the true philosophical knowledge of the Deity as he is.

3 *The pure Ones*: 'The text has on *śucáyaḥ*, the pure : the Scholiast supplies *Maruts*, for whom, it is said, seven platters are placed at the Agnicayana ceremony ; and they are severally invoked by the appellations Idṛś, Anyādṛś, Tādṛś, Pratidṛś, Mitaḥ, Sammitaḥ, and others. In consequence of this participation, with Agni, of sacrificial offerings, they exchanged their perishable, for immortal, bodies, and obtained heaven. The Maruts are, therefore, like the Ṛbhus, deified mortals.' Wilson.
Three autumn seasons : during three years. Ludwig observes that the period of three years in connexion with religious vows or ceremonies is mentioned elsewhere also.

4 *The powers of Rudra* : Rudra here is a name of Agni.
The mortal band : the Maruts, so called as not having been originally immortal.

6 Soon as the holy beings had discovered the thrice-seven mystic things contained within thee,
With these, one-minded, they preserve the Amṛta : guard thou the life of all their plants and cattle.

7 Thou, Agni, knower of men's works, hast sent us good food in constant course for our subsistence :
Thou deeply skilled in paths of Gods becamest an envoy never wearied, offering-bearer.

8 Knowing the Law, the seven strong floods from heaven, full of good thought, discerned the doors of riches.
Saramā found the cattle's firm-built prison whereby the race of man is still supported.

9 They who approached all noble operations making a path that leads to life immortal,
To be the Bird's support, the spacious mother, Aditi, and her great Sons stood in power.

10 When Gods immortal made both eyes of heaven, they gave to him the gift of beauteous glory.
Now they flow forth like rivers set in motion : they knew the Red Steeds coming down, O Agni.

HYMN LXXIII. *Agni.*

1. HE who gives food, like patrimonial riches and guides aright like some wise man's instruction,
Loved like a guest who lies in pleasant lodging,—may he, as Priest, prosper his servant's dwelling.

2 He who like Savitar the God, true-minded, protecteth with his power all acts of vigour,
Truthful, like splendour, glorified by many, like breath joy-giving,—all must strive to win him.

3 He who on earth dwells like a king surrounded by faithful friends, like a God all-sustaining,
Like heroes who preside, who sit in safety : like as a blameless dame dear to her husband.

4 Thee, such, in settlements secure, O Agni, our men serve ever kindled in each dwelling.
On him have they laid splendour in abundance : dear to all men, bearer be he of riches.

5 May thy rich worshippers win food, O Agni, and princes gain long life who bring oblation.
May we get booty from our foe in battle, presenting to the Gods their share for glory.

6 The cows of holy law, sent us by Heaven, have swelled with laden udders, loudly lowing;
Soliciting his favour, from a distance the rivers to the rock have flowed together.

7 Agni, with thee, soliciting thy favour, the holy Ones have gained glory in heaven.
They made the Night and Dawn of different colours, and set the black and purple hues together.

8 May we and those who worship be the mortals whom thou, O Agni, leadest on to riches.
Thou hast filled earth and heaven and air's mid-region, and followest the whole world like a shadow.

9 Aided by thee, O Agni, may we conquer steeds with steeds, men with men, heroes with heroes,
Lords of the wealth transmitted by our fathers : and may our princes live a hundred winters.

---

6 *The thrice-seven mystic things* the secret or mysterious rites by which heaven is to be obtained; offerings of various kinds, food, clarified butter, Soma juice etc., arranged in three classes of seven. All these offerings require fire, and so are contained in Agni.

They preserve the Amṛta : the nectar or drink of the Gods; by the performance of these sacrifices they secure the fall of rain in due season.

8 *Saramā found the cattle's firm-built prison* : see I. 62. 3.

9 *To be the Bird's support* : the Bird is the Sun. *Aditi* is infinite Nature, and *her great Sons* are the Ādityas.

10 *Both eyes of heaven* : the Sun and Moon. *The deR Steeds* : the Sun's rays.

6 *The cows of holy law* : the cows whose milk is used in the various sacrifices offered in accordance with the eternal ordinance.

The rivers : the water used in sacrifice which flows or is brought to *the rock* or stone with which the Soma juice is expressed.

7 Through Agni's favour *the holy Ones*, the immortal Gods, receive the oblations which strengthen them for the performance of the great deeds which bring them glory.

8 *Like a shadow* : averting distress, as the shade of a great rock or tree wards off the oppressive heat of the sun.

9 *May our princes* : may the wealthy men who institute our sacrifices live to the greatest age usually allotted to man.

10 May these our hymns of praise, Agni,
Ordainer, be pleasant to thee in thy
heart and spirit.
May we have power to hold thy steeds of
riches, laying on thee the God-sent
gift of glory.

HYMN LXXIV.   *Agni.*

1. As forth to sacrifice we go, a hymn to
Agni let us say,
Who hears us even when afar ;
2 Who, from of old, in carnage, when the
people gathered, hath preserved
His household for the worshipper.
3 And let men say, Agni is born, e'en he
who slayeth Vṛtra, he
Who winneth wealth in every fight.
4 Him in whose house an envoy thou lovest
to taste his offered gifts,
And strengthenest his sacrifice,
5 Him, Aṅgiras, thou Son of Strength, all
men call happy in his God,
His offerings, and his sacred grass.
6 Hitherward shalt thou bring these Gods to
our laudation and to taste.
These offered gifts, fair-shining One.
7 When, Agni, on thine embassage thou
goest not a sound is heard of steed or
straining of thy car.
8 Aided by thee uninjured, strong, one after
other, goes he forth :
Agni, the offerer forward steps.
9 And splendid strength, heroic, high, Agni,
thou grantest from the Gods,
Thou God, to him who offers gifts.

HYMN LXXV.   *Agni.*

1. ACCEPT our loudest-sounding hymn, food
most delightful to the Gods,
Pouring our offerings in thy mouth.
2 Now, Agni, will we say to thee, O wisest
and best Aṅgiras,
Our precious, much-availing prayer.
3 Who, Agni, is thy kin, of men? who is thy
worthy worshipper ?
On whom dependent ? who art thou ?
4 The kinsman, Agni, of mankind, their well
beloved Friend art thou,
A Friend whom friends may supplicate.

---

10 *To hold thy steeds of riches* : to retain by us thy
horses which bring wealth, that is, coutinue to receive
and keep the riches which thou sendest.

This Hymn and the nineteen following are ascribed to the Ṛṣi Gotama, son of Rahūgaṇa.
3 *Who slayeth Vṛtra* : Agni may here be identified
with Indra.
5 *Aṅgiras* ; a name of Agni. See I. I. 6,

---

5 Bring to us Mitra, Varuṇa, bring the Gods
to mighty' sacrifice.
Bring them, O Agni, to thine home.

HYMN LXXVI.   *Agni.*

1. How may the mind draw nigh to please
thee, Agni? What hymn of praise shall
bring us greatest blessing?
Or who hath gained thy power by sacrifices ? or with what mind shall we
bring thee oblations?
2 Come hither, Agni ; sit thee down as
Hotar ; be thou who never wast deceived our leader.
May Heaven and Earth, the all-pervading,
love thee : worship the Gods to win for
us their favour.
3 Burn thou up all the Rākṣasas, O Agni;
ward thou off curses from our sacrifices.
Bring hither with his Bays the Lord of
Soma : here is glad welcome for the
Bounteous Giver.
4 Thou Priest with lip and voice that
bring us children hast been invoked.
Here with the Gods be seated.
Thine is the task of Cleanser and Presenter : waken us, Wealth-bestower and
Producer.
5 As with oblations of the priestly Manus
thou worshippedst the Gods, a Sage
with sages,
So now, O truthfullest Invoker, Agni,
worship this day with joy-bestowing
ladle.

HYMN LXXVII.   *Agni.*

1. How shall we pay oblation unto Agni?
What hymn, Godloved, is said to him
refulgent ?
Who, deathless, true to Law, mid men a
herald, bringeth the Gods as best of
sacrificers ?
2 Bring him with reverence hither, most
propitious in sacrifices, true to Law, the
herald ;

---

3 *The Lord of Soma* : Indra.
4 Agni, the prie·t or bearer of oblations, has
been invoked with a hymn which will bring the blessing of children.
The cleanser (Potar) and *the Presenter* or Invoker
(Hotar) are two of the sixteen officiating priests.
5 *Manus* : another form of the word Manu, Man,
the great fore-father of men.
With joy-bestowing ladle : with the sacrificial ladle
used in pouring the holy oil or clarified butter into the
fire, an offering especially pleasing to the Gods.

For Agni, when he seeks the Gods for
mortals, knows them full well and worships them in spirit.

3 For he is mental power, a man, and perfect; he is the bringer, friend-like, of the
wondrous.
The pious Āryan tribes at sacrifices address
them first to him who doeth marvels.

4 May Agni, foe-destroyer, manliest Hero,
accept with love our hymns and our
devotion.
So may the liberal lords whose strength is
strongest, urged by their riches, stir our
thoughts with vigour.

5 Thus Agni Jātavedas, true to Order, hath
by the priestly Gotamas been lauded.
May he augment in them splendour and
vigour : observant, as he lists, he gathers
increase.

HYMN LXXVIII.   Agni.

1. O Jātavedas, keen and swift, we Gotamas
with sacred song exalt thee for thy glories' sake.

2 Thee, as thou art, desiring wealth Gotama
worships with his song :
We laud thee for thy glories' sake.

3 As such, like Aṅgiras we call on thee
best winner of the spoil :
We laud thee for thy glories' sake.

4 Thee, best of Vṛtra-slayers, thee who
shakest off our Dasyu foes :
We laud thee for thy glories' sake.

5 A pleasant song to Agni we, sons of
Rahūgaṇa, have sung :
We laud thee for thy glories' sake.

HYMN LXXIX.   Agni.

1. He in mid-air's expanse hath golden tresses ; a raging serpent, like the rushing
tempest :

3 *The wondrous* : extraordinary wealth.
4 *Liberal lords* : wealthy patrons whose gifts will
encourage and strengthen the devotions of the priests :

---

3 *Like Aṅgiras* : after the manner of Aṅgiras, one
of the earliest performers of sacrifice.
4 *Best of Vṛtra-slayers* : here again Agni is identified
with Indra.

---

1 Agni is here spoken of in his three forms, the
golden-haired Sun, the serpentine lightning, and the
household fire for religious purposes and ordinary use.
He is said to know the morning as being re-kindled for
sacrifice at day-break, and is compared to an active
matron on account of his employment to domestic purposes.

Purely refulgent, knowing well the morning ; like honourable dames, true, active
workers.

2 Thy well-winged flashes strengthen in
their manner, when the black Bull hath
bellowed round about us.
With drops that bless and seem to smile
he cometh : the waters fall, the clouds
utter their thunder.

3 When he comes streaming with the milk
of worship, conducting by directest
paths of Order,
Aryaman, Mitra, Varuṇa, Parijman fill the
hide full where lies the nether press-stone.

4 O Agni, thou who art the Lord of wealth
in kine, thou Son of Strength,
Vouchsafe to us, O Jātavedas, high renown.

5 He, Agni, kindled, good and wise, must be
exalted in our song :
Shine, thou of many forms, shine radiantly
on us.

6 O Agni, shining of thyself by night and
when the morning breaks,
Burn, thou whose teeth are sharp, against
the Rākṣasas.

7 Adorable in all our rites, favour us, Agni,
with thine aid,
When the great hymn is chanted forth.

8 Bring to us ever-conquering wealth, wealth,
Agni, worthy of our choice,
In all our frays invincible.

9 Give us, O Agni, through thy grace
wealth that supporteth all our life,
Thy favour so that we may live.

10 O Gotama, desiring bliss present thy songs
composed with care
To Agni of the pointed flames.

11 May the man fall, O Agni, who near or
afar assaileth us :
Do thou increase and prosper us.

12 Keen and swift Agni, thousand-eyed,
chaseth the Rākṣasas afar :
He singeth, herald meet for lauds.

HYMN LXXX.   Indra.

1. Thus in the Soma, in wild joy the Brahman hath exalted thee :

2 *The black Bull hath bellowed* : the dark rain-
clouds have thundered.
3 *When he comes* to the Gods with *the milk of
worship*, the rich sacrificial offering, the Gods send
copious rain. *Parijman*, the Wanderer, the circumambient,
is in this place the stormy Wind. *The nether press-stone*
(which rests upon an ox-hide) is here the earth, the
heaven being the upper stone. Wilson, following Sāyaṇa,
translates : 'pierce through the (investing) membrane
into the womb of the cloud.'

---

1 *The Dragon* : the great serpent Ahi, one of the
demons of drought.

Thou, mightiest, thunder-armed, hast driven by force the Dragon from the earth, lauding thine own imperial sway.

2 The mighty flowing Soma-draught, brought by the Hawk, hath gladdened thee,
That in thy strength, O Thunderer, thou hast struck down Vṛtra from the floods, lauding thine own imperial sway.

3 Go forward, meet the foe, be bold; thy bolt of thunder is not checked.
Manliness, Indra, is thy might : slay Vṛtra, make the waters thine, lauding thine own imperial sway.

4 Thou smotest Vṛtra from the earth, smotest him, Indra, from the sky.
Let these life-fostering waters flow attended by the Marut host, lauding thine own imperial sway.

5 The wrathful Indra with his bolt of thunder rushing on the foe,
Smote fierce on trembling Vṛtra's back, and loosed the waters free to run, lauding his own imperial sway.

6 With hundred-jointed thunderbolt Indra hath struck him on the back,
And, while rejoicing in the juice, seeketh prosperity for friends, lauding his own imperial sway.

7 Indra, unconquered might is thine, Thunderer, Caster of the Stone;
For thou with thy surpassing power smotest to death the guileful beast, lauding thine own imperial sway.

8 Far over ninety spacious floods thy thunderbolts were cast abroad :
Great, Indra, is thy hero might, and strength is seated in thine arms, lauding thine own imperial sway.

9 Laud him a thousand all at once, shout twenty forth the hymn of praise.
Hundreds have sung aloud to him, to Indra hath the prayer been raised, lauding his own imperial sway.

10 Indra hath smitten down the power of Vṛtra,—might with stronger might.
This was his manly exploit, he slew Vṛtra and let loose the floods, lauding his own imperial sway.

11 Yea, even this great Pair of Worlds trembled in terror at thy wrath,

When, Indra, Thunderer, Marut-girt, thou slewest Vṛtra in thy strength, lauding thine own imperial sway.

12 But Vṛtra scared not Indra with his shaking or his thunder roar.
On him that iron thunderbolt fell fiercely with its thousand points, lauding his own imperial sway.

13 When with the thunder thou didst make thy dart and Vṛtra meet in war,
Thy might, O Indra, fain to slay the Dragon, was set firm in heaven, lauding thine own imperial sway.

14 When at thy shout, O Thunder-armed, each thing both fixed and moving shook,
E'en Tvaṣṭar trembled at thy wrath and quaked with fear because of thee, lauding thine own imperial sway.

15 There is not, in our knowledge, one who passeth Indra in his strength :
In him the Deities have stored manliness, insight, power and might, lauding his own imperial sway.

16 Still as of old, whatever rite Atharvan, Manus sire of all,
Dadhyach performed, their prayer and praise united in that Indra meet, lauding his own imperial sway.

HYMN LXXXI.   *Indra.*

1. THE men have lifted Indra up, the Vṛtra-slayer, to joy and strength :
Him, verily, we invoke in battles whether great or small : be he our aid in deeds of might.

2 Thou, Hero, art a warrior, thou art giver of abundant spoil.
Strengthening e'en the feeble, thou aidest the sacrificer, thou givest the offerer ample wealth.

3 When war and battles are on foot, booty is laid before the bold.
Yoke thou thy wildly-rushing Bays. Whom wilt thou slay and whom enrich ? Do thou, O Indra, make us rich.

4 Mighty through wisdom, as he lists, terrible, he hath waxed in strength.

---

16 Atharvan is the priest who first obtained fire and offered Soma and prayers to the Gods. Dadhyac is his son. Manus or Manu is the progenitor of mankind.
The refrain, 'lauding his own imperial sway,' is not always in syntactical connexion with the verse of which it forms the conclusion.

2 *Brought by the Hawk* : the Soma is said to have been brought from heaven by a hawk or falcon. Cf. I. 93. 6.

7 *The guileful beast* : the demon Vṛtra.
8 *Ninety spacious floods* : the many waters obstructed by Vṛtra.

1 *The men* : the ministering priests who exalt and strengthen with oblations.

Lord of Bay Steeds, strong-jawed, sublime,
he in joined hands for glory's sake hath
grasped his iron thunderbolt.

5 He filled the earthly atmosphere and
pressed against the lights in heaven.
None like thee ever hath been born, none,
Indra, will be born like thee. Thou hast
waxed mighty over all.

6 May he who to the offerer gives the
foeman's man-sustaining food,
May Indra lend his aid to us. Deal forth
—abundant is thy wealth—that in thy
bounty I may share.

7 He, righteous-hearted, at each time of
rapture gives us herds of kine.
Gather in both thy hands for us treasures
of many hundred sorts. Sharpen thou
us, and bring us wealth.

8 Refresh thee, Hero, with the juice out-
poured for bounty and for strength.
We know thee Lord of ample store, to
thee have sent our hearts' desires : be
therefore our Protector thou.

9 These people, Indra, keep for thee all that
is worthy of thy choice.
Discover thou, as Lord, the wealth of
men who offer up no gifts : bring thou
to us this wealth of theirs.

HYMN LXXXII.   *Indra.*

1. GRACIOUSLY listen to our songs, Maghavan,
be not negligent.
As thou hast made us full of joy and
lettest us solicit thee, now, Indra, yoke
thy two Bay Steeds.

2 Well have they eaten and rejoiced ; the
friends have risen and passed away.
The sages luminous in themselves have
praised thee with their latest hymn.
Now, Indra, yoke thy two Bay Steeds.

3 Maghavan, we will reverence thee who
art so fair to look upon.
Thus praised, according to our wish come
now with richly laden car. Now, Indra,
yoke thy two Bay Steeds.

4 He will in very truth ascend the powerful
car that finds the kine,
Who thinks upon the well-filled bowl, the
Tawny Coursers' harnesser. Now, Indra,
yoke thy two Bay Steeds.

9 *These people* : thy worshippers here.

———

1 *Maghavan* : Indra, the rich and liberal.
2 *Well have they eaten* : they, meaning the worshippers.

5 Let, Lord of Hundred Powers, thy Steeds
be harnessed on the right and left.
Therewith in rapture of the juice, draw
near to thy beloved Spouse. Now, Indra,
yoke thy two Bay Steeds.

6 With holy prayer I yoke thy long-maned
pair of Bays : come hitherward ; thou
holdest them in both thy hands.
The stirring draughts of juice outpoured
have made thee glad : thou, Thunderer,
hast rejoiced with Pūṣan and thy
Spouse.

HYMN LXXXIII.   *Indra.*

1. INDRA, the mortal man well guarded by
thine aid goes foremost in the wealth of
horses and of kine.
With amplest wealth thou fillest him, as
round about the waters clearly seen afar
fill Sindhu full.

2 The heavenly Waters come not nigh the
priestly bowl : they but look down and
see how far mid-air is spread :
The Deities conduct the pious man to
them : like suitors they delight in him
who loveth prayer.

3 Praiseworthy blessing hast thou laid upon
the pair who with uplifted ladle serve
thee, man and wife.
Unchecked he dwells and prospers in thy
law : thy power brings blessing to the
sacrificer pouring gifts.

4 First the Aṅgirases won themselves vital
power, whose fires were kindled through
good deeds and sacrifice.
The men together found the Paṇi's hoard-
ed wealth, the cattle, and the wealth in
horses and in kine.

5 Atharvan first by sacrifices laid the paths ;
then, guardian of the Law, sprang up
the loving Sun.
Uśanā Kāvya straightway hither drove
the kine. Let us with offerings honour
Yama's deathless birth.

5 *Thy Spouse* : Indrāṇī. See I. 22. 12.

3 *Man and wife* : the text has only *mithunā*, a
couple. The word apparently means here the offerer of
the sacrifice and his wife, who took part in the ceremony. Sāyaṇa explains it as the grain and the butter of
oblation.

4 *The Paṇi* : is the illiberal demon who withholds
the rain.

5 *The paths* : for the rising Sun to travel.
Uśanā Kāvya is the name of a celebrased ancient Ṛṣi.
See I. 51. 10. The meaning of the latter half of the
second verse is obscure. Ludwig renders it 'Seek we to
win by sacrifice the immortality which has sprung from
Yama.' Yama seems here to represent the rising Sun.
See Ehni, Der Mythus des Yama, p. 62.

6 When sacred grass is trimmed to aid the auspicious work, or the hymn makes its voice of praise sound to the sky.
Where the stone rings as 'twere a singer skilled in laud,—Indra in truth delights when these come near to him.

HYMN LXXXIV.   *Indra.*

1. THE Soma hath been pressed for thee, O Indra ; mightiest, bold One, come.
May Indra-vigour fill thee full, as the Sun fills mid-air with rays.

2 His pair of Tawny Coursers bring Indra of unresisted might
Hither to Rṣis' songs of praise and sacrifice performed by men.

3 Slayer of Vṛtra, mount thy car ; thy Bay Steeds have been yoked by prayer.
May, with its voice, the pressing-stone draw thine attention hitherward.

4 This poured libation, Indra, drink, immortal, gladdening, excellent.
Streams of the bright have flowed to thee here at the seat of holy Law.

5 Sing glory now to Indra, say to him your solemn eulogies.
The drops poured forth have made him glad : pay reverence to his might supreme.

6 When, Indra, thou dost yoke thy Steeds, there is no better charioteer :
None hath surpassed thee in thy might, none with good steeds o'ertaken thee.

7 He who alone bestoweth on mortal man who offereth gifts,
The ruler of resistless power, is Indra, sure.

8 When will he trample, like a weed, the man who hath no gift for him?
When, verily, will Indra hear our songs of praise ?

9 He who with Soma juice prepared amid the many honours thee,—
Verily Indra gains thereby tremendous might.

10 The juice of Soma thus diffused, sweet to the taste, the bright cows drink,
Who for the sake of splendour close to mighty Indra's side rejoice, good in their own supremacy.

11 Craving his touch the dappled kine mingle the Soma with their milk.
The milch-kine dear to Indra send forth his death-dealing thunderbolt, good in their own supremacy.

12 With veneration, passing wise, honouring his victorious might,
They follow close his many laws to win them due preëminence, good in their own supremacy.

13 With bones of Dadhyac for his arms, Indra, resistless in attack,
Struck nine-and-ninety Vṛtras dead.

14 He, searching for the horse's head, removed among the mountains, found
At Śaryaṇāvān what he sought.

15 Then verily they recognized the essential form of Tvaṣṭar's Bull,
Here in the mansion of the Moon.

16 Who yokes to-day unto the pole of Order the strong and passionate steers of checkless spirit,
With shaft-armed mouths, heart-piercing, health-bestowing ?
Long shall he live who richly pays their service.

11 *Send forth* : the cows, that is, their milk, exalt and strengthen Indra, and incite him to battle with the demons. The meaning of the refrain of this triad (verses 10, 11, 12) is not very clear. Wilson, following Sāyaṇa, translates it : 'abiding (in their stalls) expectant of his sovereignty.'

13 *Dadhyac*, or in a later form, Dadhīca, was a Rṣi, son of Atharvan, he and his father being regarded as the first founders of sacrifice. He is described as having the head of a horse given to him by the Aśvins which was afterwards cut off by Indra. With his bones or, as the legend says, the bones of this horse's head, converted into a thunderbolt, Indra slew the Vṛtras or demons who withheld the rain. The Vedic legend, which was modified and amplified in later times, appears to have been connected in its origin with that of Dadhikrās, often mentioned in the Veda and described as a kind of divine horse, probably a personification of the morning Sun in his rapid course. Dadhyac may be the old Moon whose bones, when he dies, become the stars with which Indra slays the fiends of darkness.

14 *Mountains* : the morning clouds. *Śaryaṇāvān* : said to be a lake and district in Kurukṣetra, near the modern Delhi.

15 *Tvaṣṭar's Bull* : an obscure expression for the Sun. The purport of the verse may be that when, after the rains, the bright moonlight nights came, men recognized the fact that the light was borrowed from the Sun. Wilson, following Sāyaṇa, translates the verse : 'The (solar rays) found, on this occasion the light of Tvaṣṭṛ, verily, concealed in the mansion of the moving moon.' See Hymns of the Atharva-veda, XX. 41.

16 *The strong and passionate steers* : the zealous and indefatigable priests, who are yoked to the chariot-pole of Order or employed in the performance of sacrifice ordained by eternal Law. The words of the priests are the arrows with which their mouths are armed.

4 *The bright* : Soma juice. *The seat of holy Law* : the place where sacrifice, rdained by ṛtá, or eternal Law, is performed.

10 *The bright cows* : the pure and glossy milk which absorbs or drinks the Soma juice with which it is mixed, and which is close to, or united with, Indra when offered to and accepted by him in libation.

17 Who fleeth forth? who suffereth? who
   feareth? Who knoweth Indra present,
   Indra near us ?
   Who sendeth benediction on his offspring,
   his household, wealth and person, and
   the people ?

18 Who with poured oil and offering honours
   Agni, with ladle worships at appointed
   seasons ?
   To whom to the Gods bring oblation quickly? What offerer, God-favoured,
   knows him thoroughly ?

19 Thou as a God, O Mightiest, verily blessest
   mortal man.
   O Maghavan, there is no comforter but
   thou : Indra, I speak my words to thee.

20 Let not thy bounteous gifts, let not thy
   saving help fail us, good Lord, at any
   time ;
   And measure out to us, thou lover of mankind, all riches hitherward from men.

HYMN LXXXV.   *Maruts.*

1. THEY who are glancing forth, like women,
   on their way, doers of mighty deeds,
   swift racers, Rudra's Sons,
   The Maruts have made heaven and earth
   increase and grow : in sacrifices they
   delight, the strong and wild.

2 Grown to their perfect strength greatness
   have they attained ; the Rudras have
   established their abode in heaven.
   Singing their song of praise and generating
   might, they have put glory on, the Sons
   whom Pṛśni bare.

3 When, Children of the Cow, they shine in
   bright attire, and on their fair limbs lay
   their golden ornaments,
   They drive away each adversary from their
   path, and, following their traces, fatness
   floweth down,

4 When, mighty Warriors, ye who glitter with
   your spears, o'erthrowing with your
   strength e'en what is ne'er o'erthrown,
   When, O ye Maruts, ye the host that send
   the rain, had harnessed to your cars the
   thought-fleet spotted deer.

5 When ye have harnessed to your cars the
   spotted deer, urging the thunderbolt, O
   Maruts, to the fray,
   Forth rush the torrents of the dark-red stormy cloud, and moisten, like a skin, the
   earth with water-floods.

6 Let your swift-gliding coursers bear you
   hitherward with their fleet pinions.
   Come ye forward with your arms.
   Sit on the grass; a wide seat hath been
   made for you : delight yourselves, O
   Maruts, in the pleasant food.

7 Strong in their native strength to greatness
   have they grown, stepped to the firmament and made their dwelling wide.
   When Viṣṇu saved the Soma bringing
   wild delight, the Maruts sate like birds
   on their dear holy grass.

8 In sooth like heroes fain for fight they rush
   about, like combatants fame-seeking have
   they striven in war.
   Before the Maruts every creature is afraid:
   the men are like to Kings, terrible to
   behold.

9 When Tvaṣṭar deft of hand had turned
   the thunderbolt, golden, with thousand
   edges, fashioned more skilfully,
   Indra received it to perform heroic
   deeds. Vṛtra he slew, and forced the
   flood of water forth.

10 They with their vigorous strength pushed
   the well up on high, and clove the
   cloud in twain though it was passing
   strong.
   The Maruts, bounteous Givers, sending
   forth their voice, in the wild joy of Soma
   wrought their glorious deeds.

11 They drave the cloud transverse directed
   hitherward, and poured the fountain
   forth for thirsting Gotama.

17 The answer to these questions is, the priests, who
represent the feelings of the man who institutes the
sacrifice.

18 The second line of this verse is rendered by
Wilson, following Sāyaṇa : 'To whom do the gods,
quickly bring (the wealth) that has been called for ?'
This would be intelligible enough ; but *homa* (oblation)
can hardly bear the interpretation thus forced upon it.

1 *Rudra's Sons* : the Maruts, or Storm-Gods, are
the sons of Rudra and of Pṛśni, the earth or the speckled
cloud.

2 *The Rudras* : the sons of Rudra.

3 *Children of the Cow* : that is, of Pṛśni or the cloud
under that type.

Fatness floweth down : the clouds drop fatness ; the
fertilizing rain descends.

4 The glittering spears are the flashes of lightning.
The chariot of the Maruts is said to be drawn by
spotted deer or antelopes.

6 *Sit on the grass* : on the sacred grass trimmed and
strewn for the Gods.

7 *When Viṣṇu saved the Soma* : Viṣṇu prepared the
Soma and brought it to Indra, and the Maruts, Indra's
companions, sat down with him to enjoy it.

8 *The men* : the Maruts. *Kings* : that is, warriors.

10 *The well* : here the cloud, as a reservoir of
water.

11 *Gotama* : the Ṛṣi to whom the hymn was
revealed.

Shining with varied light they come to him
with help : they with their might fulfilled the longing of the sage.

12 The shelters which ye have for him who
lauds you, bestow them threefold on
the man who offers.
Extend the same boons unto us, ye Maruts.
Give us, O Heroes, wealth with noble
offspring.

HYMN LXXXVI.   *Maruts.*

1. THE best of guardians hath that man within whose dwelling place ye drink,
O Maruts, giants of the sky.

2 Honoured with sacrifice or with the worship of the sages' hymns,
O Maruts, listen to the call.

3 Yea, the strong man to whom ye have
vouchsafed to give a sage, shall move
Into a stable rich in kine.

4 Upon this hero's sacred grass Soma is
poured in daily rites :
Praise and delight are sung aloud.

5 Let the strong Maruts hear him, him surpassing all men : strength be his
That reaches even to the Sun.

6 For, through the swift Gods' loving help,
in many an autumn, Maruts, we
Have offered up our sacrifice.

7 Fortunate shall that mortal be, O Maruts
most adorable,
Whose offerings ye bear away.

8 O Heroes truly strong, ye know the toil
of him who sings your praise,
The heart's desire of him who loves.

9 O ye of true strength, make this thing
manifest by your greatness : strike
The demon with your thunderbolt.

10 Conceal the horrid darkness, drive far
from us each devouring fiend.
Create the light for which we long.

HYMN LXXXVII.   *Maruts.*

1. LOUD Singers, never humbled, active, full
of strength, immovable, impetuous, manliest, best-beloved,
They have displayed themselves with glittering ornaments, a few in number only,
like the heavens with stars.

2 When, Maruts, on the steeps ye pile the
moving cloud, ye are like birds on whatsoever path it be.
Clouds everywhere shed forth the rain upon
your cars. Drop fatness, honey-hued,
for him who sings your praise.

3 Earth at their racings trembles as if weak
and worn, when on their ways they
yoke their cars for victory.
They, sportive, loudly roaring, armed with
glittering spears, shakers of all, themselves admire their mightiness.

4 Self-moving is that youthful band, with
spotted steeds; thus it hath lordly sway,
endued with power and might.
Truthful art thou, and blameless, searcher-
out of sin : so thou, Strong Host, wilt
be protector of this prayer.

5 We speak by our descent from our primeval Sire ; our tongue, when we behold
the Soma, stirs itself.
When, shouting, they had joined Indra in
toil of fight, then only they obtained
their sacrificial names.

6 Splendours they gained for glory, they
who wear bright rings; rays they obtained, and men to celebrate their praise.
Armed with their swords, impetuous and
fearing naught, they have possessed the
Maruts' own beloved home.

HYMN LXXXVIII.   *Maruts.*

1. COME hither, Maruts, on your lightning-
laden cars, sounding with sweet songs,
armed with lances, winged with steeds.
Fly unto us with noblest food, like birds,
O ye of mighty power.

---

3 *Shall move into a stable rich in kine* : shall become
the wealthy possessor of many cows.

8 *Of him who loves* : of the suppliant who loves
and prays to you.

10 *Devouring fiend* : 'Atrin, which stands for
attrin, is one of the many names assigned to the
powers of darkness and mischief. It is derived from
atra, which means, tooth or jaw, and therefore meant
originally an ogre with large teeth or jaws, a
devourer.'—Max Müller See Vedic Hymns, Part I.
(Sacred Books of the East, XXXII.) for a translation
and full explanation of this and other Hymns to the
Maruts.

1 *A few in number only* : 'refers to the Maruts, who
are represented as gradually rising or just showing
themselves, as yet only a few in number, like the
first stars in the sky.—' Max Müller.

5 The Soma juice inspires us, and we are guided
by the tradition received from our ancestors.
The Maruts obtained divine honours only as a
reward for assisting Indra in his battle with the
demon Vṛtra.

6 *They have possessed the Maruts' own beloved home* :
'have established themselves in what became afterwards known as their own abode, their own place
among the gods invoked at the sacrifice.'—Max Müller.

2 With their red-hued or, haply, tawny
coursers which speed their chariots on,
they come for glory.
Brilliant like gold is he who holds the
thunder. Earth have they smitten with
the chariot's felly.

3 For beauty ye have swords upon your
bodies. As they stir woods so may
they stir our spirits.
For your sake, O ye Maruts very mighty
and well-born, have they set the stone,
in motion.

4 The days went round you and came back
O yearners, back, to this prayer and to
this solemn worship.
The Gotamas making their prayer with
singing have pushed the well's lid up to
drink the water.

5 No hymn was ever known like this aforetime which Gotama sang forth for you,
O Maruts,
What time upon your golden wheels he
saw you, wild boars rushing about with
tusks of iron.

6 To you this freshening draught of Soma
rusheth, O Maruts, like the voice of one
who prayeth.
It rusheth freely from our hands as these
libations wont to flow.

HYMN LXXXIX. *Viśvedevas.*

1. MAY powers auspicious come to us from
every side, never deceived, unhindered,
and victorious,
That the Gods ever may be with us for our
gain, our guardians day by day unceasing
in their care.

2 May the auspicious favour of the Gods be
ours, on us descend the bounty of the
righteous Gods.
The friendship of the Gods have we devoutly sought : so may the Gods extend
our life that we may live.

3 We call them hither with a hymn of olden
time, Bhaga, the friendly Dakṣa, Mitra,
Aditi,
Aryaman, Varuṇa, Soma, the Aśvins. May
Sarasvatī, auspicious, grant felicity.

4 May the Wind waft to us that pleasant
medicine, may Earth our Mother give
it, and our Father Heaven,
And the joy-giving stones that press the
Soma's juice. Aśvins, may ye, for whom
our spirits long, hear this.

5 Him we invoke for aid who reigns supreme,
the Lord of all that stands or moves,
inspirer of the soul,
That Pūṣan may promote the increase of
our wealth, our keeper and our guard
infallible for our good.

6 Illustrious far and wide, may Indra prosper
us : may Pūṣan prosper us, the Master
of all wealth.
May Tārkṣya with uninjured fellies prosper us: Bṛhaspati vouchsafe to us prosperity.

7 The Maruts, Sons of Pṛśni, borne by spotted steeds, moving in glory, oft visiting
holy rites,
Sages whose tongue is Agni, brilliant as the
Sun,—hither let all the Gods for our
protection come.

8 Gods, may we with our ears listen to what
is good, and with our eyes see what is
good, ye Holy Ones.
With limbs and bodies firm may we extolling you attain the term of life appointed
by the Gods.

9 A hundred autumns stand before us, O ye
Gods, within whose space ye bring our
bodies to decay;
Within whose space our sons become fathers
in turn. Break ye not in the midst our
course of fleeting life.

---

2 *He who holds the thunder* : the holder of the
thunder or thunderbolt is Indra.

3 *Have they set the stone in motion* : men have pressed
out the Some juice and offered libations to you.

4 *And to this solemn worship* : (*vārkāryām ca devīm*)
'The most likely supposition is that vārkāryā was the
name given to some famous hymn, some paean or
song of triumph belonging to the Gotamas. The purport
of the whole line then would be that many days have
gone for the Maruts as well as for the famous hymn
addressed to them, or, in other words, that the
Gotamas have long been devoted to the Maruts....The
pushing up of the lid of the well for to drink, means
that they obtained rain from the cloud, which is here,
as before, represented as a covered well.'—Max Müller.

6 This verse is very obscure. I follow M.M.'s
translation which 'is to a great extent conjectural.'

3 *Bhaga*, enumerated by Yāska among the deities
of the highest sphere, is an Āditya regarded in the
Veda as bestowing wealth and instituting or presiding
over love and marriage. *Dakṣa* is a creative power
associated with Aditi, and therefore sometimes identified with Prajāpati.

4 *Our Father Heaven*: pitā Dyaús=Pater Ζεús,
Jupiter.

6 *Tārkṣya* : usually described as a divine horse
and probably a personification of the Sun, *Bṛhaspati* :
Lord of Prayer.

7 *Whose tongue is Agni* : who receive oblations
through Agni or fire.

9 *A hundred autumns* : regarded as the natural length
of human life. Cf. Isaiah, LXV. 20 'There shall be
no more thence an infant of days, nor an old man
that hath not filled his days : for the child shall die
an hundred years old.'

10 Aditi is the heaven, Aditi is mid-air, Aditi
is the Mother and the Sire and Son.
Aditi is all Gods, Aditi five-classed men,
Aditi all that hath been born and shall
be born.

HYMN XC.   *Viśvedevas.*

1. MAY Varuṇa with guidance straight, and
Mitra lead us, he who knows,
And Aryaman in accord with Gods.

2 For they are dealers forth of wealth, and,
not deluded, with their might
Guard evermore the holy laws.

3 Shelter may they vouchsafe to us, Immortal
Gods to mortal men,
Chasing our enemies away.

4 May they mark out our paths to bliss, Indra,
the Maruts, Pūṣan, and
Bhaga, the Gods to be adored.

5 Yea, Pūṣan, Viṣṇu, ye who run your
course, enrich our hymns with kine;
Bless us with all prosperity.

6 The winds waft sweets, the rivers pour
sweets for the man who keeps the Law :
So may the plants be sweet for us.

7 Sweet be the night and sweet the dawns,
sweet the terrestrial atmosphere;
Sweet be our Father Heaven to us.

8 May the tall tree be full of sweets for us,
and full of sweets the Sun :
May our milch-kine be sweet for us.

9 Be Mitra gracious unto us, and Varuṇa
and Aryaman:
Indra, Bṛhaspati be kind, and Viṣṇu of
the mighty stride.

HYMN XCI.   *Soma.*

1. Thou, Soma, art preëminent for wisdom;
along the straightest path thou art our
leader.
Our wise forefathers by thy guidance, Indu,
dealt out among the Gods their share
of treasure.

2 Thou by thine insight art most wise, O
Soma, strong by thine energies and all-
possessing,
Mighty art thou by all thy powers and
greatness, by glories art thou glorious,
guide of mortals.

3 Thine are King Varuṇa's eternal statutes,
lofty and deep, O Soma, is thy glory.
All-pure art thou like Mitra the beloved,
adorable, like Aryaman, O Soma.

4 With all thy glories on the earth, in
heaven, on mountains, in the plants,
and in the waters,—
With all of these, well-pleased and not in
anger, accept, O royal Soma, our
oblations.

5 Thou, Soma, art the Lord of heroes, King,
yea, Vṛtra-slayer thou :
Thou art auspicious energy.

6 And, Soma, let it be thy wish that we may
live and may not die :
Praise-loving Lord of plants art thou.

7 To him who keeps the law, both old and
young, thou givest happiness,
And energy that he may live.

8 Guard us, King Soma, on all sides from
him who threatens us : never let
The friend of one like thee be harmed.

9 With those delightful aids which thou hast,
Soma, for the worshipper,—
Even with those protect thou us.

10 Accepting this our sacrifice and this our
praise, O Soma, come,
And be thou nigh to prosper us.

11 Well-skilled in speech we magnify thee,
Soma, with our sacred songs :
Come thou to us, most gracious One.

12 Enricher, healer of disease, wealth-finder,
prospering our store,
Be, Soma, a good Friend to us.

13 Soma, be happy in our heart, as milch-
kine in the grassy meads,
As a young man in his own house.

14 O Soma, God, the mortal man who in thy
friendship hath delight,
Him doth the mighty Sage befriend.

15 Save us from slanderous reproach, keep us,
O Soma, from distress:
Be unto us a gracious Friend.

16 Soma, wax great. From every side may
vigorous powers unite in thee :
Be in the gathering-place of strength.

17 Wax, O most gladdening Soma, great
through all thy rays of light, and be

---

10 *Aditi* : the Infinite, infinite Nature.

9 *Viṣṇu of the mighty stride* : as the Sun, striding
over or traversing the three worlds.

1 *Indu* : another name of Soma, here identified
with the Moon who teaches men the proper seasons
at which to worship the Manes or deified Fathers.
See 1. 43. 8, note.

3 *Thine are King Varuṇa's eternal statutes* : thy laws
are the same as Varuṇa's laws have their origin in
thee.

14 *The mighty Sage* : Soma himself.
16 *Be in the gathering place of strength* : be thou the
central point and source of all power.

17 *Through all thy rays of light* : through all thy
stalks, according to Ludwig who takes Soma to be the
plant. Wilson, following Sāyaṇa, translates : 'Increase
with all twining plants.'

A Friend of most illustrious fame to prosper us.

18 In thee be juicy nutriments united, and powers and mighty foe-subduing vigour,
Waxing to immortality, O Soma : win highest glories for thyself in heaven.

19 Such of thy glories as with poured oblations men honour, may they all invest our worship.
Wealth-giver, furtherer with troops of heroes, sparing the brave, come, Soma, to our houses.

20 To him who worships Soma gives the milch-cow, a fleet steed and a man of active knowledge,
Skilled in home duties, meet for holy synod, for council meet, a glory to his father.

21 Invincible in fight, saver in battles, guard of our camp, winner of light and water,
Born amid hymns, well-housed, exceeding famous, victor, in thee will we rejoice, O Soma.

22 These herbs, these milch-kine, and these running waters, all these, O Soma, thou hast generated.
The spacious firmament hast thou expanded, and with the light thou hast dispelled the darkness.

23 Do thou, God Soma, with thy Godlike spirit, victorious, win for us a share of riches.
Let none prevent thee : thou art Lord of valour. Provide for both sides in the fray for booty.

HYMN XCII. *Dawn.*

1. THESE Dawns have raised their banner; in the eastern half of the mid-air they spread abroad their shining light.
Like heroes who prepare their weapons for the war, onward they come bright red in hue, the Mother Cows.

2 Readily have the purple beams of light shot up ; the Red Cows have they harnessed, easy to be yoked.
The Dawns have brought distinct percept-

ion as before : red-hued, they have attained their fulgent brilliancy.

3 They sing their song like women active in their tasks, along their common path hither from far away,
Bringing refreshment to the liberal devotee, yea, all things to the worshipper who pours the juice.

4 She, like a dancer, puts her broidered garments on : as a cow yields her udder so she bares her breast.
Creating light for all the world of life, the Dawn hath laid the darkness open as the cows their stall.

5 We have beheld the brightness of her shining; it spreads and drives away the darksome monster.
Like tints that deck the Post at sacrifices, Heaven's Daughter hath attained her wondrous splendour.

6 We have o'erpast the limit of this darkness; Dawn breaking forth again brings clear perception.
She like a flatterer smiles in light for glory, and fair of face hath wakened to rejoice us.

7 The Gotamas have praised Heaven's radiant Daughter, the leader of the charm of pleasant voices.
Dawn, thou conferrest on us strength with offspring and men, conspicuous with kine and horses.

8 O thou who shinest forth in wondrous glory, urged onward by thy strength, auspicious Lady,
Dawn, may I gain that wealth, renowned and ample, in brave sons, troops of slaves, far-famed for horses.

9 Bending her looks on all the world, the Goddess shines, widely spreading with her bright eye westward.
Waking to motion every living creature, she understands the voice of each adorer.

---

22 *These milch-kine* : the milk which is to be mixed with the Soma juice.

1 *These Dawns* : 'We have the term Uṣasaḥ, in the plural, intending, according to the Commentator, the divinities that preside over the morning : but, according to Yāska, the plural is used honorifically only, for the singular personification.'—Wilson.
The Mother Cows : the Dawns, with their red clouds, who have just given birth to the day.
2 *The Red Cows* : the red clouds of morning.

3 *Who pours the juice* : presses out and offers libations of Soma juice.

4 *Hath laid the darkness open* : the meaning, rather obscurely expressed with a harsh zeugma or ellipsis, is, Dawn, with her bright clouds, has opened and emerged from the darkness which surrounded her, in the same manner as cows leave the dark pen or stable in which they have been shut up, as soon as it is opened in the early morning.

5 *Like tints that deck the Post* : the sacrificial post or pillar, to which the victims were tied, was anointed by the priests.

7 *Pleasant voices* : of the newly-awakened birds, other animals, and human beings.

10 Ancient of days, again again born newly,
   decking her beauty with the self-same
   raiment.
   The Goddess wastes away the life of
   mortals, like a skilled hunter cutting
   birds in pieces.

11 She hath appeared discovering heaven's
   borders: to the far distance she drives
   off her Sister.
   Diminishing the days of human creatures,
   the Lady shines with all her lover's
   splendour.

12 The bright, the blessed One shines forth
   extending her rays like kine, as a flood
   rolls his waters.
   Never transgressing the divine commandments, she is beheld visible with the
   sunbeams.

13 O Dawn enriched with ample wealth,
   bestow on us the wondrous gift
   Wherewith we may support children and
   children's sons.

14 Thou radiant mover of sweet sounds, with
   wealth of horses and of kine
   Shine thou on us this day, O Dawn
   auspiciously.

15 O Dawn enriched with holy rites, yoke
   to thy car thy purple steeds,
   And then bring thou unto us all felicities.

16 O Aśvins wonderful in act, do ye unanimous direct
   Your chariot to our home wealthy in kine
   and gold.

17 Ye who brought down the hymn from
   heaven, a light that giveth light to man,
   Do ye, O Aśvins, bring strength hither unto us.

18 Hither may they who wake at dawn bring,
   to drink Soma, both the Gods,
   Health-givers, Wonder-Workers, borne on
   paths of gold.

HYMN XCIII.   Agni-Soma.

1 AGNI and Soma, mighty Pair, graciously
   hearken to my call,
   Accept in friendly wise my hymn, and
   prosper him who offers gifts.

2 The man who honours you to-day, Agni
   and Soma, with this hymn,
   Bestow on him heroic strength, increase of
   kine, and noble steeds.

3 The man who offers holy oil and burnt
   oblations unto you,
   Agni and Soma, shall enjoy great strength,
   with offspring, all his life.

4 Agni and Soma, famed is that your prowess wherewith ye stole the kine, his
   food, from Paṇi.
   Ye caused the brood of Bṛsaya to perish;
   ye found the light, the single light for
   many.

5 Agni and Soma, joined in operation ye
   have set up the shining lights in heaven.
   From curse and from reproach, Agni and
   Soma, ye freed the rivers that were
   bound in fetters.

6 One of you Mātariśvan brought from
   heaven, the Falcon rent the other from
   the mountain.
   Strengthened by holy prayer Agni and
   Soma have made us ample room for
   sacrificing.

7 Taste, Agni, Soma, this prepared oblation;
   accept it, Mighty Ones, and let it
   please you.
   Vouchsafe us good protection and kind
   favour: grant to the sacrificer health and
   riches.

8 Whoso with oil and poured oblation honours, with God-devoted heart, Agni and
   Soma,—
   Protect his sacrifice, preserve him from
   distress, grant to the sacrificer great
   felicity.

---

10 *Like a skilled hunter cutting birds in pieces* :
Sāyaṇa takes *śvaghnī* for a fowler's wife', and *vijaḥ* for
'birds.' Benfey takes *vijaḥ* for 'dice,' and explains the
clause as denoting a cunning gambler who tampers
with the dice by shaving them down...The phrase
vijaḥ iva ā mināti occurs again in RV,II. 12. 5, where
Sāyaṇa takes *vijaḥ* for *udvejakaḥ* 'a vexer.' So uncertain
are his explanations '—J. Muir, *O.S. Texts*, V. 186.

11 *Her sister* : Night. *Her lover* : the Sun.

12 *Never transgressing* : always obedient to the
eternal Law or divine order of the universe.

18 *They who wake at dawn* : according to Sāyaṇa,
the horses of the Aśvins. The expression may apply,
with at least equal propriety, to the priests who rise
at day-break to perform the morning sacrifices.

1 *Agni and Soma* : or, O Aṇgi-Soma, the two
Gods forming a dual deity *dgniṣomau*.

4 *Ye stole the kine* : recovered the cows (the rain-
clouds, or rays of light) which the niggard demon had
carried off and concealed. *Bṛsaya* : the name of a
demon or savage enemy.

5 *From curse and from reproach* : according to
Sāyaṇa, 'the rivers were defiled by the dead body of
Vṛtra, which had fallen into them ; their waters were,
consequently, unfit to bear any part in sacred rites,
until they were purified by Agni and Soma, that is,
by oblations to fire and libations of Soma Juice.'—
Wilson.

6 *Mātariśvan*, or in the nominative case, Mātariśvā,
brought Agni or fire from heaven, and the Falcon
brought Soma from the mountain or cloud, that is,
says Sāyaṇa, from Svarga on the top of Mount Meru.

9 Invoked together, mates in wealth, Agni-
Soma, accept our hymns:
Together be among the Gods.

10 Agni and Soma, unto him who worships
you with holy oil
Shine forth an ample recompense.

11 Agni and Soma, be ye pleased with these
oblations brought to you,
And come, together, nigh to us.

12 Agni and Soma, cherish well our horses,
and let our cows be fat who yield oblations.
Grant power to us and to our wealthy
patrons, and cause our holy rites to be
successful.

HYMN XCIV.   *Agni*

1 FOR Jātavedas worthy of our praise will
we frame with our mind this eulogy as
'twere a car.
For good, in his assembly, is this care of
ours. Let us not, in thy friendship,
Agni, suffer harm.

2 The man for whom thou sacrificest prospereth, dwelleth without a foe, gaineth
heroic might.
He waxeth strong, distress never approacheth him. Let us not, in thy friendship, Agni, suffer harm.

3 May we have power to kindle thee. Fulfil our thoughts. In thee the Gods eat
the presented offering,
Bring hither the Ādityas, for we long for
them. Let us not in thy friendship,
Agni, suffer harm.

4 We will bring fuel and prepare burnt
offerings, reminding thee at each successive festival.
Fulfil our thought that so we may prolong our lives. Let us not in thy friendship, Agni, suffer harm.

5 His ministers move forth, the guardians
of the folk, protecting quadruped and
biped with their rays.

Mighty art thou, the wondrous herald of
the Dawn. Let us not in thy friendship, Agni, suffer harm.

6 Thou art Presenter and the chief Invoker,
thou Director, Purifier, great High Priest
by birth.
Knowing all priestly work thou perfectest
it, Sage. Let us not in thy friendship,
Agni, suffer harm.

7 Lovely of form art thou, alike on every
side; though far, thou shinest brightly
as if close at hand.
O God, thou seest through even the dark
of night. Let us not in thy friendship,
Agni, suffer harm.

8 Gods, foremost be his car who pours
libations out, and let our hymn prevail
o'er evil-hearted men.
Attend to this our speech and make it prosper well. Let us not in thy friendship,
Agni, suffer harm.

9 Smite with thy weapons those of evil speech
and thought, devouring demons, whether
near or far away.
Then to the singer give free way for sacrifice. Let us not in thy friendship, Agni,
suffer harm.

10 When to thy chariot thou hadst yoked two
red steeds and two ruddy steeds, wind-
sped, thy roar was like a bull's.
Thou with smoke-bannered flame attackest
forest trees. Let us not in thy friendship,
Agni, suffer harm.

11 Then at thy roar the very birds are terrified, when, eating-up the grass, thy sparks
fly forth abroad.
Then is it easy for thee and thy car to pass.
Let us not in thy friendship, Agni, suffer
harm.

12 He hath the power to soothe Mitra and
Varuṇa: wonderful is tht Maruts' wrath
when they descend.
Be gracious: let their hearts be turned to
us again. Let us not in thy friendship,
Agni, suffer harm.

---

12 *Who yield oblations* : who supply milk to be mixed
with Soma juice.

Our wealthy patrons : the rich house-holders who
institute the sacrifices.

———

This Hymn and the four following are attributed
to the Ṛṣi Kutsa, the son of Aṅgiras.
1 *Jātavedas* : Agni. See I. 44. 1.
As 'twere a car : as a carpenter constructs a car
or wain.
In his assembly : among those who have met
together to worship him. The meaning might also
be : good, or auspicious, is his providence or loving
care of us.
3 *Bring hither the Ādityas* : the sons of Aditi ; all
the Gods, according to Sāyaṇa.
5 *His ministers* : his beams of light.

6 'Agni is here identified with the chief of the
sixteen priests engaged at solemn sacrifices. He is
Adhvaryu usually called the reciter of the *Yajus*—here
defined, by the scholiast, as the presenter of the
offerings : he is the *Hotṛ*, or invoking priest : he is
the *Praśāstṛ* or the *Maitravaruṇa*, whose duty it is to
direct the other priests what to do, and when to perform their functions : he is the *potṛ*, or priest so termed
and the family or hereditary *purohita* : or *purohita* may
be the same as the *Brahma* of a ceremony'—being, to
men, what *Bṛhaspati* is to the gods'.—Wilson.

12 *He hath the power* : Agni persuades Mitra and
Varuṇa to send the rain and protects men from the
fury of the Storm-Gods.

13 Thou art a God, thou art the wondrous Friend of Gods, the Vasu of the Vasus, fair in sacrifice.
Under, thine own most wide protection may we dwell. Let us not in thy friendship, Agni, suffer harm.

14 This is thy grace that, kindled in thine own abode, invoked with Soma thou soundest forth most benign,
Thou givest wealth and treasure to the worshipper. Let us not in thy friendship, Agni, suffer harm.

15 To whom thou, Lord of goodly riches, grantest freedom from every sin with perfect wholeness,
Whom with good strength thou quikenest, with children and wealth—may we be they, Eternal Being.

16 Such, Agni, thou who knowest all good fortune, God, lengthen here the days of our existence.
This prayer of ours may Varuṇa grant, and Mitra, and Aditi and Sindhu, Earth and Heaven.

HYMN XCV.   *Agni*

1. To fair goals travel Two unlike in semblance: each in succession nourishes an infant.
One bears a Godlike Babe of golden colour; bright and fair-shining is he with the other.

2 Tvaṣṭar's ten daughters, vigilant and youthful, produced this Infant borne to sundry quarters.
They bear around him whose long flames are pointed, fulgent among mankind with native splendour.

3. Three several places of his birth they honour, in mid-air, in the heaven, and in the waters.
Governing in the east of earthly regions, the seasons hath he stablished in their order.

4 Who of you knows this secret One ? The Infant by his own nature hath brought forth his Mothers.
The germ of many, from the waters' bosom he goes forth, wise and great, of Godlike nature.

5 Visible, fair, he grows in native brightness uplifted in the lap of waving waters.
When he was born both Tvaṣṭar's worlds were frightened: they turn to him and reverence the Lion.

6 The Two auspicious Ones, like women, tend him: like lowing cows they seek him in their manner.
He is the Lord of Might among the mighty; him, on the right, they balm with their oblations.

7 Like Savitar his arms with might he stretches; awful, he strives grasping the world's two borders.
He forces out from all a brilliant vesture, yea, from his Mothers draws he forth new raiment.

8 He makes him a most noble form of splendour, decking him in his home with milk and waters.
The Sage adorns the depths of air with wisdom : this is the meeting where the Gods are worshipped.

9 Wide through the firmament spreads forth triumphant the far-resplendent strength of thee the Mighty.

13 *The Vasu of the Vasus* best of the class of Gods called Vasus ; or 'the good among the good.'

16 The second line of this verse terminates the following hymns, with two exceptions, as far as the hundred and first *Sūkta*. Mitra, Varuṇa, and Aditi have been before noticed. By *Sindhu* is to be understood the divinity presiding over, or identified with, flowing water, and it may mean either the sea or flowing streams collectively, or the river Indus. *Pṛthivi* and *Div* are the personified earth and heaven. These are requested to *honour*, meaning, to preserve, or perpetuate, whatever blessing has been asked for (*tat...mām-ahantām*) ; from *mah*, to venerate or worship.'-Wilson.

1 The *Two* are Day and Night, and the infant that each suckles in turn is Agni, as the Sun by day and Fire, or the Moon, by night.

2 *Tvaṣṭar's ten daughters* : the fingers, called daughters of the artist of the Gods on account of the skill and speed with which they perform their work, generate Agni by the attrition of the fire-sticks, and then the newly-born babe is carried about hither and thither to light the various sacrificial fires.

3 In his character of the Sun he rules especially in the east, and has established and regulates the seasons of the year.

4 *This secret One* : Agni latent in the waters, in the woods etc. '*Agni*, in the form of lightning, may be considered as the son of waters collected in the clouds ; and those waters he is said to generate by the oblations he conveys.'—Wilson.

5 *Both Tvaṣṭar's worlds* : heaven and earth, formed by the divine artist represented as the Creator. Sāyaṇa takes *tvaṣṭuḥ* as an epithet of Agni, and accordingly Wilson translates : 'Both (heaven and earth) are alarmed, as the radiant Agni is born.'

6 *The Two auspicious Ones* : Heaven and Earth.

On the right : standing on the right side of the altar, the priests anoint him with offerings of clarified butter.

7 *Savitar* : the Sun. According to Sāyaṇa the Sun is called Savitar before rising, and Sūrya from his rising till his setting. *His Mothers* : are the Waters.

8 *The Sage* : Agni. *This is the meeting* : all this is the reason why men assemble to worship the Gods.

Kindled by us do thou preserve us, Agni,
with all thy self-bright undiminished
succours.

10 In dry spots he makes stream, and course,
and torrent, and inundates the earth
with floods that glisten.

All ancient things within his maw he
gathers, and moves among the new
fresh-sprouting grasses.

11 Fed with our fuel, purifying Agni, so blaze
to us auspiciously for glory.

This prayer of ours may Varuṇa grant,
and Mitra, and Aditi and Sindhu, Earth
and Heaven.

HYMN XCVI. *Agni.*

1. HE in the ancient way by strength engendered, lo ! straight hath taken to himself all wisdom.

The waters and the bowl have made him
friendly. The Gods possessed the wealth-
bestowing Agni.

2 At Āyu's ancient call he by his wisdom
gave all this progeny of men their being,

And, by refulgent light, heaven and the
waters. The Gods possessed the wealth-
bestowing Agni.

3 Praise him, ye Āryan folk, as chief performer of sacrifice adored and ever toiling,

Well-tended, Son of Strength, the constant
Giver. The Gods possessed the wealth-
bestowing Agni.

4 That Mātariśvan rich in wealth and
treasure, light-winner, finds a pathway
for his offspring,

Guard of our folk, Father of earth and
heaven. The Gods possessed the wealth-
bestowing Agni.

5 Night and Dawn, changing each the
other's colour, meeting together suckle
one same Infant :

1 *By strength engendered* : produced by violent
agitation of the fire-sticks.

Possessed : before he was visible to men.

The bowl : the Soma juice contained in the
dhiṣdṇā, or bowl. *Dhiṣdṇā* may be otherwise explained. Sāyaṇa, who is followed by Wilson, takes it
to mean *vāk*, speech. Ludwig renders it by 'wish, or
Wish-Goddess Dhiṣaṇā;' Grassmann by 'sacrificial
offerings.'

2 *At Āyu's ancient call* : at the invitation of Āyu
(living man) said by Sāyaṇa to be another name of
Manu, the progenitor of mankind.

4 *Mātariśvan* : usually the name of the divine
being who brought Agni from heaven (see I. 31.8),
said by Sāyaṇa to mean in this place Agni himself.

5 *One same Infant* : Agni (see I.95.1.) whom
they nourish with the oblation offered by men.

Golden : as the Sun.

Golden between the heaven and earth he
shineth. The Gods possessed the wealth-
bestowing Agni.

6 Root of wealth, gathering-place of treasures,
banner of sacrifice, who grants the suppliant's wishes :

Preserving him as their own life immortal,
the Gods possessed the wealth-bestowing
Agni.

7 Now and of old the home of wealth, the
mansion of what is born and what was
born aforetime,

Guard of what is and what will be hereafter,—the Gods possessed the wealth-
bestowing Agni.

8 May the Wealth-Giver grant us conquering riches; may the Wealth-Giver grant
us wealth with heroes.

May the Wealth-Giver grant us food with
offspring, and length of days may the
Wealth-Giver send us.

9 Fed with our fuel, purifying Agni, so blaze
to us auspiciously for glory.

This prayer of ours may Varuṇa grant,
and Mitra, and Aditi and Sindhu,
Earth and Heaven.

HYMN XCVII. *Agni.*

1. CHASING with light our sin away, O Agni,
shine thou wealth on us.

May his light chase our sin away.

2 For goodly fields, for pleasant homes, for
wealth we sacrifice to thee.

May his light chase our sin away.

3 Best praiser of all these be he ; foremost,
our chiefs who sacrifice.

May his light chase our sin away.

4 So that thy worshippers and we, thine,
Agni, in our sons may live.

May his light chase our sin away.

5 As ever-conquering Agni's beams of splendour go to every side,

May his light chase our sin away.

6 To every side thy face is turned, thou art
triumphant everywhere.

May his light chase our sin away.

7 O thou whose face looks every way, bear
us past foes as in a ship.

May his light chase our sin away.

8 As in a ship, convey thou us for our advantage o'er the flood.

May his light chase our sin away.

3 May he, that is Kutsa, the Ṛṣi of the hymn,
be preëminent among these who celebrate thy praises,
and may the householders who have instituted this
sacrifice be similarly distinguished.

HYMN XCVIII.   *Agni.*

1. STILL in Vaiśvānara's grace may we continue : yea, he is King supreme o'er all things living.
Sprung hence to life upon this All he looketh. Vaiśvānara hath rivalry with Sūrya.

2 Present in heaven, in earth, all-present Agni,—all plants that grow on ground hath he pervaded.
May Agni, may Vaiśvānara with vigour, present, preserve us day and night from foemen.

3 Be this thy truth, Vaiśvānara, to us-ward : let wealth in rich abundance gather round us.
This prayer of ours may Varuṇa grant, and Mitra, and Aditi and Sindhu, Earth and Heaven.

HYMN XCIX.   *Agni.*

1. FOR Jātavedas let us press the Soma : may he consume the wealth of the malignant.
May Agni carry us through all our troubles, through grief as in a boat across the river.

HYMN C.   *Indra.*

1. MAY he who hath his home with strength, the Mighty, the King supreme of earth and spacious heaven,
Lord of true power, to be invoked in battles,—may Indra, girt by Maruts, be our succour.

2 Whose way is unattainable like Sūrya's : he in each fight is the strong Vṛtra-slayer,
Mightiest with his Friends in his own courses. May Indra, girt by Maruts, be our succour.

3 Whose paths go forth in their great might resistless, forthmilking, as it were, heaven's genial moisture.
With manly strength triumphant, foe-subduer,—may Indra, girt by Maruts, be our succour.

4 Among Aṅgirases he was the chiefest, a Friend with friends, mighty amid the mighty.
Praiser mid praisers, honoured most of singers. May Indra, girt by Maruts, be our succour.

5 Strong with the Rudras as with his own children, in manly battle conquering his foemen,
With his close comrades doing deeds of glory,—may Indra, girt by Maruts, be our succour.

6 Humbler of pride, exciter of the conflict, the Lord of heroes, God invoked of many,
May he this day gain with our men the sunlight. May Indra, girt by Maruts, be our succour.

7 His help hath made him cheerer in the battle, the folk have made him guardian of their comfort.
Sole Lord is he of every holy service. May Indra, girt by Maruts, be our succour.

8 To him the Hero, on high days of prowess, heroes for help and booty shall betake them.
He hath found light even in the blinding darkness. May Indra, girt by Maruts, be our succour.

9 He with his left hand checketh even the mighty, and with his right hand gathereth up the booty.
Even with the humble he acquireth riches. May Indra, girt by Maruts, be our succour.

10 With hosts on foot and cars he winneth treasures : well is he known this day by all the people.
With manly might he conquereth those who hate him. May Indra, girt by Maruts, be our succour.

11 When in his ways with kinsmen or with strangers he speedeth to the fight, invoked of many,

1 *Vaiśvānara*, is an epithet of Agni or Fire as present with, common to, or benefiting, all men.
Sprung hence to life : produced from these two *araṇis* or fire-sticks.

This Hymn, consisting of a single stanza, is ascribed to the Ṛṣi Kaśyapa, the son of Marīci.

This Hymn is ascribed to the regal Ṛṣis the Vārṣāgiras, the five sons of the Rājā .Vṛṣāgir, whose names are mentioned in the seventeenth stanza.
3 *Whose paths* : *pánthāsaḥ*, paths, is explained as 'rays' by Sāyaṇa. Indra is here represented as the God of light and rain.

5 *Rudras* : the Maruts, sons of Rudra the chief Storm-God. They are the *close comrades* or faithful companions of Indra, who regards them not as his equals but as his children.
6 *The sunlight* : the hymn is addressed to Indra for aid in approaching battle. Sāyaṇa says that the Vārṣāgiras pray that they may have daylight and that their enemies may fight in the dark.
7 Indra is regarded as their helper and inspiriter in battle and their protector in peace. He also presides over all acts of worship, and as such rewards those who serve him.
9 *Even the humble* : not the strong only, but the feeble man also acquires riches with his help.

For gain of waters, and of sons and grandsons, may Indra, girt by Maruts, be our
succour.

12 Awful and fierce, fiend-slayer, thunder-
wielder, with boundless knowledge,
hymned by hundreds, mighty,
In strength like Soma, guard of the Five
Peoples, may Indra, girt by Maruts, be
our succour.

13 Winning the light, hitherward roars his
thunder like the terrific mighty voice of
Heaven.
Rich gifts and treasures evermore attend
him. May Indra, girt by Maruts, be
our succour.

14 Whose home eternal through his strength
surrounds him on every side, his laud,
the earth and heaven,
May he, delighted with our service, save
us. May Indra, girt by Maruts, be our
succour.

15 The limit of whose power not Gods by
Godhead, nor mortal men have reached, nor yet the Waters.
Both Earth and Heaven in vigour he surpasseth. May Indra, girt by Maruts,
be our succour.

16 The red and tawny mare, blaze-marked,
high standing, celestial who, to bring
Rjrāśva riches,
Drew at the pole the chariot yoked with
stallions, joyous, among the hosts of
men was noted.

17 The Vārṣāgiras unto thee, O Indra, the
Mighty One, sing forth this laud to
please thee,
Rjrāśva with his fellows, Ambarīṣa,
Surādhas, Sahadeva, Bhayamāna.

18 He, much invoked, hath slain Dasyus and
Śimyus, after his wont, and laid them
low with arrows.

12 *Guard of the Five Peoples* : of the five classes of
beings, according to Sāyaṇa, that is, Gods, Gandharvas,
Apsarases, Asuras and Rākṣasas. Probably the five
Ārya tribes are intended See I, 7.9.

14 *The Earth and Heaven*, his dwelling-place, are his
everlasting song of praise because they have been
established and regulated by him. This is Ludwig's
explanation of this obscure verse.

16 The epithets in this stanza are taken by 'Ludwig as names of the six horses with which Rjrāśva
drove to battle and conquered. The last four verses
of the hymn appear to have been added after the
victory.

18 *Dasyus and Śimyus* : men of indigenous hostile
races.

His fair-complexioned friends : explained by Sāyaṇa
as the glittering Maruts, means probably the Āryan
invaders as opposed to the dark-skinned races of the
country.

———

The mighty Thunderer with his fair-complexioned friends won the land, the
sunlight, and the waters.

19 May Indra evermore be our protector,
and unimperilled may we win the booty.
This prayer of ours may Varuṇa grant,
and Mitra, and Aditi and Sindhu, Earth
and Heaven.

HYMN CI.   *Indra.*

1. SING, with oblation, praise to him who
maketh glad, who with Rjiśvan drove
the dusky brood away.
Fain for help, him the strong whose right
hand wields the bolt, him girt by
Maruts we invoke to be our Friend.

2 Indra, who with triumphant wrath smote
Vyaṁsa down, and Śambara, and Pipru
the unrighteous one;
Who extirpated Śuṣṇa the insatiate,—
him girt by Maruts we invoke to be
our Friend.

3 He whose great work of manly might is
heaven and earth, and Varuṇa and
Sūrya keep his holy law ;
Indra, whose law the rivers follow as they
flow,—him girt by Maruts we invoke
to be our Friend.

4 He who is Lord and Master of the steeds
and kine, honoured—the firm and sure—
at every holy act;
Slayer even of the strong who pours no
offering out,— him girt by Maruts we
invoke to be our Friend.

5 He who is Lord of all the world that
moves and breathes, who for the Brāhman first before all found the Cows;
Indra who cast the Dasyus down beneath
his feet,—him girt by Maruts we invoke
to be our Friend.

6 Whom cowards must invoke and valiant
men of war, invoked by those who conquer and by those who flee;
Indra, to whom all beings turn their
constant thought,—him girt by Maruts
we invoke to be our Friend.

This Hymn and the following thirteen are ascribed
to the Ṛṣi Kutsa.

1 *Rjiśvan* : a king, favoured and protected by
Indra. See I. 51.5 ; 53.8.

The dusky brood : the dark aborigines who opposed
the Āryans.

2 *Vyaṁsa, Śambara*, and *Śuṣṇa* are names of fiends
of drought.

5 *Who for the Brāhman* : according to Sāyaṇa,
who recovered for the Aṅgirases the cows that had
been carried off by the Paṇis. See I. 32. 11.

7 Refulgent in the Rudras' region he proceeds,
and with the Rudras through the wide
space speeds the Dame.
The hymn of praise extols Indra the far-
renowned : him girt by Maruts we invoke
to be our Friend.

8 O girt by Maruts, whether thou delight
thee in loftiest gathering-place or lowly
dwelling,
Come thence unto our rite, true boon-best-
ower : through love of thee have we
prepared oblations.

9 We, fain for thee, strong Indra, have
pressed Soma, and, O thou sought with
prayer, have made oblations.
Now at this sacrifice, with all thy Maruts,
on sacred grass, O team-borne God,
rejoice thee.

10 Rejoice thee with thine own Bay Steeds, O
Indra, unclose thy jaws and let thy lips
be open.
Thou with the fair cheek, let thy Bay
Steeds bring thee : gracious to us, be
pleased with our oblation.

11 Guards of the camp whose praisers are the
Maruts, may we through Indra, get ourselves the booty.
This prayer of ours may Varuṇa grant,
and Mitra, and Aditi and Sindhu, Earth
and Heaven.

HYMN CII. *Indra.*

1. To thee the Mighty One I bring this
mighty hymn, for thy desire hath been
gratified by my laud.
In Indra, yea in him victorious through
his strength, the Gods have joyed at
feast and when the Soma flowed.

2 The Seven Rivers bear his glory far and
wide, and heaven and sky and earth display his comely form.
The Sun and Moon in change alternate
run their course, that we, O Indra, may
behold and may have faith.

3 Maghavan, grant us that same car to bring
us spoil, thy conquering car in which
we joy in shock of fight.
Thou, Indra, whom our hearts praise highly

in the war, grant shelter, Maghavan, to
us who love thee well.

4 Encourage thou our side in every fight:
may we, with thee for our ally, conquer
the foeman's host.
Indra, bestow on us joy and felicity:
break down, O Maghavan, the vigour of
our foes.

5 For here in divers ways these men invoking thee, holder of treasures, sing thee
hymns to win thine aid.
Ascend the car that thou mayest bring
spoil to us, for, Indra, thy fixt mind
winneth the victory.

6 His arms win kine, his power is boundless,
in each act best, with a hundred helps,
waker of battle's din
Is Indra : none may rival him in mighty
strength. Hence, eager for the spoil,
the people call on him.

7 Thy glory, Maghavan, exceeds a hundred,
yea, more than a hundred, than a thousand mid the folk,
The great bowl hath inspirited thee bound-
lessly : so mayst thou slay the Vṛtras,
breaker-down of forts !

8 Of thy great might there is a threefold
counterpart, the three earths, Lord of
men and the three realms of light.
Above this whole world, Indra, thou hast
waxen great : without a foe art thou, by
nature, from of old.

9 We invocate thee first among the Deities :
thou hast become a mighty Conqueror
in fight.
May Indra fill with spirit this our singer's
heart, and make our car impetuous,
foremost in attack.

10 Thou hast prevailed, and hast not kept
the booty back, in trifling battles or
in those of great account.
We make thee keen, the Mighty One, to
succour us : inspire us, Maghavan, when
we defy the foe.

11 May Indra evermore be our Protector, and
unimperilled may we win the booty.

---

7 *The Dame* : Ludwig suggests that Rodasī, the
wife of Rudra, is intended, and refers to the Old-
German myth of the Wind's Bride.

11 *Guards of the camp* : may we who are the
guardians of the camp or new settlement, praised and
favoured by the Maruts, win the spoil. The words
marutstotrasya vṛjánasya are somewhat obscure.

---

2 *The Seven Rivers* : the chief rivers in the neighbourhood of the earliest Āryan settlements. See I, 32,
12.

7 *The great bowel* : the vessel containing the
exhilarating Soma juice, or the mighty libation itself.
The *forts* are the cloud-castles of the demons of the
air which Indra destroys with his lightning : 'the
clouds whose moving turrets make the bastions of the
storm.'-Shelley, *Witch of Atlas.*

8 *The three earths* : perhaps the earth, the atmosphere, and the heaven.

The three realms of light : or according to Sāyaṇa,
the three fires or fire in three forms, as the sun in
heaven, the lightning in mid-air, and terrestrial fire on
earth. See also I. 105, 5.

This prayer of ours may Varuṇa grant and Mitra, and Aditi and Sindhu, Earth and Heaven.

HYMN CIII. *Indra.*

1. THAT highest Indra-power of thine is distant : that which is here sages possessed aforetime.
  This one is on the earth, in heaven the other, and both unite as flag with flag in battle.

2 He spread the wide earth out and firmly fixed it, smote with his thunderbolt and loosed the waters.
  Maghavan with his puissance struck down Ahi, rent Rauhiṇa to death and slaughtered Vyaṁsa.

3 Armed with his bolt and trusting in his prowess he wandered shattering the forts of Dāsas.
  Cast thy dart, knowing, Thunderer, at the Dasyu ; increase the Ārya's might and glory, Indra.

4 For him who thus hath taught these human races, Maghavan, bearing a fame-worthy title,
  Thunderer, drawing nigh to slay the Dasyus, hath given himself the name of Son for glory.

5 See this abundant wealth that he possesses, and put your trust in Indra's hero vigour.
  He found the cattle, and he found the horses, he found the plants, the forests and the waters.

6 To him the truly strong, whose deeds are many, to him the strong Bull let us pour the Soma.
  The Hero, watching like a thief in ambush, goes parting the possessions of the godless.

7 Well didst thou do that hero deed, O Indra, in waking with thy bolt the slumbering Ahi.
  In thee, delighted, Dames divine rejoiced them, the flying Maruts and all Gods were joyful.

8 As thou hast smitten Śuṣṇa, Pipru, Vṛtra and Kuyava, and Śambara's forts O Indra.
  This prayer of ours may Varuṇa grant, and Mitra, and Aditi and Sindhu, Earth and Heaven.

HYMN CIV. *Indra.*

1. THE altar hath been made for thee to rest on : come like a panting courser and be seated.
  Loosen thy flying Steeds, set free thy Horses who bear thee swiftly nigh at eve and morning.

2 These men have come to Indra for assistance : shall he not quickly come upon these pathways ?
  May the Gods quell the fury of the Dāsa, and may they lead our folk to happy fortune.

3 He who hath only wish as his possession casts on himself, casts foam amid the waters.
  Both wives of Kuyava in milk have bathed them : may they be drowned within the depth of Śiphā.

4 This hath his kinship checked who lives beside us : with ancient streams forth speeds and rules the Hero,

7 *Dames divine* : the Consorts of the Gods.
8 *Kuyava* : meaning, probably, 'causing bad harvests,' is the name of another of the demons of drought.

---

1 *That highest Indra-power* : Benfey explains this verse as meaning : Indra's might is in a certain way divided : one part of it is possessed by the sages who by their hymns, sacrifices and libations of Soma juice give him complete power to perform his great deeds. Sāyaṇa says that the Sun and fire are equally the lustre of Indra, one in heaven and the other on earth : and that by day fire is combined with the Sun, and by night the Sun is combined with fire.

2 *Rauhiṇa*, said to be a demon, is, like the other fiends of drought, a purple cloud that withholds the rain.

3 *Dāsas* : or Dasyus, the non-Āryan inhabitants of the land.

Knowing : distinguishing the Āryan from the barbarian.

4 The meaning of this verse appears to be, as Ludwig says, that Indra, in preparing to slay the Dasyus, has become, as it were, a son to the pious worshipper who has proclaimed his great deeds to men.

2 *The Dāsa* : explained by Sāyaṇa as the destroying demon. It apparently means here a chief of non-Āryan race whom the suppliants were going to attack.

3 Sāyaṇa explains : the Asura, or demon, Kuyava, who knows the wealth of others carries it away of himself, and being present in the water he carries off the water with the foam. In this water which has been carried away Kuyava's two wives bathe. Benfey takes the foamy water to mean the fertilizing rain. Ludwig's explanation is : While the poor Ārya who can only wish for the wealth which he does not possess has not even ordinary water to wash himself in, the wives of the enemy, in the insolent pride of their riches, bathe in milk.

Kuyava : perhaps a name given by the Āryans to one of the non-Āryan chieftains.

Śiphā, is said by Sāyaṇa to be the name of a river.

4 This stanza is very obscure. The meaning appears to be that the friendship of Indra, who sends down the rain as before, has put an end to the

Añjasī, Kuliśī, and Vīrapatnī, delighting him, bear milk upon their waters.

5 Soon as this Dasyu's traces were discovered, as she who knows her home, he sought the dwelling.

Now think thou of us, Maghavan, nor cast us away as doth a profligate his treasure.

6 Indra, as such, give us a share of sunlight, of waters, sinlessness, and reputation.

Do thou no harm to our yet unborn offspring: our trust is in thy mighty Indra-power.

7 Now we, I think, in thee as such have trusted : lead us on, Mighty One, to ample riches.

In no unready house give us, O Indra invoked of many, food and drink when hungry.

8 Slay us not, Indra; do not thou forsake us: steal not away the joys which we delight in.

Rend not our unborn brood, strong Lord of Bounty ! our vessels with the life that is within them.

9 Come to us; they have called thee Soma-lover : here is the pressed juice. Drink thereof for rapture.

Widely-capacious, pour it down within thee, and, invocated, hear us like a Father.

HYMN CV.   *Viśvedevas.*

1. WITHIN the waters runs the Moon, he with the beauteous wings in heaven.

insolence of Kuyava. See Ludwig, Ueber die neuesten Arbeiten auf dem Gebiete der Rgveda-forschung.

The signification of the three rivers in the second line is obscure. Benfey considers the names to be feminine personifications of the clouds.

Vīrapatnī, 'the hero's wife,' occurs, as Dr. Hall has pointed out, in VI. 49. 7, as an epithet of Sarasvatī the Goddess, and it may possibly here mean the river Sarasvatī.

5 *As she who knows her dwelling* : as a cow who knows her stall.

7 *In no unready house* : that is, in a house well supplied and furnished.

8 *The joys which we delight in* : probably, our children.

Our vessels : our wives with their unborn babes. Sāyaṇa gives other explanations of the expression.

This Hymn is ascribed either to Tṛta or to Kutsa. It is addressed to the Viśvedevas on behalf of Tṛta who had been imprisoned in a well. See I. 52.5. But see Macdonell, *J.R.A.S.*, July, 1893, pp. 422 note 2, and 460.

1 *Within the waters* : in the ocean of air. *He with the beauteous wings* : the Sun.

Mark this my woe : the text has only *vittam me asyd rodasī,* 'know of this of me, O Heaven and Earth,'

Ye lightnings with your golden wheels, men find not your abiding-place. Mark this my woe, ye Earth and Heaven.

2 Surely men crave and gain their wish. Close to her husband clings the wife.

And, in embraces intertwined, both give and take the bliss of love. Mark this my woe, ye Earth and Heaven.

3 O never may that light , ye Gods, fall from its station in the sky.

Ne'er fail us one like Soma sweet, the spring of our felicity. Mark this my woe ye Earth and Heaven.

4 I ask the last of sacrifice. As envoy he shall tell it forth.

Where is the ancient law divine ? Who is its new diffuser now ? Mark this my woe, ye Earth and Heaven.

5 Ye Gods who yonder have your home in the three lucid realms of heaven,

What count ye truth and what untruth ? Where is mine ancient call on you ? Mark this my woe, ye Earth and Heaven.

6 What is your firm support of Law ? What Varuṇa's observant eye ?

How may we pass the wicked on the path of mighty Aryaman ? Mark this my woe, ye Earth and Heaven.

7 I am the man who sang of old full many a laud when Soma flowed.

Yet torturing cares consume me as the wolf assails the thirsty deer. Mark this my woe, ye Earth and Heaven.

8 Like rival wives on every side enclosing ribs oppress me sore.

O Śatakratu, biting cares devour me, singer of thy praise, as rats devour the weaver's threads. Mark this my woe, ye Earth and Heaven.

which means, according to Sāyaṇa, either 'be aware of this my affliction,' or 'attend to this my hymn.'

4 *I ask the last* : the latest or youngest of the Gods, Agni, as being continually reproduced.

5 *The three lucid realms of heaven* : the world is divided into earth, sky, and heaven, and each of these, again, is sometimes spoken of as threefold.

6 *The path of mighty Aryaman* : probably the milky way, regarded as the path to heaven.—Ludwig. The general meaning of the questions in this and the two preceding verses is : Is there no longer any distinction between right and wrong ? Is there no moral government of the world ? If there be, why am I, a faithful worshipper, allowed to suffer this undeserved misery?

8 *Enclosing ribs* : according to Sāyaṇa, the walls of the well in which Tṛta was confined. *Weaver's threads* : the meaning of *śiśnā* thus explained by Sāyaṇa is uncertain. Ludwig is of opinion that wooden phallus-idols are intended. The line recurs in X. 33.3.

9 Where those seven rays are shining, thence
my home and family extend.
This Tṛta Āptya knoweth well, and
speaketh out for brotherhood. Mark
this my woe, ye Earth and Heaven.

10 May those five Bulls which stand on high
full in the midst of mighty heaven,
Having together swiftly borne my praises
to the Gods, return. Mark this my woe,
ye Earth and Heaven.

11 High in the mid ascent of heaven those
Birds of beauteous pinion sit.
Back from his path they drive the wolf as
he would cross the restless floods. Mark
this my woe, ye Earth and Heaven.

12 Firm is this new-wrought hymn of praise,
and meet to be told forth, O Gods.
The flowing of the floods is Law, Truth
is the Sun's extended light. Mark this
my woe, ye Earth and Heaven.

13 Worthy of laud, O Agni, is that kinship
which thou hast with Gods.
Here seat thee like a man : most wise,
bring thou the Gods for sacrifice. Mark
this my woe, ye Earth and Heaven.

14 Here seated, man-like as a priest shall
wisest Agni to the Gods
Speed onward our oblations, God among
the Gods, intelligent. Mark this my woe,
ye Earth and Heaven.

15 Varuṇa makes the holy prayer. To him
who finds the path we pray.
He in the heart reveals his thought. Let
sacred worship rise anew. Mark this
my woe, ye Earth and Heaven.

16 That pathway of the Sun in heaven, made
to be highly glorified,
Is not to be transgressed, O Gods. O
mortals, ye behold it not. Mark this
my woe, ye Earth and Heaven.

17 Tṛta, when buried in the well, calls on
the Gods to succour him.
That call of his Bṛhaspati heard and
released him from distress. Mark this
my woe, ye Earth and Heaven.

18 A ruddy wolf beheld me once, as I was
faring on my path.
He, like a carpenter whose back is aching
crouched and slunk away. Mark this
my woe, ye Earth and Heaven.

19 Through this our song may we, allied
with Indra, with all our heroes conquer
in the battle.
This prayer of ours may Varuṇa grant,
and Mitra, and Aditi and Sindhu, Earth
and Heaven.

HYMN CVI. *Viśvedevas.*

1. CALL we for aid on Indra, Mitra, Varuṇa
and Agni and the Marut host and
Aditi.
Even as a chariot from a difficult ravine,
bountiful Vasus, rescue us from all
distress.

2 Come ye Ādityas for our full prosperity,
in conquests of the foe, ye Gods, bring
joy to us.
Even as a chariot from a difficult ravine,
bountiful Vasus, rescue us from all
distress.

---

9 *Those seven rays* : of the Sun, says Sāyaṇa. But
probably, as Ludwig suggests, the rays are the flames
of Agni. That is, Agni with his bright beams, or the
worship of Agni, is the central point through which I
and all the members of my family are connected and
held together.

Tṛta Āptya : A mythical being who dwells in the
remotest part of the heavens, and who knows the
celestial origin of the human race.

10 *Those five Bulls* : the stars of some constellation.
According to Sāyaṇa, Indra, Varuṇa, Agni, Aryaman,
and Savitar, or Fire, Wind, Sun, Moon, and Lightning.
Sāyaṇa explains *ukṣṇaḥ*, bulls or oxen, as 'shedders of
benefits.'

11 *Those Birds of beauteous pinion* : the stars.

The wolf ; darkness or eclipse of the Moon.

12 *Law (ṛtám.)* eternal order. 'The meaning of the
word as applied to the natural world connects itself
with the alternation of day and night, the regular
passage of the sun through the heavens, or the
unswerving motion of the rain in its fall from heaven
and of the streams along their courses. This last
application of the word may have determined its
special sense of 'water' in the later language. Wallis,
Cosmology of the Ṛgveda, p. 93.

16 *That pathway of the Sun* : according to Benfey,
the way of truth, right, eternal order, as in verse 12.
According to Ludwig the path of the Sun between the
tropics is meant. The Gods, says Sāyaṇa, must not
disregard the path of the Sun, because their existence
depends upon him as regulator of the seasons at which
sacrifices are offered to them. Still less may men
disregard it, who as sinners do not behold or understand it aright.

17 *Bṛhaspati* ; the Lord of Prayer.

18 *Like a carpenter* : the comparison is not very
clear. It apparently means that the wolf crept away,
arching his back or contracting his limbs, like a
carpenter bending over his work till his back aches.
Sāyaṇa suggests also an alternative and totally different
explanation of the whole passage, by interpreting
vṛka, the wolf, as the Moon, and reading *māsakṛt*,
maker of months, instead of *mā sakṛt*, me once. See
Ludwig, Uber die neuesten Arbeiten auf dem Gebiete
der Ṛgveda-forschung.

---

1 *Vasus* : originally meaning 'the good' is sometimes used, as in this place to designate Gods in
general.

3 May the most glorious Fathers aid us, and
the two Goddesses, Mothers of the
Gods, who strengthen Law.
Even as a chariot from a difficult ravine,
bountiful Vasus, rescue us from all
distress.

4 To mighty Narāśaṁsa, strengthening his
might, to Pūṣan, ruler over men, we
pray with hymns.
Even as a chariot from a difficult ravine,
bountiful Vasus, rescue us from all
distress.

5 Bṛhaspati, make us evermore an easy path:
we crave what boon thou hast for men
in rest and stir.
Like as a chariot from a difficult ravine,
bountiful Vasus, rescue us from all
distress.

6 Sunk in the pit the Ṛṣi Kutsa called, to
aid, Indra the Vṛtra-slayer, Lord of
power and might.
Even as a chariot from a difficult ravine,
bountiful Vasus, rescue us from all
distress.

7 May Aditi the Goddess guard us with the
Gods : may the protecting God keep us
with ceaseless care.
This prayer of ours may Varuṇa grant,
and Mitra, and Aditi and Sindhu, Earth
and Heaven.

HYMN CVII. Viśvedevas.

1. THE sacrifice obtains the Gods' acceptance:
be graciously inclined to us, Ādityas.
Hitherward let your favour be directed,
and be our best deliverer from trouble.

2 By praise-songs of Aṅgirases exalted, may
the Gods come to us with their protection.
May Indra with his powers, Maruts with
Maruts, Aditi with Ādityas grant us
shelter.

3 This laud of ours may Varuṇa and Indra,
Aryaman, Agni, Savitar find pleasant.
This prayer of ours may Varuṇa grant,
and Mitra, and Aditi and Sindhu, Earth
and Heaven.

---

3 *The Fathers* : the Manes or spirits of departed
ancestors.
The two Goddesses : Heaven and Earth.
4 *Narāśaṁsa* : a mystical name of Agni, 'the
Praise of Men.'
Pūṣan : the God who nourishes men and flocks
and herds.
6 *Sunk in the pit* : perhaps figuratively for 'in
distress.' Kutsa is the Ṛṣi to whom the hymn is
ascribed.

---

2 *Maruts with Maruts* : that is, all the Maruts
together, or Maruts with their winds and storm.

HYMN CVIII. *Indra-Agni.*

1. ON that most wondrous car of yours, O
Indra and Agni, which looks round on
all things living,
Take ye your stand and come to us to-
gether, and drink libations of the flowing
Soma.

2 As vast as all this world is in its compass,
deep as it is, with its far-stretching
surface,
So let this Soma be, Indra and Agni, made
for your drinking till your soul be sated.

3 For ye have won a blessed name together:
yea, with one aim ye strove, O Vṛtra-
slayers.
So Indra-Agni, seated here together, pour
in, ye Mighty Ones, the mighty Soma.

4 Both stand adorned, when fires are duly
kindled, spreading the sacred grass, with
lifted ladles.
Drawn by strong Soma juice poured forth
around us, come, Indra-Agni, and
display your favour.

5 The brave deeds ye have done, Indra
and Agni, the forms ye have displayed
and mighty exploits,
The ancient and auspicious bonds of friendship,—for sake of these drink of the flowing Soma.

6 As first I said when choosing you, in battle
we must contend with Asuras for this
Soma.
So came ye unto this my true conviction,
and drank libations of the flowing Soma.

7 If in your dwelling, or with prince or
Brāhman, ye, Indra-Agni, Holy Ones,
rejoice you,
Even from thence, ye mighty Lords, come
hither, and drink libation of the flowing
Soma.

8 If with the Yadus, Turvaśas, ye sojourn,
with Druhyus, Anus, Pūrus, Indra-Agni !
Even from thence, ye mighty Lords, come
hither, and drink libations of the flowing
Soma.

---

4 'We have, merely, in the text, the epithets in
the dual number : the commentator supplies the
Adhvaryu and his assistant priest.'—Wilson. Benfey
refers the dual epithets to Indra and Agni, translating
them severally by 'honoured,' 'for whom sacred grass
has been strewn', 'towards whom the ladles have been
uplifted.'

8 This verse contains the names of the five well-
known Āryan tribes or families, said to be descendants
of the five similarly named sons of Yayāti. See I.7.9.

9 Whether, O Indra-Agni, ye be dwelling in lowest earth, in central, or in highest.
Even from thence, ye mighty Lords, come hither, and drink libations of the flowing Soma.

10 Whether, O Indra-Agni, ye be dwelling in highest earth, in central, or in lowest,
Even from thence, ye mighty Lords, come hither, and drink libations of the flowing Soma.

11 Whether ye be in heaven, O Indra-Agni, on earth, on mountains, in the herbs, or waters,
Even from thence, ye mighty Lords, come hither, and drink libations of the flowing Soma.

12 If, when the Sun to the mid-heaven hath mounted, ye take delight in food, O Indra-Agni,
Even from thence, ye mighty Lords, come hither, and drink libations of the flowing Soma.

13 Thus having drunk your fill of our libation, win us all kinds of wealth, Indra and Agni.
This prayer of ours may Varuṇa grant, and Mitra, and Aditi and Sindhu, Earth and Heaven.

HYMN CIX.   *Indra-Agni.*

1. LONGING for weal I looked around, in spirit, for kinsmen, Indra–Agni, or for brothers.
No providence but yours alone is with me : so have I wrought for you this hymn for succour.

2 For I have heard that ye give wealth more freely than worthless son-in-law or spouse's brother.
So offering to you this draught of Soma, I make you this new hymn, Indra and Agni,

3 Let us not break the cords : with this petition we strive to gain the powers of our forefathers.

For Indra-Agni the strong drops are joyful, for here in the bowl's lap are both the press-stones.

4 For you the bowl divine, Indra and Agni, presses the Soma gladly to delight you.
With hands auspicious and fair arms, ye Aśvins, haste, sprinkle it with sweetness in the waters.

5 You, I have heard, were mightiest, Indra-Agni, when Vṛtra fell and when the spoil was parted.
Sit at this sacrifice, ye ever active, on the strewn grass, and with the juice delight you.

6 Surpassing all men where they shout for battle, ye Twain exceed the earth and heaven in greatness.
Greater are ye than rivers and than mountains, O Indra-Agni, and all things beside them.

7 Bring wealth and give it, ye whose arms wield thunder : Indra and Agni, with your powers protect us.
Now of a truth these be the very sunbeams wherewith our fathers were of old united.

8 Give, ye who shatter forts, whose hands wield thunder : Indra and Agni, save us in our battles.
This prayer of ours may Varuṇa grant, and Mitra, and Aditi and Sindhu, Earth and Heaven.

HYMN CX.   *Ṛbhus.*

1. THE holy work I wrought before is wrought again : my sweetest hymn is sung to celebrate your praise.

our ancestors and continued to our time. Or, as Sāyaṇa explains, let us not cut or break off the long line of posterity, but ask for and obtain 'descendants endowed with the vigour of their progenitors.'

The strong drops : the exhilarating Soma.

In the bowl's lap : close to the vessel which receives the juice. But see Ludwig, Ueber die neuesten Arbeiten, etc. pp. 85-88.

4 *Ye Aśvins* : here called upon to perform the duties of the Adhvaryu and his assistant priest, to mix the sweetness, or Soma, with water to be offered to Indra and Agni.

7 *These be the very sunbeams* : The meaning of the line may be that the worship of Indra and Agni is the great bond which has kept the Ṛṣi's ancestors united. Wilson, following Sāyaṇa translates : 'May those rays of the Sun, by which our forefathers have attained, together, a heavenly region, shine also upon us.'

1 *This sea for all the Gods* : this vessel containing Soma juice for all the Gods, or for the particular class of Gods called Viśvedevāḥ or Viśvedevas.

The hallowing word : Svāhā (Ave ! Hail !) ; an exclamation used in making oblations to the Gods.

9 *In lowest earth, in central, or in highest* : in earth, mid-air, or heaven, the word earth being used loosely for sphere or world. Or the reference may be to the fanciful threefold division of the earth.

2 *Than worthless son-in-law or spouse's brother* : the worthless or defective son-in-law, or suitor, who has not, as Yāska explains the necessary qualifications, is obliged to win the consent of his future father-in-law by very liberal gifts. The maiden's brother gives her rich presents out of natural affection.

3 *Let us not break the cords* : let us not break or interrupt the long series of religious rites observed by

Here, O ye Ṛbhus, is this sea for all
the Gods : sate you with Soma offered
with the hallowing word.

2 When, seeking your enjoyment onward
from afar, ye, certain of my kinsmen,
wandered on your way,
Sons of Sudhanvan, after your long
journeying, ye came unto the home of
liberal Savitar.

3 Savitar therefore gave you immortality,
because ye came proclaiming him
whom naught can hide ;
And this the drinking-chalice of the Asura,
which till that time was one, ye made
to be fourfold.

4 When they had served with zeal at sacrifice
as priests, they, mortal as they were,
gained immortality.
The Ṛbhus, children of Sudhanvan, bright
as suns, were in a year's course made
associate with prayers.

5 The Ṛbhus, with a rod measured, as 'twere
a field, the single sacrificial chalice
wide of mouth,
Lauded of all who saw, praying for
what is best, desiring glorious fame
among Immortal Gods.

6 As oil in ladles, we through knowledge will
present unto the Heroes of the firmament our hymn,—
The Ṛbhus who came near with this
great Father's speed, and rose
to heaven's high sphere to eat the
strengthening food.

7 Ṛbhu to us is Indra freshest in his might,
Ṛbhu with powers and wealth is giver
of rich gifts.

2 *Seeking your enjoyment* : desirous of enjoying
libation of Soma juice.
My kinsmen : Sudhanvan, father of the Ṛbhus,
was a descendant of Aṅgiras, as was also Kutsa the Ṛṣi
of the hymn.
3 *Him whom naught can hide* : or, from whom
nothing can be hidden, that is, Savitar as the Sun.
The drinking-chalice of the Asura : the cup that had
been made by the Asura or immortal God Tvaṣṭar.
See 1. 20. 6. This chalice appears to be the moon
which contains the Amṛta or nectar of the Gods. The
legend seems to mean that Tvaṣṭar as God of the
year created it uniformly bright, and that the Ṛbhus,
as Gods of the seasons, made it fourfold or diversified
with four phases. See Hillebrandt. Vedische
Mythologie, I. p. 515.
4 *Associate with prayers* : 'connected with the
ceremonies (appropriated to the different seasons) of
the year.'—Wilson.
5 *Measured* : in order to divide it into four, as is
said in verse 3.
6 *This great Father* : Savitar as the Sun, the
source of all life. *Strengthening food* : Soma.

Gods, through your favour may we on
the happy day quell the attacks of
those who pour no offerings forth.

8 Out of a skin, O Ṛbhus, once ye formed
a cow, and brought the mother close
unto her calf again.
Sons of Sudhanvan, Heroes, with surpassing skill ye made your aged Parents
youthful as before.

9 Help us with strength where spoil is won,
O Indra : joined with the Ṛbhus give
us varied bounty.
This prayer of ours may Varuṇa grant,
and Mitra, and Aditi and Sindhu, Earth
and Heaven.

HYMN CXI.   *Ṛbhus.*

1. WORKING with skill they wrought the
lightly rolling car : they wrought the
Bays who bear Indra and bring great
gifts.
The Ṛbhus for their Parents made life
young again ; and fashioned for the calf
a mother by its side.

2 For sacrifice make for us active vital power ;
for skill and wisdom food with noble
progeny.
Grant to our company this power most
excellent, that with a family all-heroic
we may dwell.

3 Do ye, O Ṛbhus, make prosperity for us,
prosperity for car, ye Heroes, and for
steed.
Grant us prosperity victorious evermore,
conquering foes in battle, strangers or
akin.

4 Indra, the Ṛbhus' Lord, I invocate for aid,
the Ṛbhus, Vājas, Maruts to the Soma
draught.
Varuṇa, Mitra, both, yea, and the Aśvins
Twain : let them speed us to wealth,
wisdom, and victory.

5 May Ṛbhu send prosperity for battle, may
Vāja conquering in the fight protect us.
This prayer of ours may Varuṇa grant,
and Mitra, and Aditi and Sindhu, Earth
and Heaven.

8 *A skin* : perhaps the dried-up earth. *A cow* :
the earth refreshed by the Rains. *The mother* : the
earth. *Her calf* : the autumn Sun. *Parents* : Heaven and Earth.

4 *Vājas* that is, Vāja and his two brothers Ṛbhu
and Vibhvan, more usually called collectively the
Ṛbhavaḥ or Ṛbhus. Similarly, in this line *the
Ṛbhus* are Ṛbhu and his brothers.

HYMN CXII. *Aśvins.*

1 To give first thought to them, I worship
Heaven and Earth, and Agni, fair bright
glow, to hasten their approach.
Come hither unto us, O Aśvins, with those
aids wherewith in fight ye speed the
war-cry to the spoil.

2 Ample, unfailing, they have mounted as it
were an eloquent car that ye may think
of us and give.
Come hither unto us, O Aśvins, with
those aids wherewith ye help our
thoughts to further holy acts.

3 Ye by the might which heavenly nectar
giveth you are in supreme dominion
Lords of all these folk.
Come hither unto us, O Aśvins, with
those aids wherewith ye, Heroes, made
the barren cow give milk.

4 The aids wherewith the Wanderer through
his offspring's might, or the Two-
Mothered Son shows swiftest mid the
swift ;
Wherewith the sapient one acquired his
triple lore,—Come hither unto us, O
Aśvins, with those aids.

5 Wherewith ye raised from waters, prisoned
and fast bound, Rebha, and Vandana to
look upon the light ;
Wherewith ye succoured Kaṇva as he strove
to win,—Come hither unto us, O Aśvins,
with those aids.

6 Wherewith ye rescued Antaka when lang-
uishing deep in the pit, and Bhujyu with
unfailing help.
And comforted Karkandhu, Vayya, in
their woe,—Come hither unto us, O
Aśvins, with those aids.

7 Wherewith ye gave Śucanti wealth and
happy home, and made the fiery pit
friendly for Atri's sake ;
Wherewith ye guarded Purukutsa, Pṛśnigu,
—Come hither unto us, O Aśvins, with
those aids.

8 Mighty Ones, with what powers ye gave
Parāvṛj aid what time ye made the blind
and lame to see and walk ;
Wherewith ye set at liberty the swallowed
quail,—Come hither unto us, O Aśvins,
with those aids.

9 Wherewith ye quickened the most sweet
exhaustless flood, and comforted
Vasiṣṭha, ye who ne'er decay ;
And to Śrutarya, Kutsa, Narya gave your
help,—Come hither unto us, O Aśvins,
with those aids.

10 Wherewith ye helped, in battle of a
thousand spoils, Viśpalā seeking booty,
powerless to move.
Wherewith ye guarded friendly Vaśa,
Aśva's son,—Come hither unto us, O
Aśvins, with those aids.

1 *To give first thought to them* : Heaven and
Earth are to be the first objects of invocation. Agni,
with his signal of bright fire, is also called upon to
hasten the approach of the Aśvins to the sacrifice.

2 *They* : our offerings. *An eloquent car* : the
chariot of our hymns.

3 *Heavenly nectar* : the Soma. *The barren cow* :
of the Ṛṣi Śayu.

4 *The Wanderer* : according to Sāyaṇa, the Wind.
Agni is called his offspring as having been excited in-
to flame by the wind. Or Mātariśvan may be intended
(See I. 31.3), who brought Agni from heaven.

The Two-Mothered Son : Agni sprung from the
two fire-sticks.

The sapient one : said to be the Ṛṣi Kakṣīvān.
His triple lore : knowledge of sacrificial food, oblations
of clarified butter, and libations of Soma juice. The
meaning of the passage is uncertain.

5 *Rebha* and *Vandana* are said to have been thrown
into wells by the Asuras or demons, Kaṇva was somewhat similarly treated. 'In these, and similar instances
subsequently noticed,' says Wilson, 'we may possibly
have allusions to the dangers undergone by some of
the first teachers of Hinduism among the people whom
they sought to civilize.'

6 *Antaka* : said to have been a Rājarṣi or regal
Ṛṣi, *Bhujyu* : a Rājarṣi, son of Tugra, rescued when
in danger of drowning. *Vayya* : see II. 13,12 ; IV.
19.6.

7 *Purukutsa* : see I. 63.7. Of *Śucanti* and *Pṛśnigu*
nothing more is related.

Atri : see I. 45.3 ; 51.3. He is said to have
been thrown by the Asuras into a fiery pit.

8 *Parāvṛj* : according to Sāyaṇa, the name of a
man. Benfey explains the word as the setting Sun (side-
ways departing), called *blind* because his light is nearly
gone, and *lame* because he no longer travels. *The
swallowed quail* : swallowed, or seized, by a wolf. The
quail is said by Yāska, as quoted by Sāyaṇa, to signify
the Dawn seized and swallowed by the bright Sun.
Benfey takes it to mean the Sun after setting.

9 As the earliest bringers of light, the Aśvins may
be said to quicken and animate by their coming the
streams of the ocean of air. We are not told how
the famous *Vasiṣṭha* was comforted; and *Śrutarya, Kutsa*
and *Narya* are merely said by Sāyaṇa to be three
Ṛṣis. Kutsa has been mentioned before. See I. 33. 14;
51. 6; 63. 3.

10 *Viśpalā* : a lady who was wounded in battle,
and made whole by the Aśvins. See I. 116. 15; 117.
11; 118. 8; X. 39. 8. *Powerless to move* : pierced through
with a lance, according to Ludwig. The meaning of
atharuyám is uncertain. *Vaśa* : a celebrated Ṛṣi, the seer
of Hymn VIII. 46.

11 Whereby the cloud, ye Bounteous Givers,
shed sweet rain for Dīrghaśravas, for the
merchant Auśija,
Wherewith ye helped Kakṣīvān, singer of
your praise,—Come hither unto us, O
Aśvins, with those aids.

12 Wherewith ye made Rasā swell full with
water-floods, and urged to victory the
car without a horse ;
Wherewith Triśoka drove forth his recovered cows,—Come hither unto us, O
Aśvins, with those aids.

13 Wherewith ye compass round the Sun
when far away, strengthened Mandhātar
in his tasks as lord of lands,
And to sage Bharadvāja gave protecting
help,—Come hither unto us, O Aśvins,
with those aids.

14 Wherewith, when Śambara was slain, ye
guarded well great Atithigva, Divodāsa,
Kaśoju,
And Trasadasyu when the forts were
shattered down,—Come hither unto us,
O Aśvins, with those aids.

15 Wherewith ye honoured the great drinker
Vamra, and Upastuta and Kali when
he gained his wife,

And lent to Vyaśva and to Pṛthi favouring
help,—Come hither unto us, O Aśvins,
with those aids.

16 Wherewith, O Heroes, ye vouchsafed deliverance to Śayu, Atri, and to Manu
long ago ;
Wherewith ye shot your shafts in Syūmaraśmi's cause.—Come hither unto us,
O Aśvins, with those aids.

17 Wherewith Patharvā, in his majesty of
form, shone in his course like to a
gathered kindled fire ;
Wherewith ye helped Śaryāta in the mighty
fray,—Come hither unto us, O Aśvins,
with those aids.

18 Wherewith, Aṅgirases ! ye triumphed in
your heart, and onward went to liberate
the flood of milk ;
Wherewith ye helped the hero Manu
with new strength,—Come hither unto
us, O Aśvins, with those aids.

11 *Dīrghaśravas* : said to be a Ṛṣi who traded
for his livelihood. *Auśija* is a patronymic meaning son
of Uśij. *Kakṣīvān* is also said to have been a son of
Uśij. See I. 18. 1.

12 *Rasā* : 'The Rasā, known to the Zoroastrians
as the Raṇhā, was originally the name of a real river,
but when the Āryas moved away from it into the
Punjāb, it assumed a mythical character, and became
a kind of Okeanos, surrounding the extreme limits of
the earth.'—M. Müller, *Vedic Hymns*, I. 323. No
further account is given of the events mentioned in
this verse.

13 Aśvins are said to compass the Sun in order to
save him from eclipse.

Mandhātar : a Rājarṣi or regal Ṛṣi. See VIII.
39. 8.

Bharadvāja : a very celebrated Ṛṣi, said to be
the son of Bṛhaspati.

14 *Śambara* : one of the demons of drought slain
by Indra. Sāyaṇa takes *atithigvám* and *kaśojum* as
epithets of Divodāsa the king who was aided by the
Aśvins : 'the hospitable Divodāsa as he sought the
water (through fear of the Asuras).' *Trasadasyu* : a
prince renowned for his victories and liberality, and
for the favour shown him by the Gods. See IV. 42. 9;
VII. 19. 3; VIII. 9. 21; 19.36; 36. 7.

15 *Vamra* : called a Ṛṣi, son of Vikhanas, by
Sāyaṇa. 'The text calls him *vipipānā*, drinking much
and variously, which the Scholiast explains, drinking,
especially earthly moisture or dew.'—Wilson. Benfey
thinks that Indra is intended under the name Vamra.

Upastuta : taken by Sāyaṇa as an epithet of
Vamra, 'praised by all around him.'

Kali : a Ṛṣi, mentioned again in X. 39. 8. The
Aśvins may have restored him to youth.

Vyaśva : taken by Sāyaṇa as an epithet of Pṛthi,

'horseless, or who had lost his horse.' *Pṛthi* is said to
have been a Rājarṣi.

16 *Śayu* : see note on verse 3 of this Hymn; see
also I. 116. 22; 117. 20.

Atri : see note on verse 7 ; also I. 116.8.

Manu : this Manu is said by Sāyaṇa to have
been a Rājarṣi whom the Aśvins taught to sow barley
and other grain.

Syūmaraśmi : said to have been a Ṛṣi, seer of
hymns 77, 78, Book X.

17 *Patharvā* : said by Sāyaṇa to have been a
Rājarṣi. Benfey thinks that the word *pátharvan*, is a
dialectical form of *pátrārvan*, 'having winged horses.'
Ludwig considers Sāyaṇa's explanation (which I have
followed) to be erroneous and impossible. He thinks
that Pathurū was the name of some stronghold which
the Aśvins saved from burning, either through the instru-
mentality of a man called Jaṭhara or by means of the
rain-clouds. He accordingly renders : 'By means of
which, at Pathurū, through the power of Jaṭhara
(violence of the rain-clouds) the fire did not flame up,
though prepared and lighted on the way.' The passage
is difficult, and the interpretations put upon the words
by Sāyaṇa certainly appear to be forced, but on the
whole I think it safer to follow his guidance. I may
observe here that 'na' which in the Veda means both
'not' and 'like' sometimes makes the meaning of a
passage uncertain. In this line Sāyaṇa takes it in the
latter sense, and Ludwig in the former.

Śaryāta : perhaps the same as Śaryāti, a son of
Manu Vaivasvata.

18 *Aṅgirases* : the text has Aṅgiras only in the
singular form, which may stand, as Ludwig remarks,
for the dual. Wilson, following Sāyaṇa, translates :
'Aṅgiras, (praise the Aśvins).' Sāyaṇa supposes the
Ṛṣi to address himself by this title. Benfey joins Aṅgiras
with the following word, making *aṅgirománasā*, 'through
affection for the Aṅgirases.'

The flood of milk : the cows shut up in the cave,
that is, the rain-clouds prevented from pouring out
their water.

Manu : see verse 16.

19 Wherewith ye brought a wife for Vimada
   to wed, wherewith ye freely gave the
   ruddy cows away ;
   Wherewith ye brought the host of k ind
   Gods to Sudās—Come hither unto us,
   O Aśvins, with those aids.

20 Wherewith ye bring great bliss to him
   who offers gifts, wherewith ye have
   protected Bhujyu, Adhrigu,
   And good and gracious Subharā and
   Ṛtastup,—Come hither unto us, O
   Aśvins, with those aids.

21 Wherewith ye served Kṛśānu where the
   shafts were shot, and helped the young
   man's horse to swiftness in the race ;
   Wherewith ye bring delicious honey to the
   bees,—Come hither unto us, O Aśvins,
   with those aids.

22 Wherewith ye speed the hero as he fights
   for kine in hero battle, in the strife for
   land and sons,
   Wherewith ye safely guard his horses and
   his car,—Come hither unto us, O Aśvins
   with those aids.

23 Wherewith ye, Lords of Hundred Powers,
   helped Kutsa, son of Ārjuni, gave
   Turvīti and Dabhīti strength,
   Favoured Dhvasanti and lent Puruṣanti
   help,—Come hither unto us, O Aśvins,
   with those aids.

24 Make ye our speech effectual, O ye Aśvins,
   and this our hymn, ye mighty Wonder-
   Workers.
   In luckless game I call on you for succour :
   strengthen us also on the field of battle.

19 *Vimada* : a Ṛṣi, whose name occurs again in
I. 116. I; 117. 20; VIII. 9. 15; X. 20. 10; and X.
23. 7. The wife is said to have been the daughter of
Purumitra.
   The ruddy cows : perhaps the red rain-clouds.
   Sudās : son of Pijavana. See I. 47.7.
   20 *Bhujyu* : see note on verse 6, *Adhrigu*, taken
by Sāyaṇa as a proper name, is said to have been a
sacrificer of the Gods. *Ṛtastup* is called a Ṛṣi. Sāyaṇa
takes *subhárām* as an adjective, but has to supply *iṣam*
food, for it to qualify.
   21 *Kṛśānu* : the Kereśāni of the Avesta; one of
the guardians of the celestial Soma. See IV. 27. 3.
   The young man : whose horse was aided, was
Purukutsa.
   23 *Kutsa* : has been mentioned before as a
favourite of Indra. See I. 51. 6. *Turvīti* : see I. 36. 18
Dabhīti : see II. 13. 9; 15. 9; IV. 30. 21; VI. 20. 13;
26. 6. *Puruṣanti* : a liberal prince. See IX. 5. 8.3.
   24 *Luckless game* : a metaphor borrowed from
dicing; that is, in a time of difficulty, perhaps the
eve of a desperate battle. Sāyaṇa, following a different
derivation of the word, explains it, in the absence of
light, or in the last watch of night, when the Aśvins
are especially to be worshipped.

25 With undiminished blessings, O ye Aśvins,
   for evermore both night and day protect us.
   This prayer of ours may Varuṇa grant,
   and Mitra, and Aditi and Sindhu, Earth
   and Heaven.

HYMN CXIII.   *Dawn.*

1. THIS light is come, amid all lights the
   fairest ; born is the brilliant, far-extending brightness.
   Night, sent away for Savitar's uprising,
   hath yielded up a birth-place for the
   Morning.

2 The Fair, the Bright is come with her
   white offspring ; to her the Dark One
   hath resigned her dwelling.
   Akin, immortal, following each other,
   changing their colours both the heavens
   move onward.

3 Common, unending is the Sisters' pathway ; taught by the Gods, alternately
   they travel.
   Fair-formed, of different hues and yet
   one-minded, Night and Dawn clash not,
   neither do they tarry.

4 Bright leader of glad sounds, our eyes
   behold her ; splendid in hue she hath
   unclosed the portals.
   She, stirring up the world, hath shown us
   riches : Dawn hath awakened every
   living creature.

5 Rich Dawn, she sets afoot the coiled-up
   sleeper, one for enjoyment, one for
   wealth or worship,
   Those who saw little for extended vision.
   All living creatures hath the Dawn
   awakened.

6 One to high sway, one to exalted glory,
   one to pursue his gain, and one his
   labour :
   All to regard their different vocations, all
   moving creatures hath the Dawn
   awakened.

7 We see her there, the Child of Heaven
   apparent, the young Maid, flushing in
   her shining raiment.

   1. *Savitar* : the Sun.
   2 *Her white offspring* : white clouds that attend
her. Or the word in the text may be rendered 'bright
offspring, the Sun whom she precedes.'
   Both the heavens : or Day and Night.
   4 *Leader of glad sounds* : awakener of 'the charm
of earliest birds' and the joyful voices of other animals.
   5 *Those who saw little* : during the darkness of
night.
   6 This verse apparently alludes to a division into
four castes or classes, regal and military, priestly, mercantile, and servile. But verses 4,5,6 seem to be
separated by their refrain from the rest of the hymn,
and may perhaps be a later addition to it.

Thou sovran Lady of all earthly treasure, flush on us here, auspicious Dawn, this morning.

8 She, first of endless morns to come here-after, follows the path of morns that have departed.
Dawn, at her rising, urges forth the living : him who is dead she wakes not from his slumber.

9 As thou, Dawn, hast caused Agni to be kindled, and with the Sun's eye hast revealed creation.
And hast awakened men to offer worship, thou hast performed, for Gods, a noble service.

10 How long a time, and they shall be to-gether,—Dawns that have shone and Dawns to shine hereafter ?
She yearns for former Dawns with eager longing, and goes forth gladly shining with the others.

11 Gone are the men who in the days before us looked on the rising of the earlier Morning.
We, we the living, now behold her bright-ness and they come nigh who shall hereafter see her.

12 Foe-chaser, born of Law, the Law's protectress, joy-giver, waker of all pleasant voices,
Auspicious, bringing food for Gods' enjoy-ment, shine on us here, most bright, O Dawn, this morning.

13 From days eternal hath Dawn shone, the Goddess, and shows this light to-day, endowed with riches.
So will she shine on days to come ; immortal she moves on in her own strength, undecaying.

14 In the sky's borders hath she shone in splendour : the Goddess hath thrown off the veil of darkness.
Awakening the world with purple horses, on her well-harnessed chariot Dawn approaches.

15 Bringing all life-sustaining blessings with her, showing herself she sends forth brilliant lustre.
Last of the countless mornings that have vanished, first of bright morns to come hath Dawn arisen.

16 Arise ! the breath, the life, again hath reached us : darkness hath passed away and light approacheth.
She for the Sun hath left a path to travel : we have arrived where men prolong existence.

17 Singing the praises of refulgent Mornings with his hymn's web the priest, the poet rises.
Shine then to-day, rich Maid, on him who lauds thee, shine down on us the gift of life and offspring.

18 Dawns giving sons all heroes, kine and horses, shining upon the man who brings oblations,—
These let the Soma-presser gain when ending his glad songs louder than the voice of Vāyu.

19 Mother of Gods, Aditi's form of glory, ensign of sacrifice, shine forth exalted.
Rise up, bestowing praise on our devotion : all-bounteous, make us chief among the people.

20 Whatever splendid wealth the Dawns bring with them to bless the man who offers praise and worship,
Even that may Mitra, Varuṇa vouchsafe us, and Aditi and Sindhu, Earth and Heaven.

HYMN CXIV.   Rudra.

1. To the strong Rudra bring we these our songs of praise, to him the Lord of Heroes, with the braided hair,
That it be well with all our cattle and our men, that in this village all be healthy and well-fed.

9 *Caused Agni to be kindled* : daybreak being the proper time for lighting the sacrificial fires.

10 The meaning appears to be : How long have we to live ? When will all our future Dawns be with those that have passed away ? Wilson, following Sāyaṇa translates : 'For how long a period is it that the dawns have risen ? For how long a period will they rise ?'

She yearns : the Dawn that now shines as the first of Dawns to come is already eager to join those that have past.

12 Evil spirits vanish when Dawn appears. She comes in accordance with the eternal law of the universe which she observes and guards. Her coming is the signal for men to offer oblations to the Gods.

16. *Where men prolong existence* : a new life begins at the return of day-light.

17 *His hymn's web* : the words which he weaves, or carefully composes.

18 *Louder than the voice of Vāyu* : louder even than the roaring of the wind. Wilson translates : 'At the conclusion of his praises,' (enunciated) like the wind, (with speed).'

———

1 *Rudra* : generally explained as the Roarer, from the sound of stormy winds, the God of tempests and father of the Maruts. He is called *Kapardin* as wearing hair braided and knotted like a cowry shell (*kaparda*). Prof. Pischel (Vedische Studien, I. 55. sqq.) derives *Rudra* (the Red, the Brilliant) from a lost root *rud*, to be red.

2 Be gracious unto us, O Rudra, bring us joy : thee, Lord of Heroes, thee with reverence will we serve.
Whatever health and strength our father Manu won by sacrifice may we, under thy guidance, gain.

3 By worship of the Gods may we, O Bounteous One, O Rudra, gain thy grace, Ruler of valiant men.
Come to our families, bringing them bliss : may we, whose heroes are uninjured, bring thee sacred gifts.

4 Hither we call for aid the wise, the wanderer, impetuous Rudra, perfecter of sacrifice.
May he repel from us the anger of the Gods : verily we desire his favourable grace.

5 Him with the braided hair we call with reverence down, the wild-boar of the sky, the red, the dazzling shape.
May he, his hand filled full of sovran medicines, grant us protection, shelter, and a home secure.

6 To him the Maruts' Father is this hymn addressed, to strengthen Rudra's might, a song more sweet than sweet.
Grant us, Immortal One, the food which mortals eat : be gracious unto me, my seed, my progeny.

7 O Rudra, harm not either great or small of us, harm not the growing boy, harm not the full-grown man.
Slay not a sire among us, slay no mother here, and to our own dear bodies, Rudra, do not harm.

8 Harm us not, Rudra, in our seed and progeny, harm us not in the living, nor in cows or steeds,
Slay not our heroes in the fury of thy wrath. Bringing oblations evermore we call to thee.

9 Even as a herdsman I have brought thee hymns of praise : O Father of the Maruts, give us happiness.
Blessed is thy most favouring benevolence, so, verily, do we desire thy saving help.

10 Far be thy dart that killeth men or cattle : thy bliss be with us, O thou Lord of Heroes.
Be gracious unto us, O God, and bless us, and then vouchsafe us doubly-strong protection.

11 We, seeking help, have spoken and adored him : may Rudra, girt by Maruts, hear our calling.
This prayer of ours may Varuṇa grant, and Mitra, and Aditi and Sindhu, Earth and Heaven.

HYMN CXV.   Sūrya.

1. THE brilliant presence of the Gods hath risen, the eye of Mitra, Varuṇa and Agni.
The soul of all that moveth not or moveth, the Sun hath filled the air and earth and heaven.

2 Like as a young man followeth a maiden, so doth the Sun the Dawn, refulgent Goddess :
Where pious men extend their generations, before the Auspicious One for happy fortune.

3 Auspicious are the Sun's Bay-coloured Horses, bright, changing hues, meet for our shouts of triumph.
Bearing our prayers, the sky's ridge have they mounted, and in a moment speed round earth and heaven.

4 This is the Godhead, this might of Sūrya : he hath withdrawn what spread o'er work unfinished.
When he hath loosed his Horses from their station, straight over all Night spreadeth out her garment.

5 In the sky's lap the Sun this form assumeth that Varuṇa and Mitra may behold it.
His Bay Steeds well maintain his power eternal, at one time bright and darksome at another.

---

2 The exact meaning of the second line is somewhat uncertain. As I have rendered it, in accordance with Ludwig, it reminds one of Shelley's 'Man, the imperial shape, then multiplied His generations under the pavilion Of the Sun's throne.' Wilson, following Sāyaṇa paraphrases, 'At which season pious men perform (the ceremonies established for) ages.' Sāyaṇa proposes an alternative rendering by taking yugani (generations, ages,) to mean 'yokes for ploughs'; for, at this season, men seeking to propitiate the gods by the profit which agriculture yields, equip their ploughs.'

4 He hath withdrawn : that is, says Wilson, 'the cultivator or artisan desists from his labour, although unfinished, upon the setting of the sun'; when the sun 'has withdrawn (into himself) the diffused (light which has been shed) upon the unfinished task.'

5 His power eternal, as maker and ruler of day and night.

---

2 Won by sacrifice : that is, as an institutor of earliest sacrifice, enabled us to obtain by offerings to the Gods.

9 Even as a herdsman : as a herdsman prays for the well-being of his cattle, so the poet prays for the prosperity of those for whom he speaks.

6 This day, O Gods, while Sūrya is ascending, deliver us from trouble and dishonour.

This prayer of ours may Varuṇa grant, and Mitra, and Aditi and Sindhu, Earth and Heaven.

HYMN CXVI.   Aśvins.

1. I TRIM like grass my song for the Nāsatyas and send their lauds forth as the wind drives rain-clouds,

Who, in a chariot rapid as an arrow, brought to the youthful Vimada a consort.

2 Borne on by rapid steeds of mighty pinion, or proudly trusting in the Gods' incitements.

That stallion ass of yours won, O Nāsatyas, that thousand in the race, in Yama's contest.

3 Yea, Aśvins, as a dead man leaves his riches, Tugra left Bhujyu in the cloud of waters.

Ye brought him back in animated vessels, traversing air, unwetted by the billows.

4 Bhujyu ye bore with winged things, Nāsatyas, which for three nights, three days full swiftly travelled,

To the sea's farther shore, the strand of ocean, in three cars, hundred-footed, with six horses.

5 Ye wrought that hero exploit in the ocean which giveth no support, or hold or station,

What time ye carried Bhujyu to his dwelling, borne in a ship with hundred oars, O Aśvins.

6 The white horse which of old ye gave Aghāśva, Aśvins, a gift to be his wealth for ever,—

Still to be praised is that your glorious present, still to be famed is the brave horse of Pedu.

7 O Heroes, ye gave wisdom to Kakṣīvān who sprang from Pajra's line, who sang your praises.

Ye poured forth from the hoof of your strong charger a hundred jars of wine as from a strainer.

8 Ye warded off with cold the fire's fierce burning ; food very rich in nourishment ye furnished.

Atri, cast downward in the cavern, Aśvins ye brought, with all his people, forth to comfort.

9 Ye lifted up the well, O ye Nāsatyas, and set the base on high to open downward.

Streams flowed for folk of Gotama who thirsted, like rain to bring forth thousand-fold abundance.

10 Ye from the old Cyavāna, O Nāsatyas, stripped, as 'twere mail, the skin upon his body,

Lengthened his life when all had left him helpless, Dasras ! and made him lord of youthful maidens.

11 Worthy of praise and worth the winning, Heroes, is that your favouring succour O Nāsatyas,

What time ye, knowing well his case, delivered Vandana from the pit like hidden treasure.

12 That mighty deed of yours, for gain, O Heroes, as thunder heraldeth the rain, I publish,

---

This Hymn and the five following are ascribed to the Ṛṣi Kakṣīvān.

1 *Grass* : the sacred grass which is spread on the altar.

Nāsatyas : a common name of the Aśvins. See I. 3.3.

Vimada : the Aśvins assisted Vimada, who was attacked when returning Surya in marriage with newly-won bride, whom they carried to his house in their own chariot. Most of the deeds ascribed to the Aśvins in this hymn have been mentioned in I. 112.

2 *Stallion ass* : that draws the car of the Aśvins. See I. 34. 9.

Yama's contest : apparently the race instituted by the Gods when Prajāpati (here represented by Yama) gave his daughter Suryā in marriage to King Soma, the Moon, as related in Aitareya-Brāhmaṇa, IV. 2, See Ehni, Der Mythus des Yama, p. 160.

3 *Bhujyu* : see I. 112. 6.

5 'This', observes Wilson, 'is a rather unintelligible account of a sea-voyage, although the words of the text do not admit of any other rendering.'

6 *Aghāśva* : another name of Pedu ; or an epithet of Pedu 'having bad or vicious horses.' Pedu was a royal Ṛṣi who worshipped the Aśvins and was thus rewarded.

7 *Kakṣīvān* : a famous Ṛṣi, (see I. 18. 1,) a descendant of the Pajras or Aṅgirases. *Strong charger* : that is, the rushing rain-cloud, from which the Aśvins poured down copious showers. Cf. the Greek myth of the horse Pegasus and the fountain Hippocrene.

8 *Atri* : see I. 112. 7.

9 *The well* : that is the watery cloud. This deed is ascribed to the Maruts in I. 85. 11.

10 *Dasras* : a name of the Aśvins; Wonder-Workers, or Mighty Ones.

11 *Vandana* : see I. 112. 5.

12 *By the horse's head* : 'Indra, having taught the sciences called *Pravargyavidyā* and *Madhuvidyā* to Dadhyac, threatened that he would cut off his head if ever he taught them to any one else. The Aśvins prevailed upon him to teach them the prohibited knowledge, and, to evade Indra's threat, took off the head of the sage, replacing it by that of a horse.'—Wilson. See I. 84. 13.

When, by the horse's head, Atharvan's offspring Dadhyac made known to you the Soma's sweetness.

13 In the great rite the wise dame called, Nāsatyas, you, Lords of many treasures, to assist her.
Ye heard the weakling's wife, as 'twere an order, and gave to her a son Hiraṇyahasta.

14 Ye from the wolf's jaws, as ye stood together, set free the quail, O Heroes, O Nāsatyas.
Ye, Lords of many treasures, gave the poet his perfect vision as he mourned his trouble.

15 When in the time of night, in Khela's battle, a leg was severed like a wild bird's pinion,
Straight ye gave Viśpalā a leg of iron that she might move what time the conflict opened.

16 His father robbed Rjrāśva of his eyesight who for the she-wolf slew a hundred wethers.
Ye gave him eyes, Nāsatyas, Wonder-Workers, Physicians, that he saw with sight uninjured.

17 The Daughter of the Sun your car ascended, first reaching as it were the goal with coursers.
All Deities within their hearts assented, and ye, Nāsatyas, are close linked with glory.

18 When to his house ye came, to Divodāsa, hasting to Bharadvāja, O ye Aśvins,
The car that came with you brought splendid riches : a porpoise and a bull were yoked together.

19 Ye, bringing wealth with rule, and life with offspring, life rich in noble heroes; O Nāsatyas,
Accordant came with strength to Jahnu's children who offered you thrice every day your portion.

20 Ye bore away at night by easy pathways Jāhuṣa compassed round on every quarter,
And, with your car that cleaves the foe asunder, Nāsatyas never decaying ! rent the mountains.

21 One morn ye strengthened Vaśa for the battle, to gather spoils that might be told in thousands.
With Indra joined ye drove away misfortunes, yea foes of Pṛthuśravas, O ye mighty.

22 From the deep well ye raised on high the water, so that Ṛcatka's son, Śara, should drink it ;
And with your might, to help the weary Śayu, ye made the barren cow yield milk, Nāsatyas.

23 To Viśvaka, Nāsatyas ! son of Kṛṣṇa, the righteous man who sought your aid and praised you,
Ye with your powers restored, like some lost creature, his son Viṣṇāpū for his eyes to look on.

24 Aśvins, ye raised, like Soma in a ladle Rebha, who for ten days and ten nights, fettered.
Had lain in cruel bonds, immersed and wounded, suffering sore affliction, in the waters.

25 I have declared your wondrous deeds, O Aśvins : may this be mine, and many kine and heroes.
May I, enjoying lengthened life, still seeing, enter old age as 'twere the house I live in.

HYMN CXVII. Aśvins.

1. Aśvins, your ancient priest invites you hither to gladden you with draughts of meath of Soma.

13 *The weakling's wife* : or Vadhrimatī, which has that meaning.

14 *Set free the quail* : see I. 112. 8.

15 *Khela's battle* : the Commentator says that Khela was a Rāja, whose relative Viśpalā lost a foot in battle and received an iron leg from the Aśvins at the prayer of Agastya, Khela's family priest. See I. 112. 10.

16 *Rjrāśva*, mentioned in I. 101. 17, was one of the sons of Vṛṣāgir. The she-wolf for whom he slaughtered the sheep was one of the asses of the Aśvins in disguise, and the Aśvins consequently restored to him the eyesight of which his angry father' had deprived him.

17 *The Daughter of the Sun* : 'Sūrya, it is related, was desirous of giving his daughter Sūryā to Soma; but all the gods desired her as a wife. They agreed that he who should first reach the sun, as a goal, should wed the damsel. The Aśvins were victorious ; and Sūryā, well-pleased by their success, rushed immediately into their chariot.'—Wilson. See note on verse 2 of this hymn.

18 *Divodāsa* : see I. 112. 14. His family priest was one of the Bharadvājas. The Aśvins, it is said, yoked the porpoise and the bull together as a proof of power.

19 *Jahnu's children* : Jahnu was a Maharṣi or great Ṛṣi.

21 *Vaśa* : see I. 112. 10. *Pṛthuśravas* appears to be identical with Pṛthuśravas Kāṇīta, mentioned in VIII. 46. 21, whose family priest was Vaśa.

22 *Śayu* : has been mentioned in I. 112. 16. Of Śara in this verse and of Viśvaka, Kṛṣṇa, and Viṣṇāpū in the next we are only told that they were Ṛṣis.

24 *Rebha* : see I. 112. 5.

25 *May this be mine* : may I be master of this place or district, a substantive of some such signification being understood.

Our gift is on the grass, our song apportioned : with food and strength come hither, O Nāsatyas.

2 That car of yours, swifter than thought, O Aśvins, which drawn by brave steeds cometh to the people,
Whereon ye seek the dwelling of the pious,—come ye thereon to our abode, O Heroes.

3 Ye freed sage Atri, whom the Five Tribes honoured, from the strait pit, ye Heroes with his people,
Baffling the guiles of the malignant Dasyu, repelling them, ye Mighty in succession.

4 Rebha the sage, ye mighty Heroes, Aśvins ! whom, like a horse, vile men had sunk in water,—
Him, wounded, with your wondrous power ye rescued : your exploits of old time endure for ever.

5 Ye brought forth Vandana, ye Wonder-Workers, for triumph, like fair gold that hath been buried,
Like one who slumbered in destruction's bosom, or like the Sun when dwelling in the darkness.

6 Kakṣīvān, Pajra's son, must laud that exploit of yours, Nāsatyas, Heroes, ye who wander !
When from the hoof of your strong horse ye showered a hundred jars of honey for the people.

7 To Kṛṣṇa's son, to Viśvaka who praised you, O Heroes, ye restored his son Viṣṇāpū.
To Ghoṣā, living in her father's dwelling, stricken in years, ye gave a husband, Aśvins.

8 Ruṣatī, of the mighty people, Aśvins, ye gave to Śyāva of the line of Kaṇva.
This deed of yours, ye Strong Ones should be published, that ye gave glory to the son of Nṛṣad.

9 O Aśvins, wearing many forms at pleasure, on Pedu ye bestowed a fleet-foot courser,

Strong, winner of a thousand spoils, resistless the serpent slayer, glorious, triumphant.

10 These glorious things are yours, ye Bounteous Givers ; prayer, praise in both worlds are your habitation.
O Aśvins, when the sons of Pajra call you, send strength with nourishment to him who knoweth.

11 Hymned with the reverence of a son, O Aśvins ye Swift Ones giving booty to the singer,
Glorified by Agastya with devotion, established Viśpalā again, Nāsatyas.

12 Ye Sons of Heaven, ye Mighty, whither went ye, sought ye, for his fair praise the home of Kāvya.
When, like a pitcher full of gold, O Aśvins, on the tenth day ye lifted up the buried ?

13 Ye with the aid of your great powers, O Aśvins, restored to youth the ancient man Cyavāna.
The Daughter of the Sun with all her glory, O ye Nāsatyas, chose your car to bear her.

14 Ye, ever-youthful Ones, again remembered Tugra, according to your ancient manner :
With horses brown of hue that flew with swift wings ye brought back Bhujyu from the sea of billows.

15 The son of Tugra had invoked you, Aśvins ; borne on he went uninjured through the ocean.
Ye with your chariot swift as thought, well-harnessed, carried him off, O Mighty Ones, to safety.

16 The quail had invocated you, O Aśvins, when from the wolf's devouring jaws ye freed her.
With conquering car ye cleft the mountain's ridges : the offspring of Viśvāc ye killed with poison.

17 He whom for furnishing a hundred wethers to the she-wolf, his wicked father blinded,—

3 *Atri* : see I. 116. 8. *The Five Tribes* : are the confederate Āryan families named in the note to I. 7. 9.
4 *Rebha* : see I. 112. 5. *Like a horse* : sunk deep in water like a horse when he is bathed in a river.
5 *Vandana* : see I. 116. 11.
6 *Kakṣīvān*: see I. 116. 7. *Strong horse* : see I. 116.7.
7 *Ghoṣā* : Kakṣīvān's daughter, said to have been afflicted with leprosy and healed by the Aśvins, who found her a husband.
8 *Śyāva* : a Ṛṣi whom the Aśvins cured of leprosy and enabled to marry Ruṣatī. *The son of Nṛṣad* : Kaṇva or his descendant Śyāva.
9 *Pedu* : see I. 116. 6. *The serpent-slayer* : see IX. 88. 4, and Hymns of the Atharva-veda, X. 4. 47.

11 *Agastya* : the family priest of Khela. See I.116. 15.
12 *Kāvya* : Uśanā, son of Kavi, See I. 83. 6. *The buried* : Rebha. The meaning is, 'why did ye delay so long the rescue of Rebha?'

13 *Cyavāna* : see I. 116. 10. *The Daughter of the Sun* : see I. 116. 17.

14 *Ye brought back Bhujyu* : see I. 116. 3.

16 *The quail* : see I. 116. 14. *Viśvāc* : said to be an Asura or fiend.

17 *Ṛjrāśva* : see I. 116. 16.

To him, Ṛjrāśva, gave ye eyes, O Aśvins ;
light to the blind ye sent for perfect
vision.

18 To bring the blind man joy thus cried
the she-wolf : O Aśvins, O ye Mighty
Ones, O Heroes,
For me Ṛjrāśva, like a youthful lover,
hath cut piecemeal one and a hundred
wethers.

19 Great and weal-giving is your aid, O
Aśvins, ye, objects of all thought, made
whole the cripple.
Purandhi also for this cause invoked you,
and ye, O mighty, came to her with
succours.

20 Ye, Wonder-Workers, filled with milk for
Śayu the milkless cow, emaciated,
barren ;
And by your powers the child of Purumitra ye brought to Vimada to be his
consort.

21 Ploughing and sowing barley, O ye
Aśvins, milking out food for men, ye
Wonder-Workers,
Blasting away the Dasyu with your
trumpet, ye gave far-spreading light
unto the Ārya.

22 Ye brought the horse's head, Aśvins, and
gave it unto Dadhyac the offspring of
Atharvan.
True, he revealed to you, O Wonder-
Workers, sweet Soma, Tvaṣṭar's secret,
as your girdle.

23 O Sages, evermore I crave your favour :
be gracious unto all my prayers, O
Aśvins.
Grant me, Nāsatyas, riches in abundance,
wealth famous and accompanied with
children.

24 With liberal bounty to the weakling's
consorts ye, Heroes, gave a son Hiraṇyahasta ;
And Śyāva, cut into three several pieces,
ye brought to life again, O bounteous
Aśvins.

25 These your heroic exploits, O ye Aśvins,
done in the days of old, have men
related.

19 *Purandhi* : or as Sāyaṇa explains, 'the wise maid,'
Ghoṣā.
20 *Śayu* : see I. 112. 16; and I. 116. 22. *Vimada* :
see I. 112. 19.
22 *Dadhyac* : see I. 116. 12. *As your girdle* : to
strengthen and support you.
24 *The weakling's consort* : see I. 116. 13. *Śyāva* : cut
to pieces by the Asuras, was made whole by the Aśvins.
25 *The synod* : the congregation of worshippers.

May we, addressing prayer to you, ye
Mighty, speak with brave sons about
us to the synod.

HYMN CXVIII. *Aśvins.*

1. FLYING, with falcons, may your chariot,
Aśvins, most gracious, bringing friendly
help, come hither,—
Your chariot, swifter than the mind of
mortal, fleet as the wind, three-seated,
O ye Mighty.

2 Come to us with your chariot triple seated,
three-wheeled, of triple form, that rolleth
lightly.
Fill full our cows, give mettle to our
horses, and make each hero son grow
strong, O Aśvins.

3 With your well-rolling car, descending
swiftly, hear this the press-stone's song,
ye Wonder-Workers.
How then have ancient sages said, O
Aśvins, that ye most swiftly come to stay
affliction ?

4 O Aśvins, let your falcons bear you
hither, yoked to your chariot, swift,
with flying pinions,
Which, ever active, like the airy eagles,
carry you, O Nāsatyas, to the banquet.

5 The youthful Daughter of the Sun,
delighting in you, ascended there your
chariot, Heroes.
Borne on their swift wings let your
beauteous horses, your birds of ruddy
hue, convey you near us.

6 Ye raised up Vandana, strong Wonder-
Workers ! with great might, and with
power ye rescued Rebha.
From out the sea ye saved the son of
Tugra, and gave his youth again unto
Cyavāna.

7 To Atri, cast down to the fire that
scorched him, ye gave, O Aśvins,
strengthening food and favour.
Accepting his fair praises with approval,
ye gave his eyes again to blinded
Kaṇva.

8 For ancient Śayu in his sore affliction ye
caused his cow to swell with milk, O
Aśvins.
The quail from her great misery ye
delivered, and a new leg for Viśpalā
provided.

5 In this and the following verses most of the wonderful deeds of the Aśvins mentioned in the preceding hymn
are briefly referred to.

9 A white horse, Aśvins, ye bestowed on
　　Pedu, a serpent-slaying steed sent down
　　by Indra,
　　Loud-neighing, conquering the foe, high-
　　mettled, firm-limbed and vigorous,
　　winning thousand treasures,

10 Such as ye are, O nobly born, O Heroes,
　　we in our trouble call on you for
　　succour.
　　Accepting these our songs, for our well-
　　being come to us on your chariot
　　treasure-laden.

11 Come unto us combined in love, Nāsatyas ;
　　come with the fresh swift vigour of the
　　falcon.
　　Bearing oblations I invoke you, Aśvins,
　　at the first break of everlasting morning.

HYMN CXIX.　　　　　　　　*Aśvins.*

1. HITHER, that I may live, I call unto the
　　feast your wondrous car, thought-swift,
　　borne on by rapid steeds.
　　With thousand banners, hundred treasures,
　　pouring gifts, promptly obedient, bestow-
　　ing ample room.

2 Even as it moveth near my hymn is
　　lifted up, and all the regions come
　　together to sing praise.
　　I sweeten the oblations ; now the helpers
　　come. Ūrjānī hath, O Aśvins, mounted
　　on your car.

3 When striving man with man for glory
　　they have met, brisk, measureless, eager
　　for victory in fight,
　　Then verily your car is seen upon the
　　slope when ye, O Aśvins, bring some
　　choice boon to the prince.

4 Ye came to Bhujyu while he struggled in
　　the flood, with flying birds, self-yoked,
　　ye bore him to his sires.
　　Ye went to the far-distant home, O Mighty
　　Ones ; and famed is your great aid to
　　Divodāsa given.

5 Aśvins, the car which you had yoked for
　　glorious show your own two voices urged
　　directed to its goal.
　　Then she who came for friendship, Maid
　　of noble birth, elected you as Husbands,
　　you to be her Lords.

2 Ūrjānī : strength, personified. According to
Sāyaṇa, Ūrjānī is Sūryā the daughter of the Sun.

3 *Upon the slope* : that is, of the sky.

4 *Bhujyu,* and other persons and incidents referred
to in this hymn have been mentioned in I. 116.

5 *She who came for friendship* : Sūryā. The meaning
seems to be, as Ludwig says, that she came intending to
avail herself of the services of the Aśvins as bridesmen,
and that they became her bridegrooms instead.

6 Rebha ye saved from tyranny ; for Atri's
　　sake ye quenched with cold the fiery
　　pit that compassed him.
　　Ye made the cow of Śayu stream refreshing
　　milk, and Vandana was holpen to
　　extended life.

7 Doers of marvels, skilful workers, ye restored
　　Vandana, like a car, worn out with length
　　of days.
　　From earth ye brought the sage to life in
　　wondrous mode; be your great deeds
　　done here for him who honours you.

8 Ye went to him who mourned in a far dis-
　　tant place, him who was left forlorn by
　　treachery of his sire.
　　Rich with the light of heaven was then the
　　help ye gave, and marvellous your suc-
　　cour when ye stood by him.

9 To you in praise of sweetness sang the
　　honey-bee : Auśija calleth you in Soma's
　　rapturous joy.
　　Ye drew unto yourselves the spirit of Dadh-
　　yac, and then the horse's head uttered
　　his words to you.

10 A horse did ye provide for Pedu, excellent,
　　white, O ye Aśvins, conqueror of com-
　　batants,
　　Invincible in war by arrows, seeking heaven
　　worthy of fame, like Indra, vanquisher
　　of men.

HYMN CXX.　　　　　　　　*Aśvins.*

1. AŚVINS, what praise may win your grace?
　　Who may be pleasing to you both ?
　　How shall the ignorant worship you?

2 Here let the ignorant ask the means of you
　　who know—for none beside you knoweth
　　aught —

8 *To him who mourned* : Bhujyu.

9 *The honey-bee* : meaning Auśija or the son of Uśij,
the sage Kakṣīvān.

———

With regard to the legends recounted in these hymns
to the Aśvins, Mr. Muir remarks (*O. S. Texts,* V. 248):
'The deliverances of Rebha, Vandana, Parāvṛj, Bhujyu,
Cyavāna, and others are explained by Professor Benfey
(following Dr. Kuhn and Professor Müller,) as referring
to certain physical phenomena with which the Aśvins
are supposed by these scholars to be connected. But
this allegorical method of interpretation seems
unlikely to be correct, as it is difficult to suppose that
the phenomena in question should have been alluded to
under such a variety of names and circumstances. It
appears, therefore, to be more probable that the ṛṣis
merely refer to certain legends which were popularly
current of interventions of the Aśvins in behalf of the
persons whose names are mentioned.'

———

Parts of this Hymn are difficult and obscure. The
first nine stanzas are in nine different metres.

2 In line 2 I adopt Ludwig's emendation *akratau* for
dkrau of the text.

Not of a spiritless mortal man.

3 Such as ye are, all-wise, we call you. Ye
wise, declare to us this day accepted
prayer.

Loving you well your servant lauds you.

4 Simply, ye Mighty Ones, I ask the Gods
of that wondrous oblation hallowed by
the mystic word.

Save us from what is stronger, fiercer than
ourselves.

5 Forth go the hymn that shone in Ghoṣa
Bhṛgu's like, the song wherewith the son
of Pajra worships you,

Like some wise minister.

6 Hear ye the song of him who hastens
speedily. O Aśvins, I am he who sang
your praise.

Hither, ye Lords of Splendour, hither turn
your eyes.

7 For ye were ever nigh to deal forth ample
wealth, to give the wealth that ye had
gathered up.

As such, ye Vasus, guard us well, and
keep us safely from the wicked wolf.

8 Give us not up to any man who hateth
us, nor let our milch-cows stray, whose
udders give us food,

Far from our homes without their calves.

9 May they who love you gain you for their
Friends. Prepare ye us for opulence
with strengthening food,

Prepare us for the food that floweth from
our cows.

10 I have obtained the horseless car of
Aśvins rich in sacrifice,

And I am well content therewith.

11 May it convey me evermore : may the
light chariot pass from men

To men unto the Soma draught.

12 It holdeth slumber in contempt. and the
rich who enjoyeth not :

Both vanish quickly and are lost.

HYMN CXXI.   *Indra.*

1. WHEN will men's guardians hasting hear
with favour the song of Aṅgiras's pious
childern ?

4 *Hallowed by the mystic word* : by the exclamation
vdṣat, used in making an oblation to a God with fire.
This word is of the most essential importance in sacrifice
but if carelessly and inconsiderately used its effects are
deadly, and against these the Ṛṣi prays for protection.

5 *Ghoṣa* : Sāyaṇa says that Suhastya, the son of
Ghoṣā, is intended.

The son of Pajra : one of the descendants of the
Aṅgirases ; here, according to Sāyaṇa, the Ṛṣi Kakṣīvān.

In this Hymn, as in the preceding, there are several
very obscure passages which can only conjecturally be
translated and explained.

When to the people of the home he cometh
he strideth to the sacrifice, the Holy.

2 He stablished heaven ; he poured forth,
skilful worker, the wealth of kine, for
strength, that nurtures heroes.

The Mighty One his self-born host regarded, the horse's mate, the mother of the
heifer.

3 Lord of red dawns, he came victorious,
daily to the Aṅgirases' former invocation.

His bolt and team hath he prepared, and
stablished the heaven for quadrupeds
and men two-footed.

4 In joy of this thou didst restore, for worship, the lowing company of hidden
cattle.

When the three-pointed one descends with
onslaught he opens wide the doors that
cause man trouble.

5 Thine is that milk which thy swift-moving
Parents brought down, a strengthening
genial gift for conquest;

When the pure treasure unto thee they
offered, the milk shed from the cow who
streameth nectar.

6 There is he born. May the Swift give us
rapture, and like the Sun shine forth
from yonder dawning,

Indu, even us who drank, whose toils are
offerings, poured from the spoon, with
praise, upon the altar.

2 *The Mighty One* : Indra is here said to have regarded or looked on the host born from, or produced by him,
that is, perhaps, the heaven and the earth in general.
Specially has he regarded the animals in which the wealth
of the people chiefly consists, among which the mare and
the cow naturally hold the chief place. Ludwig would
read *mātaram gām* instead of *mātáram goḥ*. He thinks that
the mate of the horse (Sūrya) is the earth, the motherly
cow. Sāyaṇa says that Indra in sport made a mare bring
forth a calf, and Wilson following him translates : 'he
made the female of the horse unnaturally the mother of
the cow.'

4 *In joy of this* : in the rapture arising from drinking
this Soma juice.

The lowing company of hidden cattle : the rain-clouds
carried off and kept concealed by the Paṇis.

The three-pointed one : apparently the thunderbolt.
Sāyaṇa takes it to mean Indra (elevated as a triple crest
in the three worlds). *He* : Indra.

5 *Thy swift-moving Parents* : Heaven and Earth.

6 *The Swift* : the swiftly flowing and efficacious Indu
or Soma.

Whose toils are offerings : whose drops of sweat, as we
labour in our sacred duties, count as oblations to the
Gods we serve.

From yonder dawning : probably an indication of time
only.

7 When the wood-pile, made of good logs, is ready, at the Sun's worship to bind fast the Bullock,
Then when thou shinest forth through days of action for the Car-borne, the Swift, the Cattle-seeker.

8 Eight steeds thou broughtest down from mighty heaven, when fighting for the well that giveth splendour,
That men might press with stones the gladdening yellow, strengthened with milk, fermenting, to exalt them.

9 Thou hurledst forth from heaven the iron missile, brought by the Skilful, from the sling of leather,
When thou, O Much-invoked, assisting Kutsa with endless deadly darts didst compass Śuṣṇa.

10 Bolt-armed, ere darkness overtook the sunlight, thou castest at the veiling cloud thy weapon,
Thou rentest, out of heaven, though firmly knotted, the might of Śuṣṇa that was thrown around him.

11 The mighty Heaven and Earth, those bright expanses that have no wheels, joyed, Indra, at thine exploit.
Vṛtra, the boar who lay amid the waters, to sleep thou sentest with thy mighty thunder.

12 Mount Indra, lover of the men thou guardest, the well-yoked horses of the wind, best bearers.
The bolt which Kāvya Uśanā erst gave thee, strong, gladdening, Vṛtra-slaying, hath he fashioned.

13 The strong Bay Horses of the Sun thou stayedst: this Etaśa drew not the wheel, O Indra.

Casting them forth beyond the ninety rivers thou dravest down into the pit the godless.

14 Indra, preserve thou us from this affliction Thunder-armed, save us from the misery near us.
Vouchsafe us affluence in chariots, founded on horses, for our food and fame and gladness.

15 Never may this thy loving-kindness fail us; mighty in strength, may plenteous food surround us.
Maghavan, make us share the foeman's cattle : may we be thy most liberal feast companions.

HYMN CXXII.   Viśvedevas.

1. SAY, bringing sacrifice to bounteous Rudra, This juice for drink to you whose wrath is fleeting!
With Dyaus the Asura's Heroes I have lauded the Maruts as with prayer to Earth and Heaven.

2 Strong to exalt the early invocation are Night and Dawn who show with varied aspect.
The Barren clothes her in wide-woven raiment, and fair Morn shines with Sūrya's golden splendour.

3 Cheer us the Roamer round, who strikes at morning, the Wind delight us, pourer forth of waters !

7 *To bind fast the Bullock* : the Bullock is the Sun himself : the sacrifice is to secure the blessings of sunlight. Sāyaṇa explains : the priest is competent for the attachment of the animal to the stake.
The Car-borne, the Swift, the Cattle-seeker : apparently appellations of Indra.
8 *The well that giveth splendour* : the cloud that sheds fertilizing rain.
The yellow : the Soma juice.
9 *The Skilful* : Tvaṣṭar.
Kāvya Uśanā : see I.51. 10.
13 The first hemistich of this stanza is most difficult, and I do not see how it can be satisfactorily translated and explained. I have followed Grassmann who translates : 'Du liessest ruhn der Sonne starke Rosse, nicht zog der Renner mehr ihr Rad, O Indra.' If this be the meaning, the reference may be, perhaps, to an eclipse of the sun.
Etaśa : appears in a double character, first as a sacrificer who offered Soma juice to Indra and was aided and favoured by that God (I. 51. 15), and secondly, Etaśa is the name of the horses or of one of the horses, or of the single horse, of Sūrya or the Sun, especially, it seems,

of the horse who, during the night, draws back the chariot of the Sun from the west to the east. In this verse, according to M. Bergaigne, Etaśa himself or his substitute (the word 'na' which I have taken to mean 'not' being understood in its alternative sense of 'like or as') is represented as drawing the wheel when Indra has stayed the course of the Harits or Bay Horses of the Sun. It is not difficult, says M. Bergaigne, to reconcile these two different conceptions of the role of Etaśa. A sacrificer especially favoured by Indra may represent either the sacrificial fire or the Soma juice that is prepared, consecrated, and offered to the God, and Soma, in the Veda, is frequently represented as a horse. See Bergaigne, *La Religion Vedique*, Vol. II. 330—333.

1 The meaning of this very difficult verse appears to be, that the offering of Soma juice is presented to Rudra and to his sons the fierce but easily appeased Maruts or Storm-Gods, whom the poet has lauded as the Heroes of Dyaus, the Immortal, and has at the same time supplicated the Deities Heaven and Earth. Wilson, following Sāyaṇa, paraphrases the second hemistich : 'I praise him who with his heroic (followers) as (with shafts) from a quiver expelled (the *Asuras*) from heaven : and (I praise) the *Maruts*, (who abide) between heaven and earth.'
2 *The barren* : the unfruitful Night; in which no work is done.
3 *The Roamer round* : 'the circumambient divinity', the Wind.'
Who strikes at morning : perhaps, blows away all evil spirits of the night.
Parvata : the presiding Genius of the mountains and ruler of the clouds, frequently associated with Indra.

Sharpen our wits, O Parvata and Indra.
May all the Gods vouchsafe to us this
favour.

4 And Auśija shall call for me that famous
Pair who enjoy and drink, who come to
brighten.
Set ye the Offspring of the Floods before
you; both Mothers of the Living One
who beameth.

5 For you shall Auśija call him who thunders,
as, to win Arjuna's assent, cried Ghoṣā.
I will invoke, that Pūṣan may be bounteous to you, the rich munificence of
Agni.

6 Hear, Mitra-Varuṇa, these mine invocations, hear them from all men in the
hall of worship.
Giver of famous gifts, kind hearer, Sindhu
who gives fair fields, listen with all his
waters !

7 Praised, Mitra, Varuṇa ! is your gift, a
hundred cows to the Pṛkṣayāmas and
the Pajra.
Presented by car-famous Priyaratha, supplying nourishment, they came directly.

8 Praised is the gift of him the very wealthy:
may we enjoy it, men with hero children:
His who hath many gifts to give the
Pajras, a chief who makes me rich in
cars and horses.

9 The folk, O Mitra-Varuṇa, who hate you,
who sinfully hating pour you no libations,
Lay in their hearts, themselves, a wasting
sickness, whereas the righteous gaineth
all by worship.

10 That man, most puissant, wondrously
urged onward, famed among heroes,
liberal in giving,
Moveth a warrior, evermore undaunted
in all encounters even with the mighty.

11 Come to the man's, the sacrificer's calling:
hear, Kings of Immortality, joy-givers!
While ye who speed through clouds decree
your bounty largely, for fame, to him
the chariot rider.

12 Vigour will we bestow on that adorer
whose tenfold draught we come to taste,
so spake they.
May all in whom rest splendour and great
riches obtain refreshment in these sacrifices.

13 We will rejoice to drink the tenfold present
when the twicefive come bearing sacred
viands.
What can he do whose steeds and reins
are choicest? These, the all-potent, urge
brave men to conquest.

14 The sea and all the Deities shall give us
him with the golden ear and neck be-
jewelled.
Dawns, hasting to the praises of the pious,
be pleased with us. both offerers and
singers.

15 Four youthful sons of Maśarśāra vex me,
three, of the king, the conquering
Āyavasa.
Now like the Sun, O Varuṇa and Mitra,
your car hath shone, long-shaped and
reined with splendour.

HYMN CXXIII. *Dawn.*

1. THE Dakṣiṇā's broad chariot hath been
harnessed : this car the Gods Immortal
have ascended.

11 *Kings of Immortality* : Varuṇa and Mitra.

12 *Tenfold draught* : Soma juice offered in ten ladles,
the *twice-five* of the following verse.

14. *Him with the golden ear* : perhaps the Sun; but the
meaning of the hemistich is uncertain.

15 There is no verb in the first hemistich, and I follow
Sāyaṇa in supplying 'vex.' But *śiśvaḥ* may mean 'young
horses' as well as 'youthful sons,' and the verb to be
supplied may be 'carry,' as suggested by Grassmann.
The whole hymn, as Wilson observes, 'is very elliptical
and obscure', and much of it is at present unintelligible.

4 *Auśija* : the son of *Uśij*, that is, Kakṣīvān himself,
the Ṛṣi of the hymn.

That famous Pair : the Aśvins. *The Offspring of the
Flood* : Agni.

The Living One who beameth : or praiseth. Agni
appears to be meant.

5 *Him who thunders* : Indra. *Ghoṣā*, in I. 117. 5, is
said to have been provided with a husband by the Aśvins.
Arjuna, in this verse, may perhaps have been the husband's
name. The meaning of the passage is uncertain. Sāyaṇa
takes *arjuna* to mean white skin, or leprosy, from which
Ghoṣā prayed to be made free.

6 *Sindhu* : the Indus; the Deity presiding over waters.

7 Who the *Pṛkṣayāmas*, or drivers of swift horses are,
is uncertain.

The Pajra : the Ṛṣi Kakṣīvān himself, a member
of the priestly family of the Pajras.

1 *The Dakṣiṇā's broad chariot* : the Dakṣiṇā itself, that
is the honorarium or fee presented by the institutor of
a sacrifice to the priests who perform the ceremony. The
meaning of the first hemistich appears to be that all preparations have been made for the morning sacrifice, and
especially that the foe for its performance—a most essential element—is ready, and that the Gods are coming to
the rite. The word *dākṣiṇāyāḥ* is considered by Sāya a
to be an epithet of *uṣodevatāyāḥ*, understood, that is,
'of the Goddess Uṣas or Dawn.' Wilson accordingly,
translates, 'the spacious chariot of the graceful
(*Dawn*)'; Ludwig renders the word by 'friendly,'
and Grassmann by 'wealth,' both scholars
applying the epithet to Uṣas or Dawn who is not mentioned in the text. I have followed M. Bergaigne who
says : 'The interpretation of the word *dakṣiṇā* in the

Fain to bring light to homes of men the noble and active Goddess hath emerged from darkness.

2 She before all the living world hath wakened, the Lofty One who wins and gathers treasure.
Revived and ever young on high she glances. Dawn hath come first unto our morning worship.

3 If, Dawn, thou Goddess nobly born, thou dealest fortune this day to all the race of mortals,
May Savitar the God, Friend of the homestead, declare before the Sun that we are sinless.

4 Showing her wonted form each day that passeth, spreading the light she visiteth each dwelling.
Eager for conquest, with bright sheen she cometh. Her portion is the best of goodly treasures.

5 Sister of Varuṇa, sister of Bhaga, first among all sing forth, O joyous Morning.
Weak be the strength of him who worketh evil : may we subdue him with our car the guerdon.

6 Let our glad hymns and holy thoughts rise upward, for the flames brightly burning have ascended.
The far-refulgent Mornings make apparent the lovely treasures which the darkness covered.

7 The one departeth and the other cometh: unlike in hue day's halves march on successive.
One hides the gloom of the surrounding Parents. Dawn on her shining chariot is resplendent.

8 The same in form to-day, the same to-morrow, they still keep Varuṇa's eternal statute.
Blameless, in turn they traverse thirty regions, and dart across the spirit in a moment.

9 She who hath knowledge of the first day's nature is born refulgent white from out the darkness.
The Maiden breaketh not the law of Order, day by day coming to the place appointed.

10 In pride of beauty like a maid thou goest, O Goddess, to the God who longs to win thee,
And smiling, youthful, as thou shinest brightly, before him thou discoverest thy bosom.

11 Fair as a bride embellished by her mother thou showest forth thy form that all may see it.
Blessed art thou, O Dawn. Shine yet more widely. No other Dawns have reached what thou attainest.

12 Rich in kine, horses, and all goodly treasures, in constant operation with the sunbeams,
The Dawns depart and come again assuming their wonted forms that promise happy fortune.

13 Obedient to the rein of Law Eternal give us each thought that more and more shall bless us.
Shine thou on us to-day, Dawn, swift to listen. With us be riches and with chiefs who worship.

HYMN CXXIV. *Dawn.*

1. The Dawn refulgent when the fire is kindled, and the Sun rising, far diffuse their brightness.
Savitar, God, hath sent us forth to labour, each quadruped, each biped, to be active.

---

sense of sacrificial salary, in the first verse of our hymn as also in the fifth, is, not only *possible* but the *only possible* one, for the reason that this word has no other sense in the Ṛg-Veda than that of "salary, recompense," given either by the earthly *maghavan*, that is to say by those who pay the priest for performing the sacrifice, or by the heavenly *maghavan*, Indra, who in his turn pays for the sacrifice by favours of every kind to the man who causes it to be offered.' See *La Religion Vedique*, Vol. III, pp. 283, ff., for M. Bergaigne's translation of, and polemical commentary on, this hymn.

The noble and active Goddess : Uṣas, Aurora, or Dawn. The word Goddess is not in the text.

3 *May Savitar* : the all-seeing deity Savitar who presides over, but is sometimes distinguished from, the Sun, is appealed to as the best judge of the suppliant's innocence.

5 *Our car the guerdon* : may the liberal fee given for the performance of the sacrifice be to us as a war-chariot to enable us to overpower those who would injure us.

7 *Day's halves* : day and night. *The surrounding Parents* are the all en-compassing Heaven and Earth : the nightly darkness which envelops them is hidden or dispelled by the day.

8 *They traverse thirty regions* : I follow M. Bergaigne in understanding the thirty regions or spaces to be an indefinite expression for the whole universe. A more elaborate attempt at explanation will be found in Wilson's Translation in a Note from Bentley's *Hindu Astronomy*. *They* are the Dawns, and they may be said to pass across or through the spirit, to enlighten it. The second hemistich is very difficult and obscure, and can be translated only provisionally.

10 *The God who longs to win thee* : the Sun, the lover of Dawn.

13 *Chiefs who worship* : the wealthy institutors of sacrifices.

---

1 *The fire* : the sacrificial fire lighted for the morning rites.

2 Not interrupting heavenly ordinances, although she minisheth human generations.

The last of endless morns that have departed, the first of those that come, Dawn brightly shineth.

3 There in the eastern region she, Heaven's Daughter, arrayed in garments all of light, appeareth.

Truly she followeth the path of Order, nor faileth, knowing well, the heavenly quarters.

4 Near is she seen, as 'twere the Bright One's bosom: she showeth sweet things like a new song-singer.

She cometh like a fly awaking sleepers, of all returning dames most true and constant.

5 There in the east half of the watery region the Mother of the Cows hath shown her ensign.

Wider and wider still she spreadeth onward, and filleth full the laps of both her Parents.

6 She, verily, exceeding vast to look on debarreth from her light nor kin nor stranger.

Proud of her spotless form she, brightly shining, turneth not from the high nor from the humble.

7 She seeketh men as she who hath no brother, mounting her car, as 'twere to gather riches.

Dawn, like a loving matron for her husband, smiling and well attired, unmasks her beauty.

8 The Sister quitteth, for the elder Sister, her place, and having looked on her departeth.

She decks her beauty, shining forth with sunbeams, like women trooping to the festal meeting.

9 To all these Sisters who ere now have vanished a later one each day in course succeedeth.

So, like the past, with days of happy fortune, may the new Dawns shine forth on us with riches.

10 Rouse up, O Wealthy One, the liberal givers; let niggard traffickers sleep on unwakened :

Shine richly, Wealthy One, on those who worship, richly, glad.

Dawn while wasting, on the singer.

11 This young Maid from the east hath shone upon us ; she harnesseth her team of bright red oxen.

She will beam forth, the light will hasten hither, and Agni will be present in each dwelling.

12 As the birds fly forth from their resting places, so men with store of food rise at thy dawning.

Yea, to the liberal mortal who remaineth at home, O Goddess Dawn, much good thou bringest.

13 Praised through my prayer be ye who should be lauded. Ye have increased our wealth, ye Dawns who love us.

Goddesses, may we win by your good favour wealth to be told by hundreds and by thousands.

HYMN CXXV. *Svanaya.*

1. COMING at early morn he gives his treasure ; the prudent one receives and entertains him.

Thereby increasing still his life and offspring, he comes with brave sons to abundant riches.

2 Rich shall he be in gold and kine and horses. Indra bestows on him great vital power,

Who stays thee, as thou comest, with his treasure, like game caught in the net, O early comer.

3 Longing, I came this morning to the pious, the son of sacrifice, with car wealthladen.

Give him to drink juice of the stalk that gladdens ; prosper with pleasant hymns the Lord of Heroes.

4 Health-bringing streams, as milch-cows,

10 *While wasting* : as in verse 2.
12 *With store of food* : we should expect 'who seek their food,' and so Sāyaṇa explains *pitubhājaḥ*. The wealthy may be meant who share their store with others and must work to replenish it.

____

This hymn is a dialogue between a wandering priest and a pious liberal prince. For the explanatory legend, which is cited by Sāyaṇa, see the note in Wilson's translation.

1 The priest (Kakṣīvān) speaks. *His treasure* : the wealth that will follow sacrifice. *The prudent one* : the prince.

2 The prince (Svanaya) speaks.

3 The priest speaks. *Him* : Indra.

2. *She minisheth* : by marking the lapse of man's allotted time. Cf. I. 92. 10, 11.

4 *Like a fly* : admasán ná; see Geldner, Vedische Studien, II. 179.

5 *The watery region* : the misty sky. *The Cows* : rays of light.
Both her Parents : Heaven and Earth.

7 *She seeketh men* : this is not very clear. Perhaps the Sun, her lover or husband, is intended.

8 *The elder Sister* : Day, for whom Night makes room.

flow to profit him who hath worshipped, him who now will worship.

To him who freely gives and fills on all sides full streams of fatness flow and make him famous.

5 On the high ridge of heaven he stands exalted, yea, to the Gods he goes, the liberal giver.

The streams, the waters flow for him with fatness : to him this guerdon ever yields abundance.

6 For those who give rich meeds are all these splendours, for those who give rich meeds suns shine in heaven.

The givers of rich meeds are made immortal ; the givers of rich fees prolong their lifetime.

7 Let not the liberal sink to sin and sorrow, never decay the pious chiefs who worship !

Let every man besides be their protection, and let affliction fall upon the niggard.

HYMN CXXVI.   *Bhāvayavya.*

1. WITH wisdom I present these lively praises of Bhāvya dweller on the bank of Sindhu ;

For he, unconquered King, desiring glory, hath furnished me a thousand sacrifices.

2 A hundred necklets from the King, beseeching, a hundred gift-steeds I at once accepted ;

Of the lord's cows a thousand, I Kakṣīvān. His deathless glory hath he spread to heaven.

3 Horses of dusky colour stood beside me, ten chariots, Svanaya's gift, with mares to draw them.

Kine numbering sixty thousand followed after. Kakṣīvān gained them when the days were closing.

4 Forty bay horses of the ten cars' master before a thousand lead the long procession.

Reeling in joy Kakṣīvān's sons and Pajra's have grounded the coursers decked with pearly trappings.

---

1 *Bhāvya* : the prince Svanaya of the preceding hymn is here again eulogized for his munificence under the name of his father Bhāvya or Bhāvayavya, who lived on the bank of Sindhu or the Indus.

3 *With mares to draw them* : or, with damsels or female slaves. Cf. VI. 27. 8.

4 *Pajra* : the founder of the priestly family from which Kakṣīvān was descended.

The sixth stanza of the hymn is ascribed to Svanaya, and the seventh to his wife Romaśā. They have no apparent connexion with what precedes, and are in a different metre. They seem to be a fragment of a popular song. See Appendix.

---

5 An earlier gift for you have I accepted eight cows, good milkers, and three harnessed horses,

Pajras, who with your wains with your great kinsman, like troops of subjects, have been fain for glory.

HYMN CXXVII.   *Agni.*

1. AGNI I hold as herald, the munificent, the gracious, Son of Strength, who knoweth all that live, as holy Singer, knowing all,

Lord of fair rites, a God with form erected turning to the Gods,

He, when the flame hath sprung forth from the holy oil, the offered fatness, longeth for it with his glow.

2 We, sacrificing, call on thee best worshipper, the eldest of Aṅgirases, Singer, with hymns, thee, brilliant One ! with singers' hymns ;

Thee, wandering round as 't were the sky, who art the invoking Priest of men,

Whom, Bull with hair of flame, the people must observe, the people that he speed them on.

3 He with his shining glory blazing far and wide, he verily it is who slayeth demon foes, slayeth the demons like an axe :

At whose close touch things solid shake, and what is stable yields like trees.

Subduing all, he keeps his ground and flinches not, from the skilled archer flinches not.

4 To him, as one who knows, even things solid yield : unrough fire-sticks heated hot he gives his gifts to aid. Men offer Agni gifts for aid.

He deeply piercing many a thing hews it like wood with fervent glow.

Even hard and solid food he crunches with his might, yea, hard and solid food

---

This hymn, and the twelve that follow it, are attributed to the Ṛṣi Parucchepa. They are generally very obscure and frequently unintelligible. One of their peculiarities is 'to reiterate a leading word which occurs the third or fourth from the end of the first line, and sometimes also of the third, and to repeat it as the last word of the line. Thus we have here *sānum sahaso, Jātavedasam vipram na Jātavedasam*; this is little else than a kind of verbal alliterative jingle, but the Scholiast thinks it necessary to assign to the repeated word a distinct signification.'—Wilson.

2 *Eldest of Aṅgirases* : see I. 1.6.

3 *From the skilled archer flinches not* : not even a strong man armed with his bow can turn him from his course.

4 *Fire-sticks* : the two pieces of wood which are still used to produce the sacrificial fire.

with might.

5 Here near we place the sacrificial food for
him who shines forth fairer in the night
than in the day, with life then stronger
than by day.
His life gives sure and firm defence as
that one giveth to a son.
The during fires enjoy things given and
things not given, the during fires enjoy
as food.

6 He, roaring very loudly like the Maruts'
host, in fertile cultivated fields adorable,
in desert spots adorable,
Accepts and eats our offered gifts, ensign
of sacrifice by desert ;
So let all, joying, love his path when he
is glad, as men pursue a path for bliss.

7 Even as they who sang forth hymns,
addressed to heaven, the Bhṛgus with
their prayer and praise invited him, the
Bhṛgus rubbing, offering gifts.
For radiant Agni, Lord of all these treasures, is exceeding strong.
May he, the wise, accept the grateful
coverings, the wise accept the coverings.

8 Thee we invoke, the Lord of all our settled
homes, common to all, the household's
guardian, to enjoy, bearer of true
hymns, to enjoy.
Thee we invoke, the guest of men, by
whose mouth, even as a sire's,
All these Immortals come to gain their
food of life, oblations come to Gods as
food.

9 Thou, Agni, most victorious with thy
conquering strength, most Mighty One,
art born for service of the Gods, like
wealth for service of the Gods.
Most mighty is thine ecstasy, most splendid
is thy mental power.
Therefore men wait upon thee, undecaying
One, like vassals, undecaying One.

10 To him the mighty, conquering with
victorious strength, to Agni walking with
the dawn, who sendeth kine, be sung
your laud, to Agni sung ;
As he who with oblation comes calls him
aloud in every place.
Before the brands of fire he shouteth singer-
like, the herald, kindler of the brands.

11 Agni, beheld by us in nearest neighbourhood, accordant with the Gods, bring

us, with gracious love, great riches with
thy gracious love.
Give us O Mightiest, what is great, to
see and to enjoy the earth.
As one of awful power, stir up heroic
might for those who praise thee, Bounteous Lord !

HYMN CXXVIII. *Agni.*

1. By Manu's law was born this Agni, Priest
most skilled, born for the holy work of
those who yearn therefore, yea, born
for his own holy work.
All ear to him who seeks his love and
wealth to him who strives for fame,
Priest ne'er deceived, he sits in Iḷā's holy
place, girt round in Iḷā's holy place.

2 We call that perfecter of worship by the
path of sacrifice; with reverence rich in
offerings, with worship rich in offerings.
Through presentation of our food he
grows not old in this his from ;
The God whom Mātariśvan brought from
far away, for Manu brought from far
away.

3 In ordered course forthwith he traverses
the earth, swift-swallowing, bellowing
Steer, bearing the genial seed, bearing
the seed and bellowing.
Observant with a hundred eyes the God
is conqueror in the wood :
Agni, who hath his seat in broad plains
here below, and in the high lands far
away.

4 That Agni, wise High-Priest, in every
house takes thought for sacrifice and
holy service, yea, takes thought, with
mental power, for sacrifice.
Disposer, he with mental power shows all
things unto him who strives;
Whence he was born a guest enriched
with holy oil, born as Ordainer and as
Priest.

5 When through his power and in his
strong prevailing flames the Maruts'
gladdening boons mingle with Agni's
roar, boons gladdening for the active
One,
Then he accelerates the gift, and by the
greatness of his wealth,
Shall rescue us from overwhelming misery,
from curse and overwhelming woe.

---

5 *Things given and things not given* : both sacrificial
offerings and the grass brushwood of the jungle.

7 *The Bhṛgus* : descendants of Bhṛgu, the earliest
cherisher of Agni, or kindler of fire. *Rubbing* : agitating
the fire-sticks. *The coverings* : according to Sāyaṇa, the
oblations of clarified butter, etc.

1 *Iḷā's holy place* : the altar ; Iḍā or Iḷā is personified
Prayer and Worship.

2 *Mātariśvan* : see I. 31. 3.

5 *The Maruts' gladdening boons* : storm and rain.

6 Vast, universal, good he was made messenger ; the speeder with his right hand hath not loosed his hold, through love of fame not loosed his hold.

He bears oblations to the Gods for whosoever supplicates.

Agni bestows a blessing on each pious man, and opens wide the doors for him.

7 That Agni hath been set most kind in camp of men, in sacrifice like a Lord victorious, like a dear Lord in sacred rites.

His are the oblations of mankind when offered up at Iḷā's place.

He shall preserve us from Varuṇa's chastisement, yea, from the great God's chastisement.

8 Agni the Priest they supplicate to grant them wealth : him, dear, most thoughtful, have they made their messenger, him, offering-bearer have they made,

Beloved of all, who knoweth all, the Priest, the Holy one, the Sage—

Him, Friend, for help, the Gods when they are fain for wealth, him, Friend, with hymns, when fain for wealth.

HYMN CXXIX   *Indra.*

1. THE car which Indra, thou, for service of the Gods, though it be far away, O swift One, bringest near, which, Blameless One, thou bringest near,

Place swiftly nigh us for our help : be it thy will that it be strong.

Blameless and active, hear this speech of orderers, this speech of us like orderers.

2 Hear, Indra, thou whom men in every fight must call to show thy strength, for cry of battle with the men, with men of war for victory.

He who with heroes wins the light, who with the singers gains the prize,

Him the rich seek to gain even as a swift strong steed, even as a courser fleet and strong.

3 Thou, Mighty, pourest forth the hide that holds the rain, thou keepest far away, Hero, the wicked man, thou shuttest out the wicked man.

Indra, to thee I sing, to Dyaus, to Rudra glorious in himself,

To Mitra, Varuṇa I sing a far-famed hymn to the kind God a far-famed hymn.

4 We wish our Indra here that he may further you, the Friend, beloved of all,

the very strong ally, in wars the very strong ally

In all encounters strengthen thou our prayer to be a help to us.

No enemy—whom thou smitest down—subdueth thee, no enemy, whom thou smitest down.

5 Bow down the overweening pride of every foe with succour like to kindling-wood in fiercest flame, with mighty succour, Mighty One.

Guide us, thou Hero, as of old, so art thou counted blameless still.

Thou drivest, as a Priest, all sins of man away, as Priest, in person, seeking us.

6 This may I utter to the present Soma-drop, which, meet to be invoked, with power, awakes the prayer, awakes the demon-slaying prayer.

May he himself with darts of death drive far from us the scorner's hate.

Far let him flee away who speaketh wickedness and vanish like a mote of dust.

7 By thoughtful invocation this may we obtain, obtain great wealth, O Wealthy One, with Hero sons, wealth that is sweet with hero sons.

Him who is wroth we pacify with sacred food and eulogies,

Indra the Holy with our calls inspired and true, the Holy One with calls inspired.

8 On, for your good and ours, come Indra with the aid of his own lordliness to drive the wicked hence, to rend the evil-hearted ones !

The weapon which devouring fiends cast at us shall destroy themselves.

Struck down, it shall not reach the mark; hurled forth, the fire-brand shall not strike.

9 With riches in abundance, Indra, come to us, come by an unobstructed path, come by a path from demons free.

Be with us when we stray afar, be with us when our home is nigh.

Protect us with thy help both near and far away : protect us ever with thy help.

10 Thou art our own, O Indra, with victorious wealth : let might accompany thee, the Strong, to give us aid, like Mitra, to give mighty aid.

O strongest saviour, helper thou, Immortal ! of each warrior's car.

Hurt thou another and not us, O Thunder-armed, one who would hurt, O Thunder-armed !

11 Save us from injury, thou who art well
extolled : ever the warder-off art thou
of wicked ones, even as a God, of
wicked ones ;
Thou slayer of the evil fiend, saviour of
singer such as I.
Good Lord, the Father made thee slayer
of the fiends, made thee, good Lord,
to slay the fiends.

HYMN CXXX. *Indra.*

1. COME to us, Indra, from afar, conducting
us even as a lord of heroes to the
gatherings, home, like a King, his heroes'
lord.
We come with gifts of pleasant food, with
juice poured forth, invoking thee,
As sons invite a sire, that thou mayst get
thee strength, thee, bounteousest, to get
thee strength.

2 O Indra, drink the Soma juice pressed
out with stones, poured from the reservoir, as an ox drinks the spring, a very
thirsty bull the spring.
For the sweet draught that gladdens thee,
for mightiest freshening of thy strength.
Let thy Bay Horses bring thee hither as
the Sun, as every day they bring the
Sun.

3 He found the treasure brought from heaven
that lay concealed, close-hidden, like the
nestling of a bird, in rock, enclosed in
never-ending rock.
Best Aṅgiras, bolt-armed, he strove to win,
as 'twere, the stall of kine ;
So Indra hath disclosed the food concealed, disclosed the doors, the food that
lay concealed.

4 Grasping his thunderbolt with both hands,
Indra made its edge most keen, for
hurling, like a carving-knife for Ahi's
slaughter made it keen.
Endued with majesty and strength, O
Indra, and with lordly might,
Thou crashest down the trees, as when a
craftsman fells, crashest them down as
with an axe.

5 Thou, Indra, without effort hast let loose
the floods to run their free course down,

like chariots, to the sea, like chariots
showing forth their strength.
They, reaching hence away, have joined
their strength for one eternal end,
Even as the cows who poured forth every
thing for man, yea, poured forth all
things for mankind.

6 Eager for riches, men have formed for thee
this song, like as a skilful craftsman
fashioneth a car, so have they wrought
thee to their bliss ;
Adorning thee, O Singer, like a generous
steed for deeds of might,
Yea, like a steed to show his strength and
win the prize, that he may bear each
prize away.

7 For Pūru thou hast shattered, Indra !
ninety forts, for Divodāsa thy boon
servant with thy bolt, O Dancer, for
thy worshipper.
For Atithigva he, the Strong, brought
Śambara from the mountain down,
Distributing the mighty treasures with his
strength, parting all treasures with his
strength.

8 Indra in battles help his Āryan worshipper,
he who hath hundred helps at hand in
every fray, in frays that win the light of
heaven.
Plaguing the lawless he gave up to Manu's
seed the dusky skin ;
Blazing, 'twere, he burns each covetous
man away, he burns, the tyrannous
away.

9 Waxed strong in might at dawn he tore
the Sun's wheel off. Bright red, he
steals away their speech, the Lord of
Power, their speech he steals away from
them,
As thou with eager speed, O Sage, hast
come from far away to help,
As winning for thine own all happiness of
men, winning all happiness each day.

---

11 *The Father* : Janitā, the Latin genitor; the Supreme God, the Maker and Father of the Universe.

---

3 *He found the treasure* : the Soma. *The food concealed* :
according to Sāyaṇa, in the first place the rain enclosed
in the clouds, and in the second place the seeds shut up
in the earth which await the rain to make them germi-
nate.

5 *For man* : or for Manu, the great progenitor of the
human race.

7 *Pūru* : the name of a prince protected by Indra.
Divodāsa : called also *Atithigva*. See I. 92, 191.

Dancer : thou who dancest in battle; dancer of the
war-dance.

Śambara : a demon of the air ; or perhaps in this
place some human adversary of Atithigva.

9 *He tore the Sun's wheel off* : according to Sāyaṇa,
Brahmā had promised the Asuras or fiends that Indra's
thunderbolt should never destroy them. Indra, accordingly, cast at them the wheel of the Sun's chariot and
slew them therewith.

He steals their speech : Sāyaṇa thinks that the meaning
is that Indra deprived his enemies of life.

O Sage : O Indra.

10 Lauded with our new hymns, O vigorous
in deed, save us with strengthening
help, thou Shatterer of the Forts !
Thou, Indra, praised by Divodāsa's clansmen, as heaven grows great with days,
shalt wax in glory.

HYMN CXXXI.   *Indra.*

1. To Indra Dyaus the Asura hath bowed
him down, to Indra mighty Earth with
wide-extending tracts, to win the light,
with wide-spread tracts.
All Gods of one accord have set Indra in
front preëminent.
For Indra all libations must be set apart,
all man's libations set apart.

2 In all libations men with hero spirit urge
the Universal One, each seeking several
light, each fain to win the light apart.
Thee, furthering like a ship, will we set to
the chariot-pole of strength,
As men who win with sacrifices Indra's
thought, men who win Indra with their
lauds.

3 Couples desirous of thine aid are storming
thee, pouring their presents forth to win
a stall of kine, pouring gifts, Indra,
seeking thee.
When two men seeking spoil or heaven
thou bringest face to face in war,
Thou showest, Indra, then the bolt thy
constant friend, the Bull that ever waits
on thee.

4 This thine heroic power men of old time
have known, wherewith thou breakest
down, Indra, autumnal forts, breakest
them down with conquering might.
Thou hast chastised, O Indra, Lord of
Strength, the man who worships not,
And made thine own this great earth and
these water-floods ; with joyous heart
these waterfloods.

5 And they have bruited far this hero-might
when thou, O Strong One, in thy joy

helpest thy suppliants, who sought to
win thee for their Friend.
Their battle-cry thou madest sound
victorious in the shocks of war.
One stream after another have they gained
from thee, eager for glory have they
gained.

6. Also this morn may he be well inclined to
us, mark at our call our offerings and
our song of praise, our call that we
may win the light.
As thou, O Indra Thunder-armed, wilt, as
the Strong One, slay the foe,
Listen thou to the prayer of me a later
sage, hear thou a later sage's prayer.

7 O Indra, waxen strong and well-inclined
to us, thou very mighty, slay the man
that is our foe, slay the man, Hero !
with thy bolt.
Slay thou the man who injures us : hear
thou, as readiest to hear.
Far be malignity, like mischief on the
march, afar be all malignity.

HYMN CXXXII.   *Indra.*

1. Helped, Indra Maghavan, by thee in war
of old, may we subdue in fight the men
who strive with us, conquer the men
who war with us.
This day that now is close at hand bless
him who pours the Soma juice.
In this our sacrifice may we divide the
spoil, showing our strength, the spoil of
war.

2 In war which wins the light, at the free-
giver's call, at due oblation of the
early-rising one, oblation of the active
one,
Indra slew, even as we know—whom each
bowed head must reverence.
May all thy bounteous gifts be gathered
up for us, yea, the good gifts of thee
the Good.

3 This food glows for thee as of old at
sacrifice, wherein they made thee
chooser of the place, for thou choosest
the place of sacrifice.
Speak thou and make it known to us :
they see within with beams of light.

---

10 *By Divodāsa's clansmen :* by me, Paruçchepa, a
member of the house or family of Divodāsa.

3 *Couples :* sacrificers and their wives who are associated with them in offering oblations.
The Bull : the fiercely rushing thunderbolt.

4 *Autumnal forts :* strongholds on high ground, occupied as places of refuge during the heavy rains, or 'the
brilliant battlemented cloud-castles, which are so often
visible in the Indian sky at this period of the year.' —
Muir, O. S. Texts, II. 379.

Men of old time : I have followed Sāyaṇa here.
But *pūrvaḥ* probably means the Pūrus, one of the
five great Āryan tribes or clans.

---

1 *This day :* the hymn is addressed to Indra just
before an expected battle.
May we divide the spoil : divide it in anticipation ;
secure it by our sacrifice.
2 *The early-rising* and *active one* is the offerer of the
sacrifice.
3 *They made thee chooser of the place :* the meaning
appears to be that Indra is present at such sacrifices only
as he chooses to favour.

Indra, indeed, is found a seeker after spoil, spoil-seeker for his own allies.

4 So now must thy great deed be lauded as of old, when for the Aṅgirases thou openedst the stall, openedst, giving aid, the stall.
In the same manner for us here fight thou and be victorious :
To him who pours the juice give up the lawless man, the lawless who is wroth with us.

5 When with wise plan the Hero leads the people forth, they conquer in the order-ed battle, seeking fame, press, eager, onward seeking fame.
To him in time of need they sing for life with offspring and with strength.
Their hymns with Indra find a welcome place of rest : the hymns go forward to the Gods.

6 Indra and Parvata, our champions in the fight, drive ye away each man who fain would war with us, drive him far from us with the bolt.
Welcome to him concealed afar shall be the lair that he hath found.
So may the Render rend our foes on every side, rend them, O Hero, every-where.

HYMN CXXXIII.   *Indra.*

1. WITH sacrifice I purge both earth and heaven : I burn up great she-fiends who serve not Indra,
Where throttled by thy hand the foes were slaughtered, and in the pit of death lay pierced and mangled.

2 O thou who castest forth the stone, crushing the sorceresses' heads,
Break them with thy wide-spreading foot, with thy wide-spreading mighty foot.

3 Do thou, O Maghavan, beat off these sorceresses' daring strength.
Cast them within the narrow pit, within the deep and narrow pit.

4 Of whom thou hast ere now destroyed thrice-fifty with thy fierce attacks.
That deed they count a glorious deed, though small to thee, a glorious deed.

5 O Indra, crush and bray to bits the fearful fiery-weaponed fiend :
Strike every demon to the ground.

6 Tear down the mighty ones. O Indra, hear thou us. For heaven hath glowed like earth in fear, O Thunder-armed, as dreading fierce heat, Thunder-armed !
Most Mighty mid the Mighty Ones thou speedest with strong bolts of death.
Not slaying men, unconquered Hero ! with the brave, O Hero, with the thrice-seven brave.

7 The pourer of libations gains the home of wealth, pouring his gift conciliates hostilities, yea, the hostilities of Gods.
Pouring, he strives, unchecked and strong, to win him riches thousandfold.
Indra gives lasting wealth to him who pours forth gifts, yea, wealth he gives that long shall last.

HYMN CXXXIV.   *Vāyu.*

1. VĀYU, let fleet-foot coursers bring thee speedily to this our feast, to drink first of the juice we pour, to the first draught of Soma juice.
May our glad hymn, discerning well, uplifted, gratify thy mind.
Come with thy team-drawn car, O Vāyu, to the gift, come to the sacrificer's gift.

2 May the joy-giving drops, O Vāyu gladden thee, effectual, well prepared, directed to the heavens, strong, blent with milk and seeking heaven ;
That aids, effectual to fulfil, may wait upon our skilful power.
Associate teams come hitherward to grant our prayers : they shall address the hymns we sing.

3 Two red steeds Vāyu yokes, Vāyu two purple steeds, swift-footed, to the chariot, to the pole to draw, most able, at the pole, to draw.
Wake up intelligence, as when a lover wakes his sleeping love.
Illumine heaven and earth, make thou the Dawns to shine, for glory make the Dawns to shine.

Speak thou and make it known : Wilson, following Sāyaṇa, paraphrases : 'do thou declare that (rite), that men may thence behold the intermediate (firmament bright) with the rays (of the sun).' I find the passage unintelligible.

4 The man *who pours the juice* is the worshipper of Indra, and *the lawless man* is the non-Āryan inhabitant of the country, the natural enemy of the new settlers.

6 *Parvata* : the presiding Genius of mountains and clouds, frequently associated with Indra, or, according to Sāyaṇa, another form of that God. Cf. II 122. 3.

This hymn is a prayer for the destruction of witches, goblins, and evil spirits of various sorts.

2 *Who castest forth the stone* : hurlest the thunderbolt.

---

6 *Not slaying men* : that is destroying evil spirits only. *The thrice-seven brave* : the Maruts, Indra's allies. These were forty-nine in number, and thrice-seven is used inde-finitely for a larger multiple of seven.

1 *Vāyu* : the God of wind.

4 For thee the radiant Dawns in the far-
distant sky broaden their lovely
garments forth in wondrous beams,
bright-coloured in their new-born beams.
For thee the nectar-yielding Cow pours
all rich treasures forth as milk.
The Marut host hast thou engendered
from the womb, the Maruts from the
womb of heaven.

5 For thee the pure bright quickly-flowing
Soma-drops, strong in their heightening
power, hasten to mixthemselves, hasten
to the water to be mixed.
To thee the weary coward prays for luck
that he may speed away.
Thou by thy law protectest us from every
world, yea, from the world of highest
Gods.

6 Thou, Vāyu, who hast none before thee,
first of all hast right to drink these
offerings of Soma juice, hast right to
drink the juice out-poured,
Yea, poured by all invoking tribes who
free themselves from taint of sin,
For thee all cows are milked to yield the
Soma-milk, to yield the butter and the
milk.

HYMN CXXXV. *Vāyu, Indra-Vāyu.*

1. STREWN is the sacred grass ; come Vāyu,
to our feast, with team of thousands,
come, Lord of the harnessed team, with
hundreds, Lord of harnessed steeds !
The drops divine are lifted up for thee,
the God, to drink them first.
The juices rich in sweets have raised them
for thy joy, have raised themselves to
give thee strength.

2 Purified by the stones the Soma flows for
thee, clothed with its lovely splendours,
to the reservoir, flows clad in its refulgent light.
For thee the Soma is poured forth, thy
portioned share mid.Gods and men.
Drive thou thy horses, Vāyu, come to us
with love, come well-inclined and loving
us.

3 Come thou with hundreds, come with
thousands in thy team to this our
solemn rite, to taste the sacred food,
Vāyu, to taste the offerings.
This is thy seasonable share, that comes
co-radiant with the Sun.

Brought by attendant priests pure juice is
offered up, Vāyu, pure juice is offered
up.

4 The chariot with its team of horses bring
you both, to guard us and to taste the
well-appointed food, Vāyu, to taste the
offerings !
Drink of the pleasant-flavoured juice :
the first draught is assigned to you.
O Vāyu, with your splendid bounty come
ye both, Indra, with bounty come ye
both.

5 May our songs bring you hither to our
solemn rites : these drops of mighty
vigour have they beautified, like a swift
steed of mighty strength.
Drink of them well-inclined to us, come
hitherward to be our help.
Drink, Indra-Vāyu, of these juices pressed
with stones, Strength-givers ! till they
gladden you.

6 These Soma juices pressed for you in
waters here, borne by attendant priests,
are offered up to you : bright, Vāyu,
are they offered up.
Swift through the strainer have they
flowed, and here are shed for both
of you,
Soma-drops, fain for you, over the wether's
fleece, Somas over the wether's fleece.

7 O Vāyu, pass thou over all the slumberers,
and where the press-stone rings enter
ye both that house, yea, Indra, go ye
both within.
The joyous Maiden is beheld, the butter
flows. With richly laden team come to
our solemn rite, yea, Indra, come ye to
the rite.

8 Ride hither to the offering of the pleasant
juice, the holy Fig-tree which victorious
priests surround : victorious be they
still for us.
At once the cows yield milk, the barley-
meal is dressed. For thee,
O Vāyu, never shall the cows grow thin,
never for thee shall they be dry.

9 These Bulls of thine, O Vāyu with the
arm of strength, who swiftly fly within

---

4 *Nectar-yielding Cow* : Sabardughā; yielding amṛta,
ambrosia, nectar, or food for the Gods.
6 *The Soma-milk* : the libation consisting of Soma
juice mixed with milk.

6 *The wether's fleece* : the filter or strainer made of
wool, used in purifying the Soma juice. See I. 2. 1.

7 *Where the press-stone rings* : where men are pressing
out the Soma juice. *The joyous Maiden* : probably Uṣas
or Dawn.

8 *The holy Fig-tree* : the vessel for holding the Soma
juice, made of the wood of the A vattha or Ficus Religiosa; or, as Sāyaṇa explains it here, the Soma itself.
The barley-meal : forming a part of the offering.
9 *Bulls* : blasts of wind

the current of thy stream, the Bulls increasing in their might,
Horseless, yet even through the waste swift-moving, whom no shout can stay,
Hard to be checked are they, like sunbeams, in their course. hard to be checked by both the hands.

HYMN CXXXVI. *Mitra-Varuṇa.*

1. BRING adoration ample and most excellent, hymn, offerings, to the watchful Twain, the bountiful, your sweetest to the bounteous Ones.
Sovrans adored with streams of oil and praised at every sacrifice.
Their high imperial might may nowhere be assailed, ne'er may their Godhead be assailed.

2 For the broad Sun was seen a path more widely laid, the path of holy law hath been maintained with rays, the eye with Bhaga's rays of light.
Firm-set in heaven is Mitra's home, and Aryaman's and Varuṇa's.
Thence they give forth great vital strength which merits praise, high power of life that men shall praise.

3 With Aditi the luminous, the celestial, upholder of the people, come ye dāy by day, ye who watch sleepless, day by day.
Resplendent might have ye obtained, Ādityas, Lords of liberal gifts.
Movers of men, mild both, are Mitra, Varuṇa, mover of men is Aryaman.

4 This Soma be most sweet to Mitra, Varuṇa : he in the drinking-feasts, shall have a share thereof, sharing, a God, among the Gods.
May all the Gods of one accord accept it joyfully to-day.
Therefore do ye, O Kings, accomplish what we ask, ye Righteous Ones, what-e'er we ask.

2 *Bhaga's rays of light* : 'the ancient god, Bhaga,' says Mr. Wallis, 'has become in the Ṛgveda little more than a source from which descriptions of the functions of other gods are obtained, or a standard of comparison by which their greatness is enhanced. His name has survived in the Slavonic languages as a general name for god, a sense which it also has in the Avesta. To judge from the Ṛgveda, Bhaga would seem to be a survival from an ancient Sun-worship.' *The Cosmology of the Ṛgveda,* p. 11. It is difficult to explain every expression in the verse; but the general meaning appears to be that the heaven has been lighted by the Sun, and that there is the home of the Gods who thence show forth the powers which men should glorify.

3 *Aditi* and *Ādityas* : see I. 14. 3.

4 *He* : Soma himself, meaning perhaps the Moon

5 Whoso with worship serves Mitra and Varuṇa, him guard ye carefully, uninjured, from distress, guard from distress the liberal man.
Aryaman guards him well who acts uprightly following his law,
Who beautifies their service with his lauds, who makes it beautiful with songs of praise.

6 Worship will I profess to lofty Dyaus, to Heaven and Earth, to Mitra and to bounteous Varuṇa, the Bounteous, the Compassionate.
Praise Indra, praise thou Agni, praise Bhaga and heavenly Aryaman.
Long may we live and have attendant progeny, have progeny with Soma's help.

7 With the Gods' help, with Indra still beside us, may we be held self-splendid with the Maruts.
May Agni, Mitra, Varuṇa give us shelter : this may we gain, we and our wealthy princes.

HYMN CXXXVII. *Mitra-Varuṇa.*

1. WITH stones have we pressed out : O come ; these gladdening drops are blent with milk, these Soma-drops which gladden you.
Come to us, Kings who reach to heaven, approach us, coming hitherward.
These milky drops are yours, Mitra and Varuṇa, bright Soma juices blent with milk.

2 Here are the droppings ; come ye nigh ; the Soma-droppings blent with curd, juices expressed and blent with curd.
Now for the wakening of your Dawn together with the Sun-God's rays,
Juice waits for Mitra and for Varuṇa to drink, fair juice for drink, for sacrifice.

3 As 'twere a radiant-coloured cow, they milk with stones the stalk for you, with stones they milk the Soma-plant.
May ye come nigh us, may ye turn hither to drink the Soma juice.
The men pressed out this juice, Mitra and Varuṇa, pressed out this Soma for your drink.

HYMN CXXXVIII. *Pūṣan.*

4. STRONG Pūṣan's majesty is lauded evermore, the glory of his lordly might is never faint, his song of praise is never faint.

1 *Pūṣan* : see I. 14. 3, and 42. 1.

Seeking felicity I laud him nigh to help,
the source of bliss,
Who, Vigorous one, hath drawn to him
the hearts of all, drawn them, the
Vigorous One, the God.

2 Thee, then, O Pūṣan, like a swift one
on his way, I urge with lauds that
thou mayst make the foemen flee, drive,
camel-like, our foes afar.
As I, a man, call thee, a God, giver of
bliss, to be my Friend,
So make our loudly-chanted praises glorious, in battles make them glorious.

3 Thou, Pūṣan, in whose friendship they
who sing forth praise enjoy advantage,
even in wisdom, through thy grace, in
wisdom even they are advanced.
So, after this most recent course, we come
to thee with prayers for wealth.
Not stirred to anger, O Wide-Ruler, come
to us, come thou to us in every fight.

4 Not stirred to anger, come, Free-giver,
nigh to us, to take this gift of ours,
thou who hast goats for steeds, Goat-
borne ! their gift who long for fame.
So, Wonder-Worker ! may we turn thee
hither with effectual lauds.
I slight thee not, O Pūṣan, thou Resplendent One : thy friendship may not
be despised.

HYMN CXXXIX.   *Viśvedevas.*

1. HEARD be our prayer ! In thought I
honour Agni first : now straightway we
elect this heavenly company, Indra and
Vāyu we elect.
For when our latest thought is raised and
on Vivasvān centred well,
Then may our holy songs go forward on
their way, our songs as 'twere unto the
Gods.

2 As there ye, Mitra, Varuṇa, above the
true have taken to yourselves the untrue

with your mind, with wisdom's mental
energy,
So in the seats wherein ye dwell have we
beheld the Golden One,
Not with our thoughts or spirit, but with
these our eyes, yea, with the eyes that
Soma gives.

3 Aśvins, the pious call you with their hymns
of praise, sounding their loud song forth
to you, these living men, to their oblations, living men.
All glories and all nourishment, Lords of
all wealth ! depend on you.
The fellies of your golden chariot scatter
drops, Mighty Ones ! of your golden
car.

4 Well is it known, O Mighty Ones : ye
open heaven ; for you the chariot-
steeds are yoked for morning rites, unswerving steeds for morning rites.
We set you on the chariot-seat, ye Mighty,
on the golden car.
Ye seek mid-air as by a path that leads
aright, as by a path that leads direct.

5 O Rich in Strength, through your great
power vouchsafe us blessings day and
night.
The offerings which we bring to you shall
never fail, gifts brought by us shall
never fail.

6 These Soma-drops, strong Indra ! drink
for heroes, poured, pressed out by
pressing-stones, are welling forth for
thee, for thee the drops are welling
forth.
They shall make glad thy heart to give, to
give wealth great and wonderful.
Thou who acceptest praise come glorified
by hymns, come thou to us benevolent.

7 Quickly, O Agni, hear us : magnified by
us thou shalt speak for us to the Gods
adorable, yea, to the Kings adorable :
When, O ye Deities, ye gave that Milch-
cow to the Aṅgirases,
They milked her : Aryaman, joined with
them, did the work : he knoweth her
as well as I.

---

2 *Camel-like* : Sāyaṇa explains : 'as a camel carries
away his load, so carry away our enemies from the battle.'
The meaning is obscure.

4 *Thou who hast goats for steeds* : Pūṣan's chariot,
like Thorr's in the Edda, is said to be drawn by a team
of goats.

---

1 *Vivasvān* : the radiant celestial Agni.

2 This verse is exceedingly difficult. Ludwig's explanation, if I have understood him rightly, is to the
following effect : The Golden One, which is in the home
of Mitra and Varuṇa, is the Sun which is only the image
or copy of the transcendental reality, the golden shell that
covers the face of the *satyam* or verity. This apparent
Sun Mitra and Varuṇa have taken to themselves in
addition to their real essence. As this real essence is
perceived not with the eyes of the body but by the eyes

of the spirit strengthened by the elevating Soma-draught,
so on the other hand the apparent Sun is not an object of
spiritual perception. Consequently the poet says : 'With
our bodily eyes we have seen the Sun, but enlightened by
the Soma juice we have recognized it as being only an
image of you.' *The untrue* is the Sun; *the true* is the transcendental essence of the God.

7 *That Milch-cow* : according to Sāyaṇa, the Cow
of Plenty. M. Bergaigne (La Religion Vedique, I. 135,
310) thinks that prayer is meant, 'the ancient prayer of
the Fathers.' The meaning of the latter part of the verse
is uncertain.

8 Ne'er may these manly deeds of yours
for us grow old, never may your bright
glories fall into decay, never before our
time decay.
What deed of yours, new every age, wondrous, surpassing man, rings forth,
Whatever, Maruts! may be difficult to
gain, grant us, whate'er is hard to
gain.

9 Dadhyac of old, Aṅgiras, Priyamedha
these, and Kaṇva, Atri, Manu knew my
birth, yea, those of ancient days and
Manu knew.
Their long line stretcheth to the Gods,
our birth-connexions are with them.
To these, for their high station, I bow
down with song, to Indra, Agni, bow
with song.

10 Let the Invoker bless : let offerers bring
choice gifts ; Bṛhaspati the Friend doth
sacrifice with Steers, Steers that have
many an excellence.
Now with our ears we catch the sound of
the press-stone that rings afar.
The very Strong hath gained the waters
by himself, the strong gained many a
resting-place.

11 O ye Eleven Gods whose home is heaven,
O ye Eleven who make earth your
dwelling,
Ye who with might, Eleven, live in waters,
accept this sacrifice, O Gods, with
pleasure.

HYMN CXL. Agni.

1. To splendid Agni seated by the altar,
loving well his home, I bring the food
as 'twere his place of birth.

I clothe the bright One with my hymn
as with a robe, him with the car of
light, bright-hued, dispelling gloom.

2 Child of a double birth he grasps at triple
food ; in the year's course what he hath
swallowed grows anew.
He, by another's mouth and tongue a
noble Bull, with other, as an elephant,
consumes the trees.

3 The pair who dwell together, moving in
the dark bestir themselves : both parents
hasten to the babe,
Impetuous-tongued, destroying, springing
swiftly forth, one to be watched and
cherished, strengthener of his sire.

4 For man, thou Friend of men, these steeds
of thine are yoked, impatient, lightly
running, ploughing blackened lines,
Discordant-minded, fleet, gliding with easy
speed, urged onward by the wind and
rapid in their course.

5 Dispelling on their way the horror of
black gloom, making a glorious show
these flames of his fly forth,
When o'er the spacious tract he spreads
himself abroad, and rushes panting on
with thunder and with roar.

6 Amid brown plants he stoops as if adorning them, and rushes bellowing like
a bull upon his wives.
Proving his might, he decks the glory of
his form, and shakes his horns like one
terrific, hard to stay.

7 Now covered, now displayed, he grasps
as one who knows, having his resting-
place in those who know him well.

---

9 *Dadhyac of old* : all these ancient sages have been
mentioned in former hymns. As predecessors of Parucchepa, the Ṛṣi of this hymn, they are said to have
known his ancestry.

10 *Let the Invoker bless* : let the Hotar, or invoking
priest utter the *Yājyā*, words of consecration used at sacrifice.

Bṛhaspati : see I. 14. 3.

With Steers : according to Sāyaṇa, a metaphorical
expression for strong and copious libations of Soma juice.

The very Strong : the Soma. The resting-places are
the different receptacles into which the juice flows.

11 *O ye Eleven Gods* : on this Sāyaṇa remarks :
'Although, according to the text, 'There are only three
gods', (Nirukta, vii. 5), the deities who represent the
earth, etc., are but three, still through their greatness,
i. e. their respective varied manifestations, they amount to
thirty-three, according to the saying, 'other manifestations of Him exist in different places.'—J. Muir, *O. S.
Texts*, v. 10.

This and the twenty-four following hymns are ascribed
to the Ṛṣi Dīrghatamas, the son of Ucathya.

1 *The food as 'twere his place of birth* : the oblation of
clarified butter which makes the fire spring up into fresh
life.

2 *Child of a double birth* : born first from the fire-sticks
and then anew by consecration.

Triple food : clarified butter, fried cakes, Soma juice.

By another's mouth : according to Sāyaṇa, 'he receives
the oblation by means of the ladle of the ministering
priests, and in another form, that is the fire that burns
forests, he consumes the trees.'

3 *The pair who dwell together* : the two fire-sticks from
which Agni is produced by friction. *His sire* : said to be
the institutor of the sacrifice.

4 In this and the four following stanzas Agni is
described not in his sacrificial form but as the fire that
destroys the jungle and prepares the way for new settlements.

6 *As adorning them* : with the glory of his flame.

7 *As one who knows* : because, coming from heaven
with the waters, he makes the plants grow, and is said
to live within them.

Change their Parents' form : perhaps, as Ludwig suggests the plants alter the appearance of the earth, and
Agni or fire that of the sky.

A second time they wax and gather Godlike power, and blending both together
change their Parents' form.

8 The maidens with long tresses hold him in
embrace ; dead, they rise up again to
meet the Living One.
Releasing them from age with a loud roar
he comes, filling them with new spirit,
living, unsubdued.

9 Licking the mantle of the Mother, far and
wide he wanders over fields with beasts
that flee apace.
Strengthening all that walk, licking up all
around, a blackened path, forsooth, he
leaves where'er he goes.

10 O Agni, shine resplendent with our
wealthy chiefs, like a loud-snorting bull,
accustomed to the house.
Thou casting off thine infant wrappings
blazest forth as though thou hadst put
on a coat of mail for war.

11 May this our perfect prayer be dearer
unto thee than an imperfect prayer
although it please thee well.
With the pure brilliancy that radiates
from thy form, mayest thou grant to
us abundant store of wealth.

12 Grant to our chariot, to our house, O
Agni, a boat with moving feet and
constant oarage,
One that may further well our wealthy
princes and all the folk, and be our
certain refuge.

13 Welcome our laud with thine approval,
Agni. May earth and heaven and freely-
flowing rivers
Yield us long life and food and corn and
cattle, and may the red Dawns choose
for us their choicest.

HYMN CXLI.   *Agni.*

1. YEA, verily, the fair effulgence of the God
for glory was established, since he sprang
from strength.
When he inclines thereto successful is the
hymn : the songs of sacrifice have
brought him as they flow

8 *The maidens with long tresses* : the curling flames.
9 *The Mother* : the earth, whose vesture of grass and
shrubs he licks and consumes.
Strengthening all that walk : giving them strength and
speed to fly before him.
10 *Thine infant wrappings* : the waters that enveloped
the 'Child of the Floods.'
11 *This our perfect prayer* : see Vedic Hymns, I. 225.
12 *A boat* : according to Sāyaṇa, the sacrifice, with
priests for oars, and Gods, prayers and offerings, for feet.

1 *From strength* : from violent agitation of the fire-
stick.

2 Wonderful, rich in nourishment, he dwells
in food ; next, in the seven auspicious
Mothers is his home.
Thirdly, that they might drain the treasures of the Bull, the maidens brought
forth him for whom the ten provide.

3 What time from out the deep, from the
Steer's wondrous form, the Chiefs who
had the power produced him with their
strength ;
When Mātariśvan rubbed forth him who
lay concealed, for mixture of the sweet
drink, in the days of old.

4 When from the Highest Father he is
brought to us, amid the plants he rises
hungry, wondrously.
As both together join to expedite his birth,
most youthful he is born resplendent in
his light.

5 Then also entered he the Mothers, and
in them pure and uninjured he increased
in magnitude.
As to the first he rose, the vigorous from
of old, so now he runs among the
younger lowest ones.

6 Therefore they choose him Herald at the
morning rites, pressing to him as unto
Bhaga, pouring gifts,
When, much-praised, by the power and
will of Gods, he goes at all times to his
mortal worshipper to drink.

7 What time the Holy One, wind-urged,
hath risen up, serpent-like winding
through the dry grass unrestrained,
Dust lies upon the way of him who burneth
all, black-winged and pure of birth who
follows sundry paths.

8 Like a swift chariot made by men who
know their art, he with his red limbs
lifts himself aloft to heaven.
Thy worshippers become by burning black

2 *He dwells in food* : he is the cause of the production
of men's food, as sender of rain and as sacrificial fire.
The seven auspicious Mothers : according to Sāyaṇa,
the rains which fertilize the seven *lokas* or worlds.
The Bull : Agni. *The maidens*, and *the ten*, are the
fingers which produce the fire by attrition and tend it
afterwards.
3 Agni appears here to have been partly produced
by the Chiefs, the Sūris or Gods, from the depth of the
atmosphere, from Parjanya the rainy cloud symbolically
represented as a bull, and partly generated by Mātariśvan
(see I. 31. 3) by attrition, and brought by him to the
earth to receive libations of Soma juice.
4 *The Highest Father* : Dyaus. *Both together* : Heaven
and Earth.
5 *The Mothers* : the waters. *The younger lowest ones* :
the plants in which also he dwells.
6 *Herald* : or, Hotar.   *Bhaga* : see I. 136. 2.

of hue : their strength flies as before a hero's violence.

9 By thee, O Agni, Varuṇa who guards the Law, Mitra and Aryaman, the Bounteous, are made strong ;
For, as the felly holds the spokes, thou with thy might pervading hast been born encompassing them round.

10 Agni, to him who toils and pours libations, thou, Most Youthful ! sendest wealth and all the host of Gods.
Thee, therefore, even as Bhaga, will we set anew, young Child of Strength, most wealthy ! in our battle-song.

11 Vouchsafe us riches turned to worthy ends, good luck abiding in the house, and strong capacity,
Wealth that directs both worlds as they were guiding-reins, and, very Wise, the Gods' assent in sacrifice.

12 May he, the Priest resplendent, joyful, hear us, he with the radiant car and rapid horses.
May Agni, ever wise, with best directions to bliss and highest happiness conduct us.

13 With hymns of might hath Agni now been lauded, advanced to height of universal kingship.
Now may these wealthy chiefs and we together spread forth as spreads the Sun above the rain-clouds.

HYMN CXLII.   *Âpris.*

1. KINDLED, bring, Agni, Gods to-day for him who lifts the ladle up.
Spin out the ancient thread for him who sheds, with gifts, the Soma juice.

2 Thou dealest forth, Tanūnapāt, sweet sacrifice enriched with oil,
Brought by a singer such as I who offers gifts and toils for thee.

3 He wondrous, sanctifying, bright, sprinkles the sacrifice with mead,
Thrice, Narāśaṁsa from the heavens, a God mid Gods adorable.

4 Agni, besought, bring hitherward Indra the Friend, the Wonderful,
For this my hymn of praise, O sweet of tongue, is chanted forth to thee.

5 The ladle-holders strew trimmed grass at this well-ordered sacrifice ;

A home for Indra is adorned, wide, fittest to receive the Gods.

6 Thrown open be the Doors Divine, unfailing, that assist the rite,
High, purifying, much-desired, so that the Gods may enter in.

7 May Night and Morning, hymned with lauds, united, fair to look upon,
Strong Mothers of the sacrifice, seat them together on the grass.

8 May the two Priests Divine, the sage, the sweet-voiced lovers of the hymn,
Complete this sacrifice of ours, effectual, reaching heaven to-day.

9 Let Hotrā pure, set among Gods, amid the Maruts Bhāratī, Iḷā, Sarasvatī, Mahī, rest on the grass, adorable.

10 May Tvaṣṭar send us genial dew abundant, wondrous, rich in gifts,
For increase and for growth of wealth, Tvaṣṭar our kinsman and our Friend.

11 Vanaspati, give forth, thyself, and call the Gods to sacrifice.
May Agni, God intelligent, speed our oblation to the Gods.

12 To Vāyu joined with Pūṣan, with the Maruts, and the host of Gods,
To Indra who inspires the hymn cry Glory ! and present the gift.

13 Come hither to enjoy the gifts prepared with cry of Glory ! Come,
O Indra, hear their calling ; they invite thee to the sacrifice.

HYMN CXLIII.   *Agni.*

1. To Agni I present a newer mightier hymn, I bring my words and song unto the Son of Strength,
Who, Offspring of the Waters, bearing precious things sits on the earth, in season, dear Invoking Priest.

2 Soon as he sprang to birth that Agni was shown forth to Mātariśvan in the highest firmament.
When he was kindled, through his power and majesty his fiery splendour made the heavens and earth to shine.

---

1 *The ladle* : the sacrificial ladle containing the oblation.

Spin out the ancient thread : perform the sacrifice ordained of old.

2 *Tanūnapāt* : Son of Thyself; Agni. See I. 13. 2.

3 *Narāśaṁsa* : a name of Agni. See I. 13. 2.

6 *The Doors Divine* : of the hall of sacrifice. See I. 13. 6.

8 *The two Priests Divine* : see I. 13. 8.

9 *Hotrā* : a Goddess of sacrifice, regarded as the consort of Agni.
Bhāratī : a Goddess of sacred speech.
Iḷā, Sarasvatī, Mahī : see I. 13. 9.

11 *Vanaspati* : the sacrificial post said to be a form of Agni.

12 *Cry Glory !* : Svāhā ! the sacred word uttered at the end of sacrificial invocations.

---

2 *Mātariśvan* : see I. 31. 3.

3 His flames that wax not old, beams fair
to look upon of him whose face is lovely,
shine with beauteous sheen.
The rays of Agni, him whose active force
is light, through the nights glimmer
sleepless, ageless, like the floods.

4 Send thou with hymns that Agni to his
own abode, who rules, one Sovran Lord
of wealth, like Varuṇa,
Him, All-possessor, whom the Bhṛgus
with their might brought to earth's
central point, the centre of the world.

5 He whom no force can stay, even as the
Maruts' roar, like to a dart sent forth,
even as the bolt from heaven,
Agni with sharpened jaws chews up and
eats the trees, and conquers them as
when the warrior smites his foes.

6 And will not Agni find enjoyment in our
praise, will not the Vasu grant our wish
with gifts of wealth ?
Will not the Inspirer speed our prayers to
gain their end ? Him with the radiant
glance I laud with this my song.

7 The kindler of the flame wins Agni as a
Friend, promoter of the Law, whose face
is bright with oil.
Inflamed and keen, refulgent in our gatherings, he lifts our hymn on high clad in
his radiant hues.

8 Keep us incessantly with guards that cease
not, Agni, with guards auspicious, very
mighty.
With guards that never slumber, never
heedless, never beguiled, O Helper,
keep our children.

HYMN CXLIV.   *Agni.*

1. THE Priest goes forth to sacrifice, with
wondrous power sending aloft the hymn
of glorious brilliancy.
He moves to meet the ladles turning to
the right, which are the first to kiss
the place where he abides.

2 To him sang forth the flowing streams of
Holy Law, encompassed in the home
and birth-place of the God.
He, when he dwelt extended in the waters'
lap, absorbed those Godlike powers for
which he is adored.

3 Seeking in course altern to reach the
selfsame end the two copartners strive
to win this beauteous form.
Like Bhaga must he be duly invoked by
us, as he who drives the car holds fast
the horse's reins.

4 He whom the two copartners with observance tend, the pair who dwell together
in the same abode,
By night as in the day the grey one was
born young, passing untouched by eld
through many an age of man.

5 Him the ten fingers, the devotions. animate:
we mortals call on him a God to give
us help.
He speeds over the sloping surface of the
land : new deeds hath he performed
with those who gird him round.

6 For, Agni, like a herdsman, thou by thine
own might rulest o'er all that is in heaven
and on the earth ;
And these two Mighty Ones, bright, golden
closely joined, rolling them round are
come unto thy sacred grass.

7 Agni, accept with joy, be glad in this our
prayer, joy-giver, self-sustained, strong,
born of Holy Law !
For fair to see art thou turning to every
side, pleasant to look on as a dwelling
filled with food.

HYMN CXLV.   *Agni.*

1. ASK ye of him for he is come, he knoweth
it ; he, full of wisdom, is implored, is
now implored.
With him are admonitions and with him
commands : he is the Lord of Strength,
the Lord of Power and Might.

2 They ask of him : not all learn by their
questioning what he, the Sage, hath
grasped, as 'twere, with his own mind.
Forgetting not the former nor the later
word, he goeth on, not careless, in his
mental power.

3 To him these ladles go, to him these
racing mares : he only will give ear to
all the words I speak.

---

4 *Earth's central point* : the altar.
6 *The Vasu* : the God Agni.

1 *The place where he abides* : Agni's dwelling-place ;
the altar.
2 *Of Holy Law* : flowing in accordance with the
order of the universe.

---

3 *The two copartners* : the two priests, Hotar and
Adhvaryu, according to Sāyaṇa. Perhaps Day and
Night are intended, as Ludwig suggests.
4 *The grey one* : Agni. Cf. I. 164, 1.
5 *Him the ten fingers* : see I. 141. 2. *Those who gird
him round* : his worshippers.
6 *These two Mighty Ones* : Heaven and Earth.

3 *These racing mares* : these libations that quickly reach
Agni.
The Babe with flawless help : the ever-youthful Agni
who protects his worshippers.

All-speeding, victor, perfecter of sacrifice,
the Babe with flawless help hath mus-
tered vigorous might.

4 Whate'er he meets he grasps and then runs
farther on, and straightway, newly born,
creeps forward with his kin.

He stirs the wearied man to pleasure and
great joy what time the longing gifts
approach him as he comes.

5 He is a wild thing of the flood and forest :
he hath been laid upon the highest
surface.

He hath declared the lore of works to
mortals, Agni the Wise, for he knows
Law, the Truthful.

HYMN CXLVI. *Agni.*

1. I LAUD the seven-rayed, the triple-headed,
Agni all-perfect in his Parents' bosom,

Sunk in the lap of all that moves and
moves not, him who hath filled all
luminous realms of heaven.

2 As a great Steer he grew to these his
Parents ; sublime he stands, untouched
by eld, far-reaching.

He plants his footsteps on the lofty ridges
of the broad earth : his red flames lick
the udder.

3 Coming together to their common youngling both Cows, fairshaped, spread forth
in all directions,

Measuring out the paths that must be
travelled, entrusting all desires to him
the Mighty.

4 The prudent sages lead him to his dwelling, guarding with varied skill the
Ever-Youthful.

Longing, they turned their eyes unto the
River : to these the Sun of men was
manifested.

5 Born noble in the regions, aim of all
mens' eyes to be implored for life by
great and small alike,

Far as the Wealthy One hath spread
himself abroad, he is the Sire all-visible
of this progeny.

HYMN CXLVII. *Agni.*

1. How, Agni, have the radiant ones, aspiring, endued thee with the vigour of the
living,

So that on both sides fostering seed and
offspring, the Gods may joy in Holy
Law's fulfilment ?

2 Mark this my speech, Divine One, thou,
Most Youthful! offered to thee by him
who gives most freely.

One hates thee, and another sings thy
praises : I thine adorer laud thy form,
O Agni.

3 Thy guardian rays, O Agni, when they saw
him, preserved blind Māmateya from
affliction.

Lord of all riches, he preserved the pious :
the foes who fain would harm them did
no mischief.

4 The sinful man who worships not, O
Agni, who, offering not, harms us with
double-dealing,—

Be this in turn to him a heavy sentence :
may he distress himself by his revilings.

5 Yea, when a mortal knowingly, O Victor,
injures with double tongue a fellow-
mortal,

From him, praised Agni ! save thou him
that lauds thee : bring us not into
trouble and affliction.

HYMN CXLVIII. *Agni.*

1. WHAT Mātariśvan, piercing, formed by
friction, Herald of all the Gods, in
varied figure,

Is he whom they have set mid human
houses, gay-hued as light and shining
forth for beauty.

2 They shall not harm the man who brings
thee praises : such as I am, Agni my
help approves me.

---

5 *Upon the highest surface* : the meaning is not clear,
but the reference appears to be to celestial Agni in the
firmament rather than to the sacrificial fire upon the
altar.

---

1 'The three heads may be the three daily sacrifices,
or the three household fires, or the three regions, earth,
heaven and mid-air. The seven rays are the seven flames
of fire.'—Wilson.

His Parents' bosom : the lap of Heaven and Earth.

2 *The udder* : the clouds of the sky.

3 *Both Cows* : apparently Heaven and Earth ;
according to Sāyaṇa, the institutor of the rite and the
priest or the sacrificer and his wife.

4 *The River* : Agni, whose bounties flow like streams
of water.

The Wealthy One : the rich and mighty Agni.

---

1 *The radiant ones* : thy bright rays.

On both sides : both in men and women ; or (offspring)
of both sexes.

3 *Māmateya* : Dīrghatamas, the R̥ṣi of the hymn, son
of Mamatā, the wife of Ucathya.

---

1 Wilson, following Sāyaṇa, translates : 'The wind,
penetrating (amidst the fuel) has excited (Agni) the
invoker (of the gods) the multiform, the minister of all
the deities.' But then *yát*, what or when is left untranslated, and the explanation of Mātariśvan as Vāyu or
wind cannot be justified by any R̥gveda text.

All acts of mine shall they accept with
pleasure, laudation from the singer who
presents it.

3 Him in his constant seat men skilled in
worship have taken and with praises
have established.
As, harnessed to a chariot   fleet-foot
horses, at his command let bearers lead
him forward.

4 Wondrous, full many a thing he chews and
crunches : he shines amid the wood
with spreading brightness.
Upon his glowing flames the wind blows
daily, driving them like the keen shaft
of an archer.

5 Him, whom while yet in embryo the
hostile, both skilled and fain to harm,
may never injure,
Men blind and sightless through his
splendour hurt not : his never-failing
lovers have preserved him.

HYMN CXLIX.   *Agni.*

1. Hither he hastens to give, Lord of great
riches, King of the mighty, to the place
of treasure.
The pressing-stones shall serve him
speeding near us.

2 As Steer of men so Steer of earth and
heaven by glory, he whose streams all
life hath drunken,
Who hasting forward rests upon the altar.

3 He who hath lighted up the joyous castle,
wise Courser like the Steed of cloudy
heaven,
Bright like the Sun, with hundredfold
existence.

4 He, doubly born, hath spread in his
effulgence through the three luminous
realms, through all the regions,
Best sacrificing Priest where waters gather.

5 Priest doubly born, he through his love of
glory hath in his keeping all things worth
the choosing,
The man who brings him gifts hath noble
offspring.

1 *The place of treasure* : the altar, where riches are
obtained by sacrifice and prayer.
2 *As Steer of men* : preëminent, like a strong bull,
among men.
3 *The joyous castle* : or the castle Nârmiṇî; meaning,
probably, the proud stronghold of some demon.
4 *Where waters gather* : according to Sāyaṇa, in the
place of sacrifice where water is collected for ceremonial
purpose. But the reference is probably to Agni's appearance in the firmament, the waters above the earth, in
the form of lightning.
5 *Doubly born* : from the fire-sticks and again at
consecration.

HYMN CL.   *Agni.*

1. Agni, thy faithful servant I call upon thee
with many a gift,
As in the keeping of the great inciting
God ;

2 Thou who ne'er movest thee to aid the
indolent, the godless man,
Him who though wealthy never brings an
offering.

3 Splendid, O Singer, is that man, mightiest
of the great in heaven.
Agni, may we be foremost, we thy
worshippers.

HYMN CLI.   *Mitra and Varuṇa*

1. Heaven and earth trembled at the might
and voice of him, whom, loved and
Holy One, helper of all mankind,
The wise who longed for spoil in fight for
kine brought forth with power, a
Friend, mid waters, at the sacrifice.

2 As these, like friends, have done this
work for you, these prompt servants of
Purumiḷha Soma-offerer,
Give mental power to him who sings the
sacred song, and hearken, Strong Ones,
to the master of the house.

3 The folk have glorified your birth from
Earth and Heaven, to be extolled,
ye Strong Ones, for your mighty power.
Ye, when ye bring to singer and the rite,
enjoy the sacrifice performed with holy
praise and strength.

4 The people prospers, Asuras ! whom ye
dearly love : ye, Righteous Ones,
proclaim aloud the Holy Law.
That efficacious power that comes from
lofty heaven, ye bind unto the work, as
to the pole an ox.

5 On this great earth ye send your treasure
down with might : unstained by dust,
the crowding kine are in the stalls.

3 *That man* : who propitiates thee by sacrifice and
praise.
O Singer : singer of hymns, sage, or priest.

1 *Of him* : Agni.
2 *As these* : the priests. *Purumiḷha* : the prince who
offers the sacrifice. *Strong Ones* : ye mighty Gods, Mitra
and Varuṇa.
3 *When ye bring* : him, Agni, to the sacrifice.
4 *Asuras* : immortal Gods, especially the ancient
deities.
That efficacious power : as Wilson observes, the meaning
is not very obvious, although it is clear that the adequacy
of worship or sacrifice to effect its objects, or realize its
rewards, is intended.

Here in the neighbourhood they cry
unto the Sun at morning and at evening,
like swift birds of prey.

6 The flames with curling tresses serve your
sacrifice, whereto ye sing the song,
Mitra and Varuṇa.
Send down of your free will, prosper our
holy songs : ye are sole Masters of the
singer's hymn of praise.

7 Whoso with sacrifices toiling brings you
gifts, and worships, sage and priest,
fulfilling your desire,—
To him do ye draw nigh and taste his
sacrifice. Come well-inclined to us
unto our songs and prayer.

8 With sacrifices and with milk they deck
you first, ye Righteous Ones, as if
through stirrings of the mind.
To you they bring their hymns with their
collected thought, while ye with earnest
soul come to us gloriously.

9 Rich strength of life is yours : ye, Heroes,
have obtained through your surpassing
powers rich far-extending might.
Not the past days conjoined with nights,
not rivers, not the Paṇis have attained
your Godhead and your wealth.

HYMN CLII. *Mitra-Varuṇa.*

1. THE robes which ye put on abound with
fatness : uninterrupted courses are your
counsels.
All falsehood, Mitra-Varuṇa ! ye conquer,
and closely cleave unto the Law
Eternal.

2 This might of theirs hath no one comprehended. True is the crushing word
the sage hath uttered.
The fearful four-edged bolt smites down
the three-edged, and those who hate
the Gods first fall and perish.

3 The Footless Maid precedeth footed
creatures. Who marketh, Mitra-Varuṇa,

this your doing ?
The Babe Unborn supporteth this world's
burthen, fulfilleth Law and overcometh
falsehood.

4 We look on him the darling of the
Maidens, always advancing, never
falling downward,
Wearing inseparable, wide-spread raiment,
Mitra's and Varuṇa's delightful glory.

5 Unbridled Courser, born but not of horses,
neighing he flieth on with back uplifted.
The youthful love mystery thought-
surpassing, praising in Mitra-Varuṇa,
its glory.

6 May the milch-kine who favour Māmateya
prosper in this world him who loves
devotion.
May he, well skilled in rites, beg food,
and calling Aditi with his lips give us
assistance.

7 Gods, Mitra-Varuṇa, with love and
worship, let me make you delight in
this oblation.
May our prayer be victorious in battles,
may we have rain from heaven to make
us prosper.

HYMN CLIII. *Mitra-Varuṇa.*

1. WE worship with our reverence and oblations you, Mitra Varuṇa, accordant,
mighty,
So that with us, ye Twain whose backs
are sprinkled with oil, the priests with
oil and hymns support you.

2 Your praise is like a mighty power, an
impulse : to you, Twain Gods, a
well-formed hymn is offered,
As the priest decks yon, Strong Ones, in
assemblies, and the prince fain to
worship you for blessings.

9 *The Paṇis* : the envious demons who carry away
and conceal the cows or rays of light.

1 *The robes which ye put on* : the oblations of clarified
butter with which the Gods may be said to be clothed.
Uninterrupted courses are your counsels : your designs
are always fully carried into effect. Or the meaning may
be as Wilson, following Sāyaṇa, renders it : 'your natures
are to be regarded as without defect.'
2 *The fearful four-edged bolt* : Ludwig suggests an
emendation of the text and then translates : 'thrice strikes
the edge (of Indra's thunderbolt), four times the fearful
edge.' I give the literal English of the words as they stand,
the sense being, according to Sāyaṇa, that he who has
more arms is stronger than he who has fewer, the arms
intended being, perhaps sacrifice and prayer.
3 *The Footless Maid* : Dawn. *The Babe Unborn* :
the Sun before his appearance in heaven.

4 *The darling of the Maidens* : the Sun, the lover of
the Dawns.
5 *The mystery thought-surpassing* : the mystery of the
Sun's motion excites wonder, and Mitra and Varuṇa are
praised in connexion with it.
6 *Māmateya* : the son of Mamatā, Dīrghatamas the
Ṛṣi of the hymn.
Him who loves devotion : apparently Purumīḷha the
institutor of the sacrifice, mentioned in stanza 6 of the
preceding hymn.
May he beg food : the food that remains after the oblations have been presented and consumed.
Aditi : I follow Ludwig in taking Aditi in the usual
signification. Sāyaṇa takes it as meaning 'a perfect
ceremony' which is to be completed, and Grassmann as
famine, dearth, or want, which is to be averted.
The hymn is full of difficulties, and cannot at present
be satisfactorily translated.

2 *The prince* : the wealthy man who institutes the
sacrifice.

3 O Mitra-Varuṇa, Aditi the Milch-cow
streams for the rite, for folk who bring
oblation,
When in the assembly he who worships
moves you, like to a human priest,
with gifts presented.

4 So may the kine and heavenly Waters
pour you sweet drink in families that
make you joyful.
Of this may he, the ancient House-Lord,
give us. Enjoy, drink of the milk the.
cow provideth.

HYMN CLIV.　　　*Viṣṇu.*

1. I WILL declare the mighty deeds of
Viṣṇu, of him who measured out the
earthly regions,
Who propped the highest place of
congregation, thrice setting down his
footstep, widely striding.

2 For this his mighty deed is Viṣṇu lauded,
like some wild beast, dread, prowling,
mountain-roaming ;
He within whose three wide-extended
paces all living creatures have their
habitation.

3 Let the hymn lift itself as strength to
Viṣṇu, the Bull far-striding, dwelling on
the mountains,
Him who alone with triple step hath
measured this common dwelling-place,
long, far extended.

4 Him whose three places that are filled
with sweetness, imperishable, joy as it
may list them,
Who verily alone upholds the threefold,
the earth, the heaven, and all living
creatures.

5 May I attain to that his well-loved
mansion where men devoted to the
Gods are happy.
For there springs, close akin to the Wide-
Strider, the well of meath in Viṣṇu's
highest footstep.

6 Fain would we go unto your dwelling-
places where there are many-horned
and nimble oxen,
For mightily, there, shineth down upon us
the widely-striding Bull's sublimest
mansion.

HYMN CLV.　　　*Viṣṇu-Indra.*

1. To the great Hero, him who sets his mind
thereon, and Viṣṇu, praise aloud in
song your draught of juice,—
Gods ne'er beguiled, who borne as 'twere
by noble steed, have stood upon the
lofty ridges of the hills.

2 Your Soma-drinker keeps afar your furious
rush, Indra and Viṣṇu, when ye come
with all your might.
That which hath been directed well at
mortal man, bow-armed Kṛṣānu's arrow,
ye turn far aside.

3 These offerings increase his mighty manly
strength : he brings both Parents down
to share the genial flow.
He lowers, though a son, the Father's
highest name ; the third is that which
is high in the light of heaven.

4 We laud this manly power of him the
Mighty One, preserver, inoffensive,
bounteous and benign ;
His who strode, widely pacing, with three
steppings forth over the realms of earth
for freedom and for life.

5 A mortal man, when he beholds two steps
of him who looks upon the light, is
restless with amaze.
But his third step doth no one venture to
approach, no, nor the feathered birds of
air who fly with wings.

---

3 *Aditi, the Milch-cow* : aditi regarded as the source
of rewards for the pious; or Aditi may be taken as an
epithet, 'the exhaustless,' qualifying Milch-cow.
4 *The ancient House-Lord* : Agni, the guardian of the
homestead.

1 *The highest place of congregation* : heaven, where the
Gods are assembled.
Thrice setting down his footstep : see I. 22. 16.
2 *For this his mighty deed* : I have followed Sāyaṇa
who takes the active verb in a passive signification. Prof.
Peterson translates : 'Viṣṇu makes loud boast of this,'
which is perhaps a more accurate rendering.
5 *Meath* : or nectar, or honey ; meaning celestial
Soma.

6 *Your dwelling-places* : Viṣṇu's and probably Indra's.
Many-horned and nimble oxen : the stars with their ever-
twinkling rays. Cf. I. 105. 10; Vālakhilya 7. 2.

1 *To the great Hero* : Indra. *Who sets his mind thereon* :
who loves praise.
2 *Your Soma-drinker* : you gently approach your devout worshipper and do him no harm.
Kṛṣānu : one of the guardians of the heavenly Soma,
apparently a demon of drought who prevents men from
enjoying the ambrosial rain.
3 *Both Parents* : Heaven and Earth. *The genial flow* :
the sacrificial offering, the libation of Soma juice.
He lowers, though a son : the meaning appears to be
that Viṣṇu takes rank in the sacrifice above his own father
Dyaus, and that Agni has the third place.
5 'His (Viṣṇu's) path on earth and in the firmament is within mortal observation ; not so that in heaven.'
—Wilson. *His third step* : in the highest heaven. Cf. I.
154. 5.

6 He, like a rounded wheel, hath in swift
motion set his ninety racing steeds together with the four.
Developed, vast in form, with those who
sing forth praise, a youth, no more a
child, he cometh to our call.

HYMN CLVI. *Viṣṇu.*

1. FAR-SHINING, widely famed, going thy
wonted way, fed with the oil, be
helpful, Mitra-like, to us.
So, Viṣṇu, e'en the wise must swell thy
song of praise, and he who hath
oblations pay thee solemn rites.

2 He who brings gifts to him the Ancient
and the Last, to Viṣṇu who ordains,
together with his Spouse,
Who tells the lofty birth of him the Lofty
One, shall verily surpass in glory e'en
his peer.

3 Him have ye satisfied, singers, as well as
ye know, primeval germ of Order even
from his birth.
Ye, knowing e'en his name, have told it
forth: may we, Viṣṇu, enjoy the grace
of thee the Mighty One.

4 The Sovran Varuṇa and both the Aśvins
wait on this the will of him who guides
the Marut host.
Viṣṇu hath power supreme and might
that finds the day, and with his Friend
unbars the stable of the kine.

5 Even he the Heavenly One who came for
fellowship, Viṣṇu to Indra, godly to the
godlier,
Who Maker, throned in three worlds, helps
the Āryan man, and gives the worshipper
his share of Holy Law.

6 This verse is not very intelligible. Wilson following
Sāyaṇa, gives the following explanation : 'Viṣṇu is here
identified with Time, comprising ninety-four periods:
the year, two solstices, five seasons, twelve months,
twenty-four half months, thirty days, eight watches, and
twelve zodiacal signs. Ludwig translates the first hemistich : 'and under four names (of the four seasons)
he, like a round wheel, hath set in motion ninety spokes.'
The steeds, or spokes, are the days of the solar year, ninety
in each of the four seasons.

2 *Together with his Spouse* : sumájjānaye ; explained by
Sāyaṇa to mean 'self-born', and by Ludwig 'very delightful '

4 *With his Friend* : assists his friend Indra in releasing
the rain imprisoned in the mountains of cloud, or the
rays of light that have been stolen.

5 *His share of Holy Law* : his share of the blessings
which follow the performance of sacrifice.

HYMN CLVII. *Aśvins.*

1. AGNI is wakened: Sūrya riseth from the
earth. Mighty, refulgent Dawn hath
shone with all her light.
The Aśvins have equipped their chariot for
the course. God Savitar hath moved the
folk in sundry ways.

2 When, Aśvins, ye equip your very mighty
car, bedew, ye Twain, our power with
honey and with oil.
To our devotion give victorious strength
in war: may we win riches in the heroes'
strife for spoil.

3 Nigh to us come the Aśvins' lauded three-
wheeled car, the car laden with meath
and drawn by fleet-foot steeds,
Three-seated, opulent, bestowing all delight:
may it bring weal to us, to cattle and
to men.

4 Bring hither nourishment for us, ye Aśvins
Twain; sprinkle us with your whip
that drops with honey-dew.
Prolong our days of life, wipe out our trespasses; destroy our foes, be our companions and our Friends.

5 Ye store the germ of life in female creatures, ye lay it up within all living beings.
Ye have sent forth, O Aśvins passing
mighty, the fire, the sovrans of the wood,
the waters,

6 Leeches are ye with medicines to heal
us, and charioteers are ye with skill in
driving.
Ye Strong, give sway to him who brings
oblation and with his heart pours out
his gift before you.

HYMN CLVIII. *Aśvins.*

1. YE Vasus Twain, ye Rudras full of
counsel, grant us, Strong Strengtheners,
when ye stand beside us,
What wealth Aucathya craves of you,
great Helpers when ye come forward
with no niggard succour.

1 *Savitar* : the Sun as the great cause of life.

3 *Three-wheeled car* : see I. 34. 5.

4 *Your whip* : see Hymns of the Atharva-veda, IX. 1.
which is a glorification of the Aśvins' Honey-Whip, signifying, perhaps, the early stimulating and life-giving
breeze which accompanies the first appearance of these
Lords of Light and Heralds of Dawn.

5 *The sovrans of the wood* : the tall trees of the forest.

1 *Ye Vasus Twain, ye Rudras* : the Aśvins are addressed
as identical with these two classes of Gods. See I. 31. 3.
and 34. 11.

Aucathya : the son of Ucathya, Dīrghatamas the
Ṛṣi of the hymn.

2 Who may give you aught, Vasus, for
your favour, for what, at the Cow's place,
ye grant through worship?
Wake for us understanding full of riches,
come with a heart that will fulfil our
longing.

3 As erst for Tugra's son your car, sea-
crossing, strong, was equipped and set
amid the waters,
So may I gain your shelter and protection
as with winged course a hero seeks
his army.

4 May this my praise preserve Ucathya's
offspring: let not these Twain who fly
with wings exhaust me.
Let not the wood ten times up-piled
consume me, when fixed for you it bites
the ground it stands on.

5 The most maternal streams, wherein the
Dāsas cast me securely bound, have not
devoured me.
When Traitana would cleave my head
asunder, the Dāsa wounded his own
breast and shoulders.

6 Dīrghatamas the son of Mamatā hath
come to length of days in the tenth age
of human kind.
He is the Brahman of the waters as they
strive to reach their end and aim: their
charioteer is he.

HYMN CLIX.
Heaven and Earth.

1. I PRAISE with sacrifices mighty Heaven
and Earth at festivals, the wise, the
Strengtheners of Law.
Who, having Gods for progeny, conjoined
with Gods, through wonder-working
wisdom bring forth choicest boons.

2 With invocations, on the gracious Father's
mind, and on the Mother's great inherent
power I muse.
Prolific Parents, they have made the world
of life, and for their brood all round
wide immortality.

2 *The Cow's place* : according to Sāyaṇa, the altar;
the Cow being the earth.
3 *Tugra's son* : see I. 116. 3.
4 *Ucathya's offspring* : the poet himself *These
Twain* : day and night. From this and the following
verse it would appear that Dīrghatamas had been subjected to the ordeals of fire, water, and single combat with
a man called Traitana, and preserved in all three by
the Aśvins. See Ludwig, Der Ṛg-veda, IV. p. 44.
6 *The tenth age* : perhaps the tenth decade. The
meaning of the verse, which appears to be a later addition, is obscure.

3 These Sons of yours well skilled in work,
of wondrous power, brought forth to life
the two great Mothers first of all.
To keep the truth of all that stands and
all that moves, ye guard the station of
your Son who knows no guile.

4 They with surpassing skill, most wise, have
measured out the Twins united in their
birth and in their home.
They, the refulgent Sages, weave within
the sky, yea, in the depths of sea, a
web for ever new.

5 This is to-day the goodliest gift of Savitar:
this thought we have when now the
God is furthering us.
On us with loving-kindness Heaven and
Earth bestow riches and various wealth
and treasure hundredfold!

HYMN CLX.
Heaven and Earth.

1. THESE, Heaven and Earth, bestow pros-
perity on all, sustainers of the region,
Holy Ones and wise,
Two Bowls of noble kind: between these
Goddesses the God, the fulgent Sun,
travels by fixed decree.

2 Widely-capacious Pair, mighty, that never
fail, the Father and the Mother keep all
creatures safe:
The two world-halves, the spirited, the
beautiful, because the Father hath clothed
them in goodly forms.

3 Son of these Parents, he the Priest with
power to cleanse, Sage, sanctifies the
worlds with his surpassing power.
Thereto for his bright milk he milked
through all the days the party-coloured
Cow and the prolific Bull.

3 *These Sons of yours* : the Ṛbhus, who restored their
Parents' youth. See I. 20. 4. *The two great Mothers* : the
Parents of all, Heaven and Earth.
Your Son who knows no guile : Sūrya, or the Sun, who
is regarded as the symbol of truth. 'Solem quis dicere
falsum Audeat?'
4 *The Twins* : Heaven and Earth. *In the depths of
sea* : in the aerial ocean or atmosphere.

1 *Two Bowls* : so called from their hemispherical
appearance. But see Hillebrandt, Vedische Mythologie, I. p. 177, and Ludwig, Ueber die N. A. auf dem
G. der Ṛgveda-forschung, p. 87.
2 *The Father* : Dyaus, or perhaps Tvaṣṭar.
3 *Son of these Parents* : the Sun, the offspring of Heaven
and Earth.
For his bright milk : he has drawn the dew as milk
from his mother Earth, and obtained his light from
Heaven his father.

4 Among the skilful Gods most skilled is he,
who made the two world-halves which
bring prosperity to all;
Who with great wisdom measured both
the regions out, and stablished them
with pillars that shall ne'er decay.

5 Extolled in song, O Heaven and Earth,
bestow on us, ye mighty Pair, great
glory and high lordly sway,
Whereby we may extend ourselves ever
over the folk; and send us strength that
shall deserve the praise of men.

HYMN CLXI. *Ŗbhus.*

1 WHY hath the Best, why hath the Youngest come to us ? Upon what embassy
comes he ? What have we said ?
We have not blamed the chalice of illustrious birth. We, Brother Agni, praised
the goodness of the wood.

2 The chalice that is single make ye into
four: thus have the Gods commanded;
therefore am I come.
If, O Sudhanvan's Children, ye will do
this thing ye shall participate in sacrifice
with Gods.

3 What to the envoy Agni in reply ye spake,
A courser must be made, a chariot
fashioned here,
A cow must be created, and the Twain
made young. When we have done these
things, Brother, we turn to you.

4 When thus, O Ŗbhus, ye had done ye
questioned thus, Whither went he who
came to us a messenger ?
Then Tvaṣṭar, when he viewed the four
wrought chalices, concealed himself
among the Consorts of the Gods.

5 As Tvaṣṭar thus had spoken, Let us slay
these men who have reviled the chalice,
drinking-cup of Gods,

They gave themselves new names when
Soma juice was shed, and under these
new names the Maiden welcomed them.

6 Indra hath yoked his Bays, the Aśvins'
car is horsed, Bŗhaspati hath brought
the Cow of every hue.
Ye went as Ŗbhu, Vibhvan, Vāja to the
Gods, and skilled in war, obtained your
share in sacrifice.

7 Ye by your wisdom brought a cow from
out a hide ; unto that ancient Pair ye
gave again their youth.
Out of a horse, Sudhanvan's Sons, ye
formed a horse : a chariot ye equipped,
and went unto the Gods.

8 Drink ye this water, were the words ye
spake to them ; or drink ye this, the
rinsing of the Muñja-grass.
If ye approve not even this, Sudhanvan's
Sons, then at the third libation gladden
ye yourselves.

9 Most excellent are waters, thus said one
of you ; most excellent is Agni, thus
another said.
Another praised to many a one the
lightning cloud. Then did ye shape
the cups, speaking the words of truth.

10 One downward to the water drives the
crippled cow, another trims the flesh
brought on the carving-board.
One carries off the refuse at the set of
sun. How did the Parents aid their
children in their task !

11 On the high places ye have made the grass
for man, and water in the valleys, by
your skill, O Men.
Ŗbhus, ye iterate not to-day that act of
yours, your sleeping in the house of
him whom naught can hide.

---

4 *Most skilled is he* : Sāyaṇa observes that having
magnified Heavan and Earth by praising their son, the
poet now magnifies them by lauding their maker. See
Muir, *O. S. Texts*, v. 30.

The Ŗbhus ask Agni why he comes to them. *The
chalice* : see I. 20. 6.

3 *A courser must be made, etc.* : See I. 20. 2, 3, 4, and
I. 110 and 111.

4. *Then Tvaṣṭar* : represented as hiding himself for
shame among the Goddesses—probably the Celestial
Waters—when he saw this alteration of his work, and
in anger proposing to slay the Ŗbhus who had thus dis-
graced him.

5 *New names* : probably Ŗtus, Seasons, in place of
Ŗbhus.—Ludwig. *The Maiden* : apparently the daughter
of Tvaṣṭar, meaning, perhaps, as Ludwig suggests, the
first Dawn of the year, of which Tvaṣṭar is the God.

6 *The Cow of every hue* : the fruitful earth restored to
youth by the Gods of the Seasons.

8 *The rinsing of the Muñja-grass* : or Soma juice which
has been filtered through a strainer made of that grass.
'The two first alternatives intimate that the Ŗbhus may
be participant of the libations offered at dawn or at noon;
the third applies to the evening sacrifice ; the right of
the Ŗbhus to share in this being elsewhere acknowledged.'
—Wilson.

9 The meaning of these sayings in this place is not
clear.

10 The restoration to youth of the aged Parents,
Heaven and Earth, appears to be symbolically described
under the figure of a sacrifice.

How did the Parents aid? : weak and exhausted with
age they were unable to give any assistance.

11 *In the house of him whom naught can hide* : in the
mansion of the Sun, to whom the Ŗbhus went to obtain
immortality. In this and the remaining stanza, according to Sāyaṇa, the Ŗbhus are identified with the rays
of the sun.

12 As, compassing them round, ye glided
   through the worlds, where had the
   venerable Parents their abode ?
   Ye laid a curse on him who raised his
   arm at you : to him who spake aloud
   to you ye spake again.

13 When ye had slept your fill, ye Ṛbhus,
   thus ye asked, O thou whom naught
   may hide, who now hath wakened us ?
   The goat declared the hound to be
   your wakener. That day, in a full
   year, ye first unclosed your eyes.

14 The Maruts move in heaven, on earth
   this Agni ; through the mid-firmament
   the Wind approaches.
   Varuṇa comes in the sea's gathered
   waters, O Sons of Strength, desirous
   of your presence.

HYMN CLXII.   *The Horse.*

1. SLIGHT us not Varuṇa, Aryaman, or
   Mitra, Ṛbhukṣan, Indra, Āyu, or the
   Maruts,
   When we declare amid the congregation
   the virtues of the strong Steed, God-
   descended.

2 What time they bear before the Courser,
   covered with trappings and with wealth,
   the grasped oblation,
   The dappled goat goeth straightforward,
   bleating, to the place dear to Indra and
   to Pūṣan.

3 Dear to all Gods, this goat, the share of
   Pūṣan, is first led forward with the
   vigorous Courser,
   While Tvaṣṭar sends him forward with

---

13 *When ye had slept* : in the mansion of the Sun.

The goat declared the hound to be your wakener : the
meaning is obscure. Sāyaṇa's rendering is, 'the Sun
replied that the awakener was the wind.'

That day : Wilson, following Sāyaṇa, explains : 'you
have made this world to-day luminous, after the year
has expired ; that is, the rainy season being past, the
rays of the sun and moon are again visible.'

14 *Sons of Strength* : ye powerful Ṛbhus.

---

1 *Ṛbhukṣan* : a name of Indra, as lord of the Ṛbhus.

Āyu : said by both commentators, Sāyaṇa and Mahīdhara, to be used in this place for Vāyu, the God of Wind.
Āyu is probably Agni.

Amid the congregation : at sacrifice.

God-descended : sprung from the Gods, or, according
to Sāyaṇa, born as the type of various deities.

2 *Grasped oblation* : the offering that is to be made for
the horse, and which has been taken from the remains
of the butter-offering made the night before.

The dappled goat : this goat is to be tied to the horse
at the sacrificial post. *Pūṣan* here is said by Sāyaṇa to
stand for Agni.

---

the Charger, acceptable for sacrifice, to
   glory.

4 When thrice the men lead round the
   Steed, in order, who goeth to the Gods
   as meet oblation,
   The goat precedeth him, the share of
   Pūṣan, and to the Gods the sacrifice
   announceth.

5 Invoker, ministering priest, atoner, fire-
   kindler, Soma-presser, sage, reciter,
   With this well ordered sacrifice, well
   finished, do ye fill full the channels of
   the rivers.

6 The hewers of the post and those who
   carry it, and those who carve the knob
   to deck the Horse's stake ;
   Those who prepare the cooking-vessels for
   the Steed,—may the approving help of
   these promote our work.

7 Forth, for the regions of the Gods, the
   Charger with his smooth back is come ;
   my prayer attends him.
   In him rejoice the singers and the sages.
   A good friend have we won for the
   Gods' banquet.

8 May the fleet Courser's halter and his
   heel-ropes, the head-stall and the girths
   and cords about him.
   And the grass put within his mouth to
   bait him,—among the Gods, too, let
   all these be with him.

9 What part of the Steed's flesh the fly hath
   eaten, or is left sticking to the post or
   hatchet,
   Or to the slayer's hands and nails adhe-
   reth,—among the Gods, too, may all this
   be with thee.

10 Food undigested steaming from his belly,
   and any odour of raw flesh remaining,
   This let the immolators set in order and
   dress the sacrifice with perfect cooking.

11 What from thy body which with fire is
   roasted, when thou art set upon the
   spit, distilleth,
   Let not that lie on earth or grass neglected,
   but to the longing Gods let all be
   offered.

12 They who observing that the Horse is

---

4 *Who goeth to the Gods* : the object of the sacrifice
is to send the horse to the Gods that he may obtain wealth
and other blessings for his sacrificers.

5 *Invoker, etc* : these are the designations of eight of
the sixteen priests employed at solemn rites. The *sage*
(*suvipraḥ*, a priest of profound knowledge) is the superintendent of the whole ceremony.

Fill full the channels : obtain abundance of rain; or
perhaps offer oblations in abundance.

ready call out and say, the smell is good ; remove it ;

And, craving meat, await the distribution,
—may their approving help promote our labour.

13 The trial-fork of the flesh-cooking caldron, the vessels out of which the broth is sprinkled,
The warming-pots, the covers of the dishes, hooks, carving-boards,—all these attend the Charger.

14 The starting-place, his place of rest and rolling, the ropes wherewith the Charger's feet were fastened,
The water that he drank, the food he tasted,—among the Gods, too, may all these attend thee.

15 Let not the fire, smoke-scented, make thee crackle, nor glowing caldron smell and break to pieces.
Offered, beloved, approved, and consecrated,—such Charger do the Gods accept with favour.

16 The robe they spread upon the Horse to clothe him, the upper covering and the golden trappings,
The halters which restrain the Steed, the heel-ropes,—all these, as grateful to the Gods, they offer.

17 If one, when seated, with excessive urging hath with his heel or with his whip distressed thee,
All these thy woes, as with the oblations' ladle at sacrifices, with my prayer I banish.

18 The four-and-thirty ribs of the swift Charger, kin to the Gods, the slayer's hatchet pierces.
Cut ye with skill, so that the parts be flawless, and piece by piece declaring them dissect them.

19 Of Tvaṣṭar's Charger there is one dissector,—this is the custom—two there are who guide him.
Such of his limbs as I divide in order, all these, amid the balls, in fire I offer.

20 Let not thy dear soul burn thee as thou comest, let not the hatchet linger in thy body.

Let not a greedy clumsy immolator, missing the joints, mangle thy limbs unduly.

21 No, here thou diest not, thou art not injured : by easy paths unto the Gods thou goest.
Both Bays, both spotted mares are now thy fellows, and to the ass's pole is yoked the Charger.

22 May this Steed bring us all-sustaining riches, wealth in good kine, good horses, manly offspring.
Freedom from sin may Aditi vouchsafe us : the Steed with our oblations gain us lordship !

HYMN CLXIII. *The Horse.*

1. WHAT time, first springing into life, thou neighedst, proceeding from the sea or upper waters,
Limbs of the deer hadst thou, and eagle pinions. O Steed, thy birth is high and must be lauded.

2 This Steed which Yama gave hath Trita harnessed, and him, the first of all, hath Indra mounted.
His bridle the Gandharva grasped. O Vasus, from out the Sun ye fashioned forth the Courser.

3 Yama art thou, O Horse ; thou art Āditya ; Trita art thou by secret operation.
Thou art divided thoroughly from Soma. They say thou hast three bonds in heaven that hold thee.

4 Three bonds, they say, thou hast in heaven that bind thee, three in the waters, three within the ocean.

21 *Both Bays* : thou art now associated in heaven with the two bay horses of Indra, the two spotted mares of the Maruts, and the ass that draws the chariot of the Aśvins.
A full description of an Aśvamedha or Horse-sacrifice in later times may be found in the Rāmāyaṇa, Book I., Cantos 10-13.

1 *From the sea* : the Sacrificial Horse is here identified with the Sun in the ocean of air.
2 *Yama* : here said to mean Agni, as a solar deity. *Trita* : as God of the remote birth-place of the Sun. See I. 187, note.
The Gandharva : Viśvāvasu, a heavenly being who dwells in the region of the air and guards the celestial Soma.
3 *Āditya* : the Sun.
By secret operation : by the mysterious effect of the sacrifice.
Soma : here, perhaps, the Moon; but the meaning is uncertain.
4 The *three bonds* in heaven are said by Sāyaṇa to be his 'media of origin; that is the Vasus, Āditya, and Heaven.' By the waters, it is said that the habitable world is intended, and that the three *bonds* therein are tillage, rain, and seed. In *the ocean*, that is the firmament, they are cloud, lightning, and thunder. *Varuṇa* : on account of the three bonds (see I.24. 15).

18 *Four-and-thirty* : so many out of the thirty-six. As the Sacrificial Horse is the symbol of the heavens, the thirty-four ribs represent the sun, the moon, the five planets, and the twenty-seven *nakṣatras* or lunar asterisms. See Ludwig, Der Ṛgveda, III. p. 186. *Piece by piece declaring them* : the dissectors are to name the several parts as they divide them, each part being sacred to a separate divinity.
19 *Amid the balls* : the meat made up into balls.
20 *Burn thee* : make thee sad.

To me thou seemest Varuṇa, O Courser, there where they say is thy sublimest birth-place.

5 Here, Courser, are the places where they groomed thee, here are the traces of thy hoofs as winner.

Here have I seen the auspicious reins that guide thee, which those who guard the holy Law keep safely.

6 Thyself from far I recognized in spirit,—a Bird that from below flew through the heaven.

I saw thy head still soaring, striving upward by paths unsoiled by dust, pleasant to travel.

7 Here I beheld thy form, matchless in glory, eager to win thee food at the Cow's station.

Whene'er a man brings thee to thine enjoyment, thou swallowest the plants most greedy eater.

8 After the, Courser, come the car, the bridegroom, the kine come after, and the charm of maidens.

Full companies have followed for thy friendship : the pattern of thy vigour Gods have copied.

9 Horns made of gold hath he : his feet are iron : less fleet than he, though swift as thought, is Indra.

The Gods have come that they may taste the oblation of him who mounted, first of all, the Courser.

10 Symmetrical in flank, with rounded haunches, mettled like heroes, the Celestial Coursers

Put forth their strength, like swans in lengthened order, when they, the Steeds, have reached the heavenly causeway.

11 A body formed for flight hast thou, O Charger ; swift as the wind in motion is thy spirit.

Thy horns are spread abroad in all directions : they move with restless beat in wildernesses.

---

6 In this and the following stanza the horse is regarded as identical with the Sun in his course through heaven, and as accepting the oblations offered by the worshipper. *The Cow's station* : the chief place of earth, the Cow, is the altar.

7 *Most greedy eater* : regarded as a mere earthly horse.

9 *Horns made of gold* : according to Sāyaṇa, the word *horns* is used figuratively for mane. The Sun's rays are probably intended.

Who mounted, first of all, the Courser : Indra, as is said in verse 2.

10 The horses of the Sun are said to be spoken of. The exact meaning of the words is uncertain.

11 *Thy horns* : meaning, here, perhaps hoofs.

---

12 The strong Steed hath come forward to the slaughter, pondering with a mind directed God-ward.

The goat who is his kin is led before him : the sages and the singers follow after.

13 The Steed is come unto the noblest mansion, is come unto his Father and his Mother.

This day shall he approach the Gods, most welcome : then he declares good gifts to him who offers.

HYMN CLXIV.   *Viśvedevas.*

1. OF this benignant Priest, with eld greycoloured, the brother midmost of the three is lightning.

The third is he whose back with oil is sprinkled. Here I behold the Chief with seven male children.

2 Seven to the one-wheeled chariot yoke the Courser; bearing seven names the single Courser draws it.

Three-naved the wheel is, sound and undecaying, whereon are resting all these worlds of being.

3 The seven who on the seven-wheeled car are mounted have horses, seven in tale, who draw them onward.

Seven Sisters utter songs of praise together, in whom the names of the seven Cows are treasured.

---

13 *His Father and his Mother* : Heaven and Earth.

Wilson remarks : 'Although more mystical than the preceding hymn, especially in regard to the intimations of the identity of the horse with the sun, there is nothing in it incompatible with the more explicit description in the former *Sūkta* of the actual sacrifice of a horse.'

1 The *priest* is Āditya, the Sun. His next brother is lightning, another form of fire, and the third brother is *Agni Gārhapatya*, the western sacred fire maintained by each householder, and fed with oblations of clarified butter.

The *seven male children* are probably the priests.

2 *Seven* : priests. *The one-wheeled chariot* : the Sun. *Seven names* : perhaps the seven solar rays. *Three-naved* : with reference, probably, to the three seasons, the hot weather, the rains, and the cold weather. On this wheel of the Sun all existing things depend.

3 *The seven* : according to Sāyaṇa, the seven solar rays, or the seven divisions of the year, solstice, season, month, fortnight, day, night, hour. The seven wheels of the chariot and the seven horses may also, according to Sāyaṇa, be the solar rays.

Seven Sisters: probably the seven celestial rivers, which, as emblems of fertility may bear the name of cows. Sāyaṇa explains the *seven Sisters* as the solar rays, or the six seasons and the year, or the six pairs of months with the intercalary month, and *the seven Cows* as the seven notes of music as employed in chanting the praises of the Sun.

4 Who hath beheld him as he sprang to
   being, seen how the boneless One supports the bony?
   Where is the blood of earth, the life, the
   spirit? Who may approach the man
   who knows, to ask it?

5 Unripe in mind, in spirit undiscerning, I
   ask of these the Gods' established places;
   For up above the yearling Calf the sages,
   to form a web, their own seven threads
   have woven.

6 I ask, unknowing, those who know, the
   sages, as one all ignorant for sake of
   knowledge,
   What was that ONE who in the Unborn's
   image hath stablished and fixed firm
   these worlds' six regions.

7 Let him who knoweth presently declare it,
   this lovely Bird's securely founded station.
   Forth from his head the Cows draw milk,
   and, wearing his vesture, with their foot
   have drunk the water.

8 The Mother gave the Sire his share of
   Order : with thought, at first, she wedded him in spirit.
   She, the coy Dame, was filled with dew
   prolific : with adoration men approached to praise her.

9 Yoked was the Mother to the boon Cow's
   car-pole : in the dank rows of cloud the
   Infant rested.

Then the Calf lowed, and looked upon
   the Mother, the Cow who wears all
   shapes in three directions.

10 Bearing three Mothers and three Fathers,
   single he stood erect : they never make
   him weary.
   There on the pitch of heaven they speak
   together in speech all-knowing but not
   all-impelling.

11 Formed with twelve spokes, by length of
   time, unweakened, rolls round the
   heaven this wheel of during Order.
   Herein established, joined in pairs together, seven hundred Sons and twenty
   stand, O Agni.

12 They call him in the farther half of heaven
   the Sire five-footed, of twelve forms,
   wealthy in watery store.
   These others say that he, God with far-
   seeing eyes, is mounted on the lower
   seven-wheeled, six-spoked car.

13 Upon this five-spoked wheel revolving
   ever all living creatures rest and are
   dependent.
   Its axle, heavy-laden, is not heated : the
   nave from ancient time remains unbroken.

14 The wheel revolves, unwasting, with its
   felly : ten draw it, yoked to the far-
   stretching car-pole.
   The Sun's eye moves encompassed by the
   region : on him dependent rest all
   living creatures.

15 Of the co-born they call the seventh
   single-born ; the six twin pairs are
   called Ṛṣis, Children of Gods.

---

4 *How the boneless One supports the bony* : or in more
conventional and less literal words, how the unsubstantial
one (feminine) supports that (masculine) which is
endowed with substance.
   The *boneless* or unsubstantial is Prakṛti, Nature, the
original source of the substantial, that is the material and
visible world. According to Hillebrandt, Vedische
Mythologie, I. p. 338, the *boneless* One is the Sun and the
bony the Moon. See M. Müller, India, What can it Teach
us ? pp. 245, 246.
   5 *The yearling Calf* : probably the Sun, in reference
to his yearly course. What the *seven threads* are is uncertain, Sāyaṇa says they are the seven forms of the Soma
sacrifice, or the seven metres of the Vedas. Ludwig
thinks that the general meaning of the stanza is : I (the
poet) content myself with asking for information about
the places or traces of the Gods in our world; but the
sages talk about things which are beyond my power of
comprehension.
   6 *In the Unborn's image* : in the form of Aja or the
Unborn Creator, represented by the Sun. Cf. VIII. 41. 10.
   7 *This lovely Bird's...station* : the place of the Sun.
   The Cows draw milk: 'The solar rays, although especial
agents in sending down rain, are equally active in its
re-absorption.'—Wilson.
   8 The mother Earth gave the father Heaven his
share in the great work of cosmical production.
   Dew prolific : the fertilizing rain.
   9 *Yoked was the Mother* : Earth undertook the functions of the cow who supplies milk for sacrifices.
   The Infant : the young Sun.

The Calf lowed : the cloud thundered. *In three directions* : heaven, mid-air, and earth.
   10 *Three Mothers and three Fathers* : the three earths
and the three heavens. This fanciful threefold division
has occurred before. See I. 105. 5.
   They speak : the Gods converse together about the
Sun, says Sāyaṇa, in speech that knows all but does not
extend to or impress all.
   11 The wheel formed with twelve spokes is the year
with its twelve months. The seven hundred and twenty
sons, joined in pairs, are the days and nights of the year,
three hundred and sixty of each.
   12 *Five-footed* : the five feet are, Sāyaṇa says, the five
seasons, the dewy and cold seasons being counted as one.
The twelve forms are the months of the year. The seven
wheels of the car are said to be the seven solar rays, and
the six spokes of each wheel are the six seasons. I find the
stanza unintelligible.
   13 *The five-spoked wheel* : in reference, perhaps, to the
five seasons, as in verse 12.
   14 *Ten draw it* : probably the ten regions of space.
   The region : the firmament, mid-air.
   15 *The co-born* : the six pairs of months, or six seasons
of two months each. The *single-born* is the thirteenth
and intercalary month. Sāyaṇa explains ṛṣayaḥ, Ṛṣis,
in this stanza as gantāraḥ, goers; but in what sense is uncertain.

Their good gifts sought of men are ranged in order due, and various in their form move for the Lord who guides.

16 They told me these were males, though truly females : he who hath eyes sees this, the blind discerns not.
The son who is a sage hath comprehended : who knows this rightly is his father's father.

17 Beneath the upper realm, above this lower, bearing her calf at foot the Cow hath risen.
Witherward, to what place hath she departed ? Where calves she ? Not amid this herd of cattle.

18 Who, that the father of this Calf discerneth beneath the upper realm, above the lower,
Showing himself a sage, may here declare it ? Whence hath the Godlike spirit had its rising ?

19 Those that come hitherward they call departing, those that depart they call directed hither.
And what so ye have made, Indra and Soma, steeds bear as 'twere yoked to the region's car-pole.

20 Two Birds with fair wings, knit with bonds of friendship, in the same sheltering tree have found a refuge.
One of the twain eats the sweet Fig-tree's fruitage ; the other eating not regardeth only.

21 Where those fine Birds hymn ceaselessly their portion of life eternal, and the sacred synods,
There is the Universe's mighty Keeper, who, wise, hath entered into me the simple.

22 The, tree whereon the fine Birds eat the sweetness, where they all rest and procreate their offspring,—
Upon its top they say the fig is luscious : none gaineth it who knoweth not the Father.

23 How on the Gāyatrī the Gāyatrī was based, how from the Triṣṭup they fashioned the Triṣṭup forth,
How on the Jagatī was based the Jagatī,- they who know this have won themselves immortal life.

24 With Gāyatri he measures out the praise-song, Sāma with praise-song, triplet with the Triṣṭup.
The triplet with the two or four-foot measure, and with the syllable they form seven metres.

16 *They told me these were males* : Wilson observes : 'This is a piece of grammatical mysticism ; *raśmi*, a ray of the sun, here personified as a female, is properly a noun masculine.' But this is just the reverse of the explanation required. The meaning is obscure.
Grassmann suggests that the meaning is that Night and Morning, both feminine, have received the masculine name of Day.
The son who is a sage : 'According to the Scholiast, the Sun is to be considered as the father of the rays of light, which again, in their collective capacity, being the cause of rain, are the fosterers or parents of the earth : the Sun is therefore father of the father, and he who knows this is identical with the Sun.'—Wilson. The meaning of the last semi-hemistich is probably that an intelligent son may be called the parent of an ignorant father as being his superior in knowledge.
17 Uṣas or Dawn hath risen between heaven and earth, carrying with her the young Sun her offspring. *This herd of cattle* : the visible world.
18 Uṣas is the mother, but who is able to say who the father of the Sun is ?
19 This stanza may refer to the planets which change their relative position as they revolve. Indra is here the Sun, and Soma the Moon.
20 Sāyaṇa says that the *two Birds* are the vital and the Supreme Spirit, dwelling in one body. The vital spirit enjoys the fruit or rewards of actions while the Supreme Spirit is merely a passive spectator.

21 The *fine Birds* here are perhaps tne priests, and the Keeper of the Universe may be Soma.
22 Sāyaṇa explains *suparṇā*, well-winged, in this and the preceding stanza as smooth-gliding (*rays*). *Their offspring* is, he says, the light, and *the Father* is the cherishing and protecting Sun. All explanations of these three stanzas can be only conjectural. Ludwig is of opinion that they are originally unconnected fragments and that they have been inserted together in this hymn merely because the word *suparṇā* (used apparently in various senses) has a prominent place in each stanza.
Suparṇā (dual) has been explained by different scholars as two species of souls; day and night, Sun and Moon; (plural) as rays of light ; stars; metres, spirits of the dead; pri ests; and *the tree* on which they rest as the body; the orb or region of the Sun ; the sacrificial post ; the world: and the mythical World-Tree. A generally satisfactory explanation is scarcely to be hoped for.
23 Wilson, following Sāyaṇa, paraphrases this stanza as follows : 'They who know the station of Agni upon the earth; the station of Vāyu that was fabricated from the firmament, and that station of the Sun which is placed in heaven, obtain immortality.' He observes that the purport of the phraseology, borrowed from the several metres Gāyatrī, Tri ṭubh, and Jagatī, is not very clear, and that it may be merely an obscure and mystic reference to the text of the Veda, a knowledge of which is essential to final felicity. The meaning seems to be that those who are thoroughly acquainted with the appropriate rewards which follow the employment of each of the sacred metres named are on the right road to immortal life.
24 *Triplet* : the word in the text *vāká* is said to mean either two or three connected stanzas.
Two or four-foot measure : consisting of two or four *pādas* or semi-hemistichs.
And with the syllable : they form the seven generic metres of the Veda with the syllable, which is the chief element of metre, the Gāyatrī consisting of eight syllables, the Triṣṭup of eleven, and the Jagatī of twelve. See Wilson's note.

25 With Jagatī the flood in heaven he stablished, and saw the Sun in the Rathantara Sāman.
Gāyatrī hath, they say, three brands for kindling : hence it excels in majesty and vigour.

26 I invocate the milch-cow good for milking so that the milker, deft of hand, may drain her.
May Savitar give goodliest stimulation. The caldron is made hot ; I will proclaim it.

27 She, lady of all treasure, is come hither yearning in spirit for her calf and lowing.
May this cow yield her milk for both the Aśvins, and may she prosper to our high advantage.

28 The cow hath lowed after her blinking youngling ; she licks his forehead, as she lows, to form it.
His mouth she fondly calls to her warm udder, and suckles him with milk while gently lowing.

29 He also snorts, by whom encompassed round the Cow lows as she clings unto the shedder of the rain.
She with her shrilling cries hath humbled mortal man, and, turned to lightning, hath stripped off her covering robe.

30 That which hath breath and speed and life and motion lies firmly stablished in the midst of houses.
Living, by offerings to the Dead he moveth, Immortal One, the brother of the mortal.

31 I saw the Herdsman, him who never stumbles, approaching by his pathways and departing.
He, clothed with gathered and diffusive splendour, within the worlds continually travels.

32 He who hath made him doth not comprehend him : from him who saw him surely is he hidden.
He, yet enveloped in his Mother's bosom, source of much life, hath sunk into destruction.

33 Dyaus is my Father, my begetter : kinship is here. This great earth is my kin and Mother.
Between the wide-spread world-halves is the birth-place : the Father laid the Daughter's germ within it.

34 I ask thee of the earth's extremest limit, where is the centre of the world, I ask thee.
I ask thee of the Stallion's seed prolific, I ask of highest heaven where Speech abideth.

35 This altar is the earth's extremest limit ; this sacrifice of ours is the world's centre.
The Stallion's seed prolific is the Soma ; this Brahman highest heaven where Speech abideth.

36 Seven germs unripened yet are heaven's prolific seed : their functions they maintain by Viṣṇu's ordinance.
Endued with wisdom through intelligence and thought, they compass us about present on every side.

37 What thing I truly am I know not clearly : mysterious, fettered in my mind I wander.
When the first-born of holy Law approached me, then of this speech I first obtain a portion.

38 Back, forward goes he, grasped by strength inherent, the Immortal born the brother of the mortal.

25 *He* : Brahmā, according to Sāyaṇa.

Rathantara : one of the most important Sāma-hymns; Sāmaveda II. i. i. 11 = Ṛgveda VII. 32. 22, 23.

Three brands : the three *pādas*, divisions, or lines of the verse being fancifully likened to the sticks with which the sacrificial fire is kindled.

26 The milch-cow in this and the two following stanzas may be the cow who supplies milk for the sacrifice. But Sāyaṇa says that the cow may be the rain-cloud, the milk being the rain and the milker Vāyu the God of Wind who causes it to flow. The calf, Sāyaṇa says, is the world longing for the rain to fall.

29 *He also* : probably Parjanya, the personified Storm-Cloud. The Cow here is undoubtedly a cloud.

30 The subject of the first hemistich is apparently Agni. The Moon, sustained by sacrificial offerings to the Departed, appears to be the subject of the second. But see Hymns of the Atharva-veda IX. 10. 8.

31 *The Herdsman* : the Sun, the guardian of the world.

32 *Lightning*, the immediate cause of rain, with his countless offspring the fertilizing rain-drops, appears to be alluded to.

33 *World-halves* : literally bowls or vessels into which the Soma is poured, a figurative expression for heaven and earth. The firmament or space between these two is, as the region of the rain, the womb of all beings. The Father is Dyaus and the daughter is Earth whose fertility depends upon the germ of rain laid in the firmament.

35 *The earth's extremest limit* : the altar, as the place nearest to heaven, the place where the Gods visit men.
The Stallion : Dyaus, or Father Heaven.
This Brahman : The priest so named who recites the texts of the Veda.

36 This stanza, as Ludwig remarks, is one of the most unintelligible in the whole Veda. *The seven*, according to Sāyaṇa, are the solar rays, and Viṣṇu is said to be the Sun.

37 *The first-born of holy Law* : according to Sāyaṇa, the first-born (perceptions) of the truth. Soma may be intended, as suggested by Bergaine, Religion Védique, I. 150.

38 This stanza appears to refer to the Sun in his daily course from east to west and his nightly return to the

Ceaseless they move in opposite directions :
men mark the one and fail to mark the
other.

39 Upon what syllable of holy praise-song, as
'twere their highest heaven, the Gods
repose them,—

Who knows not this, what will he do with
praise-song? But they who know it
well sit here assembled.

40 Forunate mayst thou be with goodly pasture, and may we also be exceeding
wealthy.

Feed on the grass, O Cow, at every season,
and coming hitherward drink limpid
water.

41 Forming the water-floods, the buffalo hath
lowed, one-footed or two-footed or four-
footed, she,

Who hath become eight-footed or hath
got nine feet, the thousand-syllabled in
the sublimest heaven.

42 From her descend in streams the seas of
water ; thereby the world's four regions
have their being.

Thence flows the imperishable flood and
thence the universe hath life.

43 I saw from far away the smoke of fuel
with spires that rose on high o'er that
beneath it.

The Mighty Men have dressed the spotted
bullock. These were the customs in the
days aforetime.

44 Three with long tresses show in ordered
season. One of them sheareth when the
year is ended.

One with his powers the universe

regardeth: of one the sweep is seen, but
his figure.

45 Speech hath been measured out in four
divisions, the Brāhmans who have understanding know them.

Three kept in close concealment cause no
motion ; of speech, men speak only the
fourth division.

46 They call him Indra, Mitra, Varuṇa, Agni,
and he is heavenly nobly-winged Garutmān.

To what is One, sages give many a title :
they call it Agni, Yama, Mātariśvan.

47 Dark the descent : the birds are golden-
coloured ; up to the heaven they fly
robed in the waters.

Again descend they from the seat of Order,
and all the earth is moistened with their
fatness.

48 Twelve are the fellies, and the wheel is
single ; three are the naves. What man
hath understood it ?

Therein are set together spokes three hundred and sixty, which in nowise can be
loosened.

49 That breast of thine exhaustless, spring
of pleasure, wherewith thou feedest all
things that are choicest,

Wealth-giver, treasure-finder, free bestower,—bring that, Sarasvatī, that we may
drain it.

50 By means of sacrifice the Gods accomplished their sacrifice : these were the
earliest ordinances.

These Mighty Ones attained the height of
heaven, there where the Sādhyas, Gods
of old, are dwelling.

east, the former visible to men and the latter invisible.
They, in this case, would mean the Sun by day and
the Sun by night.

39 The syllable is the *Praṇava*, the mystical sacred
syllable OM. This syllable is set forth in the Upaniṣads
as the object of profound religious meditation, and the
highest spiritual efficacy is attributed to it.

40 This stanza is addressed to the cow who supplies
the milk for libations.

41 *The buffalo hath lowed* : the great rain-cloud has
thundered. Sāyaṇa explains *one-footed*, as sounding from
the cloud; *two-footed*, from cloud and sky; *four-footed*,
from the four cardinal points; *eight-footed*, from the four
points and the four-intermediate points ; *nine-footed*, from
these points and the zenith. *Gaurī*, the buffalo, is, according to Sāyaṇa, *Vāk*, Speech, the voice of heaven.

42 *From her* : from the buffalo, or cloud, *The world's
four regions* : the whole world.

43 *The smoke of fuel* : arising from burning cow-dung.
The Mighty Men : the Heroes, the Gods. *The spotted
bullock* : the Soma. The whole may, perhaps, be a
figurative description of the gathering of the rain-clouds.

44 The three are Agni who burns up the vegetation,
the all-seeing Sun, and the invisible Vāyu or Wind.

45 *Three kept in close concealment* : the *three* might mean
the three Vedas; but this interpretation does not suit the
rest of the half-line. *The fourth division* : ordinary language. See Wilson for Sāyaṇa's elaborate explanation
of this stanza, and Muir, O. S. Texts, II. 155.

46 *Garutmān* : the Celestial Bird, the Sun. All these
names says the poet, are names of one and the same Divine
Being, the One Supreme Spirit under various manifestations.

47 *Dark the descent* : the rays of light descend into the
darkness of the earth when wrapped in night, and rise
again to heaven with the moisture which they have absorbed to descend again in the form of fertilizing rain.

48 The single wheel is the year ; the twelve spokes
are the months; the three naves are the three seasons of
four months each; and the spokes are the days of the
luni-solar year. The stanza is out of place here.

49 *Sarasvatī* : See I. 3. 10.

50 *The Sādhyas* : said by Yāska to be 'the Gods whose
dwelling-place is the sky.' They are named among the
minor divinities in the *Amarakośa*, and, as Wilson observes,
'it would seem that in Sāyaṇa's day the purport of the
designation had become uncertain.'

51 Uniform, with the passing days, this water
   mounts and falls again.
   The tempest-clouds give life to earth, and
   fires re-animate the heaven.

52 The Bird Celestial, vast with noble pinion,
   the lovely germ of plants, the germ of
   waters,
   Him who delighteth us with rain in
   season, Sarasvān I invoke that he may
   help us.

HYMN CLXV.   Indra. Maruts.

1. WITH what bright beauty are the Maruts
   jointly invested, peers in age, who dwell
   together ?
   From what place have they come? With
   what intention ? Sing they their strength
   through love of wealth, these Heroes ?

2 Whose prayers have they, the Youthful
   Ones, accepted ? Who to his sacrifice
   hath turned the Maruts ?
   We will delay them on their journey sweeping—with what high spirit !—through
   the air like eagles.

3 Whence comest thou alone, thou who art
   mighty, Indra, Lord of the Brave ? What
   is thy purpose ?
   Thou greetest us when meeting us the
   Bright Ones. Lord of Bay Steeds, say
   what thou hast against us.

4 Mine are devotions, hymns ; sweet are
   libations. Strength stirs, and hurled
   forth is my bolt of thunder.
   They call for me, their lauds are longing
   for me. These my Bay Steeds bear me
   to these oblations.

5 Therefore together with our strong companions, having adorned our bodies,
   now we harness,

51 *Fires re-animate the heaven* : the oblations offered in
sacrificial fires delight and strengthen the gods.

52 *Sarasvān* : or Sarasvat, is the name of a River-
God usually assigned as a consort to Sarasvatī. In this
place the Sun is meant, and *sārasvantam* may be taken
as a mere epithet, 'rich in water' which he absorbs.

Indra, the Maruts, and the great sage Agastya are
regarded as the Ṛṣis of this hymn, which appears to be,
as Wilson observes, a vindication of 'the separate, or
at least preferential, worship of Indra, without comprehending, at the same time, as a matter of course, the
adoration of the Maruts. The hymn is translated and
fully explained in Prof. Max Müller's *Vedic Hymns*,
Part I.

1 Indra speaks.

3 Here the Maruts address Indra whom they meet
alone, unattended by them as was usual.

4 Indra replies.

5 The Maruts again speak.

Our spotted deer with might, for thou,
O Indra, hast learnt and understood our
Godlike nature.

6 Where was that nature then of yours, O
  Maruts, that ye charged me alone to
  slay the Dragon ?
  For I in truth am fierce and strong and
  mighty. I bent away from every foeman's weapons.

7 Yea, much hast thou achieved with us for
  comrades, with manly valour like thine
  own, thou Hero.
  Much may we too achieve, O mightiest
  Indra, with our great power, we
  Maruts, when we will it.

8 Vṛtra I slew by mine own strength, O
  Maruts, having waxed mighty in mine
  indignation.
  I with the thunder in my hand created for
  man these lucid softly flowing waters.

9 Nothing, O Maghavan, stands firm before
  thee ; among the Gods not one is found
  thine equal.
  None born or springing into life comes
  nigh thee. Do what thou hast to do,
  exceeding mighty ?

10 Mine only be transcendent power, whatever I, daring in my spirit, may accomplish.
   For I am known as terrible, O Maruts :
   I, Indra, am the Lord of what I ruined.

11 Now, O ye Maruts, hath your praise
   rejoiced me, the glorious hymn which
   ye have made me, Heroes !
   For me, for Indra, champion strong in
   battle, for me, yourselves, as lovers for
   a lover.

12 Here, truly, they send forth their sheen
   to meet me, wearing their blameless glory
   and their vigour.
   When I have seen you, Maruts, in gay
   splendour, ye have delighted me, so now
   delight me.

13 Who here hath magnified you, O ye Maruts ? speed forward, O ye lovers, to
   your lovers.
   Ye Radiant Ones, assisting their devotions,
   of these my holy rites be ye regardful.

6 Indra claims for himself the glory of the victory
over Vṛtra.

11 'In this verse Indra, after having declined with no
uncertain sound the friendship of the Maruts, repents himself of his unkindn ss towards his old friends. The words
of praise which they addressed to him in verse 9, in spite
of the rebuff which they had received from Indra, have
touched his heart, and we may suppose that, after this,
their reconciliation was complete.'—Max Müller.

14 To this hath Mānya's wisdom brought us,
    so as to aid, as aids the poet him who
    worships.
  Bring hither quick ! On to the sage, ye
    Maruts ! These prayers for you the sin-
    ger hath recited.

15 May this your praise, may this your song,
    O Maruts, sung by the poet, Māna's
    son, Māndārya,
  Bring offspring for ourselves with food to
    feed us. May we find strengthening
    food in full abundance !

HYMN CLXVI.   *Maruts.*

1. Now let us publish, for the vigorous com-
    pany the herald of the Strong One,
    their primeval might.
  With fire upon your way, O Maruts loud
    of voice, with battle, Mighty Ones,
    achieve your deeds of strength.

2 Bringing the pleasant meath as 'twere their
    own dear son, they sport in sportive
    wise gay at their gatherings.
  The Rudras come with succour to the
    worshipper ; self-strong they fail not him
    who offers sacrifice.

3 To whomsoever, bringer of oblations, they
    immortal guardians, have given plente-
    ous wealth,
  For him, like loving friends, the Maruts
    bringing bliss bedew the regions round
    with milk abundantly.

4 Ye who with mighty powers have stirred
    the regions up, your coursers have sped
    forth directed by themselves.
  All creatures of the earth, all dwellings
    are afraid, for brilliant is your coming
    with your spears advanced.

5 When they in dazzling rush have made
    the mountains roar, and shaken heaven's
    high back in their heroic strength,
  Each sovran of the forest fears as ye drive
    near, and the shrubs fly before you swift
    as whirling wheels.

6 Terrible Maruts, ye with ne'er-diminished
    host, with great benevolence fulfil our
    heart's desire.
  Where'er your lightning bites armed with
    its gory teeth it crunches up the cattle
    like a well-aimed dart.

7 Givers of during gifts whose bounties
    never fail, free from ill-will, at sacrifices
    glorified,
  They sing their song aloud that they may
    drink sweet juice : well do they know
    the Hero's first heroic deeds.

8 With castles hundredfold, O Maruts, guard
    ye well the man whom ye have loved
    from ruin and from sin,—
  The man whom ye the fierce, the Mighty
    Ones who roar, preserve from calumny
    by cherishing his seed.

9 O Maruts, in your cars are all things that
    are good : great powers are set as 'twere
    in rivalry therein.
  Rings are upon your shoulders when ye
    journey forth : your axle turns together
    both the chariot wheels.

10 Held in your manly arms are many goodly
    things, gold chains are on your chests,
    and glistering ornaments,
  Deer-skins are on their shoulders, on their
    fellies knives : they spread their glory
    out as birds spread out their wings.

11 Mighty in mightiness, pervading, passing
    strong, visible from afar as 'twere with
    stars of heaven,
  Lovely with pleasant tongues, sweet singers
    with their mouths, the Maruts, joined
    with Indra, shout forth all around.

12 This is your majesty, ye Maruts nobly
    born, far as the sway of Aditi your
    bounty spreads.

---

14 This verse is exceedingly difficult, and its translation at present can be only conjectural.

   Mānya, apparently, means the son of Māna.

15 *Māndārya,* probably the name of the poet, but explained differently by Sāyaṇa and Mahīdhara.

   I borrow three-fourths of this verse from Prof. M.
Müller.

   This hymn and the twenty-five following are ascribed
to the Ṛṣi Agastya, who appears in the Rāmāyaṇa as the
friend and counsellor of Rāma. He is one of those inde-
finable mythic personages who are found in the ancient
traditions of many nations, and in whom cosmogonical
or astronomical notions are generally figured. Thus
it is related of Agastya that the Vindhyan mountains
prostrated themselves before him; and yet the same
Agastya is believed to be the regent of the star Canopus.

1 *The Strong One* : Indra, who is preceded by the
Maruts.

2 *The Rudras* : the Maruts, sons of the Strong-God
Rudra.

3 *Milk* : fertilizing rain.

5 *As ye drive near* : similar abrupt changes of person
are common in the Veda.

10 *On their fellies knives* : their war-chariots have sharp
scythe-like blades attached to their wheels, or sharp
edges to their fellies.

11 *Sweet singers* : the Maruts' song in the music of
the winds.

12 *The sway of Aditi* : What the poet says is simply this,
that the bounty of the Maruts extends as far as the realm
of Aditi, i. e. is endless, or extends everywhere, Aditi
being in its original conception the deity of the unbounded
world beyond, the earliest attempt at expressing the
Infinite.'—Max Müller.

   This also is one of the hymns translated and fully
explained by Prof. Max Müller in *Vedic Hymns,* Part I.

Even Indra by desertion never disannuls the boon bestowed by you upon the pious man.

13 This is your kinship, Maruts, that, Immortals, ye were oft in olden time regardful of our call,
Having vouchsafed to man a hearing through this prayer, by wondrous deeds the Heroes have displayed their might.

14 That, O ye Maruts, we may long time flourish through your abundant riches, O swift movers,
And that our men may spread in the encampment, let me complete the rite with these oblations.

15 May this your laud, may this your song, O Maruts, sung by the poet, Māna's son, Māndārya,
Bring offspring for ourselves with food to feed us. May we find strengthening food in full abundance.

HYMN CLXVII. *Indra. Maruts.*

1. A THOUSAND are thy helps for us, O Indra : a thousand, Lord of Bays, thy choice refreshments.
Wealth of a thousand sorts hast thou to cheer us : may precious goods come nigh to us in thousands.

2 May the most sapient Maruts, with protection, with best boons brought from lofty heaven, approach us,
Now when their team of the most noble horses speeds even on the sea's extremest limit.

3 Close to them clings one moving in seclusion, like a man's wife, like a spear carried rearward,
Well grasped, bright, decked with gold ; there is Vāk also, like to a courtly, eloquent dame, among them.

4 Far off the brilliant, never-weary Maruts cling to the young Maid as a joint possession.
The fierce Gods drave not Rodasī before them, but wished for her to grow their friend and fellow.

5 When chose immortal Rodasī to follow— she with loose tresses and heroic spirit—
She climbed her servant's chariot, she like Sūryā with cloud-like motion and refulgent aspect.

6 Upon their car the young men set the Maiden wedded to glory, mighty in assemblies,
When your song, Maruts, rose, and, with oblation, the Soma-pourer sang his hymn in worship.

7 I will declare the greatness of these Maruts, their real greatness, worthy to be lauded,
How, with them, she though firm, strong-minded, haughty, travels to women happy in their fortune.

8 Mitra and Varuṇa they guard from censure: Aryaman too, discovers worthless sinners
Firm things are overthrown that ne'er were shaken : he prospers, Maruts, who gives choice oblations.

9 None of us, Maruts, near or at a distance, hath ever reached the limit of your vigour.
They in courageous might still waxing boldly have compassed round their foemen like an ocean.

10 May we this day be dearest friends of Indra, and let us call on him in fight to-morrow.
So were we erst. New might attend us daily ! So be with us Ṛbhukṣan of the Heroes !

11 May this your laud, may this your song, O Maruts, sung by the poet, Māna's son, Māndārya,
Bring offspring for ourselves with. food to feed us. May we find strengthening food in full abundance.

HYMN CLXVIII. *Maruts.*

1. SWIFT gain is his who hath you near at every rite : ye welcome every song of him who serves the Gods.

2 *The sea's extremest limit* : the skirts of the sea of air, the firmament.

3 Sāyaṇa says that the lightning is spoken of, moving in the clouds, as if in secret, like the well-attired wife who remains in the women's apartment, but sometimes showing itself, like the hymn or prayer recited at religious ceremonies. The comparisons are scarcely intelligible. Vāk here is the voice of Heaven, the thunder. See Max Müller, *Vedic Hymns*, Part I.

5 *Rodasī* : usually regarded as the consort of Rudra, said by Sāyaṇa to mean here the lightning, the bride of the Maruts.
Sūryā : the daughter of the Sun, who mounted the chariot of the Aśvins. See I. 116. 17.

7 *She* : Rodasī. In the second hemistich there is no substantive, only adjectives in the feminine gender. Wilson, following Sāyaṇa, renders the last half-line by 'supports a flourishing progeny.' Ludwig thinks that Rodasī appears as Eileithuia of the Greek pantheon, the Goddess who presides over childbirth.

10 The hymn appears to have been recited on the eve of an expected battle.
Ṛbhukṣan : a name of Indra, as lord of the Ṛbhus.

1 The text of the first line is manifestly corrupt and translation is conjectural. See Max Müller, Sacred Books of the East, XXXII, p. 281.

So may I turn you hither with fair
hymns of praise to give great succour
for the weal of both the worlds.

2 Surrounding, as it were, self-born, self-
powerful, they spring to life the shakers-
down of food and light ;
Like as the countless undulations of the
floods, worthy of praise when near, like
bullocks and like kine.

3 They who, like Somas with their well-
grown stalks pressed out, imbibed within the heart, dwell there in friendly
wise.
Upon their shoulders rests as 'twere a
warrior's spear, and in their hand they
hold a dagger and a ring.

4 Self-yoked they have descended lightly
from the sky. With your own lash,
Immortals, urge yourselves to speed.
Unstained by dust the Maruts, mighty in
their strength, have cast down e'en firm
things, armed with their shining spears.

5 Who among you, O Maruts armed with
lightning-spears, moveth you by himself,
as with the tongue his jaws ?
Ye rush from heaven's floor as though ye
sought for food, on many errands like
the Sun's diurnal Steed.

6 Say where, then, is this mighty region's
farthest bound, where, Maruts, is the
lowest depth that ye have reached,
When ye cast down like chaff the firmly
stablished pile, and from the mountain
send the glittering water-flood ?

7 Your winning is with strength, dazzling,
with heavenly light, with fruit mature,
O Maruts, full of plenteousness.
Auspicious is your gift like a free giver's
meed, victorious, spreading far, as of
immortal Gods.

8 The rivers roar before your chariot fellies
when they are uttering the voice of
rain-clouds.

2 *The shakers-down* : violently sending down the rain
which is followed by sunlight and fertility.
When near : terrific in appearance at a distance, but
gentle when propitiated with worship.
3 The first hemistich is obscure. Perhaps the meaning is that the beneficial effects of the storm are lasting
like the inspiring influence of Soma juice.
Warrior's spear : 'Rambhiṇī I now take with Sāyaṇa
in the sense of a wife clinging to the shoulders of her
husband, though what is meant is the spear, or some
other weapon, slung over the shoulders See I. 167, 3.
—M. Müller, *Vedic Hymns*, I. 283.
5 What, asks the poet, is the moving principle of the
Maruts ? Who gives them their first impulse, as a man
when he wishes moves his tongue and jaws? 'This stanza,'
remarks Wilson, 'is exceedingly elliptical and obscure:
Sāyaṇa's completion of the text is entirely conjectural.'

The lightnings laugh upon the earth beneath them, what time the Maruts
scatter forth their fatness.

9 Pṛśni brought forth, to fight the mighty
battle, the glittering army of the restless
Maruts.
Nurtured together they begat the monster,
and then looked round them for the
food that strengthens.

10 May this your laud, may this your song
O Maruts, sung by the poet Māna's son,
Māndārya,
Bring offspring for ourselves with food to
feed us. May we find strengthening food
in full abundance.

HYMN CLXIX.   *Indra.*

1. As, Indra, from great treason thou protectest, yea, from great treachery these
who approach us,
So, marking well, Controller of the Maruts
grant us their blessings, for they are thy
dearest.

2 The various doings of all mortal people
by thee are ordered, in thy wisdom,
Indra.
The host of Maruts goeth forth exulting
to win the light-bestowing spoil of battle.

3 That spear of thine sat firm for us, O
Indra : the Maruts set their whole
dread power in motion.
E'en Agni shines resplendent in the brushwood : the viands hold him as floods
hold an island.

4 Vouchsafe us now that opulence, O Indra,
as guerdon won by mightiest donation.
May hymns that please thee cause the
breast of Vāyu to swell as with the
mead's refreshing sweetness.

5 With thee, O Indra, are most bounteous
riches that further every one who lives
uprightly.
Now may these Maruts show us loving-
kindness, Gods who of old were ever
prompt to help us.

6 Bring forth the Men who rain down
boons, O Indra : exert thee in the
great terrestrial region;

9 *Pṛśni* : the mother of the Maruts. See I. 24. 3.
The monster : the mass of dark storm-clouds.

1 *These who approach us* : the Maruts.
3 *Sat firm* : was firmly and properly held by the
Warrior-God.
6 *The Men* : the Maruts. Their chariot is drawn
by spotted deer.

For their broad-chested speckled deer are
standing like a King's armies on the
field of battle.

7 Heard is the roar of the advancing
Maruts, terrific, glittering, and swiftly
moving,
Who with their rush o'erthrow as 'twere
a sinner the mortal who would fight
with those who love him

8 Give to the Mānas, Indra with Maruts,
gifts universal, gifts of cattle foremost.
Thou, God, art praised with Gods who
must be lauded. May we find strengthening food in full abundance.

HYMN CLXX. *Indra. Maruts.*

1. NAUGHT is to-day, to-morrow naught.
Who comprehends the mystery?
We must address ourselves unto another's
thought, and lost is then the hope we
formed.

2 The Maruts are thy brothers. Why, O
Indra, wouldst thou take our lives?
Agree with them in friendly wise, and do
not slay us in the fight.

3 Agastya, brother, why dost thou neglect
us, thou who art our friend?
We know the nature of thy mind. Verily
thou wilt give us naught.

4 Let them prepare the altar, let them kindle
fire in front : we two
Here will spread sacrifice for thee, that
the Immortal may observe.

5 Thou, Lord of Wealth, art Master of all
treasures, thou, Lord of friends, art thy
friends' best supporter.
O Indra, speak thou kindly with the
Maruts, and taste oblations in their
proper season.

HYMN CLXXI. *Maruts.*

1. To you I come with this mine adoration,
and with a hymn I crave the Strong
Ones' favour,

A hymn that truly makes you joyful,
Maruts. Suppress your anger and unyoke
your horses.

2 Maruts, to you this laud with prayer and
worship, formed in the mind and heart,
ye Gods, is offered.
Come ye to us, rejoicing in your spirit, for
ye are they who make our prayer effecr
tive.

3 The Maruts, praised by us, shall show us
favour; Maghavan, lauded, shall be most
propitious.
Maruts, may all our days that are to
follow be very pleasant, lovely and
triumphant.

4 I fled in terrror from this mighty Indra,
my body trembling in alarm, O Maruts.
Oblations meant for you had been made
ready; these have we set aside : for this
forgive us.

5 By whom the Mānas recognize the day-
springs, by whose strength at the dawn
of endless mornings,
Give us, thou Mighty, glory with Maruts.
fierce with the fierce, the Strong who
givest triumph.

6 Do thou, O Indra, guard the conquering
Heroes, and rid thee of thy wrath
against the Maruts,
With them, the wise, victorious and bestowing. May we find strengthening
food in full abundance.

HYMN CLXXII. *Maruts.*

1. WONDERFUL let your coming be, wondrous
with help, ye Bounteous Ones,
Maruts, who gleam as serpents gleam.

2 Far be from us, O Maruts, ye free givers,
your impetuous shaft;
Far from us be the stone ye hurl.

3 O Bounteous Givers, touch ye not, O
Maruts, Tṛṇaskanda's folk;
Lift ye us up that we may live.

---

8 *The Mānas* : men of the family of the poet Māna.

1 *Lost is then the hope we formed* : Indra appears to
have appropriated to himself the sacrifice intended for
the Maruts, who complain, accordingly, of their depen-
dence on another's will and of their disappointed hopes.
2 This is spoken by Agastya, who offered the sacrifice.
3 The Maruts complain that Agastya does not support their claim.
4 Spoken by Agastya to Indra. *We* : Agni and I.
The Immortal : Agni.
5 Agastya continues his conciliatory speech.

---

1 *Unyoke your horses* : stay with us and enjoy the
sacrifice. 'This hymn, again,' as Wilson remarks, 'indicates a sort of trimming between the worship of Indra
and the Maruts.'

---

3 Unable to translate the second hemistich satisfactorily, I have followed Sāyaṇa who takes *vdnāni* as an
adjective, lovely. Grassmann translates : 'May all our
days stand upright like beautiful trees,' and Ludwig suggests 'battling ? spears ? for *komyā vdnāni*. 'May our
trees (our lances) through our valour stand always erect.'
—Max Müller.
4 Agastya apologizes for having allowed Indra to
enjoy the offerings intended for the Maruts.
5 *By whom* : thou, Indra, by whom, etc.

---

1 *Who gleam as serpents gleam* : referring to the flashes
of lightning that accompany the Gods of storm.
2 *The stone* : the thunderbolt.
3 *Tṛṇaskanda's folk* : Tṛṇaskanda appears to be
the name of some chief not elsewhere mentioned. Wilson,
following Sāyaṇa, translates : 'protect my people (although I be) as insignificant as grass.'

HYMN CLXXIII. *Indra.*

1. THE praise-song let him sing forth bursting bird-like: sing we that hymn which like heaven's light expandeth,
   That the milk-giving cows may, unimpeded call to the sacred grass the Gods' assembly.

2 Let the Bull sing with Bulls whose toil is worship, with a loud roar like some wild beast that hungers.
   Praised God ! the glad priest brings his heart's devotion; the holy youth presents twofold oblation.

3 May the Priest come circling the measured stations, and with him bring the earth's autumnal fruitage.
   Let the Horse neigh led near, let the Steer bellow : let the Voice go between both worlds as herald,

4 To him we offer welcomest oblations, the pious bring their strength-inspiring praises.
   May Indra, wondrous in his might, accept them, car-borne and swift to move like the Nāsatyas.

5 Praise thou that Indra who is truly mighty, the car-borne Warrior, Maghavan the Hero;
   Stronger in war than those who fight against him, borne by strong steeds, who kills enclosing darkness;

6 Him who surpasses heroes in his greatness: the earth and heavens suffice not for his girdles.
   Indra endues the earth to be his garment, and, God-like, wears the heaven as 'twere a frontlet,

7 Thee, Hero, guardian of the brave in battles, who roamest in the van,—to draw thee hither,

Indra, the hosts agree beside the Soma, and joy, for his great actions, in the Chieftain.

8 Libations in the sea to thee are pleasant, when thy divine Floods come to cheer these people.
   To thee the Cow is sum of all things grateful when with the wish thou seekest men and princes.

9 So may we in this One be well befriended, well aided as it were through praise of chieftains,
   That Indra still may linger at our worship, as one led swift to work, to hear our praises.

10 Like men in rivalry extolling princes, our Friend be Indra, wielder of the thunder.
   Like true friends of some city's lord within them held in good rule with sacrifice they help him.

11 For every sacrifice makes Indra stronger, yea, when he goes around angry in spirit ;
   As pleasure at the ford invites the thirsty, as the long way brings him who gains his object.

12 Let us not here contend with Gods, O Indra, for here, O Mighty One, is thine own portion,
   The Great, whose Friends the bounteous Maruts honour, as with a stream, his song who pours oblations.

13 Addressed to thee is this our praise, O Indra : Lord of Bay Steeds, find us hereby advancement.
   So mayst thou lead us on, O God, to comfort. May we find strengthening food in full abundance.

---

1 *Let him sing* : let the Udgātar priest sing the Sāman or metrical hymn of praise, which spreads and blesses like the light of heaven.

2 *The Bull* : perhaps the institutor of the sacrifice; or Indra himself may be intended. Sāyaṇa offers both explanations.

The *Bulls* : the officiating priests.

Praised God ! : addressed to Indra. The meaning of the hemistich is obscure. The word *mithunā* (literally, pairs) which I have rendered in accordance with Sāyaṇa and Wilson, means according to Grassmann, 'both the worlds,' and according to Ludwig, 'the couples consisting of the sacrificers and the respective wives.'

3 *The Priest* : Agni, who is also the *Horse* and the *Steer*. *The measured stations* : the different fire-altars. *Fruitage* : grain for the oblation. *The Voice* : thunder.

4 *The Nāsatyas* : the Aśvins, whose chariot is famed for swiftness.

8 *In the sea* : reaching thee in the sea of air; or 'the sea' may mean the large reservoir of Soma juice. *The wish* : granting all their desires.

9 *In this One* : this one true friend Indra.

10 The stanza is difficult. Wilson, following Sāyaṇa, translates: 'Emulous in commendation like (those contending for the favour) of men, may Indra, the wielder of the thunderbolt, be equally (a friend) to us : like those who, desirous of his friendship (conciliate) the lord of a city (ruling) with good government, so do our intermediate (representatives) propitiate (Indra) with sacrifices.

11 Indra will come at last although he tarries now. We must wait patiently. The thirsty traveller comes to the stream and reaches his journey's end at last.

Wilson observes with truth that 'this hymn is in general elliptical and obscure.' A translator has to endeavour to give the probable meaning of the words as they stand, without venturing on conjectural completion of fancied ellipses and the insertion of words at pleasure after the manner of Sāyaṇa.

HYMN CLXXIV. *Indra.*

1. THOU art the King of all the Gods, O
   Indra : protect the men, O Asura,
   preserve us.
   Thou Lord of Heroes, Maghavan, our
   saver, art faithful, very rich, the victory-
   giver.

2 Indra, thou humbledst tribes that spake
   with insult by breaking down seven
   autumn forts, their refuge.
   Thou stirredst, Blameless ! billowy floods,
   and gavest his foe a prey to youthful
   Purukutsa.

3 With whom thou drivest troops whose
   lords are heroes, and bringest daylight
   now, much worshipped Indra,
   With them guard lion-like wasting active
   Agni to dwell in our tilled fields and in
   our homestead.

4 They through the greatness of thy spear,
   O Indra, shall, to thy praise, rest in
   this earthly station.
   To loose the floods, to seek, for kine, the
   battle, his Bays he mounted boldly
   seized the booty.

5 Indra, bear Kutsa, him in whom thou
   joyest : the dark-red horses of the Wind
   are docile.
   Let the Sun roll his chariot wheel anear
   us, and let the Thunderer go to meet
   the foemen.

6 Thou Indra, Lord of Bays, made strong
   by impulse, hast slain the vexers of thy
   friends, who give not.
   They who beheld the Friend beside the
   living were cast aside by thee as they
   rode onward.

7 Indra, the bard sang forth in inspiration:
   thou madest earth a covering for the
   Dāsa.

Maghavan made the three that gleam
with moisture, and to his home brought
Kuyavāc to slay him.

8 These thine old deeds new bards have
   sung, O Indra. Thou conqueredst,
   boundest many tribes for ever.
   Like castles thou hast crushed the godless
   races, and bowed the godless scorner's
   deadly weapon.

9 A Stormer thou hast made the stormy
   waters flow down, O Indra, like the
   running rivers.
   When o'er the flood thou broughtest them,
   O Hero, thou keptest Turvaśa and
   Yadu safely.

10 Indra, mayst thou be ours in all occasions,
   protector of the men, most gentle-
   hearted,
   Giving us victory over all our rivals. May
   we find strengthening food in full
   abundance.

HYMN CLXXV. *Indra.*

1. GLAD thee : thy glory hath been quaffed,
   Lord of Bay Steeds, as 'twere the bowl's
   enlivening mead.
   For thee the Strong there is strong drink,
   mighty, omnipotent to win.

2 Let our strong drink, most excellent, exhilarating, come to thee,
   Victorious, Indra ! bringing gain, immortal
   conquering in fight,

3 Thou, Hero, winner of the spoil, urgest
   to speed the car of man.
   Burn, like a vessel with the flame, the
   lawless Dasyu, Conqueror !

4 Empowered by thine own might, O Sage,
   thou stolest Sūrya's chariot wheel.
   Thou barest Kutsa with the steeds of
   Wind to Śuṣṇa as his death.

5 Most mighty is thy rapturous joy, most
   splendid is thine active power,
   Wherewith, foe-slaying, sending bliss, thou
   art supreme in gaining steeds.

1 *The men* : the priests. *Us* : thy worshippers.
Asura : immortal and divine.

2 *Autumn forts* : probably strongholds on high ground
occupied in the rainy season. *Purukutsa* : has been mentioned before. See I. 63. 7.

3 *With whom* : the Maruts.

4 *They* : the enemy, *He* : Indra.

5 *Kutsa* : the Ṛṣi of that name. Wilson paraphrases
after Sāyaṇa : 'Bear (the sage) Kutsa to that ceremony
(to which) thou desirest (to convey him).'

6 *Who give not* : who offer no oblations; barbarians
who do not worship the Gods of the Āryans. *The Friend* :
Indra. *Beside the living* : Āyu, the living, may perhaps
be a proper name here.

7 *The three that gleam with moisture* : what the three
are is not clear. Wilson translates : 'has made the three
(regions) marvellous by his gifts.' Some reference to
three mornings appears to be intended. *Kuyavāc* :
probably the name of a demon, or barbarian.

9 *Turvaśa* and *Yadu* : eponymi of Āryan tribes. See
I. 36. 8.

1 *Thy glory hath been quaffed* : thou hast drunk what
incites thee to glorious deeds, namely the Soma juice
contained in the bowl.

4 *Thou stolest Sūrya's chariot wheel* : Indra is said to
have taken the wheel of the chariot of the Sun and to have
cast it like a quoit against the demon of drought.
Kutsa : the Ṛṣi mentioned in the preceding hymn.
Indra defended him against Śuṣṇa, or protected mankind from drought. See I. 51. 6.

5 *Most mighty is thy rapturous joy* : Wilson translates ;
'Thy inebriety is most intense.' See I. 51. 2,

6 As thou, O Indra, to the ancient singers
wast ever joy, as water to the thirsty,
So unto thee I sing this invocation. May
we find strengthening food in full
abundance.

HYMN CLXXVI. *Indra.*

1. CHEER thee with draughts to win us
bliss : Soma, pierce Indra in thy strength.
Thou stormest trembling in thy rage,
and findest not a foeman nigh.

2 Make our songs penetrate to him who is
the Only One of men;
For whom the sacred food is spread, as the
steer ploughs the barley in.

3 Within whose hands deposited all the Five
Peoples' treasures rest.
Mark thou the man who injures us and
kill him like the heavenly bolt.

4 Slay everyone who pours no gift, who,
hard to reach, delights thee not.
Bestow on us what wealth he hath : this
even the worshipper awaits.

5 Thou helpest him the doubly strong whose
hymns were sung unceasingly.
When Indra fought, O Soma, thou helpest
the mighty in the fray.

6 As thou, O Indra, to the ancient singers
wast ever joy, like water to the thirsty,
So unto thee I sing this invocation. May
we find strengthening food in full
abundance.

HYMN CLXXVII. *Indra.*

1. THE Bull of men, who cherishes all
people, King of the Races, Indra, called
of many,
Fame-loving, praised, hither to me with
succour turn having yoked both vigorous
Bay Horses !

2 Thy mighty Stallions, yoked by prayer,
O Indra, thy Coursers to thy mighty
chariot harnessed,—
Ascend thou these, and borne by them
come hither : with Soma juice out-
poured, Indra, we call thee.

3 Ascend thy mighty car : the mighty
Soma is poured for thee and sweets are
sprinkled round us.
Come down to us-ward, Bull of human
races, come, having harnessed them,
with strong Bay Horses.

4 Here is God-reaching sacrifice, here the
victim; here, Indra, are the prayers,
here is the Soma.
Strewn is the sacred grass : come hither,
Śakra; seat thee and drink : unyoke
thy two Bay Coursers.

5 Come to us, Indra, come thou highly lauded to the devotions of the singer Māna.
Singing, may we find early through thy
succour, may we find strengthening food
in full abundance.

HYMN CLXXVIII. *Indra.*

1. IF, Indra, thou hast given that gracious
hearing wherewith thou helpest those
who sang thy praises.
Blast not the wish that would exalt us :
may I gain all from thee, and pay all
man's devotions.

2 Let not the Sovran Indra disappoint us in
what shall bring both Sisters to our
dwelling.
To him have run the quickly flowing
waters. May Indra come to us with life
and friendship.

3 Victorious with the men, Hero in battles,
Indra, who hears the singer's supplication,
Will bring his car nigh to the man who
offers, if he himself upholds the songs
that praise him.

4 Yea, Indra, with the men, through love of
glory consumes the sacred food which
friends have offered.
The ever-strengthening song of him who
worships is sung in fight amid the clash
of voices.

5 Aided by thee, O Maghavan, O Indra,
may we subdue our foes who count
them mighty.
Be our protector, strengthen and increase
us. May we find strengthening food
in full abundance.

HYMN CLXXX. *Aśvins.*

1. LIGHTLY your coursers travel through the
regions when round the sea of air your
car is flying.

---

3. *The Five Peoples' treasures* : the wealth of all the
Āryans. See I. 7. 9.

1 *The Bull* : the hero, or chief distinguished by
superior strength.

2—3 The word here rendered by 'mighty' (*vṛṣan*)
is commonly applied in the Veda to living beings and
things preëminent for strength, and the Vedic poets
delight in repeating it and its compounds and derivatives.
'But this is nothing yet,' observes Prof. Max Müller.
'compared to other passages, when the poet cannot get
enough of vṛṣan and vṛṣabha.' Cf. II. 16. 6; V. 36. 5;
V. 40 2, 3; VIII. 13. 31—33.

2 *Both Sisters* : Night and Morning. *The quickly
flowing waters* : for the libations.

For Hymn CLXXIX. See Appendix.

Your golden fellies scatter drops of moisture : drinking the sweetness ye atend the Mornings.

2 Ye as ye travel overtake the Courser who flies apart, the Friend of man, most holy.
The prayer is that the Sister may convey you, all praised, meath-drinkers ! to support and strengthen.

3 Ye have deposited, matured within her, in the raw cow the first milk of the milch-cow,
Which the bright offerer, shining like a serpent mid trees, presents to you whose form is perfect.

4 Ye made the fierce heat to be full of sweetness for Atri at his wish, like streaming water.
Fire-offering thence is yours, O Aśvins, Heroes : your car-wheels speed to us like springs of honey.

5 Like Tugra's ancient son may I, ye Mighty, bring you to give your gifts with milk-oblations.
Your greatness compasseth Earth, Heaven, and Waters : decayed for you is sorrow's net, ye Holy.

6 When, Bounteous Ones, ye drive your yoked team downward, ye send, by your own natures, understanding.
Swift as the wind let the prince please and feast you : he, like a pious man, gains strength for increase.

7 For verily we truthful singers praise you : the niggard trafficker is here excluded.
Now, even now do ye O blameless Aśvins, ye Mighty, guard the man whose God is near him.

8 You of a truth day after day, O Aśvins, that he might win the very plenteous torrent,

Agastya, famous among mortal heroes, roused with a thousand lauds like sounds of music.

9 When with the glory of your car ye travel, when we go speeding like the priest of mortals,
And give good horses to sacrificers, may we, Nāsatyas ! gain our share of riches.

10 With songs of praise we call to-day, O Aśvins, that your new chariot, for our own well-being,
That circles heaven with never-injured fellies. May we find strengthening food in full abundance.

HYMN CLXXXI.   *Aśvins*

1. WHAT, dearest Pair, is this in strength and riches that ye as Priests are bringing from the waters ?
This sacrifice is your glorification, ye who protect mankind and give them treasures.

2 May your pure steeds, rain-drinkers, bring you hither, swift as the tempest, your celestial coursers,
Rapid as thought, with fair backs, full of vigour, resplendent in their native light, O Aśvins.

3 Your car is like a torrent rushing downward : may it come nigh, broad-seated, for our welfare,—
Car holy, strong, that ever would be foremost, thought-swift, which ye, for whom we long, have mounted.

4 Here sprung to life, they both have sung together, with bodies free from stain, with signs that mark them ;
One of you Prince of Sacrifice, the Victor, the other counts as Heaven's auspicious offspring.

5 May your car-seat, down-gliding, golden-coloured, according to your wish approach our dwellings.
Men shall feed full the bay steeds of the other, and, Aśvins they with roars shall stir the regions.

6 Forth comes your strong Bull like a cloud of autumn, sending abundant food of liquid sweetness.

9 When you assist the pious chiefs in battle, and they win the spoil, let the priests who officiated at the sacrifices which won that aid receive their due share of the booty as their reward.

---

2 *The Courser* : the Sun. *The Sister* : Uṣas, Dawn.

3 *The first milk* : ye deposited the milk within the Cosmic Cow, and this is found unaltered in the cows of earth.

The bright offerer : I follow Roth in taking this to be the fire, creeping through the fuel as a snake that creeps and gleams through the bushes. But the hemistich is very difficult and the meaning is doubtful. Wilson, after Sāyaṇa, paraphrases : '(as vigilant in the midst of the ceremony) as a thief (in the midst) of a thicket.' Ludwig says that *hvārā* means neither snake nor thief, but a tub or wooden vessel.

4 *Atri* : See I. 112. 7.

5 *Tugra's ancient son* : See I. 117. 4. *Greatness* : I adopt Ludwig's conjecture *māhimā* for *māhinā*.

6 *The prince* : the institutor of the sacrifice.

8 *The very plenteous torrent* : to obtain abundance of rain. *Agastya* : the Ṛṣi of the hymn.

---

1 *From the waters* : from the firmament
6 *Your strong Bull* : your swift chariot Wilson remarks : 'This and the preceding stanza are not very explicit in the comparison which is intimated between the functions of the two Aśvins, for the use of *anyasya*, of the other, in the second half of the verse, is all that intimates that *ekasya*, of the one, is understood in the first half.'

Let them feed with the other's ways and vigour : the upper streams have come and do us service.

7 Your constant song hath been sent forth, Disposers ! that flows threefold in mighty strength, O Aśvins.

Thus lauded, give the suppliant protection : moving or resting hear mine invocation.

8 This song of bright contents for you is swelling in the men's hall where threefold grass is ready.

Your strong rain-cloud, ye Mighty Ones, hath swollen, honouring men as 'twere with milk's outpouring.

9 The prudent worshipper, like Pūṣan, Aśvins ! praises you as he praises Dawn and Agni,

When, singing with devotion, he invokes you. May we find strengthening food in full abundance.

HYMN CLXXXII.   *Aśvins.*

1. THIS was the task. Appear promptly, ye prudent Ones. Here is the chariot drawn by strong steeds : be ye glad.

Heart-stirring, longed for, succourers of Viśpalā, here are Heaven's Sons whose sway blesses the pious man.

2 Longed for, most Indra-like, mighty, most Marut-like, most wonderful in deed, car-borne, best charioteers,

Bring your full chariot hither heaped with liquid sweet : thereon, ye Aśvins, come to him who offers gifts.

3 What make ye there, ye Mighty ? Wherefore linger ye with folk who, offering not, are held in high esteem ?

Pass over them ; make ye the niggard's life decay : give light unto the singer eloquent in praise.

4 Crunch up on every side the dogs who bark at us : slay ye our foes, O Aśvins ; this ye understand.

Make wealthy every word of him who praises you : accept with favour, both Nāsatyas, this my laud.

5 Ye made for Tugra's son amid the water-floods that animated ship with wings to fly withal,

Whereon with God-devoted mind ye brought him forth, and fled with easy flight from out the mighty surge.

6 Four ships most welcome in the midst of ocean, urged by the Aśvins, save the son of Tugra,

Him who was cast down headlong in the waters, plunged in the thick inevitable darkness.

7 What tree was that which stood fixed in surrounding sea to which the son of Tugra supplicating clung ?

Like twigs, of which some winged creature may take hold, ye, Aśvins, bore him off safely to your renown.

8 Welcome to you be this the hymn of praises uttered by Mānas, O Nāsatyas, Heroes,

From this our gathering where we offer Soma. May we find strengthening food in full abundance.

HYMN CLXXXIII.   *Aśvins.*

1. MAKE ready that which passes thought in swiftness, that hath three wheels and triple seat, ye Mighty,

Whereon ye seek the dwelling of the pious, whereon, threefold, ye fly like birds with pinions.

2 Light rolls your easy chariot faring earthward, what time, for food, ye, full of wisdom, mount it.

May this song, wondrous fair, attend your glory : ye, as ye travel, wait on Dawn Heaven's Daughter.

3 Ascend your lightly rolling car, approaching the worshipper who turns him to his duties,—

Whereon ye come unto the house to quicken man and his offspring, O Nāsatyas, Heroes.

4 Let not the wolf, let not the she-wolf harm you. Forsake me not, nor pass me by for others.

---

7 *That flows threefold* : from three priests.

8 *Threefold grass* : sacred grass arranged to form three layers or seats.

9 *As he praises Dawn and Agni* : that is, at the morning sacrifice.

---

1 *This was the task* : this sacrifice is the work at which you have to preside.

Be ye glad : delight yourselves with the Soma juice.

Succourers of Viśpalā : by giving her an iron leg. See I. 116. 15. Or the word in the text may mean, as explained by Sāyaṇa, 'rich in benevolence to men.'

---

5 *Tugra's son* : see I. 116. 3, 4.

6 *In the midst of ocean* : I can make nothing of the *jaṭhalasya* of the text, and insert these words as substitute for translation.

7 *What tree was that* : figuratively of the Aśvins who saved him, as, in a sudden inundation, a tree saves the man who climbs it. An ingenious interpretation of the legend will be found in M. Bergaigne's *La Religion Védique*, III. 10. 17.

---

1 The three-wheeled chariot of the Aśvins has been mentioned before, See I. 34. 1.

4 *Let not the wolf* : let no enemy prevent your coming. Ludwig thinks that there is an ironical reference to the

Here stands your share, here is your hymn,
ye Mighty : yours are these vessels, full
of pleasant juices.

5 Gotama, Purumīḷha, Atri bringing oblations
all invoke you for protection.
Like one who goes straight to the point
directed, come, ye Nāsatyas, to mine
invocation.

6 We have passed o'er the limit of this darkness : our praise hath been bestowed
on you, O Aśvins.
Come hitherward by paths which Gods
have travelled. May we find strengthening food in full abundance.

HYMN CLXXXIV   *Aśvins.*

1. LET us invoke you both this day and
after the priest is here with lauds when
morn is breaking :
Nāsatyas, wheresoe'er ye be, Heaven's
Children, for him who is more liberal
than the godless.

2 With us, ye Mighty, let yourselves be
joyful, glad in our stream of Soma slay
the niggards.
Graciously hear my hymns and invitations,
marking, O Heroes, with your ears my
longing.

3 Nāsatyas, Pūṣans, ye as Gods for glory
arranged and set in order Sūryā's bridal.
Your giant steeds move on, sprung from
the waters, like ancient times of Varuṇa
the Mighty.

4 Your grace be with us, ye who love sweet
juices : further the hymn sung by the
poet Māna,
When men are joyful in your glorious
actions, to win heroic strength, ye
Bounteous Givers.

5 This praise was made, O liberal Lords,
O Aśvins, for you with fair adornment
by the Mānas.
Come to our house for us and for our
children, rejoicing, O Nāsatyas, in
Agastya.

6 We have passed o'er the limit of this darkness : our praise hath been bestowed on
you, O Aśvins.

wolf from whose jaws the Aśvins rescued the quail. See
I. 117. 16.

5 *Gotama, Purumīḷha, Atri* : sages favoured by the
Aśvins.

———

3 *Pūṣans* : ye who cherish men like Pūṣan himself.
Sūryā : the daughter of the Sun and the consort
of the Aśvins. See I. 116. 17. *Giant steeds* : cf. I. 46. 3.
What the times or ages of Varuṇa are is uncertain.

———

Come hitherward by paths which Gods
have travelled. May we find strengthening food in full abundance.

HYMN CLXXXV. *Heaven and Earth.*

1. WHETHER of these is elder, whether later?
How were they born? Who knoweth
it, ye sages?
These of themselves support all things
existing : as on a car the Day and Night
roll onward.

2 The Twain uphold, though motionless and
footless, a widespread offspring having
feet and moving.
Like your own son upon his parents' bosom,
protect us, Heaven and earth, from fearful danger.

3 I call for Aditi's unrivalled bounty, perfect,
celestial, deathless, meet for worship.
Produce this, ye Twain Worlds, for him
who lauds you. Protect us, Heaven and
Earth, from fearful danger.

4 May we be close to both the Worlds who
suffer no pain, Parents of Gods, who aid
with favour,
Both mid the Gods, with Day and Night
alternate. Protect us, Heaven and Earth,
from fearful danger.

5 Faring together, young, with meeting limits,
Twin Sisters lying in their Parents'
bosom,
Kissing the centre of the world together.
Protect us, Heaven and Earth, from
fearful danger.

6 Duly I call the two wide seats, the mighty,
the general Parents, with the God's protection.
Who, beautiful to look on, make the nectar.
Protect us, Heaven and Earth, from
fearful danger.

7 Wide, vast, and manifold, whose bounds
are distant,—these, reverent, I address
at this our worship,
The blessed Pair, victorious, all-sustaining.
Protect us, Heaven and Earth, from
fearful danger.

3 *Aditi's gift* : all the blessings of infinite Nature.
According to Sāyaṇa, Aditi means here the firmament,
in which case her gift would be seasonable rain and con-
sequent wealth.

4 *Parents of Gods* : as with the Greeks, Heaven and
Earth are regarded as the father and mother of the Gods.

5 The meaning is obscure. Ludwig suggests Daksa
and Aditi as the parents. *The centre of the world* means
usually the altar.

6 *With the God's protection* : to come to us with the
favouring help of the Gods. *The nectar* : the rain.

8 What sin we have at any time committed
  against the Gods, our friend, our house's
  chieftain,
  Thereof may this our hymn be expiation.
  Protect us, Heaven and Earth, from fearful danger.

9 May both these Friends of man, who
  bless, preserve me, may they attend me
  with their help and favour.
  Enrich the man more liberal than the
  godless. May we, ye Gods, be strong
  with food rejoicing.

10 Endowed with understanding, I have
  uttered this truth, for all to hear, to
  Earth and Heaven.
  Be near us, keep us from reproach and
  trouble. Father and Mother, with your
  help preserve us.

11 Be this my prayer fulfilled, O Earth and
  Heaven, wherewith, Father and Mother,
  I address you.
  Nearest of Gods be ye with your protection.
  May we find strengthening food in full
  abundance.

HYMN CLXXXVI. *Viśvedevas.*

1. LOVED of all men, may Savitar, through
  praises offered as sacred food, come to
  our synod,
  That you too, through our hymn, ye ever-
  youthful, may gladden, at your visit, all
  our people.

2 To us may all the Gods come trooped
  together, Aryaman, Mitra, Varuṇa
  concordant,
  That all may be promoters of our welfare,
  and with great might preserve our
  strength from slackness.

3 Agni I sing, the guest you love most
  dearly : the Conqueror through our
  lauds is friendly-minded :
  That he may be our Varuṇa rich in glory
  and send food like a prince praised by
  the godly.

4 To you I seek with reverence, Night and
  Morning, like a cow good to milk, with
  hope to conquer,

Preparing on a common day the praise-
  song with milk of various hues within
  this udder.

5 May the great Dragon of the Deep rejoice
  us : as one who nourishes her young
  comes Sindhu,
  With whom we will incite the Child of
  Waters whom vigorous course swift as
  thought bring hither.

6 Moreover Tvaṣṭar also shall approach us,
  one-minded with the princes at his
  visit.
  Hither shall come the Vṛtra-slayer Indra,
  Ruler of men, as strongest of the Heroes.

7 Him too our hymns delight, that yoke
  swift horses, like mother cows who lick
  their tender youngling.
  To him our songs shall yield themselves
  like spouses, to him the most delightful
  of the Heroes.

8 So may the Maruts, armed with mighty
  weapons, rest here on heaven and earth
  with hearts in concord,
  As Gods whose cars have dappled steeds
  like torrents, destroyers of the foe allies
  of Mitra.

9 They hasten on to happy termination their
  orders when they are made known by
  glory.
  As on a fair bright day the arrow flieth,
  o'er all the barren soil their missiles
  sparkle.

10 Incline the Aśvins to show grace, and
  Pūṣan, for power and might have they,
  their own possession.
  Friendly are Viṣṇu, Vāta, and Ṛbhukṣan :
  so may I bring the Gods to make us
  happy.

11 This is my reverent thought of you, ye
  Holy ; may it inspire you, make you
  dwell among us,—
  Thought, toiling for the Gods and seeking
  treasure. May we find strengthening
  food in full abundance.

Milk of various hues : the libations of milk mixed with
the yellow or brown Soma juice.
  This udder : apparently a figurative expression for the
place of sacrifice whence the milky libations flow.
  5 *Dragon of the Deep* : Ahibudhnya, a divine being
that dwells in, and presides over the firmament. *Sindhu* :
the Indus.
  The Child of Waters : Agni.
  6 *Tvaṣṭar* : the heavenly artist. *The princes* : institutors of the sacrifice.
  7 *That yoke swift horses* : that quickly bring the Gods
to the sacrifice.
  Their tender youngling : Sāyaṇa takes the epithet *tdru-
ṇam* as applying to Indra 'the ever-youthful.'
  10 *Ṛbhukṣan* : a name of Indra as Lord of the Ṛbhus.
See I. 162. 1.

1 *Savitar* : the Sun, especially regarded as the vivifier
and generator. *Ye ever youthful* : Viśvedevas, or All-
Gods.
  3 *Our Varuṇa* : our lord and protector.
  4 *Like a cow* : the singer is the cow and his hymn
the milk.
  With hope to conquer : to overcome sins, according
to Sāyaṇa.
  A common day : belonging to the past night and the
present morning.

HYMN CLXXXVII. *Praise of Food.*

1. Now will I glorify Food that upholds
   great strength,
   By whose invigorating power Trita rent
   Vṛtra limb from limb.

2 O pleasant Food, O Food of meath, thee
   have we chosen for our own,
   So be our kind protector thou.

3 Come hitherward to us, O Food, auspicious with auspicious help,
   Health-bringing, not unkind, a dear and
   guileless friend.

4 These juices which, O Food, are thine
   throughout the regions are diffused.
   Like winds they have their place in heaven.

5 These gifts of thine, O Food, O Food most
   sweet to taste,
   These savours of thy juices work like
   creatures that have mighty necks.

6 In thee, O Food, is set the spirit of great
   Gods.
   Under thy flag brave deeds were done :
   he slew the Dragon with thy help.

7 If thou be gone unto the splendour of the
   clouds,
   Even from thence, O Food of meath,
   prepared for our enjoyment, come.

8 Whatever morsel we consume from waters
   or from plants of earth, O Soma, wax
   thou fat thereby.

9 What, Soma, we enjoy from thee in milky
   food or barley-brew, Vātāpi, grow thou
   fat thereby.

10 O Vegetable, Cake of meal, be wholesome,
   firm, and strengthening :
   Vātāpi, grow thou fat thereby.

11 O Food, from thee as such have we drawn
   forth with lauds, like cows, our sacrificial
   gifts,
   From thee who banquetest with Gods, from
   thee who banquetest with us.

1 *Trita* : a mysterious ancient deity frequently mentioned in the Ṛgveda, principally in connexion with Indra, Vāyu, and the Maruts. His home is in the remotest part of heaven, and he is called Āptya, the Watery, that is, sprung from, or dwelling in the sea of cloud and vapour. By Sāyaṇa he is identified sometimes with Vāyu, sometimes with Indra as the pervader of the three worlds, and sometimes with Agni stationed in the three fire-receptacles.

2 The God addressed is the Soma.

5 *Like creatures that have mighty necks* : like strong bullocks.

6 *The spirit of great Gods* : thou incitest Indra and the Gods to perform glorious and benevolent acts.

9 *Vātāpi* : the fermenting Soma. According to Sāyaṇa, the body.

HYMN CLXXXVIII. *Āpris*

1. WINNER of thousands, kindled, thou shinest
   a God with Gods to-day.
   Bear out oblations, envoy, Sage.

2 Child of Thyself the sacrifice is for the
   righteous blent with meath,
   Presenting viands thousandfold.

3 Invoked and worthy of our praise bring
   Gods whose due is sacrifice :
   Thou, Agni, givest countless gifts.

4 To seat a thousand Heroes they eastward
   have strewn the grass with might,
   Whereon, Ādityas, ye shine forth.

5 The sovran all-imperial Doors, wide, good,
   many and manifold,
   Have poured their streams of holy oil.

6 With gay adornment, fair to see, in glorious beauty shine they forth :
   Let Night and Morning rest them here.

7 Let these two Sages first of all, heralds
   divine and eloquent,
   Perform for us this sacrifice.

8 You I address, Sarasvatī, and Bhāratī,
   and Iḷā, all :
   Urge ye us on to glorious fame.

9 Tvaṣṭar the Lord hath made all forms
   and all the cattle of the field :
   Cause them to multiply for us.

10 Send to the Gods, Vanaspati, thyself, the
   sacrificial draught :
   Let Agni make the oblations sweet.

11 Agni, preceder of the Gods, is honoured
   with the sacred song :
   He glows at offerings blest with Hail !

HYMN CLXXXIX. *Agni.*

1. BY goodly paths lead us to riches, Agni,
   God who knowest every sacred duty.
   Remove the sin that makes us stray and
   wander : most ample adoration will we
   bring thee.

The Āpris are the various forms of Agni, according to Sāyaṇa, which are invoked in the hymn.

1 *Thou* : Agni.

2 *Child of Thyself* : Agni. See I. 13.2.

4 *Ādityas* : See I. 14. 3.

5 *The sovran all-imperial Doors* : of the sacrificial hall through which Gods enter. They are types of the portals of the East through which light comes into the world. See Wallis, *Cosmology of the Ṛgveda*, p. 19.

7 *These two Sages* : heralds or invokers, because they call the Gods. See I. 13. 8.

8 *Sarasvatī and Bhāratī and Iḷā* : See I. 13. 9.

10 *Vanaspati* : see I. 13. 11.

11 *Blest with Hail* : See I. 13. 12.

This hymn, as Ludwig observes, appears to have been composed at a time of pestilence.

2 Lead us anew to happiness, O Agni; lead
us beyond all danger and affliction.

Be unto us a wide broad ample castle :
bless, prosper on their way our sons and
offspring.

3 Far from us, Agni, put thou all diseases :
let them strike lauds that have no saving
Agni.

God, make our home again to be a blessing, with all the Immortal Deities, O
Holy.

4 Preserve us, Agni, with perpetual succour,
refulgent in the dwelling which thou
lovest.

O Conqueror, most youthful, let no danger
touch him who praises thee to-day or
after.

5 Give not us up a prey to sin, O Agni, the
greedy enemy that brings us trouble ;

Not to the fanged that bites, not to the
toothless : give not us up, thou Conqueror, to the spoiler.

6 Such as thou art, born after Law, O Agni
when lauded give protection to our
bodies,

From whosoever would reproach or injure:
for thou, God, rescuest from all oppression.

7 Thou, well discerning both these classes,
comest to men at early morn, O holy
Agni.

Be thou obedient unto man at evening, to
be adorned, as keen, by eager suitors.

8 To him have we addressed our pious
speeches, I, Māna's son, to him victorious
Agni.

May we gain countless riches with the
sages. May we find strengthening food
in full abundance.

HYMN CXC.   Bṛhaspati.

1. GLORIFY thou Bṛhaspati, the scatheless,
who must be praised with hymns, sweet-
tongued and mighty,

To whom as leader of the song, resplendent, worthy of lauds, both Gods and
mortals listen.

2 On him wait songs according to the season
even as a stream of pious men set
moving.

Bṛhaspati—for he laid out the expanses—
was, at the sacrifice, vast Mātariśvan.

3 The praise, the verse that offers adoration,
may he bring forth, as the Sun sends
his arms out,

He who gives daily light through this
God's wisdom, strong as a dread wild
beast, and inoffensive.

4 His song of praise pervades the earth and
heaven : let the wise worshipper draw
it, like a courser.

These of Bṛhaspati, like hunters' arrows,
go to the skies that change their hue
like serpents.

5 Those, God, who count thee as a worthless
bullock, and, wealthy sinners, live on
thee the Bounteous,—

On fools like these no blessing thou bestowest : Bṛhaspati, thou punishest the
spiteful.

6 Like a fair path is he, where grass is
pleasant, though hard to win, a Friend
beloved most dearly.

Those who unharmed by enemies behold
us, while they would make them bare,
stood closely compassed.

1 *Bṛhaspati* : Lord of Prayer. See I. 14. 3.

2 *For he laid out the expanses* : spread out and revealed to the eyes of men the broad regions of heaven
and earth. The meaning of the second hemistich is not
clear. Wilson paraphrases : 'for that Bṛhaspati is the
manifestor (of all), the expansive wind that (diffusing)
blessings has been produced for (the diffusion of) water.'
There seems to be nothing in the Ṛgveda to justify the
identification of Mātariśvan with the wind, and only in
the later language has ṛtá the sense of water. See I.31.3.

3 *He* : Bṛhaspati. *He who gives daily light* : the
regular appearance of the Sun depends upon Bṛhaspati's
wisdom.

Inoffensive : arakṣdsaḥ, according to Sāyaṇa, 'free
from the opposition of Rākṣasas.'

4 *These of Bṛhaspati* : these sacred songs, compared
to arrows.

That change their hue like serpents : dhimāyān. See
I. 3. 9.

6 This stanza is unintelligible to me. Wilson renders
it : 'Be a (pleasant) way to him who goes well and makes
good offerings, like the affectionate friend of (a ruler
who) restrains the bad; and may those sinless men who
instruct us, although yet enveloped (by ignorance) stand
extricated from their covering'; and remarks : 'it is
not clear how those who are enveloped by ignorance
should be competent to teach : another explanation is,
let those who revile us, and are being protected, be
deprived of that protection.'

3 *That have no saving Agni* : or, which do not maintain the sacred fire ; whose inhabitants do not worship
Agni.

5 *The fanged* : venomous serpents. *The toothless* :
wild animals that do not bite, but injure with their
horns, etc.

7 *Both these classes* : worshippers and non-worship-
pers.

Be thou obedient : be a useful servant in the house.

As keen : akrdḥ, applied to Agni in all the places
where it occurs in the Ṛgveda, appears to mean hasty,
violent, eager, or keen. Ludwig thinks that it means
here a sacrificial post, and Grassmann, a banner. Wilson,
following Sāyaṇa, paraphrases : 'be compliant (with
his wishes); like an institutor of the rite, (who is directed)
by the desires (of the priests).

7 He to whom songs of praise go forth like torrents, as rivers eddying under banks flow sea-ward—

Bṛhaspati the wise, the eager, closely looks upon both, the waters and the vessel.

8 So hath Bṛhaspati, great, strong and mighty, the God exceeding powerful, been brought hither.

May he thus lauded give us kine and horses. May we find strengthening food in full abundance.

HYMN CXCI *Water. Grass. Sun.*

1. VENOMOUS, slightly venomous, or venomous aquatic worm,—

Both creatures, stinging, unobserved, with poison have infected me.

2 Coming, it kills the unobserved; it kills them as it goes away,

It kills them as it drives them off, and bruising bruises them to death.

3 Śara grass, Darbha, Kuśara, and Sairya, Muñja, Vīraṇa,

Where all these creatures dwell unseen, with poison have infected me.

4 The cows had settled in their stalls, the beasts of prey had sought their lairs,

Extinguished were the lights of men, when things unseen infected me.

5 Or these, these reptiles, are observed, like lurking thieves at evening time.

Seers of all, themselves unseen : be therefore very vigilant.

6 Heaven is your Sire, your Mother Earth, Soma your Brother, Aditi

Your Sister : seeing all, unseen, keep still and dwell ye happily.

7 Biters of shoulder or of limb, with needle-stings, most venomous,

Unseen, whatever ye may be, vanish together and be gone.

8 Slayer of things unseen, the Sun, beheld of all, mounts, eastward, up,

Consuming all that are not seen, and evil spirits of the night.

9 There hath the Sun-God mounted up, who scorches much and everything.

Even the Āditya from the hills, all-seen, destroying things unseen.

10 I hang the poison in the Sun, a wine-skin in a vintner's house,

He will not die, nor shall we die : his path is far : he whom Bay Horses bear hath turned thee to sweet meath.

11 This little bird, so very small, hath swallowed all thy poison up.

She will not die, nor shall we die : his path is far : he whom Bay Horses bear hath turned thee to sweet meath.

12 The three-times-seven bright sparks of fire have swallowed up the poison's strength.

They will not die, nor shall we die : his path is far : he whom Bay Horses bear hath turned thee to sweet meath.

13 Of ninety rivers and of nine with power to stay the venom's course,—

The names of all I have secured : his path is far : he whom Bay Horses bear hath turned thee to sweet meath.

7 This stanza also is very obscure. Bṛhaspati is said to look upon the waters and the vessel, that is the river to be crossed and the boat which is to be used, meaning perhaps the sacrifice and all that is used in performing it. Ludwig thinks that a play upon the words is intended, *āpaḥ* meaning both water and a religious ceremony and *táraḥ* both ferry-boat and prompt energy.

—

This so-called hymn is a spell or charm said to have been recited by Agastya when he suspected that he had been poisoned. Its silent repetition is said to be an effectual antidote against 'all venom in reptiles, insects, scorpions, roots, and artificial poisons.' I generally follow Sāyaṇa; but his explanations are not always satisfactory, and several passages must be left in their original obscurity.

1 The exact meaning of the words in the first line is uncertain.

Both creatures : both classes, either the venomous and the slightly venomous, or land-reptiles and water-snakes.

2 *Coming, it kills the unobserved* : the herb, used as an antidote, coming to the man who has been bitten kills the venomous creatures who secretly attacked him.

3 *Śara grass, etc.* : these are different sorts of grass in which snakes and other venomous reptiles lurk.

6 *Heaven*, or Dyaus, is here said to be the father of the snakes.

Soma : the Moon.

10 *I hang the poison in the Sun* : 'I deposit the poison in the solar orb, like a leather bottle in the house of a vendor of spirits'—Wilson. See Wilson's note in which he says that by the Sun or as Sāyaṇa paraphrases it, the orb of the Sun, 'is probably to be understood a mystical diagram, or figure wholly or partly typical of the solar orb : the Sun being considered as especially instrumental in counteracting the operation of poison.

He will not die : the Sun will not die from the effects of the poison thus applied, and we also who have been bitten shall through his favour recover.

11 *This little bird* : according to Sāyaṇa the bird which we call the francoline partridge, said to be a 'remover of poison.'

12 *Bright sparks of fire* : either, says Sāyaṇa, the seven flames of fire multiplied, or the twenty-one varieties of another kind of bird unaffected by eating poison.

13 *Of ninety rivers and of nine* : the numbers are used indefinitely for all the rivers of the country.

14 So have the peahens three-times-seven, so
   have the maiden Sisters Seven
   Carried thy venom far away, as girls
   bear water in their jars.
15 The poison-insect is so small ; I crush the
   creature with a stone.

I turn the poison hence away, departed
unto distant lands.
16 Forth issuing from the mountain's side
   the poison-insect spake and said :
   The scorpion's venom hath no strength ;
   Scorpion, thy venom is but weak.

---

14 *The peahens three-times-seven* : peafowls are regarded
as the great enemies of snakes. The number appears
to be merely fanciful and borrowed from verse 12.

The maiden Sisters Seven : the seven chief rivers of the
land.

15 As *kuṣumbha* means poison-bag, *kuṣumbhakáh* in

the text is taken by Ludwig and Grassmann to mean
venomous insect.

Sāyaṇa explains it as the *nakula*, nĕul or mungoose
whose hostility to the snake is proverbial. Wilson paraphrases : 'May the insignificant mungoose carry off
thy venom, (Poison) : if not, I will crush the vile (creature) with a stone.'

BOOK THE SECOND.

HYMN I. *Agni.*

1. Thou, Agni, shining in thy glory through the days, art brought to life from out the waters, from the stone :
From out the forest trees and herbs that grow on ground, thou, Sovran Lord of men art generatad pure.

2 Thine is the Herald's task and Cleanser's duly timed ; Leader art thou, and Kindler for the pious man.
Thou art Director, thou the ministering Priest : thou art the Brahman, Lord and Master in our home.

3 Hero of Heroes, Agni ! thou art Indra, thou art Viṣṇu of the Mighty Stride, adorable :
Thou, Brahmaṇaspati, the Brahman finding wealth : thou, O Sustainer, with thy wisdom tendest us.

4 Agni, thou art King Varuṇa whose laws stand fast ; as Mitra, Wonder-Worker, thou must be implored.
Aryaman, heroes' Lord, art thou, enriching all, and liberal Aṁśa in the synod, O thou God.

5 Thou givest strength, as Tvaṣṭar, to the worshipper : thou wielding Mitra's power hast kinship with the Dames.
Thou, urging thy fleet coursers, givest noble steeds : a host of heroes art thou with great store of wealth.

6 Rudra art thou, the Asura of mighty heaven : thou art the Maruts' host, thou art the Lord of food,
Thou goest with red winds : bliss hast thou in thine home. As Pūṣan thou thyself protectest worshippers.

7 Giver of wealth art thou to him who honours thee; thou art God Savitar, granter of precious things.
As Bhaga, Lord of men ! thou rulest over wealth, and guardest in his house him who hath served thee well.

8 To thee, the people's Lord within the house, the folk press forward to their King most graciously inclined.
Lord of the lovely look, all things belong to thee : ten, hundred, yea, a thousand are outweighed by thee.

9 Agni, men seek thee as a Father with their prayers, win thee, bright-formed, to brotherhood with holy act.
Thou art a Son to him who duly worships thee, and as a trusty Friend thou guardest from attack.

10 A Ṛbhu art thou, Agni, near to be adored ; thou art the Sovran Lord of foodful spoil and wealth.
Thou shinest brightly forth, thou burnest to bestow : pervading sacrifice, thou lendest us thine help.

11 Thou, God, art Aditi to him who offers gifts : thou, Hotrā, Bhāratī, art strengthened by the song.
Thou art the hundred-wintered Iḷā to give strength, Lord of Wealth ! Vṛtra-slayer and Sarasvatī.

12 Thou, Agni, cherished well, art highest vital power ; in thy delightful hue are glories visible.
Thou art the lofty might that furthers each design : thou art wealth manifold, diffused on every side.

The hymns of this Book, with the few exceptions that will be noted, are ascribed to the Ṛṣi Gṛtsamada. As Book I. is called the Book of the Śatarcins, that is of the seers of a hundred or large indefinite number of Ṛcas or verses, so this Book is commonly called the Gārtsamada Maṇḍala or Book of Gṛtsamada.

1 *Through the days* : for the days of sacrifice, according to Sāyaṇa.
The waters : from the waters of the firmament, as lightning.
From out the forest trees : in the frequently occurring conflagrations caused by the friction of dry branches. Agni is also said to have his home in plants, perhaps originally on account of a phosphorescent light which some plants emit.

2 Agni concentrates in himself the various functions of different classes of human priests, the most important of which are mentioned in the verse. The classification of the priests and the description of their duties are given with variations by different authorities. The Hotar or Herald invokes the Gods; the Potar, Purifier, or Cleanser, is the assistant of the Brahman or praying priest who remedies any defect in the ritual; the Neṣṭar or Leader leads forward the wife of the sacrificer ; the Agnīdh or Kindler lights the sacrificial fire; the Praśāstar or Director is the assistant of the Hotar ; and the Adhvaryu or ministering priest is the deacon who measures the ground, builds the altar, and makes all the preparations necessary for the sacrifice. The duties of the priests, however, varied at different times and according to the nature of the ceremony which they were engaged to perform.

3 *Viṣṇu of the Mighty Stride* : See I. 32. 16.

4 *Aṁśa* : the Distributor ; one of the Ādityas.

5 *The Dames* : the Consorts of the Gods.

11 *Hotrā, Bhāratī, Iḷā* are personifications of parts of religious worship. The epithet 'hundred-wintered' appears to refer to the natural duration of human life. *Sarasvatī* : See I. 3. 10.

13 Thee, Agni, have the Ādityas taken as
their mouth; the Bright Ones have
made thee, O Sage, to be their tongue.
They who love offerings cling to thee at
solemn rites : by thee the Gods devour
the duly offered food.

14 By thee, O Agni, all the Immortal guileless Gods eat with thy mouth the oblation that is offered them.
By thee do mortal men give sweetness to
their drink. Bright art thou born, the
embryo of the plants of earth.

15 With these thou art united, Agni; yea
thou, God of noble birth, surpassest
them in majesty,
Which, through the power of good, here
spreads abroad from thee, diffused
through both the worlds, throughout the
earth and heaven.

16 The princely worshippers who send to
those who sing thy praise, O Agni,
guerdon graced with kine and steeds,—
Lead thou both these and us forward to
higher bliss. With brave men in the
assembly may we speak aloud.

HYMN II.   *Agni.*

1. WITH sacrifice exalt Agni who knows all
life ; worship him with oblation and the
song of praise,
Well kindled, nobly fed; heaven's Lord,
Celestial Priest, who labours at the pole
where deeds of might are done.

2 At night and morning, Agni, have they
called to thee, like milch-kine in their
stalls lowing to meet their young.
As messenger of heaven thou lightest all
night long the families of men. thou
Lord of precious boons.

3 Him have the Gods established at the
region's base, doer of wondrous deeds,
Herald of heaven and earth;
Like a most famous car, Agni the purely
bright, like Mitra to be glorified among
the folk.

4 Him have they set in his own dwelling, in
the vault, like the Moon waxing, fulgent,
in the realm of air.

Bird of the firmament, observant with his
eyes, guard of the place as 'twere, looking to Gods and men.

5 May he as Priest encompass all the sacrifice : men throng to him with offerings
and with hymns of praise.
Raging with jaws of gold among the growing plants, like heaven with all the
stars, he quickens earth and sky.

6 Such as thou art, brilliantly kindled for
our weal, a liberal giver, send us riches
in thy shine,
For our advantage, Agni, God, bring
Heaven and Earth hither that they may
taste oblation brought by man.

7 Agni, give us great wealth, give riches
thousandfold : unclose to us, like doors,
strength that shall bring renown.
Make Heaven and Earth propitious
through the power of prayer, and like
the sky's bright sheen let mornings
beam on us.

8 Enkindled night by night at every morning's dawn, may he shine forth with red
flame like the realm of light,—
Agni adored in beauteous rites with lauds
of men, fair guest of living man and
King of all our folk.

9 Song chanted by us men, O Agni, Ancient
One, has swelled unto the deathless
Gods in lofty heaven—
A milch-cow yielding to the singer in the
rites wealth manifold, in hundreds, even
as he wills.

10 Agni, may we show forth our valour with
the steed or with the power of prayer
beyond all other men;
And over the Five Races let our glory
shine high like the realm of light and
unsurpassable.

11 Such, Conqueror ! be to us, be worthy of
our praise, thou for whom princes nobly
born exert themselves;
Whose sacrifice the strong seek, Agni,
when it shines for never-failing offspring
in thine own abode.

Guard of the place : of the most sacred place, the altar.

8 *May he* : Agni.

9 *A milch-cow* : the hymn of praise brings riches to
the worshipper.

10 *With the steed* : with the war-car in battle as well
as with prayers in sacrifices.

The Five Races : the five great Āryan tribes. See
I. 7. 9.

11 *The strong* : the wealthy worshippers.

Never-failing offspring : one of the chief rewards of the
worship of Agni.

---

16 *With brave men* : attended by brave sons, who will
support and strengthen us.

---

1 *Who labours at the pole* : who takes the chief part in
the performance of all-important sacrifice. A metaphor
from oxen drawing a car or wain.

2 *Have they called* : the priests.

3 *At the region's base* : at the altar, according to
Sāyaṇa.

4 The word *hvāre*, here rendered 'in the vault' is
difficult. Sāyaṇa explains it as 'solitary'. Roth would
alter the text.

12 Knower of all that lives, O Agni may we
both, singers of praise and chiefs, be in
thy keeping still.
Help us to wealth exceeding good and
glorious, abundant, rich in children
and their progeny.

13 The princely worshippers who send to
those who sing thy praise, O Agni,
guerdon, graced with kine and steeds,—
Lead thou both these and us forward to
higher bliss. With brave men in the
assembly may we speak aloud.

HYMN III. *Āprīs.*

1. AGNI is set upon the earth well kindled ;
he standeth in the presence of all beings.
Wise, ancient, God, the Priest and Purifier,
let Agni serve the Gods for he is worthy.

2 May Narāśaṁsa lighting up the chambers,
bright in his majesty through threefold
heaven,
Steeping the gift with oil diffusing purpose,
bedew the Gods at chiefest time of worship.

3 Adored in heart, as is thy right, O Agni,
serve the Gods first to-day before the
mortal.
Bring thou the Marut host. Ye men, do
worship to Indra seated on the grass,
eternal.

4 O Grass divine, increasing, rich in heroes,
strewn for wealth' sake, well laid upon
this altar,—
On this bedewed with oil sit ye, O Vasus,
sit all ye Gods, ye Holy, ye Ādityas.

5 Wide be the Doors, the Goddesses, thrown
open, easy to pass, invoked, through
adorations.
Let them unfold, expansive, everlasting,
that sanctify the class famed, rich in
heroes.

6 Good work for us, the glorious Night and
Morning, like female weavers, waxen
from aforetime,
Yielders of rich milk, interweave in concert the long-extended thread, the web
of worship.

7 Let the two heavenly Heralds, first, most
wise, most fair, present oblation duly
with the sacred verse,
Worshipping God at ordered seasons decking
them at three high places at the centre
of the earth.

8 Sarasvatī who perfects our devotion, Iḷā
divine, Bhāratī all surpassing,—
Three Goddesses, with power inherent,
seated, protect this holy Grass, our
flawless refuge !

9 Born is the pious hero swift of hearing,
like gold in hue, well formed, and full
of vigour.
May Tvaṣṭar lengthen our line and kindred,
and may they reach the place which
Gods inhabit.

10 Vanaspati shall stand anear and start us,
and Agni with his arts prepare oblation.
Let the skilled heavenly Immolator forward unto the Gods the offering thrice
anointed.

11 Oil has been mixt : oil is his habitation.
In oil he rests : oil is his proper province.
Come as thy wont is : O thou Steer, rejoice
thee ; bear off the oblation duly consecrated.

HYMN IV Agni.

1. FOR you I call the glorious refulgent
Agni, the guest of men, rich in oblations
Whom all must strive to win even as a
lover, God among godly people, Jātavedas.

2 *Narāśaṁsa* : 'the Praise of Men,' Agni. *The
chambers* : the receptacles of the offerings, according
to Sāyaṇa. *At chiefest time of worship* : when the oblation of clarified butter is cast into the fire.

3 *Before the mortal* : before the mortal priest.

4 *O Grass divine* : the sacred grass, strewn on the
floor of the hall of sacrifice as a seat for the Gods, is one
of the Āprīs or deified objects which are to be propitiated
in this hymn. All these are regarded as forms of Agni.

5 *The Doors* : of the hall of sacrifice. These appear
to have been regarded as types of, and even fancifully
identified with, the doors of the cosmic house, the portals
of the East through which the morning light enters into
the world. See *Cosmology of the Ṛgveda,* p. 19.

The class : the *maghavans,* the eminent and wealthy
men who institute sacrifices.

6 *Yielders of rich milk* : cheerful givers of rewards.

7 *Two heavenly Heralds* : invokers or priests. According to Sāyaṇa, the personified fire of earth and of the
firmament. See I. 13. 8.

The centre of the earth : the altar. *The three high places*
of the three fires.

8 *Three Goddesses* : presiding over different departments of worship.

9 *The pious hero* : a son devoted to the Gods.

10 *Vanaspati* : the sacrificial post, or Agni in that
form. See I. 13. 11.

The heavenly Immolator : Agni, typically so called.

11 *Oil* : the clarified butter oblation. *Thou Steer* :
mighty Agni.

Duly consecrated : offered with the holy word Svāhā.
See I. 13. 12.

This hymn and the three that follow are ascribed to
the Ṛṣi Somāhuti of the ancient priestly family of Bhṛgu,
one of the first institutors of sacrifice.

1 *Jātavedas* : Agni who knows all life. See I. 44. 1.

2 Bhṛgus who served him in the home of waters set him of old in houses of the living.
Over all worlds let Agni be the Sovran, the messenger of Gods with rapid coursers.

3 Among the tribes of men the Gods placed Agni as a dear Friend when they would dwell among them.
Against the longing nights may he shine brightly, and show the offerer in the house his vigour.

4 Sweet is his growth as of one's own possessions; his look when rushing fain to burn is lovely.
He darts his tongue forth, like a harnessed courser who shakes his flowing tail, among the bushes.

5 Since they who honour me have praised my greatness,—he gave, as 'twere, his hue to those who love him.
Known is he by his bright delightful splendour, and waxing old renews his youth for ever.

6 Like one athirst, he lighteth up the forests; like water down the chariot ways he roareth.
On his black path he shines in burning beauty, marked as it were the heaven that smiles through vapour.

7 Around, consuming the broad earth, he wanders, free roaming like an ox without a herdsman,—
Agni refulgent, burning up the bushes, with blackened lines, as though the earth he seasoned.

8 I, in remembrance of thine ancient favour have sung my hymn in this our third assembly.
O Agni, give us wealth with store of heroes and mighty strength in food and noble offspring.

9 May the Gṛtsamadas, serving in secret, through thee, O Agni, overcome their neighbours,

Rich in good heroes and subduing foemen. That vital power give thou to chiefs and singers.

HYMN V.   *Agni.*

1. HERALD and teacher was he born, a guardian for our patrons' help,
Earner by rites of noble wealth. That Strong One may we grasp and guide;

2 In whom, Leader of sacrifice, the seven reins, far extended, meet;
Who furthers, man-like, eighth in place, as Cleanser, all the work divine.

3 When swift he follows this behest, bird-like he chants the holy prayers.
He holds all knowledge in his grasp even as the felly rounds the wheel.

4 Together with pure mental power, pure, as Director, was he born.
Skilled in his own unchanging laws he waxes like the growing boughs.

5 Clothing them in his hues, the kine of him the Leader wait on him.
Is he not better than the Three, the Sisters who have come to us ?

6 When, laden with the holy oil, the Sitster by the Mother stands,
The Priest delights in their approach, as corn at coming of the rain.

7 For his support let him perform as ministrant his priestly task;
Yea, song of praise and sacrifice : we have bestowed, let us obtain.

8 That so this man well skilled, may pay worship to all the Holy Ones.
And, Agni, this our sacrifice which we have here prepared, to thee.

---

2 *Who served him in the home of waters* : existing in the form of lightning in the firmament before he was brought down to earth.

5 *Since they who honour me* : Agni appears to be the speaker of these words.

7 *As though the earth he seasoned* : as though, by burning the weeds and bushes, he dressed and prepared the ground for tillage.
8 *Third assembly* : at the third of the three daily sacrifices.

9 *Serving in secret* : by the peaceful discharge of priestly duties, not by warfare like the chiefs who institute the sacrifice.

1 *Our patrons* : the wealthy institutors of the sacrifice. *That Strong One*: Agni.

2 *The seven reins* : the seven priests engaged in their several duties.
Cleanser : Potar, one of the sixteen priests. See II. 1.2.

3 The first hemistich, as it stands, is unintelligible to me. Wilson, after Sāyaṇa, paraphrases : 'Whatever (offerings the priests) presents, whatever prayers he recites.'

4 *Director* : Praśāstar, one of the priests. See II. 1. 2.

5 The stanza is obscure. Ludwig thinks that Agni is here called the Leader because he leads the sister Dawns to the sacrifice, and that they are said to be three in number to correspond with the number of the cows.

6 *The Sister* : Uṣas or Dawn. *The Mother* : the northern altar, representing Earth.

7 *Let him* : Agni as priest.

8 *This man* : the worshipper.

HYMN VI. *Agni.*

1. AGNI, accept this flaming brand, this waiting with my prayer on thee :
Hear graciously these songs of praise.

2 With this hymn let us honour thee, seeker of horses, Son of Strength,
With this fair hymn, thou nobly born.

3 As such, lover of song, with songs, wealth-lover, giver of our wealth !
With reverence let us worship thee.

4 Be thou for us a liberal Prince, giver and Lord of precious things.
Drive those who hate us far away.

5 Such as thou art, give rain from heaven, give strength which no man may resist:
Give food exceeding plentiful.

6 To him who lauds thee, craving help, most youthful envoy ! through our song,
Most holy Herald ! come thou nigh.

7 Between both races, Agni, Sage, well skilled thou passest to and fro,
As envoy friendly to mankind.

8 Befriend us thou as knowing all. Sage, duly worship thou the Gods,
And seat thee on this sacred grass.

HYMN VII. *Agni.*

1. VASU, thou most youthful God, Bhārata, Agni, bring us wealth,
Excellent, splendid, much-desired.

2 Let no malignity prevail against us, either God's or man's :
Save us from this and enmity.

3 So through thy favour may we force through all our enemies a way,
As 'twere through streaming water-floods.

4 Thou, Purifier Agni, high shinest forth, bright, adorable,
When worshipped with the sacred oil.

5 Ours art thou, Agni, Bhārata, honoured by us with barren cows,
With bullocks and with kine in calf :

1 *This waiting with my prayer on thee* : this 'beseeching and besieging' as Milton says. Or *upasádam* taken in a special sense may mean the ceremony called Upasad which formed part of the Jyotiṣṭoma, a very important Soma ceremony.
2 *Seeker of horses* : in order to bestow them on the worshipper.
7 *Both races* : Gods and men. *Well skilled* : acquainted with both.

1 *Vasu* : one of the class of Gods so named. *Bhārata*: Agni is so called according to Sāyaṇa, either as having been produced by attrition by the priests, or as being the bearer of oblations. The meaning is, probably, specially connected with the Bharatas or Warriors.'
5 *With kine in calf* : *aṣṭāpadībhiḥ* is thus explained by Sāyaṇa, and is used in the language of the ritual for animals with young. Roth and Grassmann understood 'verses' consisting of eight feet, divisions, or syllables. According to Bergaigne, these cows represent prayers.

6 Wood-fed, bedewed with sacred oil, ancient, Invoker, excellent,
The Son of Strength, the Wonderful.

HYMN VIII. *Agni.*

1. Now praise, as one who strives for strength, the harnessing of Agni's car,
The liberal, the most splendid One;

2 Who, guiding worshippers aright, withers, untouched by age, the foe :
When worshipped fair to look upon;

3 Who for his glory is extolled at eve and morning in our homes,
Whose statute is inviolate;

4 Who shines refulgent like the Sun, with brilliance and with fiery flame,
Decked with imperishable sheen.

5 Him Atri, Agni, have our songs strengthened according to his sway :
All glories hath he made his own.

6 May we with Agni's, Indra's help, with Soma's, yea, of all the Gods,
Uninjured dwell together still, and conquer those who fight with us.

HYMN IX. *Agni.*

1. ACCUSTOMED to the Herald's place, the Herald hath seated him, bright, splendid, passing mighty,
Whose foresight keeps the Law from violation, excellent, pure-tongued, bringing thousands, Agni.

2 Envoy art thou, protector from the foeman; strong God, thou leadest us to higher blessings.
Refulgent, be an ever-heedful keeper, Agni, for us and for our seed offspring.

3 May we adore thee in thy loftiest birth-place, and, with our praises, in thy lower station.
The place whence thou issued forth I worship : to thee well kindled have they paid oblations.

4 Agni, best Priest, pay worship with oblation; quickly commend the gift to be presented ;

5 *Him Atri* : Agni appears here to be called by the name of the ancient sage Atri. Or *átrim* may be an epithet of Agni, signifying the devourer of the food with which he is supplied, as Sāyaṇa explains it.

1 *The Herald* : or Hotar; Agni, the Invoker of the Gods. The name comes, with more emphasis, at the end of the verse. *The Law* : especially sacrifice.
3 *In thy loftiest birth-place* : as the fire of the Sun in heaven. *Thy lower station* : the firmament, where Agni is born as lightning. *The place whence thou hast issued forth* : the altar where the sacrificial fire burns.

For thou art Lord of gathered wealth and treasure: of the bright song of praise thou art inventor.

5 The twofold opulence, O Wonder-Worker, of thee new-born each day never decreases.
Enrich with food the man who lauds thee, Agni : make him the lord of wealth with noble offspring.

6 May he, benevolent with this fair aspect, best sacrificer, bring the Gods to bless us.
Sure guardian, our protector from the foemen, shine, Agni, with thine affluence and splendour.

HYMN X. *Agni.*

1. AGNI, first, loudly calling, like a Father, kindled by man upon the seat of worship.
Clothed in his glory, deathless, keen of insight, must be adorned by all, the Strong, the Famous.

2 May Agni the resplendent hear my calling through all my songs, Immortal, keen of insight.
Dark steeds or ruddy draw his car, or carried in sundry ways he makes them red of colour.

3 On wood supine they got the well-formed Infant : a germ in various-fashioned plants was Agni ;
And in the night, not compassed round by darkness, he dwells exceeding wise, with rays of splendour.

4 With oil and sacred gifts I sprinkle Agni who makes his home in front of all things living,
Broad, vast, through vital power o'er all expanded, conspicuous, strong with all the food that feeds him.

5 I pour to him who looks in all directions: may he accept it with a friendly spirit.
Agni with bridegroom's grace and lovely colour may not be touched when all his form is fury.

6 By choice victorious, recognize thy portion: with thee for envoy may we speak like Manu.
Obtaining wealth, I call on perfect Agni who with an eloquent tongue dispenses sweetness.

HYMN XI. *Indra.*

1. HEAR thou my call, O Indra; be not heedless : thine may we be for thee to give us treasures ;
For these presented viands, seeking riches, increase thy strength like streams of water flowing.

2 Floods great and many, compassed by the Dragon, thou badest swell and settest free, O Hero.
Strengthened by songs of praise thou rentest piecemeal the Dāsa, him who deemed himself immortal.

3 For, Hero, in the lauds wherein thou joyedst, in hymns of praise, O Indra, songs of Rudras,
These streams in which is thy delight approach thee, even as the brilliant ones draw near to Vāyu.

4 We who add strength to thine own splendid vigour, laying within thine arms the splendid thunder—
With us mayst thou, O Indra, waxen splendid, with Sūrya overcome the Dāsa races.

5 Hero, thou slewest in thy valour Ahi concealed in depths, mysterious, great enchanter,
Dwelling enveloped deep within the waters, him who checked heaven and stayed the floods from flowing.

6 Indra, we laud thy great deeds wrought aforetime, we laud thine exploits later of achievement ;

---

5 *The twofold opulence* : enriching Gods with sacrifice and men with earthly blessings.
New-born each day : rekindled at the morning sacrifice.

---

1 *First* : chief of the Gods. *Loudly calling* : roaring as fire, or, to be invoked by all, according to Sāyaṇa. *Like a Father* : supporting the Gods by conveying oblations to them.
2 *Carried in sundry ways* : to one fire-receptable after another.
3 *On wood supine* : the lower piece of wood in which fire is produced.
A germ : latent in plants, with reference to the luminosity of some plants, See II. 1. 1.

---

6 *By choice* : according to Sāyaṇa, 'with lustre.' *Recognize thy portion* : acknowledge the sacrificial offering to be suitable.
Like Manu : with the wisdom and authority of Manu who was instructed directly by the Gods.

---

2 *Compassed by the Dragon* : obstructed by the great serpent Ahi.
The Dāsa : 'the savage or demon Ahi. See I. 32. 11.
3 *Songs of Rudras* : like those sung by the Rudras or Maruts, Indra's allies.
These streams : sacrificial waters or libations. *Vāyu*, the God of wind, was entitled to the first draught of the Soma juice. See verse 14 of this hymn.
4 *Splendid* : the word *śubhrā*, splendid, occurs in all three places in the text.
5 *Concealed in depths* : of the atmosphere.
6 *Heralds of Sūrya* : announcing the coming of the sunlight after the heavy rain which Indra has sent.

We laud the bolt that in thine arms lies
eager ; we laud thy two Bay Steeds,
heralds of Sūrya.

7 Indra, thy Bay Steeds showing forth their
vigour have sent a loud cry out that
droppeth fatness.
The earth hath spread herself in all her
fulness : the cloud that was about to
move hath rested.

8 Down, never ceasing, hath the rain-cloud
settled : bellowing, it hath wandered
with the Mothers.
Swelling the roar in the far distant limits,
they have spread wide the blast sent
forth by Indra.

9 Indra hath hurled ;down the magician
Vṛtra who lay beleaguering the mighty
river.
Then both the heaven and earth trembled
in terror at the strong Hero's thunder
when he bellowed.

10 Loud roared the mighty Hero's bolt of
thunder, when he, the Friend of man,
burnt up the monster,
And, having drunk his fill of flowing
Soma, baffled the guileful Dānava's
devices.

11 Drink thou, O Hero Indra, drink the Soma;
let the joy-giving juices make thee
joyful.
They, filling both thy flanks, shall swell thy
vigour. The juice that satisfies hath
helped Indra.

12 Singers have we become with thee, O
Indra : may we serve duly and prepare
devotion.
Seeking thy help we meditate thy praises:
may we at once enjoy thy gift of riches.

13 May we be thine, such by thy help, O
Indra, as swell thy vigour while they
seek thy favour.
Give us, thou God, the riches that we long
for, most powerful, with store of noble
children.

14 Give us a friend, give us an habitation;
Indra, give us the company of Maruts,

And those whose minds accord with theirs,
the Vāyus, who drink the first libation of
the Soma.

15 Let those enjoy in whom thou art delighted. Indra, drink Soma for thy strength
and gladness.
Thou hast exalted us to heaven, Preserver,
in battles, through the lofty hymns that
praise thee.

16 Great, verily, are they, O thou Protector,
who by their songs of praise have won
the blessing.
They who strew sacred grass to be thy
dwelling, helped by thee have got them
strength, O Indra.

17 Upon the great Trikadruka days, Hero,
rejoicing thee, O Indra, drink the Soma.
Come with Bay Steeds to drink of libation,
shaking the drops from out thy beard,
contented.

18 Hero, assume the might wherewith thou
clavest Vṛtra piecemeal, the Dānava
Aurṇavābha.
Thou hast disclosed the light to light the
Ārya : on thy left hand, O Indra, sank
the Dasyu.

19 May we gain wealth, subduing with thy
succour and with the Ārya, all our foes,
the Dasyus.
Our gain was that to Tṛta of our party
thou gavest up Tvaṣṭar's son Viśvarūpa.

20 He cast down Arbuda what time his vig-
our was strengthened by libations poured
by Tṛta.
Indra sent forth his whirling wheel like
Sūrya, and aided by the Aṅgirases rent
Vala.

7 *The loud cry that droppeth fatness* : is the thunder
that precedes the fertilizing · rain. *The earth hath spread
herself* : to receive the rain.

8 *The Mothers* : the original waters above the firmament.

They : Indra's attendants, the Maruts or Storm-Gods.

9 *The mighty river* : the great cloud that holds the
rain.

10 *The guileful Dānava's devices* : the magic arts of
the demon Vṛtra.

14 *The Vāyus* : the plural is used honorifically for
the singular.

17 *Trikadruka days* : the first three days of the Abhiplava festival.

18 *Aurṇavābha* : son of Urṇavābha, a demon *The
Dasyu* : the barbarian, the original inhabitant of the
land. According to Sāyaṇa the demon Vṛtra is meant.

19 It is difficult to make anything intelligible of this
stanza. *Trita* is said by Sāyaṇa to be a *Maharṣi* or great
Ṛṣi, and Viśvarūpa is said to be a three-headed monster
slain by Indra. See Sacred Books of the East, XII. 164.
Prof. Macdonell's interpretation of the stanza has much
to recommend it : 'That we, overcoming all our foes
by thy aids, (and) the barbarian by Āryan prowess,
might prosper, therefore for our benefit thou didst deliver over Viśvarūpa, the son of Tvaṣṭṛ, to the Tṛta of
(thy) frindship', i.e. to thy ally, the God Trita. See
J.R.A.S., July, 1893 pp. 432, 433.

20 *Arbuda* : a demon of the atmosphere. See I. 51 6.

Sent forth his whirling wheel : Indra is said to have used
a wheel of the Sun's chariot as a missile.

Vala : the brother of Vṛtra or Vṛtra himself. See
I. 11. 5.

21 Now let that wealthy Cow of thine, O
Indra, yield in return a boon to him who
lauds thee.
Give to thy praisers : let not fortune fail
us. Loud may we speak, with brave men,
in the assembly.

HYMN XII. Indra.

1. HE who, just born, chief God of lofty
spirit by power and might became the
Gods' protector,
Before whose breath through greatness of his
valour the two worlds trembled, He, O
men, is Indra.

2 He who fixed fast and firm the earth that
staggered, and set at rest the agitated
mountains,
Who measured out the air's wide middle
region and gave the heaven support, He,
men, is Indra.

3 Who slew the Dragon, freed the Seven
Rivers, and drove the kine forth from
the cave of Vala,
Begat the fire between two stones, the
spoiler in warriors' battle, He, O men,
is Indra.

4 By whom this universe was made to
tremble, who chased away the humbled
brood of demons,
Who, like a gambler gathering his winnings
seized the foe's riches, He, O men, is
Indra.

5 Of whom, the Terrible, they ask, Where
is He ? or verily they say of him, He is
not.
He sweeps away, like birds, the foe's
possessions. Have faith in him, for He,
O men, is Indra.

6 Stirrer to action of the poor and lowly, of
priest, of suppliant who sings his praises;
Who, fair-faced, favours him who presses
Soma with stones made ready, He, O
men, is Indra.

7 He under whose supreme control are
horses, all chariots, and the villages,
and cattle ;

He who gave being to the Sun and
Morning, who leads the waters, He, O
men, is Indra.

8 To whom two armies cry in close encounter, both enemies, the stronger and the
weaker ;
Whom two invoke upon one chariot
mounted, each for himself, He, O ye
men, is Indra.

9 Without whose help our people never
conquer ; whom, battling, they invoke
to give them succour ;
He of whom all this world is but the copy,
who shakes things moveless, He, O men,
is Indra.

10 He who hath smitten, ere they knew their
danger, with his hurled weapon many
grievous sinners ;
Who pardons not his boldness who provokes him, who slays the Dasyu, He, O
men, is Indra.

11 He who discovered in the fortieth autumn
Śambara as he dwelt among the mountains;
Who slew the Dragon putting forth his
vigour, the demon lying there, He, men,
is Indra.

12 Who with seven guiding reins, the Bull, the
Mighty, set free the Seven great Floods
to flow at pleasure;
Who, thunder-armed, rent Rauhiṇa in
pieces when scaling heaven, He, O ye
men, is Indra.

13 Even the Heaven and Earth bow down
before him, before his very breath the
mountains tremble.
Known as the Soma-drinker, armed with
thunder, who wields the bolt, He, O ye
men, is Indra.

14 Who aids with favour him who pours the
Soma and him who brews it, sacrificer,
singer.
Whom prayer exalts, and pouring forth of
Soma, and this our gift, He, O ye men,
is Indra.

15 Thou verily art fierce and true who sendest
strength to the man who brews and
pours libation.
So may we evermore, thy friends, O Indra,
speak loudly to the synod with our heroes.

---

21 *That wealthy Cow of thine* : meaning, probably,
Uṣas or Dawn, who brings good gifts to man. Or *sā
dakṣiṇā maghoni* may be translated 'that liberal meed'
of thine, that is the rich reward which Indra bestows
upon his worshippers, regarded as the counterpart of
the *dakṣiṇā* or honorarium given by the institutors of
sacrifices to the priests who perform the ceremonies.

---

3 *Begat the fire between two stones* : generated lightning between heaven and earth.
5 *Like birds* : as birds are captured by the fowler.
According to others 'like stakes of gamblers,' the meaning of *vijaḥ* being uncertain. See I. 92. 10, note.

7 *Who leads the waters* : brings the periodical rains.

8 *Whom two invoke.* : the warrior and the charioteer.

12 *Seven guiding reins* : or, according to Ludwig,
seven bright rays, said to mean seven forms of Indra.
Rauhiṇa: the name of a demon of drought.
15 *With our heroes*: with our brave sons around us.

HYMN XIII.   Indra.

1. THE Season was the parent, and when born
   therefrom it entered rapidly the floods
   wherein it grows.
   Thence was it full of sap, streaming with
   milky juice : the milk of the plant's stalk
   is chief and meet for lauds.

2 They come trooping together bearing milk
   to him, and bring him sustenance who
   gives support to all.
   The way is common for the downward
   streams to flow. Thou who didst these
   things first art worthy of our lauds.

3 One priest announces what the institutor
   gives : one, altering the forms, zealously
   plies his task,
   The third corrects the imperfections left
   by each. Thou who didst these things
   first art worthy of our lauds.

4 Dealing out food unto their people there
   they sit, like wealth to him who comes,
   more than the back can bear.
   Greedily with his teeth he eats the
   master's food. Thou who didst these
   things first art worthy of our lauds.

5 Thou hast created earth to look upon the
   sky : thou, slaying Ahi, settest free the
   river's paths.
   Thee, such, a God, the Gods have
   quickened with their lauds, even as a
   steed with waters : meet for praise art
   thou.

6 Thou givest increase, thou dealest to us
   our food : thou milkest from the moist
   the dry, the rich in sweets.
   Thou by the worshipper layest thy
   precious store : thou art sole Lord of
   all. Meet for our praise art thou.

7 Thou who hast spread abroad the streams
   by stablished law, and in the field the
   plants that blossom and bear seed ;
   Thou who hast made the matchless lightnings of the sky,—vast, compassing vast
   realms, meet for our praise art thou.

8 Who broughtest Nārmara with all his
   wealth, for sake of food, to slay him
   that the fiends might be destroyed,
   Broughtest the face unclouded of the
   strengthening one, performing much
   even now, worthy art thou of praise.

9 Thou boundest up the Dāsa's hundred
   friends and ten, when, at one's hearing,
   thou helpest thy worshipper.
   Thou for Dabhīti boundest Dasyus not with
   cords ; thou wast a mighty help. Worthy
   of lauds art thou.

10 All banks of rivers yielded to his manly
   might ; to him they gave, to him, the
   Strong, gave up their wealth.
   The six directions hast thou fixed, a five-
   fold view : thy victories reached afar.
   Worthy of lauds art thou.

11 Meet for high praise, O Hero, is thy
   power, that with thy single wisdom thou
   obtainest wealth,
   The life-support of conquering Jātūṣṭhira.
   Indra, for all thy deeds, worthy of
   lauds art thou.

1 *The Season* : the Rains, the most important
of the season. So monsoon, a corruption of *mousim*, any
season, means the Rains especially. *It* : the Soma-plant.

2 *They come* : probably the cows whose milk is to be
used in sacrifice.

The way is common : referring to the water used in
the Soma ceremony. Sāyaṇa explains the stanza differently, and Wilson paraphrases it thus : 'The aggregated (streams) come, bearing everywhere the water,
and conveying it as sustenance for the asylum of all rivers,
(the ocean) : the same path is assigned to all the descending (currents) to follow; and as he who has (assigned) them (their course), thou, (Indra), art especially
to be praised.'

3 According to Sāyaṇa three priests are here indicated, the Hotar who announces the sacrifice, the Adhvaryu who apportions the several pieces of the victim,
and the Brahman who corrects mistakes and remedies
defects in the ritual.

The first four stanzas are full of difficulties and in
places absolutely unintelligible. My version of stanza
3, which generally follows Sāyaṇa, will not bear critical
examination, but at present I have nothing better to
propose.

4 *There they sit* : according to Sāyaṇa, 'the house-
holders abide in their homes.' *To him who comes* : to a
guest. *He eats the master's food* : probably, Agni consumes the oblations of the householder.

6 *Thou milkest from the moist* : producest the dry nutritious grain from the moist stalk.

8 This stanza is unintelligible. *Nārmara* : said to
be a fiend slain by Indra.

The strengthening one : according to Sāyaṇa, Ūrja-
yantī is the name of a female demon or Piśācī. Grassmann takes it to mean the Sun. Ludwig thinks it is
the name of a stronghold used as a store-house of provisions.

9 The meaning of the first half-verse is uncertain,
the text being evidently corrupt. I adopt Ludwig's
emendation, *dāsasya*, in place of the unintelligible *vā
ydsya*.

Dabhīti : a Ṛṣi named in I. 112.23. *Not with cords*:
in a prison without cords, the grave.

10 *All banks of rivers* : the dams that prevented the
rivers of the clouds from flowing. *The six directions* :
above, below, before, behind, right, left. *The fivefold
view* : inasmuch as we cannot see what is below the
ground. Sāyaṇa explains the *ṣaḍ viṣṭiraḥ* as heaven,
earth, day, night, water, and plants, and the *Pañca
sandṛśaḥ* as the five races of men.

11 *Jātūṣṭhira* : a certain man of that name, says
Sāyaṇa; perhaps the institutor of the sacrifice.

12 Thou for Turvīti heldest still the flowing
floods, the river-stream for Vayya easily
to pass,
Didst raise the outcast from the depths,
and gavest fame unto the halt and
blind. Worthy of lauds art thou.

13 Prepare thyself to grant us that great
bounty, O Vasu, for abundant is thy
treasure.
Snatch up the wonderful, O Indra, daily.
Loud may we speak, with heroes, in
assembly.

HYMN XIV.   *Indra.*

1. MINISTERS, bring the Soma juice for Indra,
pour forth the gladdening liquor with
the beakers.
To drink of this the Hero longeth ever ;
offer it to the Bull, for this he willeth.

2 Ye ministers, to him who with the lightning smote, like a tree, the rain-with-
holding Vṛtra—
Bring it to him, him who is fain to taste
it, a draught of this which Indra here
deserveth.

3 Ye ministers, to him who smote Dṛbhīka,
who drove the kine forth, and discovered
Vala,
Offer this draught, like Vāta in the
region : clothe him with Soma even as
steeds with trappings.

4 Him who did Uraṇa to death, Adhvaryus !
though showing arms ninety-and-nine
in number;
Who cast down headlong Arbuda and
slew him,—speed ye that Indra to our
offered Soma.

5 Ye ministers, to him who struck down
Svaśna, and did to death Vyaṁsa and
greedy Śuṣṇa,
And Rudhikrās and Namuci and Pipru,—
to him, to Indra, pour ye forth libation.

6 Ye ministers, to him who, as with thunder
demolished Śambara's hundred ancient
castles ;
Who cast down Varcin's sons, a hundred
thousand,—to him, to Indra, offer ye
the Soma.

7 Ye ministers, to him who slew a hundred
thousand, and cast them down upon
earth's bosom ;
Who quelled the valiant men of Atithigva,
Kutsa, and Āyu,—bring to him the
Soma.

8 Ministers, men, whatever thing ye long
for obtain ye quickly bringing gifts to
Indra.
Bring to the Glorious One what hands
have cleansed ; to Indra bring, ye pious
ones, the Soma.

9 Do ye, O ministers, obey his order : that
purified in wood, in wood uplift ye.
Well pleased he longs for what your
hands have tended : offer the gladdening Soma juice to Indra.

10 As the cow's udder teems with milk,
Adhvaryus, so fill with Soma Indra,
liberal giver.
I know him : I am sure of this, the Holy
knows that I fain would give to him
more largely.

11 Him, ministers, the Lord of heavenly
treasure and all terrestrial wealth that
earth possesses,
Him, Indra, fill with Soma as a garner
is filled with barley full : be this your
labour.

12 Prepare thyself to grant us that great
booty, O Vasu, for abundant is thy
treasure.
Gather up wondrous wealth, O Indra,
daily. Loud may we speak, with heroes,
in assembly.

---

12 *Turvīti* and *Vayya* appear to have been enabled to
ford a great river by the aid of Indra. See I. 61 11.
Turvīti was the son of Vayya. See I. 54. 6.

The outcast : or Parāvṛj as a proper name. See
I. 112. 8, where the miracle is ascribed to the Aśvins.

13 *Snatch up the wonderful* : that is, gain quickly
wondrous wealth. This appears to be the literal meaning
of the words which Wilson paraphrases, after Sāyaṇa :
'mayest thou be disposed to grant us exceeding abundance.

---

1 *Ministers* : Adhvaryus, or priests, whose duty was
to make the preparations for sacrifice.

3 *Dṛbhīka* : one of the numerous demons slain by
Indra.

Like Vāta in the region : bringing rain, as the Wind-God
does.

As steeds with trappings : the meaning of *j ūḥ* is uncertain. Sāyaṇa explains it, 'as an old man (is covered)
with garments.'

4 *Uraṇa* : another demon. *Arbuda* : a demon mentioned in I. 51. 6.

5 *Śuṣṇa, Vyaṁsa*, and the rest, are demons, some of
whom have been previously mentioned.

6 *Śambara* : a fiend mentioned several times in Book. I.
Varcin : a demon who reviled Indra, and was slain
with all his sons and followers.

7 *The valiant men* : *vīrān*; heroes. Sāyaṇa supplies
'assailants,' as Atithigva, Kutsa, and Āyu appear in
Book I, as favoured by Indra. Here their battle with
Tūrvayāṇa (I. 53. 10) is referred to.

9 *In wood* : in the wooden receptacle.

HYMN XV. *Indra*

1. Now, verily, will I declare the exploits, mighty and true, of him the True and Mighty.
In the Trikadrukas he drank the Soma : then in its rapture Indra slew the Dragon.

2 High heaven unsupported in space he stablished : he filled the two worlds and the air's mid-region.
Earth he upheld, and gave it wide expansion. These things did Indra in the Soma's rapture.

3 From front, as 'twere a house, he ruled and measured ; pierced with his bolt the fountains of the rivers,
And made them flow at ease by paths far-reaching, These things did Indra in the Soma's rapture.

4 Compassing those who bore away Dabhīti, in kindled fire he burnt up all their weapons.
And made him rich with kine and cars and horses. These things did Indra in the Soma's rapture.

5 The mighty roaring flood he stayed from flowing, and carried those who swam not safely over.
They having crossed the stream attained to riches. These things did Indra in the Soma's rapture.

6 With mighty power he made the stream flow upward, crushed with his thunder-bolt the car of Uṣas,
Rending her slow steeds with his rapid coursers. These things did Indra in the Soma's rapture.

7 Knowing the place wherein the maids were hiding, the outcast showed himself and stood before them.
The cripple stood erect, the blind beheld them. These things did Indra in the Soma's rapture.

8 Praised by the Aṅgirases he slaughtered Vala, and burst apart the bulwarks of the mountain.
He tore away their deftly-built defences. These things did Indra in the Soma's rapture.

9 Thou, with sleep whelming Cumuri and Dhuni, slewest the Dasyu, keptest safe Dabhīti.
There the staff-bearer found the golden treasure. These things did Indra in the Soma's rapture.

10 Now let that wealthy Cow of thine, O Indra, yield in return a boon to him who lauds thee.
Give to thy praisers : let not fortune fail us. Loud may we speak, with brave men, in assembly.

HYMN XVI *Indra.*

1. To him, your own, the best among the good, I bring eulogy, like oblation in the kindled fire.
We invocate for help Indra untouched by eld, who maketh all decay, strengthened, for ever young.

2 Without whom naught exists, Indra the Lofty One; in whom alone all powers heroic are combined.
The Soma is within him, in his frame vast strength, the thunder in his hand and wisdom in his head.

3 Not by both worlds is thine own power to be surpassed, nor may thy car be stayed by mountains or by seas.
None cometh near, O Indra, to thy thunderbolt, when with swift steeds thou fliest over many a league.

4 For all men bring their will to him the Resolute, to him the Holy One, to him the Strong they cleave.
Pay worship with oblation, strong and passing wise. Drink thou the Soma, Indra, through the mighty blaze.

---

1 *In The Trikadrukas* : See II. 11. 17. *In its rapture* : in the exhilaration produced by drinking the fermented juice. See I. 51. 2 and note.

3 *From front, as 'twere a house* : the formation of the world is compared to the building of a house. Wilson renders : '(He it is) who has measured the eastern (quarters) with measures like a chamber.'

4 *Dabhīti* : See II. 13. 9.

5 Cf. I. 13. 12.

6 *The car of Uṣas* : the destruction of the chariot of Uṣas or Dawn by Indra is described more fully in IV. 30. 8.

7 Parāvṛj, here rendered 'the outcast,' is taken by Sāyaṇa as the name of a Ṛṣi who was lame and blind. When some girls made sport of him he prayed to Indra and was made sound.

9 *Cumuri and Dhuni* : Asuras or demons.
The staff-bearer : the door-keeper, or chamberlain, of Dabhīti. '*The golden treasure* : of Cumuri and Dhuni.

1 *Like oblation* : praise that magnifies and strengthens Indra as oblations of clarified butter cast into the fire increase the flame.

5 The vessel of the strong flows forth, the
flood of meath, unto the Strong who feeds
upon the strong, for drink,
Strong are the two Adhvaryus, strong are
both the stones. They press the Soma
that is strong for him the Strong.

6 Strong is thy thunderbolt, yea, and thy
car is strong; strong are thy Bay Steeds
and thy weapons powerful.
Thou, Indra, Bull, art Lord of the strong
gladdening drink : with the strong Soma,
Indra, satisfy thyself.

7 I, bold by prayer, come near thee in thy
sacred rites, thee like a saving ship, thee
shouting in the war.
Verily he will hear and mark this word
of ours : we will pour Indra forth as
'twere a spring of wealth.

8 Turn thee unto us ere calamity come nigh,
as a cow full of pasture turns her to
her calf.
Lord of a Hundred Powers, may we once
firmly cling to thy fair favours even as
husbands to their wives.

9 Now let that wealthy Cow of thine, O
Indra, yield in return a boon to him
who lauds thee.
Give to thy praisers : let not fortune fail
us. Loud may we speak, with heroes,
in assembly.

HYMN XVII.   *Indra.*

1. LIKE the Aṅgirases, sing this new song
forth to him, for, as in ancient days,
his mighty powers are shown,
When in the rapture of the Soma he unclosed with strength the solid firm-shut
stables of the kine.

2 Let him be even that God who, for the
earliest draught measuring out his
power, increased his majesty;
Hero who fortified his body in the wars,
and through his greatness set the heaven
upon his head.

3 Thou didst perform thy first great deed of
hero might what time thou showedst
power, through prayer, before this folk.

Hurled down by thee the car-borne Lord
of Tawny Steeds, the congregated swift
ones fled in sundry ways.

4 He made himself by might Lord of all
living things, and strong in vital power
waxed great above them all.
He, borne on high, o'erspread with light
the heaven and earth, and, sewing up
the turbid darkness, closed it in.

5 He with his might made firm the forward-
bending hills, the downward rushing of
the waters he ordained.
Fast he upheld the earth that nourisheth
all life, and stayed the heaven from falling by his wondrous skill.

6 Fit for the grasping of his arms is what
the Sire hath fabricated from all kind
of precious wealth.
The thunderbolt, wherewith, loud-roaring,
he smote down, and striking him to
death laid Krivi on the earth.

7 As she who in her parents' house is
growing old, I pray to thee as Bhaga
from the seat of all.
Grant knowledge, mete it out and bring it
to us here : give us the share wherewith thou makest people glad.

8 May we invoke thee as a liberal giver :
thou givest us, O Indra, strength and
labours.
Help us with manifold assistance, Indra :
Migthy One, Indra, make us yet more
wealthy.

9 Now may that wealthy Cow of thine, O
Indra, give in return a boon to him who
lauds thee.
Give to thy praisers : let not fortune fail
us. Loud may we speak, with heroes,
in assembly.

HYMN XVIII   *Indra*

1. THE rich new car hath been equipped at
morning; four yokes it hath, three whips,
seven reins to guide it :

4 *Borne on high* : or perhaps 'luminous,' as Prof.
Max Müller renders it.

5 *Forward-bending* : ready to fall until Indra fixed
them.

6 *Krivi* : originally 'a leather bag' and metaphorically
'a cloud', said by Sāyaṇa to be an Asura or demon.

7 *As Bhaga* : as the God who distributes wealth, and
also presides over love and marriage. *From the seat of all* :
from the hall of sacrifice where seats of sacred grass are
provided for all the Gods.

---

5 *The vessel of the strong* : the reservoir containing
the strong Soma. In reference to the repetition of the
word 'strong' in this and the following stanza see I. 177.
2, 3.
Both the stones : for pressing out the Soma juice.

1 Praise Indra after the manner of the ancient Aṅgirases with a new song, because his ancient deeds are
continually renewed for our advantage.
2 *Fortified his body* : protected it with a coat of mail.
3 *The congregated swift ones* : according to Sāyaṇa,
the Asuras or enemies of the Gods. According to Roth
the waters of the heaven.

1 *The rich new car* is the morning sacrifice which travels
to the Gods and obtains wealth for the worshipper. The
four yokes are the four pair of stones for pressing out the
Soma juice; the *three whips* are the three tones of

Ten-sided, friendly to mankind, light-winner, that must be urged to speed with prayers and wishes.

2 This is prepared for him the first, the second, and the third time : he is man's Priest and Herald.

Others get offspring of another parent : he goeth, as a noble Bull, with others.

3 To Indra's car the Bay Steeds have I harnessed, that new well-spoken words may bring him hither.

Here let not other worshippers detain thee, for among us are many holy singers.

4 Indra, come hitherward with two Bay Coursers, come thou with four, with six when invocated.

Come thou with eight, with ten, to drink the Soma. Here is the juice, brave Warrior : do not scorn it.

5 O Indra, come thou hither having harnessed thy car with twenty, thirty, forty horses.

Come thou with fifty well trained coursers, Indra, sixty or seventy, to drink the Soma.

6 Come to us hitherward, O Indra, carried by eighty, ninety, or an hundred horses.

This Soma juice among the Śunahotras hath been poured out, in love, to glad thee, Indra.

7 To this my prayer, O Indra, come thou hither : bind to thy car's pole all thy two Bay Coursers.

Thou art to be invoked in many places : Hero, rejoice thyself in this libation.

8 Ne'er be my love from Indra disunited : still may his liberal Milch-cow yield us treasure.

So may we under his supreme protection, safe in his arms, succeed in each forthgoing.

9 Now may that wealthy Cow of thine, O Indra, give in return a boon to him who lauds thee.

Give to thy praisers : let not fortune fail us. Loud may we speak, with heroes, in assembly.

HYMN XIX   Indra.

1. DRAUGHTS of this sweet juice have been drunk for rapture, of the wise Soma-presser's offered dainty,

Wherein, grown mighty in the days aforetime, Indra hath found delight, and men who worship.

2 Cheered by this meath Indra, whose hand wields thunder, rent piecemeal Ahi who barred up the waters,

So that the quickening currents of the rivers flowed forth like birds unto their resting-places.

3 Indra, this Mighty One, the Dragon's slayer, sent forth the flood of waters to the ocean.

He gave the Sun his life, he found the cattle, and with the night the works of days completed.

4 To him who worshippeth hath Indra given many and matchless gifts. He slayeth Vṛtra.

Straight was he to be sought with supplications by men who struggled to obtain the sunlight.

5 To him who poured him gifts he gave up Sūrya,—Indra, the God, the Mighty, to the mortal;

---

prayer; the *seven reins* are the seven metres. The meaning of *ddāritraḥ*, 'ten-sided,' is not clear. Sāyaṇa explains *aritrāḥ* as 'preservers from enemies, i. e. sins,' the planets. Grassman thinks that wheels are meant.

2 *The first, the second, and the third time* : the three daily sacrifices are referred to. *He is man's Priest* : Agni must be meant.

The second hemistich is obscure. Wilson, after Sāyaṇa, paraphrases: 'Other (priests) engender the embryo of a different (rite), but this victorious (sacrifice), the showerer (of benefits) combines with other (ceremonies).'

4 *With two Bay Coursers* : this is the usual number. The progressive multiplication in this and the following stanzas is perhaps intended to indicate the ever increasing rapidity with which the eager worshipper prays Indra to approach. The Scholiast says that by their supernatural power the two horses of Indra multiply themselves indefinitely.

6 *The Śunahotras* : apparently a family so called; etymologically 'those who sacrifice with happy result.' According to Sāyaṇa, *śunahotrāḥ* means certain vessels into which the Soma juice was poured.

1 *Have been drunk* : by Indra.

3 *And with the night* : perhaps, by giving the night for rest enabled men to perform the labours of the day. Or, as *aktunā* may mean 'by light.' 'effected the manifestation of the days by light, as Wilson renders it after Sāyaṇa.

5 See I. 61. 15. The legend says that a certain King who wished for son worshipped Sūrya who, to grant his prayer, was born himself as the King's son. Afterwards when some dispute arose between this King's son who was named Sūrya and the Ṛṣi Etaśa, Indra sided with the latter. In I. 61. 15, a chariot race appears to be referred to, and I have translated the passage accordingly, following Sāyaṇa in taking Sūrya to be the name of a man. If, however, as is very possible, Sūrya there is the Sun-God the meaning is that Indra, in order to favour his faithful worshipper Etaśa, compelled Sūrya or the Sun to bring back his chariot and horses to the east; that is the return of day on some particular occasion is attributed to Indra's intervention on behalf of his favourite. This appears to be the meaning of this verse also. See also I. 121. 13.

For Etaśa with worship brought him riches that keep distress afar, as 'twere his portion.

6 Once to the driver of his chariot, Kutsa, he gave up greedy Śuṣṇa, plague of harvest;
And Indra, for the sake of Divodāsa demolished Śambara's nine-and-ninety castles.

7 So have we brought our hymn to thee, O Indra, strengthening thee and fain ourselves for glory.
May we with best endeavours gain this friendship, and mayst thou bend the godless scorner's weapons.

8 Thus the Gṛtsamadas for thee, O Hero, have wrought their hymn and task as seeking favour.
May they who worship thee afresh, O Indra, gain food and strength, bliss, and a happy dwelling.

9 Now may that wealthy Cow of thine, O Indra, give in return a boon to him who lauds thee,
Give to thy praisers : let not fortune fail us. Loud may we speak, with heroes, in assembly.

HYMN XX   Indra.

1. As one brings forth his car when fain for combat, so bring we power to thee— regard us, Indra—
Well skilled in song, thoughtful in spirit, seeking great bliss from one like thee amid the Heroes.

2 Indra, thou art our own with thy protection, a guardian near to men who love thee truly,
Active art thou, the liberal man's defender, his who draws near to thee with right devotion.

3 May Indra, called with solemn invocations, the young, the Friend, be men's auspicious keeper,
One who will further with his aid the singer, the toiler, praiser, dresser of oblations.

4 With laud and song let me extol that Indra in whom of old men prospered and were mighty.
May he, implored, fulfil the prayer for plenty of him who worships, of the living mortal.

5 He, Indra whom the Aṅgirases' praise delighted, strengthened their prayer and made their goings prosper.
Stealing away the mornings with the sunlight, he, lauded, crushed even Aśna's ancient powers.

6 He verily, the God, the glorious Indra, hath raised him up for man, best Wonder-Worker.
He, self-reliant, mighty and triumphant, brought low the dear head of the wicked Dāsa.

7 Indra theVṛtra-slayer, Fort-destroyer, scattered the Dāsa hosts who dwelt in darkness.
For men hath he created earth and waters, and ever helped the prayer of him who worships.

8 To him in might the Gods have ever yielded, to Indra in the tumult of the battle.
When in his arms they laid the bolt, he slaughtered the Dasyus and cast down their forts of iron.

9 Now may that wealthy Cow of thine, O Indra, give in return a boon to him who lauds thee.
Give to thy praisers : let not fortune fail us. Loud may we speak, with heroes, in assembly.

As 'twere his portion : as (a father gives) his portion (to a son), according to Sāyaṇa.

6 *Kutsa* and *Divodāsa*, favourites of Indra, and *Śuṣṇa* and *Śambara*, demons of drought, have occurred frequently in Book I.

---

1 *For combat* : or, perhaps, for the race.
3 *The toiler* : the man who labours in the discharge of religious duties.

4 *The living mortal* : the present worshipper, as distinguished from the men of old.

5 *Made their goings prosper* : by recovering for them the stolen cows, frequently mentioned in Book I. *Aśna*, 'the voracious,' said to be the name of a demon, one of the many foes overthrown by Indra.

6 *Dāsa* : said by Sāyaṇa to be an Asura, or demon of that name. The word is frequently applied to the foes of the Āryas, to the malignant demons of the air as well as to the barbarous and hostile inhabitants of the land, and it is not always clear whether human or superhuman enemies are intended.
The dear head : the Dāsa's own head.

7 *The Dāsa hosts who dwelt in darkness* : the words thus rendered are variously explained. It is uncertain whether the aborigines of the country are meant, or the demons of air who dwell in the dark clouds.

8 *The Dasyus* : the Asuras or demons, according to Sāyaṇa.

HYMN XXI

1. To him the Lord of all, the Lord of wealth,
   of light; him who is Lord for ever, Lord
   of men and tilth,
   Him who is Lord of horses, Lord of kine,
   of floods, to Indra, to the Holy bring
   sweet Soma juice.

2. To him the potent One, who conquers and
   breaks down, the Victor never vanquished
   who disposes all,
   The mighty-voiced, the rider, unassailable,
   to Indra everconquering speak your
   reverent prayer.

3. Still Victor, loved by mortals, ruler over
   men, o'erthrower, warrior, he hath waxen
   as he would;
   Host-gatherer, triumphant, honoured mid
   the folk. Indra's heroic deeds will I tell
   forth to all.

4. The strong who never yields, who slew
   the furious fiend, the deep, the vast, of
   wisdom unattainable;
   Who speeds the good, the breaker-down,
   the firm, the vast,—Indra whose rites
   bring joy hath made the light of Dawn.

5. By sacrifice the yearning sages sending
   forth their songs found furtherance from
   him who speeds the flood.
   In Indra seeking help with worship and
   with hymn, they drew him to themselves
   and won them kine and wealth.

6. Indra, bestow on us the best of treasures,
   the spirit of ability and fortune;
   Increase of riches, safety of our bodies,
   charm of sweet speech, and days of
   pleasant weather.

HYMN XXII.   Indra.

1. At the Trikadrukas the Great and Strong
   hath drunk drink blent with meal. With
   Viṣṇu hath he quaffed the poured out
   Soma juice, all that he would.
   That hath so heightened him the Great,
   the Wide, to do his mighty work.
   So may the God attain the God, true
   Indu Indra who is true.

2. So he resplendent in the battle overcame
   Krivi by might. He with his majesty
   hath filled the' earth and heaven, and
   waxen strong.
   One share of the libation hath he swal-
   lowed down : one share he left.
   So may the God attend the God, true
   Indu Indra who is true.

3. Brought forth together with wisdom and
   mighty power thou grewest great; with
   hero deeds subduing the malevolent,
   most swift in act;
   Giving prosperity, and lovely wealth to
   him who praiseth thee. So may the God
   attend the God, true Indu Indra who is
   true.

4. This, Indra, was thy hero deed, Dancer,
   thy first and ancient work, worthy to be
   told forth in heaven,
   What time thou sentest down life with a
   God's own power, freeing the floods.
   All that is godless may he conquer with
   his might, and, Lord of Hundred Powers,
   find for us strength and food.

HYMN XXIII.   Brahmaṇaspati.

1. WE call thee, Lord and Leader of the
   heavenly hosts, the wise among the wise,
   the famousest of all,
   The King supreme of prayers, O Brahmaṇaspati : hear us with help ; sit
   down in place of sacrifice.

2. Bṛhaspati, God immortal ! verily the Gods
   have gained from thee, the wise, a share
   in holy rites.
   As with great light the Sun brings forth
   the rays of morn, so thou alone art
   Father of all sacred prayer.

3. When thou hast chased away revilers and
   the gloom, thou mountest the refulgent
   car of sacrifice ;
   The awful car, Bṛhaspati, that quells the
   foe, slays demons, cleaves the stall of
   kine, and finds the light.

4 Dancer : active in battle, dancer of the war-dance.

1 The Lord : literally, conqueror of all, of wealth, etc.
2 Mighty-voiced : Sāyaṇa gives two explanations,
'having a full throat,' or 'praised by many.' Rider :
borne through the sky.
4 The furious fiend : Vṛtra.
6 Ability : to perform sacred ceremonies, according
to Sāyaṇa.

1 The Trikadrukas : the first three days of the Abhiplava ceremony.
Indu : a drop, especially of Soma juice, another name
of the deified Soma.
2 Krivi : a demon, See II. 17. 6.

1 Brahmaṇaspati : alternating with Bṛhaspati, the
Deity in whom the action of the worshipper upon the
Gods is personified. See I. 14. 3. A comparatively recent
God, as the representative of the hierarchy, he is gradually
encroaching on the jurisdiction of Indra the Worrior God
of the Kṣatriyas, claiming his achievements as his own
and assuming his attributes. See Weber, Uber den
Vājapeya, Sitzungsberichte der K. P. Academie der
Wissenschaften, 1892, XXXIX, p. 15.
3 Revilers : blaspheming demons of darkness. Cleaves
the stall of kine : opens the prison where the cows or rays
of light have been shut up.

4 Thou leadest with good guidance and preservest men ; distress o'ertakes not him who offers gifts to thee.

Him who hates prayer thou punishest, Bṛhaspati, quelling his wrath : herein is thy great mightiness.

5 No sorrow, no distress from any side, no foes, no creatures double-tongued have overcome the man,—

Thou drivest all seductive fiends away from him whom, careful guard, thou keepest Brahmaṇaspati.

6 Thou art our keeper, wise, preparer of our paths : we, for thy service, sing to thee with hymns of praise.

Bṛhaspati, whoever lays a snare for us, him may his evil fate, precipitate, destroy.

7 Him, too, who threatens us without offence of ours, the evilminded, arrogant, rapacious man,—

Him turn thou from our path away, Bṛhaspati : give us fair access to this banquet of the Gods.

8 Thee as protector of our bodies we invoke, thee, saviour, as the comforter who loveth us.

Strike, O Bṛhaspati, the Gods' revilers down, and let not the unrighteous come to highest bliss.

9 Through thee, kind prosperer, O Brahmaṇaspati, may we obtain the wealth of men which all desire :

And all our enemies, who near or far away prevail against us, crush, and leave them destitute.

10 With thee as our own rich and liberal ally may we, Bṛhaspati, gain highest power of life.

Let not the guileful wicked man be lord of us :- still may we prosper, singing goodly hymns of praise.

11 Strong, never yielding, hastening to the battle-cry, consumer of the foe, victorious in the strife,

Thou art sin's true avenger, Brahmaṇspati, who tamest e'en the fierce, the wildly passionate.

12 Whoso with mind ungodly seeks to do us harm, who, deeming him a man of might mid lords, would slay,—

Let not his deadly blow reach us, Bṛhaspati ; may we humiliate the strong ill-doer's wrath.

13 The mover mid the spoil, the winner of all wealth, to be invoked in fight and reverently adored,

Bṛhaspati hath overthrown like cars of war all wicked enemies who fain would injure us.

14 Burn up the demons with thy fiercest flaming brand, those who have scorned thee in thy manifested might.

Show forth that power that shall deserve the hymn of praise : destroy the evil speakers, O Bṛhaspati.

15 Bṛhaspati, that which the foe deserves not which shines among the folk effectual, splendid,

That, Son of Law ! which is with might refulgent—that treasure wonderful bestow thou on us.

16 Give us not up to those who, foes in ambuscade, are greedy for the wealth of him who sits at ease,

Who cherish in their heart abandonment of Gods. Bṛhaspati, no further rest shall they obtain.

17 For Tvaṣṭar, he who knows each sacred song, brought thee to life, preëminent o'er all the things that be.

Guilt-scourger, guilt-avenger is Bṛhaspati, who slays the spoiler and upholds the mighty Law.

18 The mountain, for thy glory, cleft itself apart when, Aṅgiras ! thou openedst the stall of kine.

Thou, O Bṛhaspati, with Indra for ally didst hurl down water-floods which gloom had compassed round.

19 O Brahmaṇaspati, be thou controller of this our hymn and prosper thou our children.

All that the Gods regard with love is blessed. Loud may we speak, with heroes, in assembly.

HYMN XXIV.   *Brahmaṇaspati.*

1. BE pleased with this our offering, thou who art the Lord ; we will adore thee with this new and mighty song.

---

16 This stanza is difficult, and the translation is conjectural. Wilson observes that Sāyaṇa's explanation is not very intelligible.

18 *Aṅgiras* : Bṛhaspati is here called by the name of the ancient patriarch as Agni is in I. 1. 6 According to the *Bhāgavata Purāṇa* Bṛhaspati is the son of Aṅgiras.

Thou......didst hurl down : the deed usually ascribed to Indra is here attributed to Bṛhaspati as the Lord of effectual prayer. See I. 14. 3, and 62 3.

---

1 *Thy friend, our liberal patron* : the institutor of the sacrifice, the faithful worshipper of the God and the rewarder of the priests.

---

7 *This banquet of the Gods* : sacrifice in general, and especially the sacrifice which he is performing.

15 *Son of Law* : who hast thy being in accordance with ṛtá, truth or eternal Law and Order.

As this thy friend, our liberal patron, praises thee, do thou, Bṛhaspati, fulfil our hearts' desire.

2 He who with might bowed down the things that should be bowed, and in his fury rent the holds of Śambara :
Who overthrew what shook not, Brahmaṇaspati,—he made his way within the mountain stored with wealth.

3 That was a great deed for the Godliest of the Gods : strong things were loosened and the firmly fixed gave way.
He drave the kine forth and cleft Vala through by prayer, dispelled the darkness and displayed the light of heaven.

4 The well with mouth of stone that poured a flood of meath, which Brahmaṇaspati hath opened with his might—
All they who see the light have drunk their fill thereat : together they have made the watery fount flow forth.

5 Ancient will be those creatures, whatsoe'er they be ; with moons, with autumns, doors unclose themselves to you.
Effortless they pass on to perfect this and that, appointed works which Brahmaṇaspati ordained.

6 They who with much endeavour searching round obtained the Paṇis' noblest treasure hidden in the cave,—
Those sages, having marked the falsehoods, turned them back whence they had come, and sought again to enter in.

7 The pious ones when they had seen the falsehoods turned them back, the sages stood again upon the lofty ways.
Cast down with both their arms upon the rock they left the kindled fire, and said, No enemy is he.

8 With his swift bow, strung truly, Brahmaṇaspati reaches the mark whate'er it be that he desires.
Excellent are the arrows wherewithal he shoots, keen-eyed to look on men and springing from his ear.

9 He brings together and he parts, the great High Priest ; extolled is he, in battle Brahmaṇaspati.
When, gracious, for the hymn he brings forth food and wealth, the glowing Sun untroubled sends forth fervent heat.

10 First and preëminent, excelling all besides are the kind gifts of liberal Bṛhaspati.
These are the boons of him the Strong who should be loved, whereby both classes and the people have delight.

11 Thou who in every way supreme in earthly power, rejoicing, by thy mighty strength hast waxen great,—
He is the God spread forth in breadth against the Gods : he, Brahmaṇaspati, encompasseth this All.

12 From you, twain Maghavans, all truth proceedeth : even the waters break not your commandment.
Come to us, Brahmaṇaspati and Indra, to our oblation like yoked steeds to fodder.

13 The sacrificial flames most swiftly hear the call : the priest of the assembly gaineth wealth for hymns.
Hating the stern, remitting at his will the debt, strong in the shock of fight is Brahmaṇaspati.

14 The wrath of Brahmaṇaspati according to his will had full effect when he would do a mighty deed.
The kine he drave forth and distributed to heaven, even as a copious flood with strength flows sundry ways.

15 O Brahmaṇaspati, may we be evermore masters of wealth well-guided, full of vital strength.

---

2 *The holds of Śambara* : great black clouds before they pour their rain.

The mountain stored with wealth : the cloud full of precious rain.

5 This stanza is difficult. Ludwig takes *tā bhuvanā*, 'those creatures,' whose nature is imperfectly known, to be the sun and moon, the parents of months and years, which without any effort on their part bring to pass whatever Brahmaṇaspati decrees.

6 The Paṇis are the robber-fiends who carry off and hide the cows or rays of light. *Those sages* : the Aṅgirases, to whom the stolen cows are said to have belonged. *Having marked the falsehoods* : having seen through the guiles of the fiends who sought to mislead them.

7 *They left the kindled fire* : the cows, or waters and the light which follows their effusion, were set free by fire-oblations of which the A girases are regarded as the earliest institutors. *No enemy* : that is, man's greatest friend. The stanza is obscure, and Sāyaṇa's explanation is unsatisfactory.

8 *Springing from his ear* : the bow-string being drawn to the right ear. The word may, perhaps mean also, 'finding their home in, *i. e.* reaching the ears of men, and might be translated 'levelled to the ear.'

9 *He brings together and he parts* : brings friends together in worship, and disperses enemies in battle.

10 *Both classes* : according to Sāyaṇa, the institutors of the sacrifice and the priests, or Gods and men.

11 *In breadth against the Gods* : in his mightiness the representative of all the Gods.

12 *Even the waters* : all nature, even the strong and rapid water floods.

Heroes on heroes send abundantly to us,
when thou omnipotent through prayer
seekest my call.

16 O Brahmaṇaspati, be thou controller of
this our hymn, and prosper thou our
children.

All that the Gods regard with love is blessed. Loud may we speak, with heroes,
in assembly.

HYMN XXV.   *Brahmaṇaspati.*

1. He lighting up the flame shall conquer
enemies : strong shall he be who offers
prayer and brings his gift.

He with his seed spreads forth beyond
another's seed, whomever Brahmaṇaspati
takes for his friend.

2 With heroes he shall overcome his hero
foes, and spread his wealth by kine :
wise by himself is he.

His children and his children's children
grow in strength, whomever Brahmaṇaspati takes for his friend.

3 He, mighty like a raving river's billowy
flood, as a bull conquers oxen, overcomes with strength.

Like Agni's blazing rush he may not be
restrained, whomever Brahmaṇaspati takes
for his friend.

4 For him the floods of heaven flow never
failing down : first with the heroes he
goes forth to war for kine.

He slays in unabated vigour with great
might, whomever Brahmaṇaspati takes
for his friend.

5 All roaring rivers pour their waters down
for him, and many a flawless shelter
hath been granted him.

Blest with the happiness of Gods he prospers well, whomever Brahmaṇaspati takes
for his friend.

HYMN XXVI.   *Brahmaṇaspati.*

1. The righteous singer shall o'ercome his
enemies, and he who serves the Gods
subdue the godless man.

The zealous man shall vanquish the invincible, the worshipper share the food of
him who worships not.

2 Worship, thou hero, chase the arrogant
afar : put on auspicious courage for the
fight with foes.

Prepare oblation so that thou mayst have
success : we crave the favouring help of
Brahmaṇaspati.

___

2 *Worship, thou hero* : the Ṛṣi addresses the exhortation to himself.
3 *The Father of the Gods* : Sāyaṇa explains *pitáram,*
father, by *pālayitáram,* protector.

3 He with his folk, his house, his family, his
sons, gains booty for himself, and, with
the heroes, wealth,

Who with oblation and a true believing
heart serves Brahmaṇaspati the Father
of the Gods.

4 Whoso hath honoured him with offerings
rich in oil, him Brahmaṇaspati leads
forward on his way,

Saves him from sorrow, frees him from his
enemy, and is his wonderful deliverer
from woe.

HYMN XXVII.   *Ādityas.*

1. These hymns that drop down fatness, with
the ladle I ever offer to the Kings
Ādityas.

May Mitra, Aryaman, and Bhaga hear us,
the mighty Varuṇa Dakṣa, and Aṁśa.

2 With one accord may Aryaman and Mitra
and Varuṇa this day accept this praise-
song—

Ādityas bright and pure as streams of
water, free from all guile and falsehood,
blameless, perfect.

3 These Gods, Ādityas, vast, profound, and
faithful, with many eyes, fain to deceive
the wicked,

Looking within behold the good and evil :
near to the Kings is even the thing
most distant.

4 Upholding that which moves and that
which moves not, Ādityas, Gods, protectors of all being,

Provident, guarding well the world of spirits,
true to eternal Law, the debt-exactors.

5 May I, Ādityas, share in this your favour
which, Aryaman, brings profit e'en in
danger.

Under your guidance, Varuṇa and Mitra,
round troubles may I pass, like rugged
places.

___

1 *With the ladle* : that is, with my tongue that utters
praises as the sacrificial ladle pours out the oblations of
clarified butter.

Ādityas : See I. 14. 3.

Bhaga : the name of this ancient God still survives in
the Slavonic languages as a general name for God. He
is frequently invoked together with Pūṣan and the
Ādityas. See I. 14. 3.

Dakṣa : active energy, spiritual power personified,
and called an Āditya or son of Aditi. Sāyaṇa takes the
word as an epithet of Aṁśa, powerful.

Aṁśa : another of the Ādityas, the Distributor. See
II. 1. 4.

3 *Looking within* : into the hearts of men.

4 *The debt-exactors* : the punishers of sin.

6 Smooth is your path, O Aryaman and
Mitra ; excellent is it, Varuṇa, and
thornless.
Thereon, Ādityas, send us down your blessing : grant us a shelter hard to be
demolished.

7 Mother of Kings, may Aditi transport us,
by fair paths Aryaman, beyond all
hatred.
May we uninjured, girt by many heroes,
win Varuṇa's and Mitra's high protection.

8 With their support they stay three earths,
three heavens ; three are their functions
in the Gods' assembly.
Mighty through Law, Ādityas, is your
greatness ; fair is it, Aryaman, Varuṇa,
and Mitra.

9 Golden and splendid, pure like streams of
water, they hold aloft the three bright
heavenly regions.
Ne'er do they slumber, never close their
eyelids, faithful, far-ruling for the righteous mortal.

10 Thou over all, O Varuṇa, art Sovran, be
they Gods, Asura ! or be they mortals.
Grant unto us to see a hundred autumns :·
ours be the blest long lives of our forefathers.

11 Neither the right nor left do I distinguish,
neither the east nor yet the west, Ādityas.
Simple and guided by your wisdom, Vasus !
may I attain the light that brings no
danger.

12 He who bears gifts unto the Kings, true
Leaders, he whom their everlasting blessings prosper,
Moves with his chariot first in rank and
wealthy, munificent and lauded in
assemblies.

13 Pure, faithful, very strong, with heroes
round him, he dwells beside the waters
rich with pasture.
None slays, from near at hand or from
a distance, him who is under the Ādityas'
guidance.

14 Aditi, Mitra, Varuṇa, forgive us however
we have erred and sinned against you.
May I obtain the broad light free from
peril : O Indra, let not during darkness
seize us.

15 For him the Twain united pour their fulness, the rain from heaven : he thrives
most highly favoured.
He goes to war mastering both the mansions : to him both portions of the world
are gracious.

16 Your guiles, ye Holy Ones, to quell oppressors, your snares spread out against
the foe, Ādityas,
May I car-borne pass like a skilful horse-
man : uninjured may we dwell in spacious shelter.

17 May I not live, O Varuṇa, to witness my
wealthy, liberal, dear friend's destitution.
King, may I never lack well-ordered
riches. Loud may we speak, with heroes,
in assembly.

HYMN XXVIII.   *Varuṇa*

1. THIS laud of the self-radiant wise Āditya
shall be supreme o'er all that is in greatness.
I beg renown of Varuṇa the Mighty, the
God exceeding kind to him who worships.

2. Having extolled thee, Varuṇa, with thoughtful care may we have high fortune
in thy service,
Singing thy praises like the fires at coming,
day after day, of mornings rich in
cattle.

3 May we be in thy keeping, O thou Leader
wide-ruling Varuṇa, Lord of many
heroes.
O sons of Aditi, for ever faithful, pardon
us, Gods, admit us to your friendship.

4 He made them flow, the Āditya, the Sustainer : the rivers run by Varuṇa's
commandment.

7 *Mother of Kings* : Aditi, the Infinite, mother of the
Ādityas.

8 *Three are their functions* : perhaps the absorption,
retention, and effusion of rain.

10 *Asura* : a divine and immortal being; apparently
a higher title than *devāḥ*, Gods or Bright Ones.

11 I know nothing of myself and cannot attain to the
light of day, or the light of true knowledge, without your
assistance.

14 *During darkness*; death, night, darkness are to be
dreaded : daylight is comparatively free from danger.

15 *The Twain united* : heaven and earth which together
make up the world.

Both the mansions : that is, he retains possession of his
own dwelling and gains possession of that of his enemy.

Both portions of the world : heaven and earth.

17 May I never see my wealthy patron, the institutor of the ceremony reduced to poverty.

1 *This laud* : the poet magnifies the importance of
the worship which he offers to the Āditya Varuṇa, the
great King over all, the God of natural, peaceful, moral
order as contrasted with Indra, the God of battles.

These feel no weariness, nor cease from flowing : swift have they flown like birds in air around us.

5 Loose me from sin as from a bond that binds me : may we swell, Varuṇa, thy spring of Order.
Let not my thread, while I weave song, be severed, nor my work's sum, before the time, be shattered.

6 Far from me, Varuṇa, remove all danger : accept me graciously, thou Holy Sovran.
Cast off, like cords that hold a calf, my troubles : I am not even mine eyelid's lord without thee.

7 Strike us not, Varuṇa, with those dread weapons which, Asura, at thy bidding wound the sinner.
Let us not pass away from light to exile. Scatter, that we may live, the men who hate us

8 O mighty Varuṇa, now and hereafter, even as of old, will we speak forth our worship.
For in thyself, invincible God, thy statutes ne'er to be moved are fixed as on a mountain.

9 Move far from me what sins I have committed : let me not suffer, King, for guilt of others.
Full many a morn remains to dawn upon us : in these, O Varuṇa, while we live direct us.

10 O King, whoever, be he friend or kinsman, hath threatened me affrighted in my slumber—
If any wolf or robber fain would harm us, therefrom, O Varuṇa, give thou us protection.

11 May I not live O Varuṇa, to witness my wealthy, liberal dear friend's destitution.
King, may I never lack well-ordered riches. Loud may we speak, with heroes, in assembly.

HYMN XXIX.   *Viśvedevas.*

1. UPHOLDERS of the Law, ye strong Ādityas, remove my sin like her who bears in secret.
You, Varuṇa, Mitra and all Gods who listen, I call to help me, I who know your goodness.

2 Ye, Gods, are providence and ye are power : remove ye utterly all those who hate us.
As givers of good things deal with us kindly : this day be gracious to us and hereafter.

3 What service may we do you with our future, what service, Vasus, with our ancient friendship ?
O Aditi, and Varuṇa and Mitra, Indra and Maruts, make us well and happy.

4 Ye, O ye Gods, are verily our kinsmen ; as such be kind to me who now implore you.
Let not your car come slowly to our worship : of kinsmen such as you ne'er let us weary.

5 I singly have sinned many a sin against you, and ye chastised me as a sire the gambler.
Far be your nets, far, Gods, be mine offences : seize me not like a bird upon her offspring.

6 Turn yourselves hitherward this day, ye Holy, that fearing in my heart I may approach you.
Protect us, God ; let not the wolf destroy us. Save us, ye Holy, from the pit and falling.

7 May I not live, O Varuṇa, to witness my wealthy, liberal, dear friend's destitution.
King, may I never lack well-ordered riches. Loud may we speak, with heroes, in assembly.

HYMN XXX.   *Indra and Others.*

1. THE streams unceasing flow to Indra, slayer of Ahi, Savitar, God, Law's fulfiller,
Day after day goes on the sheen of waters. What time hath past since they were first set flowing ?

2 His Mother—for she knew—spake and proclaimed him who was about to cast his bolt at Vṛtra.
Cutting their paths according to his pleasure day after day flow to their goal the rivers.

---

5 *Swell......thy spring of Order* : observe and strengthen thy statutes and ordinances from which life and all blessings flow.

---

1 *Like her who bears in secret* : as an unwedded mother abandons her secretly born child in some distant place.

---

5 *As a sire the gambler* : as a father punishes his son for gambling.
Your nets : the nooses or snares which ye spread for the wicked.

---

1 *Savitar* : the Sun, as identical with Indra. The Scholiast explains the word here as the instigator or impeller of all.
What time hath past ? : meaning that the waters are eternal.

3 Aloft he stood above the airy region, and
against Vṛtra shot his deadly missile.
Enveloped in a cloud he rushed upon him.
Indra subdued the foe with sharpened
weapons.

4 As with a bolt, Bṛhaspati, fiercely flaming,
pierce thou Vṛkadvaras', the Asura's,
heroes.
Even as in time of old with might thou
slewest, so slay even now our enemy,
O Indra.

5 Cast down from heaven on high thy bolt
of thunder wherewith in joy thou smitest
dead the foeman.
For gain of children make us thine, O
Indra, of many children's children and
of cattle.

6 Whomso ye love, his power ye aid and
strengthen ; ye Twain are the rich worshipper's advancers.
Graciously favour us, Indra and Soma ;
give us firm standing in this time of
danger.

7 Let it not vex me, tire me, make me
slothful, and never let us say, Press not
the Soma ;
For him who cares for me, gives gifts,
supports me, who comes with kine to me
who pour libations.

8 Sarasvatī, protect us : with the Maruts
allied thou boldly conquerest our foemen,
While Indra does to death the daring
chieftain of Śaṇḍikas exulting in his
prowess.

9 Him who waylays, yea, him who would
destroy us,—aim at him, pierce him
with thy sharpened weapon.
Bṛhaspati, with arms thou slayest foemen :
O King, give up the spoiler to destruction.

10 Perform, O Hero, with our valiant heroes
the deeds heroic which thou hast to
finish.
Long have they been inflated with presump-
tion : slay them, and bring us hither
their possessions.

11 I craving joy address with hymn and
homage your heavenly host, the company
of Maruts,
That we may gain wealth with full store
of heroes, each day more famous, and
with troops of children.

HYMN XXXI. *Viśvedevas.*

1. HELP, Varuṇa and Mitra, O ye Twain
allied with Vasus, Rudras, and Ādityas,
help our car,
That, as the wild birds of the forest from
their home, our horses may fly forth,
glad, eager for renown.

2 Yea, now ye Gods of one accord speed
on our car what time among the folk
it seeks an act of might ;
When, hasting through the region with the
stamp of hoofs, our swift steeds trample
on the ridges of the earth.

3 Or may our Indra here, the Friend of
all mankind, coming from heaven, most
wise, girt by the Marut host,
Accompany, with aid untroubled by a
foe, our car to mighty gain, to win the
meed of strength.

4 Or may this Tvaṣṭar, God who rules the
world with power, one-minded with the
Goddesses speed forth our car ;
Iḷā and Bhaga the celestial, Earth and
Heaven, Pūṣan, Purandhi, and the
Aśvins, ruling Lords.

5 Or, seen alternate, those two blessed Goddesses, Morning and Night who stir all
living things to act :
While with my newest song I praise you
both, O Earth, that from what moves
not ye may spread forth threefold food.

6 Your blessing as a boon for suppliants we
desire : the Dragon of the Deep, and
Aja-Ekapād,

1 *Help our car* : in the chariot-race. According to
Prof. Windisch, 'car' is a figurative expression for 'hymn
of praise.' See that scholar's exhaustive discussion of
this hymn in Festgruss an Rudolf von Roth, 1893 pp.
139—144.
4 *Purandhi* : meaning the bold, or the intelligent,
may be either an epithet of Pūṣan or the name of a
separate deity.
5 *I praise you both, O Earth*: i.e. O Heaven and Earth;
the pair being always regarded as closely connected, the
mention of one is sufficient.
From what moves not : from plants as distinguished
from animals.
6 *The Dragon of the Deep* : Ahibudhnya, who dwells
in the depth of air. See I. 186. 5. *Aja-Ekapād* : 'the
unborn one-footed,' the Sun. See VI. 50. 14, note.
Trita : a Vedic God, appearing in connexion with Indra.
The Floods' swift Child : Agni. For the other names see
Index.

2 The first hemistich is obscure. I follow Ludwig's
conjectural interpretation (Der Ṛgveda, V. 63), who
reads *viduṣi* for *viduṣe*, and refers to the legend related
in IV. 18. *His Mother* : Aditi, the mother of Indra.
3 *Aloft he stood* : Indra. See I.32. *Enveloped in a cloud*:
referring to Vṛtra.
4 *Vṛkadvaras* : supposed by Ludwig to be the King
of the Śaṇḍikas, the hymn being a prayer for victory in
an approaching battle with him. *The Asura* would then
mean King.
7 *Comes with kine* : referring to Indra who rewards
his worshippers with gifts of cattle.

Trita, Ṛbhukṣan, Savitar shall joy in us,
and the Floods' swift Child in our worship and our prayer.

7 These earnest prayers I pray to you, ye
Holy : to pay you honour, living men
have formed them,
Men fain to win the prize and glory. May
they win, as a car-horse might the goal,
your notice.

HYMN XXXII. *Various Deities.*

1. GRACIOUSLY further, O ye Heaven and
Earth, this speech striving to win reward,
of me your worshipper.
First rank I give to you, Immortal, high
extolled ! I, fain to win me wealth, to
you the mighty Pair.
2 Let not man's guile annoy us, secret or
by day : give not us up a prey to these
calamities.
Sever not thou our friendship : think thereon for us. This, with a heart that
longs for bliss, we seek from thee.
3 Bring hither with benignant mind the
willing Cow teeming with plenteous
milk, full, inexhaustible.
O thou invoked by many, day by day I
urge thee with my word, a charger
rapid in his tread.
4 With eulogy I call on Rākā swift to hear :
may she, auspicious, hear us, and herself observe.
With never-breaking needle may she sew
her work, and give a hero son most
wealthy, meet for praise.
5 All thy kind thoughts, O Rākā, lovely in
their form, wherewith thou grantest
wealth to him who offers gifts—
With these come thou to us this day benevolent, O Blessed One, bestowing food
of thousand sorts.
6 O broad-tressed Sinīvālī, thou who art the
Sister of the Gods,
Accept the offered sacrifice, and, Goddess, grant us progeny.
7 With lovely fingers, lovely arms, prolific
Mother of many sons—
Present the sacred gifts to her, to Sinīvālī
Queen of men.

8 Her, Sinīvālī, her, Gungū, her, Rākā, her,
Sarasvatī, Indrāṇī to mine aid I call,
and Varuṇānī for my weal.

HYMN XXXIII.   *Rudra.*

1. FATHER of Maruts, let thy bliss approach
us : exclude us not from looking on the
sunlight.
Gracious to our fleet courser be the Hero :
may we transplant us, Rudra, in our
children.
2 With the most saving medicines which
thou givest, Rudra, may I attain a
hundred winters.
Far from us banish enmity and hatred, and
to all quarters maladies and trouble.
3 Chief of all born art thou in glory, Rudra,
armed with the thunder, mightiest of
the mighty.
Transport us over trouble to well-being :
repel thou from us all assaults of mischief.
4 Let us not anger thee with worship, Rudra,
ill praise, Strong God ! or mingled
invocation.
Do thou with strengthening balms incite
our heroes : I hear thee famed as best
of all physicians.
5 May I with praise-songs win that Rudra's
favour who is adored with gifts and
invocations.
Ne'er may the tawny God, fair-cheeked,
and gracious, swifthearing, yield us to
this evil purpose.
6 The Strong, begirt by Maruts, hath refreshed me, with most invigorating food,
imploring.
As he who finds a shade in fervent sunlight may I, uninjured, win the bliss
of Rudra.
7 Where is that gracious hand of thine, O
Rudra, the hand that giveth health and
bringeth comfort,

2 *These calamities* : some pressing troubles or immi-
nent dangers not further specified. *From thee* : probably Indra.

4 *Rākā* : the Goddess presiding over the actual day
of full moon, and apparently associated with child-
birth.

6 *Sinīvālī* : a similar lunar Goddess, who aids the
birth of children.

8 *Gungū* : identified by Sāyaṇa with Kuhū, another lunar Goddess, or the day of conjunction when the
moon rises invisible. *Indrāṇī* and *Varuṇānī* are the consorts respectively of Indra and Varuṇa.

1 *The Hero* : Rudra. According to Ludwig : Let
our brave son be mighty with the charger.

4 *With worship* : with imperfect worship. *mingled
invocation* : in which other Gods also, who have no claim
to the particular oblation, are addressed.

5 *Yield us to this evil purpose* : give us up to the malice
of our enemy.

6 *The Strong* : or the Bull, Rudra, accompanied by
his sons the Maruts.

Remover of the woe that Gods have sent
us ? O Strong One, look thou on me
with compassion.

8 To him the strong, great, tawny, fair-complexioned, I utter forth a mighty hymn
of praises.
We serve the brilliant God with adorations,
we glorify the splendid name of Rudra.

9 With firm limbs, multiform, the strong,
the tawny adorns himself with bright
gold decorations :
The strength of Godhead ne'er departs
from Rudra, him who is Sovran of this
world, the mighty.

10 Worthy, thou carriest thy bow and arrows,
worthy, thy manyhued and honoured
necklace.
Worthy, thou cuttest here each fiend to
pieces : a mightier than thou there is
not, Rudra.

11 Praise him the chariot-borne, the young,
the famous, fierce, slaying like a dread
beast of the forest.
O Rudra, praised, be gracious to the
singer : let thy hosts spare us and smite
down another.

12 I bend to thee as thou approachest, Rudra,
even as a boy before the sire who
greets him.
I praise thee Bounteous Giver, Lord of
heroes : give medicines to us as thou
art lauded.

13 Of your pure medicines, O potent Maruts,
those that are wholesomest and health-
bestowing,
Those which our father Manu hath selected, I crave from Rudra for our gain
and welfare.

14 May Rudra's missile turn aside and spare
us, the great wrath of the impetuous
One avoid us.
Turn, Bounteous God, thy strong bow from
our princes, and be thou gracious to
our seed and offspring.

15 O tawny Bull, thus showing forth thy
nature, as neither to be wroth, O God,
nor slay us.

8 *Fair-complexioned* : the white complexion of Śiva,
the later representative of Rudra, has, therefore, as Wilson
observes, its origin in the Ṛgveda.

13 *Those which our father Manu hath selected* : Wilson
observes that 'this alludes to the vegetable seeds which
Manu, according to the *Mahābhārata*, was directed to
take with him into the vessel in which he was preserved at
the time of the deluge.'

14 *Our princes* : our wealthy patrons, the institutors
of our sacrifices.

───────

Here, Rudra, listen to our invocation.
Loud may we speak, with heroes, in
assembly.

HYMN XXXIV.   *Maruts*

1. THE Maruts of resistless might who love
the rain, resplendent, terrible like wild
beasts in their strength,
Glowing like flames of fire, impetuous in
career, blowing the wandering rain-
cloud, have disclosed the kine.

2 They gleam with armlets as the heavens
are decked with stars, like cloud-born
lightnings shine the torrents of their rain.
Since the strong Rudra, O Maruts with
brilliant chests, sprang into life for you
in Pṛśni's radiant lap.

3 They drip like horses in the racings of
swift steeds; with the stream's rapid ears
they hasten on their way.
Maruts with helms of gold, ye who make
all things shake, con e with your spotted
deer, one-minded, to our food.

4 They have bestowed of Mitra all that live,
to feed, they who for evermore cause
their swift drops to flow;
Whose steeds are spotted deer, whose riches
never fail, like horses in full speed, bound
to the pole in work.

5 With brightly-flaming kine whose udders
swell with milk, with glittering lances
on your unobstructed paths,
O Maruts, of one mind, like swans who
seek their nests, come to the rapturous
enjoyment of the meath.

6 To these our prayers, O Maruts, come
unanimous, come ye to our libations
like the praise of men.

1 *Have disclosed the kine* : 'give vent to its (collected)
rain.'—Wilson.

2 *Pṛśni's radiant lap* : Pṛśni the mother of the Maruts,
probably 'the speckled cloud,' is, according to Sāyaṇa,
the Earth who in the form of a brindled cow was impreg-
nated by Rudra.

3 *With the stream's rapid ears* : 'The waves raised by
the storm may be regarded as the ears with which the
stream listens to the roaring of the tempest.'—Ludwig.
Wilson, after Sāyaṇa, paraphrases : 'and they rush along
with swift (horses) on the skirts of the sounding (cloud).'

4 The meaning of the first line is not clear. Wilson
renders it; 'The prompt-giving Maruts ever confer upon
the (offerer of sacrificial) food, as upon a friend, all these
(world-supporting) waters.'
Bound to the pole in works : carrying on their appointed
duties as horses draw the chariot to whose pole they are
harnessed.

5 *With brightly-flaming kine* : clouds that emit flashes
of lightning before they pour down their stores of fertilizing rain

6 *Like the praise of men* : which attends pious
worshippers.

Make it swell like a mare, in udder like a
cow, and for the singer grace the song
with plenteous strength.

7 Give us a steed, O Maruts mighty in
the car; prevailing prayer that brings
remembrance day by day;
Food to your praisers, to your bard in
deeds of might give winning wisdom,
power uninjured, unsurpassed.

8 When the bright-chested Maruts, lavish
of their gifts, bind at the time of bliss
their horses to the cars,
Then, as the milch-cow feeds her ealf
within the stalls, they pour forth food for
all oblation-bringing men.

9 Save us, O Maruts, Vasus, from the injurer,
the mortal foe who makes us looked
upon as wolves.
With chariot all aflame compass him round
about: O Rudras, cast away the foeman's
deadly bolt.

10 Well-known, ye Maruts, is that wondrous
course of yours, when they milked
Prśni's udder, close akin to her.
Or when to shame the bard who lauded,
Rudra's Sons, ye O infallible brought
Trita to decay.

11 We call you, such, great Maruts, following wonted ways, to the oblation paid
to Vişņu Speeder-on.
With ladles lifted up, with prayer, we
seek of them preëminent, golden-hued,
the wealth which all extol.

12 They, the Daśagvas, first of all brought
sacrifice : they at the break of mornings
shall inspirit us.

Make it swell : make our sacred song effectual, metaphorically full of milk. Prof. M. Müller would read
asvām instead of *dívām* : 'Fulfil (our prayer) like the
udder of a barren cow.'

7 *Brings remembrance* : makes the Gods remember us.
10 Prśni here is the firmament, and her udder is
the cloud from which the Maruts drew the rain. There
is a very abrupt change from the second person to the
third, from 'ye' to 'they.'

I can make nothing of the second hemistich. Wilson
paraphrases it : 'You (destroyed) the reviler of your
worshipper, and (came), irresistible sons of Rudra, to
Trita for the destruction of his enemies.' Trita is said by
Sāyaṇa to be a Ṛṣi. Ludwig in his note on the passage
takes Trita to be a name of the Soma.

11 *Vişņu Speeder-on* : who runs his rapid course round
heaven. Sāyaṇa explains Vişņu to mean 'the diffusive
and desirable Soma.' Perhaps, as Ludwig thinks, sacrifice in general is intended, of which Vişņu is the representative.

12 *The Daśagvas* : the Maruts are here said to have
been the first performers of sacrifice, the true Daśagvas.
The priests so called belonged originally to the race or
school of Aṅgiras.

Dawn with her purple beams uncovereth
the nights, with great light glowing like
a billowy sea of milk.

13 The Rudras have rejoiced them in the
gathered bands at seats of worship as in
purple ornaments.
They with impetuous vigour sending down
the rain have taken to themselves a
bright and lovely hue.

14 Soliciting their high protection for our help,
with this our adoration we sing praise
to them,
Whom, for assistance, like the five terrestrial priests, Trita hath brought to aid us
hither on his car.

15 So may your favouring help be turned to
us-ward, your kindness like a lowing cow
approach us,
Wherewith ye bear your servant over
trouble, and free your worshipper from
scoff and scorning.

HYMN XXXV.   *Son of Waters.*

1. EAGER for spoil my flow of speech I utter:
may the Floods' Child accept my songs
with favour.
Will not the rapid Son of Waters make
them lovely, for he it is who shall enjoy
them ?

2 To him let us address the song well-
fashioned, forth from the heart. Shall
he not understand it ?
The friendly Son of Waters by the greatness of Godhead hath produced all
things existing.

3 Some floods unite themselves and others
join them : the sounding rivers fill one
common storehouse.
On every side the bright Floods have
encompassed the bright resplendent
Offspring of the Waters.

4 The never-sullen waters, youthful Maidens,
carefully decking, wait on him the
youthful.
He with bright rays shines forth in splendid beauty, unfed with wood. in waters,
oil-enveloped.

5 To him three Dames are offering food to
feed him, Goddesses to the God whom
none may injure.

---

14 The second hemistich is very obscure. Sāyaṇa's
explanation (see Wilson) is altogether unsatisfactory.

---

1 *The Floods' Child* : or Son of the Waters, Apāṁnapāt, a name of Agni as born in the form of lightning
from the waters of the aerial ocean or firmament.
Make them lovely : grace them with acceptance.

Within the waters hath he pressed, as
  hollows, and drinks their milk who now
  are first made mothers.

6 Here was the horse's birth; his was the
  sunlight. Save thou our princes from the
  oppressor's onslaught.
Him, indestructible, dwelling at a distance
  in forts unwrought lies and ill spirits
  reach not.

7 He, in whose mansion is the teeming
  Milch-cow, swells the Gods' nectar and
  eats noble viands.
The Son of Waters, gathering strength in
  waters, shines for his worshipper to give
  him treasures.

8 He who in waters with his own pure
  Godhead shines widely, law-abiding,
  everlasting—
The other worlds are verily his branches,
  and plants are born of him with all their
  offspring.

9 The Waters' Son hath risen, and clothed
  in lightning ascended up unto the curled
  cloud's bosom;
And bearing with them his supremest glory
  the Youthful Ones, gold-coloured, move
  around him.

10 Golden in form is he, like gold to look on,
  his colour is like gold, the Son of Waters.
When he is seated fresh from golden birth-
  place those who present their gold give
  food to feed him.

11 This the fair name and this the lovely
  aspect of him the Waters' Son increase
  in secret.
Whom here the youthful Maids together
  kindle, his food is sacred oil of golden
  colour.

12 Him, nearest Friend of many, will we
  worship with sacrifice and reverence and
  oblation.
I make his back to shine, with chips provide
  him; I offer food and with my songs
  exalt him.

13 The Bull hath laid his own life-germ
  within them. He sucks them as an
  infant, and they kiss him.
He, Son of Waters, of unfading colour,
  hath entered here as in another's body.

14 While here he dwelleth in sublimest
  station, resplendent with the rays that
  never perish,
The Waters, bearing oil to feed their
  offspring, flow, Youthful Ones, in wan-
  derings about him.

15 Agni, I gave good shelter to the people,
  and to the princes goodly preparation.
Blessed is all that Gods regard with favour.
  Loud may we speak, with heroes, in
  assembly.

HYMN XXXVI   *Various Gods.*

1. WATER and milk hath he endued, sent
  forth to thee : the men have drained
  him with the filters and the stones.
Drink, Indra, from the Hotar's bowl—
  first right is thine—Soma hallowed and
  poured with Vaṣaṭ and Svāhā.

2 Busied with sacrifice, with spotted deer
  and spears, gleaming upon your way
  with ornaments, yea, our Friends,
Sitting on sacred grass, ye Sons of Bharata,
  drink Soma from the Potar's bowl, O
  Men of heaven.

5 *Three Dames* : Iḷā, Sarasvatī, and Bhāratī, the
personifications of sacred prayer and worship. *Within
the waters* : Agni dwelt within the waters as their unborn
babe.

6 *Here was the horse's birth* : the production of the
rapid lightning, or perhaps of the Sun ; but the meaning
is doubtful. The expression may, as Ludwig suggests,
refer to the creation of the natural horse as a descendant
of the original heavenly horse. *His was the sunlight* :
Apāṁnapāt's or Agni's. *In forts unwrought* : in the
castles of the clouds as opposed to the stone strongholds of
men.

9 *The Youthful Ones* : the rivers or waters of the aerial
ocean.

10 *Golden in form* : when wearing the shape of
lightning. *Those who present their gold* : the institutors
of sacrifice who reward tte priests.

11 *In secret* : Apāṁnapāt, the celestial Agni, increases and grows strong without men seeing the process.
The terrestrial Agni is kindled and tended by the sister
fingers and fed with oil or clarified butter.

12 *Nearest Friend of many* : lowest down, and so nearest
to men, of all the Gods. *Make his back to shine* : with
butter offered in sacrifice.

13 *Within them* : within the waters. *The Bull* :
apparently Agni himself.

As in another's body : that is, fire originally celestial
as Apāṁnapāt, has come to men as terrestrial and
sacrificial fire, contained in the wooden drill from which
it is produced by friction.

15 As the result of my hymns to Agni our people have
dwelt safely, and our wealthy men have been enabled
to offer well-conducted sacrifices.

1 The Soma juice has been pressed out with the
stones, strained through the filters, and then mixed with
water and milk before it is offered to Indra, The *Hotar's
bowl* : the sacred vessel held by the Hotar or Hotr, one
of the chief officiating priests.

Vaṣaṭ and *Svāhā*, meaning respectively 'may he
(Agni) bear it (to the Gods)' and Ave ! or Hail ! are
words of consecration and blessing used when oblations
are offered.

2 *Sons of Bharata* : the Maruts, sons of Rudra the
Warrior. *Potar* : etymologically Cleanser, the title of
another of the priests.

3 Come unto us, ye swift to listen : as at
home upon the sacred grass sit and enjoy
yourselves.
And, Tvaṣṭar, well-content be joyful in
the juice with Gods and Goddesses in
gladsome company.

4 Bring the Gods hither, Sage, and offer
sacrifice : at the three altars seat thee
willingly, O Priest.
Accept for thy delight the proffered Soma
meath : drink from the Kindler's bowl
and fill thee with thy share.

5 This is the strengthener of thy body's
manly might : strength, victory for all
time are placed within thine arms.
Pressed for thee, Maghavan, it is offered
unto thee : drink from the chalice of
this Brahman, drink thy fill.

6 Accept the sacrifice; mark both of you, my
call : the Priest hath seated him after
the ancient texts.
My prayer that bids them come goes forth
to both the Kings: drink ye the Soma
meath from the Director's bowl.

HYMN XXXVII.   *Various Gods.*

1. ENJOY thy fill of meath out of the Hotar's
cup : Adhvaryus, he desires a full
draught poured for him.
Bring it him : seeking this he gives.
Granter of Wealth, drink Soma with
the Ṛtus from the Hotar's cup.

2 He whom of old I called on, him I call
on now. He is to be invoked; his name
is He who Gives.
Here brought by priests is Soma meath.
Granter of Wealth, drink Soma with
the Ṛtus from the Potar's cup.

3 Fat may the horses be wherewith thou
speedest on : Lord of the Wood, unhar-
ming, strengthen thou thyself.
Drawing and seizing, Bold One, thou
who grantest wealth, drink Soma with
the Ṛtus from the Neṣṭar's cup.

4 From Hotar's cup and Potar's he hath
drunk and joyed : the proffered food

hath pleased him from the Neṣṭar's
bowl.
The fourth cup undisturbed, immortal, let
him drink who giveth wealth, the cup
of the wealth-giving God.

5 Yoke, O ye Twain, to-day your hero-bearing car, swift-moving hitherward : your
loosing-place is here.
Mix the oblations, then come hither with
the meath, and drink the Soma, ye rich
in abundant strength.

6 Agni, accept the fuel and our offered gift:
accept the prayer of man, accept our
eulogy.
Do thou with all, with Ṛtu, O thou
Excellent, fain, make the great Gods
all fain taste the gift we bring.

HYMN XXXVIII.   *Savitar.*

1. UPRISEN is Savitar, this God, to quicken,
Priest who neglects not this most constant
duty.
To the Gods, verily, he gives rich treasure,
and blesses him who calls them to the
banquet.

2 Having gone up on high, the God broad-
handed spreads his arms widely forth
that all may mark him.
Even the waters bend them to his service:
even this wind rests in the circling
region.

3 Though borne by swift steeds he will yet
unyoke them: e'en the fleet chariot
hath he stayed from going.
He hath checked e'en their haste who
glide like serpents. Night closely followed
Savitar's dominion.

4 What was spread out she weaves afresh,
re-weaving : the skilful leaves his labour
half-completed.

5 *O ye Twain* : Aśvins.

6. *With all, with Ṛtu* : the meaning is, apparently,
with all the Ṛtus ; but Ṛtu in the text is in the singular
number.

---

1 *To quicken* : the meaning of Savitar, as a náme of
the Sun, being the great generator or vivifier. *Priest* :
váhniḥ; or, perhaps, the supporter, or, the luminous.

3 *Their haste who glide like serpents* : the speed of the
fleet-footed horses who draw the chariot of the Sun.

4 The meaning of this stanza is obscure. I have
given what appears to be the sense of the words as they
stand, but the verse, as a whole, is scarcely intelligible.
Wilson, following Sāyaṇa, paraphrases it thus : 'She
(Night), enwraps the extended (world) like (a woman)
weaving (a garment) : the prudent man lays aside
the work he is able (to execute) in the midst (of his
labour) : but all spring up (from repose) when the
divine, unwearied Sun, who has divided the seasons,
again appears.' Roth takes *arámatiḥ*, which I have

---

4 *Sage* : Agni. *The Kindler* : the Agnīdh, the priest
who lights the fire. *The three altars* : of the Gārhapatya,
Āhavanīya, and Dakṣiṇa fires.

6 *Both the Kings* : Mitra and Varuṇa. *The Director* :
Praśāstar, another priest, first assistant of the Hotar.

---

1 Agni is addressed as Draviṇodās or Wealth-giver.
Adhvaryus : ministering priests. *The Ṛtus* : the Seasons
or the deities presiding over the Seasons. See I. 15.

3 *Lord of the Wood* : Agni, regarded as the King of
plants. *The Neṣṭar's cup* : the Neṣṭar is the priest who
leads forward the wife of the sacrificer.

He hath arisen from rest, and parted seasons : Savitar hath approached, God, holy-minded.

5 Through various dwellings, through entire existence, spreads, manifest, the household light of Agni.
The Mother gives her Son the goodliest portion, and Savitar hath sped to meet his summons.

6 He comes again, unfolded, fain for conquest: at home was he, the love of all things moving.
Each man hath come leaving his evil doings, after the Godlike Savitar's commandment.

7 The wild beasts spread through desert places seeking their watery share which thou hast set in waters.
The woods are given to the birds. These statutes of the God Savitar none disobeyeth.

8 With utmost speed, in restless haste at sunset Varuṇa seeks his watery habitation.
Then seeks each bird his nest, each beast his lodging. In due place Savitar hath set each creature.

9 Him whose high law not Varuṇa nor Indra, not Mitra, Aryaman, nor Rudra breaketh,
Nor evil-hearted fiends, here for my welfare him I invoke, God Savitar, with worship.

10 May they who strengthen bliss, and thought and wisdom, and the Dames' Lord and Narāśaṁsa aid us.

That good may come to us and wealth be gathered, may we be Savitar the God's beloved.

11 So come to us our hearts' desire, the bounty bestowed by thee, from heaven and earth and waters,
That it be well with friends and those who praise thee, and, Savitar, with the loud-lauding singer.

HYMN XXXIX.   *Aśvins.*

1. SING like the two press-stones for this same purpose; come like two misers to the tree of treasure;
Like two laud-singing Brahmans in the assembly, like the folk's envoys called in many places.

2 Moving at morning like two car-borne heroes, like to a pair of goats ye come electing ;
Like two fair dames embellishing their bodies, like a wise married pair among the people.

3 Like to a pair of horns come first to us-ward, like to a pair of hoofs with rapid motion ;
Come like two Cakavās in the grey of morning, come like two chariot wheels at dawn, ye Mighty.

4 Bear us across the rivers like two vessels, save us as ye were yokes, naves, spokes and fellies.
Be like two dogs that injure not our bodies ; preserve us, like two crutches, that we fall not.

5 Like two winds ageing not, two confluent rivers, come with quick vision like two eyes before us.

---

rendered by holy-minded, as a substantive, the Genius of Devotion, and translates : 'Again had the Weaver (Aramati) drawn in what she had spun out (the web or tissue of devotion and sacrifice), the devout man had left off in the midst of his task (at the approach of night); then Aramati arises anew and arranges the seasons : the divine Savitar is present (i. e. morning returns).'

5 *The Mother* : Uṣas or Dawn assigns to *her Son* Agni the Agnihotra rite which is performed at day-break, and Savitar, or the rising Sun, is present at the ceremony after the lighting of the sacrificial fire. Thus Agni is honoured by deities in heaven as well as by men on earth.

6 *He comes again* : Agni, re-kindled in the morning, resumes his full power, He whom all living beings love, was present, but latent, during the night.

7 Savitar provides for the wild beasts of the desert and for the birds of the air.

8 Though not generally regarded in the Veda as the God of the ocean, Varuṇa is yet frequently connected with the waters, either of the firmament or of earth.

10 *They who strengthen bliss* : the Gods in general. *The Dames' Lord* : the guardian of the consorts of the Gods, Tvaṣṭar, who is generally represented as attending or attended by them.

Narāśaṁsa : 'the Praise of Men,' a name of Agni.

---

1 In this hymn the Aśvins are compared to a number of objects animate and inanimate, in many of which the only point of resemblance is duality.

Sing like the two press-stones : may your auspicious brightness as you approach be as clear as the ringing-sound of the press-stones, and may similar blessings reward the worshippers.

Like two misers to the tree of treasure : as misers come to dig up the gold they have buried at the foot of a tree, so come ye to the libation made of the juice of the precious Soma plant. *The folk's envoys*: the messengers whom the institutors of sacrifices send to the priests when they wish to secure their services.

2 *Ye come electing* : to choose and accept the offerings made.

3 *Cakavās* : the Cakravāka, or as it is now called in Hindi, the Cakavā, is a bird frequently mentioned in later poetry as a type of love and constancy. The male bird and his mate are condemned to spend their nights on opposite banks of a river, and are allowed to meet again in the early morning. The English name of the bird is Brahmany duck. Cakavā is properly the male bird, and Cakavī the female.

Come like two hands most helpful to the body, and guide us like two feet to what is precious.

6 Even as two lips that with the mouth speak honey, even as two breasts that nourish our existence,
Like the two nostrils that protect our being, be to us as our ears that hear distinctly.

7 Like two hands give ye us increasing vigour ; like heaven and earth constrain the airy regions.
Aśvins, these hymns that struggle to approach you, sharpen ye like an axe upon a whetstone.

8 These prayers of ours exalting you, O Aśvins, have the Gṛtsamadas, for a laud, made ready.
Welcome them, O ye Heroes, and come hither. Loud may we speak. with brave men, in assembly.

HYMN XL. *Soma and Pūṣan.*

1 SOMA and Pūṣan, Parents of all riches, Parents of earth and Parents of high heaven,
You Twain, brought forth as the whole world's protectors, the Gods have made centre of life eternal.

2 At birth of these two Gods all Gods are joyful : they have caused darkness, which we hate, to vanish.
With these, with Soma and with Pūṣan, Indra generates ripe warm milk in the raw milch-cows.

3 Soma and Pūṣan, urge your chariot hither, the seven-wheeled car that measures out the region,
That stirs not all, that moves to every quarter, five-reined and harnessed by the thought, ye Mighty.

4 One in the heaven on high hath made his dwelling, on earth and in the firmament the other.
May they disclose to us great store of treasure, much-longed for, rich in food, source of enjoyment.

5 One of you Twain is Parent of all creatures, the other journeys onward all-beholding.
Soma and Pūṣan, aid my thought with favour : with you may we o'ercome in all encounters.

6 May Pūṣan stir our thought, the all-impelling, may Soma Lord of riches grant us riches.
May Aditi the perfect Goddess aid us. Loud may we speak, with heroes, in assembly.

HYMN XLI.   *Various Deities.*

1. O VĀYU, come to us with all the thousand chariots that are thine,
Team-borne, to drink the Soma juice.

2 Drawn by thy team, O Vāyu, come ; to thee is offered this, the pure.
Thou visitest the presser's house.

3 Indra and Vāyu, drawn by teams, ye Heroes, come today and drink.
Of the bright juice when blent with milk.

4 This Soma hath been shed for you, Law-strengtheners, Mitra-Varuṇa !
Listen ye here to this my call.

5 Both Kings who never injure aught seat them in their supremest home,
The thousand-pillared, firmly-based.

6 Fed with oblation, Sovran Kings, Ādityas, Lords of liberal gifts.
They wait on him whose life is true.

7 With kine, Nāsatyas, and with steeds, come, Aśvins, Rudras, to the house
That will protect its heroes well ;

8 Such, wealthy Gods ! as none afar nor standing nigh to us may harm,
Yea, no malicious mortal foe.

9 As such, O longed-far Aśvins, lead us on to wealth of varied sort,
Wealth that shall bring us room and rest.

10 Verily Indra, conquering all, driveth e'en mighty fear away,
For firm is he and swift to act.

11 Indra be gracious unto us : sin shall not reach us afterward,
And good shall be before us still.

---

1 *Soma* : addressed in this hymn is the God who represents and animates the juice of the Soma plant. See I. 18. 4.

Pūṣan : a solar deity who protects and multiplies cattle and other property. See I. 42.

2 *Ripe warm milk* : see I. 62. 9.

3 *That stirs not all* : that moves and influences the highest beings only.

4 *One in the heaven on high* : Pūṣan, as a celestial God. *The other* : Soma, who dwells on earth in plants, and in the firmament as the Moon.

5 *One of you* : Soma. With allusion, perhaps, to the libations of Soma juice which produce the rain upon which the production and growth of all creatures depend. *All-beholding* : as a solar deity, or the Sun.

1 Vāyu, the God of wind, is addressed in the first two stanzas. In those that follow the poet invokes Indra and Vāyu, Mitra and Varuṇa, the Aśvins, Indra, the Viśvedevas, Sarasvatī, and Heaven and Earth.

12 From all the regions of the world let
   Indra send security,
   The foe-subduer, swift to act.

13 O all ye Gods, come hitherward : hear
   this mine invocation, seat
   Yourselves upon this sacred grass.

14 Among the Śunahotras strong for you is
   this sweet gladdening draught.
   Drink ye of this delightsome juice.

15 Ye Martus led by Indra, Gods with
   Pūṣan for your bounteousest,
   Hear all of you this call of mine.

16 Best Mother, best of Rivers, best of Goddesses, Sarasvatī, We are, as 'twere, of
   no repute and dear Mother, give thou us
   renown.

17 In thee, Sarasvatī, divine, all generations
   have their stay.
   Be, glad with Śunahotra's sons : O
   Goddess grant us progeny.

18 Enriched with sacrifice, accept Sarasvatī,
   these prayers of ours,
   Thoughts which Gṛtsamadas beloved of
   Gods bring, Holy One, to thee.

19 Ye who bless sacrifice, go forth, for verily
   we choose you both,
   And Agni who conveys our gifts.

20 This our effectual sacrifice, reaching the
   sky, shall Heaven and Earth
   Present unto the Gods to-day.

21 In both your laps, ye guileless Ones, the
   Holy Gods shall sit them down
   To-day to drink the Soma here.

HYMN XLII   *Kapiñjala.*

1. TELLING his race aloud with cries repeated,
   he sends his voice out as his boat a
   steersman.

O Bird, be ominous of happy fortune :
from no side may calamity befall thee.

2 Let not the falcon kill thee, nor the eagle :
let not the arrow-bearing archer reach
thee.
Still crying in the region of the Fathers,
speak here auspicious, bearing joyful
tidings.

3 Bringing good tidings, Bird of happy
omen, call thou out loudly southward
of our dwellings,
So that no thief, no sinner may oppress
us. Loud may we speak, with heroes,
in assembly.

HYMN XLIII.   *Kapiñjala.*

1. HERE on the right sing forth chanters of
hymns of praise, even the winged birds
that in due season speak.
He, like a Sāma-chanter utters both the
notes, skilled in the mode of Tṛṣṭup
and of Gāyatrī.

2 Thou like the chanter-priest chantest the
Sāma, Bird ; thou singest at libations like
a Brahman's son.
Even as a vigorous horse when he comes
near the mare, announce to us good
fortune, Bird, on every side, proclaim in
all directions happy luck, O Bird.

3 When singing here, O Bird. announce
good luck to us, and when thou sittest
still think on us with kind thoughts.
When flying off thou singest thou art
like a lute. With brave sons in
assembly may we speak aloud.

---

14 *Among the Śunahotras* : the family of which Gṛtsamada, the Ṛṣi of the hymn, was a member. Cf. II. 18.
6, note.

15 *With Pūṣan for your bounteousest* : that is, among
whom Pūṣan is the most liberal giver of good gifts; or the
meaning may be, whose benefactor is Pūṣan.

16 *Sarasvatī* : see I. 3. 10.

19 *Ye who bless sacrifice* : according to Sāyaṇa, the
two *havirdhānas* or vehicles on which the Soma and other
offerings are put, and which are supposed to represent
Heaven and Earth, are addressed. It is more likely, as
Ludwig suggests, that Agni and the human priest are
intended. 'We choose you both, thee, the human priest,
and Agni the God.'

This Hymn is said to be addressed to Indra in the
form of a kapiñjala, the bird which we call the Francoline
partridge.

1 *He* : the kapiñjala.

2 *In the region of the Fathers* : towards the quarter
where the Fathers Pitaras, or spirits of deceased ancestors dwell, that is, the south the cry of birds from that
quarter being regarded as auspicious.

This Hymn is said to be addressed, like the preceding,
to Indra in the form of a kapiñjala or Francoline partridge.

1 *Sāma-chanter* : the Udgātar, one of the four chief
priests whose duty is to chant the hymns of the Sāmaveda
Both the notes : a high and a middle. *Triṣṭup* : the
measure consisting of forty-four syllables in a verse or
stanza; four Pādas or demi-hemistichs of eleven syllables
each. *Gāyatrī* : the measure consisting of twenty-four
syllables in a stanza, three lines of eight syllables each,
or one line of sixteen and one of eight.

2 *A Brahman's son* : the Brahmaputra, or Brāhman-
priest's son, is said to be the same as the Brāhmaṇāc-
chhaṁsī, one of the sixteen priests who recites the *mantra*
that is not to be sung or chanted.

BOOK THE THIRD

HYMN I. *Agni.*

1. THOU, Agni, who wilt have the strong, hast made me the Soma's priest, to worship in assembly.

   Thou shinest to the Gods, I set the press-stones. I toil ; be joyful in thyself, O Agni.

2. East have we turned the rite ; may the hymn aid it. With wood and worship shall they honour Agni.

   From heaven the synods of the wise have learnt it : e'en for the quick and strong they seek advancement.

3. The Prudent, he whose will is pure, brought welfare, allied by birth to Heaven and Earth in kinship.

   The Gods discovered in the midst of waters beautiful Agni with the Sisters' labour.

4. Him, Blessed One, the Seven strong Floods augmented, him white at birth and red when waxen mighty.

   As mother mares run to their new-born youngling, so at his birth the Gods wondered at Agni.

5. Spreading with radiant limbs throughout the region, purging his power with wise purifications,

Robing himself in light, the life of waters, he spreads abroad his high and perfect glories.

6. He sought heaven's Mighty Ones, the un-consuming, the unimpaired, not clothed and yet not naked.

   Then they, ancient and young, who dwell together, Seven sounding Rivers, as one germ received him.

7. His piles, assuming every form, are scatte-red where flow sweet waters, at the spring of fatness ;

   There stood the milch-kine with full-laden udders, and both paired Mighty Mothers of the Wondrous.

8. Carefully cherished, Son of Strength, thou shonest assuming lasting and refulgent beauties.

   Full streams of fatness and sweet juice descended, there where the Mighty One grew strong by wisdom.

9. From birth he knew even his Father's bosom, he set his voices and his streams in motion ;

   Knew him who moved with blessed Friends in secret, with the young Dames of heaven. He stayed not hidden.

10. He nursed the Infant of the Sire and Maker : alone the Babe sucked many a teeming bosom.

    Guard, for the Bright and Strong, the fellow-spouses friendly to men and bound to him in kinship.

11. The Mighty One increased in space un-bounded ; full many a glorious flood gave strength to Agni.

The Hymns of Book III. are ascribed to the Ṛṣi Viśvāmitra or to members of his family. Viśvāmitra holds an important place in Indian tradition, according to which he was born a Kṣatriya, but by the virtue of his intense austerities raised himself to the Brāhman caste. The rivalry between Viśvāmitra and the Ṛṣi Vasiṣṭha is alluded to in many passages of the Ṛgveda, and, it is thought that as caste distinctions had not at that time become fixed, the later stories on the subject of this rivalry may have rested on a Vedic legend which says that King Sudās, having employed Vasiṣṭha as his domestic priest, allowed on various occasions Viśvāmitra also to officiate, which led to jealousies and quarrel between these two functionaries. The story of Viśvāmitra is told at full length in the *Rāmāyaṇa*, I. 51—55, (Schlegel's edition, and Griffith's translation).

The first and eleven following hymns are ascribed to Viśvāmitra himself.

1 *East have we turned the rite* : towards the region of the Gods ; 'we have performed a successful sacrifice.' —Wilson.

2 *The quick and strong* : Agni, according to Sāyaṇa. Ludwig suggests that 'the quick, or clever' may mean the priest, and 'the strong' the warrior, the Maghavan or institutor of the sacrifice.

3 *The Prudent* : all-knowing Agni, son of Heaven and Earth.

With the Sisters' labour : the meaning is not clear. Ludwig suggests *upasi* instead of *apási* ; 'in the sisters' 'bosom,' in the depth of the sister rivers.

6 *Heaven's mighty Ones* : the waters above the firma-ment, the seven rivers of the next hemistich. *Not clothed and yet not naked* : having only the lucid waters for robes.

7 *His piles* : the heaped clouds. *Spring of fatness* : the place whence the fertilizing rain flows. *The milch kine* also are the laden clouds, and the *paired Mighty Mothers* are Heaven and Earth, the parents of *the Wondrous* Agni.

9 *His Father's bosom* : his father, according to Sāyaṇa, is the firmament ; but as the firmament is not represented in the Veda as a God, Dyaus, or Tvaṣṭar, is probably intended, as Ludwig suggests.

The *blessed Friends* must be the Ṛbhus, and *the young Dames* the Gnās or consorts of the Gods. *He stayed not hidden* : refers not to Agni but to his father, Tvaṣṭar.

10 *He* : the father, *Many a swelling bosom* : of the celestial Waters.

The Bright and Strong : Agni. *The fellow-spouses* : Heaven and Earth, or Night and Morning.

11 *In the Sister Rivers' service* : or in their bosom, if *upasi* may be read for *apási*.

Friend of the house, within the lap of Order lay Agni, in the Sister Rivers' service.

12 As keen supporter where great waters gather, light-shedder whom the brood rejoice to look on ;
He who begat, and will beget, the dawn-lights, most manly, Child of Floods, is youthful Agni.

13 Him, varied in his form, the lovely Infant of floods and plants the blessed wood hath gendered.
Gods even, moved in spirit, came around him, and served him at his birth, the Strong, the Wondrous.

14 Like brilliant lightnings, mighty luminaries accompany the light-diffusing Agni,
Waxen, as 'twere in secret, in his dwelling, while in the boundless stall they milk out Amṛta.

15 I sacrificing serve thee with oblations and crave with longing thy good-will and friendship.
Grant, with the Gods, thy grace to him who lauds thee, protect us with thy rays that guard the homestead.

16 May we, O Agni, thou who leadest wisely, thy followers and masters of all trea-sures,
Strong in the glory of our noble offspring, subdue the godless when they seek the battle.

17 Ensign of Gods hast thou become, O Agni, joy-giver, knower of all secret wisdom.
Friend of the homestead, thou hast lighte-ned mortals : carborne thou goest to the Gods, fulfilling.

18 Within the house hath sate the King immortal of mortals, filling full their sacred synods.
Bedewed with holy oil he shineth widely, Agni, the knower of all secret wisdom.

19 Come unto us with thine auspicious friend-ship, come speeding, Mighty, with thy mighty succours.
Grant us abundant wealth that saves from danger, that brings a good repute, a glorious portion.

20 To thee who art of old these songs, O Agni, have I declared, the ancient and the later.
These great libations to the Strong are offered : in every birth is Jātavedas stablished.

21 Stablished in every birth is Jātavedas, kindled perpetual by the Viśvāmitras.
May we rest ever in the loving-kindness, in the auspicious grace of him the Holy.

22 This sacrifice of ours do thou, O Mighty, O truly Wise, bear to the Gods rejoi-cing.
Grant us abundant food, thou priestly Herald, vouchsafe to give us ample wealth, O Agni.

23 As holy food, Agni, to thine invoker give wealth in cattle, lasting, rich in marvels.
To us be born a son, and spreading offspring. Agni, be this thy gracious will to us-ward.

HYMN II. *Agni.*

1. To him, Vaiśvānara, who strengthens Holy Law, to Agni we present our praise like oil made pure.
With thoughtful insight human priests bring him anear, our Herald from of old, as an axe forms a car.

2 He made the heaven and earth resplendent by his birth : Child of two Mothers he was meet to be implored,
Agni, oblation-bearer, gracious, ever-young, infallible, rich in radiant light, the guest of men.

3 Within the range of their surpassing power, by might, the Gods created Agni with inventive thought.
I, eager to win strength, address him, like a steed, resplendent with his brilliance, with his ample light.

4 Eager to gain, we crave from him the friendly God strength confident, choice-worthy, meet to be extolled :

20 *Songs* : literally, births; that is, productions. *In every birth is Jātavedas stablished* : Agni who knows all life is appointed in every generation as the great high priest who mediates between Gods and men.

---

1 *Vaiśvānara* : Agni who belongs to all men ; the God of all Āryan families.
Our praise : literally 'the wish,' explained by Sāyaṇa as *stutim*, that is the praise which thou wishest for and which we now offer.
2 *Child of two Mothers* : of Heaven and Earth, or of the two fire-sticks.
4 *The Bhṛgus' bounty* : Agni, the treasure which the Bhṛgus received from Mātariśvan and bestowed on other men.

---

12 *The brood* : *par excellence*, the host of Maruts.
13 *The blessed wood* : one of the fire-sticks by which Agni is kindled.
14 *The boundless stall* : limitless aerial space. *Amṛta* : water, according to Sāyaṇa.
17 *Thou goest to the Gods, fulfilling* : completing our sacrifices and making them effectual.

The Bhṛgus' bounty, willing, strong with sages' lore, even Agni shining forth with light that comes from heaven.

5 For happiness, men, having trimmed the sacred grass, set Agni glorious for his strength before them here ;
Yea, with raised ladles, him bright, dear to all the Gods, perfecting aims of works, Rudra of solemn rites.

6 Around thy dwelling-place, O brightly-shining Priest, are men at sacrifice whose sacred grass is trimmed.
Wishing to do thee service, Agni, they are there, desirous of thy friendship : grant them store of wealth.

7 He hath filled heaven and earth and the great realm of light, when at his birth the skilful held him in their hold.
He like a horse is led forth to the sacrifice Sage, graciously inclined, that he may win us strength.

8 Honour the oblation-bearer, him who knows fair rites, serve ye the Household Friend who knows all things that be.
He drives the chariot of the lofty ordinance : Agni most active, is the great High Priest of Gods.

9 They who are free from death, fain for him, purified three splendours of the mighty Agni, circling all.
To man, for his enjoyment, one of these they gave : the other two have passed into the sister sphere.

10 Man's sacrificial food hath sharpened like an axe, for brightness, him the Sage of men, the people's Lord,
Busied with sacred rites he mounts and he descends. He hath laid down his vital germ within these worlds.

11 He stirs with life in wombs dissimilar in kind, born as a Lion or a loudly-bellowing Bull :
Vaiśvānara immortal with wide-reaching might, bestowing goods and wealth on him who offers gifts.

12 Vaiśvānara, as of old, mounted the cope of heaven, heaven's ridge, well greeted, by those skilled in noble songs.
He, as of old, producing riches for the folk, still watchful, traverses the common way again.

13 For new prosperity we seek to Agni, him whose course is splendid, gold-haired, excellently bright,
Whom Mātariśvan stablished, dweller in the heaven, meet for high praise and holy, sage and true to Law.

14 As pure and swift of course, beholder of the light, who stands in heaven's bright sphere a sign, who wakes at dawn,
Agni, the head of heaven, whom none may turn aside—to him the Powerful with mighty prayer we seek.

15 The cheerful Priest, the pure, in whom no guile is found, Friend of the House, praise-worthy, dear to all mankind,
Fair to behold for beauty like a splendid car,—Agni the Friend of men we ever seek for wealth.

HYMN III. *Agni.*

1. To him who shines afar, Vaiśvānara, shall bards give precious things that he may go on certain paths :
For Agni the Immortal serves the Deities, and therefore never breaks their ever-lasting laws.

2 He, wondrous envoy, goes between the earth and heaven, firm seated as the Herald, great High Priest of men.
He compasseth with rays the lofty dwelling-place, Agni, sent forward by the Gods, enriched with prayer.

3 Sages shall glorify Agni with earnest thoughts, ensign of sacrifice, who fills the synod full :
In whom the singers have stored up their holy acts to him the worshipper looks for joy and happiness.

4 The Sire of sacrifice, great God of holy bards, Agni, the measure and the symbol of the priests,

5 *Rudra* : here a synonym of Agni. See I. 27. 10.
7 *He* : Agni. *The skilful* : the priests.
8 *He drives the chariot* : he is the leader of sacrifice ordained by holy law.
9 *They who are free from death* : the immortal Gods. *Three splerdours* : with reference to his appearance as the Sun, the lightning, and domestic fire, the last of which is given to man as his own special possession.
10 *Within these worlds* : the germ of fire is always latent in the fire-sticks or two pieces of wood which are employed to produce the flame.
11 *Born as a Lion* : destructive and voracious, and as *a loudly-bellowing Bull*, with reference to his strength and the roar of his flames.

12 *The common way* : the path of the Gods, which as the Sun he travels.
14 *Who wakes at dawn* : when re-kindled for the morning sacrifice.

———

1 *That he may go on certain paths* : may constantly visit men.
2 *The lofty dwelling-place* : the hall or chamber in which sacrifice is celebrated.

Hath entered heaven and earth that show
in varied form : the Sage whom many
love rejoiceth in his might.

5 Bright Agni with the bright car, Lord of
green domains, Vaiśvānara dweller in
the floods, who finds the light,
Pervading, swift and wild, encompassed
round with powers, him very glorious
have the Gods established here.

6 Agni, together with the Gods and Manu's
folk by thought extending sacrifice in
varied form,
Goes, car-borne, to and fro with those
who crown each rite, the fleet, the
Household Friend, who turns the curse
aside.

7 Sing, Agni, for long life to us and noble
sons : teem thou with plenty, shine
upon us store of food.
Increase the great man's strength, thou
ever-vigilant : thou, longing for the
Gods, knowest their hymns full well.

8 The Mighty One, Lord of the people and
their guest, the leader of their thoughts,
devoted Friend of priests,
Our solemn rites' announcer, Jātavedas,
men with worship ever praise, with urgings for their weal.

9 Agni the God resplendent, giver of great
joy, hath on his lovely car compassed
the lands with might.
Let us with pure laudations in his house
approach the high laws of the nourisher
of multitudes.

10 I celebrate thy glories, O Vaiśvānara,
wherewith thou, O farsighted God, has
found the light.
Thou filledst at thy birth both worlds,
the earth and heaven : all this, O
Agni, hast thou compassed of thyself.

11 By his great skill the Sage alone hath
brought to pass a great deed, mightier
than Vaiśvānara's wondrous acts.
Agni sprang into being, magnifying both
his Parents, Heaven and Earth, rich in
prolific seed.

---

5 *Lord of green domains* : who has dominion over
bushes and trees.

6 *To and fro* : between heaven and earth. *Those
who crown each rite* : the Gods who make sacrifice effectual.

7 *The great man's strength* : the strength of the eminent man who is the institutor of the sacrifice.

9 *Approach the high laws* : perform the sacrifices—
—M. Müller.

11 The first hemistich of this stanza is somewhat obscure. Sāyaṇa's paraphrase as given by Wilson is :
'From acts that are acceptable to Vaiśvānara comes great
(wealth) ; for he, the sage (Agni) alone, bestows (the
reward) of zeal in (the performance of) his worship.

HYMN IV   *Āpris.*

1. BE friendly with each kindled log of fuel,
with every flash bestow the boon of
riches.
Bring thou the Gods, O God, unto our
worship : serve, well-inclined, as Friend
thy friends, O Agni.

2 Agni whom daily Varuṇa and Mitra the
Gods bring thrice a day to this our
worship,
Tanūnapāt, enrich with meath our service
that dwells with holy oil, that offers
honour.

3 The thought that bringeth every boon proceedeth to worship first the Priest of the
libation,
That we may greet the Strong One with
our homage. Urged, may he bring the
Gods, best Sacrificer.

4 On high your way to sacrifice was made
ready ; the radiant flames went upward
to the regions.
Full in the midst of heaven the Priest is
seated : strew we the sacred grass where
Gods may rest them.

5 Claiming in mind the seven priests' burnt-
oblations, inciting all, they came in
settled order.
To this our sacrifice approach the many
who show in hero beauty at assemblies.

6 Night and Dawn, lauded, hither come
together, both smiling, different are their
forms in colour,
That Varuṇa and Mitra may accept us,
and Indra, girt by Maruts, with his
glories.

7 I crave the grace of heaven's two chief
Invokers : the seven swift steeds joy in
their wonted manner.

The Āpris who are said to be the deities of this hymn
are the divine or deified beings and objects to which the
propitiatory verses are addressed. The hymn, as Wilson
remarks, 'is more complicated and obscure than any
of the preceding addressed to the Āpris, except Sûkta
III, of the Second Maṇḍala (II. 3), to which it bears
the nearest analogy : they are both perhaps of somewhat later date than the others.'

2 *Tanūnapāt* : a name of Agni 'Child of Thyself.'
See I. 12. 2

4 *Your way* : a path for Agni and the *Barhis* or sacred
grass, the God and the deified object addressed in the
stanza.

In the midst of heaven : in the centre of the radiant hall
of sacrifice, as Sāyaṇa explains it.

5 This stanza refers to the deified doors of the hall of
sacrifice, and to the deities who preside over them.

7 *Heaven's two chief Invokers* : Agni and perhaps
Varuṇa. See I. 13. 8.

These speak of truth, praising the truth
eternal, thinking on Order as the guards
of Order.

8 May Bhāratī with all her Sisters, Iḷā accordant with the Gods, with mortals Agni,
Sarasvatī with all her kindred Rivers, come
to this grass, Three Goddesses, and seat
them.

9 Well pleased with us do thou O God, O
Tvaṣṭar, give ready issue to our procreant
vigour,
Whence springs the hero, powerful, skilled
in action, lover of Gods, adjuster of the
press-stones.

10 Send to the Gods the oblation, Lord of
Forests ; and let the Immolator, Agni,
dress it.
He as the truer Priest shall offer worship,
for the Gods' generations well he knoweth.

11 Come thou to us, O Agni, duly kindled,
together with the potent Gods and
Indra.
On this our grass sit Aditi, happy Mother,
and let our Hail delight the Gods
Immortal.

HYMN V.   *Agni.*

1. AGNI who shines against the Dawns is
wakened. The holy Singer who precedes the sages.
With far-spread lustre, kindled by the
pious, the Priest hath thrown both gates
of darkness open.

2 Agni hath waxen mighty by laudations,
to be adored with hymns of those who
praise him.
Loving the varied shows of holy Order at
the first flush of dawn he shines as
envoy.

3 Amid men's homes hath Agni been established, fulfilling with the Law, Friend,
germ of waters.

Loved and adored, the height he hath
ascended, the Singer, object of our invocations.

4 Agni is Mitra when enkindled duly, Mitra
as Priest, Varuṇa, Jātavedas ;
Mitra as active minister, and House-Friend,
Mitra of flowing rivers and of mountains.

5 The Earth's, the Bird's dear lofty place he
guardeth, he guardeth in his might the
course of Sūrya,
Guardeth the Seven-headed in the centre,
guardeth sublime the Deities enjoyment.

6 The skilful God who knows all forms of
knowledge made for himself a fair form,
meet for worship.
This Agni guards with care that never
ceases the Soma's skin, the Bird's place
rich in fatness.

7 Agni hath entered longingly the longing
shrine rich with fatness, giving easy
access.
Resplendent, pure, sublime and purifying,
again, again he renovates his Mothers.

8 Born suddenly, by plants he grew to
greatness, when tender shoots with holy
oil increased him,
Like waters lovely when they hasten downward may Agni in his Parents' lap protect us.

9 Extolled, the Strong shone forth with
kindled fuel to the earth's centre, to the
height of heaven.
May Agni, Friend, adorable Mātariśvan,
as envoy bring the Gods unto our worship.

The seven swift steeds : seven ministering priests.

8 *Bhāratī, Iḷā,* and *Sarasvatī* are Goddesses presiding
over different departments of religious worship. See I.
13. 9. The name of Agni is inserted somewhat unconnec-
tedly.

10 *Lord of Forests* : Vanaspati, a large tree ; here the
sacrificial post which is said to be a form of Agni.

Truer Priest as compared with human priests.

11 *Happy Mother* : literally, having excellent sons,
the Ādityas.

---

1 *Who shines against the Dawns* : rekindled for the
morning sacrifices.
Who precedes the sages : as their guide and teacher.
The Priest : Agni.
3 *The height* : the place called the north altar, says
Sāyaṇa. Perhaps the height of heaven may be intended.

4 Agni is here identified with Mitra, the Sun, and
both these Gods are identified with Varuṇa.

5 *The dear lofty place* of the earth may be the altar,
or the eastern point. *The Bird* is the Sun who flies
through heaven. *The Seven-headed,* said by Sāyaṇa to be
the host of Maruts, is more probably the Sun drawn by
his seven horses.

6 *The Soma's skin* : the meaning of the words *sasásya
cárma* is not clear. An envelope or a covering, which
in some mystical way is supposed to conceal the Soma-
plant, appears to be intended. *The Bird's place* : the
station of the Sun, who is adored with oblations of clarified butter.

7 *His Mothers* : or his parents, Heaven and Earth,
who are strengthened and restored to their youth by
sacrifice.
The *plants* are the twigs used as fuel, and the *tender
shoots* are the bunch of grass used in sprinkling the clarified butter over the fire.

9 *The earth's centre* : earth's most important place,
the altar.
In the second hemistich Agni is identified with
Mātariśvan the divine or semi-divine being who brought
him from heaven.

10 Best of all luminaries lofty Agni supported
   with his flame the height of heaven,
   When, far from Bhṛgus, Mātariśvan
   kindled the oblation-bearer where he lay
   in secret.

11 As holy food, Agni to thine invoker give
   wealth in cattle, lasting, rich in marvels.
   To us be born a son and spreading offspring. Agni, be this thy gracious will
   to us-word.

HYMN VI.   *Agni.*

1. URGED on by deep devotion, O ye singers,
   bring, pious ones, the God-approaching
   ladle.
   Borne onward to the right it travels eastward, and, filled with oil, to Agni
   bears oblation.

2 Thou at thy birth didst fill both earth
   and heaven, yea, Most Adorable, thou
   didst exceed them.
   Even through the heaven's and through
   the earth's expanses let thy swift seven-
   tongued flames roll on, O Agni.

3 Both Heaven and Earth and Gods who
   should be worshipped establish thee as
   Priest for every dwelling,
   Whenever human families, God-devoted,
   bringing oblations; laud thy splendid
   lustre.

4 Firm in the Gods' home is the Mighty
   seated, between vast Heaven and Earth
   the well-beloved—
   Those Cows who yield, unharmed, their
   nectar, Spouses of the Far-Strider, ever-
   young, united.

5 Great are the deeds of thee, the Great, O
   Agni : thou by thy power hast spread
   out earth and heaven.
   As soon as thou wast born thou wast an
   envoy, thou, Mighty One, was Leader
   of the people.

6 Bind to the pole with cords of holy Order
   the long-maned ruddy steeds who
   sprinkle fatness.

Bring hither, O thou God, all Gods together : provide them noble worship,
Jātavedas.

7 Even from the sky thy brilliant lights
  shone hither : still hast thou beamed
  through many a radiant morning,
  That the Gods praised their joyous Herald's
  labour eagerly burning, Agni, in the
  forests.

8 The Gods who take delight in air's wide
  region, or those the dwellers in heaven's
  realm of brightness,
  Or those, the Holy, prompt to hear, our
  helpers, who, carborne, turn their horses
  hither, Agni—

9 With these, borne on one car, Agni,
  approach us, or borne on many, for thy
  steeds are able.
  Bring, with their Dames, the Gods, the
  Three and-Thirty, after thy Godlike
  nature, and be joyful.

10 He is the Priest at whose repeated worship
   even wide Heaven and Earth sing out
   for increase.
   They fair and true and holy coming forward stand at his sacrifice who springs
   from Order.

11 As holy food, Agni, to thine invoker give
   wealth in cattle, lasting, rich in marvels.
   To us be born a son and spreading offspring. Agni, be this thy gracious will to us-
   ward.

HYMN VII.

1. THE seven tones risen from the white-
   backed viand have made their way
   between the pair of Mothers.
   Both circumjacent Parents come together :
   to yield us length of days they hasten
   forward.

---

10 *Far from Bhṛgus* : the words in the text would seem
to mean that Mātariśvan took the fire from the Bhṛgus ;
but as Ludwig suggests, *pári* perhaps implies separation.
Sāyaṇa explains *Bhṛgus* in this place by rays of the Sun.

---

1 *The God-approaching ladle* : the sacrificial ladle with
which the oblation of clarified butter or oil is offered to
the Gods.

Borne onward to the right : or to the south of the fire-
altar. According to Ludwig, bearing the sacrificial gift.

4 *The Mighty* : Agni. *Those Cows* : Heaven and
Earth who yield all blessings, here called also the spouses of Viṣṇu, the God of the mighty stride, that is,
the Sun, or as Sāyaṇa says, of the far-extending Agni.

9 *The Three-and-Thirty* : See 1. 34. 11.
This hymn and the five following are ascribed to
the Ṛṣi Viśvāmitra.

---

1 *The seven tones* are the hymns sung in seven
tones, or metres. *The white-backed wand* is the Soma
mingled with milk, and *the pair of Mothers* or Mother
and Father are heaven and Earth whose intermediate
space the hymns have reached. The *circumjacent Parents*
are heaven and Earth. The construction in the first
half of the stanza is difficult, the masculine form *ye*
being apparently used for the feminine. Sāyaṇa inserts
raśmayaḥ, rays, which he makes the subject of the first
sentence, and explains *dhāsi*, viand, by 'the all-sustaining Agni,' and *saptá váṇīḥ*, seven voices or tones, by 'the
flowing rivers.' The hymn is full of difficulties ; 'an
intentionally obscure hymn, says Professor Grassmann,
'whose partially corrupt text cannot, on account of this
obscurity, be satisfactorily re-established.'

2 The Male who dwells in heaven hath
Mares and Milchkine : he came to Goddesses who bring sweet treasure.
To thee safe resting in the seat of Order
the Cow alone upon her way proceedeth.

3 Wise Master, wealthy finder-out of riches,
he mounted those who may with ease
be guided.
He, dark-backed, manifold with varied
aspect, hath made them burst forth
from their food the brush-wood.

4 Strength-giving streams bear hither him
eternal, fain to support the mighty work·
of Tvaṣṭar.
He, flashing in his home with all his
members, hath entered both the worlds
as they were single.

5 They know the red Bull's blessing, and are
joyful under the flaming-coloured Lord's
dominion :
They who give shine from heaven with
fair effulgence, whose lofty song like Ilā
must be honoured.

6 Yea, by tradition from the ancient sages
they brought great strength from the
two mighty Parents,
To where the singer's Bull, the night's
dispeller, after his proper law hath
waxen stronger.

7 Seven holy singers guard with five Adhvaryus the Bird's beloved firmly-settled
station.
The willing Bulls, untouched by old, rejoice
them : as Gods themselves the ways of
Gods they follow.

8 I crave the grace of heaven's two chief
Invokers : the seven swift steeds joy in
their wonted manner.
These speak of truth, praising the Truth
Eternal, thinking on Order as the guards
of Order.

9 The many seek the great Steed as a stallion : the reins obey the Lord of varied
colour.
O heavenly Priest, most pleasant, full of
wisdom, bring the great Gods to us, and
Earth and Heaven.

10 Rich Lord, the Mornings have gleamed
forth in splendour, fair-rayed, fair-speak-
ing, worshipped with all viands,
Yea, with the glory of the earth, O Agni.
Forgive us, for our weal, e'en sin committed.

11 As holy food, Agni, to thine invoker, give
wealth in cattle, lasting, rich in marvels.
To us be born a son, and spreading offspring
Agni, be this thy gracious will to us-
ward.

HYMN VIII   Sacrificial Post.

1. GOD-SERVING men, O Sovran of the Forest,
with heavenly meath at sacrifice anoint
thee.
Grant wealth to us when thou art standing upright as when reposing on this
Mother's bosom.

2 Set up to eastward of the fire enkindled,
accepting prayer that wastes not, rich
in hero.
Driving far from us poverty and famine,
lift thyself up to bring us great good
fortune.

3 Lord of the Forest, raise thyself up on the
loftiest spot of earth.

2 *The Male who dwells in heaven* : celestial Agni.
The *Mares and Milch-kine* are the Goddesses of the air :
To thee : to Agni.
The Cow : Vāk the Goddess of Speech, i.e., speech
itself, prayer.

3 *Wise Master* : Agni. *Those* : his mares, the rapidly
advancing flames that bear him onward. *Dark-backed* :
with smoke.

4 *Strength-giving streams* : the waters of the air which
bring down the embryo Agni in rain. *The mighty work
of Tvaṣṭar* : the whole creation, or, as there is no
substantive expressed, the sun of Tvaṣṭar, the Sun, may
be intended. *As they were single* : hath pervaded and
illumined heaven and earth simultaneously, as though
they were one world.

5 *The red Bull* : Agni. *They* : perhaps the Gods.
Ilā : Prayer or Praise.

6 *They* : the men who first honoured Agni who is
called *the singer's Bull*, the strong God who protects his
worshipper.

7 *Adhvaryus* : ministering priests. *The Bird* : the
rapidly-flying Agni. *The willing Bulls* : the zealous priests,
who in this stanza are boldly called Gods. Cf. 'Is it not
written in your law, I said, Ye are Gods ?' (St. John,
x. 11).

8 *Heaven's two chief Invokers* : or Hotars ; according to
Sāyaṇa, the celestial and the terrestrial Agni. This
stanza is repeated from III. 4. 7.

9 *The many* : the adjective is feminine and has no
substantive expressed. The Dawns may be intended, or
perhaps libations.

10 This concluding stanza is the burden of several
hymns of this Book, and there is considerable variation
in Sāyaṇa's interpretation of it in the different places in
which it occurs.

———

1 *O Sovran of the Forest* : the tall tree (*vánaspáti*)
out of which is made the sacrificial post to which the
victim is tied. The post when consecrated is a deified
object and is regarded as a form of Agni.

With heavenly meath : or balm ; sacred oil or clarified butter. For a full account of the ceremony of
anointing the Sacrificial Post, see Haug's Aitareya
Brāhmaṇa. Vol. II. pp. 74-78.

3 *The loftiest spot of earth* : the altar.

Give splendour, fixt and measured well,
to him who brings the sacrifice.

4 Well-robed, enveloped he is come, the
youthful : springing to life his glory
waxeth greater.
Contemplative in mind and God-adoring,
sages of high intelligence upraise him.

5 Sprung up he rises in the days' fair
weather, increasing in the men-frequen-
ted synod.
With song the wise and skilful consecrate
him : his voice the God-adoring singer
utters.

6 Ye whom religious men have firmly planted; thou Forest Sovran whom the axe
hath fashioned,—
Let those the Stakes divine which here
are standing be fain to grant us wealth
with store of children.

7 O men who lift the ladles up, these hewn
and planted in the ground,
Bringing a blessing to the field, shall bear
our precious gift to Gods.

8 Ādityas, Rudras, Vasus, careful leaders,
Earth, Heaven, and Pṛthivi and Air's
mid-region,
Accordant Deities, shall bless our worship
and make our sacrifice's ensign lofty.

9 Like swan's that flee in lengthened line,
the Pillars have come to us arrayed in
brilliant colour.
They, lifted up on high, by sages, eastward, go forth as Gods to the God's
dwelling-places.

10 Those Stakes upon the earth with rings
that deck them seem to the eye like
horns of horned creatures;
Or, as upraised by priests in invocation,
let them assist us in the rush to battle.

11 Lord of the Wood, rise with a hundred
branches : with thousand branches may
we rise to greatness,
Thou whom this hatchet, with an edge
well whetted for great felicity, hath
brought before us.

4 *Well-robed, enveloped* : with a cord or garland.

5 *In the days' fair weather* : when the periodical
Rains are over.

7 *These hewn and planted* : apparently splinters cut
from the tree.

8 *Pṛthivi* : Earth regarded as single, and not as
one of the constantly connected pair Heaven and Earth.

9 *Pillars* : apparently chips or splinters (cf. stanza
7), which fall from the tree, as it is cut to form the
Sacrificial Stake, like white or grey birds alighting on
the ground.

HYMN IX.

1. WE as thy friends have chosen thee, mortals a God, to be our help,
The Waters' Child, the blessed, the resplendent One, victorious and beyond
compare.

2 Since thou delighting in the woods hast
gone unto thy mother streams,
Not to be scorned, Agni, is that return of
thine when from afar thou now art here.

3 O'er pungent smoke host thou prevailed,
and thus art thou benevolent.
Some go before, and others round about
thee sit, they in whose friendship thou
hast place.

4 Him who had passed beyond his foes,
beyond continual pursuits, Him the
unerring Ones, observant, found in floods,
couched like a lion in his lair.

5 Him wandering at his own free will, Agni
here hidden from our view,
Him Mātariśvan brought to us from far
away produced by friction, from the
Gods.

6 O Bearer of Oblations, thus mortals received
thee from the Gods,
Whilst thou, the Friend of man, guardest
each sacrifice with thine own power,
Most Youthful One.

7 Amid thy wonders this is good, yea, to
the simple is it clear,
When gathered round about thee, Agni,
lie the herds where thou art kindled in
the morn.

8 Offer to him who knows fair rites, who
burns with purifying glow,
Swift envoy, active, ancient, and adorable:
serve ye the God attentively.

9 Three times a hundred Gods and thrice
a thousand, and three times ten and nine
have worshipped Agni,

2 *That return of thine* : thy descent from the celestial waters in which thou art born as lightning.

3 *Some* : according to Sāyaṇa, the Adhvaryus ;
others : the Sāma-priests who sit and recite the prayers
and hymns.

4 *The unerring Ones* : The Gods, who followed and
found the fugitive Agni.

5 *Mātariśvan* : the divine or semi-divine being who
brought Agni to men. See Index.

7 *In the morn* : before the cattle are sent out to
graze. *The herds*, according to the Scholiast, include
men as well as quadrupeds.

9 In the Vaiśvadeva Nivid or Hymn of Invitation
to the Viśvedevas, the number of the Gods is said to
be 3 times 11, then 33, then 303, then 3003. By adding
together $33 + 303 + 3003$ the number 3339 is obtained.
See Haug's Aitareya Brāhmaṇa, II. p. 212, note.

For him spread sacred grass, with oil bedewed him, and stablished him as Priest
and Sacrificer.

HYMN X.   *Agni.*

1. THEE Agni, God, Imperial Lord of all
mankind, do mortal men
With understanding kindle at the sacrifice.
2 They laud thee in their solemn rites, Agni,
as Minister and Priest,
Shine forth in thine own home as guardian
of the Law.
3 He, verily, who honours thee with fuel,
Knower of all life,
He, Agni! wins heroic might, he prospers
well.
4 Ensign of sacrifices, he, Agni, with Gods
is come to us,
Decked by the seven priests, to him who
bringeth gifts.
5 To Agni, the Invoking Priest, offer your
best, your lofty speech,
To him Ordainer-like who brings the light
of songs.
6 Let these our hymns make Agni grow,
whence, meet for laud, he springs to
life,
To mighty strength and great possession,
fair to see.
7 Best Sacrificer, bring the Gods, O Agni,
to the pious man :
A joyful Priest, thy splendour drive our
foes afar !
8 As such, O Purifier, shine on us heroic
glorious might :
Be nearest Friend to those who laud thee,
for their weal.
9 So, wakeful, versed in sacred hymns, the
holy singers kindly thee.
Oblation-bearer, deathless, cherisher of
strength.

HYMN XI.   *Agni.*

1. AGNI is Priest, the great High Priest of
sacrifice, most swift in act :
He knows the rite in constant course.
2 Oblation-bearer, deathless, well inclined,
an eager messenger,
Agni comes nigh us with the thought.
3 Ensign of sacrifice from of old, Agni well
knoweth with his thought
To prosper this man's aim and hope.

4 Agni, illustrious from old time, the Son
of Strength who knows all life,
The Gods have made to their Priest.
5 Infallible is Agni, he who goes before the
tribes of men,
A chariot swift and ever new.
6 Strength of the Gods which none may
harm, subduing all his enemies,
Agni is mightiest in fame.
7 By offering sacred food to him the mortal
worshipper obtains.
A home from him whose light makes pure.
8 From Agni, by our hymns, may we gain
all things that bring happiness,
Singers of him who knows all life.
9 O Agni, in our deeds of might may we
obtain all precious things :
The Gods are centred all in thee.

HYMN XII.   *Indra-Agni.*

1. MOVED, Indra-Agni, by our hymn, come
to the juice, the precious dew:
Drink ye thereof, impelled by song.
2 O Indra-Agni, with the man who lauds
you comes the wakening rite :
So drink ye both this juice assured.
3 Through force of sacrifice I choose Indra-
Agni who love the wise :
With Soma let these sate them here.
4 Indra and Agni I invoke, joint-victors,
bounteous, unsubdued,
Foe-slayers, best to win the spoil.
5 Indra and Agni, singers skilled in melody
hymn you, bringing lauds :
I choose you for the sacred food.
6 Indra and Agni, ye cast down the ninety
forts which Dāsas held,
Together, with one mighty deed.
7 To Indra-Agni reverent thoughts go forward from the holy task
Along the path of sacred Law.
8 O Indra-Agni, powers are yours, and
dwellings and delightful food :
Good is your readiness to act.
9 Indra and Agni, in your deeds of might
ye deck heaven's lucid realms :
Famed is that hero strength of yours.

---

3 *This man's* : who institutes the sacrifice.

---

6 *The ninety forts* : ninety is used indefinitely for
a large number. The forts are the strongholds of the
non-Āryan inhabitants of the country.

7 *The holy task* : sacrifice.

---

5 *Who brings the light of songs* : Who brightens and
inspires our hymns.

---

2 *With the thought* : or, through our prayer.

HYMN XIII. *Agni.*

1. To Agni, to this God of yours I sing
   aloud with utmost power.
   May he come to us with the Gods, and
   sit, best Offerer, on the grass.

2 The Holy, whose are earth and heaven,
   and succour waits upon his strength;
   Him men who bring oblations laud, and
   they who wish to gain, for grace.

3 He is the Sage who guides these men,
   Leader of sacred rites is he.
   Him your own Agni, serve ye well, who
   winneth and bestoweth wealth.

4 So may the gracious Agni grant most goodly
   shelter for our use ;
   Whence in the heavens or in the floods he
   shall pour wealth upon our lands.

5 The singers kindle him, the Priest, Agni
   the Lord of tribes of men,
   Resplendent and without a peer through
   his own excellent designs.

6 Help us, thou Brahman, best of all invo-
   kers of the Gods in song.
   Beam, Friend of Maruts, bliss on us, O
   Agni, a most liberal God.

7 Yea, grant us treasure thousandfold with
   children and with nourishment,
   And, Agni, splendid hero strength, exalted,
   wasting not away.

HYMN XIV. *Agni.*

1 THE pleasant Priest is come into the synod,
   true, skilled in sacrifice, most wise,
   Ordainer.
   Agni, the Son of Strength, whose car is
   lightning, whose hair is flame, hath
   shown on earth his lustre.

2 To thee I offer reverent speech : accept
   it : to thee who markest it, victorious,
   faithful !
   Bring, thou who knowest, those who
   know, and seat thee amid the sacred
   grass, for help, O Holy.

3 The Two who show their vigour, Night
   and Morning, by the wind's paths shall
   haste to thee, O Agni.
   When men adorn the Ancient with
   oblations, these seek, as on two chariot-
   seats, the dwelling.

4 To thee, strong Agni ! Varuṇa and Mitra
   and all the Maruts sang a song of
   triumph,
   What time unto the people's lands thou
   camest, spreading them as the Sun of
   men, with lustre.

5 Approaching with raised hands and
   adoration, we have this day fulfilled
   for thee thy longing.
   Worship the Gods with most devoted
   spirit, a Priest with no unfriendly
   thought, O Agni.

6 For, Son of Strength, from thee come
   many succours, and powers abundant
   that a God possesses.
   Agni, to us with speech that hath no
   falsehood grant riches, real, to be told
   in thousands.

7 Whatever, God, in sacrifice we mortals
   have wrought is all for thee, strong,
   wise of purpose !
   Be thou the Friend of each good chariot's
   master. All this enjoy thou here,
   immortal Agni.

HYMN XV. *Agni.*

1. RESPLENDENT with thy wide-extending
   lustre, dispel the terrors of the fiends
   who hate us
   May lofty Agni be my guide and shelter,
   the easily-invoked, the good Protector.

2 Be thou to us, while now the morn is
   breaking, be thou a guardian when
   the Sun hath mounted.
   Accept, as men accept a true-born infant, my laud, O Agni nobly born in
   body.

3 Bull, who beholdest men, through many
   mornings, among the dark ones shine
   forth red, O Agni.
   Lead us, good Lord, and bear us over
   trouble : Help us who long, Most
   Youthful God, to riches.

4 Shine forth, a Bull invincible, O Agni,
   winning by conquest all the forts and
   treasures,
   Thou Jātavedas who art skilled in
   guiding, the chief high saving sacrifice's
   Leader.

The hymn and that which follows are ascribed to
the Ṛṣi Ṛṣabha, a son of Viśvāmitra.

6 *Thou Brahman* : Agni is here addressed as the
Brahman or praying priest.

---

2 *Those who know* : the Gods.
3 *The Ancient* : Agni.

4 *Spreading them* : causing Āryan men to spread as
the sun spreads his rays.

5 *Thy longing* : for oblations.

7 *All this* : all our sacrificial offerings.

---

3 *Among the dark ones* : in the darkness of the
nights.

5 Lighting Gods hither, Agni, wisest Singer,
bring thou to us many and flawless
shelters.
Bring vigour, like a car that gathers
booty : bring us, O Agni, beauteous
Earth and Heaven.

6 Swell, O thou Bull and give those powers
an impulse, e'en Earth and Heaven
who yield their milk in plenty,
Shining, O God, with Gods in clear
effulgence. Let not a mortal's evil
will obstruct us.

7 Agni, as holy food to thine invoker, give
wealth in cattle, lasting, rich in marvels.
To us be born a son and spreading
offspring. Agni, be this thy gracious
will to us-ward.

HYMN XVI.   *Agni.*

1. THIS Agni is the Lord of great felicity
and hero strength ; Lord of wealth
in herds of kine ; Lord of the battles
with the foe.

2 Wait, Maruts, Heroes, upon him the
Prosperer in whom is bliss-increasing
wealth ;
Who in fights ever conquer evil-hearted
men, who overcome the enemy.

3 As such, O Agni, deal us wealth and
hero might, O Bounteous One !
Most lofty, very glorious, rich in progeny,
free from disease and full of power.

4 He who made all that lives, who passes
all in might, who orders service to the
Gods,
He works among the Gods, he works in
hero strength, yea, also in the praise
of men.

5 Give us not up to indigence, Agni, nor
want of hero sons,
Nor, Son of Strength, to lack of cattle, nor
to blame. Drive thou our enemies away.

6 Help us to strength, blest Agni ! rich in
progeny, abundant, in our sacrifice.
Flood us with riches yet more plenteous,
bringing weal, with high renown, most
Glorious One !

HYMN XVII.   *Agni.*

1. DULY enkindled after ancient customs,
bringing all treasures, he is balmed
with unguents,—

Flame-haired, oil-clad, the purifying Agni,
skilled in fair rites, to bring the Gods
for worship.

2 As thou, O Agni, skilful Jātavedas, hast
sacrificed as Priest of Earth, of Heaven,
So with this offering bring the Gods, and
prosper this sacrifice today as erst for
Manu.

3 Three are thy times of life, O Jātavedas,
and the three mornings are thy births,
O Agni.
With these, well-knowing, grant the
Gods' kind favour, and help in stir
and stress the man who worships.

4 Agni most bright and fair with song we
honour, yea, the adorable, O Jātavedas.
Thee, envoy, messenger, oblation-bearer,
the Gods have made centre of life
eternal.

5 That Priest before thee, yet more skilled
in worship, stablished of old, health-
giver by his nature,—
After his custom offer, thou who knowest,
and lay our sacrifice where Gods may
taste it.

HYMN XVIII.   *Agni.*

1. AGNI, be kind to us when we approach
thee, good as a friend to friend, as sire
and mother.
The races of mankind are great oppressors :
burn up malignity that strives against
us.

2 Agni, burn up the unfriendly who are
near us, burn thou the foeman's curse
who pays no worship.
Burn, Vasu, thou who markest well, the
foolish : let thine eternal nimble beams
surround thee.

3 With fuel, Agni, and with oil, desirous,
mine offering I present for strength and
conquest,
With prayer, so far as I have power,
adoring—this hymn divine to gain a
hundred treasures.

---

3 *Their milk* : rain and all fertilizing influence.

2 *Who* : referring to the Maruts : the verbs being
in the third person.

3 *Most lofty etc.* : these epithets qualify wealth and
hero might.

3 *Three are thy times of life* : the existence of Agni
upon earth is said to be threefold as dependent on
the supply of fuel, clarified butter, and Soma. *The
three mornings* : Agni is re-born every morning, and the
number three appears to be used merely for the sake
of accordance with the three times of life previously
mentioned.

5 *That Priest before thee* : Agni's more skilful
predecessor is probably the celestial Agni, the high
priest who sacrifices for the Gods. The terrestrial Agni
is to take him for his model.

4 Give with thy glow, thou Son of Strength,
   when lauded, great vital power to
   those who toil to serve thee.
   Give richly, Agni, to the Viśvāmitras in
   rest and stir. Oft have we decked thy
   body.

5 Give us, O liberal Lord, great store of
   riches, for, Agni, such art thou when
   duly kindled.
   Thou in the happy singer's home
   bestowest, amply with arms extended,
   things of beauty.

HYMN XIX. *Agni.*

1. AGNI, quick, sage, infallible, all-knowing,
   I choose to be our Priest at this
   oblation.
   In our Gods' service he, best skilled,
   shall worship : may he obtain us boons
   for strength and riches.

2 Agni, to thee I lift the oil-fed ladle,
   bright, with an offering, bearing our
   oblation.
   From the right hand, choosing the Gods'
   attendance, he with rich presents hath
   arranged the worship.

3 Of keenest spirit is the man thou aidest :
   give us good offspring, thou who givest
   freely.
   In power of wealth most rich in men. O
   Agni, of thee, the Good, may we sing
   forth fair praises.

4 Men as they worship thee the God, O
   Agni, have set on thee full many a
   brilliant aspect.
   So bring, Most Youthful One, the Gods'
   assembly, the Heavenly Host which
   thou to-day shalt honour.

5 When Gods anoint thee Priest at their
   oblation, and seat thee for thy task as
   Sacrificer,
   O Agni, be thou here our kind defender,
   and to ourselves vouchsafe the gift of
   glory.

HYMN XX *Agni.*

1. WITH lauds at break of morn the priest
   invoketh Agni, Dawn, Dadhikrās, and
   both the Aśvins.
   With one consent the Gods whose light

is splendid, longing to taste our sacrifice, shall hear us.

2 Three are thy powers, O Agni, three thy
   stations, three are thy tongues, yea,
   many, Child of Order !
   Three bodies hast thou which the Gods
   delight in : with these protect our
   hymns with care unceasing.

3 O Agni, many are the names thou
   bearest, Immortal, God, Divine, and
   Jātavedas .
   And many charms of charmers, All-
   Inspirer ! have they laid in thee, Lord
   of true attendants !

4 Agni, like Bhaga, leads the godly people,
   he who is true to Law and guards the
   seasons.
   Ancient, all-knowing, he the Vṛtra-slayer
   shall bear the singer safe through every
   trouble.

5 I call on Savitar the God, on Morning,
   Bṛhaspati, and Dadhikrās, and Agni,
   On Varuṇa and Mitra, on the Aśvins,
   Bhaga, the Vasus, Rudras and Ādityas.

HYMN XXI. *Agni.*

1. SET this our sacrifice among the Immortals : be pleased with these our
   presents, Jātavedas.
   O Priest, O Agni, sit thee down before
   us, and first enjoy the drops of oil and
   fatness.

2 For thee, O Purifier, flow the drops of
   fatness rich in oil.
   After thy wont vouchsafe to us the choicest
   boon that Gods may feast.

3 Agni, Most Excellent ! for thee the Sage
   are drops that drip with oil.
   Thou art enkindled as the best of Seers.
   Help thou the sacrifice.

4 To thee, O Agni, mighty and resistless, to
   thee stream forth the drops of oil and
   fatness.
   With great light art thou come, O praised
   by poets ! Accept our offering, O thou
   Sage.

---

4 *Full many a brilliant aspect* : bright appearance,
or splendid presence.

---

1 *Dadhikrās* : or Dadhikrā, is a mythical being
described as a kind of divine horse, and probably a
personification of the morning Sun. He is invoked in
the morning together with Agni, Uṣas and the
Aśvins.

2 *Three are thy powers* : or three kinds of strengthening food, clarified butter, fuel, and Soma. *Three thy
stations* : Three altars, or the three worlds. *Three are thy
tongues* : the three fires, Gārhapatya, Āhavanīya and
Dakṣiṇā, *Three bodies* : or forms as Pāvaka, Pavamāna,
and Śuci.

3 *The names thou bearest* : or the natures thou
possessest. *Many charms* : or supernatural powers.

5 Fatness exceeding rich, extracted from the
 midst,—this as our gift we offer thee.
 Excellent God, the drops run down upon
 thy skin. Deal them to each among the
 Gods.

HYMN XXII.   *Agni.*

1. THIS is that Agni whence the longing
 Indra took the pressed Soma deep with-
 in his body.
 Winner of spoils in thousands, like a
 courser, with praise art thou exalted,
 Jātavedas.

2 That light of thine in heaven and earth,
 O Agni, in plants, O Holy One, and
 in the waters,
 Wherewith thou hast spread wide the
 air's mid-region—bright is that splendour, wavy, man-beholding.

3 O Agni, to the sea of heaven thou goest:
 thou hast called hither Gods beheld in
 spirit.
 The waters, too, come hither, those up·
 yonder in the Sun's realm of light, and
 those beneath it.

4 Let fires that dwell in mist, combined
 with those that have their home in
 floods,
 Guileless accept our sacrifice, great viands
 free from all disease.

5 Agni, as holy food to thine invoker give
 wealth in cattle, lasting, rich in
 marvels.
 To us be born a son and spreading
 offspring. Agni, be this thy gracious
 will to us-ward.

HYMN XXIII.   *Agni.*

1. RUBBED into life, well stablished in the
 dwelling, Leader of sacrifice, the Sage,
 the youthful,
 Here in the wasting fuel Jātavedas, eternal,
 hath assumed immortal being.

2 Both Bhāratas, Devaśravas, Devavāta, have
 strongly rubbed to life effectual Agni.

O Agni, look thou forth with ample
 riches : be, every day, bearer of food
 to feed us.

3 Him nobly born of old the fingers ten
 produced, him whom his Mothers
 counted dear.
 Praise Devavāta's Agni, thou Devaśravas,
 him who shall be the people's Lord.

4 He set thee in the earth's most lovely
 station, in Iḷā's place, in days of fair
 bright weather.
 On man, on Āpayā, Agni ! on the rivers
 Dṛṣadvatī, Sarasvatī, shine richly.

5 Agni, as holy food to thine invoker give
 wealth in cattle, lasting, rich in marvels.
 To us be born a son and spreading offspring Agni, be this thy gracious will to
 us-ward

HYMN XXIV.   *Agni.*

1. AGNI, subdue opposing bands, and drive
 our enemies away.
 Invincible, slay godless foes : give splendour
 to the worshipper.

2 Lit with libation, Agni, thou, deathless,
 who callest Gods to feast,
 Accept our sacrifice with joy.

3 With splendour, Agni, Son of Strength,
 thou who art worshipped, wakeful One.
 Seat thee on this my sacred grass.

4 With all thy fires, with all the Gods, Agni,
 exalt the songs we sing.
 And living men in holy rites.

5 Grant, Agni, to the worshipper wealth
 rich in heroes, plenteous store,
 Make thou us rich with many sons.

HYMN XXV.   *Agni.*

1. THOU art the sapient Son of Dyaus, O
 Agni, yes and the Child of Earth, who
 knowest all things.
 Bring the Gods specially, thou Sage, for
 worship.

3 *His Mothers* : the two fire-sticks from which Agni
springs to life.

4 *He* : the worshipper. *Earth's most lovely station* :
according to Sāyaṇa, on the northern altar. *Iḷā's place* :
the place of prayer and praise.

Dṛṣadvatī and *Sarasvatī* (see Book I 3 10) are
well known streams : *Āpayā* which is not mentioned
elsewhere, appears to have been a little stream in the
same neighbourhood, near the earlier settlements of
the Aryan immigrants.

5 *Fatness exceeding rich, extracted from the midst* : this
hymn, Sāyaṇa says, is suitable for animal sacrifices.
The fatness here spoken of is, as Professor Wilson
remarks, the same that is described in Leviticus, IV,
9, as 'the fat that covereth the inwards, and all the
fat that is upon the inwards.'

1 *Whence* : literally, wherein: that is poured out
on whom or which.

2 *Both Bhāratas* : sons of Bharata, the two Ṛṣis
of the hymn.

This hymn and the eight following are ascribed
to the Ṛṣi Viśvāmitra.

2. Agni the wise bestows the might of heroes
grants strengthening food, preparing it
for nectar.
Thou who art rich in food bring the Gods
hither.

3 Agni, infallible, lights Earth and Heaven,
immortal Goddesses gracious to all men,-
Lord through his strength, splendid through
adorations.

4 Come to the sacrifice, Agni and Indra :
come to the offerer's house who hath
the Soma.
Come, friendly-minded, Gods, to drink the
Soma.

5 In the floods' home art thou enkindled,
Agni, O Jātavedas, Son of Strength, eternal,
Exalting with thine help the gathering-
places.

HYMN XXVI. *Agni.*

1. REVERING in our heart Agni Vaiśvānara,
the finder of the light, whose promises
are true,
The liberal, gladsome, car-borne God
we Kuśikas invoke him with oblation,
seeking wealth with songs.

2 That Agni, bright, Vaiśvānara, we invoke
for help, and Mātariśvan worthy of the
song of praise;
Bṛhaspati for man's observance of the
Gods, the Singer prompt to hear, the
swiftly-moving guest.

3 Age after age Vaiśvānara, neighing like
a horse, is kindled with the women by
the Kuśikas.
May Agni, he who wakes among Immortal
Gods, grant us heroic strength and wealth
in noble steeds.

4 Let them go forth, the strong, as flames
of fire with might. Gathered for victory
they have yoked their spotted deer.
Pourers of floods, the Maruts, Masters of
all wealth, they who can ne'er be
conquered, make the mountains shake.

5 The Maruts, Friends of men, are glorious
as the fire : their mighty and resplendent succour we implore.
Those storming Sons of Rudra clothed in
robes of rain, boon-givers of good gifts,
roar as the lions roar.

6 We, band on band and troop following
troop, entreat with fair lauds Agni's
splendour and the Maruts' might,
With spotted deer for steeds, with wealth
that never fails, they, wise Ones, come
to sacrifice at our gatherings.

7 Agni am I who know, by birth, all
creatures. Mine eye is butter, in my
mouth is nectar.
I am light threefold, measurer of the region
exhaustless heat am I, named burnt-
oblation.

8 Bearing in mind a thought with light
accordant, he purified the Sun with
three refinings;
By his own nature gained the highest
treasure, and looked abroad over the
earth and heaven.

9 The Spring that fails not with a hundred
streamlets, Father inspired of prayers
that men should utter,
The Sparkler, joyous in his Parents'
bosom,—him, the Truth-speaker, sate
ye, Earth and Heaven.

HYMN XXVII. *Agni.*

1. IN ladle dropping oil your food goes in
oblation up to heaven,
Goes to the Gods in search of bliss.

2 Agni I laud, the Sage inspired, crowner
of sacrifice through song,
Who listens and gives bounteous gifts.

3 O Agni, if we might obtain control of thee
the potent God,
Then should we overcome our foes.

---

5 *In the floods' home* : in the firmament, the home
of the aerial waters.
The gathering places: the worlds or regions inhabited
by living beings, according to Sāyaṇa.

1 *Vaiśvānara* : common to, dear to, or dwelling
with, all Āryan men.
Kuśikas : men of the family of the Ṛṣi Kuśika.
2 *Mātariśvan* : said here by Sāyaṇa to mean Agni
as God of the lightning; but the usual sense of the
word is appropriate enough.
3 *With the women* : the fingers, elsewhere called
the damsels, and the sisters, which agitate the fire-
stick.
4 *Let them go forth* : the Maruts, or Storm-Gods.

7 Here Agni speaks and declares his universality
as the Soul of all. He knows all living creatures. His
eye, or in his eye, is the light which is fed with offerings
of sacred oil. The amṛta, nectar, or ambrosia, which
is the reward of piety, is obtained by burnt-offerings
or through the mouth of Agni. He traverses or
measures out the firmament, and as light he shines as
the sun in heaven, the lightning in mid-air, and fire
on earth. See note on the passage in Wilson's Translation.

8 *With three refinings* : according to Sāyaṇa, with
his three purifying forms as Agni, Vāyu, and Sūrya,
or fire, wind, and sun. But *Pavitraiḥ* may mean 'with
mental divisions, and the sense would be that Agni
divided light into three, sun, lightning and fire.

9 *His Parents' bosom* : in close connexion with
Heaven and Earth.

4 Kindled at sacrifices he is Agni, hallower,
   meet for praise,
With flame for hair : to him we seek.

5 Immortal Agni, shining far, enrobed with
   oil, well worshipped, bears
The gifts of sacrifice away.

6 The priests with ladles lifted up, worshipping here with holy thought,
Have brought this Agni for our aid.

7 Immortal, Sacrificer, God, with wondrous
   power he leads the way,
Urging the great assembly on.

8 Strong, he is set on deeds of strength. In
   sacrifices led in front,
As Singer he completes the rite.

9 Excellent, he was made by thought. The
   Germ of beings have I gained,
Yea, and the Sire of active strength.

10 Thee have I stablished, Excellent, O
   strengthened by the sage's prayer,
Thee, Agni, longing, nobly bright.

11 Agni, the swift and active One, singers,
   at time of sacrifice,
Eagerly kindle with their food.

12 Agni the Son of Strength who shines up
   to the heaven in solemn rites,
The wise of heart, I glorify.

13 Meet to be lauded and adored, showing in
   beauty through the dark,
Agni, the Strong, is kindled well.

14 Agni is kindled as a bull, like a horse-
   bearer of the Gods:
Men with oblations worship him.

15 Thee will we kindle as a bull, we who
   are Bulls ourselves, O Bull.
Thee, Agni, shining mightily.

HYMN XXVIII.   *Agni.*

1. Agni who knowest all, accept our offering
   and the cake of meal,
At dawn's libation, rich in prayer !

2 Agni, the sacrificial cake hath been prepared
   and dressed for thee :
Accept it, O Most Youthful God.

3 Agni, enjoy the cake of meal and our
   oblation three days old:
Thou, Son of Strength, art stablished at
   our sacrifice.

9 *He was made by thought* : by holy thought, or
devotion.

15 *We who are Bulls ourselves* : Priests are frequently
called bulls, on account of their great power. Cf.
III. 7. 7.

---

3 *Our oblation three days old* : the Soma juice
prepared the day before yesterday and left to ferment.

4 Here at the midday sacrifice enjoy thou
   the sacrificial cake, wise, Jātavedas!
Agni, the sages in assemblies never minish
   the portion due to thee the Mighty.

5 O Agni, at the third libation take with
   joy the offered cake of sacrifice, thou,
   Son of Strength.
Through skill in song bear to the Gods our
   sacrifice, watchful and fraught with
   riches, to Immortal God.

6 O waxing Agni, knower, thou, of all,
   accept our gifts, the cake,
And that prepared ere yesterday.

HYMN XXIX.   *Agni.*

1. HERE is the gear for friction, here tinder
   made ready for the spark.
Bring thou the Matron : we will rub Agni
   in ancient fashion forth.

2 In the two fire-sticks Jātavedas lieth, even
   as the well-set germ in pregnant women,
Agni who day by day must be exalted by
   men who watch and worship with oblations.

3 Lay this with care on that which lies
   extended : straight hath she borne the
   Steer when made prolific.
With his red pillar—radiant is his splendour
   —in our skilled task is born the Son
   of Ilā.

4 In Ilā's place we set thee down, upon the
   central point of earth,
That, Agni Jātavedas, thou mayst bear our
   offerings to the Gods.

5 Rub into life, ye men, the Sage, the guileless, Immortal, very wise and fair to look
   on.
O men, bring forth the most propitious
   Agni, first ensign of the sacrifice to
   eastward.

6 When with their arms they rub him
   straight he shineth forth like a strong
   courser, red in colour, in the wood.

1 *Here is the gear for friction* : the word *adhimānthanam*
means the upper fire stick and the string used in
agitating it. The tinder is a tuft of dry Kuśa grass
placed so as to catch the flame produced by attrition.

The Matron : the lower piece of wood in which the
spark is generated. Sāyaṇa explains the word *viśpátnim*,
feminine of *viśpáti*, lord of the people, as protectress of
men by means of the sacrifices which are performed
with the help of the fire which she produces.

3 *Lay this with care* : place the upper fire-stick,
which is to be turned rapidly round, upon the lower
piece of wood which is prepared to receive it. *The
Son of Ilā* : Agni.

4 *In Ilā's place* : on the northern altar, the place
of worship and libation, or prayer and praise.

Bright, checkless, as it were upon the
Aśvins' path, he passeth by the stones
and burneth up the grass.

7 Agni shines forth when born, observant,
mighty, the bountiful, the Singer praised
by sages;
Whom, as adorable and knowing all things,
Gods set at solemn rites as offering-
bearer.

8 Set thee, O Priest, in thine own place,
observant : lay down the sacrifice in the
home of worship.
Thou, dear to Gods, shalt serve them with
oblation : Agni, give long life to the
sacrificer.

9 Raise ye a mighty smoke, my fellow-
workers ! Ye shall attain to wealth without obstruction.
This Agni is the battle-winning Hero by
whom the Gods have overcome the
Dasyus.

10 This is thine ordered place of birth whence
sprung to life thou shonest forth.
Knowing this, Agni, sit thee down, and
prosper thou the songs we sing.

11 As Germ Celestial he is called Tanūnapāt,
and Narāśaṁsa born diffused in varied
shape.
Formed in his Mother he is Mātariśvan;
he hath, in his course, become the rapid
flight of wind.

12 With strong attrition rubbed to life, laid
down with careful hand, a Sage,
Agni, make sacrifices good, and for the
pious bring the Gods.

13 Mortals have brought to life the God
Immortal, the Conqueror with mighty
jaws, unfailing.
The sisters ten, unwedded and united,
together grasp the Babe, the new-born
Infant.

14 Served by the seven priests, he shone forth
from ancient time, when in his Mother's
bosom, in her lap, he glowed.
Giving delight each day he closeth not his
eye, since from the Asura's body he was
brought to life.

15 Even as the Maruts' onslaughts who attack
the foe, those born the first of all knew
the full power of prayer.
The Kuśikas have made the glorious
hymn ascend, and, each one singly in
his home, have kindled fire.

16 As we, O Priest observant, have elected
thee this day, what time the solemn
sacrifice began,
So surely hast thou worshipped, surely hast
thou toiled : come thou unto the Soma,
wise and knowing all.

HYMN XXX. *Indra.*

1. THE friends who offer Soma long to find
thee : they pour forth Soma and present
their viands.
They bear unmoved the cursing of the
people, for all our wisdom comes from
thee, O Indra.

2 Not far for thee are mid-air's loftiest
regions : start hither, Lord of Bays,
with thy Bay Horses.
Made for the Firm and Strong are these
libations. The pressing-stones are set
and fire is kindled.

3 Fair cheeks hath Indra, Maghavan, the
Victor, Lord of a great host, Stormer,
strong in action.
What once thou didst in might when
mortals vexed thee,—where now, O Bull,
are those thy hero exploits ?

4 For, overthrowing what hath ne'er been
shaken, thou goest forth alone destroying
Vṛtras.
For him who followeth thy Law the
mountains and heaven and earth stand
as if firmly stablished.

5 Yea, Much-invoked ! in safety through
thy glories alone thou speakest truth as
Vṛtra's slayer.
E'en these two boundless worlds to thee,
O Indra, what time thou graspest them,
are but a handful.

6 Forthwith thy Bay steeds down the
steep, O Indra, forth, crushing foemen,
go thy bolt of thunder !
Slay those who meet thee, those who flee,
who follow : make all thy promise true;
be all completed.

7 The man to whom thou givest as Provider
enjoys domestic plenty undivided.

---

6 *As it were upon the Aśvins' path* : with the speed
of the Aśvins' chariot.

8 *In thine own place* : the centre of the north altar.

11 *As Germ Celestial* : or child of the Asura Dyaus,
that is, in the form of lightning. *In his Mother* : according to Sāyaṇa, in the maternal atmosphere.

13 *The sisters ten* : the fingers used in producing fire.

14 *The Asura's body* : the Asura is, apparently, Dyaus.
Professor Wilson, following Sāyaṇa translates, 'from
the interior of the (spark) emitting wood.

15 *Those born the first of all* : the most ancient Ṛṣis
such as Kuśika and his sons.

Blest, Indra, is thy favour dropping fatness: thy worship, Much-invoked ! brings gifts in thousands.

8 Thou, Indra, Much-invoked ! didst crush to pieces Kunāru handless fiend who dwelt with Dānu.

Thou with might, Indra, smotest dead the scorner, the footless Vṛtra as he waxed in vigour.

9 Thou hast established in her seat, O Indra, the level earth, vast, vigorous, unbounded.

The Bull hath propped the heaven and air's mid-region. By thee sent onward let the floods flow hither.

10 He who withheld the kine, in silence yielded in fear before thy blow, O Indra.

He made paths easy to drive forth the cattle. Loud-breathing praises helped the Much-invoked One.

11 Indra alone filled full the earth and heaven, the Pair who meet together, rich in treasures.

Yea, bring thou near us from the air's mid-region strength, on thy car, and wholesome food, O Hero.

12 Sūrya transgresses not the ordered limits set daily by the Lord of Tawny Coursers.

When to the goal he comes, his journey ended, his Steeds he looses: this is Indra's doing.

13 Men gladly in the course of night would look on the broad bright front of the refulgent Morning;

And all acknowledge, when she comes in glory, the manifold and goodly works of Indra.

14 A mighty splendour rests upon her bosom: bearing ripe milk the Cow, unripe, advances.

All sweetness is collected in the Heifer, sweetness which Indra made for our enjoyment.

15 Barring the way they come. Be firm, O Indra; aid friends to sacrifice and him who singeth.

These must be slain by thee, malignant

mortals, armed with ill arts, our quiver-bearing foemen.

16 A cry is heard from enemies most near us : against them send thy fiercest-flaming weapon.

Rend them from under, crush them and subdue them. Slay, Maghavan, and make the fiends our booty.

17 Root up the race of Rākṣasas, O Indra ; rend it in front and crush it in the middle.

How long hast thou behaved as one who wavers ? Cast thy hot dart at him who hates devotion :

18 When borne by strong Steeds for our weal, O Leader, thou seatest thee at many noble viands.

May we be winners of abundant riches. May Indra be our wealth with store of children.

19 Bestow on us resplendent wealth. O Indra ; let us enjoy thine overflow of bounty.

Wide as a sea our longing hath expanded, fulfil it, O thou Treasure-Lord of treasures.

20 With kine and horses satisfy this longing ; with very splendid bounty skill extend it.

Seeking the light, with hymns to thee, O Indra, Kuśikas have brought their gift, the singers.

21 Lord of the kine, burst the kine's stable open : cows shall be ours, and strength that wins the booty.

Hero, whose might is true, thy home is heaven : to us, O Maghavan, grant gifts of cattle.

22 Call we on Maghavan, auspicious Indra, best Hero in this fight where spoil is gathered,

The Strong who listens, who gives aid in battles, who slays the Vṛtras, wins and gathers riches.

HYMN XXXI. _Indra._

1. WISE, teaching, following the thought of Order, the sonless gained a grandson from his daughter.

8 _Kunāru_ : the name of a demon. _Dānu_ : mother of Vṛtra. See I. 32. 9.

9 _The Bull_ : the mighty Indra.

10 _In silence_ : I adopt Prof. M. Müller's interpretation (Vedic Hymns, I. pp. 227, 228) of the difficult word _alātṛṇaḥ_, 'which had evidently become unintelligible even at the time of Yāska.'

12 _Set daily_ : with reference, perhaps, as Professor Ludwig remarks, to the apparent change in the sun's place of rising.

14 _The Cow_, and the _Heifer_ : beneficent Uṣas or Morning.

15 _They come_ : those who revile and hinder the worship of Indra.

1 I am unable to give a satisfactory or even an intelligible version or explanation of the first two stanzas which appear to attribute, in a very obscure manner, to Agni and the Gods in heaven the customs or laws of succession to property among men. In the first stanza _vāhviḥ_, which usually means an oblation-bearer, a sacrificer, a priest, or one who is borne along as a God in a celestial car, is said by Sāyaṇa to mean sonless, the father of a daughter only, because he transfers his property through his married daughter into another family. The sonless father, according to Sāyaṇa, 'stipulates that his daughter's son, his grandson, shall be his son, a mode of affiliation recognized by law; and, relying on an

Fain, as a sire, to see his child prolific,
he sped to meet her with an eager spirit.

2 The Son left not his portion to the
brother, he made a home to hold him
who should gain it.
What time his Parents gave the Priest
his being, of the good pair one acted,
one promoted.

3 Agni was born trembling with tongue
that flickered, so that the Red's great
children should be honoured.
Great is their germ, that born of them is
mighty, great the Bays' Lord's approach
through sacrifices.

4 Conquering bands upon the Warrior
waited : they recognized great light
from out the darkness.
The conscious Dawns went forth to meet
his coming, and the sole Master of the
kine was Indra.

5 The sages freed them from their firm-
built prison : the seven priests drove
them forward with their spirit.
All holy Order's pathway they discovered ;
he, full of knowledge, shared these
deeds through worship.

6 When Saramā had found the mountain's
fissure, that vast and ancient place she
plundered thoroughly.
In the floods' van she led them forth,
light-footed : she who well knew came
first unto their lowing.

7 Longing for friendship came the noblest
singer : the hill poured forth its treasure
for the pious.
The Hero with young followers fought
and conquered, and straightway Aṅgiras
was singing praises,

8 Peer of each noble thing, yea, all excelling,
all creatures doth he know, he slayeth
Śuṣṇa.
Our leader, fain for war, singing from
heaven, as Friend he saved his lovers
from dishonour.

9 They sate them down with spirit fain for
booty, making with hymns a way to
life eternal.
And this is still their place of frequent
session, whereby they sought to gain
the months through Order.

10 Drawing the milk of ancient seed prolific,
they joyed as they beheld their own
possession.
Their shout of triumph heated earth and
heaven. When the kine showed, they
bade the heroes rouse them.

11 Indra drove forth the kine, that Vṛtra-
slayer, while hymns of praise rose up
and gifts were offered.
For him the Cow, noble and far-extending,
poured pleasant juices, bringing oil and
sweetness.

---

heir thus obtained, and one who can perform his funeral rites, he is satisfied.' This may be intelligible, but what it has to do with Agni or with the rest of the the hymn is not clear. Grassmann takes *váhniḥ* to mean the upper fire-stick, and the daughter to mean the lower piece of wood.

2 *The Son left not his portion to the brother* : Wilson, following Sāyaṇa translates : '(a son) born of the body does not transfer (paternal) wealth to a sister.' Ludwig takes the meaning to be : the bodily son (of Dyaus, or of the heavenly waters) did not transmit his inheritance (that is, sacrifice) to a brother. *A home* : the plants which receive and hold Agni, who obtains the inheritance of sacrifice. *His Parents* : perhaps the fire-sticks, one of which by agitation produces the flame in the other. *The good pair* : the terrestrial offerer who performs the sacrifice, and the celestial offerer who makes it effectual. See Bergaigne, *La Religion Védique*, I. 284.

Ludwig allows that the meaning of the first two stanzas is problematical, and Wilson says of his own translation : 'these two verses, if rightly interpreted, are wholly unconnected with the subject of the *Sūkta*, and come in without any apparent object : they are very obscure, and are only made somewhat intelligible by interpretations which seem to be arbitrary, and are very unusual, although not peculiar to Sāyaṇa, his explanations being based on those of Yāska.

3 *The Red's great children* : the hot rays of the glowing fire. *That born of them* : Indra's coming, which is caused by the kindling of sacrificial fire.

4 *Conquering lands* : the ever-victorious Maruts. *The Warrior* : Indra, their leader. *Master of the kine* : recoverer of the vanished rays of light.

5 *The sages* and *the seven priests* : are the Aṅgirases.

6 *Saramā* : the hound of Indra. See I. 62. 3. *In the floods' van* : hastening out of the mountain cavern in advance of the liberated waters. *Them* : the cows, the waters and the rays of light.

7 *The noblest singer* : as a noun of multitude, all the Aṅgirases.

The Hero : Indra with his allies the Maruts.

9 *They* : the Aṅgirases, who had been eager to recover the cows. *To gain the months* : to acquire the power of keeping the monthly festivals.

10 Or, 'They joyed to see them, as their own possession, yielding the milk of ancient seed prolific.' The Aṅgirases rejoiced as they again beheld the rays of light, shedding what originates and supports all life ' Sāyaṇa's rendering of this difficult stanza is thus given by Wilson : 'Contemplating their own (cattle) giving milk to their former progeny (the *Aṅgirasas*) were delighted; their shouts spread through heaven and earth; they replaced the recovered kine in their places, and stationed guards over the cows.'

12 They made a mansion for their Father,
deftly provided him a great and glorious
dwelling ;
With firm support parted and stayed the
Parents, and, sitting, fixed him there
erected, mighty.

13 What time the ample chalice had impelled
him, swift waxing, vast, to pierce the
earth and heaven,—
Him in whom blameless songs are all
united : all powers invincible belong to
Indra.

14 I crave thy powers, I crave thy mighty
friendship : full many a team goes to
the Vṛtra-slayer.
Great is the laud, we seek the Princes'
favour. Be thou, O Maghavan, our guard
and keeper.

15 He, having found great, splendid, rich
dominion, sent life and motion to his
friends and lovers.
Indra who shone together with the Heroes
begot the song, the fire, and Sun and
Morning.

16 Vast, the House-Friend, he set the waters
flowing, all-lucid, widely spread, that
move together.
By the wise cleansings of the meath made
holy, through days and nights they
speed the swift streams onward.

17 To thee proceed the dark, the treasure-
holders, both of them sanctified by
Sūrya's bounty.
The while thy lovely storming Friends,
O Indra, fail to attain the measure of
thy greatness.

18 Be Lord of joyous songs, O Vṛtra-slayer,
Bull dear to all, who gives the power of
living.
Come unto us with thine auspicious friendship, hastening, Mighty One, with mighty
succours.

19 Like Angiras I honour him with worship,
and renovate old song for him the
Ancient.
Chase thou the many godless evil creatures, and give us, Maghavan,
heaven's light to help us.

20 Far forth are spread the purifying waters :
convey thou us across them unto
safety.
Save us, our Charioteer, from harm,
O Indra, soon, very soon, make us
win spoil of cattle.

21 His kine their Lord hath shown, e'en
Vṛtra's slayer, through the black hosts
he passed with red attendants.
Teaching us pleasant things by holy
Order, to us hath he thrown open all
his portals.

22 Call we on Maghavan, auspicious Indra,
best Hero in this fight where spoil is
gathered.
The Strong who listens, who gives aid
in battles, who slays the Vṛtras, wins
and gathers riches.

HYMN XXXII.   *Indra*

1. DRINK thou this Soma, Indra, Lord of
Soma ; drink thou the draught of
noonday which thou lovest.
Puffing thy cheeks, impetuous, liberal
Giver, here loose thy two Bay Horses
and rejoice thee.

2 Quaff it pure, meal-blent, mixt with milk,
O Indra ; we have poured forth the
Soma for thy rapture.
Knit with the prayer-fulfilling band of
Maruts, yea, with the Rudras, drink
till thou art sated ;

---

12 *For their Father* : according to Sāyaṇa, for their
protector Indra. But Agni may be meant, the mansion
being the place of sacrifice. *The Parents* : Heaven and
Earth, parents of all things.

13 *The ample chalice* : the bowl of Soma juice. But
according to Ludwig, *dhiṣaṇā* here and elsewhere,
means earnest wish, longing.

14 *Full many a team* : hymns sent forth like teams
of horses.

16 *By the wise cleansings* : or according to Sāyaṇa,
the wise purifiers, that is, Agni, Vāyu, and Sūrya, who
act as purifiers of the libation of Soma juice.

17 *The dark, the treasure-holders* : or, the dark one
and the treasure-holder; Night and Day. *Storming
Friends* : the Maruts.

20 *The purifying waters* : the epithet *pāvakāḥ*, purifying, is entirely out of place here Ludwig suggests
pāpakāḥ, wicked, which would be more suitable.

21 *Kine* : rays of light. *Red attendan's* : the Maruts.
'Many of the verses in this hymn,' Prof. Wilson
observes, 'are of more than usual obscurity.' Prof.
Grassmann places the hymn in his Appendix.

---

1 *Puffing thy cheeks* : meaning, apparently, smacking
thy lips in anticipation of the Soma-draught. Sāyaṇa
explains it as, 'filling their (Indra's horses') jaws with
fodder.' *Impetuous* : this appears to be the meaning of
the epithet *ṛjīṣin* as derived from the root *ṛj*, rather
than, as Sāyaṇa explains it, 'drinker of the spiritless
residue of the Soma.' The latter meaning, however, is
admissible, and is supported by good authority.

3 Those who gave increase to thy strength and vigour ; the Maruts singing forth thy might, O Indra.
Drink thou, O fair of cheek, whose hand wields thunder, with Rudras banded, at our noon libation.

4 They, even the Maruts who were there, excited with song the meath-created strength of Indra.
By them impelled to act he reached the vitals of Vṛtra, though he deemed that none might wound him.

5 Pleased, like a man, with our libation, Indra, drink, for enduring hero might, the Soma.
Lord of Bays, moved by sacrifice come hither : thou with the Swift Ones stirrest floods and waters.

6 When thou didst loose the streams to run like racers in the swift contest, having smitten Vṛtra
With flying weapon where he lay, O Indra, and, godless, kept the Goddesses encompassed.

7 With reverence let us worship mighty Indra, great and sublime, eternal, ever-youthful,
Whose greatness the dear world-halves have not measured, no, nor conceived the might of him the Holy.

8 Many are Indra's nobly wrought achievements, and none of all the Gods transgress his statutes.
He beareth up this earth and heaven, and, doer of marvels, he begot the Sun and Morning.

9 Herein, O Guileless One, is thy true greatness, that soon as born thou drankest up the Soma.
Days may not check the power of thee the Mighty, nor the nights, Indra, nor the months, nor autumns.

10 As soon as thou wast born in highest heaven thou drankest Soma to delight thee, Indra ;
And when thou hadst pervaded earth and heaven thou wast the first supporter of the singer.

11 Thou, puissant God, more mighty, slewest. Ahi showing his strength when couched around the waters.
The heaven itself attained not to thy greatness when with one hip of thine the earth was shadowed.

12 Sacrifice, Indra, made thee wax so mighty, the dear oblation with the flowing Soma.
O Worshipful, with worship help our worship, for worship helped thy bolt when slaying Ahi.

13 With sacrifice and wish have I brought Indra ; still for new blessings may I turn him hither,
Him magnified by ancient songs and praises, by lauds of later time and days yet recent.

14 I have brought forth a song when longing seized me : ere the decisive day will I laud Indra ;
Then may he safely bear us over trouble, as in a ship, when both sides invocate him.

15 Full is his chalice : Glory ! Like a pourer I have filled up the vessel for his drinking.
Presented on the right, dear Soma juices have brought us Indra, to rejoice him, hither.

16 Not the deep-flowing flood, O Much-invoked One ! not hills that compass thee about restrain thee,
Since here incited, for thy friends, O Indra, thou breakest e'en the firm built stall of cattle.

17 Call we on Maghavan, auspicious Indra, best Hero in this fight where spoil is gathered,
The Strong who listens, who gives aid in battles, who slays the Vṛtras, wins and gathers riches.

---

3 *The Maruts singing forth thy might* : the song of the Maruts is the music of 'The winged storms, chanting their thunder-psalm.'—Shelley.

5 *Like a man* : or, as thou wast pleased with the libation of Manu.
The Swift Ones : the Maruts.
6 *The Goddesses* : the heavenly waters.
7 *The dear world-halves* : heaven and earth.

11 *When with one hip of thine the earth was shadowed* : Prof. Wilson, following Sāyaṇa, translates : as thou remainedst concealing the earth by one of (the) flames,' and observes that meaning is not very clear. But *sphigī* means a hip and not a flame, and the poet appears to mean that a portion of Indra's body shadowed or covered the earth while the rest was in the heavens. So, in Book X. 119. 11, Indra is represented as saying when exhilarated by Soma : *diví me anyáḥ pakṣo 'dho anyám acikṛṣam,* one side of me is in the sky, and I have drawn the other down.

14 *Ere the decisive day* : on the eve of an important battle.

HYMN XXXIII.   *Indra.*

1. FORTH from the bosom of the mountains, eager as two swift mares with loosened rein contending,
Like two bright mother cows who lick their youngling, Vipāś and Śutudrī speed down their waters.

2 Impelled by Indra whom ye pray to urge you, ye move as 'twere on chariots to the ocean.
Flowing together, swelling with your billows, O lucid Streams, each of you seeks the other.

3 I have attained the most maternal River, we have approached Vipāś, the broad, the blessed.
Licking as 'twere their calf the pair of Mothers flow onward to their common home together.

4 We two who rise and swell with billowy waters move forward to the home which Gods have made us.
Our flood may not be stayed when urged to motion. What would the singer, calling to the Rivers ?

5 Linger a little at my friendly bidding ; rest, Holy Ones, a moment in your journey.
With hymn sublime soliciting your favour Kuśika's son hath called unto the River.

6 Indra who wields the thunder dug our channels : he smote down Vṛtra, him who stayed our currents.

Savitar, God, the lovely-handed, led us, and at his sending forth we flow expanded.

7 That hero deed of Indra must be lauded for ever that he rent Ahi in pieces.
He smote away the obstructors with his thunder, and eager for their course forth flowed the waters.

8 Never forget this word of thine, O singer, which future generations shall reëcho.
In hymns, O bard, show us thy loving kindness. Humble us not mid men. To thee be honour !

9 List quickly, Sisters, to the bard who cometh to you from far away with car and wagon.
Bow lowly down ; be easy to be traversed : stay, Rivers, with your floods below our axles.

10 Yea, we will listen to thy words, O singer. With wain and car from far away thou comest.
Low, like a nursing mother, will I bend me, and yield me as a maiden to her lover.

11 Soon as the Bharatas have fared across thee, the warrior band, urged on and sped by Indra,
Then let your streams flow on in rapid motion. I crave your favour who deserve our worship.

12 The warrior host, the Bharatas, fared over : the singer won the favour of the Rivers.
Swell with your billows, hasting, pouring riches. Fill full your channels, and roll swiftly onward.

13 So let your wave bear up the pins, and ye, O Waters, spare the thongs ;
And never may the pair of Bulls, harmless and sinless, waste away.

The hymn is a dialogue between Viśvāmitra and the rivers Vipāś and Śutudrī who are regarded severally as the Ṛṣis or seers of the verses ascribed to them. The legend cited by Sāyaṇa says that Viśvāmitra, the Purohita or family priest of King Sudās, having obtained wealth by means of his office, took the whole of it and came to the confluence of the Vipāś and the Śutudrī. Others followed. In order to make the rivers fordable he lauded them with the first three verses of the hymn. The hymn has some poetical beauty, and is interesting as a relic of the traditions of the Āryans regarding their progress eastward in the Land of the Five Rivers.

1 *Vipāś* : considered to be identical with the Hyphasis of Arrian, is the modern Beās which rises in the Himālayas and falls into the Sutlej, the *Śatudrī* of the text, a little to the south-east of Amritsar.

4 The rivers speak in reply to Viśvāmitra's address.

5 Viśvāmitra speaks again. *At my friendly bidding* : according to the Scholiasts, Yāska and Sāyaṇa, the meaning of *me vácase somyāya* is, 'to my speech importing the Soma ;' that is, the object of my address is that I may cross over and gather the Soma-plant. The word *somya*, consisting of, connected with, or inspired by, Soma, appears to have here its more general meaning of lovely, pleasant, or friendly. *Kuśika's son* : Viśvāmitra.

6 The rivers speak. *Savitar* : said by Sāyaṇa to be used here as an epithet of Indra, 'the impeller of the whole world.'

7 Viśvāmitra speaks.

8 The rivers speak.

9 Viśvāmitra speaks.

10 The rivers speak.

11 Viśvāmitra speaks. *The Bharatas* : the family of Viśvāmitra.

13 This verse, in a different metre, is manifestly a later addition. *The pins* : of the yokes. *The pair of Bulls* : the two strong rushing rivers. Cf Horace's *tauriformis Aufidus*. Prof. Wilson, following Sāyaṇa, gives a somewhat different version of the stanza : 'Let your waves (rivers) so flow that the pin of the yoke may be above (their) waters : leave the trace full, and may (the two streams) exempt from misfortune or defect, and uncensured, exhibit no (present) increase.'

HYMN XXXIV.   *Indra.*

1. FORT-RENDER, Lord of Wealth, dispelling foemen, Indra with lightnings hath o'ercome the Dāsa.
Impelled by prayer and waxen great in body, he hath filled earth and heaven, the Bounteous Giver.

2 I stimulate thy zeal, the Strong, the Hero, decking my song of praise for thee Immortal.
O Indra, thou art equally the Leader of heavenly hosts and human generations.

3 Leading his band Indra encompassed Vṛtra ; weak grew the wily leader of enchanters.
He who burns fierce in forests slaughtered Vyaṁsa, and made the Milch-kine of the nights apparent.

4 Indra, light-winner, days' Creator, conquered, victorious, hostile bands with those who loved him.
For man the days' bright ensign he illumined, and found the light for his joy and gladness.

5 Forward to fiercely falling blows pressed Indra, herolike doing many hero exploits.
These holy songs he taught the bard who praised him, and widely spread these Dawns' resplendent colour.

6 They laud the mighty acts of him the Mighty, the many glorious deeds performed by Indra.
He in his strength, with all-surpassing prowess, through wondrous arts crushed the malignant Dasyus.

7 Lord of the brave, Indra who rules the people gave freedom to the Gods by might and battle.
Wise singers glorify with chanted praises these his achievements in Vivasvān's dwelling.

8 Excellent, Conqueror, the victory-giver, the winner of the light and Godlike Waters,

He who hath won this broad earth and this heaven,—in Indra they rejoice who love devotions.

9 He gained possession of the Sun and Horses, Indra obtained the Cow who feedeth many.
Treasure of gold he won ; he smote the Dasyus, and gave protection to the Āryan colour.

10 He took the plants and days for his possession ; he gained the forest trees and air's mid-region.
Vala he cleft, and chased away opponents : thus was he tamer of the overweening.

11 Call we on Maghavan, auspicious Indra, best Hero in the fight where spoil is gathered,
The Strong, who listens, who gives aid in battles, who slays the Vṛtras, wins and gathers treasures.

HYMN XXXV   *Indra.*

1. MOUNT the Bay Horses to thy chariot harnessed, and come to us like Vāyu with his coursers.
Thou, hastening to us, shalt drink the Soma. Hail, Indra. We have poured it for thy rapture.

2 For him, the God who is invoked by many, the two swift Bay Steeds to the pole I harness,
That they in fleet course may bring Indra hither, e'en to this sacrifice arranged completely.

3 Bring the strong Steeds who drink the warm libation, and, Bull of Godlike nature, be thou gracious.
Let thy Steeds eat ; set free thy Tawny Horses, and roasted grain like this consume thou daily.

4 Those who are yoked by prayer I harness, fleet friendly Bays who take their joy together.
Mounting thy firm and easy car, O Indra, wise and all-knowing come thou to the Soma.

---

1 *Fort-render* : breaker-down of the cloud-castles of the demons who withhold the rain as well as of the hostile non-Āryan tribes.

3 *He who burns fierce in forests* : perhaps the thunderbolt. *Vyaṁsa* : the name of one of the demons of drought. See I. 101. 2, and 103 . 2.
Made the Milch-kine of the nights apparent : according to Sāyaṇa, made manifest the (stolen) cows (that had been hidden) in the night ; that is, recovered the rays of light.

7 *In Vivasvān's dwelling* : in the sacrificial chamber, in the home of the worshipper who represents Vivasvān, the Radiant God, regarded as the Celestial Sacrificer.

9 *The Āryan colour* : or, race of Āryas ; according to S yaṇa, the noblest tribe or order, meaning the first three classes or castes.

---

2 *I harness* : my prayer causes Indra to harness.

3 *Who drink the warm libation* : or, according to Sāyaṇa, 'who protect us from our enemies. *Roasted grain* : fried barley, according to Sāyaṇa. The grain would appear to be intended for Indra's horses. See stanza 7.

5 No other worshippers must stay beside them thy Bays, thy vigorous and smooth-backed Coursers.
  Pass by them all and hasten onward hither : with Soma pressed we will prepare to feast thee.

6 Thine is this Soma : hasten to approach it. Drink thou thereof, benevolent, and cease not.
  Sit on the sacred grass at this our worship, and take these drops into thy belly, Indra.

7 The grass is strewn for thee, pressed is the Soma ; the grain is ready for thy Bays to feed on.
  To thee who lovest them, the very mighty, strong, girt by Maruts, are these gifts presented.

8 This the sweet draught, with cows, the men, the mountains, the waters, Indra, have for thee made ready.
  Come, drink thereof, Sublime One, friendly-minded, foreseeing, knowing well the ways thou goest.

9 The Maruts, they with whom thou sharedst Soma, Indra, who made thee strong and were thine army,—
  With these accordant, eagerly desirous drink thou this Soma with the tongue of Agni.

10 Drink, Indra, of the juice by thine own nature, or by the tongue of Agni, O thou Holy.
  Accept the sacrificial gift, O Sakra, from the Adhvaryu's hand or from the Hotar's.

11 Call we on Maghavan, auspicious Indra, best Hero in the fight where spoil is gathered,
  The Strong, who listens, who gives aid in battles, who slays the Vṛtras, wins and gathers riches.

HYMN XXXVI.   Indra.

1. WITH constant succours, fain thyself to share it, make this oblation which we bring effective.
  Grown great through strengthening gifts at each libation, he hath become renowned by mighty exploits.

2 For Indra were the Somas erst-discovered, whereby he grew strong-jointed, vast, and skilful.
  Indra, take quickly these presented juices : drink of the strong, that which the strong have shaken.

3 Drink and wax great. Thine are the juices, Indra, both Somas of old time and these we bring thee.
  Even as thou drankest, Indra, earlier Somas, so drink to-day, a new guest, meet for praises.

4 Great and impetuous, mighty-voiced in battle, surpassing power is his, and strength resistless.
  Him the broad earth hath never comprehended when Somas cheered the Lord of Tawny Coursers.

5 Mighty and strong he waxed for hero exploit : the Bull was furnished a Sage's wisdom.
  Indra is our kind Lord ; his steers have vigour ; his cows are many with abundant offspring.

6 As floods according to their stream flow onward, so to the sea, as borne on cars, the waters.
  Vaster is Indra even than his dwelling, what time the stalk milked out, the Soma, fills him.

7 Eager to mingle with the sea, the rivers carry the well-pressed Soma juice to Indra.
  They drain the stalk out with their arms, quick-handed, and cleanse it with a stream of mead and filters.

8 Like lakes appear his flanks filled full with Soma : yea, he contains libations in abundance.
  When Indra had consumed the first sweet viands, he, after slaying Vṛtra, claimed the Soma.

---

8 *With cows* : that is, with the milk which is mixed with Soma. *The men* : who make all preparations for the sacrifice. *The mountains* : on which the Soma grows ; or perhaps the pressing-stones brought from the hillside. *The waters* : used to purify the Soma.

10 *By thine own nature* : by thine own strength, or effort ; spontaneously. *Sakra* : Mighty One ; a common name of Indra.

---

2 *Drink of the strong* : that is, of the strong Soma juice, which has been *shaken*, i. e. violently pressed out, by *the strong* pressing-stones.

4 *Mighty-voiced* : the exact meaning of *virapśin* is uncertain. Prof. Wilson renders it, after Sāyaṇa, by 'defier of foes.'

5 *His cows* : I follow Sāyaṇa, Roth, Ludwig, and Grassmann in giving this meaning to *dākṣiṇāḥ*, as the meaning 'guerdons,' 'donations,' does not suit the passage.

6 As rivers increase the size of the ocean, so libations of Soma juice augment the greatness of Indra until he is too vast for his home the heaven to contain him.

7 *The sea* : perhaps the sacrificial reservoir. *The rivers* : waters used in the Soma ceremonies.
They drain : that is the officiating priests.

9 Then bring thou hither, and let none
  prevent it : we know thee well, the
  Lord of wealth and treasure.
  That splendid gift which is thine own, O
  Indra, vouchsafe to us, Lord of the
  Tawny Coursers.
10 O Indra, Maghavan, impetuous mover,
  grant us abundant wealth that brings
  all blessings.
  Give us a hundred autumns for our life-
  time : give us, O fair-cheeked Indra,
  store of heroes.
11 Call we on Indra, Maghavan, auspicious,
  best Hero in the fight where spoil is
  gathered,
  The Strong, who listens, who gives aid in
  battles, who slays the Vṛtras, wins and
  gathers riches.

HYMN XXXVII. *Indra.*

1. O INDRA, for the strength that slays Vṛtra
  and conquers in the fight,
  We turn thee hitherward to us.
2 O Indra, Lord of Hundred Powers, may
  those who praise thee hitherward.
  Direct thy spirit and thine eye.
3 O Indra, Lord of Hundred Powers, with
  all our songs we invocate
  Thy names for triumph over foes.
4 We strive for glory through the powers
  immense of him whom many praise,
  Of Indra who supports mankind.
5 For Vṛtra's slaughter I address Indra
  whom many invocate,
  To win us booty in the wars.
6 In battles be victorious. We seek thee,
  Lord of Hundred Powers,
  Indra, that Vṛtra may be slain.
7 In splendid combats of the hosts, in glories
  where the fight is won.
  Indra, be victor over foes.
8 Drink thou the Soma for our help, bright,
  vigilant, exceeding strong,
  O Indra, Lord of Hundred Powers.
9 O Śatakratu, powers which thou mid the
  Five Races hast displayed—
  These, Indra, do I claim of thee.

9 *Bring thou hither* : bring the wealth for which we
pray.
10 *A hundred autumns* : See I. 89. 9.

2 *Those who praise thee* : the institutors of the
sacrifice.
8 *Vigilant* : according to Sāyaṇa, Soma prevents
sleep.
9 *Śatakratu* : Lord of a hundred, or countless,
powers.
The Five Races : Indra is the special protector of
the five Āryan tribes.

10 Indra, great glory hast thou gained. Win
  splendid fame which none may mar :
  We make thy might perpetual.
11 Come to us either from anear, or, Śakra,
  come from far away.
  Indra, wherever be thy home, come to us
  thence, O Thunder-armed.

HYMN XXXVIII. *Indra.*

1. HASTING like some strong courser good at
  drawing, a thought have I imagined
  like a workman.
  Pondering what is dearest and most noble,
  I long to see the sages full of wisdom.
2 Ask of the sages' mighty generations :
  firm-minded and devout they framed
  the heaven.
  These are thy heart-sought strengthening
  directions, and they have come to be
  sky's upholders.
3 Assuming in this world mysterious natures,
  they decked the heaven and earth for
  high dominion,
  Measured with measures, fixed their broad
  expanses, set the great worlds apart held
  firm for safety.
4 Even as he mounted up they all adorned
  him : self-luminous he travels clothed
  in splendour.
  That is the Bull's, the Asura's mighty
  figure : he, omniform, hath reached the
  eternal waters.
5 First the more ancient Bull engendered
  offspring : these are his many draughts
  that lent him vigour.
  From days of old ye Kings, two Sons of
  Heaven, by hymns of sacrifice have won
  dominion.
6 Three seats ye Sovrans, in the Holy synod,
  many, yea, all, ye honour with your
  presence.

This hymn is ascribed to the Ṛṣi Prajāpati, of
the family of Viśvāmitra, or Prajāpati, son of Vāk, or
both together, or Viśvāmitra himself. The deity is said
to be Indra, although he is mentioned only in the
concluding verse. The hymn is intentionally obscure,
and in parts unintelligible.
1 *Like a workman* : as a carpenter prepares his wood.
I long to see the sages : that I may learn from them
what I wish to know.
3 *For high dominion* : that Indra might rule over
them.
4 *Even as he mounted up* : that is, Indra as the Sun.
The eternal waters : or, according to Prof. Roth, 'the
forces of eternity.'
5 *The more ancient Bull* : Indra as the Sun.
Two Sons of Heaven : or of Dyaus ; Varuṇa and
perhaps Mitra.
6 *The three seats* are heaven, the firmament or mid-
air, and the earth. The poet appears to mean, by the

There saw I, going thither in the spirit,
Gandharvas in their course with wind-
blown tresses.

7 That same companionship of her, the
Milch-cow, here with the strong Bull's
divers forms they stablished.
Enduing still some new celestial figure, the
skilful workers shaped a form around
him.

8 Let no one here debar me from enjoying
the golden light which Savitar diffuses.
He covers both all-fostering worlds with
praises even as a woman cherishes her
children.

9 Fulfil, ye twain, his work, the Great, the
Ancient: as heavenly blessing keep your
guard around us.
All the wise Gods behold his varied
actions who stands erect, whose voice is
like a herdsman's.

10 Call we on Indra, Maghavan, auspicious,
best Hero in the fight where spoil is
gathered,
The Strong, who listens, who gives aid in
battles, who slays the Vṛtras, wins and
gathers riches.

HYMN XXXIX.   Indra.

1. To Indra from the heart the hymn proceedeth, to him the Lord, recited, built
with praises ;
The wakening song sung forth in holy
synod : that which is born for thee,
O Indra, notice.

2 Born from the heaven e'en in the days
aforetime, wakening, sung aloud in
holy synod,

Auspicious, clad in white and shining
raiment, this is the ancient hymn of
our forefathers.

3 The Mother of the Twins hath borne
Twin Children : my tongue's tip raised
itself and rested silent.
Killing the darkness at the light's foundation, the Couple newly born attain
their beauty.

4 Not one is found among them, none of
mortals, to blame our sires who fought
to win the cattle.
Their strengthener was Indra the Majestic :
he spread their stalls of kine the
Wonder-Worker.

5 Where as a Friend with friendly men,
Navagvas, with heroes, on his knees he
sought the cattle.
There, verily with ten Daśagvas Indra
found the Sun lying hidden in the
darkness.

6 Indra found meath collected in the milch-
cow, by foot and hoof, in the cow's
place of pasture.
That which lay secret, hidden in the
waters, he held in his right hand, the
rich rewarder.

7 He took the light, discerning it from
darkness : may we be far removed from
all misfortune.
These songs, O Soma-drinker, cheered by
Soma, Indra, accept from thy most
zealous poet.

8 Let there be light through both the
worlds for worship : may we be far
from most overwhelming evil.
Great woe comes even from the hostile
mortal, piled up ; but good at rescue
are the Vasus.

9 Call we on Maghavan, auspicious Indra,
best Hero in the fight where spoil is
gathered,
The Strong, who listens, who gives aid
in battles, who slays the Vṛtras, wins
and gathers riches.

---

words that follow, that no place of sacrifice is duly
consecrated unless these Gods are present.

The *Gandharvas,* according to the Scholiast, are the
guardians of the Soma. Here, probably, they are
merely sunbeams.

7 The *Milch-cow* is Dawn, and *the strong Bull* is
apparently Indra as the Sun. 'This stanza,' Professor
Wilson remarks, 'is singularly obscure, and is very
imperfectly explained by the commentators.'

8 This stanza also is hardly intelligible.

9 *Ye Twain* : apparently Mitra and Varuṇa. *The
Great, the Ancient* : Dyaus.

Whose voice is like a herdsman's : Professor Wilson
renders this, 'blandly-speaking.' The meaning appears
to be, using his voice for the protection of man, like a
herdsman who calls out to his cattle.

This hymn and the following thirteen are ascribed
to the Ṛṣi Viśvāmitra.

2 *Clad in white and shining raiment* : clothed with
energy and splendour.

3 *The Mother of the Twins* : according to Sāyaṇa,
Uṣas or Dawn. *Twin Children* : the Aśvins. *My tongue's tip raised itself* : I prepared to praise the Aśvins,
but was unequal to the task.

4 See M. Müller, Chips, IV. 29 (Edition of 1895).

5 *Navagvas* : a mythological family often associated
with the Aṅgirases and described as sharing in Indra's
battles. See I. 33. 6, and 62. 4.

Daśagvas : members of, or priestly allies connected
with, the family of Aṅgiras. See I. 62. 4.

6 *Indra found meath* : sweet rain. *By foot and hoof* :
tracking the cows by their foot-marks. *That which lay
secret* : the rain which was imprisoned in the clouds.

HYMN XL. *Indra.*

1. THEE, Indra, we invoke, the Bull, what
time the Soma is expressed.
So drink thou of the savoury juice.

2 Indra, whom many laud, accept the
strength-conferring Soma juice :
Quaff, pour down drink that satisfies.

3 Indra, with all the Gods promote our
wealth-bestowing sacrifice,
Thou highly-lauded Lord of men.

4 Lord of the brave, to thee proceed these
drops of Soma juice expressed,
The bright drops to thy dwelling-place.

5 Within thy belly, Indra, take juice, Soma
the most excellent : Thine are the drops
celestial.

6 Drink our libation, Lord of hymns : with
streams of meath thou art bedewed :
Our glory, Indra, is thy gift.

7 To Indra go the treasures of the worshipper, which never fail :
He drinks the Soma and is strong

8 From far away, from near at hand, O
Vṛtra-slayer, come to us :
Accept the songs we sing to thee.

9 When from the space between the near
and far thou art invoked by us,
Thence, Indra. come thou hitherward.

HYMN XLI. *Indra.*

1. INVOKED to drink the Soma juice, come
with thy Bay Steeds, Thunder-armed !
Come, Indra, hitherward to me.

2 Our priest is seated, true to time ; the
grass is regularly strewn ;
The pressing-stones were set at morn.

3 These prayers, O thou who hearest prayer
are offered : seat thee on the grass.
Hero, enjoy the offered cake.

4 O Vṛtra-slayer, be thou pleased with these
libations, with these hymns,
Song-loving Indra, with our lauds.

5 Our hymns caress the Lord of Strength,
vast, drinker of the Soma's juice,
Indra, as mother-cows their calf.

6 Delight thee with the juice we pour for
thine own great munificence :
Yield not thy singer to reproach.

7 We, Indra, dearly loving thee, bearing
oblation, sing thee hymns :
Thou, Vasu, dearly lovest us.

9 *The space between the near and far*: the firmament
or mid-air, between the earth and the distant sky.

8 O thou to whom thy Bays are dear, loose
not thy Horses far from us :
Here glad thee, Indra, Lord divine.

9 May long-maned Coursers, dropping oil,
bring thee on swift car hitherward,
Indra, to seat thee on the grass.

HYMN XLII. *Indra.*

1. COME to the juice that we have pressed,
to Soma, Indra, blent with milk :
Come, favouring us, thy Bay-drawn car !

2 Come, Indra, to this gladdening drink,
placed on the grass, pressed out with
stones :
Wilt thou not drink thy fill thereof ?

3 To Indra have my songs of praise gone
forth, thus rapidly sent hence,
To turn him to the Soma-draught.

4 Hither with songs of praise we call Indra
to drink the Soma juice :
Will he not come to us by lauds ?

5 Indra, these Somas are expressed. Take
them within thy belly, Lord
Of Hundred Powers, thou Prince of
Wealth.

6 We know thee winner of the spoil, and
resolute in battles, Sage !
Therefore thy blessing we implore.

7 Borne hither by thy Stallions, drink, Indra,
this juice which we have pressed,
Mingled with barley and with milk.

8 Indra, for thee, in thine own place, I
urge the Soma for thy draught :
Deep in thy heart let it remain,

9 We call on thee, the Ancient One, Indra,
to drink the Soma juice,
We Kuśikas who seek thine aid.

HYMN XLIII. *Indra.*

1. MOUNTED upon thy chariot-seat approach
us : thine is the Soma-draught from
days aforetime.
Loose for the sacred grass thy dear
companions. These men who bring
oblation call thee hither.

2 Come our true Friend, passing by many
people ; come with thy two Bay Steeds
to our devotions ;
For these our hymns are calling thee,
O Indra, hymns formed for praise,
soliciting thy friendship.

9 *We Kuśikas* : members of the family of Kuśika
who was the father or the grandfather of Viśvāmitra,
the Ṛṣi of the hymn.

1 *Thy dear companions* : thy horses.

3 Pleased, with thy Bay Steeds, Indra, God,
  come quickly to this our sacrifice that
  heightens worship ;
  For with my thoughts, presenting oil to
  feed thee, I call thee to the feast of
  sweet libations.

4 Yea, let thy two Bay Stallions bear thee
  hither, well limbed and good to draw,
  thy dear companions.
  Pleased with the corn-blent offering
  which we bring thee, may Indra, Friend,
  hear his friend's adoration.

5 Wilt thou not make me guardian of the
  people, make me, impetuous Maghavan,
  their ruler ?
  Make me a Ṛṣi having drunk of Soma ?
  Wilt thou not give me wealth that
  lasts for ever ?

6 Yoked to thy chariot, led thy tall Bays,
  Indra, companions of thy banquet, bear
  thee hither,
  Who from of old press to heaven's farthest
  limits, the Bull's impetuous and well-
  groomed Horses.

7 Drink of the strong pressed out by strong
  ones, Indra, that which the Falcon
  brought thee when thou longedst ;
  In whose wild joy thou stirrest up the
  people, in whose wild joy thou didst
  unbar the cow-stalls.

8 Call we on Indra, Maghavan, auspicious,
  best Hero in the fight where spoi is
  gathered ;
  The Strong, who listens, who gives aid in
  battles, who slays the Vṛtras, wins and
  gathers riches.

HYMN XLIV.   *Indra.*

1. May this delightsome Soma be expressed
   for thee by tawny stones.
   Joying thereat, O Indra, with thy Bay
   Steeds come : ascend thy golden-
   coloured car.

2 In love thou madest Uṣas glow, in love
  thou madest Sūrya shine.
  Thou, Indra, knowing, thinking, Lord of
  Tawny Steeds, above all glories waxest
  great.

7 *The strong* : the Soma juice. *The strong ones* :
the press-stones.

That which the Falcon brought thee : the Soma is said
to have been brought from heaven by a falcon. See I.
80. 2, and 93. 6.

Throughout the hymn the poet rings the changes
on words said to be derivatives of the root *h i* to take,
as *haryatá*, delightsome, *haryán*, loving, *hári*, bay or
tawny, *hárit*, green, yellow, or gold-coloured.

3 The heaven with streams of golden hue,
  earth with her tints of green and gold—
  The golden Pair yield Indra plenteous
  nourishment : between them moves the
  golden One.

4 When born to life the golden Bull illumines all the realm of light.
  He takes his golden weapon, Lord of
  Tawny Steeds, the golden thunder in
  his arms.

5 The bright, the well-loved thunderbolt,
  girt with the bright, Indra disclosed,
  Disclosed the Soma juice pressed out by
  tawny stones, with tawny steeds drave
  forth the kine.

HYMN XLV.   *Indra.*

1. Come hither, Indra, with Bay Steeds,
   joyous, with tails like peacocks' plumes.
   Let no men check thy course as fowlers
   stay the bird : pass o'er them as o'er
   desert lands.

2 He who slew Vṛtra, burst the cloud,
  brake the strongholds and drave the
  floods,
  Indra who mounts his chariot at his Bay
  Steeds' cry, shatters e'en things that
  stand most firm.

3 Like pools of water deep and full, like
  kine thou cherishest thy might ;
  Like the milch-cows that go well-guarded
  to the mead, like water-brooks that
  reach the lake.

4 Bring thou us wealth with power to
  strike, our share, 'gainst him who calls
  it his.

3 *The golden One* : the Sun.
4 *The golden Bull* : Indra as the Sun.
5 *Girt with the bright* : surrounded by flashes of
light. *With tawny steeds* : or by means of the tawny
pressing-stones, *i. e.*, inspirited by draughts of the expressed Soma juice.

----

1 *Tails like peacock's plumes* : trailing clouds with
fringes of purple and gold.

2 *Like pools of water* : the meaning appears to be,
as Prof. Ludwig suggests : thy mental power is as
inexhaustible as the water in deep springs, as safe from
harm as carefully guarded cows that go without straying
to their pasture, and ever full like streams that pour
water into a lake. Professor Wilson, following Sāyaṇa,
paraphrases thus : 'Thou cherishest the celebrator of
the pious rite as (thou fillest) the deep seas (with water)
or as a careful herdsman (cherishes) the cows : thou
imbibest the Soma) as cows (obtain) fodder, and the
juices flow into thee) as rivulets flow into a lake.'
Kratu, which I have, rendered by 'might,' means power,
either mental or bodily, and sometimes also, especially
in later works, a sacrificial ceremony. Sāyaṇa has
filled up supposed ellipses in the most arbitrary way.

Shake, Indra, as with hooks, the tree
for ripened fruit, for wealth to satisfy
our wish.

5 Indra, self-ruling Lord art thou, good
Leader, of most glorious fame.
So, waxen in thy strength, O thou
whom many praise, be thou most swift to
hear our call.

HYMN XLVI.   *Indra.*

1. OF thee, the Bull, the Warrior, Sovran
Ruler, joyous and fierce, ancient and
ever youthful,
The undecaying One who wields the thunder, renowned and great, great are the
exploits, Indra.

2 Great art thou, Mighty Lord, through
manly vigour, O fierce One, gathering
spoil, subduing others,
Thyself alone the universe's Sovran : so
send forth men to combat and to rest
them.

3 He hath surpassed all measure in his
brightness, yea, and the Gods, for none
may be his equal.
Impetuous Indra in his might exceedeth
wide vast mid-air and heaven and earth
together.

4 To Indra, even as rivers to the ocean,
flow forth from days of old the Soma
juices ;
To him wide deep and mighty from his
birth-time, the well of holy thoughts,
all-comprehending.

5 The Soma, Indra, which the earth and
heaven bear for thee as a mother bears
her infant,
This they send forth to thee, this, vigorous
Hero ! Adhvaryus purify for thee to
drink of.

HYMN XLVII.   *Indra.*

1. DRINK, Indra, Marut-girt, as Bull, the
Soma, for joy, for rapture even as thou
listest.
Pour down the flood of meath within thy
belly : thou from of old art King of
Soma juices.

2 Indra, accordant, with the banded Maruts,
drink Soma, Hero, as wise Vṛtra-
slayer.

---

3 *Impetuous* : or, according to 'Sāyaṇa, whom
Professors Wilson and Ludwig follow, 'drinker of the
spiritless Soma juice, 'er des auch dis somatrester.'

Slay thou our foemen, drive away assailants
and make us safe on every side from
danger.

3 And, drinker at due seasons, drink in
season, Indra, with friendly Gods, our
pressed-out Soma.
The Maruts following, whom thou madest
sharers, gave thee the victory, and thou
slewest Vṛtra.

4 Drink Soma, Indra, banded with the
Maruts who, Maghavan, strengthened
thee at Ahi's slaughter,
'Gainst Śambara, Lord of Bays ! in winning cattle, and now rejoice in thee,
the holy Singers.

5 The Bull whose strength hath waxed,
whom Maruts follow, free-giving Indra,
the celestial Ruler,
Mighty, all-conquering, the victory-giver,
him let us call to grant us new protection.

HYMN XLVIII.   *Indra.*

1. SOON as the young Bull sprang into existence he longed to taste the pressed-
out Soma's liquor.
Drink thou thy fill, according to thy longing, first, of the goodly mixture blent
with Soma.

2 That day when thou wast born thou, fain
to taste it, drankest the plant's milk
which the mountains nourish.
That milk thy Mother first, the Dame
who bare thee, poured for thee in thy
mighty Father's dwelling.

3 Desiring food he came unto his Mother,
and on her breast beheld the pungent
Soma.
Wise, he moved on, keeping aloof the
others, and wrought great exploits in
his varied aspects.

---

4 *In winning cattle* : in recovering the stolen kine,
the vanished rays of light, or, generally, in battle with
the demons of drought.

5 This stanza recurs in VI. 19. 11.

---

1 *The young Bull* : Indra.

2 *Which the mountains nourish* : the Soma plant is
said to have grown on the hills. *Thy Mother* : Aditi.
Thy mighty Father : according to the later mythology
Kaśyapa was the husband of Aditi and father of Indra
and the other deities, and Sāyaṇa says that in this
passage Kaśyapa is intended. But it seems almost
certain that Tvaṣṭar, whom Indra conquered at his
birth, is here referred to as his mighty Father. See
Bergaigne, *La Religion Védique*, III. 58 ff.

4 Fierce, quickly conquering, of surpassing vigour, he framed his body even as he listed.

E'en from his birth-time Indra conquered Tvaṣṭar, bore off the Soma and in beakers drank it.

5 Call we on Maghavan, auspicious Indra, best Hero in the fight where spoil is gathered ;

The Strong, who listens, who gives aid in battles, who slays the Vṛtras, wins and gathers riches.

HYMN XLIX. *Indra.*

1. GREAT Indra will I laud, in whom all people who drink the Soma have attained their longing ;

Whom, passing wise, Gods, Heaven and Earth, engendered, formed by a Master's hand, to crush the Vṛtras.

2 Whom, most heroic, borne by Tawny Coursers, verily none subdueth in the battle ;

Who, reaching far, most vigorous, hath shortened the Dasyu's life with Warriors bold of spirit.

3 Victor in fight, swift mover like a war-horse, pervading both worlds, rainer down of blessings,

To be invoked in war like Bhaga, Father, as 'twere, of hymns, fair, prompt to hear, strength-giver.

4 Supporting heaven, the high back of the region, his car is Vāyu with his team of Vasus.

Illumining the nights, the Sun's creator, like Dhiṣaṇā he deals forth strength and riches.

5 Call we on Maghavan, auspicious Indra, best Hero in the fight where spoil is gathered ;

The Strong, who listens, who gives aid in battles, who slays the Vṛtras, wins and gathers treasure.

1 *Formed by a Master's hand* : or fashioned by Vibhvan one of the Ṛbhus. According to Sāyaṇa, appointed by Brahmā for the government of the world. *The Vṛtras* : Vṛtra and similar fiends, or, generally, the enemies of the Gods and Āryans.

2 *With Warriors bold of spirit* : his allies the Maruts.

4 *His car is Vāyu* : the construction of the first hemistich is difficult and the sense is doubtful. The meaning may be, as Vāyu the God of wind moves like a chariot on high drawn by the coursers of the air, so Indra moves accompanied by the Vasus or Maruts.

Like Dhiṣaṇā : the Wish-Goddess, a deity presiding over prosperity. See I. 96. 1, note ; IV. 34. 1 ; V. 41. 8.

HYMN L. *Indra.*

1. LET Indra drink, All-hail ! for his is Soma,—the mighty Bull come, girt by Maruts, hither.

Far-reaching, let him fill him with these viands, and let our offering sate his body's longing.

2 I yoke thy pair of trusty Steeds for swiftness, whose faithful service from of old thou lovest.

Here, fair of cheek ! let thy Bay Coursers place thee : drink of this lovely well-effused libation.

3 With milk they made Indra their good Preserver, lauding for help and rule the bounteous rainer.

Impetuous God, when thou hast drunk the Soma, enraptured send us cattle in abundance.

4 With kine and horses satisfy this longing ; with very splendid bounty still extend it.

Seeking the light, with hymns to thee, O Indra, the Kuśikas have brought their gift, the singers.

5 Call we on Maghavan, auspicious Indra, best Hero in the fight where spoil is gathered ;

The Strong, who listens, who gives aid in battles, who slays the Vṛtras, wins and gathers riches.

HYMN LI. *Indra.*

1. HIGH hymns have sounded forth the praise of Maghavan, supporter of mankind, of Indra meet for lauds ;

Him who hath waxen great, invoked with beauteous songs, Immortal One, whose praise each day is sung aloud.

2 To Indra from all sides go forth my songs of praise, the Lord of Hundred Powers, strong, Hero, like the sea,

Swift, winner of the booty, breaker-down of forts, faithful and ever-glorious, finder of the light.

1 *All-hail* : I take *svāhā* here as an exclamation addressed to Indra. Sāyaṇa explains the word by *svāhākṛtamimam somam*, (let Indra drink) this Soma offered with Svāhā.

3 *With milk* : with libations of Soma juice mingled with milk.

4 This stanza is found also in Hymn XXX. 20 of this Book.

3 Where battle's spoil is piled the singer
   winneth praise, for Indra taketh care of
   matchless worshippers.
   He in Vivasvān's dwelling findeth his
   delight : praise thou the ever-conquering slayer of the foe.

4 Thee, valorous, most heroic of the heroes,
   shall the priests glorify with songs and
   praises.
   Full of all wondrous power he goes to
   conquest : worship is his, sole Lord
   from days aforetime.

5 Abundant are the gifts he gives to mortals : for him the earth bears a rich
   store of treasures.
   The heavens, the growing plants, the
   living waters, the forest trees preserve
   their wealth for Indra.

6 To thee, O Indra, Lord of Bays, for ever
   are offered prayers and songs : accept
   them gladly.
   As Kinsman think thou of some fresh
   assistance ; good Friend, give strength
   and life to those who praise thee.

7 Here, Indra, drink thou Soma with the
   Maruts, as thou didst drink the juice
   beside Śāryāta.
   Under thy guidance, in thy keeping, Hero,
   the singers serve, skilled in fair sacrifices.

8 So eagerly desirous drink the Soma, our
   juice, O Indra, with thy friends the
   Maruts,
   Since at thy birth all Deities adorned thee
   for the great fight, O thou invoked of
   many.

9 He was your comrade in your zeal, O
   Maruts : they, rich in noble gifts, rejoiced in Indra.
   With them together let the Vṛtra-slayer
   drink in his home the worshipper's
   libation.

10 So, Lord of affluent gifts, this juice hath
   been expressed for thee with strength :
   Drink of it, thou who lovest song.

11 Incline thy body to this juice which suits
   thy Godlike nature well :
   May it cheer thee who lovest it.

12 Brave Indra, let it work through both thy

flanks, and through thy head by prayer,
And through thine arms, to prosper us.

HYMN LII.   *Indra.*

1. INDRA, accept at break of day our Soma
   mixt with roasted corn,
   With groats with cake, with eulogies.

2 Accept, O Indra, and enjoy the well-dressed sacrificial cake : Oblations are
   poured forth to thee.

3 Consume our sacrificial cake, accept the
   songs of praise we sing,
   As he who woos accepts his bride.

4 Famed from of old, accept the cake at our
   libation poured at dawn,
   For great, O Indra, is thy power.

5 Let roasted corn of our midday libation,
   and sacrificial cake here please thee,
   Indra,
   What time the lauding singer, keen of
   purpose and eager as a bull, with hymns
   implores thee.

6 At the third sacrifice, O thou whom many
   praise, give glory to the roasted corn
   and holy cake.
   With offered viands and with songs may
   we assist thee, Sage, whom Vāja and
   the Ṛbhus wait upon.

7 The groats have we prepared for thee with
   Pūṣan, corn for thee, Lord of Bay
   Steeds, with thy horses.
   Eat thou the meal-cake, banded with the
   Maruts, wise Hero, Vṛtra-slayer, drink
   the Soma.

8 Bring forth the roasted corn to meet him
   quickly, cake for the bravest Hero mid
   the heroes.
   Indra, may hymns accordant with thee
   daily strengthen thee, Bold One, for the
   draught of Soma.

---

3 *In Vivasvān's dwelling* : in the sacrificial chamber
of the worshipper. See III. 34. 7.
   Śāryāta : said by Sāyaṇa to have been a Rājā son
of Śaryāta who was perhaps the same as Śaryāti, a son
of Manu Vaivasvata. See 1. 51. 12; 112. 17
   8 *For the great fight* : the battle with Vṛtra and the
demons of drought.

1 *With groats, with cake* : *karambhiṇam apūpávantam* ;
karambhá is coarsely ground corn, or meal mixed with
curds, a kind of gruel : *apūpá* is a cake made of
flour.
   Stanzas 1—4, in Gāyatrī metre, accompany the
morning offering; stanza 5, in Trṣṭup, the offering of
noon; and 6, in Jagatī, the evening libation.
   6 *Give glory* : honour by accepting. *Vāja and the
Ṛbhus* : the three Ṛbhus.
   7 *With Pūṣan* : because *karambhá*, groats or gruel, is
the usual offering to that God. *Corn* : for Indra's horses.

HYMN LIII. *Indra, Parvata, Etc.*

1. On a high car, O Parvata and Indra,
   bring pleasant viands, with brave heroes,
   hither.
   Enjoy the gifts, Gods, at our sacrifices :
   wax strong by hymns, rejoice in our
   oblation.

2. Stay still, O Maghavan, advance no farther:
   a draught of well-pressed Soma will I
   give thee.
   With sweetest song I grasp, O Mighty
   Indra, thy garment's hem as a child
   grasps his father's.

3. Adhvaryu, sing we both ; sing thou in
   answer : make we a laud acceptable to
   Indra.
   Upon this sacrificer's grass be seated : to
   Indra shall our eulogy be uttered.

4. A wife, O Maghavan is home and dwelling : so let thy Bay Steeds yoked convey
   thee hither.
   Whenever we press out for thee the Soma,
   let Agni as our Herald speed to call
   thee.

5. Depart, O Maghavan ; again come hither :
   both there and here thy goal is Indra,
   Brother,
   Where thy tall chariot hath a place to rest
   in, and where thou loosest thy loud-
   neighing Courser.

6. Thou hast drunk Soma, Indra, turn thee
   homeward ; thy joy is in thy home, thy
   gracious Consort ;
   Where thy tall chariot hath a place to rest
   in, and thy strong Courser is set free
   with guerdon.

7. Bounteous are these, Angirases, Virūpas :
   the Asura's Heroes and the Sons of
   Heaven.

They, giving store of wealth to Viśvāmitra,
prolong his life through countless Soma-
pressings.

8. Maghavan weareth every shape at pleasure,
   effecting magic changes in his body,
   Holy One, drinker out of season, coming
   thrice, in a moment, through fit prayers,
   from heaven.

9. The mighty sage, God-born and God-inci-
   ted, who looks on men, restrained the
   billowy river.
   When Viśvāmitra was Sudās's escort, then
   Indra through the Kuśikas grew friendly.

10. Like swans, prepare a song of praise with
    pressing-stones, glad in your hymns with
    juice poured forth in sacrifice.
    Ye singers, with the Gods, sages who look
    on men, ye Kuśikas drink up the Soma's
    savoury meath.

11. Come forward, Kuśikas, and be attentive ;
    let loose Sudās's horse to win him riches.
    East, west, and north, let the King slay
    the foeman, then at earth's choicest
    place perform his worship.

12. Praises to Indra have I sung, sustainer of
    this earth and heaven. This prayer of
    Viśvāmitra keeps secure the race of
    Bharatas.

13. The Viśvāmitras have sung forth this pra-
    yer to Indra Thunder-armed :
    So let him make us prosperous.

14. Among the Kīkaṭas what do thy cattle ?
    They pour no milky draught, they heat
    no caldron.

In addition to Indra and his frequent associate
Parvata, the Genius of the mountains and clouds, the
Goddess Vāk or Speech (stanzas 15, 16), and the
several parts of the chariot or wain (17—20) are regarded as the deities or objects reverently mentioned or
addressed in this hymn.

1 *With brave heroes* : accompanied, or followed by
heroic sons.

3 *Adhvaryu, sing we both* : the Hotar calls on the
Adhvaryu to join him in the performance of the ceremony.

4 *A wife......is home and dwelling* : or, perhaps, 'Wife,
Maghavan, is home, so is this chamber; that is, Indra is
to regard the sacrificial chamber as his home for the
present, until he returns to his consort and his other
home in heaven.

6 *Thy gracious Consort* : Indrāṇī. *With guerdon* :
with corn and water.

7 Professor Wilson, following Sāyaṇa, paraphrases :
'These sacrificers are (*Bhojas*), of whom the diversified
Angirases (are the priests): and the heroic sons of the
expeller (of the foes of the Gods) from heaven, bestowing

riches upon Viśvāmitra at the sacrifice of a thousand
(victims), prolong his life.' The Bhojas (bounteous
ones) are said to be the Kṣatriya descendants of Sudās,
and the diversified Angirases Medhātithi and the rest of
the race of Angiras. 'The Asura,' explained by Sāyaṇa
as the expeller of the foes of the Gods from heaven, is
said to be Rudra, and his sons are the Maruts. The
Virūpas are connected with Angiras in X. 62. 5., and
a Virūpa is mentioned in I. 45. 3. and VIII. 64. 6.

8 *Drinker out of season* : drinking the celestial Soma
whenever he wishes, irrespectively of the appointed times
for libations on earth. *Thrice* : to the three daily libations.

9 *The mighty sage* : Viśv. mitra. See III. 33, note.

11 In this and the two following stanzas the priests
implore the aid of Indra for King Sudās who is going
forth to battle.
Earth's choicest place : the altar.

12 *The race of Bharatas* : the descendants of Viśvāmitra, Bharata being the son of the celebrated Śakuntalā
who was Viśvāmitra's daughter by the Apsaras Menā.
See *Vedic India* (Story of the Nations series), pp.
319 ff.

14 *The Kīkaṭas* : the non-Āryan inhabitants of a
country (probably Kośala or Oudh) usually identified
with South Bihār. The meaning is that the cows bestowed by Indra are unprofitable when in the possession
of men who do not worship the Āryan Gods. *Pramaganda*
the prince of the Kīkaṭas ; according to Sāyaṇa the
word means 'the son of the usurer.

Bring thou to us the wealth of Pramaganda ; give up to us, O Maghavan, the low-born.

15 Sasarparī, the gift of Jamadagnis, hath lowed with mighty voice dispelling famine.
The Daughter of the Sun hath spread our glory among the Gods, imperishable, deathless.

16 Sasarparī brought glory speedily to these, over the generations of the Fivefold Race ;
Daughter of Pakṣa, she bestows new vital power, she whom the ancient Jamadagnis gave to me.

17 Strong be the pair of oxen, firm the axles, let not the pole slip nor the yoke be broken.
May Indra keep the yoke-pins from decay-

ing : attend us, thou whose fellies are uninjured.

18 O Indra, give our bodies strength, strength to the bulls who draw the wains,
Strength to our seed and progeny that they may live, for thou art he who giveth strength.

19 Enclose thee in the heart of Khayar timber, in the car wrought of Śiṃśapā put firmness.
Show thyself strong, O Axle, fixed and strengthened : throw us not from the car whereon we travel.

20 Let not this sovran of the wood leave us forlorn or injure us.
Safe may we be until we reach our homes and rest us and unyoke.

21 With various aids this day come to us, Indra, with best aids speed us, Maghavan, thou Hero.
Let him who hateth us fall headlong downward : him whom we hate let vital breath abandon.

22 He heats his very axe, and then cuts a mere Semal blossom off.
O Indra, like a caldron cracked and seething, so he pours out foam.

---

15 *Sasarparī, the gift of Jamadagnis* : according to Sāyaṇa, Sasarparī (swiftly moving or gliding everywhere), is a name or an epithet of Vāk, Voice or Speech, the daughter of Sūrya or the Sun. The following is Dr. Muir's translation of Sāyaṇa's quotation from Ṣaḍgurśiṣya's Commentary on the Anukramaṇikā, as given with an addition in Weber's *Indische Studien* : 'Regarding the two verses beginning "Sasarparīḥ" those acquainted with antiquity tell a story. At a sacrifice of king Saudāsa the power and speech of Viśvāmitra were completely vanquished by Śakti, son of Vasiṣṭha ; and the son of Gādhi (Viśvāmitra) being so overcome, became dejected. The Jamadagnis drew from the abode of the sun a voice called "Sasarparī," the daughter of Brahmā, or of the sun, and gave her to him. Then that Voice somewhat dispelled the disquiet of the Jamadagnis (or, according to the reading of the line given by Sāyaṇa, "that Voice, being intelligence, dispelled the unintelligence of the Kuśikas"). Viśvāmitra then incited the Kuśikas with the words *upapreta* 'approach' (see verse 11). And being gladdened by receiving the Voice, he paid homage to the Jamadagnis praising them with the two verses beginning 'Sasarparīḥ'.—*O. S. Texts*, I. 343. Prof Ludwig is inclined to agree with Prof. Roth who thinks that sasarparī may mean a war-trumpet, which inspirits the combatants and dispels their fear of the enemy. Prof. Grassmann argues that *mimāya*, hath lowed, is applicable only to a cow or bull, and thinks that sasarparī means the mystic cow Sabardughā, the cow who lets her milk flow abundantly. I am inclined to prefer the explanation of the Indian commentator, although it cannot be regarded as entirely satisfactory.
The *Jamadagnis*, according to Sāyaṇa are Rṣis who maintain a blazing fire.

16 *The Fivefold Race* : the five tribes of Āryan men ; according to Sāyaṇa, the four castes, and barbarians or non-Āryans.
Daughter of Pakṣa : that is, of the Sun who causes the light and dark periods of the moon.

17 In this and the three following stanzas Viśvāmitra being about to depart from King Sudās's sacrificial hall blesses, or invokes good luck for, the several parts of the chariot or wain on which he is going to travel.
Attend us : the chariot is here addressed.

19 *Khayar timber* : the hard wood of the Khadira, or Acacia Catechu, of which the pin of the axle was made. *Śiṃśapā* : Dalbergia Sisu, also a common timber-tree.

20 *This sovran of the wood* : the timber of which the body of the car is made.

21 Prof. Roth is of opinion that this hymn consists of fragments composed by Viśvāmitra or his descendants at different dates, and that the verses (9—13), in which that Rṣi represents himself and the Kuśikas as being the priests of Sudās are earlier than the concluding verses (21—24), which consist of imprecations directed against Vasiṣṭha. These last verses, he remarks, contain an expression of wounded pride, and threaten vengeance against an enemy who had come into possession of some power or dignity which Viśvāmitra himself had previously enjoyed. With regard to the relations between Viśvāmitra and Vasiṣṭha as priests of Sudās, see Muir's *Original Sanskrit Texts*, I. pp. 371 ff.

22 Professor Wilson remarks : 'The construction is elliptical: the ellipse is supplied by the scholiast, as the tree is cut down by the axe so may the enemy be cut down : as one cuts off without difficulty the flower of the *Simbala*, so may he be destroyed : as the cauldron when struck, and thence leaking, scatters foam or breath from its mouth, so may that hater, struck by the flower of my prayer, vomit foam from his mouth.' The phrases are probably, as Ludwig explains merely proverbial expressions for threats full of sound and fury followed by insignificant results.
The *Semal* (Śimbala) is the Silk-cotton tree.

23 Men notice not the arrow, O ye people ;
   they bring the red beast deeming it a
   bullock.
   A sluggish steed men run not with the
   courser, nor ever lead an ass before a
   charger.
24 These men, the sons of Bharata, O Indra,
   regard not severance or close connexion.
   They urge their own steed as it were
   another's, and take him, swift as the
   bow's string, to battle.

HYMN LIV.   *Viśvedevas.*

1. To him adorable, mighty, meet for synods,
   this strengthening hymn, unceasing, have
   they offered.
   May Agni hear us with his homely splendours, hear us, Eternal One, with heavenly lustre.
2 To mighty Heaven and Earth I sing forth
   loudly : my wish goes out desirous and
   well knowing
   Both, at whose laud in synods, showing

favour, the Gods rejoice them with the
living mortal.
3 O Heaven and Earth, may your great law
  be faithful: be ye our leaders for our
  high advantage.
  To Heaven and Earth I offer this my
  homage, with food, O Agni, as I pray
  for riches.
4 Yea, holy Heaven and Earth, the ancient
  sages whose word was ever true had
  power to find you;
And brave men in the fight where heroes
  conquer, O Earth, have known you well
  and paid you honour.
5 What pathway leadeth to the Gods ? Who
  knoweth this of a truth, and who will
  now declare it ?
  Seen are their lowest dwelling-places only,
  but they are in remote and secret regions.
6 The Sage who looketh on mankind hath
  viewed them bedewed, rejoicing in the
  seat of Order.
  They make a home as for a bird, though
  parted, with one same will finding themselves together.
7 Partners though parted, with far-distant
  limits, on one firm place both stand for
  ever watchful,
  And, being young for evermore, as sisters,
  speak to each other names that are
  united.
8 All living things they part and keep
  asunder; though bearing up the mighty
  Gods they reel not.

---

23 *Men notice not the arrow* : or, according to
Sāyaṇa, men heed not the destroyer', i.e. the power of
Viśvāmitra who will destroy his enemies is not known to,
or regarded by, his opponents.
   They bring the red beast : the meaning of *lodhám* is
uncertain. Sāyaṇa explains it as *lubdham*, desirous (that)
his penance might not be frustrated). Prof. Roth
suggests that *lodhám* means red, and denotes an animal
of some kind contrasted with *paśu* (a tame or sacrificial
animal, a bullock), so that the clause would have somewhat the same meaning as 'they look on the wolf as if
it were a hare.' Durga, the commentator on the
Nirukta, says : 'The text in which this word (*lodhá*)
occurs is a verse expressing hatred of Vasiṣṭha.
But I am a Kāpiṣṭhala of the family of Vasiṣṭha; and
therefore do not interpret it.' See Muir's *O.S. Texts*,
I. pp. 344, 372.
   Deeming it a bullock : according to Sāyaṇa, thinking
the sage, Viśvāmitra, who kept silence of his own
accord to be merely stupid like some inferior animal.
In the second line the rivalry of Vasiṣṭha with himself
appears to be ridiculed.
   24 *The son of Bharata* : descendants and adherents
of Viśvāmitra. Prof. Wilson, following Sāyaṇa, paraphrases the the stanza : 'These sons of Bharata, Indra,
understand severance (from the Vasiṣṭhas), not association (with them) ; they urge their steeds (against them)
as against a constant foe : they bear a stout bow (for
their destruction) in battle.' The word *áraṇam*, strange,
foreign, another's, gives no intelligible sense. Prof.
Ludwig suggests in its place *karaṇam*, an ever-ready
helper. Dr. Muir suggests that the word may mean
'as if to a distance.'

---

1 *To him* : Agni. *Meet for synods* : to be worshipped
in sacrificial assemblies. *May Agni hear us* : both as
terrestrial fire used for sacrifice and domestic purposes
and as celestial fire in the form of the Sun. *They* :
the priestly singers.
   2 *Knowing both* : recognizing the greatness of Heaven
and Earth. *The living mortal* : men as worshippers.

5 *Seen are their lowest dwelling-places* : the constellations ; but the Gods are also in mysterious and higher
realms beyond, and who knows the path that leads
thither ?
   6 *The Sage who looketh on mankind* : the all-seeing
and omniscient Sun. *Them* : Heaven and Earth.
Bedewed : with the water above the firmament and rain
respectively. *In the seat of Order* : in the place which
the eternal Order of the Universe has assigned to them.
They make a home : though meeting together, they
leave a space, like a bird's nest, between them.
   7 *Speak to each other names that are united* : address
each other or perhaps, are addressed, by dual appellations, such as *urvī*, the Two Spacious Ones, *dyāvāpṛthivī*,
Heaven-Earth, etc.
   8 *One All* : 'We find mention in one hymn of a
primordial substance or unit out of which the universe
was developed. This is 'the one thing' (*ekam*) which
we have met with in connection with Aja, the Unborn
(Book I. 164, 6, 46.), and which is also used synony-
mously with the universe in accordance with the principle which is the key to much of the later mysticism that
cause and effect are identical. The poet endeavours, in
a strain which preludes the philosophy of the Upaniṣads, to picture to himself the first state of the world,
and the first signs of life and growth in it.'—Wallis,
Cosmology of the Ṛgveda, p. 58.

One All is Lord of what is fixed and moving, that walks, that flies, this multiform creation.

9 Afar the Ancient from of old I ponder, our kinship with our mighty Sire and Father,—

Singing the praise whereof the Gods by custom stand on the spacious far-extended pathway.

10 This laud, O Heaven and Earth, to you I utter: let the kind-hearted hear, whose tongue is Agni,

Young, Sovran Rulers, Varuṇa and Mitra, the wise and very glorious Ādityas.

11 The fair-tongued Savitar, the golden-handed, comes thrice from heaven as Lord in our assembly.

Bear to the Gods this song of praise, and send us, then, Savitar, complete and perfect safety.

12 Deft worker, skiful-handed, helpful, holy, may Tvaṣṭar, God, give us these things to aid us.

Take your delight, ye Ṛbhus joined with Pūṣan: ye have prepared the rite with stones adjusted.

13 Borne on their flashing car, the spear-armed Maruts, the nimble Youths of Heaven, the Sons of Order,

The Holy, and Sarasvatī, shall hear us: ye Mighty, give us wealth with noble offspring.

14 To Viṣṇu rich in marvels, songs and praises shall go as singers on the road of Bhaga,—

The Chieftain of the Mighty Stride, whose Mothers, the many young Dames, never disregard him.

15 Indra, who rules through all his powers heroic, hath with his majesty filled earth and heaven.

Lord of brave hosts, Fort-crusher, Vṛtra-slayer, gather thou up and bring us store of cattle.

16 My Sires are the Nāsatyas, kind to kinsmen : the Aśvins' kinship is a glorious title.

For ye are they who give us store of riches: ye guard your gift uncheated by the bounteous.

17 This is, ye Wise, your great and glorious title, that all ye Deities abide in Indra.

Friend, Much-invoked ! art thou with thy dear Ṛbhus : fashion ye this our hymn for our advantage.

18 Aryaman, Aditi deserve our worship: the laws of Varuṇa remain unbroken.

The lot of childlessness remove ye from us, and let our course be rich in kine and offspring.

19 May the Gods' envoy, sent to many a quarter, proclaim us sinless for our perfect safety.

May Earth and Heaven, the Sun, the waters, hear us, and the wide firmament and constellations.

20 Hear us the mountains which distil the rain-drops, and, resting firm, rejoice in freshening moisture.

May Aditi with the Ādityas hear us, and Maruts grant us their auspicious shelter.

21 Soft be our path for ever, well-provisioned: with pleasant meath, O Gods, the herbs besprinkle.

Safe be my bliss, O Agni, in thy friend-ship : may I attain the seat of foodful riches,

22 Enjoy the offering : beam thou strength upon us; combine thou for our good all kinds of glory.

Conquer in battle, Agni, all those foemen, and light us every day with loving-kindness.

HYMN LV. *Viśvedevas.*

1. AT the first shining of the earliest Mornings, in the Cow's home was born the Great Eternal.

---

9 *Singing the praise whereof* : that is, with reference to which kinship with our father Dyaus or Heaven the Gods themselves bear witness to its existence.

11 *Comes thrice* : at the three daily sacrifices.

12 *These things* : for which we pray.

14 *On the road of Bhaga* : or on the path of good fortune or felicity.

The Chieftain of the Mighty Stride : Viṣṇu as the Sun. *The Mothers*, according to Sāyaṇa, are the regions of space which generate all beings. Sāyaṇa supplies *ājñām*, command, after *ydsya*, whose, and Prof. Wilson, renders the passage accordingly, 'whose commands the many-blending regions of space, the generators (of all being) do not disobey.'

16 *My Sires are the Nāsatyas* : the Aśvins regard me with fatherly affection, *Te* : the Aśvins. *Uncheated by the bounteous* ; never deceived by liberal men like us.

17 *Abide in Indra* : not as Sāyaṇa explains. in the sphere or world of Indra. The meaning is, as Professor Ludwig points out, that the glory of the Gods consists in their recognition as forming a part of the true, supreme and all-embracing divine principle, in which, as the Absolute God, all their individual attributes are absorbed and vanish.

Fashion ye : perhaps merely, give a favourable issue to.

19 *The Gods' envoy* : Agni.

21 *With pleasant meath* : with refreshing rain.

---

1 *In the Cow's home* : in the firmament or heaven, the place of the mystical Cosmic Cow. *The Great Eternal* : the two adjectives are in the neuter gender

Now shall the statutes of the Gods be valid. Great is the Gods' supreme and sole dominion.

2 Let not the Gods here injure us, O Agni, nor Fathers of old time who know the region,
Nor the sign set between two ancient dwellings. Great is the Gods' supreme and sole dominion.

3 My wishes fly abroad to many places : I glance back to the ancient sacrifices.
Let us declare the truth when fire is kindled. Great is the Gods' supreme and sole dominion.

4 King Universal, born to sundry quarters, extended through the wood he lies on couches.
One Mother rests: another feeds the Infant. Great is the Gods' supreme and sole dominion.

5 Lodged in old plants, he grows again in younger, swiftly within the newly-born and tender.
Though they are unimpregned, he makes them fruitful. Great is the Gods' supreme and sole dominion.

6 Now lying far away, Child of two Mothers, he wanders unrestrained, the single youngling.
These are the laws of Varuṇa and Mitra. Great is the Gods' supreme and sole dominion.

7 Child of two Mothers, Priest, sole Lord in synods, he still precedes while resting as foundation.
They who speak sweetly bring him sweet addresses. Great is the Gods' supreme and sole dominion.

8 As to a friendly warrior when he battles, each thing that comes anear is seen to meet him.
The hymn commingles with the cow's oblation. Great is the Gods' supreme and sole dominion.

9 Deep within these the hoary envoy pierceth; mighty, he goeth to the realm of splendour,
And looketh on us, clad in wondrous beauty. Great is the Gods' supreme and sole dominion.

10 Viṣṇu, the guardian, keeps the loftiest station, upholding dear, immortal dwelling-places.
Agni knows well all these created beings. Great is the Gods' supreme and sole dominion.

11 Ye, variant Pair, have made yourselves twin beauties: one of the Twain is dark, bright shines the other;
And yet these two, the dark, the red, are Sisters. Great is the Gods' supreme and sole dominion.

12 Where the two Cows, the Mother and the Daughter, meet and give suck yielding their lordly nectar,
I praise them at the seat of law eternal. Great is the Gods' supreme and sole dominion.

13 Loud hath she lowed, licking the other's youngling. On what world hath the Milch-cow laid her udder ?

without a substantive. Sāyaṇa supplies *jyotiḥ*, light, in the form of the Sun. *Great is*, etc. 'Great and incomparable is the divine nature of the gods.'—Muir.

2 The meaning of the stanza is, as Professor Ludwig says : May we be able to calculate correctly the time of the Sun's approach, that is, the moment of his rising, when we should begin our sacred ceremonies. Let not the Gods lead us astray, or allow us to err, in this matter; let not the Fathers, or spirits of the departed, who are acquainted with the region in which the Sun first appears, and who have transmitted their knowledge to their descendants, nor the Sun himself (or, per haps, Agni) deceive us. *Two ancient dwellings* : heaven and earth, the homes respectively of Gods and men.

3 *I glance back* : so Prof. M. Müller translates the passage.

4 *King Universal* : Agni, the God of all Āryan men. *To sundry quarters* : to various altars, for sacrificial purposes.
One Mother : the earth. *Another* : the heaven. Or, as Prof. Ludwig suggests, the lower of the two fire-sticks remains still while the upper stick, which is agitated, gives him life and strength.

5 Agni is latent in all plants, and from those that are old decaying he passes into the young and tender ones.

6 *Far away* : or, in the west, as Sūrya or the Sun when he has set.

He wanders : when he has risen again.

7 *Priest* : Agni, the herald who calls the Gods, the *hotar* or invoker.

As foundation : as the root and basis of every religious act.

8 Agni is here represented as a champion who draws men to meet him as a friend. *The hymn commingles* : penetrates, as it were, and accompanies the libation of milk and Soma juice.

9 *Within these* : plants in general. *The hoary envoy* : Agni, the ancient messenger between Gods and man. *To the realm of splendour* : to heaven as the Sun.

10 *Loftiest station* : in the zenith. Cf. I. 154. 5, 6.

11 *Ye, variant Pair* : Day and Night.

12 *The two Cows* : Earth and Heaven, according to Sāyaṇa ; more probably Night and Morning are intended. *The seat of law eternal* : the altar, the place of sacrifice appointed by everlasting law or *ṛtd*.

13 *Loud hath she lowed* : Heaven, as the rain pours down *The other's youngling*, or calf, is Agni. *On what world* : no one knows where the rain comes from. *This Iḷā* : a name of the earth ; or *Iḷā* may mean, with the freshening draught (of rain).

This Iḷā streameth with the milk of Order. Great is the Gods' supreme and sole dominion.

14 Earth weareth beauties manifold: uplifted, licking her Calf of eighteen months, she standeth.
Well-skilled I seek the seat of law eternal. Great is the Gods' supreme and sole dominion.

15 Within a wondrous place the Twain are treasured : the one is manifest, the other hidden.
One common pathway leads in two directions. Great is the Gods' supreme and sole dominion.

16 Let the milch-kine that have no calves storm downward, yielding rich nectar, streaming, unexhausted,
These who are ever new and fresh and youthful. Great is the Gods' supreme and sole dominion.

17 What time the Bull bellows in other regions, another herd receives the genial moisture;
For he is Bhaga, King, the earth's Protector. Great is the Gods' supreme and sole dominion.

18 Let us declare the Hero's wealth in horses, O all ye folk: of this the Gods have knowledge.
Sixfold they bear him, or by fives are harnessed. Great is the Gods' supreme and sole dominion.

19 Tvaṣṭar the God, the omniform Creator, begets and feeds mankind in various manner.

His, verily, are all these living creatures. Great is the Gods' supreme and sole dominion.

20 The two great meeting Bowls hath he united: each of the Pair is laden with his treasure.
The Hero is renowned for gathering riches. Great is the Gods' supreme and sole dominion.

21 Yea, and on this our earth the All-Sustainer dwells like a King with noble friends about him.
In his protection heroes rest in safety. Great is the Gods' supreme and sole dominion.

22 Rich in their gifts for thee are herbs and waters, and earth brings all her wealth for thee, O Indra.
May we as friends of thine share goodly treasures. Great is the Gods' supreme and sole dominion.

HYMN LVI.   *Viśvedevas.*

1. Not men of magic skill, not men of wisdom impair the Gods' first steadfast ordinances.
Ne'er may the earth and heaven which know not malice, nor the fixed hills, be bowed by sage devices.

2 One, moving not away, supports six burthens : the Cows proceed to him the true, the Highest.
Near stand three Mighty Ones who travel swiftly: two are concealed from sight, one is apparent.

---

14 *Earth : pádyā,* according to Sāyaṇa, has this meaning. *Uplifted.........she standeth* : apparently, Heaven, but according to Sāyaṇa, the Earth elevated in the northern altar.
Her calf of eighteen months : or according to Sāyaṇa's alternative explanation, her calf who protects the three worlds.' The calf is the Sun.

15 *Within a wondrous place* : when Morning comes, Night is concealed in some mysterious place to which Morning or Day also retires in turn when Night succeeds. From this mysterious prison Morning and Night come to us by the same path, one departing as the other approaches.

16 *The milch-kine that have no calves* : the heavy clouds which pour out their fertilizing rain as cows yield their refreshing milk, but which are unlike cows inasmuch as they have no calves.

17 *The Bull* : Indra as Parjanya the God of the rain cloud.
Another herd : the fertilizing shower falls in other regions.

18 The number of Indra's horses is variously stated. Here he is said to be drawn by six horses, the six seasons of the year, or by five at a time, or the seasons regarded as five by the combination of *hemanta* and *śiśira* the cold and the dewy seasons.

20 *The two great meeting Bowls* : the heaven and earth, hemispherical in appearance, which meet at the horizon. So the author of *The Witness of the Sun* speaks of 'the great bowl of the earth, which hollowed to the horizon.'

22 *The All-Sustainer* : Indra.

1 The statutes of the Gods are unalterable ; they stand fixed for ever like the benignant heaven and earth and like the mountains that never can be moved.

2 The meaning of the stanza is uncertain. According to Sāyaṇa, the *one, moving not away,* is the stationary year which sustains the load of the six seasons, and *the Cows* are the solar rays which pervade the year, or the Sun as its representative. Professor Ludwig thinks that Tvaṣṭar may be intended, and that the cows may be the consorts of the Gods who are generally represented as bearing him company. *Three Mighty Ones* : according to Sāyaṇa, heaven, the firmament, and the earth, of which the earth is fully visible and the first two are only seen imperfectly. *Who travel swiftly* : this is Sāyaṇa's explanation of *átyāḥ* coursers ; but the meaning is not clear.

3 The Bull who wears all shapes, the triple-
breasted, three-uddered, with a brood
in many places,
Ruleth majestic with his triple aspect, the
Bull, the Everlasting Ones' impregner.

4 When nigh them, as their tracer he observed them : he called aloud the dear name
of Ādityas.
The Goddesses, the Waters, stayed to meet
him : they who were wandering separate
enclosed him.

5 Streams ! the wise Gods have thrice three
habitations. Child of three Mothers, he
is Lord in synods.
Three are the holy Ladies of the Waters,
thrice here from heaven supreme in
our assembly.

6 Do thou, O Savitar, from heaven thrice
hither, three times a day, send down thy
blessings daily.
Send us, O Bhaga, triple wealth and
treasure; cause the two worlds to prosper
us, Preserver !

7 Savitar thrice from heaven pours down
abundance, and the fair-handed Kings
Varuṇa, Mitra;
And spacious Heaven and Earth, yea,
and the Waters, solicit wealth that
Savitar may send us.

8 Three are the bright realms, best, beyond
attainment, and three, the Asura's Heroes,
rule as Sovrans,
Holy and vigorous, never to be injured.
Thrice may the Gods from heaven attend
our synod.

HYMN LVII.   *Viśvedevas.*

1. My thought with fine discernment hath
discovered the Cow who wanders free
without a herdsman,
Her who hath straightway poured me
food in plenty: Indra and Agni therefore are her praisers.

2 Indra and Pūṣan, deft of hand and
mighty, well-pleased have drained the
heaven's exhaustless udder.
As in this praise the Gods have all delighted, may I win blessing here from you,
O Vasus.

3 Fain to lend vigour to the Bull, the sisters
with reverence recognize the germ within
him.
The Cows come lowing hither to the
Youngling, to him endued with great
and wondrous beauties.

4 Fixing with thought, at sacrifice, the press-
stones, I bid the well-formed Heaven
and Earth come hither ;
For these thy flames, which give men boons
in plenty, rise up on high, the beautiful, the holy.

5 Agni, thy meath-sweet tongue that tastes
fair viands, which among Gods is called
the far-extended,—
Therewith make all the Holy Ones be
seated here for our help, and feed them
with sweet juices.

6 Let thy stream give us drink, O God, O
Agni, wonderful and exhaustless like the
rain-clouds.

3 *The Bull* : the God who presides over the year.
The three breasts and the three udders are probably
heaven, the firmament, and the earth. *His triple aspect*:
the six seasons, reduced by combination to three, the hot
season, the rains, and the cold season. *The Everlasting
Ones*, according to Sāyaṇa. are the plants : but the
three Mighty Ones, or the Waters, may be intended.

4 *He* : probably, as Professor Ludwig says, Agni
as Savitar, the God presiding over the year. *The
Ādityas* here appear to be the months.

5 *Thrice three habitations* : each of the three worlds
having three subdivisions. *Child of three Mothers* : Agni
as Savitar appears to be meant, the three mothers
being, perhaps, the three seasons. According to
Sāyaṇa, *trimītā* here means 'the measurer of the three
(worlds), the Sun. *Ladies of the Waters* : Iḷā, Sarasvatī,
and Bhāratī. *Thrice* : at the three daily sacrifices.

6 *Cause the two worlds* : I follow Prof. Ludwig in
taking *dhiṣaṇe* as an accusative.

8 *The bright realms* : heaven, divided into three.
The Asura's Heroes : according to Sāyaṇa, Agni, Vāyu,
and Sūrya.

This hymn and the five following are attributed to
the Ṛṣi Viśvāmitra.

1 *With fine discernment* : the participle *vivikvān* in the
masculine form appears to be used instead of the feminine form with *maniṣā*, thought. Sāyaṇa reads *mani-
ṣām* in the accusative case and following him, Professor
Wilson translates : 'May the discriminating Indra
apprehend my glorification (of the Gods), which is free
as a milch-cow grazing alone, without a cowherd.'
The Cow : Vāk, Voice or Speech, the voice of prayer
and praise which the poet proceeds to appropriate and
employ, and which Indra and Agni are said to approve
and praise by their acceptance.

2 *As in this praise* : there is no substantive in the
text. Sāyaṇa supplies *vedyām*, altar.

3 *The Bull* : Agni. *The sisters* : the fingers which
produce the fire by friction. *The germ within him* : Agni's
fructifying power. *The Youngling* : Agni. According to
Sāyaṇa the *Cows* are the plants which spring up in the
vegetable world, adorned with its various products, as
cows go eagerly to their calves.

4 *Thy flames* : O Agni.

6 *Jātavedas* : knowing all things that live or exist.

Thus care for us, O Vasu Jātavedas, show us thy loving-kindness, reaching all men.

HYMN LVIII. *Aśvins.*

1. THE Ancient's Milch-cow yields the things we long for : the Son of Dakṣiṇā travels between them.
She with the splendid chariot brings refulgence. The praise of Uṣas hath awoke the Aśvins.

2 They bear you hither by well-orderd statute : our sacred offerings rise as if to parents.
Destroy in us the counsel of the niggard : come hitherward, for we have shown you favour.

3 With lightly-rolling car and well-yoked horses hear this, the press-stone's song, ye Wonder-Workers.
Have not the sages of old time, ye Aśvins, called you most prompt to come and stay misfortune ?

4 Remember us, and come to us, for ever men, as their wont is, invocate the Aśvins.
Friends as it were have offered you these juices, sweet, blent with milk at the first break of morning.

5 Even through many regions, O ye Aśvins— high praise is yours among mankind, ye Mighty—
Come, helpers, on the paths which Gods have travelled : here your libations of sweet meath are ready.

6 Ancient your home, auspicious is your friendship : Heroes, your wealth is with the house of Jahnu.
Forming again with you auspicious friendship, let us rejoice with draughts of meath together.

7 O Aśvins, Very Mighty ones, with Vāyu and with his steeds, one-minded, ever-youthful,

Nāsatyas, joying in the third day's Soma, drink it, not hostile, Very Bounteous Givers.

8 Aśvins, to you are brought abundant viands in rivalry with sacred songs, unceasing.
Sprung from high Law your car, urged on by press-stones, goes round the earth and heaven in one brief moment.

9 Aśvins, your Soma sheds delicious sweetness : drink ye thereof and come unto our dwelling.
Your car, assuming many a shape, most often goes to the Soma-presser's place of meeting.

HYMN LIX. *Mitra.*

1. MITRA, when speaking, stirreth men to labour : Mitra sustaineth both the earth and heaven.
Mitra beholdeth men with eyes that close not. To Mitra bring, with holy oil, oblation.

2 Foremost be he who brings thee food, O Mitra, who strives to keep thy sacred Law, Āditya.
He whom thou helpest ne'er is slain or conquered, on him, from near or far, falls no affliction.

3 Joying in sacred food and free from sickness, with knees bent lowly on the earth's broad surface,
Following closely the Āditya's statute, may we remain in Mitra's gracious favour.

4 Auspicious and adorable, this Mitra was born with fair dominion, King, Disposer.
May we enjoy the grace of him the Holy, yea, rest in his propitious loving-kindness.

5 The great Āditya, to be served with worship, who stirreth men, is gracious to the singer.
To Mitra, him most highly to be lauded, offer in fire oblation that he loveth.

6 The gainful grace of Mitra, God, supporter of the race of man,
Gives splendour of most glorious fame.

7 Mitra whose glory spreads afar, he who in might surpasses heaven,
Surpasses earth in his renown.

8 All the Five Races have repaired to Mitra, ever strong to aid,
For he sustaineth all the Gods.

1 *The Ancient's Milch-cow* : bounteous Uṣas or Dawn, daughter of ancient Dyaus or Heaven. *Dakṣiṇā* : the sacrificial guerdon, personified. Her son is Agni, the Sun who travels between heaven and earth.

2 *They* : our offerings of prayer and praise. *Destroy in us* : remove from us all illiberal thoughts, and let us be bounteous in our worship of the Gods.

5 *Even through many regions* : come to us even from far away, although many other worshippers also will try to detain us.

6 *The house of Jahnu* : the family of the Kuśikas, of whom Jahnu was the ancestor. 'Jahnu's children' are mentioned as having been favoured worshippers of the Aśvins in Book I. 116. 19.

7 *The third day's Soma* : pressed out the day before yesterday, and in the meantime left to ferment.

1 *Stirreth men to labour* : Mitra being the God of Day. Cf. VII. 362.

8 *All the Five Races* : all Āryan men.

9 Mitra to Gods, to living men, to him who
    strews the holy grass,
  Gives food fulfilling sacred Law.

HYMN LX.   *Rbhus.*

1. HERE is your ghostly kinship, here, O
      Men : they came desirous to these holy
      rites with store of wealth,
    With wondrous arts, whereby, with sche-
      mes to meet each need,
    Ye gained, Sudhanvan's Sons ! your share
      in sacrifice.

2 The mighty powers wherewith· ye formed
    the chalices, the thought by which ye
    drew the cow from out the hide,
  The intellect wherewith ye wrought the
    two Bay Steeds,—through these, O
    Rbhus, ye attained divinity.

3 Friendship with Indra have the Rbhus,
    fully gained : grandsons of Manu, they
    skilfully urged the work.
  Sudhanvan's Children won them ever-
    lasting life, serving with holy rites, pious
    with noble acts.

4 In company with Indra come ye to the
    juice, then gloriously shall your wishes
    be fulfilled.
  Not to be paragoned, ye Priests, are your
    good deeds, nor your heroic acts,
    Rbhus, Sudhanvan's Sons.

5 O Indra, with the Rbhus, Mighty Ones,
    pour down the Soma juice effused, well-
    blent, from both thy hands.
  Maghavan, urged by song, in the drink-
    offerer's house rejoice thee with the
    Heroes, with Sudhanvan's Sons.

6 With Rbhu near, and Vāja, Indra, here
    exult, with Sacī, praised of many, in
    the juice we pour.
  These homes wherein we dwell have
    turned themselves to thee,—devotions to
    the Gods, as laws of men ordain.

7 Come with the mighty Rbhus, Indra,
    come to us, strengthening with thy help
    the singer's holy praise ;

At hundred eager calls come to the living
  man, with thousand arts attend the act
  of sacrifice.

HYMN LXI.   *Usas.*

1. O Usas, strong with strength, endowed
      with knowledge, accept the singer's
      praise, O wealthy Lady.
    Thou, Goddess, ancient, young, and full
      of wisdom, movest, all-bounteous ! as
      the Law ordaineth.

2 Shine forth, O Morning, thou auspicious
    Goddess, on thy bright car awaking
    pleasant voices.
  Let docile horses of far-reaching splendour
    convey thee hitherward, the golden-
    coloured.

3 Thou, Morning, turning thee to every
    creature, standest on high as ensign of
    the Immortal,
  To one same goal ever and ever wending :
    now, like a wheel, O newly-born, roll
    hither.

4 Letting her reins drop downward, Mor-
    ning cometh, the wealthy Dame, the
    Lady of the dwelling ;
  Bringing forth light, the Wonderful, the
    Blessed hath spread her from the bounds
    of earth and heaven.

5 Hither invoke the radiant Goddess Mor-
    ning, and bring with reverence your
    hymn to praise her.
  She, dropping sweets, hath set in heaven
    her brightness, and, fair to look on,
    hath beamed forth her splendour.

6 From heaven, with hymns, the Holy One
    was wakened : brightly to both worlds
    came the wealthy Lady.
  To Morning, Agni, when she comes reful-
    gent, thou goest forth soliciting fair
    riches.

7 On Law's firm base the speeder of the
    Mornings, the Bull, hath entered mighty
    earth and heaven.
  Great is the power of Varuna and Mitra,
    which, bright, hath spread in every
    place its splendour.

---

9 *Gives food fulfilling sacred Law* : the food which
enables men to offer the appointed sacrifices.

---

1 *Here is your ghostly kinship* : here, in the sacrificial
chamber where the deities are worshipped, ye, Rbhus,
originally men, are spiritually connected with the Gods
as partakers of sacrificial offerings. *They* : the Rbhus.
With store of wealth : their great skill; the 'wondrous
arts' of the following line.

  2 See I. 20, 2, 3, 6,

  6 *Sacī* : Might, personified, the Consort of Indra.

  7 *The living man* : the worshipper.

---

3 *The Immortal* : the Sun.

4 *Letting her reins drop* : perhaps, sending down rays
of light.

7 *The Bull* : the Sun, who, as following the Dawns,
may be said to urge them onward.

HYMN LXII. *Indra and Others.*

1. YOUR well-known prompt activities aforetime needed no impulse from your faithful servant.
   Where, Indra-Varuṇa, is now that glory
   wherewith ye brought support to those
   who loved you ?

2 This man, most diligent, seeking after
riches, incessantly invokes you for your
favour.
   Accordant, Indra-Varuṇa, with Maruts,
   with Heaven and Earth, hear ye mine
   invocation.

3 O Indra-Varuṇa, ours be this treasure,
ours be wealth, Maruts, with full store
of heroes.
   .May the Varūtrīs with their shelter aid
   us, and Bhāratī and Hotrā with the
   Mornings.

4 Be pleased ! with our oblations, thou loved
of all Gods, Bṛhaspati :
   Give wealth to him who brings thee gifts.

5 At sacrifices, with your hymns worship
the pure Bṛhaspati—
   I pray for power which none may bend—

6 The Bull of men, whom none deceive, the
wearer of each shape at will,
   Bṛhaspati Most Excellent.

7 Divine, resplendent Pūṣan, this our
newest hymn of eulogy,
   By us is chanted forth to thee.

8 Accept with favour this my song, be gracious to the earnest thought,

Even as a bridegroom to his bride.

9 May he who sees all living things, sees
them together at a glance,—
   May he, may Pūṣan be our help.

10 May we attain that excellent glory of
Savitar the God :
   So May he stimulate our prayers.

11 With understanding, earnestly, of Savitar
the God we crave
   Our portion of prosperity.

12 Men, singers worship Savitar the God
with hymn and holy rites,
   Urged by the impulse of their thoughts.

13 Soma who gives success goes forth, goes to
the gathering place of Gods,
   To seat him at the seat of Law.

14 To us and to our cattle may Soma give
salutary food,
   To biped and to quadruped.

15 May Soma, strengthening our power of
life, and conquering our foes,
   In our assembly take his seat.

16 May Mitra-Varuṇa, sapient Pair, bedew
our pasturage with oil,
   With meath the regions of the air.

17 Far-ruling, joyful when adored, ye reign
through majesty of might,
   With pure laws everlastingly.

18 Lauded by Jamadagni's song, sit in the
place of holy Law :
   Drink Soma, ye who strengthen Law.

The hymn consists of six *ṛcas* or triplets, the deities
of which are severally (1) Indra and Varuṇa, (2)
Bṛhaspati, (3) Pūṣan, (4) Savitar, (5) Soma, (6)
Mitra and Varuṇa.

1 This stanza is difficult on account of the uncertainty of the meaning of *bhḷmáyaḥ* in the first line and
of *sinam* in the second. Professor Wilson renders it :
Indra and Varuṇa, may these people who are relying
upon you, and wandering about (in alarm), sustain
no injury from a youthful (adversary); for where is
that reputation (you enjoy) on account that you bestow
sustenance on your friends ?' Professor Ludwig's translation is to the following effect : 'These that are counted
yours, these whirling weapons, were made not to be
hurled at your dependent. Varuṇa, Mitra, Where is this
your glory, wherewith against your friends   end
your missile?' My version follows Professor Roth's
interpretation in the St. Petersburg Lexicon.

2 *This man* : the worshipper.

3 *The Varūtrīs* : guardian Goddesses; the Consorts
of the Gods, according to the Commentator. *Bhāratī
and Hotrā* : Goddesses presiding over different departments of religious worship.

4 *Bṛhaspati* : Lord of Prayer.

10 This stanza is the Sāvitrī, the Gāyatrī *par excellence,* 'the celebrated verse of the Vedas which forms
part of the daily devotions of the Brahmans, and was
first made known to English readers by Sir W. Jones's
translation of a paraphrastic interpretation; he renders
it, Let us adore the supremacy of that divine sun,
the godhead, who illuminates all, from whom all
proceed, to whom all must return, whom we invoke to
direct our understandings aright in our progress towards
his holy seat—Wilson. See *Rgveda Sanhitā,* Vol. III.
p. 111.

13 *The gathering-place of Gods* : the sacrificial chamber.
The seat of Law : the place where sacrifice ordained by
eternal Law is performed.

16 *With oil* : with clarified butter, with fatness, that
is, with fertilizing rain. *With meath* : or with honey,
that is with sweet refreshing dew.

18 *Jamadagni,* may, according to Sāyaṇa, be in this
place an epithet of Viśvāmitra, and mean 'by whom the
fire has been kindled; or *Jamadagni* may be another
Ṛṣi and the seer of the hymn.

BOOK THE FOURTH

HYMN I. *Agni.*

1. THEE Agni, have the Gods, ever of one
accord, sent hither down, a God, appointed messenger, yea, with their wisdom
sent thee down.
  The Immortal, O thou Holy One, mid
  mortal men, the God-devoted God, the
  wise, have they brought forth, brought
  forth the omnipresent God-devoted Sage.

2 As such, O Agni, bring with favour to the
Gods thy Brother Varuṇa who loveth
sacrifice,
  True to the Law, the Āditya who supporteth men, the King, supporter of
  mankind.

3 Do thou, O Friend, turn hither him who
is our Friend, swift as a wheel, like two
car-steeds in rapid course, Wondrous! to
us in rapid course.
  O Agni, find thou grace for us with Varuṇa,
  with Maruts who illumine all.
  Bless us, thou Radiant One, for seed and
  progeny, yea, bless us, O thou Wondrous
  God.

4 Do thou who knowest Varuṇa, O Agni,
put far away from us the God's displeasure.
  Best Sacrificer, brightest One, refulgent
  remove thou far from us all those who
  hate us.

5 Be thou, O Agni, nearest us with succour,
our closest Friend while now this Morn
is breaking.
  Reconcile to us Varuṇa, be bounteous :
  enjoy the gracious juice; be swift to
  hear us.

6 Excellent is the glance, of brightest splendour, which the auspicious God bestows
on mortals,—
  The God's glance, longed-for even as the
  butter, pure, heated, of the cow, the
  milch-cow's bounty.

7 Three are those births, the true, the most
exalted, eagerly longed-for, of the God,
of Agni.

He came invested in the boundless region,
pure, radiant, friendly, mightily resplendent.

8 This envoy joyeth in all seats of worship,
borne on his golden car, sweet-tongued
Invoker:
  Lovely to look on, with red steeds, effulgent, like a feast rich in food, joyous
  for ever.

9 Allied by worship, let him give man
knowledge : by an extended cord they
lead him onward.
  He stays, effectual in this mortal's dwelling, and the God wins a share in his
  possessions.

10 Let Agni—for he knows the way—conduct
us to all that he enjoys of God-sent
riches,
  What all the Immortals have prepared
  with wisdom, Dyaus, Sire, Begetter,
  raining down true blessings.

11 In houses first he sprang into existence,
at great heaven's base, and in this
region's bosom;
  Footless and headless, both his ends concealing, in his Bull's lair drawing himself together.

12 Wondrously first he rose aloft, defiant, in
the Bull's lair, the home of holy Order,
  Longed-for, young, beautiful, and far-resplendent : and seven dear friends sprang
  up unto the Mighty.

13 Here did our human fathers take their
places, fain to fulfil the sacred Law of
worship.

8 *Sweet-tongued* : with tasting the oblations; or,
perhaps, pleasant-voiced.

9 *By an extended cord* : by virtue of the endless
chain or series of regularly performed sacrifices. *Effectual*:
perfecting the sacrifices, or fulfilling all the
desires of the worshipper.
  A share in his possessions : because the wealth of
the worshipper depends upon the favour of Agni.

11 *Footless and headless* : without distinguishable head
or feet.
  His Bull's lair . apparently the fuel in which he
grows strong; according to Sāyaṇa, 'in the nest of the
rain cloud.'

12 *The home of holy Order* : the altar, the place of
law-appointed sacrifices. *Seven dear friends* : seven minor
priests; or the frequently mentioned seven tongues or
rays of fire.

13 *Our human fathers* : the Angirases. *Teeming Milch-
kine* : the rays of light.

This hymn, and the following forty, are ascribed
to the Ṛṣi Vāmadeva, son of Gotama.

7 *Three are those births* : the manifestations of Agni
in heaven as the Sun in the firmament as lightning,
and on earth as sacrificial and domestic fire.

Forth drave they, with loud call, Dawn's
teeming Milch-kine hid in the mountain-
stable, in the cavern.

14 Splendid were they when they had rent
the mountain : others, around, shall tell
forth this their exploit.

They sang their song, prepared to free the
cattle : they found the light; with holy
hymns they worshipped.

15 Eager, with thought intent upon the booty,
the men with their celestial speech threw
open,

The solid mountain firm, compact, enclosing, confining Cows, the stable full of
cattle.

16 The Milch-cow's earliest name they comprehended : they found the Mother's
thrice-seven noblest titles.

This the bands knew, and sent forth accla-
mation : with the Bull's sheen the Red
One was apparent.

17 The turbid darkness fled, the heaven was
splendid : up rose the bright beam of
celestial Morning.

Sūrya ascended to the wide expanses, beholding deeds of men both good and evil.

18 Then, afterwards they looked around,
awakened, when first they held that
Heaven allotted treasure.

Now all the Gods abide in all their
dwellings. Varuṇa, Mitra, be the prayer
effective.

19 I will call hither brightly-beaming Agni,
the Herald, all-supporting, best at worship.

14 *Splendid* : illumined by the recovered rays of
light.

15 *The booty* : the Cows, the rays of light. *Their
celestial speech* : prayer.

16 *The Milch-cow's* : here, according to Sāyaṇa, Vāk
or Voice, Speech, or especially prayer. It is uncertain
what is meant by *the Mother's thrice-seven noblest* (titles,
names, forms, or some similar word being necessarily
understood). Professor Wilson, following Sāyaṇa,
renders the passage : 'knowing the thrice-seven excellent (forms) of the maternal (rhythm), 'that is, the
twenty-one metres of the Vedas; or, he adds, the
passage may refer 'to the ancient nomenclature of
cattle, as uttered by the *Angirases* as *Ehi, surabhi,
guggulu, gandhinī,* etc.'

With the Bull's sheen : with the splendour of the
Sun. *The Red One* : Uṣas or Dawn.

18 *That Heaven-allotted treasure* : the recovered rays
of light.

19 Sāyaṇa's explanation of the second line of this
stanza is different, and Professor Wilson, following him
translates: 'without milking the pure udder (of the
cow), without purified food of the *Soma* offered in
libation,' implying according to the Scholiast, 'that no
offering is made to Agni on the occasion; praise alone
is addressed to him.' *Nā*, in the Veda, it may be
remembered, means both *not* and *like*, and in some
passages it is difficult to determine in which of its
senses the word is to be taken.

He hath disclosed, like the milch cows'
pure udder, the Soma's juice when
cleansed and poured from beakers.

20 The freest God of all who should be worshipped, the guest who is received in all
men's houses,

Agni who hath secured the Gods' high
favour,—may he be gracious, to us
Jātavedas.

HYMN II. *Agni.*

1. THE Faithful One, Immortal among
mortals, a God among the Gods, appointed envoy,

Priest, best at worship, must shine forth
in glory : Agni shall be raised high with
man's oblations.

2 Born for us here this day, O Son of
Vigour, between both races of born
beings, Agni,

Thou farest as an envoy, having harnessed,
Sublime One!thy strong-muscled radiant
stallions.

3 I laud the ruddy steeds who pour down
blessing, dropping oil, fleetest through
the thought of Order.

Yoking red horses to and fro thou goest
between you Deities and mortal races.

4 Aryaman, Mitra, Varuṇa, and Indra with
Viṣṇu, of the Gods, Maruts and Aśvins—

These, Agni, with good car and steeds,
bring hither, most bountiful, to folk with
fair oblations.

5 Agni, be this our sacrifice eternal, with
brave friends, rich in kine and sheep and
horses,

Rich, Asura ! in sacred food and children,
in full assembly, wealth broad-based
and during.

6 The man who, sweating, brings for thee
the fuel, and makes his head to ache,
thy faithful servant,—

Agni, to him be a self-strong Protector :
guard him from all who seek to do him
mischief.

2 *Between both races of born beings* : between Gods
and men, the Gods also being called *jātāḥ* or born, as
sons of Heaven and Earth.

3 *The thought of Order* : the thought of Law-appointed sacrifice.

You Deities : the Gods of whom thou, Agni, art
one.

6 *Makes his head to ache* : with the load of wood
which he carries on it.

7 Who brings thee food, though thou hast food in plenty, welcomes his cheerful guest and speeds him onward,
Who kindles thee devoutly in his dwelling,—to him be wealth secure and freely giving.

8 Whoso sings praise to thee at eve or morning, and, with oblation, doth the thing thou lovest,—
In his own home, even as a gold-girt courser, rescue him from distress, the bounteous giver.

9 Whoso brings gifts to thee Immortal, Agni, and doth thee service with uplifted ladle,—
Let him not, sorely toiling, lose his riches; let not the sinner's wickedness enclose him.

10 Whose well-wrought worship thou acceptest, Agni, thou God a mortal's gift, thou liberal Giver,—
Dear be his sacrifice to thee, Most Youthful ! and may we strengthen him when he adores thee.

11 May he who knows distinguish sense and folly of men, like straight and crooked backs of horses.
Lead us, O God, to wealth and noble offspring : keep penury afar and grant us plenty.

12 This Sage the Sages, ne'er deceived, commanded, setting him down in dwellings of the living.
Hence mayst thou, friendly God, with rapid footsteps behold the Gods, wonderful, fair to look on.

13 Good guidance hast thou for the priest, O Agni, who, Youngest God ! with outpoured Soma serves thee.
Ruler of men, thou joyous God, bring treasure splendid and plentiful to aid the toiler.

14 Now all that we, thy faithful servants, Agni, have done with feet, with hands, and with our bodies,
The wise, with toil, the holy rite have guided, as those who frame a car with manual cunning.

15 May we, seven sages first in rank, engender, from Dawn the Mother, men to be ordainers.
May we, Angirases, be sons of Heaven, and, radiant, burst the wealth-containing mountain.

16 As in the days of old our ancient Fathers, speeding the work of holy worship, Agni,
Sought pure light and devotion, singing praises; they cleft the ground and made red Dawns apparent.

17 Gods, doing holy acts, devout, resplendent, smelting like ore their human generations.
Enkindling Agni and exalting Indra, they came encompassing the stall of cattle.

18 Strong One ! he marked them—and the Gods before them—like herds of cattle in a foodful pasture.
There they moaned forth their strong desire for mortals, to aid the True, the nearest One, the Living.

19 We have worked for thee, we have laboured nobly—bright Dawns have shed their light upon our worship—
Adding a beauty to the perfect Agni, and the God's beauteous eye that shines for ever.

20 Agni, Disposer, we have sung these praises to thee the Wise: do thou accept them gladly.
Blaze up on high and ever make us richer. Give us great wealth, O thou whose boons are many.

---

7 *Freely giving* : enabling the possessor to be bountiful in turn.

11 *He who knows* : the wise Agni. *Like straight and crooked backs* : *aśvānām*, of horses, is supplied by Sāyaṇa; as a horse-keeper or groom distinguishes between well-shaped and ill-shaped backs. *Keep penury afar* : I follow Professor Roth in his interpretation of *ditim* and *dditim* in this passage. Professor Wilson, following Sāyaṇa, translates : 'be bountiful to the liberal giver ; shun him who gives not.' 'Give us this life on earth, keep off the life to come.'—Max Müller.

12 *This Sage* : Agni. *The Sages* : the other Gods. *Commanded* : ordered to become a priestly herald or invoker. *With rapid footsteps* : I follow Sāyaṇa ; but the correctness of his explanation is doubtful. According to Pischel, *paḍbhiḥ* here means 'with (thine) eyes.'

15 'Again, through the identification of the fathers with the light they are brought into connection with the metaphor of generation......The fathers are united with the Dawn, and desire with her to beget male children. In a hymn to Soma they are mentioned along with the morning Sun as having placed the germ in the earth ; and the fruitfulness of heaven and earth, which give birth to gods and men, is described as produced by the fathers.'—Wallis, *Cosmology of the Rgveda*, p. 72.

The wealth-containing mountain : the cloud with its store of rain, or the cave in which the cows or rays of light were imprisoned.

17 *Gods* : the godlike Angirases. *Smelting like ore* : purifying their humanity, as ore is purified by smelting.

18 *Strong One* : O mighty Agni. *He marked them* : Indra saw the kine of the Angirases, the stolen rays of light. *The True, the Nearest One, the Living* : Agni appears to be meant.

———

HYMN III.   *Agni.*

1. WIN, to assist you, Rudra, Lord of worship, Priest of both worlds, effectual Sacrificer,
Agni, invested with his golden colours, before the thunder strike and lay you senseless.

2 This shrine have we made ready for thy coming, as the fond dame attires her for her husband.
Performer of good work, sit down before us, invested while these flames incline to meet thee.

3 A hymn, O Priest, to him who hears, the gentle, to him who looks on men, exceeding gracious,
A song of praise sing to the God Immortal, whom the stone, presser of the sweet juice, worships.

4 Even as true knower of the Law, O Agni, to this our solemn rite be thou attentive.
When shall thy songs of festival be sung thee? When is thy friendship shown within our dwelling?

5 Why this complaint to Varuṇa, O Agni? And why to Heaven? for what is our transgression?
How wilt thou speak to Earth and bounteous Mitra? What wilt thou say to Aryaman and Bhaga?

6 What, when thou blazest on the lesser altars, what to the mighty Wind who comes to bless us,
True, circumambient? what to Earth, O Agni, what wilt thou say to man-destroying Rudra?

7 How to great Pūṣan who promotes our welfare,— to honoured Rudra what, who gives oblations?

What sin of ours to the far-striding Viṣṇu, what, Agni, wilt thou tell the Lofty Arrow.

8 What wilt thou tell the truthful band of Maruts, how answer the great Sun when thou art questioned?
Before the Free, before the Swift, defend us: fulfil heaven's work, all-knowing Jātavedas.

9 I crave the cow's true gift arranged by Order: though raw, she hath the sweet ripe juice, O Agni.
Though she is black of hue with milk she teemeth, nutritious, brightly shining, all-sustaining.

10 Agni the Bull, the manly, hath been sprinkled with oil upon his back, by Law eternal.
He who gives vital power goes on unswerving. Pṛṣni the Bull hath milked the pure white udder.

11 By Law the Angirases cleft the rock asunder, and sang their hymns together with the cattle.
Bringing great bliss the men encompassed Morning: light was apparent at the birth of Agni.

12 By Law the Immortal Goddesses the Waters, with meath-rich waves, O Agni, and uninjured,
Like a strong courser lauded in his running, sped to flow onward swiftly and for ever.

13 Go never to the feast of one who harms us, the treacherous neighbour or unworthy kinsman.
Punish us not for a false brother's trespass. Let us not feel the might of friend or foeman.

14 O Agni, keep us safe with thy protection, loving us, honoured God! and ever guarding.
Beat thou away, destory severe affliction: slay e'en the demon when he waxes mighty.

---

1 *Rudra* : here meaning Agni. *Before the thunder strike* : before death overtakes you. Professor Ludwig refers to the Atharvaveda, XII. 2. 9, where Agni Kravyād, or Agni in his most terrific form, is spoken of as the God of Death who stupefies men with his thunderbolt.

2 *The flames* : there is no substantive in the text. Sāyaṇa supplies 'flames or songs of praise,' or 'ladles' may be the word understood. Professor Ludwig supplies *viśaḥ* or *prajāḥ* 'families or people,' and Professor Grassmann 'libations'.

5 *Why this complaint* : why dost thou accuse us of sin ?

6 *On the lesser altars* : on the *dhiṣṇyās*, siac-altars, or heaps of earth covered with sand on which the fire is placed. *Man-destroying* : the destroyer of wicked men, says the Scholiast. Rudra is generally represented as a benevolent God.

7 *The Lofty Arrow* : the lightning.

8 *How answer the great Sun* : the sense of stanzas 5—8 appears to be, as Professor Ludwig observes : thou hast no grounds for complaining of us to any one of the Gods : be, rather, our advocate if Sūrya comes forward as our accuser.
Before the Free, before the Swift : the Sun.

9 The first line is difficult. 'I solicit the milk of the cow essential for the sacrifice.'—Wilson. *Through raw* : this opposition of the uncooked cow and the milk cooked or ripened in her udder has been noticed before. See I. 62. 9.

10 *Pṛṣni* : here said to be Sūrya or the Sun, who draws his light from the sky. But see Benfey, Vedica und Verwandtes, pp. 74, 75.

15 Through these our songs of praise be
gracious, Agni; moved by our prayers,
O Hero, touch our viands.

Accept, O Angiras, these our devotions,
and let the praise which Gods desire
address thee.

16 To thee who knowest, Agni, thou Disposer,
all these wise secret speeches have I
uttered,

Sung to thee, Sage, the charming words
of wisdom, to thee, O Singer, with my
thoughts and Praises.

HYMN IV. *Agni.*

1. Put forth like a wide-spreading net thy
vigour; go like a mighty King with his
attendants.

Thou, following thy swift net, shootest
arrows : transfix the fiends with darts
that burn most fiercely.

2 Forth go in rapid flight thy whirling
weapons : follow them closely, glowing
in thy fury.

Spread with thy tongue the winged flames,
O Agni; unfettered, cast thy firebrands
all around thee.

3 Send thy spies forward, fleetest in thy
motion ; be, ne'er deceived, the guardian of this people

From him who, near or far, is bent on
evil, and let no trouble sent from thee
o'ercome us.

4 Rise up, O Agni, spread thee out before
us : burn down our foes, thou who hast
sharpened arrows.

Him, blazing Agni ! who hath worked
us mischief, consume thou utterly like
dried-up stubble.

5 Rise, Agni, drive off those who fight
against us : make manifest thine own
celestial vigour.

Slacken the strong bows of the demon-
driven : destroy our foemen whether
kin or stranger.

6 Most Youthful God, he knoweth well thy
favour who gave an impulse to this
high devotion.

All fair days and magnificence of riches
hast thou beamed forth upon the good
man's portals.

7 Blest, Agni, be the man, the liberal
giver, who with his lauds and regular
oblation

Is fain to please thee for his life and
dwelling. May all his days be bright :
be this his longing.

8 I praise thy gracious favour : sing in
answer. May this my song sing like a
loved one with thee.

Lords of good steeds and cars may we
adorn thee, and day by day vouchsafe
thou us dominion.

9 Here of free choice let each one serve thee
richly, resplendent day by day at eve
and morning.

So may we honour thee, content and
joyous, passing beyond the glories of
the people.

10 Whoso with good steeds and fine gold,
O Agni, comes nigh thee on a car laden
with treasure,

His Friend art thou, yea, thou art his
Protector whose joy it is to entertain
thee duly.

11 Through words and kinship I destroy the
mighty : this power I have from Gotama
my father.

Mark thou this speech of ours, O thou
Most Youthful, Friend of the House,
exceeding wise, Invoker.

12 Knowing no slumber, speedy and propitious,
alert and ever friendly, most unwearied,

May thy protecting powers, unerring Agni,
taking their places here, combined, preserve us.

13 Thy guardian rays, O Agni, when they
saw him, preserved blind Māmateya from
affliction.

Lord of all riches, he preserved the pious:
the foes who fain would harm them did no
mischief.

This hymn is said by Sāyaṇa to be addressed to
Agni as slayer of the Rāksasas, that is, as God of the
fire with which the immigrant Āryans burnt the jungle,
drove back the hostile aborigines, and cleared the
ground for encampment or permanent settlement.

3 *Thy spies* : thy first flames, sent forward as if to
reconnoitre.

5 *The demon-driven* : those whom evil spirits incite
to attack us.

8 *Sing in answer* : with the auspicious sound of thy
crackling flames.

11 *Through words and kinship* : that is, through my
close alliance with Agni, effected by the prayers with
which my fathers and I have worshipped him.

The mighty : the Rākṣasas or demons, according
to Sāyaṇa.

13 This stanza has occurred before, I. 147. 3.
Blind Māmateya : the Ṛṣi Dīrghatamas. *Lord of all
riches* : Agni.

14 Aided by thee with thee may we be
  wealthy, may we gain strength with thee
  to guide us onward.
  Fulfil the words of both, O Ever Truthful:
  straightway do this, thou God whom power
  emboldens.

15 O Agni, with this fuel will we serve thee;
  accept the laud we sing to thee with favour.
  Destroy the cursing Rākṣasas: preserve us,
  O rich in friends, from guile and scorn
  and slander.

HYMN V. *Agni.*

1. How shall we give with one accord oblation
  to Agni, to Vaiśvānara the Bounteous?
  Great light, with full high growth hath he
  uplifted, and, as a pillar bears the roof,
  sustains it.

2 Reproach not him who, God and self-
  reliant, vouchsafed this bounty unto me a
  mortal,—
  Deathless, discerner, wise, to me the simple,
  Vaiśvānara most manly, youthful Agni.

3 Sharp-pointed, powerful, strong, of boundless
  vigour, Agni who knows the lofty hymn,
  kept secret
  As the lost milch-cow's track, the doubly
  Mighty,—he hath declared to me this
  hidden knowledge.

4 May he with sharpened teeth, the Bounteous
  Giver, Agni, consume with flame most
  fiercely glowing.
  Those who regard not Varuṇa's command-
  ments and the dear stedfast laws of sapient
  Mitra.

5 Like youthful women without brothers,
  straying, like dames who hate their lords,
  of evil conduct,
  They who are full of sin, untrue, unfaithful,
  they have engendered this abysmal
  station.

6 To me, weak, innocent, thou, luminous
  Agni, hast boldly given as 'twere a heavy
  burthen,
  This Pṛṣṭha hymn, profound and strong
  and mighty, of seven elements, and with
  offered dainties.

7 So may our song that purifies, through
  wisdom reach in a moment him the Universal,
  Established on the height, on earth's best
  station, above the beauteous grassy skin
  of Pṛṣṇi.

8 Of this my speech what shall I utter further?
  They indicate the milk stored up in secret
  When they have thrown as 'twere the cows'
  stalls open. The Bird protects earths' best
  and well-loved station.

9 This is the Great Ones' mighty apparition
  which from of old the radiant Cow hath
  followed.
  This, shining brightly in the place of Order,
  swift, hasting on in secret, she discovered.

10 He then who shone together with his
  Parents remembered Pṛṣṇi's fair and
  secret treasure,
  Which, in the Mother Cow's most lofty
  station, the Bull's tongue, of the flame
  bent forward, tasted.

11 With reverence I declare the Law, O Agni;
  what is, comes by thine order, Jātavedas.
  Of this, whate'er it be, thou art the Sovran,
  yea, all the wealth that is in earth or
  heaven.

12 What is our wealth therefrom, and what our
  treasure? Tell us O Jātavedas, for thou
  knowest,
  What is our best course in this secret
  passage: we, unreproached, have reached a place far distant.

---

14 *The words of both* : the wishes of Gods and men.
Sāyaṇa gives a different explanation, and Professor
Wilson translates accordingly : 'destroy both (sorts of
calumniators.)'

The Ṛṣi Vāmadeva, as Professor Roth observes,
'profess to make known a mysterious and recondite
wisdom which had been revealed to him by Agni,' and
the language of the hymn is correspondingly difficult
and obscure.

1 *Vaiśvānara* : common God of all Āryan men.

2 *This bounty* : the gift of this mysterious knowledge.

5 *This abysmal station* : that is, says Sāyaṇa,
narakasthānam or hell The wicked are the cause of
the existence of the place of punishment prepared for
them.

6 *This Pṛṣṭha hymn* : Pṛṣṭha is the name of a particular arrangement of Sāmans employed at the mid-day
oblation.

7 *The Universal* : Vaiśvānara Agni. *Established on
the height* : according to this conjectural translation,
which follows a suggestion of Professor Ludwig, the
reference is to Agni placed on the altar, above the
surface of the earth (Pṛṣṇi). But the meaning of
jábāru (on the height) is uncertain. Professor Wilson
translates : 'whose swift-ascending brilliant (orb) is
stationed on the east of the earth, to mount,' like the
sun, above the immoveable heaven.'

8 This stanza appears to allude to the Angirases
recovering the lost rays of light, *the milk stored up in
secret.* *The Bird* : the Sun who flies through heaven.

9 *The Great Ones' mighty apparition* : the solar orb;
the Great Ones being the Sun's rays. *The radiant Cow* :
Uṣas or Dawn who discovers the Sun as he travels in
secret, or by night, from west to east, and follows him
till he is about to rise.

10 *He* : Agni. *His Parents* : Heaven and Earth.
Pṛṣṇi is the Cow whose milk is used in the oblation
which Agni, the Bull, devours.

13 What is the limit, what the rules, the
   guerdon ? Like fleet-foot coursers speed
   we to the contest.
   When will the Goddesses, the Immortal's
   Spouses, the Dawns, spread over us the
   Sun-God's splendour?

14 Unsatisfied, with speech devoid of vigour,
   scanty and frivolous and inconclusive,
   Wherefore do they address thee here, O
   Agni? Let these who have no weapons
   suffer sorrow.

15 The majesty of him the Good, the Mighty,
   aflame, hath shone for glory in the
   dwelling.
   He, clothed in light, hath shone most fair
   to look on, wealthy in boons, as a home
   shines with riches.

HYMN VI.   *Agni.*

1. PRIEST of our rite, stand up erect, O Agni,
   in the Gods' service best of sacrificers,
   For over every thought thou art the Ruler:
   thou furtherest e'en the wisdom of the
   pious.

2 He was set down mid men as Priest
   unerring, Agni, wise, welcome in our
   holy synods.
   Like Savitar he hath lifted up his splendour,
   and like a builder raised his smoke to
   heaven.

3 The glowing ladle, filled with oil, is lifted;
   choosing Gods' service to the right he
   circles.
   Eager he rises like the new-wrought pillar
   which, firmly set and fixed, anoints the
   victims.

4 When sacred grass is strewn and Agni
   kindled, the Adhvaryu rises to his task
   rejoicing.
   Agni the Priest, like one who tends the
   cattle, goes three times round, as from of
   old he wills it.

5 Agni himself, the Priest, with measured
   motion, goes round, with sweet speech,
   cheerful, true to Order.
   His fulgent flames run forth like vigorous
   horses; all creatures are affrighted when
   he blazes.

14 *These who have no weapons* : who are unprovided
with the necessary elements of sacrifice, and therefore
unable to please Agni.

2 *Like a builder* : as the builder of a house raises a
pillar.

3 *To the right he circles* : is carried round to the
altars. *Anoints the victims* : smears them with the
clarified butter with which it (the sacrificial post) has
been previously anointed.

6 Beautiful and auspicious is thine aspect, O
   lovely Agni, terrible when spreading.
   Thy splendours are not covered by the
   darkness : detraction leaves no stain
   upon thy body.

7 Naught hindered his production, Bounteous
   Giver : his Mother and his Sire were free
   to send him.
   Then as Friend benevolent, refulgent, Agni
   shone forth in human habitations.

8 He, Agni, whom the twice-five sisters,
   dwelling together, in the homes of men
   engendered,
   Bright like a spear's tooth, wakened in the
   morning, with powerful mouth and like
   an axe well-sharpened.

9 These thy Bay Coursers, Agni, dropping
   fatness, ruddy vigorous, speeding
   straightly forward,
   And red steeds, wonderful, of mighty
   muscle, are to this service of the Gods
   invited :

10 These brightly-shining flames of thine, O
   Agni, that move for ever restless, all-
   subduing,
   Like falcons hasting eagerly to the quarry,
   roar loudly like the army of the Maruts.

11 To thee, O flaming God, hath prayer been
   offered. Let the priest laud thee: give to
   him who worships.
   Men have established Agni as Invoker, fain
   to adore the glory of the living.

HYMN VII.   *Agni.*

1. HERE by ordainers was this God appointed
   first Invoker, best at worship, to be
   praised at rites:
   Whom Apnavāna, and the Bhṛgus caused
   to shine bright-coloured in the wood,
   spreading from home to home.

2 When shall thy glory as a God, Agni, be
   suddenly shown forth.

7 *His Mother and his Sire* : Earth and Heaven.
To send him : to be messenger between men and Gods.

8 *The twice-five sisters* : the priest's fingers which
produce the sacrificial fire.

9 *Bay Coursers* : *harítaḥ* ; Harits; the prototype (the
word being feminine) of the Greek 'Charites.' See M.
Müller, Chips from a German Workshop, IV. 141 (new
edition).

11 *The glory of the living* : Agni as Narāśansa, the
Praise or Glory of Men.

1 *Here* : at this ceremony. *Ordainers* : the regulators
of the sacrifice. *Apnavāna* : a Ṛsi of the family of
Bhigu.

For mortal men have held thee fast,
adorable in all their homes,

3 Seeing thee faithful to the Law, most sapient,
like the starry heaven,
Illumining with cheerful ray each solemn
rite in every house.

4 Vivasvān's envoy living men have taken as
their ensign, swift,
The ruler over all mankind, moving like
Bhṛgu in each home.

5 Him the intelligent have they placed duly
as Invoking Priest,
Welcome, with sanctifying flame, best
worshipper, with sevenfold might;

6 In his Eternal Mothers, in the wood, concealed and unapproached,
Kept secret though his flames are bright
seeking on all sides, quickly found.

7 That as food spreads forth in this earthly
udder, Gods may rejoice them in the
home of Order,
Great Agni, served with reverence and
oblation, flies ever to the sacrifice, the
Faithful.

8 Bird of each rite, skilled in an envoy's
duties, knowing both worlds and that
which lies between them,
Thou goest from of old a willing Herald,
knowing full well heaven's innermost
recesses.

9 Bright God, thy path is black: light is before
thee: thy moving splendour is the chief
of wonders.
When she, yet unimpregnate, hath conceived thee, even when newly born
thou art an envoy.

10 Yet newly born, his vigour is apparent
when the wind blows upon his fiery
splendour,
His sharpened tongue he layeth on the
brushwood, and with his teeth e'en
solid food consumeth.

11 When he hath borne off food with swift
flame swiftly, strong Agni makes himself
a speedy envoy,
Follows the rustling of the wind, consuming,
and courser-like, speeds, drives the swift
horse onward.

HYMN VIII.   Agni.

1. YOUR envoy who possesses all, Immortal,
bearer of your gifts,
Best worshipper, I woo with song.

2 He, Mighty, knows the gift of wealth, he
knows the deep recess of heaven :
He shall bring hitherward the Gods.

3 He knows, a God himself, to guide Gods
to the righteous in his home :
He gives e'en treasures that we love.

4 He is the Herald : well-informed, he doth
his errand to and fro,
Knowing the deep recess of heaven.

5 May we be they who gratify Agni with
sacrificial gifts,
Who cherish and enkindle him.

6 Illustrious for wealth are they, and hero
deeds, victorious,
Who have served Agni reverently.

7 So unto us, day after day, may riches
craved by many come,
And power and might spring up for us.

8 That holy Singer in his strength shoots
forth his arrows swifter than
The swift shafts of the tribes of men.

HYMN IX.   Agni.

1. AGNI, show favour : great art thou who
to this pious man art come,
To seat thee on the sacred grass.

2 May he the Immortal, Helper, hard to
be deceived among mankind,
Become the messenger of all.

---

4 *Vivasvān's envoy* : according to Sāyaṇa, the messenger of the worshipper. *Moving like Bhṛgu* : or shining;
Bhṛgu being originally a personification of lightning.

5 *Sevenfold might* : Agni's seven flames.

6 *Eternal Mothers* : the Celestial Waters. *Seeking on
all sides* : roaming at will in search of food.

7 *In this earthly udder* : here on earth, and especially
at the altar from which oblations come. Only when the
elements of sacrifice are forthcoming can Agni invite and
bring the Gods. *The home of Order* : the place of law-
ordained sacrifice.

8 *Bird of each rite* : attending all sacrifices. *That
which lies between them*: the firmament or mid-air between
heaven and earth.

9 *She, yet unimpregnate* : the piece of wood in which
fire is produced.

---

11 *When he hath borne off food* : I follow Sāyaṇa,
but am not satisfied with his explanation. *Courser-like* :
Agni, himself a courser, drives on the wind as it were
a courser. Professor Ludwig suggests that *árvā* here
may mean a rider, not a courser.

---

2 *Knows the gift of wealth* : how to enrich his worshippers.

---

4 *Doth his errand to and fro* : bears to the Gods
the prayers, praises, and oblations of their worshippers,
and brings them down to the sacrifice.

---

8 *That holy Singer* : Agni the Priest. The stanza is
difficult. Professor Wilson, following Sāyaṇa, translates :
'May the wise Agni entirely obviate by his power the
removeable (ills) of men the descendants of Manu'.
I have adopted Professor Ludwig's interpretation.

3 Around the altar is he led, welcome Chief
    Priest at solemn rites,
  Or as the Potar sits him down.
4 Agni in fire at sacrifice, and in the house
    as Lord thereof,
  And as a Brahman takes his seat.
5 Thou comest as the guide of folk who cele-
    brate a sacrifice,
  And tó oblations brought by men.
6 Thou servest as his messenger whose sacri-
    fice thou lovest well,
  To bear the mortal's gifts to heaven.
7 Accept our solemn rite ; be pleased, Angi-
    ras, with our sacrifice :
  Give ear and listen to our call.
8 May thine inviolable car, wherewith thou
    guardest those who give,
  Come near to us from every side.

HYMN X.   *Agni.*

1. THIS day with praises, Agni, we bring thee
    that which thou lovest.
  Right judgment, like a horse, with our
    devotions.
2 For thou hast ever been the Car-driver,
    Agni, of noble
  Strength, lofty sacrifice, and rightful judg-
    ment.
3 Through these our praises come thou to
    meet us, bright as the sunlight,
  O Agni, well disposed, with all thine
    aspects.
4 Now may we serve thee singing these
    lauds this day to thee, Agni.
  Loud as the voice of Heaven thy blasts
    are roaring.
5 Just at this time of the day and the night
    thy look is the sweetest :
  It shineth near us even as gold for glory.
6 Spotless thy body, brilliant as gold, like
    clarified butter :
  This gleams like gold on thee, O Self-
    dependent.
7 All hate and mischief, yea, if committed,
    Agni, thou turnest,
  Holy One, from the man who rightly
    worships.
8 Agni, with you Gods, prosperous be our
    friendships and kinships.

3 *Chief Priest* : Hotar, the presenter of the oblation.
The Potar : literally, Cleanser or Purifier, another of the
sixteen priests usually employed.
    4 I read *utắgnắ* as proposed by Prof. Max Müller
and Prof. Ludwig in place of the almost impossible *utá
gnắḥ* of the text.   — — —
    2 *Car-driver* : promoter.
    6 *This* : thy splendour.
    8 *This altar* : literally, this udder ; that is, the
place whence oblations proceed.

Be this our bond here by this place, thine
    altar.

HYMN XI.   *Agni.*

1. THY blessed majesty, victorious Agni,
    shines brightly in the neighbourhood of
    Sūrya.
  Splendid to see, it shows even at night-
    time, and food is fair to look on in thy
    beauty.
2 Agni, disclose his thought for him who
    singeth, the well, Strong God ! while
    thou art praised with fervour.
  Vouchsafe to us that powerful hymn, O
    Mighty, which, Radiant One ! with
    all the Gods thou lovest.
3 From thee, O Agni, springs poetic wisdom,
    from thee come thoughts and hymns of
    praise that prosper ;
  From thee flows wealth, with heroes to
    adorn it, to the true-hearted man who
    gives oblation.
4 From thee the hero springs who wins the
    booty, bringer of help, mighty, of real
    courage.
  From thee comes wealth, sent by the
    Gods, bliss-giving ; Agni, from thee the
    fleet impetuous charger.
5 Immortal Agni, thee whose voice is plea-
    sant, as first in rank, as God, religious
    mortals
  Invite with hymns ; thee who removest
    hatred, Friend of the Home, the house-
    hold's Lord, unerring.
6 Far from us thou removest want and
    sorrow, far from us all ill-will when
    thou protectest.
  Son of Strength, Agni, blest is he at
    evening, whom thou as God attendest
    for his welfare.

HYMN XII.   *Agni.*

1. WHOSO enkindles thee, with lifted ladle,
    and thrice this day offers thee food, O
    Agni,
  May he excel, triumphant through thy
    splendours, wise through thy mental
    power, O Jātavedas.
2 Whoso with toil and trouble brings thee
    fuel, serving the majesty of mighty Agni,

1 *In the neighbourhood of Sūrya* : by day, in the
sunshine.
    2 *The well* : the source of sacred song.
    4 *The hero* : or the strong horse.

He, kindling thee at evening and at morning, prospers, and comes to wealth, and slays his foemen.

3 Agni is Master of sublime dominion, Agni is Lord of strength and lofty riches.
Straightway the self-reliant God, Most Youthful, gives treasures to the mortal who adores him.

4 Most Youthful God, whatever sin, through folly, we here, as human beings, have committed,
In sight of Aditi make thou us sinless : remit, entirely, Agni, our offences.

5 Even in the presence of great sin, O Agni, free us from prison of the Gods or mortals.
Never may we who are thy friends be injured : grant health and strength unto our seed and offspring.

6 Even as ye here, Gods Excellent and Holy, have loosed the cow that by the foot was tethered,
So also set us free from this affliction : long let our life, O Agni, be extended.

HYMN XIII. *Agni.*

1. AGNI hath looked, benevolently-minded, on the wealth-giving spring of radiant Mornings.
Come, Aśvins, to the dwelling of the pious : Sūrya the God is rising with his splendour.

2 Savitar, God, hath spread on high his lustre, waving his flag like a spoil-seeking hero.
Their stablished way go Varuṇa and Mitra, what time they make the Sun ascend the heaven.

3 Him whom they made to drive away the darkness, Lords of sure mansions, constant to their object,

4 *Aditi* : apparently the great omnipresent Power which controls the forces of the universe, and from which no sins are hidden.

5 *Prison of the Gods or mortals* : actual imprisonment by men and corresponding chastisement by the Gods.

6 *The cow* : the cow-buffalo, tied to a post, representing symbolically the man who is in the bonds of sin. Cf. X. 126. 6.

2 *Waving his flag* : according to Sāyaṇa, 'scattering the dew.' But there can be no doubt that *drapsá*, the Zend *drafsha*, means a banner in this place. Sāyaṇa explains *sátvā*, a hero, as 'a bull,' but this interpretation cannot be accepted.

Their stablished way : the course appointed for them in the eternal order of the universe.

3 *Coursers* : *haritaḥ*; Harits. Cf. IV. 6.9.

Him who beholds the universe, the Sun-God, seven strong and youthful Coursers carry onward.

4 Spreading thy web with mightiest Steeds thou comest, rending apart, thou God, the black-hued mantle.
The rays of Sūrya tremulously shining sink, like a hide, the darkness in the waters.

5 How is it that, unbound and not supported, he falleth not although directed downward ?
By what self-power moves he ? Who hath seen it ? He guards the vault of heaven, a close-set pillar.

HYMN XIV. *Agni.*

1. THE God hath looked, even Agni Jātavedas, to meet the Dawns refulgent in their glories.
Come on your chariot, ye who travel widely, come to this sacrifice of ours, Nāsatyas.

2 Producing light for all the world of creatures, God Savitar hath raised aloft his banner.
Making his presence known by sunbeams, Sūrya hath filled the firmament and earth and heaven.

3 Red Dawn is come, riding with brightness onward, distinguished by her beams, gay-hued and mighty.
Dawn on her nobly-harnessed car, the Goddess, awaking men to happiness, approacheth.

4 May those most powerful steeds and chariot bring you, O Aśvins, hither at the break of morning.
Here for your draught of meath are Soma juices : at this our sacrifice rejoice, ye Mighty.

5 How is it that, unbound and unsupported, he falleth not although directed downward ?
By what self-power moves he ? Who hath seen it ? He guards the vault of heaven, a close-set pillar ?

HYMN XV. *Agni.*

1. AGNI the Herald, like a horse, is led forth at our solemn rite,

This hymn is an imitation of the preceding. The last stanza is adopted word for word.

5 *He* : in the text *ayam*, this, that is Sūrya, the Sun, mentioned in stanza 2.

1 *Is led forth* : implying the formal bringing of fire from the household fire to light the sacrificial fire.

God among Gods adorable.

2 Three times unto our solemn rite comes
  Agni like a charioteer,
  Bearing the viands to the Gods.

3 Round the oblations hath he paced, Agni
  the Wise, the Lord of Strength,
  Giving the offerer precious boons.

4 He who is kindled eastward for Sṛñjaya,
  Devavāta's son,
  Resplendent, tamer of the foe.

5 So mighty be the Agni whom the mortal
  hero shall command,
  With sharpened teeth and bountiful.

6 Day after day they dress him, as they
  clean a horse who wins the prize,
  Dress the red Scion of the Sky.

7 When Sahadeva's princely son with two
  bay horses thought of me,
  Summoned by him I drew not back.

8 And truly those two noble bays I straightway took when offered me,
  From Sahadeva's princely son.

9 Long, O ye Aśvins, may he live, your
  care, ye Gods, the princely son.
  Of Sahadeva, Somaka.

10 Cause him the youthful prince, the son of
  Sahadeva, to enjoy
  Long life, O Aśvins, O ye Gods.

HYMN XVI.   *Indra.*

1. IMPETUOUS, true, let Maghavan come hither,
  and let his Tawny Coursers speed to
  reach us.
  For him have we pressed juice exceeding
  potent : here, praised with song, let
  him effect his visit.

2 Unyoke, as at thy journey's end, O Hero,
  to gladden thee today at this libation.

Like Uśanā, the priest a laud shall utter,
  a hymn to thee, the Lord Divine, who
  markest.

3 When the Bull, quaffing, praises our libation, as a sage paying holy rites in
  secret,
  Seven singers here from heaven hath he
  begotten, who e'en by day have
  wrought their works while singing.

4 When heaven's fair light by hymns was
  made apparent (they made great splendour shine at break of morning),
  He with his succour, best of Heroes, scattered the blinding darkness so that men
  saw clearly.

5 Indra, Impetuous One, hath waxed im-
  mensely : he with his vastness hath
  filled earth and heaven.
  E'en beyond this his majesty extendeth
  who hath exceeded all the worlds in
  greatness.

6 Śakra who knoweth well all human actions
  hath with his eager Friends let loose the
  waters.
  They with their songs cleft e'en the mountain open and willingly disclosed the
  stall of cattle.

7 He smote away the floods' obstructer,
  Vṛtra ; Earth, conscious, lent her aid to
  speed thy thunder.
  Thou sentest forth the waters of the ocean,
  as Lord through power and might, O
  daring Hero.

8 When, Much-invoked ! the water's rock
  thou cleftest, Saramā showed herself and
  went before thee.
  Hymned by Aṅgirases, bursting the cow-
  stalls, much strength thou foundest for
  us as our leader.

9 Come, Maghavan, Friend of Man, to aid
  the singer imploring thee in battle for
  the sunlight.
  Speed him with help in his inspired invokings : down sink the sorcerer, the
  prayerless Dasyu.

2 *Three times* : with reference to the three sacrifices.
4 *Eastward* : on the *uttaravedi* or north altar.
Sṛñjaya : a certain Soma-sacrificer *kaścit somayājī*, says
Sāyaṇa. Professor Wilson observes : 'We have several
princes of the name in the Purāṇas, but none distinguished by this patronymic : the *Sṛñjayas* are also a people
in the west of India.'
6 *The red Scion of the Sky* : or, Aruṣa, the Child
of Heaven, i.e. the Sun.

7 *Sahadeva's princely son* : Somaka, the institutor of
the sacrifice, son of a Rājā named Sahadeva. *With
two bay horses* : which were to be the priest's honorarium.

9 *Your care* : there is no substantive in the text.
Sāyaṇa supplies *tarpakaḥ* satisfier, i.e. worshipper.
Professor Ludwig regards *vām* as a dativus ethicus.

1 *Impetuous* : according to Sāyaṇa, *ṛjīṣī*, the word in
the text, means accepter, or drinker, of the spiritless
Soma, of the Soma when its essence or strength has
passed away. Professor Ludwig follows Sāyaṇa.

2 *Like Uśanā* : the Ṛṣi Uśanā, or Uśanas, called
also Kāvya or Kavi's son, appears in the Veda as the
especial friend of Indra. See I. 51. 10 ; 33, 5 ; 117, 12.

3 *The Bull* : the mighty Indra. *Seven singers* : the
meaning of this line is not clear. Professor Wilson,
following Sāyaṇa, translates : 'and this generates the
seven efficient (rays) from heaven, which, being
glorified, have made (manifest) the objects of (human)
perception.'

4 *Scattered, etc.* : or, fashioned blind turbid darkness
so that men saw clearly.

6 *Śakra* : Indra, the powerful. *His eager Friends* :
the Maruts.

8 *Saramā* : the hound of Indra, who tracked the
stolen cows. See I. 62. 3, and 72. 8.

10 Come to our home resolved to slay the
Dasyu : Kutsa longed eagerly to win thy
friendship.
Alike in form ye both sate in his dwelling :
the faithful Lady was in doubt between
you.

11 Thou comest, fain to succour him, with
Kutsa,—a goad that masters both the
Wind-God's horses,
That, holding the brown steeds like spoil
for capture, the sage may on the final
day be present.

12 For Kutsa, with thy thousand, thou at
day-break didst hurl down greedy Śuṣṇa,
foe of harvest.
Quickly with Kutsa's friend destroy the
Dasyus, and roll the chariot-wheel of
Sūrya near us.

13 Thou to the son of Vidathin, Ṛjiṣvan,
gavest up mighty Mṛgaya and Pipru.
Thou smotest down the swarthy fifty thousand, and rentest forts as age consumes
a garment.

14 What time thou settest near the Sun thy
body, thy form, Immortal One, is seen
expanding :
Thou a wild elephant with might invested,
like a dread lion as thou wieldest weapons.

15 Wishes for wealth have gone to Indra,
longing for him in war for light and
at libation,
Eager for glory, labouring with praise-
songs : he is like home, like sweet and
fair nutrition.

16 Call we for you that Indra, prompt to
listen, him who hath done so much for
men's advantage ;
Who, Lord of envied bounty, to a singer
like me brings quickly booty worth the
capture.

17 When the sharp-pointed arrow, O thou
Hero, flieth mid any conflict of the
people,
When, Faithful One, the dread encounter
cometh, then be thou the Protector of
our body.

18 Further the holy thoughts of Vāmadeva ;
be thou a guileless Friend in fight for
booty.
We come to thee whose providence protects us : wide be thy sway for ever
for thy singer.

19 O Indra, with these men who love thee
truly, free givers, Maghavan, in every
battle,
May we rejoice through many autumns,
quelling our foes, as days subdue the
nights with splendour.

20 Now, as the Bhṛgus wrought a car, for
Indra the Strong, the Mighty, we our
prayer have fashioned,
That he may, ne'er withdraw from us his
friendship, but be our bodies' guard and
strong defender.

21 Now, Indra ! lauded, glorified with praises,
let power swell high like rivers for the
singer.
For thee a new hymn, Lord of Bays, is
fashioned. May we, car-borne, through
song be victors ever.

HYMN XVII.　　　　　　　　　*Indra.*

1. GREAT art thou, Indra ; yea, the earth,
with gladness, and heaven confess to
thee thine high dominion.
Thou in thy vigour having slaughtered
Vṛtra didst free the floods arrested by
the Dragon.

2 Heaven trembled at the birth of thine
effulgence ; Earth trembled at the fear
of thy displeasure.

10 *Kutsa* : a Rājarṣi or royal Ṛṣi, frequently mentioned as the favoured friend of Indra.

The faithful Lady : even Kutsa's wife could hardly
distinguish one from the other; or, as Sāyaṇa explains,
Indra took Kutsa to his own home where Śacī his
consort was uncertain which of the two was Indra.

11 *The sage* : Kutsa. *The final day* : the decisive
day of battle.

12 *With thy thousand* : thy many followers. *Foe of
harvest* : or Kuyava may be the name of another fiend
or barbarous enemy. See I. 104. 3. *Kutsa's friend* : the
thunderbolt, according to Sāyaṇa. *Roll the chariot-wheel
of Sūrya near us* : bring back the daylight.

13 *Ṛjiṣvan* : a prince mentioned before as protected
by Indra. See I. 51. 5. *Mṛgaya and Pipru* : demons of
the air. *The swarthy fifty thousand* : black Rakṣasas,
fiends, or hostile aborigines.

14 *What time thou settest near the Sun thy body* : perhaps, as Professor Ludwig suggests, a poetical explanation
of an eclipse of the sun.

15 *Eager for glory* : a transition from 'wishes' to
'wishers' implied therein. *Nutrition* : according to Sāyaṇa,
like Lakṣmī the Goddess of prosperity.

19 *Free givers* : liberal institutors of sacrifice.

20 *As the Bhṛgus* : according to Sāyaṇa = splendid
carpenters ; but the reference must be to the celebrated
priestly family, and 'car' may be used metaphorically
for the hymn which rapidly reaches the Gods.

1 *The Dragon* : Ahi, the serpent-demon who stays
the rain from falling.

The stedfast mountains shook in agitation : the waters flowed, and desert spots were flooded.

3 Hurling his bolt with might he cleft the mountain, while, putting forth his strength, he showed his vigour.

He slaughtered Vṛtra with his bolt, exulting, and, their lord slain, forth flowed the waters swiftly.

4 Thy Father Dyaus esteemed himself a hero : most noble was the work of Indra's Maker,

His who begat the strong bolt's Lord who roareth, immovable like earth from her foundation.

5 He who alone o'erthrows the world of creatures, Indra the peoples' King, invoked of many—

Verily all rejoice in him, extolling the boons which Maghavan the God hath sent them.

6 All Soma juices are his own for ever, most gladdening draughts are ever his, the Mighty,

Thou ever wast the Treasure-Lord of treasures : Indra, thou lettest all folk share thy bounty.

7 Moreover, when thou first wast born, O Indra, thou struckest terror into all the people.

Thou, Maghavan, rentest with thy bolt the Dragon who lay against the waterfloods of heaven.

8 The ever-slaying, bold and furious Indra, the bright bolt's Lord, infinite, strong and mighty,

Who slayeth Vṛtra and acquireth booty, giver of blessings, Maghavan the bounteous:

9 Alone renowned as Maghavan in battles, he frighteneth away assembled armies.

He bringeth us the booty that he winneth : may we, well-loved, continue in his friendship.

10 Renowned is he when conquering and when slaying : 'tis he who winneth cattle in the combat.

When Indra hardeneth his indignation all that is fixed and all that moveth fear him.

11 Indra hath won all kine, all gold, all horses,—Maghavan, he who breaketh forts in pieces ;

Most manly with these men of his who help him, dealing out wealth and gathering the treasure.

12 What is the care of Indra for his Mother, what cares he for the Father who begat him ?

His care is that which speeds his might in conflicts, like wind borne onward by the clouds that thunder.

13 Maghavan makes the settled man unsettled : he scatters dust that he hath swept together,

Breaking in pieces like Heaven armed with lightning : Maghavan shall enrich the man who lauds him.

14 He urged the chariot-wheel of Sūrya forward : Etaśa, speeding on his way, he rested.

Him the black undulating cloud bedeweth, in this mid-air's depth, at the base of darkness,

15 As in the night the sacrificing priest.

16 Eager for booty, craving strength and horses, we-singers stir Indra, the strong, for friendship,

Who gives the wives we seek, whose succour fails not, to hasten, like a pitcher to the fountain.

4 *Esteemed himself a hero* : as being the father of such a son.

5 *Extolling* : I follow Professor Wilson in taking *gṛṇatáḥ* as a nominative plural, a lightened form for *gṛṇantáḥ*. Otherwise it is difficult to make sense out of the second line.

8 *Indra* : in this stanza is in the accusative case without a subject or a governing verb. Sāyaṇa supplies *vayam stotāraḥ stumeti*, 'we singers praise.'

11 *Who breaketh forts in pieces* : as it seems impossible to make any sense out of *pūrvíḥ*, I have adopted Professor Grassmann's conjecture, which is somewhat reluctantly accepted by Professor Ludwig and read *pūrbhíd* instead of the word in the text. Sāyaṇa supplies *śatrusenāḥ*, 'armies of enemies.' *These men* : who sing his praises and so increase his strength.

12 *His care is*: there are no corresponding words in the text, but it is necessary to supply something of the kind. The meaning is, Indra is independent of, and cares nothing about, his parents, but he does care for his dear ally the thunderbolt.

13 *Scatters dust* : causes commotion and keeps the world in a state of unrest.

14 This difficult stanza appears to refer to an eclipse of the Sun. Indra was urging on the Sun's chariot when suddenly he rested or stopped Etaśa the horse that drew it, and threw him back into the black moist cloud of the darkness of night. See 1. 121. 13, and A. Kuhn, Mythologische Studien, 1. pp. 58—60.

15 *The sacrificing priest* : lets the fire shine, understood. Sāyaṇa explains, 'as the sacrificer sprinkles Soma upon the invoking priest Agni,' taking *hotā*, a nominative case, as *hotāram*, an accusative. Professor Grassmann thinks that the single Pāda was originally a gloss on the preceding stanza.

16 *Who gives the wives we seek* : perhaps referring as, Professor Ludwig observes, to the forcible abduction of women after a victory.

17 Be thou our guardian, show thyself our
kinsman, watching and blessing those
who pour the Soma ;
As Friend, as Sire, most fatherly of fathers,
giving the suppliant vital strength and
freedom.

18 Be helping Friend of those who seek thy
friendship : give life, when lauded,
Indra, to the singer.
For, Indra, we the priests have paid thee
worship, exalting thee with these our
sacrifices.

19 Alone, when Indra Maghavan is lauded,
he slayeth many ne'er-resisted Vṛtras.
Him in whose keeping is the well-loved
singer never do Gods or mortals stay
or hinder.

20 E'en so let Maghavan, the loud-voiced
Indra, give us true blessings, foeless,
men's upholder.
King of all creatures, give us glory amply,
exalted glory due to him who lauds
thee.

21 Now, Indra ! lauded, glorified with praises, let power swell high like rivers for
the singer.
For thee a new hymn, Lord of Bays ! is
fashioned. May we, car-borne, through
song be victors ever.

HYMN XVIII. *Indra and Others.*

1. THIS is the ancient and accepted pathway by which all Gods have come into
existence.
Hereby could one be born though waxen
mighty. Let him not, otherwise, destroy his Mother.

2 Not this way go I forth : hard is the
passage. Forth from the side obliquely
will I issue.

Indra, Aditi, and Vāmadeva are said to be the
Ṛṣis or seers as well as the deities of the hymn, as it
consists of conversation in which all bear part. The
hymn appears to be made up of somewhat incoherent
fragments, and the Commentators do not seem to have
been successful in their apportionment of the stanzas to
the several speakers. See Prof. Pischel's Excursus (Vedische Studien, II pp. 42—54), and Prof. Ludwig's
criticism thereon, Ueber die neuesten Arbeiten auf dem
Gebiete der Ṛgveda-forschung, pp. 142 sqq.

1 The main subject is the birth and infancy of
Indra. He refuses to be born in the usual manner and
insists on coming into the world in another way. The
speaker—Vyaṁsa his father, Aditi his mother, or some
other—dissuades him, eventually, it seems, (stanza 3)
with success. The Commentators erroneously take the
stanza as referring to the birth of Vāmadeva.

2 Indra, as yet unborn, is the speaker. *One* :
perhaps Vṛtra. *The other* : perhaps Viṣṇu, whom he
addresses in stanza 11.

Much that is yet undone must I accomplish ; one must l combat and the other
question.

3 He bent his eye upon the dying Mother :
My word I now withdraw. That way
I follow.
In Tvaṣṭar's dwelling Indra drank the
Soma, a hundredworth of juice pressed
from the mortar.

4 What strange act shall he do, he whom
his Mother bore for a thousand months
and many autumns ?
No peer hath he among those born already, nor among those who shall be
born hereafter.

5 Deeming him a reproach, his mother hid
him, Indra, endowed with all heroic
valour.
Then up he sprang himself, assumed his
vesture, and filled, as soon as born, the
earth and heaven.

6 With lively motion onward flow these
waters, the Holy Ones, shouting, as
'twere, together.
Ask them to tell thee what the floods are
saying, what girdling rock the waters
burst asunder.

7 Are they addressing him with words of
welcome ? Will the floods take on them
the shame of Indra ?
With his great thunderbolt my Son hath
slaughtered Vṛtra, and set these rivers
free to wander.

8 I cast thee from me, mine,—thy youthful mother: thee, mine own offspring,
Kuśavā hath swallowed.

3 Indra, who has changed his mind, speaks the
second half of the first line.

4 It is not clear who the speaker is. Professor
Wilson observes : '*Aditi* defends her son upon the plea
that, as his period of gestation was marvellous, his
actions are not to be compared with those of any others.'

5 *Deeming him a reproach* : either because he appeared to be weak, or because, as Sāyaṇa says, he was born
in a chamber in privacy unworthy of so great a God.

6 *What girdling rock* : an allusion to the prison of
thick cloud from which Indra freed the waters.

7 *Words of welcome* : nivids, sentences or short formularies inserted in a liturgy and containing epithets
or short invocations of the Gods.
The shame of Indra : his fancied guilt incurred in
slaying Vṛtra. See I. 32. 14.

8 *Mine* : Sāyaṇa explains *mámat* as 'exulting.'
Professor Roth, whom Professor Grassmann and the
translators of the *Siebenzig Lieder* follow, renders it by
now—now. I have preferred Professor Ludwig's interpretation, originally due to Benfey, and taken the
word as another form of *máma*. The word is important
as expressing Aditi's acknowledgment of Indra as her
son. *Kuśavā* : according to Sāyaṇa, a Rākṣasī or
female demon who swallowed Indra at his birth ;
according to von Roth, the name of a river.

To him, mine infant, were the waters gracious. Indra, my Son, rose up in conquering vigour.

9 Thou art mine own, O Maghavan, whom Vyaṁsa struck to the ground and smote thy jaws in pieces.
But, smitten through, the mastery thou wonnest, and with thy bolt the Dāsa's head thou crushedst.

10 The Heifer hath brought forth the Strong, the Mighty, the unconquerable Bull, the furious Indra.
The Mother left her unlicked Calf to wander, seeking himself, the path that he would follow.

11 Then to her mighty Child the Mother turned her, saying, My son, these Deities forsake thee.
Then Indra said, about to slaughter Vṛtra, O my friend Viṣṇu, stride full boldly forward.

12 Who was he then who made thy Mother widow? Who sought to slay thee lying still or moving?
What God, when by the foot thy Sire thou tookest and slewest, was at hand to give thee comfort?

13 In deep distress I cooked a dog's intestines. Among the Gods I found not one to comfort.
My consort I beheld in degradation. The Falcon then brought me the pleasant Soma.

---

10 *The Heifer* ; Aditi, the young mother of Indra.

11 *Stride full boldly forward* : that is, assist me in my battle with Vṛtra. Professor Grassmann and the translators of the *Siebenzig Lieder* render the passage differently 'O Vischnu, Freund, geh etwas doch zur Seite,' and, 'Viṣṇu mein Freund geh etwas aus dem Wege ; that is, 'step aside,' or 'out of the way,' and let me conquer Vṛtra without thy aid.

12 This appears to be Viṣṇu's answer. Why dost thou ask me to help thee now? Didst thou not slay thine own father, thy father who sought to kill thee when yet unborn and when coming to the birth? Vyaṁsa appears to be the father whom Indra slew (stanza 9). Sāyaṇa merely says that the allusions are variously explained by the followers of the Taittirīya school of the Yajurveda.

13 This appears to be Vāmadeva's excuse for having in his utmost need cooked and eaten, or desired to eat, impure flesh. 'So *Manu* has, Vāmadeva who well knew right and wrong, was by no means rendered impure, though desirous, when oppressed with hunger, of eating the flesh of dogs for the preservation of his life, X. 106.'—Wilson. According to Ludwig, Bergaigne, and Hillebrandt, the stanza is spoken by Indra. *The Falcon* : alluding to the way in which the Soma was first brought from heaven. Sāyaṇa explains it as 'Indra coming swiftly as a falcon.'

HYMN XIX.   *Indra.*

1. THEE, verily, O Thunder-wielding Indra, all the Gods here, the Helpers swift to listen,
And both the worlds elected, thee the Mighty, High, waxen strong, alone to slaughter Vṛtra.

2 The Gods, as worn witheld, relaxed their efforts : thou, Indra, born of truth, wast Sovran Ruler.
Thou slewest Ahi who besieged the waters, and duggest out their all-supporting channels.

3 The insatiate one, extended, hard to waken, who slumbered in perpetual sleep, O Indra,—
The Dragon stretched against the seven prone rivers, where no joint was, thou rentest with thy thunder.

4 Indra with might shook earth and her foundation as the wind stirs the water with its fury.
Striving, with strength he burst the firm asunder, and tore away the summits of the mountains.

5 They ran to thee as mothers to their offspring : the clouds, like chariots, hastened forth together.
Thou didst refresh the streams and force the billows : thou, Indra, settest free obstructed rivers.

6 Thou for the sake of Vayya and Turvīti didst stay the great stream, flowing, all-sustaining :
Yea, at their prayer didst check the rushing river and make the floods easy to cross, O Indra.

7 He let the young Maids skilled in Law, unwedded, like fountains, bubbling, flow forth streaming onward.
He inundated thirsty plains and deserts, and milked the dry Cows of the mighty master.

---

2 *Relaxed their efforts* : or abdicated their functions as protectors and made over to Indra the duty of slaying the oppressor Vṛtra.

3 *Where no joint was* : that would have facilitated his dismemberment.

5 *The clouds* : according to Sāyaṇa *ádrayaḥ*, mountains or clouds, here means the Maruts.

6 *Vayya and Turvīti* : Turvīti has been mentioned frequently in Book I. as having been protected by Indra, and Vayya is said to have been his father and companion. See I. 54. 6 ; II. 13. 12.

7 *The young Maids skilled in Law* : the rivers that know and follow the law of their being, the Order of the universe.

He milked the dry Cows : he drew rain from the clouds which had hitherto been prevented by their mighty master Vṛtra from yielding their stores.

8 Through many a morn and many a lovely
autumn, having slain Vṛtra, he set
free the rivers.

Indra hath set at liberty to wander on
earth the streams encompassed pressed
together.

9 Lord of Bay Steeds, thou broughtest from
the ant-hill the unwedded damsel's son
whom ants were eating.

The blind saw clearly, as he grasped the
serpent, rose, brake the jar : his joints
again united.

10 To the wise man, O Sage and Sovran
Ruler, the man who knoweth all thine
ancient exploits.

Hath told these deeds of might as thou
hast wrought them, great acts, spontaneous, and to man's advantage.

11 Now, Indra ! lauded, glorified with praises,
let powers swell high, like rivers, for
the singer.

For thee a new hymn, Lord of Bays ! is
fashioned. May we, car-borne, through
song be victors ever.

HYMN XX.   Indra.

1. FROM near or far away may mighty Indra,
giver of succour, come for our protection,
Lord of men, armed with thunder, with
the Strongest, slaying his foes in conflict,
in the battles.

2 May Indra come to us with Tawny
Coursers, inclined to us, to favour and
enrich us.

May Maghavan, loud-voiced and wielding
thunder, stand by us at this sacrifice, in
combat.

3 Thou, honouring this our sacrifice, O Indra,
shalt give us strength and fill us full of
courage.

To win the booty, Thunder-armed ! like
hunters may we with thee subdue in
fight our foemen.

4 Loving us well, benevolent, close beside
us, drink, Godlike Indra, of the well-
pressed Soma.

Drink of the meath we offer, and delight
thee with food that cometh from the
mountain ridges.

5 Him who is sung aloud by recent sages,
like a ripe-fruited tree, a scythe-armed
victor,—

I, like a bridegroom thinking of his consort, call hither Indra, him invoked of
many;

6 Him who in native strength is like a mountain, the lofty Indra born of old for
conquest,

Terrific wielder of the ancient thunder.
filled full with splendour as a jar with
water.

7 Whom from of old there is not one to
hinder, none to curtail the riches of his
bounty.

Pouring forth freely, O thou Strong and
Mighty, vouchsafe us riches, God invoked
of many !

8 Of wealth and homes of men thou art the
ruler, and opener of the stable of the
cattle.

Helper of men, winner of spoil in combats,
thou leadest to an ample heap of riches.

9 By what great might is he renowned as
strongest, wherewith the Lofty One stirs
up wild battles ?

Best soother of the worshipper's great
sorrow, he gives possessions to the man
who lauds him.

10 Slay us not; bring, bestow on us the ample
gift which thou hast to give to him who
offers.

At this new gift, with this laud sung before
thee, extolling thee, we, Indra, will
declare it.

11 Now, Indra ! lauded, glorified with praises,
let power swell high, like rivers, for the
singer.

---

9 Sāyaṇa says that Agrū (unwedded) was a woman
of that name, whose son was hidden in an ant-hill,
whence Indra rescued him, restored his sight, and re-
united his broken joints.

Brake the jar : broke through the ant-hill in which
he was confined. Professor Ludwig thinks that the son
of the unwedded damsel is the lightning which burst
forth from the parent cloud. The passage is obscure.

1 *With the Strongest* : the most powerful Maruts.

4 *That cometh from the mountain ridges* : where the
Soma was said especially to grow. According to Sāyaṇa's interpretation, the translation would be, 'with the
food brought thee with the hymn of noonday,' *Pṛṣṭha*

means both 'back, or high ridge,' and 'a hymn employed at the midday oblation,' and the meaning of the
adjective *pṛṣṭhya* is similarly ambiguous.

5 *A scythe-armed victor* : the meaning is uncertain.
Sāyaṇa explains *sṛṇyaḥ* as 'armed with a hook or sickle,'
'skilled in the use of arms'. Professor Ludwig translates,
'wie ein fassender haken,' 'like a grasping hook'. Professor Aufrecht thinks that *sṛṇyo ná jetā* may perhaps
mean, 'like a winner of sickles (as a prize).' Professor
Grassmann thinks that a reaper, cutting down corn
with his sickle, is intended.

6 *Wielder of the ancient thunder* : I follow Sāyaṇa,
but am not satisfied with his explanation. Professor
Grassmann follows Bollensen in reading *vrajám*, cowpen,
instead of *vájram*, thunderbolt, and this is the reading
given also in the St. Petersburg Lexicon. If this alteration were adopted the translation would be, 'the fierce
discloser of the firm-built cow-stall.'

A new hymn, Lord of Bays ! for thee is
fashioned. May we, car-born, through
song be victors ever.

HYMN XXI. *Indra.*

1. MAY Indra come to us for our protection;
here be the Hero, praised, our feast-
companion.
May he whose powers are many, waxen
mighty, cherish, like Dyaus, his own
supreme dominion.

2 Here magnify his great heroic exploits,
most glorious One, enriching men with
bounties,
Whose will is like a Sovran in assembly,
who rules the people, Conqueror, all-
surpassing.

3 Hither let Indra come from earth or
heaven, hither with speech from firmament or ocean;
With Maruts, from the realm of light to
aid us, or from a distance, from the
seat of Order.

4 That Indra will we laud in our assemblies,
him who is Lord of great and lasting
riches,
Victor with Vāyu where the herds are
gathered, who leads with boldness on to
higher fortune.

5 May the Priest, Lord of many blessings,
striving,—who fixing reverence on
reverence, giving
Vent to his voice, inciteth men to worship—
with lauds bring Indra hither to our
dwellings.

6 When sitting pondering in deep devotion
in Auśija's abode they ply the press-
stone,
May he whose wrath is fierce, the mighty
bearer, come as the house-lord's priest
within our chambers.

7 Surely the power of Bhārvara the mighty
for ever helpeth to support the singer;

That which in Auśija's abode lies hidden,
to come forth for delight and for devotion.

8 When he unbars the spaces of the mountains, and quickens with his floods the
water-torrents,
He finds in lair the buffalo and wild-ox
when the wise lead him on to vigorous
exploit.

9 Auspicious are thy hands, thine arms well-
fashioned which proffer bounty, Indra,
to thy praiser.
What sloth is this ? Why dost thou not
rejoice thee ? Why dost thou not delight
thyself with giving ?

10 So Indra is the truthful Lord of treasure.
Freedom he gave to man by slaying
Vṛtra.
Much-lauded ! help us with thy power to
riches : may I be sharer of thy Godlike
favour.

11 Now, Indra ! lauded, glorified with praises,
let power swell high, like rivers, for the
singer.
For thee a new hymn, Lord of Bays ! is
fashioned. May we, care-borne, through
song be victors ever.

HYMN XXII. *Indra.*

1. THAT gift of ours which Indra loves and
welcomes, even that he makes for us,
the Great and Strong One.
He who comes wielding in his might the
thunder, Maghavan, gives prayer, praise,
and laud, and Soma.

2 Bull, hurler of the four-edged rain-producer
with both his arms, strong, mighty,
most heroic;

---

3 *From a distance, from the seat of Order* : perhaps,
from the farthest limit of the ordered universe. According to Sāyaṇa, from the region of cloud, *meghalokāt*.

4 *Where the herds are gathered* : in places where
cattle, the prize of victory, abound.

5 *The Priest* : apparently Agni. *Fixing reverence on
reverence* : urging man to continual adoration.

6 *Auśija* is generally a patronymic of the Ṛṣi
Kakṣivān and others. According to Sāyaṇa the instruc-
tor of the sacrifice is meant. The stanza is obscure.

7 *Bhārvara* : according to sāyaṇa, a name of Indra
as son of Bhārvara, the supporter of the world, that is
Prajāpati. Professor Grassmann thinks that Agni is
meant and Professor Ludwig considers it tolerably clear
that Bhārvara is identical with Auśija. The exact
meaning of the stanza is doubtful, but its general
purport appears to be that Bhārvara, whether he be

Auśija, or Indra, or Agni, has a store of wealth or
power to protect the worshipper and assist him in the
performance of his religious duties.

8 *When he unbars* : when Indra lays open the interior of the mountain of clouds within which the rain
is imprisoned.

The buffalo and wild-ox : the Gaura (Bos gaurus)
and the Gavaya (Bos gavaeus) are two kinds of wild
cattle. The *gaurásya* and *gavayásya* of the text must be
taken as partitive genitives after *viddí*, he finds. 'The
purport of the expression, according to the scholiast, is,
that Indra obtains these two animals *tau dvau paśū
labhate*, either for himself as sacrificial flesh, or for his
worshippers, some of whom, at least, even now, would
not object to eat the flesh of the wild oxen.--Wilson.

---

2 *Rain-producer* : the thunderbolt or lightning which
is supposed to cause rain by opening the cloud.
Paruṣṇī : one of the rivers of the Panjāb, called
in later times Irāvatī, the modern Rāvī. Indra appears
to be represented as clothing himself in the wool-like
waves, or fleecy vapours, of the river, and lovingly
covering or uniting in one stream her several joints,
limbs, or branches. 'The phraseology here,' Professor
Wilson remarks, 'is somewhat obscure and the scholiast
does not materially enlighten us.'

Wearing as wool Paruṣṇī for adornment, whose joints for sake of friendship he hath covered.

3 God who of all the Gods was born divinest, endowed with ample strength and mighty powers,
And bearing in his arms the yearning thunder, with violent rush caused heaven and earth to tremble.

4 Before the High God, at his birth, heaven trembled, earth, many floods and all the precipices.
The Strong One bringeth nigh the Bull's two Parents : loud sing the winds, like men, in air's mid-region.

5 These are thy great deeds, Indra, thine, the Mighty, deeds to be told aloud at all libations,
That thou, O Hero, bold and boldly daring, didst with thy bolt, by strength, destroy the Dragon.

6 True are all these thy deeds, O Most Heroic. The Milch-kine issued from the streaming udder.
In fear of thee, O thou of manly spirit, the rivers swiftly set themselves in motion.

7 With joy, O Indra, Lord of Tawny Coursers, the Sisters then, these Goddesses, extolled thee,
When thou didst give the prisoned ones their freedom to wander at their will in long succession.

8 Pressed is the gladdening stalk as 'twere a river : so let the rite, the toiler's power, attract thee
To us-ward, of the Bright One, as the courser strains his exceedingly strong leather bridle.

9 Ever by us perform thy most heroic, thine highest, best victorious deeds, O Victor.
For us make Vṛtras easy to be conquered : destroy the weapon of our mortal foeman.

10 Graciously listen to our prayer, O Indra, and strength of varied sort bestow thou on us.
Send to us all intelligence and wisdom : O Maghavan, be he who gives us cattle.

11 Now, Indra ! lauded, glorified with praises, let wealth swell high like rivers to the singer.
For thee a new hymn, Lord of Bays ! is fashioned. May we, car-borne, through song be victors ever.

HYMN XXIII. *Indra.*

1. How, what priest's sacrifice hath he made mighty, rejoicing in the Soma and its fountain ?
Delighting in juice, eagerly drinking, the Lofty One hath waxed for splendid riches.

2 What hero hath been made his feast-companion ? Who hath been partner in his loving-kindness ?
What know we of his wondrous acts ? How often comes he to aid and speed the pious toiler ?

3 How heareth Indra offered invocation ? How, hearing, marketh he the invoker's wishes ?
What are his ancient acts of bounty ? Wherefore call they him One who filleth full the singer ?

4 How doth the priest who laboureth, ever longing, win for himself the wealth which he possesseth ?
May he, the God, mark well my truthful praises, having received the homage which he loveth.

5 How, and what bond of friendship with a mortal hath the God chosen as this morn is breaking ?
How, and what love hath he for those who love him, who have entwined in him their firm affection ?

6 Is then thy friendship with thy friends most mighty ? Thy brotherhood with us, —when may we tell it ?

---

4 The meaning of the second line is, Indra brings near, but holds apart, the heaven and the earth, the parents of the mighty Sun, and the winds sing in the intermediate space which has thus provided for them.

6 *The Milch-kine* : streams of fertilizing rain. The *udder* is the cloud.

7 *The Sisters* : the rivers.

8 The construction of the middle portion of the stanza is very difficult.
The general meaning appears to be, 'The Soma has been pressed and the juice flows copiously. Let our sacrifice draw thee hither with all the strength of a hard-pulling horse.' Who '*the Bright One*' is not clear; probably Agni is meant.

1 *Mighty* : effectual. *Its fountain* : more literally, udder; the sacrifice, the source from which the Soma flows as milk from the udder of the cow.
For splendid riches : in order to bestow splendid wealth on the sacrificer, according to Sāyaṇa.

2 *What hero*, etc. : no one is allowed to share the offerings made to Indra or to know his benevolent intentions.

6 *The stream of milk* : this line is difficult. Indra's close connexion with the Sun is referred to, and the general purport may be, as Professor Ludwig suggests : When thou risest up as the Sun, then we declare thy brotherhood with us ; or in other words, Indra's beauty

The streams of milk move, as most wondrous sunlight, the beauty of the Lovely One for glory.

7 About to slay the Indra-less destructive spirit he sharpens his keen arms to strike her.
Whereby the Strong, although our debts' exactor, drives in the distant mornings that we know not.

8 Eternal Law hath varied food that strengthens ; thought of eternal Law, removes transgressions.
The praise-hymn of eternal Law, arousing, glowing, hath oped the deaf ears of the living.

9 Firm-seated are eternal Law's foundations ; in its fair form are many splendid beauties.
By holy Law long lasting food they bring us ; by holy Law have cows come to our worship.

10 Fixing eternal Law he, too, upholds it : swift moves the might of Law and wins the booty.
To Law belong the vast deep Earth and Heaven : Milch-kine supreme, to Law their milk they render.

11 Now, Indra ! lauded, glorified with praises, let power swell high like rivers to the singer.
For thee a new hymn, Lord of Bays, is fashioned. May we, car-borne, through song be victors ever.

---

is made known as the light of the sun. Sāyaṇa explains *sárgāḥ* as, the efforts, (*udyogāḥ*), *goḥ*, of the moving one (Indra).

7 *Spirit* : the Druh, or mischievous female sprite who does not acknowledge Indra. The purport of the second line is: Indra, although the punisher of our sins, does not suffer us to be destroyed by evil spirits, but continuing to rise as the Sun, urges on a succession of mornings in the light of which the demons of the night disappear.

8 *Eternal Law* : here, Sāyaṇa says, the word *ṛtá* means Āditya, or Indra, or sacrifice. Its meaning varies slightly in this and the two following stanzas, but the original idea of regularity, conformity to, or establishment by, eternal order or law, is found throughout. In the second line *eternal Law* is the regular law-ordained sacrifice. *Glowing* : brilliant, or clearly sounding. *The living* : the worshipper.

9 *They bring us* : that is, the cows which *have come to our worship*, to be presented to the priests as payment of their services.

10 *Fixing eternal Law* : the establisher of the law is also its upholder or administrator. Professor Wilson translates : 'The (worshipper) subjecting Ṛta (to his will) verily enjoys Ṛta.'
To Law belong : or, were made for the sake of order or law-ordained sacrifice. *Milch-kine supreme* : bounteous heaven and earth, which cherish and support sacrifice or eternal order in general.

HYMN XXIV.   *Indra.*

1. WHAT worthy praise will bring before us Indra, the Son of Strength, that he may grant us riches ;
For he the Hero, gives the singer treasures : he is the Lord who sends us gifts, ye people.

2 To be invoked and hymned in fight with Vṛtra, that well-praised Indra gives us real bounties.
That Maghavan brings comfort in the foray to the religious man who pours libations.

3 Him, verily, the men invoke in combat ; risking their lives they make him their protector,
When heroes, foe to foe, give up their bodies, fighting, each side, for children and their offspring.

4 Strong God ! the folk at need put forth their vigour, striving together in the whirl of battle.
When warrior bands encounter one another some in the grapple quit themselves like Indra.

5 Hence many a one worships the might of Indra : hence let the brew succeed the meal-oblation.
Hence let the Soma banish those who pour not : even hence I joy to pay the Strong One worship.

6 Indra gives comfort to the man who truly presses, for him who longs for it, the Soma,
Not disaffected, with devoted spirit this man he takes to be his friend in battles.

7 He who this day for Indra presses Soma, prepares the brew and fries the grains of barley—
Loving the hymns of that devoted servant, to him may Indra give heroic vigour.

8 When the impetuous chief hath sought the conflict, and the lord looked upon the long-drawn battle,

---

1 *The Son of Strength* : the Mighty One.

5 *Let the brew succeed the meal-oblation* : or, let the offering of cooked viands follow that of the sacrificial cake; let varied offerings be made in rapid succession. *Let the Soma banish* : let those who pour no Soma libations to Indra be kept at a distance from those who thus worship him.

8 When the chieftain has gone out to fight, his wife calls on Indra to protect him. According to Sāyaṇa, the 'impetuous chief,' 'the lord,' is Indra whom his consort recalls to drink the Soma juice which has been prepared for him by men.

The matron calls to the Strong God whom pressers of Soma have encouraged in the dwelling.

9 He bid a small price for a thing of value : I was content, returning, still unpurchased.
He heightened not his insufficient offer. Simple and clever, both milk out the udder.

10 Who for ten milch-kine purchaseth from me this Indra who is mine ?
When he hath slain the Vṛtras let the buyer give him back to me.

11 Now, Indra ! lauded, glorified with praises, let wealth swell high like rivers for the singer.
For thee a new hymn, Lord of Bays, is fashioned. May we, car-borne, through song be victors ever.

HYMN XXV.   *Indra.*

1. WHAT friend of man, God-loving, hath delighted, yearning therefor, this day in Indra's friendship ?
Who with enkindled flame and flowing Soma laudeth him for his great protecting favour ?

2 Who hath with prayer bowed to the Soma-lover ? What pious man endues the beams of morning ?
Who seeks bond, friendship, brotherhood with Indra ? Who hath recourse unto the Sage for succour ?

3 Who claims to-day the Deities' protection, asks Aditi for light, or the Ādityas ?
Of whose pressed stalk of Soma drink the Aśvins, Indra, and Agni, well-inclined in spirit ?

4 To him shall Agni Bhārata give shelter : long shall he look upon the Sun uprising,
Who sayeth, Let us press the juice for Indra, man's Friend, the Hero manliest of heroes.

9 *I was content* : spoken by Indra. *Both milk out the udder* : both the simple, or needy, buyer and the shrewd seller make as much as they can out of the bargain ; that is, the buying and selling of Indra, meaning the settlement of the fee to be paid to the priest for obtaining Indra's favour by sacrifice. Professor Grassmann banishes stanzas 9 and 10 to an appendix, as not originally belonging to the hymn.

2 *Endues the beams of morning* : the expression means, apparently, 'betakes himself to prayer at day-break.' Sāyaṇa's interpretation is, 'Who covers that is, supports, the cows given by Indra?'

4 *Agni Bhāra'a* : Agni as the especial God of the Bharata family to which Vāmadeva the Ṛṣi of the hymn belonged.

5 Him neither few men overcome, nor many : to him shall Aditi give spacious shelter.
Dear is the pious, the devout, to Indra ; dear is the zealous, dear the Soma-bringer.

6 This Hero curbs the mighty for the zealous : the presser's brew Indra possesses solely:
No brother, kin, or friend to him who pours not, destroyer of the dumb who would resist him.

7 Not with the wealthy churl who pours no Soma doth Indra, Soma-drinker, bind alliance.
He draws away his wealth and slays him naked, own Friend to him who offers, for oblation.

8 Highest and lowest, men who stand between them, going, returning, dwelling in contentment,
Those who show forth their strength when urged to battle—these are the men who call for aid on Indra.

HYMN XXVI.   *Indra.*

1. I WAS aforetime Manu, I was Sūrya : I am the sage Kakṣivān, holy singer.
Kutsa the son of Ārjuni I master. I am the sapient Uśanā behold me.

2 I have bestowed the earth upon the Ārya, and rain upon the man who brings oblation.
I guided forth the loudly-roaring waters, and the Gods moved according to my pleasure.

3 In the wild joy of Soma I demolished Śambara's forts, ninety-and-nine, together;
And, utterly, the hundredth habitation, when helping Divodāsa Atithigva.

6 *Curbs the mighty* : the meaning of *prāśuṣāṭ* is somewhat uncertain ; 'prompt discomfiter of foes.'—Sāyaṇa. 'Bridling, leading, driving or having swift horses.'—Prof. Roth. 'Conqueror of the mighty.'—Prof. Ludwig. *The dumb* : the man who has no voice to praise him.

7 *Naked* : stripped of all his property ; destitute. *To him who offers, for oblation* : according to Sāyaṇa, 'to the man who pours the libation and prepares the dressed food; 'to him who presents the libation and oblation.'— Wilson.

The deity of the first three stanzas is said to be either Indra or Paramātmā the Supreme Spirit or Soul of the universe): the deity or deified object of the other stanzas is the Śyena or Falcon.

1 Indra is the speaker of the first three verses, although it is not clear what he means by saying that he is Kakṣivān and Uśanā, unless he intends to identify himself with all existence.

3 *Śambara* ; *Divodāsa*; *Atithigva* (here an adname or epithet of Divodāsa):see Index of Names.

4 Before all birds be ranked this Bird, O
   Maruts ; supreme of falcons be this
   fleet-winged Falcon,
  Because, strong-pinioned, with no car to
   bear him, he brought to Manu the God-
   loved oblation.
5 When the Bird brought it, hence in rapid
   motion sent on the wide path fleet as
   thought he hurried.
  Swift he returned with sweetness of the
   Soma, and hence the Falcon hath acquired his glory.
6 Bearing the stalk, the Falcon speeding onward, Bird bringing from afar the draught that gladdens,
  Friend of the Gods, brought, grasping
   fast, the Soma which he had taken from
   yon loftiest heaven.
7 The Falcon took and brought the Soma,
   bearing thousand libations with him, yea,
   ten thousand.
  The Bold One left Malignities behind
   him, wise, in wild joy of Soma, left
   the foolish.

HYMN XXVII.   *The Falcon.*

1. I, As I lay within the womb, considered
   all generations of these Gods in order.
  A hundred iron fortresses confined me but
   forth I flew with rapid speed a Falcon.
2 Not at his own free pleasure did he bear
   me : he conquered with his strength and
   manly courage.
  Straightway the Bold One left the fiends
   behind him and passed the winds as he
   grew yet more mighty.
3 When with loud cry from heaven down
   sped the Falcon, thence hasting like the
   wind he bore the Bold One.

---

4 *With no car to bear him* : literally, 'with his own
wheel-less nature,' that is, by his own natural impulse.
Oblation : the Soma.
6 *The draught that gladdens* : the plant that yields
the exhilarating juice.
7 *The Bold One* : Indra.

---

1 *The womb* : of the rain cloud. *A hundred fortresses*:
cf. 'Śambara's hundred ancient castles' (II. 14. 6,)
Considered: or reviewed, in hope of finding a deliverer.
  The speaker is Agni, that is, the lightning which
rends the cloud and brings down the sweet rain—the
fleet Falcon who brings Soma from heaven. See Prof.
Bloomfield, The Myth of Soma and the Eagle, Festgruss an Rudolf von Roth, 1893, pp 149—155. Cf.
Hymns of the Atharva-veda, VI. 48. 1.
2 *Not at his own free pleasure* : the falcon's mere
will was not enough, says Soma ; he had first-to fight
and conquer my keepers.
  The Bold One : Indra. See stanza 7 of the preceding hymn.
3 *The Bold One* : meaning Soma. The construction
of the first line is difficult. *Kṛṣānu* : one of the guards
of the celestial Soma. See I. 155. 2.

Then, wildly raging in his mind, the
   archer Kṛśānu aimed and loosed the
   string to strike him.
4 The Falcon bore him from heaven's lofty
   summit as the swift car of Indra's Friend
   bore Bhujyu.
  Then downward hither fell a flying feather
   of the Bird hasting forward in his
   journey.
5 And now let Maghavan accept the beaker,
   white, filled with milk, filled with the
   shining liquid;
  The best of sweet meath which the priests
   have offered : that Indra to his joy may
   drink, the Hero, that he may take and
   drink it to his rapture.

HYMN XXVIII.   *Indra-Soma.*

1. ALLIED with thee, in this thy friendship,
   Soma, Indra for man made waters flow
   together,
  Slew Ahi, and sent forth the Seven Rivers,
   and opened as it were obstructed fountains.
2 Indu, with thee for his confederate, Indra
   swiftly with might pressed down the
   wheel of Sūrya.
  What rolled, all life's support, on heaven's
   high summit was separated from the great
   oppressor.
3 Indra smote down, Agni consumed, O
   Indu, the Dasyus ere the noontide in the
   conflict.
  Of those who gladly sought a hard-won
   dwelling he cast down many a thousand
   with his arrow.
4 Lower than all besides hast thou, O Indra,
   cast down the Dasyus, abject tribes of
   Dāsas.

---

4 The allusion in the first line is to the rescue of
Bhujyu, by the Aśvins (see I. 112. 6), and we should
therefore expect *índrāvatoḥ*, 'of Indra's two friends,'
instead of *índrāvato*. *Feather* : *parṇám* ; which became
on earth the sacred Parṇa or Palāśa tree, the beautiful
Butea Frondosa.
5 The metrical form and the ritual application
indicate the comparatively recent addition of this
stanza to the ancient hymn.

  The hymn has been discussed by Weber, Vedische
Beiträge, pp. 4 ff.
1 *The Seven Rivers* : perhaps the five rivers of the
Panjāb, the Indus, and the Sarasvat . See I. 32. 12.
2 *Pressed down the wheel of Sūrya* : probably an
eclipse of the sun is intended. *What rolled* : the sun's
wheel. From the *great oppressor* : 'maho druho, prabhū-
tasya drogdhuḥ, of the very mighty oppressor or tyrant,
alluding probably to his heat.'—Wilson. Cf. VI. 20 5.
Indu : a drop, especially a drop of Soma juice, is a
frequently occurring name of the God Soma.
3 *Ere the noontide* : in the forenoon, when they
have inspirited themselves with draughts of Soma juice.

Ye drave away, ye put to death the foemen, and took great vengeance with your
murdering weapons.

5 So, of a truth, Indra and Soma, Heroes,
ye burst the stable of the kine and horses,
The stable which the bar of stone obstructed; and piercing through set free the
habitations.

HYMN XXIX.   *Indra.*

1. COME, lauded, unto us with powers and
succours, O Indra, with thy Tawny
Steeds; exulting,
Past even the foeman's manifold libations,
glorified with our hymns, true Wealth-
bestower.

2 Man's Friend, to this our sacrifice he
cometh marking how he is called by
Soma-pressers.
Fearless, and conscious that his Steeds are
noble, he joyeth with the Soma-pouring
heroes.

3 Make his ears hear, that he may show his
vigour and may be joyful in the way
he loveth.
May mighty Indra pouring forth in bounty
bestow on us good roads and perfect
safety;

4 He who with succour comes to his implorer,
the singer here who with his song invites
him;
He who himself sets to the pole swift Coursers, he who hath hundreds, thousands,
Thunder-wielder.

5 O Indra Maghavan, by thee protected
may we be thine, princes and priests
and singers,
Sharing the riches sent from lofty heaven
which yields much food, and all desire
its bounty.

---

5 *Ye burst the stable of the king and horses*: liberated
the kine, that is, the imprisoned waters which fertilized
the earth and caused cattle and horses to multiply.

---

1 *Past*: or, over, that is, let not the offerings of our
enemies detain thee.

2 *Heroes*: eminent men who institute sacrifices.

4 *Hundreds, thousands*: apparently, of treasures, and
not horses as Sāyaṇa explains.

5 *Princes*: the institutors of the sacrifice, the *Sūris*.
The phraseology of the second line is somewhat obscure.
Professor Wilson renders it 'participant with thee for the
sake of distributing brilliant wealth, and abundant food,
entitled to (our) commendation.' Professor Ludwig in
his Commentary suggests that the meaning may be
that the institutors of the sacrifice are to distribute the
wealth, and the priests to receive it.

HYMN XXX.   *Indra.*

1. O INDRA, Vṛtra-slayer, none is better,
mightier than thou:
Verily there is none like thee.

2 Like chariot-wheels these people all together follow after thee:
Thou ever art renowned as Great.

3 Not even all the gathered Gods conquered
thee, Indra, in the war,
When thou didst lengthen days by night.

4 When for the sake of those oppressed, and
Kutsa as he battled,
Thou stolest away the Sun's car-wheel.

5 When, fighting singly, Indra, thou o'erca-
mest all the furious Gods, thou slewest
those who strove with thee.

6 When also for a mortal man, Indra, thou
speddest forth the Sun,
And holpest Etaśa with might.

7 What? Vṛtra-slayer, art not thou,
Maghavan, fiercest in thy wrath?
So hast thou quelled the demon too.

8 And this heroic deed of might thou, Indra,
also hast achieved,
That thou didst smite to death the Dame,
Heaven's Daughter, meditating ill.

9 Thou, Indra, Mighty One, didst crush
Uṣas, though Daughter of the Sky.
When lifting up herself in pride.

10 Then from her chariot Uṣas fled, affrighted, from her ruined car.
When the strong God had shattered it.

11 So there this car of Uṣas lay, broken to
pieces, in Vipāś,
And she herself fled far away.

---

3 This seems to be the meaning of the text,—a
contest between Indra and the rest of the Gods—and
stanza 5 appears to confirm this interpretation. Professor Wilson, following Sāyaṇa, translates: 'Verily all
the gods with thee (for) their strength, have warred
(with the *Asuras*); wherefore thou hast destroyed them
by day and by night.'
When thou didst lengthen days: didst prolong the day
into the night. Cf. Joshua X 1.3.

4 *Stolest away the Sun's car-wheel*: an eclipse of the
Sun, perhaps, is intended; or the meaning may be
merely that the Sun's course was stayed, as in stanza 3.

5 *All the furious Gods*: according to Sāyaṇa, 'all
those who strove against the Gods.'

6 *And holpest Etaśa*: that is, the return of day on
some particular occasion is attributed to Indra's intervention on behalf of his favourite. See Index.

7 *The demon*: Vṛtra, the son of Danu.

8 The destruction by Indra of the chariot of Uṣas
or Dawn appears to mean the extinction of her light
after the rising of the Sun. So in II. 15. 6. Indra is
said to have 'crushed with his thunderbolt the car of
Uṣas, rending her slow steeds with his rapid Coursers.'
The myth is alluded to in other passages also. See X.
138. 5.

11 *In Vipāś*: or on the bank of that river.

12 Thou, Indra, didst with magic power
   resist the overflowing stream
   Who spread her waters o'er the land.

13 Valiantly didst thou seize and take the
   store which Śuṣṇa had amassed,
   When thou didst crush his fortresses.

14 Thou, Indra, also smotest down Kulitara's
   son Śambara,
   The Dāsa, from the lofty hill.

15 Of Dāsa Varcin's thou didst slay the
   hundred thousand and the five,
   Crushed like the fellies of a car.

16 So Indra, Lord of Heroes, Powers, caused
   the unwedded damsel's son,
   The castaway, to share the lauds.

17 So sapient Indra, Lord of Might, brought
   Turvaśa and Yadu, those
   Who feared the flood, in safety o'er.

18 Arṇa and Citraratha, both Āryas, thou,
   Indra, slewest swift,
   On yonder side of Sarayu.

19 Thou, Vṛtraslayer, didst conduct those
   two forlorn, the blind, the lame:
   None may attain this bliss of thine.

20 For Divodāsa, him who brought oblations,
   Indra overthrew
   A hundred fortresses of stone.

21 The thirty thousand Dāsas he with magic
   power and weapons sent
   To slumber, for Dabhīti's sake.

22 As such, O Vṛtra-slayer, thou art general
   Lord of kine for all,
   Thou Shaker of all things that be.

23 Indra, whatever deed of might thou hast
   this day to execute,
   None be there now to hinder it.

24 O Watchful One, may Aryaman the God
   give thee all goodly things.
   May Pūṣan, Bhaga, and the God Karūḷatī
   give all things fair.

HYMN XXXI.   Indra.

1. WITH what help will he come to us,
   wonderful, ever-waxing Friend;
   With what most mighty company?

2 What genuine and most liberal draught
   will spirit thee with juice to burst
   Open e'en strongly-guarded wealth?

3 Do thou who art Protector of us thy
   friends who praise thee
   With hundred aids approach us.

4 Like as a courser's circling wheel, so turn
   thee hitherward to us,
   Attracted by the hymns of men.

5 Thou seekest as it were thine own stations
   with swift descent of powers:
   I share thee even with the Sun.

6 What time thy courage and his wheels
   together, Indra, run their course
   With thee and with the Sun alike,

7 So even, Lord of Power and Might, the
   people call thee Maghavan,
   Giver, who pauses not to think.

8 And verily to him who toils and presses
   Soma juice for thee
   Thou quickly givest ample wealth.

---

12 *The overflowing stream* : or, possibly, some stream called Vibāli, the exact meaning of the word being doubtful.

14 *Kulitara's son* : this is Sāyaṇa's explanation of *kaulitarám.*

15 *Of Dāsa Varcin's*): of the followers of the demon or savage Varcin. See II. 14. 6. *And the five* : the position of *pañca* in the stanza seems to indicate that it is taken separately. Sāyaṇa prefixes it to *śatá,* making the number slain a thousand and five hundred.

Crushed like the fellies of a car : '(surrounding) him like the fellies (round the spokes of a wheel).'—Wilson.

The unwedded damsel's son : the son of Agrū, according to Sāyaṇa. See IV. 19. 9.

17 *Turvaśa and Yadu* : so I. 174. 9 'When o'er the flood thou broughtest them, O Hero, thou keptest Turvaśa and Yadu safely.'

Who feared the flood : literally, 'non-bathers' (*asnātārā*), meaning probably unable to swim.

18 *Arṇa and Citraratha* : two kings, says the Scholiast, 'presuming on their dignity as Āryas and devoid of faith in, or devotion to, Indra.' *Sarayu* here is probably some river in the Panjāb, and not the Sarayu of Oudh the modern Sarjū. Turvaśa and Yadu may perhaps have crossed the river, and under the protection of Indra conquered two Āryan chiefs whose lands lay beyond it.

19 *The blind, the lame* : see II. 13. 12. where one man only, the outcast, of Parāvṛj, is spoken of as 'the halt and blind.'

20 *Divodāsa* : see Index.

21 *Dabhīti* : a Ṛṣi favoured by Indra. See Index.

24 *Karūḷatī* : from the position of the word in the stanza would appear to be the name of a separate God, but Sāyaṇa (who is followed by Professors Roth and Grassmann as well as Wilson) takes it as an epithet of Pūṣan, i.e. the broken-toothed or toothless God. 'According to the Purāṇas, Pūṣan had his teeth knocked out by Vīrabhadra's followers at Dakṣa's sacrifice.'—Wilson. The institutor of the sacrifice appears to be addressed in this verse which is probably a later addition to the original hymn.

---

2 *Genuine and most liberal* : producing good results and causing thee to be most bountiful. *Strongly-guarded wealth*: to burst open the treasure-houses of our enemies and give us their contents ; or the allusion may be to the waters shut up in the clouds.

4 *By the hymns* : literally, 'by the teams,' *niyudbhiḥ,* that is, strings of verses, hymns, or praises.

5 *With swift descent of powers* : by the natural and spontaneous outflow of divine strength, as water pours down a precipice.

I share thee : 'I glorify thee together with the Sun.'—Wilson.

7 *Maghavan* : the rich and munificent One.

9 No, not a hundred hinderers can check thy
   gracious bounty's flow,
   Nor thy great deeds when thou wilt act.

10 May thine assistance keep us safe, thy
   hundred and thy thousand aids :
   May all thy favours strengthen us.

11 Do thou elect us this place for friendship
   and prosperity,
   And great celestial opulence.

12 Favour us, Indra, evermore with overflowing store of wealth:
   With all thy succours aid thou us.

13 With new protections, Indra, like an
   archer, open thou for us
   The stables that are filled with kine.

14 Our chariot, Indra, boldly moves endued
   with splendour, ne'er repulsed,
   Winning for us both kine and steeds.

15 O Sūrya, make our fame to be most excellent among the Gods,
   Most lofty as the heaven on high.

HYMN XXXII.   *Indra.*

1. O THOU who slewest Vṛtra, come, O
   Indra, hither to our side,
   Mighty One with thy mighty aids.

2 Swift and impetuous art thou, wondrous
   amid the well-dressed folk:
   Thou doest marvels for our help.

3 Even with the weak thou smitest down him
   who is stronger, with thy strength
   The mighty, with the Friends thou hast.

4 O Indra, we are close to thee; to thee we
   sing aloud our songs:
   Help and defend us, even us.

5 As such, O Caster of the Stone, come with
   thy succours wonderful,
   Blameless, and irresistible.

6 May we be friends of one like thee, O
   Indra, with the wealth of kine,
   Comrades for lively energy.

7 For thou, O Indra, art alone the Lord of
   strength that comes from kine :
   So grant thou us abundant food.

8 They turn thee not another way, when,
   lauded, Lover of the Song,
   Thou wilt give wealth to those who praise.

9 The Gotamas have sung their song of
   praise to thee that thou mayst give,
   Indra, for lively energy.

10 We will declare thy hero deeds, what Dāsa
   forts thou brakest down,
   Attacking them in rapturous joy.

11 The sages sing those manly deeds which,
   Indra, Lover of the Song,
   Thou wroughtest when the Soma flowed.

12 Indra, the Gotamas who bring thee praises
   have grown strong by thee.
   Give them renown with hero sons.

13 For, Indra, verily thou art the general
   treasure even of all :
   Thee, therefore, do we invocate.

14 Excellent Indra, turn to us : glad thee
   among us with the juice
   Of Somas, Soma-drinker thou.

15 May praise from us who think on thee,
   O Indra, bring thee near to us.
   Turn thy two Bay Steeds hitherward.

16 Eat of our sacrificial cake : rejoice thee
   in the songs we sing.
   Even as a lover in his bride.

17 To Indra for a thousand steeds well-trained
   and fleet of foot we pray,
   And hundred jars of Soma juice.

18 We make a hundred of thy kine, yea, and
   a thousand, hasten nigh :
   So let thy bounty come to us.

19 We have obtained, a gift from thee, ten
   water-ewers wrought of gold :
   Thou, Vṛtra-slayer, givest much.

20 A bounteous Giver, give us much, bring
   much and not a trifling gift :
   Much, Indra, wilt thou fain bestow.

21 O Vṛtra-slayer, thou art famed in many a
   place as bountiful
   Hero, thy bounty let us share.

22 I praise thy pair of Tawny Steeds, wise
   Son of him who giveth kine
   Terrify not the cows with these.

---

10 *In rapturous joy* : in exhilaration produced by the
Soma juice.

17 *Jars* : a *khārī* is properly a measure of grain, and
by metonymy a vessel, jar, or pitcher, containing that
quantity, which is said to be equal to about three of
our bushels.

22. *Wise Son of him who giveth kine* : Indra himself is
the special giver of cattle, and this attribute of his may
perhaps, as Professor Ludwig conjectures, be personified in
an imaginary father Goṣā, the winner or bestower of kine.
Sāyaṇa would force on *naṭāt*, son, the meaning *na pātayitaḥ*
'thou who dost not cast down' (thy worshippers). *With
these* : two horses of thine. The meaning of this last
Pāda is uncertain.

---

2 *Amid the well-dressed folk* : the adjective *chitriṇīṣu*,
feminine plural in the locative case, stands without a
substantive, and Sāyaṇa supplies *prajāsu*, people ; well-
dressed, perhaps, for a religious ceremony, or possibly,
armed for war.

5 *Caster of the Stone* : wielder of the thunderbolt.

23 Like two slight images of girls, unrobed,
    upon a new-wrought post,
  So shine the Bay Steeds in their course.

24 For me the Bays are ready when I start,
    or start not, with the dawn, Innocuous
    in the ways they take.

HYMN XXXIII.   *Ṛbhus.*

1. I SEND my voice as herald to the Ṛbhus;
    I crave the white cow for the overspreading.
  Wind-sped, the Skilful Ones in rapid motion
    have in an instant compassed round the
    heaven.

2 What time the Ṛbhus had with care and
    marvels done proper service to assist
    their Parents,
  They won the friendship of the Gods; the
    Sages carried away the fruit of their
    devotion.

3 May they who made their Parents, who
    were lying like posts that moulder, young
    again for ever,—
  May Vāja, Vibhvan, Ṛbhu, joined with
    Indra, protect our sacrifice, the Soma-
    lovers.

4 As for a year the Ṛbhus kept the Milch-
    cow, throughout a year fashioned and
    formed her body,
  And through a year's space still sustained
    her brightness, through these their labours
    they were made immortal.

5 Two beakers let us make,—thus said the
    eldest. Let us make three,—this was the
    younger's sentence.
  Four beakers let us make,—thus spoke the
    youngest. Tvaṣṭar approved this rede
    of yours, O Ṛbhus.

6 The men spake truth and even so they
    acted : this Godlike way of theirs the
    Ṛbhus followed.
  And Tvaṣṭar, when he looked on the four
    beakers resplendent as the day, was moved
    with envy.

7 When for twelve days the Ṛbhus joyed
    reposing as guests of him who never
    may be hidden,
  They made fair fertile fields, they brought
    the rivers. Plants spread o'er deserts,
    waters filled the hollows.

8 May they who formed the swift car, bear-
    ing Heroes, and the Cow omniform and
    all-impelling,
  Even may they form wealth for us,—the
    Ṛbhus, dexterous-handed, deft in work
    and gracious.

9 So in their work the Gods had satisfaction,
    pondering it with thought and mental
    insight.
  The Gods' expert artificer was Vāja,
    Indra's Ṛbhukṣan, Varuṇa's was Vibhvan.

10 They who, made glad with sacrifice and
    praises, wrought the two Bays, his docile
    Steeds, for Indra,—
  Ṛbhus, as those who wish a friend to
    prosper, bestow upon us gear and growth
    of riches.

11 This day have they set gladdening drink
    before you. Not without toil are Gods
    inclined to friendship.
  Therefore do ye who are so great, O
    Ṛbhus, vouchsafe us treasures at this
    third libation.

HYMN XXXIV.   *Ṛbhus.*

1. To this our sacrifice come Ṛbhu, Vibhvan,
    Vāja, and Indra with the gift of riches,
  Because this day hath Dhiṣaṇā the God-
    dess set drink for you : the gladdening
    draughts have reached you.

---

23 *Images of girls* : perhaps as caryatids, but the
passage is obscure. Professor Wilson translates : 'Like
two puppets on an arranged, new, and slender stage '

24 According to Sāyaṇa, Let thy inoffensive bay
horses give me a sufficiency at sacrifices whether I go
to them in a car drawn by oxen or without a car so
drawn, that is, on foot.

---

1 *For the overspreading* : a technical expression for
pouring the milk into or over the Soma juice. 'For the
dilution (of the *Soma* libation).'—Wilson. For the
Ṛbhus, see Index.

5 *Two beakers* : or sacrificial ladles. See I. 20. 6.

---

7 *Him who never may be hidden* : the Sun; Savitar.

8 *The swift car* : the three-wheeled chariot which
bears the Aśvins.

The Cow omniform : or of every hue. 'Indra hath
yoked his Bays, the Aśvins' car is horsed, Bṛhaspati
hath brought the Cow of every hue.'—I. 161. 6.

11 *At this third libation* : in the evening, the proper
time for drink-offerings to the Ṛbhus.

  The myth of the Ṛbhus is exceedingly obscure.
They are regarded as ancient sacrificers who attained
immortality as the reward of their pious labours. The
parents whom they restored to youth appear to be the
universal parents, heaven and earth, rejuvenated each
morning and especially in the spring. The milch-cow
(stanza 4) is perhaps the earth, regarded as the productive soil. The twelve days (stanza 7) are perhaps, as
Ludwig suggests, the twelve nights *vratyāḥ prajāpateḥ*, or
'holy to Prajāpati.' See Hymns of the Atharva-veda,
IV. 11. 11. For careful study and ingenious interpretations of the myth, see F. Nève, *Essai sur le mythe
des Ṛbhavas* : Paris : 1847 : and M. Bergaigne, *La
Religion Védique*, II. 406—413; III. 51—55.

Dhiṣaṇā : a divinity closely connected with Soma
and presiding over prosperity.

2 Knowing your birth and rich in gathered
treasure, Ṛbhus, rejoice together with
the Ṛtus.
   The gladdening draughts and wisdom have
   approached you : send ye us riches with
   good store of heroes.
3 For you was made this sacrifice, O Ṛbhus,
which ye, like men, won for yourselves
aforetime.
   To you come all who find in you their
   pleasure : ye all were—even the two
   elder—Vājas.
4 Now for the mortal worshipper, O Heroes,
for him who served you, was the gift
of riches.
   Drink, Vājas, Ṛbhus ! unto you is offered,
   to gladden you, the third and great
   libation.
5 Come to us, Heroes, Vājas and Ṛbhukṣans, glorified for the sake of mighty
treasure.
   These draughts approach you as the day
   is closing, as cows, whose calves are
   newly-born, their stable.
6 Come to this sacrifice of ours, ye Children
of Strength, invoked with humble
adoration.
   Drink of this meath, Wealth-givers, joined
   with Indra with whom ye are in full
   accord, ye Princes.
7 Close knit with Varuṇa drink the Soma,
Indra; close-knit, Hymn-lover ! with
the Maruts drink it :
   Close-knit with drinkers first, who drink
   in season; close-knit with heavenly
   Dames who give us treasures.
8 Rejoice in full accord with the Ādityas,
in concord with the Parvatas, O Ṛbhus;
   In full accord with Savitar, Divine One;
   in full accord with floods that pour forth
   riches.

9 Ṛbhus, who helped their Parents and the
Aśvins, who formed the Milch-cow and
the pair of horses,
   Made armour, set the heaven and earth
   asunder,—far-reaching Heroes, they
   have made good offspring.
10 Ye who have wealth in cattle and in
booty, in heroes, in rich sustenance and
treasure,
   Such, O ye Ṛbhus, first to drink, rejoicing, give unto us and those who laud
   our present.
11 Ye were not far : we have not left you
thirsting, blameless in this our sacrifice,
O Ṛbhus.
   Rejoice you with the Maruts and with
   Indra, with the Kings, Gods ! that ye
   may give us riches.

HYMN XXXV.   *Ṛbhus.*

1. COME hither, O ye Sons of Strength, ye
Ṛbhus; stay not afar, ye Children of
Sudhanvan.
   At this libation is your gift of treasure.
   Let gladdening draughts approach you
   after Indra's.
2 Hither is come the Ṛbhus' gift of riches;
here was the drinking of the well-pressed
Soma,
   Since by dexterity and skill as craftsmen
   ye made the single chalice to be fourfold.
3 Ye made fourfold the chalice that was
single : ye spake these words and said,
O Friend, assist us;
   Then, Vājas ! gained the path of life
   eternal, deft-handed Ṛbhus, to the Gods'
   assembly.
4 Out of what substance was that chalice
fashioned which ye made fourfold by
your art and wisdom?
   Now for the gladdening draught press out
   the liquor, and drink, O Ṛbhus, of the
   meath of Soma.
5 Ye with your cunning made your Parents
youthful; the cup, for Gods to drink,
ye formed with cunning;
   With cunning, Ṛbhus, rich in treasure,
   fashioned the two swift Tawny Steeds
   who carry Indra.

2 *Knowing your birth* : knowing how you have
attained immortality and deification. *The Ṛtus* : the
seasons personified and honoured as deities. The Ṛbhus
as cosmic powers are closely connected with them.

3 *Vājas* : that is, although Vāja is strictly the
name of the youngest of the three only, you are all
entitled to that appellation which means active, strong,
or spirited. Professor Grassmann translates : 'ihr alle
seid die ersten hier, O Vadscha's;' ye are all the first
(entitled to precedence) here, O V. jas; but the word
utá is then left untranslated.

4 *The third and great libation* : see the preceding
hymn, stanza 11.

5 *Ṛbhukṣans* : Ṛbhukṣan is another name of Ṛbhu,
the eldest of the three.

7 *Drinkers first* : those who claim and receive the
libation first ; here, apparently, the Ṛtus or Seasons.

8 *Parvatas* : Gods presiding over mountains and
clouds.

9 *Made armour* : for the Gods.
10 *Those who laud our present* : who accompany
with hymns, and so recommend to the Gods, our
oblation.
11 *The Kings* : the other Gods, or the Gods in
general.

———

1 *After Indra's* : libations having been offered to
Indra at dawn and at noonday. See stanza 7.

3 *O Friend* : Agni.

5 *Cunning* : power and skill as craftsmen ; *śácyā.*

6 Whoso pours out for you, when days are
closing, the sharp libation for your joy,
O Vājas,
For him, O mighty Ṛbhus, ye, rejoicing,
have fashioned wealth with plenteous
store of heroes.

7 Lord of Bay Steeds, at dawn the juice thou
drankest : thine, only thine, is the noonday libation.
Now drink thou with the wealth-bestowing
Ṛbhus, whom for their skill thou madest
friends, O Indra.

8 Ye, whom your artist skill hath raised to
Godhead have set you down above
in heaven like falcons.
So give us riches, Children of Sudhanvan,
O Sons of Strength; ye have become
immortal.

9 The third libation, that bestoweth treasure,
which ye have won by skill, ye dexter-
ous-handed,—
This drink hath been effused for you, O
Ṛbhus : drink it with high delight,
with joy like Indra's.

HYMN XXXVI.   Ṛbhus.

1. THE car that was not made for horses or
for reins, three-wheeled, worthy of lauds,
rolls round the firmament.
That is the great announcement of your
Deity, that, O ye Ṛbhus, ye sustain the
earth and heaven.

2 Ye Sapient Ones who made the lightly-
rolling car out of your mind, by thought,
the car that never errs,
You, being such, to drink of this drink-
offering, you, O ye Vājas, and ye Ṛbhus,
we invoke.

3 O Vājas, Ṛbhus, reaching far, among the
Gods this was your exaltation gloriously
declared,
In that your aged Parents, worn with
length of days, ye wrought again to
youth so that they moved at will.

4 The chalice that was single ye have made
fourfold, and by your wisdom brought
the Cow forth from the hide.
So quickly, mid the Gods, ye gained immortal life. Vājas and Ṛbhus, your great
work must be extolled.

6 *Fashioned wealth* : made or fabricated as craftsmen.

1 *The car* : the three-wheeled chariot of the Aśvins,
drawn by asses, *i.e.* the grey clouds of morning
twilight.
3 *Ye wrought again to youth* : forms of the verb
takṣ, to form, fabricate, fashion, as a carpenter does
with wood, are used in this and other hymns to the
Ṛbhus, the artificers, instead of words signifying, restoring, giving, producing, and the like.

5 Wealth from the Ṛbhus is most glorious
in renown, that which the Heroes, famed
for vigour, have produced.
In synods must be sung the car which
Vibhvan wrought: that which ye favour,
Gods ! is famed among mankind.

6 Strong is the steed, the man a sage in
eloquence, the bowman is a hero hard
to beat in fight,
Great store of wealth and manly power
hath he obtained whom Vāja, Vibhvan,
Ṛbhus have looked kindly on.

7 To you hath been assigned the fairest ornament, the hymn of praise : Vājas and
Ṛbhus, joy therein;
For ye have lore and wisdom and poetic
skill : as such, with this our prayer we
call on you to come.

8 According to the wishes of our hearts may
ye, who have full knowledge of all the
delights of men,
Fashion for us, O Ṛbhus, power and
splendid wealth, rich in high courage,
excellent, and vital strength.

9 Bestowing on us here riches and offspring,
here fashion fame for us befitting heroes.
Vouchsafe us wealth of splendid sort, O
Ṛbhus, that we may make us more
renowned than others.

HYMN XXXVII.   Ṛbhus.

1. COME to our sacrifice, Vājas, Ṛbhukṣans,
Gods, by the paths which Gods are wont
to travel,
As ye, gay Gods, accept in splendid
weather the sacrifice among these folk
of Manus.

2 May these rites please you in your heart
and spirit; may the drops clothed in oil
this day approach you.
May the abundant juices bear you onward
to power and strength, and, when
imbibed, delight you.

3 Your threefold going near is God-appointed, so praise is given you, Vājas and
Ṛbhukṣans.

5 *The car which Vibhvan wrought* : or the sacrificial
cup; the text has only *vibhvataṣṭḍh*, that which was
fabricated by Vibhvan, or as Sāyaṇa says, by the
Ṛbhus.
8 *According to the wishes of our hearts* : or, according
to S yaṇa, on account of the praises which we have
offered to you.

1 *In splendid weather* : after the rains, when pro-
tracted sacrifices are not interrupted by storms. *These
folk of Manus* : Aryan men.
3 *Threefold going near* : coming to the altar at the
three daily sacrifices.

So, Manus-like, mid younger folk I offer,
  to you who are aloft in heaven, the
  Soma.
4 Strong, with fair chains of gold and jaws
  of iron, ye have a splendid car and well-
  fed horses.
  Ye Sons of Strength, ye progeny of Indra,
  to you the best is offered to delight
  you.
5 Ṛbhukṣans ! him, for handy wealth, the
  mightiest comrade in the fight,
  Him, Indra's equal, we invoke, most
  bounteous ever, rich in steeds.
6 The mortal man whom, Ṛbhus, ye and
  Indra favour with your help,
  Must be successful, by his thoughts, at
  sacrifice and with the steed.
7 O Vājas and Ṛbhukṣans, free for us the
  paths to sacrifice,
  Ye Princes, lauded, that we may press forward to each point of heaven.
8 O Vājas and Ṛbhukṣans, ye Nāsatyas,
  Indra, bless this wealth,
  And, before other men's, the steed, that
  ample riches may be won.

HYMN XXXVIII.   *Dadhikrās.*

1. FROM you two came the gifts in days
  aforetime which Trasadasyu granted to
  the Pūrus.
  Ye gave the winner of our fields and
  plough-lands, and the strong smiter who
  subdued the Dasyus.

5 *Him* : Ṛbhu, as representing his brothers also.
6 *By his thoughts* : referring to the worshipper who
by his devout thoughts and acts will obtain success in
sacrifice. *With the steed* : referring to the warrior who
will be victorious in battle with his war-chariot.
7 *Press onward to each point of heaven* : that is, be
everywhere victorious, achieve, what was in later times
the object of great kings' highest ambition, the *digvijaya*
or conquest of lands in every direction.
8 *Nāsatyas* : Aśvins. *The steeds* : either the war-
horses in general, or, as Professor Ludwig suggests, a
particular horse that is to be sacrificed.

Dadhikrās, in the nominative case, or Dadhikrā in
the crude form, is the name of a mythical being
often mentioned in the Ṛgveda and the actual subject
of this hymn and three others. He is described as a kind
of divine horse and probably, like Tārkṣya, is a personification of the morning sun ; sometimes he is
considered as a creation of heaven and earth, sometimes
of Mitra Varuṇa, and is invoked in the morning together with Agni, Uṣas, and the Aśvins. The name is
probably derived from *dadhi*, thickened milk, and *kṛī*
to scatter, in allusion to the rising sun spreading dew
and hoar-frost like milk. Aeschylus. See St. P.
Lexicon, or M. Williams's Dictionary. Professor
Ludwig thinks that the hymn is a fragment, referring
not to the mythical being but to an actual war-horse
bearing his name.
1 *From you two* : Mitra and Varuṇa, according to

2 And ye gave mighty Dadhikrās, the giver
  of many gifts, who visiteth all people,
  Impetuous hawk, swift and of varied
  colour, like a brave King whom each
  true man must honour.
3 Whom, as 'twere down a precipice, swift
  rushing, each Pūru praises and his heart
  rejoices,—
  Springing forth like a hero fain for battle,
  whirling the car and flying like the
  tempest.
4 Who gaineth precious booty in the combats
  and moveth, winning spoil, among the
  cattle;
  Shown in bright colour, looking on the
  assemblies, beyond the churl, to worship
  of the living.
5 Loudly the folk cry after him in battles,
  as 'twere a thief who steals away a
  garment;
  Speeding to glory, or a herd of cattle,
  even as a hungry falcon swooping downward.
6 And, fain to come forth first amid these
  armies, this way and that with rows of
  cars he rushes,
  Gay like a bridesman, making him a garland, tossing the dust, champing the rein
  that holds him.
7 And that strong Steed, victorious and faithful, obedient with his body in the
  combat,
  Speeding straight on amid the swiftly
  pressing, casts o'er his brows the dust
  he tosses upward.
8 And at his thunder, like the roar of heaven,
  those who attack tremble and are
  affrighted;
  For when he fights against embattled
  thousands, dread is he in his striving;
  none may stay him.

stanza 2 of the following hymn ; Heaven and Earth,
according to Sāyaṇa. *Trasadasyu* : the king has been
mentioned before (I. 112. 14.) as a favourite of the
Aśvins. Professor Ludwig points out that, to accord
with what is said in IV. 42. 8., the reading should be
Trasadasyum ; 'ye who gave Trasadasyu to the Pūrus,'
the verb *nitoṣé* standing for the dual *nitoṣetne.. The Pūrus* :
one of the Āryan tribes. See Index.
4 *Beyond the churl* : passing by the niggard who
offers no oblations, and looking kindly on the sacrifice
of the living man or devout worshipper. The word
aratim apparently = *drātim*.
5 *Speeding* : referring to Dadhikrās seeking fame
and booty.
6 *Making him a garland* : of the chariots that
surround him.
7 *Amid the swiftly pressing* : the text has no substantive : *senāsu*, hosts, or *vikṣu*, people, may be understood.

9 The people praise the overpowering swiftness of this fleet Steed who giveth men
abundance.
Of him they say when drawing back from
battle. Dadhikrās hath sped forward with
his thousands.

10 Dadhikrās hath o'erspread the Fivefold
People with vigour, as the Sun lightens
the waters.
May the strong Steed who winneth hundreds, thousands, requite with sweetness
these my words and praises.

HYMN XXXIX   *Dadhikrās.*

1. Now give we praise to Dadhikrās the
rapid, and mention in our laud the
Earth and Heaven.
May the Dawns flushing move me to
exertion, and bear me safely over every
trouble.

2 I praise the mighty Steed who fills my
spirit, the Stallion Dadhikrāvan rich in
bounties,
Whom, swift of foot and shining bright as
Agni, ye, Varuṇa and Mitra, gave to
Pūrus.

3 Him who hath honoured, when the flame
is kindled at break of dawn, the Courser
Dadhikrāvan,
Him, of one mind with Varuṇa and Mitra
may Aditi make free from all transgression.

4 When we remember mighty Dadhikrāvan
our food and strength, then the blest
name of Maruts,
Varuṇa, Mitra, we invoke for welfare, and
Agni, and the thunder-wielding Indra.

5 Both sides invoke him as they call on
Indra when they stir forth and turn to
sacrificing.
To us have Varuṇa and Mitra granted
the Courser Dadhikrās, a guide for
mortals.

6 So have I glorified with praise strong
Dadhikrāvan, conquering Steed.
Sweet may he make our mouths ; may he
prolong the days we have to live.

2 *Dadhikrāvan* : a lengthened, interchangeable form
of Dadhikrās.
3 *Aditi* : here a male deity, probably Agni.
5 *When they stir forth and turn to sacrificing* : when
men who are going out on a foray, or to battle, offer
sacrifices for their success. Or the meaning may be,
both those who go out to battle and those who remain
at home and sacrifice.
6 *Sweet may he make our mouths* : purify our lips if
we have spoken wicked words.

HYMN XL.   *Dadhikrāvan.*

1. LET us recite the praise of Dadhikrāvan :
may all the Mornings move me to
exertion ;
Praise of the Lord of Waters, Dawn, and
Agni, Bṛhaspati Son of Aṅgiras, and
Sūrya.

2 Brave, seeking war and booty, dwelling
with the good and with the swift, may
he hasten the food of Dawn.
May he be the true, the fleet, the lover of
the course, the bird-like Dadhikrāvan,
bring food, strength, and light.

3 His pinion, rapid runner, fans him on his
way, as of a bird that hastens onward
to its aim,
And, as it were a falcon's gliding through
the air, strikes Dadhikrāvan's side as he
speeds on with might.

4 Bound by the neck and by the flanks and
by the mouth, the vigorous Courser lends
new swiftness to his speed.
Drawing himself together, as his strength
allows, Dadhikrās springs along the
windings of the paths.

5 The Haṁsa homed in light, the Vasu in
mid-air, the priest beside the altar, in
the house the guest,
Dweller in noblest place, mid men, in
truth, in sky, born of flood, kine, truth,
mountain, he is holy Law.

HYMN XLI.   *Indra-Varuṇa.*

1. WHAT laud, O Indra-Varuṇa, with oblation, hath like the Immortal Priest
obtained your favour ?

1. *The Lord* : literally, the conqueror, that is, the
winner, the obtainer.
2 *Hasten the food of Dawn* : 'accept the (sacrificial)
food at the time of the desirable dawn.'—Wilson. This
line is difficult, and the meaning is somewhat obscure.
4 *Lends new swiftness to his speed* : I adopt Sāyaṇa's
interpretation, *tvarayati, gantum*. Prof Eggeling translates
more literally 'speedeth after the whip' (Satapatha-
Brāhmaṇa, V. 1. 5. 19).
5 In this stanza Dadhikrās is identified with the
eternal Law of the universe and with all types or forms
of the Supreme Being. He is the Haṁsa, the Swan
of heaven, or the Sun, the Vasu in mid-air or the
Wind, Agni as the priest and guest of men. As the
Sun he is born from, or amid, kine or rays of light and
springs up from the celestial ocean and the mountains
of cloud behind which he rises. See Professor Wilson's
note on the passage. The stanza is explained also in
Śatapatha Brāhmaṇa VI. 7. 3. 11 (Sacred Books of
the East, XLI. p. 281).

The hymn is addressed to Indra-Varuṇa, that is,
Indra and Varuṇa, conjointly.
1 *The Immortal Priest* : Agni.

Hath our effectual laud, addressed with homage, touched you, O Indra-Varuṇa, in spirit ?

2 He who with dainty food hath won you, Indra and Varuṇa, Gods, as his allies to friendship,
layeth the Vṛtras and his foes in battles, and through your mighty favours is made famous.

3 Indra and Varuṇa are most liberal givers of treasure to the men who toil to serve them,
When they, as Friends inclined to friendship, honoured with dainty food, delight in flowing Soma.

4 Indra and Varuṇa, ye hurl, O Mighty, on him your strongest flashing bolt of thunder
Who treats us ill, the robber and oppressor : measure on him your overwhelming vigour.

5 O Indra-Varuṇa, be ye the lovers of this my song, as steers who love the milch-cow.
Milk may it yield us as, gone forth to pasture, the great Cow pouring out her thousand rivers.

6 For fertile fields, for worthy sons and grandsons, for the Sun's beauty and for steer-like vigour,
May Indra-Varuṇa with gracious favours work marvels for us in the stress of battle.

7 For you, as Princes, for your ancient kindness, good comrades of the man who seeks for booty,
We choose to us for the dear bond of friendship, most liberal Heroes bringing bliss like parents.

8 Showing their strength, these hymns for grace, Free-givers ! have gone to you, devoted, as to battle,
For glory have they gone, as milk to Soma, to Indra-Varuṇa my thoughts and praises.

9 To Indra and to Varuṇa, desirous of gaining wealth have these my thoughts proceeded.
They have come nigh to you as treasure-lovers, like mares, fleet-footed, eager for the glory.

10 May we ourselves be lords of during riches, of ample sustenance for car and horses.
So may the Twain who work with newest succours bring yoked teams hitherward to us and riches.

11 Come with your mighty succours, O ye Mighty ; come, Indra-Varuṇa, to us in battle.
What time the flashing arrows play in combat, may we through you be winners in the contest.

HYMN XLII.   *Indra-Varuṇa.*

1. I AM the royal Ruler, mine is empire, as mine who sway all life are all Immortals.
Varuṇa's will the Gods obey and follow. I am the King of men's most lofty cover.

2 I am King Varuṇa. To me were given these first existing high celestial powers.
Varuṇa's will the Gods obey and follow. I am the King of men's most lofty cover.

3 I Varuṇa am Indra : in their greatness, these the two wide deep fairly-fashioned regions,
These the two world-halves have I, even as Tvaṣṭar knowing all beings, joined and held together.

4 I made to flow the moisture-shedding waters, and set the heaven firm in the seat of Order.
By Law the Son of Aditi, Law Observer, hath spread abroad the world in three-fold measure.

5 Heroes with noble horses, fain for battle, selected warriors, call on me in combat.
I Indra Maghavan, excite the conflict ; I stir the dust, Lord of surpassing vigour.

6 All this I did. The Gods' own conquering power never impedeth me whom none opposeth.

---

11 The hymn is a prayer for aid in a coming battle.

———

Varuṇa and his supersessor Indra severally urge their claims to superiority, and the poet decides between them. Cf. X. 124.

1 Varuṇa is the speaker of the first four stanzas. *Men's most lofty cover* : the highest heaven.

3 *Indra* : all that Indra represents, Prince and King of all.
As Tvaṣṭar : or, as their great artificer.

4 *In the seat of Order* : in the place appointed by Law or the eternal Order of the universe. *The Son of Aditi* : I, Varuṇa.

5 Indra is the speaker of this and of the following stanza.

---

5 *Milk may it yield us* : bring us a rich reward. *The great Cow* : of plenty.

6 *For the Sun's beauty* : for long life wherein we may continue to see the glory of the sun.

8 *For glory* : to glorify you.

9 *Eager for the glory* : of winning the prize in the chariot-race.

When lauds and Soma juice have made
me joyful, both the unbounded regions
are affrighted.

7 All beings know these deeds of thine :
thou tellest this unto Varuṇa, thou great
Disposer !
Thou art renowned as having slain the
Vṛtras. Thou madest flow the floods
that were obstructed.

8 Our fathers then were these, the Seven
Ṛṣis, what time the son of Durgaha
was captive.
For her they gained by sacrifice Trasadasyu, a demi-god, like Indra, conquering
foemen.

9 The spouse of Purukutsa gave oblations to
you, O Indra-Varuṇa, with homage.
Then unto her ye gave King Trasadasyu,
the demi-god, the slayer of the foeman.

10 May we, possessing much, delight in riches,
Gods in oblations and the kine in
pasture ;
And that Milch-cow who shrinks not
from the milking, O Indra-Varuṇa,
give to us daily.

HYMN XLIII.   *Aśvins.*

1. WHO will hear, who of those who merit
worship, which of all Gods take pleasure
in our homage?
On whose heart shall we lay this laud
celestial, rich with fair offerings, dearest
to Immortals ?

2 Who will be gracious ? Who will come
most quickly of all the Gods ? Who will
bring bliss most largely ?
What car do they call swift with rapid
coursers ? That which the Daughter of
the Sun elected.

3 So many days do ye come swiftly hither,
as Indra to give help in stress of battle.
Descended from the sky, divine, strong-
pinioned, by which of all your powers
are ye most mighty ?

4 What is the prayer that we should bring
you, Aśvins, whereby ye come to us
when invoked ?
Whether of you confronts e'en great
betrayal ? Lovers of sweetness, Dasras,
help and save us.

5 In the wide space your chariot reacheth
heaven, what time it turneth hither from
the ocean.
Sweets from your sweet shall drop, lovers
of sweetness ! These have they dressed
for you as dainty viands.

6 Let Sindhu with his wave bedew your
horses : in fiery glow have the red birds
come hither.
Observed of all was that your rapid going,
whereby ye were the Lords of Sūrya's
Daughter.

7 Whene'er I gratified you here together,
your grace was given us, O ye rich in
booty.
Protect, ye Twain, the singer of your
praises : to you, Nāsatyas, is my wish
directed.

HYMN XLIV.   *Aśvins.*

1. WE will invoke this day your car, far-
spreading, O Aśvins, even the gathering,
of the sunlight,—
Car praised in hymns, most ample, rich in
treasure, fitted with seats, the car that
beareth Sūryā.

2 Aśvins, ye gained that glory by your Godhead, ye Sons of Heaven, by your own
might and power.
Food followeth close upon your bright
appearing when stately horses in your
chariot draw you.

3 Who bringeth you to-day for help with
offered oblation, or with hymns to drink
the juices ?
Who, for the sacrifice's ancient lover, turneth you hither, Aśvins, offering homage?

7 The poet speaks.

8 *Our fathers then were these* : 'The seven *Ṛṣis* were
the protectors of this our (kingdom).'—Wilson. The
meaning is obscure. Professor Grassmann banishes
stanzas 8, 9, and 10 to the appendix as late additions
to the hymn. Sāyaṇa says that Purukutsa, son of
Durgaha, being in captivity, his wife propitiated the
Seven Ṛṣis, who by the favour of Indra and Varuṇa
obtained for her a son named Trasadasyu. *For her* :
the wife of Purukutsa.

10 *That Milch-cow* : wealth.

2 *The Daughter of the Sun* : Sūryā, bride of the
Aśvins. See I. 116. 17.

4 *Dasras* : workers of marvels, mighty ones, a
common appellation of the Aśvins.

6 *Birds* : flying steeds. Cf. IV. 45. 4.

1 *The gathering of the sunlight* : Professor Wilson
translates, after Sāyaṇa, 'the associator of the solar ray,'
and observes : '*Saṅgatim goh*, is only explained, *goh
saṅgamayitāram*, the bringer into union, or associator, of
Go : what the latter is intended for is not explained,
and the translation is purely conjectural, founded upon
the connection of the Aśvins with light or the sun.'
Professor Grassmann translates : 'der zur Milch eilt,'
'which hastens to the milk.'

4 Borne on your golden car, ye omnipresent ! come to this sacrifice of ours, Nāsatyas. Drink of the pleasant liquor of the Soma : give riches to the people who adore you.

5 Come hitherward to us from earth, from heaven, borne on your golden chariot rolling lightly. Suffer not other worshippers to stay you : here are ye bound by earlier bonds of friendship.

6 Now for us both, mete out, O Wonder-Workers, riches exceeding great with store of heroes, Because the men have sent you praise, O Aśvins, and Ajamīlhas come to the laudation.

7 Whene'er I gratified you here together, your grace was given us, O ye rich in booty. Protect, ye Twain, the singer of your praises : to you, Nāsatyas, is my wish directed.

HYMN XLV. *Aśvins*

1. YONDER goes up that light : your chariot is yoked that travels round upon the summit of this heaven. Within this car are stored three kindred shares of food, and a skin filled with meath is rustling as the fourth.

2 Forth come your viands rich with store of pleasant meath, and cars and horses at the flushing of the dawn, Stripping the covering from the surrounded gloom, and spreading through mid-air bright radiance like the Sun.

3 Drink of the meath with lips accustomed to the draught ; harness for the meath's sake the chariot that ye love. Refresh the way ye go, refresh the paths with meath : hither, O Aśvins, bring the skin that holds the meath.

4 The swans ye have are friendly, rich in store of meath, gold-pinioned, strong to draw, awake at early morn, Swimming the flood, exultant, fain for draughts that cheer : ye come like flies to our libations of the meath.

5 Well knowing solemn rites and rich in meath, the fires sing to the morning Aśvins at the break of day, When with pure hands the prudent energetic priest hath with the stones pressed out the Soma rich in meath.

6 The rays advancing nigh, chasing with day the gloom, spread through the firmament bright radiance like the Sun ; And the Sun harnessing his horses goeth forth : ye through your Godlike nature let his paths be known.

7 Devout in thought I have declared, O Aśvins, your chariot with good steeds, which lasts for ever, Wherewith ye travel swiftly through the regions to the prompt worshipper who brings oblation.

HYMN XLVI. *Vāyu. Indra-Vāyu*

1. DRINK the best draught of Soma juice, O Vāyu, at our holy rites : For thou art he who drinketh first.

2 Come, team-drawn, with thy hundred helps, with Indra seated in the car, Vāyu, and drink your fill of juice.

3 May steeds a thousand bring you both, Indra and Vāyu, hitherward To drink the Soma, to the feast.

4 For ye, O Indra-Vāyu, mount the golden-seated car that aids The sacrifice, that reaches heaven.

5 On far-refulgent chariot come unto the man who offers gifts : Come, Indra-Vāyu, hitherward.

6 Here, Indra-Vāyu, is the juice : drink it, accordant with the Gods, Within the giver's dwelling-place.

7 Hither, O Indra-Vāyu, be your journey : here unyoke your steeds, Here for your draught of Soma juice.

HYMN XLVII. *Vāyu. Indra-Vāyu.*

1. VĀYU, the bright is offered thee, best of the meath at holy rites. Come thou to drink the Soma juice, God, longed-for, on thy team-drawn car.

---

6 *Both* : priests and patrons. *Ajamīlhas* : men of the Ṛṣi's family

---

The Ṛṣi of this and the remaining hymns of this Book is Vāmadeva.

1 *Three kindred shares* : shares of similar food, for both Aśvins and Sūryā, the skin of meath being intended for earthly beings.—Ludwig.

4 *Swans* : the Aśvins, chariot-steeds.

---

6 *The rays advancing nigh* : I follow the interpretation of Sāyaṇa who supplies 'the rays' and 'the gloom;' but the exact meaning of the half-line is uncertain.

2 *Drink your fill* : the verb is in the dual number, Indra being included.

1 *The bright* : juice, understood.

2 O Vāyu, thou and Indra are meet
drinkers of these Soma-draughts,
For unto you the drops proceed as waters
gather to the vale.

3 O Indra-Vāyu, mighty Twain, speeding
together, Lords of Strength,
Come to our succour with your team, that
ye may drink the Soma juice.

4 The longed-for teams which ye possess, O
Heroes, for the worshipper,
Turn to us, Indra-Vāyu, ye to whom the
sacrifice is paid.

HYMN XLVIII.   *Vāyu.*

1. TASTE offerings never tasted yet, as bards
enjoy the foeman's wealth.
O Vāyu, on refulgent car come to the
drinking of the juice.

2 Removing curses, drawn by teams, with
Indra seated by thy side,
O Vāyu, on refulgent car come to the
drinking of the juice.

3 The two dark treasuries of wealth that wear
all beauties wait on thee.
O Vāyu, on refulgent car come to the
drinking of the juice.

4 May nine-and-ninety harnessed steeds who
yoke them at thy will bring thee.
O Vāyu, on refulgent car come to the
drinking of the juice.

5 Harness, O Vāyu, to thy car a hundred
well-fed tawny steeds,
Yea, or a thousand steeds, and let thy
chariot come to us with might.

HYMN XLIX.   *Indra-Bṛhaspati.*

1. DEAR is this offering in your mouth, O
Indra and Bṛhaspati :
Famed is the laud, the gladdening draught.

2 This lovely Soma is effused, O Indra and
Bṛhaspati,
For you, to drink it and rejoice.

3 As Soma-drinkers to our house come, Indra
and Bṛhaspati—and Indra—to drink
Soma juice.

4 Vouchsafe us riches hundredfold, O Indra
and Bṛhaspati,
With store of horses, thousandfold.

5 O Indra and Bṛhaspati, we call you when
the meath is shed,
With songs, to drink the Soma juice.

6 Drink, Indra and Bṛhaspati, the Soma in
the giver's house :
Delight yourselves abiding there.

HYMN L.   *Bṛhaspati.*

1. HIM who with might hath propped earth's
ends, who sitteth in threefold seat,
Bṛhaspati, with thunder,
Him of the pleasant tongue have ancient
sages, deep-thinking, holy singers, set
before them.

2 Wild in their course, in well-marked wise
rejoicing were they, Bṛhaspati, who
pressed around us.
Preserve Bṛhaspati, the stall uninjured, this
company's raining, ever-moving birth-
place.

3 Bṛhaspati, from thy remotest distance have
they sat down who love the law eternal.
For thee were dug wells springing from the
mountain, which murmuring round about
pour streams of sweetness.

4 Bṛhaspati, when first he had his being
from mighty splendour in supremest
heaven,
Strong, with his sevenfold mouth, with
noise of thunder, with his seven rays,
blew and dispersed the darkness.

---

3 *And Indra :* the words *indraśca* of the text are
manifestly superfluous.

As bards enjoy the foeman's wealth : vipo ná rāyó aryáḥ:
Sāyaṇa explains *vipo ná* as 'like a king who makes his
enemies tremble, and *rāyo aryáḥ* as 'bestow wealth upon
the worshipper.' Professor Grassmann translates :
'gleich Reisern spriess des Frommen Gut,' 'May the pious
man's wealth sprout like twigs or suckers.' *Vipo*
(*vipaḥ*) may mean either inspired singers, bards, or
twigs, and *ariḥ*, of which *aryaḥ* is the genitive, means
both an enemy and a pious man, a worshipper. I
follow Professor Ludwig's interpretation. The 'bards'
are the inspired singers of the victorious party who
share the booty after the battle.

3 *The two dark treasuries of wealth* : heaven and
earth, not yet illuminated by the sun.

Indra and Bṛhaspati conjointly are the deities of
stanzas 10 and 11, which, with 7, 8, and 9, are
evidently a late addition to the original hymn.
1 *In threefold seat* : heaven, mid-air, and earth.
Set before them : for adoration ; or given them the
foremost place in sacrifice.
2 *They...who pressed around us* : apparently the
Maruts. *The stall* : like the boundless stall' of III. 1
14, the aerial home of the Maruts.
This company's : the text has only *asya*, 'of this.' I
follow Professor Ludwig in his interpretation of this very
difficult stanza, and supply *gaṇasya*, troop or company,
i.e. of the Maruts. According to Sāyaṇa, Bṛhaspati is
asked to protect the worshipper or institutor of the
sacrifice.
3 *Have they sat down* : probably the Maruts are
intended, and not horses as Sāyaṇa says. *Wells springing from the mountain* : reservoirs of Soma juice, pressed
out by the stones, have been prepared.

5 With the loud-shouting band who sang
his praises, with thunder, he destroyed
obstructive Vala.
  Bṛhaspati thundering drave forth the cattle,
  the lowing cows who make oblations
  ready.

6 Serve we with sacrifices, gifts, and homage
even thus the Steer of all the Gods, the
Father.
  Bṛhaspati, may we be lords of riches, with
  noble progeny and store of heroes.

7 Surely that King by power and might
heroic hath made him lord of all his
foes' possessions,
  Who cherishes Bṛhaspati well-tended,
  adorns and worships him as foremost
  sharer.

8 In his own house he dwells in peace and
comfort : to him for ever holy food
flows richly.
  To him the people with free will pay
  homage—the King with whom the
  Brahman hath precedence.

9 He, unopposed, is master of the riches of
his own subjects and of hostile people.
  The Gods uphold that King with their
  protection who helps the Brahman when
  he seeks his favour.

10 Indra, Bṛhaspati, rainers of treasure, rejoicing at this sacrifice drink the Soma.
  Let the abundant drops sink deep within
  you : vouchsafe us riches with full store
  of heroes.

11 Bṛhaspati and Indra, make us prosper :
may this be your benevolence to us-
ward.
  Assist our holy thoughts, wake up our
  spirit : weaken the hatred of our foe
  and rivals.

HYMN LI.   Dawn.

1. FORTH from the darkness in the region
eastward this most abundant splendid
light hath mounted.
  Now verily the far-refulgent Mornings,
  Daughters of Heaven, bring welfare to
  the people.

Sevenfold mouth ..seven rays : as identified with Agni.
  5 *Obstructive* : or retentive; the meaning of *phaligám*
is somewhat uncertain : probably, reservoir, i.e. holder
and withholder of the rain. *The loudshouting band* : the
Maruts.

10 *Rainers of treasure* : the meaning of *vṛṣaṇvasū*
is uncertain ; 'strong or excellent as bulls,' according
to Ludwig and Grassmann. Perhaps 'strong with
treasures.'

2 The richly-coloured Dawns have mounted
eastward, like pillars planted at our
sacrifices,
  And, flushing far, splendid and purifying,
  unbarred the portals of the fold of
  darkness.

3 Dispelling gloom this day the wealthy
Mornings urge liberal givers to present
their treasures.
  In the unlightened depth of darkness round
  them let niggard traffickers sleep un-
  awakened.

4 O Goddesses, is this your car, I ask you,
ancient this day, or is it new, ye Mornings,
  Wherewith, rich Dawns, ye seek with
  wealth Navagva, Daśagva Aṅgira, the
  seven-toned singer ?

5 With horses harnessed by eternal Order,
Goddesses, swiftly round the worlds ye
travel,
  Arousing from their rest, O Dawns, the
  sleeping, and all that lives, man, bird,
  and beast, to motion.

6 Which among these is eldest, and where
is she through whom they fixed the
Ṛbhus' regulations ?
  What time the splendid Dawns go forth
  for splendour, they are not known apart,
  alike, unwasting.

7 Blest were these Dawns of old, shining
with succour, true with the truth that
springs from holy Order ;
  With whom the toiling worshipper, by
  praises, hymning and lauding, soon
  attained to riches.

8 Hither from eastward all at once they travel,
from one place spreading in the self-
same manner.
  Awaking, from the seat of holy Order
  the Godlike Dawns come nigh like
  troops of cattle.

3 *Niggard traffickers* : wealthy churls who offer no
sacrifices.
  4 *Navagva, Daśagva* : individual members of the so-
named mythical priestly families which are frequently
associated with the Aṅgirases. *Aṅgira* : a member of
the family of Aṅgiras. *Seven-toned* : literally, 'seven-
mouthed,' using in his hymns the seven metres of the
Veda, or repeating hymns of seven kinds .
  6 *The Ṛbhus' regulations* : the seasons of the year,
the Ṛbhus being cosmic powers and closely connected
with the Ṛtus.
  8 *Like troops of cattle* : going forth to pasture at
day-break.

9 Thus they go forth with undiminished colours, these Mornings similar, in self-same fashion,
  Concealing the gigantic might of darkness with radiant bodies bright and pure and shining.
10 O Goddesses, O Heaven's refulgent Daughters, bestow upon us wealth with store of children.
  As from our pleasant place of rest ye rouse us may we be masters of heroic vigour.
11 Well-skilled in lore of sacrifice, ye Daughters of Heaven, refulgent Dawns, I thus address you.
  May we be glorious among the people. May Heaven vouchsafe us this, and Earth the Goddess.

HYMN LII.   Dawn.

1. THIS Lady, giver of delight, after her Sister shining forth, Daughter of Heaven, hath shown herself.
2 Unfailing, Mother of the Kine, in colour like a bright red mare,
  The Dawn became the Aśvins' Friend.
3 Yea, and thou art the Aśvins' Friend, the Mother of the Kine art thou :
  O Dawn thou rulest over wealth.
4 Thinking of thee, O Joyous One, as her who driveth hate away,
  We woke to meet thee with our lauds.
5 Our eyes behold thy blessed rays like troops of cattle loosed to feed.
  Dawn hath filled full the wide expanse.
6 When thou hast filled it, Fulgent One ! thou layest bare the gloom with light.
  After thy nature aid us, Dawn.
7 Thou overspreadest heaven with rays, the dear wide region of mid-air.
  With thy bright shining lustre, Dawn.

HYMN LIII.   Savitar.

1. OF Savitar the God, the sapient Asura, we crave this great gift which is worthy of our choice,
  Wherewith he freely grants his worshipper defence. This with his rays the Great God hath vouchsafed to us.

2 Sustainer of the heaven, Lord of the whole world's life, the Sage, he putteth on his golden-coloured mail.
  Clear-sighted, spreading far, filling the spacious realm, Savitar hath brought forth bliss that deserveth laud.
3 He hath filled full the regions of the heaven and earth : the God for his own strengthening waketh up the hymn.
  Savitar hath stretched out his arms to cherish life, producing with his rays and lulling all that moves.
4 Lighting all living creatures, ne'er to be deceived, Savitar, God, protects each holy ordinance.
  He hath stretched out his arms to all the folk of earth, and, with his laws observed, rules his own mighty course.
5 Savitar thrice surrounding with his mightiness mid-air, three regions, and the triple sphere of light,
  Sets the three heavens in motion and the threefold earth, and willingly protects us with his triple law.
6 Most gracious God, who brings to life and lulls to rest, he who controls the world, what moves not and what moves,
  May he vouchsafe us shelter,—Savitar the God,—for tranquil life, with triple bar against distress.
7 With the year's seasons hath Savitar, God, come nigh : may he prosper our home, give food and noble sons.
  May he invigorate us through the days and nights, and may he send us opulence with progeny.

HYMN LIV.   Savitar.

1. Now must we praise and honour Savitar the God : at this time of the day the men must call to him,
  Him who distributes wealth to Manu's progeny, that he may grant us here riches most excellent.
2 For thou at first producest for the holy Gods the noblest of all portions, immortality :
  Thereafter as a gift to men, O Savitar, thou openest existence, life succeeding life.

1 *After her Sister* : when Night has departed.
3 *The Kine* : the early rays of light, or fleecy clouds of morning. *Friend of the Aśvins*: as being worshipped at the same time.
4 *Driveth hate away* : especially the malignity of the evil spirits of the night.

1 *Savitar* : the Sun as the great vivifier, generator, and producer.

3 *Lulling* : the word in the text, *niveśdyan*, means 'bringing to rest.' Sāyaṇa explains it by 'establishing in their several duties.'
5 *Triple law* : according to Sāyaṇa, his functions as distributor of heat, rain, and cold. *Three heavens* : See I. 105. 5.

3 If we, men as we are, have sinned against
the Gods through want of thought, in
weakness, or through insolence,
Absolve us from the guilt and make us free
from sin, O Savitar, alike among both
Gods and men.

4 None may impede that power of Savitar
the God whereby he will maintain the
universal world.
What the fair-fingered God brings forth
on earth's expanse or in the height of
heaven, that work of his stands sure.

5 To lofty hills thou sendest those whom
Indra leads, and givest fixed abodes with
houses unto these.
However they may fly and draw themselves
apart, still, Savitar, they stand obeying
thy behest.

6 May the libations poured to thee thrice
daily, day after day, O Savitar, bring
us blessing.
May Indra, Heaven, Earth, Sindhu with
the Waters, Aditi with Ādityas, give us
shelter.

HYMN LV.　　　　　*Viśvedevas.*

1. WHO of you, Vasus, saveth ? who protecteth ? O Heaven and Earth and Aditi,
preserve us,
Varuṇa, Mitra, from the stronger mortal.
Gods, which of you at sacrifice giveth
comfort ?

2 They who with laud extol the ancient
statutes, when they shine forth infallible
dividers,
Have ordered as perpetual Ordainers, and
beamed as holy-thoughted Wonder-
Workers.

3 The Housewife Goddess, Aditi, and Sindhu,
the Goddess Svasti I implore for friendship :
And may the unobstructed Night and

Morning both, day and night, provide
for our protection.

4 Aryaman, Varuṇa have disclosed the
pathway, Agni as Lord of Strength the
road to welfare.
Lauded in manly mode may Indra-Viṣṇu
grant us their powerful defence and
shelter.

5 I have besought the favour of the Maruts,
of Parvata, of Bhaga God who rescues.
From trouble caused by man the Lord
preserve us; from woe sent by his friend
let Mitra save us.

6 Agree, through these our watery oblations,
Goddesses, Heaven and Earth, with
Ahibudhnya.
As if to win the sea, the Gharma-heaters
have opened, as they come anear, the
rivers.

7 May Goddess Aditi with Gods defend us,
save us the saviour God with care
unceasing.
We dare not stint the sacred food of
Mitra and Varuṇa upon the back of
Agni.

8 Agni is Sovran Lord of wealth, Agni of
great prosperity :
May he bestow these gifts on us.

9 Hither to us, rich pleasant Dawn, bring
many things to be desired,
Thou who hast ample store of wealth.

10 So then may Bhaga, Savitar, Varuṇa, Mitra,
Aryaman, Indra, with bounty come to us.

HYMN LVI.　　　　*Heaven and Earth.*

1. MAY mighty Heaven and Earth, most
meet for honour, be present here with
light and gleaming splendours;

---

5 *To lofty hills* : 'Thou elevatest those, of whom
Indra is chief, above the vast clouds : for these, (thy
worshippers), thou providest dwelling (places) filled
with habitations.'—Wilson. 'The difficulties in connection with this verse are very great, and perhaps insuper-
able,' says Professor Peterson, in whose *Hymns from the
Rgveda* (Bombay Sanskrit Series, No. XXXVI.) the
Sanskrit student will find a full statement of these
difficulties, and the interpretations proposed by Sāyaṇa
and by European scholars, not one of which is convincing.

2 *They* : the deities of light ; 'dividers, as separating
day from night, and Ordainers, as fixing and regulating
the year and the seasons.

3 *Housewife Goddess* : as being the mother of the
Gods. *Svasti* : Prosperity.

5 *The Lord* : Varuṇa. *Sent by his Friend* : Varuṇa,
as the great chastiser of men. Professor Roth, whom
Professor Grassmann follows, takes *jányāt* to mean
caused by strangers, and *mitríyāt* caused by friends.

6 This stanza is difficult and its meaning is obscure.
The words *ápyebhir iṣṭaíḥ* 'through watery oblations'
are rendered by Professor Grassmann, 'nebst den
erwünschten Wassergottern,' 'together with the wished-
for Water-Gods.' *Ahibudhnya* : the Dragon of the Deep,
is a divine being who dwells in the depths of the ocean
of air. Cf. I. 186. 5 ; II. 31. 6. *As if to win the sea* :
as if wishing to gain the ocean of abundant wealth. *The
Gharma-heaters* : the priests who prepare the oblation of
hot milk or other hot beverage which is offered especially to the Aśvins. Or Gharma may mean the
cauldron or vessel in which the oblation is boiled. The
meaning seems to be, as Professor Ludwig explains it,
that the priests, sacrificing, and hymning lead down
towards themselves the rivers of the ocean of plenty.

7 *The saviour God* : Indra. *Upon the back of Agni* :
poured upon the flames.

1 *The Steer* : according to Sāyaṇa, Parjanya the God
of rain-clouds.

When, fixing them apart, vast, most extensive, the Steer roars loudly in far-reaching courses.

2 The Goddesses with Gods, holy with holy, the Two stand pouring out their rain, exhaustless:
Faithful and guileless, having Gods for children, leaders of sacrifice with shining splendours.

3 Sure in the worlds he was a skilful Craftsman, he who produced these Twain the Earth and Heaven.
Wise, with his power he brought both realms, together spacious and deep, well-fashioned, unsupported.

4 O Heaven and Earth, with one accord promoting, with high protection as of Queens, our welfare,
Far-reaching, universal, holy, guard us. May we, car-borne, through song be victors ever.

5 To both of you, O Heaven and Earth, we bring our lofty song of praise,
Pure Ones ! to glorify you both.

6 Ye sanctify each other's form, by your own proper might ye rule,
And from of old observe the Law.

7 Furthering and fulfilling, ye, O Mighty, perfect Mitra's Law.
Ye sit around our sacrifice.

HYMN LVII.   *Kṣetrapati, Etc.*

1. WE through the Master of the Field, even as through a friend, obtain
What nourisheth our kine and steeds. In such may he be good to us.

2 As the cow yieldeth milk, pour for us freely, Lord of the Field, the wave that beareth sweetness,
Distilling meath, well-purified like butter, and let the Lords of holy Law be gracious.

2 *Pouring out their rain* : bestowing good gifts.
4 *As of Queens* : I follow with some hesitation Professor Ludwig's interpretation of *pátnivadbh r*. Professor Wilson, following Sāyaṇa, translates, 'with our spacious dwellings, *inhabited by our wives*.'
5 These three concluding verses form in reality another hymn.

In this hymn various agricultural personifications are addressed, the deity of the first three stanzas being called Kṣetrapati, of the fourth Suna, of the fifth and eighth Sunāsira, of the sixth and seventh Sitā. 'It is said in the Gṛhya-Sūtras that each verse is to be silently repeated, with an oblation to fire, at the commencement of ploughing.'—Wilson.
1 *The Master of the Field* : Kṣetrapati, the popular Genius Loci, said to mean either Rudra or Agni.

3 Sweet be the plants for us, the heavens, the waters, and full of sweets for us be air's mid-region.
May the Field's Lord for us be full of sweetness, and may we follow after him uninjured.

4 Happily work our steers and men, may the plough furrow happily.
Happily be the traces bound; happily may he ply the goad.

5 Suna and Sīra, welcome ye this laud, and with the milk which ye have made in heaven
Bedew ye both this earth of ours.

6 Auspicious Sītā, come thou near : we venerate and worship thee
That thou mayst bless and prosper us and bring us fruits abundantly.

7 May Indra press the furrow down, may Pūṣan guide its course aright.
May she, as rich in milk, be drained for us through each succeeding year.

8 Happily let the shares turn up the plough-land, happily go the ploughers with the oxen.
With meath and milk Parjanya make us happy. Grant us prosperity, Suna and Sīra.

HYMN LVIII.   *Ghṛta.*

1. FORTH from the ocean sprang the wave of sweetness : together with the stalk it turned to Amṛta,

5 *Suna and Sīra* : two deities or deified objects who bless or are closely connected with agriculture. According to Yāska Suna (the auspicious) is Vāyu, and Sīra (plough) is Āditya or the Sun. Professor Roth conjectures that the words mean here ploughshare and plough. Professor Grassmann translates; 'O Pflug und Lenker,' 'plough and ploughman.'
6 *Sītā* : the Furrow or Husbandry personified and addressed as a deity ; in after time the heroine of the Rāmāyaṇa.
7 *Indra* : as the God who sends the necessary rain, Indra is prayed to bless the work by pressing down and deepening the furrow 'May Indra take hold of Sitā.'—Wilson. *May she, as rich in milk* : according to the Scholiast, *sá*, she, here means the sky.

The hymn is in praise of *Ghṛta*, the clarified butter or oil used in sacrifices, but a choice of deities is offered in the Index—Agni or Sūrya, Waters, Cows, or Ghṛta. It is, as Professor Wilson observes, 'a good specimen of Vaidik vagueness, and mystification, and of the straits to which commentators are put to extract an intelligible meaning from the text.'
1 It would be fruitless, as Professor Ludwig remarks, to repeat all the various explanations which Sāyaṇa gives of the first line of this stanza : they only show the utter uncertainty of tradition in reference to the passage. For instance, *samudrá*, ocean, is said to mean, sacrificial

That which is holy oil's mysterious title:
but the Gods' tongue is truly Amṛta's
centre.

2 Let us declare aloud the name of Ghṛta,
and at this sacrifice hold it up with
homage.
So let the Brahman hear the praise we
utter. This hath the four-horned Buffalo
emitted.

3 Four are his horns, three are the feet that
bear him; his heads are two, his hands
are seven in number.
Bound with a triple bond the Steer roars
loudly : the mighty God hath entered
in to mortals.

4 That oil in triple shape the Gods discovered
laid down within the Cow, concealed
by Paṇis.

Indra produced one shape, Sūrya another:
by their own power they formed the
third from Vena.

5 From inmost reservoir in countless channels
flow down these rivers which the foe
beholds not.
I look upon the streams of oil descending,
and lo ! the Golden Reed is there among
them.

6 Like rivers our libations flow together,
cleansing themselves in inmost heart
and spirit.
The streams of holy oil pour swiftly downward like the wild beasts that fly before
the bowman.

7 As rushing down the rapids of a river,
flow swifter than the wind the vigorous
currents,
The streams of oil in swelling fluctuation
like a red courser bursting through the
fences.

8.Like women at a gathering fair to look
on and gently smiling, they incline to
Agni.
The streams of holy oil attain the fuel,
and Jātavedas joyfully receives them.

9 As maidens deck themselves with gay adornment to join the bridal feast, I now
behold them.
Where Soma flows and sacrifice is ready,
thither the streams of holy oil are
running.

10 Send to our eulogy a herd of cattle :
bestow upon us excellent possessions.
Bear to the Gods the sacrifice we offer :
the streams of oil flow pure and full of
sweetness.

11 The universe depends upon thy power and
might within the sea, within the heart,
within all life.
May we attain that sweetly-flavoured
wave of thine, brought, at its gathering,
o'er the surface of the floods.

fire ; or celestial fire ; or the firmament; or the udder
of the cow; and *ūrmi,* wave, may accordingly mean
reward; or rain; or butter. Professor Ludwig thinks
that the sense of the stanza may be : the life-giving
essence which develops itself out of the world-ocean
turns into Soma in the Moon, but it is neither of
these two, but the tongue of the Gods (Agni?) from
which the Amṛta proceeds and to which it returns.
But see A. Hillebrandt. Vedische Mythologie, I. 321,
322.

The Brahman : according to Mahīdhara, the *ṛtvij* or
priest. Probably Agni is meant. The last half-line of
the stanza is translated, after Sāyaṇa, by Professor
Wilson : 'the fair-complexioned deity perfects this rite,'
the epithet 'four-horned' being transferred to 'Brahman.'
The God may be called a *buffalo* (*gaurá*, Bos Gaurus)
as a type of extraordinary strength. Mahīdhara explains
gaurá by *yajña,* sacrifice, having four horns, that is, four
officiating priests.

3 *Four are his horns* : the four horns of Agni as
identified with sacrifice are said by Sāyaṇa to be the
four Vedas, and, if identified with Āditya, the four
cardinal points. The *three feet* are, in the former case,
the three daily sacrifices, in the latter, morning, noon,
and evening. The two heads are, in the former case,
the *Brahmaudana* and the *Pravargya* ceremonies, in the
latter, day and night. Similarly, the *seven hands* are
explained, alternatively, as the seven metres of the
Veda or the seven rays of the Sun ; and the *triple bond*
as the *Mantra, Kalpa,* and *Brāhmaṇa,* prayer, ceremonial,
and rationale, of the Veda, or the three regions,
heaven, firmament, and earth. The *Steer* is, either as
sacrifice of Āditya, the pourer down of rewards, and
the loud roaring is the sound of the repetition of the
texts of the Veda. Mahīdhara's explanation differs
from that of Sāyaṇa. The four horns are priests ; or
nouns, verbs, prepositions, and particles ; the three
feet are the Vedas, or the first, second, and third persons, or the past, present, and future tenses ; the two
heads are two sacrifices, or the agent and object ; the
seven hands are the metres or the cases of the noun ;
and the three bonds are the three daily sacrifices,
or the singular, dual, and plural numbers. See Wilson's
note.

4 *In triple-shape* : as milk, curds, and butter,
according to Sāyaṇa. The meaning seems to be that
Indra, Sūrya, and Vena (who is probably Agni),
restored the power of the elements of sacrifice respecti-

vely in heaven the firmament, and the earth, after they
had been rendered ineffectual for a time by the malignant Paṇis.

5 *The Golden Reed* : Celestial Agni.

10 *Send to our eulogy a herd of cattle* : this is Sāyaṇa's
interpretation. The Gods are addressed, and asked to
reward the singers.

11 *Thy power* : Agni's. *In the sea* : in the aerial
ocean, the firmament, in which Agni is present as lightning. *Within the heart* : as Vaiśvānara. belonging to all
men. *Within all life* : as the vital principle, or heat.
The *wave* is the butter of the oblation.

BOOK THE FIFTH

HYMN I. *Agni.*

1. AGNI is wakened by the people's fuel to meet the Dawn who cometh like a milch-cow.

Like young trees shooting up on high their branches, his flames are rising to the vault of heaven.

2 For worship of the Gods the Priest was wakened : at morning gracious Agni hath arisen.

Kindled, his radiant might is made apparent, and the great Deity set free from darkness.

3 When he hath stirred the line of his attendants, with the pure milk pure Agni is anointed.

The strength-bestowing gift is then made ready, which spread in front, with tongues, erect, he drinketh.

4 The spirits of the pious turn together to Agni, as the eyes of all to Sūrya.

He, when both Dawns of different hues have borne him, springs up at daybreak as a strong white charger.

5 The noble One was born at days' beginning, laid red in colour mid the well-laid fuel.

Yielding in every house his seven rich treasures, Agni is seated, Priest most skilled in worship.

6 Agni hath sat him down, a Priest most skilful, on a sweet-smelling place, his Mother's bosom.

Young, faithful, sage, preëminent o'er many, kindled among the folk whom he sustaineth.

7 This Singer excellent at sacrifices, Agni the Priest, they glorify with homage.

Him who spread out both worlds by Law Eternal they balm with oil, strong Steed who never faileth.

8 He, worshipful House-Friend, in his home is worshipped, our own auspicious guest, lauded by sages.

That strength the Bull with thousand horns possesses. In might, O Agni, thou excellest others.

9 Thou quickly passest by all others, Agni, for him to whom thou hast appeared most lovely,

Wondrously fair, adorable, effulgent, the guest of men, the darling of the people.

10 To thee, Most Youthful God ! to thee, O Agni from near and far the people bring their tribute.

Mark well the prayer of him who best extols thee. Great, high, auspicious, Agni, is thy shelter.

11 Ascend to-day thy splendid car, O Agni, in splendour, with the Holy Ones around it.

Knowing the paths by mid-air's spacious region bring hither Gods to feast on our oblation.

12 To him adorable, sage, strong and mighty we have sung forth our song of praise and homage.

Gaviṣṭhira hath raised with prayer to Agni this laud far-reaching, like gold light to heaven.

HYMN II. *Agni.*

1. THE youthful Mother keeps the Boy in secret pressed to her close, nor yields him to the Father.

But, when he lies upon the arm, the people see his unfading countenance before them.

---

8 *The Bull with thousand horns* : Agni as the Sun with his countless rays.

---

1 The kindling of the sacrificial fire is figuratively described. The lower piece of wood retains the latent spark and will not give it up to the *yajamāna* or worshipper until he has generated it by attrition. When the fire has been produced, and is shown like a child that is carried on the arm, its brightness is apparent to all. This seems to be the meaning of the stanza ; but to arrive at it *aratnau* must be read instead of the *aratau* of the text ; and this or some similar alteration is required by the metre. But see Ludwig's Commentary.

---

1 *Young trees* : the meaning of '*yahvāḥ*' here is uncertain. 'Like birds (?) flying up (or like strong men reaching up) to a branch' (M. Müller).

3 *The line of his attendants* : the row of ministering priests, the people of st. 1. But the exact meaning of the words of the text is uncertain.

4 *To Sūrya* : to the Sun. *Both Dawns* : Night and Morning.

5 *Seven rich treasures* : wealth of various sorts.
His Mother's bosom : the altar raised above the ground.

2 What child is this thou carriest as handmaid, O Youthful One ? The Consort-
Queen hath borne him.
The Babe unborn increased through many
autumns. I saw him born what time
his Mother bare him.

3 I saw him from afar gold-toothed, bright-
coloured, hurling his weapons from his
habitation,
What time I gave him Amṛta free from
mixture. How can the Indraless, the
hymnless harm me ?

4 I saw him moving from the place he dwells
in, even as with a herd, brilliantly shining.
These seized him not : he had been born
already. They who were grey with age
again grow youthful.

5 Who separate my young bull from the
cattle, they whose protector was in truth
no stranger ?
Let those whose hands have seized upon
them free them. May he, observant,
drive the herd to us-ward.

6 Mid mortal men godless have secreted the
King of all who live, home of the people.
So may the prayers of Atri give him freedom. Reproached in turn be those who
now reproach him.

7 Thou from the stake didst loose e'en
Śunaḥśepa bound for a thousand ; for
he prayed with fervour.

So, Agni, loose from us the bonds that bind
us, when thou art seated here, O Priest
who knowest.

8 Thou hast sped from me, Agni, in thine
anger : this the protector of Gods' Laws
hath told me.
Indra who knoweth bent his eye upon thee:
by him instructed am I come, O Agni.

9 Agni shines far and wide with lofty splendour, and by his greatness makes all
things apparent.
He conquers godless and malign enchantments, and sharpens both his horns to
gore the Rakṣas.

10 Loud in the heaven above be Agni's
roarings with keen-edged weapons to
destroy the demons.
Forth burst his splendours in the Soma's
rapture. The godless bands press round
but cannot stay him.

11 As a skilled craftsman makes a car, a
singer I, Mighty One ! this hymn for
thee have fashioned.
If thou, O Agni, God, accept it gladly,
may we obtain thereby the heavenly
Waters.

12 May he, the strong-necked Steer, waxing
in vigour, gather the foeman's wealth
with none to check him.
Thus to this Agni have the Immortals
spoken. To man who spreads the grass
may he grant shelter, grant shelter to the
man who brings oblation.

2 The meaning is obscure. The *handmaid* and the
Consort-Queen (*mdhiṣī*) are perhaps the two fire-sticks.
The fire thus produced is not the genuine Agni, who is
born as lightning from the cloud.

3 I offered sweet libations of Soma juice to Agni
when I beheld him in the form of lightning, and
consequently the godless who do not acknowledge
Indra are unable to injure me.

4 *Even as with a herd* : Agni is here represented
as the Sun with his host of rays. *These seized him not* :
the Dawns could not detain him : the Sun was too
powerful. But the meaning of *tāḥ*, 'these,' without a
substantive, is somewhat uncertain. *They who were grey* :
the ancient flames of the Sun recover their youth and
strength. Or the half-line may be rendered : 'The
Dawns, the youthful Maidens, grow decrepit'. This is
Professor Ludwig's interpretation, and it has much to
recommend it.

5 This stanza is extremely obscure. It may refer to
some actual occurrence to which a mythical colouring
has been added. 'What enemies have despoiled my
kingdom ?' is Sāyaṇa's explanation of the first half-line.

6 This stanza appears to refer to some contention
between the descendants of Atri and some other priestly
family, perhaps the Bhṛgus, as Professor Ludwig thinks,
regarding the worship of Agni. *Home of the people* :
Agni ; the asylum of men.'—Wilson.

7 *Śunaḥśepa* : see I. 24. *Bound for a thousand*: bought
for a thousand cows in order that he might be bound to
the sacrificial post. Sāyaṇa, who is followed by Professors

Wilson, Roth, and Grassmann, take *sahásrādyūpād* together, 'from a thousand stakes.'

9 *Rakṣas* : a collective noun signifying the whole
race of Rākṣasas ; originally, harm, injury.

1 *Varuṇa* : regarded as the type of royalty. *Mitra* :
the friendly, beneficent God. *Indra* : the chief of all
the Gods.

2 *Ary man* : in connexion with marriage ; *aryaman*
meaning also a companion, especially a friend who asks
a girl in marriage for another, and Agni being, as the
Sun, the regulator of the season for marriage, and it,
consecrator as the sacrificial fire.

HYMN III. Agni.

1. THOU at thy birth art Varuṇa, O Agni ;
when thou art kindled thou becomest
Mitra.
In thee, O Son of Strength, all Gods are
centred. Indra art thou to man who
brings oblation.

2 Aryaman art thou as regardeth maidens :
mysterious · is thy name, O Self-sustainer.
As a kind friend with streams of milk they

balm thee what time thou makest wife and lord one-minded.

3 The Maruts deck their beauty for thy glory, yea, Rudra ! for thy birth fair, brightly-coloured.

That which was fixed as Viṣṇu's loftiest station—therewith the secret of the Cows thou guardest.

4 Gods through thy glory, God who art so lovely ! granting abundant gifts gained life immortal.

As their own Priest have men established Agni ; and serve him fain for praise from him who liveth.

5 There is no priest more skilled than thou in worship; none Self-sustainer pass thee in wisdom.

The man within whose house as guest thou dwellest, O God, by sacrifice shall conquer mortals.

6 Aided by thee, O Agni may we conquer through our oblation, fain for wealth, awakened :

May we in battle, in the days' assemblies, O Son of Strength, by riches conquer mortals.

7 He shall bring evil on the evil-plotter whoever turns against us sin and outrage.

Destroy this calumny of him, O Agni, whoever injures us with double-dealing.

8 At this dawn's flushing, God ! our ancient fathers served thee with offerings, making thee their envoy,

When, Agni, to the store of wealth thou goest, a God enkindled with good things by mortals.

9 Save, thou who knowest, draw thy father near thee, who counts as thine own son, O Child of Power.

O sapient Agni, when wilt thou regard us ? When, skilled in holy Law, wilt thou direct us ?

10 Adoring thee he gives thee many a title, when thou, Good Lord ! acceptest this as Father.

And doth not Agni, glad in strength of Godhead, gain splendid bliss when he hath waxen mighty ?

11 Most Youthful Agni, verily thou bearest thy praiser safely over all his troubles.

Thieves have been seen by us and open foemen : unknown have been the plottings of the wicked.

12 To thee these eulogies have been directed: or to the Vasu hath this sin been spoken.

But this our Agni, flaming high, shall never yield us to calumny, to him who wrongs us.

HYMN IV.   *Agni.*

1. O AGNI, King and Lord of wealth and treasures, in thee is my delight at sacrifices.

Through thee may we obtain the strength we long for, and overcome the fierce attacks of mortals.

2 Agni, Eternal Father, offering-bearer, fair to behold, far-reaching, far-refulgent,

From well-kept household fire beam food to feed us, and measure out to us abundant glory.

3 The Sage of men, the Lord of human races, pure, purifying Agni, balmed with butter,

Him the Omniscient as your Priest ye stablish : he wins among the Gods things worth the choosing.

4 Agni, enjoy, of one accord with Iḷā, striving in rivalry with beams of Sūrya,

Enjoy, O Jātavedas, this our fuel, and bring the Gods to us to taste oblations.

5 As dear House-Friend, guest welcome in the dwelling, to this our sacrifice come thou who knowest.

---

3 *Rudra* : here, as in other places, a name of Agni. *Viṣṇu's loftiest station* : the height of the firmament, which supplies milk to the celestial Cows, and, as mysteriously connected with them, to the cows of earth. *The secret of the Cows* : apparently, their udder—the cloud—is meant by *guhyam nāma gonām*, 'the cows' secret name.'

4 *Gained life immortal* : Agni alone, it is said, was originally immortal, and the other Gods obtained immortality through him.

From him who liveth : Agni, the special representant of vital power.

6 *In the days' assemblies* : gatherings on days appointed for sacrifice.

8 *The store of wealth* : according to Sāyaṇa, the place containing the riches of sacrificial offerings.

9 *Thy father* : the sacrificer, who supports Agni with oblations, and in his turn is loved and cherished as a son.

10 *Acceptest this* : the homage of the worshipper. *When he hath waxen mighty* : or been exalted by our praise.

11 *Thieves have been seen* : although we have seen thieves and enemies we have been saved by Agni from suffering injury from their evil designs.

12 *Hath this sin been spoken* : if my praise be not acceptable to Agni, it is an offence and a sin. Or the meaning may be, this sin of our enemies who plot against us has been declared to Agni.

---

4. *Iḷā* : prayer and praise, personified. *With beams of Sūrya* : putting forth thy power at day-break and so vying with the sun.

And, Agni, having scattered all assailants,
   bring to us the possessions of our foemen.
6 Drive thou away the Dasyu with thy
   weapon. As, gaining vital power for
   thine own body,
   O Son of Strength, the Gods thou satisfiest,
   so in fight save us, most heroic Agni.
7 May we, O Agni, with our lauds adore
   thee, and with our gifts, fair-beaming
   Purifier !
   Send to us wealth containing all things
   precious : bestow upon us every sort of
   riches.
8 Son of Strength, Agni, dweller in three
   regions, accept our sacrifice and our
   oblation.
   Among the Gods may we be counted pious:
   protect us with a triply-guarding shelter.
9 Over all woes and dangers, Jātavedas,
   bear us as in a boat across a river.
   Praised with our homage even as Atri
   praised thee, O Agni, be the guardian
   of our bodies.
10 As I, remembering thee with grateful
   spirit, a mortal, call with might on thee
   Immortal,
   Vouchsafe us high renown, O Jātavedas,
   and may I be immortal by my children.
11 The pious man, O Jātavedas Agni, to
   whom thou grantest ample room and
   pleasure,
   Gaineth abundant wealth with sons and
   horses, with heroes and with kine for
   his well-being.

HYMN V.   *Āpris.*

1. To Agni, Jātavedas, to the flame, the
   well-enkindled God,
   Offer thick sacrificial oil.
2 He, Narāśaṁsa, ne'er beguiled, inspiriteth
   this sacrifice :
   For sage is he, with sweets in hand.
3 Adored, O Agni, hither bring Indra the
   Wonderful, the Friend,
   On lightly-rolling car to aid.

4 Spread thyself out, thou soft as wool !
   The holy hymns have sung to thee.
   Bring gain to us, O beautiful !
5 Open yourselves, ye Doors Divine, easy
   of access for our aid :
   Fill, more and more, the sacrifice.
6 Fair strengtheners of vital power, young
   Mothers of eternal Law,
   Morning and Night we supplicate.
7 On the wind's flight come, glorified, ye
   two celestial Priests of man :
   Come ye to this our sacrifice.
8 Ilā, Sarasvatī, Mahī, three Goddesses who
   bring us weal,
   Be seated harmless on the grass.
9 Rich in all plenty, Tvaṣṭar, come auspicious of thine own accord :
   Help us in every sacrifice.
10 Vanaspati, wherever thou knowest the
   Gods' mysterious names,
   Send our oblations thitherward.
11 To Agni and to Varuṇa, Indra, the
   Maruts, and the Gods,
   With Svāhā be oblation brought.

HYMN VI.   *Agni.*

1. I VALUE Agni that good Lord, the home
   to which the kine return :
   Whom fleet-foot coursers seek as home,
   and strong enduring steeds as home.
   Bring food to those who sing thy praise.
2 'Tis Agni whom we laud as good, to whom
   the milch-kine come in herds,
   To whom the chargers swift of foot, to
   whom our well-born princes come.
   Bring food to those who sing thy praise.
3 Agni the God of all mankind, gives, verily,
   a steed to man.
   Agni gives precious gear for wealth, treasure he gives when he is pleased. Bring
   food to those who sing thy praise.
4 God, Agni, we will kindle thee, rich in
   thy splendour, fading not,

---

6 *As, gaining vital power* : as the oblations of men
which thou carriest to the Gods increase thine own
strength also. Sāyaṇa takes the second half-line in
connexion with the first : 'Drive thou away the Dasyu
with thy weapon, obtaining vital strength for thine
own body.'

8 *Dweller in three regions* : heaven, firmament and
earth, as the sun, the lightning, and terrestrial fire.

9 *Atri* : the famous Ṛṣi, ancestor of Vasuśruta the
Ṛṣi or seer of this hymn.

Āpris : is the collective name of the Gods and
deified objects addressed in the hymn. See I, 13; 142;
188; II. 3 ; III. 4.

4 *Thou soft as wool* : the Barhis or sacred grass, on
which the Gods are to sit, is addressed.

5 *Doors Divine* : of the sacrificial hall, types of the
portals of the East. See I. 188. 5.

Eternal Law : law-ordained sacrifice.

7 *Two celestial Priests* : See I. 13. 8.

10 *Vanaspati* : the sacrificial stake, regarded as a form
of Agni.

11 *S āhā* : Hail ! Glory ! is here an Āprī, as a
personification of Agni. See I. 13. 12.

1 *Strong enduring steeds* : or constant worshippers,
according to Sāyaṇa : and this interpretation is
supported by stanza 2, which is a slightly-varied
repetition of this stanza.

So that this glorious fuel may send forth
by day its light for thee. Bring food to
those who sing thy praise.

5 To thee the splendid, Lord of flame, bright,
wondrous, Prince of men, is brought.
Oblation with the holy verse, O Agni,
bearer of our gifts.
Bring food to those who sing thy praise.

6 These Agnis in the seats of the fire nourish
each thing most excellent.
They give delight, they spread abroad,
they move themselves continually. Bring
food to those who sing thy praise.

7 Agni, these brilliant flames of thine wax
like strong chargers mightily,
Who with the treadings of their hoofs go
swiftly to the stalls of kine. Bring food
to those who sing thy praise.

8 To us who laud thee, Agni, bring fresh
food and safe and happy homes.
May we who have sung hymns to thee
have thee for envoy in each house.
Bring food to those who sing thy praise.

9 Thou, brilliant God, within thy mouth
warmest both ladles of the oil.
So fill us also, in our hymns, abundantly,
O Lord of Strength. Bring food to those
who sing thy praise.

10 Thus Agni have we duly served with sacrifices and with hymns.
So may he give us what we crave, store
of brave sons and fleet-foot steeds.
Bring food to those who sing thy praise.

HYMN VII. *Agni.*

1. OFFER to Agni, O my friends, your
seemly food, your seemly praise;
To him supremest o'er the folk, the Son
of Strength, the mighty Lord:

2 Him in whose presence, when they meet
in full assembly, men rejoice;
Even him whom worthy ones inflame, and
living creatures bring to life.

3 When we present to him the food and
sacrificial gifts of men,

He by the might of splendour grasps the
holy Ordinance's rein.

4 He gives a signal in the night even to him
who is afar,
When he, the Bright, unchanged by eld,
consumes the sovrans of the wood.

5 He in whose service on the ways they offer
up their drops of sweat,
On him as their high kin have they mounted, as ridges on the earth.

6 Whom, sought of many, mortal man hath
found to be the Stay of all;
He who gives flavour to our food, the
home of every man that lives.

7 Even as a herd that crops the grass he
shears the field and wilderness,
With flashing teeth and beard of gold,
deft with his unabated might.

8 For him, to whom, bright as an axe he,
as to Atri, hath flashed forth,
Hath the well-bearing Mother borne,
producing when her time is come.

9 Agni to whom the oil is shed by him thou
lovest to support,
Bestow upon these mortals fame and splendour and intelligence.

10 Such zeal hath he, resistless one: he gained
the cattle given by thee.
Agni, may Atri overcome the Dasyus who
bestow no gifts, subdue the men who
give no food.

HYMN VIII. *Agni.*

1. O AGNI urged to strength, the men of
old who loved the Law enkindled thee,
the Ancient, for their aid,
Thee very bright, and holy, nourisher of
all, most excellent, the Friend and
Master of the home.

---

6 *These Agnis* : the original flames of Agni manifested in the three fire-altars, each fire being regarded as
an independent representative of Agni.

7 *To the stalls of kine* : the flames of Agni who
longs for oblations of milk and butter are compared to
the horses of raiders who seize the cattle of their
enemies.

The Ṛṣi of this and of the following hymn is
said to be iṣa of the family of Atri. But this name
appears to have been formed from the word iṣám (food)
in stanza 1, or iṣáḥ in stanza 1, and not to be the
name of a real person.

3 *Grasps the holy Ordinance's rein* : assumes the
direction of the sacrifice as invoker of the Gods and
conveyer of men's oblations.

5 *On the ways* : in the course of sacrifice. The toil
of the ministering priests is often regarded as their
offering to the Gods. *On him* : the meaning of this
line is obscure. Professor Wilson, following Sāyaṇa,
translates : 'and (the drops) mount upon the fire as
if they were its own numerous offspring as (boys
ride) upon the back (of a father).' The meaning may
be that the drops mount upon Agni, who bears the
oblations to heaven, as the backs or ridges (of the
hills) raise themselves above the ground. My version,
which follows Professor Ludwig's explanation, is only
conjectural.

8 This stanza also is obscure. *The well-bearing
Mother* is the lower fire-stick which at the proper time
produces the spark for the man to whom Agni, keen
and bright as an axe, is manifested as he was to the
ancient sage Atri, the ancestor of the Ṛṣi of the hymn.

10 The last Pāda is difficult. Professor Wilson,
after Sāyaṇa, renders it : 'may iṣa overcome (hostile)
men.' But iṣaḥ is evidently 'food', and not the name
of a man.

2 Thee, Agni, men have stablished as their
guest of old, as Master of the household,
thee, with hair of flame;
High-bannered, multiform, distributor of
wealth, kind helper, good protector, drier
of the floods.

3 The tribes of men praise thee, Agni, who
knowest well burnt offerings, the
Discerner, lavishest of wealth,
Dwelling in secret, Blest One ! visible to
all, loud-roaring, skilled in worship,
glorified with oil.

4 Ever to thee, O Agni, as exceeding strong
have we drawn nigh with songs and
reverence singing hymns.
So be thou pleased with us, Angiras ! as
a God enkindled by the noble with man's
goodly light.

5 Thou, Agni ! multiform, God who art
lauded much ! givest in every house
subsistence as of old.
Thou rulest by thy might o'er food of
many a sort : that light of thine when
blazing may not be opposed.

6 The Gods, Most Youthful Agni, have made
thee, inflamed, the bearer of oblations
and the messenger.
Thee, widely-reaching, homed in sacred
oil, invoked, effulgent, have they made
the Eye that stirs the thought.

7 Men seeking joy have lit thee worshipped
from of old, O Agni, with good fuel
and with sacred oil.
So thou, bedewed and waxing mighty by
the plants, spreadest thyself abroad over
the realms of earth.

HYMN IX.   *Agni.*

1. BEARING oblations mortal men, O Agni,
worship thee the God.
I deem thee Jātavedas : bear our offerings,
thou, unceasingly.

2 In the man's home who offers gifts, where
grass is trimmed, Agni is Priest,
To whom all sacrifices come and strengthenings that win renown.

3 Whom, as an infant newly-born, the
kindling-sticks have brought to life,

Sustainer of the tribes of men, skilled in
well-ordered sacrifice.

4 Yea, very hard art thou to grasp, like
offspring of the wriggling snakes,
When thou consumest many woods like an
ox, Agni, in the mead.

5 Whose flames, when thou art sending forth
the smoke, completely reach the mark,
When Trta in the height of heaven, like
as a smelter fanneth thee, e'en as a
smelter sharpeneth thee.

6 O Agni, by thy succour and by Mitra s
friendly furtherance,
May we, averting hate, subdue the wickedness of mortal men.

7 O Agni, to our heroes bring such riches,
thou victorious God.
May he protect and nourish us, and help
in gaining strength : be thou near us
in fight for our success.

HYMN X.   *Agni.*

1. BRING us most mighty splendour thou,
Agni, resistless on thy way.
With overflowing store of wealth mark
out for us a path to strength.

2 Ours art thou, wondrous Agni, by wisdom
and bounteousness of power.
The might of Asuras rests on thee, like
Mitra worshipful in act.

3 Agni, increase our means of life, increase
the house and home of these,
The men, the princes who have won great
riches through our hymns of praise.

4 Bright Agni, they who deck their songs
for thee have horses as their meed.
The men are mighty in their might, they
whose high laud, as that of heaven,
awakes thee of its own accord.

5 O Agni, those resplendent flames of thine
go valorously forth,
Like lightnings flashing round us, like a
rattling car that seeks the spoil.

6 Now, Agni, come to succour us; let priests
draw nigh to offer gifts;

---

3 *Dwelling in secret* : latent in the fire-sticks, or
dwelling in men's hearts.

4 *The noble* : the patron of the sacrifice.

7 *Bedewed* : anointed with clarified butter. *By the
plants* which supply fuel.

---

1 *I deem thee Jātavedas* : I hold thee to be the
knower of all created beings.

---

4 *Like an ox* : as an ox eats up the grass.

5 *Trta* : here perhaps Vāyu, the Wind. According
to Sāyaṇa, Trta here means Agni himself *diffused in the
three regions.* See Macdonell, J.R.A.S. July, 1893,
p. 446.

---

4 *Awakes thee of its own accord* : the meaning of
this last Pāda is doubtful. Sāyaṇa disconnects *bodhati
tmánā* from the preceding words and supplies the
name of the Ṛṣi Gaya : Gaya of his own accord
arouses thee.

6 *Subdue all regions of the earth* : an allusion to the
digvijaya, universal conquest, or subjugation of all
neighbouring princes. Sāyaṇa explains *āśāḥ* alternatively as 'wishes' ; 'compass all their desires.'

And let the patrons of our rites subdue
all regions of the earth.

7 Bring to us, Agni, Aṅgiras, lauded of old
and lauded now,

Invoker ! wealth to quell the strong, that
singers may extol thee. Be near us in fight
for our success.

HYMN XI.   *Agni.*

1. THE watchful Guardian of the people hath
been born, Agni, the very strong, for
fresh prosperity.

With oil upon his face, with high heaven-
touching flame, he shineth splendidly,
pure, for the Bharatas.

2 Ensign of sacrifice, the earliest Household-
Priest, the men have kindled Agni in
his threefold seat,

With Indra and the Gods together on the
grass let the wise Priest sit to complete
the sacrifice.

3 Pure, unadorned, from thy two Mothers
art thou born: thou camest from Vivasvān
as a charming Sage.

With oil they strengthened thee, O Agni,
worshipped God : thy banner was the
smoke that mounted to the sky.

4 May Agni graciously come to our sacrifice.
The men bear Agni here and there in
every house.

He hath become an envoy, bearer of our
gifts : electing Agni, men choose one
exceeding wise.

5 For thee, O Agni, is this sweetest prayer
of mine : dear to thy spirit be this
product of my thought.

As great streams fill the river so our songs
of praise fill thee, and make thee yet
more mighty in thy strength.

6 O Agni, the Aṅgirases discovered thee
what time thou layest hidden, fleeing
back from wood to wood.

Thou by attrition art produced as conquering might, and men, O Aṅgiras, call
thee the Son of Strength.

HYMN XII.   *Agni.*

1. To Agni, lofty Asura, meet for worship,
Steer of eternal Law, my prayer I offer;

I bring my song directed to the Mighty
like pure oil for his mouth at sacrifices.

2 Mark the Law, thou who knowest, yea,
observe it : send forth the full streams
of eternal Order.

I use no sorcery with might or falsehood :
the sacred Law of the Red Steer I
follow.

3 How hast thou, follower of the Law eternal,
become the knower of a new song,
Agni ?

The God, the Guardian of the seasons,
knows me : the Lord of him who won
this wealth I know not.

4 Who, Agni, in alliance with thy foeman,
what splendid helpers won for them
their riches ?

Agni, who guard the dwelling-place of
falsehood ? Who are protectors of the
speech of liars ?

5 Agni, those friends of thine have turned
them from thee : gracious of old, they
have become ungracious.

They have deceived themselves by their
own speeches, uttering wicked words
against the righteous.

6 He who pays sacrifice to thee with homage,
O Agni, keeps the Red Steer's Law
eternal;

Wide is his dwelling. May the noble
offspring of Nahuṣa who wandered forth
come hither.

HYMN XIII.   *Agni.*

1. WITH songs of praise we call on thee, we
kindle thee with songs of praise,

Agni, with songs of praise, for help.

2 Eager for wealth, we meditate Agni's
effectual praise to-day,

Praise of the God who touches heaven.

3 May Agni, Priest among mankind, take
pleasure in our songs of praise,

And worship the Celestial Folk.

4 Thou, Agni, art spread widely forth, Priest
dear and excellent; through thee

Men make the sacrifice complete.

---

1 *For the Bharatas* : for the sake of the priests,
according to Sāyaṇa and Mahīdhara.

2 *In his threefold seat* ; the three fire-altars.

3 *Thy two Mothers* : the fire-sticks. *Vivasvān* : the
sacrificer, according to Sāyaṇa. But see Index.

4 *Here and there* : or in different places ; from
one altar to another.

6 *Thou layest hidden* : alluding to the legend of
the flight and capture of Agni. See 1. 65. 1.

3 *Knower of a new song* : according to Professor
Ludwig, the new song is one in which for the first
time we have been obliged to remind thee of thy
duties as the champion of eternal Law, whereas formerly
we had only thanks and prayers to offer thee. *The
Guardian of the seasons* : thou, Agni, who, as the Sun,
regulatest the seasons, knowest me ; but I know
nothing of the God who has befriended my wealthy
enemy.

4 Who are the Gods who have enriched the
wicked who hate both thee and me ?

6 The meaning of the second line is obscure.
Professor Wilson, following Sāyaṇa, translates : 'and
may a virtuous successor of the man who diligently
worships thee come in his place.' I adopt Professor
Ludwig's rendering.

5 Singers exalt thee, Agni, well lauded, best
giver of our strength :
So grant thou us heroic might.

6 Thou, Agni, as the felly rings the spokes,
encompassest the Gods.
I yearn for bounty manifold.

HYMN XIV. *Agni.*

1. ENKINDLING the Immortal, wake Agni with
song of praise : may he bear our oblations to the Gods.

2 At high solemnities mortal men glorify him
the Immortal, best
At sacrifice among mankind.

3 That he may bear their gifts to heaven,
all glorify him Agni, God,
With ladle that distilleth oil.

4 Agni shone bright when born, with light
killing the Dasyus and the dark :
He found the Kine, the Floods, the Sun.

5 Serve Agni, God adorable, the Sage whose
back is balmed with oil :
Let him approach, and hear my call.

6 They have exalted Agni, God of all
mankind, with oil and hymns
Of praise, devout and eloquent.

HYMN XV. *Agni.*

1. To him, the far-renowned, the wise
Ordainer, ancient and glorious, a song
I offer.
Enthroned in oil, the Asura, bliss-giver,
is Agni, firm support of noble riches.

2 By holy Law they kept supporting Order,
by help of sacrifice, in loftiest heaven,—
They who attained with born men to the
unborn, men seated on that stay, heaven's
firm sustainer.

3 Averting woe, they labour hard to bring
him, the ancient, plenteous food as
power resistless.
May he, born newly, conquer his assailants:
round him they stand as round an
angry lion.

4 When, like a mother, spreading forth to
nourish, to cherish and regard each
man that liveth,—

The Ṛṣi of Hymn XV, is said to be Dharuṇa of
the family of Atri, but this name is evidently taken from
the words *dharuṇaḥ* (firm) in stanza 1, and *dharuṇam* in
stanza 2.

2 *They who attained* : our ancestors, or the Fathers,
who with, or by the aid of, the priests, were raised to
seats in the firmament.

4 *Thou wanderest round* : seeking fresh wood to burn
in order to restore thy exhausted strength.

Consuming all the strength that thou hast
gotten, thou wanderest round, thyself,
in varied fashion.

5 May strength preserve the compass of
thy vigour, God ! that broad stream of
thine that beareth riches.
Thou, like a thief who keeps his refuge
secret, hast holpen Atri to great wealth,
by teaching.

HYMN XVI. *Agni.*

1. GREAT power is in the beam of light,
sing praise to Agni, to the God
Whom men have set in foremost place
like Mitra with their eulogies.

2 He by the splendour of his arms is Priest
of every able man.
Agni conveys oblation straight, and deals,
as Bhaga deals, his boons.

3 All rests upon the laud and love of him
the rich, high-flaming God,
On whom, loud-roaring, men have laid
great strength as on a faithful friend.

4 So, Agni, be the Friend of these with
liberal gift of hero strength.
Yea, Heaven and Earth have not surpassed
this Youthful One in glorious fame.

5 O Agni, quickly come to us, and, glorified,
bring precious wealth.
So we and these our princes will assemble
for the good of all. Be near in fight to
prosper us.

HYMN XVII. *Agni.*

1. GOD, may a mortal call the Strong
hither, with solemn rites, to aid,
A man call Agni to protect when sacrifice
is well prepared.

2 Near him thou seemest mightier still in
native glory, set to hold
Apart yon flame-hued vault of heaven,
lovely beyond the thought of man.

5 *May strength preserve* : mayest thou ever find fresh
fuel or strengthening food.

Thou, like a thief : 'This may, perhaps, imply that
the wealth bestowed upon the *Ṛṣi* is deposited in a
secure receptacle, like the hidden booty of a thief, but
the whole *Sukta* is obscurely worded.'—Wilson.

1 *Like Mitra* : or as a friend.

2 *Every able man* : who has means, will, and skill
as a sacrificer.

4 *Of these* : institutors of the sacrifice. *This Youthful One* : Agni. The exact meaning of the second line
is somewhat uncertain.

1 *The Strong* : Agni.

2 *Near him* : Sūrya.

3 Yea, this is by the light of him whom
   powerful song hath bound to act,
Whose beams of splendour flash on high
   as though they sprang from heavenly
   seed.

4 Wealth loads the Wonder-Worker's car
   through his, the very wise One's power.
Then, meet to be invoked among all tribes,
   is Agni glorified.

5 Now, too, the princes shall obtain excellent riches by our lips.
Protect us for our welfare : lend thy
   succour, O thou Son of Strength. Be
   near in fight to prosper us.

HYMN XVIII.   *Agni.*

1. AT dawn let Agni, much-beloved guest of
   the house, be glorified;
Immortal who delights in all oblations
   brought by mortal men.

2 For Dvita who receives through wealth
   of native strength maimed offerings,
Thy praiser even gains at once the Soma-
   drops, Immortal Gods !

3 Nobles, with song I call that car of yours
   that shines with lengthened life,
For, God who givest steeds ! that car
   hither and thither goes unharmed.

4 They who have varied ways of thought,
   who guard the lauds within their lips,

And strew the grass before the light, have
   decked themselves with high renown.

5 Immortal Agni, give the chiefs, heroes who
   institute the rite,
Heroes' illustrious, lofty fame, who at the
   synod met for praise presented me with
   fifty steeds.

HYMN XIX.   *Agni.*

1. ONE state begets another state : husk is
   made visible from husk :
Within his Mother's side he speaks.

2 Discerning, have they offered gifts : they
   guard the strength that never wastes.
To a strong fort have they pressed in.

3 Śvaitreya's people, all his men, have
   gloriously increased in might.
A gold chain Bṛhaduktha wears, as, through
   this Soma, seeking spoil.

4 I bring, as 'twere, the longed-for milk, the
   dear milk of the Sister-Pair.
Like to a caldron filled with food is he,
   unconquered, conquering all.

5 Beam of light, come to us in sportive
   fashion, finding thyself close to the wind
   that fans thee.
These flames of his are wasting flames,
   like arrows keen-pointed, sharpened, on
   his breast.

---

3 *This is by the light of him* : this Sūrya, or the
Sun, shines only by the light of Agni.

4 When the wonder-working Sun brings us wealth,
the merit is due to Agni.—Ludwig. According to
Sāyaṇa, the meaning is, as given by Professor Wilson :
'By the worship of him who is pleasing of aspect
the provident (heap) wealth in their cars.' The absence
of a verb makes the exact meaning uncertain.

The hymn is ascribed to a Ṛṣi Dvita of the family
of Atri, but the name seems to be borrowed from the
Dvita of stanza 2.

2 The meaning of this stanza is obscure. According to Sāyaṇa, Dvita is the Ṛṣi of the hymn, and the
first line is rendered by Professor Wilson : 'Be (willing
to make) a grant of thine own strength to Dvita, the
bearer of the pure libation.' But *mṛktávāhase* must mean
the bearer or receiver of a maimed or imperfect oblation,
and Dvita then would be the mythical personage of
that name to whom, together with Tṛta, it, was
customary to wish away and consign any threatened
calamity or unpleasantness (To Tṛta and to Dvita, Dawn!
bear thou away the evil dream RV. X. 47. 16). In
the present case, any possible imperfection in the offering made to Agni is previously removed by a libation
to Dvita. See Professor Ludwig's Commentary, Part
I. 338. M. Bergaigne (Religion Vedique, II. 327) gives
a different explanation.

3 *Nobles* : wealthy institutors of the sacrifice ;
Maghavans. *That car of yours* : apparently Agni, who
carries oblations to the Gods.

4 *Varied ways of thought* : manifold modes of showing
their devotion. *Guard the lauds* : perpetuate hymns of

praise by frequent repetition. *Before the light* : according
to Sāyaṇa, *svárṇare* means, 'in the sacrifice which leads
man to heaven.' Professor Grassmann renders the word
by 'Dem Glanzesherrn,' for the Lord of Light.'

---

1 We know only outward forms and circumstances,
and the real nature of the God is concealed from us.
   The God speaks only in the bosom of his mother.
—Ludwig. Sāyaṇa gives a totally different interpretation, the word *vavrí* (husk or covering) in the first
stanza being taken as the name of the Ṛṣi of the hymn.

2 *Discerning* : perhaps, as Prof. Ludwig suggests,
distinguishing thy essence from thy appearance. The
strong fort which the worshippers have entered and
settled in is, perhaps, their religious knowledge.

3 Śvaitreya's people have conquered, and their
priest Bṛhaduktha has been rewarded for his services
with a chain of gold, won for him by the Soma-libations
which he has offered.—Ludwig. Śvaitreya (son of Śvitrā
See I. 33. 14) and Bṛhaduktha are, apparently, proper
names. Sāyaṇa explains the former as Agni or lightning
'abiding in the white firmament,' and the latter as
'zealously or highly praising.'

4 *The dear milk of the Sister-Pair* : the Soma dear
to Heaven and Earth. The exact meaning of the line
is uncertain.

5 This stanza is very difficult, and, like much of
the rest of the hymn, can be only conjecturally
translated.

HYMN XX.   *Agni.*

1. AGNI, best winner of the spoil, cause us to praise before the Gods
As our associate meet for lauds, wealth which thou verily deemest wealth.

2 Agni, the great who ward not off the anger of thy power and might
Stir up the wrath and hatred due to one who holds an alien creed.

3 Thee, Agni, would we choose as Priest, the perfecter of strength and skill;
We who bring sacred food invoke with song thee Chief at holy rites.

4 Here as is needful for thine aid we toil, O Conqueror, day by day,
For wealth, for Law. May we rejoice, Most Wise One ! at the feast, with kine, rejoice, with heroes, at the feast.

HYMN XXI.   *Agni.*

1. WE stablish thee as Manus used, as Manus used we kindle thee.
Like Manus, for the pious man, Aṅgiras, Agni, worship Gods.

2 For well, O Agni, art thou pleased when thou art kindled mid mankind.
Straight go the ladles unto thee, thou high-born God whose food is oil.

3 Thee have all Gods of one accord established as their messenger.
Serving at sacrifices men adore thee as a God, O Sage.

4 Let mortal man adore your God, Agni, with worship due to Gods.
Shine forth enkindled, Radiant One. Sit in the chamber of the Law, sit in the chamber of the food.

HYMN XXII.   *Agni.*

1. LIKE Atri, Viśvasāman ! sing to him of purifying light,

The Ṛṣis of the hymn are said to be certain members of the family of Atri called Prayasvats, that is, bringers or possessors of sacred food, a word which occurs in stanza 3.
2 *Who holds on alien creed* : who follows other than Vedic observances.
4 *For Law* : to maintain the holy law, and especially the eternally-ordained sacrifice. *With kine* : possessing plenty of cattle. *With heroes* : with brave sons about us.

———

The hymn is ascribed to a Ṛṣi Sasa, this name being taken from the word *sasásya* in the last Pāda of stanza 4.
1 *Manus* another form of Manu.
4 *The chamber of the Law* : the sacrificial chamber or hall. *Of the food* : or, as Professor Roth explains it, where the sacred grass is strewn ; according to Sāyaṇa, of Sasa, the supposed Ṛṣi of the hymn.

———

The Ṛṣi is Viśvasāman, of the family of Atri.

Who must be praised in holy rites, the Priest most welcome in the house.

2 Set Jātavedas in his place, Agni the God and Minister.
Let sacrifice proceed to-day duly, comprising all the Gods.

3 All mortals come to thee for aid, the God of most observant mind.
Of thine excelling favour we bethink us as we long for it.

4 Mark with attention this our speech, O Agni, thou victorious One.
Thee, Strong-jawed ! as the homestead's Lord, the Atris with their lauds exalt, the Atris beautify with songs.

HYMN XXIII.   *Agni.*

1. BY thy fair splendour's mighty power, O Agni, bring victorious wealth,
Wealth that o'ercometh all mankind, and, near us, conquereth in fight.

2 Victorious Agni, bring to us the wealth that vanquisheth in war;
For thou art wonderful and true, giver of strength in herds of kine.

3 For all the folk with one accord, whose sacred grass is trimmed and strewn,
Invite thee to their worship-halls, as a dear Priest, for choicest wealth.

4 For he, the God of all men, hath gotten him might that quelleth foes.
O Agni, in these homes shine forth, bright God ! for our prosperity, shine, Purifier ! splendidly.

HYMN XXIV.   *Agni.*

1. O AGNI, be our nearest Friend, be thou a kind deliverer and a gracious Friend.

2 Excellent Agni, come thou nigh to us, and give us wealth most splendidly renowned.

3 So hear us, listen to this call of ours, and keep us far from every sinful man.

4 To thee then, O Most Bright, O Radiant God, we come with prayer for happiness for our friends.

———

The Ṛṣi is said to be Dyumna Viśvacarṣaṇi— both these names being words occurring in the hymn.
1 *By thy fair splendour's mighty power* : the words of the text are *dyumnásya prāsahā.*
4 *The God of all men* : *viśvácarṣaṇiḥ,* a common epithet of Agni.

The legend connected with this hymn is discussed by Prof Max Müller in Journal of the Royal Asiatic Society, New Series, II. 441 f. See Lanman's Sanskrit Reader, p. 368.

HYMN XXV. *Agni.*

1. I WILL sing near, for grace, your God
   Agni, for he is good to us.
   Son of the Brands, may he give gifts, and,
   righteous, save us from the foe.

2 For he is true, whom men of old enkindled, and the Gods themselves,
   The Priest with the delicious tongue, rich
   with the light of glorious beams.

3 With wisdom that surpasseth all, with
   gracious will most excellent,
   O Agni, worthy of our choice, shine wealth
   on us through hymns of praise.

4 Agni is King, for he extends to mortals
   and to Gods alike.
   Agni is bearer of our gifts. Worship ye
   Agni with your thoughts.

5 Agni gives to the worshipper a son, the
   best, of mightiest fame,
   Of deep devotion, ne'er subdued, bringer
   of glory to his sire.

6 Agni bestows the hero-lord who conquers
   with the men in fight.
   Agni bestows the fleet-foot steed, the victor
   never overcome.

7 The mightiest song is Agni's : shine on
   high, thou who art rich in light.
   Like the Chief Consort of a King, riches
   and strength proceed from thee.

8 Resplendent are thy rays of light : loud
   is thy voice like pressing-stones.
   Yea, of itself thy thunder goes forth like
   the roaring of the heaven.

9 Thus, seeking riches, have we paid homage
   to Agni Conqueror.
   May he, most wise, as with a ship, carry
   us over all our foes.

The Ṛṣis of the hymn are members of the family
of Atri called Vasūyus (seekers of riches). Cf. stanza 9.

1 *I will sing near* : I will invite and bring near
with my song.

2 *For he is true* : the faithful rewarder of his
worshippers.

7 The exact meaning of the stanza is uncertain.
Professor Wilson, following Sāyaṇa, paraphrases the
first line : 'That (praise) which best conveys (our
veneration is due) to Agni : affluent in splendour,
grant us, (Agni), great (wealth).'

Like the Chief Consort of a King : as the chief
queen proceeds from her home in royal state. Professor
Ludwig translates *mā́ iṣiva* by 'as a strong cow,' but
gives in his Commentary the alternative rendering 'as a
king's wife.' Sāyaṇa makes *mahiṣi* an adjective agreeing with *rayiḥ*, and says that *iva* like, is pleonastic. I
have followed Mahīdhara.

8 *Loud is thy voice* : the meaning of this half-line
is not certain.

HXMN XXVI. *Agni.*

1. O AGNI, Holy and Divine, with splendour
   and thy pleasant tongue
   Bring hither and adore the Gods.

2 We pray thee, thou who droppest oil,
   bright-rayed ! who lookest on the Sun,
   Bring the Gods hither to the feast.

3 We have enkindled thee, O Sage, bright
   caller of the Gods to feast.
   O Agni, great in Sacrifice.

4 O Agni, come with all the Gods, come
   to our sacrificial gift :
   We choose thee as Invoking Priest.

5 Bring, Agni, to the worshipper who pours
   the juice, heroic strength :
   Sit with the Gods upon the grass.

6 Victor of thousands, Agni, thou, enkindled, cherishest the laws,
   Laud-worthy, envoy of the Gods.

7 Set Agni Jātavedas down, the bearer of
   our sacred gifts,
   Most Youthful, God and Minister.

8 Duly proceed our sacrifice, comprising all
   the Gods, to-day :
   Strew holy grass to be their seat.

9 So may the Maruts sit thereon, the Aśvins,
   Mitra, Varuṇa :
   The Gods with all their company.

HYMN XXVII. *Agni.*

1. THE Godlike hero, famousest of nobles,
   hath granted me two oxen with a wagon.
   Trvṛṣan's son Tryaruṇa hath distinguished
   himself, Vaiśvānara Agni ! with ten thousands.

2 Protect Tryaruṇa, as thou art waxing strong
   and art highly praised, Vaiśvānara Agni!
   Who granteth me a hundred kine and
   twenty, and two bay horses, good at
   draught, and harnessed.

3 So Trasadasyu served thee, God Most
   Youthful, craving thy favour for the
   ninth time, Agni ;
   Tryaruṇa who with attentive spirit accepteth many a song from me the mighty.

6 *Cherishest the laws* : especially religious ordinances,
sacrifices.

The Ṛṣis are said to be Tryaruṇa, Trasadasyu,
and Aśvamedha ; or Atri alone. The metre is Triṣṭup
in stanzas 1, 2, 3, and Anuṣṭup in 4, 5, 6 ; and,
correspondingly, the hymn is made up of two separate
and independent eulogies of munificent princes.

3 *Trasadasyu* : Terror of Dasyus ; apparently, as
Ludwig suggests, an honorary name or title of several
princes. *Accepteth* : rewards with gifts.

4 He who declares his wish to me, to Aśva-
    medha, to the Prince,
  Pays him who with his verse seeks gain,
    gives power to him who keeps the Law.
5 From whom a hundred oxen, all of speckled
    hue, delight my heart,
  The gifts of Aśvamedha, like thrice-mingled
    draughts of Soma juice.
6 To Aśvamedha who bestows a hundred
    gifts grant hero power,
  O Indra-Agni ! lofty rule like the unwast-
    ing Sun in heaven.

HYMN XXVIII.   *Agni.*

1. AGNI inflamed hath sent to heaven his
    lustre : he shines forth widely turning
    unto Morning.
  Eastward the ladle goes that brings all
    blessing, praising the Gods with homage
    and oblation.
2 Enkindled, thou art King of the immortal
    world : him who brings offerings thou
    attendest for his weal.
  He whom thou urgest on makes all posses-
    sions his : he sets before thee, Agni, gifts
    that guests may claim.
3 Show thyself strong for mighty bliss, O
    Agni, most excellent be thine effulgent
    splendours.
  Make easy to maintain our household lord-
    ship, and overcome the might of those
    who hate us.
4 Thy glory, Agni, I adore, kindled, exalted
    in thy strength.
  A Steer of brilliant splendour, thou art
    lighted well at sacred rites.
5 Agni, invoked and kindled, serve the Gods,
    thou skilled in sacrifice :
  For thou art bearer of our gifts.
6 Invoke and worship Agni while the sacri-
    ficial rite proceeds :
  For offering-bearer choose ye him.

HYMN XXIX.   *Agni.*

1. MAN's worship of the Gods hath three
    great lustres, and three celestial lights
    have they established
  The Maruts gifted with pure strength adore
    thee, for thou, O Indra, art their sapient
    Ṛṣi.
2 What time the Maruts sang their song to
    Indra, joyous when he had drunk of
    Soma juices,
  He grasped his thunderbolt to slay the
    Dragon, and loosed, that they might flow,
    the youthful Waters.
3 And, O ye Brahmans, Maruts, so may
    Indra drink draughts of this my carefully
    pressed Soma ;
  For this oblation found for man the cattle,
    and Indra, having quaffed it, slew the
    Dragon.
4 Then heaven and earth he sundered and
    supported : wrapped even in these he
    struck the Beast with terror.
  So Indra forced the Engulfer to disgorge-
    ment, and slew the Dānava panting
    against him.
5 Thus all the Gods, O Maghavan, delivered
    to thee of their free will the draught of
    Somà ;
  When thou for Etaśa didst cause to tarry
    the flying mares of Sūrya racing forward.
6 When Maghavan with the thunderbolt
    demolished his nine-and-ninety castles
    all together,
  The Maruts, where they met, glorified
    Indra : ye with the Tṛṣṭup hymn
    obstructed heaven.
7 As friend to aid a friend, Agni dressed
    quickly three hundred buffaloes, even as
    he willed it.
  And Indra, from man's gift, for Vṛtra's

---

4 The stanza is difficult. Aśvamedha apparently
says that the man who requests him to institute a
sacrifice is by so doing the enricher of the priests.
  5 *Thrice-mingled* : mixed with milk, curds, and
parched grain.

The hymn is ascribed to a supposed Viśvavārā, a
lady of the family of Atri.
  1 *The ladle* : the sacrificial ladle with which the oil
or clarified butter is taken up and poured out. The
text has the feminine adjective *ghṛtācī* only, *juhū* being
understood. *That brings all blessing* : Sāyaṇa takes
viśvavārā to be the name of a woman. *Praising the
Gods* : said figuratively of the ladle held by the priest
who praises.
  3 *Make easy to maintain* : or, to follow Sāyaṇa :
Perfect the well-knit bond of wife and husband.

---

1 *Three great lustres* : this is Sāyaṇa's explanation of
the *tryaryamā* of the text. Professor Ludwig suggests
that human relationships, such as *Maghavans* or nobles,
priests, and *viśas* or the people, may be intended. *The
three celestial lights* : the Sun, the Wind, the Fire, according to Sāyaṇa. *They* : the Maruts, says Sāyaṇa. *Ṛṣi* :
here meaning beholder, according to Sāyaṇa.
  3 *Brahmans* : priests. Sāyaṇa explains the word as
meaning lofty or mighty in this passage.
  4 *The Beast* : the demon Vṛtra. *The Engulfer* :
Vṛtra, who had swallowed the celestial waters. *The
Dānava* : the son of Danu, Vṛtra.
  For *Etaśa* : See II. 19. 5.
  6 *His nine-and-ninety castles* : the aerial castles of
Śambara, the demon of drought. *Obstructed heaven* :
made the loud hymn strike the sky.

slaughter, drank off at once three lakes of pressed-out Soma.

8 When thou three hundred buffaloes' flesh hadst eaten, and drunk, as Maghavan, three lakes of Soma,
All the Gods raised as 'twere a shout of triumph to Indra praise because he slew the Dragon.

9 What time ye came with strong steeds swiftly speeding, O Uśanā and Indra, to the dwelling,
Thou camest thither conquering together with Kutsa and the Gods : thou slewest Śuṣṇa.

10 One car-wheel of the Sun thou rolledst forward, and one thou settest free to move for Kutsa.
Thou slewest noseless Dasyus with thy weapon, and in their home o'erthrewest hostile speakers.

11 The lauds of Gaurivīti made thee mighty : to Vidathin's son, as prey, thou gavest Pipru.
Rjiśvan drew thee into friendship dressing the sacred food, and thou hast drunk his Soma.

12 Navagvas and Daśagvas with libations of Soma juice sing hymns of praise to Indra.
Labouring at their task the men laid open the stall of Kine though firmly closed and fastened.

13 How shall I serve thee, Maghavan, though knowing full well what hero deeds thou hast accomplished ?
And the fresh deeds which thou wilt do, Most Mighty ! these, too, will we tell forth in sacred synods.

14 Resistless from of old through hero courage, thou hast done all these many acts, O Indra.
What thou wilt do in bravery, Thunder-wielder ! none is there who may hinder this thy prowess.

7 *Three lakes* : large vessels or tubs are probably intended.

9 *Uśanā* : Indra's special friend. See Index. *To the dwelling* : of Kutsa.

10 *One car wheel* : an eclipse of the sun appears to be referred to. *Noseless* : that is, the flat-nosed barbarians, *a-nāsaḥ* ; or the word may be, as Sāyaṇa explains it, *an-āsaḥ*, i.e. mouthless, voiceless, unintelligibly speaking. See Muir, *Original Sanskrit Texts*, II. 377.

11 *Gaurivīti* : the Ṛ i of the hymn. *Vidathin's son* : Ṛjiśvan, mentioned in Book I, as a favourite of Indra.

12 *Navagvas and Daśagvas* : priestly families connected or identified with the Aṅgirases.

15 Indra, accept the prayers which now are offered, accept the new prayers, Mightiest ! which we utter.
Like fair and well-made robes, I, seeking riches, as a deft craftsman makes a car, have wrought them.

HYMN XXX.   *Indra.*

1. WHERE is that Hero ? Who hath looked on Indra borne on light-rolling car by Tawny Coursers,
Who, Thunderer, seeks with wealth the Soma-presser, and to his house goes, much-invoked, to aid him ?

2 I have beheld his strong and secret dwelling, longing have sought the Founder's habitation.
I asked of others, and they said in answer, May we, awakened men, attain to Indra.

3 We will tell, Indra, when we pour libation, what mighty deeds thou hast performed to please us.
Let him who knows not learn, who knows them listen : hither rides Maghavan with all his army.

4 Indra, when born, thou madest firm thy spirit : alone thou seekest war to fight with many.
With might thou clavest e'en the rock asunder, and foundest out the stable of the Milch-kine.

5 When thou wast born supremest at a distance, bearing a name renowned in far-off regions,
Since then e'en Gods have been afraid of Indra : he conquered all the floods which served the Dāsa.

6 These blissful Maruts sing their psalm to praise thee, and pour to thee libation of the Soma.
Indra with wondrous powers subdued the Dragon, the guileful lurker who beset the waters.

7 Thou, Maghavan, from the first didst scatter foemen, speeding, while joying in the milk, the Giver.

2 *I have beheld* : meaning, perhaps, I have tried to behold, I have looked for. *The Founder's habitation* : the dwelling-place of Indra who established the world.

5 *Which served the Dāsá* : which were subject to the demon Vṛtra.

7 *The giver* : the offerer of oblations. But the meaning of *dánam* is uncertain. Professor Ludwig translates it by 'the splitting (thunderbolt),' and Sāyaṇa explains it as 'the assailant of the Gods (Vṛtra).'
Namuci : one of the malignant demons of the atmosphere who withhold the rain.

There, seeking man's prosperity, thou
torest away the head of Namuci the
Dāsa.

8 Pounding the head of Namuci the Dāsa,
me, too thou madest thine associate,
Indra !
Yea, and the rolling stone that is in heaven
both worlds, as on a car, brought to
the Maruts.

9 Women for weapons hath the Dāsa taken.
What injury can his feeble armies do
me ?
Well he distinguished his two different
voices, and Indra then advanced to fight
the Dasyu.

10 Divided from their calves the Cows went
lowing around, on every side, hither and
thither.
These Indra re-united with his helpers,
what time the well-pressed Soma made
him joyful.

11 What time the Somas mixed by Babhru
cheered him, loud the Steer bellowed in
his habitations.
So Indra drank thereof, the Fort-destroyer, and gave him guerdon, in return,
of milch-kine.

12 This good deed have the Ruśamas done,
Agni ! that they have granted me four
thousand cattle.
We have received Rṇañcaya's wealth, of
heroes the most heroic, which was freely
offered.

13 The Ruśamas, O Agni, sent me homeward with fair adornment and with
kine in thousands.
The strong libations have made Indra joyful, when night, whose course was ending,
changed to morning.

14 Night, well-nigh ended, at Rṇañcaya's
coming, King of the Ruśamas, was
changed to morning.
Like a strong courser, fleet of foot, urged
onward, Babhru hath gained four thousand as his guerdon.

15 We have received four thousand head of
cattle presented by the Ruśamas, O
Agni.
And we, the singers, have received the
caldron of metal which was heated for
Pravargya.

HYMN XXXI.　　　　　Indra.

1. MAGHAVAN Indra turns his chariot downward, the strength-displaying car which
he hath mounted.
Even as a herdsman driveth forth his
cattle, he goeth, first, uninjured, fain
for treasure.

2. Haste to us, Lord of Bays; be not ungracious : visit us, lover of gold-hued
oblation.
There is naught else better than thou art,
Indra : e'en to the wifeless hast thou
given spouses.

3 When out of strength arose the strength
that conquers, Indra displayed all
powers that he possesses.
Forth from the cave he drove the milky
mothers, and with the light laid bare
investing darkness.

4. Anus have wrought a chariot for thy
Courser, and Tvaṣṭar, Much-invoked !
thy bolt that glitters.
The Brahmans with their songs exalting
Indra increased his strength that he
might slaughter Ahi.

5 When heroes sang their laud to thee the
Hero, Indra ! and stones and Aditi accordant,

8 *The rolling stone* : perhaps the thunderbolt ; or if
the thunderbolt is supposed to be the speaker of this
stanza, as Professor Ludwig is inclined to think, the
Sun must be meant ; that is, heaven and earth brought
the Sun to the Maruts to aid Indra in his fight with
the demon.

9 Indra is the speaker of the first line. *Women* :
perhaps the subject waters. *His two different voices* :
the meaning may be that Indra heard the voices of the
women as well as the voice of Namuci, and so knew
that he had not an army of demon-warriors to
fight against. Professor Wilson, following Sāyaṇa,
translates : 'the two his best beloved, (Indra) confined
in the inner apartments.'

10 *With his helpers* : with the aid of the Maruts.

11 *Babhru* : the Ṛṣi of the hymn, who appears to
have assisted the Ruśamas, a neighbouring people, in
a successful foray, and to have been rewarded with a
large portion of the booty. Rṇañcaya was the king of
of this people.

15 *Heated for Pravargya*: a ceremony introductory
to the Soma-sacrifice, in which fresh milk was poured
into a heated vessel called *mahāvīrá* or, as in this place,
gharmá.

———

1 *Even as a herdsman dri eth forth his cattle* : so, says
Sāyaṇa, Indra drives his enemies before him. *Fain for
treasure* : wishing to obtain the riches of his enemies.

2 *Gold-hued oblation* : consisting of yellow Soma
juice. *Spouses* : carried off in raids favoured by the
Warrior-God.

4 *Anus* : probably meaning Bhṛgus, who belonged
to that tribe.

The Brahmans : according to Sāyaṇa, the Aṅgirases,
or the Maruts.

5 *Stones*: used for pressing the Soma juice. *Without or steed or chariot* : that is, the worshippers of Indra
overcame their enemies by prayer and the favour of
their God.

Without or steed or chariot were the fellies which, sped by Indra, rolled upon the Dasyus.

6 I will declare thine exploits wrought aforetime, and, Maghavan, thy deeds of late achievement,
When, Lord of Might, thou sunderedst earth and heaven, winning for man the moistly-gleaming waters.

7 This is thy deed, e'en this, Wonderful ! Singer ! that, slaying Ahi, here thy strength thou showedst,
Didst check and stay e'en Śuṣṇa's wiles and magic, and, drawing nigh, didst chase away the Dasyus.

8 Thou, Indra, on the farther bank for Yadu and Turvaśa didst stay the gushing waters.
Ye both assailed the fierce : thou barest Kutsa : when Gods and Uśanā came to you together.

9 Let the steeds bring you both, Indra and Kutsa, borne on the chariot within hear-ing-distance.
Ye blew him from the waters, from his dwelling, and chased the darkness from the noble's spirit.

10 Even this sage hath come looking for suc-cour even to Vāta's docile harnessed horses.
Here are the Maruts, all. thy dear compa-nions : prayers have increased thy power and might, O Indra.

11 When night was near its close he carried forward e'en the Sun's chariot backward in its running.
Etaśa brought his wheel and firmly stays it : setting it eastward he shall give us courage.

12 This Indra, O ye men, hath come to see you, seeking a friend who hath expressed the Soma.

8 *Yadu and Turvaśa*: See Index. *Ye both* : Indra and Kutsa. *The fierce* : Śuṣṇa, a demon of drought. *Thou barest Kutsa* : to his home.

9 *Ye blew him from the waters* : drave Śuṣṇa from the atmosphere in which he dwelt, and thus removed the grief of the eminent men who instituted sacrifices.

10 *Looking for succour* : Sāya ta takes *avasyuḥ* here as the name of a Ṛṣi the seer of the hymn.

11 The return of the lingering morning sun appears to be attributed, on some particular occasion, to the special intervention of Indra on his favourite's behalf. The stanza is hardly intelligible as it stands. Sāyaṇa explains Etaśa by 'for Etaśa' The verse is discussed by Prof. Geldner (Vedische Studien, II. 162f) and his explanation is criticised by Prof. Ludwig (Ueber die Neuesten Arbeiten &c. p. 171).

12 *The creaking stone* : the upper press-stone.

———

The creaking stone is laid upon the altar, and the Adhvaryus come to turn it quickly.

13 Let mortals who were happy still be happy ; let them not come to sorrow, O Immortal.
Love thou the pious, and to these thy people—with whom may we be number-ed—give thou vigour.

HYMN XXXII.   *Indra.*

1. THE well thou clavest, settest free the fountains, and gavest rest to floods that were obstructed.
Thou, Indra, laying the great mountain open, slaying the Dānava, didst loose the torrents.

2 The fountain-depths obstructed in their seasons, thou, Thunderer ! madest flow, the mountain's udder.
Strong Indra, thou. by slaying e'en the Dragon that lay extended there hast shown thy vigour.

3 Indra with violence smote down the weapon, yea, even of that wild and mighty crea-ture.
Although he deemed himself alone un-equalled, another had been born e'en yet more potent.

4 Him, whom the heavenly food of these delighted, child of the mist, strong wax-ing, couched in darkness,
Him the bolt-hurling Thunderer with his lightning smote down and slew, the Dānava's wrath-fire, Śuṣṇa.

5 Though he might ne'er be wounded still his vitals felt that, the God's bolt, which his powers supported,
When, after offered draughts, Strong Lord, thou laidest him, fain to battle, in the pit in darkness.

6 Him as he lay there huge in length extended, still waxing in the gloom which no sun lightened,
Him, after loud-voiced threats, the Hero Indra, rejoicing in the poured libation, slaughtered.

7 When 'gainst the mighty Dānava his weapon Indra uplifted, power which none could combat,
When at the hurling of his bolt he smote him, he made him lower than all living creatures.

1 *The well* : the rain-cloud. *The fountains* : the sources of the waters of the firmament. *The mountain* : the massive cloud.
   The Dānava : Vṛtra, the son of Danu.
4 *Of these* : of living creatures.

8 The fierce God seized that huge and restless coiler, insatiate, drinker of the
sweets, recumbent,
And with his mighty weapon in his dwelling
smote down the footless evil-speaking
ogre.

9 Who may arrest his strength or check his
vigour ? Alone, resistless, he bears off
all riches.
Even these Twain, these Goddesses, through
terror of Indra's might, retire from his
dominion.

10 E'en the Celestial Axe bows down before
him, and the Earth, lover-like, gives way
to Indra.
As he imparts all vigour to these people,
straightway the folk bend them to him
the Godlike.

11 I hear that thou wast born sole Lord of
heroes of the Five Races, famed among
the people.
As such my wishes have most lately
grasped him, invoking Indra both at
eve and morning.

12 So, too, I hear of thee as in due season
urging to action and enriching singers.
What have thy friends received from thee,
the Brahmans who, faithful, rest their
hopes on thee, O Indra?

HYMN XXXIII. Indra.

1. GREAT praise to Indra, great and strong
mid heroes, I ponder thus, the feeble
to the Mighty,
Who with his band shows favour to this
people, when lauded, in the fight where
spoil is gathered.

2 So made attentive by our hymns, Steer !
Indra ! thou fastenedst the girth of thy
Bay Coursers,
Which, Maghavan, at thy will thou drivest
hither. With these subdue for us the men
who hate us.

3 They were not turned to us-ward, lofty
Indra ! while yet through lack of prayer
they stood unharnessed.
Ascend this chariot, thou whose hand
wields thunder, and draw the rein, O
Lord of noble horses.

4 Thou, because many lauds are thine, O
Indra, wast active warring in the fields
for cattle.
For Sūrya in his own abode thou, Hero,
formedst in fights even a Dāsa's nature.

5 Thine are we, Indra; thine are all these
people, conscious of might, whose cars
are set in motion.
Some hero come to us, O Strong as Ahi !
beauteous in war, to be invoked like
Bhaga.

6 Strength much to be desired is in thee,
Indra : the Immortal dances forth his
hero exploits.
Such, Lord of Treasure, give us splendid
riches. I praise the Friend's gift, his
whose wealth is mighty.

7 Thus favour us, O Indra, with thy succour; Hero, protect the bards who sing
thy praises.
Be friendly in the fray to those who offer
the skin of beautiful and well-pressed
Soma.

8 And these ten steeds which Trasadasyu gives
me, the goldrich chief, the son of Purukutsa,
Resplendent in their brightness shall convey
me. Gairikṣita willed it and so came I
hither.

9 And these, bestowed as sacrificial guerdon,
the powerful tawny steeds of Mārutāśva;
And thousands which kind Cyavatāna
gave me, abundantly bestowed for my
adornment.

10 And these commended horses, bright and
active, by Dhvanya son of Lakṣmaṇa
presented,
Came unto me, as cows into the Ṛṣi
Saṁvaraṇa's stall, with magnitude of
riches.

---

9 *These Goddesses* : Heaven and Earth.

10 *E'en the Celestial Axe* : perhaps the thunderbolt,
which is one of the meanings assigned to *svádhitiḥ.*
Sāyaṇa explains the word in this passage as 'the self-
supported heaven,' and Professor Roth thinks that a
tree of very hard wood, called Svadhiti, is intended, as
we might say, even the oak bends down before him.

11 *Of the Five Races* : belonging to the five Āryan
tribes. But see Muir, *Original Sanskrit Texts*, Vol I.
178.

4 The second half of the stanza refers to an eclipse
of the sun. Indra is said to have formed for Sūrya
in his own abode, that is, in the eastern heaven, the
nature of a Dāsa, *i. e.* made him a slave or dark.

6 *Dances forth his hero exploits* : battle being regarded as a war dance, as in the Old German poetry, and
in Homer's.—Ludwig.

8 *Son of Purukutsa* : Paurukutsya and Gairikṣita are
both patronymics of Trasadasyu.

9 This stanza is obscure. Nothing further is known
of Mārutāśva or Cyavatāna.

10 Dhvanya and his father Lakṣmaṇa are also
unknown to fame. These three concluding stanzas are
banished to the appendix by Professor Grassmann as
being a later addition to the original hymn.

HYMN XXXIV.   *Indra.*

1. BOUNDLESS and wasting not, the heavenly food of Gods goes to the foeless One, doer of wondrous deeds.
Press out, make ready, offer gifts with special zeal to him whom many laud, accepter of the prayer.

2 He who filled full his belly with the Soma's juice, Maghavan, was delighted with the meath's sweet draught,
When Uśanā, that he might slay the monstrous beast, gave him the mighty weapon with a thousand points.

3 Illustrious is the man whoever presseth out Soma for him in sunshine or in cloud and rain.
The mighty Maghavan who is the sage's Friend advanceth more and more his beauteous progeny.

4 The Strong God doth not flee away from him whose sire, whose mother or whose brother he hath done to death.
He, the Avenger, seeketh this man's offered gifts : this God, the source of riches, doth not flee from sin.

5 He seeks no enterprise with five or ten to aid, nor stays with him who pours no juice though prospering well.
The Shaker conquers or slays in this way or that, and to the pious gives a stable full of kine.

6 Exceeding strong in war he stays the chariot wheel, and, hating him who pours not, prospers him who pours.
Indra the terrible, tamer of every man, as Ārya leads away the Dāsa at his will.

7 He gathers up for plunder all the niggards' gear : excellent wealth he gives to him who offers gifts.
Not even in wide stronghold may all the folk stand firm who have provoked to anger his surpassing might.

8 When Indra Maghavan hath marked two wealthy men fighting for beauteous cows with all their followers,
He who stirs all things takes one as his close ally, and, Shaker, with his Heroes, sends the kine to him.

9 Agni ! I laud the liberal Āgniveśi, Śatri the type and standard of the pious.
May the collected waters yield him plenty, and his be powerful and bright dominion.

HYMN XXXV.   *Indra.*

1. INDRA, for our assistance bring that most effectual power of thine,
Which conquers men for us, and wins the spoil, invincible in fight.

2 Indra, whatever aids be thine, four be they, or, O Hero, three,
Or those of the Five Tribes of men, bring quickly all that help to us.

3 The aid most excellent of thee the Mightiest hitherward we call,
For thou wast born with hero might, conquering, Indra, with the Strong.

4 Mighty to prosper us wast thou born, and mighty is the strength thou hast.
In native power thy soul is firm : thy valour, Indra, slays a host.

5 O Śatakratu, Lord of Strength, O Indra, Caster of the Stone.
With all thy chariot's force assail the man who shows himself thy foe.

6 For, Mightiest Vṛtra-slayer, thee, fierce, foremost among many, folk
Whose sacred grass is trimmed invite to battle where the spoil is won.

7 Indra, do thou protect our car that mingles foremost in the fights,
That bears its part in every fray, invincible and seeking spoil.

---

2 *Uśanā* : See I. 51. 10. *The monstrous beast* : Vṛtra or Ahi ; according to Sāyaṇa, a demon called Mṛga.

3 The meaning of the second half of this stanza is somewhat uncertain. Professor Wilson, following Sāyaṇa, renders it : 'Śakra disregards the man who is proud of his descendants and vain of his person, and who, though wealthy, is a friend of the base.' Professor Grassmann, following Professor Roth's interpretation of the doubtful words, translates similarly : 'Den Prahler stösst zurück der starke, mächtige den eitlen Stutzer, der dem Kargen sich gesellt.' Professor Ludwig, whom I here follow with hesitation, explains *kavāsakhāḥ*, or *kavā sakhā* (like Agnāviṣṇu, Agnāmarut, Nabhānediṣṭha, etc.) as, friend with the wise.

4 Śakra or the Strong God does not fear the vengeance of those whose nearest relations he has killed for neglect of his worship.

Doth not flee from sin : perhaps, as Dr. Muir suggests, does not fear to punish the offender against him.

5 *The Shaker* : he who makes his enemies tremble, according to Sāyaṇa.

6 *The chariot wheel* : of his enemies.

9 *Āgniveśi* : son of Agniveśa, Śatri, a prince or chief whose name does not occur again in the Ṛgveda.
—— ——
2 *Four be they* : according to Sāyaṇa, the favours or succours given to the four castes : *three*, similarly meaning the succours given to the three worlds.

3 *With the Strong* : the Maruts.

8 Come to us, Indra, and protect our car
  with thine intelligence.
  May we, O Mightiest One, obtain excellent fame at break of day, and meditate
  our hymn at dawn.

HYMN XXXVI.   *Indra.*

1. MAY Indra come to us, he who knows
   rightly to give forth treasures from his
   store of riches.
   Even as a thirsty steer who roams the
   deserts may he drink eagerly the milked-
   out Soma.

2 Lord of Bay Horses, Hero, may the Soma
  rise to thy cheeks and jaws like moun-
  tain-ridges.
  May we, O King, as he who driveth
  coursers, all joy in thee with hymns,
  invoked of many !

3 Invoked of many, Caster of the Stone !
  my heart quakes like a rolling wheel
  for fear of penury.
  Shall not Purūvasu the singer give thee
  praise, O ever-prospering Maghavan,
  mounted on thy car ?

4 Like the press-stone is this thy praiser,
  Indra. Loudly he lifts his voice with
  strong endeavour.
  With thy left hand, O Maghavan, give
  us riches : with thy right, Lord of Bays,
  be not reluctant.

5 May the strong Heaven make thee the
  Strong wax stronger : Strong, thou art
  borne by thy two strong Bay Horses.
  So, fair of cheek, with mighty chariot,
  mighty, uphold us, strong-willed, thunder-
  armed, in battle.

6 Maruts, let all the people in obeisance
  bow down before this youthful Śrutaratha,
  Who, rich in steeds, gave me two dark
  red horses together with three hundred
  head of cattle.

HYMN XXXVII.   *Indra.*

1. BEDEWED with holy oil and meetly worshipped, the Swift One vies with Sūrya's
   beam in splendour.
   For him may mornings dawn without
   cessation who saith, Let us press Soma
   out for Indra.

2 With kindled fire and strewn grass let
  him worship, and, Soma-presser, sing
  with stones adjusted :
  And let the priest whose press-stones ring
  forth loudly, go down with his oblation
  to the river.

3 This wife is coming near who loves her
  husband who carries to his home a
  vigorous consort.
  Here may his car seek fame, here loudly
  thunder, and his wheel make a thousand
  revolutions.

4 No troubles vex that King in whose home
  Indra drinks the sharp Soma juice with
  milk commingled.
  With heroes he drives near, he slays the
  foeman : Blest, cherishing that name,
  he guards his people.

5 May he support in peace and win in
  battle : he masters both the hosts that
  meet together.
  Dear shall he be to Sūrya, dear to Agni,
  who with pressed Soma offers gifts to
  Indra.

HYMN XXXVIII.   *Indra.*

1. WIDE, Indra Śatakratu, spreads the bounty
   of thine ample grace :
   So, Lord of fair dominion, Friend of all
   men, give us splendid wealth.

2 The food which, Mightiest Indra, thou
  possessest worthy of renown
  Is bruited as most widely famed, invincible, O Golden-hued !

3 O Darter of the Stone, the powers which
  readily obey thy will,—
  Divinities, both thou and they, ye rule,
  to guard them, earth and heaven.

4 And from whatever power of thine, O
  Vṛtra-slayer, it may be,
  Bring thou to us heroic strength : thou
  hast a man's regard for us.

5 In thy protection, with these aids of
  thine, O Lord of Hundred Powers,
  Indra, may we be guarded well, Hero,
  may we be guarded well.

---

2 *To the river* : for ablution before sacrificing.

3 *This wife* : according to Sāyaṇa, the wife of
Indra who accompanies him to the sacrifice.

The foeman : or the wicked man, or his enemy,
pāpam vairiṇam vā.—Sāyaṇa.

---

3 *The powers* : according to Sāyaṇa, the strong
Maruts.

---

3 *Purūvasu* : I, the Ṛṣi ; apparently the same as
Prabhūvasu, the seer of the hymn.

---

1 *The Swift One* : Agni.

HYMN XXXIX. *Indra.*

1. STONE-DARTING Indra. Wondrous One,
   what wealth is richly given from thee,
   That bounty, Treasure-Finder ! bring filling
   both thy hands, to us.

2 Bring what thou deemest worth the wish,
   O Indra, that which is in heaven.
   So may we know thee as thou art, bound-
   less in thy munificence.

3 Thy lofty spirit, far-renowned as fain to
   give and prompt to win,—
   With this thou rendest e'en the firm,
   Stone-Darter ! so to gain thee strength.

4 Singers with many songs have made
   Indra propitious to their fame,
   Him who is King of human kind, most
   liberal of your wealthy ones.

5 To him, to Indra must be sung the poet's
   word, the hymn of praise.
   To him, accepter of the prayer, the Atris
   raise their songs on high, the Atris
   beautify their songs.

HYMN XL. *Indra. Sūrya. Atri.*

1. COME thou to what the stones have
   pressed, drink Soma, O thou Soma's
   Lord,
   Indra best Vṛtra-slayer Strong One, with
   the Strong.

2 Strong is the stone, the draught is strong,
   strong is this Soma that is pressed,
   Indra, best Vṛtra-slayer, Strong One with
   the Strong.

3 As strong I call on thee the Strong, O
   Thunder-armed, with various aids,
   Indra, best Vṛtra-slayer, Strong One with
   the Strong.

4 Impetuous, Thunderer, Strong, quelling
   the mighty, King, potent, Vṛtra-slayer,
   Soma-drinker,
   May he come hither with his yoked Bay
   Horses; may Indra gladden him at the
   noon libation.

5 O Sūrya, when the Asura's descendant,
   Svarbhānu, pierced thee through and
   through with darkness,
   All creatures looked like one who is
   bewildered, who knoweth not the place
   where he is standing.

The hymn is not homogeneous. The first part
(1—4) is a separate invocation of Indra, and the subject
of the second part is the Sun's eclipse by Svarbhānu
and release by Atri.

1 *With the Strong* : together with the Maruts.

5 *Svarbhānu* : the Asura or demon who causes
eclipses of the sun and moon, the Rāhu of later times.
The name does not occur again in the Ṛgveda.

6 What time thou smotest down Svarbhānu's
   magic that spread itself beneath the
   sky, O Indra,
   By his fourth sacred prayer Atri discovered
   Sūrya concealed in gloom that stayed
   his function.

7 Let not the oppressor with this dread,
   through anger swallow me up, for I am
   thine, O Atri.
   Mitra art thou, the sender of true blessings:
   thou and King Varuṇa be both my
   helpers.

8 The Brahman Atri, as he set the press-
   stones, serving the Gods with praise and
   adoration,
   Established in the heaven the eye of Sūrya,
   and caused Svarbhānu's magic arts to
   vanish.

9 The Atris found the Sun again, him whom
   Svarbhānu of the brood
   Of Asuras had pierced with gloom. This
   none besides had power to do.

HYMN XLI. *Viśvedevas*

1. WHO, Mitra-Varuṇa, is your pious servant
   to give you gifts from earth or mighty
   heaven ?
   Preserve us in the seat of holy Order, and
   give the offerer power that winneth
   cattle.

2 May Mitra, Varuṇa, Aryaman, and Āyu,
   Indra Ṛbhukṣan, and the Maruts, love
   us,
   And they who of one mind with bounteous
   Rudra accept the hymn and laud with
   adorations.

3 You will I call to feed the car-horse, Aśvins,
   with the wind's flight swiftest of those
   who travel :

6 *By his fourth sacred prayer* : according to Sāyaṇa,
by four stanzas (5—8) of this hymn. Probably, as
Ludwig suggests, a fourth prayer in addition to the
usual liturgy of three prayers against an eclipse. Prof.
Lanman discusses and translates the latter portion of the
hymn in Festgruss an R. von Roth, pp, 187 f. and
adduces an interesting Buddhist parallel from the
Saṁyutta Nikāya, I. ii. 1.

7 Sūrya or the Sun is the speaker. *The oppressor* :
Svarbhānu.

9 *Of the brood of Asuras* : the word *āsurāḥ* in this
hymn means belonging to, or descendant of, Asuras,
demons or evil spirits. This use of the word is unknown in the earliest portions of the Ṛgveda.

2 *Āyu* : here said to mean Vāyu, the God of wind.
See I. 162. I. The celestial Agni is probably intended.
Ṛbhu ṣan : a name of Indra, as Lord of the Ṛbhus.
   And they who : the Maruts especially, as being
Rudra's sons.

3 *The Asura of heaven* : or the Lord of heaven.
According to Sāyaṇa, Asura means here either the
destroyer of life, Rudra, or the giver of life, Sūrya or
Vāyu.

Or also to the Asura of heaven, Worshipful, bring a hymn as 'twere libation.

4 The heavenly Victor, he whose priest is
Kanva, Trta with Dyaus accordant,
Vata, Agni,
All-feeding Pūṣan, Bhaga sought the
oblation, as they whose steeds are fleetest
seek the contest.

5 Bring ye your riches forward borne on
horses : let thought be framed for help
and gain of treasure.
Blest be the priest of Auśija through
courses, the courses which are yours the
fleet, O Maruts.

6 Bring hither him who yokes the car, your
Vāyu, who praises with his songs, the
God and Singer;
And, praying and devout, noble and pru-
dent, may the Gods' Spouses in their
thoughts retain us.

7 I speed to you with powers that should be
honoured, with songs distinguishing
Heaven's mighty Daughters,
Morning and Night, the Two, as 'twere
all-knowing : these bring the sacrifice
unto the mortal.

8 You I extol, the nourishers of heroes,
bringing you gifts, Vāstoṣpati and
Tvaṣṭar—
Rich Dhiṣaṇā accords through our obeisance—and Trees and Plants, for the
swift gain of riches.

9 Ours be the Parvatas, even they, for offspring, free-moving, who are Heroes
like the Vasus.
May holy Āptya, Friend of man, exalted,
strengthen our word for ever and be
near us.

10 Trta praised him, germ of the earthly
hero, with pure songs him the Offspring
of the Waters.

Agni with might neighs loudly like a
charger : he of the flaming hair destroys
the forests.

11 How shall we speak to the great might
of Rudra? How speak to Bhaga who
takes thought for riches?
May Plants, the Waters, and the Sky
preserve us, and Woods and Mountains
with their trees for tresses.

12 May the swift Wanderer, Lord of refreshments, listen to our songs, who speeds
through cloudy heaven :
And may the Waters, bright like castles,
hear us, as they flow onward from the
cloven mountain.

13 We know your ways, ye Mighty Ones :
receiving choice meed, ye Wonderful,
we will proclaim it.
Even strong birds descend not to the
mortal who strives to reach them with
swift blow and weapons.

14 Celestial and terrestrial generations, and
Waters will I summon to the feasting.
May days with bright dawns cause my
songs to prosper, and may the conquered
streams increase their waters.

15 Duly to each one hath my laud been offered. Strong be Varūtrī with her powers
to succour.

---

12 *Swift Wanderer* : Vāyu, God of the circumambient wind.
   As they flow onward : the text has *pári sruco*.
Sāyaṇa explains *sruco* (ladles) by *saraṇaśīlāḥ*, inclined
or accustomed to flow. Professor Ludwig suggests
parisruto (flowing round or over) as the original reading.
   Cloven mountain : according to Sāyaṇa, the increasing, *i. e.* the towering, or swelling, mountain, or cloud.

13 This stanza is exceedingly difficult. I follow
Professor Ludwig in his interpretation, and understand
the meaning to be : we know what your ways are, and
we glorify you because you reward us for doing so. If
you appeared to us only as hostile and terrible deities we
should not praise you any more than birds allow themselves to be lured down by the man who shoots at them.
Professor Wilson, following Sāyaṇa, paraphrases the
stanza : 'Mighty Maruts, of goodly aspect, quickly hear
(the praises) that we who repair to you repeat, offering
acceptable (oblations) : (the Maruts) coming hither,
well disposed, come down to us (destroying) with their
weapons the mortals opposed to them, (overcome) by
agitation.

14 *The conquered streams* : won from the hostile
barbarians.

15 *Varūtrī* : one of a class of guardian Goddesses.
See I. 2.10. and III. 62. 3
   Rasā a mythical stream which flows round the
earth and the atmosphere, here personified as a benignant Goddess : earth, according to Sāyaṇa. See I.
112. 12. *Straight-handed* : holding out her hand to
guide and help us.

---

4 *The heavenly Victor* : Indra. *Trta* : according to
Sāyaṇa Trta here is not the name of a separate deity
(Trta Āptya), but an epithet of Vāyu, 'pervading the
three regions of earth, firmament, and heaven.'
   5 *The priest of Auśija* : Atri, the ministrant priest
of Kakṣivān the son of Uśij.—Sāyaṇa.
   8 *Vāstoṣpati* : Lord of the Homestead, Indra.
   Dhiṣaṇā : a Goddess presiding over prosperity and
gain ; according to Sāyaṇa, Vāgdevatā, the Goddess of
speech.
   9 *The Parvatas* : the genii who preside over
mountains and clouds. *For offspring* : that they may
give us children and children's children.
   Holy Āptya : Trta Āptya, a divinity or mythical
being who dwells in the remotest part of the heavens.
   10 *Germ of the earthly hero* : Agni, the Offspring of
the Waters, who develops into the strong God, or
Hero, who appears on earth in the form of terrestrial
fire.

May the great Mother Rasā here befriend us, straight-handed, with the princes, striving forward.

16 How may we serve the Liberal Ones with worship, the Maruts swift of course in invocation, the Maruts far-renowned in invocation ?

Let not the Dragon of the Deep annoy us, and gladly may he welcome our addresses.

17 Thus thinking, O ye Gods, the mortal wins you to give him increase of his herds of cattle : the mortal wins him, O ye Gods, your favour.

Here he wins wholesome food to feed this body : as for mine old age, Nirṛti consume it !

18 O Gods, may we obtain from you this favour, strengthening food through the Cow's praise, ye Vasus.

May she who gives good gifts, the gracious Goddess, come speeding nigh to us for our well-being.

19 May Ilā, Mother of the herds of cattle, and Urvaśī with all the streams accept us;

May Urvaśī in lofty heaven accepting, as she partakes the oblation of the living,

20 Visit us while she shares Ūrjavya's food.

HYMN XLII.   *Viśvedevas.*

1. Now may our sweetest song with deep devotion reach Varuṇa, Mitra, Aditi, and Bhaga.

May the Five Priests' Lord, dwelling in oblations, bliss-giving Asura, hear, whose paths are open.

2 May Aditi welcome, even as a mother her dear heart-gladdening son, my song that lauds her.

The prayer they love, bliss-giving, God-appointed, I offer unto Varuṇa and Mitra.

3 Inspirit him, the Sagest of the Sages; with sacrificial oil and meath bedew him.

So then let him, God Savitar, provide us excellent, ready, and resplendent treasures.

4 With willing mind, Indra, vouchsafe us cattle, prosperity, Lord of Bays ! and pious patrons;

And, with the sacred prayer by Gods appointed, give us the holy Deities' loving-kindness.

5 God Bhaga, Savitar who deals forth riches, Indra, and they who conquer Vṛtra's treasures,

And Vāja and Ṛbhukṣan and Purandhi, the Mighty and Immortal Ones, protect us !

6 Let us declare his deeds, the undecaying unrivalled Victor whom the Maruts follow.

None of old times, O Maghavan, nor later, none of these days hath reached thy hero prowess.

7 Praise him the Chief who gives the boon of riches, Bṛhaspati distributor of treasures,

Who, blessing most the man who sings and praises, comes with abundant wealth to his invoker.

8 Tended, Bṛhaspati, with thy protections, the princes are unharmed and girt by heroes.

Wealth that brings bliss is found among the givers of horses and of cattle and of raiment.

9 Make their wealth flee who, through our hymns enjoying their riches, yield us not an ample guerdon.

Far from the sun keep those who hate devotion, the godless, prospering in their vocation.

10 With wheelless chariots drive down him, O Maruts, who at the feasts of Gods regards the demons.

May he, though bathed in sweat, form empty wishes, who blames his sacred rite who toils to serve you.

11 Praise him whose bow is strong and sure his arrow, him who is Lord of every balm that healeth.

---

16 *The Dragon of the Deep* : Áhibudhnya, the regent of the depths of the firmament.

17 *Nirṛti* : the Goddess of destruction. 'May Nirṛti (he thinks) swallow up my old age (not me).' —Ludwig.

Ilā : here meaning Earth, according to Sāyaṇa. *Urvaśī* : apparently Fervour or Enthusiasm personified as a divine being.

20 *Ūrjavya's food* : the viands provided by Ūrjavya, the prince or patron who institutes the sacrifice.

The hymn is generally difficult and obscure ; and parts of the translation are, and must at present be, conjectural.

---

1 *The Five Priests' Lord* : apparently Varuṇa, the five priests who serve him being five Ādityas. According to Sāyaṇa Vāyu is meant.

3 *The Sagest of the Sages* : Savitar, perhaps as identified with Agni.

5 *Ṛbhukṣan* : in this place is said by Sāyaṇa to mean Ṛbhu, and *Purandhi* (the intelligent) to mean Vibhvan.

11 *Praise him* : Rudra.

Worship thou Rudra for his great good favour : adore the Asura, God, with salutations.

12 May the House-friends, the cunning-handed Artists, may the Steer's Wives, the streams carved out by Vibhvan,

And may the fair Ones honour and befriend us, Sarasvatī, Bṛhaddivā, and Rākā.

13 My newest song, thought that now springs within me, I offer to the Great, the Sure Protector,

Who made for us this All, in fond love laying each varied form within his Daughter's bosom.

14 Now, even now, may thy fair praise, O Singer, attain Iḍaspati who roars and thunders,

Who, rich in clouds and waters with his lightning speeds forth bedewing both the earth and heaven.

15 May this my laud attain the troop of Maruts, those who are youths in act, the Sons of Rudra.

The wish calls me to riches and well-being: praise the unwearied Ones whose steeds are dappled.

16 May this my laud reach earth and air's mid-region, and forest trees and plants to win me riches.

May every Deity be swift to listen, and Mother Earth with no ill thought regard me.

17 Gods, may we dwell in free untroubled bliss.

18 May we obtain the Aśvins' newest favour, and gain their health-bestowing happy guidance.

Bring riches hither unto us, and heroes, and all felicity and joy, Immortals !

HYMN XLIII.   *Viśvedevas.*

1. MAY the Milch-cows who hasten to their object come harmless unto us with liquid sweetness.

The Singer, lauding, calls, for ample riches, the Seven Mighty Ones who bring enjoyment.

2 With reverence and fair praise will I bring hither, for sake of strength, exhaustless Earth and Heaven.

Father and Mother, sweet of speech, fairhanded, may they, far-famed, in every fight protect us.

3 Adhvaryus, make the sweet libations ready, and bring the beautiful bright juice to Vāyu.

God, as our Priest, be thou the first to drink it : we give thee of the mead to make thee joyful.

4 Two arms—the Soma's dexterous immolators—and the ten fingers set and fix the press-stone.

The stalk hath poured, fair with its spreading branches, the mead's bright glittering juice that dwells on mountains.

5 The Soma hath been pressed for thee, its lover, to give thee power and might and high enjoyment.

Invoked, turn hither in thy car, O Indra, at need, thy two well-trained and dear Bay Horses.

6 Bring by God-traversed paths, accordant, Agni, the great Aramati, Celestial Lady,

Exalted, worshipped with our gifts and homage, who knoweth holy Law, to drink sweet Soma.

7 As on his father's lap the son, the darling, so on the fire is set the sacred caldron,

Which holy singers deck, as if extending and heating that which holds the fatty membrane.

8 Hither, as herald to invite the Aśvins, come the great lofty song, most sweet and pleasant !

Come in one car, Joy-givers ! to the

---

12 *The cunning-handed Artists* : the Ṛbhus. *The Steer's Wives* : the spouses of the mighty Indra. *Carved out by Vibhvan* : whose channels were formed by him as the artificer of Varuṇa.

Bṛhaddivā : a Goddess frequently associated with Iḷā, Sarasvatī, and others. Sāyaṇa takes the word in this place as an epithet, 'very brilliant,' of *Rākā*, the Goddess who presides over the day of full moon.

13 *The Great, the Sure Protector* : Indra. *His Daughter*: Earth. Here, as Ludwig observes, we have the germ of the myth of Prajāpati and his daughter. Cf. X .61.

14 *Iḍaspati* : the Lord of the libation; here Parjanya, God of the rain-clouds.

1 *The Milch-cows* : the rivers. *The Seven Mighty*

Ones : probably the Indus, the five rivers of the Panjāb, and the Sarasvatī, or the Kubhā. See I. 32.12.

4 *Immolators* : or preparers.

6 *Aramati* : the Goddess who presides over worship and active piety, and also personifies the Earth ; the Spenta-Armaiti, or Holy Piety, and Spirit of Earth, of the Zoroastrians.

7 *As if extending* : perhaps, stretching (over the fire) and so roasting, as Prof. Roth explains. *Heating that which holds the fatty membrane* : 'roasting a marrowyielding animal.'—Wilson. The *vapā* is the omentum or membrane enfolding the intestines of the victim, specially offered to Gods in the *Vapāhuti* sacrifice.

8 *Joy-givers* : ye beneficent Aśvins. *Like the bolt* : 'As the cart cannot move if the axle of the wheel is not fastened by the pin or bolt, so the offering of the Soma is without efficacy unless the Aśvins be present.'— Wilson, from Sāyaṇa.

banquet, like the bolt binding pole and nave, come hither.

9 I have declared this speech of adoration to mightiest Pūṣan and victorious Vāyu, Who by their bounty are the hymns' inspirers, and of themselves give power as a possession.

10 Invoked by us bring hither, Jātavedas ! the Maruts all under their names and figures.

Come to the sacrifice with aid all Maruts, all to the songs and praises of the singer !

11 From high heaven may Sarasvatī the Holy visit our sacrifice, and from the mountain.

Eager, propitious, may the balmy Goddess hear our effectual speech, our invocation.

12 Set in his seat the God whose back is dusky, Bṛhaspati the lofty, the Disposer.

Him let us worship, set within the dwelling, the red, the golden-hued, the all-resplendent.

13 May the Sustainer, high in heaven, come hither, the Bounteous One, invoked, with all his favours,

Dweller with Dames divine, with plants, unwearied, the Steer with triple horn, the life-bestower.

14 The tuneful eloquent priests of him who liveth have sought the Mother's bright and loftiest station.

As living men, with offered gifts and homage they deck the most auspicious Child to clothe him.

15 Agni, great vital power is thine, the mighty: pairs waxing old in their devotion seek thee.

May every Deity be swift to listen, and Mother Earth with no ill thought regard me.

16 Gods, may we dwell in free untroubled bliss.

17 May we obtain the Aśvins' newest favour, and gain their health-bestowing happy guidance.

Bring riches hither unto us, and heroes, and all felicity and joy, Immortals !

HYMN XLIV. *Viśvedevas.*

1. As in the first old times, as all were wont, as now, he draweth forth the power turned hitherward with song,

The Princedom throned on holy grass, who findeth light, swift, conquering in the plants wherein he waxeth strong.

2 Shining to him who leaves heaven's regions undisturbed, which to his sheen who is beneath show fair in light,

Good guardian art thou, not to be deceived, Most Wise ! Far from deceits thy name dwelleth in holy Law.

3 Truth waits upon oblation present and to come : naught checks him in his way, this victory-bringing Priest :

The Mighty Child who glides along the sacred grass, the undecaying Youth set in the midst of plants.

4 These come, well-yoked, to you for furtherance in the rite : down come the twin-born strengtheners of Law for him,

16 This line and the following stanza are identical with 17 and 18 of the preceding hymn.

1 *He draweth forth* : the Agnidh, or priest who kindles the sacrificial fire, draws, or literally milks out, Agni from the fire-sticks by attrition. I follow Professor Ludwig in taking *dohase* and *várdhase* as third persons singular. Professor Grassmann banishes to his Appendix this 'most bombastic and intentionally obscure hymn,' which he considers to be a later interpolation. *The Princedom* : the Prince, Agni; *jyeṣṭátātim* the abstract being used for the concrete.

2 *Shining to him* : apparently, to the Sun ; but the meaning is uncertain.

Who is beneath : the Sun when he is setting, or perhaps Agni. *Thou* : Indra.

3 *Truth waits upon oblation* : the hopes and wishes of the sacrificer are realized. It seems impossible to get any meaning out of *átyam* (courser) and I follow Professor Ludwig in reading *satyám* (truth or realization). *The victory-bringing Priest, the Mighty Child, the undecaying Youth,* is Agni.

4 *These come, well-yoked* : probably the priests, closely associated in their sacred duties, who bring the waters used in the preparation of the Soma and so are called *strengtheners of Law, i. e.* furtherers of the law-appointed sacrifice *for him,* for Agni the Child of the Waters.

The hide stealeth away their names : according to Sāyaṇa, Āditya or the Sun steals (that is, absorbs) the waters in low places ; or Agni appropriates the offerings presented to him. Professor Ludwig is of opinion.

11 *Balmy* : literally, filled with, or sprinkling *ghṛta*, oil, fatness, or fertilizing fluid. 'The showerer of water.'—Wilson.

12 *Whose back is dusky* : darkened by enveloping smoke, Bṛhaspati being here identified with Agni.

13 *The Sustainer* : or the very strong One, Agni. *With triple horn* : according to Sāyaṇa, having horns or flames of three colours, red, white, and black (with smoke).

14 *Eloquent* : the meaning of *rāspírdsaḥ* is uncertain. Sāyaṇa explains it by 'holders of sacrificial ladles.' *The Mother* is the earth, and her *loftiest station* is the altar. *Of him who liveth* : of the living man, the worshipper. *The Child* is Agni.

15 *Pairs* : human pairs of worshippers; husbands and wives. The second half of this stanza is repeated from stanza 16 of the preceding hymn.

With reins easily guided and commanding all. In the deep fall the hide stealeth away their names.

5 Thou, moving beauteously in visibly pregnant ones, snatching with trees the branching plant that grasps the juice,
Shinest, true Singer ! mid the upholders of the voice. Increase thy Consorts thou, lively at sacrifice.

6 Like as he is beheld such is he said to be. They with effectual splendour in the floods have made
Earth yield us room enough and amply wide extent, great might invincible, with store of hero sons.

7 Sūrya the Sage, as if unwedded, with a Spouse, in battle-loving spirit moveth o'er the foes.
May he, self-excellent, grant us a sheltering home, a house that wards the fierce heat off on every side.

8 Thy name, sung forth by Rsis in these hymns of ours, goes to the loftier One with this swift mover's light.
By skill he wins the boon whereon his heart is set : he who bestirs himself shall bring the thing to pass.

9 The chief and best of these abideth in the sea, nor doth libation fail wherein it is prolonged.
The heart of him who praiseth trembleth not in fear there where the hymn is found connected with the pure.

10 For it is he : with thoughts of Kṣatra, Manasa, of Yajata, and Sadhri, and Evāvada,
With Avatsāra's sweet songs will we strive to win the mightiest strength which even he who knows should gain.

11 The Hawk is their full source, girth-stretching rapturous drink of Viśvavāra, of Māyin, and Yajata.
They ever seek a fresh draught so that they may come, know when thy time to halt and drink thy fill is near.

12 Sadāprṇa the holy, Tarya, Śrutavit, and Bāhuvṛkta, joined with you, have slain the foes.
He gains his wish in both the worlds and brightly shines—when he adores the host with well-advancing steeds.

13 The worshipper's defender is Sutambhara, producer and uplifter of all holy thoughts.
The milch-cow brought, sweet-flavoured milk was dealt around. Who speaks the bidding text knows this, not he who sleeps.

14 The sacred hymns love him who wakes and watches : to him who watches come the Sāma verses.
This Soma saith unto the man who watches, I rest and have my dwelling in thy friendship.

15 Agni is watchful, and the Rcas love him; Agni is watchful, Sāma verses seek him.
Agni is watchful, to him saith this Soma, I rest and have my dwelling in thy friendship.

---

kriviḥ (literally, leather bottle or bag, and metaphorically cloud, cistern, or well) in this place=*samudrāṇ* in its twofold signification as Soma reservoir and sea. The meaning then would be that the names of the waters, *i. e.* the waters themselves, fall into the reservoir and into the sea. According to Sāyaṇa the whole stanza refers to the Sun, the *well-yoked* being his 'well-combined rays.'

5 This stanza is addressed to Agni. *Visibly pregnant ones* : perhaps the waters. *With trees* : with burning fuel. *Thy Consorts* : the flames.

7 *As if unwedded* : Sūrya the Sun-God, although wedded to Uṣas or Dawn, is courageous as an unmarried man untroubled by care for wife and child ; may he give us assurance of security as he himself knows how delightful that is.

8 *Thy name* : the name of the institutor of the sacrifice. *The loftier One* : Sūrya. *This swift mover's light* : the flames of Agni. *He who bestirs himself* : the restless Agni.

9 *Of these* : hymns of praise. *Abideth in the sea* : is closely connected with the vat or reservoir of Soma. According to Sāyaṇa the meaning is that the best of the hymns proceed to the ocean-like Sun (*samuravatparyavasānabhūtam sūryam*).

10 *For it is he* : 'He verily (is to be glorified).'— Wilson. *Kṣatra, Manasa, etc.* are said to be the names of Rṣis associated with Avatsara to whom especially the hymn is ascribed.

11 *The Hawk*: who brought the Soma from heaven. See IV. 27. *Viśvavāra, Māyin,* and *Yajata* are said to be Rṣis.

12 *Sadāprṇa* and the others mentioned in this verse are also Rṣis. *He* : each of the Rṣis. *The host* : of Gods.

13 *Sutambhara* : said to be the name of a Rṣi. The word means the bearer of the juice or libation. Professor Ludwig says that the Hawk (st. 11) is intended.

15 *The Rcas* : the hymns and verses of the Rgveda.

The hymn is exceedingly difficult and obscure, and in parts it seems to be hopelessly unintelligible. Professor Wilson's paraphrase and Professor Grassmann's translation differ very widely from the version—founded mainly on Professor Ludwig's interpretation—which I offer as a temporary makeshift.

HYMN XLV.   *Viśvedevas.*

1. BARDS of approaching Dawn who know the heavens are come with hymns to throw the mountain open.

   The Sun hath risen and oped the stable portals: the doors of men, too, hath the God thrown open.

2. Sūrya hath spread his light as splendour : hither came the Cows' Mother, conscious, from the stable,

   To streams that flow with biting waves to deserts ; and heaven is stablished like a firm-set pillar.

3. This laud hath won the burden of the mountain. To aid the ancient birth of mighty waters

   The mountain parted, Heaven performed his office. The worshippers were worn with constant serving.

4. With hymns and God-loved words will I invoke you, Indra and Agni, to obtain your favour,

   For verily sages, skilled in sacrificing, worship the Maruts and with lauds invite them.

5. This day approach us : may our thoughts be holy, far from us let us cast away misfortune.

   Let us keep those who hate us at a distance, and haste to meet the man who sacrifices.

6. Come, let us carry out, O friends, the purpose wherewith the Mother threw the Cow's stall open,

   That wherewith Manu conquered Viśiśipra, wherewith the wandering merchant gained heaven's water.

7. Here, urged by hands, loudly hath rung the press-stone wherewith Navagvas through ten months sang praises.

   Saramā went aright and found the cattle. Aṅgiras gave effect to all their labours.

8. When at the dawning of this mighty Goddess, Aṅgirases all sang forth with the cattle,—

   Their spring is in the loftiest place of meeting,—Saramā found the kine by Order's pathway.

9. Borne by his Coursers Seven may Sūrya visit the field that spreadeth wide for his long journey.

   Down on the Soma swooped the rapid Falcon. Bright was the young Sage moving mid his cattle.

10. Sūrya hath mounted to the shining ocean when he hath yoked his fair-backed Tawny Horses.

    The wise have drawn him like a ship through water : the floods obedient have descended hither.

11. I lay upon the Floods your hymn, light-winning, wherewith Navagvas their ten months completed.

    Through this our hymn may we have Gods to guard us : through this our hymn pass safe beyond affliction.

HYMN XLVI.   *Viśvedevas.*

1. WELL knowing I have bound me, horse-like, to the pole : I carry that which bears us on and gives us help.

---

1 *Bards* : the Aṅgirases who sing the praises of Uṣas and who know the exact time when morning rites are to be celebrated. *The mountain* : the cloud in which the stolen Cows, or vanished rays of light, have been concealed.

2 *The Cows' Mother* : Dawn ; the parent of the rays of light.

3 *The burden of the mountain* : the store of water which lies like an unborn babe in the bosom of the mountain-like cloud. *Performed his office* : aided the production of the rain. *The worshippers* : the Aṅgirases.

6 *Wherewith* : I follow Professor Grassmann in taking *yā* as instrumental —*ydyā*. *The Mother* : Dawn. *Viśiśipra* : meaning, perhaps, jawless or chinless, may, Sāyaṇa says, be Vṛtra, and *Manu* here may mean Indra. Manu probably represents the victorious Āryan invader and Viśiśipra the conquered barbarian.

The wandering merchant : Sāyaṇa says that this refers to the story of Kakṣīvān to whom the Aśvins sent rain. See I. 112. 11.

7 *Through ten months* : referring to the sacrifices of nine and ten months' duration performed by the Navagvas and the Daśagvas, priestly families frequently mentioned in connexion with the Aṅgirases. These names mean, respectively, nine-month ministrants and ten-month ministrants, and are translated in the St. Petersburg Lexicon by Neuner and Zehner, Niners and Tenners. *Saramā* : see Index. *Aṅgiras* : Agni.

8 *Their spring* : the source of the Cows, that is the Cows themselves. *The loftiest place of meeting* : the height of heaven. The half-line is apparently parenthetical.

9 *The rapid Falcon* : which brought the Soma from heaven. *The young Sage* : 'ever young and far-seeing.' The Sun is intended, moving in the midst of his rays.

10 *The shining ocean* : the luminous firmament.

11 *I lay upon the floods* : I offer to the Waters. *Light-winning* : which gains for the worshipper the light of heaven.

The Consorts of the Gods are the deities of the last two stanzas.

1 : The Ṛṣi Pratikṣatra. *The pole* : a metaphorical expression for sacrificial duties. *That which bears us on* : the pole, the performance of sacrifice. 'I

I seek for no release, no turning back therefrom. May he who knows the way, the Leader, guide me straight.

2 O Agni, Indra, Varuṇa, and Mitra, give, O ye Gods, and Marut host, and Viṣṇu.
May both Nāsatyas, Rudra, heavenly Matrons, Pūṣan, Sarasvatī, Bhaga, accept us.

3 Indra and Agni, Mitra, Varuṇa, Aditi, the Waters, Mountains, Maruts, Sky, and Earth and Heaven,
Viṣṇu I call, Pūṣan, and Brahmaṇaspati, and Bhaga, Śaṁsa, Savitar that they may help.

4 May Viṣṇu also and Vāta who injures none, and Soma granter of possessions give us joy ;
And may the Ṛbhus and the Aśvins, Tvaṣṭar and Vibhvan remember us so that we may have wealth.

5 So may the band of Maruts dwelling in the sky, the holy, come to us to sit on sacred grass ;
Bṛhaspati and Pūṣan grant us sure defence, Varuṇa, Mitra, Aryaman guard and shelter us.

6 And may the Mountains famed in noble eulogies, and the fair-gleaming Rivers keep us safe from harm.
May Bhaga the Dispenser come with power and grace, and far-pervading Aditi listen to my call.

7 May the Gods' Spouses aid us of their own free will, aid us to offspring and the winning of the spoil.
Grant us protection, O ye gracious Goddesses, ye who are on the earth or in the waters' realm.

8 May the Dames, wives of Gods, enjoy our presents, Rāṭ, Aśvinī, Agnāyī, and Indrāṇī.
May Rodasī and Varuṇānī hear us, and Goddesses come at the Matrons' season.

HYMN XLVII. *Viśvedevas.*

1. URGING to toil and making proclamation, seeking Heaven's Daughter comes the Mighty Mother :
She comes, the youthful Hymn, unto the Fathers, inviting to her home and loudly calling.

2 Swift in their motion, hasting to their duty, reaching the central point of life immortal,
On every side about the earth and heaven go forth the spacious paths without a limit.

3 Steer, Sea, Red Bird with strong wings, he hath entered the dwelling-place of the Primeval Father.
A gay-hued Stone set in the midst of heaven, he hath gone forth and guards mid-air's two limits.

4 Four bear him up and give him rest and quiet, and ten invigorate the Babe for travel.
His kine most excellent, of threefold nature, pass swiftly round the boundaries of heaven.

5 Wondrous, O people, is the mystic knowledge that while the waters stand the streams are flowing :
That, separate from his Mother, Two support him, closely-united, twins, here made apparent.

---

support that transcendant and preservative load.'—Wilson. *He who knows the way* : the divine inner guide: *mārgābhijño'ntaryāmi devaḥ*—Sāyaṇa.

3 *Śaṁsa* : prayer or wish, personified. Or *śáṅsam* may be a verbal form, I praise.

8 *Rāṭ* : the name of a Goddess, or, as Sāyaṇa takes it, bright, qualifying *Aśvinī*, the Consort of the Aśvins. *Rodasī* : the Spouse of Rudra. See Index.

At the Matrons' season : at the time appointed for the celestial dames, the Consorts of the Gods.

---

1 *Heaven's Daughter* : Uṣas or Dawn. *The Mighty Mother* : perhaps, as Professor Ludwig suggests, Vāk or Speech is intended, who appears in the second line as the Hymn personified.

2 *The central point of life immortal* : the Sun. *The paths* : the long lines of light.

3 *Sea* : as the great attracter and receptacle of the waters.
He : the Sun. *The Primeval Father* : Dyaus, or Heaven.
A gay-hued Stone : Professor Ludwig would read *pṛśniraśmá*, 'with variegated rays,' instead of the *pṛśnidśmá* of the text. But the alteration seems to be unnecessary.

4 *Four* : according to Sāyaṇa, the four chief priests. Possibly Varuṇa, Mitra, Aryaman, Bhaga are intended.—Ludwig.
Ten : the regions of space ; as the Sun attracts the waters from all sides. *His kine* : his rays. *Of threefold nature* : producing heat, cold (by their absence), and rain.

5 The marvel is that the waters stand still in the sea while the rivers are continually flowing into it. Cf. Ecclesiastes, I.7. *Separate from his Mother* : Sūrya's Mother is the invisible Aditi ; and he is supported by Heaven and Earth, the closely-connected pair who are visible in this world.—Ludwig.

6 For him they lenghten prayers and acts of
worship : the Mothers weave garments
for him their offspring.
Rejoicing, for the Steer's impregning
contact, his Spouses move on paths or
heaven to meet him.

7 Be this our praise, O Varuṇa and Mitra ;
may this be health and force to us, O
Agni.
May we obtain firm ground and room
for resting : Glory to Heaven, the lofty
habitation !

HYMN XLVIII. *Viśvedevas.*

1. WHAT may we meditate for the beloved
Power, mighty in native strength and
glorious in itself,
Which as a magic energy seeking waters
spreads even to the immeasurable middle
region's cloud ?

2 O'er all the region with their uniform advance these have spread out the lore
that giveth heroes strength.
Back, with their course reversed, the others
pass away : the pious lengthens life with
those that are before.

3 With pressing-stones and with the bright
beams of the day he hurls his broadest
bolt against the Guileful One.
Even he whose hundred wander in his own
abode, driving the days afar and bringing them again.

4 I, to enjoy the beauty of his form, behold
that rapid rush of his as 'twere an axe's
edge,
What time he gives the man who calls on
him in fight wealth like a dwelling-house
filled full with store of food.

5 Four-faced and nobly clad, Varuṇa, urging
on the pious to his task, stirs himself
with the tongue.

6 *They* : worshippers. *The Mothers* : the Dawns,
or the regions of space, which clothe the Sun with light.
His Spouses : the solar rays.

7 *Firm ground and room for resting* : 'stability and
permanence.'—Wilson.

———

1 *Which as a magic energy* : or, what time the magic
energy, that is Vāk, Voice or Speech.

2 *These* : Dawns. *Before* : yet to come.

3 *With pressing-stones* : in alliance with, and strengthened by them, that is, the libations which they aid.
He : Indra. *The Guileful One* : Vṛtra. *Even he* : Indra
as the Sun. *Whose hundred* : Sāyaṇa supplies, rays.

4 *His form* : Agni's.

5 *Varuṇa* : according to Sāyaṇa, *ārvṇaḥ* here is an
adjective=*tamovārakaḥ*, darkness-repelling, and an
epithet of Agni.
With the tongue : causing the worshipper to speak
of him.

Naught by our human nature do we know
of him, him from whom Bhaga Savitar
bestows the boon.

HYMN XLIX. *Viśvedevas.*

1. THIS day I bring God Savitar to meet you,
and Bhaga who allots the wealth of
mortals.
You, Aśvins, Heroes rich in treasures,
daily seeking your friendship fain would
I turn hither.

2 Knowing full well the Asura's time of
coming, worship God Savitar with
hymns and praises.
Let him who rightly knoweth speak with
homage to him who dealeth out man's
noblest treasure.

3 Not for reward doth Pūṣan send his
blessings, Bhaga, or Aditi : his garb is
splendour.
May Indra, Viṣṇu, Varuṇa, Mitra, Agni
produce auspicious days, the Wonder-
Workers.

4 Sending the shelter which we ask, the
foeless Savitar and the Rivers shall approach us.
When I, the sacrifice's priest, invite them,
may we be lords of wealth and rich
possessions.

5 They who devote such worship to the
Vasus, singing their hymns to Varuṇa
and Mitra,
Vouchsafe them ample room, far off be
danger. Through grace of Heaven and
Earth may we be happy.

HYMN L. *Viśvedevas.*

1. LET every mortal man elect the friendship
of the guiding God.
Each one solicits him for wealth and seeks
renown to prosper him.

Naught by our human nature : all our knowledge of
the God comes by his inspiration.

Bhaga : according to Sāyaṇa *bhāgaḥ* here is an
epithet of Savitar, mighty or adorable.

———

2 *The Asura's time of coming* : the approach of the
divine Savitar.

3 *Aditi* : according to Sāyaṇa=*akhaṇḍanīyaḥ*, who
cannot be impaired, used here as an epithet of Agni,
understood, as are also *pūṣā*, 'nourishing, and *bhāgaḥ*,
'adorable.' But Sāyaṇa gives also the alternative interpretation of the words as three deities.

———

The Ṛ i is said to be Svasti (a name apparently
borrowed from *svastaye* for weal, in stanza 5).

1 *The guiding God* : Savitar.

2 These, leading God, are thine, and these
here ready to speak after us.
As such may we attain to wealth and wait
with services on thee.

3 So further honour as our guests the Hero
Gods and then the Dames.
May he remove and keep afar our foes
and all who block our path.

4 Where fire is set, and swiftly runs the
victim dwelling in the trough,
He wins, with heroes in his home, friendly
to man, like constant streams.

5 May these thy riches, Leader God ! that
rule the car, be blest to us,
Yea, blest to us for wealth and weal. This
will we ponder praising strength, this
ponder as we praise the God.

HYMN LI.   *Visvedevas.*

1. WITH all assistants, Agni, come hither to
drink the Soma-juice;
With Gods unto our sacred gifts.

2 Come to the sacrifice, O ye whose ways
are right, whose laws are true,
And drink the draught with Agni's tongue.

3 O Singer, with the singers, O Gracious,
with those who move at dawn,
Come to the Soma-draught with Gods.

4 To Indra and to Vāyu dear, this Soma,
by the mortar pressed,
Is now poured forth to fill the jar.

5 Vāyu, come hither to the feast, well-
pleased unto our sacred gifts :
Drink of the Soma juice effused : come
to the food.

6 Ye, Indra, Vāyu, well deserve to drink
the juices pressed by us.
Gladly accept them, spotless Pair : come
to the food.

7 For Indra and for Vāyu pressed are Soma
juices blent with curd,
As rivers to the lowland flow : come to
the food.

8 Associate with all the Gods, come, with
the Aśvins and with Dawn,
Agni, as erst with Atri, so enjoy the juice.

9 Associate with Varuṇa, with Mitra, Soma,
Viṣṇu, come,
Agni, as erst with Atri, so enjoy the juice.

10 Associate with Vasus, with Ādityas, Indra,
Vāyu, come, Agni as erst with Atri, so
enjoy the juice.

11 May Bhaga and the Aśvins grant us health
and wealth, and Goddess Aditi and he
whom none resist.
The Asura Pūṣan grant us all prosperity,
and Heaven and Earth most wise
vouchsafe us happiness.

12 Let us solicit Vāyu for prosperity, and
Soma who is Lord of all the world for
weal ;
For weal Bṛhaspati with all his company.
May the Ādityas bring us health and
happiness.

13 May all the Gods, may Agni the beneficent,
God of all men, this day be with us
for our weal.
Help us the Ṛbhus, the Divine Ones, for
our good. May Rudra bless and keep
us from calamity.

14 Prosper us, Mitra, Varuṇa. O wealthy
Pathyā, prosper us.
Indra and Agni, prosper us; prosper us
thou, O Aditi.

15 Like Sun and Moon may we pursue in
full prosperity our path,
And meet with one who gives again, who
knows us well and slays us not.

HYMN LII   *Maruts.*

1. SING boldly forth, Śyāvāśva, with the
Maruts who are loud in song,
Who, holy, as their wont is, joy in glory
that is free from guile.

2 *These* : worshippers.

3 *The Dames* : Consorts of the Gods. *May he* :
Savitar.

4 This stanza is obscure. *Droṇaḥ paśuḥ*, the
victim or beast connected with, or dwelling in, the
droṇa, tub or trough, is apparently the Soma. The meaning may be that the man who causes the sacrificial fire
to be kindled and libations of Soma juice to be prepared
is rewarded with brave sons and general prosperity.

1 *With all assistants* : 'with all the protecting
deities.'—Wilson.

2 *O ye* : other Gods.

3 *O Singer* . Agni. *With the singers*: with the human
priests. *Those who move at dawn* : the Gods who come
to the morning sacrifice.

8 *As erst with Atri* : as thou wast accustomed to
enjoy the libation offered by the ancient Atri, the
progenitor of the Ṛṣi of the hymn.

11 *Health and wealth* : *svasti* ; well-being, prosperity.
I have slightly varied the translation of the word,
which recurs in every line of stanzas 11—14 and in the
first line of 15. *The Asura* : the divine and immortal
being. Sāyaṇa explains the word as the expeller of
enemies, or the giver of life and strength.'

12 *With all his company* : with all the host of
heaven.

14 *Wealthy Pathyā* : 'the rich path,' personified as
a deity of happiness and welfare.

15 *Who gives again* : who repays the kindness we
have shown him when he was our guest. These, as
Professor Ludwig observes, are the wishes of a man who
is starting on a journey to a distant place.

2 For in their boldness they are friends of
firm and sure heroic strength.
They in their course, bold-spirited, guard
all men of their own accord.

3 Like steers in rapid motion they advance
and overtake the nights;
And thus the Maruts' power in heaven
and on the earth we celebrate.

4 With boldness to your Maruts let us offer
laud and sacrifice :
Who all, through ages of mankind, guard
mortal man from injury.

5 Praiseworthy, givers of good gifts, Heroes
with full and perfect strength—
To Maruts, Holy Ones of heaven, will I
extol the sacrifice.

6 The lofty Heroes cast their spears and
weapons bright with gleaming gold.
After these Maruts followed close, like
laughing lightning from the sky, a splendour of its own accord.

7 They who waxed mighty, of the earth, they
who are in the wide mid-air,
Or in the rivers' compass, or in the abode
of ample heaven.

8 Praise thou the Maruts' company, the
valorous and truly strong,
The Heroes, hasting by themselves have
yoked their deer for victory.

9 Fair-gleaming, on Parusnī they have
clothed themselves in robes of wool,
And with their chariot tires they cleave the
rock asunder in their might.

10 Whether as wanderers from the way or
speeders on or to the path,
Under these names the spreading band
tend well the sacrifice for me.

11 To this the Heroes well attend, well do
their teams attend to this.
Visible are their varied forms. Behold,
they are Pārāvatas.

12 Hymn-singing, seeking water, they, praising,
have danced about the spring.

What are they unto me? No thieves, but
helpers, splendid to behold.

13 Sublime, with lightnings for their spears,
Sages and Orderers are they.
Ṛṣi, adore that Marut host, and make
them happy with thy song.

14 Ṛṣi, invite the Marut band with offerings,
as a maid her friend.
From heaven, too, Bold Ones, in your
might haste hither glorified with songs.

15 Thinking of these now let him come, as
with the escort of the Gods,
And with the splendid Princes, famed for
rapid courses, to the gifts.

16 Princes, who, when I asked their kin,
named Pṛśni as their Mother-cow,
And the impetuous Rudra they, the Mighty
Ones, declared their Sire.

17 The mighty ones, the seven times seven,
have singly given me hundred gifts.
I have obtained on Yamunā famed wealth
in kine and wealth in steeds.

HYMN LIII.   *Maruts.*

1. Who knows the birth of these, or who
lived in the Maruts' favour in the days
of old

---

9 *Parusnī* : one of the rivers of the Panjāb, now
called the Rāvī. *Robes of wool* : the fleecy vapours
which rise from the waters. See IV. 22. 2.

11 *Pārāvatas* : a tribe who dwelt on the banks of
the Parusnī who may have been in the habit of making
sudden incursions into the country through which the
Sindhu or Indus flows.

12 *Seeking water* : this is Sāyaṇa's explanation of
kubhanyavaḥ, the meaning of which is uncertain. *The
spring* : apparently, the cloud. According to Sāyaṇa
the reference is to the water—or the well—which was
miraculously brought to the thirsting Gotama by the
Maruts. See I. 85. 11. The stanza is difficult and

14 *As a maid her friend* : this seems to be the meaning
of *mitrám ná yóṣaṇā*, which Sāyaṇa explains, as a friend
(or as Āditya, the Sun) with praise.

15 The three concluding stanzas are very difficult,
and attempts at translation and explanation must be
purely conjectural. The following is the substance of
Professor Ludwig's note. Śākins [mighty ones] in
stanza 17 are apparently a clan (yajamānāḥ, or institutors of sacrifice) whose number consisting of a multiple of seven, gave occasion to their comparison to the
Maruts, and an easy transition to the *dānastuti* or eulogy
of their liberality. The construction is : now thinking
of these sacrificers [or, Maruts] may he [the Ṛṣi]
come together, as with the escort of the Gods (invited
in stanza 14,) in company with [the Maruts or the]
Sūris to the sacrificial offerings.
Stanza 16 is to be understood figuratively as eulogy
of the Śākins who are here directly identified with the
Maruts. The priest must know the lineage of the sacrificers, because in certain ceremonies he must proclaim their
names, and here Śākins are considered to have inherited their liberality from Pṛśni as their mother and their
power from Rudra as their father.

17 *The Mighty Ones* : or the Śākins, as Professor
Ludwig explains.
The seven times seven : there are said to be seven
troops of the Maruts, each consisting of seven. The Śākins,
or powerful institutors of sacrifice, appear to be intended here (see preceding note) as compared to, or identified with the Maruts. *On Yamunā* : on the banks of
the river now known as the Jumna.

This and all Ṛgveda hymns addressed to the Maruts
have been translated and thoroughly discussed by Professor Max Müller in Vedic Hymns, Part I. (Sacred
Books of the East, Vol. XXXII.)

1 *Of these* : Gods : the Maruts.

What time their spotted deer were yoked?

2 Who, when they stood upon their cars,
hath heard them tell the way they went?
Who was the bounteous man to whom
their kindred rains flowed down with
food of sacrifice ?

3 To me they told it, and they came with
winged steeds radiant to the draught,
Youths, Heroes free from spot or stain :
Behold us here and praise thou us;

4 Who shine self-luminous with ornaments
and swords, with breastplates, armlets,
and with wreaths,
Arrayed on chariots and with bows.

5 O swift to pour your bounties down, ye
Maruts, with delight I look upon your
cars,
Like splendours coming through the rain.

6 Munificent Heroes, they have cast heaven's
treasury down for the worshipper's
behoof :
They set the storm-cloud free to stream
through both the worlds, and rainfloods
flow o'er desert spots.

7 The bursting streams in billowy flood
have spread abroad, like milch-kine,
o'er the firmament.
Like swift steeds hasting to their journey's
resting-place, to every side run glittering
brooks.

8 Hither, O Maruts, come from heaven, from
mid-air, or from near at hand :
Tarry not far away from us.

9 So let not Rasā, Krumu, or Anitabhā,
Kubhā, or Sindhu hold you back.
Let not the watery Sarayu obstruct your
way. With us be all the bliss ye give.

10 That brilliant gathering of your cars, the
company of Maruts, of the Youthful
Ones,
The rain-showers, speeding on, attend.

11 With eulogies and hymns may we follow
your army, troop by troop, and band
by band,
And company by company.

12 To what oblation-giver, sprung of noble
ancestry, have sped
The Maruts on this course to-day?

13 Vouchsafe to us the bounty, that which
we implore, through which, for child
and progeny,
Ye give the seed of corn that wasteth
not away, and bliss that reacheth to
all life.

14 May we in safety pass by those who
slander us, leaving behind disgrace and
hate.
Maruts, may we be there when ye, at
dawn, in rest and toil, rain waters
down and balm.

15 Favoured by Gods shall be the man, O
Heroes, Maruts ! and possessed of noble
sons,
Whom ye protect. Such may we be.

16 Praise the Free-givers. At this liberal
patron's rite they joy like cattle in the
mead.
So call thou unto them who come as ancient
Friends : hymn those who love thee
with a song.

HYMN LIV. *Maruts.*

1. THIS hymn will I make for the Marut
host who bright in native splendour
cast the mountains down.
Sing the great strength of those illustrious
in renown, who stay the heat, who
sacrifice on heights of heaven.

2 O Maruts, rich in water, strengtheners
of life are your strong bands with
harnessed steeds, that wander far.
Trita roars out at him who aims the
lightning-flash. The waters sweeping
round are thundering on their way.

3 They gleam with lightning, Heroes, Casters
of the Stone, wind-rapid Maruts, over-
throwers of the hills,
Oft through desire to rain coming with
storm of hail, roaring in onset, violent
and exceeding strong.

4 When, mighty Rudras, through the nights
and through the days, when through
the sky and realms of air, shakers of all,

---

9 *Rasā* : a river probably an affluent of the Sindhu
or Indus as *Anita hā* also seems to have been. *Krumu* :
a tributary of the Indus, identified by some with the
Kurum. *Kuhhā* : the Kóphén, or Kābul river which
falls into the Indus near Attock. *Sarayu* : probably a
river in the Panjāb which gave its name to the Sarayu
or Sarjū of Oudh.

---

1 *Who sacrifice on heights of heaven* : 'to whom solemn
rites are familiar ; by whom the sacrifices called
Pṛṣṭha are made.'– Wilson. The word *pṛṣṭhá* is ambiguous, signifying both height or ridge and a certain
arrangement of hymns (see IV. 20. 4). So also *gharmá*
in the same half-line signifies both heat and an oblation
of hot milk or other heated beverage, and the meaning
of the compound *gharmastubhe* is accordingly ambiguous.
2 *Trita* : the Vedic God who frequently appears
in connexion with the Maruts. According to Sāyaṇa,
Trita is the cloud or company of Maruts stationed in
three places.

When over the broad fields ye drive along
like ships, e'en to strongholds ye come,
Maruts, but are not harmed.

5 Maruts, this hero strength and majesty
of yours hath, like the Sun, extended
o'er a lengthened way,
When in your course like deer with splendour unsubdued ye bowed the hill that
gives imperishable rain.

6 Bright shone your host, ye Sages, Maruts,
when ye smote the waving tree as when
the worm consumeth it.
Accordant, as the eye guides him who
walks, have ye led our devotion onward
by an easy path.

7 Never is he, O Maruts, slain or overcome,
never doth he decay ne'er is distressed
or harmed;
His treasures, his resources, never waste
away, whom, whether he be prince or
Ṛṣi, ye direct.

8 With harnessed team like heroes overcoming troops, the friendly Maruts, laden
with their water-casks,
Let the spring flow, and when impetuous'
they roar they inundate the earth with
floods of pleasant meath.

9 Free for the Maruts is the earth with
sloping ways, free for the rushing Ones
is heaven with steep descents.
The paths of air's mid-region are precipitous, precipitous the mountains with
their running streams.

10 When, as the Sun hath risen up, ye take
delight, O bounteous radiant Maruts,
Heroes of the sky,
Your coursers weary not when speeding on
their way, and rapidly ye reach the end
of this your path.

11 Lances are on your shoulders, anklets on
your feet, gold chains are on your
breasts, gems, Maruts, on your car.
Lightnings aglow with flame are flashing
in your hands, and visors wrought of
gold are laid upon your heads.

12 Maruts, in eager stir ye shake the vault of
heaven, splendid beyond conception,
for its shining fruit.
They gathered when they let their deeds
of might flash forth. The Pious Ones
send forth a far-resounding shout.

13 Sage Maruts, may we be the drivers of the
car of riches full of life that have been
given by you.

12 *For its shining fruit* : the bright water.
13 *The drivers of the car* : that is, the controllers.
May we by our prayers and sacrifices bring down and

O Maruts, let that wealth in thousands
dwell with us which never vanishes
like Tiṣya from the sky.

14 Maruts, ye further wealth with longed-
for heroes, further the Ṛṣi skilled in
chanted verses.
Ye give the Bharata as his strength, a
charger, and ye bestow a king who
quickly listens.

15 Of you, most swift to succour ! I solicit
wealth wherewith we may spread forth
mid men like as the Sun.
Accept, O Maruts, graciously this hymn
of mine that we may live a hundred
winters through its power.

HYMN LV.   *Maruts.*

1. WITH gleaming lances, with their breasts
adorned with gold, the Maruts, rushing
onward, hold high power of life.
They hasten with swift steeds easy to be
controlled. Their cars moved onward
as they went to victory.

2 Ye, as ye wist, have gained of your own
selves your power : high, O ye Mighty
Ones, and wide ye shine abroad.
They with their strength have even measured out the sky.
Their cars moved onward as they went to
victory.

3 Strong, born together, they together have
waxed great : the Heroes more and more
have grown to majesty
Resplendent as the Sun's beams in their
light are they. Their cars moved onward as they went to victory.

4 Maruts, your mightiness deserves to be
adored, sight to be longed for like the
shining of the Sun.
So lead us with your aid to immortality.

enjoy the riches which you give.

Tiṣya : an asterism regarded as shaped like an
arrow and containing three stars. According to Sāyaṇa
Tiṣya here is synonymous with Āditya.

14 *The Bharata* : a warrior, or one of family of
Bharata. See Index. According to Sāyaṇa, Śyāvāśva
the Ṛṣi of the hymn is intended : 'to (me) the ministrant
priest.' Wilson.

Who quickly listens : to his people's prayers. Sāyaṇa
explains *śruṣṭimántam* as *sukhavantam*, happy and prosperous.

15 *A hundred winters* : a frequently occurring expression, 'from which we might infer,' says Dr. J. Muir,
'that the Indians still retained some recollection of
their having at one time occupied a colder country.'
See *Original Sanskrit Texts*, II. 323.

Their cars moved onward as they went to
victory.

5 O Maruts, from the Ocean ye uplift the
rain, and fraught with vaporous moisture
pour the torrents down.
Never, ye Wonder-Workers, are your Milch-
kine dry. Their cars moved onward as
they went to victory.

6 When to your car-poles ye have yoked
your spotted deer to be your steeds, and
put your golden mantles on,
O Maruts, ye disperse all enemies abroad.
Their cars moved onward as they went
to victory.

7 Neither the mountains nor the rivers keep
you back : whither ye have resolved
thither ye, Maruts, go.
Ye compass round about even the heaven
and earth. Their cars moved onward as
they went to victory.

Whate'er is ancient, Maruts, what of recent
time, whate'er is spoken, Vasus, what is
chanted forth,
They who take cognizance of all of this are
ye. Their cars moved onward as they
went to victory.

9 Be gracious unto us, ye Maruts, slay us not :
extend ye unto us shelter of many a
sort.
Pay due regard unto our friendship and our
praise. Their cars moved onward as they
went to victory.

10 O Maruts, lead us on to higher fortune :
deliver us, when lauded, from afflictions.
Accept, ye Holy Ones, the gifts we bring
you. May we be masters of abundant
riches.

HYMN LVI.   *Maruts.*

1. AGNI, that valorous company adorned with
ornaments of gold,
The people of the Maruts, I call down
to-day even from the luminous realm of
heaven.

2 Even as thou thinkest in thy heart, thither
my wishes also tend.
Those who have come most near to thine
invoking calls, strengthen them fearful to
behold.

3 Earth, like a bounteous lady, liberal of her
gifts, struck down and shaken, yet exultant, comes to us.

5 *Your Milch-kine* : the rain-clouds.

2 *Strengthen them* : that is, the Maruts, with oblations.
3 The exact meaning of the first line is somewhat
uncertain. Sāyaṇa explains it : 'As the earth—that is

Impetuous as a bear, O Maruts, is your
rush terrible as a dreadful bull.

4 They who with mighty strength o'erthrow
like oxen difficult to yoke,
Cause e'en the heavenly stone to shake,
yea, shake the rocky mountain as they
race along.

5 Rise up ! even now with lauds I call the
very numerous company,
Unequalled, of these Maruts, like a herd of
kine, grown up together in their strength.

6 Bind to your car the bright red mares, yoke
the red coursers to your car.
Bind to the pole, to draw, the fleet-foot
tawny steeds, the best at drawing, to the
pole.

7 Yea, and this loudly-neighing bright red
vigorous horse who hath been stationed,
fair to see,
Let him not cause delay, O Maruts, in your
course, urge ye him onward in your cars.

8 The Maruts' chariot, ever fain to gather
glory, we invoke,
Which Rodasī hath mounted, bringing
pleasant gifts, with Maruts in her company.

9 I call that brilliant band of yours, adorable,
rapid on the car
Whereon the bounteous Dame, auspicious,
nobly born, shows glorious with the
Marut host.

HYMN LVII.   *Maruts.*

1. OF one accord, with Indra, O ye Rudras,
come borne on your golden car for our
prosperity.
An offering from us, this hymn is brought
to you, as, unto one who thirsts for
water, heavenly springs.

the people of the earth—having a powerful master,
when oppressed by others, has recourse to him her own
master, so the army of Maruts comes exulting to us.'
But *miḍhuṣmatī* (bounteous, liberal, bringing forth abundant fruit) cannot mean *prabalasvāmikā*, having a powerful master.

Struck down : by the rain sent by the Maruts.

7 *Who hath been stationed* : or harnessed to the car.
8 *Rodasī* : the Consort of Rudra and mother of the
Maruts.

9 *The bounteous Dame* : Rodasī. *Shows glorious* : or,
is glorified.

1 *O ye Rudras* : or Sons of Rudra. *For our prosperity*:
'to the accessible (sacrifice).'—Wilson. *Heavenly springs* :
an allusion, says Sāyaṇa, to the well, that is, the cloud
which was brought by the Maruts to thirsty Gotama.
See I. 85. 11.

2 Armed with your daggers, full of wisdom, armed with spears, armed with your quivers, armed with arrows, with good bows,

Good horses and good cars have ye, O Pṛśni's Sons : ye, Maruts, with good weapons go to victory.

3 From hills and heaven ye shake wealth for the worshipper : in terror at your coming low the woods bow down.

Ye make the earth to tremble, Sons of Pṛśni, when for victory ye have yoked, fierce Ones ! your spotted deer.

4 Bright with the blasts of wind, wrapped in their robes of rain, like twins of noble aspect and of lovely form,

The Maruts, spotless, with steeds tawny-hued and red, strong in their mightiness and spreading wide like heaven.

5 Rich in adornment, rich in drops, munificent, bright in their aspect, yielding bounties that endure,

Noble by birth, adorned with gold upon their breasts, the Singers of the sky have won immortal fame.

6 Borne on both shoulders, O ye Maruts, are your spears : within your arms is laid your energy and strength.

Bold thoughts are in your heads, your weapons in your cars, all glorious majesty is moulded on your forms.

7 Vouchsafe to us, O Maruts, splendid bounty in cattle and in steeds, in cars and heroes.

Children of Rudra, give us high distinction : may I enjoy your Godlike help and favour.

8 Ho ! Maruts, Heroes, skilled in Law, immortal, be gracious unto us, ye rich in treasures,

Ye hearers of the truth, ye sage and youthful, grown mighty, dwelling on the lofty mountains.

HYMN LVIII.   *Maruts.*

1. Now do I glorify their mighty cohort, the company of these the youthful Maruts,

Who ride impetuous on with rapid horses, and radiant in themselves, are Lords of Amṛta.

2 The mighty glittering band, arm-bound with bracelets, givers of bliss, unmeasured in their greatness,

With magical powers, bountiful, ever-roaring,—these, liberal Heroes, venerate thou singer.

3 This day may all your water-bringers, Maruts, they who impel the falling rain, approach us.

This fire, O Maruts, hath been duly kindled ; let it find favour with you, youthful Sages.

4 Ye raise up for the folk an active ruler whom, Holy Ones ! a Master's hand hath fashioned.

Ye send the fighter hand to hand, arm-mighty, and the brave hero, Maruts ! with good horses.

5 They spring forth more and more, strong in their glories, like days, like spokes where none are last in order.

Highest and mightiest are the Sons of Pṛśni. Firm to their own intention cling the Maruts.

6 When ye have hastened on with spotted coursers, O Maruts, on your cars with strong-wrought fellies,

The waters are disturbed, the woods are shattered. Let Dyaus the Red Steer send his thunder downward.

7 Even Earth hath spread herself wide at their coming, and they as husbands have with power impregned her.

They to the pole have yoked the winds for coursers: their sweat have they made rain, these Sons of Rudra.

8 Ho ! Maruts, Heroes, skilled in Law, immortal, be gracious unto us, ye rich in treasures,

Ye hearers of the truth, ye sage and youthful, grown mighty, dwelling on the lofty mountains.

---

4 *Like twins* : all alike.

5 *The Singers of the sky* : chanters of their thunder-psalm.

6 *Bold thoughts* : Sāyaṇa explains *nṛmṇā = nṛmṇāni* as golden tiaras. The word *ṇṛmṇd* in one or another of its cases occurs some thirty times in the Ṛgveda, and always in the sense of manly power, valour, or valorous deed.

8 *Ye hearers of the truth* : or, famous for your truth, for the realization of your promises.

---

1 *Lords of Amṛta* : controllers of the sweet life-giving rain.

2 *Arm-bound with bracelets* : or, rather, 'adorned with quoits on their hands.'—M. Müller.

4 *Whom...a Master's hand hath fashioned* : according to Sāyaṇa *vibhvataṣṭám* means fabricated or modelled by Vibhvan, the second of the three Ṛbhus, i. e. *atyanta-rūpavantam* or exceedingly handsome. *The fighter hand to hand* : the man who fights on foot is your gift as well as the warrior who is borne to battle in a chariot.

HYMN LIX. *Maruts.*

1. YOUR spy hath called to you to give prosperity. I sing to Heaven and Earth and offer sacrifice.
They bathe their steeds and hasten through the firmament : they spread abroad their radiance through the sea of cloud.

2 Earth shakes and reels in terror at their onward rush, like a full ship which, quivering, lets the water in.
Marked on their ways are they, visible from afar : the Heroes press between in mighty armament.

3 As the exalted horn of bulls for splendid might, as the Sun's eye set in the firmament's expanse,
Like vigorous horses ye are beauteous to behold, and for your glory show like bridegrooms, O ye Men.

4 Who, O ye Maruts, may attain the mighty lore of you the mighty, who may reach your manly deeds?
Ye, verily, make earth tremble like a ray of light what time ye bring your boons to give prosperity.

5 Like steeds of ruddy colour, scions of one race, as foremost champions they have battled in the van.
The Heroes have waxed strong like well-grown manly youths; with floods of rain they make the Sun's eye fade away.

6 Having no eldest and no youngest in their band, no middlemost, preeminent they have waxed in might,
These Sons of Prśni, sprung of noble ancestry : come hitherward to us, ye bridegrooms of the sky.

7 Like birds of air they flew with might in lengthened lines from heaven's high ridges to the borders of the sky.
The steeds who carry them, as Gods and mortals know, have caused the waters of the mountains to descend.

8 May Dyaus, the Infinite, roar for our banquet : may Dawns toil for us, glittering with moisture.

Lauded by thee, these Maruts, Sons o Rudra, O Ṛṣi, have sent down the heavenly treasure.

HYMN LX. *Maruts.*

1. I LAUD with reverence the gracious Agni : here may he sit and part our meed among us.
As with spoil-seeking cars I bring oblation : turned rightward I will swell the Marut's praise-song.

2 The Maruts, yea, the Rudras, who have mounted their famous spotted deer and cars swift-moving,—
Before you, fierce Ones ! woods bow down in terror : Earth, even the mountain, trembles at your coming.

3 Though vast and tall, the mountain is affrighted, the height of heaven is shaken at your roaring
When, armed with lances, ye are sporting, Maruts, and rush along together like the waters.

4 They, like young suitors, sons of wealthy houses, have with their golden natures decked their bodies.
Strong on their cars, the lordly Ones, for glory, have set their splendours on their forms for ever.

5 None being eldest, none among them youngest, as brothers they have grown to happy fortune.
May their Sire Rudra, young and deft, and Prśni pouring much milk, bring fair days to the Maruts.

6 Whether, O blessed Maruts, ye be dwelling in highest, midmost, or in lowest heaven,
Thence, O ye Rudras, and thou also, Agni, notice the sacrificial food we offer.

7 O Maruts, Lords of all, when Agni and when ye drive downward from sublimest heaven along the heights,
Shakers of all, rejoicing, slayers of the foe, give riches to the Soma-pressing worshipper.

---

1 *Your spy* : Agni, as the lightning. According to Sāyaṇa *spát* is for *sprasṭá*, one who touches (the oblation), the Hotar or presenting priest.

2 *Press between* : rush through the air between heaven and earth.

7 *Gods and mortals* : the text has only *ubhdye*, both (sides or parties). The word generally means Gods and men; but perhaps, as Professor Ludwig suggests, Heaven and Earth may be intended here.

8 *Dyaus. the Infinite* : Cf. X. 63. 3.

1 *Turned rightward* : making reverential salutation by circumambulation from left to right ; the Gaelic *deasil*.

4 *With their golden natures* : with some hesitation I follow Professor Ludwig in taking *hiraṇyaih,* as an old form of the feminine, with *svad dbhiḥ.* Professor Wilson, following Sāyaṇa, translates : 'with golden (ornaments) and purifying waters.'

5 *Pouring much milk* : Prśni, the mother of the Maruts, the cloud of the firmament, being represented as a cow.

Bring fair days to the Maruts : perhaps the bright weather which follows the Rains. 'Grant favourable days for (the sake of) the Maruts.'—Wilson.

8 O Agni, with the Maruts as they gleam
and sing, gathered in troop, rejoicing
drink the Soma juice;
With these the living ones who cleanse
and further all, joined with thy banner,
O Vaiśvānara, from of old.

HYMN LXI.   *Maruts.*

1. O HEROES lordliest of all, who are ye
that have singly come
Forth from a region most remote?

2 Where are your horses, where the reins?
How came ye? how had ye the power?
Rein was on nose and seat on back.

3 The whip is laid upon the flank. The
heroes stretch their thighs apart,
Like women when the babe is born.

4 Go ye, O Heroes, far away, ye bridegrooms with a lovely Spouse
That ye may warm you at the fire.

5 May she gain cattle for her meed,
hundreds of sheep and steeds and kine,
Who threw embracing arms around the
hero whom Śyāvāśva praised.

6 Yea, many a woman is more firm and
better than the man who turns
Away from Gods, and offers not.

7 She who discerns the weak and worn, the
man who thirsts and is in want :
She sets her mind upon the Gods.

8 And yet full many a one, unpraised, mean
niggard, is entitled man :
Only in weregild is he such.

9 And she, the young, the joyous-spirited,
divulged the path to Śyāva, yea, to me.
Two red steeds carried me to Purumīḷha's
side, that sage of far-extended fame,

10 Him who, like Vaidadaśvi, like Taranta,
hath bestowed on me
A hundred cows in liberal gift.

11 They who are borne by rapid steeds,
drinking the meath that gives delight,
They have attained high glories here.

12 They by whose splendour both the worlds
are over-spread they shine on cars
As the gold gleams above in heaven.

13 That Marut band is ever young, borne on
bright cars, unblamable,
Moving to victory, checked by none.

14 Who knoweth, verily, of these where the
All-shakers take delight,
Born, spotless, after sacred Law ?

15 Guides are ye, lovers of the song to mortal
man through holy hymn,
And hearers when he cries for help.

16 Do ye, destroyers of the foe, worshipful
and exceeding bright,
Send down the treasures that we crave.

17 O Ūrmyā, bear thou far away to Dārbhya
this my hymn of praise,
Songs, Goddess, as if chariot-borne.

18 From me to Rathavīti say, when he hath
pressed the Soma juice,
The wish I had departeth not.

19 This wealthy Rathavīti dwells among the
people rich in kine,
Among the mountains, far withdrawn.

HYMN LXII.   *Mitra-Varuṇa.*

1. By your high Law firm order is esta-
blished there where they loose for travel
Sūrya's horses.
Ten hundred stood together : there I
looked on this the most marvellous
Deities' one chief glory.

2 This, Mitra-Varuṇa, is your special greatness : floods that stood there they with
the days attracted.

11 This stanza is apparently the beginning of a
separate hymn, in honour of the Maruts.
12 *As the gold* : the golden Sun.
17 *Ūrmyā* : Goddess of Night. *Dārbhya* : Rathavīti,
son of Darbha.
18 *The wish I had* : to perform a sacrifice for the
rich and liberal Rathavīti.

8 *Joined with thy banner* : closely connected with thy
ensign or banner of flame.

4 *With a lovely Spouse* : apparently Rodasī, who is
sometimes regarded as the wife of the whole band of
Maruts.

5 *She* : according to Sāyaṇa, the wife of Taranta
(stanza 10) who is 'the hero whom Śyāvāśva praised.'

6 *More firm* : the word thus rendered, *śdśīyasī*, is
taken by Sāyaṇa to be the name of Taranta's wife.

8 *Only in weregild* : only as regards the fine to be
paid for manslaughter, either by him or for him, can he
be accounted a man. The verse is obscure. See Vedic
Hymns (Sacred Books of the East), Part I. p. 360, and
Ludwig. Ueber die neuesten Arbeiten, &c., p. 40.

9 *And she* : Taranta's wife. *Śyāva* = Śyāvāśva, the
Ṛṣi of the hymn.

10 *Vaidadaśvi* : Purumīḷha, son of Vidadaśva.

1 *By your high Law* : the eternal order of the universe, which in the region of the Sun regulates the
starting and the journeying of his horses, depends on, or
is identical with, the everlasting statutes of Mitra and
Varuṇa. *Ten hundred* : rays of the Sun. *One chief glory* :
the orb of the Sun, the noblest visible form of Agni and
other Gods.

2 *Floods that stood there* : they, that is the sunbeams,
have in the course of days milked out or attracted to themselves the waters that stood apart from the Sun *Tasthuṣīḥ*
(standing, stationary) has no substantive expressed, and
the meaning of the milch-kine of the firmament. The
voices are probably the thunder and the roar of the

Ye cause to flow all voices of the cow-
pen : your single chariotfelly hath rolled
hither.

3 O Mitra-Varuṇa, ye by your greatness,
both Kings, have firmly stablished earth
and heaven,
Ye caused the cows to stream, the plants
to flourish, and, scattering swift drops,
sent down the rain-flood.

4 Let your well-harnessed horses bear you
hither : hitherward let them come with
reins drawn tightly.
A covering cloud of sacred oil attends you,
and your streams flow to us from days
aforetime.

5 To make the lustre wider and more famous,
guarding the sacred grass with veneration,
Ye, Mitra-Varuṇa, firm, strong, awe-inspi-
ring, are seated on a throne amid oblations.

6 With hands that shed no blood, guarding
the pious, whom, Varuṇa, ye save amid
oblations.
Ye Twain, together, Kings of willing
spirit, uphold dominion based on thousand pillars.

7 Adorned with gold, its columns are of
iron : in heaven it glitters like a whip
for horses;
Or stablished on a field deep-spoiled and
fruitful. So may we share the meath
that loads your car-seat.

8 Ye mount your car gold-hued at break of
morning, and iron-pillared when the
Sun is setting,
And from that place, O Varuṇa and
Mitra, behold infinity and limitation.

9 Bountiful guardians of the world ! the
shelter that is impenetrable, strongest,
flawless,
Aid us with that, O Varuṇa and Mitra,
and when we long to win may we be
victors.

HYMN LXIII.   Mitra-Varuṇa.

1. GUARDIANS of Order, ye whose Laws are
ever true, in the sublimest heaven your
chariot ye ascend.
O Mitra-Varuṇa whomsoe'er ye favour,
here, to him the rain with sweetness
streameth down from heaven.

2 This world's imperial Kings, O Mitra-
Varuṇa, ye rule in holy synod, looking
on the light.
We pray for rain, your boon, and immortality. Through heaven and over earth the
thunderers take their way.

3 Imperial Kings, strong, Heroes, Lords of
earth and heaven, Mitra and Varuṇa,
ye ever active Ones,
Ye wait on thunder with the many-tinted
clouds, and by the Asura's magic power
cause Heaven to rain.

4 Your magic, Mitra-Varuṇa, resteth in the
heaven. The Sun, the wondrous weapon,
cometh forth as light.
Ye hide him in the sky with cloud and
flood of rain, and water-drops, Parjanya!
full of sweetness flow.

5 The Maruts yoke their easy car for victory,
O Mitra-Varuṇa, as a hero in the wars.
The thunderers roam through regions
varied in their hues. Imperial Kings,
bedew us with the milk of heaven.

6 Refreshing is your voice, O Mitra-Varuṇa :
Parjanya sendeth out a wondrous mighty
voice.
With magic power the Maruts clothe them
with the clouds. Ye Two cause Heaven
to rain, the red, the spotless One.

rushing rain. *Your single chariot-felly* : the circumference
or felly of the wheel being, by metonymy, put for the
chariot.

4 *A covering cloud of sacred oil* : of ghṛta, butter, *i. e.*
fertilizing rain.

5 *On a throne* : or on your car.

6 *Ye save amid oblations* : the sacrificial hall with its
precincts being regarded as an inviolable asylum.

7 *Adorned with gold* :—the chariot of Mitra and
Varuṇa. *Like a whip for horses* : according to Sāyaṇa,
the whip is the lightning and the horses are the flying
clouds.

Or stablished : the meaning of this third Pāda is
not clear. Professor Wilson, following Sāyaṇa, translates :
'may we load the vehicle with the libation in an
auspicious pace, or in the sacrificial hall, (where the
columns) are erected.'

8 *Iron-pillared* : the chariot which shines like gold
in the light of the rising sun looks dim and dark like
bronze or iron at sunset.

Infinity and limitation : *áditim ditim ca* ; according
to Sāyaṇa, Aditi or the Earth as an indivisible whole,

and Diti as representing the divisible people and living
creatures inhabiting it. Aditi appears to mean infinite
Nature, and Diti to be a Goddess connected with
Aditi without any distinct conception, and merely as a
contrast to her. The two words may perhaps mean
the eternal and the perishable, yonder boundless space
and the bounded space near us, or Sky and Earth, or
Nature by day and Nature by night. 'At all events, as
Dr. Muir observes, 'the two together appear to be put by
the poet for the entire aggregate of visible nature.' See
Original Sanskrit Texts, V. pp. 42, 43.

The hymn is a prayer for rain.

2 *The thunderers* : the roaring winds.

3 *The Asura's magic power* : the Asura or divine
Being here is either Dyaus or Parjanya.

7 Wise, with your Law and through the
Asura's magic power ye guard the
ordinances, Mitra-Varuṇa.
Ye by eternal Order govern all the world.
Ye set the Sun in heaven as a refulgent
car.

HYMN LXIV.   Mitra-Varuṇa

1. You, foeman-slaying Varuṇa and Mitra,
we invoke with song,
Who, as with penfold of your arms, encompass round the realm of light.

2 Stretch out your arms with favouring love
unto this man who singeth hymns,
For in all places is sung forth your ever-
gracious friendliness.

3 That I may gain a refuge now, may my
steps be on Mitra's path.
Men go protected in the charge of this
dear Friend who harms us not.

4 Mitra and Varuṇa, from you may I, by
song, win noblest meed.
That shall stir envy in the homes of
wealthy chiefs and those who praise.

5 With your fair splendours, Varuṇa and
Mitra, to our gathering come,
That in their homes the wealthy chiefs
and they who are your friends may
thrive.

6 With those, moreover, among whom ye
hold your high supremacy,
Vouchsafe us room that we may win
strength for prosperity and wealth.

7 When morning flushes, Holy Ones ! in
the Gods' realm where white Cows
shine,
Supporting Arcanānas, speed, ye Heroes,
with your active feet hither to my
pressed Soma juice.

HYMN LXV.   Mitra-Varuṇa.

1. FULL wise is he who hath discerned : let
him speak to us of the Gods,—
The man whose praise-songs Varuṇa the
beautiful, or Mitra, loves.

1 *With penfold of your arms* : I follow Professor
Ludwig in taking *vrajá* as an instrumental case.
3 *May my steps be* : may I walk in the way of
Mitra, that is, may I keep his holy law.
5 *The wealthy chiefs* : the institutors of sacrifice.
Your friends : we, the priests.
6 *With those* : with the Gods.
7 *White Cows* : the white clouds of early morning.
Arcanānas : the Ṛṣi of the hymn. *With your active feet*:the
literal translation of *hastibhiḥ paḍbhiḥ* would be, with feet
provided with hands : 'With rapid steeds.' —Wilson. See
M. Bloomfield, Contributions to the Interpretation of the
Veda, Second Series, p. 35.

1 *Of the Gods* : regarding Mitra and Varuṇa.

2 For they are Kings of noblest might, of
glorious fame most widely spread;
Lords of the brave, who strengthen Law,
the Holy Ones with every race.

3 Approaching you with prayer for aid, to-
gether I address you first
We who have good steeds call on you,
Most Sage, to give us strength besides.

4 E'en out of misery Mitra gives a way to
dwelling at our ease,
For he who worships hath the grace of
Mitra, fighter in the van.

5 In Mitra's shelter that extends to utmost
distance may we dwell,
Unmenaced, guarded by the care, ever as
sons of Varuṇa.

6 Ye, Mitra, urge this people on, and to one
end direct their ways.
Neglect not ye the wealthy chiefs, neglect
not us the Ṛṣis : be our guardians when
ye quaff the milk.

HYMN LXVI.   Mitra-Varuṇa.

1. O SAPIENT man, call the Two Gods, the
very wise, who slay the foe.
For Varuṇa, whose form is Law, place
offerings for his great delight.

2 For they have won unbroken sway in full
perfection, power divine.
And, like high laws, the world of man
hath been made beautiful as light.

3 Therefore we praise you that your cars may
travel far in front of ours—
You who accept the eulogy of Rātahavya
with his hymns.

4 And ye show wisdom, Wondrous Gods !
with fulness of intelligence.
By men's discernment are ye marked, O ye
whose might is purified.

5 *As sons of Varuṇa* : or perhaps, as Professor Ludwig
suggests, with Varuṇa as our son, that is with kingly
descendants.
6 *Ye, Mitra* : and Varuṇa.
When ye quaff the milk : 'in the presenting of the
libation.'—Wilson.

1 *O Sapient man* : thou who knowest how to praise
the Gods.
Whose form is Law : according to Sāyaṇa, 'whose
form is water.'
2 *Like high laws* : Professor Ludwig would read
vratena instead of *vratéva*, that is, through holy ordinance.
3 *Rātahavya* : the Ṛṣi of the hymn. I can make
nothing out of this stanza, and I follow Sāyaṇa in
despair of finding a reasonable interpretation.
4 This stanza also is difficult and obscure.

5 This is the Law sublime, O Earth : to aid
the Ṛṣis' toil for fame

The Two, wide-spreading, are prepared.
They come with ample overflow.

6 Mitra, ye Gods with wandering eyes, would
that the worshippers and we
Might strive to reach the realm ye rule,
most spacious and protected well.

HYMN LXVII.   Mitra-Varuṇa.

1. YE Gods, Ādityas, Varuṇa, Aryaman, Mitra,
verily
Have here obtained supremest sway, high,
holy, set apart for you.

2 When, Varuṇa and Mitra, ye sit in your
golden dwelling-place,
Ye Twain, supporters of mankind, foe-
slayers, give felicity.

3 All these, possessors of all wealth, Varuṇa,
Mitra, Aryaman,
Follow their ways, as if with feet, and
guard from injury mortal man.

4 For they are true, they cleave to Law,
held holy among every race,
Good leaders, bounteous in their gifts,
deliverers even from distress.

5 Which of your persons, Varuṇa or Mitra,
merits not our praise ?
Therefore our thought is turned to you,
the Atris' thought is turned to you.

HYMN LXVIII.   Mitra-Varuṇa.

1. SING forth unto your Varuṇa and Mitra
with a song inspired.
They, Mighty Lords, are lofty Law :

2 Full springs of fatness, Sovran Kings, Mitra
and Varuṇa, the Twain,
Gods glorified among the Gods.

5 *O Earth* : Pṛthivī, or Earth, is quite out of place
here. Professor Ludwig suspects a corruption of the
text, and Professor Grassmann thinks that the whole
stanza has been inserted by mistake. The two wide-
spreading or far-reaching Gods, Mitra and Varuṇa, are
said to be ready to listen to the Ṛṣis' prayers and so to
increase their renown. The copious fall of rain is proof
that their prayers have been heard.
6 *Ye Gods* : Mitra and Varuṇa, Mitra only being
named.

———

2 *Your golden dwelling-place* : the delightful place of
sacrifice, according to Sāyaṇa.
3 *Follow their ways* : their royal ordinances, *vratā*,
that is *vratāni*.

———

1 *They, Mighty Lords, are lofty Law* : '(come)mighty
deities, to the great sacrifice.'—Wilson.
2 *Full prings of fatness* : originators of streams of
fertilizing rain; or *ghṛtáyoni* may mean here as it does
elsewhere, dwelling or having their home with *ghṛtá*,
clarified butter or oil used in sacrifice.

3 So help ye us to riches, great terrestrial
and celestial wealth :
Vast is your sway among the Gods.

4 Carefully tending Law with Law they have
attained their vigorous might.
The two Gods wax devoid of guile.

5 With rainy skies and streaming floods, Lords
of the strength that bringeth gifts,
A lofty seat have they attained.

HYMN LXIX.   Mitra-Varuṇa.

1. THREE spheres of light, O Varuṇa, three
heavens, three firmaments ye comprehend,
O Mitra:
Waxed strong, ye keep the splendour of
dominion, guarding the Ordinance that
lasts for ever.

2 Ye, Varuṇa, have kine who yield refreshment; Mitra, your floods pour water
full of sweetness.
There stand the Three Steers, splendid in
their brightness, who fill the three
world-bowls with genial moisture.

3 I call at dawn on Aditi the Goddess, I call
at noon and when the Sun is setting.
I pray, O Mitra-Varuṇa, for safety, for
wealth and progeny, in rest and trouble.

4 Ye who uphold the region, sphere of brightness, ye who support earth's realm,
Divine Ādityas,
The Immortal Gods, O Varuṇa and Mitra,
never impair your everlasting statutes.

HYMN LXX.   Mitra-Varuṇa.

1. EVEN far and wide, O Varuṇa and Mitra,
doth your grace extend.
May I obtain your kind good-will.

2 From you, benignant Gods, may we gain
fully food for sustenance.
Such, O ye Rudras, my we be.

3 Guard us, O Rudras, with your guards,
save us, ye skilled to save, my we
Subdue the Dasyus, we ourselves,

5 *Lords of the strength that bringeth gifts* : 'lords of
sustenance, suited to the liberal donors (of oblations).'
—Wilson.

———

1 *Three firmaments* : according to Sāyaṇa, three
realms of earth, an interpretation which is more in
accordance with the second half of stanza 2.
2 *The Three Steers* : Agni as terrestrial fire on earth,
Vāyu as the wind in the firmament, and Sūrya as the
Sun in heaven. *World bowls* : Ludwig explains differently. See his Ueber die neuesten Arbeiten auf dem
Gebiete der Ṛgveda forschung, p. 85. *Genial moisture* :
the fertilizing rain.

———

2 *O ye Rudras* : O Mitra and Varuṇa.

4 Or ne'er may we, O Wondrous Strong,
enjoy another's solemn feast,
Ourselves, our sons, or progeny.

HYMN LXXI.   *Mitra-Varuṇa.*

1. O VARUṆA and Mitra, ye who slay the
foemen, come with might
To this our goodly sacrifice.

2 For, Varuṇa and Mitra, ye Sages are
Rulers over all. Fill full our songs, for
this ye can.

3 Come to the juice that we have pressed.
Varuṇa, Mitra, come to drink
This Soma of the worshipper.

HYMN LXXII.   *Mitra-Varuṇa.*

1 To Varuṇa and Mitra we offer with songs,
as Atri did. Sit on the sacred grass to
drink the Soma juice.

2 By Ordinance and Law ye dwell in peace
secure, bestirring men.
Sit on the sacred grass to drink the
Soma juice.

3 May Varuṇa and Mitra, for our help,
accept the sacrifice.
Sit on the sacred grass to drink the Soma
juice.

HYMN LXXIII.   *Aśvins.*

1. WHETHER, O Aśvins, ye this day be far
remote or near at hand,
In many spots or in mid-air, come hither,
Lords of ample wealth.

2 These here, who show o'er widest space,
bringing full many a wondrous act,
Resistless, lovingly I seek, I call the
Mightiest to enjoy.

3 Another beauteous wheel have ye fixed
there to decorate your car.
With others through the realms ye roam in
might unto the neighbouring tribes.

4 That deed of yours that is extolled,
Viśvas ! hath all been done with this.
Born otherwise, and spotless, ye have
entered kinship's bonds with us.

5 When Sūryā mounted on your car that
rolls for ever rapidly,
Birds of red hue were round about and
burning splendours compassed you.

6 Atri bethinks himself of you, O Heroes,
with a friendly mind,
What time, Nāsatyas, with his mouth he
stirs the spotless flame for you.

7 Strong is your swiftly moving steed, famed
his exertion in the course
When by your great deeds, Aśvins, Chiefs,
Atri is brought to us again.

8 Lovers of sweetness, Rudras, she who
streams with sweetness waits on you.
When ye have travelled through the seas
men bring you gifts of well-dressed food.

9 Aśvins, with truth they call you Twain
bestowers of felicity ;
At sacrifice most prompt to hear, most
gracious ye at sacrifice.

10 Most pleasing to the Aśvins be these
prayers which magnify their might,
Which we have fashioned, even as cars :
high reverence have we spoken forth.

3 *There* : the third wheel of their chariot, standing by
itself in front, is especially emphasized. *With others* :
Sāyaṇa explains *anyā* by *anyena cakreṇa, i. e.* with
another, or the other, wheel ; but the two hind wheels
must be intended, or *anyā* must be in agreement with
yugā. The neighbouring tribes : the meaning of *nāhuṣā
yugā* is not clear. Professor Ludwig translates the
words by 'zu den geschlechtern der Nahuṣa,' 'to the
tribes of the [people called] Nahuṣas.' Professor
Wilson, following Sāyaṇa, translates the stanza differently : 'You have arrested one luminous wheel of (your)
car for illumining the form (of the sun), whilst with
the other you traverse the spheres (to regulate) by your
power the ages of mankind.'

4 *Viśvas* ! : Sāyaṇa explains *viśvā,* by *vyāptau,* the
two who spread through or pervade : 'universal
(deities).'—Wilson. *With this* : according to Sāyaṇa,
with this Paura (the Ṛṣi of the hymn). Or 'this' may
mean, as Professor Ludwig thinks, the third of the car,
in which mysterious virtue more especially resides. *Born
otherwise* : of divine and not human origin.

5 *Sūryā* : the Daughter of the Sun. See I. 116. 17.

7 *Atri is brought to us again* : See I. 112. 7.

8 *She who streams with sweetness* : Vāk, Voice or
Speech, or our praise, *stutirasmatkṛtā.* 'Our nutritious
(adoration).'—Wilson. *The seas* : of air.

4 *Or ne'er may we* : I adopt Professor Ludwig's
explanation. We will overcome the Dasyus by our
own power, or we will never again participate in any
man's solemn festival held in honour of the Gods : a
self-imprecation in case of failing to carry out their
purpose.

1 *With might* : Sāyaṇa explains *barhāṇā* as *hantārau
śatrūṇām,* destroyers of enemies.

2 *Fill full our songs* : let them overflow with, or
produce abundantly, the results for which we pray.

1 *As Atri did* : after the manner of Atri, the founder
of our family.

1 *In many spots* : the *purū* in the text is thus explained by Sāyaṇa.

2 *To enjoy* : the libation offered to you. According
to Sāyaṇa, *bhujé* here means for enjoyment, or for
protection.

HYMN LXXIV.   *Aśvins.*

1. WHERE in the heavens are ye to-day,
   Gods, Aśvins, rich in constancy ?
   Hear this, ye excellent as Steers : Atri
   inviteth you to come.

2 Where are they now ? Where are the
   Twain, the famed Nāsatyas, Gods in
   heaven ?

   Who is the man ye strive to reach ? Who
   of your suppliants is with you ?

3 Whom do ye visit, whom approach ? to
   whom direct your harnessed car ?
   With whose devotions are ye pleased ?
   We long for you to further us.

4 Ye, Strengtheners, for Paura stir the filler
   swimming in the flood,
   Advancing to be captured like a lion to
   the ambuscade.

1 *Rich in constancy* : faithful friends of your worshippers. *Excellent as Steers* : 'liberal showerers (of
benefits).'—Wilson.

2 *Of your suppliants* : this, although not entirely
satisfactory, seems to be the only possible explanation
of *nadīnām* in this place. Professor Ludwig remarks,
truly enough, that if *ko* (quis ?) could be taken as *kā*
(quae), the passage would present no difficulty. The
meaning would then be, which of the rivers (of the
Panj b) rejoices in your presence ? Sāyaṇa paraphrases the passage : *kaḥ stotā vām yuvayornadīnām stutīnām sacā
sahāyaḥ syāt* ; 'what praiser may be the associate of the
praises of you twain' ?

4 This stanza is desperately difficult. Professor
Wilson translates in accordance with Sāvaṇa's explanation: '*Pauras, send* to Paura the rain-shedding cloud; drive
it to him who is engaged in sacrifice, as (hunters chase)
a lion in a forest.' Professor Wilson remarks : 'The name
of the Ṛṣi is here, according to the scholiast, arbitrarily
applied, first to the *Aśvins*, because they are in relation
with *Paura* as the author of the *Sūkta* ; and although
the text gives *Paura* in the vocative singular, it is to be
understood in the dual *Paura*, therefore, being *Aśvins* :
next it implies, as *Pauram*, a cloud, from its being
solicited by the *Ṛṣi* for the fall of rain, as implied by
the last term, *Paurāya*, to me the Ṛṣi so called.' Professor Roth is of opinion that Paúra, in the vocative
case, means the Aśvins, as fillers, increasers or strengtheners ; and that *paurām*, in the accusative case, means
the Soma, the filler or satisfying juice (cf. II. 11. 11,
The juice that satisfies hath holpen Indra), said to be
swimming in the flood, *i. e.* mixed with water. The
second half of the stanza would then probably mean
that the Soma flows on in order to be taken up and used
in libations as a lion goes to the place where men lie
in wait to capture him or where a pitfall has been
prepared to entrap him. Still there remains the very
great difficulty of Paúra in the singular being used
instead of the dual Paurau. Professor Ludwig remarks :
'Paura : S. etad aśvinoḥ sambodhanam ; but it is to
be taken direct as a cry of warning. Paura is to
mean the Aśvins, Paura is to mean the Ṛṣi of the
hymn, Paura is to mean the cloud. This is naturally
too much. The word udaprutam (swimming in water)
shows that Paura had been enticed to a place where
his enemies intended to drown him. He had gone to
the spot as unsuspiɔiously as a lion approaches the pitfall,

5 Ye from cyavāna worn with age removed his skin as 'twere a robe.
   So, when ye made him young again, he
   stirred the longing of a dame.

6 Here is the man who lauds you both : to
   see your glory are we here.
   Now hear me, come with saving help, ye
   who are rich in store of wealth.

7 Who among many mortal men this day
   hath won you to himself ?
   What bard, accepters of the bard ? Who,
   rich in wealth ! with sacrifice ?

8 O Aśvins, may your car approach, most
   excellent of cars for speed.
   Through many regions may our praise
   pass onward among mortal men.

9 May our laudation of you Twain, lovers
   of meath ! be sweet to you.
   Fly hitherward, ye wise of heart, like
   falcons with your winged steeds.

10 O Aśvins, when at any time ye listen to
   this call of mine,
   For you is dainty food prepared : they
   mix refreshing food for you.

HYMN LXXV.   *Aśvins.*

1. To meet your treasure-bringing car, the
   mighty car most dear to us,
   Aśvins, the Ṛṣi is prepared, your praiser,
   with his song of praise. Lovers of sweetness, hear my call.

2 Pass, O ye Aśvins, pass away beyond all
   tribes of selfish men,
   Wonderful, with your golden paths, most
   gracious, bringers of the flood. Lovers
   of sweetness, hear my call.

3 Come to us, O ye Aśvin Pair, bringing
   your precious treasures, come
   Ye Rudras, on your paths of gold, rejoicing, rich in store of wealth. Lovers of
   sweetness, hear my call.

and was already in the water when the Aśvins called
out to him and stopped him. According to this explanation the translation would be : 'For Paura ye cried,
Paura ! and saved him when swimming in the flood,
Him who had reached the ambush as a lion to the
capture goes.

5 *Cyavāna* : See I. 116. 10.

6 *Rich in store of wealth* : 'affluent in food,'—Wilson,
after Sāyaṇa ; 'lords of swift horses,'—Roth; 'possessors
of excellent mares,'—Ludwig.

1 *Lovers of sweetness* : drinkers of the sweet Soma
juice : according to Sāyaṇa, masters of the Madhuvidyā, or knowledge of sweetness, that is, the knowledge
that teaches where the Soma is to be found. See I. 84.
13.

2 *Selfish men* : reading *ahaṁsanāḥ* for *ahaṁ sanā*.
See Aufrecht, Ṛ. V. II. XLII. note.

3 *Rich in store of wealth* : or, Lords of rapid steeds.
See note on stanza 6 of the preceding hymn.

4 O strong and Good, the voice of him who
   lauds you well cleaves to your car.
   And that great beast, your chariot-steed,
   fair, wonderful, makes dainty food.
   Lovers of sweetness, hear my call.

5 Watchful in spirit, born on cars, impetuous, listing to his cry,
   Aśvins, with winged steeds ye speed down
   to cyavāna void of guile. Lovers of
   sweetness, hear my call.

6 Hither, O Heroes, let your steeds, of dappled hue, yoked at the thought,
   Your flying steeds, O Aśvins, bring you
   hitherward, with bliss, to drink. Lovers of sweetness, hear my call.

7 O Aśvins, hither come to us ; Nāsatyas,
   be not disinclined.
   Through longing for the pious turn out of
   the way to reach our home. Lovers of
   sweetness, hear my call.

8 Ye Lords of Splendour, free from guile,
   come, stand at this our sacrifice.
   Beside the singer, Aśvins, who longs for
   your grace and lauds you both. Lovers
   of sweetness, hear my call.

9 Dawn with her white herd hath appeared,
   and in due time hath fire been placed.
   Harnessed is your immortal car, O Wonder-
   Workers, strong and kind. Lovers of
   sweetness, hear my call.

HYMN LXXVI.   Aśvins

1. AGNI, the bright face of the Dawns, is shining ; the singers' pious voices have
   ascended.
   Borne on your chariot, Aśvins, turn you
   hither, and come unto our full and rich
   libation.

2 Most frequent guests, they scorn not what
   is ready : even now the lauded Aśvins
   are beside us.
   With promptest aid they come at morn
   and evening, the worshipper's most
   blessed guards from trouble.

3 Yea, come at milking-time, at early morning, at noon of day and when the Sun
   is setting,
   By day, by night, with favour most auspicious. Not only now the draught hath
   drawn the Aśvins.

4 For this place, Aśvins, was of old your
   dwelling, these were your houses, this
   your habitation.
   Come to us from high heaven and from
   the mountain. Come from the waters
   bringing food and vigour.

5 May we obtain the Aśvins' newest favour,
   and gain their health-bestowing happy
   guidance.
   Bring riches hither unto us, and heroes, and
   all felicity and joy, Immortals !

HYMN LXXVII.   Aśvins.

1. FIRST worship those who come at early
   morning : let the Twain drink before
   the giftless niggard.
   The Aśvins claim the sacrifice at day-
   break : the sages yielding the first share
   extol them.

2 Worship at dawn and instigate the
   Aśvins : nor is the worshipper at eve
   rejected.
   Besides ourselves another craves and worships : each first in worship is most
   highly favoured.

3 Covered with gold, meath-tinted, dropping
   fatness, your chariot with its freight of
   food comes hither,
   Swift as thought, Aśvins, rapid as the
   tempest, wherewith ye travel over all
   obstructions.

4 He who hath served most often the Nāsatyas, and gives the sweetest food at
   distribution,

---

4 *And that great beast* : the chariot of the Aśvins is
sometimes said to be drawn by a stallion ass (see I.
34. ; 116. 2; 162. 21), the dun-coloured animal
representing the grey tints of early morning.

5 *Cyavāna* : See I 116. 10.

8 *Who longs for your grace* : Sāyana takes *avasyum*
here to be a proper name, Avasyu, who is said to be
the Ṛṣi of the hymn.

9 *In due time* : for the morning libation.

1 *The bright face* : making his first appearance at
early morning. *Libation* : *gharmám*, the offering of hot
milk or other heated beverage.

3 'The Aśvins are invited to come at different
times, at morning, mid-day and sunset ; and in VII.
22. 14, it is similarly said that they are invoked in the
evening as well as at dawn. It need not, however,
surprise us that they should be invited to attend the
different ceremonies of the worshippers, and therefore
conceived to appear at hours distinct from the supposed
natural periods of their manifestation.'—J. Muir, *O.
Sanskrit Texts*, V. 239.

5 This stanza is identical with V. 42. 18.

1 *Before the giftless nigga d* : 'before the greedy
withholders (of the offering).'—Wilson.

2 *Nor is the worshipper at eve rejected* : literally, a
thing unaccepted or rejected. Sāyana explains differently : 'the evening is not for the gods; it is unaccep-
table to them.'—Wilson. This explanation, though
supported by the text *pūrvāhṇo vai devānām*, the forenoon
verily belongs to the Gods, is not in accordance with
the use of Vedic times.

Furthers with his own holy works his offspring, and ever passes those whose
flames ascend not.

5 May we obtain the Aśvins' newest favour,
and gain their health-bestowing happy
guidance.
Bring riches hither unto us, and heroes,
and all felicity and joy, Immortals !

HYMN LXXVIII. *Aśvins.*

1. YE Aśvins, hither come to us : Nāsatyas,
be not disinclined.
Fly hither like two swans unto the juice
we shed.

2 O Aśvins, like a pair of deer, like two wild
cattle to the mead :
Fly hither like two swans unto the juice
we shed.

3 O Aśvins rich in gifts, accept our sacrifice
to prosper it :
Fly hither like two swans unto the juice
we shed.

4 As Atri when descending to the cavern
called on you loudly like a wailing
woman,
Ye came to him, O Aśvins, with the
freshest and most auspicious fleetness of
a falcon.

5 Tree, part asunder like the side of her
who bringeth forth a child.
Ye Aśvins, listen to my call : loose Saptavadhri from his bonds.

6 For Saptavadhri, for the seer affrighted
when he wept and wailed,
Ye, Aśvins, with your magic powers rent
up the tree and shattered it.

7 Like as the wind on every side ruffles a
pool of lotuses,
So stir in thee the babe unborn, so may
the ten-month babe descend.

8 Like as the wind, like as the wood, like
as the sea is set astir,
So also, ten-month babe, descend together
with the after-birth.

9 The child who hath for ten months' time
been lying in his mother's side,—

2 *Wild cattle* : Gauras, or Boves Cauri.
4 *The cavern* : the abyss or deep pit into which
he was cast by Asuras or evil spirits. See I. 112. 7;
116. 8; 117. 3.
5 *Tree, part asunder* : Saptavadhri appears to have
got his hand or foot jammed in a split tree, and to have
been extricated when he called on the Aśvins to aid
him.
9 'This and the two stanzas preceding are termed
by Sāyaṇa the *garbhasrāvinyupaniṣad*, the liturgy of
child-birth.'—Wilson.
The connexion between 1—6, and 7—9 is not

May he come forth alive, unharmed, yea,
living from the living dame.

HYMN LXXIX. *Dawn.*

1. O HEAVENLY Dawn, awaken us to ample
opulence to-day
Even as thou hast wakened us with Satyaśravas, Vayya's son, high-born ! delightful with thy steeds !

2 Daughter of Heaven, thou dawnedst on
Sunītha Śucadratha's son,
So dawn thou on one mightier still, on
Satyaśravas, Vayya's son, high-born !
delightful with thy steeds !

3 So, bringing treasure, dawn to-day on us
thou Daughter of the Sky,
As thou, O mightier yet, didst shine for
Satyaśravas, Vayya's son, high-born !
delightful with thy steeds !

4 Here round about thee are the priests
who laud thee, Bright One, with their
hymns,
And men with gifts, O Bounteous Dame,
splendid with wealth and offering much,
high-born ! delightful with thy steeds !

5 Whatever these thy bands perform to please
thee or to win them wealth,
E'en fain they gird us round and give
rich gifts which ne'er are reft away,
high-born ! delightful with thy steeds !

clear. By *yoṣā nādhamānā* (a wailing woman) a parturient woman may perhaps, Professor Ludwig thinks,
be intended. Atri, as he descended into the pit, invoked the Aśvins that they might release him as a woman
releases the child she bears. A tree—which is much
harder and firmer than a woman's body—unclosed itself when Saptavadhri invoked the Aśvins. So shall the
parturient woman bring forth her child through the
help of the Aśvins and at Atri's intercession. A connexion may thus be established, though here and there
it would be rather forced.

———

1 *Satyaśravas* : the Ṛṣi of the hymn. *Delightful with
thy steeds* : pleasant to those whom thou favourest on
account of the horses which thou bestowest. The word
áśvasūṃṛte is variously rendered *e. g.* by Professor
Wilson, after Sāyaṇa, 'praised sincerely for (the gift of)
horses;' by Prof. Ludwig, 'an rossen trefliches besitzende,'
'having an excellent possession in horses;' by Prof. Roth
'vom jubel der Rosse begleitete,' 'accompanied by the
joyous neigh of horses;' and by Prof. Grassmann,
'rossereiche,' 'rich in horses.'

4 *Men with gifts* : the Maghavans, or wealthy
householders, who institute the sacrifice and provide
offerings for the Gods and presents for the officiating
priests.

5 *These thy bands* : the congregation of worshippers.
Which ne'er are reft away : or which are never in vain,
never fail to obtain their due reward from heaven :
'Sāyaṇa,' Professor Wilson remarks, 'seems rather
dubious as to the proper sense of several of these
words :...........the sum of the meaning, agreeably to

6 Give to these wealthy patrons fame, O
affluent Dawn, with hero sons,
To these our princes who have brought
rich gifts ne'er to be reft away, high-
born ! delightful with thy steeds !

7 Bring lofty and resplendent fame, O thou
munificent Dawn, to these
Our wealthy patrons who bestow rich
gifts on us of steeds and kine, high-born!
delightful with thy steeds !

8 Bring us, O Daughter of the Sky, subsistence in our herds of kine,
Together with the sunbeams, with the
shine of pure refulgent flames, high-
born ! delightful with thy steeds !

9 O Daughter of the Sky, shine forth ; delay
not to perform thy task.
Let not the Sun with fervent heat consume
thee like a robber foe, high-born !
delightful with the steeds !

10 So much, and more exceedingly, O Dawn,
it suits thee to bestow,
Thou Radiant One who ceasest not to shine
for those who sing thy praise, high-
born ! delightful with thy steeds !

HYMN LXXX.   *Dawn.*

1. THE singers welcome with their hymns
and praises the Goddess Dawn who
bringeth in the sunlight,
Sublime, by Law true to eternal Order,
bright on her path, red-tinted, far-
refulgent.

2 She comes in front, fair, rousing up the
people, making the pathways easy to
be travelled.
High, on her lofty chariot, all-impelling,
Dawn gives her splendour at the days'
beginning.

3 She, harnessing her car with purple oxen,
injuring none, hath brought perpetual
riches.
Opening paths to happiness, the Goddess
shines, praised by all, giver of every
blessing.

4 With changing tints she gleams in double
splendour while from the eastward she
displays her body.

She travels perfectly the path of Order,
nor fails to reach, as one who knows,
the quarters.

5 As conscious that her limbs are bright
with bathing, she stands, as 'twere, erect
that we may see her.
Driving away malignity and darkness,
Dawn, Child of Heaven, hath come to
us with lustre.

6 The Daughter of the Sky, like some chaste
woman, bends, opposite to men, her
forehead downward.
The Maid, disclosing boons to him who
worships, hath brought again the daylight as aforetime.

HYMN LXXXI.   *Savitar.*

1. THE priests of him the lofty Priest well-
skilled in hymns harness their spirit, yea,
harness their holy thoughts.
He only knowing works assigns their priestly tasks. Yea, lofty is the praise of
Savitar the God.

2 The Sapient One arrays himself in every
form : for quadruped and biped he hath
brought forth good.
Excellent Savitar hath looked on heaven's
high vault, and shineth after the outgo-
ing of the Dawn.

3 Even he, the God whose going-forth and
majesty the other Deities have followed
with their might,
He who hath measured the terrestrial
regions out by his great power, he is the
Courser Savitar.

4 To the three spheres of light thou goest,
Savitar, and with the rays of Sūrya thou
combinest thee.
Around, on both sides thou encompassest
the night : yea, thou, O God, art Mitra
through thy righteous laws.

---

5 *With bathing* : in the dews of heaven.

---

1. *The lofty Priest* : Savitar. *Knowing works* : skilled
in rules which regulate religious functions, or perhaps
understanding the intentions or wishes of the worshippers : 'he alone knowing their functions directs the
priests.'—Wilson.

2 *Arrays himself in every form* : makes all eternal
objects clearly visible at sunrise.

3 *The Courser Savitar* : Sāyaṇa explains *étaśaḥ* as
white, bright shining. It also means a horse, especially one of the horses of the Sun, and here designates
the Sun himself under that form. See Śatapatha-
Brāhmaṇa, VI. 3. 1. 18; Sacred Books of the East,
XLI. p. 19 .

4 According to Sāyaṇa, Savitar is especially the
Sun before rising, and Sūrya is the Sun in general.

---

the scholiast, is, all they who, offering oblations, worship
the dawn receive the reward for the benefit of us, of
me, that is the author of the hymn, *ye tvám havir-dadataḥ
stuvanti te sarve apy-asmadartham phalaṁ dhārayanti.'*

9 *Delay not to perform thy task* : 'delay not our
(sacred) rite.'—Wilson.

2 *In front* of the Sun ; *sūryasya purastāt.*—Sāyaṇa.

4 *The quarters* : the regions of the sky which she
visits in obedience to the eternal law of the universe.

5 Over all generation thou art Lord alone :
Pūṣan art thou, O God, in all thy
goings-forth.
Yea, thou hast domination over all this
world. Śyāvāśva hath brought praise
to thee, O Savitar.

HYMN LXXXII. *Savitar.*

1. WE crave of Savitar the God this treasure
much to be enjoyed.
The best, all-yielding, conquering gift of
Bhaga we would gladly win.

2 Savitar's own supremacy, most glorious
and beloved of all,
No one diminisheth in aught.

3 For Savitar who is Bhaga shall send riches
to his worshipper.
That wondrous portion we implore.

4 Send us this day, God Savitar, prosperity
with progeny.
Drive thou the evil dream away.

5 Savitar, God, send far away all sorrows
and calamities,
And send us only what is good.

6 Sinless in sight of Aditi through the God
Savitar's influence,
May we obtain all lovely things.

7 We with our hymns this day elect the
general God, Lord of the good,
Savitar whose decrees are true.

8 He who for ever vigilant precedes these
Twain, the Day and Night,
Is Savitar the thoughtful God.

9 He who gives glory unto all these living
creatures with the song,
And brings them forth, is Savitar.

HYMN LXXXIII. *Parjanya.*

1. SING with these songs thy welcome to the
Mighty, with adoration praise and call
Parjanya.
The Bull, loud roaring, swift to send his
bounty, lays in the plants the seed for
germination.

2 He smites the trees apart, he slays the
demons : all life fears him who wields
the mighty weapon.
From him exceeding strong flees e'en the
guiltless, when thundering Parjanya
smites the wicked.

3 Like a car-driver whipping on his horses,
he makes the messengers of rain spring
forward.
Far off resounds the roaring of the lion,
what time Parjanya fills the sky with
rain-cloud.

4 Forth burst the winds, down come the
lightning-flashes : the plants shoot up,
the realm of light is streaming.
Food springs abundant for all living creatures, what time Parjanya quickens earth
with moisture.

5 Thou at whose bidding earth bows low
before thee, at whose command hoofed
cattle fly in terror,
At whose behest the plants assume all
colours, even thou Parjanya, yield us
great protection.

6 Send down for us the rain of heaven, ye
Maruts, and let the Stallion's flood
descend in torrents.
Come hither with this thunder while thou
pourest the waters down, our heavenly
Lord and Father.

7 Thunder and roar : the germ of life deposit. Fly round us on thy chariot water-
laden.
Thine opened water-skin draw with thee
downward, and let the hollows and the
heights be level.

8 Lift up the mighty vessel, pour down water,
and let the liberated streams rush forward.

---

3 *Shall send* : *suvāti*, from the root *su* or *sū*, from
which Savitar also is formed. The principal signifi-
cations of the root are (1) to generate or bring forth;
(2) to pour forth a libation ; and (3) to send or impel.
See Muir, *O. S. Texts*, V. 165.

4 *Send us* : *sāviḥ*, from the same root : *Drive thou
away* : *párā suva*.

5 *Send far away* : *párā suva*.

6 *Influence* : *savé*.

7 *The general God* : *viśvádevam* : 'who possesses all
divine attributes.'—Muir; '(identical with) all the
gods,'—Wilson; 'den allgott,' 'the all-god,'—Ludwig;
'den allgottlichen,' 'the all-divine,'—Grassmann. *Whose
decrees are true* : *satyásavam* : 'who possesses true energy.'
—Muir.

9 *He who gives glory* : 'he who by his creative power
produces the objects of the song of praise.'—Ludwig.

---

1 *Parjanya* : God of thunderstorms and rain, the
generator and nourisher of plants and living creatures.
See Muir. *O. S. Texts*, V. 140 ff., and, especially, M.
Müller, India, What can it Teach us pp. 186—194.

2 *The wicked* : *duṣkṛtaḥ*, evil-doers. 'There does
not seem to be any sufficient reason to understand
evil-doers here, and, in verse 9, of the cloud demons,
or simply of the malignant clouds, as Sāyaṇa in his
explanation of verse 9 does. The poet may naturally
have supposed that it was exclusively or principally the
wicked who were struck down by thunderbolts.'—
Muir, *O. S. Texts*, V. 141.

Saturate both the earth and heaven with fatness, and for the cows let there be drink abundant.

9 When thou, with thunder and with roar, Parjanya, smitest sinners down,
This universe exults thereat, yea, all that is upon the earth.

10 Thou hast poured down the rain-flood : now withhold it. Thou hast made desert places fit for travel.
Thou hast made herbs to grow for our enjoyment : yea, thou hast won thee praise from living creatures.

HYMN LXXXIV.   *Pṛthivī.*

1. THOU, of a truth, O Pṛthivī, bearest the tool that rends the hills :
Thou rich in torrents, who with might quickenest earth, O Mighty One.

2 To thee, O wanderer at will, ring out the lauds with beams of day,
Who drivest, like a neighing steed, the swelling cloud, O bright of hue.

3 Who graspest with thy might on earth· e'en the strong sovrans of the wood,
When from the lightning of thy cloud the rain-floods of the heaven descend.

HYMN LXXXV.   *Varuṇa.*

1. SING forth a hymn sublime and solemn, grateful to glorious Varuṇa, imperial Ruler,
Who hath struck out, like one who slays the victim, earth as a skin to spread in front of Sūrya.

2 In the tree-tops the air he hath extended, put milk in kine and vigorous speed in horses,

Set intellect in hearts, fire in the waters, Sūrya in heaven and Soma on the mountain.

3 Varuṇa lets the big cask, opening downward, flow through the heaven and earth and air's mid-region.
Therewith the universe's Sovran waters earth as the shower of rain bedews the barley.

4 When Varuṇa is fain for milk he moistens the sky, the land, and earth to her foundation.
Then straight the mountains clothe them in the rain-cloud : the Heroes, putting forth their vigour, loose them.

5 I will declare this mighty deed of magic, of glorious Varuṇa the Lord Immortal,
Who standing in the firmament hath meted the earth out with the Sun as with a measure.

6 None, verily, hath ever let or hindered this the most wise God's mighty deed of magic,
Whereby with all their flood, the lucid rivers fill not one sea wherein they pour their waters.

7 If we have sinned against the man who loves us, have ever wronged a brother, friend, or comrade,
The neighbour ever with us, or a stranger, O Varuṇa, remove from us the trespass.

8 If we, as gamesters cheat at play, have cheated, done wrong unwittingly or sinned of purpose,
Cast all these sins away like loosened fetters, and, Varuṇa let us be thine own beloved.

HYMN LXXXVI.   *Indra-Agni.*

1. THE mortal man whom ye, the Twain, Indra and Agni, help in fight,

---

10 *Thou hast won thee praise* : or, perhaps, 'thou hast fulfilled the longing of the people.'

---

1. *Pṛthivī* : in this place not the Goddess Earth or earth personified, but a deity of the middle air or firmament. '*Dvirūpā Pṛthivī*,' says Sāyaṇa, 'Pṛthivī has two forms.' *The tool that rends the hills* : the instrument that strikes and pierces the mountains and opens the water-springs, the thunderbolt or the power that produces similar results.

2 *The swelling cloud* : *perum* ; the exact meaning of the word is doubtful Professor Ludwig thinks that the lightning is intended.

---

1 *Sing forth* : *prá......arcā.* The Ṛṣi addresses himself. Or *arcā* may be the first person singular, I sing. *Like one who slays the victim* : 'not the ordinary Immolator, but the priest who spreads out the skin of the slaughtered victim to receive its disjointed members.' —Ludwig.

2 *In the tree-tops* : *váneṣu,* explained by Sāyaṇa as *vṛkṣāgreṣu* : 'in the clouds,' according to the St. Peters-

burg Lexicon. *Soma on the mountain* : 'the Soma creeper.' *Mahīdhara* observes, grows in the clefts of the stones of mountains, *parvatānām páṣṇa and iṣu somavallyā utpādya-mānatvāt.*'—Wilson.

4 *Is fain for milk* : wishes for libations of milk ; or the meaning may be, when he wishes to draw forth the milk, the fertilizing rain, of the clouds. *Earth to her foundation* : the text has only *pṛthivīm,* meaning earth in its full extent (terra) as distinguished from *bhūmim,* the land, soil, or ground (humus or solum), Or *pṛthivīm* may perhaps mean the firmament here as Sāyaṇa explains it. See note on *Pṛthivī* in the preceding hymn. *The Heroes* : the strong Maruts. *Loose them* : loosen the roots of the mountains and make them tremble.

5 *Deed of magic* : *māyām* : or the word may be rendered by 'device' or design.' See Wallis, *Cosmology of the Rgveda,* pp. 102, 103.

Breaks through e'en strongly-guarded
wealth as Tṛta burst his way through
reeds.

2 The Twain invincible in war, worthy to
be renowned in frays,
Lords of the Fivefold People, these, Indra
and Agni, we invoke.

3 Impetuous is their strength, and keen the
lightning of the mighty Pair,
Which from their arms speeds with the
car to Vṛtra's slayer for the kine.

4 Indra and Agni, we invoke you both, as
such, to send your cars :
Lords of quick-coming bounty, ye who
know, chief lovers of the song.

5 These who give increase day by day, Gods
without guile for mortal man,
Worthy themselves, I honour most, Two
Gods as partners, for my horse.

6 The strength-bestowing offering thus to
Indra-Agni hath been paid, as butter,
purified by stones.
Deal to our princes high renown, deal
wealth to those who sing your praise,
deal food to those who sing your praise.

HYMN LXXXVII. *Maruts.*

1. To Viṣṇu, to the Mighty whom the Maruts
follow let your hymns born in song go
forth, Evayāmarut;
To the impetuous, strong band, adorned
with bracelets, that rushes on in joy and
ever roars for vigour.

2 They who with might were manifest, and
who willingly by their own knowledge
told it forth, Evayāmarut.
Maruts, this strength of yours no wisdom
comprehendeth : through their gifts'
greatness they are moveless as the
mountains.

3 Who by the psalm they sing are heard,
from lofty heaven, the strong, the
brightly shining Ones, Evayāmarut;
In whose abode there is no mightier one
to move them, whose lightnings are as
fires, who urge the roaring rivers.

4 He of the Mighty Stride forth strode,
Evayāmarut, out of the spacious dwelling-place, their home in common.
When he, himself, hath yoked his emulous
strong horses on heights, he cometh forth,
joy-giving, with the Heroes.

5 Like your tremendous roar, the rainer
with light flashing, strong, speeding,
hath made all tremble, Evayāmarut,
Wherewith victorious ye, self-luminous,
press onward, with strong reins, decked
with gold, impetuous and well-weaponed.

6 Unbounded is your greatness, ye of mighty
power : may your bright vigour be
our aid, Evayāmarut;
For ye are visible helpers in the time of
trouble : like fires, aglow with light,
save us from shame and insult.

7 So may the Rudras, mighty warriors,
Evayāmarut, with splendid brilliancy,
like fires, be our protectors;

1 *Through reeds* : so Professor Roth interprets the *vāṇīḥ* of the text. See I. 52. 5. According to Sāyaṇa the meaning is, as Tṛta the Ṛṣi breaks down and refutes the words or arguments of his opponents. See Macdonell, J.R.A.S, July 1893, p. 426.

2 *The Fivefold People* : the five Āryan tribes.

5 *I honour most* : *puró dadhé* ; I set in front, in the most honourable place. *For my horse* : that I may win the chariot-race. 'For (the sake of obtaining) horses.'—Wilson.

6 *As butter* : Sāyaṇa explains *ghṛtám*, sacrificial oil or clarified butter, by Soma juice ; but *pūtám*, purified, qualifies *havyám*, the offering, and not *ghṛtám*. The libation of Soma juice which has been purified by the operation of the press-stones, strainer, etc., has been offered like clarified butter or holy oil.

The hymn is ascribed to a Ṛṣi Evayāmarut, a name which is evidently borrowed from the refrain.

1 *Born in song* : developing themselves and taking form in song : *vāci niṣpannā* :—Sāyaṇa. 'Voice-born.' —Wilson. Or *girijā* may have its usual meaning, mountain-born, with reference to the close connexion of the hymns with the pressing-stones which came from the hills. *Evayāmarut* : Professor Wilson, following Sāyaṇa translates : 'May the voice-born praises of Evayāmarut reach you, Viṣṇu, attended by the Maruts,' and observes that 'the name of the Ṛṣi, *Evayāmarut*, remains unalter-

ed in its case termination, whatever may be its syntac-tical connexion with the rest of the sentence.' This is manifestly impossible, and the word is certainly not a proper name. *Evayā*, in I. 156. I. 'going thy wonted way,' is an epithet of Viṣṇu, and Professor Roth thinks that *Evayāmarut* is an exclamation meaning, O Viṣṇu and Maruts ! or, O Maruts who speed around ! But in both these cases it would be necessary to change the accent, both in this hymn and in the Sāmaveda where stanza 1 occurs again. Professor Grassmann suggests, 'speeding (like Viṣṇu) is the Marut host,' or, 'The speeding Viṣṇu is the true Marut, or lord of the Maruts,' as the probable meaning of the word. I find *Evayāmarut* unintelligible, and, as Professor Ludwig has done, leave it untranslated, as a mere sacrificial exclama-tion. See Vedic Hymns (Sacred Books of the East) Part .1. p. 365.

4 *He of the Mighty Stride* : Viṣṇu. According to Sāyaṇa, the wide-spreading (band of Maruts). *Their home* : Viṣṇu's and Indra's. *With the Heroes* : with the Maruts.

6 *In the time of trouble* : the meaning of *prásitau* is uncertain. Professor Wilson, after Sāyaṇa, translates : 'for you are regulators for overseeing (what is fit for) the limits of the sacrifice.'

They whose terrestrial dwelling-place is wide-extended, whom none suspect of sin, whose bands have lofty courage.

8 Come in a friendly spirit, come to us, O Maruts, and hear his call who praises you, Evayāmarut.

Like car-borne men, one-minded with the mighty Viṣṇu, keep enmity far from us with your deeds of wonder.

9 Come to our sacrifice, ye Holy Ones, to bless it, and, free from demons, hear our call, Evayāmarut.

Most excellent, like mountains in the air's mid-region, be irresistible, ye Wise, to this man's hater.

9 *This man's hater* : him who hates the institutor of the sacrifice, or derides and reviles the holy ceremony.

BOOK THE SIXTH

HYMN I. *Agni.*

1. THOU, first inventor of this prayer, O
Agni, Worker of Marvels, hast become
our Herald.
   Thou, Bull, hast made us strength which
none may conquer, strength that shall
overcome all other prowess.

2 As Priest thou sattest at the seat of worship,
furthering us, best Offerer, meet for
honour.
   So first to thee have pious men resorted,
turning thy mind to thoughts of ample
riches.

3 In thee, still watching, they have followed
riches, who goest with much wealth
as with an army,
   The radiant Agni, lofty, fair to look on,
worshipped with marrow, evermore
resplendent.

4 They who approached the God's abode
with homage, eager for glory, won them
perfect glory :
   Yea, they gained even sacrificial titles,
and found delight in thine auspicious
aspect.

5 On earth the people magnify thee greatly,
thee their celestial and terrestrial riches.
   Thou, Helper, must be known as our
Preserver, Father and Mother of mankind
for ever.

6 Dear priest among mankind, adorable Agni
hath seated him, joy-giver, skilled in
worship.
   Let us approach thee shining in thy dwelling, kneeling upon our knees, with
adoration.

7 Longing for bliss, pure-minded, God-devoted, Agni, we seek thee, such, meet to
be lauded.
   Thou, Agni, leddest forth our men to
battle, refulgent with the heaven's
exalted splendour.

8 Sage of mankind, all peoples' Lord and
Master, the Bull of men, the sender
down of blessings,
   Still pressing on, promoting, purifying,
Agni the Holy One, the Lord of riches.

9 Agni, the mortal who hath toiled and
worshipped, brought thee oblations with
his kindled fuel,
   And well knows sacrifice with adoration,
gains every joy with thee to guard and
help him.

10 Mightily let us worship thee the Mighty,
with reverence, Agni! fuel and oblations,
   With songs, O Son of Strength, with hymns,
with altar : so may we strive for thine
auspicious favour.

11 Thou who hast covered heaven and earth
with splendour and with thy glories,
glorious and triumphant.
   Continue thou to shine on us, O Agni,
with strength abundant, rich, and long-
enduring.

12 Vouchsafe us ever, as man needs, O Vasu,
abundant wealth of kine for son and
offspring.
   Food noble, plenteous, far from sin and
evil, be with us, and fair fame to make
us happy.

13 May I obtain much wealth in many places
by love of thee and through thy grace,
King Agni;
   For in thee, Bounteous One, in thee the
Sovran, Agni, are many boons for him
who serves thee.

HYMN II. *Agni.*

1. THOU, Agni, even as Mitra, hast a princely
glory of thine own.
   Thou, active Vasu, makest fame increase
like full prosperity.

2 For, verily, men pray to thee with sacrifices and with songs.
   To thee the Friendly Courser, seen of all,
comes speeding through the air.

3 Of one accord men kindle thee Heaven's
signal of the sacrifice,
   When, craving bliss, this race of man invites thee to the solemn rite.

The Ṛṣi of the hymn is Bharadvāja, to whom, with
a few exceptions, all the hymns of this Book are
attributed.

1 *Our Herald* : or Invoking Priest who calls the
Gods to the sacrifice.

3 *Worshipped with marrow* : to whom especially the
fat covering of the inwards of the victims was offered.

4 *They who approached the God's abode* : the Ṛbhus,
Maruts, or Aṅgirases may be meant.

5 *Their celestial and terrestrial riches* : rāyáḥ ubhdyāsaḥ;
literally, riches of both kinds. According to Sāyaṇa,
consisting in cattle and in possessions other than cattle.

8 *Sage of mankind, etc.* : Sage, Lord, Bull, etc.

are in the accusative case, in apposition with 'thee' in
stanza 7, though separated by an intervening half-stanza.

—

2 *The Friendly Courser* : the Sun.

3 Or, possibly, as suggested by Professor Ludwig,
'The men accordant with the heaven light thee the sign
of sacrifice;' that is, understanding the signs in heaven
and so knowing the proper time for the ceremony.

4 Let the man thrive who travails sore, in prayer, far thee the Bountiful.
He with the help of lofty Dyaus comes safe through straits of enmity.

5 The mortal who with fuel lights thy flame and offers unto thee,
Supports a house with many a branch, Agni, to live a hundred years.

6 Thy bright smoke lifts itself aloft, and far-extended shines in heaven.
For, Purifier ! like the Sun thou beamest with thy radiant glow.

7 For in men's houses thou must be glorified as a well-loved guest,
Gay like an elder in a fort, claiming protection like a son.

8 Thou, Agni, like an able steed, art urged by wisdom in the wood.
Thou art like wind; food, home art thou, like a young horse that runs astray.

9 E'en things imperishable, thou, O Agni, like a grazing ox,
Eatest, when hosts, Eternal One ! of thee the Mighty rend the woods.

10 Agni, thou enterest as Priest the home of men who sacrifice.
Lord of the people, prosper them. Accept the offering, Aṅgiras !

11 O Agni, God with Mitra's might, call hither the favour of the Gods from earth and heaven.
Bring weal from heaven, that men may dwell securely. May we o'ercome the foe's malign oppressions, may we o'ercome them, through thy help o'ercome them.

HYMN III.   *Agni.*

1. TRUE, guardian of the Law, thy faithful servant wins ample light and dwells in peace, O Agni,
Whom thou, as Varuṇa in accord with Mitra, guardest, O God, by banishing his trouble.

2 He hath paid sacrifices, toiled in worship, and offered gifts to wealth-increasing Agni.

Him the displeasure of the famous moves not, outrage and scorn affect not such a mortal.

3 Bright God, whose look is free from stain like Sūrya's, thou, swift, what time thou earnestly desirest,
Hast gear to give us. Come with joy at evening, where, Child of Wood, thou mayest also tarry.

4 Fierce is his gait and vast his wondrous body : he champeth like a horse with bit and bridle,
And, darting forth his tongue, as 'twere a hatchet, burning the woods, smelteth them like a smelter.

5 Archer-like, fain to shoot, he sets his arrow, and whets his splendour like the edge of iron :
The messenger of night with brilliant pathway, like a tree-roosting bird of rapid pinion.

6 In beams of morn he clothes him like the singer, and bright as Mitra with his splendour crackles.
Red in the night, by day the men's possession : red, he belongs to men by day, Immortal.

7 Like Heaven's when scattering beams his voice was uttered : among the plants the radiant Hero shouted,
Who with his glow in rapid course came hither to fill both worlds, well-wedded Dames, with treasure.

8 Who, with supporting streams and rays that suit him, hath flashed like lightning with his native vigour.

---

7 *Gay like an elder* : Agni must be respected and cared for like a father as well as protected like a son.

8 *In the wood* : wherein fire is produced by attrition. The exact meaning of the stanza is somewhat uncertain. *Like wind* : moving everywhere.

9 *Eatest* : this or some similar verb must be supplied.

---

1 *As Varuṇa in accord with Mitra* : that is, Agni, Varuṇa, and Mitra as one.—Ludwig.

3 I gratefully adopt Professor Pischel's interpretation of this very difficult stanza which I had regarded as hopelessly obscure. See *Vedische Studien*, I. pp. 37—50.

4 *With bit and bridle* : *yamasānd āsā*; 'champing fodder with his mouth.'—Wilson. *As 'twere a hatchet* : Agni, and not his tongue, is likened to the hatchet.

5 *Of iron* : or metal, the exact meaning of *áyas* being uncertain.

6 *In beams of morn* : the light of early morning shines on the fire and the singer alike and simultaneously. *Bright as Mitra* : 'diffusing friendly light.'—Wilson. *The men's possession* : I take *nṛīn* as a shortened form of *nṛṇắm* ; but it is difficult to make sense of the half-stanza. Professor Wilson, following Sāyaṇa, translates : '(he it is) who is luminous by night, and who lights men (to their work) by day ; who is immortal and radiant ; who lights men by day.' The verb is supplied by Sāyaṇa.

7 *Like Heaven's* : like the voice of Dyaus, the thunder. *Well-wedded Dames* : having excellent Lords, perhaps Indra and Agni.

Like the deft Maker of the band of
Maruts, the bright impetuous One
hath shone refulgent.

HYMN IV. *Agni.*

1. As at man's service of the Gods, Invoker,
thou, Son of Strength, dost sacrifice and
worship,
So bring for us to-day all Gods together,
bring willingly the willing Gods, O
Agni.

2 May Agni, radiant Herald of the morning, meet to be known, accept our
praise with favour.
Dear to all life, mid mortal men Immortal,
our guest, awake at dawn, is Jātavedas.

3 Whose might the very heavens regard with
wonder : bright as the Sun he clothes
himself with lustre.
He who sends forth, Eternal Purifier, hath
shattered e'en the ancient works of
Aśna.

4 Thou art a Singer, Son ! our feast-companion : Agni at birth prepared his
food and pathway.
Therefore vouchsafe us strength, O Strength-
bestower. Win like a King : foes trouble
not thy dwelling.

5 Even he who eats his firm hard food with
swiftness, and overtakes the nights as Vāyu
kingdoms.
May we o'ercome those who resist thine
orders, like a steed casting down the
flying foemen.

6 Like Sūrya with his fulgent rays, O Agni,
thou overspreadest both the worlds with
splendour.
Decked with bright colour he dispels the
darkness, like Auśija, with clear flame
swiftly flying.

7 We have elected thee as most delightful
for thy beams' glow : hear our great
laud, O Agni.
The best men praise thee as the peer of
Indra in strength, mid Gods, like Vāyu
in thy bounty.

8 Now, Agni, on the tranquil paths of riches
come to us for our weal : save us from
sorrow.
Grant chiefs and bard this boon. May we
live happy, with hero children, through
a hundred winters.

HYMN V. *Agni.*

1. I INVOCATE your Son of Strength, the
Youthful, with hymns, the Youngest
God, whose speech is guileless;
Sage who sends wealth comprising every
treasure, bringer of many boons, devoid
of malice.

2 At eve and morn thy pious servants bring
thee their precious gifts, O Priest of
many aspects,
On whom, the Purifier, all things living,
as on firm ground their happiness have
stablished.

3 Thou from of old hast dwelt among these
people, by mental power the charioteer
of blessings.
Hence sendest thou, O sapient Jātavedas,
to him who serves thee treasures in
succession.

4 Agni, whoever secretly attacks us, the
neighbour, thou with Mitra's might !
who harms us,
Burn him with thine own Steers for ever
youthful, burning with burning heat,
thou fiercest burner.

5 He who serves thee with sacrifice and fuel,
with hymn, O Son of Strength, and
chanted praises,
Shines out, Immortal ! in the midst of
mortals, a sage, with wealth, with splendour and with glory.

---

8 *The deft Maker of the band of Maruts* : Dyaus is
probably intended.

---

1 *Invoker* : *Hotar*, herald or inviter of the Gods.

3 *Aśna* : apparently one of the demons of drought.

4 *His food and pathway* : or his pathway to his food
may be intended.

5 *His firm hard food* : *vāraṇám ánnam*; the food of
elephants, i. e. trees, according to Professor Ludwig.
Professor Wilson, following Sāyaṇa, translates the first
half-line : 'He who whets his (gloom)—dispersing
(radiance), who eats the (offered) oblation.' *As Vāyu
kingdoms* : *rāṣṭrī* standing, perhaps, for *rāṣṭryā (rāṣṭryāṇi)*,
but the exact meaning is uncertain. Perhaps, as Professor Ludwig suggests, as Vāyu or the wind blows
uninterrupted through the whole land, so Agni is
kindled at night-fall and again at early dawn before
the night has entirely passed away.

6 *Like Auśija* : perhaps some contemporary priest,
who is regarded as bringing back the daylight by
prayer and sacrifice. 'Like the adored (sun).'—Wilson.

8 *Tranquil* : *avṛkebhiḥ*; literally untroubled by wolves,
or enemies. *Grant chiefs and bard* : the wealthy men
who institute the sacrifice and the priest who sings.
Or it may be rendered, 'Grant the chiefs' bard,' that
is, the priest who sings for his wealthy patrons. *A
hundred winters* : see V. 54. 15, note.

2 *Priest of many aspects* : *purvaṇīka*, having many
faces, aspects, or manifestations. According to Sāyaṇa,
having many flames instead of faces.

4 *Thine own Steers* : thy strong flames. *Burn him,
etc.* : *tápā tapiṣṭhadḍpasā tápasvān.*

6 Do this, O Agni, when we urge thee, quickly, triumphant in thy might subdue our foemen.

When thou art praised with words and decked with brightness, accept this chanted hymn, the singer's worship.

7 Help us, that we may gain this wish, O Agni, gain riches, Wealthy One ! with store of heroes.

Desiring strength from thee may we be strengthened, and win, Eternal ! thine eternal glory.

HYMN VI.   *Agni.*

1. He who seeks furtherance and grace to help him goes to the Son of Strength with newest worship,

Calling the heavenly Priest to share the banquet, who rends the wood, bright, with his blackened pathway.

2 White-hued and thundering he dwells in splendour, Most Youthful, with the loud-voiced and eternal—

Agni, most variform, the Purifier, who follows crunching many ample forests.

3 Incited by the wind thy flames, O Agni, move onward, Pure One ! pure, in all directions.

Thy most destructive heavenly Navagvas break the woods down and devastate them boldly.

4 Thy pure white horses from their bonds are loosened : O Radiant One, they shear the ground beneath them,

And far and wide shines out thy flame, and flickers rapidly moving over earth's high ridges.

5 Forth darts the Bull's tongue like the sharp stone weapon discharged by him who fights to win the cattle.

Agni's fierce flame is like a hero's onset: dread and resistless he destroys the forests.

6 Thou with the sunlight of the great Impeller hast boldly over-spread the earth's expanses.

So drive away with conquering might all perils : fighting out foemen burn up those who harm us.

7 Wondrous ! of wondrous power ! give to the singer wealth wondrous, marked, most wonderful, life-giving.

Wealth bright, O Bright One, vast, with many heroes, give with thy bright flames to the man who lauds thee.

HYMN VII.   *Agni.*

1. Him, messenger of earth and head of heaven, Agni Vaiśvānara, born in holy Order,

The Sage, the King, the guest of men, a vessel fit for their mouths, the Gods have generated.

2 Him have they praised, mid-point of sacrifices, great cistern of libations, seat of riches.

Vaiśvānara, conveyer of oblations, ensign of worship, have the Gods engendered.

3 From thee, O Agni, springs the mighty singer, from thee come heroes who subdue the foeman.

O King, Vaiśvānara, bestow thou on us excellent treasures worthy to be longed for.

4 To thee, Immortal ! when to life thou springest, all the Gods sing for joy as to their infant.

They by thy mental powers were made immortal, Vaiśvānara, when thou shonest from thy Parents.

5 Agni Vaiśvānara, no one hath ever resisted these thy mighty ordinances,

When thou, arising from thy Parents' bosom, foundest the light for days' appointed courses.

6 The summits of the heaven are traversed through and through by the Immortal's light, Vaiśvānara's brilliancy.

All creatures in existence rest upon his head. The Seven swift-flowing Streams have grown like branches forth,

7 Vaiśvānara, who measured out the realms of air, Sage very wise who made the lucid spheres of heaven,

---

7 *Sá citra citrám citáyantam asme citrakṣatra citrátamam vasodhám* | *C ndrám rayim puruviram bṛhántam cándra candrábhir gṛṇaté yuvasva.*

---

2 *The loud-voiced and eternal* : the Maruts.

3 *Nava vas* : the flames of fire being regarded as the ministers of Agni, who is the best or oldest of the Aṅgirases of whom the Navagvas are a class.

4 *Earth's high ridges* : *ádhi sānu pṛśneḥ*; Pṛśni here being the multiform earth.

5 *Who fights to win the cattle* : Indra who wars with demons of drought and darkness.

6 *The great Impeller* : Sūrya, the vivifying Sun.

1 *A vessel fit for their mouths* : through whose means they receive men's offerings.

2 *Mid-point of sacrifices* : 'the bond of sacrifices.'—Wilson. Agni or fire is essential in all sacrifices.

6 *The Seven swift-flowing Streams* : the five rivers of the Panjāb, the Indus and the Sarasvatī or the Kubhā. *Have grown* : from Vaiśvānara Agni.

7 *Of immortality* : according to Sāyaṇa, of water which is the cause of immortality 'Of ambrosial (rain).'—Wilson.

The Undeceivable who spread out all the worlds, keeper is he and guard of immortality.

HYMN VIII.   *Agni.*

1. AT Jātavedas' holy gathering I will tell aloud the conquering might of the swift red-hued Steer.
A pure and fresher hymn flows to Vaiśvā-nara, even as for Agni lovely Soma is made pure.

2 That Agni, when in loftiest heaven he sprang to life, Guardian of Holy Laws, kept and observed them well.
Exceeding wise, he measured out the firmament. Vaiśvānara attained to heaven by mightiness.

3 Wonderful Mitra propped the heaven and earth apart, and covered and concealed the darkness with his light.
He made the two bowls part asunder like two skins. Vaiśvānara put forth all his creative power.

4 The Mighty seized him in the bosom of the floods : the people waited on the King who should be praised.
As envoy of Vivasvān Mātariśvan brought Agni Vaiśvānara hither from far away.

5 In every age bestow upon the singers wealth, worthy of holy synods, glorious, ever new.
King, undecaying, as it were with sharpened bolt, smite down the sinner like a tree with lightning-flash.

6 Do thou bestow, O Agni, on our wealthy chiefs, rule, with good heroes, undecaying, bending not.
So may we win for us strength, O Vaiśvā-nara, hundredfold, thousandfold, O Agni, by thy help.

7 O thou who dwellest in three places, Helper, keep with effective guards our princely patrons.
Keep our band, Agni, who have brought thee presents. Lengthen their lives, Vaiśvānara, when lauded.

3 *The two bowls* : the heaven and earth, called *dhiṣáṇe* or bowls from their hemispherical appearance.

4 *The Mighty* : the Gods who followed and found the fugitive Agni. *The people* : or the subjects, *viśaḥ*. *Of Vivasvān* : according to Sāyaṇa, from Āditya or the Sun.

7 *Who dwellest in three places* : in heaven as the Sun, in the firmament as lightning, and on earth as fire.

HYMN IX.   *Agni.*

1. ONE half of day is dark, and bright the other : both atmospheres move on by sage devices.
Agni Vaiśvānara, when born as Sovran, hath with his lustre overcome the darkness.

2 I know not either warp or woof, I know not the web they weave when moving to the contest.
Whose son shall here speak words that must be spoken without assistance from the Father near him?

3 For both the warp and woof he under-standeth, and in due time shall speak what should be spoken,
Who knoweth as the immortal world's Protector, descending, seeing with no aid from other.

4 He is the Priest, the first of all : behold him. Mid mortal men he is the light immortal.
Here was he born, firm-seated in his station, Immortal, ever waxing in his body.

5 A firm light hath been set for men to look on : among all things that fly the mind is swiftest.

The hymn is somewhat obscure; but the general purport appears to be; Agni is the priests' guide and teacher. As sunlight dispels the darkness so he enlightens our understandings. I know nothing of the mysteries of sacrifice ; but I look to Agni for light, and prepare the ear and eye of my mind to receive knowledge and inspiration from him.

1 *Both atmospheres* : the *rájas* or atmosphere is divided into two parts, one half belonging to the sky and the other to the earth. See Wallis, *The Cosmology of the Ṛgveda*, pp. 115, 116.

2 *I know not either warp or woof* : 'The first half of the stanza...implies, according to those who know tradition, *samp adāyavidaḥ*, says *Sāyaṇa*, a figurative allusion to the mysteries of sacrifice : the threads of the warp, *tantu*, are the metres of the Vedas, those of the woof, *otu*, the liturgic prayers and ceremonial, the combination of which two is the cloth, or sacrifice : the *ātmavi-daḥ*, or, *Vedāntis*, understand it as alluding to the mysteries of creation, the threads of the warp being the subtle elements, those of the woof the gross, and their com ination the universe.'—Wilson. Professor Grassmann and the translators of the *Siebenzig Lieder* think that a young singer is preparing himself for a contest with older bards, and, being distrustful of his own unaided powers to find material for his song, expresses his reliance upon Agni, and seeks inspiration from him. *To the contest* : the sacrifice is here intended : a meeting for religious worship; *saṅgamane devayajane*.—Sāyaṇa,
Whose son : Agni is the Father whose aid every one requires, however excellent his own human father may be.

5 *A firm light* : Agni remains in his place, and the effectual performance of the sacrifice depends upon the activity of his mind.
'According to the *Vedānti* view of the text, the light is *Brahma*, seated spontaneously in the heart as

All Gods of one accord, with one intention, move unobstructed to a single purpose.

6 Mine ears unclose to hear, mine eye to see him ; the light that harbours in my spirit broadens.

Far roams my mind whose thoughts are in the distance. What shall I speak, what shall I now imagine ?

7 All the Gods bowed them down in fear before thee, Agni, when thou wast dwelling in the darkness.

Vaiśvānara be gracious to assist us, may the Immortal favour us and help us.

HYMN X.   *Agni.*

1. INSTALL at sacrifice, while the rite advances, your pleasant, heavenly Agni, meet for praises.

With hymns—for he illumines us—install him. He, Jātavedas, makes our rites successful.

2 Hear this laud, Radiant Priest of many aspects, O Agni with the fires of man enkindled,

Laud which bards send forth pure as sacred butter, strength to this man, as 'twere for self-advantage.

3 Mid mortal men that singer thrives in glory who offers gifts with hymns of praise to Agni,

And the God, wondrous bright, with wondrous succours helps him to win a stable filled with cattle.

4 He, at his birth, whose path is black behind him, filled heaven and earth with far-apparent splendour :

And he himself hath been, through night's thick darkness, made manifest by light, the Purifier.

5 With thy most mighty aid, confer, O Agni, wonderful wealth on us and on our princes,

Who stand preëminent, surpassing others in liberal gifts, in fame, and hero virtues.

6 Agni, accept this sacrifice with gladness, which, seated here, the worshipper presenteth.

Fair hymns hadst thou among the Bharadvājas, and holpest them to gain abundant vigour.

7 Scatter our foes, increase our store. May we be glad a hundred winters with brave sons.

HYMN XI.   *Agni.*

1. EAGERLY sacrifice thou, most skilful, Agni ! Priest, pressing on as if the Maruts sent thee.

To our oblation bring the two Nāsatyas, Mitra and Varuṇa and Earth and Heaven.

2 Thou art our guileless, most delightful Herald, the God, among mankind, of holy synods.

A Priest with purifying tongue, O Agni, sacrifice with thy mouth to thine own body.

3 For even the blessed longing that is in thee would bring the Gods down to the singer's worship,

When the Aṅgirases' sagest Sage, the Poet, sings the sweet measure at the solemn service.

4 Bright hath he beamed, the wise, the far-refulgent. Worship the two wide-spreading Worlds, O Agni,

Whom as the Living One rich in oblations the Five Tribes, bringing gifts, adorn with homage.

5 When I with reverence clip the grass for Agni, when the trimmed ladle, full of oil, is lifted,

Firm on the seat of earth is based the altar : eye-like, the sacrifice is directed Sun-ward.

---

the means of true knowledge, to which all the senses, together with the mind and consciousness, refer, as to the one cause of creation, or *Paramātmā,* supreme spirit.'— Wilson. The stanza is translated by Prof. Wilson, after Sāyaṇa : 'A steady light, swifter than thought, stationed among moving beings to show (the way) to happiness : all the gods being of one mind and of like wisdom, proceed respectfully to the presence of the one (chief) agent. (Vaiśvānara)'.

1 *Install :* establish him as your *Purohita* or Chief Priest ; or set him in front as the Āhavan ya fire.

2 *Strength to this man :* the hymn is to give strength to the worshipper, and the priests are to sing with vigour as though their own interests were immediately concerned. Sāyaṇa takes *mamdtā* (out of self-interest) as a proper name, 'As Mamatā (formerly offered it).'— Wilson.

3 *A stable filled with cattle :* the expression includes the waters of heaven, the light of day, and booty in cattle-lifting expeditions.

6 *Bharadvājas :* the family of the great Ṛṣi to whom the hymn was revealed.

7 *A hundred winters :* See note on VI. 4. 8.

2 *Of holy synods :* I follow Professor Ludwig in taking *viddthā* as an old genitive plural, and not = *viddthe,* as Sāyaṇa does. *Sacrifice......to thine own body :* or, sa rifice......thy proper body ; or, (keep thine own body near us to be worshipped.

6 Enrich us, O thou Priest of many aspects,
with the Gods, Agni, with thy fires,
enkindled.
O Son of Strength, clad in the robe of
riches, may we escape from woe as from
a prison.

HYMN XII. *Agni.*

1. KING of trimmed grass, Herald within the
dwelling, may Agni worship the
Impeller's World-halves.
He, Son of Strength, the Holy, from a
distance hath spread himself abroad with
light like Sūrya.

2 In thee, most wise, shall Dyaus, for full
perfection, King ! Holy One ! pronounce
the call to worship.
Found in three places, like the Speeder's
footstep, come to present men's riches as
oblations !

3 Whose blaze most splendid, sovran in the
forest, shines waxing on his way like the
·Impeller.
He knows himself, like as a guileless smelter,
not to be stayed among the plants,
Immortal.

4 Our friends extol him like a steed for
vigour, even Agni in the dwelling,
Jātavedas.
Tree-fed, he fights with power as doth
a champion, like Dawn's Sire to be
praised with sacrifices.

5 Men wonder at his shining glows when,
paring the woods with ease, o'er the
broad earth he goeth,
And, like a rushing flood, loosed quickly,
burneth, swift as a guilty thief, o'er
desert places.

6 So mighty thou protectest us from slander,
O Champion, Agni ! with all fires enkindled.

1 *The Impeller's World-halves* : the heaven and earth,
illumined by, and so belonging to, the all-vivifying
Sun.
2 *In thee* : or by thee, in thy lightning form, Dyaus
or Heaven shall pronounce the *yājyā*, the consecrating
text used at sacrifices and thus invite the Gods to be
present. *Found in three places* : in heaven, atmosphere,
and earth, and in the corresponding fire-receptacles at
sacrifice. *The Speeder's footstep* : the threefold step of
Viṣṇu as the Sun, traversing the three worlds of earth,
air, and sky.
3 *A guileless smelter* : he knows his power to consume what he attacks, like a melter of metal who
knows what he can do and does not deceive himself.
According to Sāyaṇa, *dravitā* here means runner, 'rushing
like the innoxious (wind).'—Wilson.
4 *Dawn's Sire* : Dyaus or Heaven, the Father of
Uṣas or Dawn.

Bring opulence and drive away affliction.
May brave sons gladden us through
a hundred winters.

HYMN XIII. *Agni.*

1. FROM thee, as branches from a tree, O
Agni, from thee, Auspicious God ! spring
all our blessings—
Wealth swiftly, strength in battle with our
foemen, the rain besought of heaven,
the flow of waters.

2 Thou art our Bhaga to send wealth :
thou dwellest, like circumambient air,
with wondrous splendour.
Friend art thou of the lofty Law, like
Mitra, Controller, Agni ! God ! of
many a blessing.

3 Agni ! the hero slays with might his foeman ; the singer bears away the Paṇi's
booty—
Even he whom thou, Sage, born in Law,
incitest by wealth, accordant with the
Child of Waters.

4 The man who, Son of Strength ! with
sacrifices, hymns, lauds, attracts thy
fervour to the altar,
Enjoys each precious thing, O God, O
Agni, gains wealth of corn and is the
lord of treasures.

5 Grant, Son of Strength, to men for their
subsistence such things as bring high
fame and hero children.
For thou with might givest much food
in cattle even to the wicked wolf
when he is hungry.

6 Eloquent, Son of Strength, Most Mighty,
Agni, vouchsafe us seed and offspring,
full of vigour.
May I by all my songs obtain abundance.
May. brave sons gladden us through
a hundred winters.

HYMN XIV. *Agni.*

1. WHOSO to Agni hath endeared his thought
and service by his hymns,
That mortal eats before the rest, and finds
sufficiency of food.

3 *His foeman* : *vṛtrám* signifying any enemy : *dvara-
kam śatrum*—Sāyaṇa. *The Child of Waters* : here said to
mean the lightning, born of the watery cloud.
5 *To the wicked wolf* : or, perhaps, even to the
foe Vṛka. Cf. VII. 68. 8.

1 *That mortal eats before the rest* : 'May the mortal...
quickly become distinguished as first (amongst men).'—
Wilson.

2 Agni, in truth, is passing wise, most skilled in ordering, a Seer.
At sacrifices Manus' sons glorify Agni as
their Priest.

3 The foeman's wealth in many a place,
Agni, is emulous to help.
Men fight the fiend, and seek by rites to
overcome the riteless foe.

4 Agni bestows the hero chief, winner of
waters, firm in fray.
Soon as they look upon his might his enemies tremble in alarm.

5 For with his wisdom Agni, God, protects
the mortal from reproach,
Whose conquering wealth is never checked,
is never checked in deeds of might.

6 O Agni, God with Mitra's might call
hither the favour of the Gods from
earth and heaven.
Bring weal from heaven that men may
dwell securely. May we o'ercome the
foe's malign oppressions, may we
o'ercome them, through thy help o'ercome them.

HYMN XV.   *Agni.*

1. WITH this my song I strive to reach this
guest of yours, who wakes at early
morn, the Lord of all the tribes.
Each time he comes from heaven, the
Pure One from of old : from ancient
days the Child eats everlasting food.

2 Whom, well-disposed, the Bhṛgus stablished as a Friend, whom men must
glorify, high-flaming in the wood.
As such, most friendly, thou art every day
extolled in lauds by Vītahavya, O thou
wondrous God.

3 Be thou the foeless helper of the skilful
man, subduer of the enemy near or far
away.
Bestow a wealthy home on men, O Son
of Strength. Give Vitahavya riches
spreading far and wide, give Bharadvāja
wide-spread wealth.

4 Him, your refulgent guest, Agni who
comes from heaven, the Herald of
mankind, well-skilled in sacred rites,

Who, like a holy singer, utters heavenly
words, oblation-bearer, envoy, God, I
seek with hymns.

5 Who with his purifying, eye-attracting
form hath shone upon the earth as with
the light of Dawn ;
Who speeding on, as in the fight of Etaśa,
cometh, untouched by age, as one
athirst in heat.

6 Worship ye Agni, Agni, with your log of
wood; praise your beloved, your beloved
guest with songs.
Invite ye the Immortal hither with your
hymns. A God among the Gods, he
loveth what is choice, loveth our service,
God mid Gods.

7 Agni inflamed with fuel in my song I
sing, pure, Cleanser, steadfast, set in
front at sacrifice.
Wise Jātavedas we implore with prayers
for bliss the Priest, the holy Singer,
bounteous, void of guile.

8 Men, Agni, in each age have made thee,
Deathless One, their envoy, offering-
bearer, guard adorable.
With reverence Gods and mortals have
established thee, the ever-watchful,
omnipresent Household Lord.

9 Thou, Agni, ordering the works and
ways of both, as envoy of the Gods
traversest both the worlds.
When we lay claim to thy regard and
gracious care, be thou to us a thrice-
protecting friendly guard.

10 Him fair of face, rapid, and fair to look
on, him very wise may we who know
not follow.
Let him who knows all rules invite for
worship, Agni announce our offering to
the Immortals.

11 Him, Agni, thou deliverest and savest who
brings him prayer to thee the Wise,
O Hero,
The end of sacrifice or its inception ; yea,
thou endowest him with power and
riches.

12 Guard us from him who would assail us,

---

2 *Most skilled in ordering* : the chief regulator of
religious rites.
3 *Emulous to hlep* : waiting for us to seize and use.

---

1 *The Child* : born of the fire sticks, or of Heaven
and Earth. *Everlasting food* : the Amṛta contained in
the sacrificial offerings.
2 *Vitahavya* : either the name of the Ṛṣi, as Sāyaṇa
takes it, or an epithet 'whose oblations are enjoyed,'
qualifying Bharadvāja understood.

---

5 *In the fight of Etaśa* : when he contended with
Sūrya. See II. 19. 5, where Indra is said to have
assisted Etaśa.

9 *Of both* : of Gods and men.

11 The second half of the stanza is not clear. Professor Wilson paraphrases it after Sāyaṇa : 'thou rewar-
dest with strength and with riches him (who undertakes)
the institution, (who effects) the accomplishment, of the
sacrifice.

Agni ; preserve us, O thou Victor, from dishonour.

Here let the place of darkening come upon thee : may wealth be ours, desirable in thousands.

13 Agni, the Priest, is King, Lord of the homestead, he, Jātavedas, knows all generations.

Most skilful worshipper mid Gods and mortals, may he begin the sacrifice, the Holy.

14 Whate'er to-day thou, bright-flamed Priest, enjoyest from the man's rite—for thou art sacrificer—

Worship, for duly dost thou spread in greatness : bear off thine offerings of to-day, Most Youthful.

15 Look thou upon the viands duly laid for thee. Fain would he set thee here to worship Heaven and Earth.

Help us, O liberal Agni, in the strife for spoil, so that we may o'ercome all things that trouble us, o'ercome, o'ercome them with thy help.

16 Together with all Gods, O fair-faced Agni, be seated first upon the wool-lined altar,

Nest-like, bedewed with oil. Bear this our worship to Savitar who sacrifices rightly.

17 Here the arranging priests, as did Atharvan, rub this Agni forth,

Whom, not bewildered, as he moved in winding ways, they brought from gloom.

18 For the Gods' banquet be thou born, for full perfection and for weal.

Bring the Immortal Gods who strengthen holy Law : so let our sacrifice reach the Gods.

19 O Agni, Lord and Master of men's homesteads, with kindled fuel we have made thee mighty.

Let not our household gear be found defective. Sharpen us with thy penetrating splendour.

HYMN XVI.   Agni.

1. PRIEST of all sacrifices hast thou been appointed by the Gods,
Agni, amid the race of man.

2 So with thy joyous tongues for us sacrifice nobly in this rite.
Bring thou the Gods and worship them.

3 For well, O God, Disposer, thou knowest, straight on, the paths and ways,
Agni, most wise in sacrifice.

4 Thee, too, hath Bharata of old, with mighty men, implored for bliss.
And worshipped thee the worshipful.

5 Thou givest these abundant boons to Divodāsa pouring forth,
To Bharadvāja offering gifts.

6 Do thou, Immortal Messenger, bring hither the Celestial Folk;
Hearing the singer's eulogy.

7 Mortals with pious thought implore thee, Agni, God, at holy rites,
To come unto the feast of Gods.

8 I glorify thine aspect and the might of thee the Bountiful.
All those who love shall joy in thee,

9 Invoker placed by Manus, thou, Agni, art near, the wisest Priest :
Pay worship to the Tribes of Heaven.

10 Come, Agni, lauded, to the feast ; come to the offering of the gifts.
As Priest be seated on the grass.

11 So, Aṅgiras, we make thee strong with fuel and with holy oil.
Blaze high, thou youngest of the Gods.

12 For us thou winnest, Agni, God, heroic strength exceeding great,
Far-spreading and of high renown.

---

12 *The place of darkening* : this passage is very obscure. Professor Ludwig thinks that the time of battle is meant. May the foes who attack us find that they have to deal with thee as our ally. Sāyaṇa explains *pāthaḥ* as food offered in sacrifice, and *dhvasmanvát* as *dhvastadoṣam*, freed from defects : 'May the food reach thee free from imperfection.' Professor Grassmann translates : 'Es dring mit dir dein rauchumhüllter Gang vor;' 'Thy smoke-enveloped course press forward with thee.'

13 *Knows all generations* : *viśvā veda jánimā* ; etymology of Jātavedas.—Ludwig.

14 *The man's* : who institutes the sacrifice.

15 *Fain would he* : the patron of the sacrifice.

The original hymn seems to end with this stanza, as the repetition, o'ercome...o'ercome, o'ercome, *tarema...tarema......tarema* also indicates.

16 *Wool-lined altar* : built up like the nest of a bird with layers of wool, in which wool and resins for incense are placed. See Aitareya-Brāhmaṇa, I. 5. 28 (Haug's translation p. 62). *To Savitar* : according to Sāyaṇa, Savitar means the originator, the institutor of the sacrifice, and the dative case is used in the sense of the genitive, 'the sacrifice of the institutor of the rite.' In another place he explains *savitre yájamānāya* by 'for the sake of the benefit of the sacrificing institutor of the ceremony.'

17 *Atharvan* : the priest who first obtained fire and offered Soma and prayers to the Gods. *As he moved in winding ways* : when he fled and tried to hide himself from the Gods.

4 *Bharata* : according to Sāyaṇa the King of that name, son of Duṣyanta and Śakuntalā.

13 Agni, Atharvan brought thee forth, by
rubbing, from the lotus-flower,
The head of Viśva, of the Priest.

14 Thee. Vṛtra's slayer, breaker down of
castles, hath Atharvan's son,
Dadhyac the Ṛṣi, lighted up.

15 The hero Pāthya kindled thee the Dasyus'
most destructive foe,
Winner of spoil in every fight.

16 Come, here, O Agni, will I sing verily
other songs to thee,
And with these drops shalt thou grow
strong.

17 Where'er thy mind applies itself, vigour
preëminent hast thou :
There wilt thou gain a dwelling-place.

18 Not for a moment only lasts thy bounty,
good to many a one !
Our service therefore shalt thou gain.

19 Agni, the Bhārata, hath been sought, the
Vṛtra-slayer, marked of all,
Yea, Divodāsa's Hero Lord.

20 For he gave riches that surpass in greatness all the things of earth,
Fighting untroubled, unsubdued.

21 Thou, Agni, as in days of old, with
recent glory, gathered light,
Hast overspread the lofty heaven.

22 Bring to your Agni, O my friends, boldly
your laud and sacrifice :
Give the Disposer praise and song.

23 For as sagacious Herald he hath sat
through every age of man,
Oblation-bearing messenger.

24 Bring those Two Kings whose ways are
pure, Ādityas, and the Marut host,
Excellent God ! and Heaven and Earth.

25 For strong and active mortal man, excellent, Agni, is the look
Of thee Immortal, Son of Strength !

26 Rich through his wisdom, noblest be the
giver serving thee to-day :

The man hath brought his hymn of
praise.

27 These, Agni, these are helped by thee,
who strong and active all their lives,
O'ercome the malice of the foe, fight down
the malice of the foe.

28 May Agni with his pointed blaze cast
down each fierce devouring fiend :
May Agni win us wealth by war.

29 O active Jātavedas, bring riches with
store of hero sons :
Slay thou the demons, O Most Wise.

30 Keep us, O Jātavedas, from the troubling
of the man of sin :
Guard us thou Sage who knowest prayer.

31 Whatever sinner, Agni, brings oblations
to procure our death,
Save us from woe that he would work.

32 Drive from us with thy tongue, O God,
the man who doeth evil deeds,
The mortal who would strike us dead.

33 Give shelter reaching far and wide to
Bharadvāja, conquering Lord !
Agni, send wealth most excellent.

34 May Agni slay the Vṛtras,—fain for riches,
through the lord of song,
Served with oblation, kindled, bright.

35 His Father's Father, shining in his
Mother's everlasting side,
Set on the seat of holy Law.

36 O active Jātavedas, bring devotion that
wins progeny, Agni, that it may shine
to heaven.

37 O Child of Strength, to thee whose look
is lovely we with dainty food,
O Agni, have poured forth our songs.

38 To thee for shelter are we come, as to the
shade from fervent heat,
Agni, who glitterest like gold.

39 Mighty as one who slays with shafts, or
like a bull with sharpened horn,
Agni, thou breakest down the forts.

40 Whom, like an infant newly born,
devourer, in their arms they bear,
Men's Agni, skilled in holy rites.

41 Bear to the banquet of the Gods the God
best finder-out of wealth,
Let him be seated in his place.

13 *The lotus-flower* : apparently a figurative expression for heaven. *Viśva* : Heaven, personified.

14 *Dadhyac* : See I. 84. 13, note.

15 *Pāthya* : probably some celebrated sacrificer. Dr.
Garbe (Vaitāna-Sūtra II. 14) translates *pāthyo vṛṣā*
in this text by 'der Hengst auf der Strasse, the Stallion
on the way.'

18 *Not for a moment only lasts thy bounty* : Sāyaṇa
understands this differently : 'Let not thy full (blaze)
be distressing to the eye.'—Wilson.

19 *The Bhārata* : the especial protector of the
Bharatas. According to Sāyaṇa the word means either
'descended from the priests called Bharatas,' or 'the
bearer of oblations.'

24 *Those Two Kings* : Mitra and Varuṇa.

35 *His Father's Father* : 'here, as before, the mother
of *Agni* is the earth, the father is heaven : Agni is said
to be the father or fosterer of his parent heaven by
transmitting to it the flame and smoke of burnt-offerings.'
—Wilson.

37 *Child of Strength* : sahaskṛta ; literally, made or
produced by strength, i.e. the violent agitation of the
fire-stick.

42 In Jātavedas kindle ye the dear guest who hath now appeared
In a soft place, the homestead's Lord.

43 Harness, O Agni, O thou God, thy steeds which are most excellent :
They bear thee as thy spirit wills.

44 Come hither, bring the Gods to us to taste the sacrificial feast,
To drink the draught of Soma juice.

45 O Agni of the Bharatas, blaze high with everlasting might,
Shine forth and gleam, Eternal One.

46 The mortal man who serves the God with banquet, and, bringing gifts at sacrifice, lauds Agni,
May well attract, with prayer and hands uplifted, the Priest of Heaven and Earth, true Sacrificer.

47 Agni, we bring thee, with our hymn, oblation fashioned in the heart.
Let these be oxen unto thee, let these be bulls and kine to thee.

48 The Gods enkindle Agni, best slayer of Vṛtra, first in rank,
The Mighty One who brings us wealth and crushes down the Rākṣasas.

HYMN XVII. *Indra.*

1. DRINK Soma, Mighty One, for which, when lauded, thou breakest through the cattle-stall, O Indra ;
Thou who, O Bold One, armed with thunder smotest Vṛtra with might, and every hostile being.

2 Drink it thou God who art impetuous victor, Lord of our hymns, with beauteous jaws, the Hero,
Render of kine-stalls, car-borne, thunder-wielding, so pierce thy way to wondrous strength, O Indra.

3 Drink as of old, and let the draught delight thee : hear thou our prayer and let our songs exalt thee.
Make the Sun visible, make food abundant, slaughter the foes, pierce through and free the cattle.

4 These gladdening drops, O Indra, Self-sustainer, quaffed shall augment thee in thy mighty splendour.

Yea, let the cheering drops delight thee greatly, great, perfect, strong, powerful, all-subduing.

5 Gladdened whereby, bursting the firm enclosures, thou gavest splendour to the Sun and Morning.
The mighty rock that compassed in the cattle, ne'er moved, thou shookest from its seat, O Indra.

6 Thou with thy wisdom, power, and works of wonder, hast stored the ripe milk in the raw cows' udders,
Unbarred the firm doors for the kine of Morning, and, with the Angirases, set free the cattle.

7 Thou hast spread out wide earth, a mighty marvel, and, high thyself, propped lofty heaven, O Indra.
Both worlds, whose Sons are Gods, thou hast supported, young, Mothers from old time of holy Order.

8 Yea, Indra, all the Deities installed thee their one strong Champion in the van for battle.
What time the godless was the Gods' assailant, Indra they chose to win the light of heaven.

9 Yea, e'en that heaven itself of old bent backward before thy bolt, in terror of its anger,
When Indra, life of every living creature, smote down within his lair the assailing Dragon.

10 Yea, Strong One ! Tvaṣṭar turned for thee, the Mighty, the bolt with thousand spikes and hundred edges,
Eager and prompt at will, wherewith thou crushedst the boasting Dragon, O impetuous Hero.

11 He dressed a hundred buffaloes, O Indra, for thee whom all accordant Maruts strengthen.
He, Pūṣan Viṣṇu, poured forth three great vessels to him, the juice that cheers, that slaughters Vṛtra.

---

6 *The ripe milk* : the cows are called raw as contrasted with the warm milk matured in their udders. See 1. 62. 9. This miracle is ascribed to the Aśvins also. See I. 180. 3.

7 *Whose Sons are Gods* : Heaven and Earth are frequently called the parents of the Gods. So in Greek mythology the Gods sprang from the union of Uranus and Gaia. 'Cent mythologies,' M. Réville remarks, 'sont fondées sur le mariage du ciel et de la terre.' See Muir, *O. S. Texts*, V. p. 24.

8 *The godless* : the demon Vṛtra.

11 *He* : Agni. See V. 29. 7. *Three great vessels* : literally, lakes. See V. 29. 7. *That slaughters Vṛtra* : inspirits Indra to slay him.

---

42 *In Jātavedas kindle ye* : the meaning is said to be, that the fire of burnt-offerings is to be kindled by the fire produced by attrition.

46 *True Sacrificer* : whose sacrifices are always effectual.

47 *Let these be oxen* : let our oblations be as acceptable to thee as herds of cattle are to men.

12 Thou settest free the rushing wave of
waters, the floods' great swell encompassed and obstructed.
Along steep slopes their course thou
turnedst, Indra, directed downward,
speeding to the ocean.

13 So may our new prayer bring thee to
protect us, thee well-armed Hero with
thy bolt of thunder,
Indra, who made these worlds, the Strong,
the Mighty, who never groweth old,
the victory-giver.

14 So, Indra, form us brilliant holy singers
for strength, for glory, and for food and
riches.
Give Bharadvāja hero patrons, Indra!
Indra, be ours upon the day of trial.

15 With this may we obtain strength God-
appointed, and brave sons gladden us
through a hundred winters.

HYMN XVIII.   *Indra.*

1. GLORIFY him whose might is all-surpassing,
Indra the much-invoked who fights
uninjured.
Magnify with these songs the never-van-
quished, the Strong, the Bull of men, the
Mighty Victor.

2 He, Champion, Hero, Warrior, Lord of
battles, impetuous, loudly roaring, great
destroyer,
Who whirls the dust on high, alone, o'erthrower, hath made all races of mankind
his subjects.

3 Thou, thou alone, hast tamed the Dasyus;
singly thou hast subdued the people for
the Ārya.
In this, or is it not, thine hero exploit,
Indra? Declare it at the proper season.

4 For true, I deem, thy strength is, thine
the Mighty, thine, O Most Potent, thine
the Conquering Victor;
Strong, of the strong, Most Mighty, of the
mighty, thine, driver of the churl to acts
of bounty.

5 Be this our ancient bond of friendship
with you and with Aṅgirases here who
speak of Vala.
Thou, Wondrous, Shaker of things firm,
didst smite him in his fresh strength,
and force his doors and castles.

6 With holy thoughts must he be called,
the Mighty, showing his power in the
great fight with Vṛtra.
He must be called to give us seed and offspring, the Thunderer must be moved
and sped to battle.

7 He in his might, with name that lives for
ever, hath far surpassed all human
generations.
He, most heroic, hath his home with
splendour, with glory and with riches
and with valour.

8 Stranger to guile, who ne'er was false or
faithless, bearing a name that may be
well remembered,
Indra crushed Cumuri, Dhuni, Śambara,
Pipru, and Śuṣṇa, that their castles fell
in ruin.

9 With saving might that must be praised
and lauded, Indra, ascend thy car to
smite down Vṛtra.
In thy right hand hold fast thy bolt of
thunder, and weaken, Bounteous Lord,
his art and magic.

10 As Agni, as the dart burns the dry forest,
like the dread shaft burn down the
fiends, O Indra;
Thou who with high deep-reaching spear
hast broken, hast covered over mischief
and destroyed it.

11 With wealth, by thousand paths come
hither, Agni, paths that bring ample
strength, O thou Most Splendid.
Come, Son of Strength, o'er whom, Invoked of many! the godless hath no power
to keep thee distant.

12 From heaven, from earth is bruited forth
the greatness of him the firm, the fiery,
the resplendent.
No foe hath he, no counterpart, no refuge
is there from him the Conqueror full
of wisdom

13 This day the deed that thou hast done
is famous, when thou, for him, with
many thousand others
Laidest low Kutsa, Āyu, Atithigva, and
boldly didst deliver Tūrvayāṇa.

---

14 *The day of trial*: the decisive day of battle.
15 *With this*: *stutyā*, praise, is understood.

---

3 *At the proper season*: show that thou hast this
power by aiding us before it is too late and when our
enemies have conquered us.

5 *With you*: with Indra and his allies, the Maruts.

---

8 *Cumuri, etc.*: demons of drought. See Index.

10 The exact meaning of the second half-stanza is
uncertain, as *gambhriḍyā* and *ṛṣvḍyā*, deep and high,
have no substantive.

13 *For him*: for Tūrvayāṇa: who appears to have
been an especial favourite of Indra. According to
Sāyaṇa, *tūrvayāṇa*, 'quickly going,' is an epithet of
Divodāsa. Sāyaṇa represents the exploit as having
been achieved *for* Kutsa, Āyu, and Atithigva, but
this is not the meaning of the words of the text. *A new
hymn*: of praise for some new favour shown to us.

14 In thee, O God, the wisest of the Sages,
all Gods were joyful when thou slewest
Ahi.
When, lauded for thyself, thou gavest
freedom to sore-afflicted Heaven and to
the people.

15 This power of thine both heaven and
earth acknowledge, the deathless Gods
acknowledge it, O Indra.
Do what thou ne'er hast done, O Mighty
Worker : beget a new hymn at thy
sacrifices.

HYMN XIX. *Indra.*

1. GREAT, hero-like controlling men is Indra,
unwasting in his powers, doubled in
vastness.
He, turned to us, hath grown to hero
vigour : broad, wide, he hath been
decked by those who serve him.

2 The bowl made Indra swift to gather booty,
the High, the Lofty, Youthful, Undecaying,
Him who hath waxed by strength which
none may conquer, and even at once
grown to complete perfection.

3 Stretch out those hands of thine, extend
to us-ward thy wide capacious arms,
and grant us glory.
Like as the household herdsman guards the
cattle, so move thou round about us in
the combat.

4 Now, fain for strength, let us invite your
Indra hither, who lieth hidden with his
Heroes,—
Free from all blame, without reproach,
uninjured, e'en as were those who sang,
of old, his praises.

5 With steadfast laws, wealth-giver, strong
through Soma, he hath much fair and
precious food to feed us.
In him unite all paths that lead to riches,
like rivers that commingle with the
ocean.

6 Bring unto us the mightiest might, O Hero,
strong and most potent force, thou
great Subduer !
All splendid vigorous powers of men vouchsafe us, Lord of Bay Steeds, that they
may make us joyful.

7 Bring us, grown mighty in its strength,
O Indra, thy friendly rapturous joy that
wins the battle,
Wherewith by thee assisted and triumphant,
we may laud thee in gaining seed and
offspring.

8 Indra, bestow on us the power heroic,
skilled and exceeding strong, that wins
the booty,
Wherewith, by thine assistance, we may
conquer our foes in battle, be they
kin or stranger.

9 Let thine heroic strength come from behind us, before us, from above us or
below us.
From every side may it approach us, Indra.
Give us the glory of the realm of
splendour.

10 With most heroic aid from thee, like heroes,
Indra, may we win wealth by deeds of
glory.
Thou, King, art Lord of earthly, heavenly
treasure : vouchsafe us riches vast,
sublime, and lasting.

11 The Bull, whose strength hath waxed,
whom Maruts follow, free-giving Indra,
the Celestial Ruler,
Mighty, all-conquering, the victory-giver,
him let us call to grant us new protection.

12 Give up the people who are high and
haughty to these men and to me, O
Thunder-wielder !
Therefore upon the earth do we invoke
thee, where heroes win, for sons and
kine and waters.

13 Through these thy friendships, God invoked of many ! may we be victors
over every foeman.
Slaying both kinds of foe, may we, O
Hero, be happy, helped by thee, with
ample riches.

HYMN XX. *Indra.*

1. GIVE us wealth, Indra, that with might,
as heaven o'ertops the earth, o'ercomes
our foes in battle,
Wealth that brings thousands and that
wins the corn-lands, wealth, Son of
Strength ! that vanquishes the foeman.

---

1 *Controlling men* : or, satisfier of men. 'Fulfiller
(of the desires) of men.'—Wilson.
2 *The bowl* : that is, the libation of Soma juice.
But see Ludwig, Ueber die neuesten Arbeiten, &c., p.
87.
4 *Who lieth hidden* : Sāyaṇa explains *catinam* as
śatrūṇām cātakam nāśakam ; 'the destroyer (of enemies)'.
—Wilson.

9 *From behind us, etc.* : or, from the west, from the
north, from the south, from the east
11 .This stanza has occurred in III. 47. 5.
12 *Where heroes win* : *śūrasātau* ; in battle.
13 *Both kinds of foe* : kinsmen and strangers. See
stanza 8.

—

2 Even as the power of Dyaus, to thee, O
Indra, all Asura sway was by the Gods
entrusted,
When thou, Impetuous ! leagued with
Viṣṇu, slewest Vṛtra the Dragon who
enclosed the waters.

3 Indra, Strong, Victor, Mightier than the
mighty, addressed with prayer and perfect in his splendour,
Lord of the bolt that breaketh forts in
pieces, became the King of the sweet
juice of Soma.

4 There, Indra, while the light was won, the
Paṇis fled, 'neath a hundred blows, for
wise Daśoni,
And greedy Śuṣṇa's magical devices :
nor left he any of their food remaining.

5 What time the thunder fell and Śuṣṇa
perished, all life's support from the great
Druh was taken.
Indra made room for his car-driver Kutsa
who sate beside him, when he gained
the sunlight.

6 As the Hawk rent for him the stalk that
gladdens, he wrenched the head from
Namuci the Dāsa.
He guarded Nam, Sayya's son, in slumber,
and sated him with food, success, and
riches.

7 Thou, thunder-armed, with thy great might
hast shattered Pipru's strong forts who
knew the wiles of serpents.
Thou gavest to thy worshipper Rjiśvan
imperishable wealth, O Bounteous Giver.

8 The crafty Vetasu, the swift Daśoni, and
Tugra speedily with all his servants,
Hath Indra, gladdening with strong assistance, forced near as 'twere to glorify
the Mother.

9 Resistless, with the hosts he battles, bearing
in both his arms the Vṛtra-slaying
thunder.
He mounts his Bays, as the car-seat an
archer : yoked at a word they bear the
lofty Indra.

10 May we, O Indra, gain by thy new favour:
so Pūrus laud thee, with their sacrifices,
That thou hast wrecked seven autumn forts,
their shelter, slain Dāsa tribes and aided
Purukutsa.

11 Favouring Uśanā the son of Kavi, thou
wast his ancient strengthener, O Indra.
Thou gavest Navavāstva as a present, to
the great father gavest back his grandson.

12 Thou, roaring Indra, drovest on the waters
that made a roaring sound like rushing
rivers,
What time, O Hero, o'er the sea thou
broughtest, in safety broughtest Turvaśa
and Yadu.

13 This Indra, was thy work in war : thou
sentest Dhuni and Cumuri to sleep and
slumber.
Dabhīti lit the flame for thee, and worshipped with fuel, hymns, poured Soma,
dressed oblations.

HYMN XXI. *Indra. Viśvedevas.*

1. THESE the most constant singer's invocations call thee who art to be invoked,
O Hero;
Hymns call anew the chariot-borne, Eternal:
by eloquence men gain abundant riches.

2 I praise that Indra, known to all men,
honoured with songs, extolled with
hymns at sacrifices,
Whose majesty, rich in wondrous arts,
surpasseth the magnitude of earth, and
heaven in greatness.

3 He hath made pathways, with the Sun

4 *For wise Daśoni* : Daśoni would appear in this
place to be the name of some man whom Indra
protected. Sāyaṇa says that the dative case is put for the
ablative, and that the meaning is, 'from the sage who
offers many oblations,' that is, from Kutsa. Ludwig
takes Da oṇi here to be the priest of the Paṇis : 'fled
or fell for or to him' meaning that he was powerless to
save them.

5 *Druh* : or, oppressor. Cf. IV. 28. 2.

6 *The Hawk* : which brought the Soma from
heaven. See I. 93. 6; IV. 27. *Nami* : See X. 48. 9.

8 Vetasu, Daśoni, and Tugra appear to be names
of enemies conquered by Indra. But *swift, tūtujim*,
may be a Proper Name. T tuji Tuji (VI. 26. 4), and
Daśoni (*daśoṇim*) may be an adjective, 'having ten arms
or helpers.' Cf. X. 49. 4, and see Ludwig, Der
Ṛgveda, III. p. 1 6. *As 'twere to glorify the Mother* :
Sāyaṇa takes *dyotanāya* as the name of a rājā, and
according to his interpretation Indra compelled the
conquered foes to approach Dyotana submissively as
a son comes before a mother. *The Mother* : the great
Mother Aditi.

10 *Autumn forts* : probably strong places on elevated ground occupied by the Dāsas or original inhabitants
during the rains and autumn. According to Sāyaṇa,
cities or strongholds of Śarat, a demon.

11 *Navavāstva* : an Asura, or a mysterious being who
perhaps represents the Sun, released from captivity or
eclipse by Indra and by him restored to his own or to
Indra's father—apparently to Uśanā or Heaven. Cf.
X. 49. 6 : Bergaigne, II. 223; Pischel (Vedische Studien,
II. 128); Ludwig, Ueber dien. Arbeiten auf dem
Gebiete der Ṛgveda-forschung, 160.

12 See I. 174. 9.

13 *Dhuni and Cumuri* : Asuras or demons, sent to
sleep, that is slain, by Indra. 'Thou, with sleep
whelming Cumuri and Dhuni, 'slewest the Dasyu,
keptest safe Dabhīti' (II. 15. 9). Cf. VI. 18. 8.

to aid 'him, throughout the darkness that extended pathless.

Mortals who yearn to worship ne'er dishonour, O Mighty God, thy Law who art Immortal.

4 And he who did these things, where is that Indra ? among what tribes? what people doth he visit ?

What sacrifice contents thy mind and wishes ? What priest among them all? what hymn, O Indra ?

5 Yea, here were they who, born of old, have served thee, thy friends of ancient time, thou active Worker.

Bethink thee now of these, Invoked of many ! the midmost and the recent, and the youngest.

6 Inquiring after him, thy later servants, Indra, have gained thy former old traditions.

Hero, to whom the prayer is brought, we praise thee as great for that wherein we know thee mighty.

7 The demon's strength is gathered fast against thee : great as that strength hath grown, go forth to meet it.

With thine own ancient friend and companion, the thunderbolt, brave Champion ! drive it backward.

8 Hear, too, the prayer of this thy present beadsman, O Indra, Hero, cherishing the singer.

For thou wast aye our fathers' Friend aforetime, still swift to listen to their supplication.

9 Bring to our help this day, for our protection, Varuṇa, Mitra, Indra, and the Maruts,

Pūṣan and Viṣṇu, Agni and Purandhi, Savitar also, and the Plants and Mountains.

10 The singers here exalt with hymns and praises thee who art very Mighty and Most Holy.

Hear, when invoked, the invoker's invocation. Beside thee there is none like thee, Immortal !

11 Now to my words come quickly thou who knowest, O Son of Strength, with all who claim our worship,

Who visit sacred rites, whose tongue is Agni, Gods who made Manu stronger than the Dasyu.

12 On good and evil ways be thou our Leader, thou who art known to all as Pathpreparer.

Bring power to us, O Indra, with thy Horses, Steeds that are best to draw, broad-backed, unwearied.

HYMN XXII.   *Indra.*

1. WITH these my hymns I glorify that Indra who is alone to be invoked by mortals,

The Lord, the Mighty One, of manly vigour, victorious, Hero, true, and full of wisdom.

2 Our sires of old, Navagvas, sages seven, while urging him to show his might, extolled him,

Dwelling on heights, swift, smiting down opponents, guileless in word, and in his thoughts most mighty.

3 We seek that Indra to obtain his riches that bring much food, and men, and store of heroes.

Bring us, Lord of Bay Steeds, to make us joyful, celestial wealth, abundant, undecaying.

4 Tell thou us this, if at thy hand aforetime the earlier singers have obtained good fortune,

What is thy share and portion, Strong Subduer, Asura-slayer, rich, invoked of many ?

5 He who for car-borne Indra, armed with thunder, hath a hymn, craving, deeplypiercing, fluent,

Who sends a song effectual, firmly-grasping, and strength-bestowing, he comes near the mighty.

6 Strong of thyself, thou by this art hast shattered, with thought-swift Parvata, him who waxed against thee,

And, Mightiest ! roaring ! boldly rent in pieces things that were firmly fixed and never shaken.

7 Him will we fit for you with new devotion, the strongest Ancient One, in ancient manner.

2 *Navagvas* : here, apparently, identified with the Aṅgirases.

4 *What is thy share and portion* : 'what is the portion, what the offering (due) to thee.'—Wilson. *Asura-slayer:* possibly, the smiter and conqueror of the Asura Dyaus.

5 *Comes near the mighty* : 'encounters (with confidence) the malevolent.'—Wilson.

6 *Parvata* : the Genius of the mountains and clouds, frequently associated with Indra. According to Sāyaṇa (*bahuparvaṇā vajreṇa*), the many-knotted thunderbolt is intended. *Him who waxed against thee* : Vṛtra.

9 *Purandhi* : 'the intelligent,' or 'the bold' may be either an epithet of Agni or the name of a separate deity.

So may that Indra, boundless, faithful
Leader, conduct us o'er all places hard
to traverse.

8 Thou for the people who oppress hast
kindled the earthly firmament and that
of heaven.
With heat, O Bull, on every side consume
them : heat earth and flood for him who
hates devotion.

9 Of all the Heavenly Folk, of earthly creatures thou art the King, O God of
splendid aspect.
In thy right hand, O Indra, grasp the
thunder : Eternal ! thou destroyest all
enchantments.

10 Give us confirmed prosperity, O Indra,
vast and exhaustless for the foe's subduing.
Strengthen therewith the Ārya's hate and
Dāsa's, and let the arms of Nahuṣas be
mighty.

11 Come with thy team which brings all blessings hither, Disposer, much-invoked,
exceeding holy.
Thou whom no fiend, no God can stay or
hinder, come swiftly with these Steeds in
my direction.

HYMN XXIII.   *Indra.*

1. Thou art attached to pressed-out Soma,
Indra, at laud, at prayer, and when the
hymn is chanted ;
Or when with yoked Bays, Maghavan,
thou comest, O Indra, bearing in thine
arms the thunder.

2 Or when on that decisive day thou holpest
the presser of the juice at Vṛtra's slaughter ;
Or when thou, while the strong one feared,
undaunted, gavest to death, Indra, the
daring Dasyus.

3 Let Indra drink the pressed-out Soma,
Helper and mighty Guide of him who
sings his praises.
He gives the hero room who pours oblations, and treasure even to the lowly
singer.

4 E'en humble rites with his Bay steeds he
visits : he wields the bolt, drinks Soma,
gives us cattle.

He makes the valiant rich in store of
heroes, accepts our praise and hears the
singer's calling.

5 What he hath longed for we have brought
to Indra, who from the days of old hath
done us service.
While Soma flows we will sing hymn, and
laud him, so that our prayer may strengthen Indra's vigour.

6 Thou hast made prayer the means of thine
exalting, therefore we wait on thee with
hymns, O Indra.
May we, by the pressed Soma, Soma-
drinker ! bring thee, with sacrifice,
blissful sweet refreshment.

7 Mark well our sacrificial cake, delighted :
Indra, drink Soma and the milk commingled.
Here on the sacrificer's grass be seated :
give ample room to thy devoted servant.

8 O Mighty One, be joyful as thou willest.
Let these our sacrifices reach and find
thee ;
And may this hymn and these our invocations turn thee, whom many men invoke,
to help us.

9 Friends, when the juices flow, replenish duly
your own, your bounteous Indra with
the Soma.
Will it not aid him to support us ? Indra
spares him who sheds the juice to win
his favour.

10 While Soma flowed, thus Indra hath been
lauded, Ruler of nobles, mid the
Bharadvājas,
That Indra may become the singer's
patron and give him wealth in every
kind of treasure.

HYMN XXIV.   *Indra.*

1. Strong rapturous joy, praise, glory are
with Indra : impetuous God, he quaffs
the juice of Soma :
That Maghavan whom men must laud
with singing, Heaven-dweller, King of
songs, whose help is lasting.

2 He, Friend of man, most wise, victorious
Hero, hears, with far-reaching aid, the
singer call him.
Excellent, Praise of Men, the bard's
Supporter, Strong, he gives strength,
extolled in holy synod.

---

8 *The people who oppress* : the Rākṣasas and other
enemies.

10 *Nahuṣas* : See VI. 46. 7, note.

1 *Strong rapturous joy* : produced by drinking Soma-
libations.

2 *Praise of Men* : *śáṁso narām*, as Agni is called
Narāśaṁsa.

3 The lofty axle of thy wheels, O Hero, is
not surpassed by heaven and earth in
greatness.
Like branches of a tree, Invoked of many !
manifold aids spring forth from thee,
O Indra.

4 Strong Lord, thine energies, endowed with
vigour, are like the paths of kine
converging homeward.
Like bonds of cord, Indra, that bind the
younglings, no bonds are they, O thou
of boundless bounty.

5 One act to-day, another act tomorrow :
oft Indra makes what is not yet existent.
Here have we Mitra, Varuṇa, and Pūṣan
to overcome the foeman's domination.

6 By song and sacrifice men brought the
waters from thee, as from a mountain's
ridge, O Indra.
Urging thy might, with these fair lauds
they seek thee, O theme of song, as
horses rush to battle.

7 That Indra whom nor months nor autumn
seasons wither with age, nor fleeting
days enfeeble,—
Still may his body wax, e'en now so mighty,
glorified by the lauds and hymns that
praise him.

8 Extolled, he bends not to the strong, the
steadfast, nor to the bold incited by the
Dasyu.
High mountains are as level plains to
Indra : even in the deep he finds
firm ground to rest on.

9 Impetuous Speeder through all depth and
distance, give strengthening food, thou
drinker of the juices.
Stand up erect to help us, unreluctant,
what time the gloom of night brightens
to morning.

10 Hasting to help, come hither and protect
him, keep him from harm when he is
here, O Indra.
At home, abroad, from injury preserve
him. May brave sons gladden us through
a hundred winters.

HYMN XXV. *Indra.*

1. WITH thine assistance, O thou Mighty
Indra, be it the least, the midmost,
or the highest,—
Great with those aids and by these powers
support us, Strong God ! in battle that
subdues our foemen.

2 With these discomfit hosts that fight
against us, and check the opponent's
wrath, thyself uninjured.
With these chase all our foes to every
quarter : subdue the tribes of Dāsas to
the Ārya.

3 Those who array themselves as foes to
smite us, O Indra, be they kin or be
they strangers,—
Strike thou their manly strength that it
be feeble, and drive in headlong flight
our foemen backward.

4 With strength of limb the hero slays
the hero, when bright in arms they range
, them for the combat.
When two opposing hosts contend in battle
for seed and offspring, waters, kine, or
corn-lands.

5 Yet no strong man hath conquered thee,
no hero, no brave, no warrior trusting
in his valour.
Not one of these is match for thee, O Indra.
Thou far surpassest all these living
creatures.

6 He is the Lord of both these armies'
valour when the commanders call them
to the conflict :

---

4 *Converging homeward* : all Indra's great deeds indicate their divine author as the tracks made by grazing
cows may be traced back to the common pen from
which they have come forth.

Like bonds : the ties by which Indra's worshippers
are bound to him are ties of love and not fetters of
slavery. There is a play on the word *dāman* in the
text which derived from *dā*, to give, means gift or
bounty, and derived from *dā*, to bind, means, cord,
rope, bond, or fetter : *vatsānām ná tantáyaḥ te Indra
ḍámanvantaḥ adamānaḥ sudā́man* (Pada text). The word
vatsá also means a youngling, especially a calf, and a
dear child, a darling, so that Indra's favoured worshippers are also intended.

5 *Here* : that is, in Indra we have a champion
equal to the three Gods mentioned.

10 *Hasting to help* : I follow Professor Pischel
(*Vedische Studien*, I. p. 41) in his explanation of *nāyám*
in this passage. Professor Ludwig translates somewhat
similarly. Sāyaṇa (followed by Professors Wilson and
Grassmann) takes *nāyám* in the signification of leader ;
'accompany the leader.' Professor Roth thinks it may
be a proper name. *Him* : the institutor of the sacrifice.

The poet prays for victory in a coming battle.

1 *By these powers* : on account of, or by means of,
the sacrificial food which increases thy strength.

6 *He is the Lord* : Indra can give valour and victory
to either side as he chooses. Sāyaṇa explains the first
half-stanza differently : 'Of both these (disputants),
that one acquires wealth whose priests invoke (Indra) at
the sacrifice.'—Wilson.

When with their ranks expanded they are
fighting with a great foe or for a home
with heroes.

7 And when the people stir themselves for
battle, be thou their saviour, Indra, and
protector,
And theirs, thy manliest of our friends,
the pious, the chiefs who have installed
us priests, O Indra.

8 To thee for high dominion hath been
given, for evermore, for slaughtering
the Vṛtras,
All lordly power and might, O Holy
Indra, given by Gods for victory in
battle.

9 So urge our hosts together in the combats : yield up the godless bands that
fight against us.
Singing, at morn may we find thee with
favour, yea, Indra, and e'en now, we
Bharadvājas.

HYMN XXVI. *Indra.*

1. O INDRA, hear us. Raining down the
Soma, we call on thee to win us mighty
valour.
Give us strong succour on the day of
trial, when the tribes gather on the field
of battle.

2 The warrior, son of warrior sire, invokes
thee, to gain great strength that may
be won as booty :
To thee, the brave man's Lord, the fiends'
subduer, he looks when fighting hand
to hand for cattle.

3 Thou didst impel the sage to win the
daylight, didst ruin Śuṣṇa for the pious
Kutsa.
The invulnerable demon's head thou
clavest when thou wouldst win the praise
of Atithigva.

4 The lofty battle-car thou broughtest
forward; thou holpest Daśadyu the
strong when fighting.
Along with Vetasu thou slewest Tugra,
and madest Tuji strong, who praised
thee, Indra.

5 Thou madest good the laud, what time
thou rentest a hundred thousand fighting foes, O Hero,

Slewest the Dāsa Śambara of the mountain,
and with strange aids didst succour
Divodāsa.

6 Made glad with Soma-draughts and faith,
thou sentest Cumuri to his sleep, to
please Dabhīti.
Thou, kindly giving Raji to Piṭhīnas.
slewest with might, at once, the sixty
thousand.

7 May I too, with the liberal chiefs, O
Indra, acquire thy bliss supreme and
domination,
When, Mightiest ! Hero-girt ! Nahuṣa
heroes boast them in thee, the triply-
strong Defender.

8 So may we be thy friends, thy best
beloved, O Indra, at this holy invocation.
Best be Prātardani, illustrious ruler, in
slaying foemen and in gaining riches.

HYMN XXVII. *Indra.*

1 WHAT deed hath Indra done in the wild
transport, in quaffing or in friendship
with, the Soma ?
What joys have men of ancient times or
recent obtained within the chamber of
libation ?

2 In its wild joy Indra hath proved him
faithful, faithful in quaffing, faithful in
its friendship.
His truth is the delight that in this
chamber the men of old and recent
times have tasted.

3 All thy vast power, O Maghavan, we
know not, know not the riches of thy
full abundance.
No one hath seen that might of thine,
productive of bounty every day renewed,
O Indra.

4 This one great power of thine our eyes
have witnessed, wherewith thou slewest
Varaśikha's children,

---

3 *The sage* : *bhārgavam ṛṣim* : Sāyaṇa ; the Ṛṣi,
descendant of Bhṛgu.

4 *Vetasu* : according to Sāyaṇa, either a king aided
by him or a demon slain by him. Cf. VI. 20. 8.
Tuji : a rājā of that name, says Sāyaṇa.

6 *Raji* : a maiden of that name.—Sāyaṇa. *Piṭhīnas* :
a man so called.—Sāyaṇa.

8 *Prātardani* : son of a prince named Pratardana.
The other names have occurred before. See Index.

The liberality of Abhyāvartin Cāyamāna is said
to be the deified object of stanza 8.

1 'According to Sāyaṇa the Ṛṣi here expresses his
impatience at the delay of the reward of his praises :
in the next verse he sings his recantation.'—Wilson.

4 *Varaśikha* : a certain Asura or demon, says
Sāyaṇa. He seems to have been the leader of the
Vṛcīvans.

When by the force of thy descending
thunder, at the mere sound, their boldest
was demolished.

5 In aid of Abhyāvartin Cāyamāna, Indra
destroyed the seed of Varaśikha.
At Hariyūpīyā he smote the vanguard of
the Vṛcīvans, and the rear fled frighted.

6 Three thousand, mailed, in quest of fame,
together, on the Yavyāvatī, O much-
sought Indra,
Vṛcīvan's sons, falling before the arrow,
like bursting vessels went to their
destruction.

7 He, whose two red Steers, seeking goodly
pasture, plying their tongues move on
'twixt earth and heaven,
Gave Turvaśa to Sṛñjaya, and, to aid
him, gave the Vṛcīvans up to Daivavāta.

8 Two wagon-teams, with damsels, twenty
oxen, O Agni, Abhyāvartin Cāyamāna,
The liberal Sovran, giveth me. This
guerdon of Pṛthu's seed is hard to win
from others.

HYMN XXVIII. *Cows.*

1. THE Kine have come and brought good
fortune : let them rest in the cow-pen
and be happy near us.
Here let them stay prolific, many-coloured,
and yield through many morns their milk
for Indra.

2 Indra aids him who offers sacrifice and
gifts : he takes not what is his, and gives
him more thereto.
Increasing ever more and ever more his
wealth, he makes the pious dwell within
unbroken bounds.

3 These are ne'er lost, no robber ever injures them : no evil-minded foe attempts
to harass them.
The master of the Kine lives many a year
with these, the Cows whereby he pours
his gifts and serves the Gods.

4 The charger with his dusty brow o'ertakes
them not, and never to the shambles
do they take their way.
These Cows, the cattle of the pious worshipper, roam over widespread pasture
where no danger is.

5 To me the Cows seem Bhaga, they seem
Indra, they seem a portion of the first-
poured Soma.
These present Cows, they, O ye men, are
Indra. I long for Indra with my heart
and spirit.

6 O Cows, ye fatten e'en the worn and
wasted, and make the unlovely beautiful
to look on.
Prosper my house, ye with auspicious
voices. Your power is glorified in our
assemblies.

7 Crop goodly pasturage and be prolific :
drink pure sweet water at good drinking-
places.
Never be thief or sinful man your master,
and may the dart of Rudra still avoid
you.

8 Now let this close admixture be close
intermigled with these Cows,
Mixt with the Steer's prolific flow, and,
Indra, with thy hero might.

HYMN XXIX. *Indra.*

1. YOUR men have followed Indra for his
friendship, and for his loving-kindness
glorified him.

5 *Abhyāvartin Cāyamāna* : a king, apparently the leader of the Pārthavas, the enemies of Varaśikha and the Vṛcīvans.

Hariyūpīyā : (having golden sacrificial posts), the name of a town, or, according to others, of a river.

Vṛcīvān's : Vṛcīvan is said to have been the eldest son of Varaśikha, and to have given his name to the family or tribe. The name does not occur again in the Hymns.

6 *Yavyāvatī* : the name of a river, according to Sāyaṇa identical with the Hariyūpīyā of stanza 5.

7 *He* : Indra. *Red Steers* : bright horses, according to Sāyaṇa.

Gave Turvaśa to Sṛñjaya : gave up the Turvaśas, a tribe apparently settled in the north-west of India, to their neighbours and enemies the Sṛñjayas. *Daivavāta* : Abhyāvartin Cāyamāna, son of Devavāta.

8 *With damsels* : accompanied with slave-girls ; or, drawn by mares. Cf. I. 126 3. *Of Pṛthu's seed* : or 'bestowed by Pārthavas,' that is, presented by Abhyā-vartin, one of the descendants of Pṛthu.

3 *Are ne'er lost ; ná tá naśanti* : Sāyaṇa assigns an imperative meaning to *naśanti* and the other verbs in the indicative mood which occur in this and the following stanzas : 'Let not the Cows be lost : let no thief, etc.'—Wilson.

4 *The charger......o'ertakes them not* : they are not, or, according to Sāyaṇa, let them not be, carried off in predatory incursions.

5 The worshipper regards the Cows as the deities, Bhaga and Indra, who bring him happiness. *They, O ye men, are Indra* : an allusion, apparently, to the refrain of hymn 12 of Book II., He, O men, is Indra.

7 *May the dart of Rudra still avoid you* : so, I. 114. 10. 'Far be thy dart that killeth men or cattle,' and II. 33. 14. 'May Rudra's missile turn aside and spare us, the great wrath of the Impetuous One avoid us.'

8 This stanza appears to refer to the mingling of the milk (the cows) with the juice of strong Soma (the steer), which when offered as a libation to Indra will increase his heroic strength. But the phraseology is somewhat obscure.

For he bestows great wealth, the Thunder-
wielder : worship him, Great and Kind,
to win his favour.

2 Him to whose hand, men closely cling,
and drivers stand on his golden chariot
firmly stationed.
With his firm arms he holds the reins;
his Horses, the Stallions, are yoked ready
for the journey.

3 Thy devotees embrace thy feet for glory.
Bold, thunder-armed, rich, through thy
strength, in guerdon,
Robed in a garment fair as heaven to
look on, thou hast displayed thee like
an active dancer.

4 That Soma when effused hath best consis-
tence, for which the food is dressed
and grain is mingled;
By which the men who pray, extolling
Indra, chief favourites of Gods, recite
their praises.

5 No limit of thy might hath been appointed, which by its greatness sundered
earth and heaven.
These the Prince filleth full with strong
endeavour, driving, as 'twere, with help
his flocks to waters.

6 So be the lofty Indra prompt to listen,
Helper unaided, golden-visored Hero.
Yea, so may he, shown forth in might
unequalled, smite down the many Vṛtras
and the Dasyus.

HYMN XXX.   *Indra.*

1. INDRA hath waxed yet more for hero
prowess, alone, Eternal, he bestoweth
treasures.
Indra transcendeth both the worlds in
greatness : one half of him equalleth
earth and heaven.

2 Yea, mighty I esteem his Godlike nature :
none hindereth what he hath on ce
determined.
Near and afar he spread and set the
regions, and every day the Sun became
apparent.

3 E'en now endures thine exploit of the
Rivers, when, Indra, for their floods
thou clavest passage.
Like men who sit at meat the mountains
settled: by thee, Most Wise ! the regions
were made steadfast.

4 This is the truth, none else is like thee,
Indra, no God superior to thee, no
mortal.
Thou slewest Ahi who besieged the waters,
and lettest loose the streams to hurry
seaward.

5 Indra, thou breakest up the floods and
portals on all sides, and the firmness of
the mountain.
Thou art the King of men, of all that
liveth, engendering at once Sun, Heaven,
and Morning.

HYMN XXXI.   *Indra.*

1. SOLE Lord of wealth art thou, O Lord
of riches : thou in thine hands hast held
the people, Indra !
Men have invoked thee with contending
voices for seed and waters, progeny
and sunlight.

2 Through fear of thee, O Indra, all the
regions of earth, though naught may
move them, shake and tremble.
All that is firm is frightened at thy coming,—the earth, the heaven, the mountain, and the forest.

3 With Kutsa, Indra ! thou didst conquer
Śuṣṇa, voracious, bane of crops, in
fight for cattle.

---

5 *The Prince* : Indra appears to be meant. *Driving...
his flocks* : cp. I. 10. 2. 'And the Ram hastens with
his troop,' that is, Indra comes with his band of Maruts.
Sāyaṇa takes *sūriḥ* in its more usual signification of worshipper or institutor of the sacrifice ; and Professor
Wilson translates : 'the pious worshipper, hastening
(to sacrifice), and earnestly performing worship, gratifies
thee with the offering, as (the cowkeeper satisfies) the
herds with water.'

6 *Helper unaided* : this seems to be the meaning of
ūti dnūti, with help that needs no other help. Sāyaṇa
explains the words, 'by coming or by not coming,'
whether he be present or absent.

Golden-visored : 'Azure-chinned.'—Wilson. 'With
yellow-coloured jaws.'—Ludwig. I have followed Professor Roth.

---

1 Indra hath grown stronger and stronger for the
performance of his mighty deeds.

3 *Like men who sit at meat* : or, perhaps, like flies
who settle on food. See Geldner, Vedische Studien,
II. 180.

---

1 *Men......with contending voices* : the combatants on
both sides invoke Indra's aid in battle.
According to Prof. Pischel, *Vedische Studien,* I. 34,
the meaning is as follows : —
Alone wast thou, Lord of all wealth and riches, yet
hast thou made the folk submissive, Indra,
When with uplifted voice the tribes invoked thee
for water, sons, posterity and sunlight.'
'The folk,' *kṛṣṭih* meaning the speaker's enemies,
and 'the tribes, *carṣaṇáyo*, meaning the five Āryan
tribes.

3 *Kutsa* : the special favourite of Indra. *Bane of
crops* : or Kuyava may be the name of another demon
of drought or savage enemy. See Index. *Thou rentest*

In the close fray thou rentest him : thou stolest the Sun's wheel and didst drive away misfortunes.

4 Thou smotest to the ground the hundred castles, impregnable, of Śambara the Dasyu,
When, Strong, with might thou holpest Divodāsa who poured libations out, O Soma-buyer, and madest Bharadvāja rich who praised thee.

5 As such, true Hero, for great joy of battle mount thy terrific car, O Brave and Manly.
Come with thine help to me, thou distant Roamer, and, glorious God, spread among men my glory.

HYMN XXXII. *Indra.*

1. I WITH my lips have fashioned for this Hero words never matched, most plentiful and auspicious,
For him the Ancient, Great, Strong, Energetic, the very mighty Wielder of the Thunder.

2 Amid the sages, with the Sun he brightened the Parents : glorified, he burst the mountain;
And, roaring with the holy-thoughted singers, he loosed the bond that held the beams of Morning.

3 Famed for great deeds, with priests who kneel and laud him, he still hath conquered in the frays for cattle,
And broken down the forts, the Fort-destroyer, a Friend with friends, a Sage among the sages.

4 Come with thy girthed mares, with abundant vigour and plenteous strength to him who sings thy praises.
Come hither, borne by mares with many heroes, Lover of song ! Steer ! for the people's welfare.

5 Indra with rush and might, sped by his Coursers, hath swiftly won the waters from the southward.
Thus set at liberty the rivers daily flow to their goal, incessant and exhaustless.

HYMN XXXIII. *Indra.*

1. GIVE us the rapture that is mightiest, Indra, prompt to bestow and swift to aid, O Hero,
That wins with brave steeds where brave steeds encounter, and quells the Vṛtras and the foes in battle.

2 For with loud voice the tribes invoke thee, Indra, to aid them in the battle-field of heroes.
Thou, with the singers, hast pierced through the Paṇis : the charger whom thou aidest wins the booty.

3 Both races, Indra, of opposing foemen, O Hero, both the Ārya and the Dāsa,
Hast thou struck down like woods with well-shot lightnings : thou rentest them in fight, most manly Chieftain !

4 Indra, befriend us with no scanty succour, prosper and aid us, Loved of all that liveth,
When, fighting for the sunlight, we invoke thee, O Hero, in the fray, in war's division.

5 Be ours, O Indra, now and for the future, be graciously inclined and near to help us.
Thus may we, singing, sheltered by the Mighty, win many cattle on the day of trial.

HYMN XXXIV. *Indra.*

1. FULL many songs have met in thee, O Indra, and many a noble thought from thee proceedeth.
Now and of old the eulogies of sages, their

---

him : literally, 'bittest' : *ddśa*, according to Sāyaṇa, standing for *adaśaḥ*. *Stolest the Sun's wheel* : see I. 175. 4.

Misfortunes : according to Sāyaṇa, 'disturbing or injurious Rākṣasas, etc.

4 *The hundred castles* : probably the castles of cloud which retain the rain. So, II. 19. 6, 'And Indra, for the sake of Divodāsa, demolished Śambara's nine-and-ninety castles '

4 *Soma-buyer* : purchaser of Soma-libations with the help which he gives to the worshipper.

———

2 *He brightened the Parents* : illuminated the universal parents, Heaven and Earth. *The sages* : the Aṅgirases, *the holy-thoughted singers* of the next line.

4 *With thy girthed mares* : the meaning of *nīvyābhiḥ*, a feminine plural adjective in the instrumental case, standing without a substantive, is uncertain. Sāyaṇa

explains the word by *navyābhirnavatarābhiḥ*, 'very new or young,' and supplies *vaḍavābhiḥ*, 'mares.' Professor Roth thinks that *nīvyābhiḥ* may be a substantive meaning 'with garments,' and Professor Grassmann translates 'mit Gaben,' 'with gifts,' that is, presents carried in a *nīvi* or apron. *With many heroes* : *puruvīrābhiḥ* again is an adjective without a substantive, in the same gender, number, and case as *nīvyābhiḥ*. According to Sāyaṇa, it also qualifies *vaḍavābhiḥ*, 'with mares,' understood, and means 'having many colts.'

5 *From the southward* : from the quarter whence the Rains come.

———

1 *Give us the rapture* : let us be benefited by the transport which draughts of Soma juice produce in thee.

———

holy hymns and lauds, have yearned
for Indra.

2 He, praised of many, bold, invoked of
many, alone is glorified at sacrifices.
Like a car harnessed for some great
achievement, Indra must be the cause
of our rejoicing.

3 They make their way to Indra and exalt
him, him whom no prayers and no
laudations trouble;
For when a hundred or a thousand singers
laud him who loves the song their praise
delights him.

4 As brightness mingles with the Moon in
heaven, the offered Soma yearns to mix
with Indra.
Like water brought to men in desert places,
our gifts at sacrifice have still refreshed
him.

5 To him this mighty eulogy, to Indra hath
this our laud been uttered by the poets,
That in the great encounter with the
foemen, Loved of all life, Indra may
guard and help us.

HYMN XXXV.   *Indra.*

1. WHEN shall our prayers rest in thy car
beside thee ? When dost thou give the
singer food for thousands?
When wilt thou clothe this poet's laud
with plenty, and when wilt thou enrich
our hymns with booty ?

2 When wilt thou gather men with men, O
Indra, heroes with heroes, and prevail
in combat ?
Thou shalt win triply kine in frays for
cattle, so, Indra, give thou us celestial
glory.

---

3 *They make their way* : that is, prayers and laudations reach Indra and strengthen him. They do not
vex him as they would vex a man who would be
unable to fulfil the prayers and would be conscious
that he did not deserve the laudations.

4 *As brightness mingles with the Moon* : I follow
Professor Ludwig in his interpretation of this difficult
passage; but its exact meaning still seems doubtful.
'*Arcā* is the nominative singular. We have here the
later Jyotsnā or Kaumudī as the wife or feminine
power of the Moon. Sūryā, the daughter of the Sun,
i. e. the Moon's lght which is borrowed from the Sun
is an earlier conception.'—Ludwig.

5 *By the poets* : by those who sing hymns of praise.
Matibhiḥ=stotṛbhiḥ—Sāyaṇa. *In the great encounter with
the foemen*: *mahati vṛtratūrye* : in the great victory over
Vṛtra : that is, generally, in battle with enemies ;
saṅgrāme.—Sāyaṇa.

---

1 *Rest in thy car beside thee* ? : when shall our prayers
reach thee as thou standest on thy chariot ? The poet
expresses impatience at Indra's inattention to his petitions.

3 Yea, when wilt thou, O Indra, thou Most
Mighty, make the prayer all-sustaining
for the singer?
When wilt thou yoke, as we yoke songs,
thy Horses, and come to offerings that
bring wealth in cattle ?

4 Grant to the Singer food with store of
cattle, splendid with horses and the
fame of riches.
Send food to swell the milch-cow good at
milking : bright be its shine among the
Bharadvājas.

5 Lead otherwise this present foeman, Śakra!
Hence art thou praised as Hero, foe-
destroyer
Him who gives pure gifts may I praise
unceasing. Sage, quicken the Āṅgirases
by devotion.

HYMN XXXVI.   *Indra.*

1. THY raptures ever were for all men's profit:
so evermore have been thine earthly
riches.
Thou still hast been the dealer-forth of
vigour, since among Gods thou hast
had power and Godhead.

2 Men have obtained his strength by sacrificing, and ever urged him on to hero
valour.

---

5 I find this stanza hopelessly obscure, and do not
attempt to translate it, giving instead of a conjectural
translation a reproduction of the substance of Sāyaṇa's
absolutely worthless paraphrase. *Lead otherwise* : according to Sāyaṇa, 'consign to death, to a course different
from that of living beings.'—Wilson.

The Āṅgirases : the descendants of Aṅgirases, that
is the Bharadvājas.

Professor Ludwig translates : 'Also at another time
(I wish) hither this strong (defence), when thou as a
hero, Śakra, singest open [aufsingst] the doors; may I
never lose the cow that yields bright juice , cause thou
her to hasten through the prayer of the Āṅgirases. In
his Commentary Prof. Ludwig alters 'lose the cow,
etc.' into 'lose the seed-pouring (bull) of the milch-cow.'
Professor Aufrecht would read *vrijanam* instead of
vṛjanam and *vṛṇiṣe* instead of *gṛṇiṣe*, and Prof. Grassmann
translates accordingly : 'Now too, as formerly, I choose
for myself this man, when, Strong One, as hero thou
openest the doors. Never then may the steer whose seed
streams fail me. Quicken, O Sage, the singers through
prayer.'

---

1 *Thy raptures* : produced by drinking the Soma
juice. *Power and Godhead* : *asuryám* : Asura-hood, the
nature and power of an Asura or High God. Some
give a different meaning to *dhāráyathāḥ* : 'thou maintainest
vigour among the gods.'—Wilson. 'Indra is said to give
divine power to the other gods.'—Muir, *O. S. T.*, V. 92.

2 *His strength* : the powerful aid of Indra. *Charger* :
Indra, impetuous as a war-horse who takes the bit
between his teeth. Sāyaṇa explains *syūma gṛbhe* : as
'seizer of enemies who are in uninterrupted lines'. 'They
offer sacrifices to him as seizer of an uninterrupted series

For the rein-seizing, the impetuous Charger
they furnished power even for Vṛtra's
slaughter.

3 Associate with him, as teams of horses,
help, manly might, and vigour follow
Indra.

As rivers reach the sea, so, strong with
praises, our holy songs reach him the
Comprehensive.

4 Lauded by us, let flow the spring, O
Indra, of excellent and brightly-shining
riches.

For thou art Lord of men, without an
equal : of all the world thou art the
only Sovran.

5 Hear what thou mayst hear, thou who,
fain for worship, as heaven girds earth,
guardest thy servant's treasure;

That thou mayst be our own, joying in
power, famed through thy might in
every generation.

HYMN XXXVII   *Indra.*

1. LET thy Bay Horses, yoked, O mighty
Indra, bring thy car hither fraught
with every blessing.

For thee, the Heavenly, e'en the poor
invoketh : may we this day, thy feast-
companions, prosper.

2 Forth to the vat the brown drops flow for
service, and purified proceed directly
forward.

May Indra drink of this, our guest aforetime, Celestial King of the strong
draught of Soma.

3 Bringing us hitherward all-potent Indra
on well-wheeled chariot, may the Steeds
who bear him

Convey him on the road direct to glory,
and ne'er may Vāyu's Amṛta cease and
fail him.

4 Supreme, he stirs this man to give the

guerdon,—Indra, most efficacious of the
princes,—

Wherewith, O Thunderer, thou removest
sorrow, and, Bold One ! partest wealth
among the nobles.

5 Indra is he who gives enduring vigour :
may our songs magnify the God Most
Mighty.

Best Vṛtra-slayer be the Hero Indra :
these things he gives as Prince, with
strong endeavour.

HYMN XXXVIII.   *Indra.*

1. HE hath drunk hence, Most Marvellous,
and carried away our great and splendid
call on Indra.

The Bounteous, when we serve the Gods,
accepteth song yet more famous and the
gifts we bring him.

2 The speaker filleth with a cry to Indra his
ears who cometh nigh e'en from a
distance.

May this my call bring Indra to my
presence, this call to Gods composed in
sacred verses.

3 Him have I sung with my best song and
praises, Indra of ancient birth and
Everlasting.

For prayer and songs in him are concentrated : let laud wax mighty when
addressed to Indra :

4 Indra, whom sacrifice shall strengthen,
Soma, and song and hymn, and praises
and devotion,

Whom Dawns shall strengthen when the
night departeth, Indra whom days shall
strengthen, months, and autumns.

5 Him, born for conquering might in full
perfection, and waxen strong for bounty
and for glory,

Great, Powerful, will we to-day, O singer,
invite to aid us and to quell our foemen.

---

of foes, their assailant, their subduer, and also for the
destruction of Vṛtra.—Wilson.

---

1 *Thee, the Heavenly* : svarvān appears to apply to
tvā, thee, Indra, and to stand for svarvantam. See
Pischel, *Vedische Studien*, I. 198, 218.

3 *To glory* : 'to the prize of battle.'—Grassmann.
'To our rite.'—Wilson.

Vāyu's Amṛta : 'Vāyu is possessor of the Amṛta
probably as being Tvaṣṭar's son-in-law. VIII. 26. 21.
—Ludwig.

4 *This man* : the institutor of the sacrifice. *Wherewith* : on account of which guerdon. The liberal
guerdon given by the nobles who defray the expenses of
the sacrifice causes Indra in his turn to be gracious and
liberal of his gifts to them.

---

5 *With strong endeavour* : exerting his power on
behalf of his worshippers.

---

1 *He hath drunk hence* : Professor Ludwig thinks that
the first line must refer to Agni, who receives the
libation *hence*, that is, from the priest's cup, and conveys to Indra the invocation addressed to him. But
Indra himself may be intended in the first line as well
as in the second.

3 *Let laud wax mighty* : when the power of Indra is
celebrated, the song should be lofty as the dignity of
the subject demands.

5 *To quell our foemen* : or, to conquer Vṛtras, that
is, Vṛtra and similar fiends.

HYMN XXXIX   *Indra.*

1. Of this our charming, our celestial Soma,
   eloquent,   wise,   Priest,   with inspired
   devotion,
   Of this thy close attendant, hast thou
   drunken. God, send the singer food with
   milk to grace it.

2 Craving the kine, rushing against the
   mountain led on by Law, with holy-
   minded comrades,
   He broke the never-broken ridge of Vala.
   With words of might Indra subdued
   the Paṇis..

3 This Indu lighted darksome nights, O
   Indra, throughout the years, at morning
   and at evening.
   Him have they stablished as the days'
   bright ensign. He made the Mornings
   to be born in splendour.

4 He shone and caused to shine the worlds
   that shone not. By Law he lighted up
   the host of Mornings.
   He moves with Steeds yoked by eternal
   Order, contenting men with nave that
   finds the sunlight.

5 Now, praised, O Ancient King ! fill thou
   the singer with plenteous food that he
   may deal forth treasures.
   Give waters, herbs that have no poison,
   forests, and kine, and steeds, and men,
   to him who lauds thee.

HYMN XL.   *Indra*

1. Drink, Indra ; juice is shed to make thee
   joyful : loose thy Bay Steeds and give
   thy friends their freedom.
   Begin the song, seated in our assembly.
   Give strength for sacrifice to him who
   singeth.

2 Drink thou of this whereof at birth,
   O Indra, thou drankest, Mighty One !
   for power and rapture.

---

1 *Our celestial Soma* : as Professor Wilson observes,
'Several of the epithets in the text are unusual, and
agreeably to European notions, very inapplicable to a
beverage.' The Soma is called *eloquent* and *wise* as giving
eloquence and wisdom, and *priest* because it is employed
in offerings to the Gods.
   With milk to grace it : that is, of which milk and
butter constitute the most excellent part.
   2 *Holy-minded comrades* : the Aṅgirases. *Vala* : a
demon who stole away the cows of the Gods, *i. e.* the
rays of light. See Index.
   3 *This Indu* : Indu is here the Moon, which is
identified with Soma.
   The days' bright ensign : the standard by which time
is measured.
   4 *Nave* : used by synecdoche for chariot.

---

1 *Thy friends* : thy dear horses.

The men, the pressing-stones, the cows,
the waters have made this Soma ready
for thy drinking.

3 The fire is kindled, Soma pressed, O Indra:
let thy Bays, best to draw, convey
thee hither.
With mind devoted, Indra, I invoke thee.
Come, for our great prosperity approach
us.

4 Indra, come hither : evermore thou camest
through our great strong desire to drink
the Soma.
Listen and hear the prayers which now
we offer, and let this sacrifice increase
thy vigour.

5 Mayst thou, O Indra, on the day of trial,
present or absent, wheresoe'er thou
dwellest,
Thence, with thy team, accordant with
the Maruts, Song-lover ! guard our
sacrifice, to help us.

HYMN XLI.   *Indra.*

1. Come gracious to our sacrifice, O Indra :
   pressed Soma-drops are purified to ple ase
   thee.
   As cattle seek their home, so, Thunder-
   wielder, come, Indra, first of those who
   claim our worship.

2 With that well-formed most wide-extending
   palate, wherewith thou ever drinkest
   streams of sweetness,
   Drink thou; the Adhvaryu standeth up
   before thee : let thy spoil-winning
   thunderbolt attend thee.

3 This drop, steer-strong and omniform, the
   Soma, hath been made ready for
   the Bull, for Indra.
   Drink this, Lord of the Bays, thou Strong
   Supporter, this that is thine of old, thy
   food for ever.

4 Soma when pressed excels the unpressed
   Soma, better, for one who knows, to
   give him pleasure.
   Come to this sacrifice of ours, O Victor :
   replenish all thy powers with this
   libation.

---

1 *Gracious* : more   literally, 'without anger'.
'Unirascible.'—Wilson.
   2 *The Adhvaryu* : the ministering priest.
   3 *Supporter* : *sthātar*=Stator in Jupiter Stator, one
who causes to stay or stand, rallier of men in battle.
   4 *Replenish all thy powers* : or, 'give us all powers in
full.'

5 We call on thee, O Indra : come thou
hither : sufficient be the Soma for thy
body.
Rejoice thee, Śatakratu ! in the juices :
guard us in wars, guard us among our
people.

HYMN XLII. *Indra.*

1. Bring sacrificial gifts to him, Omniscient,
for he longs to drink,
The Wanderer who comes with speed, the
Hero ever in the van.

2 With Soma go ye nigh to him chief drinker
of the Soma's juice :
With beakers to the Impetuous God, to
Indra with the drops effused.

3 What time, with Soma, with the juice
effused, ye come before the God,
Full wise he knows the hope of each, and,
Bold One, strikes this foe and that.

4 To him, Adhvaryu ! yea, to him give
offerings of the juice expressed.
Will he not keep us safely from the
spiteful curse of each presumptuous
high-born foe ?

HYMN XLIII. *Indra.*

1. In whose wild joy thou madest once
Śambara Divodāsa's prey,
This Soma is pressed out for thee, O
Indra : drink !

2 Whose gladdening draught, shed from the
points, thou guardest in the midst and
end,
This Soma is pressed out for thee, O Indra :
drink !

3 In whose wild joy thou settest free the kine
held fast within the rock,
This Soma is pressed out for thee, O
Indra : drink !

4 This, in whose juice delighting thou gainest
the might of Maghavan,
This Soma is pressed out for thee, O Indra :
drink !

HYMN XLIV. *Indra.*

1. That which is wealthiest, Wealthy God !
in splendours most illustrious,
Soma is pressed : thy gladdening draught,
Indra ! libation's Lord ! is this.

2 Effectual, Most Effectual One ! thine, as
bestowing wealth of hymns,
Soma is pressed : thy gladdening draught,
Indra ! libation's Lord ! is this.

3 Wherewith thou art increased in strength,
and conquerest with thy proper aids,
Soma is pressed : thy gladdening draught,
Indra ! libation's Lord ! is this.

4 Him for your sake I glorify as Lord of
Strength who wrongeth none,
The Hero Indra, conquering all, Most
Bounteous, God of all the tribes.

5 Those Goddesses, both Heaven and Earth,
revere the power and might of him,
Him whom our songs increase in strength,
the Lord of bounty swift to come.

6 To seat your Indra, I will spread abroad
with power this song of praise.
The saving succours that abide in him, like
songs, extend and grow.

7 A recent Friend, he found the skilful
priest : he drank, and showed forth
treasure from the Gods.
He conquered, borne by strong all-shaking
mares, and was with far-spread power his
friends' Protector.

8 In course of Law the sapient juice was
quaffed : the Deities to glory turned
their mind.
Winning through hymns a lofty title, he,

---

3 *Strikes this foe and that* : there is no substantive
in the text. Sāyana makes *tám tam* refer to *kāmam*,
hope or wish : 'And the suppressor (of enemies)
assuredly grants it, whatever it may be '—Wilson.

1 *Śambara* : a demon of draught. *Divodāsa* : called
also Atithigva : 'Thou savedst Kutsa when Śusna was
smitten down ; to Atithigva gavest Śambara for a prey.'
—I. 51. 6.

2 *From the points* : from the sharp ends of the
branchlets of the plant. See Hillebrandt, V. Mythologie, p. 232. *In the midst and end* : according to
Sāyana, at noon and at the evening libation.

---

4 *Gainest the might of Maghavan* : Indra acquires
his power from libations of Soma juice.

---

6 *To seat your Indra* : as Indra's seat is on the
barhis or sacred grass that is spread on the floor of the
chamber of sacrifice, so the hymn also, as his spiritual
seat, is supposed to have the power of inducing him
to come.

7 *He found the skilful priest* : 'Indra appreciates him
who is skilled (in holy rites),'—Wilson. The word
yaṣṭāram, sacrificer, is supplied by Sāyana.

Borne by strong, all-shaking mares : this is Sāyana's
first explanation of *staulābhir dhantáribhih*, two feminine
plurals in the instrumental case, *vadavābhih*, 'with
mares, being understood. Brought by his robust
agitators (of the earth, his steeds).'—Wilson. Or, Sāyana
says, although the words are feminine, the Maruts
may be intended. Other conjectural explanations have
been attempted, but they are not convincing.

the Lovely, made his beauteous form apparent.

9 Bestow on us the most illustrious strength : ward off men's manifold malignities.
Give with thy might abundant vital force, and aid us graciously in gaining riches.

10 We turn to thee as Giver, liberal Indra. Lord of the Bay Steeds, be not thou ungracious.
No friend among mankind have we to look to : why have men called thee him who spurs the niggard ?

11 Give us not up, Strong Hero ! to the hungry : unharmed be we whom thou, so rich, befriendest.
Full many a boon hast thou for men : demolish those who present no gifts nor pour oblations.

12 As Indra thundering impels the rain-clouds, so doth he send us store of kine and horses.
Thou art of old the Cherisher of singers : let not the rich who bring no gifts deceive thee.

13 Adhvaryu, hero, bring to mighty Indra— for he is King thereof—the pressed-out juices ;
To him exalted by the hymns and praises, ancient and modern, of the singing Ṛṣis.

14 In the wild joy of this hath Indra, knowing full many a form, struck down resistless Vṛtras.
Proclaim aloud to him the savoury Soma so that the Hero, strong of jaw, may drink it.

15 May Indra drink this Soma poured to please him, and cheered therewith slay Vṛtra with his thunder.
Come to our sacrifice even from a distance, good lover of our songs, the bard's Supporter.

16 The cup whence Indra drinks the draught is present : the Amṛta dear to Indra hath been drunken,
That it may cheer the God to gracious favour, and keep far from us hatred and affliction.

17 Therewith enraptured, Hero, slay our foemen, the unfriendly, Maghavan ! be they kin or strangers,
Those who still aim their hostile darts to smite us, turn them to flight, O Indra, crush and kill them.

18 O Indra Maghavan, in these our battles win easy paths for us and ample freedom.
That we may gain waters and seed and offspring, set thou our princes on thy side, O Indra.

19 Let thy Bay Stallions, harnessed, bring thee hither, Steeds with strong chariot and strong reins to hold them,
Strong Horses, speeding hither, bearing thunder, well-harnessed, for the strong exciting potion.

20 Beside the vat, Strong God ! stand thy strong Horses, shining with holy oil, like waves exulting.
Indra, they bring to thee, the Strong and Mighty, Soma of juices shed by mighty press-stones.

21 Thou art the Bull of earth, the Bull of heaven, Bull of the rivers, Bull of standing waters.
For thee, the Strong, O Bull, hath Indu swollen. juice pleasant, sweet to drink, for thine election.

22 This God, with might, when first he had his being, with Indra for ally, held fast the Paṇi.
This Indu stole away the warlike weapons, and foiled the arts of his malignant father.

23 The Dawns he wedded to a glorious Consort, and set within the Sun the light that lights him.

---

10 *Who spurs the niggard* : urges even the niggardly to be liberal. See Pischel, *Vedische Studien*, I. p. 124.

12 *The Cherisher of singers* : or, 'he whom the singers nourish, that is, strengthen by their hymns.

14 *Knowing full many a form* : detecting and not deceived by the various forms assumed by the demon Vṛtra and his crew.

15 *The bard's Supporter* : or, 'whom singers nourish,' as in stanza 12.

19 In this and the two following stanzas we have the repetition, so dear to some of the Vedic poets, of *vṛṣa* in composition, *vṛṣan* and *vṛṣabhá*, so commonly applied in the hymns to living beings and things preëminent for strength.

22 *This God* : Indu or Soma, the Moon. *Of his malignant father* : Tvaṣṭar appears to be meant. Sāyaṇa's paraphrase is non-natural : 'of the malignant secreter of (the stolen) wealth, (the cattle).'—Wilson. Sāyaṇa makes *pituh*, as derived from *pā*, to protect,= *pālayituḥ*, 'the safe keeper, and *svásya*=Lat. *sui*, 'of his property. This safe keeper, secreter, and robber would be the demon Vala.

23 *Glorious Consort* : the Sun. *In the third lucid regions* : perhaps, as Professor Ludwig suggests, in the spheres of the Sun, the Moon, and the stars. 'According to the scholiast, this may merely mean that the Soma becomes as it were ambrosia when received or concealed in the vessels at the three diurnal ceremonies, which ambrosia is properly deposited with the gods

He found in heaven, in the third lucid regions, the threefold Amṛta in its close concealment.

24 He stayed and held the heaven and earth asunder : the chariot with the seven-fold reins he harnessed.
This Soma set with power within the milch-kine a spring whose ripe contents ten fingers empty.

HYMN XLV. *Indra.*

1. THAT Indra is our youthful Friend, who with his trusty guidance led
Turvaśa, Yadu from afar.

2 Even to the dull and uninspired Indra gives vital power, and wins
Even with slow steed the offered prize.

3 Great are his ways of guiding us, and manifold are his eulogies :
His kind protections never fail.

4 Friends, sing your psalm and offer praise to him to whom the prayer is brought:
For our great Providence is he.

5 Thou, Slaughterer of Vṛtra, art Guardian and Friend of one and two,
Yea, of a man like one of us.

6 Beyond men's hate thou leadest us, and givest cause to sing thy praise :
Good Hero art thou called by men.

7 I call with hymns, as 'twere a cow to milk, the Friend who merits praise,
The Brahman who accepts the prayer.

8 Him in whose hands they say are stored all treasures from the days of old,
The Hero, conquering in the fight.

9 Lord of Strength, Caster of the Stone, destroy the firm forts built by men,
And foil their arts, unbending God !

10 Thee, thee as such, O Lord of Power, O Indra, Soma-drinker, true,

We, fain for glory, have invoked.

11 Such as thou wast of old, and art now to be called on when the prize
Lies ready, listen to our call.

12 With hymns and coursers we will gain, Indra, through thee, both steeds and spoil
Most glorious, and the proffered prize.

13 Thou, Indra, Lover of the Song, whom men must stir to help, hast been
Great in the contest for the prize.

14 Slayer of foes, whatever aid of thine imparts the swiftest course,
With that impel our car to speed.

15 As skilfullest of those who drive the chariot, with our art and aim,
O Conqueror, win the proffered prize.

16 Praise him who, Matchless and Alone, was born the Lord of living men,
Most active, with heroic soul.

17 Thou who hast been the singers' Friend, a Friend auspicious with thine aid,
As such, O Indra, favour us.

18 Grasp in thine arms the thunderbolt, O Thunder-armed, to slay the fiends :
Mayst thou subdue the foemen's host.

19 I call the ancient Friend, allied with wealth, who speeds the lowly man,
Him to whom chiefly prayer is brought.

20 For he alone is Lord of all the treasures of the earth : he speeds
Hither, chief Lover of the Song.

21 So with thy yoked teams satisfy our wish with power and wealth in steeds
And cattle, boldly, Lord of kine !

22 Sing this, what time the juice is pressed, to him your Hero, Much-invoked,
To please him as a mighty Steer.

23 He, Excellent, withholdeth not his gift of power and wealth in kine,
When he hath listened to our songs.

24 May he with might unclose for us the cow's stall, whosesoe'er it be,
To which the Dasyu-slayer goes.

25 O Indra Śatakratu, these our songs have called aloud to thee,
Like mother cows to meet their calves.

abiding in the third bright sphere, or in heaven.—Wilson.

24 *The chariot* : of the Sun, drawn by seven horses. *Whose ripe contents ten fingers empty* : this appears to be the meaning of the *pakvám dáṣayantram utsam* of the text, literally, 'the ripe spring with ten engines.' 'The mature deeply-organized secretion.'—Wilson.

1 *Turvaśa, Yadu* : the names of these two eponymi of Āryan tribes are frequently associated. See Index. An expedition against Divodāsa appears to be referred to.

2 *Even to the dull and uninspired* : he favours whom he will, and the race is not always to the swift.

7 *As 'twere a cow to milk* : like the cow that is brought to give the milk that is to be mingled with the Soma libation. *The Brahman* : Indra regarded as a Priest.

11 *When the prize lies ready* : to be given to the victor in the chariot race, the chief object of the hymn being to secure victory in the approaching contest through the favour of the God.

24 *Whosesoe'er it be* ; the meaning of *kuvitsasya* here is somewhat uncertain. Sāyaṇa explains it as, of Kuvitsa, a certain person who does much harm. The meaning appears to be, may Indra open for us the cow-stall and give us the cattle of any Dasyu whom he, that is, we under his guidance, may attack.

26 Hard is thy love to win : thou art a Steer
    to him who longs for steers :
    Be to one craving steeds a Steed.

27 Delight thee with the juice we pour for
    thine own great munificence :
    Yield not thy singer to reproach.

28 These songs with every draught we pour
    come, Lover of the Song, to thee,
    As milch-kine hasten to their young :

29 To thee most oft invoked, amid the many
    singers' rivalry
    Who beg with all their might for wealth.

30 Nearest and most attractive may our laud,
    O Indra, come to thee.
    Urge thou us on to ample wealth.

31 Bṛbu hath set himself above the Paṇis,
    o'er their highest head,
    Like the wide bush on Gaṅgā's bank.

32 He whose good bounty, thousandfold, swift
    as the rushing of the wind,
    Suddenly offers as a gift.

33 So all our singers ever praise the pious
    Bṛbu's noble deed,
    Chief, best to give his thousands, best to
    give a thousand liberal gifts.

HYMN XLVI. *Indra.*

1. THAT we may win us wealth and power
    we poets, verily, call on thee :
    In war men call on thee, Indra, the hero's
    Lord, in the steed's race-course call on
    thee.

26 *Thou art a Steer* : *gavām pradātā,*, 'a giver of
cattle.'—Sāyaṇa. *A Steed* : *aśvapradaḥ,* a giver of
horses.—Sāyaṇa.

27 This stanza is repeated, word for word, from III.
41. 6.

31 *Bṛbu* : according to Sāyaṇa, the carpenter or
artificer of the Paṇis.

The Paṇis here are, in accordance with the original
meaning of the words, merchants or traders, and the
merchant Bṛbu is eulogized for his piety and liberality,
qualities which were not the usual characteristics of the
class to which he belonged. A legend, referred to by
Sāyaṇa, and recorded in the *Mānava-dharma-śāstra* or
Laws of Manu, 10. 107, relates that Bharadvāja, when
distressd by hunger in a lonely forest, accepted many
cows from the carpenter Bṛbu ; the moral being that
men of inferior caste and low condition may distinguish
themselves by their liberality. See Wilson's Note, Vol.
III. p. 466. *The wide bush* : the belt of underwood.
Others would read *uruukakṣaḥ* as one word instead of
uruh kākṣaḥ, and explain it as the name of a man, son
of a woman called Gaṅgā.

33 *Chief* : *sūri,* as institutor of the sacrifice. See,
on stanzas 31—33, Prof. Weber's Episches im vedischen
Ritual (Sitzungsberichte der K. P. Akademie der
Wissenschaften, XXXVIII. pp. 28 sqq.), and M.
Müller, Chips from a German Workshop, IV. 138
(new edition).

2 As such, O Wonderful, whose hand holds
    thunder, praised as mighty, Caster of
    the Stone !
    Pour on us boldly, Indra, kine and chariot-
    steeds, ever to be the conqueror's
    strength.

3 We call upon that Indra, who, most active,
    ever slays the foe :
    Lord of the brave, Most Manly, with a
    thousand powers, help thou and prosper
    us in fight.

4 Ṛcīṣama, thou forcest men as with a bull,
    with anger, in the furious fray.
    Be thou our Helper in the mighty battle
    fought for sunlight, water, and for life.

5 O Indra, bring us name and fame, enrich-
    ing, mightiest, excellent,
    Wherewith, O Wondrous God, fair-visored,
    thunder-armed, thou hast filled full this
    earth and heaven.

6 We call on thee, O King, Mighty amid
    the Gods, Ruler of men, to succour us.
    All that is weak in us, Excellent God,
    make firm: make our foes easy to subdue.

7 All strength and valour that is found,
    Indra, in tribes of Nahuṣas, and all
    the splendid fame that the Five Tribes
    enjoy
    Bring, yea, all manly powers at once.

8 Or, Maghavan, what vigorous strength in
    Tṛkṣi lay, in Druhyus or in Pūru's folk,
    Fully bestow on us, that, in the conquer-
    ing fray, we may subdue our foes in
    fight.

9 O Indra, grant a happy home, a triple
    refuge triply strong.
    Bestow a dwelling-place on the rich lords
    and me, and keep thy dart afar from
    these.

3 *With a thousand powers* : *sáhasramuṣka,* literally,
mille testiculos habens. The reading of the Sāmaveda,
sáhasramanyu, full of boundless ardour, is, as Professor
Ludwig remarks, much more aesthetic.

4 *Ṛcīṣama* : or, worthy of praise ! But the exact
meaning of the epithet is somewhat uncertain.

5 *Fair-visored* : or, fair of cheek.

7 *Nahuṣas* : people, apparently distinct from the
five Āryan tribes *par excellence,* and dwellers on or near
the Indus. According to Sāyaṇa, human beings in
general and men, and Professor Roth explains the
word as men generally, but with the special sense of
stranger, or neighbour. See Muir, *O.S. Texts,* I. 179,
180.

8 *Tṛkṣi* : a king so named, says Sāyaṇa. In
another place (VIII. 22. 7) he has the patronymic
Trāsadasyava, son i. e. peer of, Trasadasyu. *In Druhyus*
or *in Pūru's folk* : literally, 'in Druhyu or in Pūru,' the
names of the eponymi of these tribes being used for the
tribes themselves.

10 They who with minds intent on spoil
subdue the foe, boldly attack and smite
him down,—
From these, O Indra Maghavan who
lovest song, be closest guardian of our
lives.

11 And now, O Indra, strengthen us : come
near and aid us in the fight,
What time the feathered shafts are flying
in the air, the arrows with their sharpened points.

12 Give us, where heroes strain their bodies
in the fight, the shelter that our fathers
loved.
To us and to our sons give refuge : keep
afar all unobserved hostility.

13 When, Indra, in the mighty fray thou
urgest chargers to their speed,
On the uneven road and on a toilsome
path, like falcons, eager for renown,

14 Speeding like rivers rushing down a steep
descent, responsive to the urging call,
That come like birds attracted to the
bait, held in by reins in both the
driver's hands.

HYMN XLVII. *Indra, Etc.*

1. YEA, this is good to taste and full of
sweetness, verily it is strong and rich
in flavour.
No one may conquer Indra in the battle
when he hath drunken of the draught
we offer.

2 This sweet juice here had mightiest power
to gladden : it boldened Indra when
he slaughtered Vṛtra,
When he defeated Śambara's many
onslaughts, and battered down his nine-
and ninety ramparts.

3 This stirreth up my voice when I have
drunk it : this hath aroused from sleep
my yearning spirit.
This Sage hath measured out the six
expanses from which no single creature
is excluded.

4 This, even this, is he who hath created
the breadth of earth, the lofty height of
heaven.

He formed the nectar in three headlong
rivers. Soma supports the wide mid-air
above us.

5 He found the wavy sea of brilliant colours
in forefront of the Dawns who dwell in
brightness.
This Mighty One, the Steer begirt by
Maruts, hath propped the heavens up
with a mighty pillar.

6 Drink Soma boldly from the beaker, Indra,
in war for treasures, Hero, Vṛtra-slayer !
Fill thyself full at the mid-day libation,
and give us wealth, thou Treasury of
riches.

7 Look out for us, O Indra, as our Leader,
and guide us on to gain yet goodlier
treasure.
Excellent Guardian, bear us well through
peril, and lead us on to wealth with
careful guidance.

8 Lead us to ample room, O thou who
knowest, to happiness, security, and
sunlight.
High, Indra, are the arms of thee the
Mighty : may we betake us to their lofty
shelter.

9 Set us on widest chariot-seat, O Indra,
with two steeds best to draw, O Lord
of Hundreds !
Bring us the best among all sorts of viands :
let not the foe's wealth, Maghavan,
subdue us.

10 Be gracious, Indra, let my days be
lengthened : sharpen my thought as
'twere a blade of iron
Approve whatever words I speak, dependent on thee, and grant me thy divine
protection.

11 Indra the Rescuer, Indra the Helper, Hero
who listens at each invocation,
Śakra I call, Indra invoked of many.
May Indra Maghavan prosper and bless
us.

12 May helpful Indra as our good Protector,
Lord of all treasures, favour us with
succour,

---

12 *To us and to our sons give refuge* : the Commentator takes *acittam* 'unobserved' with *cardiḥ*, and
explains the words as 'armour unknown by the enemies.'

---

3 *This Sage hath measured out* : the creative acts
of Indra are ascribed to Soma which inspirits him to
perform them. *The six expanses*, are the two worlds,
heaven and earth, and the three subdivisions of each;
or, according to the Commentator, heaven, earth, day,
night, water, and plants.

---

4 *In three headlong rivers* : perhaps the three
unknown rivers Añjasī, Kuliśī, and Vīrapatnī, of I.
104. 4, which Benfey considers to be personifications of
the clouds; but the meaning of the half-line is uncertain.
'This Soma has deposited the ambrosia in its three
principal (receptacles).'—Wilson. Soma in stanzas 4 and
5 is probably the Moon-God.

9 *Let not the foe's wealth, Maghavan, subdue us* : it
seems necessary to follow Professor Ludwig in taking
rāyaḥ in the plural as the subject of the singular verb
tārīt. Other examples of such an irregularity are
found in the Veda.

Baffle our foes, and give us rest and safety,
and may we be the lords of hero vigour.

13 May we enjoy the grace of him the Holy,
yea, may we dwell in his auspicious
favour.
May helpful Indra as our good Preserver
drive from us, even from afar, our
foemen.

14 Like rivers rushing down a slope, O Indra,
to thee haste songs and prayers and
linked verses.
Thou gatherest, Thunderer ! like wide-
spread bounty, kine, water, drops, and
manifold libations.

15 Who lauds him, satisfies him, pays him
worship ? E'en the rich noble still hath
found him mighty.
With power, as when one moves his feet
alternate, he makes the last precede,
the foremost follow.

16 Famed is the Hero as each strong man's
tamer, ever advancing one and then
another.
King of both worlds, hating the high and
haughty, Indra protects the men who
are his people.

17 He loves no more the men he loved
aforetime : he turns and moves away
allied with others.
Rejecting those who disregard his worship,
Indra victorious lives through many
autumns.

18 In every figure he hath been the model :
this is his only form for us to look on.
Indra moves multiform by his illusions;
for his Bay Steeds are yoked, ten times
a hundred.

19 Here Tvaṣṭar, yoking to the car the Bay
Steeds, hath extended sway.

Who will for ever stand upon the foeman's
side, even when our princes sit at ease ?

20 Gods, we have reached a country void
of pasture the land, though spacious,
was too small to hold us.
Brhaspati, provide in war for cattle; find
a path, Indra, for this faithful singer.

21 Day after day far from their seat he drove
them, alike, from place to place, those
darksome creatures.
The Hero slew the meanly-huckstering
Dāsas, Varcin and Śambara, where the
waters gather.

22 Out of thy bounty, Indra, hath Prastoka
bestowed ten coffers and ten mettled
horses.
We have received in turn from Divodāsa
Śambara's wealth, the gift of Atithigva.

23 Ten horses and ten treasure-chests, ten
garments as an added gift,
These and ten lumps of gold have I received
from Divodāsa's hand.

24 Ten cars with extra steed to each, for the
Atharvans hundred cows,
Hath Aśvatha to Pāyu given.

25 Thus Sṛnjaya's son honoured the Bharadvājas, recipients of all noble gifts and
bounty.

26 Lord of the wood, be firm and strong in
body : be, bearing us, a brave victorious
hero
Show forth thy strength, compact with
straps of leather, and let thy rider win
all spoils of battle.

27 Its mighty strength was borrowed from
the heaven and earth : its conquering
force was brought from sovrans of the
wood.
Honour with holy gifts the Car like Indra's
bolt, the Car bound round with straps,
the vigour of the floods.

13 This stanza is apparently the conclusion of the
original hymn ; a new hymn or fragment of a hymn
begins with the following stanza.—Ludwig.

15 *With power* : he rules the fortunes of men
according to his pleasure, setting up one and putting
down another, making the first last and the last first.

18 '*Indra* presents himself as *Agni, Viṣṇu,* or *Rudra,*
or any other deity who is the actual object of worship,
and is really the deity to be adored : he is identifiable
with each.'—Wilson.

Ten times a hundred : 'His chariots and horses are
multiplied according to the forms in which he manifests himself : agreeably to the *Vaidāntika* interpretation
of the stanza, *Indra* is here identified with Parameśvara,
the supreme first cause, identical with creation.'—Wilson.

19 *Tvaṣṭar* : supposed by the Commentator to be
identified with Indra ; but this is unnecessary. The *sway*
may be merely the authority which Tvaṣṭar exercises
in yoking the chariot-steeds for Indra.

Who will for ever stand upon the foeman's side ? :
that is, Indra will not always favour our enemies, even
when, as is now the case, our nobles are not engaged in
war.—Ludwig.

21 Indra is represented as having put to flight the
dark aborigines and slain the niggardly demons or
savages Varcin and Śambara. See IV. 30. 14, 15.

22 *Prastoka, Divodāsa,* and *Atithigva* are names of
one and the same prince, who is called also Aśvatha,
and Sārñjaya or son of Sṛnjaya.

24 *For the Atharvans* : for the Ṛṣis of the family of
Atharvan, says Sāyṇa. *Pāyu* : the brother of Garga
the Ṛṣi of the hymn.
This stanza consists of two Pādas only instead of
four.

26 *Lord of the wood* : forest tree, that is the timber
of which the car is made. This car is the deified object
of this and the two following stanzas.

28 Thou Bolt of Indra, Vanguard of the
Maruts, close knit to Varuṇa and Child
of Mitra,—
As such, accepting gifts which here we
offer, receive, O Godlike Chariot, these
oblations.

29 Send forth thy voice aloud through earth
and heaven, and let the world in all
its breadth regard thee;
O Drum, accordant with the Gods and
Indra, drive thou afar, yea, very far, our
foemen.

30 Thunder out strength and fill us full of
vigour : yea, thunder forth and drive
away all dangers.
Drive hence, O War-drum, drive away
misfortune : thou art the Fist of Indra :
show thy firmness.

31 Drive hither those, and these again bring
hither : the War-drum speaks aloud as
battle's signal.
Our heroes, winged with horses, come together. Let our car-warriors, Indra, be
triumphant.

HYMN XLVIII.   *Agni and Others.*

1. SING to your Agni with each song, at every
sacrifice, for strength.
Come, let us praise the Wise and Everlasting God, even as a well-beloved
Friend,

2 The Son of Strength; for is he not our
gracious Lord ? Let us serve him who
bears our gifts.
In battle may he be our help and strengthener, yea, be the saviour of our
lives.

3 Agni, thou beamest forth with light, great
Hero, never changed by time.
Shining, pure Agni ! with a light that
never fades, beam with thy fair beams
brilliantly.

4 Thou worshippest great Gods : bring
them without delay by wisdom and thy
wondrous power.

O Agni, make them turn hither to succour
us. Give strength, and win it for thyself.

5 He whom floods, stones, and trees support,
the offspring of eternal Law;
He who when rubbed with force is brought
to life by men upon the lofty height
of earth;

6 He who hath filled both worlds full with
his brilliant shine, who hastens with his
smoke to heaven;
He made himself apparent through the
gloom by night, the Red Bull in the
darksome nights, the Red Bull in the
darksome nights.

7 O Agni, with thy lofty beams, with thy
pure brilliancy, O God,
Kindled, Most Youthful One ! by Bharadvāja's hand, shine on us, O pure God,
with wealth, shine, Purifier ! splendidly.

8 Thou art the Lord of house and home of
all the tribes, O Agni, of all tribes of
men.
Guard with a hundred forts thy kindler
from distress, through hundred winters,
Youngest God ! and those who make
thy singers rich.

9 Wonderful, with thy favouring help, send
us thy bounties, gracious Lord.
Thou art the Charioteer, Agni, of earthly
wealth : find rest and safety for our
seed.

10 With guards unfailing never negligent
speed thou our children and our progeny.
Keep far from us, O Agni, all celestial
wrath and wickedness of godless men.

11 Hither, O friends, with newest song drive
her who freely pours her milk;
Loose her who never turns away;

12 Who, for the host of Maruts bright with
native sheen, hath shed immortal fame
like milk;
Whom the impetuous Maruts look upon
with love, who moves in splendour on
their ways.

29 *O Drum* : the *dundubhī* addressed and glorified in
these concluding verses was a sort of loud kettle-drum,
like that still used.

31 Drive to us the cows of the enemy and send
our own cows home in safety. *Gāḥ*, cows, is understood
with *amū́ḥ*, those, and *imā́ḥ* these.

1 *Come, let us sing* : it seems necessary to take the
singular verb with the plural pronoun.

2 *Who bears our gifts* : conveys our sacrificial offerings
to the Gods.

5 *Floods, stones, and trees* : the waters that are mixed
with the Soma juice, the press-stones which crush the
plant, and the wood which, produces the fire by attrition or feeds it as fuel. *The lofty height of earth* : the altar.

11 *Who freely pours her milk* : *sabárdughā* ; the
general name of the cow or cows milked at sacrifices.

12 The sacrificial cow is here identified with Pṛ́sni‘
the mother of the Maruts.

13 For Bharadvāja she poured down in days
of old
The milch-cow yielding milk for all, and
food that gives all nourishment.

14 Your friend like Indra passing wise, with
magic power like Varuṇa.
Like Aryaman joy-giving, bringing plenteous food like Viṣṇu for my wish, I
praise,

15 Bright as the host of Maruts mighty in
their roar. May they bring Pūṣan free
from foes;
May they bring hither hundreds, thousands
for our men : may they bring hidden
stores to light, and make wealth easy to
be found.

16 Haste to me, Pūṣan, in thine ear, bright
Deity : I fain would speak :
Most sinful is our foeman's hate.

17 Tear not up by the roots the Kākambīra
tree : destroy thou all malignity.
Let them not snare by day the neck of
that Celestial Bird the Sun.

18 Uninjured let thy friendship be, like the
smooth surface of a skin,
A flawless skin, containing curds, full to
the mouth, containing curds.

19 For thou art high above mankind, in
glory equal to the Gods.
Therefore, O Pūṣan, look upon us in the
fight : now help us as in days of old.

20 May the kind excellence of him the Kind,
loud Roarers ! be our guide,
Be it the God's, O Maruts, or a mortal
man's who worships, ye impetuous Ones!

21 They whose high glory in a moment like
the God, the Sun, goes round the space
of heaven,

The Maruts have obtained bright strength,
a sacred name, strength that destroys
the Vṛtras, strength Vṛtra-destroying
excellent.

22 Once, only once, the heaven was made,
once only once, the earth was formed-
Once, only Pṛśni's milk was shed : no
second, after this, is born.

HYMN XLIX.   Viśvedevas.

1. I LAUD with newest songs the Righteous
People, Mitra and Varuṇa who make
us happy.
Let them approach, here let them listen,—
Agni, Varuṇa, Mitra, Lords of fair
dominion.

2 Him, to be praised at each tribe's sacrifices,
the Two young Matrons' sober-minded
Herald,
The Son of Strength, the Child of Heaven,
the signal of sacrifice, red Agni will
I worship.

3 Unlike in form are the Red God's two
Daughters : one is the Sun's, and stars
bedeck the other.
Apart, the Sanctifiers, in succession, come
to the famed hymn, praised in holy
verses.

4 I with a lofty song call hither Vāyu, all-
bounteous, filler of his car, most wealthy.
Thou, Sage, with bright path, Lord of
harnessed horses, impetuous, promptly
honourest the prudent.

5 That chariot of the Aśvins, fair to look
on, pleaseth me well, yoked with a
thought, refulgent,
Wherewith, Nāsatyas, Chiefs, ye seek our
dwelling, to give new strength to us and
to our children.

6 Bulls of the Earth, O Vāta and Parjanya,
stir up for us the regions of the water.

---

13 According to my version, which follows that of
Professor Ludwig, Pṛśni should be the deity of this
stanza. Sāyaṇa explains it differently : O Maruts, milk,
etc.

14 Your friend : Pūṣan. For my wish : that I may
obtain my wish ; 'for the distribution of wealth,'—
Wilson.

17 The Kākambīra tree : according to Sāyaṇa,
kākambīra means literally 'crow-bearer:' 'with its
progeny of crows.'—Wilson. It is apparently the name
of some umbrageous tree, and in this place implies
metaphorically Śamyu the Ṛṣi of the hymn with his
many branches of sons and grandsons.

Let them not snare : let not our enemies deprive
us of the sunlight : the Sun being frequently called a
bird, those who would deprive the speaker of the light
of day are regarded as fowlers.

18 Containing curds : 'Such a skin of curds, Sāyaṇa
says, is always carried in Pūṣan's chariot.'—Wilson.

20 The God's : Agni's.

22 Heaven and Earth, having once been made or
brought forth, are permanent. Pṛśni, the mother of the
Maruts, has once for all given birth to her brood.
No second : śardhaḥ, host (of Maruts) is understood with
anyáḥ.

---

2 The Two young Matrons : Heaven and Earth. The
Child of Heaven : or of Dyaus or Dyu.

3 Two Daughters : Day and Night.

4 Filler of his car : with wealth to reward his worshippers. The prudent : the wise worshipper.

6 Bulls of the Earth : or of Pṛthivī as identified with
Pṛśni. Vāta is another name of Vāyu, the Wind-God;
and Parjanya is the Rain-cloud personified. Hearers of
truth : the Maruts are thus addressed, as making true
or realizing the prayers of men to which they listen.
I follow Sāyaṇa's interpretation of the second half of
the stanza.

Hearers of truth, ye, Sages, World-Supporters, increase his living wealth whose songs delight you.

7 So may Sarasvatī, the Hero's Consort, brisk with rare life, the lightning's Child, inspire us,
And, with the Dames accordant, give the singer a refuge unassailable and flawless.

8 I praise with eloquence him who guards all pathways. He, when his love impelled him, went to Arka.
May he vouchsafe us gear with gold to grace it : may Pūṣan make each prayer of ours effective.

9 May Herald Agni, fulgent, bring for worship Tvaṣṭar adored, in homes and swift to listen,
Glorious, first to share, the life-bestower, the ever active God, fair-armed, fair-handed.

10 Rudra by day, Rudra at night we honour with these our songs, the Universe's Father.
Him great and lofty, blissful, undecaying let us call specially as the Sage impels us.

11 Ye who are youthful, wise, and meet for· worship, come, Maruts, to the longing of the singer.
Coming, as erst to Aṅgiras, O Heroes, ye animate and quicken e'en the desert.

12 Even as the herdsman driveth home his cattle, I urge my songs to him the strong swift Hero

May he, the glorious, lay upon his body the singer's hymns, as stars bedeck the heaven.

13 He who for man's behoof in his affliction thrice measured out the earthly regions, Viṣṇu—
When one so great as thou affordeth shelter, may we with wealth and with ourselves be happy.

14 Sweet be this song of mine to Ahibudhnya, Parvata, Savitar, with Floods and Lightnings;
Sweet, with the Plants, to Gods who seek oblations. May liberal Bhaga speed us on to riches.

15 Give riches borne on cars, with many heroes, contenting men, the guard of mighty Order.
Give us a lasting home that we may battle with godless bands of men who fight against us, and meet with tribes to whom the Gods are gracious.

HYMN L.   Viśvedevas.

1. I CALL with prayers on Aditi your Goddess, on Agni, Mitra, Varuṇa for favour,
On Aryaman who gives unasked, the gracious, on Gods who save, on Savitar and Bhaga.

2 Visit, to prove us free from sin, O Sūrya, Lord of great might, the bright Gods sprung from Dakṣa,
Twice-born and true, observing sacred duties, Holy and full of light, whose tongue is Agni.

3 And, O ye Heaven and Earth, a wide dominion, O ye most blissful Worlds, our lofty shelter,

---

7 *The Hero's Consort* : *vīrāpatnī* : according to Sāyaṇa, she whose husband is the hero Prajāpati, or, the protectress of heroes. The River-God Sarasvān or Sarasvat is more usually considered to be the consort of Sarasvatī, who originally a River-Goddess, appears in this place in her later and present-day character of the Goddess of learning and eloquence. See note, borrowed from Muir, on I. 3. 10. *The Dames* : Gnās, or Consorts of the Gods.

8 *Him who guards all pathways* : Pūṣan, the special protector of travellers and guardian of roads and paths. See I. 42. *Arka* : the Sun, to whom Pūṣan appears to have gone both as an envoy on behalf of the other Gods when Sūryā was to be given in marriage, and as a suitor on his own account. Sūryā, it may be remembered, chose the Aśvins to be her husbands. See I. 116. 17. I follow Professor Pischel (*Vedische Studien*, I. pp. 1—52) in his interpretation of this difficult stanza.

10 *The Sage* : the wise, that is, wisdom-giving, Soma.

11 *As erst to Aṅgiras* : *aṅgirasvát* ; 'like rays (of light).'—Wilson; 'like the Aṅgirasas.'—Roth ; 'like messengers of the Gods.'—Grassmann.

12. *The strong swift Hero* : Viṣṇu seems to be intended, and not the company of Maruts as Sāyaṇa explains the passage, taking *vīrya* as an adjective=heroic or powerful.

14 *Ahibudhnya* : the Dragon of the Deep, or 'leviathan of the Sea of Heaven,' the distant, invisible and deified being who presides over the firmament.

15 *The guard of mighty Order* : the wealth that enables men to institute the law-ordained sacrifices. *To whom the Gods are gracious* : 'to whom the Gods come to accept libations.' I follow Sāyaṇa in thus distinguishing *ddevīḥ* from *ddevīḥ*, godless.

2 *Visit, to prove us free from sin* : visit and invite the Gods to come and bear witness to our innocence before the all-seeing Sun. The word *anāgāstve*. in the locative case (in sinlessness) is used with a dative signification. *Sprung from Dakṣa* : Dakṣa is a creative Power associated with Aditi, and therefore sometimes identified with Prajāpati. Sāyaṇa explains *dākṣapitṛin* in his commentary on VII. 66. 2, as 'preservers or lords of strength,' and the compound may mean Lords of vigour, or fathers of strength in this passage also. *Twice-born* : having two births or manifestations, dwelling in heaven and appearing also on earth : *Whose tongue is Agni* : who consume oblations by means of fire.

Give ample room and freedom for our
dwelling, a home, ye Hemispheres, which
none may rival.

4 This day invited may the Sons of Rudra,
resistless, excellent, stoop down to meet
us;
For, when beset with slight or sore affliction,
we ever call upon the Gods, the Maruts;

5 To whom the Goddess Rodasī clings
closely, whom Pūṣan follows bringing
ample bounty.
What time ye hear our call and come, O
Maruts, upon your separate path all
creatures tremble.

6 With a new hymn extol, O thou who
singest, the Lover of the Song, the Hero
Indra.
May he, exalted, hear our invocation, and
grant us mighty wealth and strength
when lauded.

7 Give full protection, Friends of man, ye
Waters, in peace and trouble, to our
sons and grandsons.
For ye are our most motherly physicians,
parents of all that standeth, all that
moveth.

8 May Savitar come hither and approach
us, the God who rescues, Holy, golden-
handed,
The God who, bounteous as the face of
Morning, discloses precious gifts for him
who worships.

9 And thou, O Son of Strength, do thou
turn hither the Gods to-day to this our
holy service.
May I for evermore enjoy thy bounty,
and, Agni, by thy grace be rich in
heroes.

10 Come also to my call, O ye Nāsatyas, yea,
verily, through my prayers, ye Holy
Sages.
As from great darkness ye delivered Atri,
protect us, Chiefs, from danger in the
conflict.

11 O Gods, bestow upon us riches, splendid
with strength and heroes, bringing food
in plenty.
Be gracious, helpful Gods of earth, of
heaven, born of the Cow, and dwellers
in the waters.

12 May Rudra and Sarasvatī, accordant,
Viṣṇu and Vāyu, pour down gifts and
bless us;
Ṛbhukṣan, Vāja, and divine Vidhātar,
Parjanya, Vāta make our food abundant.

13 May this God Savitar, the Lord, the
Offspring of Waters, pouring down his
dew be gracious,
And, with the Gods and Dames accordant,
Tvaṣṭṛ; Dyaus with the Gods and
Pṛthivī with oceans.

14 May Aja-Ekapād and Ahibudhnya, and
Earth and Ocean hear our invocation;
All Gods who strengthen Law, invoked and
lauded, and holy texts uttered by sages,
help us.

15 So with my thoughts and hymns of praise
the children of Bharadvāja sing aloud to
please you.
The Dames invoked, and the resistless
Vasus, and all ye Holy Ones have been
exalted.

HYMN LI.　　　　　*Viśvedevas.*

1. THAT mighty eye of Varuṇa and Mitra,
infallible and dear, is moving upward.
The pure and lovely face of holy Order
hath shone like gold of heaven in its
arising.

2 The Sage who knows these Gods' three
ranks and orders, and all their generations near and distant,
Beholding good and evil acts of mortals,
Sūra marks well the doing of the pious.

12 This and the four following stanzas form a new
hymn, or are a recapitulation, with additions, of the
preceding verses. *And divine Vidhātar:* or 'the divine
Disposer.'

14 *Aja-Ekapād;* according to Roth, probably a
genius of the storm, 'the stormer of one foot. See II.
31. 6. But *ajá* may signify 'unborn' rather than 'driver,'
and the Sun may be intended, in accordance with the
explanation of the Commentators. Aja-Ekapād is called
in X. 65. 13. the bearer of heaven, 'and the ascription
of one foot to the Sun might be due to his appearance
alone in the sky as opposed to the Dawns and Aśvins.'
See Wallis, *Cosmology of the Ṛgveda,* p. 54. M. Bergaigne
says: 'Aja-Ekapād, then is the 'unborn who has only
one foot,' that is to say, 'who dwells in the single
isolated world, the place of mystery,' in opposition to
the god who manifests himself in divers worlds, to Agni
or Soma in their various visible forms.' See *La Religion
Védique,* III. pp. 20—25.

15 Sāyaṇa interprets the first line somewhat differently: 'Thus do my sons the Bharadvājas worship the
Gods with sacred rites and hymns'

1 *Eye of Varuṇa and Mitra:* the Sun.

2 *Three ranks and orders:* according to Sāyaṇa, the
three cognizable worlds or stations of the Gods, the
earth of the Vasus, the firmament of the Rudras, and
heaven of the Ādityas. *Sūra:* Sūrya; the Sun.

3 *Ye Hemispheres: dhiṣaṇe;* literally, 'two bowls,' a
frequently-occurring expression for heaven and earth.

5 *Rodasī:* the Consort of Rudra.

11 *Born of the Cow:* the Maruts, sons of the Cow
P. śni, according to Sāyaṇa. The Gods of heaven are
said to be the Ādityas, those of earth the Vasus, and
those of water, that is, the firmament, the Rudras.
Roth explains *gojātāḥ* as 'born of the starry heaven.'

3 I praise you Guards of mighty Law eternal,
　　Aditi, Mitra, Varuna, the noble,
　Aryaman, Bhaga, all whose thoughts are
　　faithful : hither I call the Bright who
　　share in common.

4 Lords of the brave, infallible, foe-destroyers,
　　great Kings, bestowers of fair homes to
　　dwell in,
　Young, Heroes, ruling heaven with strong
　　dominion, Ādityas, Aditi I seek with
　　worship.

5 O Heaven our Father, Earth our guileless
　　Mother, O Brother Agni, and ye Vasus,
　　bless us.
　Grant us, O Aditi and ye Ādityas, all of
　　one mind, your manifold protection.

6 Give us not up to any evil creature, as
　　spoil to wolf or she-wolf, O ye Holy.
　For ye are they who guide aright our
　　bodies, ye are the rulers of our speech
　　and vigour.

7 Let us not suffer for the sin of others, nor
　　do the deed which ye, O Vasus, punish.
　Ye, Universal Gods ! are all-controllers :
　　may he do harm unto himself who hates
　　me.

8 Mighty is homage : I adopt and use it.
　　Homage hath held in place the earth
　　and heaven.
　Homage to Gods ! Homage commands
　　and rules them. I banish even commit-
　　ted sin by homage.

9 You Furtherers of Law, pure in your spirit,
　　infallible, dwellers in the home of Order,
　To you all Heroes mighty and far-seeing
　　I bow me down, O Holy Ones, with
　　homage.

10 For these are they who shine with noblest
　　splendour; through all our troubles
　　these conduct us safely—
　Varuna, Mitra, Agni, mighty Rulers, true-
　　minded, faithful to the hymn's con-
　　trollers.

11 May they, Earth, Aditi, Indra, Bhaga,
　　Pūṣan increase our laud, increase the
　　Fivefold people.

Giving good help, good refuge, goodly
　　guidance, be they our good deliverers,
　　good protectors.

12 Come now, O Gods, to your celestial
　　station : the Bharadvājas' priest entreats
　　your favour.
　He, sacrificing, fain for wealth, hath
　　honoured the Gods with those who sit
　　and share oblations.

13 Agni, drive thou the wicked foe, the
　　evil-hearted thief away,
　Far, far, Lord of the brave ! and give us
　　easy paths.

14 Soma, these pressing-stones have called
　　aloud to win thee for our Friend.
　Destroy the greedy Paṇi, for a wolf is he.

15 Ye, O most bountiful, are they who, led
　　by Indra, seek the sky.
　Give us good paths for travel : guard us
　　well at home.

16 Now have we entered on the road that
　　leads to bliss, without a foe,
　The road whereon a man escapes all
　　enemies and gathers wealth.

HYMN LII.　　　　　　*Viśvedevas.*

1. THIS I allow not in the earth or heaven,
　　at sacrifice or in these holy duties.
　May the huge mountains crush him
　　down : degraded be Atiyāja's sacrificing
　　patron.

2 Or he who holds us in contempt, O
　　Maruts, or seeks to blame the prayer
　　that we are making,
　May agonies of burning be his portion.
　May the sky scorch the man who hates
　　devotion.

3 Why then, O Soma, do they call thee
　　keeper of prayer ? Why then our
　　guardian from reproaches ?

---

12 This stanza is difficult, and I do not thoroughly
understand it.

14 *Paṇi* : either one of the envious demons who steal
away the light, or the avaricious and niggardly trafficker
who offers no sacrifices to the Gods.

15 *Ye, O Most Bountiful* : all ye Gods.

16 These four concluding stanzas, in changed metres,
are a prayer for protection on a journey. Professor
Grassmann banishes them, together with stanzas 11 and
12, to the Appendix as being in his opinion later additions to the original hymn.

---

3 *Who share in common* : sadhanyāḥ; ; according to
Sāyaṇa, dhanasahitān, 'accompanied by wealth.'

7 *Let us not suffer for the sin of others* : so, VII. 86.
5. 'Loose us from sins committed by our fathers.' Compare also Taittirīya Brāhmaṇa, III. 7. 12. 3. cited by
Muir, O. S. T., V. 66. 'May Agni free me from the sin
which my mother or my father committed when I was
a babe unborn.'

10 *The hymn's controllers* : 'those who are prominent
in (their) praise.'—Wilson.

11 *The Fivefold People* : pánca jánāḥ ; the five Āryan
tribes ; 'the five orders of beings.'—Wilson.

1 According to Sāyaṇa Ṛjiśvan curses a rival Ṛṣi
Atiyāja : but the name Atiyāja (from *ati* and *yaj*)
seems to be employed expressly to signify one who over-
sacrifices, that is, sacrifices more than is necessary or
prescribed, superfluity, as well as deficiency, being a
fault that causes a sacrifice to fail. See Ludwig, IV. 220.

3 *Soma* : the Moon-God.

Why then beholdest thou how men revile us ? Cast thy hot dart at him who hates devotion.

4 May Mornings as they spring to life protect me, and may the Rivers as they swell preserve me.

My guardians be the firmly-seated mountains : the Fathers, when I call on Gods, defend me !

5 Through all our days may we be healthy-minded, and look upon the Sun when he arises.

Grant this the Treasure-Lord of treasures, coming, observant, oftenest of Gods, with succour !

6 Most near, most oft comes Indra with protection, and she Sarasvatī, who swells with rivers :

Parjanya, bringing health with herbs, and Agni, well lauded swift to listen, like a father.

7 Hear this mine invocation ; come hither, O Universal Gods,

Be seated on this holy grass.

8 To him who comes to meet you, Gods, with offerings bathed in holy oil—

Approach ye, one and all, to him.

9 All Sons of Immortality shall listen to the songs we sing,

And be exceeding good to us.

10 May all the Gods who strengthen Law, with Ṛtus, listening to our call,

Be pleased with their appropriate draught.

11 May Indra with the Marut host, with Tvaṣṭar, Mitra, Aryaman,

Accept the laud and these our gifts.

12 O Agni, Priest, as rules ordain, offer this sacrifice of ours,

Remembering the Heavenly Folk.

13 Listen, All-Gods, to this mine invocation, ye who inhabit heaven, and air's mid-regions,

All ye, O Holy Ones, whose tongue is Agni, seated upon this sacred grass, be joyful.

14 May the All-Gods who claim our worship hear my thought; may the two World-halves hear it, and the Waters' Child.

Let me not utter words that ye may disregard. Closely allied with you may we rejoice in bliss.

15 And those who, Mighty, with the wiles of serpents, were born on earth, in heaven, where waters gather—

May they vouchsafe us life of full duration. May the Gods kindly give us nights and mornings.

16 At this my call, O Agni and Parjanya, help, swift to hear, my thought and our laudation.

One generates holy food, the other offspring, so grant us food enough with store of children.

17 When holy grass is strewn and fire enkindled, with hymn and lowly homage I invite you.

All-Gods, to day in this our great assembly rejoice, ye Holy, in the gifts we offer.

HYMN LIII.   *Pūṣan.*

1. LORD of the path, O Pūṣan, we have yoked and bound thee to our hymn,

Even as a car, to win the prize.

2 Bring us the wealth that men require, a manly master of a house,

Free-handed with the liberal meed.

3 Even him who would not give, do thou, O glowing Pūṣan, urge to give,

And make the niggard's soul grow soft.

4 Clear paths that we may win the prize; scatter our enemies afar.

Strong God, be all our thoughts fulfilled.

5 Penetrate with an awl, O Sage, the hearts of avaricious churls,

And make them subject to our will.

6 Thrust with thine awl, O Pūṣan : seek that which the niggard's heart holds dear,

And make him subject to our will.

---

15 *With the wiles of serpents* : *dhimāyāḥ* : according to Sāyaṇa, 'possessed of the wisdom or knowledge that kills.' Cf. I. 3. 9, note.

16 *The other offspring*: Parjanya, the personified Rain-cloud, produces corn and food offered in sacrifice, and Agni promotes the procreation of children.

1 *Lord of the path* : custodian of roads and guide of travellers. *To win the prize* : or, to win us wealth or food.

2 *Master of a house* : a householder who will institute sacrifices and liberally reward the officiating priests.

4 *Win the prize* : or win us wealth, or food.

5 *With an awl* : 'with a goad.'—Wilson.

---

5 *Treasure-Lord of treasures* : Agni, from whom, or through whom, all blessings come to the pious.

9 *Sons of Immortality* : according to the Scholiast, 'sons of the immortal' (Prajāpati, regarded as the progenitor of Gods and men).

10 *With Ṛtus* : together with the Seasons personified ; or, at the prescribed seasons, as Sāyaṇa explains.

13 *All Gods* : Viśve devāḥ, or Universal Gods.

7 Tear up and rend in pieces, Sage, the
  hearts of avaricious churls,
  And make them subject to our will.

8 Thou, glowing Pūṣan, carriest an awl
  that urges men to prayer;
  Therewith do thou tear up and rend to
  shreds the heart of every one.

9 Thou bearest, glowing Lord ! a goad with
  horny point that guides the cows :
  Thence do we seek thy gift of bliss.

10 And make this hymn of ours produce kine,
   horses, and a store of wealth
   For our delight and use as men.

HYMN LIV.   *Pūṣan.*

1. O Pūṣan, bring us to the man who knows,
   who shall direct us straight,
   And say unto us, It is here.

2 May we go forth with Pūṣan who shall
  point the houses out to us,
  And say to us, These same are they.

3 Unharmed is Pūṣan's chariot wheel; the
  box ne'er falleth to the ground,
  Nor doth the loosened felly shake.

4 Pūṣan forgetteth not the man who serveth
  him with offered gift :
  That man is first to gather wealth.

5 May Pūṣan follow near our kine; may
  Pūṣan keep our horses safe :
  May Pūṣan gather gear for us.

6 Follow the kine of him who pours libations
  out and worships thee;
  And ours who sing thee songs of praise.

7 Let none be lost, none injured, none sink
  in a pit and break a limb.
  Return with these all safe and sound.

8 Pūṣan who listens to our prayers, the
  Strong whose wealth is never lost,
  The Lord of riches, we implore.

9 Secure in thy protecting care, O Pūṣan,
  never may we fail :
  We here are they who sing thy praise.

10 From out the distance, far and wide, may
   Pūṣan stretch his right hand forth,
   And drive our lost again to us.

HYMN LV.   *Pūṣan.*

1. Son of Deliverance, come, bright God !
   Let us twain go together : be our
   charioteer of sacrifice.

2 We pray for wealth to thee most skilled
  of charioteers, with braided hair,
  Lord of great riches, and our Friend.

3 Bright God whose steeds are goats, thou
  art a stream of wealth, a treasure-heap,
  The Friend of every pious man.

4 Pūṣan, who driveth goats for steeds, the
  Strong and Mighty, who is called
  His Sister's lover, will we laud.

5 His Mother's suitor I address. May he who
  loves his Sister hear,
  Brother of Indra, and my Friend.

6 May the sure-footed goats come nigh, conveying Pūṣan on his car,
  The God who visiteth mankind.

---

9 *With horny point* : the exact meaning of *goopaṣā*
is uncertain. Others explain it as 'director of cattle,'
'furnished with leathern thongs;' 'cow tailed.'

This hymn and the five following have been translated by Dr. Muir, *Original Sanskrit Texts*, V. 176—
180. Professor Peterson also gives a translation of Hymns
LIII—LVII in his *Hymns from the Rgveda* (Bombay
Sanskrit Series No. XXXVI).

1 This stanza, Sāyaṇa says, is to be muttered by
one who seeks his lost property. *The man who knows* :
the wise man or wizard.

2 *These same are they* : these are the houses in
which the stolen property is concealed.

3 *The box* : basket, or inner part of the car. Professor Wilson, following Sāyaṇa, translates : 'The discus
of Pūṣan does not destroy ; its sheath is not discarded,
its edge harms not us.' But the three things mentioned
are evidently parts of Pūṣan's chariot.

7 *With these* : cows.

---

8 We pray to Pūṣan for the safety of our property
because he is the Lord of wealth ; he himself loses
nothing that is his, and he always listens to our prayers.

---

1 *Son of Deliverance* : that is, 'Deliverer,' one who
gives men ample room and freedom. Sāyaṇa explains
vimuco napāt in another place as 'offspring of the cloud.'
See I. 42. 1. Here, he says, the meaning is, 'son of
Prajāpati, who at the creation sends forth from himself
all creatures'. Roth explains *vimuc* as 'unyoking' horses
at the end of a journey. Pūṣan would then be 'the son
of return,' the God who brings travellers safely home,
which is one of his especial functions.

2 *With braided hair* : *kapardínam* ; an epithet of
Rudra also. See I. 114. 1.

3 *Whose steeds are goats* : cf. I. 138. 4.

4 *His Sister's lover* : according to Sāyaṇa, Pūṣan's
sister is Uṣas or Dawn.

5 *His Mother's suitor* : Sāyaṇa explains *mātur didhiṣum*
as *rātreḥ patim*, lord or husband of Night. Probably
Sūryā is intended. See Bergaigne, *La Religion Védique*,
II. 428. Compare also Book VI. 48. 8. *Brother of Indra*
as an Āditya or son of Aditi.

6 *Sure-footed* : *niṣṭmbhdḥ* : this word does not occur
elsewhere and its meaning is uncertain. Wilson renders
it 'harnessed,' and other explanations have been proposed, but as Dr. Muir observes : 'All seems guess work,'

HYMN LVI.   *Pūṣan.*

1. WHOSO remembers Pūṣan as eater of mingled curd and meal
Need think no more upon the God.
2 And he is best of charioteers. Indra, the
hero's Lord, allied
With him as Friend, destroys the foes.
3 And there the best of charioteers hath
guided through the speckled cloud
The golden wheel of Sūra's car.
4 Whate'er we speak this day to thee, Wise,
Wondrous God whom many praise,
Give thou fulfilment of our thought.
5 Lead on this company of ours, that longs
for kine, to win the spoil:
Thou, Pūṣan, art renowned afar.
6 Prosperity we crave from thee, afar from
sin and near to wealth,
Tending to perfect happiness both for to-
morrow and to-day.

HYMN LVII.   *Indra and Pūṣan.*

1. INDRA and Pūṣan will we call for friendship and prosperity
And for the winning of the spoil.
2 One by the Soma sits to drink juice which
the mortar hath expressed:
The other longs for curd and meal.
3 Goats are the team that draws the one :
the other hath Bay Steeds at hand;
With both of these he slays the fiends.
4 When Indra, wondrous strong, brought

down the streams, the mighty water-
floods,
Pūṣan was standing by his side.
5 To this, to Pūṣan's favouring love, and
Indra's, may we closely cling,
As to a tree's extended bough.
6 As one who drives a car draws in his
reins, may we draw Pūṣan near,
And Indra, for our great success.

HYMN LVIII.   *Pūṣan.*

1. LIKE heaven art thou : one form is bright,
one holy, like Day and Night dissimilar
in colour.
All magic powers thou aidest, self-dependent ! Auspicious be thy bounty here,
O Pūṣan.
2 Goat-borne, the guard of cattle, he whose
home is strength, inspirer of the hymn,
set over all the world;
Brandishing here and there his lightly-
moving goad, beholding every creature,
Pūṣan, God, goes forth.
3 O Pūṣan, with thy golden ships that
travel across the ocean, in the air's
mid-region,
Thou goest on an embassy to Sūrya,
subdued by love, desirous of the glory.
4 Near kinsman of the heaven and earth
is Pūṣan, liberal, Lord of food, of wondrous lustre,
Whom strong and vigorous and swiftly-
moving, subdued by love, the Deities
gave to Sūryā.

HYMN LIX.   *Indra-Agni.*

1. I WILL declare, while juices flow, the
manly deeds that ye have done :

---

1 *Eater of mingled curd and meal* : *karambhāt* ; *karambhá* was some soft food, a sort of gruel offered especially
to Pūṣan.

I have followed Professor Ludwig in my translation
of this difficult passage, the meaning seeming to be that
in setting before Pūṣan the food that he loves the worshipper has done all that is necessary to secure his help.
Sāyaṇa's explanation is much the same if 'a God' be
substituted for 'the God' in line 2, that is, Pūṣan alone
is sufficient : the worshipper need think upon no other
God.

3 Pūṣan seems to be intended. He is said to have
driven the Sun's wheel *paruṣe gávi*, literally, 'in the
brindled bull,' meaning apparently, the speckled cloud,
or train of variegated clouds. He, the impeller, the chief
of charioteers (Pūṣan), ever urges on that golden wheel
(of his car) for the radiant Sun. While the others
think that the verse refers to Indra's pressing down
the wheel of the Sun from the mountain of cloud and
bringing back the light. See Peterson, *Hymns from the
Ṛgveda*, p. 171.

---

3 *The fiends* : the Vṛtras, the demons of drought,
or enemies in general.

---

1 *One holy* : 'venerable'.—Wilson. This is apparently a euphemism for 'dark.' Pūṣan is here regarded
as the Sun present by day and even in his absence
regulating the night also. According to Professor
Ludwig, he is represented as the summer Sun and the
winter Sun. *Thou aidest* : 'thou exercisest.'—Muir.

3 *Subdued by love* : of Sūryā, the daughter of the
Sun. See VI. 49. 8. *Of the glory* : of winning Sūryā
for his bride.

4 *The Deities gave to Sūryā* : 'the formula of the
verse gives the idea rather of a birth than of a marriage.
But Pūṣan is the lover of his mother, VI. 55. 5; Sūryā
then might be the spouse as well as the mother of
Pūṣan. She is doubtlessly also the sister with whom
Pūṣan is united, VI. 55. 4.5.'—Bergaigne, *La Religion
Védique*, II. 428.

Your Fathers, enemies of Gods, were smitten down, and, Indra-Agni, ye survive.

2 Thus, Indra-Agni, verily your greatness merits loftiest praise,
Sprung from one common Father, brothers, twins are ye; your Mother is in every place.

3 These who delight in flowing juice, like fellow horses at their food,
Indra and Agni, Gods armed with the thunderbolt, we call this day to come with help.

4 Indra and Agni, Friends of Law, served with rich gifts, your speech is kind
To him who praises you while these libations flow : that man, O Gods, ye ne'er consume.

5 What mortal understands, O Gods, Indra and Agni, this your way ?
One of you, yoking Steeds that move to every side, advances in your common car.

6 First, Indra-Agni, hath this Maid come footless unto those with feet.
Stretching her head and speaking loudly with her tongue, she hath gone downward thirty steps.

7 E'en now, O Indra-Agni, men hold in their arms and stretch their bows.
Desert us not in this great fray, in battles for the sake of kine.

8 The foeman's sinful enmities, Indra and Agni, vex me sore.
Drive those who hate me far away, and keep them distant from the Sun.

9 Indra and Agni, yours are all the treasures of the heavens and earth.
Here give ye us the opulence that prospers every living man.

10 O Indra-Agni, who accept the laud, and hear us for our praise,
Come near us, drawn by all our songs, to drink of this our Soma juice.

HYMN LX. *Indra-Agni.*

1. HE slays the foe and wins the spoil who worships Indra and Agni, strong and mighty Heroes,
Who rule as Sovrans over ample riches, victorious, showing forth their power in conquest.

2 So battle now, O Indra and thou, Agni, for cows and waters, sunlight, stolen Mornings.
Team-borne, thou makest kine thine own, O Agni : thou, Indra, light, Dawns, regions, wondrous waters.

3 With Vṛtra-slaying might, Indra and Agni, come, drawn by homage, O ye Vṛtra-slayers.
Indra and Agni, show yourselves among us with your supreme and unrestricted bounties.

4 I call the Twain whose deeds of old have all been famed in ancient days :
O Indra-Agni, harm us not.

5 The Strong, the scatterers of the foe, Indra and Agni, we invoke;
May they be kind to one like me.

6 They slay our Ārya foes, these Lords of heroes, slay our Dasyu foes :
And drive our enemies away.

7 Indra and Agni, these our songs of praise have sounded forth to you :
Ye who bring blessings ! drink the juice.

8 Come, Indra-Agni, with those teams, desired of many, which ye have,

---

1 *Your Fathers......were smitten down :* hatáso vām *pitáro :* the meaning is obscure. Sāyaṇa explains *pitáro* as Asuras or demons, deriving the word from a root *pi*, to injure : 'The Pitṛs the enemies of the gods, have been slain by you.'—Wilson. Prof. Grassmann reads, conjecturally, *píyavo,* 'scorners,' instead of the unsuitable *pitáro.* Gods of an elder generation, the fathers of Indra and Agni, appear to be intended, and the words as they stand can hardly bear any other meaning. *Hatáso* then would mean, 'not were slain,' but were struck down, degraded, and deprived of their power, like the earlier Hellenic Gods. Professor Ludwig suggests other possible explanations. See also Bergaigne, La Religion Védique, III. 75, and Ehni, Der Mythus des Yama, p. 80.

2 *One common Father :* Dyaus. According to Sāyaṇa, Prajāpati.

Your Mother : Aditi, infinite and omnipresent ; according to Sāyaṇa, identified with the wide-extended earth. But see Ehni, Der Mythus des Yama, p. 79.

4 *Ye ne'er consume :* Prof. Ludwig suggests the reading *bhartsathaḥ,* 'threaten,' instead of *bhasáthaḥ.*

5 *One of you :* Indra, as the Sun, whose horses here are the spreading beams of light, pursues his appointed way through heaven.

6 *This Maid :* the text has only the feminine pronoun *idám* (haec); Uṣas or Dawn is intended. *Footless :* moving unsupported in the sky. Cf. I. 152. 3. *Stretching her head :* according to one of Sāyaṇa's explanations, 'having abandoned the head, being herself headless,' which is hardly consistent with what follows. *Thirty steps :* the thirty divisions of the Indian day and night through which Dawn passes before she reappears. But cf. I. 123. 8.

7 The hymn is a prayer for aid in a fray.

---

2 *Stolen Mornings :* the Dawns and light that have been carried away and concealed by the Paṇis or demons of darkness.

3 *Vṛtra-slaying :* or, generally, 'foeman slaying.'

O Heroes, for the worshipper.

9 With those to this libation poured, ye
    Heroes, Indra-Agni, come :
    Come ye to drink the Soma juice.

10 Glorify him who compasses all forests with
    his glowing flame,
    And leaves them blackened with his tongue.

11 He who gains Indra's bliss with fire enkin-
    dled finds an easy way
    Over the floods to happiness.

12 Give us fleet coursers to convey Indra
    and Agni, and bestow
    Abundant strengthening food on us.

13 Indra and Agni, I will call you hither
    and make you joyful with the gifts I
    offer.
    Ye Twain are givers both of food and
    riches : to win me strength and vigour
    I invoke you.

14 Come unto us with riches, come with
    wealth in horses and in kine.
    Indra and Agni, we invoke you both, the
    Gods, as Friends for friendship, bringing
    bliss.

15 Indra and Agni, hear his call who worships·
    with libations poured.
    Come and enjoy the offerings, drink the
    sweetly-flavoured Soma juice.

HYMN LXI.   *Sarasvati.*

1. To Vadhryaśva when· he worshipped her
    with gifts she gave fierce Divodāsa,
    canceller of debts.
    Consumer of the churlish niggard, one
    and all, thine, O Sarasvatī, are these
    effectual boons.

2 She with her might, like one who digs for
    lotus-stems, hath burst with her strong
    waves the ridges of the hills.

10 *Glorify* : addressed to the *stotar* or praise-singer.
11 *Over the floods* : the dangers and troubles that
bar his way.
12 *To convey Indra and Agni* : to bring you, Indra
and Agni, to our sacrifice.

1 *Vadhryaśva* : a celebrated Ṛṣi. See X. 69. *She* :
Sarasvatī, the River Goddess. *Gave* : as a son.
Canceller of debts : acquitting, by his birth, the debt
which his father owed to his progenitors, the religious
obligation of begetting a son who should perform the
ceremonies which they require. *Churlish niggard* : who
offers no sacrifices. The meaning of *avasám* is uncertain. Sāyaṇa explains it as 'gratifying himself only.'
Professor Ludwig regards it as compounded of *a* +*vasā*=
thin or meagre. *These effectual boons* : the gift of a
son.
2 *She* : Sarasvatī as the river! The description
given in the text can hardly apply to the small stream
generally known under that name; and from this and
other passages which will be noticed as they occur it
seems probable that Sarasvatī is also another name of
Sindhu or the Indus. See Zimmer, *Altindisches Leben,*
pp. 6 ff. *Pārāvatas* : See V. 52. 11.

Let us invite with songs and holy hymns
for help Sarasvatī who slayeth the
Pārāvatas.

3 Thou castest down, Sarasvatī, those who
    scorned the Gods, the brood of every
    Bṛsaya skilled in magic arts.
    Thou hast discovered rivers for the tribes
    of men, and, rich in wealth ! made
    poison flow away from them.

4 May the divine Sarasvatī, rich in her
    wealth, protect us well,
    Furthering all our thoughts with might ;

5 Whoso, divine Sarasvatī, invokes thee
    where the prize is set,
    Like Indra when he smites the foe.

6 Aid us, divine Sarasvatī, thou who art
    strong in wealth and power :
    Like Pūṣan, give us opulence.

7 Yea, this divine Sarasvatī, terrible with
    her golden path,
    Foe-slayer, claims our eulogy.

8 Whose limitless unbroken flood, swift-
    moving with a rapid rush,
    Comes onward with tempestuous roar.

9 She hath spread us beyond all foes, beyond
    her Sisters, Holy One,
    As Sūrya spreadeth out the days.

10 Yea, she most dear amid dear streams,
    Seven-sistered, graciously inclined,
    Sarasvatī hath earned our praise.

11 Guard us from hate Sarasvatī, she who
    hath filled the realms of earth,
    And that wide tract, the firmament !

12 Seven-sistered, sprung from threefold source,
    the Five Tribes' prosperer, she must be
    Invoked in every deed of might.

13 Marked out by majesty among the Mighty
    Ones, in glory swifter than the other
    rapid Streams,
    Created vast for victory like a chariot,
    Sarasvatī must be extolled by every
    sage.

14 Guide us, Sarasvatī, to glorious treasure :
    refuse us not thy milk, nor spurn us
    from thee.
    Gladly accept our friendship and obedi-
    ence : let us not go from thee to dis-
    tant countries.

3 *Every Bṛsaya* : every demon like Bṛsaya, who is
said to have been the father of Vṛtra. See I. 93. 4.
Rich in wealth : *vājinīvati* : according to Sāyaṇa, 'giver
of sustenance.'
9 *Her Sisters* : the other rivers of the Panjāb.
12 *Sprung from threefold source* : 'abiding in the three
worlds,' that is, pervading heaven, earth, and hell,
according to Sāyaṇa, like Gaṅgā in later times.

HYMN LXII. *Aśvins.*

1. I LAUD the Heroes Twain, this heaven's Controllers : singing with songs of praise I call the Aśvins,
Fain in a moment, when the morns are breaking, to part the earth's ends and the spacious regions.

2 Moving to sacrifice through realms of lustre they light the radiance of the car that bears them.
Traversing many wide unmeasured spaces, over the wastes ye pass, and fields, and waters.

3 Ye to that bounteous path of yours, ye mighty, have ever borne away our thoughts with horses,
Mind-swift and full of vigour, that the trouble of man who offers gifts might cease and slumber.

4 So ye, when ye have yoked your chariot-horses, come to the hymn of the most recent singer.
Our true and ancient Herald Priest shall bring you, the Youthful, bearing splendour, food, and vigour.

5 With newest hymn I call those Wonder-Workers, ancient and brilliant, and exceeding mighty,
Bringers of bliss to him who lauds and praises, bestowing varied bounties on the singer.

6 So ye, with birds, out of the sea and waters bore Bhujyu, son of Tugra, through the regions.
Speeding with winged steeds through dustless spaces, out of the bosom of the flood they bore him.

7 Victors, car-borne, ye rent the rock asunder: Bulls, heard the calling of the eunuch's consort.
Bounteous, ye filled the cow with milk for Śayu: thus, swift and zealous Ones, ye showed your favour.

8 Whate'er from olden time, Heaven, Earth! existeth great object of the wrath of Gods and mortals,
Make that, Ādityas, Vasus, sons of Rudra, an evil brand to one allied with demons.

9 May he who knows, as Varuṇa and Mitra, air's realm, appointing both the Kings in season,
Against the secret fiend cast forth his weapon, against the lying words that strangers utter.

10 Come to our home with friendly wheels, for offspring; come on your radiant chariot rich in heroes.
Strike off, ye Twain, the heads of our assailants who with man's treacherous attack approach us.

11 Come hitherward to us with teams of horses, the highest and the midmost and the lowest.
Bountiful Lords, throw open to the singer doors e'en of the firm-closed stall of cattle.

HYMN LXIII. *Aśvins.*

1. WHERE hath the hymn with reverence, like an envoy, found both fair Gods to-day, invoked of many—
Hymn that hath brought the two Nāsatyas hither ? To this man's thought be ye, both Gods, most friendly.

2 Come readily to this mine invocation, lauded with songs, that ye may drink the juices.
Compass this house to keep it from the foeman, that none may force it, either near or distant.

3 Juice in wide room hath been prepared to feast you : for you the grass is strewn, most soft to tread on.
With lifted hands your servant hath adored you. Yearning for you the press-stones shed the liquid.

---

1 *To part the earth's ends* : as heralds of light to define the limits of earth and sky and so separate one from the other.

3 This stanza is very obscure. Sāyaṇa's paraphrase is inconsistent with the plain meaning of several of the words of the text. 'Fierce Aśvins, from that humble mansion to which (you have repaired), you have ever borne with your desirable horses, as swift as thought, the pious worshippers in some manner (to heave : Let the injurer of the liberal man (be consigned by you) to (final) repose.'—Wilson.

6 *Bhujyu* : See I. 116. 3—5.

7 *The eunuch's consort* : Vadhrimatī. See I. 116.
13. *Śayu* : See I. 116. 22.

9 Mitra and Varuṇa appear here as comprehended in a third God, who must be the Asura Dyaus. He, comprising the heaven of night as well as the heaven of day, assigns to Mitra and Varuṇa the charge, respectively of day and night. See Ludwig's Commentary.

10 *For offspring* : *tánayāya* ; to give us offspring. The second line of the stanza might be rendered : 'Turn back, ye Twain, the heads, with secret onslaught, even of those who seek to harm the mortal.'

11 *The highest and the midmost or the lowest* : or, as Professor Ludwig translates ; 'the earliest, the midmost, and the latest.'

---

2 *Either near or distant* : neighbour or stranger.

3 *In wide room* : where there is ample space for the sacrificial ceremonies.

4 Agni uplifts him at your sacrifices : forth
   goes the oblation dropping oil and
   glowing.
   Up stands the grateful-minded priest,
   elected, appointed to invoke the two
   Nāsatyas.

5 Lords of great wealth ! for glory ᵥ Sūrya's
   Daughter mounted your car that brings
   a hundred succours.
   Famed for your magic arts were ye, magi-
   cians ! amid the race of Gods, ye
   dancing Heroes !

6 Ye Twain, with these your glories fair to
   look on, brought, to win victory, rich
   gifts for Sūryā.
   After you flew your birds, marvels of
   beauty : dear to our hearts ! the song,
   well lauded, reached you.

7 May your winged coursers, best to draw.
   Nāsatyas ! convey you to the object of
   your wishes.
   Swift as the thought, your car hath been
   sent onward to food of many a sort and
   dainty viands.

8 Lords of great wealth, manifold is your
   bounty : ye filled our cow with food
   that never faileth.
   Lovers of sweetness ! yours are praise and
   singers, and poured libations which have
   sought your favour.

9 Mine were two mares of Puraya, brown,
   swift-footed; a hundred with Sumīdha,
   food with Peruk
   Śaṇḍa gave ten gold-decked and well-
   trained horses, tame and obedient and
   of lofty stature.

10 Nāsatyas ! Purupanthās offered hundreds,
   thousands of steeds to him who sang
   your praises,
   Gave, Heroes ! to the singer Bharadvāja.
   Ye-Wonder-Workers, let the fiends be
   slaughtered.

11 May I with princes share your bliss in
   freedom.

HYMN LXIV.   *Dawn.*

1. THE radiant Dawns have risen up for
   glory, in their white splendour like the
   waves of waters.
   She maketh paths all easy, fair to travel,
   and, rich, hath shown herself benign
   and friendly.

2 We see that thou art good : far shines
   thy lustre ; thy beams, thy splendours
   have flown up to heaven.
   Decking thyself, thou makest bare thy
   bosom, shining in majesty, thou Goddess
   Morning.

3 Red are the kine and luminous that bear
   her the Blessed One who spreadeth
   through the distance.
   The foes she chaseth like a valiant archer,
   like a swift warrior she repelleth
   darkness.

4 Thy ways are easy on the hills : thou
   passest Invincible ! Self-luminous !
   through waters.
   So lofty Goddess with thine ample pathway,
   Daughter of Heaven, bring wealth to
   give us comfort.

5 Dawn, bring me wealth : untroubled,
   with thine oxen thou bearest riches at
   thy will and pleasure ;
   Thou who, a Goddess, Child of Heaven,
   hast shown thee lovely through bounty
   when we called thee early.

6 As the birds fly forth from their resting-
   places, so men with store of food rise at
   thy dawning.

5 *Sūrya's Daughter* : See I. 116. 17. *Dancing Heroes* :
ye who dance through the air. Cf. VIII. 20. 22, and
'Day's harbinger comes dancing from the east' (Milton—
Song On May Morning).

6 *Rich gifts for Sūryā* : who chose the Aśvins to be
her husbands.

9 This and the following stanza eulogize the
liberality of several wealthy institutors of sacrifice ; but
it is difficult to make out what were the gifts they
gave as the verses are filled with epithets without nouns.
Vaḍave, mares, suits the dual epithets *ṛjre*, and *raghvī*,
brown and swift. After *śatám*, a hundred. Sāyaṇa
supplies *gávaḥ*, cows. Instead of 'well-trained' Sāyaṇa's
rendering is 'handsome,' and he supplies *aśvān*, 'horses,'
or *rathān*, 'chariots' for the absent noun. 'Obedient,
gallant, and well-favoured servants' would represent his
rendering of the last half-line of the stanza. The
translations given by Professors Ludwig and Grassmann
differ from each other and from Sāyaṇa's version. As
Professor Wilson remarks : 'If we render the stanza
literally, it is utterly unintelligible : the greater part of
the *Sūkta* is very obscure.' Puraya, Sumīdha, and
Peruka are the names of liberal patrons.

10 *Purupanthās* : another of these generous nobles.
In this case *dśvānām*, of horses, appears in the text.

11 *Your bliss* : the felicity which the Aśvins bestow.

1 *Dawns* : the plural may be honorific, or may
signify Dawn and her rays of light.

3 *Warrior* : borne on a chariot.

4 *Through waters* : of the firmament.

6 This stanza occurs in a hymn to Dawn ascribed
to the Ṛṣi Kakṣīvān I. 124. 12. *With store of food* :
pitubhājḍḥ, 'enjoying or sharing food,' is explained by
Sāyaṇa as *annasyopāyakāḥ*, 'who have to gain their
sustenance.' The wealthy may be meant, who sharet
their store with others and must work to replenish it.

Yea, to the liberal mortal who remaineth
at home, O Goddess Dawn, much good
thou bringest.

HYMN LXV. *Dawn.*

1. SHEDDING her light on human habitations
this Child of Heaven hath called us
from our slumber;
She who at night-time with her argent
lustre hath shown herself e'en through
the shades of darkness.

2 All this with red-rayed steeds have they
divided : the Dawns on bright cars
shine in wondrous fashion.
They, bringing near the stately rite's
commencement, drive far away the
night's surrounding shadows.

3 Dawns, bringing hither, to the man who
worships, glory and power and might
and food and vigour,
Opulent, with imperial sway like heroes,
favour your servant and this day enrich
him.

4 Now is there treasure for the man who
serves you, now for the hero, Dawns !
who brings oblation;
Now for the singer when he sings the
praise-song. Even to one like me ye
brought aforetime.

5 O Dawn who standest on the mountain
ridges, Aṅgirases now praise thy stalls
of cattle.
With prayer and holy hymn they burst
them open : the heroes' calling on the
Gods was fruitful.

6 Shine on us as of old, thou Child of Hea-
ven, on him, rich Maid ! who serves like
Bharadvāja.
Give to the singer wealth with noble

heroes, and upon us bestow wide-spreading glory.

HYMN LXVI. *Maruts.*

1. E'EN to the wise let that be still a wonder
to which the general name of Cow is
given.
The one hath swelled among mankind for
milking : Pṛśni hath drained but once
her fair bright udder.

2 They who like kindled flames of fire are
glowing, the Maruts, twice and thrice
have waxen mighty.
Golden and dustless were their cars, invested with their great strength and their
heroic vigour.

3 They who are Sons of the rain-pouring
Rudra, whom the long-lasting One had
power to foster:
The Mighty Ones whose germ great Mother
Pṛśni is known to have received for
man's advantage.

4 They shrink not from the birth; in this
same manner still resting there they
purge away reproaches.
When they have streamed forth, brilliant,
at their pleasure, with their own splendour they bedew their bodies.

5 Even those who bear the brave bold name
of Maruts, whom not the active quickly
wins for milking.
Even the liberal wards not off those fierce
ones, those who are light and agile in
their greatness.

6 When, strong in strength and armed with
potent weapons, they had united well-
formed earth and heaven,

The liberal mortal : the man who sacrifices to the Gods.
To bring out this meaning more clearly the last line
may be translated : 'To him who stays at home and
pours oblations, O Goddess Dawn, thou givest ample
riches.'

---

1 *At night-time* : an allusion, perhaps, to the 'false
dawn' before the appearance of the real dawn, although this faint glimmer can hardly be called lustre.
Or the light of stars may be intended, as belonging to
Dawn rather than to Night.

2 *All this......have they divided* : separated light
from darkness. *The stately rite* : the Agnihotra, or great
morning sacrifice.

5 *Aṅgirases here praise* : 'What we are doing here
is in reality only a repetition of what the Aṅgirasas did
in ancient times.'—Ludwig.

6 *Bharadvāja* : the great ancestor of the priestly
family of which the Ṛṣi of the hymn was a member.

---

1 This meaning may be that while things of
different nature are designated by the name of Cow,
all that is so called has a claim to our wonder and
admiration. The Cow of earth yields her milk frequently and in abundance : Pṛśni, the Cow of the firmament, has given milk but once, when she brought forth
her offspring, the Maruts. 'Once only Pṛśni's milk was
shed : no second, after this, is born' (VI. 48. 22).
Sāyaṇa's interpretation is utterly inconsistent with the
plain meaning of the words of the text.

2 *Twice and thrice* : perhaps in relation to earth and
heaven, and to earth, firmament, and heaven.

4 *Still resting there* : while yet unborn they free
their mother from the reproach of barrenness.

5 *Wins for milking* : persuades to grant his petitions.
The version of the second line is merely conjectural as
the meaning of *staundḥ* (explained by Sāyaṇa as=*stenāḥ*
robbers) is unknown. 'The liberal donor pacifies the
angry Maruts who are otherwise in their might the
resistless plunderers of their wealth).'—Wilson.

6 *United* : by obscuring the horizon with cloud
and rain.

Rodasī stood among these furious Heroes
like splendour shining with her native
brightness.

7 No team of goats shall draw your car,
O Maruts, no horse no charioteer be he
who drives it.
Halting not, reinless, through the air it
travels, speeding alone its paths through
earth and heaven.

8 None may obstruct, none overtake, O
Maruts, him whom ye succour in the
strife of battle
For sons and progeny, for kine and waters:
he bursts the cow-stall on the day of
trial.

9 Bring a bright hymn to praise the band of
Maruts, the Singers, rapid, strong in
native vigour,
Who conquer mighty strength with strength
more mighty: earth shakes in terror at
their wars, O Agni.

10 Bright like the flashing flames of sacrifices,
like tongues of fire impetuous in their
onset,
Chanting their psalm, singing aloud, like
heroes, splendid from birth, invincible,
the Maruts.

11 That swelling band I call with invocation,
the brood of Rudra, armed with glittering lances.
Pure hymns are meet for that celestial
army : like floods and mountains have
the Strong Ones battled.

HYMN LXVII. *Mitra-Varuna.*

1. Now Mitra-Varuṇa shall be exalted high
by your songs, noblest of all existing;
They who, as 'twere with reins are best
Controllers, unequalled with their arms
to check the people.

7 No feeble or ordinary team must convey you ;
no common charioteer must drive your chariot.

8 *Bursts the cow-stall* : carries away the enemy's
cattle.

10 *Singing aloud* : 'causing their opponents to
tremble,' according to Sāyaṇa, who derives the word
from the root *dhū*, to shake. Derived from *dhvan*, to
sound, *dhunayaḥ* means singers, musicians, minstrels,
leaders of the wild music of the wind and storm
(stürmer.—Ludwig). See *Vedische Studien*, I. 269.

11 *Like floods and mountains* : perhaps, with the
impetuosity of rushing waters and the firm strength of
mountains. But the meaning of this last half-line, as
of many other passages of the hymn, is very obscure.

The hymn has been translated and thoroughly discussed by Peter von Bradke (Festgrutss an R. von Roth,
1893, pp. 117—125). See also Vedic Hymns, I. 368—
372 (Sacred Books of the East, XXXII).

2 To you Two Gods is this my thought
extended, turned to the sacred grass with
loving homage.
Give us, O Mitra-Varuṇa, a dwelling safe
from attack, which ye shall guard, Boon-
Givers !

3 Come hither, Mitra-Varuṇa, invited with
eulogies and loving adoration,
Ye who with your might, as Work-Control-
lers, urge even men who quickly hear
to labour.

4 Whom, of pure origin, like two strong
horses, Aditi bore as babes in proper
season,
Whom, Mighty at your birth, the Mighty
Goddess brought forth as terrors to the
mortal foeman.

5 As all the Gods in their great joy and
gladness gave you with one accord your
high dominion,
As ye surround both worlds, though wide
and spacious, your spies are ever true
and ne'er bewildered.

6 So, through the days maintaining princely
power, ye prop the height as 'twere
from loftiest heaven.
The Star of all the Gods, established,
filleth the heaven and earth with food
of man who liveth.

7 Take the strong drink, to quaff till ye are
sated, when he and his attendants fill
the chamber.
The young Maids brook not that none
seeks to win them, when, Quickeners of
all ! they scatter moisture.

8 So with your tongue come ever, when
your envoy, faithful and very wise, attends
our worship.
Nourished by holy oil ! be this your
glory : annihilate the sacrificer's trouble.

9 When, Mitra-Varuṇa, they strive against
you and break the friendly laws ye have
established,
They, neither Gods nor men in estimation,
like Api's sons have godless sacrifices.

5 *Your spies* : messengers or angels, probably the
rest of the Ādityas. See I. 25. 13.

6 *The height* : the high ridge or summit of heaven.
The Star of all the Gods : representing all the Gods :
the Sun. He draws up the waters which descend to
fertilize the earth.

7 *He* : the worshipper ; or, perhaps, Soma. *The
chamber* : of sacrifice. *The Young Maids* : the water,
necessary for the preparation of the Soma libation, is
ready and impatiently waiting to be used.

8 *With your tongue* : Agni, by whose tongue of fire
they consume the oblations. *Your envoy* : Agni.

9 *Like Api's sons* : 'sons of the Waters.'—Grassmann.
The meaning is uncertain. *Godless sacrifices* : unattended by Gods, and therefore fruitless.

10 When singers in their song uplift their
   voices, some chant the Nivid texts with
   steady purpose.
   Then may we sing you lauds that shall
   be fruitful : do ye not rival all the
   Gods in greatness?
11 O Mitra-Varuṇa, may your large bounty
   come to us hither, near to this our
   dwelling,
   When the kine haste to us, and when
   they harness the fleet-foot mettled stallion
   for the battle.

HYMN LXVIII.   *Indra-Varuṇa.*

1. HIS honouring rite whose grass is trimmed
   is offered swiftly to you, in Manu's
   wise, accordant,
   The rite which Indra-Varuṇa shall carry
   this day to high success and glorious
   issue.
2 For at Gods' worship they are best through
   vigour; they have become the strongest
   of the Heroes;
   With mighty strength, most liberal of the
   Princes, Chiefs of the host, by Law made
   Vṛtra's slayers.
3 Praise those Twain Gods for powers that
   merit worship, Indra and Varuṇa, for
   bliss, the joyous.
   One with his might and thunderbolt
   slays Vṛtra; the other as a Sage stands
   near in troubles.
4 Though dames and men have waxen strong
   and mighty, and all the Gods self-
   praised among the Heroes,
   Ye, Indra-Varuṇa, have in might surpassed
   them, and thus were ye spread wide,
   O Earth and Heaven.
5 Righteous is he, and liberal and helpful
   who, Indra-Varuṇa, brings you gifts
   with gladness.
   That bounteous man through food shall
   conquer foemen, and win him opulence
   and wealthy people.

6 May wealth which ye bestow in food
   and treasure on him who brings you
   gifts and sacrifices,
   Wealth, Gods ! which breaks the curse of
   those who vex us, be, Indra-Varuṇa, e'en
   our own possession.
7 So also, Indra-Varuṇa, may our princes
   have riches swift to save, with Gods to
   guard them—
   They whose great might gives victory in
   battles, and their triumphant glory spreads
   with swiftness.
8 Indra and Varuṇa, Gods whom we are
   lauding, mingle ye wealth with our
   heroic glory.
   May we, who praise the strength of what
   is mighty, pass dangers, as with boats
   we cross the waters.
9 Now will I sing a dear and far-extending
   hymn to Varuṇa the God, sublime,
   imperial Lord,
   Who, mighty Governor, Eternal, as with
   flame, illumines both wide worlds with
   majesty and power.
10 True to Law, Indra-Varuṇa, drinkers of
   the juice, drink this pressed Soma which
   shall give you rapturous joy.
   Your chariot cometh to the banquet of the
   Gods, to sacrifice, as it were home, that
   ye may drink.
11 Indra and Varuṇa, drink your fill, ye
   Heroes, of this invigorating sweetest
   Soma.
   This juice is shed by us that ye may quaff
   it : on this trimmed grass be seated,
   and rejoice you

HYMN LXIX.   *Indra-Viṣṇu*

1. INDRA and Viṣṇu, at my task's completion
   I urge you on with food and sacred
   service.
   Accept the sacrifice and grant us riches,
   leading us on by unobstructed pathways.
2 Ye who inspire all hymns, Indra and
   Viṣṇu, ye vessels who contain the Soma
   juices,
   May hymns of praise that now are sung
   address you, the lauds that are recited
   by the singers.

10 *Nivid texts* : short formularies of invocation inserted
in a liturgy.
11 *When the kine haste to us* : when the cattle of the
men whom we are about to attack are ready and eager
to be carried off. Sāyaṇa's interpretation of the last
line is totally different : 'when (your) praises are uttered,
and the sacrificers add in the ceremony the *Soma* that
inspires straightforwardness and resolution, and is the
showerer (of benefits).)'—Wilson.

———

3 *In troubles* : 'in deeds of might.'—Ludwig. 'With
snares, or nooses,' according to Professor Geldner, *Vedische
studien* I. 142.
4 *Self-praised* : on account of their own deeds, or
their own nature.

8 *Of what is mighty* : apparently, riches.
9 This stanza, in honour of Varuṇa alone, appears
to be the beginning of another hymn. Professor
Grassmann banishes stanzas 9 and 10 to his Appendix.

———

1 *At my task's completion* : when all arrangements
for the sacrifice have been made.
2 *Who inspire* : literally, 'the generators,' *janitdrá.
By the singers* : or, 'with laudations.'

3 Lords of joy-giving draughts, Indra and Visnu, come, giving gifts of treasure, to the Soma.
   With brilliant rays of hymns let chanted praises, repeated with the lauds, adorn and deck you.

4 May your foe-conquering horses bring you hither, Indra and Viṣṇu, sharers of the banquet.
   Of all our hymns accept the invocations : list to my prayers and hear the songs I sing you.

5 This your deed, Indra-Viṣṇu, must be lauded : widely ye strode in the wild joy of Soma.
   Ye made the firmament of larger compass, and made the regions broad for our existence.

6 Strengthened with sacred offerings, Indra-Viṣṇu, first eaters, served with worship and oblation,
   Fed with the holy oil, vouchsafe us riches : ye are the lake, the vat that holds the Soma.

7 Drink of this meath, O Indra, thou, and Viṣṇu; drink ye your fill of Soma, Wonder-Workers.
   The sweet exhilarating juice hath reached you. Hear ye my prayers, give ear unto my calling.

8 Ye Twain have conquered, ne'er have ye been conquered : never hath either of the Twain been vanquished.
   Ye, Indra-Viṣṇu, when ye fought the battle, produced this infinite with three divisions.

### HYMN LXX.					*Heaven and Earth.*

1. FILLED full of fatness, compassing all things that be, wide, spacious, dropping meath, beautiful in their form,
   The Heaven and the Earth by Varuṇa's decree, unwasting, rich in germs, stand parted each from each.

2 The Everlasting Pair, with full streams, rich in milk, in their pure rule pour fatness for the pious man.
   Ye who are Regents of this world, O Earth

and Heaven, pour into us the genial flow that prospers men.

3 Whoso, for righteous life, pours offerings to you, O Heaven and Earth, ye Hemispheres, that man succeeds.
   He in his seed is born again and spreads by Law : from you flow things diverse in form, but ruled alike.

4 Enclosed in fatness, Heaven and Earth are bright therewith : they mingle with the fatness which they still increase.
   Wide, broad, set foremost at election of the priest, to them the singers pray for bliss to further them.

5 May Heaven and Earth pour down the balmy rain for us, balm-dropping, yielding balm, with balm upon your path,
   Bestowing by your Godhead sacrifice and wealth, great fame and strength for us and good heroic might.

6 May Heaven and Earth make food swell plenteously for us, all-knowing Father, Mother, wondrous in their works.
   Pouring out bounties, may, in union, both the Worlds, all beneficial, send us gain, and power, and wealth.

### HYMN LXXI.					*Savitar.*

1. FULL of effectual wisdom Savitar the God hath stretched out golden arms that he may bring forth life.
   Young and most skilful, while he holds the region up, the Warrior sprinkles fatness over both his hands.

2 May we enjoy the noblest vivifying force of Savitar the God, that he may give us wealth :
   For thou art mighty to produce and lull to rest the world of life that moves on two feet and on four.

3 Protect our habitation, Savitar, this day, with guardian aids around, auspicious, firm and true.
   God of the golden tongue, keep us for newest

---

8 *Produced this infinite* : brought into existence the world with all its creatures, the three divisions being heaven, firmament, and earth. See Professor Wilson's note for Sāyaṇa's explanation of the passage.

The deities are Dyāvāpṛthivī, that is Dyaus, Heaven, and Pṛthivī, Earth, combined in a compound dual.

---

1 *Full of fatness* : containing *ghṛta, ghi,* clarified butter, fatness in general, especially the fertilizing rain.

---

3 *Ye Hemispheres* : *dhiṣaṇe* ; two bowls. 'Firm-set,' —Wilson. *By Law* : in the course of nature.

4 *Set foremost at election of the priest* : 'first propitiated at the sacrifice.'—Wilson.

---

vi 1 *Savitar* : the Sun as the great generator or viisfier. *Sprinkles fatness* : Professor Ludwig thinks that thn may be somewhat ironical. 'The god sprinkles his haids, probably, as a preparation for the hard work whch he is about to perform; but there is an underlying thought that a good deal of the fatness [in the shape of fertilizing rain] also falls down to the earth.'

bliss : let not the evil-wisher have us in his power.

4 This Savitar the God, the golden-handed, Friend of the home, hath risen to meet the twilight.
With cheeks of brass, with pleasant tongue, the Holy, he sends the worshipper rich gifts in plenty.

5 Like a Director, Savitar hath extended his golden arms, exceeding fair to look on.
He hath gone up the heights of earth and heaven, and made each monster fall and cease from troubling.

6 Fair wealth, O Savitar, to-day, to-morrow, fair wealth produce for us each day that passes.
May we through this our song be happy gainers, God, of a fair and spacious habitation.

HYMN LXXII. Indra-Soma.

1. GREAT is this might of yours, Indra and Soma : the first high exploits were your own achievements.
Ye found the Sun, ye found the light of heaven : ye killed all darkness and the Gods' blasphemers.

2 Ye, Indra-Soma, gave her light to Morning, and led the Sun on high with all his splendour.
Ye stayed the heaven with a supporting pillar, and spread abroad apart, the Earth, the Mother.

3 Ye slew the flood-obstructing serpent Vrtra, Indra and Soma : Heaven approved your exploit.
Ye urged to speed the currents of the rivers, and many seas have ye filled full with waters.

4 Ye in the unripe udders of the milch-kine have set the ripe milk, Indra, thou, and Soma.

Ye have held fast the unimpeded whiteness within these many-coloured moving creatures.

5 Verily ye bestow, Indra and Soma, wealth, famed, victorious, passing to our children.
Ye have invested men, ye Mighty Beings, with manly strength that conquers in the battle.

HYMN LXXIII. Bṛhaspati.

1. SERVED with oblations, first-born, mountain-render, Aṅgiras' son, Bṛhaspati, the Holy,
With twice-firm path, dwelling in light, our Father, roars loudly, as a bull, to Earth and Heaven.

2 Bṛhaspati, who made for such a people wide room and verge when Gods were invocated,
Slaying his enemies, breaks down their castles, quelling his foes and conquering those who hate him.

3 Bṛhaspati in war hath won rich treasures, hath won, this God, the great stalls filled with cattle.
Striving to win waters and light, resistless, Bṛhaspati with lightning smites the foeman.

HYMN LXXIV. Soma-Rudra.

1. HOLD fast your Godlike sway, O Soma-Rudra : let these our sacrifices quickly reach you.
Placing in every house your seven great treasures, bring blessing to our quadrupeds and bipeds.

2 Soma and Rudra, chase to every quarter the sickness that hath visited our dwelling.
Drive Nirṛti away into the distance, and give us excellent and happy glories.

3 Provide, O Soma-Rudra, for our bodies all needful medicines to heal and cure us.

4 *To meet the twilight*: 'at the close of night.'—Wilson. *Cheeks of brass* : *áyohanuḥ*; according to Sāyaṇa. 'golden-jawed.'

5 *A Director* ; a priest who directs others. Or, perhaps, 'an Invoker,' as Professor Ludwig suggests. *Each monster* : every terror of the night. Sāyaṇa's interpretation of the last line is totally different : 'and,' moving along, delights every thing that is.'—Wilson.

----

4 *Ye in the unripe udders* : the unripe, that is raw, udders are contrasted with the warm milk that is cooked or matured in them. See I. 62. 9. *The unimpeded whiteness* : the milk which is not prevented from flowing. The colour of the milk is contrasted with the colour of the cows that produce it.

----

1 *Bṛhaspati* : Lord of Prayer ; the Deity in whom the action of the worshipper upon the Gods is personified. See I. 14. 3. *Mountain-render* : 'Bṛhaspati *cleft the mountain*' (I. 62. 3). *Dwelling in light* : or, perhaps, in the Sun. The meaning of *prāgharmasád* is uncertain.

2 *Such a people* : so good a people. *When Gods were invocated* : in battle.

3 *With lightning* : or with Sunlight : 'with sacred prayers.'—Wilson.

----

1 *Quadrupeds and bipeds* : or, 'bless all of us, men and four-footed creatures.

2 *Nirṛti* : the Goddess of Death and Destruction.

Set free and draw away the sin committed which we have still inherent in our persons.

4 Armed with keen shafts and weapons, kind and loving, be gracious unto us, Soma and Rudra.
Release us from the noose of Varuṇa; keep us from sorrow, in your tender loving-kindness.

HYMN LXXV.   *Weapons of War.*

1. THE warrior's look is like a thunderous rain-cloud's, when, armed with mail, he seeks the lap of battle.
Be thou victorious with unwounded body: so let the thickness of thy mail protect thee.

2 With Bow let us win kine, with Bow the battle, with Bow be victors in our hot encounters.
The Bow brings grief and sorrow to the foeman : armed with the Bow may we subdue all regions.

3 Close to his ear, as fain to speak, She presses, holding her well-loved Friend in her embraces.
Strained on the Bow, She whispers like a woman—this Bowstring that preserves us in the combat.

4 These, meeting like a woman and her lover, bear, mother-like, their child upon their bosom.
May the two Bow-ends, starting swift asunder, scatter, in unison, the foes who hate us.

5 With many a son, father of many daughters, He clangs and clashes as he goes to battle.
Slung on the back, pouring his brood, the Quiver vanquishes all opposing bands and armies.

6 Upstanding in the Car the skilful Charioteer guides his strong Horses on whithersoe'er he will.

See and admire the strength of those controlling Reins which from behind declare the will of him who drives.

7 Horses whose hoofs rain dust are neighing loudly, yoked to the Chariots, showing forth their vigour,
With their forefeet descending on the foemen, they, never flinching, trample and destroy them.

8 Car-bearer is the name of his oblation, whereon are laid his Weapons and his Armour.
So let us here, each day that passes, honour the helpful Car with hearts exceeding joyful.

9 In sweet association lived the fathers who gave us life, profound and strong in trouble,
Unwearied, armed with shafts and wondrous weapons, free, real heroes, conquerors of armies.

10 The Brāhmans, and the Fathers meet for Soma-draughts, and, graciously inclined, unequalled Heaven and Earth.
Guard us from evil, Pūṣan, guard us strengtheners of Law : let not the evil-wisher master us.

11 Her tooth a deer, dressed in an eagle's feathers, bound with cow-hide, launched forth, She flieth onward.
There where the heroes speed hither and thither, there may the Arrows shelter and protect us.

12 Avoid us thou whose flight is straight, and let our bodies be as stone.
May Soma kindly speak to us, and Aditi protect us well.

---

4 *The noose of Varuṇa* : Varuṇa, the moral Governor of the world, is represented as armed with a noose or lasso for the capture and destruction of the wicked.

---

3 *She* : the bowstring. *Her well-loved friend* : the arrow. *Whispers like a woman* : 'twangs like the scream of a woman.'—Muir. But the faint sound made by the string while it is being drawn to the ear is intended. Homer likens the sound to the voice of a swallow.

4 *These* : the two ends of the bow. *Like a woman and her lover* : or, 'drawing close like two women to their lovers'. *Their child* : the arrow.

5 *With many a son* : the quiver is called the father of sons and daughters, it is said, because the words signifying arrow are both masculine and feminine.

8 *Car-bearer* : *rathavdhanam* : a platform, stand, or truck on which the chariot is placed when not in use. The word seems in this place to mean also the oblation offered by the warrior to the ideal war-chariot personified, or to a tutelary deity of chariots.

9 There is no verb in this stanza, and the only substantive, *pitáraḥ*, fathers, is explained by both Commentators as *pālayitāraḥ*, guards, defenders, that is, apparently, those who attend the chariot of the chief. Professor Wilson, following Sāyaṇa, translates : 'The guards (of the chariot), revelling in the savoury (spoil, distributors of food, protectors in calamity, armed with spears, resolute, beautifully arranged, strong in arrows, invincible, of heroic valour, robust, and conquerors of numerous hosts.'

10 *The Brāhmans and the Fathers* : or, perhaps, the sacerdotal Fathers. The stanza, which is grammatically difficult, seems out of place.

11 *Her tooth a deer* : the point of the arrow is made of a piece of deer's horn attached to the shaft with leather strings. The butt of the arrow is feathered.

13 He lays his blows upon their backs, he
deals his blows upon their thighs.

Thou, Whip, who urgest horses, drive
sagacious horses in the fray.

14 It compasses the arm with serpent windings,
fending away the friction of the bowstring:
So may the Brace, well-skilled in all its
duties, guard manfully the man from
every quarter.

15 Now to the Shaft with venom smeared,
tipped with deer-horn, with iron mouth,
Celestial, of Parjanya's seed, be this great
adoration paid.

16 Loosed from the Bowstring fly away, thou
Arrow, sharpened by our prayer.
Go to the foemen, strike them home, and
let not one be left alive.

17 There where the flights of Arrows fall like
boys whose locks are yet unshorn.
Even there may Brahmanaspati, and Aditi
protect us well, protect us well through
all our days.

18 Thy vital parts I cover with thine Armour:
with immortality King Soma clothe thee.
Varuṇa give thee what is more than ample,
and in thy triumph may the Gods be
joyful.

19 Whoso would kill us, whether he be a
strange foe or one of us,
May all the Gods discomfit him. My
nearest, closest Mail is prayer.

---

13 *He* : the whip.
14 *It* : the brace or guard worn on the archer's
left arm, fastened on with leather straps.

15 *With venom smeared* : by the Laws of Manu,
that is, the ideal Code of the Mānavas, Ksatriyas
were forbidden to poison their arrows. Arrows appear
to have been of two kinds, one, the older and less
effective, *tipped with deer-horn*, and the other *with iron
mouth*, pointed with *áyas*, bronze or iron. *Celestial, of
Parjanya's seed* : made of the tall reeds that grow in
the Rains under the influence of Parjanya the God of
the rain-cloud.

16 *Sharpened by our prayer* : 'whetted by charm.'—
Wilson.

17 *Like boys whose locks are yet unshorn*: : 'the point
of the comparison is not very obvious, but it may
mean that the arrows fall where they list, as boys
before they are left with the lock of hair, before the
religious tonsure, play about wherever they like'—
Wilson. Professor Roth separates *viśikhā* from *kumārd*,
and translates : 'Where the arrows fly, young and
old : that is, feathered and unfeathered.'

18 *Thy vital parts* : the *várman*, or coat of mail,
protected the shoulders, back, chest, and lower parts of
the body. If not made of metal, it was strengthened
and adorned with metal of some kind. The Indians in
the army of Xerxes are said by Herodotus to have
worn clothes made out of the bark of trees (VII. 65);
but he probably meant the common soldiers only, and
not the chiefs. For a full description of the arms, offen-
sive and defensive, used in Vedic times, see Muir,
O. S. Texts, V. 469 ; *Altindisches Leben*, pp. 293—301;
or Dutt's *History of Civilization in Ancient India*, I. p. 88.

BOOK THE SEVENTH

HYMN I. *Agni.*

1. THE men from fire-sticks, with their hands' swift movement, have, in deep thought, engendered glorious Agni,
Far-seen, with pointed flame, Lord of the homestead.

2 The Vasus set that Agni in the dwelling, fair to behold, for help from every quarter :
Who, in the home for ever, must be honoured.

3 Shine thou before us, Agni, well-enkindled, with flame, Most Youthful God, that never fadeth.
To thee come all our sacrificial viands.

4 Among all fires these fires have shone most brightly, splendid with light, begirt by noble heroes,
Where men of lofty birth sit down together.

5 Victorious Agni, grant us wealth with wisdom, wealth with brave sons, famous and independent,
Which not a foe who deals in magic conquers.

6 To whom, the Strong, at morn and eve comes, maid-like, the ladle dropping oil, with its oblation :
Wealth-seeking comes to him his own devotion.

7 Burn up all malice with those flames, O Agni, wherewith of old thou burntest up Jarūtha,
And drive away in silence pain and sickness.

8 With him who lighteth up thy splendour, Agni, excellent, pure, refulgent, Purifier,
Be present, and with us through these our praises.

9 Agni, the patriarchal men, the mortals who have in many places spread thy lustre,—
Be gracious to us here for their sake also.

10 Let these men, heroes in the fight with foemen, prevail against all godless arts of magic,—
These who approve the noble song I sing thee.

11 Let us not sit in want of men, O Agni, without descendants, heroless, about thee :
But, O House-Friend, in houses full of children.

12 By sacrifice which the Steeds' Lord ever visits, there make our dwelling rich in seed and offspring,
Increasing still with lineal successors.

13 Guard us, O Agni, from the hated demon, guard us from malice of the churlish sinner :
Allied with thee may I subdue assailants.

14 May this same fire of mine surpass all others, this fire where offspring, vigorous and firm-handed,
Wins, on a thousand paths, what ne'er shall perish.

15 This is that Agni, saviour from the foeman, who guards the kindler of the flame from sorrow :
Heroes of noble lineage serve and tend him.

16 This is that Agni, served in many places, whom the rich lord who brings oblation kindles,
And round him goes the priest at sacrifices.

17 Agni, may we with riches in possession bring thee continual offerings in abundance,
Using both means to draw thee to our worship.

18 Agni, bear thou, Eternal, these most welcome oblations to the Deities' assembly :
Let them enjoy our very fragrant presents.

19 Give us not up, Agni, to want of heroes, to wretched clothes, to need, to destitution.

All the hymns of this Book are ascribed to the Ṛṣi Vasiṣṭha, with whom his sons are associated as the seers of parts of two hymns.

1 *In deep thought* : 'with their fingers,' according to Sāyaṇa, this meaning having been attributed without any philological grounds to the word *dīdhitibhiḥ* from its use in this and similar passages.

6 *His own devotion* : the worship which belongs especially to him.

7 *Jarūtha* : a Rākṣasa or demon with a loud harsh voice.—Sāyaṇa.

12 *Tho Steeds' Lord* : Agni, whose swift flames are called horses.

17 *Both means* : prayer and praise.

Yield us not, Holy One, to fiend or hunger; injure us not at home or in the forest.

20 Give strength and power to these my prayers, O Agni; O God, pour blessings on our chiefs and nobles.

Grant that both we and they may share thy bounty. Ye Gods, protect us evermore with blessings.

21 Thou Agni, swift to hear, art fair of aspect : beam forth, O Son of Strength, in full effulgence.

Let me not want, with thee, a son for ever : let not a manly hero ever fail us.

22 Condemn us not to indigence, O Agni, beside these flaming fires which Gods have kindled;

Nor, even after fault, let thy displeasure, thine as a God, O Son of Strength, o'ertake us.

23 O Agni, fair of face, the wealthy mortal who to the Immortal offers his oblation.

Hath him who wins him treasure by his Godhead, to whom the prince, in need, goes supplicating.

24 Knowing our chief felicity, O Agni, bring hither ample riches to our nobles,

Wherewith we may enjoy ourselves, O Victor, with undiminished life and hero children.

25 Give strength and power to these my prayers, O Agni; O God, pour blessings on our chiefs and nobles.

Grant that both we and they may share thy bounty. Ye Gods, protect us evermore with blessings.

HYMN II. *Âpris.*

1. GLADLY accept, this day, our fuel, Agni : send up thy sacred smoke and shine sublimely.

Touch the celestial summits with thy columns, and overspread thee with the rays of Sūrya.

2 With sacrifice to these we men will honour the majesty of holy Narāśaṁsa—

To these the pure, most wise, the thought-inspirers, Gods who enjoy both sorts of our oblations.

3 We will extol at sacrifice for ever, as men may do, Agni whom Manu kindled,

Your very skilful Asura, meet for worship, envoy between both worlds, the truthful speaker.

4 Bearing the sacred grass, the men who serve him strew it with reverence, on their knees, by Agni.

Calling him to the spotted grass, oil-sprinkled, adorn him, ye Adhvaryus, with oblation.

5 With holy thoughts the pious have thrown open Doors fain for chariots in the Gods' assembly.

Like two full mother cows who lick their youngling, like maidens for the gathering, they adorn them.

6 And let the two exalted Heavenly Ladies, Morning and Night, like a cow good at milking,

Come, much-invoked, and on our grass be seated, wealthy, deserving worship, for our welfare.

7 You, Bards and Singers at men's sacrifices, both filled with wisdom, I incline to worship.

Send up our offerings when we call upon you, and so among the Gods obtain us treasures.

8 May Bhāratī with all her Sisters, Ilā accordant with the Gods, with mortals Agni,

Sarasvatī with all her kindred Rivers, come to this grass, Three Goddesses, and seat them.

---

21 *For ever*: *nitye*; perpetual ; who shall live for ever in his posterity.
22 *Which Gods have kindled* : lighted by the ministering priests.
23 *Hath him* : possesses, or enjoys the favour of, Agni. 'That deity (Agni) favours the presenter of (sacrificial) wealth.'—Wilson.
24 *Knowing our chief felicity* : understanding what we want to make us happy, that is, riches.

The Āpris are the divine or deified beings and objects to which the propitiatory verses are addressed. For other Āpri hymns see I. 13; 188; II. 3; III. 4; V. 5; IX. 5; X. 70; 110.

2 *Narāśaṁsa* : 'the Praise of Men' ; Agni. *Both sorts of our oblations* : offerings of ghṛta, ghi, or clarified butter, and libations of Soma juice.

---

5 *Doors* : the deified doors of the hall of sacrifice where the Gods assemble. *Fain for chariots* : welcoming the approach of the cars in which the priests come to the ceremony. The latter half of the stanza is obscure : (the ladles) placed to the east are plying the fire with *ghi* at sacrifices, as the mother cows lick the calf, or as rivers (water the fields).'—Wilson.

6 *Like a cow* : the dual *dhenū*, two cows, instead of *dhenúh*, would, as Ludwig suggests, seem to us to be preferable.

7 *Bards and Singers* : the *hotārā*, or 'two Invokers' of I. 13. 8; perhaps Agni and Varuṇa and Āditya.

8 Stanzas 8—11 are identical with stanzas 8—11 of Book III. 4.

9 Well pleased with us do thou, O God, O
   Tvaṣṭar, give ready issue to our
   procreant vigour,
   Whence springs the hero, powerful, skilled
   in action, lover of Gods, adjuster of
   the press-stones.

10 Send to the Gods the oblation, Lord of
   Forests, and let the Immolator, Agni,
   dress it.
   He as the truer Priest shall offer worship,
   for the God'sgenerations well he
   knoweth.

11 Come thou to us, O Agni, duly kindled,
   together with the potent Gods and
   Indra.
   On this our grass sit Aditi, happy Mother,
   and let our Hail ! delight the Gods
   Immortal.

HYMN III.   *Agni.*

1. ASSOCIATE with fires, make your God Agni
   envoy at sacrifice, best skilled in worship,
   Established firm among mankind, the
   Holy, flame-crowned and fed with oil,
   the Purifier.

2 Like a steed neighing eager for the
   pasture, when he hath stepped forth
   from the great enclosure :
   Then the wind following blows upon his
   splendour, and, straight, the path
   is black which thou hast travelled.

3 From thee a Bull but newly born, O Agni,
   the kindled everlasting flames rise
   upward.
   Aloft to heaven thy ruddy smoke ascendeth : Agni, thou speedest to the Gods
   as envoy.

4 Thou whose fresh lustre o'er the earth
   advanceth when greedily with thy jaws
   thy food thou eatest.
   Like a host hurried onward comes thy
   lasso : fierce, with thy tongue thou
   piercest, as 'twere barley.

5 The men have decked him both at eve
   and morning, Most Youthful Agni, as
   they tend a courser.

1 *Associate* : *sajóṣāḥ* being a shortened form of
sajóṣasaḥ, the nominative plural. Sāyaṇa explains it as
an accusative singular, qualifying Agni.

2 *From the great enclosure* : 'from the vast enclosing
(forest).'—Wilson. Others understand it as the enclosure in which the horse is confined.

4 *Thou piercest as 'twere barley* : the comparison is
somewhat compressed : the meaning is, thou penetratest
and fellest the trees of the forest with thy tongue as
men cut down barley with a reaping-hook.

They kindle him, a guest within his
dwelling : bright shines the splendour
of the worshipped Hero.

6 O fair of face, beautiful is thine aspect
when, very near at hand, like gold thou
gleamest,
Like Heaven's thundering roar thy might
approaches, and like the wondrous Sun
thy light thou showest.

7 That we may worship, with your Hail to
Agni ! with sacrificial cakes and fat
oblations,
Guard us, O Agni, with those boundless
glories as with a hundred fortresses
of iron.

8 Thine are resistless songs for him who
offers, and hero-giving hymns wherewith
thou savest;
With these, O Son of Strength, O Jātavedas, guard us, preserve these princes
and the singers.

9 When forth he cometh, like an axe new-
sharpened, pure in his form, resplendent
in his body,
Sprung, sought with eager longing, from
his Parents, for the Gods' worship,
Sage and Purifier :

10 Shine this felicity on us, O Agni : may
we attain to perfect understanding.
All happiness be theirs who sing and
praise thee. Ye Gods, preserve us
evermore with blessings.

HYMN IV.   *Agni.*

1. BRING forth your gifts to his refulgent
   splendour, your hymn as purest offering
   to Agni,
   To him who goes as messenger with knowledge between all songs of men and
   Gods in heaven.

2 Wise must this Agni be, though young
   and tender, since he was born, Most
   Youthful, of his Mother;
   He who with bright teeth seizeth fast the
   forests, and eats his food, though
   plenteous, in a moment.

3 Before his presence must we all assemble,
   this God's whom men have seized in
   his white splendour.

9 *From his Parents* : the two fire-sticks.

———

3 *Must we all assemble* : I follow Ludwig in his
interpretation of *saṁsddi* : as we are forsaken, and our
protector is far away (st. 6, 7, 8), we must crowd to
the God of Fire for defence.

This Agni who hath brooked that men should seize him hath shone for man with glow insufferable.

4 Far-seeing hath this Agni been established, deathless mid mortals, wise among the foolish.
Here, O victorious God, forbear to harm us : may we for ever share thy gracious favour.

5 He who hath occupied his God-made dwelling, Agni, in wisdom hath surpassed Immortals.
A Babe unborn, the plants and trees support him, and the earth beareth him the All-sustainer.

6 Agni is Lord of Amṛta in abundance, Lord of the gift of wealth and hero valour,
Victorious God, let us not sit about thee like men devoid of strength, beauty, and worship.

7 The foeman's treasure may be won with labour : may we be masters of our own possessions.
Agni, no son is he who springs from others: lengthen not out the pathways of the foolish.

8 Unwelcome for adoption is the stranger, one to be thought of as another's offspring,
Though grown familiar by continual presence. May our strong hero come, freshly triumphant.

9 Guard us from him who would assail us, Agni; preserve us O thou Victor, from dishonour.
Here let the place of darkening come upon thee : may wealth be ours, desirable, in thousands.

10 Shine this felicity on us, O Agni : may we attain to perfect understanding.
All happiness be theirs who sing and praise thee. Ye Gods, preserve us evermore with blessings.

6 In the second line I have borrowed from Prof. Max Müller, *Vedic Hy.ms*, I. p. 80.

7 Let us remain in undisturbed possession of our own property, and let us have sons of our own begetting and not the adopted children of others.

8 Men do not look with pleasure and affection on adopted sons ; but we are longing to see our absent protector return to us.—Ludwig. Others explain the last half-verse differently : 'therefore let there come to us (a son) new-born, possessed of food, victorious over foes.'—Wilson.

9 This stanza is a repetition of VI. 15, 12, where see note.

10 Repeated from stanza 10 of the preceding hymn.

HYMN V.   *Agni.*

1. BRING forth your song of praise to mighty Agni, the speedy messenger of earth and heaven,
Vaiśvānara, who, with those who wake, hath waxen great in the lap of all the Gods Immortal.

2 Sought in the heavens, on earth is Agni stablished, leader of rivers, Bull of standing waters.
Vaiśvānara, when he hath grown in glory, shines on the tribes of men with light and treasure.

3 For fear of thee forth fled the dark-hued races, scattered abroad, deserting their possessions,
When, glowing, O Vaiśvānara, for Pūru, thou Agni didst light up and rend their castles.

4 Agni Vaiśvānara, both Earth and Heaven submit them to thy threefold jurisdiction.
Refulgent in thine undecaying lustre thou hast invested both the worlds with splendour.

5 Agni, the tawny horses, loudly neighing our resonant hymns that drop with oil, attend thee;
Lord of the tribes, our Charioteer of riches, Ensign of days, Vaiśvānara of mornings.

6 In thee, O bright as Mitra, Vasus seated the might of Asuras, for they loved thy spirit.
Thou dravest Dasyus from their home, O Agni, and broughtest forth broad light to light the Ārya.

7 Born in the loftiest heaven thou in a moment reachest, like wind, the place where Gods inhabit.
Thou, favouring thine offspring, roaredst loudly when giving life to creatures, Jātavedas.

The hymn is addressed to Agni as Vaiśvānara, the God who is present with, and benefits, all Āryan men.
1 *With those who wake* : tended by the priests. According to Sāyaṇa 'associated with the wakened Gods.'

2 *Bull of standing waters* : the meaning of *stiyānām* is uncertain. Perhaps, as Ludwig suggests, plants and bushes are intended which Agni like a bull levels with the ground.

3 *The dark-hued races* : according to von Roth, the spirits of darkness. *For Pūru* : or, for man.

4 *Threefold jurisdiction* : in heaven, mid-air, and earth.

5 *The tawny horses* : the hymns that hasten to Agni like eager horses. Ludwig translates the *haritaḥ* of the text by 'gold-yellow,' qualifying 'hymn's; that is, hymns with libations of yellow Soma juice.

6 *Thou dravest* : cf. I. 117. 21.

8 Send us that strength, Vaiśvānara, send
it, Agni, that strength, O Jātavedas, full
of splendour,
Wherewith, all-bounteous God, thou pourest
riches, as fame wide-spreading, on the
man who offers.

9 Agni, bestow upon our chiefs and nobles
that famous power, that wealth which
feedeth many.
Accordant with the Vasus and the Rudras,
Agni, Vaiśvānara, give us sure protection.

HYMN VI.   Agni.

1. Praise of the Asura, high imperial Ruler,
the Manly One in whom the folk shall
triumph—
I laud his deeds who is as strong as Indra,
and lauding celebrate the Fort-destroyer.

2 Sage, Sing, Food, Light,—they bring him
from the mountain, the blessed Sovran
of the earth and heaven.
I decorate with songs the mighty actions
which Agni, Fort-destroyer, did aforetime.

3 The foolish, faithless, rudely-speaking
niggards, without belief or sacrifice or
worship,—
Far far sway hath Agni chased those
Dasyus, and, in the east, hath turned the
godless westward.

4 Him who brought eastward, manliest with
his prowess, the Maids rejoicing in the
western darkness,
That Agni I extol, the Lord of riches,
unyielding tamer of assailing foemen.

5 Him who brake down the walls with
deadly weapons, and gave the Mornings
to a noble Husband,
Young Agni, who with conquering strength
subduing the tribes of Nahus made them
bring their tribute.

6 In whose protection all men rest by
nature, desiring to enjoy his gracious
favour—

Agni Vaiśvānara in his Parents' bosom
hath found the choicest seat in earth
and heaven.

7 Vaiśvānrara the God, at the sun's setting,
hath taken to himself deep-hidden
treasures :
Agni hath taken them from earth and
heaven, from the sea under and the sea
above us.

HYMN VII.   Agni.

1. I send forth even your God, victorious
Agni, like a strong courser, with mine
adoration.
Herald of sacrifice be he who knoweth :
he hath reached Gods, himself, with
measured motion.

2 By paths that are thine own come hither,
Agni, joyous, delighting in the Gods'
alliance,
Making the heights of earth roar with thy
fury, burning with eager teeth the woods
and forests.

3 The grass is strewn; the sacrifice advances :
adored as Priest, Agni is made
propitious,
Invoking both All-boon-bestowing Mothers
of whom, Most Youthful ! thou wast
born to help us.

4 Forthwith the men, the best of these for
wisdom, have made him leader in the
solemn worship.
As Lord in homes of men is Agni stablished,
the Holy One, the joyous, sweetly
speaking.

5 He hath come, chosen bearer, and is
seated in man's home, Brahman, Agni,
the Supporter,
He whom both Heaven and Earth exalt
and strengthen,whom, Giver of all boons,
the Hotar worships.

6 These have passed all in glory, who, the
manly, have wrought with skill the
hymn of adoration ;

---

1 *Fort-destroyer* : demolisher of the cloud-castles of
the demons of drought, or of the strongholds of the non-
Āryan tribes.
2 *Form the mountain* : from the cloud, as lightning.
3 *Westward* : into the darkness of night.
4 *Who brought eastward* : brought back the vanished
lights of dawn.
5 *To a noble Husband* : the Sun, or Agni himself.
The tribes of Nahus . or, according to von Roth, neighbouring people.

---

7 Agni becomes the representative of the Sun, and
in his absence gives light and other blessings to man.
The sea above us : the ocean of air.

———

1 *Like a strong courser* : glorified with my praises,
like a horse that has been groomed and adorned. Or,
perhaps, merely, rapid as a horse. *With measured motion* :
or, a speedy runner. Sāyana explains the word *mitedruḥ*,
in this place as 'consumer of trees,' but in IV. 6. 5 as
parimitagatiḥ, 'with measured motion.'

3 *Both......Mothers* : Heaven and Earth.

Who, listening, have advanced the people's
welfare, and set their thoughts on this
my holy statute.

7 We, the Vasiṣṭhas, now implore thee,
Agni, O Son of Strength, the Lord of
wealth and treasure.
Thou hast brought food to singers and to
nobles. Ye Gods, preserve us evermore
with blessings.

HYMN VIII.   *Agni*

1. THE King whose face is decked with oil is
kindled with homage offered by his
faithful servant.
The men, the priests adore him with
oblations. Agni hath shone forth when
the dawn is breaking.

2 Yea, he hath been acknowledged as most
mighty, the joyous Priest of men, the
youthful Agni.
He, spreading o'er the earth, made
light around him, and grew among the
plants with blackened fellies.

3 How dost thou decorate our hymn, O
Agni ? What power dost thou exert
when thou art lauded ?
When, Bounteous God, may we be lords
of riches, winners of precious wealth
which none may conquer ?

4 Far famed is this the Bharata's own Agni :
he shineth like the Sun with lofty
splendour.
He who hath vanquished Pūru in the
battle, the heavenly guest hath glowed
in full refulgence.

5 Full many oblations are in thee collected :
with all thine aspects thou hast waxen
gracious.
Thou art already famed as praised and
lauded, yet still, O nobly born, increase
thy body.

6 Be this my song, that winneth countless
treasure, engendered with redoubled
force for Agni,

That, splendid, chasing sickness, slaying
demons, it may delight our friend and
bless the singers.

7 We, the Vasiṣṭhas, now implore thee, Agni,
O Son of Strength, the Lord of wealth
and riches.
Thou hast brought food to singers and to
nobles. Ye Gods, preserve us evermore
with blessings.

HYMN IX.   *Agni.*

1. ROUSED from their bosom is the Dawns'
beloved, the joyous Priest, most sapient,
Purifier.
He gives a signal both to Gods and
mortals, to Gods oblations, riches to the
pious.

2 Most wise is he who, forcing doors of
Paṇis, brought the bright Sun to us
who feedeth many.
The cheerful Priest, men's Friend and
home-companion, through still night's
darkness he is made apparent.

3 Wise, ne'er deceived, uncircumscribed,
refulgent, our gracious guest, a Friend
with good attendants,
Shines forth with wondrous light before
the Mornings ; the young plants hath
he entered, Child of Waters.

4 Seeking our gatherings, he, your Jātavedas,
hath shone adorable through human
ages,
Who gleams refulgent with his lovely
lustre : the kine have waked to meet
him when enkindled.

5 Go on thy message to the Gods, and fail
not, O Agni, with their band who pray
and worship.
Bring all the Gods that they may give us
riches, Sarasvatī, the Maruts, Aśvins,
Waters.

6 Vasiṣṭha, when enkindling thee, O Agni,
hath slain Jarūtha. Give us wealth in
plenty.
Sing praise in choral song, O Jātavedas.
Ye Gods, preserve us evermore with
blessings.

---

6 *Who set their thoughts on this my holy statute* : that
is, apparently, who duly observe the law which requires
us to worship Agni. 'Who are glorifiers of this truthful
(deity).'—Wilson.

2 *With blackened fellies* : leaving black tracks behind him : 'dark-pathed.'—Wilson.

4 *The Bharata* : Vasiṣṭha, the *purohita* of the
Bharatas. *Pūru* : the Pūrus, (one of the Five Āryan
Tribes) who opposed the Bharatas.

6 *Countless treasure* : literally, hundreds, thousands.
Our friend : the institutor of the sacrifice.

---

1. *The Dawns' beloved* : Agni, as lighted up at day-
break. *A signal* : of sacrifice, which men are to offer
and Gods are to receive.

6 *Jarūtha* : See VII. 1. 7, where the destruction of
Jarūtha, is ascribed to Agni himself. Jarūtha, said by
Sāyaṇa to have been a Rākṣasa or demon, was
probably an enemy who was slain in a battle at which
Vasiṣṭha was present as *purohita*.—Ludwig.

HYMN X.   *Agni.*

1. HE hath sent forth, bright, radiant, and
   refulgent, like the Dawn's Lover, his
   far-spreading lustre.
   Pure in his splendour shines the golden
   Hero : our longing thoughts hath he
   aroused and wakened.
2. He, like the Sun, hath shone while Morn
   is breaking, and priests who weave the
   sacrifice sing praises,
   Agni, the God, who knows their generations and visits Gods, most bounteous,
   rapid envoy.
3. Our songs and holy hymns go forth to
   Agni, seeking the God and asking him
   for riches,
   Him fair to see, of goodly aspect, mighty,
   men's messenger who carries their oblations.
4. Joined with the Vasus, Agni, bring thou
   Indra bring hither mighty Rudra with
   the Rudras,
   Aditi good to all men with Ādityas,
   Bṛhaspati All-bounteous, with the
   Singers.
5. Men eagerly implore at sacrifices Agni,
   Most Youthful God, the joyous Herald.
   For he is Lord and Ruler over riches, and
   for Gods' worship an unwearied envoy.

HYMN XI.   *Agni.*

1. GRAET art thou, Agni, sacrifice's Herald :
   not without thee are deathless Gods
   made joyful.
   Come hither with all Deities about thee :
   here take thy seat, the first, as Priest, O
   Agni.
2. Men with oblations evermore entreat thee,
   the swift, to undertake an envoy's duty.
   He on whose sacred grass with Gods thou
   sittest, to him, O Agni, are the days
   propitious.
3. Three times a day in thee are shown the
   treasures sent for the mortal who presents
   oblation.

1 *Like the Dawn's Lover* : the Sun. See I. 69. 1.
2 *And priests* : I adopt Sāyaṇa's interpretation of
this half-line.
4 *Singers* : or Ṛkvans, deities who attend and sing
the praises of some God : 'the adorable (Aṅgirasas).'—
Wilson.

3 *Three times a day* : at the morning, the noon,
and the evening libation. Or the meaning may be, in
the three fire-receptacles. *Like a man* : acting like a
human priest. The Commentators explain *manuṣvát* by
'as (at the sacrifice) of Manu.'

Bring the Gods hither like a man, O Agni :
be thou our envoy, guarding us from
curses.
4. Lord of the lofty sacrifice is Agni, Agni is
   Lord of every gift presented.
   The Vasus were contented with his wisdom,
   so the Gods made him their oblation-
   bearer.
5. O Agni, bring the Gods to taste our
   presents : with Indra leading, here let
   them be joyful.
   Convey this sacrifice to Gods in heaven.
   Ye Gods, preserve us evermore with
   blessings.

HYMN XII.   *Agni.*

1. WE with great reverence have approached The Youngest who hath shone
   forth well-kindled in his dwelling,
   With wondrous light between wide earth
   and heaven, well-worshipped, looking
   forth in all directions.
2. Through his great might o'ercoming all
   misfortunes, praised in the house is
   Agni Jātavedas.
   May he protect us from disgrace and
   trouble, both us who laud him and our
   noble patrons.
3. O Agni, thou art Varuṇa and Mitra :
   Vasiṣṭhas with their holy hymns exalt
   thee.
   With thee be most abundant gain of
   treasure. Ye Gods, preserve us evermore
   with blessings.

HYMN XIII.   *Agni.*

1. BRING song and hymn to Agni, Asura-
   slayer, enlightener of all and thought-
   bestower.
   Like an oblation on the grass, to please
   him, I bring this to Vaiśvānara, hymn-
   inspirer.
2. Thou with thy flame, O Agni, brightly
   glowing, hast at thy birth filled full
   the earth and heaven.
   Thou with thy might, Vaiśvānara
   Jātavedas, settest the Gods free from
   the curse that bound them.

1 *The Youngest* : Agni. most youthful of the Gods,
as being continually reproduced.

2 *The curse that bound them* : the Gods seem to have
been subject to the infirmities of old age until Indra, or,
as is here said, Agni, freed them. See IV. 19. 2.

3 Agni, when, born thou lookedst on all
creatures, like a brisk herdsman moving
round his cattle.
The path to prayer, Vaiśvānara, thou
foundest. Ye Gods, preserve us evermore
with blessings.

HYMN XIV   *Agni.*

1. WITH reverence and with offered gifts
serve we the God whose flame is bright:
Let us bring Jātavedas fuel, and adore
Agni when we invoke the Gods.

2 Agni, may we perform thy rites with fuel,
and honour thee, O Holy one, with
praises :
Honour thee, Priest of sacrifice ! with
butter, thee, God of blessed light ! with
our oblation.

3 Come, Agni, with the Gods to our invoking, come, pleased, to offerings sanctified
with Vaṣaṭ.
May we be his who pays thee, God, due
honour. Ye Gods, preserve us evermore
with blessings.

HYMN XV.   *Agni.*

1. OFFER oblations in his mouth, the bounteous God's whom we must serve.
His who is nearest kin to us :

2 Who for the Fivefold People's sake hath
seated him in every home,
Wise, Youthful, Master of the house.

3 On all sides may that Agni guard our
household folk and property;
May he deliver us from woe.

4 I have begotten this new hymn for Agni,
Falcon of the sky :
Will he not give us of his wealth ?

5 Whose glories when he glows in front of
sacrifice are fair to see,
Like wealth of one with hero sons.

6 May he enjoy this hallowed gift, Agni
accept our songs, who bears
Oblations, best of worshippers.

7 Lord of the house, whom men must
seek, we set thee down, O Worshipped
One!
Bright, rich in heroes, Agni ! God !

8 Shine forth at night and morn : through
thee with fires are we provided well.
Thou, rich in heroes, art our Friend.

9 The men come near thee for their gain,
the singers with their songs of praise :
Speech, thousandfold, comes near to thee.

10 Bright, Purifier, meet for praise, Immortal with refulgent glow,
Agni drives Rākṣasas away.

11 As such, bring us abundant wealth, young
Child of Strength, for this thou canst :
May Bhaga give us what is choice.

12 Thou, Agni, givest hero fame : Bhaga
and Savitar the God,
And Diti give us what is good.

13 Agni, preserve us from distress : consume
our enemies, O God,
Eternal, with the hottest flames.

14 And, irresistible, be thou a mighty iron
fort to us,
With hundred walls for man's defence.

15 Do thou preserve us, eve and morn, from
sorrow, from the wicked men,
Infallible ! by day and night.

HYMN XVI.   *Agni.*

1. WITH this my reverent hymn I call
Agni for you, the Son of Strength,
Dear, wisest envoy, served with noble
sacrifice, immortal messenger of all.

2 His two red horses, all-supporting, let him
yoke : let him, well-worshipped, urge
them fast.
Then hath the sacrifice good prayers and
happy end, and heavenly gift of wealth
to men.

3 The flame of him the Bountiful, the Much-
invoked, hath mounted up,
And his red-coloured smoke-clouds reach
and touch the sky : the men are kindling Agni well.

4 Thee, thee Most Glorious One we make
our messenger. Bring the Gods hither to
the feast.
Give us, O Son of Strength, all food that
feedeth man : give that for which we
pray to thee.

5 Thou, Agni, art the homestead's Lord, our
Herald at the sacrifice.

9 *Speech* : *ákṣarā*, the imperishable ; here speech in
the shape of praise and prayer.

12 *Diti* : generally regarded as the opposite of Aditi,
which may have been the word used by the poet,
changed by later reciters, who considered the metre
irregular, into Diti. *See Vedic Hymns*, I. p. 256.

3 *Sanctified with Vaṣaṭ*: Vaṣaṭ (may he bear it to
the Gods) is the exclamation used at the moment of
pouring the sacrificial oil or clarified butter on the fire.

5 *Herald* : *Hotar*, or invoking priest. *Cleanser* : *Potar*,
or purifier, another of the officiating priests. Agni performs the duties of all human priests.

Lord of all boons, thou art the Cleanser
and a Sage. Pay worship, and enjoy
the good.

6 Give riches to the sacrificer, O Most Wise,
for thou art he who granteth wealth.
Inspire with zeal each priest at this our
solemn rite; all who are skilled in singing praise.

7 O Agni who art worshipped well, dear let
our princes be to thee,
Our wealthy patrons who are governors of
men, who part, as gifts, their stalls of
kine.

8 They in whose home, her hand bearing
the sacred oil, Ilā sits down well-
satisfied—
Guard them, Victorious God, from slander
and from harm : give us a refuge famed
afar.

9 Do thou, a Priest with pleasant tongue,
most wise, and very near to us,
Agni, bring riches hither to our liberal
chiefs, and speed the offering of our gifts.

10 They who bestow as bounty plenteous
wealth of steeds, moved by desire of
great renown—
Do thou with saving help preserve them
from distress, Most Youthful ! with a
hundred forts.

11 The God who gives your wealth demands
a full libation poured to him.
Pour ye it forth, then fill the vessel full
again : then doth the God pay heed
to you.

12 Him have the Gods appointed Priest of
sacrifice, oblation-bearer, passing wise.
Agni gives wealth and valour to the worshipper, to folk who offer up their gifts.

HYMN XVII.   *Agni.*

1. AGNI, be kindled well with proper fuel, and
let the grass be scattered wide about
thee.

2 Let the impatient Portals be thrown open :
bring thou the Gods impatient to come
hither.

3 Taste, Agni : serve the Gods with our
oblation. Offer   good   sacrifices,
Jātavedas !

---

8 *Ilā* : the Goddess who is regarded as the sacrificial food or oblation personified : *annarūpā havirlakṣaṇā
devī.*—Sāyaṇa.

2 *The impatient Portals* : the doors of the sacrificial
chamber which long to bear their part in the holy ceremony.

4 Let Jātavedas pay fair sacrifices, worship
and gratify the Gods Immortal.

5 Wise God, win for us things that are all-
goodly, and let the prayers we pray to-
day be fruitful.

6 Thee, even thee, the Son of Strength, O
Agni, those Gods have made the bearer
of oblations.

7 To thee the God may we perform our
worship : do thou, besought, grant us
abundant riches.

HYMN XVIII.   *Indra.*

1. ALL is with thee, O Indra, all the treasures
which erst our fathers won who sang
thy praises.
With thee are milch-kine good to milk,
and horses : best winner thou of riches
for the pious.

2 For like a King among his wives thou
dwellest : with glories, as a Sage,
surround and help us.
Make us, thy servants, strong for wealth,
and honour our songs with kine and
steeds and decoration.

3 Here these our holy hymns with joy and
gladness in pious emulation have
approached thee.
Hitherward come thy path that leads to
riches : may we find shelter in thy
favour, Indra.

4 Vasiṣṭha hath poured forth his prayers,
desiring to milk thee like a cow in
goodly pasture.
All these my people call thee Lord of
cattle : may Indra come unto the
prayer we offer.

5 What though the floods spread widely,
Indra made them shallow and easy for
Sudās to traverse.
He, worthy of our praises, caused the
Simyu, foe of our hymn, to curse the
rivers' fury.

---

6 *Those Gods* : the famous Gods.

The hymn glorifies Indra as the protector of Sudās,
the King of the Tṛtsus, and praises the liberality of
that prince. See *Vedic India* (Story of the Nations
Series), pp. 319—332.
4 *Vasiṣṭha* : the Ṛṣi of the hymn and the chief
priest who had accompanied the warlike expedition
of Sudās. *To milk thee* : to obtain riches through
thy favour by means of my hymn, as men milk the
cow at sacrifice for the milk which is required for
libations.
5 The poet begins to recount the events of Sudās's
victorious expedition. These are not always intelligible
partly on account of the obscure phraseology employed,
and partly on account of our ignorance of details
which are vaguely alluded to. In this stanza Sudās,
king or chief of the Tṛtsu tribe, has, with the aid of

6 Eager for spoil was Turvaśa Puroḍās, fain
to win wealth, like fishes urged by
hunger.
The Bhṛgus and the Druhyus quickly
listened : friend rescued friend mid the
two distant peoples.

7 Together came the Pakthas, the Bhalānas,
the Alinas, the Śivas, the Viṣāṇins.
Yet to the Tṛtsus came the Ārya's Comrade,
through love of spoil and heroes' war, to
lead them.

8 Fools, in their folly fain to waste her
waters, they parted inexhaustible
Paruṣṇī.
Lord of the Earth, he with his might re-
pressed them : still lay the herd and the
affrighted herdsman.

9 As to their goal they sped to their destruction : they sought Paruṣṇī ; e'en the
swift returned not.
Indra abandoned, to Sudās the manly, the
swiftly flying foes, unmanly babblers.

10 They went like kine unherded from the
pasture, each clinging to a friend as
chance directed.

Indra, crossed a deep river (the Paruṣṇī which is now
called the Rāvī), and put the Śimyus to flight, some of
the fugitives being drowned in its waters. The Śimyus
are mentioned together with the Dasyus, in I. 100.
18, as hostile barbarians slain by Indra. The second
half of the stanza is difficult, the meaning of two of
the words being uncertain.

6 *Turvaśa Puroḍās* : Turvaśa appears here as one
of the enemies of Sudās. I follow, with much hesitation, Ludwig in taking Puroḍās as an appellative of
Turvaśa : 'Turvaśa, who was preceding (at solemn
rites).'—Wilson. *The Bhṛgus and the Druhyus* : here,
apparently, allies of Turvaśa. *Friends* : according to
others, Matsyas, a people.

7 *The Pakthas*, and the rest mentioned in the first
line of the stanza appear to have been non-Āryan
tribes opposed to the Tṛtsus. According to the Scholiast
these names are the denominations of various ministers
at religious rites, and following this interpretation
Wilson translates the stanza as follows : 'Those who
dress the oblation, those who pronounce auspicious words,
those who abstain from penance, those who bear horns
(in their hands), those who bestow happiness (on the
world by sacrifice), glorify that Indra who recovered
the cattle of the *Ārya* from the plunderers, who slew
the enemies in battle,' *The Ārya's Comrade* : Indra, the
ally of Tṛtsu against the non-Āryan confederacy.

8 The confederates, who were on the right or
farther bank of the Paruṣṇī, intending to attack Sudās
and the Tṛtsus, appear to have attempted to make the
river fordable by digging channels and so diverting the
water, which, it seems, rushed back into its natural bed
and drowned the men who were crossing the stream.
The second line of the stanza is obscure and the translation is conjectural. Wilson translates : 'but he by his
greatness pervades the earth, Kavi, the son of Caya-
māna, like a falling victim, sleeps (in death).' *The
herd* and *the herdsman* are, of course, the hostile band and
its leader.

They who drive spotted steeds, sent down
by Pṛśni, gave ear, the Warriors and
the harnessed horses.

11 The King who scattered one-and-twenty
people of both Vaikarṇa tribes through
lust of glory—
As the skilled priest clips grass within the
chamber, so hath the Hero Indra
wrought their downfall.

12 Thou, thunder-armed, o'erwhelmedst in
the waters famed ancient Kavaṣa and
then the Druhyu.
Others here claiming friendship to their
friendship, devoted unto thee, in thee
were joyful.

13 Indra at once with conquering might
demolished all their strong places and
their seven castles.
The goods of Anu's son he gave to Tṛtsu.
May we in sacrifice conquer scornful
Pūru.

14 The Anavas and Druhyus, seeking booty,
have slept, the sixty hundred, yea, six
thousand,
And six-and-sixty heroes. For the pious
were all these mighty exploits done by
Indra.

15 These Tṛtsus under Indra's careful
guidance came speeding like loosed
waters rushing downward.
The foemen, measuring exceeding closely,
abandoned to Sudās all their provisions.

10 *They went* : the fugitives who escaped drowning.
They who drive spotted steeds : the Maruts, sent down by
their mother Pṛśni to aid Sudās.

11 *People* : or, houses, *i. e.* families. *Both Vaikarṇa
tribes* : perhaps some allies of the Druhyus ; but the
meaning of *vaikarṇáyoḥ* is uncertain. See Zimmer, *Altindisches Leben.* p. 103. Ludwig thinks that the reference
is to a mythic battle at some place called Vaikar-
ṇau between Indra (the King) and the Maruts (the
one-and-twenty people). *Clips grass* : with one clean cut.

12 *Kavaṣa* : perhaps the priest of one of the two
Vaikarṇa tribes which Zimmer is inclined to identify
with the Kuru-Krivis. See *Altindisches Leben*, p. 127.
Others here : 'for they, Indra, who are devoted to thee
and glorify thee, preferring thy friendship, enjoy it.'—
Wilson. The exact meaning is uncertain.

13 *To Tṛtsu* : to Sudās, the King of the Tṛtsus.

14 *The Anavas* : men of the Anu tribe. *The sixty
hundred* : 'The enumeration is very obscurely expressed,
ṣaṣṭiḥ śatā ṣaṭsahasrā ṣaṣṭir adhi ṣaṭ, literally, six
hundreds, six thousands, sixty, with six more : Sāyaṇa
understands by *śatāni*, thousands, *sahasrāṇityarthaḥ.*'—
Wilson. 'Sixty-six thousand six hundred and six.'
Ludwig suggests that *daśa* should be read instead of
śatā, which would make the number 6666. See Benfey,
Vedica und Linguistica, pp. 139—162.

15 *Measuring exceeding closely* : though taking great
care of their goods and reluctantly giving them up.

16 The hero's side who drank the dressed
oblation, Indra's denier, far o'er earth
he scattered.
Indra brought down the fierce destroyer's
fury. He gave them various roads,
the path's Controller.

17 E'en with the weak he wrought this
matchless exploit : e'en with a goat he
did to death a lion.
He pared the pillar's angles with a needle.
Thus to Sudās Indra gave all provisions.

18 To thee have all thine enemies submitted:
e'en the fierce Bheda hast thou made
thy subject.
Cast down thy sharpened thunderbolt,
O Indra, on him who harms the men
who sing thy praises.

19 Yamunā and the Tṛtsus aided Indra.
There he stripped Bheda bare of all
his treasures.
The Ajas and the Śigrus and the Yakṣus
brought in to him as tribute heads of
horses.

20 Not to be scorned, but like Dawns past
and recent, O Indra, are thy favours
and thy riches.
Devaka, Manyamāna's son, thou slewest,
and smotest Śambara from the lofty
mountain.

21 They who, from home, have gladdened
thee, thy servants Parāśara, Vasiṣṭha,
Śatayātu,
Will not forget thy friendship, liberal
Giver. So shall the days dawn prosperous
for the princes.

22 Priest-like, with praise, I move around
the altar, earning Paijavana's reward,
O Agni,
Two hundred cows from Devavān's descendant, two chariots from Sudās with
mares to draw them.

23 Gift of Paijavana, four horses bear me in
foremost place, trained steeds with pearl
to deck them.
Sudās's brown steeds, firmly-stepping, carry
me and my son for progeny and glory.

24 Him whose fame spreads between wide
earth and heaven, who, as dispenser,
gives each chief his portion,
Seven flowing Rivers glorify like Indra.
He slew Yudhyāmadhi in close encounter.

25 Attend on him O ye heroic Maruts as on
Sudās's father Divodāsa.
Further Paijavana's desire with favour.
Guard faithfully his lasting firm domi-
nion.

HYMN XIX.   *Indra.*

1. HE like a bull with sharpened horns,
terrific, singly excites and agitates all
the people :
Thou givest him who largely pours libations
his goods who pours not, for his own
possession.

2 Thou, verily, Indra, gavest help to Kutsa,
willingly giving ear to him in battle,
When, aiding Ārjuneya, thou subduedst
to him both Kuyava and the Dāsa
Śuṣṇa.

3 O Bold One, thou with all thine aids hast
boldly holpen Sudās whose offerings
were accepted,
Pūru in winning land and slaying foemen,
and Trasadasyu son of Purukutsa.

---

16 *The hero's side* : the party of the hostile leader,
the non-Āryans who denied Indra, and themselves
devoured the oblations that should have been presented
to him. *He gave them various roads* : made them fly in
all directions.

17 *E'en with a goat* : impossible deeds mentioned as
illustrations of Indra's miraculous power.

18 *Bheda* : an enemy of Sudās, or an unbeliever,
says Sāyaṇa.

19 *Yamunā* : the Jumna. But it is not easy to see
how the expedition reached so far. The Ajas, Śigrus,
and Yakṣus were perhaps subject to Bheda, but nothing
is known regarding them. *Heads of horses* : which had
been killed in battle.

20 *Like Dawns* : renewed every day. *Devaka* : not
mentioned elsewhere. According to Grassmann *devakam
mānyamānám* refers to Śambara 'thinking himself a God.'

21 *Parāśara* is said by one authority to have been
the son, and by another the grandson of the Ṛṣi
Vasiṣṭha. *Śatayātu* is said to be Śakti, Vasiṣṭha's son.

22 Here begins the *dānastuti* or praise of the prince's
liberality. *Paijavana* : Sudās, descendant of Pijavana.
Devavān's descendant : Sudās, Devavān being either the
same as Divodāsa, the father of Sudās, or one of his
forefathers.

24 *Seven flowing Rivers glorify* : the seven chief rivers
of the Panjāb glorify him as they glorify Indra. Or,
they (men) praise him as the seven rivers praise Indra.
'The seven rivers bear his glory far and wide' (I. 102-2).
Yudhyāmidhi : not mentioned elsewhere.

25 *Maruts* : here, perhaps, the Maghavans or wealthy
nobles are intended who stand in the same relation to
Sudās as the Maruts to Indra.

---

1 *Excites and agitates* : as God of battles. *Thou:*
Indra. This abrupt change from the third person to
the second is not unusual in the Veda.

2 *Ārjuneya* : Kutsa, descendant of Arjuna. See I.
112. 23. *Kuyava* : See I. 103.8.

4 At the Gods' banquet, hero-souled ! with Heroes, Lord of Bay Steeds, thou slewest many foemen.
Thou sentest in swift death to sleep the Dasyu, both Cumuri and Dhuni, for Dabhīti.

5 These were thy mighty powers that, Thunder-wielder, thou swiftly crushedst nine-and-ninety castles :
Thou capturedst the hundredth in thine onslaught; thou slewest Namuci, thou slewest Vṛtra.

6 Old are the blessings, Indra, which thou gavest Sudās the worshipper who brought oblations.
For thee, the Strong, I yoke thy strong Bay Horses : may our prayers reach thee and win strength, Most Mighty !

7 Give us not up, Lord of Bay Horses, Victor, in this thine own assembly, to the wicked.
Deliver us with true and faithful succours: dear may we be to thee among the princes.

8 May we men, Maghavan, the friends thou lovest, near thee be joyful under thy protection.
Fain to fulfil the wish of Atithigva humble the pride of Turvaśa and Yādva.

9 Swiftly, in truth, O Maghavan, about thee men skilled in hymning sing their songs and praises.
Elect us also into their assembly who by their calls on thee despoiled the niggards.

10 Thine are these lauds, O manliest of heroes, lauds which revert to us and give us riches.
Favour these, Indra, when they fight with foemen, as Friend and Hero and the heroes' Helper.

11 Now, lauded for thine aid, Heroic Indra,

sped by our prayer, wax mighty in thy body.
Apportion to us strength and habitations. Ye Gods, protect us evermore with blessings.

HYMN XX. *Indra.*

1. STRONG, Godly-natured, born for hero exploit, man's Friend, he doth whatever deed he willeth.
Saving us e'en from great transgression, Indra, the Youthful, visiteth man's home with favour.

2 Waxing greatness Indra slayeth Vṛtra : the Hero with his aid hath helped the singer.
He gave Sudās wide room and space, and often hath granted wealth to him who brought oblations.

3 Soldier unchecked, war-rousing, battling Hero, unconquered from of old, victorious ever,
Indra the very strong hath scattered armies; yea, he hath slain each foe who fought against him.

4 Thou with thy greatness hast filled full, O Indra, even both the worlds with might, O thou Most Mighty.
Lord of Bays, Indra, brandishing his thunder, is gratified with Soma at the banquet.

5 A Bull begat the Bull for joy of battle, and a strong Mother brought forth him the manly.
He who is Chief of men, their armies' Leader, is strong Hero, bold, and fain for booty.

6 The people falter not, nor suffer sorrow, who win themselves this God's terrific spirit.
He who with sacrifices worships Indra is lord of wealth, law-born and law's protector.

7 Whene'er the elder fain would help the younger the greater cometh to the lesser's present.

---

4 *For Cumuri, Dhuni, and Dabhīti.* See Vol. I. Index.

5 *Namuci :* another demon of drought. See I. 53. 7. *In thine onslaught :* according to Sāyaṇa, for thy dwelling : 'thou hast occupied the hundredth as a place of abode.'—Wilson.

6 *Sudās :* the King of the Tṛtsus, celebrated in the preceding hymn.

8 *Atithigva :* probably a descendant of Sudās who must have lived long before the composition of this hymn, as the favour bestowed upon him by Indra is spoken of as old in stanza 6. *Yādva :* or Yadu's son.

9 *Elect us also :* that is, let us share the blessings which thou withholdest from the illiberal churls who offer no oblations and givest to those who call upon thee and worship thee.

---

5 *A Bull begat the Bull :* 'A vigorous (god) begot a vigorous (son).'—Muir. The father of Indra is Kaśyapa, according to Sāyaṇa; but probably Dyaus is intended. *A strong Mother :* Aditi.

6 *Law-born :* born in accordance with the law.

7 The relations between Gods and men resemble those between elders and juniors, superiors and inferiors among men. The inferior comes to his superior with some offering in his hand and is assisted by him in return. So Indra should accept our oblations, and reward us with wealth.

Shall the Immortal sit aloof' inactive? O Wondrous Indra, bring us wondrous riches.

8 Thy dear folk, Indra, who present oblations, are, in chief place, thy friends, O Thunder-wielder.
May we be best content in this thy favour, sheltered by One who slays not, but preserves us.

9 To thee the mighty hymn hath clamoured loudly, and, Maghavan, the eloquent hath besought thee.
Desire of wealth hath come upon thy singer : help us then, Śakra, to our share of riches.

10 Place us by food which thou hast given, O Indra, us and the wealthy patrons who command us.
Let thy great power bring good to him who lauds thee. Ye Gods, preserve us evermore with blessings.

HYMN XXI. *Indra.*

1. PRESSED is the juice divine with milk commingled : thereto hath Indra ever been accustomed.
We wake thee, Lord of Bays, with sacrifices: mark this our laud in the wild joy of Soma.

2 On to the rite they move, the grass they scatter, these Soma-drinkers eloquent in synod.
Hither, for men to grasp, are brought the press-stones, far-thundering, famous, strong, that wait on heroes.

3 Indra, thou settest free the many waters that were encompassed, Hero, by the Dragon.
Down rolled, as if on chariots borne, the rivers : through fear of thee all things created tremble.

4 Skilled in all manly deeds the God terrific hath with his weapons mastered these opponents.
Indra in rapturous joy shook down their castles he slew them in his might, the Thunder-wielder.

5 No evil spirits have impelled us, Indra, nor fiends, O Mightiest God, with their devices.

Let our true God subdue the hostile rabble: let not the lewd approach our holy worship.

6 Thou in thy strength surpassest Earth and Heaven : the regions comprehend not all thy greatness.
With thine own power and might thou slewest Vṛtra : no foe hath found the end of thee in battle.

7 Even the earlier Deities submitted their powers to thy supreme divine dominion.
Indra wins wealth and deals it out to others : men in the strife for booty call on Indra.

8 The humble hath invoked thee for protection, thee, Lord of great felicity, O Indra.
Thou with a hundred aids hast been our Helper: one who brings gifts like thee hath his defender.

9 May we, O Indra, be thy friends for ever, eagerly, Conqueror, yielding greater homage.
May, through thy grace, the strength of us who battle quell in the shock the onset of the foeman.

10 Place us by food which thou hast given, O Indra, us and the wealthy patrons who command us.
Let thy great power bring good to him who lauds thee. Ye Gods, preserve us evermore with blessings.

HYMN XXII *Indra.*

1. DRINK Soma, Lord of Bays, and let it cheer thee : Indra, the stone, like a well-guided courser,
Directed by the presser's arms hath pressed it.

2 So let the draught of joy, thy dear companion, by which, O Lord of Bays, thou slayest foemen,
Delight thee, Indra, Lord of princely treasures.

3 Mark closely, Maghavan, the words I utter, this eulogy recited by Vasiṣṭha :
Accept the prayers I offer at thy banquet.

5 *The lewd* : those who do not follow Vedic observances, according to Yāska. For a full discussion of the meaning of *śiṣnádeváḥ*, see Muir. *O. S. Texts*, IV. 406—411.

8 *One who brings gifts like thee* : Sāyaṇa interprets differently : 'be our defender against every overpowering (assailant) like to thee.'—Wilson.

9 *The eloquent* :*stámuḥ* ; according to Ludwig, mouthy, talkat've, and, in a good sense, fluent eloquent. The Commentators explain the word as 'praiser.'

1 *We wake thee* : or. we think of thee, serve thee.
4 *These opponents* : according to Sāyaṇa. the demons of the air. The text has no noun for 'these.'

4 Hear thou the call of the juice-drinking
   press-stone : hear thou the Brahman's
   hymn who sings and lauds thee.
   Take to thine inmost self these adorations.

5 I know and ne'er forget the hymns and
   praises of thee, the Conqueror, and thy
   strength immortal.
   Thy name I ever utter. Self-Refulgent !

6 Among mankind many are thy libations,
   and many a time the pious sage invokes
   thee.
   O Maghavan, be not long distant from
   us.

7 All these libations are for thee, O Hero :
   to thee I offer these my prayers that
   strengthen.
   Ever, in every place, must men invoke
   thee.

8 Never do men attain, O Wonder-Worker,
   thy greatness, Mighty One, who must
   be lauded,
   Nor, Indra, thine heroic power and bounty.

9 Among all Ṛṣis, Indra, old and recent,
   who have engendered hymns as sacred
   singers,
   Even with us be thine auspicious friendships. Ye Gods, preserve us evermore
   with blessings.

HYMN XXIII.   *Indra.*

1. PRAYERS have been offered up through
   love of glory : Vasiṣṭha, honour Indra
   in the battle.
   He who with might extends through all
   existence hears words which I, his faithful servant, utter.

2 A cry was raised which reached the Gods,
   O Indra, a cry to them to send us strength
   in combat.
   None among men knows his own life's
   duration : bear us in safety over these
   our troubles.

3 The Bays, the booty-seeking car I harness:
   my prayers have reached him who
   accepts them gladly.
   Indra, when he had slain resistless foemen,
   forced with his might the two world-
   halves asunder.

4 Like barren cows, moreover, swelled the
   waters : the singers sought thy holy
   rite, O Indra.
   Come unto us as with his team comes
   Vāyu : thou, through our solemn hymns
   bestowest booty.

5 So may these gladdening draughts rejoice
   thee, Indra, the Mighty, very bounteous
   to the singer.
   Alone among the Gods thou pitiest mortals:
   O Hero, make thee glad at this libation.

6 Thus the Vasiṣṭhas glorify with praises
   Indra the Powerful whose arm wields
   thunder.
   Praised, may he guard our wealth in kine
   and heroes. Ye Gods, preserve us evermore with blessings.

HYMN XXIV.   *Indra.*

1. A HOME is made for thee to dwell in,
   Indra : O Much-invoked, go thither with
   the heroes.
   That thou, to prosper us, mayst be our
   Helper, vouchsafe us wealth, rejoice
   with draughts of Soma.

2 Indra, thy wish, twice-strong, is comprehended : pressed is the Soma, poured
   are pleasant juices.
   This hymn of praise, from loosened tongue,
   made perfect, draws Indra to itself with
   loud invoking.

3 Come, thou Impetuous; God, from earth
   or heaven; come to our holy grass to
   drink the Soma.
   Hither to me let thy Bay Horses bring
   thee to listen to our hymns and make
   thee joyful.

4 Come unto us with all thine aids, accordant, Lord of Bay Steeds, accepting
   our devotions,
   Fair-helmeted, o'ercoming with the mighty,
   and lending us the strength of bulls,
   O Indra.

5 As to the chariot pole a vigorous courser,
   this laud is brought to the great strong
   Upholder.
   This hymn solicits wealth of thee : in
   heaven, as 'twere above the sky, set
   thou our glory.

---

4 *Juice-drinking* : that presses out the juice of the
plant, and so may be said to drink it. The Scholiast
inserts *mama*, of me : 'Hear the invocation of the
(grinding) stone (of me) repeatedly drinking (the
Soma).'—Wilson.

---

2 *A cry was raised* : I follow Pischel's interpretation
of this very difficult stanza. See *Vedische Studien*, I. pp.
34—36.

---

4 *Barren cows* : which are fatter than others.

---

1 *A home* : in the sacrificial chamber. *Heroes* : or,
men ; the priests.

4 *Fair-helmeted* : or fair-cheeked, or handsome-
chinned.

6 With precious things. O Indra, thus content us : may we attain to thine exalted favour.

Send our chiefs plenteous food with hero children. Preserve us evermore, ye Gods, with blessings.

HYMN XXV. *Indra.*

1

WHEN with thy mighty help, O potent Indra, the armies rush together in their fury.

When from the strong man's arm the lightning flieth, let not the mind go forth to side with others.

2 O Indra, where the ground is hard to traverse, smite down our foes, the mortals who assail us,

Keep far from us the curse of the reviler: bring us accumulated store of treasures.

3 God of the fair helm, give Sudās a hundred succours, a thousand blessings, and thy bounty.

Strike down the weapon of our mortal foeman : bestow upon us splendid fame and riches.

4 I wait the power of one like thee, O Indra, gifts of a Helper such as thou art, Hero.

Strong, Mighty God, dwell with me now and ever : Lord of Bay Horses, do not thou desert us.

5 Here are the Kutsas supplicating Indra for might, the Lord of Bays for God-sent conquest.

Make our foes ever easy to be vanquished: may we, victorious, win the spoil, O Hero.

6 With precious things, O Indra, thus content us: may we attain to thine exalted favour.

Send our chiefs plenteous food with hero children. Preserve us evermore, ye Gods, with blessings.

HYMN XXVI. *Indra.*

1. SOMA unpressed ne'er gladdened liberal Indra, no juices pressed without a prayer have pleased him.

The battle has begun, and the singer prays to Indra for aid.
1 *The lightning* : the swift and flashing arrow. *Others* : the enemy.
3 *Sudās* : according to Sāyaṇa, 'the liberal donor (of oblations).' Wilson.
5 *The Kutsas* : apparently the priests of the hostile party.

---

1 *Soma unpressed* : cp. VI. 41. 4, Soma when

I generate a laud that shall delight him, new and heroic, so that he may hear us.

2 At every laud the Soma gladdens Indra : pressed juices please him as each psalm is chanted,

What time the priests with one united effort call him to aid, as sons invoke their father.

3 These deeds he did; let him achieve new exploits, such as the priests declare at their libations.

Indra hath taken and possessed all castles, like as one common husband doth his spouses.

4 Even thus have they declared him. Famed is Indra as Conqueror, sole distributer of treasures;

Whose many succours come in close succession. May dear delightful benefits attend us.

5 Thus, to bring help to men, Vasiṣṭha laudeth Indra, the peoples' Hero, at libation.

Bestow upon us strength and wealth in thousands. Preserve us evermore, ye Gods, with blessings.

HYMN XXVII. *Indra.*

1. MEN call on Indra in the armed encounter that he may make the hymns they sing decisive.

Hero, rejoicing in thy might, in combat give us a portion of the stall of cattle,

2 Grant, Indra Maghavan, invoked of many, to these my friends the strength which thou possessest.

Thou, Maghavan, hast rent strong places open : unclose for us, Wise God, thy hidden bounty.

3 King of the living world, of men, is Indra, of all in varied form that earth containeth.

Thence to the worshipper he giveth riches: may he enrich us also when we laud him.

4 Maghavan Indra, when we all invoke him, bountiful ever sendeth strength to aid us :

(properly) pressed excels the unpressed (or ill-pressed) Soma. Not only must the juice be duly expressed, but it must be expressed and offered with prayer.
3 *All castles* : all the strongholds of the demons of drought, the cloud-castles in which the rain is imprisoned.

---

1 *Give us a portion, etc.* : aid us to capture and carry off the cattle of the enemy.

Whose perfect guerdon, never failing, bringeth wealth to the men, to friends the thing they covet.

5 Quick, Indra, give us room and way to riches, and let us bring thy mind to grant us treasures,

That we may win us cars and steeds and cattle. Preserve us evermore, ye Gods, with blessings.

HYMN XXVIII.   *Indra.*

1. COME to our prayers, O Indra, thou who knowest : let thy Bay Steeds be yoked and guided hither.

Though mortal men on every side invoke thee, still give thine ear to us, O All-impeller.

2 Thy greatness reacheth to our invocation, the sages' prayer which, Potent God, thou guardest.

What time thy hand, O Mighty, holds the thunder, awful in strength thou hast become resistless.

3 What time thou drewest both world-halves together, like heroes led by thee who call each other—

For thou wast born for strength and high dominion—then e'en the active over-threw the sluggish.

4 Honour us in these present days, O Indra, for hostile men are making expiation.

Our sin that sinless Varuṇa discovered, the Wondrous-Wise hath long ago forgiven.

5 We will address this liberal Lord, this Indra, that he may grant us gifts of ample riches,

Best favourer of the singer's prayer and praises. Preserve us evermore, ye Gods, with blessings.

2 *Thy greatness reacheth to our invocation* : thou hast the power to come to our call if thou wilt.

3 *Drewest both world-halves together* : settest heaven and earth opposite to each other, like armies arrayed for battle. *E'en the active* : the meaning of the half-line is doubtful, and *cit*, even, seems to be out of place. Wilson translates, after Sāyaṇa : 'whence the presenter of offerings overcomes him who offers them not.' According to Professor Grassmann, 'the active' is Indra, and 'the inactive' is the sluggish demon. Ludwig suggests an alteration of the text.

4 *Are making expiation* : or, possibly, set themselves in order, that is, equip and prepare themselves for battle. *The Wondrous-Wise* : *māyī*; Varuṇa.

HYMN XXIX   *Indra.*

1. THIS Soma hath been pressed for thee, O Indra : come hither, Lord of Bays, for this thou lovest.

Drink of this fair, this well-effused libation: Maghavan, give us wealth when we implore thee.

2 Come to us quickly with thy Bay Steeds, Hero, come to our prayer, accepting our devotion.

Enjoy thyself aright at this libation, and listen thou unto the prayers we offer.

3 What satisfaction do our hymns afford thee? When, Maghavan ? Now let us do thee service.

Hymns, only hymns, with love for thee, I weave thee : then hear, O Indra, these mine invocations.

4 They, verily, were also human beings whom thou wast wont to hear, those earlier sages.

Hence I, O Indra Maghavan, invoke thee: thou art our Providence, even as a Father.

5 We will address this liberal Lord, this Indra, that he may grant us gifts of ample riches,

Best favourer of the singer's prayer and praises. Preserve us evermore, ye Gods, with blessings.

HYMN XXX.   *Indra.*

1. WITH power and strength, O Mighty God, approach us : be the augmenter, Indra, of these riches;

Strong Thunderer, Lord of men, for potent valour, for manly exploit and for high dominion.

2 Thee, worth invoking, in the din of battle, heroes invoke in fray for life and sun-light.

Among all people thou art foremost fighter: give up our enemies to easy slaughter.

3 When fair bright days shall dawn on us, O Indra, and thou shalt bring thy banner near in battle,

Agni the Asura shall sit as Herald, cal-

3 *Now let us do thee service* : *nūnam* : 'no time like the present.'—Ludwig.

1 *For potent valour* : that is, to give us potent valour.

2 *Foremost fighter* : caster of the spear, warrior, according to von Roth; but the meaning of *sényaḥ* is somewhat uncertain.

ling Gods hither for our great good
fortune.

4 Thine are we, Indra, thine, both these
who praise thee, and those who give rich
gifts, O God and Hero.
Grant to our princes excellent protection,
may they wax old and still be strong
and happy.

5 We will address this liberal Lord, this Indra,
that he may grant us gifts of ample riches,
Best favourer of the singer's prayer and
praises. Preserve us evermore, ye Gods,
with blessings.

HYMN XXXI.   *Indra.*

1. SING ye a song, to make him glad, to Indra,
Lord of Tawny Steeds,
The Soma-drinker, O my friends.

2 To him the Bounteous say the laud, and
let us glorify, as men May do, the Giver
of true gifts.

3 O Indra, Lord of boundless might, for us
thou winnest strength and kine,
Thou winnest gold for us, Good Lord.

4 Faithful to thee we loudly sing, heroic
Indra, songs to thee : Mark, O Good
Lord, this act of ours.

5 Give us not up to man's reproach, to
foeman's hateful calumny : In thee
alone is all my strength.

6 Thou art mine ample coat of mail, my
Champion, Vrtra-Slayer, thou :
With thee for Friend I brave the foe.

7 Yea, great art thou whose conquering
might two independent Powers confess.
The Heaven, O Indra, and the Earth.

8 So let the voice surround thee, which
attends the Maruts on their way,
Reaching thee with the rays of light.

9 Let the ascending drops attain to thee,
the Wondrous God, in heaven :
Let all the folk bow down to thee.

10 Bring to the Wise, the Great, who waxeth
mighty, your offerings, and make ready
your devotion ;
To many clans he goeth, man's controller.

11 For Indra, the sublime, the far-pervading,
have singers generated prayer and
praises :
The sages never violate his statutes.

12 The choirs have stablished Indra King
for ever, for victory, him whose anger
is resistless :

7 *Independent* : *svadhāvarī* ; 'abounding in food.'—
Wilson.

8 *The voice* : 'the praises of thine adorers.—Wilson.

And, for the Bays' Lord, strengthened
those he loveth.

HYMN XXXII.   *Indra.*

1. LET none, no, not thy worshippers, delay
thee far away from us.
Even from far away come thou unto our
feast, or listen if already here.

2 For here, like flies on honey, these who
pray to thee sit by the juice that they
have poured.
Wealth-craving singers have on Indra set
their hope, as men set foot upon a car.

3 Longing for wealth I call on him, the
Thunderer with the strong right hand,
As a son calleth on his sire.

4 These Soma juices, mixed with curd, have
been expressed for Indra here.
Come with thy Bay Steeds, Thunder-
wielder, to our home, to drink them till
they make thee glad.

5 May he whose ear is open hear us. He is
asked for wealth : will he despise our
prayer ?
Him who bestows at once a hundred
thousand gifts none shall restrain when
he would give.

6 The hero never checked by men hath
gained his strength through Indra, he
Who presses out and pours his deep
libations forth, O Vrtra-slayer, unto
thee.

7 When thou dost drive the fighting men
together be, thou Mighty One, the
mighty's shield.
May we divide the wealth of him whom
thou hast slain : bring us, Unreachable,
his goods.

8 For Indra, Soma-drinker, armed with
thunder, press the Soma juice.
Make ready your dressed meats : cause
him to favour us. The Giver blesses
him who gives.

12 *Strengthened* : 'barhayā : for abarhayan, as is clear
from what precedes.'—Ludwig. Sāyaṇa takes *barhayā* as
the imperative : 'urge thy kinsmen, (worshipper, to
glorify) the lord of bay steeds.'—Wilson.

I am indebted to Max Müller's translation of this
hymn in his *Ancient Sanskrit Literature* for many of the
renderings which I have adopted.

3 *With the strong right hand* : or giver of good gifts.

7 *The mighty's shield* : 'the shield of the mighty
(Vasiṣṭhas).'—M.M.; 'a protection of the Maghavans,'
i. e. the institutors of the sacrifice—Ludwig.

8 *The Giver blesses him who gives* : Indra rewards the
liberal worshipper.

9 Grudge not, ye Soma pourers; stir you, pay the rites, for wealth, to the great Conqueror.
Only the active conquers, dwells in peace, and thrives : not for the niggard are the Gods.

10 No one hath overturned or stayed the car of him who freely gives.
The man whom Indra and the Marut host defend comes to a stable full of kine.

11 Indra, that man when fighting shall obtain the spoil, whose strong defender thou wilt be.
Be thou the gracious helper, Hero ! of our cars, be thou the helper of our men.

12 His portion is exceeding great like a victorious soldier's spoil.
Him who is Indra, Lord of Bays, no foes subdue. He gives the Soma-pourer strength.

13 Make for the Holy Gods a hymn that is not mean, but well-arranged and fair of form.
Even many snares and bonds subdue not him who dwells with Indra through his sacrifice.

14 Indra, what mortal will attack the man who hath his wealth in thee ?
The strong will win the spoil on the decisive day through faith in thee, O Maghavan.

15 In battles with the foe urge on our mighty ones who give the treasures dear to thee,
And may we with our princes, Lord of Tawny Steeds ! pass through all peril, led by thee.

16 Thine, Indra, is the lowest wealth, thou cherishest the mid-most wealth,
Thou ever rulest all the highest : in the fray for cattle none resisteth thee.

17 Thou art renowned as giving wealth to every one in all the battles that are fought.
Craving protection, all these people of the earth, O Much-invoked, implore thy name.

18 If I, O Indra, were the Lord of riches ample as thine own,
I should support the singer, God who givest wealth ! and not abandon him to woe.

19 Each day would I enrich the man who sang my praise, in whatsoever place he were.
No kinship is there better, Maghavan, than thine : a father even is no more.

20 With Plenty for his true ally the active man will gain the spoil.
Your Indra, Much-invoked, I bend with song, as bends a wright his wheel of solid wood.

21 A moral wins no riches by unworthy praise: wealth comes not to the niggard churl.
Light is the task to give, O Maghavan, to one like me on the decisive day.

22 Like kine unmilked we call aloud, Hero, to thee, and sing thy praise,
Looker on heavenly light, Lord of this moving world, Lord, Indra, of what moveth not.

23 None other like to thee, of earth or of the heavens, hath been or ever will be born.
Desiring horses, Indra Maghavan ! and kine, as men of might we call on thee.

24 Bring, Indra, the Victorious Ones; bring, elder thou, the younger host.
For, Maghavan, thou art rich in treasures from of old, and must be called in every fight.

25 Drive thou away our enemies, O Maghavan : make riches easy to be won.
Be thou our good Protector in the strife for spoil : Cherisher of our friends be thou.

26 O Indra, give us wisdom as a sire gives wisdom to his sons.
Guide us, O Much-invoked, in this our way may we still live and look upon the light.

27 Grant that no mighty foes, unknown, malevolent, unhallowed, tread us to the ground.
With thine assistance, Hero, may we pass through all the waters that are rushing down.

HYMN XXXIII   *Vasiṣṭha.*

1. THESE who wear hair-knots on the right, the movers of holy thought, white-robed, have won me over.

20 *Plenty* : or, Spirit, Boldness.
24 *Bring, Indra, the Victorious Ones* : these would be the Maruts. 'Elder Indra, bring that (wealth to me) being the junior.'—Wilson. 'Bring all this to those who are good, O Indra, be they old or young.'—M. Müller.

The hymn is a glorification of Vasiṣṭha and his family the latter part relating his birth and the earlier verses, referring to his connexion with King Sudās.
1 *Hair-knots* : kaparda is the cúḍa or single lock of

I warned the men, when from the grass I raised me, Not from afar can my Vasiṣṭhas help you.

2 With soma they brought Indra from a distance, over Vaiśanta, from the strong libation.
Indra preferred Vasiṣṭhas to the Soma pressed by the son of Vayatā, Pāśadyumna.

3 So, verily, with these he crossed the river, in company with these he slaughtered Bheda.
So in the fight with the Ten Kings, Vasiṣṭhas ! did Indra help Sudās through your devotions.

4 I gladly, [men ! with prayer prayed by our fathers have fixed your axle : ye shall not be injured :
Since, when ye sang aloud the Śakvarī verses, Vasiṣṭhas ! ye invigorated Indra.

5 Like thirsty men they looked to heaven, in battle with the Ten Kings, surrounded and imploring.
Then Indra heard Vasiṣṭha as he praised him, and gave the Tṛtsus ample room and freedom.

6 Like sticks and staves wherewith they drive the cattle, stripped bare, the Bharatas were found defenceless:
Vasiṣṭha then became their chief and leader : then widely were the Tṛtsus' clans extended.

7 Three fertilize the worlds with genial moisture : three noble Creatures cast a light before them.

8 Like the Sun's growing glory is their splendour, and like the sea's is their unfathomed greatness.
Their course is like the wind's. Your laud, Vasiṣṭhas, can never be attained by any other.

9 They with perceptions of the heart in secret resort to that which spreads a thousand branches.
The Apsaras brought hither the Vasiṣṭhas wearing the vesture spun for them by Yama.

10 A form of lustre springing from the lightning wast thou, when Varuṇa and Mitra saw thee.
Thy one and only birth was then, Vasiṣṭha, when from thy stock Agastya brought thee hither.

11 Born of their love for Urvaśī, Vasiṣṭha thou, priest, art son of Varuṇa and Mitra ;
And as a fallen drop, in heavenly fervour, all the Gods laid thee on a lotus-blossom.

12 He, thinker, knower both of earth and heaven, endowed with many a gift, bestowing thousands,
Destined to wear the vesture spun by Yama, sprang from the Apsaras to life, Vasiṣṭha.

13 Born at the sacrifice, urged by adorations,

hair left on the head at tonsure, which, according to the Scholiast, it was characteristic of the *Vasiṣṭhas* to wear on the right of the crown of the head. *White-robed* : white-coloured, according to Sāyaṇa. *Me* : Vasiṣṭha, who is the speaker of stanzas 1—6. 'Von Roth (under the word *av*) regards Indra as the speaker. May it not be Sudās?'—Muir, *O.S. Text*, I. 319, 320, where stanzas 1—13 are translated. *From the grass* : the sacred grass laid on the floor of the sacrificial chamber.

2 *Vaiśanta* : probably the name of a river. *Pāśadyumna* : another king who was sacrificing to Indra at the same time as Sudās.

3 *The river* Yamunā See VII. 18. 19. *Ten Kings* : of the confederate tribes who opposed Sudās. See VII. 18.

4 *Śakvarī verses* : hymns of praise in the Śakvarī metre (14 × 4).

5 *Tṛtsus* : the tribe of which Sudās was King.
6 *Bharatas* : apparently the same as the Tṛtsus.

7 Indra is the speaker of the rest of the hymn. 'In explanation of this, Sāyaṇa quotes a passage from the Śatyāyana Brāhmaṇa : (1) Agni produces a fertilizing fluid on the earth, Vāyu in the air, the Sun in the sky. (2) The 'three noble creatures' are the Vasus,

Rudras, and Ādityas. The Sun is their light. (3) Agni, Vāyu, and the Sun each attend the Dawn.'—Muir. *O. S. Texts*, i. 320.

9 *That which spreads a thousand branches* : according to Ludwig's Translation, the Sun-God is meant ; according to his later view, the reference is to the mystic tree sustained by Varuṇa in the baseless region (I. 24. 7). *The vesture* ; the body. The stanza is very obscure, and Sāyaṇa's explanation, which overrides grammar, is not satisfactory : 'By the wisdom seated in the heart the *Vasiṣṭhas* traverse the hidden thousand-branched world, and the *Apsarasas* sit down, wearing the vesture spread out by Yama.'—Wilson.

10 Vasiṣṭha appears here as an embodiment of lightning, light, or fire and to have been brought down to men by Agastya who was born in the same way as Vasiṣṭha.

11 *Urvaśī* : the most celebrated of the Apsarases or nymphs of heaven *On a lotus-blossom* : or, according to others, 'in the sacred pitcher,' or water-jar used in sacrifice. 'In the lake.'—Wilson.

For a full account of this production of Vasiṣṭha, the curious reader is referred to Muir. *O. S. Texts*, I. 321. See M. Müller, *Chips*, IV. 108, 109, and Hillebrandt. *Varuṇa und Mitra*, 148, 149.

12 *The Apsaras* : Urvaśī.

both with a common flow bedewed the pitcher.

Then from the midst thereof there rose up Māna, and thence they say was born the sage Vasiṣṭha.

14 He brings the bearer of the laud and Sāman : first shall he speak bringing the stone for pressing.

With grateful hearts in reverence approach him : to you, O Pratṛdas, Vasiṣṭha cometh.

HYMN XXXIV   Viṣvedevas·

1. MAY our divine and brilliant hymn go forth, like a swift chariot wrought and fashioned well.

2 The waters listen as they flow along : they know the origin of heaven and earth.

3 Yea, the broad waters swell their flood for him : of him strong heroes think amid their foes.

4 Set ye for him the coursers to the pole: like Indra Thunderer is the Golden-armed.

5 Arouse you, like the days, to sacrifice : speed gladly like a traveller on the way.

6 Go swift to battles, to the sacrifice : set up a flag, a hero for the folk.

7 Up from his strength hath risen as 'twere a light : it bears the load as earth bears living things.

8 Agni, no demon I invoke the Gods : by law completing it, I form a hymn.

9 Closely about you lay your heavenly song, and send your voice to where the Gods abide.

10 Varuṇa, Mighty, with a thousand eyes, beholds the paths wherein these rivers run.

11 He, King of kings, the glory of the floods, o'er all that liveth hath resistless sway.

12 May he assist us among all the tribes, and make the envier's praise devoid of light.

13 May the foes' threatening arrow pass us by : may he put far from us our bodies' sin.

14 Agni, oblation-eater, through our prayers aid us : to him our dearest laud is brought.

15 Accordant with the Gods choose for our Friend the Waters' Child : may he be good to us.

16 With lauds I sing the Dragon born of floods : he sits beneath the streams in middle air.

17 Ne'er may the Dragon of the Deep harm us : ne'er fail this faithful servant's sacrifice.

18 To these our heroes may they grant renown: may pious men march boldly on to wealth.

19 Leading great hosts, with fierce attacks of these, they burn their foes as the Sun burns the earth.

20 What time our wives draw near to us, may he, left-handed Tvaṣṭar, give us hero sons.

21 May Tvaṣṭar find our hymn acceptable, and may Aramati, seeking wealth, be ours.

22 May they who lavish gifts bestow those treasures : may Rodasī and Varuṇānī listen.

May he, with the Varūtrīs, be our refuge, may bountiful Tvaṣṭar give us store of riches.

23 So may rich Mountains and the liberal Waters, so may all Herbs that grow on ground, and Heaven,

And Earth accordant with the Forest-Sovrans, and both the World-halves round about protect us.

24 To this may both the wide Worlds lend

---

13 *Māna* : said to be another name of Agastya.

14 *The bearer of the laud and Sāman* : the pressing-stone, which was worked du ing the recitation of sacred verses. *Pratṛdās* : a name used here to designate the Tṛtsus

This difficult and obscure hymn has been translated and thoroughly discussed by Geldner (*Vedische Studien*, II. pp. 129—155, criticized by Prof. Ludwig, *Ueber die neuesten Arbeiten auf dem Gebiete der Ṛgveda-forschung*, pp. 163—167).

———

2 'An allusion, perhaps, to the subsequently received cosmogony, as in *Manu*, that water was the first of created things.'- Wilson.

3 *For him* : Indra.

4 *The Golden-armed* : Savitar.

6 *A hero* : a sort of personification of the sacrifice. 'An expiatory sacrifice for (the good of) mankind.'—Wilson.

---

16 *The Dragon born of floods*: Ahibudhnya, or the Dragon of the Deep of the following stanza ; the regent of the sea of air.

18 *They* : the Gods.

19 *Of these* : Gods, or Maruts, according to the Scholiast.

21 *Aramati* : the Genius of Devotion and active piety.

22 *Varūtrīs* : protecting Goddesses.

23 *Forest-Sovrans* : tall timber trees.

———

approval, and Varuṇa in heaven, whose Friend is Indra.

May all the Maruts give consent, the Victors, that we may hold great wealth in firm possession.

25 May Indra, Varuṇa, Mitra, and Agni, Waters, Herbs, Trees accept the praise we offer.

May we find refuge in the Marut's bosom. Protect us evermore, ye Gods, with blessings.

HYMN XXXV.   *Viśvedevas.*

1. BEFRIEND us with their aids Indra and Agni, Indra and Varuṇa who receive oblations !

Indra and Soma give health, strength and comfort, Indra and Pūṣan be our help in battle.

2 Auspicious Friends to us be Bhaga, Samsa, auspicious be Purandhi and all Riches ;

The blessing of the true and well-conducted, and Aryaman in many forms apparent.

3 Kind unto us be Maker and Sustainer, and the far-reaching Pair with God-like natures.

Auspicious unto us be Earth and Heaven, the Mountain, and the Gods' fair invocations.

4 Favour us Agni with his face of splendour, and Varuṇa and Mitra and the Aśvins.

Favour us noble actions of the pious, impetuous vāta blow on us with favour.

5 Early invoked, may Heaven and Earth be friendly, and Air's mid-region good for us to look on.

To us may Herbs and Forest-Trees be gracious, gracious the Lord Victorious of the region.

6 Be the God Indra with the Vasus friendly, and, with Ādityas, Varuṇa who blesseth.

Kind, with the Rudras, be the Healer Rudra, and, with the Dames, may Tvaṣṭar kindly listen.

7 Blest unto us be Soma, and devotions, blest be the Sacrifice, the Stones for pressing.

Blest be the fixing of the sacred Pillars, blest be the tender Grass and blest the Altar.

8 May the far-seeing Sun rise up to bless us : be the four Quarters of the sky auspicious.

Auspicious be the firmly-seated Mountains, auspicious be the Rivers and the Waters.

9 May Aditi through holy works be gracious, and may the Maruts, loud in song, be friendly.

May Viṣṇu give felicity, and Pūṣan, the Air that cherisheth our life, and Vāyu.

10 Prosper us Savitar, the God who rescues, and let the radiant Mornings be propitious.

Auspicious to all creatures be Parjanya, auspicious be the field's benign Protector.

11 May all the fellowship of Gods befriend us, Sarasvatī, with Holy Thoughts, be gracious.

Friendly be they, the Liberal Ones who seek us, yea, those who dwell in heaven, on earth, in waters.

12 May the great Lords of Truth protect and aid us : blest to us be our horses and our cattle.

Kind be the pious skilful-handed Ṛbhus, kind be the Fathers at our invocations.

13 May Aja-Ekapād, the God, be gracious, gracious the Dragon of the Deep, and Ocean.

Gracious be he the swelling Child of Waters, gracious be Pṛśni who hath Gods to guard her.

14 So may the Rudras, Vasus, and Ādityas accept the new hymn which we now are making.

May all the Holy Ones of earth and heaven, and the Cow's offspring hear our invocation.

15 They who of Holy Gods are very holy, Immortal, knowing Law, whom man must worship,—

May these to-day give us broad paths to travel. Preserve us evermore, ye Gods, with blessings.

10 *The field's benign Protector* : Agni, or Rudra. See IV. 57. I.

13 *Aja-Ekapād* : the Sun. See VI. 50. 14, and footnote.

The Dragon of the Deep : Ahibudhnya, regent of the depths of the firmament.

14 *Cow's offspring* : the Maruts. According to von Roth those who are born and live in radiant heaven.

15 *Broad paths to travel* : perhaps, generally, an easy road to prosperity.

1 *Befriend us* : *śám no bhavatām.* The indeclinable word *śám*, signifying happy, auspicious, pleasant, sweet, kind, agreeable, etc., etc., is used with or without the verb *bhū*, in the first thirteen stanzas. I have varied the expression here and there.

2 *Samsa* : Prayer or Wish personified. Or it may be Narāśamsa, Agni. *Purandhi*: Plenty, or Spirit, Boldness personified.

3 *Far-reaching Pair* : Heaven and Earth.

5 *The Lord Victorious* : Indra.

HYMN XXXVI.   *Viśvedevas*

1. LET the prayer issue from the seat of Order, for Sūrya with his beams hath loosed the cattle.
With lofty ridges earth is far extended, and Agni's flame hath lit the spacious surface.

2 O Asuras, O Varuṇa and Mitra, this hymn to you, like food, anew I offer.
One of you is a strong unerring Leader, and Mitra, speaking, stirreth men to labour.

3 The movements of the gliding wind come hither : like cows, the springs are filled to overflowing.
Born in the station e'en of lofty heaven the Bull hath loudly bellowed in this region.

4 May I bring hither with my song, O Indra, wise Aryaman who yokes thy dear Bay Horses,
Voracious, with thy noble car, O Hero, him who defeats the wrath of the malicious.

5 In their own place of sacrifice adorers worship to gain long life and win his friendship.
He hath poured food on men when they have praised him; be this, the dearest reverence, paid to Rudra.

6 Coming together, glorious, loudly roaring— Sarasvatī, Mother of Floods, the seventh— With copious milk, with fair streams,

strongly flowing, full swelling with the volume of their water ;

7. And may the mighty Maruts, too, rejoicing, aid our devotion and protect our offspring.
Let not swift-moving Akṣarā neglect us: they have increased our own appropriate riches,

8 Bring ye the great Aramati before you, and Pūṣan as the Hero of the synod,
Bhaga who looks upon this hymn with favour, and, as our strength, the bountiful Purandhi.

9 May this our song of praise reach you, O Maruts, and Viṣṇu guardian of the future infant.
May they vouchsafe the singer strength for offspring. Preserve us evermore, ye Gods, with blessings.

HYMN XXXVII.   *Viśvedevas.*

1. LET your best-bearing car that must be lauded, ne'er injured, bring you Vājas and Ṛbhukṣans.
Fill you, fair-helmeted ! with mighty Soma, thrice-mixed, at our libations, to delight you.

2 Ye who behold the light of heaven, Ṛbhukṣans, give our rich patrons unmolested riches.
Drink, heavenly-natured. at our sacrifices, and give us bounties for the hymns we sing you.

3 For thou, O Bounteous One, art used to giving, at parting treasure whether small or ample.
Filled full are both thine arms with great possessions : thy goodness keeps thee not from granting riches.

4 Indra, high-famed, as Vāja and Ṛbhu-

---

1 *The seat of Order* : 'the hall of the sacrifice.'— Wilson. *The cattle* : rays of light.

2 'One of you (Varuṇa) is the lord and unassailable guide, and he who is called Mitra, (*i.e.* the friend) calls men to activity. Here so much at least is declared (and the same thing is expressed in nearly the same words in other places), that the light of day, which awakens life, and brings joy and activity into the world, is the narrower sphere of Mitra's power ; though, however, Varuṇa is not relegated to the night alone, for he continues to be the lord and the first.'—Von Roth, quoted by Muir *O. S. Texts*, V. 70. The meaning of *indḥ* translated by 'lord' in this extract, is, in the Veda, rather 'strong,' 'energetic,' and is so given in the St. Petersburg Lexicon, the meaning lord' belonging to later literature. The second half of the second line is repeated with a variation, from III. 59. 1.

3 *The springs* : the fountains of rain ; the clouds. *The Bull* : Parjanya, God of the rain-cloud. *This region* : literally, this udder ; the firmament.

4 *Voracious* : epithet of horses ; but the meaning of *dhāyú* is uncertain. According to Sāyaṇa, it means 'holding,' 'vigorous;' according to Ludwig, 'pouring forth rain;' according to Grassmann, 'thirsty.'

5 *His friendship* : Rudra's.
6 *The seventh* : with the six other celebrated rivers. See I. 32. 12.

7 *Akṣarā* : Vāk, or Voice; 'the imperishable goddess of speech.'—Wilson. Cf. VII. 15. 9.

8 *Aramati* : the personification of religious worship, or active piety. See VII. 34. 21. According to Sāyaṇa, *ardmatim* here is an epithet of *mahím*, 'the never-resting Earth.' For the various meanings assigned by Sāyaṇa to this word in the various places in which it occurs, See Muir, *O. S. Texts*, IV. 317.

9 *Viṣṇu* : Cf. X. 184. 1.

---

1 *Vājas and Ṛbhukṣans* : that is, Ṛbhukṣan or Ṛbhu, Vibhvan, and Vāja, commonly called the Ṛbhus from the name of the first of the three. *Fair-helmeted*: 'handsome-chinned.'—Wilson ; 'Strong-jawed.'—Ludwig. *Thrice-mixed* : with milk, curds, and meal.

3 *Bounteous One* : Maghavan; Indra.

kṣan, thou goest working, singing to the dwelling.

Lord of Bay Steeds, this day may we Vasiṣṭhas offer our prayers to thee and bring oblations.

5 Thou winnest swift advancement for thy servant, through hymns, Lord of Bay Steeds, which thou hast favoured.

For thee with friendly succour have we battled, and when, O Indra, wilt thou grant us riches?

6 To us thy priests a home, as 'twere, thou givest : when, Indra wilt thou recognize our praises ?

May thy strong Steed, through our ancestral worship, bring food and wealth with heroes to our dwelling.

7 Though Nirṛti the Goddess reigneth round him, Autumns with food in plenty come to Indra.

With three close Friends to length of days he cometh, he whom men let not rest at home in quiet.

8 Promise us gifts, O Savitar : may riches come unto us in Parvata's full bounty.

May the Celestial Guardian still attend us. Preserve us evermore, ye Gods, with blessings.

HYMN XXXVIII. *Savitar.*

1. ON high hath Savitar, this God, extended the golden lustre which he spreads around him.

Now, now must Bhaga be invoked by mortals, Lord of great riches who distributes treasures.

2 Rise up, O Savitar whose hands are golden, and hear this man while sacrifice is offered,

Spreading afar thy broad and wide effulgence, and bringing mortal men the food that feeds them.

3 Let Savitar the God be hymned with praises, to whom the Vasus, even, all sing glory.

Sweet be our lauds to him whose due is worship : may he with all protection guard our princes.

4 Even he whom Aditi the Goddess praises, rejoicing in God Savitar's incitement:

Even he who praise the high imperial Rulers, Varuṇa, Mitra, Aryaman, sing in concert.

5 They who come emulous to our oblation, dispensing bounty, from the earth and heaven.

May they and Ahibudhnya hear our calling: guard us Varūtrī with the Ekadhenus.

6 This may the Lord of Life, entreated, grant us,—the wealth which Savitar the God possesses.

The mighty calls on Bhaga for protection, on Bhaga calls the weak to give him riches.

7 Bless us the Vājins when we call, while slowly they move, strong Singers, to the Gods' assembly.

Crushing the wolf, the serpent, and the demons, may they completely banish all affliction.

8 Deep-skilled in Law eternal, deathless, Singers, O Vājins, help us in each fray for booty.

Drink of this meath, be satisfied, be joyful: then go on paths which Gods are wont to travel.

HYMN XXXIX *Viśvedevas.*

1. AGNI, erect, hath shown enriching favour: the flame goes forward to the Gods' assembly.

Like car-borne men the stones their path have chosen : let the priest, quickened, celebrate our worship.

---

4 *Working* : 'the fulfiller (of wishes).'—Wilson. The first line is somewhat obscure.

7 *Nirṛti* : the Goddess of Death and Destruction, who has no power over Indra. *Three close Friends* : the Ṛbhus, who represent the year, the annual course of Indra as the Sun. Sāyaṇa's explanation is different: 'Indra, the upholder of the three regions, whom the divine Nirṛti acknowledges as ruler, whom abundant years pass over, whom mortals detain from his own abode, approaches to (recruit) his decaying strength.' —Wilson; who observes : 'the explanation is not very clear.'

8 *Parvata's full bounty* : the Genius of mountain and cloud.

3 *The Vasus* : the Gods in general, according to Sāyaṇa.

5 *Varūtrī* : 'the protectress (the goddess of speech).' —Wilson. *Ekadhenus* : the Waters are probably meant: 'excellent cattle,'—Wilson.

7 *Vājins* : a class of divinities so named, according to Sāyaṇa ; but according to Mahīdhara, horses, *i.e.* the teams which draw the chariots of the Gods. *The wolf*, or the robber. *The serpent* : or the assassin. *The demons* : the Rākṣasas. See *Śatapatha-Brāhmaṇa*, V. I. 5. 21—24, (S. Books of the East, XLI. 27) for a different version of stanzas 6 and 7.

1 *The stones* : the pressing-stones have begun their course.

2 Soft to the tread, their sacred grass is
  scattered : these go like Kings amid the
  band around them,
  At the folk's early call on Night and
  Morning,—Vāyu, and Pūṣan with his
  team, to bless us.

3 Here on their path the noble Gods proceeded : in the wide firmament the
  Beauteous decked them.
  Bend your way hither, ye who travel
  widely : hear this our envoy who hath
  gone to meet you.

4 For they are holy aids at sacrifices : all
  Gods approach the place of congregation.
  Bring these, desirous, to our worship,
  Agni, swift the Nāsatyas, Bhaga, and
  Purandhi.

5 Agni, to these men's hymns, from earth,
  from heaven, bring Mitra, Varuṇa,
  Indra, and Agni,
  And Aryaman, and Aditi, and Viṣṇu.
  Sarasvatī be joyful, and the Maruts.

6 Even as the holy wish, the gift is offered :
  may he, unsated, come when men desire
  him.
  Give never-failing ever-conquering riches :
  with Gods for our allies may we be
  victors.

7 Now have both worlds been praised by
  the Vasiṣṭhas ; and holy Mitra, Varuṇa,
  and Agni.
  May they, bright Deities, make our song
  supremest. Preserve us evermore, ye
  Gods, with blessings.

HYMN XL.   *Viśvedevas.*

1. BE gathered all the audience of the synod :
   let us begin their praise whose course
   is rapid.
   Whate'er God Savitar this day produces,
   may we be where the Wealthy One
   distributes.

2 This, dealt from heaven, may both the
  Worlds vouchsafe us, and Varuṇa, Indra,
  Aryaman, and Mitra.

2 *These go like Kings* : according to Sāyaṇa, 'may
the two lords of people (Vāyu and Pūṣan)...appear
now.'

3 *Our envoy* : Agni.

5 *Agni* ; in his own form as a celestial God, not in
that of terrestrial fire.

6 *He, unsated* : Agni.

1 *Their praise* : praise of the Gods.

2 *Dealt from heaven* : or, distributed by Dyu or
Dyaus.

May Goddess Aditi assign us riches, Vāyu
and Bhaga make them ours for ever.

3 Strong be the man and full of power, O
  Maruts, whom ye, borne on by spotted
  coursers, favour.
  Him, too, Sarasvatī and Agni further,
  and there is none to rob him of his
  riches.

4 This Varuṇa is guide of Law, he, Mitra,
  and Aryaman, the Kings, our work have
  finished.
  Divine and foeless Aditi quickly listens.
  May these deliver us unharmed from
  trouble.

5 With offerings I propitiate the branches
  of this swift-moving God, the bounteous
  Viṣṇu.
  Hence Rudra gained his Rudra-strength :
  O Aśvins, ye sought the house that
  hath celestial viands.

6 Be not thou angry here, O glowing Pūṣan,
  for what Varūtrī and the Bounteous
  gave us.
  May the swift-moving Gods protect and
  bless us, and Vāta send us rain, who
  wanders round us.

7 Now have both worlds been praised by
  the Vasiṣṭhas, and holy Mitra, Varuṇa,
  and Agni.
  May they, bright Deities, make our song
  supremest. Preserve us evermore, ye
  Gods, with blessings.

HYMN XLI.   *Bhaga.*

1. AGNI at dawn, and Indra we invoke at
   dawn, and Varuṇa and Mitra, and the
   Aśvins twain :
   Bhaga at dawn, Pūṣan, and Brahmaṇaspati,
   Soma at dawn, Rudra we will invoke
   at dawn.

4 *Our work* : the sacrifice.

5 *The branches* : 'vaydḥ, branches : all other deities
are, as it were, branches of Viṣṇu, anye devāḥ, śākhā iva
bhavanti : as by a text cited by the scholiast, Viṣṇu is
all divinities, Viṣṇu sarvā devatā iti śruteḥ.'—Wilson. This,
Ludwig remarks, gives no satisfactory interpretation ;
but I am unable to offer any thing better at present.
Grassmann alters vaydḥ into vayāma : 'we with our
offerings approach the banquet of this swift-moving
God, the bounteous Viṣṇu ; i.e. come to offer him
sacrificial food.'

The hymn is addressed chiefly to Bhaga the bountiful, whose name, slightly corrupted, survives in the
Slavonic languages as a general name for God ; but
the Gods mentioned in stanza 1, and Uṣas, Dawn or
Morning, are also regarded as the deities of the verses in
which their names occur.

2 We will invoke strong, early-conquering
  Bhaga, the Son of Aditi, the great
  supporter :
  Thinking of whom, the poor, yea, even
  the mighty, even the King himself says,
  Give me Bhaga.

3 Bhaga our guide, Bhaga whose gifts are
  faithful, favour this song, and give us
  wealth, O Bhaga.
  Bhaga, augment our store of kine and
  horses, Bhaga, may we be rich in men
  and heroes.

4 So may felicity be ours at present, and
  when the day approaches, and at noontide;
  And may we still, O Bounteous One, at
  sunset be happy in the Deities' loving-
  kindness.

5 May Bhaga verily be bliss-bestower, and
  through him, Gods! may happiness attend
  us.
  As such, O Bhaga, all with might invoke
  thee : as such be thou our Champion
  here, O Bhaga.

6 To this our worship may all Dawns incline
  them, and come to the pure place like
  Dadhikravan.
  As strong steeds draw a chariot may they
  bring us hitherward Bhaga who discovers
  treasure.

7 May blessed Mornings dawn on us for ever,
  with wealth of kine, of horses, and of
  heroes,
  Streaming with all abundance, pouring
  fatness. Preserve us evermore, ye Gods,
  with blessings.

HYMN XLII.   *Visvedevas.*

1. LET Brahmans and Angirases come forward,
   and let the roar of cloudy heaven
   surround us.
   Loud low the Milch-kine swimming in
   the waters : set be the stones that grace
   our holy service.

2 Fair, Agni, is thy long-known path to
  travel : yoke for the juice thy bay, thy
  ruddy horses,
  Or red steeds, Hero-bearing, for the
  chamber. Seated, I call the Deities'
  generations.

3 They glorify your sacrifice with worship,
  yet the glad Priest near them is left
  unequalled.
  Bring the Gods hither, thou of many
  aspects : turn hitherward Aramati the
  Holy.

4 What time the Guest hath made himself
  apparent, at ease reclining in the rich
  man's dwelling,
  Agni, well-pleased, well-placed within the
  chamber gives to a house like this wealth
  worth the choosing.

5 Accept this sacrifice of ours, O Agni;
  glorify it with Indra and the Maruts.
  Here on our grass let Night and Dawn
  be seated : bring longing Varuna and
  Mitra hither.

6 Thus hath Vasiṣṭha praised victorious
  Agni, yearning for wealth that giveth
  all subsistence.
  May he bestow on us food, strength, and
  riches. Preserve us evermore, ye Gods,
  with blessings.

HYMN XLIII.   *Visvedevas.*

1. SING out the pious at your sacrifices to
   move with adorations Earth and
   Heaven—
   The Holy Singers, whose unmatched
   devotions, like a tree's branches, part
   in all directions.

2 Let sacrifice proceed like some fleet courser:
  with one accord lift ye on high the
  ladles.
  Strew sacred grass meet for the solemn
  service : bright flames that love the
  Gods have mounted upward.

3 Like babes in arms reposing on their
  mother, let the Gods sit upon the grass's
  summit.
  Let general fire make bright the flame of

---

2 *Give me Bhaga* : or riches.

6 *The pure place* : the chamber of sacrifice *Like
Dadhikravan* : swift as Dadhikravan, the famous horse,
the type and model of racers. See IV. 39. 3; 40. 1—3.

1 *Angirases* : Rṣis so named, according to Sāyaṇa.
The Milch-kine : the clouds in the watery firmament,
with allusion also to the milk and water mixed with the
Soma juice. *The stones* : the press-stones. Sāyaṇa's
explanation is different : 'may the pious couple, (the
Yajamāna and his wife) conjointly appreciate the beauty
of the sacrifice.'—Wilson.

2 *Thy bay, thy ruddy horses* : or the Harits and the
Rohits. *Red steeds* : or Aruṣas. *Hero-bearing* : carrying
the Hero Agni. *For the chamber* : the sacrificial hall ;
'in thy stable.'—M. Müller.

3 The human priests cannot equal Agni in efficiency.
Aramati : the Genius of Devotion. See VII. 36. 8.

4 *The Guest* : Agni.

3 *Let general fire* : or, according to Sāyaṇa, 'Let
the full ladle balm the fire of worship.' The exact

worship : scorn us not, Agni, in the Gods' assembly.

4 Gladly the Gods have let themselves be honoured, milking the copious streams of holy Order.
The highest might to-day is yours, the Vasus': come ye, as many as ye are, one-minded.

5 So, Agni, send us wealth among the people: may we be closely knit to thee, O Victor,
Unharmed, and rich, and taking joy together. Preserve us evermore, ye Gods, with blessings.

HYMN XLIV.   *Dadhikrās.*

1. I CALL on Dadhikrās, the first, to give you aid, the Aśvins, Bhaga, Dawn, and Agni kindled well,
Indra, and Viṣṇu, Pūṣan, Brahmaṇaspati, Ādityas, Heaven and Earth, the Waters, and the Light.

2 When, rising, to the sacrifice we hasten, awaking Dadhikrās with adorations.
Seating on sacred grass the Goddess Ilā, let us invoke the sage swift-hearing Aśvins.

3 While I am thus arousing Dadhikrāvan I speak to Agni, Earth, and Dawn, and Sūrya,
The red, the brown of Varuṇa ever mindful : may they ward off from us all grief and trouble.

4 Foremost is Dadhikrāvan, vigorous courser; in forefront of the cars, his way he knoweth,

Closely allied with Sūrya and with Morning, Ādityas, and Aṅgirases, and Vasus.

5 May Dadhikrās prepare the way we travel that we may pass along the path of Order.
May Agni hear us, and the Heavenly Army : hear us all Mighty Ones whom none deceiveth.

HYMN XLV.   *Savitar.*

1. MAY the God Savitar, rich in goodly treasures, filling the region, borne by steeds, come hither,
In his hand holding much that makes men happy, lulling to slumber and arousing creatures.

2 Golden, sublime, and easy in their motion, his arms extend unto the bounds of heaven.
Now shall that mightiness of his be lauded: even Sūra yields to him in active vigour.

3 May this God Savitar, the Strong and Mighty, the Lord of precious wealth, vouchsafe us treasures.
May he, advancing his far-spreading lustre, bestow on us the food that feedeth mortals.

4 These songs praise Savitar whose tongue is pleasant, praise him whose arms are full, whose hands are lovely.
High vital strength, and manifold, may he grant us. Preserve us evermore, ye Gods, with blessings.

HYMN XLVI.   *Rudra.*

1. To Rudra bring these songs, whose bow is firm and strong, the self-dependent God with swiftly-flying shafts,
The Wise, the Conqueror whom none may overcome, armed with sharp-pointed weapons : may he hear our call.

2 He through his lordship thinks on beings of the earth, on heavenly beings through his high imperial sway.
Come willingly to our doors that gladly welcome thee, and heal all sickness, Rudra, in our families.

3 May thy bright arrow which, shot down by thee from heaven, flieth upon the earth, pass us uninjured by.

meaning is uncertain as both subject and object are adjectives without substantives.
4 *Milking the copious streams* : enjoying the libations of law-ordained sacrifice. 'Who are the bestowers of water, the shedders of showers.'—Wilson.

1 *Dadhikrās* : See. IV. 38. 1.
3 *Dadhikrāvan* : a lengthened form of Dadhikrās. See IV. 39. 2, and 40. *The red, the brown* : apparently the horse of Varuṇa, that is, the Sun, is intended. *Ever mindful* : 'who is mindful of his adorers.—Wilson. The meaning of the word *maṁścatoḥ*, or *māṁścatoḥ*, is uncertain. Von Roth thinks that a colour, dun or yellow is meant. Ludwig would explain it as 'knotting snares or nooses.' Grassmann translates it by, 'des Mondveracheuchers, 'who scares away the Moon.'
4 *In forefront of the cars* : according to Sāyaṇa, the chariots of the Gods are intended. But, as Pischel observes (*Vedische Studien*, I. 124), Dadhikrāvan, the famous race-horse, was for 'the gentlemen of the turf' in King Trasadasyu's time what the matchless English horse Eclipse was in recent days. It seems probable that Dadhikrāvan may have been originally only a most distinguished racer, glorified and deified by the exaggerated praises of the bards of a people who ware passionately fond of chariot-racing.

2 *Sūra* : the Sun as distinguished from, or a different form of, Savitar who is said by Sāyaṇa to be the Sun before his rising.

Thou, very gracious God, hast thousand medicines : inflict no evil on our sons or progeny.

4 Slay us not, nor abandon us, O Rudra : let not thy noose, when thou art angry, seize us.
Give us trimmed grass and fame among the living. Preserve us evermore, ye Gods, with blessings.

HYMN XLVII.   *Waters.*

1. MAY we obtain this day from you, O Waters, that wave of pure refreshment, which the pious
Made erst the special beverage of Indra, bright, stainless, rich in sweets and dropping fatness.

2 May the Floods' Offspring, he whose course is rapid, protect that wave most rich in sweets, O Waters,
That shall make Indra and the Vasus joyful. This may we gain from you to-day, we pious.

3 All-purifying, joying in their nature, to paths of Gods the Goddesses move onward.
They never violate the laws of Indra. Present the oil-rich offering to the Rivers.

4 Whom Sūrya with his bright beams hath attracted, and Indra dug the path for them to travel,
May these Streams give us ample room and freedom. Preserve us evermore, ye Gods, with blessings.

---

3 *Very gracious God* ; *svapivāta.* 'This word is not explained in the printed text of Sāyaṇa, although in the "Varietas Lectionis," appended to his preface, Prof. Müller notes that in one MS., B. 4, *svapivāta* is rendered by *jitaprāṇa,* "he by whom life (or breath) is conquered." In the Nirukta, X. 7, it is explained by *svāpta-vacana,* "thou whose words are very suitable or authoritative."—Muir, *O. S. Texts,* IV. 314, where an exhaustive note on the word will be found. Wilson renders *svapivāta* by 'wind-appeaser,' and Grassmann by 'vielbegehrter,' 'much-desired.'

4 *Give us trimmed grass :* let us share in sacrifice. *Fame among the living :* the St. Petersburg Lexicon takes *jīvaśaṁse* to mean rule over the living. Others take the word as qualifying *barhiṣi,* trimmed grass, *i.e.* sacrifice, and signifying 'desired by the living,' 'to be praised among men,' 'promising (long) life.' See *Vedic Hymns,* Part I. p. 439.

---

1 *Wave of pure refreshment :* 'sweet essence of the earth ; *'ūrmi* is said here to imply the *Soma* juice produced from the earth.'—Wilson.

3 *All-purifying :* *śatápavitrāḥ ;* literally, with a hundred, that is, countless, means of purification. *The Goddesses :* the divine Waters.

HYMN XLVIII.   *Ṛbhus.*

1. YE liberal Heroes, Vājas and Ṛbhukṣans, come and delight you with our flowing Soma.
May your strength, Vibhus, as ye come to meet us, turn hitherward your car that brings men profit.

2 May we as Ṛbhu with your Ṛbhus conquer strength with our strength, as Vibhus with the Vibhus.
May Vāja aid us in the fight for booty, and helped by Indra may we quell the foeman.

3 For they rule many tribes with high dominion, and conquer all their foes in close encounter.
May Indra, Vibhvan, Vāja, and Ṛbhukṣan destroy by turns the wicked foeman's valour.

4 Now, Deities, give us ample room and freedom : be all of you, one-minded, our protection.
So let the Vasus grant us strength and vigour. Preserve us evermore, ye Gods, with blessings.

HYMN XLIX.   *Waters.*

1. FORTH from the middle of the flood the Waters—their chief the Sea—flow cleansing, never sleeping.
Indra, the Bull, the Thunderer, dug their channels : here let those Waters, Goddesses, protect me.

2 Waters which come from heaven, or those that wander dug from the earth, or flowing free by nature,
Bright, purifying, speeding to the Ocean, here let those Waters, Goddesses, protect me.

3 Those amid whom goes Varuṇa the Sovran, he who discriminates men's truth and falsehood—
Distilling meath, the bright, the purifying, here let those Waters, Goddesses, protect me.

4 They from whom Varuṇa the King, and

---

1 *Vājas and Ṛbhukṣans :* ye three, Ṛbhu, Vibhvan, and Vāja.

2 The meaning is, may we be as powerful as Ṛbhu, as mighty as the company of the Vibhus (another name of the Ṛbhus). Sāyaṇa explains *ṛbhu* as great, and *vibhvaḥ* as powerful. *In the fight for booty :* *vájasātau ;* a play on the word and name *vája.*

4 *The Vasus :* according to Sāyaṇa *vásavaḥ* here is an epithet of *Ṛbhávaḥ,* understood; the exalted (Ṛbhus).'—Wilson.

---

1 *The flood :* the ocean of air, the firmament.

Soma, and all the Deities drink strength
and vigour,
They into whom Vaiśvānara Agni entered,
here let those Waters, Goddesses, protect
me.

HYMN L. *Various Deities.*

1. O MITRA-VARUṆA, guard and protect me
here : let not that come to me which
nests within and swells.
I drive afar the scorpion hateful to the
sight : let not the winding worm touch
me and wound my foot.

2 Eruption that appears upon the twofold
joints, and that which overspreads the
ankles and the knees,
May the refulgent Agni banish far away :
let not the winding worm touch me and
wound my foot.

3 The poison that is formed upon the
Śalmali, that which is found in streams,
that which the plants produce,
All this may all the Gods banish and drive
away : let not the winding worm touch
me and wound my foot.

4 The steep declivities, the valleys, and the
heights, the channels full of water, and
the waterless—
May those who swell with water, gracious
Goddesses, never afflict us with the Śipada
disease, may all the rivers keep us free
from Śimidā.

HYMN LI. *Ādityas.*

1. THROUGH the Ādityas' most auspicious
shelter, through their most recent succour
may we conquer.
May they, the Mighty, giving ear, establish
this sacrifice, to make us free and
sinless.

The deities are (1) Mitra and Varuṇa, (2)
Agni, (3) Viśve Devāḥ, (4) Praise of the Rivers. Each
stanza of the hymn is to be repeated as an antidote
to the poison or disease which it specifies.

1 *That which nests within and swells* : 'the insidious
and spreading (poison).—Wilson. Sāyaṇa supplies the
substantive *viṣam. The scorpion : ajakāvám* ; the exact
meaning is uncertain.

2 *Twofold joints* : of the arms and legs. Sāyaṇa's
interpretation is different: 'the poison which is generated in the manifold knots (of trees).'—Wilson.

3 *The Śalmali* : the silk-cotton tree. *All the Gods*:
or, the All-Gods or Viśvedevas.

4 *The Śipada disease* : 'perhaps the Vedic form
of *Ślipada*, the Cochin leg.'—Wilson. *Śimidā* : apparently a female demon, or a disease, attributed to her
malevolence.

2 Let Aditi rejoice and the Ādityas, Varuṇa,
Mitra, Aryaman, most righteous.
May they, the Guardians of the world,
protect us, and, to show favour, drink
this day our Soma.

3 All Universal Deities, the Maruts, all the
Ādityas, yea, and all the Ṛbhus,
Indra, and Agni, and the Aśvins, lauded.
Preserve us evermore, ye Gods, with
blessings.

HYMN LII. *Ādityas.*

1. MAY we be free from every bond, Ādityas ! a castle among Gods and men,
ye Vasus.
Winning, may we win Varuṇa and Mitra,
and, being, may we be, O Earth and
Heaven.

2 May Varuṇa and Mitra grant this blessing, our Guardians, shelter to our seed
and offspring.
Let us not suffer for another's trespass,
nor do the thing that ye, O Vasus,
punish.

3 The ever-prompt Aṅgirases, imploring
riches from Savitar the God, obtained
them.
So may our Father who is great and holy,
and all the Gods, accordant, grant this
favour.

HYMN LIII. *Heaven and Earth.*

1. As priest with solemn rites and adorations
I worship Heaven and Earth, the High
and Holy.
To them, great Parents of the Gods, have
sages of ancient time, singing, assigned
precedence.

2 With newest hymns set in the seat of
Order, those the Two Parents, born
before all others,
Come, Heaven and Earth, with the Celestial People, hither to us, for strong is
your protection.

3 Yea, Heaven and Earth, ye hold in your
possession full many a treasure for the
liberal giver.

3 *Universal Deities : viśve devāḥ* ; the All-Gods.
Lauded : the sentence is incomplete, the substantives in
the nominative case having no verb.

1 *Being* : really and truly being, rich, powerful,
and distinguished.
3 *Our Father* : Varuṇa, the father of Vasiṣṭha; or
Savitar, or Prajāpati may be intended.

3 *For the liberal giver* : or, for Sudās.

Grant us that wealth which comes in free abundance. Preserve us evermore, ye Gods, with blessings.

HYMN LIV.   *Vāstoṣpati.*

1. ACKNOWLEDGE us, O Guardian of the Homestead : bring no disease, and give us happy entrance.
Whate'er we ask of thee, be pleased to grant it, and prosper thou quadrupeds and bipeds.
2 Protector of the Home, be our promoter : increase our wealth in kine and steeds, O Indu.
May we be ever-youthful in thy friendship: be pleased in us as in his sons a father.
3 Through thy dear fellowship that bringeth welfare, may we be victors, Guardian of the Dwelling !
Protect our happiness in rest and labour. Preserve us evermore, ye Gods, with blessings.

HYMN LV.   *Vāstoṣpati.*

1. VĀSTOṢPATI, who killest all disease and wearest every form,
Be an auspicious Friend to us.
2 When, O bright Son of Saramā, thou showest, tawny-hued ! thy teeth,
They gleam like lances' points within thy mouth when thou wouldst bite ; go thou to sleep.
3 Saramā's Son, retrace thy way : bark at the robber and the thief.
At Indra's singers barkest thou ? Why dost thou seek to terrify us ? Go to sleep.
4 Be on thy guard against the boar, and let the boar beware of thee.
At Indra's singers barkest thou ? Why dost thou seek to terrify us ? Go to sleep.

Vāstoṣpati is the Genius or tutelary God of the house. In this hymn he is addressed also as Indu, another name of Soma the Moon-God.

Vāstoṣpati is the deity of the first stanza, and Indra of the rest.

The metre is Gāyatrī in stanza I, Upariṣṭādbṛhatī (8 × 3 + 12) in 2—4, and Anuṣṭup in 5—8, and the hymn appears to be made up of three corresponding pieces unconnected by their subjects.
2 *Son of Saramā* : Saramā, the hound of Indra, is mother of the two Sārameyas, the brindled watch-dogs of Yama, God of the Dead. This stanza and the two following appear to be addressed by the spirits of Indra's worshippers to one of the dogs who would prevent their entering the home of the pious.

5 Sleep mother, let the father sleep, sleep dog and master of the house.
Let all the kinsmen sleep, sleep all the people who are round about.
6 The man who sits, the man who walks, and whosoever looks on us,
Of these we closely shut the eyes, even as we closely shut this house.
7 The Bull who hath a thousand horns, who rises up from out the sea,—
By him the Strong and Mighty One we lull and make the people sleep.
8 The women sleeping in the court, lying without, or stretched on beds,
The matrons with their odorous sweets— these, one and all, we lull to sleep.

HYMN LVI.   *Maruts.*

1. WHO are these radiant men in serried rank, Rudra's young heroes borne by noble steeds ?
2 Verily no one knoweth whence they sprang : they, and they only, know each other's birth.
3 They strew each other with their blasts, these Hawks : they strove together, roaring like the wind.
4 A sage was he who knew these mysteries, what in her udder mighty Pṛśni bore.

5 This and the three following stanzas form a lullaby or sleep-song, probably sung as a charm by a lover on a secret visit to his love.
7 *The Bull who hath a thousand horns* : the Sun, whose setting brings the time of rest and sleep ; or perhaps the starry heaven is intended.
8 *With their odorous sweets* : wearing garlands of fragrant flowers on festive occasions, according to Sāyaṇa : 'decorated with holiday perfumes.'—Wilson. According to a legend mentioned by Sāyaṇa, Vasiṣṭha, having fasted for three days was entering the house of Varuṇa in hope of food, when the watch-dog set upon him and was put to sleep by the repetition of the last four verses, which are to be recited on similar occasions by thieves and house-breakers. See Wilson's note. The hymn has been discussed by Aufrecht, *Indische Studien,* IV. 337f, and by Lanman, *Sanskrit Reader,* p. 370.

3 *They strew each other with their blasts* : the meaning of *svapūbhiḥ* is uncertain. 'They go together by their own pure paths.'—Wilson. 'They plucked each other with their beaks (?)'—M. Müller. 'They bestrew each other with light.'—Grassmann. 'They scatter dust over each other with besoms.'—Roth. I follow Professor Ludwig. The meaning appears to be that the Hawks or rapid Maruts are so crowded in their onward sweep that those in front feel the quick breath of those who follow. Similarly (VIII. 20. 21), the crowded Maruts are likened to cattle who lick each other's heads or humps.
4 *What in her udder* : according to Sāyaṇa, what beings (Maruts, etc.) mighty Pṛśni bore at her udder or in the firmament.

5 Ever victorious, through the Maruts, be this band of Heroes, nursing manly strength,

6 Most bright in splendour, fleetest on their way, close-knit to glory, strong with varied power.

7 Yea, mighty is your power and firm your strength : so, potent, with the Maruts, be the band.

8 Bright is your spirit, wrathful are your minds : your bold troop's minstrel is like one inspired.

9 Ever avert your blazing shaft from us, and let not your displeasure reach us here.

10 Your dear names, conquering Maruts, we invoke, calling aloud till we are satisfied.

11 Well-armed, impetuous in their haste, they deck themselves, their forms, with oblations : to you, the pure, ornaments made of gold.

12 Pure, Maruts, pure yourselves, are your oblations: to you, the pure, pure sacrifice I offer.

By Law they came to truth, the Law's observers, bright by their birth, and pure, and sanctifying.

13 Your rings, O Maruts, rest upon your shoulders, and chains of gold are twined upon your bosoms.

Gleaming with drops of rain, like lightning-flashes, after your wont ye whirl about your weapons.

14 Wide in the depth of air spread forth your glories, far, most adorable, ye bear your titles.

Maruts, accept this thousandfold allotment of household sacrifice and household treasure.

15 If, Maruts, ye regard the praise recited here at this mighty singer invocation,

Vouchsafe us quickly wealth with noble heroes, wealth which no man who hateth us may injure.

16 The Maruts, fleet as coursers, while they deck them like youths spectators of a festal meeting,

Linger, like beauteous colts, about the dwelling, like frisking calves, these who pour down the water.

17 So may the Maruts help us and be gracious, bringing free room to lovely Earth and Heaven.

Far be your bolt that slayeth men and cattle. Ye Vasus, turn yourselves to us with blessings.

18 The priest, when seated, loudly calls you, Maruts, praising in song your universal bounty.

He, Bulls ! who hath so much in his possession, free from duplicity, with hymns invokes you.

19 These Maruts bring the swift man to a stand-still, and strength with mightier strength they break and humble

These guard the singer from the man who hates him and lay their sore displeasure on the wicked.

20 These Maruts rouse even the poor and needy : the Vasus love him as an active champion.

Drive to a distance, O ye Bulls, the darkness : give us full store of children and descendants.

21 Never, O Maruts, may we lose your bounty, nor, car-borne Lords ! be hindmost when ye deal it.

Give us a share in that delightful treasure, the genuine wealth that, Bulls ! is your possession.

22 What time the men in fury rush together for running streams, for pastures, and for houses.

Then, O ye Maruts, ye who spring from Rudra, be our protectors in the strife with foemen.

23 Full many a deed ye did for our forefathers worthy of lauds which, even of old, they sang you.

The strong man, with the Maruts, wins in battle, the charger, with the Maruts, gains the booty.

24 Ours, O ye Maruts, be the vigorous Hero, the Lord Divine of men, the strong Sustainer,

With whom to fair lands we may cross the waters, and dwell in our own home with you beside us.

---

8 *Your bold troop's minstrel* : the leader of the Maruts' thunder-psalm. *Like one inspired* : *muniriva,* like a Muni or inspired saint. 'The sounds produced by the shaking of the trees are like the varied intonations of a reciter of praises, is Sāyaṇa's explanation.'—Wilson. Lanman translates differently : Clear is your whistling. Your hearts are wrathful as the wild onward-rush of a doughty troop.'

14 *Ye bear your titles* : you make yourselves known. 'You send down (the waters) that beat down (the dust).'—Wilson. *Nāmāni,* names, according to Sāyaṇa, means waters, because they bend down the dust, *pāṁsūn namayanti.*

24 *The Lord Divine* : literally, the Asura. *We may cross the waters* : the Maruts are besought to favour an expedition for the acquisition of new settlements on the farther side of a river.

25 May Indra, Mitra, Varuṇa and Agni,
    Waters, and Plants, and Trees accept
    our praises.
    May we find shelter in the Marut's bosom.
    Preserve us evermore, ye Gods, with
    blessings.

HYMN LVII.   Maruts.

1. YEA, through the power of your sweet
    juice, ye Holy ! the Marut host is glad
    at sacrifices.
    They cause even spacious heaven and earth
    to tremble, they make the spring flow
    when they come, the Mighty.

2 The Maruts watch the man who sings
    their praises, promoters of the thought
    of him who worships.
    Seat you on sacred grass in our assembly,
    this day, with friendly minds, to share
    the banquet.

3 No others gleam so brightly as these
    Maruts with their own forms, their
    golden gauds, their weapons.
    With all adornments, decking earth and
    heaven, they heighten, for bright show,
    their common splendour.

4 Far from us be your blazing dart, O
    Maruts, when we, through human
    frailty, sin against you.
    Let us not be exposed to that, ye Holy !
    May your most loving favour still at-
    tend us.

5 May even what we have done delight the
    Maruts, the blameless Ones, the bright,
    the purifying.
    Further us, O ye Holy, with your kind-
    ness : advance us mightily that we may
    prosper.

6 And may the Maruts, praised by all their
    titles, Heroes, enjoy the taste of our
    oblations.
    Give us of Amṛta for the sake of offspring:
    awake the excellent fair stores of riches.

1 *Ye Holy* : according to Sāyaṇa, the Maruts are
addressed. *The Marut host* : *nāma Mārutam* : the Marut
name, *i.e.* those who are called Maruts.

This hymn, and all the hymns to the Maruts have
been translated and explained in Max Müller's *Vedic
Hymns*, I. (Sacred Books of the East, Vol. XXXII.)

6 *Give us of Amṛta* : the secret essence which pervades the world and nourishes and sustains all must
naturally also be the element that promotes reproduction.—Ludwig. Von Roth explains the passage differently : 'Add us to (the number of) the people of
eternity, *i.e.* to the blessed.' 'Vouchsafe our children
long life.'—Grassmann. 'Bestow water upon our
progeny.'—Wilson.

7 Hither, ye Maruts, praised, with all your
    succours, with all felicity come to our
    princes,
    Who, of themselves, a hundredfold in-
    crease us. Preserve us evermore, ye
    Gods, with blessings.

HYMN LVIII.   Maruts.

1. SING to the troop that pours down rain
    in common, the Mighty Company of
    celestial nature.
    They make the world-halves tremble with
    their greatness : from depths of earth
    and sky they reach to heaven.

2 Yea, your birth, Maruts, was with wild
    commotion, ye who move swiftly, fierce
    in wrath, terrific.
    Ye all-surpassing in your might and vigour,
    each looker on the light fears at your
    coming.

3 Give ample vital power unto our princes :
    let our fair praises gratify the Maruts.
    As the way travelled helpeth people onward,
    so further us with your delightful
    succours.

4 Your favoured singer counts his wealth by
    hundreds : the strong steed whom ye
    favour wins a thousand.
    The Sovran whom ye aid destroys the
    foeman. May this your gift, ye Shakers,
    be distinguished.

5 I call, as such, the Sons of bounteous
    Rudra : will not the Maruts turn again
    to us-ward ?
    What secret sin or open stirs their anger,
    that we implore the Swift Ones to
    forgive us.

6 This eulogy of the Bounteous hath been
    spoken : accept, ye Maruts, this our
    hymn of praises.
    Ye Bulls, keep those who hate us at a
    distance. Preserve us evermore, ye Gods,
    with blessings.

HYMN LIX.   Maruts.

1. WHOMSO ye rescue here and there, whomso
    ye guide, O Deities,

1 *From depths of earth and sky* : *nirṛti* here is said to
be synonymous with *bhūmi*, earth, and *avaṁsā*, the
unsupported, with *antarikṣa*, firmament. But *nirṛti*,
Death, Destruction, as identified with *bhūmi*, may be
the Pṛthivī of the atmosphere (See V. 84.), which must
originally have been considered to be the place of departed spirits.
2 *Each looker on the light* : *viśvaḥ svardṛk* : according to Sāyaṇa, every tree.

To him give shelter, Agni, Mitra, Varuṇa,
ye Maruts, and thou Aryaman.

2 Through your kind favour, Gods, on
some auspicious day, the worshipper
subdues his foes.
That man increases home and strengthening ample food who brings you offerings
as ye list.

3 Vasiṣṭha will not overlook the lowliest one
among you all.
O Maruts, of our Soma juice effused to-day
drink all of you with eager haste.

4 Your succour in the battle injures not the
man to whom ye, Heroes, grant your
gifts.
May your most recent favour turn to us
again. Come quickly, ye who fain would
drink.

5 Come hitherward to drink the juice, O
ye whose bounties give you joy.
These offerings are for you, these, Maruts,
I present. Go not to any place but
this.

6 Sit on our sacred grass, be graciously
inclined to give the wealth for which
we long,
To take delight, ye Maruts, Friends of all,
with Svāhā, in sweet Soma juice.

7 Decking the beauty of their forms in
secret the Swans with purple backs
have flown down hither.
Around me all the Company hath
settled, like joyous Heroes glad in our
libation.

8 Maruts, the man whose wrath is hard to
master, he who would slay us ere we
think, O Vasus,
May he be tangled in the toils of mischief;
smite ye him down with your most
flaming weapon.

9 O Maruts, ye consuming Gods, enjoy this
offering brought for you,
To help us, ye who slay the foe.

10 Sharers of household sacrifice, come,
Maruts, stay not far away,
That ye may help us, Bounteous Ones.

11 Here, Self-strong Maruts, yea, even here,
ye Sages with your sunbright skins !
I dedicate your sacrifice.

12 Tryambaka we worship, sweet augmenter
of prosperity.
As from its stem the cucumber, so may
I be released from death, not reft of
immortality.

HYMN LX. *Mitra-Varuṇa.*

1. WHEN thou, O Sun, this day, arising
sinless, shalt speak the truth to Varuṇa
and Mitra,
O Aditi, may all the Deities love us,
and thou, O Aryaman, while we are
singing.

2 Looking on man, O Varuṇa and Mitra,
this Sun ascendeth up by both the
pathways,
Guardian of all things fixt, of all that
moveth, beholding good and evil acts
of mortals.

3 He from their home hath yoked the Seven
gold Coursers who, dropping oil and
fatness, carry Sūrya.
Yours, Varuṇa and Mitra, he surveyeth
the worlds and living creatures like a
herdsman.

4 Your coursers rich in store of sweets have
mounted : to the bright ocean Sūrya hath
ascended,
For whom the Ādityas make his pathway
ready, Aryaman, Mitra, Varuṇa, accordant.

5 For these, even Aryaman, Varuṇa and
Mitra, are the chastisers of all guile
and falsehood.
These, Aditi's Sons, infallible and mighty,
have waxen in the home of law Eternal.

12 *Tryambaka* : a name of Rudra. *Sweet* : according to Sāyaṇa, *sugándhim*, sweet-smelling, means here,
'whose fame is fragrant.' 'The verse occurs in the
Yajur-Veda, 6. 30, and is, in some instances, differently
interpreted; *Tryambaka* is termed *netratrayopetam Rudram*
the triocular Rudra : *sugándhim, divyagandhopetam*, of
celestial fragrance : the *urvāruka* is said to mean the
karkandhu [fruit of the jujube-tree), which, when ripe,
falls of itself from its stalk.'—Wilson.

The hymn is addressed chiefly to Mitra and
Varuṇa, but Sūrya or the Sun is the deity of the first
stanza.

1 *Sinless* : Sāyaṇa makes *ánāgāḥ=anāgasaḥ* : 'declare
the truth...that we are void of sin.'—Wilson. But this
seems forced, and the implied meaning of the poet is
clear enough if the word is taken in its usual signification.

2 *Both the pathways* : near the earth and high in the
firmament.

4 *Injures not* : a litotes for, is of the greatest advantage to.

5 *Whose bounties give you joy* : or follow each other
closely, and are ever fresh and ready.

6 *Svāhā* : an exclamation, like Ave ! or Hail ! used
in making oblations to the Gods.

7 *With purple backs* : *nīlapṛṣṭhāḥ*: cf. Horace's 'pur-
purei olores.'

8 *Mischief* : or one of the malicious spirits called
Druhs.

6 These, Mitra, Varuṇa whom none deceiveth, with great power quicken even the fool to wisdom,
And, wakening, moreover, thoughtful insight, lead it by easy paths o'er grief and trouble,

7 They ever vigilant, with eyes that close not, caring for heaven and earth, lead on the thoughtless.
Even in the river's bed there is a shallow: across this broad expanse may they conduct us.

8 When Aditi and Varuṇa and Mitra, like guardians, give Sudās their friendly shelter,
Granting him sons and lineal succession, let us not, bold ones ! move the Gods to anger.

9 May he with offerings purify the altar from any stains of Varuṇa's reviler.
Aryaman save us from all those who hate us : give room and freedom to Sudās, ye Mighty.

10 Hid from our eyes is their resplendent meeting : by their mysterious might they hold dominion.
Heroes ! we cry trembling in fear before you, even in the greatness of your power have mercy.

11 He who wins favour for his prayer by worship, that he may gain him strength and highest riches,
That good man's mind the Mighty Ones will follow : they have brought comfort to his spacious dwelling.

12 This priestly task, Gods ! Varuṇa and Mitra ! hath been performed for you at sacrifices.
Convey us safely over every peril. Preserve us evermore, ye Gods, with blessings.

HYMN LXI.   Mitra-Varuṇa.

1. O Varuṇa and Mitra, Sūrya spreading the beauteous light of you Twain Gods ariseth.

6 *Mitra, Varuṇa* : and Aryaman, understood : the verbs are in the plural.
8 *Bold ones* : the warning is addressed to the people of Sudās, who has been frequently mentioned in preceding hymns.
9 *May he* : Agni may be intended. *Varuṇa's reviler*: those who speak evil of princes like Sudās, Varuṇa being the king's prototype.—Ludwig.
10 *Their resplendent meeting* : that of Mitra, Varuṇa, and Aryaman.
11 *Have brought comfort to his spacious dwelling* : 'bestow a spacious mansion for a dwelling upon him.'—Wilson.

He who beholdeth all existing creatures observeth well the zeal that is in mortals.

2 The holy sage, renowned afar, directeth his hymns to you, O Varuṇa and Mitra,—
He whose devotions, sapient Gods, ye favour so that ye fill, as 'twere, with power his autumns.

3 From the wide earth, O Varuṇa and Mitra, from the great lofty heaven, ye, Bounteous Givers,·
Have in the fields and houses set your warders who visit every spot and watch unceasing.

4 I praise the strength of Varuṇa and Mitra : that strength, by mightiness, keeps both worlds asunder.
Heroless pass the months of the ungodly : he who loves sacrifice makes his home enduring.

5 Steers, all infallible are these your people in whom no wondrous thing is seen, no worship.
Guile follows close the men who are untruthful : no secrets may be hidden from your knowledge.

6 I will exalt your sacrifice with homage : as priest, I, Mitra-Varuṇa, invoke you.
May these new hymns and prayers that I have fashioned delight you to the profit of the singer.

7 This priestly task, Gods ! Varuṇa and Mitra ! hath been performed for you at sacrifices.
Convey us safely over every peril. Preserve us evermore, ye Gods, with blessings.

2 *Autumns* : years of his life.

5 This stanza is difficult. Sāyaṇa's interpretation as given by Wilson is : 'Unperplexed, all-pervading showerers (of benefits), these praises are for you, in which nothing surprising, no adoration (worthy of you), is beheld : the insincere commendations of men serve as offences : eulogies of you, although offered in secret are not unappreciated.' The version of the *Seventy Hymns* is somewhat as follows : 'All your avenging spirits, O ye Mighty, follow unerringly the sinner's traces. They have no sign that men may mark, no figure. Naught is so secret that ye fail to know it.' This latter involves a slight alteration of the text. I prefer Ludwig's interpretation, although it is not absolutely convincing.

6 *To the profit of the singer* : See *Vedische Studien*, I. 43.

HYMN LXII. *Mitra-Varuṇa.*

1. Sūrya hath sent aloft his beams of splendour o'er all the tribes of men in countless places.
Together with the heaven he shines apparent, formed by his Makers well with power and wisdom.

2 So hast thou mounted up before us, Sūrya, through these our praises, with fleet dappled horses.
Declare us free from all offence to Mitra, and Varuṇa, and Aryaman, and Agni.

3 May holy Agni, Varuṇa, and Mitra send down their riches upon us in thousands.
May they, the Bright Ones, make our praise-song perfect, and, when we laud them, grant us all our wishes.

4 O undivided Heaven and Earth, preserve us, us, Lofty Ones ! your nobly-born descendants.
Let us not anger Varuṇa, nor Vāyu, nor him, the dearest Friend of mortals, Mitra.

5 Stretch forth your arms and let our lives be lengthened : with fatness dew the pastures of our cattle.
Ye Youthful, make us famed among the people : hear, Mitra-Varuṇa, these mine invocations.

6 Now Mitra, Varuṇa, Aryaman vouchsafe us freedom and room, for us and for our children.
May we find paths all fair and good to travel. Preserve us evermore, ye Gods, with blessings.

HYMN LXIII. *Mitra-Varuṇa.*

1. Common to all mankind, auspicious Sūrya, he who beholdeth all, is mounting upward ;
The God, the eye of Varuṇa and Mitra, who rolled up darkness like a piece of leather.

2 Sūrya's great ensign, restless as the billow, that urgeth men to action, is advancing :
Onward he still would roll the wheel well-rounded, which Etaśa, harnessed to the car-pole, moveth.

3 Refulgent from the bosom of the Mornings, he in whom singers take delight ascendeth.
This Savitar, God, is my chief joy and pleasure, who breaketh not the universal statute.

2 *Etaśa* : or the bright or dappled steed ; one of the horses of the Sun.
3 *Breaketh not* : faithfully observes and supports.

4 Golden, far-seeing, from the heaven he riseth : far is his goal, he hasteth on resplendent.
Men, verily, inspirited by Sūrya speed to their aims and do the work assigned them.

5 Where the immortals have prepared his pathway he flieth through the region like a falcon.
With homage and oblations will we serve you, O Mitra-Varuṇa, when the Sun hath risen.

6 Now Mitra, Varuṇa, Aryaman vouchsafe us freedom and room, for us and for our children.
May we find paths all fair and good to travel. Preserve us evermore, ye Gods, with blessings.

HYMN LXIV. *Mitra-Varuṇa.*

1. Ye Twain who rule, in heaven and earth, the region, clothed be your clouds in robes of oil and fatness.
May the imperial Varuṇa, and Mitra, and high-born Aryaman accept our presents.

2 Kings, guards of mighty everlasting Order, come hitherward, ye Princes, Lords of Rivers.
Send us from heaven, O Varuṇa and Mitra, rain and sweet food, ye who pour down your bounties.

3 May the dear God, and Varuṇa and Mitra conduct us by the most effective pathways,
That foes may say unto Sudās our chieftain, May, we, too, joy in food with Gods to guard us.

4 Him who hath wrought for you this car in spirit, who makes the song rise upward and sustains it,
Bedew with fatness, Varuṇa nd Mitra : ye Kings, make glad the pleasant dwelling-places.

5 To you this laud, O Varuṇa and Mitra is offered like bright Soma juice to Vāyu.

1 *Clothed be your clouds* : 'A covering cloud of sacred oil attends you (V. 62. 4). 'Impelled by you, (the clouds) assume the form of rain.'—Wilson.
3 The second half of the stanza is obscure. The meaning appears to be that even our foes, the godless who offer no sacrifices, shall envy the prosperity which we enjoy through the liberality of Sudās, and shall wish to follow our example, to sacrifice to the Gods and to enjoy their protection and the blessings which they send.
4 *This car* : this carefully-formed hymn which goes, like a chariot, to the Gods.
5 *To Vāyu* : who receives the first draught of Soma juice at the morning libation.

Favour our songs of praise, wake thought and spirit. Preserve us evermore, ye Gods, with blessings.

HYMN LXV.   *Mitra-Varuṇa.*

1. WITH hymns I call you, when the Sun hath risen, Mitra, and Varuṇa whose thoughts are holy,
Whose Power Divine, supreme and everlasting, comes with good heed at each man's supplication.

2 For they are Asuras of Gods, the friendly : make, both of you, our lands exceeding fruitful.
May we obtain you, Varuṇa and Mitra, wherever Heaven and Earth and days may bless us.

3 Bonds of the sinner, they bear many nooses: the wicked mortal hardly may escape them.
Varuṇa-Mitra, may your path of Order bear us o'er trouble as a boat o'er waters.

4 Come, taste our offering, Varuṇa and Mitra : bedew our pasture with sweet food and fatness.
Pour down in plenty here upon the people the choicest of your fair celestial water.

5 To you this laud, O Varuṇa and Mitra, is offered, like bright Soma juice to Vāyu.
Favour our songs of praise, wake thought and spirit. Preserve us evermore, ye Gods, with blessings.

HYMN LXVI   *Mitra-Varuṇa.*

1. LET our strong hymn of praise go forth, the laud of Mitra-Varuṇa,
With homage to that high-born Pair ;

2 The Two exceeding wise, the Sons of Dakṣa, whom the gods ordained
For lordship, excellently great.

3 Such, Guardians of our homes and us, O Mitra-Varuṇa, fulfil

The thoughts of those who sing your praise.

4 So when the Sun hath risen to-day, may sinless Mitra, Aryaman,
Bhaga, and Savitar send us forth.

5 May this our home be guarded well : forward, ye Bounteous, on the way,
Who bear us safely o'er distress.

6. And those Self-reigning, Aditi, whose statute is inviolate,
The Kings who rule a vast domain.

7 Soon as the Sun hath risen, to you, to Mitra-Varuṇa, I sing,
And Aryaman who slays the foe.

8 With wealth of gold may this my song bring unmolested power and might,
And, Brahmans, gain the sacrifice.

9 May we be thine, God Varuṇa, and with our princes, Mitra, thine :
Food and Heaven's light will we obtain.

10 Many are they who strengthen Law, Sun-eyed, with Agni for their tongue,
They who direct the three great gatherings with their thoughts, yea, all things with surpassing might.

11 They who have stablished year and month and then the day, night, sacrifice and holy verse,
Varuṇa, Mitra, Aryaman, the Kings, have won dominion which none else may gain.

12 So at the rising of the Sun we think of you with hymns to-day,
Even as Varuṇa, Mitra, Aryaman deserve: ye are the charioteers of Law.

13 True to Law, born in Law, the strengtheners of Law, terrible, haters of the false,
In their felicity which gives the best defence may we men and our princes dwell.

---

4 *Sinless* : Sāyaṇa here, as in VII. 60. 1, takes *dnāgāḥ* as = *anāgasaḥ*, as that, according to his interpretation, the translation would be : may Savitar, Mitra, Aryaman, and Bhaga send us sinless forth.

6 *Aditi* is out of place here, as there is no copulative in the text : whose mother is Aditi, seems to be intended.

8 *And, Brahmans, gain the sacrifice* : the exact meaning is uncertain : 'May it (be effective), sages, for the fulfilment of (the objects of) the sacrifice.'—Wilson.

10 *The three great gatherings* : or three assemblies. The meaning it not clear. Ludwig is of opinion that the three castes are intended.

The meaning of stanzas 10 and 11 is that although there be many deities, Varuṇa, Mitra, and Aryaman are supreme.

The hymn appears to be composed of fragments of other hymns with a few original additions. Cf. VII 63. 5; 66. 7. 12; VI. 68. 8; VII. 62. 5; III. 62. 16. See von Bradke, *Dyaus Asura*, 3—5.

1 *Power Divine* : *asuryám* : Asurahood. *Whose* : refers to Mitra and Varuṇa.

2 *Asuras of Gods* : the high or ruling Gods of all the deities.

3 *Bonds* : binders. *Many nooses* : 'Your guiles, ye Holy Ones, to quell oppressors, your snares spread out against the foe, Ādityas' (II. 27. 16).

---

2 *Sons of Dakṣa* : See VI. 50. 2. *For lordship* : literally for Asurahood.

14 Uprises, on the slope of heaven, that
marvel that attracts the sight,
As swift celestial Etaśa bears it away,
prepared for every eye to see.

15 Lord of each single head, of fixt
and moving things, equally through
the whole expanse,
The Seven sister Bays bear Sūrya on his
car, to bring us wealth and happiness.

16 A hundred autumns may we see that
bright Eye, God-ordained, arise :
A hundred autumns may we live.

17 Infallible through your wisdom, come hither,
resplendent Varuṇa,
And Mitra, to the Soma draught.

18 Come as the laws of Heaven ordain,
Varuṇa, Mitra, void of guile :
Press near and drink the Soma juice.

19 Come, Mitra, Varuṇa, accept, Heroes,
our sacrificial gift :
Drink Soma, ye who strengthen Law.

HYMN LXVII. *Aśvins.*

1. I WITH a holy heart that brings oblation
will sing forth praise to meet your car,
ye Princes,
Which, Much-desired ! hath wakened as
your envoy. I call you hither as a son
his parents.

2 Brightly hath Agni shone by us enkindled:
the limits even of darkness were
apparent.
Eastward is seen the Banner of the Morning, the Banner born to give Heaven's
Daughter glory.

3 With hymns the deft priest is about you,
Aśvins, the eloquent priest attends you
now, Nāsatyas.
Come by the paths that ye are wont to
travel, on car that finds the light, laden
with treasure.

4 When, suppliant for your help, Lovers of
Sweetness ! I seeking wealth call you
to our libation,
Hitherward let your vigorous horses bear
you : drink ye with us the well-pressed
Soma juices.

5 Bring forward, Aśvins, Gods, to its fulfilment my never-wearied prayer that asks
for riches.

Vouchsafe us all high spirit in the combat,
and with your powers, O Lords of Power,
assist us.

6 Favour us in these prayers of ours, O
Aśvins. May we have genial vigour,
ne'er to fail us.
So may we, strong in children and descendants, go, wealthy, to the banquet that
awaits you.

7 Lovers of Sweetness, we have brought this
treasure to you as 'twere an envoy sent
for friendship.
Come unto us with spirits free from anger,
in homes of men enjoying our oblation.

8 With one, the same, intention, ye swift
movers, o'er the Seven Rivers hath your
chariot travelled.
Yoked by the Gods, your strong steeds
never weary while speeding forward at
the pole they bear you.

9 Exhaustless be your bounty to our princes
who with their wealth incite the gift of
riches,
Who further friendship with their noble
natures, combining wealth in kine with
wealth in horses.

10 Now hear, O Youthful Twain, mine
invocation : come, Aśvins, to the home
where food aboundeth.
Vouchsafe us wealth, do honour to our
nobles. Preserve us evermore, ye Gods,
with blessings.

HYMN LXVIII. *Aśvins.*

1. COME, radiant Aśvins, with your noble
horses : accept your servant's hymns, ye
Wonder-Workers :
Enjoy oblations which we bring to greet
you.

2 The gladdening juices stand prepared
before you : come quickly and partake
of mine oblation.
Pass by the calling of our foe and hear
us.

3 Your chariot with a hundred aids, O
Aśvins, beareth you swift as thought
across the regions,
Speeding to us, O ye whose wealth is
Sūryā.

9 *Incite the gift of riches* : move the Gods to give
riches in return.
Friendship : or, a kinsman, meaning, apparently, the
priest.

———

3 *Whose wealth is Sūryā* : having Sūryā for your
possession or treasure. Sūryā, the daughter of the Sun,
is the consort of the Aśvins. See I. 116. 17.

15 *Sister Bays* : the Harits. See IV. 6. 9; 13.3.

18 *Come as the laws of Heaven ordain* : 'Come with
your glories from the sky.'—Sāyaṇa. 'Come hither with
the hosts of heaven.'—Grassmann.

———

1 *Much-desired* : 'adorable.'—Wilson.

4 What time this stone of yours, the Gods'
adorer, upraised, sounds forth for you
as Soma-presser,
Let the priest bring you, Fair Ones,
through oblations.

5 The nourishment ye have is, truly,
wondrous : ye gave thereof a quickening store to Atri,
Who, being dear to you, receives your
favour.

6 That gift, which all may gain, ye gave
Cyavāna, when he grew old, who
offered you oblations,
When ye bestowed on him enduring
beauty.

7 What time his wicked friends abandoned
Bhujyu, O Aśvins, in the middle of the
ocean,
Your horse delivered him, your faithful
servant.

8 Ye lent your aid to Vṛka when exhausted,
and listened when invoked to Śayu's
calling.
Ye made the cow pour forth her milk like
water, and, Aśvins, strengthened with
your strength the barren.

9 With his fair hymns this singer, too, extols you, waking with glad thoughts at
the break of morning.
May the cow nourish him with milk to
feed him. Preserve us evermore, ye
Gods, with blessings.

---

4 *The Gods' adorer* ; *devayáḥ* : literally, turning or
going to the Gods, inasmuch as it is employed in
preparing the Soma juice. *The priest* : here, perhaps,
the pressing-stone.

5 *A quickening store* : the meaning of *máhiṣvantam,*
which does not occur elsewhere, is uncertain. According
to Sāyaṇa it means a pit or cavern : ye liberated Atri
from the cavern, or, literally, ye separated the cavern
from Atri. For the legend, See I. 116. 12.

6 *Which all may gain* ; which you Aśvins are ready
to grant to every worshipper who needs it. For the
story of Cyavāna, See I. 116. 10; 117. 13; 118. 6.

7 *Bhujyu* : See Vol. I., Index. *Your horse* : this
meaning is suggested by von Roth for the uncertain
word *drāvā,* which generally appears to mean hostile or
illiberal but may perhaps stand in this passage for
arvā, a common word signifying horse. See I. 117. 14:—
'With horses brown of hue that flew with swift wings
ye brought back Bhujyu from the sea of billows.' See
also VII. 69. 7.

8 *Vṛka* : literally wolf, or robber. Some man so
named seems to be meant. *Śayu* : See I. 118. 8; VI. 13.5.

9 *This singer* : the Ṛṣi Vasiṣṭha. *The cow* : that
is brought to supply the milk required for libations.

HYMN LXIX.　　　　　　*Aśvins.*

1. MAY your gold chariot, drawn by vigorous
horses, come to us, blocking up the earth
and heaven,
Bright with its fellies while its way drops
fatness, food-laden, rich in coursers,
man's protector.

2 Let it approach, yoked by the will, three-
seated, extending far and wide o'er
fivefold beings,
Whereon ye visit God-adoring races, bending your course whither ye will, O
Aśvins.

3 Renowned, with noble horses, come ye
hither : drink, Wondrous Pair, the cup
that holds sweet juices.
Your car whereon your Spouse is wont
to travel marks with its track the farthest
ends of heaven.

4 When night was turning to the grey of
morning the Maiden, Sūrya's Daughter,
chose your splendour.
When with your power and might ye aid
the pious he comes through heat to life
by your assistance.

5 O Chariot-borne, this car of yours invested
with rays of light comes harnessed to
our dwelling.
Herewith, O Aśvins, while the dawn is
breaking, to this our sacrifice bring peace
and blessing.

6 Like the wild cattle thirsty for the lightning, Heroes, come nigh this day to our
libations.
Men call on you with hymns in many
places, but let not other worshippers
detain you.

7 Bhujyu, abandoned in the midst of ocean,
ye raised from out the water with your
horses,
Uninjured, winged, flagging not, undaunted, with deeds of wonder saving
him, O Aśvins.

8 Now hear, O Youthful Twain, mine
invocation : come, Aśvins, to the home
where food aboundeth.

---

2 *Fivefold beings* : 'sarvaprāṇinaḥ,' all living beings,
says Sāyaṇa.

3 *Your Spouse* : Sūryā, daughter of the Sun.

4 *Chose your splendour* : See I. 116. 17.

6 *Thirsty for the lightning* : which immediately
precedes, or accompanies, the rain they long for.

7 *Horses* : not in the text, but supplied by Sāyaṇa
and obviously understood. See preceding hymn, 7, note.

Vouchsafe us wealth, do honour to our nobles. Preserve us evermore, ye Gods, with blessings.

HYMN LXX. *Aśvins.*

1. RICH in all blessings, Aśvins come ye hither : this place on earth is called your own possession,
Like a strong horse with a fair back it standeth, whereon, as in a lap, ye seat you firmly.

2 This most delightful eulogy awaits you : in the man's house drink-offering hath been heated,
Which bringeth you over the seas and rivers, yoking as 'twere two well-matched shining horses.

3 Whatever dwellings ye possess, O Aśvins, in fields of men or in the streams of heaven,
Resting upon the summit of the mountain, or bringing food to him who gives oblation,

4 Delight yourselves, ye Gods, in plants and waters when Ṛṣis give them and ye find they suit you.
Enriching us with treasures in abundance ye have looked back to former generations.

5 Aśvins, though ye have heard them oft aforetime, regard the many prayers which Ṛṣis offer.
Come to the man even as his heart desireth : may we enjoy your most delightful favour.

6 Come to the sacrifice offered you, Nāsatyas, with men, oblations, and prayer duly uttered.
Come to Vasiṣṭha as his heart desireth, for unto you these holy hymns are chanted.

7 This is the thought, this is the song, O Aśvins : accept this hymn of ours, ye Steers, with favour.
May these our prayers addressed to you come nigh you. Preserve us evermore, ye Gods, with blessings.

1 *This place* : the altar.

2 *Drink-offering* : *gharmá* : the libation of hot milk; or, the caldron in which it is prepared.

4 *Ye have looked back to former generations*: Sāyaṇa explains *yugdni* differently : '(favour us) as you have favoured former couples[*i.e.* sacrificers and their wives].' —Wilson.

5 *The man* : the institutor of the sacrifice.

HYMN LXXI. *Aśvins.*

1. THE Night retireth from the Dawn her Sister ; the Dark one yieldeth to the Red her pathway.
Let us invoke you rich in steeds and cattle : by day and night keep far from us the arrow.

2 Bearing rich treasure in your car, O Aśvins, come to the mortal who presents oblation.
Keep at a distance penury and sickness; Lovers of Sweetness, day and night preserve us.

3 May your strong horses, seeking bliss, bring hither your chariot at the earliest flush of morning.
With coursers yoked by Law drive hither, Aśvins, your car whose reins are light, laden with treasure.

4 The chariot, Princes, that conveys you, moving at daylight, triple-seated, fraught with riches,
Even with this come unto us, Nāsatyas, that laden with all food it may approach us.

5 Ye freed Cyavāna from old age and weakness : ye brought the courser fleet of food to Pedu.
Ye rescued Atri from distress and darkness, and loosed for Jāhuṣa the bonds that bound him.

6 This is the thought, this is the song, O Aśvins: accept this hymn of ours, ye Steers, with favour.
May these our prayers addressed to you come nigh you. Preserve us evermore, ye Gods, with blessings.

HYMN LXXII. *Aśvins.*

1. COME, O Nāsatyas, on your car resplendent, rich in abundant wealth of kine and horses.
As harnessed steeds, all our laudations follow you whose forms shine with most delightful beauty.

2 Come with the Gods associate, come ye hither to us, Nāsatyas, with your car accordant.

1 *The Red* : the Sun. *The arrow* : of disease and death.

3 *Seeking bliss* : for men.

5 For *Cyavāna, Pedu, Atri,* and *Jāhuṣa*, See Vol. I. Index. The re-appearance, heralded by the Aśvins or Gods of Twilight, of the departed Sun appears to be symbolized in all these legends.

'Twixt you and us there is ancestral friendship and common kin : remember and regard it.

3 Awakened are the songs that praise the Aśvins, the kindred prayers and the Celestial Mornings.
Inviting those we long for, Earth and Heaven, the singer calleth these Nāsatyas hither.

4 What time the Dawns break forth in light, O Aśvins, to you the poets offer their devotions.
God Savitar hath sent aloft his splendour, and fires sing praises with the kindled fuel.

5 Come from the west, come from the east, Nāsatyas, come, Aśvins, from below and from above us.
Bring wealth from all sides for the Fivefold People. Preserve us evermore, ye Gods, with blessings.

HYMN LXXIII.   *Aśvins.*

1. WE have o'erpassed the limit of this darkness while, worshipping the Gods, we sang their praises.
The song invoketh both Immortal Aśvins far-reaching, born of old, great Wonder-Workers.

2 And, O Nāsatyas, man's dear Priest is seated, who brings to sacrifice and offers worship,
Be near and taste the pleasant juice, O Aśvins : with food, I call you to the sacrifices.

3 We choosing you, have let our worship follow its course : ye Steers, accept this hymn with favour.
Obeying you as your appointed servant, Vasiṣṭha singing hath with lauds aroused you.

4 And these Two Priests come nigh unto our people, united, demon-slayers, mighty-handed.
The juices that exhilarate are mingled. Injure us not, but come with happy fortune.

5 *The Fivefold People* : the five Āryan tribes. See I. 7. 9.

———

The first half-line has occurred before in I. 92. 6, and 183. 6.

2 *Man's dear Priest* : Agni.

4 *These Two Priests* : the Aśvins. *Demon-slayers* : slayers of Rākṣasas and evil spirits of the night which disappear at the coming of the heralds of day.

———

5 Come from the west, come from the east, Nāsatyas, come, Aśvins, from below and from above us.
Bring wealth from all sides for the Fivefold People. Preserve us evermore, ye Gods, with blessings.

HYMN LXXIV.   *Aśvins.*

1. THESE morning sacrifices call you, Aśvins, at the break of day.
For help have I invoked you rich in power and might : for, house by house ye visit all.

2 O Heroes, ye bestow wonderful nourishment: send it to him whose songs are sweet.
Accordant, both of you, drive your car down to us, and drink the savoury Soma juice.

3 Approach ye and be near to us : drink, O ye Aśvins, of the meath.
Draw forth the milk, ye Mighty, rich in genuine wealth : injure us not, and come to us.

4 The horses that convey you in their rapid flight down to the worshipper's abode,
With these your speedy coursers, Heroes, Aśvins, come, ye Gods, come well-inclined to us.

5 Yea, verily, our princes seek the Aśvins in pursuit of food.
These shall give lasting glory to our liberal lords, and, both Nāsatyas, shelter us.

6 Those who have led the way, like cars, offending none, those who are guardians of the men—
Also through their own might the heroes have grown strong, and dwell in safe and happy homes.

HYMN LXXV.   *Dawn.*

1. BORN in the heavens the Dawn hath flushed, and showing her majesty is come as Law ordaineth.
She hath uncovered fiends and hateful darkness ; best of Aṅgirases, hath waked the pathways.

2 Rouse us this day to high and happy fortune : to great felicity, O Dawn, promote us.

3 *Draw forth the milk* : milk the sweet rain from the firmament.

6 *Who have led the way, like cars* : wealthy nobles or princes, 'the heroes' of the second line.

———

1 *Best of Aṅgirases* : endowed with the noblest characteristics of the holy Aṅgirases. *Waked the pathways*: lighted them for men to use.

Vouchsafe us manifold and splendid riches,
famed among mortals, man-befriending
Goddess !

3 See, lovely Morning's everlasting splendours, bright with their varied colours,
have approached us.
Filling the region of mid-air, producing
the rites of holy worship, they have
mounted.

4 She yokes her chariot far away, and swiftly
visits the lands where the Five Tribes
are settled,
Looking upon the works and ways of
mortals, Daughter of Heaven, the world's
Imperial Lady.

5 She who is rich in spoil, the Spouse of
Sūrya, wondrously opulent, rules all
wealth and treasures.
Consumer of our youth, the seers extol
her : lauded by priests rich Dawn
shines out refulgent.

6 Apparent are the steeds of varied colour,
the red steeds carrying resplendent
Morning.
On her all-lovely car she comes, the Fair
One, and brings rich treasure for her
faithful servant.

7 True with the True and Mighty with the
Mighty, with Gods a Goddess, Holy with
the Holy,
She brake strong fences down and gave
the cattle : the kine were lowing as they
greeted Morning.

8 O Dawn, now give us wealth in kine and
heroes, and horses, fraught with manifold enjoyment.
Protect our sacred grass from man's
reproaches. Preserve us evermore, ye
Gods, with blessings.

HYMN LXXVI.   *Dawn.*

1. SAVITAR God of all men hath sent upward his light, designed for all mankind,
immortal.
Through the Gods' power that Eye was
first created. Dawn hath made all the
universe apparent.

2 I see the paths which Gods are wont to
travel, innocuous paths made ready by
the Vasus.
Eastward the flag of Dawn hath been
uplifted; she hath come hither o'er the
tops of houses.

7 *Gave the cattle* : restored the rays of light that had
been imprisoned by the demons of darkness.

3 Great is, in truth, the number of the Mornings which were aforetime at the Sun's
uprising.
Since thou, O Dawn, hast been beheld
repairing as to thy love, as one no more
to leave him.

4 They were the Gods' companions at the
banquet, the ancient sages true to Law
Eternal.
The Fathers found the light that lay in
darkness, and with effectual words begat the Morning.

5 Meeting together in the same enclosure,
they strive not, of one mind, one with
another.
They never break the Gods' eternal
statutes, and injure none, in rivalry with
Vasus.

6 Extolling thee, Blest Goddess, the Vasiṣṭhas,
awake at early morn, with lauds implore
thee.
Leader of kine and Queen of all that
strengthens, shine, come as first to us,
O high-born Morning.

7 She bringeth bounty and sweet charm of
voices. The flushing Dawn is sung by
the Vasiṣṭhas,
Giving us riches famed to distant places.
Preserve us evermore, ye Gods, with
blessings.

HYMN LXXVII.   *Dawn.*

1. SHE hath shone brightly like a youthful
woman, stirring to motion every living
creature.
Agni hath come to feed on mortals' fuel.
She hath made light and chased away
the darkness.

2 Turned to this All, far-spreading, she hath
risen and shone in brightness with white
robes about her.
She hath beamed forth lovely with golden
colours, Mother of kine, Guide of the
days she bringeth.

3 *As to thy love* : to the Sun, who is sometimes
called the lover and sometimes the husband of Uṣas or
Dawn.

4 *The Fathers* : the ancestors of the Ṛṣis in the
spirit-world are associated with the Gods as companions,
friends, and assistants. See M. Müller, *India, What can
it Teach us* ? pp. 223, 224.

5 *In the same enclosure* : the vast aerial hall in
which the Gods assemble.

1 *Agni hath come to feed on mortals' fuel* : 'Agni is
to be kindled for the good of men.'—Wilson.
2 *Kine* : rays of light.

3 Bearing the Gods' own Eye, auspicious Lady, leading her Courser white and fair to look on,
Distinguished by her beams Dawn shines apparent, come forth to all the world with wondrous treasure.

4 Draw nigh with wealth and dawn away the foeman : prepare for us wide pasture free from danger.
Drive away those who hate us, bring us riches : pour bounty, opulent Lady, on the singer.

5 Send thy most excellent beams to shine and light us, giving us lengthened days, O Dawn, O Goddess,
Granting us food, thou who hast all things precious, and bounty rich in chariots, kine, and horses.

6 O Uṣas, nobly-born, Daughter of Heaven, whom the Vasiṣṭhas with their hymns make mighty,
Bestow thou on us vast and glorious riches. Preserve us evermore, ye Gods, with blessings.

HYMN LXXVIII.   *Dawn.*

1. WE have beheld her earliest lights approaching : her many glories part, on high, asunder.
On car sublime, refulgent, wending hither, O Uṣas, bring the wealth that makes us happy.

2 The fire well-kindled sings aloud to greet her, and with their hymns the priests are chanting welcome.
Uṣas approaches in her splendour, driving all evil darkness far away, the Goddess.

3 Apparent eastward are those lights of Morning, sending out lustre, as they rise, around them.
She hath brought forth Sun, sacrifice, and Agni, and far away hath fled detested darkness.

4 Rich Daughter of the Sky, we all behold her, yea, all men look on Dawn as she is breaking.
Her car that moves self-harnessed hath she mounted, the car drawn onward by her well-yoked horses.

5 Inspired with loving thoughts this day to greet thee, we and our wealthy nobles have awakened.

3 *The Gods' own Eye,* and Dawn's *white Courser* are the Sun.

Show yourselves fruitful, Dawns, as ye are rising. Preserve us evermore, ye Gods, with blessings.

HYMN LXXIX.   *Dawn.*

1. ROUSING the lands where men's Five Tribes are settled, Dawn hath disclosed the pathways of the people.
She hath sent out her sheen with beauteous oxen. The Sun with light hath opened earth and heaven.

2 They paint their bright rays on the sky's far limits : the Dawns come on like tribes arrayed for battle.
Thy cattle, closely shutting up the darkness, as Savitar spreads his arms, give forth their lustre.

3 Wealthy, most like to Indra, Dawn hath risen, and brought forth lauds that shall promote our welfare.
Daughter of Heaven, a Goddess, she distributes, best of Aṅgirases, treasures to the pious.

4 Bestow on us, O Dawn, that ample bounty which thou didst send to those who sang thy praises;
Thou whom with bellowings of a bull they quickened : thou didst unbar the firm-set mountain's portals.

5 Impelling every God to grant his bounty sending to us the charm of pleasant voices,
Vouchsafe us thoughts, for profit, as thou breakest. Preserve us evermore, ye Gods, with blessings.

HYMN LXXX.   *Dawn.*

1 THE priests, Vasiṣṭhas, are the first awakened to welcome Uṣas with their songs and praises,
Who makes surrounding regions part asunder, and shows apparent all existing creatures.

1. *Five Tribes* : of Āryans. *Pathways* : *pathyā* here has apparently the same meaning as in VII. 75. 1. But according to the Pada text and Sāyaṇa it is an adjective agreeing with *Uṣáḥ* (Dawn), and signifying beneficial.

2 *They* : the Dawns. *For battle* : supplied by Sāyaṇa.

3 *Best of Aṅgirases* : See VII. 75. 1.

4 The second line is translated by Prof. Wilson : 'thou whom (thy worshippers) welcomed with clamour (loud as the bellowing) of a bull.'

Portals : the doors of the mountain or cloud in which the cows or rays of light were imprisoned. Uṣas is by impliation entreated to open these doors now for the singer of the hymn.

2 Giving fresh life when she hath hid the
darkness, this Dawn hath wakened there
with new-born lustre.
Youthful and unrestrained she cometh
forward : she hath turned thoughts to
Sun and fire and worship.

3 May blessed Mornings shine on us for
ever, with wealth of kine, of horses,
and of heroes,
Streaming with all abundance, pouring
fatness. Preserve us evermore, ye Gods,
with blessings.

HYMN LXXXI.   *Dawn.*

1. ADVANCING,   sending forth her rays,
the Daughter of the Sky is seen.
Uncovering, that we may see, the mighty
gloom, the friendly Lady makes the
light.

2 The Sun ascending, the refulgent Star,
pours down his beams together with the
Dawn.
O Dawn, at thine arising, and the Sun's,
may we attain the share allotted us.

3 Promptly we woke to welcome thee, O
Uṣas, Daughter of the Sky,
Thee, Bounteous One, who bringest all
we long to have, and to the offerer
health and wealth.

4 Thou, dawning, workest fain to light the
great world, yea, heaven, Goddess ! that
it may be seen.
We yearn to be thine own, Dealer of
Wealth : may we be to this Mother
like her sons.

5 Bring us that wondrous bounty, Dawn,
that shall be famed most far away.
What, Child of Heaven, thou hast of
nourishment for man, bestow thou on
us to enjoy.

6 Give to our princes opulence and immortal
fame, and strength in herds of kine
to us.
May she who prompts the wealthy, Lady
of sweet strains, may Uṣas dawn our
foes away.

HYMN LXXXII.   *Indra-Varuṇa*

1. GRANT us your strong protection, Indra-
Varuṇa, our people, and our family, for
sacrifice.
May we subdue in fight our evil-hearted
foes, him who attacks the man steadfast
in lengthened rites.

2 O Indra-Varuṇa, mighty and very rich !
One of you is called Monarch and
One Autocrat.
All Gods in the most lofty region of the
air have, O ye Steers, combined all
power and might in you.

3 Ye with your strength have pierced the
fountains of the floods : the Sun
have ye brought forward as the Lord in
heaven.
Cheered by this magic draught ye, Indra-
Varuṇa, made the dry places stream,
made songs of praise flow forth.

4 In battels and in frays we ministering
priests, kneeling upon our knees for
furtherance of our weal,
Invoke you, only you, the Lords of twofold
wealth, you prompt to hear, we bards,
O Indra-Varuṇa.

5 O Indra-Varuṇa, as ye created all these
creatures of the world by your surpas-
sing might,
In peace and quiet Mitra waits on
Varuṇa, the Other, awful, with the
Maruts seeks renown.

6 That Varuṇa's high worth may shine
preëminent, these Twain have measured
each his proper power and might.
The One subdueth the destructive enemy;
the Other with a few furthereth many
a man.

7 No trouble, no misfortune, Indra-Varuṇa,
no woe from any side assails the mortal
man
Whose sacrifice, O Gods, ye visit and
enjoy : ne'er doth the crafty guile of
mortal injure him.

8 With your divine protection, Heroes,
come to us : mine invocation hear, if
ye be pleased therewith.

2 *She hath turned thoughts* : or, with Sāyaṇa, 'she
hath made manifest sacrifice, Sun, and Agni.' Cf. VII.
78. 3.
  3 This stanza is repeated from VII. 41. 7.

6 *Lady of sweet strains* : *sūnṛtāvatī* : according to
Sāyaṇa, 'speaker of truth.' 'Possessing all that is excellent.'—Ludwig.

2 *One of you* : Varuṇa is called *samrāj* or universal
ruler (thoroughly resplendent, according to Sāyaṇa),
and Indra *svarāj*, independent ruler, or, according to
Sāyaṇa, self-resplendent.
  4 *Twofold wealth* : celestial and terrestrial.
  5 *Waits on Varuṇa* : and so acknowledges his supremacy. *The Other* : Indra.
  6 *The One* : Varuṇa.

Bestow ye upon us, O Indra-Varuṇa, your friendship and your kinship and your favouring grace.

9 In battle after battle, Indra-Varuṇa, be ye our Champions, ye who are the peoples' strength,
When both opposing bands invoke you for the fight, and men that they may gain offspring and progeny.

10 May Indra, Varuṇa, Mitra, and Aryaman vouchsafe us glory and great shelter spreading far.
We think of the beneficent light of Aditi, and Savitar's song of praise, the God who strengthens Law.

HYMN LXXXIII. *Indra-Varuṇa.*

1. Looking to you and your alliance, O ye Men, armed with broad axes they went forward, fain for spoil.
Ye smote and slew his Dāsa and his Āryan enemies, and helped Sudās with favour, Indra-Varuṇa.

2 Where heroes come together with their banners raised, in the encounter where is naught for us to love,
Where all things that behold the light are terrified, there did ye comfort us, O Indra-Varuṇa.

3 The boundaries of earth were seen all dark with dust : O Indra-Varuṇa, the shout went up to heaven.
The enmities of the people compassed me about. Ye heard my calling and ye came to me with help.

4 With your resistless weapons, Indra-Varuṇa, ye conquered Bheda and ye gave Sudās your aid.
Ye heard the prayers of these amid the cries of war : effectual was the service of the Tṛtsus' priest.

5 O Indra-Varuṇa, the wickedness of foes and mine assailants' hatred sorely trouble me.

Ye Twain are Lords of riches both of earth and heaven : so grant to us your aid on the decisive day.

6 The men of both the hosts invoked you in the fight, Indra and Varuṇa, that they might win the wealth,
What time ye helped Sudās, with all the Tṛtsu folk, when the Ten Kings had pressed him down in their attack.

7 Ten Kings who worshipped not, O Indra-Varuṇa, confederate, in war prevailed not o'er Sudās.
True was the boast of heroes sitting at the feast : so at their invocations Gods were on their side.

8 O Indra-Varuṇa, ye gave Sudās your aid when the Ten Kings in battle compassed him about,
There where the white-robed Tṛtsus with their braided hair, skilled in song worshipped you with homage and with hymn.

9 One of you Twain destroys the Vṛtras in the fight, the Other evermore maintains his holy Laws.
We call on you, ye Mighty, with our hymns of praise. Vouchsafe us your protection, Indra-Varuṇa.

10 May Indra, Varuṇa, Mitra, and Aryaman vouchsafe us glory and great shelter spreading far.
We think of the beneficent light of Aditi, and Savitar's song of praise, the God who strengthens Law.

HYMN LXXXIV. *Indra-Varuṇa.*

1. Kings, Indra-Varuṇa, I would turn you hither to this our sacrifice with gifts and homage.
Held in both arms the ladle, dropping fatness, goes of itself to you whose forms are varied.

2 Dyaus quickens and promotes your high dominion who bind with bonds not wrought of rope or cordage.
Far from us still be Varuṇa's displeasure : may Indra give us spacious room to dwell in.

Indra and Varuṇa are praised by the Vasiṣṭhas, the family priests of Sudās, King of the Tṛtsus, for having given him the victory over the ten confederate Kings. See VII. 33. 3.

1 *O ye Men* : or Heroes ; Indra and Varuṇa. *Armed with broad axes* 'armed with large sickles.'—Wilson. Ludwig maintains that the former meaning is perfectly impossible, and argues that *pṛthupárśavaḥ* must mean 'the Pṛthus and the Parśus.'

2 *Where is naught for us to love* : Prof. Grassmann, whom Prof. Peterson follows, explains differently : 'where all that is dear is at stake.'

4 *Bheda* : See VII. 18. 19.

5 *Both of earth and heaven* : or perhaps, belonging to both sides.

8 *With their braided hair* : See VII. 33. 1.

10 This stanza is repeated from the preceding hymn.

———

2 *Dyaus* : cf. VI. 62. 9. *Not wrought of rope* : moral and figurative, no material.

3 Make ye our sacrifice fair amid the assemblies : make ye our prayers approved among our princes.
May God-sent riches come for our possession : further ye us with your delightful succours.

4 O Indra-Varuna, vouchsafe us riches with store of treasure, food, and every blessing;
For the Āditya, banisher of falsehood, the Hero, dealeth wealth in boundless plenty.

5 May this my song reach Varuna and Indra, and, strongly urging, win me sons and offspring.
To the Gods' banquet may we go with riches. Preserve us evermore, ye Gods, with blessings.

HYMN LXXXV. *Indra-Varuna.*

1. FOR you I deck a harmless hymn, presenting the Soma juice to Varuna and Indra—
A hymn that shines like heavenly Dawn with fatness. May they be near us on the march and guard us.

2 Here where the arrows fall amid the banners both hosts invoke the Gods in emulation.
O Indra-Varuna, smite back those—our foemen, yea, smite them with your shaft to every quarter.

3 Self-lucid in their seats, e'en heavenly Waters endowed with Godhead Varuna and Indra.
One of these holds the folk distinct and sundered, the Other smites and slays resistless foemen.

4 Wise be the priest and skilled in Law Eternal, who with his sacred gifts and adoration.
Brings you to aid us with your might, Ādityas : let him have viands to promote his welfare.

4 *The Āditya* : Varuna.

———

1 *On the march* : the Ṛṣi prays for aid in an expected battle.

3 *With Godhead* : libations of Soma juice, with which water is mingled, support the Gods in their several stations : *somenāpyāyitā hi devatāḥ sve sve sthāne 'vatiṣṭhante.*—Sāyaṇa. *Distinct and sundered* : differently treated, rewarded or punished in accordance with their deserts. 'The other sustains the separate creatures.' —Muir. 'The one protects the tribes which are scattered abroad.'—Grassmann.

4 *Wise be the priest* : or, wise must the priest be, skilled, etc. *He* : the institutor of sacrifice. *Viands*: sacrificial food to be offered to the Gods.

5 May this my song reach Varuna and Indra, and, strongly urging, win me sons and offspring.
To the Gods' banquet may we go with riches. Preserve us evermore, ye Gods with blessings.

HYMN LXXXVI. *Varuna.*

1. WISE, verily, are creatures through his greatness who stayed even spacious heaven and earth asunder;
Who urged the high and mighty sky to motion, the Star of old, and spread the earth before him.

2 With mine own heart I commune on the question how Varuna and I may be united.
What gift of mine will he accept unangered? When may I calmly look and find him gracious ?

3 Fain to know this my sin I question others: I seek the wise, O Varuna, and ask them.
This one same answer even the sages gave me, "Surely this Varuna is angry with thee."

4 What, Varuna, hath been my chief transgression, that thou wouldst slay the friend who sings thy praises ?
Tell me, Unconquerable Lord, and quickly sinless will I approach thee with mine homage.

5 Free us from sins committed by our fathers, from those wherein we have ourselves offended.
O King, loose, like a thief who feeds the cattle, as from the cord a calf, set free Vasiṣṭha.

6 Not our own will betrayed us, but seduction, thoughtlessness, Varuna ! wine, dice, or anger.
The old is near to lead astray the younger : even sleep removeth not all evil-doing.

7 Slavelike may I do service to the Bounteous, serve, free from sin, the God inclined to anger.

1 *The Star* : the Sun.

5 *Like a thief who feeds the cattle* : who has performed penance for his theft, and, at the completion of the service, offered fodder to the stolen animal : 'who has feasted on stolen cattle '—M. Müller. But See Pischel, *Vedische Studien*, I. p. 106.

6. *Seduction* : or, as Sāyaṇa explains, 'the settled course of fate.'
The old is near : 'The stronger perverts the weaker.'—Muir. 'There is a senior [God] in the proximity of the junior [man].'—Wilson.

This gentle Lord gives wisdom to the simple : the wiser God leads on the wise to riches.

8 O Lord, O Varuṇa, may this laudation come close to thee and lie within thy spirit.
May it be well with us in rest and labour. Preserve us ever-more, ye Gods, with blessings.

HYMN LXXXVII.   *Varuṇa.*

1. Varuṇa cut a path way out for Sūrya, and led the watery floods of rivers onward.
The Mares, as in a race, speed on in order. He made great channels for the days to follow.

2 The wind, thy breath, hath sounded through the region like a wild beast that seeks his food in pastures.
Within these two, exalted Earth and Heaven, O Varuṇa, are all the forms thou lovest.

3 Varuṇa's spies, sent forth upon their errand, survey the two world-halves well formed and fashioned.
Wise are they, holy, skilled in sacrifices, the furtherers of the praise-songs of the prudent.

4 To me who understand hath Varuṇa spoken, the names borne by the Cow are three times seven.
The sapient God, knowing the place's secret, shall speak as 'twere to teach the race that cometh.

5 On him three heavens rest and are supported, and the three earths are there in sixfold order.

The wise King Varuṇa hath made in heaven that Golden Swing to cover it with glory.

6 Like Varuṇa from heaven he sinks in Sindhu, like a white-shining spark, a strong wild creature.
Ruling in depths and meting out the region, great saving power hath he, this world's Controller.

7 Before this Varuṇa may we be sinless— him who shows mercy even to the sinner—
While we are keeping Aditi's ordinances. Preserve us evermore, ye Gods, with blessings.

HYMN LXXXVIII.   *Varuṇa.*

1. Present to Varuṇa thine hymn, Vasiṣṭha, bright, most delightful to the Bounteous Giver,
Who bringeth on to us the Bull, the lofty, the Holy, laden with a thousand treasures.

2 And now, as I am come before his presence, I take the face of Varuṇa for Agni's.
So might he bring—Lord also of the darkness—the light in heaven that I may see its beauty !

3 When Varuṇa and I embark together and urge our boat into the midst of ocean,
We, when we ride o'er ridges of the

---

1 *The Mares* : the swift rivers. The half-line is difficult. 'Hastening (to his task) as a horse let loose rushes to (a flock of) mares, he divided the great nights from the days.'—Wilson. 'Like a troop (of horses) let loose, following the mares, he has made great channels for the days.'—Muir.
3 *Varuṇa's spies* : the other Ādityas, or perhaps the Fathers.
4 *The Cow* : according to Sāyaṇa, Vāk or Speech in the form of a cow having twenty-one metres attached to her breast, throat, and head, or holding the names of twenty-one kinds of sacrifice. Aditi may be intended, or Pṛśni with the thrice seven Maruts.
The sapient God : 'The wise god, though he knows them, has not revealed the mysteries of (her) place, which he desires to grant to a future generation.'—Muir. According to Sāyaṇa, *nd* in this line is not negative.
5 For the *three heavens* and *three earths*, See Vol. I., Index. *In sixfold order* : perhaps referring to the heavens and earths or else the three earths arbitrarily doubled. 'The three earths with their six seasons.'—Wilson. *That Golden Swing* : the Sun.

6 *He* : the Sun. *Sindhu* : or the sea. *Ruling in depths*: referring to Varuṇa whose dominion following the setting sun, reaches to the depths of the ocean. *Meting out the region* : or, who measured out the firmament. Sāyaṇa's interpretation of this stanza is different : '(Radiant) as the sun, Varuṇa placed the ocean (in its bed), white as a drop (of water), vigorous as an antelope, object of profound praise, distributor of water, the powerful transporter beyond sin, the ruler of this existing (world).'— Wilson.

7 *Aditi's ordinances* : according to Sāyaṇa, Aditi here means 'the Mighty.' that is, Varuṇa.

1 *The Bull* : the Sun.

2 *For Agni's* : that is it appears to me to be flaming with anger.

3 'The kernel of the hymn lies in verses 3 to 6. The singer believes that he has been forsaken by his helper Varuṇa ; with anguish he remembers his communion with the God in former times. In a vision he sees himself translated into Varuṇa's realm, he goes sailing with the God, is called to be Ṛṣi or holy singer to the God, and is in his palace with him. Now, Varuṇa has withdrawn his favour, yet let him have mercy on his singer, and not punish him so grievously for his sin. The hymn perhaps originally closed with verse 6'—Prof. von Roth's note in the *Siebenzig Lieder*, translated by Prof. Peterson. But See Hillebrandt, *Varuṇa und Mitra*, pp. 25, 26.

waters, will swing within that swing and there be happy.

4 Varuṇa placed Vasiṣṭha in the vessel, and deftly with his might made him a Ṛṣi.
When days shone bright the Sage made him a singer, while the heavens broadened and the Dawns were lengthened.

5 What hath become of those our ancient friendships, when without enmity we walked together?
I, Varuṇa, thou glorious Lord, have entered thy lofty home, thine house with thousand portals.

6 If he, thy true ally, hath sinned against thee, still, Varuṇa, he is the friend thou lovedst.
Let us not, Living One, as sinners, know thee : give shelter, as a Sage, to him who lauds thee.

7 While we abide in these fixed habitations, and from the lap of Aditi win favour,
May Varuṇa untie the bond that binds us. Preserve us evermore, ye Gods, with blessings.

HYMN LXXXIX.   *Varuṇa.*

1. LET me not yet, King Varuṇa, enter into the house of clay :
Have mercy, spare me, Mighty Lord.

2 When, Thunderer ! I move along tremulous like a wind-blown skin,
Have mercy, spare me, Mighty Lord.

3 O Bright and Powerful God, through want of strength I erred and went astray :
Have mercy, spare me, Mighty Lord.

4 Thirst found thy worshipper though he stood in the midst of water-floods :
Have mercy, spare me, Mighty Lord.

7 *Aditi* : here said to mean earth.

The hymn has been translated by Dr. Muir *O.S. Texts*, V. 67, Prof. M. Müller, *Anc. Sansk. Lit.*, 540, the authors of *Siebenzig Lieder*, p. 12, and Prof. Peterson, *Hymns from the Ṛgveda*, p. 287.

1 *The house of clay* : the grave. Cf. Atharva-veda, V. 30. 14.

2 *Thunderer* : adrivaḥ, Caster of the Stone, a common epithet of Indra, but not suitable to Varuṇa. *Tremulous* : Sāyaṇa adds *śaityena*, with cold : and Prof Wilson observes that 'the *Varuṇa-pāśa*, a kind of dropsy, seems to be referred to.' Cf. Atharva-veda, IV. 16. 7.

4 *Thirst* : avarice. *In the midst of water-floods* : when surrounded by abundant wealth. According to the Commentator, the allusion is to Vasiṣṭha's sea-voyage; or perhaps the perpetual thirst of dropsy may be intended.

5 O Varuṇa, whatever the offence may be which we as men commit against the heavenly host,
When through our want of thought we violate thy laws, punish us not, O God, for that iniquity.

HYMN XC.   *Vāyu.*

1. To you pure juices, rich in meath, are offered by priests through longing for the Pair of Heroes.
Drive, Vāyu, bring thine harnessed horses hither : drink the pressed Soma till it make thee joyful.

2 Whoso to thee, the Mighty, brings oblation, pure Soma unto thee, pure-drinking Vāyu,
That man thou makest famous among mortals : to him strong sons are born in quick succession.

3 The God whom both these worlds brought forth for riches, whom heavenly Dhiṣaṇā for our wealth appointeth,
His team of harnessed horses waits on Vāyu, and, foremost, on the radiant Treasure-bearer.

4 The spotless Dawns with fair bright days have broken; they found the spacious light when they were shining.
Eagerly they disclosed the stall of cattle: floods streamed for them as in the days aforetime.

5 These with their truthful spirit, shining brightly, move on provided with their natural insight.
Viands attend the car that beareth Heroes, your car, ye Sovran Pair, Indra and Vāyu.

6 May these who give us heavenly light, these rulers, with gifts of kine and horses, gold and treasures.
These princes, through full life, Indra and

The last three stanzas are addressed to Indra and Vāyu as a dual Deity.

1 *The Pair of Heroes* : Indra and Vāyu.

3 *The God* : apparently, Indra. *Dhiṣaṇā* : a Goddess of prosperity and gain. *The radiant Treasure-bearer* : perhaps Soma.

4 *They found* : the Aṅgirases. 'They are not named in the text, but Sāyaṇa refers the whole to them ; by their praise of *Vāyu* the dawn broke, the stolen cattle were rescued, and the obstructed rain set at liberty.'—Wilson.

5 *These* : the institutors of sacrifice.

6 *These rulers, these princes*, are the wealthy nobles who defray the expenses and reward the priests.

Vāyu ! o'ercome in battle with their steeds and heroes.

7 Like coursers seeking fame will we Vasiṣṭhas, O Indra-Vāyu, with our fair laudations.
Exerting all our power call you to aid us. Preserve us evermore, ye Gods, with blessings.

HYMN XCI.   *Vāyu.*

1. WERE not in sooth, the Gods aforetime blameless, whose pleasure was increased by adoration ?
For Vāyu and for man in his affliction they caused the Morning to arise with Sūrya.

2 Guardians infallible, eager as envoys, preserve us safe through many months and autumns.
Addressed to you, our fair praise, Indra-Vāyu, implores your favour and renewed well-being.

3 Wise, bright, arranger of his teams, he seeketh men with rich food whose treasures are abundant.
They have arranged them of one mind with Vāyu : the men have wrought all noble operations.

4 So far as native power and strength permit you, so far as men behold whose eyes have vision,
O ye pure-drinkers, drink with us pure Soma : sit on this sacred grass, Indra and Vāyu.

5 Driving down teams that bear the lovely Heroes, hitherward, Indra-Vāyu, come together.
To you this prime of savoury juice is offered : here loose your horses and be friendly-minded.

6 Your hundred and your thousand teams, O Indra and Vāyu, all-munificent, which attend you,
With these most gracious-minded come ye hither, and drink, O Heroes of the meath we offer.

Indra is associated with Vāyu in almost every stanza.

1 *For Vāyu* : I translate the *vāydve* of the text, but it is evident that *Āydve*, for Āyu, or the living one, should be read in its stead.

3 *He seeketh* : Vāyu. The meaning of the stanza is obscure.

5 *The lovely Heroes* : Indra and Vāyu.

---

7 Like coursers seeking fame will we Vasiṣṭhas, O Indra-Vāyu, with our fair laudations,
Exerting all our power, call you to aid us. Preserve us evermore, ye Gods, with blessings.

HYMN XCII.   *Vāyu.*

1. O VĀYU, drinker of the pure, be near us : a thousand teams are thine, All-bounteous Giver.
To thee the rapture-bringing juice is offered, whose first draught, God, thou takest as thy portion.

2 Prompt at the holy rites forth came the presser with Soma-draughts for Indra and for Vāyu,
When ministering priests with strong devotion bring to you Twain the first taste of the Soma.

3 The teams wherewith thou seekest him who offers, within his home, O Vāyu, to direct him,
Therewith send wealth: to us with full enjoyment, a hero son and gifts of kine and horses.

4 Near to the Gods and making Indra joyful, devout and offering precious gifts to Vāyu,
Allied with princes, smiting down the hostile, may we with heroes conquer foes in battle.

5 With thy yoked teams in hundreds and in thousands come to our sacrifice and solemn worship.
Come, Vāyu, make thee glad at this libation. Preserve us evermore, ye Gods, with blessings.

HYMN XCIII.   *Indra-Agni.*

1. SLAYERS of enemies, Indra and Agni, accept this day our new-born pure laudation.
Again, again I call you prompt to listen, best to give quickly strength to him who craves it.

2 For ye were strong to gain, exceeding mighty, growing together, waxing in your vigour.

---

1 *Drinker of the pure* : or bright, Soma.

4 *Allied* : the priests are the allies and moral supporters of the princes in war.

5 *In hundreds and in thousands* : Cf. I. 135. 3.

Lords of the pasture filled with ample riches, bestow upon us strength both fresh and lasting.

3 Yea when the strong have entered our assembly, and singers seeking with their hymns your favour,
They are like steeds who come into the race-course, those men who call aloud on Indra-Agni.

4 The singer, seeking with his hymns your favour, begs splendid riches of their first possessor.
Further us with new bounties, Indra-Agni, armed with strong thunder, slayers of the foeman.

5 When two great hosts, arrayed against each other, meet clothed with brightness, in the fierce encounter
Stand ye beside the godly, smite the godless; and still assist the men who press the Soma.

6 To this our Soma-pressing, Indra-Agni, come ye prepared to show your loving-kindness,
For not at any time have ye despised us. So may I draw you with all strengthenings hither.

7 So Agni, kindled mid this adoration, invite thou Mitra, Varuṇa, and Indra.
Forgive whatever sin we have committed : may Aryaman and Aditi remove it.

8 While we accelerate these our sacrifices, may we win strength from both of you, O Agni :
Ne'er may the Maruts, Indra, Viṣṇu slight us. Preserve us evermore, ye Gods, with blessings.

HYMN XCIV.   *Indra-Agni.*

1. As rain from out the cloud, for you, Indra and Agni, from my soul
This noblest praise hath been produced.

2 Do ye, O Indra-Agni, hear the singer's call : accept his songs.
Ye Rulers, grant his heart's desire.

3 Give us not up to poverty, ye Heroes, Indra-Agni, nor
To slander and reproach of men.

4 To Indra and to Agni we bring reverence, high and holy hymn,
And, craving help, soft words with prayer.

5 For all these holy singers here implore these Twain to succour them,
And priests that they may win   them strength.

6 Eager to laud you, we with songs invoke you, bearing sacred food,
Fain for success in sacrifice.

7 Indra and Agni, come to us with favour, ye who conquer men :
Let not the wicked master us.

8 At no time let the injurious blow of hostile mortal fall on us :
O Indra-Agni, shelter us.

9 Whatever wealth we crave of you, in gold, in cattle, or in steeds,
That, Indra-Agni, let us gain;

10 When heroes prompt in worship call Indra and Agni, Lords of steeds,
Beside the Soma juice effused.

11 Call hither with the song and lauds those who best slay the foemen, those
Who take delight in hymns of praise.

12 Slay ye the wicked man whose thought is evil of the demon kind.
Slay him who stays the waters, slay the Serpent with your deadly dart.

HYMN XCV.   *Sarasvatī.*

1. THIS stream Sarasvatī with fostering current comes forth, our sure defence, our fort of iron.
As on a car, the flood flows on, surpassing in majesty and might all other waters.

3 *The strong* : the nobles who institute sacrifices.

4 *Their first possessor* : each God who is invoked.

5 *Great hosts* : 'hosts' must be supplied. The feminine dual adjectives have no substantive in the text.

7 *Aryaman and Aditi* : Mitra and others being understood, as the verb is plural.

8 *O Agni* : that is, Indra and Agni.

1 *As rain* : the hymn of praise is copious in its flow, and is doubly beneficial, gratifying the Gods and bringing blessings to the worshipper. *From my soul* : *mánmanaḥ* : explained by the Commentator here and in the corresponding passage of the Sāmaveda by *stotuḥ*, praiser or worshipper.

11 *Call hither* : I follow Prof. Ludwig in reading *āvivāsata*, instead of *āvivāsataḥ* which involves a very harsh construction.

12 *Him who stays the waters* : *udadhím* : according to Sāyaṇa, like an *udadhíḥ*, water-holder or pitcher. *The Serpent* : *ábhogám*, 'the coiler,' explained differently by Sāyaṇa, as 'one who enjoys good things from the worshippers.'

1 *Sarasvatī* : Sindhu or Indus appears to be intended under this name. See VI. 61. 2, and *Vedic Hymns*, I. p. 60.

2 Pure in her course from mountains to the ocean, alone of streams Sarasvatī hath listened.
Thinking of wealth and the great world of creatures, she poured for Nāhuṣa her milk and fatness.

3 Friendly to man he grew among the women, a strong young Steer amid the Holy Ladies.
He gives the fleet steed to our wealthy princes, and decks their bodies for success in battle.

4 May this Sarasvatī be pleased and listen at this our sacrifice, auspicious Lady,
When we with reverence, on our knees, implore her close-knit to wealth, most kind to those she loveth.

5 These offerings have ye made with adoration : say this, Sarasvatī, and accept our praises;
And, placing us under thy dear protection, may we approach thee, as a tree, for shelter.

6 For thee, O Blest Sarasvatī, Vasiṣṭha hath here unbarred the doors of sacred Order.
Wax, Bright One, and give strength to him who lauds thee. Preserve us evermore, ye Gods, with blessings.

HYMN XCVI.   Sarasvatī.

1. I SING a lofty song, for she is mightiest, most divine of Streams.
Sarasvatī will I exalt with hymns and lauds, and, O Vasiṣṭha, Heaven and Earth.

2 When in the fulness of their strength the Pūrus dwell, Beauteous One, on thy two grassy banks,
Favour us thou who hast the Maruts for thy friends : stir up the bounty of our chiefs.

3 So may Sarasvatī auspicious send good luck; she, rich in spoil, is never niggardly in thought,
When praised in Jamadagni's way and lauded as Vasiṣṭha lauds.

4 We call upon Sarasvān, as unmarried men who long for wives,
As liberal men who yearn for sons.

5 Be thou our kind protector, O Sarasvān, with those waves of thine
Laden with sweets and dropping oil.

6 May we enjoy Sarasvān's breast, all-beautiful, that swells with streams,
May we gain food and progeny.

HYMN XCVII.   Bṛhaspati.

1. WHERE Heaven and Earth combine in men's assembly, and those who love the Gods delight in worship,
Where the libations are effused for Indra, may he come first to drink and make him stronger.

2 We crave the heavenly grace of Gods to guard us—so may Bṛhaspati, O friends, exalt us—
That he, the Bounteous God, may find us sinless, who giveth from a distance like a father.

3 That Brahmaṇaspati, most High and Gracious, I glorify with offerings and with homage.
May the great song of praise divine, reach Indra who is the King of prayer the Gods' creation.

4 May that Bṛhaspati who brings all blessings, most dearly loved, be seated by our altar.
Heroes and wealth we crave; may he bestow them, and bear us safe beyond the men who vex us.

---

2 Nāhuṣa : according to the legend, a King who prayed to Sarasvatī who gave him butter and milk sufficient for the thousand-year sacrifice which he was about to perform. The Nahuṣas, the people living on the banks of the river, are probably intended.
3 He grew : Sarasvān, the consort of Sarasvatī.
5 These offerings : this half-line is very obscure. Prof. Ludwig thinks that these words may be supposed to be spoken by Sarasvatī to her worshippers, but he is not satisfied of the correctness of his conjecture. 'Presenting to thee.,jSarasvatī these oblations with reverence (may we receive from thee affluence).'—Wilson.

---

1. Heaven and Earth : heaven as the home of the Goddess, and earth where she flows as a river.
2 The Pūrus : an Āryan tribe settled on both banks of the Sarasvatī or Indus. See Vol. I., Index. Grassy banks : this, as von Roth has suggested, seems to be the meaning of āndhasi, but the expression is difficult. See Hillebrandt, Vedische Mythologie, p. 254.

---

3 Jamadagni : a celebrated ancient Ṛṣi.

Indra is the deity of stanza I, Indra and Brahmaṇaspati are the deities of 3 and 9, Indra and Bṛhaspati of 10, and the rest of the hymn is addressed to Bṛhaspati. Bṛhaspati and Brahmaṇaspati are one and the same God, the Lord of Prayer. See I, 14. 3.

1 Where Heaven and Earth combine : where Gods and men meet at the the place of sacrifice. And make him stronger : Sāyaṇa explains vdyaśca differently : '(may his) swift (horses approach).'—Wilson.

2 Like a father : although he is far away he gives us what we ask like a father who is near at hand.—Ludwig.

3 The Gods' creation : devákṛtasya : inspired, or, literally, made, by the Gods.

5 To us these Deathless Ones, erst born,
have granted this laud of ours
which gives the Immortal pleasure.
Let us invoke Bṛhaspati, the foeless, the
clear-voiced God, the Holy One of
households

6 Him, this Bṛhaspati, his red-hued horses,
drawing together, full of strength, bring
hither.
Robed in red colour like the cloud, they
carry the Lord of Might whose friendship gives a dwelling.

7 For he is pure, with hundred wings, refulgent, with sword of gold, impetuous,
winning sunlight.
Sublime Bṛhaspati, easy of access granteth
his friends most bountiful refreshment.

8 Both Heaven and Earth, divine, the Deity's
Parents, have made Bṛhaspati increase
in grandeur.
Glorify him, O friends, who merits glory:
may he give prayer fair way and easy
passage.

9 This, Brahmaṇaspati, is your laudation :
prayer hath been made to thunder-
wielding Indra.
Favour our songs, wake up our thought
and spirit : destroy the godless and our
foemen's malice.

10 Ye Twain are Lords of wealth in earth
and heaven, thou, O Bṛhaspati, and
thou, O Indra.
Mean though he be, give wealth to him
who lauds you. Preserve us evermore,
ye Gods, with blessings.

HYMN XCVIII.   Indra.

1. PRIESTS, offer to the Lord of all the
people the milked-out stalk of Soma,
radiant-coloured.
No wild-bull knows his drinking-place
like Indra who ever seeks him who hath
pressed the Soma,

2 Thou dost desire to drink, each day that
passes, the pleasant food which thou hast
had aforetime,
O Indra, gratified in heart and spirit, drink
eagerly the Soma set before thee.

3 Thou, newly-born, for strength didst drink
the Soma; the Mother told thee of thy
future greatness.
O Indra, thou hast filled mid-air's wide
region, and given the Gods by battle
room and freedom.

4 When thou hast urged the arrogant to
combat, proud in their strength of arm,
we will subdue them.
Or, Indra, when thou fightest girt by
heroes, we in the glorious fray with thee
will conquer.

5 I will declare the earliest deeds of Indra,
and recent acts which Maghavan hath
accomplished.
When he had conquered godless wiles
and magic, Soma became his own entire
possession.

6 Thine is this world of flocks and herds
around thee, which with the eye of
Sūrya thou beholdest.
Thou, Indra, art alone the Lord of cattle;
may we enjoy the treasure which thou
givest.

7 Ye Twain are Lords of wealth in earth and
heaven, thou, O Bṛhaspati, and thou,
O Indra.
Mean though he be, give wealth to him
who lauds you. Preserve us evermore, ye Gods, with blessings.

HYMN XCIX.   Viṣṇu.

1. MEN come not nigh thy majesty who
growest beyond all bound and measure
with thy body.
Both thy two regions of the earth, O
Viṣṇu, we know : thou God, knowest
the highest also.

2 None who is born or being born, God
Viṣṇu, hath reached the utmost limit of
thy grandeur.
The vast high vault of heaven hast thou
supported, and fixed earth's eastern
pinnacle securely.

5 Our hymns of praise which are acceptable to the
immortal God have been given to us by the everlasting
deities themselves. Sāyaṇa's explanation is different :
'may the first born immortals' (by his command)
bestow upon us the food that is necessary for existence.'
—Wilson.

6 *Whose friendship gives a dwelling* : I adopt the
interpretation given by Professor Cowell in his note on
the passage in Wilson's translation.

7 *With hundred wings* : 'borne by numerous con-
veyances.'—Wilson.

8 *In grandeur* : or, by their might.

10 *Mean* : or, poor.

1 *Radiant-coloured* : *aruṇám*, red, ruddy, here explained by the Commentator as *ārocamānam*, shining.

3 *Thy future greatness* : See VI. 18. 4, where Aditi
says :—'No peer hath he among born already, nor
among those who shall be born hereafter.'

1 *Two regions of the earth*: that is, the earth and the
firmament. 'The two lower regions are within the
range of our perception ; the third belongs to Viṣṇu,
whither he stepped with the third of his ascending
strides.'—Wallis, *Cosmology of the Ṛgveda*, p. 115.

3 Rich in sweet food be ye, and rich in milch-kine, with fertile pastures, fain to do men service.

Both these worlds, Viṣṇu, hast thou stayed asunder, and firmly fixed the earth with pegs around it.

4 Ye have made spacious room for sacrificing by generating Sūrya, Dawn, and Agni.

O Heroes, ye have conquered in your battles even the bull-jawed Dāsa's wiles and magic.

5 Ye have destroyed, thou, Indra, and thou, Viṣṇu, Śambara's nine-and-ninety fenced castles.

Ye Twain smote down a hundred times a thousand resistless heroes of the royal Varcin.

6 This is the lofty hymn of praise, exalting the Lords of Mighty Stride, the strong and lofty.

I laud you in the solemn synods, Viṣṇu: pour ye food on us in our camps, O Indra.

7 O Viṣṇu, unto thee my lips cry Vaṣaṭ ! Let this mine offering, Śipiviṣṭa, please thee.

May these my songs of eulogy exalt thee. Preserve us evermore, ye Gods, with blessings.

HYMN C.   *Viṣṇu.*

1 NE'ER doth the man repent, who, seeking profit, bringeth his gift to the far-striding Viṣṇu.

He who adoreth him with all his spirit winneth himself so great a benefactor.

2 Thou, Viṣṇu, constant in thy courses, gavest good-will to all men, and a hymn that lasteth,

That thou mightst move us to abundant comfort of very splendid wealth with store of horses.

3 Three times strode forth this God in all his grandeur over this earth bright with a hundred splendours.

Foremost be Viṣṇu, stronger than the strongest : for glorious is his name who lives for ever.

4 Over this earth with mighty step strode Viṣṇu, ready to give it for a home to Manu.

In him the humble people trust for safety: he, nobly born, hath made them spacious dwellings.

5 To-day I laud this name, O Śipiviṣṭa, I, skilled in rules, the name of thee the Noble.

Yea, I the poor and weak praise thee the Mighty who dwellest in the realm beyond this region.

6 What was there to be blamed in thee, O Viṣṇu, when thou declaredst, I am Śipiviṣṭa ?

Hide not this form from us, nor keep it secret, since thou didst wear another shape in battle.

7 O Viṣṇu, unto thee my lips cry Vaṣaṭ ! Let this mine offering, Śipiviṣṭa, please thee.

May these my songs of eulogy exalt thee. Preserve us evermore, ye Gods, with blessings.

HYMN CI.   *Parjanya.*

1 SPEAK forth three words, the words which light precedeth, which milk this udder that produceth nectar.

Quickly made manifest, the Bull hath bellowed, engendering the germ of plants, the Infant.

3 *The first line appears to be Viṣṇu's blessing on heaven and earth when be parted and supported them.*

4 *Bull-jawed* : or Vṛṣaśipra may be the name of the Dāsa.

5 *Royal Varcin* : See II. 14. 6.

7 *Vaṣaṭ* : the exclamation used on making an oblation. *Śipiviṣṭa* : a name of Viṣṇu of uncertain etymology and meaning 'Invested with rays of light,' according to Sāyaṇa. See Muir, *O.S. Texts*, IV. 87, 88, *note*.

2 *A hymn that lasteth* : continually recurring occasion to praise thee.

3 *This earth* : meaning, says the Commentator, earth, firmament, and heaven.

6 This stanza is unintelligible. The Commentator on the corresponding passage of the Sāmaveda says : 'Viṣṇu formerly abandoning his own form, and assuming another artificial shape, succoured Vasiṣṭha in battle. Recognizing the god, the Ṛṣi addresses him with the verse.' *Śipiviṣṭa* is said to be a word of equivocal meaning, 'clothed with rays of light,' and 'denuded.' See Wilson's note, and *O. S. Texts*, IV. 87, 88, *note*. The passage looks like the germ of the later incarnations of the God which occur in the *Śatapatha Brāhmaṇa* and the *Purāṇas*.

1 *Three words* : or texts of the three Vedas. *Which light precedeth* : introduced by the sacred syllable OM. More probably Parjanya is addressed, the three words being his voice, the thunder (V. 63. 6), heard in heaven, air, and earth, and preceded by the lightning-flash. See Bergaigne, *Quarante Hymnes du Ṛgveda*, p. 79. *Milk this udder* : draw down the sweet rain from the cloud. *The Bull* : Parjanya. *The Infant* : Agni in the form of lightning.

2 Giver of growth to plants, the God who
ruleth over the waters and all moving
creatures,
Vouchsafe us triple shelter for our refuge,
and threefold light to succour and
befriend us.

3 Now he is sterile, now begetteth
offspring, even as he willeth doth he
change his figure.
The Father's genial flow bedews the
Mother; therewith the Sire, therewith
the son is nourished.

4 In him all living creatures have their
being, and the three heavens with triply-
flowing waters.
Three reservoirs that sprinkle down their
treasure shed their sweet streams around
him with a murmur.

5 May this my song to Sovran Lord
Parjanya come near unto his heart
and give him pleasure.
May we obtain the showers that bring
enjoyment, and God-protected plants
with goodly fruitage.

6 He is the Bull of all, and their impregner :
he holds the life of all things fixed and
moving.
May this rite save me till my hundredth
autumn. Preserve us evermore, ye Gods,
with blessings.

HYMN CII   Parjanya.

1 SING forth and laud Parjanya, son of
Heaven, who sends the gift of rain :
May he provide our pasturage.

2 Parjanya is the God who forms in kine,
in mares, in plants of earth,
And womankind, the germ of life.

3 Offer and pour into his mouth oblation
rich in savoury juice :
May he for ever give us food.

2 *Threefold light* : with reference to the divisions of
the day and the seasons.

3 *He is sterile* : sends no rain, like a barren cow
that gives no milk.
The Father's genial flow : 'The father is the sky,
earth the mother, who receives the rain from the
former, which, producing the means of offering libations
and oblations, returns again to the parent heaven, as
well as supports his offspring—all living creatures.'—
Wilson.

4 *Three reservoirs* : according to Sāyaṇa, clouds in
the east, west, and north

6 *The Bull of all* : the plants, understood.

3 *Into his mouth* : that is, Agni, who is the mouth
by which the other Gods consume the offerings that are
made to them.

HYMN CIII.   *Frogs.*

1. THEY who lay quiet for a year, the Brāhmans who fulfil their vows,
The Frogs have lifted up their voice, the
voice Parjanya hath inspired.

2 What time on these, as on a dry skin
lying in the pool's bed, the floods of
heaven descended,
The music of the Frogs comes forth in
concert like the cows lowing with their
calves beside them.

3 When at the coming of the Rains the
water has poured upon them as they
yearned and thirsted,
One seeks another as he talks and greets
him with cries of pleasure as a son his
father.

4 Each of these twain receives the other
kindly, while they are revelling in the
flow of waters,
When the Frog moistened by the rain
springs forward, and Green and Spotty
both combine their voices.

5 When one of these repeats the other's
language, as he who learns the lesson of
the teacher,
Your every limb seems to be growing larger
as ye converse with eloquence on the
waters.

6 One is Cow-bellow and Goat-bleat the
other, one Frog is Green and one of
them is Spotty.
They bear one common name, and yet
they vary, and, talking, modulate the
voice diversely.

7 As Brāhmans, sitting round the brimful
vessel, talk at the Soma-rite of
Atirātra,
So, Frogs, ye gather round the pool to
honour this day of all the year, the first
of Rain-time.

The hymn has been translated by Dr. Muir, *O. S.
Texts.* V. 436, and by Professor F. Max Müller in his
Ancient Sanskrit Literature, pp. 494f, who remarks : 'The
hymn......which is called a panegyric of the frogs, is
clearly a satire on the priests ; and it is curious to
observe that the same animal should have been
chosen by the Vedic satirist to represent the priests,
which, by the earliest satirist of Greece, was selected
as the representative of the Homeric heroes.' But see
Oldenberg, *Die Religion des Veda*, p. 70. The hymn
evidently belongs to a late period of Vedic poetry.

3 *With cries of pleasure* : akhkhalīkṛtya : uttering the
imitative exclamation akhkhala.

5 *Your every limb* : this abrupt change of person is
not unfrequent in the Veda.

7 *Atirātra* : a ceremony accompanied by three noc-
turnal recitations.

8 These Brāhmans with the Soma juice,
performing their year-long rite, have
lifted up their voices ;
And these Adhvaryus, sweating with their
kettles, come forth and show themselves,
and none are hidden.

9 They keep the twelve month's God-
appointed order, and never do the men
neglect the season.
Soon as the Rain-time in the year returneth,
these who were heated kettles gain their
freedom.

10 Cow-bellow and Goat-bleat have granted
riches, and Green and Spotty have
vouchsafed us treasure.
The Frogs who give us cows in hundreds
lengthen our lives in this most fertilizing
season.

HYMN CIV.   *Indra-Soma.*

1. INDRA and Soma, burn, destroy the demon
foe, send downward, O ye Bulls, those
who add gloom to gloom.
Annihilate the fools, slay them and burn
them up : chase them away from us,
pierce the voracious ones.

8 *Year-long rite* : 'Sāyaṇa makes it refer to *Gavām
ayanam*, a sacrificial session, which commences and ends
with the *atirātra*, and lasts a whole year.'—Cowell, in
Wilson's Translation. *Sweating with their kettles* : 'There
is a quibble on the word *gharmiṅaḥ*, having or bearing
the vessel, or performing the rite so termed; or suffering
from *gharma*, heat, or the hot season '— Wilson. *And
none are hidden* : *gúhyā ná ké cit* : some take *ná* here as
like' : 'issue forth like persons who have been hidden.'
—Muir. 'Pop out like hermits.'—M. Müller.

9 *The men*: the priest-like frogs. *These who were heated
kettles* : the frogs who had been burnt and scorched by
the hot weather.

10 *Have granted riches* : as the earliest proclaimers of
the advent of the Rains which revive and fertilize the
earth.

'It is possibly an echo of this production that we
find in a description of autumn in the Harivaṁśa, V
8803, where the poet compares the noise made by a
frog, after his rest of sixteen half months, along with his
wives, to the recitation of the Ṛgveda by a Brāhman
surrounded by his pupils...On this verse the late M.
Langlois somewhat naively remarks as follows : Dans
noe moeurs rien n' egalerait l' impertinence d' une com-
paraison dans laquelle une grenouille serait assimilee a
un respectable ecclesiastique. Les Indiens, a ce qu' il
parait, ne voyaient daus telle espece de rapproache-
ment aucune teinte d' impiete.'—Muir, *O. S. Texts*, V.
433. But See Bergaigne, *La Religion Vedique*, I. 292.

The hymn consists chiefly of imprecations directed
against demons and evil spirits, Rākṣasas and Yātudhānas. The deities are various.

1 *The demon foe* : *ráksah* : the Rākṣasas, fiends,
demons, goblins, going about at night, disturbing sacrifices and devout men, ensnaring and even devouring
human beings, and generally hostile to the human race.

2 Indra and Soma, let sin round the wicked
boil like as a caldron set amid the flames
of fire.
Against the foe of prayer, devourer of raw
flesh, the vile fiend fierce of eye, keep
ye perpetual hate.

3 Indra and Soma, plunge the wicked in the
depth, yea, cast them into darkness that
hath no support,
So that not one of them may ever thence
return : so may your wrathful might
prevail and conquer them.

4 Indra and Soma, hurl your deadly crushing
bolt down on the wicked fiend from
heaven and from the earth.
Yea, forge out of the mountains your
celestial dart wherewith ye burn to death
the waxing demon race.

5 Indra and Soma, cast ye downward out
of heaven your deadly darts of stone
burning with fiery flame,
Eternal, scorching darts ; plunge the
voracious ones within the depth, and let
them sink without a sound.

6 Indra and Soma, let this hymn control
you both, even as the girth encompasses
two vigorous steeds—
The song of praise which I with wisdom
offer you : do ye, as Lords of men,
animate these my prayers.

7 In your impetuous manner think ye both
thereon : destroy these evil beings,
slay the treacherous fiends.
Indra and Soma, let the wicked have no
bliss who evermore assails us with
malignity.

8 Whoso accuses me with words of falsehood when I pursue my way with
guileless spirit,
May he, the speaker of untruth, be,
Indra, like water which the hollowed
hand compresses.

9 Those who destroy, as is their wont, the
simple, and with their evil natures
harm the righteous,
May Soma give them over to the serpent,
or to the lap of Nirṛti consign them.

2 *The vile fiend* : *kimídine* : explained by the Commentator as one who goes about saying, *Kimidānīm* or
What now ! A quidaunc, a vile and treacherous spy
and informer. The word is used as the name of a
class of evil spirits.

5 *Without a sound* : so suddenly that they have not
time to cry out.

9 *To the serpent* : or to death by serpents' bites.
Nirṛti : Death and Destruction.

10 The fiend, O Agni, who designs to injure
the essence of our food, kine, steeds, or
bodies,
May he, the adversary, thief, and robber,
sink to destruction, both himself and
offspring.

11 May he be swept away, himself and
children : may all the three earths
press him down beneath them.
May his fair glory, O ye Gods, be
blighted, who in the day or night would
fain destroy us.

12 The prudent finds it easy to distinguish
the true and false : their words oppose
each other.
Of these two that which is the true and
honest, Soma protects, and brings the
false to nothing.

13 Never doth Soma aid and guide the
wicked or him who falsely claims
the Warrior's title.
He slays the fiend and him who speaks
untruly : both lie entangled in the
noose of Indra.

14 As if I worshipped deities of falsehood,
or thought vain thoughts about the
Gods, O Agni.
Why art thou angry with us, Jātavedas ?
Destruction fall on those who lie against
thee !

15 So may I die this day if I have harassed
any man's life or if I be a demon.
Yea, may he lose all his ten sons together
who with false tongue hath called me
Yātudhāna.

16 May Indra slay him with a mighty
weapon, and let the vilest of all
creatures perish,
The fiend who says that he is pure, who
calls me a demon though devoid of
demon nature.

17 She too who wanders like an owl
at night-time, hiding her body in her
guile and malice,
May she fall downward into endless
caverns. May press-stones with loud
ring destroy the demons.

18 Spread out, ye Maruts, search among the
people : seize ye and grind the
Rākṣasas to pieces,
Who fly abroad, transformed to birds, at
night-time, or sully and pollute our
holy worship.

19 Hurl down from heaven thy bolt of stone,
O Indra : sharpen it, Maghavan, made
keen by Soma.
Forward, behind, and from above and
under, smite down the demons with
thy rocky weapon.

20 They fly, the demon dogs, and, bent on
mischief, fain would they harm indomi-
table Indra.
Śakra makes sharp his weapon for the
wicked : now let him cast his bolt at
fiendish wizards.

21 Indra hath ever been the fiends' destroyer
who spoil oblations of the Gods'
invokers :
Yea, Śakra, like an axe that spilts the
timber, attacks and smashes them like
earthen vessels.

22 Destroy the fiend shaped like an owl or
owlet, destroy him in the form of dog
or cuckoo.
Destroy him shaped as eagle or as vulture :
as with a stone, O Indra, crush the
demon.

23 Let not the fiend of witchcraft-workers
reach us : may Dawn drive off the
couples of Kimīdins.
Earth keep us safe from earthly woe and
trouble : from grief that comes from
heaven mid-air preserve us.

---

13 *The Warrior's title* : the rank of a Kṣatriya or
prince of the military order.

The first eleven stanzas 'are considered to be a
malediction upon the *Rākṣasas* by the *Ṛṣi*. To account
for the change of tone (in 12—16), *Sāyaṇa* gives an
unusual version of the legend told in the *Mahābhārata* of
king *Kalmāṣapāda* being transformed to a *Rākṣasa*, and
devouring the 100 sons of Vasiṣṭha : here it is said
that a *Rākṣasa*, having devoured the *Ṛṣi's* sons, assumed
his shape, and said to him, "I am *Vasiṣṭha*, thou art the
Rākṣasa;" to which Vasiṣṭha replied by repeating this
verse (stanza 12), declaratory of his discriminating between truth and falsehood.'—Wilson.

'The verses may, as Professor Max Müller supposes,
have arisen out of Vasiṣṭha's contest with Viśvāmitra
[See III. 53. 21. note], and it may have been the latter
personage who brought those charges of heresy, and of
murderous and demoniacal character against his rival.'—
Muir, *O. S. Texts*, I. 327, 328.

15 *Yātudhāna* : explained by Sāyaṇa as=Rākṣasa.
The Yātudhāna probably was rather the goblin or
sorcerer while the Rākṣasa was the violent and voracious
ogre.

17 Here the malediction on evil spirits in general is
resumed and continued to the end of the hymn. *She
too* : the *Rākṣasī*, or she-fiend.

23 *Kimīdins* : or vile spirits. See note on stanza 2.

24 Slay the male demon, Indra ! slay the female, joying and triumphing in arts of magic.
Let the fools' gods with bent necks fall and perish, and see no more the Sun when he arises.

25 Look each one hither, look around : Indra and Soma, watch ye well.
Cast forth your weapon at the fiends ; against the sorcerers hurl your bolt.

24 *Fools' gods* : *mū́radevāḥ* : explained by Sāyaṇa as=*māraṇakṛíḍāḥ*, 'those who make killing their sport.' According to the St. Petersburg Lexicon, *mū́radevāḥ*= *mūladevāḥ*, a species of demons or goblins.

BOOK THE EIGHTH

HYMN I.   *Indra.*

1. GLORIFY naught besides, O friends ; so shall no sorrow trouble you.
Praise only mighty Indra when the juice is shed, and say your lauds repeatedly :

2 Even him, eternal, like a bull who rushes down, men's Conqueror, bounteous like a cow ;
Him who is cause of both, of enmity and peace, to both sides most munificent.

3 Although these men in sundry ways invoke thee to obtain thine aid,
Be this our prayer, addressed, O Indra, unto thee, thine exaltation every day.

4 Those skilled in song, O Maghavan, among these men o'ercome with might the foeman's songs.
Come hither, bring us strength in many a varied form most near that it may succour us.

5 O Caster of the Stone, I would not sell thee for a mighty price,
Not for a thousand, Thunderer ! nor ten thousand, nor a hundred, Lord of countless wealth !

6 O Indra, thou art more to me than sire or niggard brother is.
Thou and my mother, O Good Lord, appear alike, to give me wealth abundantly.

7 Where art thou ? Whither art thou gone ? For many a place attracts thy mind.
Haste, Warrior, Fort-destroyer, Lord of battle's din, haste, holy songs have sounded forth.

8 Sing out the psalm to him who breaks down castles for his faithful friend,
Verses to bring the Thunderer to destroy the forts and sit on Kaṇva's sacred grass.

9 The Horses which are thine in tens, in hundreds, yea, in thousands thine,
Even those vigorous Steeds, fleet-footed in the course, with those come quickly near to us.

10 This day I call Sabardughā who animates the holy song,
Indra the richly-yielding Milch-cow who provides unfailing food in ample stream.

11 When Sūra wounded Etaśa, with Vāta's rolling winged car.
Indra bore Kutsa Ārjuneya off, and mocked Gandharva the unconquered One.

12 He without ligature, before making incision in the neck,
Closed up the wound again, most wealthy Maghavan, who maketh whole the injured part.

13 May we be never cast aside, and strangers, as it were, to thee.
We, Thunder-wielding Indra, count ourselves as trees rejected and unfit to burn.

14 O Vṛtra-slayer, we were thought slow and unready for the fray.
Yet once in thy great bounty may we have delight, O Hero, after praising thee.

15 If he will listen to my laud, then may our Soma-drops that flow
Rapidly through the strainer gladden Indra, drops due to the Tugryas' Strengthener.

16 Come now unto the common laud of thee and of thy faithful friend.
So may our wealthy nobles' praise give

---

2 *Bounteous like a cow* : the adjective is not in the text, but must be supplied in order to make the comparison intelligible. See *Vedische Studien*, I. 103. *To both sides* : to the singers and the institutors of sacrifice.

5 *A hundred* : meaning 'infinite,' according to the Commentator.

8 *For his faithful friend* : Ludwig takes Vāvātar to be the name of a king who has been deserted by Indra and consequently defeated in battle. *Kaṇva's sacred grass* : trimmed and prepared by Medhātithi and Medhyātithi, each of whom is a son of Kaṇva.

10 *Sabardughā* : the general name of cows which supply the milk required for sacrificial purposes. See VI. 48. 11, note. Here Indra himself is intended, as is shown in the following line.

11 *Sūra* : Sūrya, the Sun-God. *Wounded* : 'harassed.' —Wilson. *Etaśa* : a *protégé* of Indra. See Vol. I. Index. *Vāta* : the Wind-God. *Kutsa* : See Vol. I., Index. *Gandharva*: the Sun. The meaning of the stanza is somewhat obscure.

12 *Closed up the wound again* : healed Etaśa who had been wounded by Sūrya.

13 *Count ourselves as trees* : or, 'count us not as trees,' the meaning of *na*, 'not' and 'like' being ambiguous.

15 *Due to the Tugryas' Strengthener* : that belong to Indra the protector of the chiefs of the race of Tugra, who appear to have been the patrons of the Ṛṣis of Kaṇva's family.

16 *Faithful friend* : See stanza 8.

joy to thee. Fain would I sing thine eulogy.

17 Press out the Soma with the stones, and in the waters wash it clean.
The men investing it with raiment made of milk shall milk it forth from out the stems.

18 Whether thou come from earth or from the lustre of the lofty heaven,
Wax stronger in thy body through my song of praise : fill full all creatures, O most Wise.

19 For Indra press the Soma out, most gladdening and most excellent.
May Śakra make it swell sent forth with every prayer and asking, as it were, for strength.

20 Let me not, still beseeching thee with earnest song at Soma rites,
Anger thee like soma wild beast. Who would not beseech him who hath power to grant his prayer ?

21 The draught made swift with rapturous joy, effectual with its mighty strength,
All-conquering, distilling transport, let him drink : for he in ecstasy gives us gifts.

22 Where bliss is not, may he, All-praised, God whom the pious glorify,
Bestow great wealth upon the mortal worshipper who sheds the juice and praises him.

23 Come, Indra, and rejoice thyself, O God, in manifold affluence.
Thou fillest like a lake thy vast capacious bulk with Soma and with draughts besides.

24 A thousand and a hundred Steeds are harnessed to thy golden car.
So may the long-maned Bays, yoked by devotion, bring Indra to drink the Soma juice.

25 Yoked to thy chariot wrought of gold, may thy two Bays with peacock tails,

Convey thee hither, Steeds with their white backs, to quaff sweet juice that makes us eloquent.

26 So drink, thou Lover of the Song, as the first drinker, of this juice.
This the outpouring of the savoury sap prepared is good and meet to gladden thee.

27 He who alone by wondrous deed is Mighty, Strong by holy works,
May he come, fair of cheek ; may he not stay afar, but come and turn not from our call.

28 Śuṣṇa's quick moving castle thou hast crushed to pieces with thy bolts.
Thou, Indra, from of old, hast followed after light, since we have had thee to invoke.

29 My praises when the Sun hath risen, my praises at the time of noon,
My praises at the coming of the gloom of night, O Vasu, have gone forth to thee.

30 Praise yea, praise him. Of princes these are the most liberal of their gifts,
These, Paramajyā, Ninditāśva, Prapathī, most bounteous, O Medhyātithi.

31 When to the car, by faith, I yoked the horses longing for the way—
For skilled is Yadu's son in dealing precious wealth, he who is rich in herds of kine.

32 May he who gave me two brown steeds together with their cloths of gold,

17 *From out the stems* : See *Vedische Studien*, I. 133, 178. Sāyaṇa explains the second line differently : '(for by so doing) the leaders (of the rain, the *Maruts*) clothing (the sky with clouds) as with a vesture of the hide of the cow, milk forth (the water) for the rivers.'—Wilson.

21 *Let him drink* : *pibatu* : supplied by the Scholiast; there being no verb in the text.

22 *Where bliss is not* : that is, in defeat and trouble. But the meaning of *śevāre* is uncertain. 'At the sacrifice,' is Sāyaṇa's explanation. Von Roth suggests 'in the treasure-chamber.' I adopt Ludwig's interpretation.

23 *With draughts besides* : with thy fellow-topers (the Maruts).'—Wilson.

26 *As the first drinker* : 'According to the Scholiast, *pūrvapāḥ* means *Vāyu*, who, having arrived first in the race, drank the *Soma* before the other gods. The allusion is to the principal *graha* libation, called *Aindravāyava*, which *Indra* and *Vāyu* share together.'—Wilson.

28 *Castle* : of cloud. *Followed after light* : to find and bring it back.

30 *Praise him* : Indra, Paramajyā, Ninditāśva, and Prapathī appear to be the names of the chiefs who are praised for their liberality. Sāyaṇa makes Āsaṅga the speaker : 'Praise me, for we are the most liberal givers : (praise me as one) who bears the best arms (*paramajyā*), follows the right path (*prapathī*), and outstrips a horse in speed (*ninditāśva*).'

31 *The horses* : presented by the prince. The sentence is incomplete. The Scholiast supplies at the end of the line *tadānīm evammām stuhi*, then praise me thus. *Yadu's son* : Āsaṅga, descendant of the ancient eponymous hero Yadu. See Vol. I., Index. *Rich in herds of kine* : *paśuḥ* which appears to be in apposition with *yādvaḥ*, is hardly intelligible here. Sāyaṇa explains it as *paśumān*, having beasts or cattle, or as a derivative of *paś*, to see, and meaning one who sees what is subtle, *sūkṣmasya draṣṭā*. Neither of these explanations has anything that Sāvaṇa's name to recommend it, but I adopt the former as a makeshift.

May he, Āsaṅga's son Svanadratha, obtain all joy and high felicities.

33 Playoga's son Āsaṅga, by ten thousand, O Agni, hath surpassed the rest in giving.
For me ten bright-hued oxen have come forward like lotus-stalks from out a lake upstanding.

34 What time her husband's perfect restoration to his lost strength and manhood was apparent,
His consort Śaśvatī with joy addressed him, Now art thou well, my lord, and shalt be happy.

HYMN II. *Indra.*

1. HERE is the Soma juice expressed; O Vasu, drink till thou art full :
Undaunted God, we give it thee.

2 Washed by the men, pressed out with stones, strained through the filter made of wool,
'Tis like a courser bathed in stream.

3 This juice have we made sweet for thee like barley, blending it with milk.
Indra, I call thee to our feast.

4 Beloved of all, Indra alone drinks up the flowing Soma juice
Among the Gods and mortal men.

5 The Friend, whom not the brilliant-hued, the badly-mixt or bitter draught,
Repels, the far-extending God;

6 While other men than we with milk chase him as hunters chase a deer,
And with their kine inveigle him.

7 For him, for Indra, for the God, be pressed three draughts of Soma juice
In the juice-drinker's own abode.

8 Three reservoirs exude their drops, filled are three beakers to the brim,
All for one offering to the God.

9 Pure art thou, set in many a place, and blended in the midst with milk
And curd, to cheer the Hero best.

10 Here, Indra, are thy Soma-draughts pressed out by us, the strong, the pure:
They crave admixture of the milk.

11 O Indra, pour in milk, prepare the cake, and mix the Soma-draught :
I hear them say that thou art rich.

12 Quaffed juices fight within the breast. The drunken praise not by their wine,
The naked praise not when it rains.

13 Rich be the praiser of one rich, munificent and famed like thee:
High rank be his, O Lord of Bays.

14 Foe of the man who adds no milk, he heeds not any chanted hymn
Or holy psalm that may be sung.

15 Give us not, Indra, as a prey unto the scornful or the proud :
Help, Mighty One, with power and might.

16 This, even this, O Indra, we implore : as thy devoted friends,
The Kaṇvas praise thee with their hymns.

17 Naught else, O Thunderer, have I praised in the skilled singer's eulogy :

---

33 *Ten bright-hued oxen* : meaning ten thousand, according to Sāyaṇa.

34 Āsaṅga, the King whose liberality, with that of his son (32), and perhaps his grandsons (30), has been eulogized in the four preceding stanzas, had, the legend says, been changed to a woman by the imprecation of the Gods and afterwards restored to his manhood in consequence of his repentance and the intercession of Medhātithi and Medhyātithi whom he richly rewarded. In this stanza Śaśvatī congratulates him on his restoration. Professors Ludwig and Grassmann have translated the stanza more literally.

---

1 *O Vasu* : Good Lord, 'Giver of dwellings,' according to Sāyaṇa.

2 *Strained through the filter made of wool* more literally 'cleansed by the tail-wool of the sheep,' the material of which the sieve, strainer, or filter used for clearing and purifying the Soma juice was made.

3 *Like barley* : or, like the sacrificial cake made of barley-meal.

4 *Alone drinks up* : he alone is to receive the entire libation, which other Gods only share among them.

5 *Brilliant-hued* : without sufficient mixture with milk to thicken it and change its colour. The meaning of this and the following stanza is : Indra prefers our libations, imperfectly prepared as they may be, to the milk-offerings with which other men endeavour to attract him.

8 *Three reservoirs* : or troughs used in the preparation of the Soma-libations. They are called severally, *droṇakalaśa, pūtabhṛt,* and *āṇavanīya.*

9 *In the midst* : 'in the middle (of the day ?).'— Hillebrandt.

12 This stanza breaks the connexion between stanzas 11 and 13, and is in itself almost unintelligible. Wilson paraphrases, after Sāyaṇa : 'The potations (of Soma) contend in thy interior (for thine exhilaration) like the ebriety caused by wine : thy worshippers praise thee (filled full of Soma) like the udder (of a cow with milk).' Sāyaṇa's explanation of *nagndḥ,* naked men, as worshippers, *stotārāḥ,* 'who do not desert the verses of the Veda,' is obviously impossible. *Ūdhaḥ* udder, frequently means the rainy sky, and it may have this meaning here ; so that the sense of the passage may possibly be, as Ludwig suggests, that neither great wealth nor abject poverty tends to make a man devout. The rich man when he drinks his wine at home and the ill-clad wretch exposed to the drenching rain are equally regardless of the Gods.

13 *Rich be the praiser of the rich* : this appears to be the continuation of 'thou art rich' of stanza 11.

14 Indra will not accept worship without oblation.

On thy laud only have I thought.

18 The Gods seek him who presses out the
   Soma; they desire not sleep :
   They punish sloth unweariedly.

19 Come hither swift with gifts of wealth—
   be not thou angry with us—like
   A great man with a youthful bride.

20 Let him not, wrathful with us, spend the
   evening far from us to-day,
   Like some unpleasant son-in-law.

21 For well we know this Hero's love, most
   liberal of the boons he gives,
   His plans whom the three worlds display.

22 Pour forth the gift which Kaṇvas bring,
   for none more glorious do we know
   Than the Strong Lord with countless
   aids.

23 O presser, offer Soma first to Indra, Hero,
   Śakra, him
   The Friend of man, that he may drink;

24 Who, in untroubled ways, is best provider,
   for his worshippers.
   Of strength in horses and in kine.

25 Pressers, for him blend Soma juice, each
   draught most excellent, for him
   The Brave, the Hero, for his joy.

26 The Vṛtra-slayer drinks the juice. May
   he who gives a hundred aids
   Approach, nor stay afar from us.

27 May the strong Bay Steeds, yoked by
   prayer, bring hither unto us our Friend,
   Lover of Song, renowned by songs.

28 Sweet are the Soma juices, come ! Blent
   are the Soma juices, come !
   Ṛṣi-like, mighty, fair of cheek, come hither
   quickly to the feast.

29 And lauds which strengthen thee for great
   bounty and valour, and exalt
   Indra who doeth glorious deeds,

30 And songs to thee who lovest song, and
   all those hymns addressed to thee—
   These evermore confirm thy might.

31 Thus he, sole doer of great deeds whose
   hand holds thunder, gives us strength,
   He who hath never been subdued.

32 Vṛtra he slays with his right hand, even
   Indra, great with mighty power,
   And much-invoked in many a place.

33 He upon whom all men depend, all
   regions, all achievements, he
   Takes pleasure in our wealthy chiefs.

34 All this hath he accomplished, yea, Indra,
   most gloriously renowned,
   Who gives our wealthy princes strength.

35 Who drives his chariot seeking spoil,
   even from afar, to him he loves :
   For swift is he to bring men wealth.

36 The Sage who, winning spoil with steeds,
   slays Vṛtra, Hero with the men,
   His servant's faithful succourer.

37 O Priyamedhas, worship with collected
   mind this Indra whom
   The Soma hath full well inspired.

38 Ye Kaṇvas, sing the Mighty One, Lord
   of the Brave, who loves renown,
   All-present, glorified by song.

39 Strong Friend, who, with no trace of feet,
   restores the cattle to the men,
   Who rest their wish and hope on him.

40 Shaped as a Ram, Stone-hurler ! once
   thou camest hither to the son
   Of Kaṇva, wise Medhyātithi.

41 Vibhindu, thou hast helped this man,
   giving him thousands four times ten,
   And afterward eight thousand more.

42 And these twain pouring streams of milk,
   creative, daughters of delight,
   For wedlock sake I glorify.

---

34 *All this hath he accomplished* : the slaughter of
Vṛtra and other great deeds ; or, he made all these
creatures.

36 *The Sage* : Indra. *With the men* : accompanied
by the Maruts.

37 *Priyamedhas* : members of the family of one of
the Ṛṣis.

39 *With no trace of feet* : without tracking the lost
cattle (the rays of light) by their footsteps.

40 *Shaped as a Ram* : See I. 51. 1. The legend is
told in the *Ṣaḍviṁśa Brāhmaṇa*, I. 1.

41 *Vibhindu* : the prince, the institutor of the sacrifice.

42 The stanza is obscure, the meaning of *mākíʼ* a
feminine dual which Sāyaṇa explains by *nirmātryau*,
makers or creators, *i.e.* heaven and earth, being uncertain. Sāyaṇa's paraphrase of the stanza is : 'I
glorify these two (heaven and earth), the augmenters
of water, the originators (of beings), the benefactors
of the worshipper, on account of their generation (of
the wealth so given to me).'—Wilson.

———

19 *A great man* : the exact meaning of *mahán*, great,
is not certain. Sāyaṇa explains it by *guṇairadhikaḥ*,
eminent on account of his good qualities. 'Be not
bashful, like the ardent husband of a new bride.'—
Wilson. 'Like a rich man, newly married.'—Grassmann.

20 *Like some unpleasant son-in-law* : who sees that his
company is unwelcome and consequently stays at home.

23 *First to Indra* : See VIII. 1. 26. *Śakra* : Indra,
the Mighty One.

HYMN III. *Indra.*

1. DRINK, Indra, of the savoury juice, and
cheer thee with our milky draught.
Be, for our weal, our Friend and sharer
of the feast, and let thy wisdom guard
us well.

2 In thy kind grace and favour may we still
be strong : expose us not to foe's attack.
With manifold assistance guard and succour
us, and bring us to felicity.

3 May these my songs of praise exalt thee,
Lord, who hast abundant wealth.
Men skilled in holy hymns, pure, with
the hues of fire, have sung them with
their lauds to thee.

4 He, with his might enhanced by Ṛṣis
thousandfold, hath like an ocean spread
himself.
His majesty is praised as true at solemn
rites, his power where holy singers rule.

5 Indra for worship of the Gods, Indra
while sacrifice proceeds,
Indra, as worshippers in battle-shock, we
call, Indra that we may win the spoil.

6 With might hath Indra spread out heaven
and earth, with power hath Indra
lighted up the Sun.
In Indra are all creatures closely held;
in him meet the distilling Soma-drops.

7 Men with their lauds are urging thee,
Indra, to drink the Soma first.
The Ṛbhus in accord have lifted up their
voice, and Rudras sung thee as the first.

8 Indra increased his manly strength at
sacrifice, in the wild rapture of this
juice.
And living men to-day, even as of old,
sing forth their praises to his majesty.

9 I crave of thee that hero strength, that
thou mayst first regard this prayer,
Wherewith thou holpest Bhṛgu and the
Yatis and Praskaṇva when the prize
was staked.

10 Wherewith thou sentest mighty waters to
the sea, that, Indra, is thy manly
strength.

For ever unattainable is this power of
him to whom the worlds have cried
aloud.

11 Help us, O Indra, when we pray to thee
for wealth and hero might.
First help thou on to strength the man
who strives to win, and aid our laud,
O Ancient One.

12 Help for us, Indra, as thou holpest Paura
once, this man's devotions bent on gain.
Help, as thou gavest Ruśama and Śyāvaka
and Svarṇara and Kṛpa aid.

13 What newest of imploring prayers shall,
then, the zealous mortal sing?
For have not they who laud his might,
and Indra-power won for themselves
the light of heaven ?

14 When shall they keep the Law and praise
thee mid the Gods? Who counts as Ṛṣi
and as sage?
When ever wilt thou, Indra Maghavan,
come nigh to presser's or to praiser's
call ?

15 These songs of ours exceeding sweet, these
hymns of praise ascend to thee,
Like ever-conquering chariots that display
their strength, gain wealth, and give
unfailing aid.

16 The Bhṛgus are like Suns, like Kaṇvas,
and have gained all that their thoughts
were bent upon.
The living men of Priyamedha's race have
sung exalting Indra with their lauds.

17 Best slayer of the Vṛtras, yoke thy Bay
Steeds, Indra, from afar.
Come with the High Ones hither,
Maghavan, to us, Mighty, to drink
the Soma juice.

18 For these, the bards and singers, have
cried out to thee with prayer, to gain
the sacrifice.
As such, O Maghavan, Indra, who lovest
song, even as a lover hear my call.

19 Thou from the lofty plains above, O
Indra, hurledst Vṛtra down.
Thou dravest forth the kine of guileful
Mṛgaya and Arbuda from the moun-
tain's hold.

---

3 *With the hues of fire* : or, radiant as Agni.

7 *The Ṛbhus* : as deities connected with the seasons
which are regulated by the Sun whom Indra has
caused to shine.

9 *Bhṛgu* : See Vol. I., Index. *Yatis* : an ancient
race of ascetics connected with the Bhṛgus, and, according to one legend, said to have taken part in the
creation of the world. *Praskaṇva* : a Ṛṣi, son of Kaṇva,
the seer of some hymns of Book I.

10 *The worlds* : all men, or all living creatures.

12 *Paura* : the son of King Puru. *Ruśama*, *Śyāvaka*,
Svarṇara, and *Kṛpa* appear to have been princes especially
favoured by Indra. Cf. stanza 2 of the following hymn.

17 *High Ones* : the Maruts.

18 *To gain the sacrifice* : to ensure its proper performance and the blessings which flow from it.

19 *Mṛgaya* : See IV. 16. 13. *Arbuda* : See Vol. I.,
Index.

20 Bright were the flaming fires, the Sun
gave forth his shine, and Soma, Indra's
juice, shone clear.
Indra, thou blewest the great Dragon from
the air : men must regard that valorous
deed.

21 The fairest courser of them all, who run-
neth on as 'twere to heaven.
Which Indra and the Maruts gave, and
Pākasthāman Kaurayāṇ.

22 To me hath Pākasthāman given, a ruddy
horse, good at the pole,
Filling his girth and rousing wealth;

23 Compared with whom no other ten strong
coursers, harnessed to the pole,
Bear Tugrya to his dwelling place.

24 Raiment is body, food is life, and healing
ointment giveth strength.
As the free-handed giver of the ruddy steed,
I have named Pākasthāman fourth.

HYMN IV.   Indra.

1. THOUGH, Indra, thou art called by men .
eastward and westward, north and
south,
Thou chiefly art with Ānava and Turvaśa,
brave Champion ! urged by men to
come.

2 Or, Indra, when with Ruma, Ruśama,
Śyāvaka, and Kṛpa thou rejoicest thee,
Still do the Kaṇvas, bringing praises, with
their prayers, O Indra, draw thee
hither : come.

3 Even as the wild-bull, when he thirsts,
goes to the desert's watery pool,
Come hither quickly both at morning and
at eve, and with the Kaṇvas drink thy
fill.

4 May the drops gladden thee, rich Indra,
and obtain bounty for him who pours
the juice.
Soma pressed in the mortar didst thou

take and drink, and hence hast won
surpassing might.

5 With mightier strength he conquered
strength, with energy he crushed their
wrath.
O Indra, Strong in youth, all those who
sought the fray bent and bowed down
to thee like trees.

6 He who wins promise of thine aid goes
girt as with a thousand mighty men
of war.
He makes his son preëminent in hero
might : he serves with reverential
prayer.

7 With thee, the Mighty, for our Friend, we
will not fear or feel fatigue.
May we see Turvaśa and Yadu : thy great
deed, O Hero, must be glorified.

8 On his left hip the Hero hath reclined
himself : the proffered feast offends him
not.
The milk is blended with the honey of
the bee : quickly come hither, haste,
and drink.

9 Indra, thy friend is fair of form and rich
in horses, cars, and kine.
He evermore hath food accompanied by
wealth, and radiant joins the company.

10 Come like a thirsty antelope to the drinking-place : drink Soma to thy heart's
desire.
Raining it down, O Maghavan, day after
day, thou gainest thy surpassing might.

11 Priest, let the Soma juice flow forth, for
Indra longs to drink thereof.
He even now hath yoked his vigorous Bay
Steeds : the Vṛtra-slayer hath come
near.

12 The man with whom thou fillest thee with
Soma deems himself a pious worshipper.
This thine appropriate food is here poured
out for thee : come, hasten forward.
drink of it.

13 Press out the Soma juice, ye priests, for
Indra borne upon his car.
The pressing-stones speak loud of Indra,
while they shed the juice which, offered,
honours him.

14 To the brown juice may his dear vigorous
Bay Steeds bring Indra, to our holy
task.

Hither let thy Car-steeds who seek the
sacrifice bring thee to our drink-offerings.

15 Pūṣan, the Lord of ample wealth, for
firm alliance we elect.
May he with wisdom, Śakra ! Looser !
Much-invoked ! aid us to riches and to
seed.

16 Sharpen us like a razor in the barber's
hands : send riches thou who settest
free.
Easy to find with thee are treasures of the
Dawn for mortal man whom thou dost
speed.

17 Pūṣan, I long to win thy love, I long to
praise thee, Radiant God.
Excellent Lord, 'tis strange to me, no wish
have I to sing the psalm that Pajra
sings.

18 My kine, O Radiant God, seek pasture
where they will, my during wealth,
Immortal One.
Be our protector, Pūṣan ! be, most liberal
Lord, propitious to our gathering
strength.

19 Rich was the gift Kuruṅga gave, a hundred
steeds at morning rites.
Among the gifts of Turvaśas we thought
of him, the opulent, the splendid King.

20 What by his morning songs Kāṇva, the
powerful, hath, with the Priyamedhas,
gained—
The herds of sixty thousand pure and
spotless kine, have I, the Ṛṣi, driven
away.

21 The very trees were joyful at my coming :
kine they obtained in plenty, steeds in
plenty.

HYMN V. *Aśvins.*

1. WHEN, even as she were present here, red
Dawn hath shone from far away,
She spreadeth light on every side.

2 Like Heroes on your will-yoked car far-
shining, Wonder-Workers ! ye

15 *Pūṣan* : may here be a name of Indra. *Looser* :
of the chariot-horses when thou comest to sacrifices ;
or, according to Sāyaṇa, liberator (from sin).

17 *Pajra* : one of the Pajras, a celebrated priestly
family, with whom the Kaṇvas appear to have been on
hostile terms.

19 *Kuruṅga* : this prince's name does not occur
again.

20 *Pure and spotless* : I follow Sāyaṇa's interpretation
of *nirmajām*, but its correctness is at least doubtful. Von
Roth suggests 'to the watering-place' as the meaning of
the word, and Ludwig 'so that none remained behind.'

Attend, O Aśvins, on the Dawn.

3 By you, O Lords of ample wealth, our
songs of praise have been observed :
As envoy have I brought the prayer.

4 Kaṇvas must praise the Aśvins dear to
many, making many glad,
Most rich, that they may succour us.

5 Most liberal, best at winning strength,
inciters, Lords of splendour who
Visit the worshipper's abode.

6 So for devout Sudeva dew with fatness
his unfailing mead,
And make it rich for sacrifice.

7 Hitherward running speedily with horses,
as with rapid hawks,
Come, Aśvins, to our song of praise :

8 Wherewith the three wide distances, and
all the lights that are in heaven.
Ye traverse, and three times of night.

9 O Finders of the Day, that we may win
us food of kine and wealth,
Open the paths for us to tread.

10 O Aśvins, bring us wealth in kine, in
noble heroes, and in cars :
Bring us the strength that horses give.

11 Ye Lords of splendour, glorified, ye
Wonder-Workers borne on paths
Of gold, drink sweets with Soma juice.

12 To us, ye Lords of ample wealth, and to
our wealth chiefs extend
Wide shelter, ne'er to be assailed.

13 Come quickly downward to the prayer of
people whom ye favour most :
Approach not unto other folk.

14 Ye Aśvins whom our minds perceive,
drink of this lovely gladdening draught,
The meath which we present to you.

15 Bring riches hither unto us in hundreds
and in thousands, source
Of plenteous food, sustaining all.

16 Verily sages call on you, ye Heroes, in
full many a place.
Moved by the priests, O Aśvins, come.

17 Men who have trimmed the sacred grass,
bringing oblations and prepared,

3 *Lords of ample wealth* : 'affluent in sacrifices.'—
Wilson. See V. 74 7. *As envoy* : as the messenger of
the patron of the sacrifice.

8 *Times of night* : *yāmas*, night-watches of three
hours each.

11 *Sweets* : or meath, *mádhu* ; here, perhaps, the
milk.—Ludwig.

16 *By the priests* : *vāghádbhiḥ* : according to Sāyaṇa,
'with horses.'

O Aśvins, are invoking you.

18 May this our hymn of praise to-day, most
powerful to bring you, be,
O Aśvins, nearest to your hearts.

19 The skin filled full of savoury meath, laid
in the pathway of your car—
O Aśvins, drink ye both therefrom.

20 For this, ye Lords of ample wealth, bring
blessing for our herd, our kine,
Our progeny, and plenteous food.

21 Ye too unclose to us like doors the strengthening waters of the sky,
And rivers, ye who find the day.

22 When did the son of Tugra serve you,
Men ? Abandoned in the sea,
That with winged steeds your car might
fly.

23 Ye, O Nāsatyas, ministered to Kaṇva with
repeated aid,
When cast into the heated pit.

24 Come near with those most recent aids of
yours which merit eulogy,
When I invoke you, Wealthy Gods.

25 As ye protected Kaṇva erst, Priyamedha
and Upastuta,
Atri, Śiñjāra, Aśvins Twain !

26 And Aṁśu in decisive fight, Agastya in the
fray for kine.
And, in his battles, Sobhari.

27 For so much bliss, or even more, O Aśvins,
Wealthy Gods, than this,
We pray white singing hymns to you.

28 Ascend your car with golden seat, O Aśvins,
and with reins of gold,
That reaches even to the sky.

29 Golden is its supporting shaft, the axle also
is of gold,
And both the wheels are made of gold.

30 Thereon, ye Lords of ample wealth, come
to us even from afar,
Come ye to this mine eulogy.

31 From far away ye come to us, Aśvins,
enjoying plenteous food
Of Dāsas, O Immortal Ones.

32 With splendour, riches, and renown, O
Aśvins, hither come to us,
Nāsatyas, shining brilliantly.

33 May dappled horses, steeds who fly with
pinions, bring you hitherward
To people skilled in sacrifice.

34 The wheel delayeth not that car of yours
accompanied by song,
That cometh with a store of food.

35 Borne on that chariot wrought of gold,
with coursers very fleet of foot,
Come, O Nāsatyas, swift as thought.

36 O Wealthy Gods, ye taste and find the
brisk and watchful wild beast good.
Associate wealth with food for us.

37 As such, O Aśvins, find for me my share
of new-presented gifts,
As Kaśu, Cedi's son, gave me a hundred
head of buffaloes, and ten thousand
kine.

38 He who hath given me for mine own ten
Kings like gold to look upon.
At Caidya's feet are all the people round
about, all those who think upon the
shield.

39 No man, not any, goes upon the path on
which the Cedis walk.
No other prince, no folk is held more
liberal of gifts than they.

19 The Aśvins appear to be invited to halt and
drink the libations prepared for them by their worshippers, and not, as Sāyaṇa explains, to drink from
the skin suspended in their own car.—Ludwig.

22 *The son of Tugra* : Bhujyu, whose rescue by the
Aśvins has frequently been related and referred to. The
meaning is, I do not honour you only when I am in
distress, as others whom you have aided have done.

23 *Ministered to Kaṇva* : See I. 112. 5, and 118. 7.

24 *Wealthy Gods* : the meaning of *vṛṣaṇvasū* is
uncertain : 'rich in showers' is Sāyaṇa's explanation,
and 'excellent as steers' Prof. Ludwig's. I follow von
Roth, but his interpretation is conjectural.

25 *Kaṇva, Priyamedha, Upastuta* and *Atri* have been
mentioned in Book I. Sāyaṇa takes *śiñjāram* to be an
epithet of Atri, 'repeating praises.'

26 *Aṁśu*: a worshipper so named.—Sāyaṇa. *Agastya:*
appears in I. 117. 11, where he is said to have been
the family-priest of Khela. The great Ṛṣi Agastya is
the seer of Hymns 166—191 of Book I. See also VII.
33. 10. *Sobhari* : a Ṛṣi, the seer of Hymns 19—22 of
this Book.

31 *Plenteous food of Dāsas* : the meaning appears to
be that even far away in the east the Dāsas or non-
Āryan inhabitants sacrifice to the Aśvins. Sāyaṇa
explains the stanza differently : 'Immortal Aśvins,
destroyers of the cities of the *Dāsas*, ye bring to us food
from afar.'—Wilson.

36 According to Sāyaṇa the *watchful wild beast* is the
Soma which must be chased or sought after by the
Gods. Ludwig would read *svapatho*, with a transitive
and causal meaning, instead of *svádatho, i. e.*, ye when
ye appear in the morning *send to sleep* the wild beasts
that have been awake all night. The stanza is obscure.

37 *Buffaloes* : or camels.

38 This stanza appears to be spoken by Kaśu who
is called Caidya or son of Cedi. *Who think upon
the shield* : who are practised in wearing armour of
leather, according to Sāyaṇa.

HYMN VI   *Indra*

1. INDRA, great in his power and might,
and like Parjanya rich in rain,
Is magnified by Vatsa's lauds.

2 When the priests, strengthening the Son
of Holy Law, present their gifts,
Singers with Order's hymn of praiser.

3 Since Kaṇvas with their lauds have made
Indra complete the sacrifice.
Words are their own appropriate arms.

4 Before his hot displeasure all the peoples,
all the men, bow down,
As rivers bow them to the sea.

5 This power of his shone brightly forth
when Indra brought together, like
A skin, the worlds of heaven and earth.

6 The fiercely-moving Vṛtra's head he severed with his thunderbolt,
His mighty hundred-knotted bolt.

7 Here are—we sing them loudly forth—our
thoughts among the best of songs.
Even lightnings like the blaze of fire.

8 When hidden thoughts, spontaneously
advancing, glow, and with the stream
Of sacrifice the Kaṇvas shine.

9 Indra, may we obtain that wealth in horses
and in herds of cows,
And prayer that may be noticed first.

10 I from my Father have received deep
knowledge of the Holy Law :
I was born like unto the Sun.

11 After the lore of ancient time I make,
like Kaṇva, beauteous songs,
And Indra's self gains strength thereby.

12 Whatever Ṛṣis have not praised thee,
Indra, or have lauded thee,
By me exalted wax thou strong.

13 When his wrath thundered, when he
rent Vṛtra to pieces, limb by limb,
He sent the waters to the sea.

14 Against the Dasyu Śuṣṇa thou, Indra,
didst hurl thy during bolt :
Thou, Dread one, hast a hero's fame.

15 Neither the heavens nor firmaments nor
regions of the earth contain
Indra, the Thunderer with his might.

16 O Indra him who lay at length staying
thy copious waters thou,
In his own footsteps, smotest down.

17 Thou hiddest deep in darkness him, O
Indra, who had set his grasp
On spacious heaven and earth conjoined.

18 Indra, whatever Yatis and Bhṛgus have
offered praise to thee,
Listen, thou Mighty, to my call.

19 Indra, these spotted cows yield thee their
butter and the milky draught;
Aiders, thereby, of sacrifice;

20 Which, teeming, have received thee as a
life-germ, Indra, with their mouth,
Like Sūrya who sustaineth all.

21 O Lord of Might, with hymns of praise the
Kaṇvas have increased thy power,
The drops poured forth have strengthened
thee.

22 Under thy guidance, Indra, mid thy praises, Lord of Thunder, shall
The sacrifice be soon performed.

23 Indra, disclose much food for us, like a
stronghold with store of kine:
Give progeny and heroic strength.

24 And, Indra, grant us all that wealth of
fleet steeds which shone bright of old
Among the tribes of Nahuṣas.

25 Hither thou seemest to attract heaven's
fold which shines before our eyes,
When, Indra, thou art kind to us.

26 Yea, when thou puttest forth thy power,
Indra, thou governest the folk.
Mighty, unlimited in strength.

27 The tribes who bring oblations call to
thee, to thee to give them help,
With drops to thee who spreadest far.

28 There where the mountains downward
slope, there by the meeting of the streams
The Sage was manifest with song.

3 *Words are their own appropriate arms* : 'they declare
all weapons needless.'—Wilson.

10 *From my Father*: 'from Indra, the true protector,'
according to Sāyaṇa.

12 *Have not praised thee* : have not praised thee yet,
that is, will praise thee hereafter.—Ludwig.

16 *In his own footsteps* : or, in the (waters) at his
feet. 'Into the rushing streams.'—Wilson.

17 *Conjoined* : like two bowls turned towards each
other.

18 *Yatis* : 'pious sages.'—Wilson. Aṅgirases, according to Sāyaṇa.

22 The stanza is unintelligible to me. Sāyaṇa says
that 'thee' means Indra in the shape of the grass which
his fertilizing energy causes to grow, and by feeding
on which the cows multiply. This energy of Indra's
is all-supporting like the sun. See Wilson's note.
Ludwig proposes an alteration of the text.

24 *Tribes of Nahuṣas* : or, perhaps, the neighbouring
tribes.

28 *The Sage* : Indra. 'Sāyaṇa's conclusion of the
purport of the verse is, that men ought to sacrifice in
those places where *Indra* is said to be manifested.'—
Wilson.

29 Thence, marking, from his lofty place
   downward he looks upon the sea,
   And thence with rapid stir he moves.

30 Then, verily, they see the light refulgent
   of primeval seed,
   Kindled on yonder side of heaven.

31 Indra, the Kaṇvas all exalt thy wisdom
   and thy manly power,
   And, Mightiest ! thine heroic strength.

32 Accept this eulogy of mine, Indra, and
   guard me carefully :
   Strengthen my thought and prosper it.

33 For thee, O Mighty, Thunder-armed, we
   singers through devotion have
   Fashioned the hymn that we may live.

34 To Indra have the Kaṇvas sung, like waters
   speeding down a slope :
   The song is fain to go to him.

35 As rivers swell the ocean, so our hymns
   of praise make Indra strong,
   Eternal, of resistless wrath.

36 Come with thy lovely Bay Steeds, come
   to us from regions far away :
   O Indra, drink this Soma juice.

37 Best slayer of Vṛtras, men whose sacred
   grass is ready trimmed
   Invoke thee for the gain of spoil.

38 The heavens and earth come after thee
   as the wheel follows Etaśa :
   To thee flow Soma-drops effused.

39 Rejoice, O Indra, in the light, rejoice in
   Śaryaṇāvān, be Glad in the sacrificer's
   hymn.

40 Grown strong in heaven, the Thunder-armed
   hath bellowed, Vṛtra-slayer, Bull,
   Chief drinker of the Soma juice.

41 Thou art a Ṛṣi born of old, sole Ruler
   over all by might :
   Thou, Indra, guardest well our wealth.

42 May thy Bay Steeds with beauteous backs,
   a hundred, bring thee to the feast,
   Bring thee to these our Soma-draughts.

43 The Kaṇvas with their hymns of praise
   have magnified this ancient thought
   That swells with streams of meath and
   oil.

44 Mid mightiest Gods let mortal man choose
   Indra at the sacrifice,
   Indra, whoe'er would win, for help.

45 Thy steeds, by Priyamedhas praised, shall
   bring thee, God whom all invoke,
   Hither to drink the Soma juice.

46 A hundred thousand have I gained from
   Parśu, from Tirindira,
   And presents of the Yādavas.

47 Ten thousand head of kine, and steeds three
   times a hundred they bestowed
   On Pajra for the Sāma-song.

48 Kakuha hath reached up to heaven, bestowing buffaloes yoked in fours,
   And matched in fame the Yādavas.

HYMN VII.   Maruts.

1. O MARUTS, when the sage hath poured the
   Tṛṣṭup forth as food for you,
   Ye shine amid the mountain-clouds.

2 When, Bright Ones, fain to show your might
   ye have determined on your course,
   The mountain-clouds have bent them down.

3 Loud roaring with the winds the Sons of
   Pṛśni have upraised themselves :
   They have poured out the streaming food.

4 The Maruts spread the mist abroad and
   make mountains rock and reel,
   When with the winds they go their way ;

5 What time the rivers and the hills before
   your coming bowed them down,
   So to sustain your mighty force.

6 We call on you for aid by night, on you
   for succour in the day,
   On you while sacrifice proceeds.

7 These, verily, wondrous, red of hue, speed
   on their courses with a roar
   Over the ridges of the sky.

8 With might they drop the loosened rein so
   that the Sun may run his course,
   And spread themselves with beams of light.

46 *From Parśu, from Tirindira* : 'from Tirindira the
son of Parśu.'—Wilson. Both names are Iranian (cf.
Tiridates, Persa). See Weber's *Episches im Vedischen
Ritual*, pp. 36—38 (Sitzungsberichte der K. P. Akademie
der Wissenschaften, 1891, XXXVIII).

Yādavas : or Yadus, descendants of the hero Yadu.

47 *Pajra* : See VIII. 4. 17.

48 *Kakuha* : or, the lofty one, meaning Tirindira.
Buffaloes : or camels.

————

1 *The Tṛṣṭup* : according to one of Sāyaṇa's three
interpretations, the Soma offering at the midday libation
accompanied by hymns in the Tṛṣṭup metre.

8 *They drop the loosened rein* : they speed forward to
prepare the way for the Sun.

29 *The sea* : the reservoir of Soma juice.

30 *The light* : the Sun which is lighted up beyond
the range of men's sight.

38 *As the wheel follows Etaśa* : as the chariot of the
Sun follows the horse that draws it.

39 *Śaryaṇāvān* : said to be a lake and district in
Kurukṣetra. See I. 84. 14, note.

9 Accept, ye Maruts, this my song, accept
ye this mine hymn of praise,
Accept, Ṛbhukṣans, this my call.

10 The dappled Cows have poured three lakes,
meath for the Thunder-wielding God,
From the great cask, the watery cloud.

11 O Maruts, quickly come to us when, longing for felicity,
We call you hither from the sky.

12 For, Rudras and Ṛbhukṣans, ye, Most
Bountiful, are in the house,
Wise when the gladdening draught is
drunk.

13 O Maruts, send us down from heaven
riches distilling rapturous joy,
With plenteous food, sustaining all.

14 When, Bright Ones, hither from the hills
ye have resolved to take your way,
Ye revel in the drops effused.

15 Man should solicit with his lauds happiness
which belongs to them,
So great a band invincible.

16 They who like fiery sparks with showers
of rain blow through the heaven and
earth,
Milking the spring that never fails.

17 With chariots and tumultuous roar, with
tempests and with hymns of praise
The Sons of Pṛśni hurry forth.

18 For wealth, we think of that whereby ye
aided Yadu, Turvaśa,
And Kaṇva who obtained the spoil.

19 May these our viands Bounteous Ones !
that flow in streams like holy oil,
With Kāṇva's hymns, increase your might.

20 Where, Bounteous Lords for whom the
grass is trimmed, are ye rejoicing
now ?
What Brahman is adoring you ?

21 Is it not there where ye of old, supplied
with sacred grass, for lauds
Inspired the strong in sacrifice ?

22 They brought together both the worlds, the
mighty waters, and the Sun,
And, joint by joint, the thunderbolt.

23 They sundered Vṛtra limb from limb and
split the gloomy mountain-clouds,
Performing a heroic deed.

24 They reinforced the power and strength
of Trita as he fought, and helped
Indra in battle with the foe.

25 They deck themselves for glory, bright,
celestial, lightning in their hands,
And helms of gold upon their heads.

26 When eagerly ye from far away came to
the cavern of the Bull,
He bellowed in his fear like Heaven.

27 Borne by your golden-footed steeds, O
Gods, come hither to receive
The sacrifice we offer you.

28 When the red leader draws along their
spotted deer yoked to the car.
The Bright Ones come, and shed the rain.

29 Suṣoma, Śaryaṇāvān, and Ārjīka full of
homes, have they,
These Heroes, sought with downward car.

30 When, Maruts, ye come to him, the singer
who invokes you thus,
With favours to your suppliant ?

31 What now ? where have ye still a friend
since ye left Indra all alone ?
Who counteth on your friendship now ?

32 The Kaṇvas sing forth Agni's praise together with our Maruts' who
Wield thunder and wear swords of gold.

33 Hither for new felicity may I attract the
Impetuous Ones,
The Heroes with their wondrous strength.

34 Before them sink the very hills deeming
themselves abysses : yea,
Even the mountains bend them down.

35 Steeds flying on their tortuous path through
mid-air carry them, and give
The man who lauds them strength and life.

24 *Trita* : a Vedic deity, perhaps Agni in his third
form, generally associated with Indra, Vāyu, and the
Maruts. See Vol. I., index. *In battle with the foe* : or,
to overcome Vṛtra.

26 *The cavern of the Bull* : perhaps, the hollow of the
rain-cloud : 'the opening of the rainy (firmament).'—
Wilson.

28 *Leader* : or side-horse.

29 *Śaryaṇāvān* : Has occurred before (See I. 84. 14
and VIII 6. 39) as the name of a lake. *Ārjīka* is said
by Sāyaṇa to be the name of a district, and he takes
Suṣoma (containing excellent Soma) to be an adjective
qualifying it, See Zimmer, *Altindisches Leben*, p. 19.

31 *Left Indra all alone* ? : This is merely a rhetorical
question meaning, ye never did desert him. The Maruts
alone stood by him when he fought with Vṛtra.

9 *Ṛbhukṣans* : Mighty Ones, according to Sāyaṇa.

10 *The dappled Cows* ; the Maruts. *Three lakes* :
three large Soma receptacles, the *Droṇakalaśa* the
Ādhavanīya, and the *Pūtabhṛt*. The meaning is, the
Maruts have poured down abundant water from the
rain-cloud.

19 *With Kāṇva's hymns* : hymns of the Ṛṣi Punar-
vatsa, a descendant of Kaṇva.

21 *The strong in sacrifice* : the *Maghavans*, wealthy
worshippers.

36 Agni was born the first of all, like Sūrya
lovely with his light :
With lustre these have spread abroad.

HYMN VIII. *Aśvins.*

1. With all the succours that are yours, O
Aśvins, hither come to us :
Wonderful, borne on paths of gold, drink
ye the meath with Soma juice.

2 Come now, ye Aśvins, on your car decked
with a sun-bright canopy,
Bountiful, with your golden forms, Sages
with depth of intellect.

3 Come hither from the Nahuṣas, come,
drawn by pure hymns, from mid-air.
O Aśvins, drink the savoury juice shed in
the Kaṇvas' sacrifice.

4 Come to us hither from the heavens, come
from mid-air, well-loved by us :
Here Kaṇva's son hath pressed for you the
pleasant meath of Soma juice.

5 Come, Aśvins, to give ear to us, to drink
the Soma, Aśvins, come.
Hail, Strengtheners of the praise-song !
speed onward, ye Heroes, with your
thoughts.

6 As, Heroes, in the olden time the Ṛṣis
called you to their aid,
So now, O Aśvins, come to us, come near
to this mine eulogy.

7 Even from the luminous sphere of heaven
come to us, ye who find the light,
Carers for Vatsa, through our prayers and
lauds, O ye who hear our call.

8 Do others more than we adore the Aśvins
with their hymns of praise ?
The Ṛṣi Vatsa, Kaṇva's son, hath magnified you with his songs.

9 The holy singer with his hymns hath called
you, Aśvins, hither-ward;
Best Vṛtra-slayers, free from stain, as such
bring us felicity.

10 What time, ye Lords of ample wealth,
the Lady mounted on your car,

Then, O ye Aśvins, ye attained all wishes
that your hearts desired.

11 Come thence, O Aśvins, on your car that
hath a thousand ornaments :
Vatsa the sage, the sage's son, hath sung
a song of sweets to you.

12 Cheerers of many, rich in goods, discoverers
of opulence,
The Aśvins, Riders through the sky, have
welcomed this my song of praise.

13 O Aśvins, grant us all rich gifts wherewith no man may interfere.
Make us observe the stated times : give us
not over to reproach.

14 Whether, Nāsatyas, ye be nigh, or whether
ye be far away,
Come thence, O Aśvins, on your car that
hath a thousand ornaments.

15 Vatsa the Ṛṣi with his songs, Nāsatyas,
hath exalted you :
Grant him rich food distilling oil, graced
with a thousand ornaments.

16 Bestow on him, O Aśvins, food that
strengthens, and that drops with oil,
On him who praises you for bliss, and,
Lords of bounty, prays for wealth.

17 Come to us, ye who slay the foe, Lords of
rich treasure, to this hymn.
O Heroes, give us high renown and these
good things of earth for help.

18 The Priyamedhas have invoked you with
all succours that are yours,
You, Aśvins, Lords of solemn rites, with
calls entreating you to come.

19 Come to us, Aśvins, ye who bring felicity,
auspicious Ones,
To Vatsa who with prayer and hymn,
lovers of song, hath honoured you.

20 Aid us, O Heroes, for those hymns for
which ye helped Gośarya erst,
Gave Vaśa, Daśavraja aid, and Kaṇva and
Medhātithi:

21 And favoured Trasadasyu, ye Heroes, in
spoil-deciding fray :
For these, O Aśvins, graciously assist us in
acquiring strength.

22 O Aśvins, may pure hymns of ours, and
songs and praises, honour you:
Best slayers everywhere of foes, as such we
fondly yearn for you.

---

36 *With lustre these have spread abroad* : 'then they
(the Maruts) stood round in their radiance.' 'The
Scholiast intimates that this verse refers to the ceremony
called *Agnimāruta*, when *Agni* is first worshipped, then
the *Maruts*.'—Wilson.

---

3 *From the Nahuṣas* : or, according to others, from
the neighbouring people.

7 *Carers for Vatsa* : ye who favour and provide for
Vatsa, the Ṛṣi of Hymn VI. of this Book.

10 *The Lady* : Sūryā, Daughter of the Sun. See, I.
116. 17.

20 *Gośarya* : said by Sāyaṇa to be a name of Śayu.
See I. 116, 22. *Vaśa* and *Daśavraja* are known only as
protégés of the Aśvins.

21 *Trasadasyu* : See Vol. I., Index.

23 Three places of the Aśvins, erst concealed,
are made apparent now.
Both Sages, with the flight of Law come
hither unto those who live.

HYMN IX.   *Aśvins.*

1. To help and favour Vatsa now, O Aśvins,
come ye hitherward.
Bestow on him a dwelling spacious and
secure, and keep malignities away.

2 All manliness that is in heaven, with the
Five Tribes, or in mid-air,
Bestow, ye Aśvins, upon us.

3 Remember Kāṇva first of all among the
singers, Aśvins, who
Have thought upon your wondrous deeds.

4 Aśvins, for you with song of praise this
hot oblation is effused,
This your sweet Soma juice, ye Lords of
ample wealth, through which ye think
upon the foe.

5 Whatever ye have done in floods, in the
tree, Wonder-Workers, and in growing
plants,
Therewith, O Aśvins, succour me.

6 What force, Nāsatyas, ye exert, whatever,
Gods, ye tend and heal,
This your own Vatsa gains not by his
hymns alone : ye visit him who offers
gifts.

7 Now hath the Ṛṣi splendidly thought out
the Aśvins' hymn of praise.
Let the Atharvan pour the warm oblation
forth, and Soma very rich in sweets.

8 Ye Aśvins, now ascend your car that lightly
rolls upon its way.

May these my praises make you speed
hitherward like a cloud of heaven.

9 When, O Nāsatyas, we this day make you
speed hither with our hymns,
Or, Aśvins, with our songs of praise,
remember Kāṇva specially.

10 As erst Kakṣīvān and the Ṛṣi Vyaśva, as
erst Dīrghatamas invoked your presence,
Or, in the sacrificial chambers, Vainya
Pṛthī, so be ye mindful of us here, O
Aśvins.

11 Come as home-guardians, saving us from
foemen, guarding our living creatures
and our bodies,
Come to the house to give us seed and
offspring,

12 Whether with Indra ye be faring, Aśvins,
or resting in one dwelling-place with
Vāyu,
In concord with the Ṛbhus or Ādityas, or
standing still in Viṣṇu's striding-places.

13 When I, O Aśvins, call on you to-day that
I may gather strength,
Or as all-conquering might in war, be
that the Aśvins' noblest grace.

14 Now come, ye Aśvins, hitherward : here
are oblations set for you;
These Soma-draughts to aid Yadu and
Turvaśa, these offered you mid Kaṇva's
Sons.

15 Whatever healing balm is yours, Nāsatyas,
near or far away,
Therewith, great Sages, grant a home to
Vatsa and to Vimada.

16 Together with the Goddess, with the
Aśvins' Speech have I awoke.
Thou, Goddess, hast disclosed the hymn,
and holy gift from mortal men.

17 Awake the Aśvins, Goddess Dawn ! Up
Mighty Lady of sweet strains !
Rise, straightway, priest of sacrifice ! High
glory to the gladdening draught !

18 Thou, Dawn, approaching with thy light
shinest together with the Sun,

23 *Three places* : according to Sāyaṇa, the three
wheels of the Aśvins' chariot are intended. The three
places can only be heaven, firmament, and earth, hidden
during the darkness of night and made visible by the
coming of the Aśvins and Dawn.

---

1 *Vatsa* : apparently another name of Śaśakarṇa,
called also Kāṇva or descendant of Kaṇva, the Ṛṣi of
the hymn.

3 *Thought upon* : or touched upon, handled.

4 *Think upon the foe* : plan the destruction of the
demon of darkness.

5 *Whatever ye have done* : Professor Wilson paraphrases after Sāyaṇa : 'preserve me with that (healing
virtue, deposited by you in the waters, in the trees,
in the herbs.'

7 *The Atharvan* : the priest who has special charge
of the fire and the Soma. I follow Ludwig in taking
átharvaṇi as a nominative and not as a locative as
Sāyaṇa does ; 'the will sprinkle the sweet-flavoured
Soma and the *gharma* (oblation) on the *Atharvan* fire.'—
Wilson.

10 *Kakṣīvān* : See I. 18. 1. *Vyaśva* : See I. 112. 15.
Dīrghatamas : See Vol. I., Index. *Vainya* : Son of Vena.
Pṛthī : the first anointed king.

11 *Our living creatures* : our dependents and our
cattle.

12 *Viṣṇu's striding-places* : from which he made his
three great strides through earth, firmament, and heaven.

13 *That* : the granting of my request.

15 *And to Vimada* : as ye did to Vimada.—Sāyaṇa.
See Vol. I., Index.

16 *The Goddess* : Dawn. *The Aśvins' Speech* : Vāk or
Speech who glorifies the Aśvins ; *i. e.* the hymn that
praises them.

And to this man-protecting home the chariot of the Aśvins comes.

19 When yellow stalks give forth the juice, as cows from udders pour their milk,
And voices sound the song of praise, the Aśvins' worshippers show first.

20 Forward for glory and for strength, protection that shall conquer men,
And power and skill, most sapient Ones !

21 When Aśvins, worthy of our lauds, ye seat you in the father's house.
With wisdom or the bliss ye bring.

HYMN X.   *Aśvins.*

1. WHETHER ye travel far away or dwell in yonder light of heaven,
Or in a mansion that is built above the sea, come thence, ye Aśvins, hitherward.

2 Or if for Manu ye prepared the sacrifice, remember also Kanva's son.
I call Bṛhaspati, Indra, Viṣṇu, all the gods, the Aśvins borne by rapid steeds.

3 Those Aśvins I invoke who work marvels, brought hither to receive,
With whom our friendship is most famed, and kinship passing that of Gods.

4 On whom the solemn rites depend, whose worshippers rise without the Sun :
These who foreknow the holy work of sacrifice, and by their Godhead drink the sweets of Soma juice.

5 Whether ye, Lords of ample wealth, now linger in the east or west,
With Druhyu, or with Anu, Yadu, Turvaśa, I call you hither; come to me.

6 Lords of great riches, whether through the firmament ye fly or speed through heaven and earth,

Or with your Godlike natures stand upon your cars, come thence, O Aśvins, hitherward.

HYMN XI.   *Agni.*

1. THOU Agni, God mid mortal men, art guard of sacred rites, thou art
To be adored at sacrifice.

2 O Mighty Agni, thou must be glorified at our festivals,
Bearing our offerings to the Gods.

3 O Jātavedas Agni, fight and drive our foes afar from us,
Them and their godless enmities.

4 Thou, Jātavedas, seekest not the worship of a hostile man,
However nigh it be to thee.

5 We sages, mortals as we are, adore the mighty name of thee,
Immortal Jātavedas' name.

6 Sages, we call the Sage to help, mortals, we call the God to aid :
We call on Agni with our songs.

7 May Vatsa draw thy mind away even from thy loftiest dwelling-place,
Agni, with song that yearns for thee.

8 Thou art the same in many a place : mid all the people thou art Lord.
In fray and fight we call on thee.

9 When we are seeking strength we call Agni to help us in the strife,
The giver of rich gifts in war.

10 Ancient, adorable at sacrifices, Priest from of old, meet for our praise, thou sittest.
Fill full and satisfy thy body, Agni, and win us happiness by offering worship.

HYMN XII.   *Indra.*

1. Joy, Mightiest Indra, known and marked, sprung most from Soma-draughts, wherewith
Thou smitest down the greedy fiend, for that we long.

---

19 *Yellow stalks* : of Soma plants.

20 *Forward for glory* : advance and come to give us glory, etc.

21 *In the father's house* : in the sacrificial hall of the father of the family, the wealthy householder who institutes the sacrifice. This stanza is a continuation of 19, although the connexion is interrupted by the intervening stanza.

———

1 *Above the sea* : above the ocean of air.

3 *To receive* : our oblations.

4 *Without the sun* : Sāyaṇa explains *asūre* differently, connecting in with *sūri* instead of *sūra* : 'of whom there are worshippers in a place where there is no worship.'—Wilson.

5 *Druhyu* and the other names stand for the tribes called after these ancient chieftains. See Vol. I., Index.

———

The hymn is translated in Max Müller's *History of Ancient Sanskrit Literature.*

2 *Bearing our offerings to the Gods* : literally, 'the charioteer of solemn rites.'

———

1 *Joy* : *mádah.* the rapturous exhilaration produced in Indra by drinking the Soma juice. *For that we long* : the short refrain or burden which generally concludes each stanza of each triplet of this hymn is sometimes rather loosely attached and cannot always be clearly brought out in the proper place in translation.

2 Wherewith thou holpest Adhrigu, the great
   Daśagva, and the God
   Who stirs the sunlight, and the sea, for
   that we long.

3 Wherewith thou dravest forth like cars
   Sindhu and all the mighty floods
   To go the way ordained by Law, for
   that we long.

4 Accept this laud for aid, made pure like
   oil, thou Caster of the Stone,
   Whereby even in a moment thou hast
   waxen great.

5 Be pleased, Song-lover, with this song :
   it flows abundant like the sea.
   Indra, with all thy succours thou hast
   waxen great.

6 The God who from afar hath sent gifts to
   maintain our friendship's bond,
   Thou, spreading them like rain from heaven,
   hast waxen great.

7 The beams that mark him have grown
   strong, the thunder rests between his
   arms,
   When, like the Sun, he hath increased
   both Heaven and Earth.

8 When, Mighty Lord of Heroes, thou didst
   eat a thousand buffaloes,
   Then grew and waxed exceeding great
   thine Indra-power.

9 Indra consumeth with the rays of Sūrya
   the malicious man :
   Like Agni conquering the woods, he hath
   grown strong.

10 This newest thought of ours that suits the
   time approaches unto thee :
   Serving, beloved in many a place it metes
   and marks.

11 The pious germ of sacrifice directly purifies
   the soul.

By Indra's lauds it waxes great, it metes
and marks.

12 Indra who wins the friend hath spread
   himself to drink the Soma-draught :
   Like worshipper's dilating praise; it metes
   and marks.

13 He whom the sages, living men, have
   gladdened, offering up their hymns,
   Hath swelled like oil of sacrifice in Agni's
   mouth.

14 Aditi also hath brought forth a hymn for
   Indra, Sovran Lord :
   The work of sacrifice for help is glorified.

15 The ministering priests have sung their
   songs for aid and eulogy :
   God, thy Bays turn not from the rite which
   Law ordains.

16 If, Indra, thou drink Soma by Viṣṇu's or
   Tṛta Āptya's side,
   Or with the Maruts take delight in flowing
   drops;

17 Or, Śakra, if thou gladden thee afar or
   in the sea of air,
   Rejoice thee in this juice of ours, in flowing
   drops.

18 Or, Lord of Heroes, if thou aid the worshipper who sheds the juice,
   Or him whose laud delights thee, and
   his flowing drops.

19 To magnify the God, the God, Indra,
   yea, Indra for your help,
   And promptly end the sacrifice—this have
   they gained.

20 With worship, him whom men adore, with
   Soma, him who drinks it most,
   Indra with lauds have they increased—
   this have they gained.

21 His leadings are with power and might
   and his instructions manifold :
   He gives the worshipper all wealth : this
   have they gained.

22 For slaying Vṛtra have the Gods set Indra
   in the foremost place.

2 *Adhrigu* : according to Sāyaṇa a Ṛṣi so named.
See I. 112. 20. *Daśagva* : one of the priestly family
connected with, or identical with, the Aṅgirases, 'the
accomplisher of the ten (months' rite).'—Wilson. Ludwig
thinks that *Daśagva* here may mean the Sun. *The sea* :
of air.

8 *Didst eat a thousand buffaloes* : the buffaloes probably represent the clouds which the Sun dissipates or
consumes.—Ludwig. 'When thou hast slain thousands
of mighty foes.'—Wilson.

10 *It metes and marks* : defines and discriminates
Indra's good qualities.—Sāyaṇa.

11 The *germ of sacrifice* is probably the wish that
prompts the offering.

Sāyaṇa explains differently : 'The devout praiser of
the adorable (Indra purifies in due succession the offering (of the Soma) ; with sacred hymns he magnifies

(the might of Indra, he verily proclaims the measure
(of his merits).

12 *Worshipper's dilating praise* : I follow Sāyaṇa : but
the stanza is unintelligible to me. 'Indra the benefactor
of his friend (the worshipper), has enlarged himself to
drink the Soma, in like manner as the pious praise
dilates and proclaims the measure of his merits.'
—Wilson. The meaning of *vdśi* (praise, according to
Sāyaṇa) is uncertain. Von Roth thinks that the two
press-stones are meant, and others explain it as the
sword, knife, or axe used in sacrifice.

16 *Tṛta Āptya* : See VIII. 7. 24, note. Here he
appears as the preparer of celestial Soma for Indra.

Indra the choral bands have sung, for
vigorous strength.

23 We to the Mighty with our might, with
lauds to him who hears our call,
With holy hymns have sung aloud, for
vigorous strength.

24 Not earth, nor heaven, nor firmaments
contain the Thunder-wielding God :
They shake before his violent rush and
vigorous strength.

25 What time the Gods, O Indra, set thee
foremost in the furious fight,
Then thy two beautiful Bay Steeds carried
thee on.

26 When Vṛtra, stayer of the floods, thou
slewest, Thunderer with might,
Then thy two beautiful Bay Steeds carried
thee on.

27 When Viṣṇu, through thine energy, strode
wide those three great steps of his,
Then thy two beautiful Bay Steeds carried
thee on.

28 When thy two beautiful Bay Steeds grew
great and greater day by day,
Even then all creatures that had life
bowed down to thee.

29 When, Indra, all the Marut folk humbly
submitted them to thee,
Even then all creatures that had life
bowed down to thee.

30 When yonder Sun, that brilliant light,
thou settest in the heaven above,
Even then all creatures that had life bowed
down to thee.

31 To thee, O Indra, with this thought the
sage lifts up this eulogy,
Akin and leading as on foot to sacrifice.

32 When in thine own dear dwelling all
gathered have lifted up the voice
Milk-streams at worship's central spot, for
sacrifice,

33 As Priest, O Indra, give us wealth in
brave men and good steeds and kine
That we may first remember thee for
sacrifice.

31 The second line is difficult. Wilson, following
Sāyaṇa, paraphrases the stanza: 'The wise (worshipper),
Indra, offers thee this gratifying sincere praise along
with pious rites at the sacrifice, as (a man places) a kinsman in (a prominent) position.'

32 *Milk-streams* : the sweetly-flowing hymns.

Wilson remarks : 'This is probably an ancient hymn,
both by its repetitions and combination of simplicity
and obscurity.'

HYMN XIII.   *Indra.*

1. INDRA, when Soma juices flow, makes his
mind pure and meet for lauds.
He gains the power that brings success,
for great is he.

2 In heaven's first region, in the seat of
Gods, is he who brings success,
Most glorious, prompt to save, who wins
the water-floods.

3 Him, to win strength, have I invoked,
even Indra mighty for the fray.
Be thou most near to us for bliss, a Friend
to aid.

4 Indra, Song-lover, here for thee the worshipper's libation flows.
Rejoicing in this sacred grass thou shinest
forth.

5 Even now, O Indra, give us that which,
pressing juice, we crave of thee.
Bring us wealth manifold which finds the
light of heaven.

6 What time the zealous worshipper hath
boldly sung his songs to thee,
Like branches of a tree up-grows what
they desire.

7 Generate songs even as of old, give ear
unto the singer's call :
Thou for the pious hast grown great at
each carouse.

8 Sweet strains that glorify him play like
waters speeding down a slope,
Yea, him who in this song is called the
Lord of Heaven;

9 Yea, who alone is called the Lord, the
single Ruler of the folk,
By worshippers seeking aid : may he joy
in the draught.

10 Praise him, the Glorious, skilled in song,
Lord of the two victorious Bays :
They seek the worshipper's abode who bows
in prayer.

11 Put forth thy strength : with dappled
Steeds come, thou of mighty intellect,
With swift Steeds to the sacrifice, for 'tis
thy joy.

12 Grant wealth to those who praise thee,
Lord of Heroes, Mightiest Indra : give
Our princes everlasting fame and opulence.

13 I call thee when the Sun is risen, I call
thee at the noon of day :
With thy car-horses, Indra, come well-
pleased to us.

7 *Generate songs* : by granting the prayers of the
singers.

14 Speed forward hither, come to us, rejoice
thee in the milky draught :
Spin out the thread of ancient time, as
well is known.

15 If, Śakra, Vṛtra-slayer, thou be far away
or near to us.
Or in the sea, thou art the guard of Soma
juice.

16 Let songs we sing and Soma-drops expressed
by us make Indra strong:
The tribes who bring oblations find
delight in him.

17 Him sages longing for his aid, with offerings brought in eager haste,
Him, even as branches, all mankind have
made to grow.

18 At the Tṛkadrukas the Gods span sacrifice
that stirred the mind :
May our songs strengthen him who still
hath strengthened us.

19 When, true to duty, at due times the worshipper offers lauds to thee,
They call him Purifier, Pure, and Wonderful.

20 That mind of Rudra, fresh and strong,
moves conscious in the ancient ways,
With reference whereto the wise have
ordered this.

21 If thou elect to be my Friend drink of
this sacrificial juice,
By help whereof we may subdue all
enemies.

22 O Indra, Lover of the song, when shall
thy praiser be most blest ?
When wilt thou grant us wealth in herds
of kine and steeds ?

23 And thy two highly-lauded Bays, strong
stallions, draw thy car who art

Untouched by age, most gladdening car
for which we pray.

24 With ancient offerings we implore the
Young and Strong whom many praise.
He from of old hath sat upon dear sacred
grass.

25 Wax mighty, thou whom many laud for
aids which Ṛṣis have extolled.
Pour down for us abundant food and
guard us well.

26 O Indra, Caster of the Stone, thou helpest
him who praises thee:
From sacrifice I send to thee a mind-
yoked hymn.

27 Here, yoking for the Soma-draught these
Horses, sharers of thy feast,
Thy Bay Steeds, Indra, fraught with wealth,
consent to come.

28 Attendants on thy glory, let the Rudras
roar assent to thee,
And all the Marut companies come to the
feast.

29 These his victorious followers hold in the
heavens the place they love,
Leagued in the heart of sacrifice, as well
we know.

30 That we may long behold the light, what
time the ordered rite proceeds,
He duly measures, as he views, the
sacrifice.

31 O Indra, strong is this thy car, and strong
are these Bay Steeds of thine :
O Śatakratu, thou art strong, strong is
our call.

32 Strong is the press-stone, strong thy joy,
strong is the flowing Soma juice :
Strong is the rite thou furtherest, strong
is our call.

33 As strong I call on thee the Strong, O
Thunderer with thy thousand aids:
For thou hast won the hymn of praise.
Strong is our call.

14 *Spin out the thread of ancient times* : 'extend the
ancient sacrifice.'—Wilson.

The due performance of sacrifice is regarded as an
unbroken thread reaching through a succession of
Ṛṣis from ancient to modern times.

15 *In the sea* : in the firmament, or ocean of air.

17 *All mankind* : kṣoṇiḥ. But see M. Müller, *Vedic
Hymns*, I. 310.

18 *At the Tṛkadrukas* : according to Sāyaṇa these
are the first three days of the Abhiplava ceremony.
According to some modern scholars they are probably
three peculiar Soma-vessels, or an oblation consisting
of three offerings of Soma. *Span sacrifice* : See above
note on 14. *That stirred the mind* : that urged others to
follow the example.

19 *Him* : a change of person, Indra being meant.

20 *Have ordered this* : song of praise, or holy ceremony.—Ludwig.

26 *Mind-yoked* : made ready by the poet's mind, as
a chariot—to which the hymn is frequently compared—
is equipped for a journey.

28 *The Rudras* : the sons of Rudra, the Maruts.

29 *The heart*, literally navel, that is the central point,
of sacrifice, is the receptacle on which oblations are placed,
or the *uttaravedī* or north altar.

31 *Strong* : vṛṣā : as has been noticed before (See
I. 177. 2.3.) some of the Vedic poets delight in the
repetition of this word and derivatives from the same
root. Sāyaṇa explains *vṛṣā* : as 'showerer of benefits,'
and Ludwig translates it by 'stierkräftig,' strong as a
bull. The original meaning of the word is male,
masculine, and, hence, strong.

HYMN XIV.   *Indra.*

1. IF I, O Indra, were, like thee, the single
Sovran of all wealth,
My worshipper should be rich in kine.

2 I should be fain, O Lord of Power, to
strengthen and enrich the sage,
Were I the Lord of herds of kine.

3 To worshippers who press the juice thy
goodness, Indra, is a cow
Yielding in plenty kine and steeds.

4 None is there, Indra, God or man, to
hinder thy munificence,
The wealth which, lauded, thou wilt give.

5 The sacrifice made Indra strong when he
unrolled the earth, and made
Himself a diadem in heaven.

6 Thine aid we claim, O Indra, thine who
after thou hast waxen great
Hast won all treasures for thine own.

7 In Soma's ecstasy Indra spread the firmament and realms of light,
When he cleft Vala limb from limb.

8 Showing the hidden he drave forth the
cows for the Aṅgirases,
And Vala he cast headlong down.

9 By Indra were the luminous realms of
heaven established and secured,
Firm and immovable from their place.

10 Indra, thy laud moves quickly like a joyous
wave of water-floods :
Bright shine the drops that gladden thee.

11 For thou, O Indra, art the God whom
hymns and praises magnify:
Thou blessest those who worship thee.

12 Let the two long-maned Bay Steeds bring
Indra to drink the Soma juice,
The Bountiful to our sacrifice.

13 With waters' foam thou torest off, Indra,
the head of Namuci,
Subduing all contending hosts.

14 The Dasyus, when they fain would climb
by magic arts and mount to heaven,
Thou, Indra, castest down to earth.

15 As Soma-drinker conquering all, thou
scatteredst to every side
Their settlement who poured no gifts.

HYMN XV.   *Indra.*

1. SING forth to him whom many men invoke,
to him whom many laud :
Invite the powerful Indra with your songs
of praise.

2 Whose lofty might—for doubly strong is
he—supports the heavens and earth,
And hills and plains and floods and light
with manly power.

3 Such, Praised by many ! thou art King :
alone thou smitest Vṛtras dead,
To gain, O Indra, spoils of war and high
renown.

4 We sing this strong and wild delight of
thine which conquers in the fray,
Which, Caster of the Stone ! gives room
and shines like gold.

5 Wherewith thou also foundest lights for
Āyu and for Manu's sake :
Now joying in this sacred grass thou
beamest forth.

6 This day too singers of the hymn praise,
as of old, this might of thine :
Win thou the waters day by day, thralls
of the strong.

7 That lofty Indra-power of thine, thy
strength and thine intelligence,
Thy thunderbolt for which we long, the
wish makes keen.

8 O Indra, Heaven and Earth augment thy
manly power and thy renown ;
The waters and thy mountains stir and
urge thee on.

9 Viṣṇu the lofty ruling Power, Varuṇa,
Mitra sing thy praise :
In thee the Maruts' company have great
delight.

10 O Indra, thou wast born the Lord of
men, most liberal of thy gifts :
Excellent deeds for evermore are all thine
own.

11 Ever, alone, O highly-praised, thou sendest
Vṛtras to their rest :
None else than Indra executes the mighty
deed.

12 Though here and there, in varied hymns,
Indra, men call on thee for aid,

---

13 *With waters' foam* : with a thunderbolt in the
form of foam, according to a later legend. See Lanman,
Sanskrit Reader, p. 375, who takes Namuci to be a
waterspout in a lake, and 'with foam' to mean 'accompanied by foam.'

---

4 *Wild delight* : Soma juice, the cause of thy
rapture.

5 *For Āyu and for Manu's sake* : that is for man.
Āyu was the son of Purūravas and Urvaśī.

6 *Thralls of the strong* : controlled and imprisoned
by Vṛtra.

7 *The wish* : our wishes expressed in prayer and
praise.

Still with our heroes fight and win the
light of heaven.

13 Already have all forms of him entered
our spacious dwelling-place :
For victory stir thou Indra, up, the Lord
of Might.

HYMN XVI.   *Indra.*

1. PRAISE Indra whom our songs must laud,
sole Sovran of mankind, the Chief
Most liberal who controlleth men.

2 In whom the hymns of praise delight, and
all the glory-giving songs.
Like the floods' longing for the sea.

3 Him I invite with eulogy, best King,
effective in the fight,
Strong for the gain of mighty spoil.

4 Whose perfect ecstasies are wide, profound,
victorious, and give
Joy in the field where heroes win.

5 Him, when the spoils of war are staked,
men call to be their advocate :
They who have Indra win the day.

6 Men honour him with stirring songs and
magnify with solemn rites :
Indra is he who giveth ease.

7 Indra is priest and Ṛṣi, he is much
invoked by many men,
And mighty by his mighty powers.

8 Meet to be lauded and invoked, true Hero
with his deeds of might,
Victorious even when alone.

9 The men, the people magnify that Indra
with their Sāma songs,
With hymns and sacred eulogies :

10 Him who advances them to wealth, sends
light to lead them in the war,
And quells their foemen in the fray.

11 May he, the saviour much-invoked, may
Indra bear us in a ship
Safely beyond all enemies.

12 As such, O Indra, honour us with gifts
of booty, further us,
And lead us to felicity.

13 *All forms of him* : the various qualities of Indra
have been celebrated.

Stir thou : the Ṛṣi addresses himself. *Lord of Might:*
śácipatim : in later literature, lord or husband of Śacī
or his might personified and regarded as his consort.

7 *Priest* : brahmā, meaning, according to Sāyaṇa,
greater than all. See VI. 45. 7, 'The Brahman who
accepts the prayer,' that is, Indra regarded as a priest.
Ṛṣi : according to Sāyaṇa, 'the beholder of all the Āryan
race.'

HYMN XVII   *Indra.*

1. COME, we have pressed the juice for thee;
O Indra, drink this Soma here :
Sit thou on this my sacred grass.

2 O Indra, let thy long-maned Bays, yoked
by prayer, bring thee hitherward :
Give ear and listen to our prayers.

3 We Soma-bearing Brāhmans call thee
Soma-drinker with thy friend,
We, Indra, bringing Soma juice.

4 Come unto us who bring the juice, come
unto this our eulogy,
Fair-visored ! drink thou of the juice.

5 I pour it down within thee, so through
all thy members let it spread :
Take with thy tongue the pleasant drink.

6 Sweet to thy body let it be, delicious be
the savoury juice :
Sweet be the Soma to thine heart.

7 Like women, let this Soma-draught,
invested with its robe, approach,
O active Indra, close to thee.

8 Indra, transported with the juice, vast in
his bulk, strong in his neck
And stout arms, smites the Vṛtras down.

9 O Indra, go thou forward, thou who
rulest over all by might :
Thou Vṛtra-slayer slay the fiends.

10 Long be thy grasping-hook wherewith
thou givest ample wealth to him
Who sheds the juice and worships thee.

11 Here, Indra, is thy Soma-draught, made
pure upon the sacred grass :
Run hither, come and drink thereof.

12 Famed for thy radiance, worshipped well !
this juice is shed for thy delight :
Thou art invoked, Ākhandala !

13 To Kuṇḍapāyya, grandson's son, grandson
of Śṛṅgavṛṣ ! to thee,

3 *With thy friend* : Indra's companion, the thunderbolt. 'With suitable praise.'—Wilson.

7 *Like women* : dressed in white garments and moving
slowly. *Its robe* : the milk that colours it.

12 *Famed for thy radiance, worshipped well* : the words
thus rendered, *śácigo* and *śácipūjana*, have not been
satisfactorily explained by the Commentator, and their
meaning is still uncertain. According to Sāyaṇa, the
former may mean 'thou whose cattle are strong,' or 'thou
whose radiance is renowned,' and the latter 'thou of
renowned adoration' or 'whose hymns are renowned.'
See Wilson's note. *Thou art invoked, Ākhandala*: or, 'Thou
O Destroyer, art invoked.' This appellation of Indra
does not occur again in the Ṛgveda. See Muir, *O. S.
Texts,* IV. 190.

13 *Kuṇḍapāyya* and *Śṛṅgavṛṣ* appear here to be names
of men. According to Sāyaṇa, *kuṇḍapāyya* is the name

To him have I addressed my thought.

14 Strong pillar thou, Lord of the home !
armour of Soma-offerers :
The drop of Soma breaketh all the strongholds down, and Indra is the Ṛṣis'
Friend.

15 Holy Pṛdākusānu, winner of the spoil,
one eminent o'er many men,
Lead on the wild horse Indra with his
vigorous grasp forward to drink the
Soma juice.

## HYMN XVIII.					Ādityas.

1. Now let the mortal offer prayer to win
the unexampled grace
Of these Ādityas and their aid to cherish
life.

2 For not an enemy molests the paths
which these Ādityas tread :
Infallible guards, they strengthen us in
happiness.

3 Now soon may Bhaga, Savitar, Varuṇa,
Mitra, Aryaman
Give us the shelter widely spread which
we implore.

4 With Gods come thou whose fostering
care none checks, O Goddesss Aditi :
Come, dear to many, with the Lords who
guard us well.

5 For well these Sons of Aditi know to
keep enmities aloof,
Unrivalled, giving ample room, they save
from woe.

6 Aditi guard our herd by day, Aditi, free
from guile, by night,
Aditi, ever strengthening, save us from
grief !

7 And in the day our hymn is this : May
Aditi come nigh to help,
With loving-kindness bring us weal and
chase our foes.

8 And may the Aśvins, the divine Pair of
Physicians, send us health :
May they remove iniquity and chase our
foes.

9 May Agni bless us with his fires, and
Sūrya warm us pleasantly :
May the pure Wind breathe sweet on us,
and chase our foes.

10 Drive ye disease and strife away, drive
ye away malignity :
Ādityas, keep us ever far from sore distress.

11 Remove from us the arrow, keep
famine, Ādityas ! far away :
Keep enmities afar from us, Lords of all
wealth !

12 Now, O Ādityas, grant to us the shelter
that lets man go free,
Yea, even the sinner from his sin, ye
Bounteous Gods !

13 Whatever mortal with the power of
demons fain would injure us,
May he, impetuous, suffer harm by his
own deeds.

14 May sin o'ertake our human foe, the
man who speaketh evil thing,
Him who would cause our misery, whose
heart is false.

15 Gods, ye are with the simple ones, ye
know each mortal in your hearts ;
Ye, Vasus, well discriminate the false
and true.

16 Fain would we have the sheltering aid of
mountains and of water-floods :
Keep far from us iniquity, O Heaven and
Earth.

17 So with auspicious sheltering aid do ye,
O Vasus, carry us
Beyond all trouble and distress, borne in
your ship.

18 Ādityas, ye Most Mighty Ones, grant to
our children and their seed
Extended term of life that they may live
long days.

---

of a particular Soma ceremony, and the offspring of
Śṛṅgavṛṣ, is Indra himself. '(Indra), who wast the
offspring of Śṛṅgavṛṣ, of whom the kuṇḍapāyya rite was
the protector, (the sages) have fixed (of old) their minds
upon this ceremony.' See Wilson's note who observes
that 'the construction is loose, and the explanation not
very satisfactory.'

14 Lord of the home : apparently the householder who
institutes the sacrifice is addressed. he vāstoṣpate gṛhapate.
—Sāyaṇa. The Ṛṣis' Friend : munīnāṁ sákhā, the friend
of the Munis, sages, saintly men or ascetics ; of us Ṛṣis,
according to Sāyaṇa.

15 Pṛdākusānu : I follow Ludwig in taking this to be
the name of the institutor of the sacrifice. According
to Sāyaṇa who explains it as 'lifting up the head or back
like a serpent,' or 'to be propitiated, as a serpent is, with
gems, charms, medicaments, etc.,' it is an epithet of
Indra; and the leader forward of Indra in the second
line is the worshipper, understood. Grassmann banishes
the last three stanzas to his Appendix as not originally
forming part of the hymn.

---

1 Ādityas : See I. 14. 3.

4 With the Lords : sūríbhiḥ ; that is, the Gods.

13 With the power of demons : 'from his diabolical
nature.'—Wilson .

19 Sacrifice, O Ādityas, is your inward
monitor : be kind,
For in the bond of kindred we are bound
to you.

20 The Maruts' high protecting aid, the
Aśvins, and the God who saves,
Mitra and Varuṇa for weal we supplicate.

21 Grant us a home with triple guard,
Aryaman, Mitra, Varuna !
Unthreatened, Maruts ! meet for praise,
and filled with men.

22 And as we human beings, O Ādityas, are
akin to death,
Graciously lengthen ye our lives that we
may live.

HYMN XIX.   *Agni.*

1. SING praise to him, the Lord of Light.
The Gods have made the God to be
their messenger,
And sent oblation to Gods.

2 Agni, the Bounteous Giver, bright with
varied flames, laud thou, O singer
Sobhari—
Him who controls this sacred food with
Soma blent, who hath first claim to
sacrifice.

3 Thee have we chosen skilfullest in sacrifice,
Immortal Priest among the Gods,
Wise finisher of this holy rite :

4 The Son of Strength, the blessed, brightly-
shining One, Agni whose light is excellent.
May he by sacrifice win us in heaven
the grace of Mitra, Varuṇa, and the
Floods.

5 The mortal who hath ministered to Agni
with oblation, fuel, ritual lore,
And reverence, skilled in sacrifice.

6 Verily swift to run are his fleet-footed
steeds, and most resplendent fame is his.
No trouble caused by Gods or wrought
by mortal man from any side o'ertaketh
him.

7 May we by thine own fires be well sup-
plied with fire, O Son of Strength, O
Lord of Might :
Thou as our Friend hast worthy men.

8 Agni, who praises like a guest of friendly
mind, is as a car that brings us gear.
Also in thee is found perfect security :
thou art the Sovran Lord of wealth.

9 That man, moreover, merits praise who
brings, auspicious Agni, sacrificial gifts :
May he win riches by his thoughts.

10 He for whose sacrifice thou standest up
erect is prosperous and rules o'er men.
He wins with coursers and with singers
skilled in song : with heroes he obtains
the prize.

11 He in whose dwelling Agni is chief
ornament, and, all-desired, loves his
laud well,
And zealously tends his offerings—

12 His, or the lauding sage's word, his, Son
of Strength ! who is most prompt with
sacred gifts,
Set thou beneath the Gods, Vasu, above
mankind, the speech of the intelligent.

13 He who with sacrificial gifts or homage
bringeth very skilful Agni nigh,
Or him who flashes fast with song,

14 The mortal who with blazing fuel, as his
laws command, adores the Perfect God,
Blest with his thoughts in splendour shall
exceed all men, as though he overpassed
the floods.

15 Give us the splendour, Agni, which may
overcome each greedy fiend in our
abode,
The wrath of evil-hearted folk.

16 That, wherewith Mitra, Varuṇa, and

---

19 *Your inward monitor* : or near remembrancer, not
suffering you to rest until you have rewarded men for
their devotions. Ludwig says that the *hiḷáḥ* of the text
is really *hi iḷaḥ* : For sacrifice, Ādityas, is your nearest
dwelling-place.

20 *The God who saves* : Indra, who is especially the
tutelary God of Āryans.

21 *With triple guard* : or, triply defending or defended.
According to Sāyaṇa, protecting from heat, cold, and wet;
or three-storeyed.

22 *Akin to death* : born subject to death.

1 *The Gods* : in the first line are, according to
Sāyaṇa, the priests, *i. e.* those who praise : *dívyanti
stávantiti devā ṛtvijo* ; but the word may be taken in its
ordinary signification.

5 *Ritual lore* : *vedena* here can hardly mean, as
Sāyaṇa explains it, 'by studying the Veda.' It may perhaps mean 'by knowledge of the proper use of the sacred

formulas,' or as M. Müller says, 'by the bundle of grass'
used in sacrifice. See *Anc. S. Literature.* p. 28, note, and
p. 205.

7 *Hast worthy men* : in us thy worshippers.

10 *With coursers and with singers* : is successful in
chariot-races and is rewarded by the Gods for his sacrifices.

12 *Set thou beneath the Gods* and *above mankind,* is said
to mean 'spread through all the sky.' The meaning of
this and the preceding stanza is somewhat obscurely
expressed.

14 *The Perfect God* : *áditim,* explained by Sāyaṇa as
akhaṇḍanīyam, indivisible, complete.

16 *That* : radiance or splendour.

Aryaman, the Aśvins, Bhaga give us
light,
That may we, by thy power finding best
furtherance, worship,
O Indra, helped by thee.

17 O Agni, most devout are they, the sages
who have set thee Sage exceeding wise,
O God, for men to look upon :

18 Who have arranged thine altar Blessed
God, at morn, brought thine oblation,
pressed the juice.
They by their deeds of strength have won
them mighty wealth, who have set all
their hope in thee.

19 May Agni worshipped bring us bliss, may
the gift, Blessed One, and sacrifice bring
bliss ;
Yea, may our praises bring us bliss.

20 Show forth the mind that brings success
in war with fiends, wherewith thou
conquerest in fight.
Bring down the many firm hopes of our
enemies, and let us vanquish with
thine aid.

21 I praise with song the Friend of man,
whom Gods sent down to be herald
and messenger,
Best worshipper, bearer of our gifts.

22 Thou unto sharp-toothed Agni, Young
and Radiant God, proclaimest with
thy song the feast—
Agni, who for our sweet strains moulds
heroic strength when sacred oil is
offered him,

23 While, served with sacrificial oil, now
upward and now downward Agni
moves his sword,
As doth the Asura his robe.

24 The God, the Friend of man, who bears
our gifts to heaven, the God with his
sweet-smelling mouth,
Distributes, skilled in sacrifice, his precious
things, Invoking Priest, Immortal God.

25 Son of Strength, Agni, if thou wert the
mortal, bright as Mitra ! worshipped
with our gifts !
And I were the Immortal God,

26 I would not give thee up, Vasu, to calumny, or misery, O Bounteous One.

My worshipper should feel no hunger
or distress, nor, Agni, should he live
in sin.

27 Like a son cherished in his father's house,
let our oblation rise unto the Gods.

28 With thine immediate aid may I, excellent
Agni, ever gain my wish,
A mortal with a God to help.

29 O Agni, by thy wisdom, by thy bounties,
by thy leading may I gather wealth.
Excellent Agni, thou art called my Providence : delight thou to be liberal.

30 Agni, he conquers by thine aid that brings
him store of noble heroes and great
strength,
Whose bond of friendship is thy choice.

31 Thy spark is black and crackling, kindled
in due time, O Bounteous, it is taken up.
Thou art the dear Friend of the mighty
Mornings : thou shinest in glimmerings
of the night.

32 We Sobharis have come to him, for succour,
who is good to help with thousand
powers,
The Sovran, Trasadasyu's Friend.

33 O Agni, thou on whom all other fires
depend, as branches on the parent stem,
I make the treasures of the folk, like
songs, mine own, while I exalt thy
sovran might.

34 The mortal whom, Ādityas, ye, Guileless,
lead to the farther bank
Of all the princes, Bounteous Ones !—

35 Whoe'er he be, Man-ruling Kings ! the
Regent of the race of men—
May we, O Mitra, Varuṇa, and Aryaman,
like him be furtherers of your law.

36 A gift of fifty female slaves hath Trasadasyu given me, Purukutsa's son,
Most liberal, kind, lord of the brave.

37 And Śyāva too for me led forth a strong
steed at Suvāstu's ford :

26 *In sin* : such as neglect of the Gods in consequence of poverty.

33 The meaning of the second line appears to be :
'I praise Agni better than other men. I overpower
their hymns and secure for myself the rewards which
they were intended to obtain.'

36 *Female slaves* : *vadhūnām* : *vadhū* means usually a
bride, a wife, a woman in general, and here handmaids
or female slaves, the wives or daughters of conquered
Dāsas, appear to be meant. According to von Roth,
mares or other female draught-animals are intended.

37 *Suvāstu* is in all probability the Soastos of
Arrian (Suwad or Swat) near the Kophen or Kābul
river. *Kine* : there is no substantive in the text. The
stanza, which has no comment in the printed edition,

20 *Bring down the many firm hopes* : there is no substantive in the text, and hopes, resolves, thoughts or something similar must be supplied.

21 *The Friend of man* : or *mānurhitam* may mean 'him
who was established by Manus.'

23 *His sword* : the flashing flame. *The Asura* : the
Sun, according to Sāyaṇa. *Robe* : outward form.

A herd of three times seventy kine, good lord of gifts, he gave to me.

HYMN XX.   *Maruts.*

1. LET none, Swift Travellers ! check you : come hither, like-spirited, stay not far away,
Ye benders even of what is firm.

2 Maruts, Ṛbhukṣans, Rudras come ye with your cars strong-fellied and exceeding bright.
Come, ye for whom we long, with food, to sacrifice, come ye with love to Sobhari.

3 For well we know the vigorous might of Rudra's Sons, the Maruts, who are passing strong,
Swift Viṣṇu's band, who send the rain.

4 Islands are bursting forth and misery is stayed : the heaven and earth are joined in one.
Decked with bright rings, ye spread the broad expanses out, when ye, Self-luminous, stirred yourselves.

5 Even things immovable shake and reel, the mountains and the forest trees at your approach,
And the earth trembles as ye come.

6 To lend free course, O Maruts, to your furious rush, heaven high and higher still gives way,
Where they, the Heroes mighty with their arms, display their gleaming ornaments on their forms.

7 After their Godlike nature they, the bull-like Heroes, dazzling and impetuous, wear
Great splendour as they show erect.

8 The pivot of the Sobharis' chariot within the golden box is balmed with milk.
May they the Well-born, Mighty, kindred of the Cow, aid us to food and to delight.

9 Bring, ye who sprinkle balmy drops. oblations to your vigorous Marut company,
To those whose leader is the Bull.

10 Come hither, O ye Maruts, on your strong-horsed car, solid in look, with solid naves.
Lightly like winged falcons, O ye Heroes, come, come to enjoy our offerings.

11 Their decoration is the same : their ornaments of gold are bright upon their arms;
Their lances glitter splendidly.

12 They toil not to defend their bodies from attack, strong Heroes with their mighty arms.
Strong are your bows and strong the weapons in your cars, and glory sits on every face.

13 Whose name extendeth like a sea, alone, resplendent, so that all have joy in it,
And life-power like ancestral might.

14 Pay honour to these Maruts and sing praise to them, for of the wheel-spokes of the car
Of these loud roarers none is last : this is their power, this moves them to give mighty gifts.

15 Blest by your favouring help was he, O Maruts, at the earlier flushings of the morn,
And even now shall he be blest.

16 The strong man to whose sacrifice, O Heroes, ye approach that ye may taste thereof,
With glories and with war that winneth spoil shall gain great bliss, ye Shakers of the world.

17 Even as Rudra's Sons, the brood of the Creator Dyaus, the Asura, desire,
O Youthful Ones, so shall it be :

is very obscure and can be only conjecturally translated. See Ludwig's Translation and Commentary, I. 427, and IV. 380.

———

4 Sāyaṇa seems to explain this verse, 'The islands fall asunder, the firmest (trees) experience distress ; they (the winds) distress heaven and earth ; the waters hurry onward, O bright weaponed, self-shining ones, when you agitate them.'—E.B.C.'s note in Wilson's Translation. The stanza is difficult. I have followed, generally, Ludwig's version. *Islands* : the higher unsubmerged grounds. *Misery* : caused by the preceding hot and dry weather. *Are joined in one* : as the heavy rain cures the horizon. *Bright rings* : worn on the arms or the ankles or carried by the Maruts on their shoulders. See I. 166. 9.

7 *Bull-like* : the exact meaning of *vṛṣapsavaḥ* is uncertain. *Show erect* : *dhrutapsavaḥ* is conjecturally translated.

8 *Box* : the interior of the chariot. *With milk* : with fertilizing rain sent by the Maruts. *The Cow* : Pṛśni.

9 *Ye who sprinkle balmy drops* : priests who offer libations. *Whose leader is the Bull* : whom Indra leads. Or, it may be, whose chariot is drawn by bulls, as in the following stanza.

10 *Solid in look* : or with bull-like, or strong look.

14 *None is last* : no part of their chariot wheel is behind the rest in speed. *This moves them to give mighty gifts* : or, this (characteristic belongs to them) through greatness of their gifts.

15 *He* : your worshipper.

18 And these the bounteous, worthy of the
   Maruts who move onward pouring down
   the rain—
   Even for their sake, O Youthful Ones,
   with kindest heart take us to you to be
   your own.

19 O Sobhari, with newest song sing out unto
   the youthful purifying Bulls,
   Even as a plougher to his steers.

20 Who, like a celebrated boxer, overcome the
   challengers in every fight :
   They who, like shining bulls, are most
   illustrious—honour those Maruts with
   thy song.

21 Allied by common ancestry, ye Maruts,
   even the Cows, alike in energy,
   Lick, all by turns, each other's head.

22 Even mortal man, ye Dancers breast-
   adorned with gold, attains to brotherhood with you.
   Mark ye and notice us, O Maruts ; evermore your friendship is secured to us.

23 O Maruts, rich in noble gifts, bring us a
   portion of the Maruts' medicine,
   Ye Coursers who are Friends to us.

24 Haters of those who serve you not, bliss-
   bringers, bring us bliss with those auspicious aids
   Wherewith ye are victorious and guard
   Sindhu well, and succour Krvi in his
   need.

25 Maruts, who rest on fair trimmed grass,
   what balm soever Sindhu or Asiknī
   hath,
   Or mountains or the seas contain.

26 Ye carry on your bodies, ye who see it
   all : so bless us graciously therewith.
   Cast, Maruts, to the ground our sick man's
   malady : replace the dislocated limb.

18 *The bounteous* : the liberal institutors of sacrifice.

19 *Purifying bulls* : the strong Maruts who send the
sweet rain.

21 *Allied by common ancestry* : as the offspring of Pṛśni.
The Cows : the Maruts. *Lick...each other's head* : as they
crowd together in their course. According to Sāyaṇa, 'the
cows severally lick up the quarters of the sky.'

22 *Ye Dancers* : ye who dance through the air.

24 *Kṛvi* : the eponymus of a warrior tribe in the
Panjāb, in later times combined with, or identical with
the Pañcālas. Sāyaṇa takes *kṛvim* here to mean a
well : 'with which you provided a well (for Gotama).'
—Wilson.

25 *Asiknī* : the Acesines of Quintus Curtius, the
Vedic name of the Candrabhāgā, the modern Cenāb.

26 *Replace the dislocated limb* : 're-establish his enfee-
bled frame.'—Wilson

HYMN XXI.   *Indra.*

1. WE call on thee, O Matchless One ! We
   seeking help, possessing nothing firm
   ourselves,
   Call on thee wonderful in fight :

2 On thee for aid in sacrifice. This youth
   of ours, the bold, the mighty, hath gone
   forth.
   We therefore, we thy friends, Indra, have
   chosen thee, free-giver, as our Guardian
   God.

3 Come hither, for the drops are here, O
   Lord of corn-lands. Lord of horses,
   Lord of kine :
   Drink thou the Soma, Soma's Lord !

4 For we the kinless singers have drawn
   hither thee, O Indra, who hast numerous kin.
   With all the forms thou hast, come thou
   of bull-like strength, come near to drink
   the Soma juice.

5 Sitting like birds beside thy meath,
   mingled with milk, that gladdeneth and
   exalteth thee,
   Indra, to thee we sing aloud.

6 We speak to thee with this our reverential
   prayer. Why art thou pondering yet
   awhile ?
   Here are our wishes ; thou art liberal,
   Lord of Bays : we and our hymns are
   present here.

7 For not in recent times alone, O Indra,
   Thunder-armed, have we obtained thine
   aid.
   Of old we knew thy plenteous wealth.

8 Hero, we knew thy friendship and thy rich
   rewards : these, Thunderer, now we crave
   of thee.
   O Vasu, for all wealth that cometh of the
   kine, sharpen our powers, fair-visored
   God.

9 Him who of old hath brought to us this
   and that blessing, him I magnify for
   you,
   Even Indra, O my friends, for help :

10 Borne by Bay Steeds, the Lord of heroes,
   ruling men, for it is he who takes
   delight.
   May Maghavan bestow on us his worshippers hundreds of cattle and of steeds.

11 Hero, may we, with thee for Friend,
   withstand the man who pants against us
   in his wrath,

2 *This youth of ours* : the noble who has instituted
the sacrifice.

In fight with people rich in kine.

12 May we be victors in the singer's battle-
song, and meet the wicked, Much-
invoked !
With heroes smite the foeman and show
forth our strength. O Indra, further
thou our thoughts.

13 O Indra, from all ancient time rivalless
ever and companionless art thou :
Thou seekest comradeship in war.

14 Thou findest not the wealthy man to be
thy friend : those scorn thee who are
flown with wine.
What time thou thunderest and gatherest,
then thou, even as a Father, art invoked.

15 O Indra, let us not, like fools who waste
their lives at home, with friendship such
as thine
Sit idly by the poured-out juice.

16 Giver of kine, may we not miss thy
gracious gifts : let us not rob thee of
thine own.
Strip even the strong places of the foe,
and bring : thy gifts can never be
made vain.

17 Indra or blest Sarasvatī alone bestows
such wealth, treasure so great, or thou,
O Citra, on the worshipper.

18 Citra is King, and only kinglings are the
rest who dwell beside Sarasvatī.
He, like Parjanya with his rain, hath
spread himself with thousand, yea, with
myriad gifts.

HYMN XXII. *Aśvins.*

1. HITHERWARD have I called to-day, for
succour, that most wondrous car
Which ye ascended, Aśvins, ye whose
paths are red, swift to give ear, for
Sūryā's sake.

13 *Thou seekest comradeship in war* : befriendest thy
worshippers when they need thine assistance in battle.

14 *Gatherest* : the clouds.—M. Müller.

17 *Citra* : the name of this king does not occur
elsewhere in the Ṛgveda.

18 *King* : *rājā. Kinglings* ; *rājakāḥ. Parjanya* : God
of the rain-cloud, regarded as the type of liberal benefi-
cence.

———

1 *Ye whose paths are red* : *rudravartanī* : this epithet
of the Aśvins is variously explained : 'having a path
which causes weeping in battle,' or 'whose paths are
praised,'—Sāyaṇa; 'advancing on the path to battle.'—
Wilson ; 'proceeding on terrible roads.'—Muir ; 'going
on Rudra's path.'—Ludwig; 'on your light path.'—Grassmann; 'going on a reddish path.'—Pischel. See *Vedische
Studien*, I., pp. 15 and 55—60. *For Sūryā's sake* : who
chose the Aśvins as her husbands. See I. 116. 17.

2 Car ever young, much longed-for, easily
invoked, soon guided, first in deeds of
might,
Which waits and serves, O Sobhari, with
benevolence, without a rival or a foe.

3 These Aśvins with our homage, these Two
Omnipresent Deities
Hitherward will we bring for kind help,
these who seek the dwelling of the
worshipper.

4 One of your chariot wheels is moving
swiftly round, one speeds for you its
onward course.
Like a milch-cow, O Lords of splendour,
and with haste let your benevolence
come to us.

5 That chariot of yours which hath a triple
seat and reins of gold,
The famous car that traverseth the heaven
and earth, thereon Nāsatyas, Aśvins,
come.

6 Ye with your plough, when favouring
Manu with your help, ploughed the first
harvest in the sky.
As such will we exalt you, Lords of
splendour, now, O Aśvins, with our
prayer and praise.

7 Come to us, Lords of ample wealth, by
paths of everlasting Law,
Whereby to high dominion ye with mighty
strength raised Tṛkṣi, Trasadasyu's son.

8 This Soma pressed with stones is yours, ye
Heroes, Lords of plenteous wealth.
Approach to drink the Soma, come, drink
in the worshipper's abode.

9 O Aśvins, mount the chariot, mount the
golden seat, ye who are Lords of
plenteous wealth,
And bring to us abundant food.

10 The aids wherewith ye helped Paktha and
Adhrigu, and Babhru severed from his
friends,—
With those, O Aśvins, come hither with
speed and soon, and heal whatever is
diseased.

4 The movements of the two wheels are not very
intelligibly decribed. See I. 30. 19, and V. 73. 3. *Like
a milch-cow* : a common type of liberality.

6 *Ploughed the first harvest* : first ploughed the ground
and sowed and reaped : that is, taught, by example,
men to do so. Cp. I. 117. 21 : 'Ploughing and sowing
barley, O ye Aśvins, milking out food for men, ye
wonder-workers, Blasting away the Dasyu with your
trumpet, ye have bestowed wide light upon the Ārya.'

7 *Tṛkṣi* : See VI. 46. 8.

10 *Paktha, Adhrigu, and Babhru* are said to have
been kings.

11 When we continually invoke the Aśvins,
the resistless, at this time of day,
We lovers of the song, with songs.

12 Through these, ye Mighty Ones, come
hither to my call which brings all
blessings, wears all forms,—
Through which, All-present Heroes, lavishest of food ye strengthened Kṛvi, come
through these.

13 I speak to both of these as such, these
Aśvins whom I reverence at this time
of day :
With homage we entreat them both.

14 Ye who are Lords of splendour, ye whose
paths are red, at eve, at morn, at
sacrifice,
Give us not utterly as prey to mortal foe,
ye Rudras, Lords of ample wealth.

15 For bliss I call the blissful car, at morn
the inseparable Aśvins with their car
I call, like Sobhari our sire.

16 Rapid as thought, and strong, and
speeding to the joy, bringing your swiftly-coming help,
Be to us a protection even from far away,
Lords of great wealth, with many aids.

17 Come, Wonder-Workers, to our home,
our home, O Aśvins, rich in cattle,
steeds, and gold,
Chief drinkers of the Soma's juice !

18 Choice-worthy strength, heroic, firm and
excellent, uninjured by the Rakṣas
foe,
At this your coming nigh, ye Lords of
ample wealth and all good things, may
we obtain.

HYMN XXIII. *Agni.*

1. WORSHIP thou Jātavedas, pray to him who
willingly accepts,
Whose smoke wanders at will, and none
may grasp his flame.

2 Thou, all men's friend, Viśvamanas,
exaltest Agni with thy song,

12 *Kṛvi* : See VIII. 20. 24.

14 *Ye Rudras* : ye red-hued or bright Gods.

17 *Rich in cattle* : proleptic; which your coming will
make rich.

———

The Ṛṣi is Viśvamanas the son of Vyaśva.

1 *Who willingly accepts* : *prativyam* : according to
Sāyaṇa, 'disposed to encounter enemies.'

2 The second line is difficult, as the adjective
viṣpardhasaḥ stands without a substantive and may be
either the accusative plural or the genitive singular :
'who is the giver of chariots to the unenvious (worshipper).'
—Wilson.

The Giver, and his flames with which no
cars contend.

3 Whose resolute assault, to win vigour and
food, deserves our praise,—
Through whose discovering power the
priest obtaineth wealth.

4 Up springs the imperishable flame, the
flame of the Refulgent One
Most bright, with glowing jaws and glory
in his train.

5 Skilled in fair sacrifice, extolled, arise in
Godlike loveliness,
Shining with lofty splendour, with effulgent
light.

6 Called straight to our oblations, come,
O Agni, through our eulogies,
As thou hast been our envoy bearing up
our gifts.

7 I call your Agni, from of old Invoking
Priest of living men :
Him with this song I laud and magnify
for you.

8 Whom, wondrous wise, they animate with
solemn rites and his fair form,
Kind as a friend to men who keep the
holy Law.

9 Him, true to Law, who perfecteth the
sacrifice, Law-loving ones !
Ye with your song have gratified in the
place of prayer.

10 May all our sacrifices go to him the truest
Aṅgiras,
Who is among mankind the most illustrious
Priest.

11 Imperishable Agni, thine are all these high
enkindled lights,
Like horses and like stallions showing
forth their strength.

12 So give us, Lord of Power and Might,
riches combined with hero strength,
And guard us with our sons and grandsons in our frays.

13 Soon as the eager Lord of men is friendly
unto Manu's race,
Agni averteth from us all the demon host.

14 O Hero Agni, Lord of men, on hearing
this new laud of mine,
Burn down the Rākṣasas, enchanters,
with thy flame.

15 No mortal foe can e'er prevail by arts of
magic over him

3 *Assault* : on the oblations which the fire consumes.

9 *Law-loving ones* : 'pious worshippers.'—Wilson.
Have gratified : or must gratify.

Who serveth Agni well with sacrificial gifts.

16 Vyaśva the sage, who sought the Bull, hath won thee, finder of good things :
As such may we enkindle thee for ample wealth.

17 Uśanā Kāvya stablished thee, O Agni, as Invoking Priest :
Thee, Jātavedas, Sacrificing Priest for man.

18 All Deities of one accord appointed thee their messenger :
Thou, God, through hearing, hadst first claim to sacrifice.

19 Him may the mortal hero make his own immortal messenger.
Far-spreading, Purifier, him whose path is black.

20 With lifted ladles let us call him splendid with his brilliant flame,
Men's ancient Agni, wasting not, adorable.

21 The man who pays the worship due to him with sacrificial gifts
Obtains both plenteous nourishment and hero fame.

22 To Jātavedas Agni, chief in sacrifices, first of all
With homage goes the ladle rich with sacred gifts.

23 Even as Vyaśva did, may we with these most high and liberal hymns
Pay worship unto Agni of the splendid flame.

24 Now sing, as Sthūrayūpa sang, with lauds to him who spreadeth far,
To Agni of the home, O Ṛṣi, Vyaśva's son.

25 As welcome guest of human kind, as offspring of the forest kings,
The sages worship ancient Agni for his aid.

26 For men's oblations brought to him who is the mighty Lord of all,
Sit, Agni, mid our homage, on the sacred grass.

27 Grant us abundant · treasures, grant the opulence which many crave,

With store of heroes, progeny, and high renown.

28 Agni, Most Youthful of the Gods, send evermore the gift of wealth
Unto Varosuṣāman and to all his folk.

29 A mighty Conqueror art thou, O Agni, so disclose to us
Food in our herds of kine and gain of ample wealth.

30 Thou, Agni, art a glorious God : bring hither Mitra, Varuṇa,
Imperial Sovrans, holy-minded, true to Law.

HYMN XXIV.   *Indra.*

1. COMPANIONS, let us learn a prayer to Indra whom the thunder arms,
To glorify your bold and most heroic Friend.

2 For thou by slaying Vṛtra art the Vṛtra-slayer, famed for might.
Thou, Hero, in rich gifts surpassest wealthy chiefs.

3 As such, when glorified, bring us riches of very wondrous fame,
Set in the highest rank, Wealth-giver, Lord of Bays !

4 Yea, Indra, thou disclosest that preëminent dear wealth of men :
Boldly, O Bold One, glorified, bring it to us.

5 The workers of destruction stay neither thy right hand nor thy left :
Nor hosts that press about thee, Lord of Bays, in fight.

6 O Thunder-armed, I come with songs to thee as to a stall with kine :
Fulfil the wish and thought of him who sings thy praise.

7 Chief Vṛtra-slayer, through the hymn of Viśvamanas think of all,
All that concerneth us, Excellent, Mighty Guide.

8 May we, O Vṛtra-slayer, O Hero, find this thy newest boon, Longed-for, and excellent, thou who art much invoked !

16 *Who sought the Bull* : the strong Agni. According to Sāyaṇa, 'the showerer (of rain).'

17 *Uśanā Kāvya* : See Vol. I., Index.

18 *Through hearing* : and, by causing the Gods to hear, men's prayers.

24 *Sthūrayūpa* : said by Sāyaṇa to be the name of of a Ṛṣi.

25 *Forest kings* : tall trees, or trees in general.

28 *Varosuṣāman* : I follow the St. Petersburg Lexicon in joining *varo* to *suṣāmṇe* and taking the whole as one word and the name of a chief. Ludwig translates somewhat as follows : 'Agni, send quickly to the folk who know the goodly Sāman well, the gift of wealth, for ever, Youngest God ! to all.' But in a later volume of his work (III. p. 162 he comes to the conclusion that Suṣāman is a proper name, and that *varo* (which may, he thinks, be an interjection) must not be combined with it.

9 O Indra, Dancer, Much-invoked ! as thy
   great power is unsurpassed,
So be thy bounty to the worshipper unchecked.

10 Most Mighty, most heroic One, for
   mighty bounty fill thee full.
Though strong, strengthen thyself to win
   wealth, Maghavan !

11 O Thunderer, never have our prayers
   gone forth to any God but thee :
So help us, Maghavan, with thine assistance now.

12 For, Dancer, verily I find none else for
   bounty, saving thee,
For splendid wealth and power, thou
   Lover of the Song.

13 For Indra pour ye out the drops ; meath
   blent with Soma let him drink :
With bounty and with majesty will he
   further us.

14 I spake to the Bay Coursers' Lord, to
   him who gives ability :
Now hear the son of Aśva as he praises
   thee.

15 Never was any Hero born before thee
   mightier than thou :
None certainly like thee in goodness and
   in wealth.

16 O ministering priest, pour out of the
   sweet juice what gladdens most :
So is the Hero praised who ever prospers
   us.

17 Indra, whom Tawny Coursers bear, praise
   such as thine, preëminent,
None by his power or by his goodness
   hath attained.

18 We, seeking glory, have invoked this
   Master of all power and might
Who must be glorified by constant
   sacrifice.

19 Come, sing we praise to Indra, friends,
   the Hero who deserves the laud,
Him who with none to aid o'ercomes all
   tribes of men.

20 To him who wins the kine, who keeps
   no cattle back, Celestial God,

Speak wondrous speech more sweet than
   butter and than meath.

21 Whose hero powers are measureless, whose
   bounty ne'er may be surpassed,
Whose liberality, like light, is over all.

22 As Vyaśva did, praise Indra, praise the
   Strong unfluctuating Guide,
Who gives the foe's possessions to the
   worshipper.

23 Now, son of Vyaśva, praise thou him
   who to the tenth time still is new,
The very Wise, whom living men must
   glorify

24 Thou knowest, Indra, Thunder-armed,
   how to avoid destructive powers,
As one secure from pitfalls each returning
   day.

25 O Indra, bring that aid wherewith of
   old, Most Wondrous ! thou didst slay
His foes for active Kutsa : send it down
   to us.

26 So now we seek thee fresh in might, Most
   Wonderful in act ! for gain :
For thou art he who conquers all our foes
   for us.

27 Who will set free from ruinous woe, or
   Ārya on the Seven Streams :
O valiant Hero, bend the Dāsa's weapon
   down.

28 As to Varosuṣāman thou broughtest
   great riches, for their gain,
To Vyaśva's sons, Blest Lady, rich in
   ample wealth !

29 Let Nārya's sacrificial meed reach
   Vyaśva's Soma-bearing sons :
In hundreds and in thousands be the
   great reward.

30 If one should ask thee, Where is he who
   sacrificed ? Whither lookest thou ?

23 *Who to the tenth time still is new* : continually
renews his liberality to us. This seems to be the
meaning of the *daśamām ndsam* (tenth new) of the text.
Sāyaṇa explains differently : 'who is the tenth (of the
pervading vital principles), the adorable.'

24 *Destructive powers* : the plural of Nirṛti, Death or
Destruction. I adopt Ludwig's interpretation of the
second line

27 *Ārya on the Seven Streams* : from any Āryan enemy
in the land of the Seven Rivers, probably the Indus,
the five rivers of the Panjāb, and the Kubhā.

28 *Varosuṣāman* : See VIII. 23. 28. *Blest Lady* : Uṣas
or Dawn is addressed.

29 *Nārya's sacrificial meed* : Nārya appears to be
the name of the institutor of the sacrifice.

30 Ludwig observes : 'This stanza clearly refers to
the greatness of the reward given by Nārya, and its
meaning is : here are so many cows (presented by
Nārya) that one might think that, in consequence of
the sacrifice, Vala had given up his cows [which he
had stolen from the Gods, and hidden in a cave],
and taken his departure.' Uṣas says also, 'my cows are
quite superfluous here, and I will drive them away to
some other place.' The stanza is addressed to Uṣas,

9 *Dancer* : of the dance of war. According to
Sāyaṇa, 'dancer, or who causes to dance, *i.e.* agitator,
exciter, Indra's faculty of internal impulse in all
beings.'—Wilson.

14 *Son of Aśva* : *i.e.* of Vyaśva, the Ṛṣi Viśvamanas.

20 *Who keeps no cattle back* : either literally who aids
his worshippers to win cattle in their raids and gives
them all the booty ; or, who sends forth all the kine
or rays of light that he has recovered from the powers
of darkness. According to Sāyaṇa, 'who rejects no
praise.'

Like Vala he hath passed away and
dwelleth now on Gomatī.

HYMN XXV.   *Mitra-Varuṇa.*

1. I WORSHIP you who guard this All, Gods,
holiest among the Gods,
You, faithful to the Law, whose power is
sanctified.

2 So, too, like charioteers are they, Mitra
and sapient Varuṇa,
Sons high-born from of old, whose holy
laws stand fast.

3 These Twain, possessors of all wealth,
most glorious, for supremest sway
Aditi, Mighty Mother, true to Law,
brought forth.

4 Great Varuṇa and Mitra, Gods, Asuras
and imperial Lords,
True to Eternal Law proclaim the high
decree.

5 The offspring of a lofty Power, Dakṣa's
Two Sons exceeding strong,
Who, Lords of flowing rain, dwell in the
place of food.

6 Ye who have gathered up your gifts,
celestial and terrestrial food,
Let your rain come to us fraught with the
mist of heaven.

7 The Twain, who from the lofty sky seem
to look down on herds below,
Holy, imperial Lords, are set to be
revered.

8 They, true to Law, exceeding strong,
have sat them down for sovran rule :
Princes whose laws stand fast, they have
obtained their sway.

9 Pathfinders even better than the eye,
with unobstructed sight,
Even when they close their lids, observant,
they perceive.

10 So may the Goddess Aditi, may the
Nāsatyas guard us well,
The Maruts guard us well, endowed with
mighty strength.

11 Do ye, O Bounteous Gods, protect our
dwelling-place by day and night :
With you for our defenders may we go
unharmed.

12 May we, unharmed, serve bountiful
Viṣṇu, the God who slayeth none :
Self-moving Sindhu hear and be the first
to mark.

13 This sure protection we elect, desirable
and reaching far,
Which Mitra, Varuṇa, and Aryaman
afford.

14 And may the Sindhu of the floods, the
Maruts, and the Aśvin Pair,
Boon Indra, and boon Viṣṇu have one
mind with us.

15 Because these warring Heroes stay the
enmity of every foe,
As the fierce water-flood repels the furious
ones.

16 Here this one God, the Lord of men,
looks forth exceeding far and wide :
And we, for your advantage, keep his
holy laws.

17 We keep the old accustomed laws, the
statutes of supremacy,
The long-known laws of Mitra and of
Varuṇa.

18 He who hath measured with his ray the
boundaries of heaven and earth,
And with his majesty hath filled the two
worlds full,

19 Sūrya hath spread his light aloft up to
the region of the sky,
Like Agni all aflame when gifts are
offered him.

20 With him who sits afar the word is lord
of food that comes from kine,
Controller of the gift of unempoisoned
food.

21 So unto Sūrya, Heaven, and Earth at
morning and at eve I speak.
Bringing enjoyments ever rise thou up for
us.

---

and the second line is the answer she is to give to the
question contained in the first. *Gomati* some affluent of
the Indus, which in later times lent its name to the
Gomatī, or Gumti, which flows through Oudh and falls
into the Ganges.

2 *Charioteers* : furtherers of eternal Law. See VII.
66. 12.

5 *Dakṣa's Two Sons* : or sons of power or energy,
according to Sāyaṇa. Dakṣa as a creative power, is
frequently associated with Aditi. *Place of food* : heaven
from which the food-producing rain comes.

12 *Sindhu* : the Indus. According to Sāyaṇa, Viṣṇu
who causes wealth to flow to his worshippers.

20 Varuṇa has only to command and men have
milk and wholesome food. Sāyaṇa explains differently:
'Raise your voice in the spacious hall of sacrifice to
him who is lord over food derived from cattle.'—Wilson

21 *Thou* : Sūrya, that is, according to Sāyaṇa, Mitra
and Varuṇa in Sūrya's shape.

22 From Ukṣaṇyāyana a bay, from Harayāṇa
   a white steed,
   And from Suṣāman we obtained a harnessed car.

23 These two shall bring me further gain of
   troops of tawny-coloured steeds,
   The carriers shall they be of active men
   of war.

24 And the two sages have I gained who
   hold the reins and bear the whip,
   And the two great strong coursers, with
   my newest song.

HYMN XXVI.   *Aśvins.*

1. I CALL your chariot to receive united praise
   mid princely men,
   Strong Gods who pour down wealth, of
   never vanquished might !

2 Ye to Varosuṣāman come, Nāsatyas, for
   this glorious rite.
   With your protecting aid, Strong Gods,
   who pour down wealth.

3 So with oblations we invoke you, rich in
   ample wealth, to-day,
   When night hath passed, O ye who send
   us plenteous food.

4 O Aśvins, Heroes, let your car, famed,
   best to travel, come to us,
   And, for his glory, mark your zealous
   servant's lauds.

5 Aśvins, who send us precious gifts, even
   when offended, think of him :
   For ye, O Rudras, lead us safe beyond our
   foes.

6 For, Wonder-Workers, with fleet steeds ye
   fly completely round this All,

22 *Suṣāman* : here without *Varo*, the prefix or interjection or whatever it may be. See VIII. 23. 28.

23 *These two* : horses.

24 *Two sages* : *viprā* : the meaning is uncertain.
According to Sāyaṇa the word is an epithet of 'coursers' :
'sagacious.'—Wilson. Ludwig thinks that the grooms
(probably enslaved enemies) are ironically called
sages, or as he translates, Brāhmans. Dr. Muir
translates the stanza differently ; 'I have celebrated at
the same time with a new hymn, these two sages
and mighty [princes], strong, swift, and carrying
whips.' But this rendering has little to recommend it.

1 *Princely men* : the *Sūris* or institutors of the sacrifice.

2 *Varosuṣāman* : See VIII. 23. 28. *Who pour down
wealth* : *vṛṣaṇvasū* ; See IV. 50. 10, note.

5 *Rudras* : bright Gods.

6 *Honey-hued* : *mádhuvarṇā* : 'of fascinating complexion.'—Wilson.

   Stirring our thoughts, ye Lords of splendour, honey-hued.

7 With all-sustaining opulence, Aśvins, come
   hitherward to us,
   Ye rich and noble Heroes, ne'er to be
   o'erthrown.

8 To welcome this mine offering, O ye
   Indra-like Nāsatyas, come
   As Gods of best accord this day with other
   Gods.

9 For we, like Vyaśva, lifting up our voice
   like oxen, call on you :
   With all your loving kindness, Sages, come
   to us.

10 O Ṛṣi, laud the Aśvins well. Will they
   not listen to thy call ?
   Will they not burn the Paṇis who are
   nearer them ?

11 O Heroes, listen to the son of Vyaśva, and
   regard me here,
   Varuṇa, Mitra, Aryaman, of one accord.

12 Gods whom we yearn for, of your gifts, of
   what ye bring to us, bestow
   By princes' hands on me, ye Mighty, day
   by day.

13 Him whom your sacrifices clothe, even
   as a woman with her robe,
   The Aśvins help to glory honouring him
   well.

14 Whoso regards your care of men as succour
   widest in its reach,
   About his dwelling go, ye Aśvins, loving
   us.

15 Come to us ye who pour down wealth,
   come to the home which men must
   guard :
   Like shafts, ye are made meet for sacrifice
   by song.

16 Most fetching of all calls, the laud, as
   envoy, Heroes, called to you :
   Be it your own, O Aśvin Pair.

17 Be ye in yonder sea of heaven, or joying
   in the home of food,
   Listen to me, Immortal Ones.

18 This river with his lucid flow attracts
   you, more than all the streams,—
   Even Sindhu with his path of gold.

19 O Aśvins, with that glorious fame come
   hither, through our brilliant song,

15 *Like shafts* : as arrows are sharpened for their
work, so the Aśvins are prepared for the sacrifice by
the Ṛṣi's hymn. The word *viṣudruhā*, explained by
Sāyaṇa as two arrows, is difficult, and other readings and
explanations have been suggested.

18 *With his lucid flow* : *śvetayāvarī* : taken by
Sāyaṇa as the name of a river.

Come ye whose ways are marked with
light.

20 Harness the steeds who draw the car,
O Vasu, bring the well-fed pair.
O Vāyu, drink thou of our meath : come
unto our drink-offerings.

21 Wonderful Vāyu, Lord of Right, thou
who art Tvaṣṭar's son-in-law,
Thy saving succour we elect.

22 To Tvaṣṭar's son-in-law we pray for
wealth whereof he hath control :
For glory we seek Vāyu, men with juice
effused.

23 From heaven, auspicious Vāyu, come ;
drive hither with thy noble steeds :
Come on thy mighty car with wide-extending seat.

24 We call thee to the homes of men,
thee wealthiest in noble food,
And liberal as a press-stone with a horse's
back.

25 So, glad and joyful in thine heart, do
thou, God, Vāyu, first of all
Vouchsafe us water, strength, and thought.

HYMN XXVII.   *Viśvedevas.*

1. CHIEF Priest is Agni at the laud, as stones
and grass at sacrifice :
With song I seek the Maruts, Brahmaṇaspati, Gods for help much to be desired.

2 I sing to cattle and to Earth, to trees, to
Dawns, to Night, to plants.
O all ye Vasus, ye possessors of all wealth,
be ye the furtherers of our thoughts.

3 Forth go, with Agni, to the Gods our
sacrifice of ancient use,

To the Ādityas, Varuṇa whose Law stands
fast, and the all-lightening Marut troop.

4 Lords of all wealth, may they be strengtheners of man, destroyers of his
enemies.
Lords of all wealth, do ye, with guards
which none may harm, preserve our
dwelling free from foes.

5 Come to us with one mind to-day, come
to us all with one accord,
Maruts with holy song, and, Goddess
Aditi, Mighty One, to our house and
home.

6 Send us delightful things, ye Maruts, on
your steeds : come ye, O Mitra, to our
gifts.
Let Indra, Varuṇa, and the Ādityas sit,
swift Heroes, on our sacred grass.

7 We who have trimmed the grass for you,
and set the banquet in array,
And pressed the Soma, call you, Varuṇa,
like men, with sacrificial fires aflame.

8 O Maruts, Viṣṇu, Aśvins, Pūṣan, haste
away with minds turned hitherward to
me.
Let the Strong Indra, famed as Vṛtra's
slayer, come first with the winners of
the spoil.

9 Ye Guileless Gods, bestow on us a refuge
strong on every side,
A sure protection, Vasus, unassailable from
near at hand or from afar.

10 Kinship have I with you, and close
alliance, O ye Gods, destroyers of our
foes.
Call us to our prosperity of former days,
and soon to new felicity.

11 For now have I sent forth to you, that I
may win a fair reward,
Lords of all wealth, with homage, this my
song of praise like a milch-cow that
faileth not.

12 Excellent Savitar hath mounted up on
high for you, ye sure and careful
Guides.
Bipeds and quadrupeds, with several

21 *Tvaṣṭar's son-in-law* : the Commentators give no
satisfactory explanation. Saraṇyū, Tvaṣṭar's daughter,
was the wife of Vivasvān, who cannot be identified with
Vāyu. See Hillebrandt, *Vedische Mythologie*, I. p. 521.

24 The second line is difficult. The press-stone
which produces the Soma juice which makes the Gods
bountiful is regarded as a type of liberality; it may be
called *áśvapṛṣṭham*, literally, horse-backed, because it
bears its load of Soma stalks like a horse. 'Sharp-backed',
'with sharp ridges', as suggested by Pischel, gives a
a better meaning.

────

1 *Chief Priest* : according to Sāyaṇa, *purohitaḥ* here
is taken in its primary sense of 'placed in front,' that
is, set by the priests on the *uttaravedi* or northern altar
or fire-receptacle. *The laud : ukthá :* a kind of religious
service consisting of the recitation of certain eulogistic
verses.

2 *I sing to :* or I glorify, in order that I may win
or propitiate them.

6 *Come ye, O Mitra* : Varuṇa and Aryaman being
understood.

7 *Like men :* manuṣvát : or after the manner of
Manus.

11 *Like a milch-cow that faileth not* : the meaning
of *ányām* here is somewhat uncertain. Sāyaṇa explains
it by *adṛṣṭapūrvām* unprecedented, and Grassmann by
'a stream that never dries up.' I have adopted Ludwig's
interpretation.

────

hopes and aims, and birds have settled to their tasks.

13 Singing their praise with God-like thought let us invoke each God for grace,
Each God to bring you help, each God to strengthen you.

14 For of one spirit are the Gods with mortal man, co-sharers all of gracious gifts.
May they increase our strength hereafter and to-day, providing ease and ample room.

15 I laud you, O ye Guileless Gods, here where we meet to render praise.
None, Varuṇa and Mitra, harms the mortal man who honours and obeys your laws.

16 He makes his house endure, he gathers plenteous food who pays obedience to your will.
Born in his sons anew he spreads as Law commands, and prospers every way unharmed.

17 E'en without war he gathers wealth, and goes his way on pleasant paths,
Whom Mitra, Varuna and Aryaman protect, sharing the gift, of one accord.

18 E'en on the plain for him ye make a sloping path, an easy way where road is none :
And far away from him the ineffectual shaft must vanish, shot at him in vain.

19 If ye appoint the rite to-day, kind Rulers, when the Sun ascends,
Lords of all wealth, at sunset or at wakingtime, or be it at the noon of day,

20 Or, Asuras, when ye have sheltered the worshipper who goes to sacrifice, at eve,
May we, O Vasus, ye possessors of all wealth, come then into the midst of you.

21 If ye to-day at sunrise, or at noon, or in the gloom of eve,
Lords of all riches, give fair treasure to the man, the wise man who hath sacrificed,

22 Then we, imperial Rulers, claim of you this boon, your wide protection, as a son.
May we, Ādityas, offering holy gifts, obtain that which shall bring us greater bliss.

HYMN XXVIII.   *Viśvedevas.*

1. THE Thirty Gods and Three besides, whose seat hath been the sacred grass,
From time of old have found and gained.

2 Varuṇa, Mitra, Aryaman, Agnis, with Consorts, sending boons,
To whom our Vaṣaṭ ! is addressed :

3 These are our guardians in the west, and northward here, and in the south,
And on the east, with all the tribe.

4 Even as the Gods desire so verily shall it be. None minisheth this power of theirs,
No demon, and no mortal man.

5 The Seven carry seven spears; seven are the splendours they possess,
And seven the glories they assume.

HYMN XXIX   *Viśvedevas.*

1. ONE is a youth brown, active, manifold : he decks the golden one with ornament.

2 Another, luminous, occupies the place of sacrifice, Sage, among the Gods.

3 One brandishes in his hand an iron knife, firm, in his seat amid the Deities.

4 Another holds the thunderbolt, wherewith he slays the Vṛtras, resting in his hand.

5 Another bears a pointed weapon : bright is he, and strong, with healing medicines.

---

1 *Thirty Gods and Three* : See I. 139. 11.

2 *Agnis* : Agni in his various forms and under different names. *With Consorts* : with the Gnās, Celestial Dames, wives of the Gods. *Vaṣaṭ* ! : the exclamation made when the oblation is offered.

4 *No demon and no mortal man* : or no mortal who presents no offerings to the Gods.

5 *The Seven* : the Maruts, seven, or seven times nine, or seven times seven in number. Sāyaṇa mentions the legend of their birth, which will be found in the *Rāmāyaṇa*, Book I., Cantos 46, 47. The meaning is merely that the Maruts carry lances, that is, their lightnings, and are splendidly adorned. See I. 37. The connexion of this stanza with the preceding is not obvious.

---

1 *One* : Soma. 'The yellow Soma juice is itself an ornament to the gold on the finger (Atharvaveda, XVIII. 3. 18, hiraṇyapāvāḥ) of the priest.'—Ludwig. According to others, Soma as the Moon is intended, who 'decorates (himself) with golden ornaments.'—Wilson.

2 *Another, luminous* : Agni.

3 *One brandishes* : Tvaṣṭar, as the Artificer of the Gods.

4 *Another holds the thunderbolt* : Indra.

5 *Another*: Rudra. See I. 43. 4.

6 Another, thief-like, watches well the ways,
and knows the places where the
treasures lie.

7 Another with his mighty stride hath made
his three steps thither where the Gods
rejoice.

8 Two with one Dame ride on with winged
steeds, and journey forth like travellers
on their way.

9 Two, highest, in the heavens have set
their seat, worshipped with holy oil,
Imperial Kings.

10 Some, singing lauds, conceived the Sāma-
hymn, great hymn whereby they caused
the Sun to shine.

HYMN XXX. *Viśvedevas.*

1. NOT one of you, ye Gods, is small, none
of you is a feeble child :
All of you, verily, are great.

2 Thus be ye lauded, ye destroyers of the
foe, ye Three-and-Thirty Deities,
The Gods of man, the Holy Ones.

3 As such defend and succour us, with
benedictions speak to us :
Lead us not from our fathers' and from
Manu's path into the distance far away.

4 Ye Deities who stay with us, and all ye
Gods of all mankind,
Give us your wide protection, give shelter
for cattle and for steed.

HYMN XXXI. *Various Deities.*

1. THAT Brahman pleases Indra well, who
worships, sacrifices, pours Libation, and
prepares the meal.

2 Śakra protects from woe the man who
gives him sacrificial cake.
And offers Soma blent with milk.

3 His chariot shall be glorious, sped by
Gods, and mighty shall he be,
Subduing all hostilities.

4 Each day that passes, in his house flows
his libation, rich in milk,
Exhaustless, bringing progeny.

5 O Gods, with constant draught of milk,
husband and wife with one accord
Press out and wash the Soma juice.

6 They gain sufficient food : they come
united to the sacred grass,
And never do they fail in strength.

7 Never do they deny or seek to hide the
favour of the Gods :
They win high glory for themselves.

8 With sons and daughters by their side
they reach their full extent of life,
Both decked with ornaments of gold.

9 Serving the Immortal One with gifts of
sacrificial meal and wealth,
They satisfy the claims of love and pay
due honour to the Gods.

10 We claim protection from the Hills, we
claim protection of the Floods,
Of him who stands by Viṣṇu's side.

11 May Pūṣan come, and Bhaga, Lord of
wealth, All-bounteous, for our weal :
Broad be the path that leads to bliss :

12 Aramati, and, free from foes, Viśva with
spirit of a God,
And the Ādityas' peerless might.

13 Seeing that Mitra, Aryaman, and Varuṇa
are guarding us,
The paths of Law are fair to tread.

14 I glorify with song, for wealth, Agni the
God, the first of you.

---

6 *Another* : Pūṣan. See I. 42.

7 *Another with his mighty stride* : Viṣṇu. *Thither* :
to his station in the height of heaven.

8 *Two with one Dame* : the Aśvins with Sūryā. See
I. 116. 17.

9 *Two, highest* : Mitra and Varuṇa.

10 *Some, singing lauds* : the Aṅgirases, or, according
to Sāyaṇa, the Atris.

---

2 *Three-and-Thirty Deities* ; See I. 139. 11. *The Gods
of man* : or, God whom Manu worshipped, which
interpretation is supported by stanza 3.

4 *Who stay with us* : or are present at this sacrifice.

---

1 *Brahman* : here any pious worshipper, not one of
the regular professional priests, but the institutor of
sacrifice who during the ceremony may be regarded as
their chief. *Prepares the meal* : paśupuroḍāśādikam pacati:
Sāyaṇa ; 'cooks the cake which is an essential part of
the animal sacrifice, etc.

---

9 *The Immortal One* : amṛtāya : Agni, or the Immortal (host), that is, the Gods in general. According to
Sāyaṇa, 'that they may obtain immortality (in their
sons and descendants).' *They satisfy* : this pāda is
considered by some, on metrical and other grounds, to
be an interpolation. According to Pischel (*Vedische
Studien*, I p. 178), the half-line refers to the beating
and preparation of the rough stalks of the Soma plant.

10 *Of him who stands by Viṣṇu's side* : of Viṣṇu and
his associate Indra.'—Ludwig.

12 *Aramati* : the Genius of Devotion. *Viśva* :
Dyaus ?—Ludwig. 'All the worshippers,' according to
Sāyaṇa.

14 *Who prospereth our fields* : kṣetrasādhasam : Sāyaṇa
explains kṣetra (the modern Hindi khet, a field) as
sacrifice ; 'the bountiful perfecter of the sacrifice.'—
Wilson.

We honour as a well-loved Friend the God who prospereth our fields.

15 As in all frays the hero, so swift moves his car whom Gods attend.
The man who, sacrificing, strives to win the heart of Deities will conquer those who worship not.

16 Ne'er are ye injured, worshipper, presser of juice, or pious man.
The man who, sacrificing, strives to win the heart of Deities will conquer those who worship not.

17 None in his action equals him, none holds him far or keeps him off.
The man who, sacrificing, strives to win the heart of Deities will conquer those who worship not.

18 Such strength of heroes shall be his, such mastery of fleet-foot steeds.
The man who, sacrificing, strives to win the heart of Deities will conquer those who worship not.

HYMN XXXII.   *Indra.*

1. KAṆVAS, tell forth with song the deeds of Indra, the Impetuous,
Wrought in the Soma's wild delight.

2 Strong God, he slew Anarśani, Sṛbinda, Pipru, and the fiend,
Ahīśuva, and loosed the floods.

3. Thou broughtest down the dwelling-place, the height of lofty Arbuda.
That exploit, Indra, must be famed.

4 Bold, to your famous Soma I call the fair-visored God for aid,
Down like a torrent from the hill.

5 Rejoicing in the Soma-draughts, Hero, burst open, like a fort,
The stall of horses and of kine.

6 If my libation gladdens, if thou takest pleasure in my laud,
Come with thy Godhead from afar.

7 O Indra, Lover of the Song, the singers of thy praise are we :
O Soma-drinker, quicken us.

8 And, taking thy delight with us bring us still undiminished food:
Great is thy wealth, O Maghavan.

9 Make thou us rich in herds of kine, in steeds, in gold : let us exert
Our strength in sacrificial gifts.

10 Let us call him to aid whose hands stretch far, to whom high laud is due.
Who worketh well to succour us.

11 He, Śatakratu, even in fight acts as a Vṛtra-slayer still :
He gives his worshippers much wealth.

12 May he, this Śakra, strengthen us, Boon God who satisfies our needs,
Indra, with all his saving helps.

13 To him, the mighty stream of wealth, the Soma-presser's rescuing Friend,
To Indra sing your song of praise ;

14 Who bringeth what is great and firm, who winneth glory in his wars,
Lord of vast wealth through power and might.

15 There liveth none to check or stay his energies and gracious deeds :
None who can say, He giveth not.

16 No debt is due by Brahmans now, by active men who press the juice :
Well hath each Soma-draught been paid.

17 Sing ye to him who must be praised, say lauds to him who must be praised,
Bring prayer to him who must be praised.

18 May he, unchecked, strong, meet for praise, bring hundreds, thousands forth to light,
Indra who aids the worshipper.

19 Go with thy God-like nature forth, go where the folk are calling thee :
Drink, Indra, of the drops we pour.

20 Drink milky draughts which are thine own, this too which was with Tugrya once,
This is it, Indra, that is thine.

21 Pass him who pours libations out in angry mood or after sin :
Here drink the juice we offer thee.

11 *Śatakratu* : Lord of a Hundred Powers.

12 *Śakra* : the Mighty.

16 The Brahmans or worshippers have, by offering libations, discharged their obligations to the Gods, and the Gods have repaid them, or will soon repay them for their offerings.

18 *Hundreds, thousands* : countless treasures for us to enjoy.

20 *Which was with Tugrya* : like that which thy favourite Bhujyu (See Vol. I, Index) formerly offered thee.

1 *The Impetuous* : *ṛjiṣiṇaḥ* : 'the drinker of the stale Soma.'—Wilson.

2 *The fiend* : the Dāsa, or savage. All the names are names of demons of drought of whom Pipru has been mentioned frequently in preceding Books.

3 *Arbuda*: See I. 51. 6; II. 11. 20; 14. 4.

4 *Like a torrent from the hill* : 'as (a traveller invokes) the water from a cloud.'—Wilson.

22 Over the three great distances, past the
   Five Peoples go thy way,
   O Indra, noticing our voice.

23 Send forth thy ray like Sūrya : let my
   songs attract thee hitherward,
   Like waters gathering to the vale.

24 Now to the Hero fair of cheek, Adhvaryu,
   pour the Soma forth :
   Bring of the juice that he may drink :

25 Who cleft the water-cloud in twain, loosed
   rivers for their downward flow,
   And set the ripe milk in the kine.

26 He, meet for praise, slew Vṛtra, slew
   Ahiśuva, Ūrṇavābha's son,
   And pierced through Arbuda with frost.

27 To him your matchless Mighty One,
   unconquerable Conqueror,
   Sing forth the prayer which Gods have
   given :

28 Indra, who in the wild delight of Soma
   juice considers here
   All holy Laws among the Gods.

29 Hither let these thy Bays who share thy
   banquet, Steeds with golden manes,
   Convey thee to the feast prepared.

30 Hither, O thou whom many laud, the
   Bays whom Priyamedha praised,
   Shall bring thee to the Soma-draught.

HYMN XXXIII.   *Indra.*

1. WE compass thee like waters, we whose
   grass is trimmed and Soma pressed.
   Here where the filter pours its stream,
   thy worshippers round thee, O Vṛtra-
   slayer, sit.

2 Men, Vasu ! by the Soma, with lauds
   call thee to the foremost place :
   When comest thou athirst unto the juice
   as home, O Indra, like a bellowing
   bull ?

3 Boldly, Bold Hero, bring us spoil in thousands for the Kaṇvas' sake :
   O active Maghavan, with eager prayer
   we crave the yellow-hued with store of
   kine.

4 Medhyātithi, to Indra sing, drink of the
   juice to make thee glad.
   Close-knit to his Bay Steeds, bolt-armed,
   beside the juice is he : his chariot is of
   gold.

5 He who is praised as strong of hand
   both right and left, most wise and bold :
   Indra who, rich in hundreds, gathers
   thousands up, honoured as breaker-
   down of forts.

6 The bold of heart whom none provokes,
   who stands in bearded confidence;
   Much-lauded, very glorious, overthrowing
   foes, strong Helper, like a bull with
   might.

7 Who knows what vital power he wins,
   drinking beside the flowing juice ?
   This is the fair-cheeked God who, joying
   in the draught, breaks down the castles
   in his strength.

8 As a wild elephant rushes on, this way and
   that way, mad with heat,
   None may compel thee, yet come hither
   to the draught : thou movest mighty
   in thy power.

9 When he, the Mighty, ne'er o'erthrown,
   steadfast, made ready for the fight,
   When Indra Maghavan lists to his praiser's
   call, he will not stand aloof, but come.

10 Yea, verily, thou art a Bull, with a bull's
   rush, whom none may stay :
   Thou, Mighty One, art celebrated as a
   Bull, famed as a Bull both near and far.

---

22 *The three great distances* : the space in front of
thee, behind thee, and at thy side. *Noticing our voice* :
hearing and attending to our invocations. Come to us
who are thy true worshippers, and pass by others who
worship thee in the hope of being avenged upon their
enemies or of obtaining pardon for some sin.

26 *Ūrṇavābha's son* : Aurṇavābha : a demon of
drought. See II. 11. 18. *With frost* : making the piercing cold of winter his weapon.

1 *The filter* : or woollen strainer through which
the Soma juice is run to purify it.

2 *As home* : as familiar to thee as thine own home.

3 *The yellow-hued* : there is no substantive, but gold
must be intended.

6 *In bearded confidence* : a conjectural paraphrase.
Smaśruṣu [in (his) beard] is said by Sāyaṇa to mean
here 'in combats,' that is, perhaps, as Ludwig suggests,
among ranks of men bristling with spears. But this can
hardly be the meaning of the word which 'is probably
an idiomatic expression for the fierce look of a warrior who
challenges the foe.'—Ludwig. So, in the Edda, Thorr,
when about to meet a foe, is said to have 'raised his
beard's voice.' See Grimm, *Teutonic Mythology*, I. 177
(English Translation).

8 *Mad with heat* : that is, *mast*, or as phonetically
spelt, *must*.

10 *Thou art a Bull* : vṛṣā : or strong and mighty.
As has been observed before (VIII. 13. 31, note),
some of the Vedic poets delight in the repetition of
this word and its derivatives.

11 Thy reins are very bulls in strength, bulls'
    strength is in thy golden whip.
    Thy car, O Maghavan, thy Bays are
    strong as bulls : thou, Śatakratu, art a
    Bull.
12 Let the strong presser press for thee.
    Bring hither, thou straight-rushing Bull.
    The mighty makes the mighty run in
    flowing streams for thee whom thy Bay
    Horses bear.
13 Come, thou most potent Indra, come to
    drink the savoury Soma juice.
    Maghavan, very wise, will quickly come
    to hear the songs, the prayer, the hymns
    of praise.
14 When thou hast mounted on thy car let
    thy yoked Bay Steeds carry thee,
    Past other men's libations, Lord of Hun-
    dred Powers, thee, Vṛtra-slayer, thee our
    Friend.
15 O thou Most Lofty One, accept our laud
    as nearest to thine heart.
    May our libations be most sweet to make
    thee glad, O Soma-drinker, Heavenly
    Lord.
16 Neither in thy decree nor mine, but in
    another's he delights,—
    The man who brought us unto this.
17 Indra himself hath said, The mind of
    woman brooks not discipline,
    Her intellect hath little weight.
18 His pair of horses, rushing on in their
    wild transport, draw his car :
    High-lifted is the stallion's yoke.
19 Cast down thine eyes and look not up.
    More closely set thy feet. Let none
    See what thy garment veils, for thou, a
    Brahman, hast become a dame.

HYMN XXXIV.   *Indra.*

1. COME hither, Indra, with thy Bays, come
    thou to Kaṇva's eulogy.
    Ye by command of yonder Dyaus, God
    bright by day ! have gone to heaven.

2 May the stone draw thee as it speaks, the
    Soma-stone with ringing voice.
    Ye by command of yonder Dyaus, etc.
3 The stones' rim shakes the Soma here like
    a wolf worrying a sheep.
    Ye, etc.
4 The Kaṇvas call thee hitherward for
    succour and to win the spoil.
    Ye, etc.
5 I set for thee, as for the Strong, the first
    draught of the juices shed.
6 Come with abundant blessings, come with
    perfect care to succour us.
7 Come, Lord of lofty thought, who hast
    infinite wealth and countless aids.
8 Adorable mid Gods, the Priest good to
    mankind shall bring thee near.
9 As wings the falcon, so thy Bays rushing
    in joy shall carry thee.
10 Come from the enemy to us, to Svāhā !
    and the Soma-draught.
11 Come hither with thine ear inclined to
    hear, take pleasure in our lauds.
12 Lord of well-nourished Horses, come with
    well-fed Steeds alike in hue.
13 Come hither from the mountains, come
    from regions of the sea of air.
14 Disclose to us O Hero, wealth in thousands
    both of kine and steeds.
15 Bring riches hitherward to us in hundreds,
    thousands, myriads.
    Ye by command of yonder Dyaus, God
    bright by day ! have gone to heaven.
16 The thousand steeds, the mightiest troop,
    which we and Indra have received
    From Vasurocis as a gift,
17 The brown that match the wind in speed,
    and bright bay coursers fleet of foot,
    Like Suns, resplendent are they all.

---

11 *Golden whip* : the lightning, with which Indra
lashes the clouds, his horses.

12 *The mighty makes the mighty run* : the priest makes
the Soma juice flow.

16 The last four stanzas of the hymn are not very
intelligible, nor is their connexion with the preceding
verses obvious. Stanzas 16 and 18 appear to be spoken
by a woman and 17 by a man. Stanza 19 is said to be
addressed by Indra to Āsaṅga son of Playoga, who had
been changed to a woman by the imprecation of the
Gods, and who was afterwards restored to manhood.

The Ṛṣi is Nipātithi of the family of Kaṇva, but
stanzas 16—18 are ascribed in the Index to the thousand Vasurociṣas who are said to have been a division
of the family of Aṅgiras.

1 The exact meaning of the second line, which is

the burden of the first fifteen stanzas, is obscure. *Ye*
probably means Indra's horses, and *God bright by day* !
(*divāvaso*) Indra himself ; that is, ye, horses and thou,
Indra, have gone to heaven. The Scholiast offers two
different explanations, in one case boldly altering two
words of the text. See Wilson's Translation, note.

8 *The Priest good to mankind* : or, the Invoking
Priest, Invoker or Herald established by Manu, namely
Agni.

10 *Svāhā* : an exclamation used in sacrifice ; Ave !
or Hail !

16 *Vasurocis* : *vásurociṣaḥ* is probably the ablative
singular, and not the nominative plural, the name
of the institutor of the sacrifice. Wilson, following
Sāyaṇa, translates : 'We, the thousand Vasurociṣas,
and Indra (our leader), when we obtain vigorous herds
of horses,—.'

18 Mid the Pārāvata's rich gifts, swift steeds
    whose wheels run rapidly,
    I seemed to stand amid a wood.

HYMN XXXV.   *Aśvins.*

1. WITH Agni and with Indra, Viṣṇu.
    Varuṇa, with the Ādityas, Rudras,
    Vasus, closely leagued ;
    Accordant, of one mind with Sūrya and
    with Dawn, O Aśvins, drink the Soma
    juice.

2 With all the Holy Thoughts, all being,
    Mighty Ones ! in close alliance with
    the Mountains, Heaven, and Earth ;
    Accordant. of one mind with Sūrya and
    with Dawn, O Aśvins, drink the Soma
    juice.

3 With all the Deities, three times eleven,
    here, in close alliance with the Maruts,
    Bhṛgus, Floods ;
    Accordant, of one mind with Sūrya and
    with Dawn, O Aśvins, drink the Soma
    juice.

4 Accept the sacrifice, attend to this my
    call : come nigh, O ye Twain Gods, to
    all libations here.
    Accordant, of one mind with Sūrya and
    with Dawn, O Aśvins, bring us streng-
    thening food.

5 Accept our praise-song as a youth accepts
    a maid. Come nigh, O ye Twain Gods,
    to all libations here.
    Accordant, of one mind with Sūrya and
    with Dawn, O Aśvins, bring us streng-
    thening food.

6 Accept the songs we sing, accept the
    solemn rite. Come nigh, O ye Twain
    Gods, to all libations here.

    Accordant, of one mind with Sūrya and
    with Dawn, O Aśvins, bring us streng-
    thening food.

7 Ye fly as starlings fly unto the forest
    trees ; like buffaloes ye seek the Soma
    we have shed.
    Accordant, of one mind with Sūrya and
    with Dawn, come thrice, O Aśvins, to
    our home.

8 Ye fly like swans, like those who travel on
    their way ; like buffaloes ye seek the
    Soma we have shed.
    Accordant, of one mind with Sūrya and
    with Dawn, come thrice, O Aśvins, to
    our home.

9 Ye fly to our oblation like a pair of
    hawks ; like buffaloes ye seek the Soma
    we have shed.
    Accordant, of one mind with Sūrya and
    with Dawn, come thrice, O Aśvins, to
    our home.

10 Come hitherward and drink and satisfy
    yourselves, bestow upon us progeny and
    affluence.
    Accordant, of one mind with Sūrya and
    with Dawn, O Aśvins, grant us vigorous
    strength.

11 Conquer your foes, protect us, praise
    your worshippers ; bestow upon us
    progeny and affluence.
    Accordant, of one mind with Sūrya and
    with Dawn, O Aśvins, grant us vigorous
    strength.

12 Slay enemies, animate men whom ye
    befriend ; bestow upon us progeny and
    affluence.
    Accordant, of one mind with Sūrya and
    with Dawn, O Aśvins, grant us vigorous
    strength.

13 With Mitra, Varuṇa, Dharma, and the
    Maruts in your company approach unto
    your praiser's call.
    Accordant, of one mind with Sūrya and
    with Dawn, and with the Ādityas,
    Aśvins ! come.

14 With Viṣṇu and the Angirases attending
    you, and with the Maruts come unto
    your praiser's call.
    Accordant, of one mind with Sūrya and
    with Dawn, and with the Ādityas,
    Aśvins ! come.

15 With Ṛbhus and with Vājas. O ye
    Mighty Ones, leagued with the Maruts
    come ye to your praiser's call.
    Accordant, of one mind with Sūrya and
    with Dawn, and with the Ādityas,
    Aśvins ! come.

16 Give spirit to our prayer and animate our
    thoughts; slay ye the Rākṣasas and
    drive away disease.

---

18 *The Pārāvata* : is Vasurocis. The Pārāvatas
are probably the Paruētai of Ptolemy, who were settled
northwards of Arachosia.—Ludwig.

---

5 *A youth* : literally two youths. 'As youths are
delighted (by the voices of maidens).'—Wilson.

---

8 Ye come eagerly to the Soma as thirsty *haṁsas*
(swans, geese, or flamingoes) travellers, and buffaloes
hasten to the water.

13 *Dharma* : Right , Justice, Law, Virtue or Duty
personified.

Accordant, of one mind with Sūrya and with Dawn, the presser's Soma, Aśvins ! drink.

17 Strengthen the Ruling Power, strengthen the men of war; slay ye the Rākṣasas and drive away disease.
Accordant, of one mind with Sūrya and with Dawn, the presser's Soma, Aśvins ! drink.

18 Give strength unto the milch-kine, give the people strength, slay ye the Rākṣasas and drive away disease.
Accordant, of one mind with Sūrya and with Dawn, the presser's Soma, Aśvins ! drink.

19 As ye heard Atri's earliest eulogy, so hear Śyāvāśva, Soma-presser, ye who reel in joy.
Accordant, of one mind with Sūrya and with Dawn, drink juice, O Aśvins, three days old.

20 Further like running streams Śyāvāśva's eulogies who presses out the Soma, ye who reel in joy.
Accordant, of one mind with Sūrya and with Dawn, drink juice, O Aśvins, three days old.

21 Seize, as ye grasp the reins, Śyāvāśva's solemn rites who presses out the Soma, ye who reel in joy.
Accordant, of one mind with Sūrya and with Dawn, drink juice, O Aśvins, three days old.

22 Drive down your chariot hitherward : drink ye the Soma's savoury juice.
Approach, ye Aśvins, come to us : I call you, eager for your aid. Grant treasures to the worshipper.

23 When sacrifice which tells our reverence hath begun. Heroes ! to drink the gushing juice,
Approach, ye Aśvins, come to us : I call you, eager for your aid. Grant treasures to the worshipper.

24 Sate you with consecrated drink, with juice effused, ye Deities.

17 *The Ruling Power* : kṣatrám : hence *Kṣatriya*, a man of the princely or military order.

18 *The people* : viśas : hence *Vaiśya*, a man of the mercantile class or order.

19 *Atri's* : as he was the progenitor of the Ṛṣi of the Hymn. See Vol. I., Index.

21 *Solemn rites* : that is, the oblations presented thereat.

24 *Consecrated drink* : libations offered with the sacrificial exclamation Svāhā ! Ave ! or Hail !

Approach, ye Aśvins, come to us : I call you, eager for your aid. Grant treasures to the worshipper.

HYMN XXXVI.   *Indra.*

1. Thou helpest him whose grass is trimmed, who sheds the juice, O Śatakratu, drink Soma to make thee glad.
The share which they have fixed for thee, thou, Indra, Victor o'er all hosts and space, begirt with Maruts, Lord of Heroes, winner of the floods.

2 Maghavan, help thy worshipper : let him help thee. O Śatakratu, drink Soma to make thee glad.
The share which they have fixed for thee, etc.

3 Thou aidest Gods with food, and that with might aids thee,
O Śatakratu, drink Soma to make thee glad.

4 Creator of the heaven, creator of the earth, O Śatakratu, drink Soma to make thee glad.

5 Father of cattle, father of all steeds art thou. O Śatakratu, drink Soma to make thee glad.

6 Stone-hurler, glorify the Atris' hymn of praise. O Śatakratu, drink Soma to make thee glad.

7 Hear thou Śyāvāśva while he pours to thee, as erst thou heardest Atri when he wrought his holy rites.
Indra, thou only gavest Trasadasyu aid in the fierce fight with heroes, strengthening his prayers.

HYMN XXXVII.   *Indra.*

1. This prayer, and those who shed the juice, in wars with Vṛtra thou holpest, Indra, Lord of Strength, with all thy succours.
O Vṛtra-slayer, from libation poured at

1 *Which they have fixed* : which all the Gods have assigned. This half-verse is the refrain of stanzas 1—6. *And space, begirt* : or, and wide space, girt. *The floods* : the waters of heaven, the rain.

2 *Let him help thee* : according to Sāyaṇa, 'protect thyself (by drinking the Soma).' 'The mutual relation between the God and his worshipper is expressed, and the translation 'help thyself' is ridiculous.'—Ludwig.

3 *Food* : sacrificial food. *That* : food, especially in the shape of Soma.

7 *Trasadasyu* : an especial favourite of Indra and the Aśvins, celebrated for his victories and liberality. See Index.

1 *O Vṛtra-slayer, etc.* : this half-verse is repeated as a refrain in the five following stanzas.

noon, drink of the Soma juice, thou blameless Thunderer.

2 Thou mighty Conqueror of hostile armaments, O Indra, Lord of Strength, with all thy saving help.

3 Sole Ruler, thou art Sovran of this world of life, O Indra, Lord of Strength, with all thy saving help.

4 Thou only sunderest these two consistent worlds, O Indra, Lord of Strength, with all thy saving help.

5 Thou art the Lord supreme o'er rest and energy, O Indra, Lord of Strength, with all thy saving help.

6 Thou helpest one to power, and one thou hast not helped, O Indra, Lord of Strength, with all thy saving aid.

7 Hear thou Śyāvāśva while he sings to thee, as erst thou heardest Atri when he wrought his holy rites.
Indra, thou only gavest Trasadasyu aid in the fierce fight with heroes, strengthening his powers.

HYMN XXXVIII.   *Indra-Agni.*

1. Ye Twain are Priests of sacrifice, winners in war and holy works :
Indra and Agni, mark this well.

2 Ye bounteous riders on the car, ye Vṛtra-slayers unsubdued :
Indra and Agni, mark this well.

3 The men with pressing-stones have pressed this meath of yours which gives delight:
Indra and Agni, mark this well.

4 Accept our sacrifice for weal, sharers of praise! the Soma shed :
Indra and Agni, Heroes, come.

5 Be pleased with these libations which attract you to our sacred gifts :
Indra and Agni, Heroes, come.

6 Accept this eulogy of mine whose model is the Gāyatrī : Indra and Agni, Heroes, come.

7 Come with the early-faring Gods, ye who are Lords of genuine wealth :
Indra-Agni, to the Soma-draught !

8 Hear ye the call of Atris, hear Śyāvāśva as he sheds the juice :
Indra-Agni to the Soma-draught !

9 Thus have I called you to our aid as sages called on you of old :
Indra-Agni to the Soma draught !

10 Indra's and Agni's grace I claim, Sarasvatī's associates
To whom this psalm of praise is sung.

HYMN XXXIX.   *Agni.*

1. The glorious Agni have I praised, and worshipped with the sacred food.
May Agni deck the Gods for us. Between both gathering-places he goes on his embassy, the Sage. May all the others die away.

2 Agni, burn down the word within their bodies through our newest speech,
All hatreds of the godless, all the wicked man's malignities. Away let the destroyers go. May all the others die away.

3 Agni, I offer hymns to thee, like holy oil within thy mouth.
Acknowledge them among the Gods, for thou art the most excellent, the worshipper's blissful messenger. Let all the others die away.

4 Agni bestows all vital power even as each man supplicates.
He brings the Vasus strengthening gifts, and grants delight, in rest and stir, for every calling on the Gods. Let all the others die away.

---

4 *Consistent worlds* : there is no substantive in the text, and *lokau* (worlds) is supplied by Sāyaṇa.

5 *Rest and energy* : or peace and war. 'Prosperity and gains.'—Wilson.

6 *To power*: *kṣatrāya* : the rule exercised by princes.

7 Repeated from the preceding hymn with the alteration of two words—*rebhataḥ,* singing, instead of *sunvatāḥ,* pouring (libations), and *kṣatrāṇi* (princely) powers instead of *brāhmaṇi,* prayers, 'as if,' observes Dr. Muir, 'the former (*brahmāṇi,*) contained a reference to the functions of the priest, and the latter to those of the prince.'— *O.S. Texts,* I. 263.

---

1 *Mark this well* : 'hear (the praise) of this (thy worshipper).'—Wilson.

2 *Bounteous*: *tośāsā* : according to Sāyaṇa, 'destroyers of foes.'

---

6 *Whose model is the Gāyatrī* : composed in Gāyatrī metre.

7 *Early-faring Gods* : 'But Thou wast up at break of day.'—George Herbert.

10 *Sarasvatī's associates* : according to Sāyaṇa, 'to whom praise belongs.'

---

1 *Deck the Gods for us* : 'brighten the gods with the oblations at our sacrifice.'—Wilson. Both *gathering-places* : heaven and earth. *All the others* : *anyaké same* : meaning, according to Sāyaṇa, all our enemies.

2 *All hatreds of the godless* : *arātīr arāvṇām* must be read instead of *arāti rarāvṇām.*—Ludwig.

5 Agni hath made himself renowned by
   wonderful victorious act.
   He is the Priest of all the tribes, chosen
   with sacrificial meeds. He urges Deities
   to receive. Let all the others die away.

6 Agni knows all that springs from Gods, he
   knows the mystery of men.
   Giver of wealth is Agni, he uncloses both
   the doors to us when worshipped with
   our newest gift. Let all the others die
   away.

7 Agni inhabiteth with Gods and men who
   offer sacrifice.
   He cherisheth with great delight much
   wisdom, as all things that be, God among
   Gods adorable. May all the others die
   away.

8 Agni who liveth in all streams, Lord of
   the Sevenfold Race of men,
   Him dweller in three homes we seek,
   best slayer of the Dasyus for Mandhātar,
   first in sacrifice. Let all the others die
   away.

9 Agni the Wise inhabiteth three gathering-
   places, triply formed.
   Decked as our envoy let the Sage bring
   hither and conciliate the Thrice Eleven
   Deities. Let all the others die away.

10 Our Agni, thou art first among the Gods,
   and first mid living men.
   Thou only rulest over wealth. Round
   about thee, as natural dams, circumfluous
   the waters run. Let all the others die
   away.

HYMN XL.   *Indra-Agni.*

1. INDRA and Agni, surely ye as Conquerors
   will give us wealth,
   Whereby in fight we may o'ercome that
   which is strong and firmly fixed, as

Agni burns the woods with wind. Let
all the others die away.

2 We set no snares to tangle you; Indra we
   worship and adore, Hero of heroes
   mightiest.
   Once may he come unto us with his Steed,
   come unto us to win us strength, and
   to complete the sacrifice.

3 For, famous Indra-Agni, ye are dwellers in
   the midst of frays.
   Sages in wisdom, ye are knit to him who
   seeketh you as friends. Heroes, bestow
   on him his wish.

4 Nabhāka-like, with sacred song Indra's
   and Agni's praise I sing,
   Theirs to whom all this world belongs,
   this heaven and this mighty earth which
   bear rich treasure in their lap.

5 To Indra and to Agni send your prayers,
   as was Nabhāka's wont,—
   Who oped with sideway opening the sea
   with its foundations seven—Indra all
   powerful in his might.

6 Tear thou asunder, as of old, like tangles
   of a creeping plant,
   Demolish thou the Dāsa's might. May we
   with Indra's help divide the treasure he
   hath gathered up.

7 What time with this same song these men
   call Indra-Agni sundry ways,
   May we with our own heroes quell those
   who provoke us to the fight, and conquer
   those who strive with us.

8 The Two refulgent with their beams rise
   and come downward from the sky.
   By Indra's and by Agni's hest, flowing
   away, the rivers run which they released
   from their restraint.

9 O Indra, many are thine aids, many thy
   ways of guiding us,

5 *With sacrificial meeds* : *dákṣiṇābhiḥ* : his *dakṣiṇās*
or honoraria as Priest are the oblations which he receives as a God.

6 *That springs from Gods*: 'the past and the present,
while *the mystery of men* is the future.'—Ludwig. *Both
the doors* : of wealth, or, perhaps of heaven also.

8 *Lord of the Sevenfold Race of men* : perhaps meaning, God of all men, like Vaiśvānara ; or the reference
may be to the seven priests : 'Who is ministered to by
seven priests.'—Wilson. 'Acting as seven priests.'—M.
Müller. Mandhātar : said to be the same as Māndhātar,
son of Yuvanāśva, and Ṛṣi of X. 134.

9 *Three gathering-places* : heaven, firmament, and
earth.

10 *Round about thee the waters run* : Cf. 'Him, pure,
resplendent, Offspring of the Waters, the waters pure
have on all sides encompassed.' (II. 35. 3).

1 *Let all the others die away* : this refrain recurs in
all stanzas of the hymn except the final.

2 *Once* : *kaddcit*: expressive of impatience.—Ludwig.

4 *Nabhāka-like* : Nabhāka may have been the
father of Nabhāka the Ṛṣi of the hymn.

5 *Who oped*: 'who overspread (with their lustre).'—
Wilson. The Commentator does not explain the
passage.

7 *This same song* : a hymn like our own, for victory
in battle.

8 *The Two refulgent with their beams* : apparently the
Sun and Moon. According to Sāyaṇa, Indra and Agni
are intended.

Lord of the Bay Steeds, Hinva's Son. To
a Good Hero come our prayers, which
soon shall have accomplishment.

10 Inspire him with your holy hymns, the
Hero bright and glorious,
Him who with might demolisheth even
the brood of Śuṣṇa, and winneth for us
the heavenly streams.

11 Inspire him worshipped with fair rites,'
the glorious Hero truly brave.
He brake in pieces Śuṣṇa's brood who still
expected not the stroke, and won for us
the heavenly streams. Let all the others
die away.

12 Thus have we sung anew to Indra-Agni,
as sang our sires, Aṅgirases, and
Mandhātar.
Guard us with triple shelter and preserve
us : may we be masters of a store of
riches.

HYMN XLI.   *Varuṇa.*

1. To make this Varuṇa come forth, sing
thou a song unto the band of Maruts
wiser than thyself,—
This Varuṇa who guardeth well the
thoughts of men like herds of kine.
Let all the others die away.

2 Him altogether praise I with the song and
hymns our fathers sang, and with
Nābhāka's eulogies,—
Him dwelling at the rivers' source, surrounded by his Sisters Seven.

3 The nights he hath encompassed, and
stablished the morns with magic art :
visible over all is he.
His dear Ones, following his Law, have
prospered the Three Dawns for him.

4 He, visible o'er all the earth, stablished
the quarters of the sky :

He measured out the eastern place, that
is the fold of Varuṇa : like a strong
herdsman is the God.

5 He who supports the worlds of life, he who
well knows the hidden names mysterious
of the morning beams,
He cherishes much wisdom, Sage, as heaven
brings forth each varied form.

6 In whom all wisdom centres,— as the nave
is set within the wheel.
Haste ye to honour Trita, as kine haste
to gather in the fold, even as they
muster steeds to yoke.

7 He wraps these regions as a robe; he
contemplates the tribes of Gods and all
the works of mortal men.
Before the home of Varuṇa all the Gods
follow his decree.

8 He is an Ocean far-removed, yet through
the heaven to him ascends the worship
which these realms possess.
With his bright foot he overthrew their
magic, and went up to heaven.

9 Ruler, whose bright far-seeing rays, pervading all three earths, have filled the
three superior realms of heaven.
Firm is the seat of Varuṇa : over the
Seven he rules as King.

10 Who, after his decree, o'erspread the
Dark Ones with a robe of light;
Who measured out the ancient seat, who

9 *Hinva's Son*: Hinva (the driver, impeller, instigator
of actions), a father invented for Indra by the poet.
To a Good Hero : to Indra. 'The meaning of the verse,
even with the help of the scholiast, is far from intelligible.'—Wilson.

1 *To make this Varuṇa come forth* : Sāyaṇa explains
prábhūtaye as an adjective=*prakṛṣṭadhanáya* : 'to that
opulent Varuṇa.'—Wilson. *Wiser* : more skilled in
singing. *The thoughts* : holy thoughts and devotions.
The refrain, Let all, etc., recurs at the end of every
stanza.

2 *Nābhāka's* : that is, mine own. *Sisters Seven* : the
five rivers of the Panjab, the Indus and perhaps the
Kubhâ. See 1. 32, note.

3 *His dear Ones* : apparently the nights, which give
place to the mornings. *Three Dawns* : according to
Sāyaṇa, morning. noon, and evening.

4 *The fold* : or, perhaps, the course, meaning the
place from which he starts.

6 *Trita* : Varuṇa, here, apparently, identified with
this ancient God who represents the expanse of heaven.
According to Sāyaṇa, (Varuṇa) 'who abides in the
three worlds.'

7 This stanza is very obscure, and my rendering is
conjectural. The commentary is defective, and von Roth
and Ludwig think that the correctness of one word in
the text is doubtful. According to the slight alteration
suggested by the latter scholar, 'under the lead' would
stand instead of 'before the home.'

8 The first line of this stanza also is difficult.
Wilson, following Sāyaṇa, translates : 'He is the hidden
ocean ; swift he mounts (the heaven) as (the sun) the
sky ; when he has placed the sacrifice in those (regions
of the firmament).' Ludwig's interpretation, which I
follow, requires *tiráh* to be read instead of *turáh* (swift).
Their magic : the magical arts of the fiends of darkness.

9 *Firm* : So Hesiod (Theog. V. 127) calls Ouranos =
Varuṇa the firm seat of the Gods. See M. Müller,
Chips from a German Workshop, IV. xx (new edition).
The Seven : rivers, understood.

10 *The Dark Ones* : the nights, which Varuṇa
turns into days. But see *Chips*, IV. xxii. *The Unborn* :
the primeval, everlasting, uncreated Divine Being.
According to Sāyaṇa, the Sun.

pillared both the worlds apart as the Unborn supported heaven. Let all the others die away.

HYMN XLII.   *Varuṇa.*

1. LORD of all wealth, the Asura propped the heavens, and measured out the broad earth's wide expanses.
He, King supreme, approached all living creatures. All these are Varuṇa's holy operations.

2 So humbly worship Varuṇa the Mighty : revere the wise Guard of World Immortal.
May he vouchsafe us triply-barred protection. O Earth and Heaven, within your lap preserve us.

3 Sharpen this song of him who strives his utmost, sharpen, God Varuṇa, his strength and insight;
May we ascend the ship that bears us safely, whereby we may pass over all misfortune.

4 Aśvins, with songs the singer stones have made you hasten hitherward,
Nāsatyas, to the Soma-draught. Let all the others die away.

5 As the sage Atri with his hymns, O Aśvins, called you eagerly,
Nāsatyas, to the Soma-draught. Let all the others die away.

6 So have I called you to our aid, even as the wise have called of old,
Nāsatyas, to the Soma-draught. Let all the others die away.

HYMN XLIII.   *Agni.*

1. THESE songs of mine go forth as lauds of Agni, the disposing Sage,
Whose worshipper is ne'er o'erthrown.

2 Wise Agni Jātavedas, I beget a song of praise for thee.
Who willingly receivest it.

3 Thy sharpened flames, O Agni, like the gleams of light that glitter through,
Devour the forests with their teeth.

4 Gold-coloured, bannered with the smoke, urged by the wind, aloft to heaven
Rise, lightly borne, the flames of fire.

5 These lightly kindled fiery flames are all around made visible,
Even as the gleamings of the Dawns.

6 As Jātavedas speeds along, the dust is black beneath his feet,
When Agni spreads upon the earth.

7 Making the plants his nourishment, Agni devours and wearies not,
Seeking the tender shrubs again.

8 Bending him down with all his tongues, he flickers with his fiery glow :
Splendid is Agni in the woods.

9 Agni, thine home is in the floods : into the plants thou forcest way,
And as their Child art born anew.

10 Worshipped with offerings shines thy flame, O Agni, from the sacred oil,
With kisses on the ladle's mouth.

11 Let us serve Agni with our hymns, Disposer, fed on ox and cow,
Who bears the Soma on his back.

12 Yea, thee, O Agni, do we seek with homage and with fuel, Priest
Whose wisdom is most excellent.

13 O worshipped with oblations, pure Agni, we call on thee as erst,
Did Bhṛgu, Manus, Aṅgiras.

14 For thou, O Agni, by the fire, Sage by the Sage, Good by the Good,
Friend by the Friend, art lighted up.

15 So wealth in thousands, food with store of heroes give thou to the sage,
O Agni, to the worshipper.

16 O Agni, Brother, made by strength, Lord of red steeds and brilliant sway,
Take pleasure in this laud of mine.

17 My praises, Agni, go to thee, as the cows seek the stall to meet,
The lowing calf that longs for milk.

---

1 *The Asura :* the High God, Varuṇa. 'The wise spirit.'—M. Müller.

2 *Of the World Immortal :* *amṛtasya :* according to Sāyaṇa, of amrita or ambrosia.

3 *The ship :* a metaphorical expression for hymn and sacrifice. Cf. I. 46. 7; 140. 12; IX. 89. 2; X. 44. 6; 63. 10; 101. 2; 105. 9.

11 *Fed on ox and cow :* 'the eater of the ox, the eater of the marrow.'—Wilson. *Who bears the Soma on his back :* *sómapṛṣṭāya :* 'on whose back the libation is poured.'—Wilson.

14 Sāyaṇa refers to the *Aitareya Brāhmaṇa,* I. 16, 'which describes how the fire produced by friction from the two *araṇis* [fire-sticks] is thrown into the Āhavanīya fire, in the Atithyeṣṭi ceremony. "In the verse *tvam hyagne* [For thou, O Agni] etc., the one *vipra* (a sage) means one Agni, the other *vipra* the other Agni ; the one *san* (being, existing) means the one, the other *san* (in *satā*) the other Agni.' (Haug's trans.).—Note by E. B. C. in Wilson's Translation. *Sán* and *satá* may also mean 'good.'

16 *Made by strength :* produced by violent agitation of the fire-stick.

18 Agni, best Aṅgiras, to thee all people
   who have pleasant homes,
   Apart, have turned as to their wish.

19 The sages skilled in holy song and thinkers with their thoughts have urged
   Agni to share the sacred feast.

20 So, Agni, unto thee the Priest, Invoker,
   strong in forays, pray
   Those who spin out the sacrifice.

21 In many a place, the same in look art
   thou, a Prince o'er all the tribes :
   In battles we invoke thine aid.

22 Pray thou to Agni, pray to him who
   blazes served with sacred oil :
   Let him give ear to this our call.

23 We call on thee as such, as one who
   hears, as Jātavedas, one,
   Agni ! who beats away our foes.

24 I pray to Agni, King of men, the Wonderful, the President
   Of holy Laws : may he give ear.

25 Him like a bridegroom, him who stirs all
   people, like a noble horse,
   Like a fleet steed, we instigate.

26 Slaying things deadly, burning up foes,
   Rākṣasas, on every side,
   Shine, Agni, with thy sharpened flame.

27 Thou whom the people kindle even as
   Manus did, best Aṅgiras !
   O Agni, mark thou this my speech.

28 O Agni, made by strength ! be thou
   born in the heavens or born in floods,
   As such we call on thee with songs.

29 Yea, all the people, all the folk who have
   good dwellings, each apart,
   Send food for thee to eat thereof.

30 O Agni, so may we, devout, gazed at by
   men, throughout our days,
   Pass lightly over all distress.

31 We venerate with cheerful hearts the
   cheerful Agni, dear to all,
   Burning, with purifying flame.

32 So thou, O Agni rich in light, beaming
   like Sūrya with thy rays
   Boldly demolishest the gloom.

33 We pray to thee for this thy gift, Victor !
   the gift that faileth not,
   O Agni, choicest wealth from thee.

HYMN XLIV.   *Agni.*

1. PAY service unto Agni with your fuel, rouse
   your Guest with oil :
   In him present your offerings.

2 Agni, do thou accept my laud, be magnified by this my song :
   Welcome my sweetly-spoken words.

3 Agni, envoy, I place in front ; the oblation-bearer I address :
   Here let him seat the Deities.

4 Agni, the lofty flames of thee enkindled
   have gone up on high,
   Thy bright flames, thou Refulgent One.

5 Beloved ! let my ladles full of sacred oil
   come near to thee :
   Agni, accept our offerings.

6 I worship Agni—may he hear !—the
   cheerful, the Invoker, Priest,
   Of varied splendour, rich in light.

7 Ancient Invoker, meet for praise, beloved
   Agni, wise and strong,
   The visitant of solemn rites.

8 Agni, best Aṅgiras, accept straightway
   these offerings, and guide
   The seasonable sacrifice.

9 Excellent God, with brilliant flames,
   enkindled bring thou hitherward,
   Knowing the way, the Heavenly Host.

10 Him, Sage and Herald, void of guile,
   ensign of sacrifices, him
   Smoke-bannered, rich in light, we seek.

11 O Agni, be our Guardian thou, God,
   against those who injure us :
   Destroy our foes, thou Son of Strength.

12 Making his body beautiful, Agni the Sage
   hath waxen by
   The singer and his ancient hymn.

13 I invocate the Child of Strength, Agni
   with purifying flame,
   At this well-ordered sacrifice.

14 So Agni, rich in many friends, with fiery
   splendour, seat thyself
   With Gods upon our sacred grass.

15 The mortal man who serves the God Agni
   within his own abode,
   For him he causes wealth to shine.

16 Agni is head and height of heaven, the
   Master of the earth is he :

---

28 *In the heavens* : as the Sun. *In floods* : in the
waters of the firmament as lightning.

30 *Gazed at by men* : objects of their admiration.
'Beholding men.'—Wilson. 'Living (among men).'—
St. Petersburg Lexicon.

---

14 *Rich in many friends* : 'thou who hast Mitra's
splendour.'—Ludwig.

15 *For him he causes wealth to shine* : or, 'To him he
shines forth opulence.' 'To him he gives riches.'—
Wilson.

He quickeneth the waters' seed.

17 Upward, O Agni, rise thy flames, pure
and resplendent, blazing high,
Thy lustres, fair effulgences.

18 For, Agni, thou as Lord of Light rulest
o'er choicest gifts : may I,
Thy singer, find defence in thee.

19 O Agni, they who understand stir thee
to action with their thoughts :
So let our songs enhance thy might.

20 We ever claim the friendship of Agni,
the singing messenger,
Of God-like nature, void of guile.

21 Agni who bears most holy sway, the holy
Singer, holy Sage,
Shines holy when we worship him.

22 Yea, let my meditations, let my songs exalt
thee evermore.
Think, Agni, of our friendly bond,

23 If I were thou and thou wert I, O Agni,
every prayer of thine
Should have its due fulfilment here.

24 For Excellent and Lord of wealth art thou
O Agni, rich in light :
May we enjoy thy favouring grace.

25 Agni, to thee whose laws stand fast our
resonant songs of praise speed forth,
As rivers hasten to the sea.

26 Agni, the Youthful Lord of men, who
stirreth much and eateth all,
The Sage, I glorify with hymns.

27 To Agni let us haste with lauds, the
Guide of sacrificial rites,
Armed with sharp teeth, the Mighty
One.

28 And let this man, good Agni, be with
thee the singer of thy praise :
Be gracious, Holy One, to him.

29 For thou art sharer of our feast, wise,
ever watchful as a Sage :
Agni, thou shinest in the sky.

30 O Agni, Sage, before our foes, before
misfortunes fall on us,
Excellent Lord, prolong our lives.

16 *The waters' seed* : as lightning, he impregnates
the waters of the air.

26 *Eateth all* : consumes the entire oblation.—
Sāyaṇa. But the meaning is probably general.

28 *This man* : the Ṛṣi or singer himself.

29 *In the sky* : or, up to heaven.

———

HYMN XLV. *Indra*

1 HITHERWARD ! they who light flame and
straightway trim the sacred grass,
Whose Friend is Indra ever young.

2 High is their fuel, great their laud, wide
is their splinter from the stake,
Whose Friend is Indra ever young.

3 Unequelled in fight the hero leads his
army with the warrior chiefs.
Whose Friend is Indra ever young.

4 The new-born Vṛtra-slayer asked his
Mother, as he seized his shaft,
Who are the fierce? Who are renowned ?

5 Śavasī answered, He who seeks thine
enmity will battle like
A stately elephant on a hill.

6 And hear, O Maghavan ; to him who
craves of thee thou grantest all :
Whate'er thou makest firm is firm.

7 What time the Warrior Indra goes to
battle, borne by noble steeds,
Best of all charioteers is he.

8 Repel, O Thunder-armed, in all directions
all attacks on us :
And be our own most glorious God.

9 May Indra set our car in front, in foremost place to win the spoil,
He whom the wicked injure not.

10 Thine enmity may we escape, and, Śakra,
for thy bounty, rich
In kine, may we come near to thee ;

11 Softly approaching, Thunder-armed !
wealthy by hundreds, rich in steeds,
Unrivalled, ready with our gifts.

12 For thine exalted excellence gives to thy
worshippers each day
Hundreds and thousands of thy boons.

13 Indra, we know thee breaker-down even of
strong forts, winner of spoil,
As one who conquers wealth for us.

14 Though thou art highest, Sage and Bold !
let the drops cheer thee when we come

2 *Splinter* : the first shaving, splinter, or strip of
wood, cut from the *yūpa* or sacrificial post, and used
in the sacrifice.

4 As soon as he was born Indra showed his warlike
disposition, and asked what worthy opponents he should
have.

5 *Śavasī*, or, the Strong Dame ; his mother Aditi.
A stately elephant : I follow Sāyaṇa who explains *dṛṣaḥ*
as *darśaniyo gajaḥ*, a beautiful elephant, although in
other places the word seems to mean beauty (I. 124 7),
and forehead (V. 80. 6). The allusion is to the size
and strength of Vṛtra, Indra's future antagonist.

To thee as to a trafficker.

15 Bring unto us the treasure of the opulent
man who, loth to give,
Hath slighted thee for gain of wealth.

16 Indra, these friends of ours, supplied with
Soma, wait and look to thee,
As men with fodder to the herd.

17 And thee who art not deaf, whose ears
are quick to listen, for our aid,
We call to us from far away.

18 When thou hast listened, make our call
one which thou never wilt forget,
And be our very nearest Friend.

19 When even now, when we have been in
trouble, we have thought of thee,
O Indra, give us gifts of kine.

20 O Lord of Strength, we rest on thee, as
old men rest upon a staff :
We long to have thee dwell with us.

21 To Indra sing a song of praise, Hero of
mighty valour, him
Whom no one challenges to war.

22 Hero, the Soma being shed, I pour the
juice for thee to drink:
Sate thee and finish thy carouse.

23 Let not the fools, or those who mock,
beguile thee when they seek thine aid :
Love not the enemies of prayer.

24 Here let them with rich milky draught
cheer thee to great munificence :
Drink as the wild-bull drinks the lake.

25 Proclaim in our assemblies what deeds,
new and ancient, far away,
The Vṛtra-slayer hath achieved.

26 In battle of a thousand arms Indra drank
Kadrū's Soma juice :
There he displayed his manly might.

27 True undeniable strength he found in
Yadu and in Turvaśa,
And conquered through the sacrifice.

28 Him have I magnified, our Lord in
common, Guardian of your folk,
Discloser of great wealth in kine ;

29 Ṛbhukṣan, not to be restrained, who
strengthened Tugra's son in lauds,
Indra beside the flowing juice;

30 Who for Triśoka clave the hill that formed
a wide receptacle,
So that the cows might issue forth.

31 Whate'er thy plan or purpose be, whate'er,
in transport, thou wouldst do,
Do it not, Indra, but be kind.

32 But little hath been heard of done upon
the earth by one like thee ;
Let thine heart, Indra, turn to us.

33 Thine then shall be this high renown,
thine shall these lofty praises be,
When, Indra, thou art kind to us.

34 Not for one trespass, not for two, O Hero,
slay us, nor for three,
Nor yet for many trespasses.

35 I fear one powerful like thee, the crusher-
down of enemies,
Mighty, repelling all attacks.

36 O wealthy God, ne'er may I live to see
my friend or son in need :
Hitherward let thy heart be turned.

37 What friend, O people, unprovoked, hath
ever said unto a friend,
He turns and leaves us in distress ?

38 Hero, insatiate enjoy this Soma juice so
near to thee,
Even as a hunter rushing down.

39 Hither I draw those Bays of thine yoked
by our hymn, with splendid car,
That thou mayst give unto the priests.

40 Drive all our enemies away, smite down
the foes who press around,

29 Ṛbhukṣan : Indra, Lord of the Ṛbhus. *Tugra's
son* : Bhujyu. According to Sāyaṇa, *tugryavṛdham* means
'augmenter of water.'

30 *The hill* is the massive rain-cloud, and *the cows*
are streams of water.

31 *Do it not* : 'Sāyaṇa understands this, "do it not
for thou hast done it for us,—only make us happy."
Could it be that the worshipper had a feeling of
nemesis ? or would he monopolize all ?'—Note by E.
B. C. in Wilson's Translation.

32 'In the following verses (32—36) the poet seems
to express disappointment at the inadequate manifestation of Indra's power, while he at the same time
entreats his grace and forgiveness.'—O. S. *Texts*, V.
p. 111.

37 This stanza is Indra's answer to the poet's complaint. The meaning seems to be : no friend without
good cause calls his friend a traitor. What then have
I done, or left undone, that thou shouldst say that I
have forsaken thee ? See Ludwig's Commentary on
the very difficult *jah kḍḥ* or *jahākaḥ*.

14 *As to a trafficker* : as to one who knows the
value of our worship and oblations and will give us
something in return.

23 *The enemies of prayer* : according to Sāyaṇa
those who hate Brāhmans.

24 *The wild-bull* : the *gaura*.

26 *Kadrū's Soma juice* : Kadrū here is apparently the
name of a Ṛṣi or of one of the officiating priests. The
St. Petersburg Lexicon takes it to mean, from a *kadrū*
or Soma vessel.

27 *Undeniable* : *ahnavāyyám*, according to Sāyaṇa, is
the name of the enemy of Turvaśa and Yadu : 'he
overcame Ahnavāyya in battle.'—Wilson.

And bring the wealth for which we long :

41 O Indra, that which is concealed in
strong firm place precipitous :
Bring us the wealth for which we long :

42 Great riches which the world of men shall
recognize as sent by thee :
Bring us the wealth for which we long.

HYMN XLVI.   *Indra.*

1. WE, Indra, Lord of ample wealth, our
Guide, depend on one like thee,
Thou driver of the Tawny Steeds.

2 For, Hurler of the Bolt, we know thee
true, the giver of our food,
We know the giver of our wealth.

3 O thou whose majesty the bards celebrate
with their songs, thou Lord,
Of hundred powers and hundred aids.

4 Fair guidance hath the mortal man whom
Aryaman, the Marut host,
And Mitra, void of guile, protect.

5 Kine, steeds, and hero strength he gains,
and prospers, by the Ādityas sped,
Ever in wealth which all desire.

6 We pray to Indra for his gift, to him the
Fearless and the Strong,
We pray to him the Lord of wealth.

7 For verily combined in him are all the
fearless powers of aid.
Him, rich in wealth, let swift Steeds
bring to us, his Bays, to Soma juice
for his carouse :

8 Yea, that most excellent carouse, Indra,
which slays most enemies,
With Heroes wins the light of heaven,
and is invincible in war :

9 Which merits fame, all-bountiful ! and,
unsubdued, hath victory in deeds of
might.
So come to our libations, Strongest !
Excellent ! May we obtain a stall of
kine.

10 Responding to our wish for cows, for
steeds, and chariots, as of old,
Be gracious, Greatest of the Great !

11 For, Hero, nowhere can I find the bounds
of thy munificence.
Still do thou favour us, O Bolt-armed
Maghavan : with strength hast thou
rewarded hymns.

12 High, glorifier of his friend, he knows all
generations, he whom many praise.
All races of mankind with ladles lifted up
invoke that Mighty Indra's aid.

13 Be he our Champion and Protector in
great deeds, rich in all wealth, the
Vṛtra-slayer, Maghavan.

14 In the wild raptures of the juice sing to
your Hero with high laud, to him the
Wise,
To Indra, glorious in his name, the
Mighty One, even as the hymn alloweth
it.

15 Thou givest wealth to me myself, thou
givest treasure, Excellent ! and the
strong steed,
O Much-invoked, in deeds of might, yea,
even now.

16 Him, Sovran Ruler of all precious things,
who even hath power o'er this fair form
of his,
As now it taketh shape, and afterward,

17 We praise, so that the Mighty One may
speed to you, Pourer of boun ies, Traveller, prepared to go.
Thou favourest the Maruts known to all,
by song and sacrifice.
With song and praise I sing to thee.

18 We in the sacrifice perform their will
whose voice is lifted high,
The worship of those Thundering Ones
who o'er the ridges of these mountains
fly in troops.

19 O Indra, Mightiest, bring us that which
crushes men of evil minds,
Wealth suited to our needs, O Stirrer of
the thought, best wealth, O thou who
stirrest thought.

13 This stanza may have been the conclusion of
one of the original hymns.

14 *As the hymn alloweth it* : in due accordance with
the metre.

16 Sāyaṇa explains the latter part of the first line
and the following part of the second as, 'who overcomes this obstructor (the enemy) as he wages war.'
I follow Ludwig's interpretation who refers to III. 53.
8, 'Maghavan weareth e.ery shape at pleasure, effecting magic changes in his body; and VI. 47. 18,
'Indra moves multiform by his illusions.'

18 *Their will* : the pleasure of the Maruts.

The hymn appears to be composed of two or more
originally separate hymns (see Pischel, *Vedische Studien*,
I. pp. 7 - 9). There are seventeen varieties of metre
(see Index of Hymns). The hymn is difficult and
obscure in parts, where only conjectural translations
can be given.

7 *Powers of aid* : or, succourers ; the Maruts may
be intended.

20 O Winner, noble winner, strong, wondrous,
  most splendid, excellent,
  Sole Lord of victory, bring all-overpower-
  ing wealth, joy-giving, chief in deeds of
  might.

21 Now let the godless man approach who
  hath received reward so great
  As Vaśa, Aśvya, when this light of
  morning dawned, received from Pṛthuśravas, from Kanīta's son.

22 Steeds sixty thousand and ten thousand
  kine, and twenty hundred camels I
  obtained ;
  Ten hundred brown in hue, and other
  ten red in three spots : in all, ten
  thousand kine.

23 Ten browns that make my wealth increase,
  fleet steeds whose tails are long and fair,
  Turn with swift whirl my chariot wheel ;

24 The gifts which Pṛthuśravas gave, Kanīta's
  son munificent.
  He gave a chariot wrought of gold : the
  prince was passing bountiful, and won
  himself most lofty fame.

25 Come thou to this great rite of ours,
  Vāyu ! to give us vigorous light.
  We have served thee that thou mightest
  give much to us, yea, mightest quickly
  give great wealth.

26 Who with thrice seven times seventy
  horses comes to us, invested with the
  rays of morn,
  Through these our Soma-draughts and
  those who press, to give, drinker of pure
  bright Soma juice.

27 Who hath inclined this glorious one,
  bounteous himself, to give me gifts.
  Borne on firm chariot with the prosperous
  Nahuṣa, wise, to a man yet more
  devout.

28 Sole Lord in beauty meet for praise, O
  Vāyu, dropping fatness down,

Hurried along by steeds, by camels, and
  by hounds, spreads forth thy train : even
  this it is.

29 So, as a prize dear to the strong, the sixty
  thousand have I gained,
  Bulls that resemble vigorous steeds.

30 To me come oxen like a herd, yea, unto
  me the oxen come.

31 And in the grazing herd he made a
  hundred camels bleat for me,
  And twenty hundred mid the white.

32 A hundred has the sage received, Dāsa
  Balbūtha's and Tarukṣa's gifts.
  These are thy people, Vāyu, who rejoice
  with Indra for their guard, rejoice with
  Gods for guards.

33 And now to Vaśa Aśvya here this stately
  woman is led forth,
  Adorned with ornaments of gold.

HYMN XLVII. *Ādityas.*

1. GREAT help ye give the worshipper,
  Varuṇa, Mitra, Mighty Ones ! No
  sorrow ever reaches him whom ye,
  Ādityas, keep from harm. Yours are
  incomparable aids, and good the succour
  they afford.

2 O Gods, Ādityas, well ye know the way
  to keep all woes afar.
  As the birds spread their sheltering wings,
  spread your protection over us.

3 As the birds spread their sheltering wings
  let your protection cover us.
  We mean all shelter and defence, ye who
  have all things for your own.

4 To whomsoever they, Most Wise, have
  given a home and means of life,
  O'er the whole riches of this man they,
  the Ādityas, have control.

5 As drivers of the car avoid ill roads, let
  sorrows pass us by.
  May we be under Indra's guard, in the
  Ādityas' favouring grace.

---

20 *O winner* : of wealth to be given to thy worshippers. 'O bountiful, most bountiful.'—Wilson.

21 *Vaśa Aśvya* : the Ṛṣi of the hymn. See I. 112. 10.
Pṛthuśravas : See I. 116. 21.

22 *In all, ten thousand kine* : the exact meaning is
not very clear. The last line is rendered differently
in Wilson's Translation : 'a thousand brown mares,—
and ten times ten thousand cows with three red patches.'

26 *Who* : apparently Vāyu, but, according to Sāyaṇa,
Pṛthuśravas.

27 *On firm chariot* : literally, on a car made of the
wood of the Araḍu tree (Calosanthes Indica). But
Sāyaṇa makes two proper names of the words, 'with
Araḍva and Akṣa.'

28 The *steeds, camels,* and *hounds* are apparently the
fantastic forms of the clouds that fly before Vāyu or
the wind.

31 *Mid the white*: herds of cows.

32 *Dāsa Balbūtha* : probably an aboriginal ally of
Pṛthuśravas. See Weber, *Episches im Vedischen Ritual,* p.
30.

33 *This stately woman* : probably the wife of the
conquered King.—Ludwig.

1 *Yours are, etc* : the refrain recurs in every verse
of the hymn.

6 For verily men sink and faint through
 loss of wealth which ye have given.
 Much hath he gained from you, O Gods,
 whom ye, Ādityas, have approached.

7 On him shall no fierce anger fall, no sore
 distress shall visit him,
 To whom, Ādityas, ye have lent your
 shelter that extendeth far.

8 Resting in you, O Gods, we are like men
 who fight in coats of mail.
 Ye guard us from each great offence, ye
 guard us from each lighter fault.

9 May Aditi defend us, may Aditi guard and
 shelter us,
 Mother of wealthy Mitra and of Aryaman
 and Varuṇa.

10 The shelter, Gods, that is secure, auspicious, free from malady,
 A sure protection, triply strong, even that
 do ye extend to us.

11 Look down on us, Ādityas, as a guide
 exploring from the bank.
 Lead us to pleasant ways as men lead
 horses to an easy ford.

12 Ill be it for the demons' friend to find us
 or come near to us.
 But for the milch-cow be it well, and for
 the man who strives for fame.

13 Each evil deed made manifest, and that
 which is concealed, O Gods,
 The whole thereof remove from us to
 Trita Āptya far away.

14 Daughter of Heaven, the dream that bodes
 evil to us or to our kine,
 Remove, O Lady of the Light, to Trita
 Āptya far away.

15 Even if, O Child of Heaven, it make a
 garland or a chain of gold,
 The whole bad dream, whate'er it be, to
 Trita Āptya we consign.

16 To him whose food and work is this, who
 comes to take his share therein,

To Trita, and to Dvita, Dawn ! bear thou
 the evil dream away.

17 As we collect the utmost debt, even the
 eighth and sixteenth part,
 So unto Āptya we transfer together all the
 evil dream.

18 Now have we conquered and obtained,
 and from our trespasses are free.
 Shine thou away the evil dream, O Dawn,
 whereof we are afraid. Yours are
 incomparable aids, and good the succour
 they afford.

HYMN XLVIII.   *Soma.*

1. WISELY have I enjoyed the savoury viand,
 religious-thoughted, best to find out
 treasure,
 The food to which all Deities and mortals,
 calling it meath, gather themselves
 together.

2 Thou shalt be Aditi as thou hast entered
 within, appeaser of celestial anger.
 Indu, enjoying Indra's friendship, bring
 us—as a swift steed the car—forward to
 riches.

3 We have drunk Soma and become
 immortal ; we have attained the light,
 the Gods discovered.
 Now what may foeman's malice do to
 harm us ? What, O Immortal, mortal
 man's deception ?

4 Absorbed into the heart, be sweet, O Indu,
 as a kind father to his son, O Soma,
 As a wise Friend to friend : do thou,
 wide-ruler, O Soma, lengthen out our
 days for living.

5 These glorious drops that give me freedom
 have I drunk. Closely they knit my
 joints as straps secure a car.
 Let them protect my foot from slipping
 on the way : yea, let the drops I drink
 preserve me from disease.

6 Make me shine bright like fire produced by
 friction : give us a clearer sight and
 make us better.

---

13 *To Trita Āptya far away* : Trita Āptya is a divinity
dwelling in the remotest part of the heavens to whom
it was customary to wish away and consign any threatened calamity or unpleasantness. As Sāyaṇa regards
Trita Āptya as the Ṛṣi of the hymn, he is compelled
to force a different interpretation on the first half of
the second line : '(let it not be found) in Trita Āptya,
keep it far from us.'—Wilson.

14 *Daughter of Heaven* : Uṣas or Dawn.

15 "The sense would then be 'even though parts of
it be pleasant, we put the whole of the evil dream
away.'"—Macdonell, Journal of R.A.S., July, 1893. p.
461.

16 *To him* : to Trita whose business it is to receive

these consignments. *To Dvita* : a similar being, sometimes associated with Trita. See V. 18. 2.

---

1 *Meath* : *mádhu* : or, sweet.

2 *Within* : within my heart. *Indu* : Soma.

3 *We have drunk Soma* : See Muir, *O. S. Texts.* III.
264, 265.

5 *From slipping on the way* : 'may they keep us from a
loosely knit worship.'—Wilson.

For in carouse I think of thee, O Soma,
Shall I, as a rich man, attain to
comfort ?

7 May we enjoy with an enlivened spirit
the juice thou givest, like ancestral
riches.

O Soma, King, prolong thou our existence
as Sūrya makes the shining days grow
longer.

8 King Soma, favour us and make us prosper :
we are thy devotees ; of this be
mindful.

Spirit and power are fresh in us, O Indu :
give us not up unto our foeman's
pleasure.

9 For thou hast settled in each joint, O
Soma, aim of men's eyes and guardian of
our bodies.

When we offend against thine holy statutes,
as a kind Friend, God, best of all, be
gracious.

10 May I be with the Friend whose heart is
tender, who, Lord of Bays ! when quaffed
will never harm me—

This Soma now deposited within me. For
this, I pray for longer life to Indra.

11 Our maladies have lost their strength and
vanished : they feared, and passed away
into the darkness.

Soma hath risen in us, exceeding mighty,
and we are come where men prolong
existence.

12 Fathers, that Indu which our hearts have
drunken, Immortal in himself, hath
entered mortals.

So let us serve this Soma with oblation,
and rest securely in his grace and
favour.

13 Associate with the Fathers thou, O Soma,
hast spread thyself abroad through earth
and heaven.

So with oblation let us serve thee, Indu,
and so let us become the lords of
riches,

14 Give us your blessing, O ye Gods, preservers. Never may sleep or idle talk
control us.

But evermore may we, as friends of Soma,
speak to the synod with brave sons
around us.

15 On all sides, Soma, thou art our life-giver :
aim of all eyes, light-finder, come within
us.

Indu, of one accord with thy protections
both from behind and from before
preserve us.

HYMN XLIX. *Agni.*

1. AGNI, come hither with thy fires ; we
choose thee as Invoking Priest.

Let the extended ladle full of oil balm
thee, best Priest, to sit on sacred
grass.

2 For unto thee, O Aṅgiras, O Son of
Strength, move ladles in the sacrifice.

To Agni, Child of Force, whose locks
drop oil, we seek, foremost in sacrificial
rites.

3 Agni, thou art Disposer, Sage, Herald,
bright God ! and worshipful,

Best offerer, cheerful, to be praised in holy
rites, pure Lord ! by singers with their
hymns.

4 Most Youthful and Eternal, bring the
longing Gods to me, the guileless, for
the feast.

Come, Vasu, to the banquet that is well-
prepared : rejoice thee, gracious, with
our songs.

5 Famed art thou, Agni, far and wide,
Preserver, righteous, and a Sage.

The holy singers, O refulgent kindled
God ! arrangers, call on thee to come .

6 Shine, Most Resplendent ! blaze, send bliss
unto the folk, and to thy worshipper :
Great art thou.

So may my princes, with good fires, subduing foes, rest in the keeping of the
Gods.

I place at the end of this Book the eleven hymns, called
the Vālakhilya, which are usually inserted after Hymn
XLVIII. These hymns are not reckoned in the division
of the Ṛgveda into Maṇḍalas (Books) and Anuvākas
(Chapters), and Sāyaṇa does not notice them in his
Commentary. See Wilson's Translation, V. p. 96, note
by Cowell. See also Max Müller's *Vedic Hymns* I,
(Sacred Books of the East, Vol. XXXII.), pp. xlvi—
xlviii.

Eleven must be added to the number of this hymn
and of all that follow in this Book to make them correspond with the numbers in Max Müller's edition of the
text.

2 *Whose locks drop oil* : 'butter-haired.'—Wilson.

5 *The arrangers* : of the ritual of sacrifice.

6 *Princes* : wealthy patrons. According to Sāyaṇa,
the Ṛṣi's own sons and others may be intended.

9 *Aim of men's eyes* : or beholder of men.

12 *Immortal in himself* : See note on I. 18. 4.

13 *Soma* : here the Moon-God, who is intimately
connected with the Pitṛs or Fathers. See *Hymns of the
Atharva-veda*, XVIII. 4. 72.

7 O Agni, as thou burnest down to earth
even high-grown underwood,
So, bright as Mitra is, burn him who
injures us, him who plots ill against thy
friend.

8 Give us not as a prey to mortal enemy,
nor to the wicked friend of fiends.
With conquering guards, auspicious, unassailable, protect us, O Most Youthful
God.

9 Protect us, Agni, through the first, protect
us through the second hymn,
Protect us through three hymns, O Lord
of Power and Might, through four
hymns, Vasu, guard thou us.

10 Preserve us from each fiend who brings
the Gods no gift, preserve thou us in
deeds of strength :
For we possess in thee the nearest Friend
of all, for service of the Gods and
weal.

11 O Holy Agni, give us wealth renowned
with men and strengthening life.
Bestow on us, O Helper, that which many
crave, more glorious still by righteous-
ness ;

12 Wherewith we may o'ercome our rivals
in the war, o'erpowering the foe's
designs.
So wax thou by our food, O Excellent in
strength. Quicken our thoughts that
find out wealth.

13 Agni is even as a bull who whets and
brandishes his horns.
Well-sharpened are his jaws which may
not be withstood : the Child of Strength
hath powerful teeth.

14 Not to be stayed, O Bull, O Agni, are thy
teeth when thou art spreading far and
wide.
Make our oblations duly offered up, O
Priest, and give us store of precious
things.

15 Thou liest in the wood : from both thy
Mothers mortals kindle thee.
Unweariedly thou bearest up the offerer's
gifts, then shinest bright among the
Gods.

16 And so the seven priests, O Agni, worship
thee, Free-giver, Everlasting One.
Thou cleavest through the rock with heat
and fervent glow. Agni, rise up above
the men.

17 For you let us whose grass is trimmed call
Agni, Agni, restless God.
Let us whose food is offered call to all
the tribes Agni the Invoking Priest of
men.

18 Agni, with noble psalm that tells his wish
he dwells, thinking on thee who guardest
him.
Speedily bring us strength of many varied
sorts to be most near to succour us.

19 Agni, Praise-singer ! Lord of men, God !
burner-up of Rākṣasas,
Mighty art thou, the ever-present House-
hold-Lord, Home-friend and Guardian
from the sky.

20 Let no fiend come among us, O thou rich
in light, no spell of those who deal in
spells.
To distant pastures drive faint hunger : far
away, O Agni, chase the demons'
friends.

HYMN L.   *Indra.*

1. BOTH boons,—may Indra, hitherward
turned, listen to this prayer of ours,
And mightiest Maghavan with thought
inclined to us come near to drink the
Soma juice.

2 For him, strong, independent Ruler,
Heaven and Earth have fashioned forth
for power and might.
Thou seatest thee as first among thy peers
in place, for thy soul longs for Soma
juice.

3 Fill thyself full, O Lord of wealth, O Indra,
with the juice we shed.
We know thee, Lord of Bay Steeds !
victor in the fight, vanquishing e'en the
invincible.

---

16 *Seven priests* : minor Hotar priests, such as the
Maitrāvaruṇa and others. *The rock* : *ádrim,* explained
by Sāyaṇa as *megham,* the cloud.

17 *The restless God* : or, 'the irresistible.'—Wilson.

18 *He dwells* : that is, the pious institutor of sacrifice.

20 *Spell of those who deal in spells* : *yāturyātumávatām:*
'torment of the evil spirits.'—Wilson.

9 The numbers probably have reference to the four
quarters of the sky.—Ludwig.

12 *Wherewith* : referring to the wealth which Agni is
asked to give.

15 *In the wood* : in the pieces of wood used for the
production of Agni.

1 *Both boons* : Indra is asked to bear the prayer
and to drink the Soma.

4 Changeless in truth, O Maghavan Indra,
let it be as thou in wisdom willest it.
May we, O fair of cheek, win booty with
thine aid, O Thunderer, swiftly seeking
it.

5 Indra, with all thy saving helps give us
assistance, Lord of power.
For after thee we follow even as glorious
bliss, thee, Hero, finder-out of wealth.

6 Increaser of our steeds and multiplying
kine, a golden well, O God, art thou,
For no one may impair the gifts laid up
in thee. Bring me whatever thing I
ask.

7 For thou,—come to the worshipper !—wilt
find great wealth to make us rich.
Fill thyself full, O Maghavan, for gain of
kine, full, Indra, for the gain of steeds.

8 Thou as thy gift bestowest many hundred
herds, yea, many thousands dost thou
give.
With singers' hymns have we brought the
Fort-render near, singing to Indra for
his grace.

9 Whether the simple or the sage, Indra,
have offered praise to thee,
He Śatakratu ! by his love hath gladdened
thee, ambitious ! ever pressing on !

10 If he the Strong of arm, the breaker-down
of forts, the great Destroyer, hear my
call,
We, seeking riches cry to Indra, Lord of
wealth, to Śatakratu with our lauds.

11 We count not then as sinners, nor as
niggardly or foolish men,
When with the Soma juice which we have
shed we make Indra, the Mighty One,
our Friend.

12 Him have we yoked in fight, the powerful
Conqueror, debt-claimer, not to be
deceived.
Best charioteer, the Victor marks each fault,
he knows the strong to whom he will
come near.

13 Indra, give us security from that whereof
we are afraid.

Help us, O Maghavan, let thy succour
give us this : drive away foes and
enemies.

14 For thou, O liberal Lord of bounty,
strengthenest his ample home who worships thee.
So Indra, Maghavan, thou Lover of the
Song, we with pressed Soma call on thee,

15 Indra is Vṛtra-slayer, guard, our best
defender from the foe.
May he preserve our last and middlemost,
and keep watch from behind us and
before.

16 Defend us from behind, below, above, in
front, on all sides, Indra, shield us well.
Keep far away from us the terror sent
from heaven : keep impious weapons far
away.

17 Protect us, Indra, each to-day, each
morrow, and each following day.
Our singers, through all days, shalt thou,
Lord of the brave, keep safely both by
day and night.

18 A crushing Warrior, passing rich is
Maghavan, endowed with all heroic
might.
Thine arms, O Śatakratu, are exceeding
strong, arms which have grasped the
thunderbolt.

HYMN LI. *Indra.*

1. OFFER ye up as praise to him that wherein
Indra takes delight.
The Soma-bringers magnify Indra's great
energy with hymns. Good are the gifts
that Indra gives.

2 Sole among chiefs, companionless, impetuous, and peerless, he
Hath waxen great o'er many folk, yea, over
all things born, in might.

3 Lord of swift bounty, he will win e'en with
a steed of worthless sort.
This, Indra, must be told of thee who wilt
perform heroic deeds.

4 Come to us hither : let us pay devotions
that enhance thy might,

9 *The simple or the sage* : 'the unskilled or the
skilled.'—Wilson.

12 *Marks each fault* : the meaning of *bhṛmám* is
uncertain : according to Ludwig it is 'his supporter or
feeder', that is, the worshipper who presents him with
sacrificial food. Sāyaṇa takes it with *vājinam* : 'the
strong racer.'—Wilson. *The strong* : the rich and powerful worshipper.

15 *Our last and middlemost* : putram, son, being understood, according to Sāyaṇa. The expression probably
means 'all of us.'

16 *The terror sent from heaven* : 'supernatural alarm.'—
Wilson.

1 *Good are*, etc: the refrain is repeated in each verse.

2 *Chiefs* : nṛbhiḥ : men, meaning Gods, according
to Sāyaṇa. *Folk* : or, tribes.

3 *He will win e'en with a steed of worthless sort* :
'He......wishes to bestow blessings (upon us) with his
unurged courser.'—Wilson.

For which, Most Potent ! thou wouldst fain bless the man here who strives for fame.

5 For thou, O Indra, makest yet more bold the spirit of the bold
Who with strong Soma serveth thee, still ready with his reverent prayers.

6 Worthy of song, he looketh down as a man looketh into wells.
Pleased with the Soma-bringer's skill he maketh him his mate and friend.

7 In strength and wisdom all the Gods, Indra, have yielded unto thee.
Be thou the Guard of all, O thou whom many praise.

8 Praised, Indra, is this might of thine, best for the service of the Gods,
That thou with power dost slay Vṛtra, O Lord of Strength.

9 He makes the races of mankind like synods of the Beauteous One.
Indra knows this his manifest deed, and is renowned.

10 Thy might, O Indra, at its birth, thee also, and thy mental power,
In thy care, Maghavan rich in kine ! they have increased exceedingly.

11 O Vṛtra-slayer, thou and I will both combine for winning spoil.
Even malignity will consent, O Bolt-armed Hero, unto us.

12 Let us extol this Indra as truthful and never as untrue.
Dire is his death who pours no gifts ; great light hath he who offers them. Good are the gifts that Indra gives.

HYMN LII.   *Indra.*

1. WITH powers of Mighty Ones hath he, Ancient, Beloved, been equipped,
Through whom the Father Manu made prayers efficacious with the Gods.

2 Him, Maker of the sky, let stones wet with the Soma ne'er forsake,
Nor hymns and prayer that must be said.

3 Indra who knew full well disclosed the kine to the Aṅgirases.
This his great deed must be extolled.

4 Indra, promoter of the song, the sage's Strengthener as of old,
Shall come to bless and succour us at presentation of this laud.

5 Now after their desire's intent the pious singers with the cry
Of Hail ! have sung loud hymns to thee, Indra, to gain a stall of kine.

6 With Indra rest all deeds of might, deeds done and yet to be performed,
Whom singers know devoid of guile.

7 When the Five Tribes with all their men to Indra have sent out their voice,
And when the priest hath strewn much grass, this is the Friend's own dwelling-place.

8 This praise is verily thine own : thou hast performed these manly deeds,
And sped the wheel upon its way.

9 At the o'erflowing of this Steer, boldly he strode for life, and took
Soma as cattle take their corn.

10 Receiving this and craving help, we, who with you are Dakṣa's sons,
Would fain exalt the Maruts' Lord.

11 Yea, Hero, with the singers we sing to the duly-coming Band.
Allied with thee may we prevail.

12 With us are raining Rudras, clouds accordant in call to battle, at the death of Vṛtra,
The strong assigned to him who sings and praises. May Gods with Indra at their head protect us.

---

6 *He looketh down* : kindly on us as a thirsty man looks eagerly into a well.

9 *Like synods of the Beauteous One* : like assemblies that meet to honour him ; but the meaning is obscure.

10 *They* : thy worshippers.

11 *Malignity* : or the malignant man. 'The niggard.' —Wilson.

12 *Dire is his death* : or, great is his destruction.

---

1 This difficult verse is variously interpreted both by Indian commentators and by European scholars. I follow partly Aufrecht's translation as given by Dr. Muir, and partly Ludwig's Commentary. See. *O.S. Texts*, I. pp. 163—164; Ludwig's *Ṛgveda*, V. pp. 167—168; and Wilson's Translation, V. p. 107. The *Ancient, Beloved* appears to be Soma and not Indra.

7 *The Friend's* : Indra's. The second line is very obscure. See Bergaigne, I. vi., and *Vedic Hymns*, I., p. 226. I adopt Ludwig's interpretation.

8 *The wheel* : the Sun.

9 *This Steer* : Soma ; that is, when abundant libations had been offered. *He* : Indra.

10 *Dakṣa's sons* : of the same origin with you. 'Lords of food,' according to Sāyaṇa.

11 *Duly-coming Band* : of Maruts, led by Indra.

12 *The strong* : perhaps the thunderbolt with which Indra aids the worshipper.

HYMN LIII.   *Indra.*

1. MAY our hymns give thee great delight.
   Display thy bounty, Thunderer.
   Drive off the enemies of prayer.

2 Crush with thy foot the niggard churls
   who bring no gifts. Mighty art thou :
   There is not one to equal thee.

3 Thou art the Lord of Soma pressed,
   Soma unpressed is also thine.
   Thou art the Sovran of the folk.

4 Come, go thou forth, dwelling in heaven
   and listening to the prayers of men :
   Thou fillest both the heavens and earth.

5 Even that hill with rocky heights, with
   hundreds, thousands, held within.
   Thou for thy worshippers brakest through.

6 We call on thee both night and day to
   taste the flowing Soma juice :
   Do thou fulfil our heart's desire.

7 Where is that ever-youthful Steer, strong-
   necked and never yet bent down ?
   What Brahman ministers to him ?

8 To whose libation doth the Steer, betake
   him with delight therein ?
   Who takes delight in Indra now ?

9 Whom, Vṛtra-slayer, have thy gift and
   hero powers accompanied ?
   Who is thy dearest in the laud ?

10 For thee among mankind, among the
   Pūrus is this Soma shed.
   Hasten thou hither : drink thereof.

11 This, growing by Suṣomā and by Śaryaṇāvān, dear to thee,
   In Ārjīkīya, cheers thee best.

12 Hasten thou hitherward, and drink this
   for munificence to-day,
   Delightful for thine eager draught.

HYMN LIV.   *Indra.*

1. THOUGH, Indra, thou art called by men
   from east and west, from north and
   south,
   Come hither quickly with fleet steeds ;

2 If in the effluence of heaven, rich in its
   light, thou takest joy,
   Or in the sea in Soma juice.

3 With songs I call thee, Great and Wide,
   even as a cow to profit us,
   Indra, to drink the Soma-draught.

4 Hither, O Indra, let thy Bays bear up and
   bring upon thy car
   Thy glory, God ! and majesty.

5 Thou, Indra, wouldst be sung and praised
   as great, strong, lordly in thy deeds :
   Come hither, drink our Soma juice.

6 We who have shed the Soma and prepared
   the feast are calling thee.
   To sit on this our sacred grass.

7 As, Indra, thou art evermore the common
   Lord of all alike,
   As such we invocate thee now.

8 The men with stones have milked for thee
   this nectar of the Soma juice :
   Indra, be pleased with it, and drink.

9 Neglect all pious men with skill in sacred
   song : come hitherward,
   With speed, and give us high renown.

10 Gods, may the mighty rest unharmed, the
   King who gives me spotted kine,
   Kine decked with golden ornaments.

11 Beside a thousand spotted kine I have
   received a gift of gold,
   Pure, brilliant, and exceeding great.

12 Durgaha's grandsons, giving me a thousand
   kine, munificent,
   Have won renown among the Gods.

---

3 *Unpressed* : in its natural state in the stalks of the
plant. Or, as Ludwig suggests, the Soma which
Indra drinks in heaven may be meant. See VII. 26. 1.

5 *That hill* : the cloud with its countless treasures
of rain.

6 *Night* : just before dawn.

10 *Among the Pūrus* : among men, or among Kings
named Pūrus.—Sāyaṇa.

11 *Suṣomā* : apparently a river which cannot now be
identified. *Ārjīkīya* : probably a country or district.
Saryaṇāvān is said to be a lake in the district of Kurukṣetra. See Vol. I., Index. For conjectures regarding
Suṣomā and Ārjīkīya, see Zimmer, *Altindisches Leben*,
pp. 12, 13. Cf. VIII. 7. 29.

---

2 *The effluence of heaven* : or the place in heaven
from which the Amṛta flows. *In the sea* : of air ; the
firmament.

3 *As a cow* : as the most useful of all animals.

9 *All pious men* : all other worshippers.

10 *The King* : who instituted the sacrifice. According to Sāyaṇa, Indra is meant ; but this is impossible.

12 *Durgaha's grandsons* : Sāyaṇa explains *durgdhasya*
by *auḥkham gāhamānasya me*, of me plunged in grief, and
ndpātaḥ (nepotes) as *arakṣitasya*, unprotected : 'Unprotected as I am, and plunged in sorrow (my dependents)
by the favour of the gods obtain food, and are blessed
with abundance in a thousand cattle.' See Wilson's
Translation, and Cowell's note.

HYMN LV. *Indra.*

1. LOUD singing at the sacred rite where
   Soma flows we priests invoke
   With haste, that he may help, as the
   bard's Cherisher, Indra who findeth
   wealth for you.

2. Whom with fair helm, in rapture of the
   juice, the firm resistless slayers hinder
   not :
   Giver of glorious wealth to him who sing
   his praise, honouring him who toils and
   pours :

3 Śakra, who like a curry-comb for horses
   or a golden goad,
   Indra, the Vṛtra-slayer, urges eagerly the
   opening of the stall of kine :

4 Who for the worshipper scatters forth
   ample wealth, even though buried, piled
   in heaps :
   May Indra, Lord of Bay Steeds, fair-helmed
   Thunderer, act at his pleasure, as he
   lists.

5 Hero whom many praise, what thou hast
   longed for, even of old, from men.
   All that we offer unto thee, O Indra, now,
   sacrifice, laud, effectual speech.

6 To Soma, Much-invoked, Bolt-armed !
   for thy carouse, Celestial, Soma-drinker !
   come.
   Thou to the man who prays and pours
   the juice hast been best giver of delightful wealth.

7 Here, verily, yesterday we let the Thunder-
   wielder drink his fill.
   So in like manner offer him the juice to-
   day. Now range you by the Glorious
   One.

8 Even the wolf, the savage beast that rends
   the sheep, follows the path of his decrees.
   So graciously accepting, Indra, this our
   praise, with wondrous thought come
   forth to us.

9 What manly deed of vigour now remains
   that Indra hath not done ?

Who hath not heard his glorious title and
his fame, the Vṛtra-slayer from his birth ?

10 How great his power resistless ! how
   invincible the Vṛtra-slayer's matchless
   might !
   Indra excels all usurers who see the day,
   excels all traffickers in strength.

11 O Indra, Vṛtra-slayer, we, thy very constant worshippers,
   Bring prayers ne'er heard before to thee,
   O Much-invoked, O Thunder-armed, to
   be thy meed.

12 O thou of mighty acts, the aids that are
   in thee call forward many an eager
   hope.
   Past the drink-offerings, Vasu, even of the
   good, hear my call, Strongest God, and
   come.

13 Verily, Indra, we are thine, we worshippers
   depend on thee.
   For there is none but only thou to show
   us grace, O Maghavan, thou much
   invoked.

14 From this our misery and famine set us
   free, from this dire curse deliver us.
   Succour us with thine help and with thy
   wondrous thought. Most Mighty, finder
   of the way.

15 Now let your Soma juice be poured ; be
   not afraid, O Kali's sons.
   This darkening sorrow goes away ; yea, of
   itself it vanishes.

HYMN LVI. *Ādityas.*

1. Now pray we to these Kṣatriyas, to the
   Ādityas for their aid,
   These who are gracious to assist.

2 May Mitra bear us o'er distress, and
   Varuṇa and Aryaman,
   Yea, the Ādityas, as they know.

3 For wonderful and meet for praise is these
   Ādityas' saving help
   To him who offers and prepares.

4 The mighty aid of you, the Great, Varuṇa,
   Mitra, Aryaman,
   We claim to be our sure defence.

1 *We priests invoke* : the construction is difficult.
I follow Ludwig and take *huvé*, an infinitive, as
equivalent to the first person plural.

3 *Curry-comb for horses* : the purifier of his worshippers and well-skilled in horses, according to Sāyaṇa.
Golden goad : wonderful and golden-bodied, according
to Sāyaṇa. The meaning of *kijaḥ*, as well as of *mṛkṣdḥ*,
is uncertain, but both seem to signify instruments connected with horses.

4 *Buried* : : as gold, precious stones etc.

8 *The wolf* : according to Sāyaṇa, the robber.
The reason of mentioning either in this place is not
obvious.

10 *Who see the day* : who live. According to Sāyaṇa,
who look upon the Sun in their present life, but will be
sunk in darkness after death.

14 *From this our misery* : the hymn was 'seen' and
employed in a time of dearth and famine. *Finder of
the way* : to prosperity.

15 *Kali's sons* : Kali is the Ṛṣi or seer of the hymn.

1 *Kṣatriyas* : royal princes.

5 Guard us, Ādityas, still alive, before the
   deadly weapon strike :
   Are ye not they who hear our call ?

6 What sheltering defence ye have for him
   who toils in pouring gifts,
   Graciously bless ye us therewith.

7 Ādityas, Gods, from sorrow there is freedom; for the sinless, wealth,
   O ye in whom no fault is seen.

8 Let not this fetter bind us fast : may he
   release us for success ;
   For strong is Indra and renowned.

9 O Gods who fain would lend your aid,
   destroy not us as ye destroy
   Your enemies who go astray.

10 And thee too, O Great Aditi, thee also,
   Goddess, I address,
   Thee very gracious to assist.

11 Save us in depth and shallow from the
   foe, thou Mother of Strong Sons :
   Let no one of our seed be harmed.

12 Far-spread ! wide-ruling ! grant that we,
   unharmed by envy, may expand :
   Grant that our progeny may live.

13 Those who, the Princes of the folk, in
   native glory, ne'er deceived,
   Maintain their statutes, void of guile—

14 As such, from mouth of ravening wolves,
   O ye Ādityas, rescue us,
   Like a bound thief, O Aditi.

15 Ādityas, let this arrow, yea, let this malignity depart
   From us or e'er it strike us dead.

16 For, Bountiful Ādityas, we have evermore
   enjoyed your help,
   Both now and in the days of old.

17 To every one, O ye Most Wise, who
   turneth even from sin to you,
   Ye Gods vouchsafe that he may live.

18 May this new mercy profit us, which, ye
   Ādityas, frees like one,
   Bound from his bonds, O Aditi.

19 O ye Ādityas, this your might is not to be
   despised by us :
   So be ye graciously inclined.

20 Let not Vivasvān's weapon nor the shaft,
   Ādityas, wrought with skill,
   Destroy us ere old age be nigh.

21 On every side dispel all sin, Ādityas, all
   hostility,
   Indigence, and combined attack.

HYMN LVII.   *Indra.*

1. EVEN as a car to give us aid, we draw
   thee hither for our bliss,
   Strong in thy deeds, checking assault, Lord,
   Mightiest Indra, of the brave !

2 Great in thy power and wisdom, Strong,
   with thought that comprehendeth all !
   Thou hast filled full with majesty.

3 Thou very Mighty One, whose hands by
   virtue of thy greatness grasp,
   The golden bolt that breaks its way.

4 Your Lord of might that ne'er hath bent,
   that ruleth over all mankind,
   I call, that he, as he is wont, may aid
   the chariots and the men.

5 Whom, ever furthering, in frays that win
   the light, in both the hosts
   Men call to succour and to help.

6 Indra, the Strong, the measureless, worthy
   of praise, Most Bountiful,
   Sole Ruler even over wealth.

7 Him, for his ample bounty, him, this
   Indra do I urge to drink,
   Who, as his praise was sung of old, the
   Dancer, is the Lord of men.

8 Thou Mighty One, whose friendship none
   of mortals ever hath obtained :
   None will attain unto thy might.

9 Aided by thee, with thee allied, in frays for
   water and for sun,
   Bolt-armed ! may we win ample spoil.

10 So seek we thee with sacrifice and songs,
   chief Lover of the Song,
   As, in our battles Indra, thou to Purumāyya gavest help.

11 O Thunderer, thou whose friendship and
   whose onward guidance both are sweet,
   Thy sacrifice must be prepared.

12 To us, ourselves, give ample room, give
   for our dwelling ample room :
   Give ample room to us to live.

---

11 *Of Strong Sons* : the Ādityas.

17 *Who turneth even from sin* : who comes to you for
forgiveness.

20 *Vivasvān's weapon* : the deadly bolt of the Sun,
or perhaps, metaphorically, of the sacrificer.

21 *Combined attack* : 'the closely drawn net.' –Wilson.

---

2 *Thou hast filled full* : the universe.

7 *The Dancer* : in the dance of war.

10 *Purumāyya* : according to Sāyaṇa, 'me (the Ṛṣi)
the possessor of much wisdom.'

13 We count the banquet of the Gods a
   spacious pathway for the men,
   And for the cattle, and the car.

14 Six men, yea, two and two, made glad
   with Soma juice, come near to me
   With offerings pleasant to the taste.

15 Two brown-hued steeds, Indrota's gift,
   two bays from Ṛkṣa's son were mine,
   From Aśvamedha's son two red.

16 From Atithigva good car-steeds; from
   Ārkṣa rein-obeying steeds,
   From Aśvamedha beauteous ones.

17 Indrota, Atithigva's son, gave me six
   horses matched with mares :
   And Pūtakratu gave besides.

18 Marked above all, amid the brown, is the
   red mare Vṛṣaṇvati,
   Obedient to the rein and whip.

19 O bound to me by deeds of might, not
   even the man who loves to blame,
   Hath found a single fault in you.

HYMN LVIII.   *Indra.*

1. I SEND you forth the song of praise for
   Indu, hero-gladdener.
   With hymn and plenty he invites you to
   complete the sacrifice.

2 Thou wishest for thy kine a bull, for those
   who long for his approach,
   For those who turn away from him, lord
   of thy cows whom none may kill.

3 The dappled kine who stream with milk
   prepare his draught of Soma juice :

Clans in the birth-place of the Gods, in
   the three luminous realms of heaven.

4 Praise, even as he is known, with song
   Indra the guardian of the kine,
   The Son of Truth, Lord of the brave.

5 Hither his Bay Steeds have been sent, red
   Steeds are on the sacred grass,
   Where we in concert sing our songs.

6 For Indra Thunder-armed the kine have
   yielded mingled milk and meath,
   What time he found them in the vault.

7 When I and Indra mount on high up to
   the Bright One's place and home,
   We, having drunk of meath, will reach
   his seat whose Friends are three times
   seven.

8 Sing, sing ye forth your songs of praise, ye
   Ṛriyamedhas, sing your songs :
   Yea, let young children sing their lauds :
   as a strong castle praise ye him.

9 Now loudly let the viol sound, the lute
   send out its voice with might,
   Shrill be the music of the string. To Indra
   is the hymn up-raised.

10 When hither speed the dappled cows,
   unflinching, easy to be milked,
   Seize quickly, as it bursts away, the Soma
   juice for Indra's drink.

11 Indra hath drunk, Agni hath drunk : all
   Deities have drunk their fill.
   Here Varuṇa shall have his home, to whom
   the floods have sung aloud as mother-
   kine unto their calves.

---

13 Sacrifice to the Gods procures freedom and security
for us and all who belong to us.

15 'These princes with their respective fathers are
the six of V. 14. The sons of *Ṛkṣa* and *Aśvamedha* had
originally commenced the sacrifice, but *Indrota* and his
father *Atithigva* came to see it and added their gifts.
The sons alone are mentioned : the son is the father's
second self, *pitṛ-putrayor abhedāt.'*—Cowell's note in
Wilson's Translation.

16 *Ārkṣa* : the son of Ṛkṣa. *Aśvamedha* : the son of
Aśvamedha.

17 *Pūtakratu* : son of Aśvamedha.

18 *Vṛṣaṇvati* : according to von Roth, 'perhaps, that
may be found among stallions.'

19 *O bound to me* : this stanza is addressed to the
princes who instituted the sacrifice and gave the rewards
which have been mentioned.

---

1 *The song of praise* : triṣṭubham : used in a general
sense for any hymn of praise. *Indu* : Soma. According
to Sāyaṇa, Indra is meant.

2 The stanza is difficult. I adopt Pischel's explanation of *nadám* and *odatīnām.*

3 *Clans*: viśaḥ: possibly the cows are meant. Eggelings
translates: 'At his birth the well-like, milking speckled one
mix the Soma (draught), the clans of the gods in the
three spheres of the heavens' (Sacred Books of the East,
XLI. p. 307). Pischel observes: 'The connexion of the first
three stanzas is probably this: Soma shall be celebrated by
you in your song of praise in order that he may liberally reward you. What thou wishest for thyself is a bull
for the cows, in order that they may be propagated and
provide Indra with milk to be mixed with his Soma
juice, while they serve the race of Gods in all three
realms of heaven. —*Vedische Studien*, I. p. 197.

6 *In the vault* : 'in the cavity of the Soma-vessel.'—
von Roth; 'on the horizon.'—Ludwig ; 'near at hand.'—
Sāyaṇa.

7 *The Bright One's place* : the station of the Sun.
Whose Friends are three times seven : Indra who is the
friend of the Maruts. I follow Ludwig in combining the
triḥ saptá sákhyuḥ of the text into one compound word.
Sāyaṇa's explanation is different : 'let us be united
in the twenty-first sphere of the (universal) friend.'—
See note in Wilson's Translation.

9 *The viol* : *gárgaraḥ* : 'a kind of musical instrument,' says Sāyaṇa. *Godhá*, originally the leather guard
worn by bowmen on the left arm, and *piṅgá* (said to
mean bowstring) are also, apparently, names of musical
instruments.

12 Thou, Varuṇa, to whom belong Seven
Rivers, art a glorious God.
The waters flow into thy throat as 'twere
a pipe with ample mouth.

13 He who hath made the fleet steeds spring,
well-harnessed, to the worshipper,
He, the swift Guide, is that fair form that
loosed the horses near at hand.

'14 Indra, the very Mighty, holds his enemies
in utter scorn.
He, far away, and yet a child, cleft the
cloud smitten by his voice.

15 He, yet a boy exceeding small, mounted
his newly-fashioned car.
He for his Mother and his Sire cooked
the wild mighty buffalo.

16 Lord of the home, fair-helmeted, ascend
thy chariot wrought of gold.
We will attend the Heavenly One, the
thousand-footed, red of hue, matchless,
who blesses where he goes.

17 With reverence they come hitherward to
him as to a Sovran lord,
That they may bring him near for this
man's good success, to prosper and
bestow his gifts.

18 The Priyamedhas have observed the offering
of the men of old,
Of ancient custom, while they strewed the
sacred grass, and spread their sacrificial
food.

HYMN LIX.   *Indra.*

1. HE who, as Sovran Lord of men, moves
with his chariots unrestrained,
The Vṛtra-slayer vanquisher, of fighting
hosts, preëminent, is praised with song.

2 Honour that Indra, Puruhanman ! for his
aid, in whose sustaining hand of old,
The splendid bolt of thunder was deposited,
as the great Sun was set in heaven.

12 Varuṇa's throat, or palate, is said to mean the sea,
into which the seven rivers flow.

15 *His Mother and his Sire* : Earth and Heaven.
The *buffalo* is the dark rain-cloud which Indra pierces
with his lightning, or perhaps the demon Vala is intended.

16 *The Heavenly One* : the Sun, which is Indra's
chariot. *Thousand-footed* : bright with countless rays of
light.

17 *This man's* : who institutes the sacrifice.

———

2 *Puruhanman* : the Ṛṣi of the hymn addresses
himself. *Sustaining* : or *vidhartári* may (with Ludwig)
be taken as a nominative with *vájraḥ*, the bolt of
thunder as a sustainer (of Order).

3 No one by deed attains to him who works
and strengthens evermore :
No, not by sacrifice, to Indra praised o
all, resistless, daring, bold in might.

4 The potent Conqueror, invincible in war,
him at whose birth the Mighty Ones,
The Kine who spread aftar, sent their loud
voices out, heavens, earths sent their
loud voices out,

5 O Indra, if a hundred heavens and if a
hundred earths were thine—
No, not a thousand Suns could match
thee at thy birth, not both the worlds,
O Thunderer.

6 Thou, Hero, hast performed thy hero
deeds with might, yea, all with strength,
O Strongest One.
Maghavan, help us to a stable full of
kine, O Thunderer, with wondrous aids.

7 Let not a godless mortal gain this food,
O thou whose life is long !
But one who yokes the bright-hued steeds,
the Etaśas, even Indra yoker of the
Bays.

8 Urge ye the Conqueror to give, your
Indra greatly to be praised,
To be invoked in shallow waters and in
depths, to be invoked in deeds of might.

9 O Vasu, O thou Hero, raise us up to
ample opulence.
Raise us to gain of mighty wealth, O
Maghavan, O Indra, to sublime renown.

10 Indra, thou justifiest us, and tramplest
down thy slanderers.
Guard thyself, valiant Hero, in thy vital
parts : strike down the Dāsa with thy
blows.

11 The man who brings no sacrifice, inhuman, godless, infidel,
Him let his friend the mountain cast to
rapid death, the mountain cast the
Dasyu down.

12 O Mightiest Indra, loving us, gather thou
up, as grains of corn,
Within thine hand, of these their kine, to
give away, yea, gather twice as loving us.

4 *The Kine* : the heavens and the earths.

7 *Etaśas* : the horses of the Sun.

10 *In thy vital parts* : literally, between thy thighs.
'Shelter us between thy thighs.'—Wilson.

11 *His friend* : in which he hopes to find refuge :
according to Sāyaṇa. Parvata (mountain) is a Ṛṣi,
the friend of Indra.

12 *Their kine* : the property of the hostile aborigines.

13 O my companions, wish for power. How
   may we perfect Śara's praise,
   The liberal princely patron, never to be
   harmed ?

14 By many a sage whose grass is trimmed
   thou art continually praised,
   That thou, O Śara, hast bestowed here
   one and here another calf.

15 The noble, Śūradeva's son, hath brought
   a calf, led by the ear to three of us.
   As a chief brings a goat to milk.

HYMN LX.   *Agni.*

1. O AGNI, with thy mighty wealth guard
   us from all malignity,
   Yea, from all hate of mortal man.

2 For over thee, O Friend from birth, the
   wrath of man hath no control :
   Nay, Guardian of the earth art thou.

3 As such, with all the Gods, O Son of
   Strength, auspicious in thy flame.
   Give us wealth bringing all things good.

4 Malignities stay not from wealth the mortal
   man whom, Agni, thou
   Protectest while he offers gifts.

5 Sage Agni, he whom thou dost urge, in
   worship of the Gods, to wealth,
   With thine assistance winneth kine.

6 Riches with many heroes thou hast for
   the man who offers gifts :
   Lead thou us on to higher bliss.

7 Save us, O Jātavedas, nor abandon us to
   him who sins,
   Unto the evil-hearted man.

8 O Agni, let no godless man avert thy
   bounty as a God :
   Over all treasures thou art Lord.

9 So, Son of Strength, thou aidest us to
   what is great and excellent.
   Those, Vasu ! Friend ! who sing thy praise.

10 Let our songs come anear to him beauteous and bright with piercing flame,
   Our offerings, with our homage, to the
   Lord of wealth, to him whom many
   praise, for help :

11 To Agni Jātavedas, to the Son of Strength, that he may give us precious gifts,
   Immortal, from of old Priest among mortal
   men, the most delightful in the house :

12 Agni, made yours by sacrifice, Agni, while
   holy rites advance ;
   Agni, the first in songs, first with the
   warrior steed ; Agni to win the land
   for us.

13 May Agni who is Lord of wealth vouchsafe us food for friendship sake.
   Agni we ever seek for seed and progeny,
   the Vasu who protects our lives.

14 Solicit with your chants, for help, Agni
   the God with piercing flame,
   For riches famous Agni, Purumīlha and
   ye men ! Agni to light our dwelling
   well.

15 Agni we laud that he may keep our foes
   afar, Agni to give us health and strength.
   Let him as Guardian be invoked in all
   the tribes, the lighter-up of glowing
   brands.

HYMN LXI.   *Agni.*

1. PREPARE oblation : let him come ; and
   let the minister serve again
   Who knows the ordering thereof.

2 Rejoicing in his friendship, let the priest
   be seated over man,
   Beside the shoot of active power.

3 Him, glowing bright beyond all thought,
   they seek among the race of man ;

---

13 *Śara's praise* : Śara must be the institutor of the
sacrifice : according to Sāyaṇa he is Indra, 'the destroyer.'

14 *Here one and here another* : *ékam-ekam* : meaning
many.

15 *Śūradeva's son* : Śara. Sāyaṇa explains *śauradevyáḥ*
as cows won in battle. 'May Maghavan, taking them
by the ears, lead the cows with their calves from our
three (destructive enemies), as the owner leads a goat
to drink.'—Wilson.

2 *Guardian of the earth* : *kṣápāvān* : 'Lord of the
night.'—Sāyaṇa.

5 *Winneth kine* : literally, is a goer among cows :
'walks (lord) among crowds of cattle.'—Wilson.

---

12 *With the warrior steed* : *árvati* : the fierce and
rapid fire that clears the jungle for the advance of the
Āryan settlers.

14 *To light our dwelling well* : I follow Ludwig's
explanation. Sāyaṇa takes *sudityé* as a proper name :
'a house for (me) Suditi.'—Wilson.

15 *The lighter-up of glowing brands* : *vásturṣṇām* :
according to Sāyaṇa, 'the giver of homes to us Ṛṣis.'

The language of the hymn is intentionally obscure,
and much of my translation (in which I generally follow
Ludwig) must be regarded as conjectural.

1 *Let him come* : Agni. *The minister* : or, the
Adhvaryu.

2 *The shoot* : Agni, according to Sāyaṇa : the
stalks of the Soma-plant, according to von Roth.

3 *They seek* : that is, the Gods.

With him for tougue they seize the food.

4 He hath inflamed the twofold plain : life-
giving, he hath climbed the wood,
And with his tongue hath struck the rock.

5 Wandering here the radiant Calf finds
none to fetter him, and seeks
The Mother to declare his praise.

6 And now that great and mighty team, the
team of horses that are his,
And traces of his car, are seen.

7 The seven milk a single cow ; the two set
other five to work,
On the stream's loud-resounding bank.

8 Entreated by Vivasvān's ten, Indra cast
down the water-jar
With threefold hammer from the sky.

9 Three times the newly-kindled flame proceeds around the sacrifice :
The priests anoint it with the meath.

10 With reverence they drain the fount that
circles with its wheel above,
Exhaustless, with the mouth below.

11 The pressing-stones are set at work : the
meath is poured into the tank,
At the out-shedding of the fount.

12 Ye cows, protect the fount : the two
Mighty Ones bless the sacrifice.
The handles twain are wrought of gold.

13 Pour on the juice the ornament which
reaches both the heaven and earth :
Supply the liquid to the Bull.

14 These know their own abiding-place : like
calves beside the mother cows
They meet together with their kin.

15 Devouring in their greedy jaws, they make
sustaining food in heaven,
To Indra, Agni light and prayer.

16 The Pious One milked out rich food,
sustenance dealt in portions seven,
Together with the Sun's seven rays.

17 I took some Soma when the Sun rose up,
O Mitra, Varuṇa.
That is the sick man's medicine.

18 From where oblations must be laid, which
is the Well-beloved's home,
He with his tongue hath compassed heaven.

HYMN LXII.   *Aśvins.*

1. ROUSE ye for him who keeps the Law,
yoke your steeds, Aśvins, to your car :
Let your protecting help be near.

2 Come, Aśvins, with your car more swift
than is the twinkling of an eye :
Let your protecting help be near.

3 Aśvins, ye overlaid with cold the fiery pit
for Atri's sake :
Let your protecting help be near.

4 Where are ye ? whither are ye gone ?
whither, like falcons, have ye flown ?
Let your protecting help be near.

5 If ye at any time this day are listening to
this my call,
Let your protecting help be near.

6 The Aśvins, first to hear our prayer, for
closest kinship I approach :
Let your protecting help be near.

7 For Atri ye, O Aśvins, made a dwelling-
place to shield him well,

4 *The twofold plain* : the expanses of earth and
heaven. *Climbed the wood* : a forest conflagration is
referred to.

5 *The radiant Calf* : Agni in the form of lightning.
Here : in the sky above us. *The Mother* : the cloud,
which will praise him with a thunder-psalm.

7 *The seven* : officiating priests, or assistants. See
II. 1. 2. *A single cow* : the text has only *ekām.*
Sāyaṇa supplies, cow, which he explains as the *gharma,*
pitcher or caldron used for heating milk, etc., in the
Pravargya ceremony. *Loud-resounding bank* : with
reference to the sacrificial exclamations, uttered by the
officiating priests. *The two* : the Adhvaryu and the
Pratiprasthātar, his Assistant, direct the five others in
the performance of the ceremony.

8 *Entreated by Vivasvān's ten* : according to Sāyaṇa,
the ten fingers of the worshipper. Ten priests are
probably meant. *Indra* : Agni or Āditya may be meant.
—Sāyaṇa. *The water-jar* : the rainy cloud. *Hammer* :
meaning, probably, the zigzag lightning. Sāyaṇa
explains it by *raśminā,* with his ray.

10 *The fount* : *avatám* : the *gharma* or *mahāvira,*
the contents of which are poured into the fire. *Its wheel* :
apparently, the circular rim on which it usually stands
and which is now inverted that all the liquid may flow
out. According to Hillebrandt (*Vedische Mythologie* 1.
325) *the fount* is the Moon.

12 *The two Mighty Ones* : Heaven and Earth. But as
the meaning of *rapsudā* is unknown, the sentence can be
only conjecturally translated : '(The two kinds of milk)
in the sacrifice are plentiful and fruit-giving.'—Wilson.

13 *The ornament* : the milk which is mingled with
the Soma. *To the Bull* : to Agni.

14 *These know* : the cows know, and come to, the
place where they are to be milked for sacrificial purposes
as well as they know their own stable.

15 *Devouring* : perhaps the flames ; but the stanza
is obscure.

16 *The Pious One* : Agni. *Dealt in portions seven* :
one for each priest.

18 *The Well-beloved's home* : 'the place which I, the
eager offerer, choose.—Wilson. *Haryatá,* 'the well-beloved,'
is perhaps the Soma.

1 *Who keeps the Law* : which enjoins sacrifice. The
Ṛṣi means himself.

3 *For Atri's sake* : See I. 116. 8.

Let your protecting help be near.

8 Ye warded off the fervent heat for Atri
  when he sweetly spake :
  Let your protecting help be near.

9 Erst Saptavadhri by his prayer obtained the
  trenchant edge of fire :
  Let your protecting help be near.

10 Come hither, O ye Lords of wealth, and
  listen to this call of mine :
  Let your protecting help be near.

11 What is this praise told forth of you as
  Elders in the ancient way ?
  Let your protecting help be near.

12 One common brotherhood is yours, Aśvins
  your kindred is the same :
  Let your protecting help be near.

13 This is your chariot, Aśvins, which speeds
  through the regions, earth and heaven :
  Let your protecting aid be near.

14 Approach ye hitherward to us with thousands both of steeds and kine :
  Let your protecting help be near.

15 Pass us not by, remember us with thousands both of kine and steeds :
  Let your protecting help be near.

16 The purple-tinted Dawn hath risen, and
  true to Law hath made the light :
  Let your protecting help be near.

17 He looked upon the Aśvins, as an axe-
  armed man upon a tree :
  Let your protecting help be near.

18 By the black band encompassed round,
  break it down, bold one, like a fort.
  Let your protecting help be near.

HYMN LXIII.   *Agni.*

1. EXERTING all our strength with thoughts of
power we glorify in speech

9 *Saptavadhri* : See V. 78. 6. His release seems to
have been effected by employing fire. But see Myrian-
theus, *Die Aśvins*, pp. 88, 90.

11 'Why is this (repeated invocation) addressed to
you as if you were decrepit like old men?'—Wilson.

12. *One common brotherhood* : as twin children of the
consort of Vivasvān, the Sun.

17 The meaning is obscure. 'Aśvins, the splendidly-
brilliant (sun cleaves the darkness) as the woodman
with his axe a tree.'—Wilson. He (the demon) looked
at the Aśvins.'—Grassmann.

18 The first line is said by Sāyaṇa to be addressed
to Saptavadhri. It seems to express self-encourage-
ment before an attack upon a Dāsa enemy. But see
Mvriantheus, *Die Aśvins*, p. 90.

1 I follow Ludwig in his interpretation of this
stanza the construction of which is difficult.

Agni your dear familiar Friend, the darling
  Guest in every home.

2 Whom, served with sacrificial oil like
  Mitra, men presenting gifts
  Eulogize with their songs of praise ;

3 Much-lauded Jātavedas, him who bears
  oblations up to heaven
  Prepared in service of the Gods.

4 To noblest Agni, Friend of man, best
  Vṛtra-slayer, are we come,
  Him in whose presence Ṛkṣa's son, mighty
  Śrutarvan, waxes great ;

5 To deathless Jātavedas, meet for praise,
  adored, with sacred oil,
  Visible through the gloom of night ;

6 Even Agni whom these priestly men worship
  with sacrificial gifts,
  With lifted ladles offering them.

7 O Agni, this our newest hymn hath been
  addressed from us to thee,
  O cheerful Guest, well-born, most wise,
  worker of wonders, ne'er deceived.

8 Agni, may it be dear to thee, most grateful, and exceeding sweet :
  Grow mightier, eulogized therewith.

9 Splendid with splendours may it be, and
  in the battle with the foe
  Add loftier glory to thy fame.

10 Steed, cow, a lord of heroes, bright like
  Indra, who shall fill the car.
  Whose high renown ye celebrate, and
  people praise each glorious deed.

11 Thou whom Gopavana made glad with
  song, O Agni Aṅgiras,
  Hear this my call, thou Holy One.

12 Thou whom the priestly folk implore to
  aid the gathering of the spoil,
  Such be thou in the fight with foes.

13 I, called to him who reels with joy, Śrutarvan, Ṛkṣa's son, shall stroke
  The heads of four presented steeds, like
  the long wool of fleecy rams.

14 Four coursers with a splendid car, Śaviṣṭha's horses, fleet of foot,
  Shall bring me to the sacred feast, as
  flying steeds brought Tugra's son.

2 *Like Mitra* : or as a friend ; or like the Sun—
Sāyana.

10 *Steed, cow* : there is no verb to govern these
accusatives. Perhaps, let it, that is, the hymn, give,
may be understood. Sāyaṇa explains *gām.* cow, by
gantāram, goer. '(Worship) ye men, the bright (Agni)
who goes like a horse and fills our chariots (with spoil).'
—Wilson.

14 *Tugra's son* : Bhujyu. See Vol. I., Index.

15 The very truth do I declare to thee,
   Paruṣṇī, mighty flood.
   Waters ! no man is there who gives
   more horses than Śaviṣṭha gives.

HYMN LXIV.   Agni.

1. YOKE, Agni, as a charioteer, thy steeds
   who best invite the Gods: As ancient
   Herald seat thyself.

2 And, God, as skilfullest of all, call for us
   hitherward the Gods:
   Give all our wishes sure effect.

3 For thou, Most Youthful, Son of Strength,
   thou to whom sacrifice is paid,
   Art holy, faithful to the Law.

4 This Agni, Lord of wealth and spoil hundredfold, thousandfold, is head
   And chief of riches and a Sage.

5 As craftsmen bend the felly, so bend at
   our general call: come nigh,
   Aṅgiras, to the sacrifice.

6 Now, O Virūpa, rouse for him, Strong God
   who shines at early morn,
   Fair praise with voice that ceases not.

7 With missile of this Agni, his who looks
   afar, will we lay low
   The thief in combat for the kine.

8 Let not the Companies of Gods fail us, like
   Dawns that float away,
   Like cows who leave the niggardly.

9 Let not the sinful tyranny of any fiercely-
   hating foe
   Smite us, as billows smite a ship.

10 O Agni, God, the people sing reverent
   praise to thee for strength :
   With terrors trouble thou the foe.

11 Wilt thou not, Agni, lend us aid in winning cattle, winning wealth ?
   Maker of room, make room for us.

12 In this great battle cast us not aside as
   one who bears a load :
   Snatch up the wealth and win it all.

13 O Agni, let this plague pursue and fright
   another and not us :
   Make our impetuous strength more strong.

14 The reverent or unwearied man whose
   holy labour he accepts,
   Him Agni favours with success.

15 Abandoning the foeman's host pass hither
   to this company :
   Assist the men with whom I stand.

16 As we have known thy gracious help, as
   of a Father, long ago,
   So now we pray to thee for bliss.

HYMN LXV.   Indra.

1. NOT to forsake me, I invoke this Indra girt
   by Maruts,
   Lord Of magic power who rules with
   might.

2 This Indra with his Marut Friends clave
   into pieces Vṛtra's head
   With hundred-knotted thunderbolt.

3 Indra, with Marut Friends grown strong,
   hath rent asunder Vṛtra, and
   Released the waters of the sea.

4 This is that Indra who, begirt by Maruts,
   won the light of heaven
   That he might drink the Soma juice.

5 Mighty, impetuous, begirt by Maruts, him
   who loudly roars,
   Indra we invocate with songs.

6 Indra begirt by Maruts we invoke after the
   ancient plan,
   That he may drink the Soma juice.

7 O liberal Indra, Marut-girt, much-lauded
   Śatakratu, drink
   The Soma at this sacrifice.

8 To thee, O Indra, Marut-girt, these Soma
   juices, Thunderer !
   Are offered from the heart with lauds.

9 Drink, Indra, with thy Marut Friends,
   pressed Soma at the morning rites,
   Whetting thy thunderbolt with strength.

10 Arising in thy might, thy jaws thou
   shookest, Indra, having quaffed
   The Soma which the mortar pressed.

11 Indra, both worlds complained to thee
   when uttering thy fearful roar,

---

15 *Paruṣṇī* : now the Rāvī, the river on whose bank
Śrutarvan offered his sacrifice.

---

1 *Ancient Herald* : or, chief Invoker.

6 *Virūpa* : the Ṛṣi of the hymn who addresses himself. *Who shines at early morn* : or, aspiring heavenward.

7 *The thief* : the hymn is a prayer for aid in an
expedition for the recovery of stolen cattle.

8 *Like Dawns that float away* : 'like cows that bathe
them in the stream,' according to the explanation given
in the St. Petersburg Lexicon. *Like cows who leave the
niggardly* : 'the kine abandon not a little (calf).'—
Wilson.

---

3 *Of the sea* : of the firmament or ocean of air.

11 *Complained to thee* : in terror. *When uttering thy
fearful roar* : the meaning of *krákṣamāṇam*, rendered
thus conjecturally, is uncertain.

What time thou smotest Dasyus dead.

12 From Indra have I measured out a song
eight-footed with nine parts,
Delicate, faithful, to the Law.

HYMN LXVI. *Indra.*

1. SCARCELY was Śatakratu born when of his
Mother he inquired,
Who are the mighty? Who are famed?

2. Then Śavasī declared to him Aurṇavābha,
Ahīśuva:
Son, these be they thou must o'erthrow.

3 The Vṛtra-slayer smote them all as spokes
are hammered into naves:
The Dasyu-killer waxed in might.

4 Then Indra at a single draught drank the
contents of thirty pails,
Pails that were filled with Soma juice.

5 Indra in groundless realms of space pierced
the Gandharva through, that he
Might make Brahmans' strength increase.

6 Down from the mountains Indra shot
hither his well-directed shaft:
He gained the ready brew of rice.

7 One only is that shaft of thine, with thousand feathers, hundred barbs,
Which, Indra, thou hast made thy friend.

8 Strong as the Ṛbhus at thy birth, therewith to those who praise thee, men
And women, bring thou food to eat.

9 By thee these exploits were achieved, the
mightiest deeds, abundantly:
Firm in thy heart thou settest them.

10 All these things Viṣṇu brought, the Lord
of ample stride whom thou hadst sent—
A hundred buffaloes, a brew of rice and
milk: and Indra slew the ravening
boar

11 Most deadly is thy bow, successful, fashioned well: good is thine arrow, decked
with gold.
Warlike and well equipped thine arms
are, which increase sweetness for him
who drinks the sweet.

HYMN LXVII. *Indra.*

1. BRING us a thousand, Indra, as our
guerdon for the Soma juice:
Hundreds of kine, O Hero, bring.

2 Bring cattle, bring us ornament, bring us
embellishment and steeds,
Give us, besides, two rings of gold.

3 And, Bold One, bring in ample store rich
jewels to adorn the ear,
For thou, Good Lord, art far renowned.

4 None other is there for the priest, Hero!
but thou, to give him gifts,
To win much spoil and prosper him.

5 Indra can never be brought low, Śakra can
never be subdued:
He heareth and beholdeth all.

6 He spieth out the wrath of man, he who
can never be deceived:
Ere blame can come he marketh it.

7 He hath his stomach full of might, the
Vṛtra-slayer, Conqueror,
The Soma-drinker, ordering all.

---

12 *Eight-footed with nine parts:* the hymn consists of triplets, each of which contains nine Pādas, parts or half-lines, of eight feet or syllables each. That is, the metre is octosyllabic (8×3), and the triplet contains three stanzas in that metre, or nine octosyllabic Pādas. *From Indra:* originating in him as its subject or inspirer. *Faithful to the Law:* closely connected with sacrifice.

---

1 Cp. VIII. 45. 4.

2 *Śavasī:* or, the Mighty One. Indra's Mother. Aurṇavābha or Urṇavābha's son. See VIII 32. 26. *These:* and other fiends, as *té*, these, is plural.

4 *Pails:* or, bowls: literally, lakes. The meaning of the word *kāṇuka* in this stanza is uncertain. It appears to be an adjective qualifying *sarāṁsi* pails or lakes. See note in Wilson's Translation.

5 *The Gandharva:* a heavenly being who dwells in the region of the air and guards the celestial Soma, that is, the rain. See I. 22. 14, and 163. 2. According to Sāyaṇa, the Gandharva is the rain-cloud itself, which Indra shattered, and so released the fertilizing water.

6 The stanza is similarly explained by Sāyaṇa. Indra smote the rain from the clouds, and obtained food for men.

7 *One only:* Indra alone is the wielder of the thunderbolt.

---

10 *All these things:* the buffaloes or dark clouds, and the rice and milk or fertilizing rain. *Slew:* the verb is supplied by Sāyaṇa. *The ravening boar:* Vṛtra. Cf. I. 61. 7, where the deed is similarly related. See Prof. A.A. Macdonell, *Journal R. A. Society,* 1895, p. 186.

11 *Which increase sweetness for him who drinks the sweet:* this is Ludwig's interpretation of two very difficult words which mean according to Wilson's Translation, 'destructively overthrowing, destructively piercing; according to the St. Petersburg Lexicon, 'like two bees delighting in sweetness;' and according to Grassmann, 'sweetness lo es thy two lips.'

---

1 *A thous nd:* cows, understood.

2 *Two rings:* the meaning of *manā* here is somewhat uncertain. See Max Müller, *India, What can it Teach us?* pp. 125, 126; Weber, *Episches im Vedichen Ritual,* p. 30; and Zimmer, *Altindisches Leben,* pp. 50, 51.

8 In thee all treasures are combined, Soma !
    all blessed things in thee,
Uninjured, easy to bestow.

9 To thee speeds forth my hope that craves
    the gift of corn, and kine and gold,
Yea, craving horses, speeds to thee.

10 Indra, through hope in thee alone even
    this sickle do I grasp.
Fill my hand, Maghavan, with all that
    it can hold of barley cut or gathered up.

HYMN LXVIII.   *Soma.*

1. THIS here is Soma, ne'er restrained, active,
    all-conquering bursting forth,
Ṛṣi and Sage by sapience.

2 All that is bare he covers o'er, all that
    is sick he medicines ;
The blind man sees, the cripple walks.

3 Thou, Soma, givest wide defence against
    the hate of alien men,
Hatreds that waste and weaken us.

4 Thou by thine insight and thy skill, Impe-
    tuous One, from heaven and earth
Drivest the sinner's enmity.

5 When to their task they come with zeal,
    may they obtain the Giver's grace,
And satisfy his wish who thirsts.

6 So may he find what erst was lost, so may
    he speed the pious man,
And lengthen his remaining life.

7 Gracious, displaying tender love, uncon-
    quered, gentle in thy thoughts,
Be sweet, O Soma, to our heart.

8 O Soma, terrify us not ; strike us not with
    alarm, O King :
Wound not our heart with dazzling flame.

9 When in my dwelling-place I see the
    wicked enemies of Gods,
King, chase their hatred far away, thou
    Bounteous One, dispel our foes.

---

8 *Soma* : here said to mean Indra himself.

10 'It would appear as if the field were a barren
one and the poet sought from *Indra* a harvest which
he had not sown.'—Wilson.

1 *Bursting forth* : according to Sāyaṇa, causing
(fruit) to spring forth.

4 *Impetuous One* : ṛjiṣin : according to Sāyaṇa,
'possessed of the remains or dregs of the Soma juice
offered in the third *savana.*'

5 *They* : the priests. *The Giver's* : bountiful Indra's.
His wish : Indra's longing for Soma-libations.

9 *The wicked enemies* : or, the enmities; that is, when
I see that the Gods are displeased with me.

HYMN LXIX.   *Indra.*

1. O ŚATAKRATU, truly I have made none else
    my Comforter.
Indra,' be gracious unto us.

2 Thou who hast ever aided us kindly of
    old to win the spoil,
As such, O Indra, favour us.

3 What now ? As prompter of the poor thou
    helpest him who sheds the juice.
Wilt thou not, Indra, strengthen us ?

4 O Indra, help our chariot on, yea, Thun-
    derer, though it lag behind :
Give this my car the foremost place.

5 Ho there ! why sittest thou at ease ?
    Make thou my chariot to be first :
And bring the fame of victory near.

6 Assist our car that seeks the prize. What
    can be easier for thee ?
So make thou us victorious.

7 Indra, be firm : a fort art thou. To thine
    appointed place proceeds
The auspicious hymn in season due.

8 Let not our portion be disgrace. Broad is
    the course, the prize is set,
The barriers are opened wide.

9 This thing we wish, that thou mayst take
    thy fourth, thy sacrificial name.
So art thou held to be our Lord.

10 Ekadyū hath exalted thee, Immortals: both
    Goddesses and Gods hath he delighted.
Bestow upon him bounty meet for praises.
    May he, enriched with prayer, come
    soon and early.

HYMN LXX.   *Indra.*

1. INDRA, God of the mighty arm, gather
    for us with thy right hand
Manifold and nutritious spoil.

2 We know thee mighty in thy deeds, of
    mighty bounty, mighty wealth,
Mighty in measure, prompt to aid.

3 Hero, when thou art fain to give, neither
    may Gods nor mortal men

---

4 The hymn is a prayer for success in a coming
chariot race.

7 *To thine appointed place* : 'to thee the repeller (of
enemies).'—Wilson.

9 *Thy fourth, thy sacrificial name* : the other three,
according to Sāyaṇa, are the constellation-names, the
secret name, and the revealed name.

10 The Gods in general are the deities of this stanza.
Ekadyū is the seer of the hymn. *He, enriched with prayer*:
Indra, exalted by our hymn.

Restrain thee like a fearful Bull.

4 Come, let us glorify Indra, Lord supreme
of wealth, Self-ruling King :
In bounty may he harm us not.

5 Let prelude sound and following chant :
so let him hear the Sāman sung,
And with his bounty answer us.

6 O Indra, with thy right hand bring, and
with thy left remember us :
Let us not lose our share of wealth.

7 Come nigh, O Bold One, boldly bring
hither the riches of the churl
Who giveth least of all the folk.

8 Indra, the booty which thou hast with
holy singers to receive,
Even that booty win with us.

9 Indra, thy swiftly-coming spoil, the booty
which rejoices all,
Sounds quick in concert with our hopes.

HYMN LXXI. *Indra.*

1. HASTE forward to us from afar, or, Vṛtra-
slayer, from anear,
To meet the offering to the meath.

2 Strong are the Soma-draughts; come nigh :
the juices fill thee with delight :
Drink boldly even as thou art wont.

3 Joy, Indra, in the strengthening food :
let it content thy wish and thought,
And be delightful to thine heart.

4 Come to us thou who hast no foe : we
call thee down to hymns of praise,
In heaven's sublimest realm of light.

5 This Soma here expressed with stones and
dressed with milk for thy carouse,
Indra, is offered up to thee.

6 Graciously, Indra, hear my call. Come
and obtain the draught, and sate
Thyself with juices blent with milk.

7 The Soma, Indra, which is shed in chalices
and vats for thee,
Drink thou, for thou art Lord thereof.

8 The Soma seen within the vats, as in the
flood the Moon is seen,
Drink thou, for thou art Lord thereof.

9 That which the Hawk brought in his
claw, inviolate, through the air to thee,
Drink thou, for thou art Lord thereof.

HYMN LXXII. *Viśvedevas.*

1. WE choose unto ourselves that high protection of the Mighty Gods
That it may help and succour us.

2 May they be ever our allies, Varuṇa,
Mitra, Aryaman,
Far-seeing Gods who prosper us.

3 Ye furtherers of holy Law, transport us
safe o'er many woes,
As over water-floods in ships.

4 Dear wealth be Aryaman to us, Varuṇa
dear wealth meet for praise :
Dear wealth we choose unto ourselves.

5 For Sovrans of dear wealth are ye, Ādityas,
not of sinner's wealth,
Ye sapient Gods who slay the foe.

6 We in our homes, ye Bounteous Ones,
and while we journey on the road,
Invoke you, Gods, to prosper us.

7 Regard us, Indra, Viṣṇu, here, ye Aśvins
and the Marut host,
Us who are kith and kin to you.

8 Ye Bounteous Ones, from time of old we
here set forth our brotherhood,
Our kinship in the Mother's womb.

9 Then come with Indra for your chief, as
early day, ye Bounteous Gods
Yea, I address you now for this.

HYMN LXXIII. *Agni.*

1. AGNI, your dearest Guest, I laud, him who
is loving as a friend,
Who brings us riches like a car.

2 Whom as a far-foreseeing Sage the
Gods have, from the olden time,
Established among mortal men.

3 Do thou, Most Youthful God, protect the
men who offer, hear their songs,
And of thyself preserve their seed.

---

5 *Let prelude sound : prá stoṣad upagāsiṣat :* let the
prastotar and the *uagātar,* two of the officiating priests at
the chanting of a Sāman, discharge their functions : the
former singing the prelude and the latter the accom-
paniment.

8 *Win with us :* make us thy allies.

9 *Sounds in concert with our hopes :* answers to our
expectation. Perhaps as Ludwig thinks, the word
'sounds' refers to the herd of cattle which probably
constituted the spoil that is spoken of.

---

8 *The Moon :* in allusion to the double meaning of
Soma, the plant and its juice, and the Moon.

9 *The Hawk :* See I. 80. 2, and 93. 6.

8 *In the Mother's womb :* as common children of Aditi
the General Mother of all living beings.

3 *And of thyself preserve their seed :* or, and guard
our offspring and ourselves.

4 What is the praise wherewith, O God,
Aṅgiras, Agni, Son of Strength,
We, after thine own wish and thought,

5 May serve thee, O thou Child of Power,
and with what sacrifice's plan ?
What prayer shall I now speak to thee ?

6 Our God, make all of us to dwell in happy
habitations, and
Reward our songs with spoil and wealth.

7 Lord of the house, what plenty fills the
songs which thou inspirest now,
Thou whose hymn helps to win the kine ?

8 Him Wise and Strong they glorify, the
foremost Champion in the fray,
And mighty in his dwelling-place.

9 Agni, he dwells in rest and peace who
smites and no one smites again:
With hero sons he prospers well

HYMN LXXIV. *Aśvins.*

1. To this mine invocation, O ye Aśvins,
ye Nāsatyas, come,
To drink the savoury Soma juice.

2 This laud of mine, ye Aśvins Twain, and
this mine invitation hear,
To drink the savoury Soma juice.

3 Here Kṛṣṇa is invoking you, O Aśvins,
Lords of ample wealth.
To drink the savoury Soma juice.

4 List, Heroes, to the singer's call, the call
of Kṛṣṇa lauding you,
To drink the savoury Soma juice.

5 Chiefs, to the sage who sings your praise
grant an inviolable home,
To drink the savoury Soma juice.

6 Come to the worshipper's abode, Aśvins,
who here is lauding you,
To drink the savoury Soma juice.

7 Yoke to the firmly jointed car the ass
which draws you, Lords of wealth.
To drink the savoury Soma juice.

8 Come hither, Aśvins, on your car of
triple form with triple seat,
To drink the savoury Soma juice.

9 O Aśvins, O Nāsatyas, now accept with
favouring grace my songs,
To drink the savoury Soma juice.

9 *He* : the faithful worshipper.

5 *To drink*: so that ye may drink.
7 *The ass* : cf. I. 34. 9; 116. 2; and 162. 21.
8 *Of triple form with triple seat* : See I. 34. 2, 9.

HYMN LXXV. *Aśvins.*

1. YE Twain are wondrous strong, well-
skilled in arts that heal, both bringers
of delight, ye both won Dakṣa's praise.
Viśvaka calls on you as such to save his
life. Break ye not off our friendship,
come and set me free.

2 How shall he praise you now who is
distraught in mind ? Ye Twain give
wisdom for the gain of what is good.
Viśvaka calls on you as such to save his
life. Break ye not off our friendship,
come and set me free.

3 Already have ye Twain, possessors of great
wealth, prospered Viṣṇāpū thus for
gain of what is good.
Viśvaka calls on you as such to save his
life. Break ye not off our friendship,
come and set me free.

4 And that Impetuous Hero, winner of the
spoil, though he is far away, we call to
succour us,
Whose gracious favour, like a father's,
is most sweet. Break ye not off our
friendship, come and set me free.

5 About the holy Law toils Savitar the God :
the horn of holy Law hath he spread
far and wide.
The holy Law hath quelled even mighty
men of war. Break ye not off our
friendship, come and set me free.

HYMN LXXVI. *Aśvins.*

1. SPLENDID, O Aśvins, is your praise. Come
fountain-like, to pour the stream.
Of the sweet juice effused—dear is it,
Chiefs, in heaven—drink like two wild
bulls at a pool.

The Ṛṣi is Viśvaka son of Kṛṣṇa.

1 *Dakṣa's praise* : on the occasion mentioned in I.
116. 2; or when the Aśvins won Sūryā for their bride,
I. 116. 17. *To save his life* : according to Sāyaṇa, 'for
the sake of his son.' *Come and set me free* : 'flying loose
(your reins and gallop hither).'—Wilson. 'Unyoke
your horses.'Grassmann.

2 *Distraught in mind* : referring either to Viśvaka
himself, or the man for whom he invokes the Aśvins'
aid. According to Sāyaṇa, Vimanāḥ (distraught in
mind) here is the name of a Ṛṣi.

3 *Viṣṇāpū* : the Ṛṣi's son or grandson.

4 *That Impetuous Hero* : Indra. 'These two verses,'
says Grassmann, 'are taken from another hymn. Verse
5 is addressed to Savitar, and verse 4, as it appears, to
Indra. The refrain, which is altogether unsuitable here,
has been added in order to connect the verses with the
preceding hymn.'

2 Drink the libation rich in sweets, O Aśvins
   Twain: sit. Heroes, on the sacred grass.
  Do ye with joyful heart in the abode of
   man preserve his life by means of
   wealth.

3 The Priyamedhas bid you come with all
   the succours that are yours.
  Come to his house whose holy grass is
   trimmed, to dear sacrifice at the morning
   rites.

4 Drink ye the Soma rich in meath, ye
   Aśvins Twain : sit gladly on the sacred
   grass.
  So, waxen mighty, to our eulogy from
   heaven come ye as wild-bulls to the pool.

5 Come to us, O ye Aśvins, now with steeds
   of many a varied hue,
  Ye Lords of splendour, wondrous, borne
   on paths of gold, drink Soma, ye who
   strengthen Law.

6 For we the priestly singers, fain to hymn
   your praise, invoke you for the gain of
   strength.
  So, wondrous, fair, and famed for great
   deeds come to us, through our hymn,
   Aśvins, when ye hear.

HYMN LXXVII.   *Indra.*

1. As cows low to their calves in stalls, so
   with our songs we glorify
  This Indra, even your Wondrous God who
   checks attack, who joys in the delicious
   juice.

2 Celestial, bounteous Giver, girt about
   with might, rich, mountain-like, in
   precious things,
  Him swift we seek for foodful booty rich
   in kine, brought hundredfold and
   thousandfold.

3 Indra, the strong and lofty hills are
   powerless to bar thy way.
  None stay that act of thine when thou
   wouldst fain give wealth to one like me
   who sings thy praise.

4 A Warrior thou by strength, wisdom, and
   wondrous deed, in might excellest all
   that is.

Hither may this our hymn attract thee to
   our help, the hymn which Gotamas have
   made.

5 For in thy might thou stretchest out
   beyond the boundaries of heaven.
  The earthly region, Indra, comprehends
   thee not. After thy Godhead hast thou
   waxed.

6 When, Maghavan, thou honourest the
   worshipper, no one is there to stay thy
   wealth.
  Most liberal Giver thou, do thou inspire
   our song of praise, that we may win the
   spoil.

HYMN LXXVIII.   *Indra.*

1. To Indra sing the lofty hymn, Maruts !
   that slays the Vṛtras best.
  Whereby the Holy Ones created for the
   God the light divine that ever wakes.

2 Indra who quells the curse blew curses far
   away, and then in splendour came to
   us.
  Indra, refulgent with thy Marut host ! the
   Gods strove eagerly to win thy love.

3 Sing to your lofty Indra, sing, Maruts,
   a holy hymn of praise.
  Let Śatakratu, Vṛtra-slayer, kill the foe
   with hundred-knotted thunderbolt.

4 Aim and fetch boldly forth, O thou whose
   heart is bold : great glory will be thine
   thereby.
  In rapid torrent let the mother waters
   spread. Slay Vṛtra, win the light of
   heaven.

5 When thou, unequalled Maghavan, wast
   born to smite the Vṛtras dead,
  Thou spreadest out the spacious earth and
   didst support and prop the heavens.

6 Then was the sacrifice produced for thee,
   the laud, and song of joy,
  Thou in thy might surpassest all, all that
   now is and yet shall be.

---

2 *The libation* : *gharmám* : the heated milk or \ other
beverage, or the vessel in which it is heated.

3 *The Priyamedhas* : Priyamedha and his family.

---

1 *As cows* : the cows who are milked for sacrificial
purposes, whose calves are shut up during the ceremony.

5 *The earthly region* : the *rajas* region, middle air,
or firmament is frequently divided into two, one half belonging to the earth and the other half to the sky. See
Wallis, *Cosmology of the Ṛgveda,* pp. 114, 115.

---

1 *Maruts* : here meaning the singers of the hymn of
praise. 'Priests.'—Wilson. *The light divine* : the Sun,
which the Viśvedevas generated or created for Indra.

7 Raw kine thou filledst with ripe milk.
Thou madest Sūrya rise to heaven.
Heat him as milk is heated with pure
Sāma hymns, great joy to him who
loves the song.

HYMN LXXIX. *Indra.*

1. MAY Indra, who in every fight must be
invoked, be near to us.
May the most mighty Vṛtra-slayer, meet
for praise, come to libations and to
hymns.

2 Thou art the best of all in sending
bounteous gifts, true art thou, lordly in
thine act.
We claim alliance with the very Glorious
One, yea, with the Mighty Son of
Strength.

3 Prayers unsurpassed are offered up to thee
the Lover of the Song.
Indra, Lord of Bay Steeds, accept these
fitting hymns, hymns which we have
thought out for thee.

4 For thou, O Maghavan, art truthful, ne'er
subdued and bringest many a Vṛtra low.
As such, O Mightiest Lord, Wielder of
Thunder, send wealth hither to the
worshipper.

5 O Indra, thou art far-renowned, impetuous, O Lord of Strength.
Alone thou slayest with the guardian of
mankind resistless never-conquered foes.

6 As such we seek thee now, O Asura, thee
most wise, craving thy bounty as our
share.
Thy sheltering defence is like a mighty
cloak. So may thy glories reach to us.

HYMN LXXX. *Indra.*

1. DOWN to the stream a maiden came, and
found the Soma by the way.
Bearing it to her home she said, For Indra
will I press thee out, for Śakra will I
press thee out.

2 Thou roaming yonder, little man, beholding
every house in turn,
Drink thou this Soma pressed with teeth,
accompanied with grain and curds, with
cake of meal and song of praise.

3 Fain would we learn to know thee well,
nor yet can we attain to thee.
Still slowly and in gradual drops, O
Indu, unto Indra flow.

4 Will he not help and work for us? Will
he not make us wealthier?
Shall we not, hostile to our lord, unite
ourselves to Indra now?

5 O Indra, cause to sprout again three
places, these which I declare,—
My father's head, his cultured field, and
this the part below my waist.

6 Make all of these grow crops of hair, you
cultivated field of ours,
My body, and my father's head.

7 Cleansing Apālā, Indra! thrice, thou
gavest sunlike skin to her,
Drawn, Śatakratu! through the hole of
car, of wagon, and of yoke.

The Ṛṣi is Apālā of the family of Atri.
1 *A maiden*: Apālā.
2 *Little man*: *virakāḥ*: according to Sāyaṇa, hero.
Indra is intended perhaps as Sūrya the Sun-God.
3 *Indu*: Soma.
4 *He*: Indra. *Hostile to our lord*: Apālā, it is said,
was afflicted with a cutaneous disease and was consequently repudiated by her husband.
7 *Sunlike*: bright and clear. 'Sāyaṇa says that Indra
dragged her through the wide hole of his chariot,
the narrower hole of the cart and the small hole of the
yoke, and she cast off three skins. The first skin became
a hedgehog, the second an alligator, the third a chame-
leon. I suppose, with Prof. Aufrecht, that the hole
or space of the chariot and cart represents the opening
between the four wheels; the hole of the yoke seems
to me to mean the opening through which the animal's
head passed, corresponding to Homer's *exuglē* II. 19.
406.'—Cowell.

For the legend from the Śātyāyana Brāhmaṇa, founded on the hints contained in this hymn and repeated
by Sāyaṇa in his Commentary, see also Wilson's Translation, Vol. V.

Prof. Aufrecht has published the text and commentary of this hymn in *Indische Studien*, IV. p. 1 sqq.
See M. Müller's Ṛgveda Saṁhitā, Vol. III., 2nd edition, p. 33 sqq.

---

7 *Raw kine*; cf. I. 62. 9; 180. 3; II. 40. 2; IV 3. 9;
VI. 72. 4; 17. 6; 44. 24; VIII. 32. 25. *Thou madest
Sūrya rise to heaven*: Sāyaṇa relates a legend that
when the Paṇis had carried off the cows of the Aṅgirases
and placed them in a mountain enveloped in darkness,
Indra, at the prayer of the Ṛṣis, set the sun in heaven
in order that he might see and recover their cattle.
Heat him as milk is heated: this line is difficult. '(Priests)
excite (Indra) with your praises as men heat the *Gharma*
with *Sāman*-hymns.'—Wilson. *Gharma* means either the
hot milk or other beverage offered in the Pravargya
ceremony, or the vessel in which it is heated. *Great joy
to him who loves the song*: or perhaps the meaning is, the
Bṛhat-Sāman (one of the most important Sāma hymns,
the first and second verses of R.V. VI. 46), is dear to
him who loves song.

---

3 *Fitting hymns*: *yojanā*: See Wilson's Translation and
note.

5 *The guardian of mankind*: Indra's thunderbolt with
which he slays the demons of drought.

HYMN LXXXI.   *Indra.*

1. INVITE ye Indra with a song to drink
   your draught of Soma juice,
   All-conquering Śatakratu, most munificent
   of all who live.

2 Lauded by many, much-invoked, leader
   of song, renowned of old :
   His name is Indra, tell it forth.

3 Indra the Dancer be to us the giver of
   abundant strength :
   May he, the mighty, bring it near.

4 Indra whose jaws are strong hath drunk
   of worshipping Sudakṣa's draught,
   The Soma juice with barley mixt.

5 Call Indra loudly with your songs of
   praise to drink the Soma juice.
   For this is what augments his strength.

6 When he hath drunk its gladdening drops,
   the God with vigour of a God
   Hath far surpassed all things that are.

7 Thou speedest down to succour us this
   ever-conquering God of yours,
   Him who is drawn to all our songs ;

8 The Warrior not to be restrained, the
   Soma-drinker ne'er o'erthrown,
   The Chieftain of resistless might.

9 O Indra, send us riches, thou Omniscient,
   worthy of our praise :
   Help us in the decisive fray.

10 Even thence, O Indra, come to us with
   food that gives a hundred powers,
   With food that gives a thousand powers.

11 We sought the wisdom of the wise. Śakra,
   Kine-giver, Thunder-armed !
   May we with steeds o'ercome in fight.

12 We make thee, Śatakratu, find enjoyment
   in the songs we sing,
   Like cattle in the pasture lands.

13 For, Śatakratu, Thunder-armed, all that
   we craved, as men are wont,

All that we hoped, have we attained.

14 Those, Son of Strength, are come to thee
   who cherish wishes in their hearts :
   O Indra, none excelleth thee.

15 So, Hero, guard us with thy care, with
   thy most liberal providence,
   Speedy, and terrible to foes.

16 O Śatakratu Indra, now rejoice with that
   carouse of thine
   Which is most splendid of them all ;

17 Even, Indra, that carouse which slays the
   Vṛtras best, most widely famed,
   Best giver of thy power and might.

18 For that which is thy gift we know, true
   Soma-drinker, Thunder-armed,
   Mighty One, amid all the folk.

19 For Indra, Lover of Carouse, loud be
   our songs about the juice :
   Let poets sing the song of praise.

20 We summon Indra to the draught, in
   whom all glories rest, in whom
   The seven communities rejoice.

21 At the Trikadrukas the Gods span sacrifice
   that stirs the mind :
   Let our songs aid and prosper it.

22 Let the drops pass within thee as the rivers
   flow into the sea :
   O Indra, naught excelleth thee.

23 Thou, wakeful Hero, by thy might hast
   taken food of Soma juice,
   Which, Indra, is within thee now.

24 O Indra, Vṛtra-slayer, let Soma be ready
   for thy maw,
   The drops be ready for thy forms.

25 Now Śrutakakṣa sings his song that cattle
   and the steed may come,
   That Indra's very self may come.

26 Here, Indra, thou art ready by our Soma
   juices shed for thee,
   Śakra, at hand that thou mayst give.

27 Even from far away our songs reach thee,
   O Caster of the Stone :
   May we come very close to thee.

3 *The Dancer* : active in battle, dancer of the war
dance. *Near* : *abhijñú* : or, up to our knees.

4 *Sudakṣa's draught.* : offered by a Ṛṣi of that name.

7 According to Sāyaṇa this stanza is addressed by
the *Yajamāna* or sacrificer to the *Stotar* or praising
priest, and he gives an imperative sense to the indicative, thou speedest down : 'Bring hither.'—Wilson.

10 *Even thence* : from where thou art ; from heaven.

11 *Of the wise* : Indra. *Kine-giver* : *godare* : perhaps,
'burster open of the cow-stall ;' 'cleaver of mountains.'
—Wilson.

12 *Like cattle* : as the cowherd refreshes his cattle.—
Sāyaṇa.

18 *Thy gift* : the wealth which thou givest. *Amid all
the folk* : among all the worshippers who offer thee
Soma.—Sāyaṇa.

20 *Seven communities* : *saptá saṁsddaḥ* : probably = all
the folk, in stanza 18 ; 'the seven associated priests.'—
Wilson.

21 *At the Trikadrukas* : See VIII. 13. 18, and note.

24 *Thy forms* : thy various bodies or splendours.—
Sāyaṇa.

25 *Śrutakakṣa* : the Ṛṣi of the hymn.

28 For so thou art the hero's Friend, a Hero,
  too, art thou, and strong :
  So may thine heart be won to us.

29 So hath the offering, wealthiest Lord,
  been paid by all the worshippers :
  So dwell thou, Indra, even with me.

30 Be not thou like a slothful priest, O Lord
  of spoil and wealth : rejoice
  In the pressed Soma blent with milk.

31 O Indra, let not ill designs surround us
  in the sunbeams' light :
  This may we gain with thee for Friend.

32 With thee to help us, Indra, let us answer
  all our enemies :
  For thou art ours and we are thine.

33 Indra, the poets and thy friends, faithful
  to thee, shall loudly sing
  Thy praises as they follow thee.

HYMN LXXXII.   *Indra.*

1. SŪRYA, thou mountest up to meet the
  Hero famous for his wealth,
  Who hurls the bolt and works for man :

2 Him who with might of both his arms
  brake nine-and-ninety castles down,
  Slew Vṛtra and smote Ahi dead.

3 This Indra is our gracious Friend. He
  sends us in a full broad stream
  Riches in horses, kine, and corn.

4 Whatever, Vṛtra-slayer ! thou, Sūrya, hast
  risen upon to-day,
  That, Indra, all is in thy power.

5 When, Mighty One, Lord of the brave,
  thou thinkest thus, I shall not die,
  That thought of thine is true indeed.

6 Thou, Indra, goest unto all Soma libations
  shed for thee,
  Both far away and near at hand.

7 We make this Indra very strong to strike
  the mighty Vṛtra dead :
  A vigorous Hero shall he be.

8 Indra was made for giving, set, most
  mighty, o'er the joyous draught.
  Bright, meet for Soma, famed in song.

9 By song as 'twere, the powerful bolt which
  none may parry was prepared :
  Lofty, invincible he grew.

10 Indra, Song-lover, lauded, make even in
  the wilds fair ways for us,
  Whenever, Maghavan, thou wilt.

11 Thou whose commandment and behest of
  sovran sway none disregards,
  Neither audacious man nor God.

12 And both these Goddesses, Earth, Heaven,
  Lord of the beauteous helm ! revere
  Thy might which no one may resist.

13 Thou in the black cows and the red and
  in the cows with spotted skin
  This white milk hast deposited.

14 When in their terror all the Gods shrank
  from the Dragon's furious might,
  Fear of the monster fell on them.

15 Then he was my Defender, then, Invincible, whose foe is not,
  The Vṛtra-slayer showed his might.

16 Him your best Vṛtra-slayer, him the
  famous Champion of mankind
  I urge to great munificence,

17 To come, Much-lauded ! Many-named !
  with this same thought that longs for
  milk,
  Whene'er the Soma juice is shed.

18 Much-honoured by libations, may the
  Vṛtra-slayer wake for us :
  May Śakra listen to our prayers.

19 O Hero, with that aid dost thou delight
  us, with what succour bring
  Riches to those who worship thee ?

20 With whose libation joys the Strong, the
  Hero with his team who quells
  The foe, to drink the Soma juice ?

21 Rejoicing in thy spirit bring thousandfold
  opulence to us :
  Enrich thy votary with gifts.

22 These juices with their wedded wives flow
  to enjoyment lovingly :

30 *Priest* : *brahmā* : Brahman or praying priest.

31 *In the sunbeams' light* : as Indra stands in the
closest relationship to the Sun.

———

2 *Nine-and-ninety castles* : cloud-castles of the demon
Śambara.

8 *Was made* : was created by Prajāpati.—Sāyaṇa.

12 *Lord of the beauteous helm* : or 'deity of the handsome jaw.'—Wilson.

13 *In the black cows* : cf I. 62. 9.

14 *The Dragon's furious might* : the fierce attack of the
demon Ahi. *Of the monster* : or, of the wild beast, Ahi.

16 *Champion* : I join *prá* to *śárdham,* as suggested in
the St. Petersburg Lexicon.

17 *To come* : that is, that thou, Indra, mayst come,
This abrupt change of person is not uncommon in the
Veda.

22 The *wedded wives*: of the Soma juices are said to be
the two waters called *vasativaryaḥ* and *ekadhanāḥ,* used in
the Soma ceremonies. *To enjoyment* : to be drunk by
Indra. *To waters speeds the restless one* : or, with Grassmann, 'The lover of the waters speeds.' The exact
meaning of *nicumpuṇḍ ḥ* is uncertain, Yāska deriving
it from *cam,* to eat, and Mahīdhara from *cup,* to
creep or move slowly. The meaning of the sentence

To waters speeds the restless one.

23 Presented strengthening gifts have sent
  Indra away at sacrifice,
  With might, unto the cleansing bath.

24 These two who share his feast, Bay Steeds
  with golden manes, shall bring him to
  The banquet that is laid for him.

25 For thee, O Lord of Light, are shed these
  Soma-drops, and grass is strewn :
  Bring Indra to his worshippers.

26 May Indra give thee skill, and lights of
  heaven, wealth to his votary
  And priests who praise him : laud ye him.

27 O Śatakratu, wondrous strength and all
  our lauds I bring to thee :
  Be gracious to thy worshippers.

28 Bring to us all things excellent, O Śatakratu,
  food and strength :
  For, Indra, thou art kind to us.

29 O Śatakratu, bring to us all blessings, all
  felicity :
  For, Indra, thou art kind to us.

30 Bearing the Soma juice we call, best Vṛtra-
  slayer, unto thee :
  For, Indra, thou art kind to us.

31 Come, Lord of rapturous joys, to our
  libation with thy Bay Steeds, come
  To our libation with thy Steeds.

32 Known as best Vṛtra-slayer erst, as Indra
  Śatakratu, come
  With Bay Steeds to the juice we shed.

33 O Vṛtra-slayer, thou art he who drinks
  these drops of Soma : come
  With Bay Steeds to the juice we shed.

34 May Indra give, to aid us, wealth handy
  that rules the Skilful Ones :
  Yea, may the Strong give potent wealth.

is, according to the Scholiast, that, at the time of the
concluding purificatory ceremony which is to atone for
errors and omissions in the principal sacrifice, the stale
Soma is thrown into the waters. See Cowell's note in
Wilson's Translation.

23 *The cleansing bath* : the *avabhṛtha*, here, apparently,
the bath or vessel in which the Soma plants were rinsed
and purified.

34 *Handy* : ṛbhúm. *That rules the Skilful Ones* :
ṛbhukṣáṇam. *The Strong* : vājí. These words are used as
plays upon the names of the Ṛbhus, or as Grassmann
says, the verse may have been taken from a hymn
addressed to the Ṛbhus. 'May Indra bring to us the
bounteous Ṛbhu Ṛbhukṣaṇa to partake of our sacrificial
viands; may he, the mighty, bring the mighty (Vāja)'—
Wilson. Cowell remarks : 'Ṛbhukṣaṇa was the eldest
and Vāja the youngest of the three brothers. The Ṛbhus
have a share in the evening libation between Prajāpati
and Savitṛ, see Ait. Brāhm. iii. 30. This verse is
addressed to the Ṛbhus in the evening libation on the
ninth day of the Dvādaśāha ceremony (*ib.* v. 21).'

HYMN LXXXIII. *Maruts.*

1. THE Cow, the famous Mother of the
  wealthy Maruts, pours her milk :
  Both horses of the cars are yoked,—

2 She in whose bosom all the Gods, and
  Sun and Moon for men to see,
  Maintain their everlasting Laws.

3 This all the pious sing to us, and sacred
  poets evermore :
  The Maruts to the Soma-draught !

4 Here is the Soma ready pressed : of this
  the Maruts drink, of this
  Self-luminous the Aśvins drink.

5 Of this, moreover, purified, set in three
  places, procreant,
  Drink Varuṇa, Mitra, Aryaman.

6 And Indra, like the Herald Priest, desirous
  of the milky juice,
  At early morn will quaff thereof.

7 When have the Princes gleamed and shone
  through waters as through troops of foes ?
  When hasten they whose might is pure ?

8 What favour do I claim this day of you
  great Deities, you who are
  Wondrously splendid in yourselves ?

9 I call, to drink the Soma, those Maruts
  who spread all realms of earth
  And luminous regions of the sky.

10 You, even such, pure in your might, you,
  O ye Maruts, I invoke
  From heaven to drink this Soma juice.

11 The Maruts, those who have sustained
  and propped the heavens and earth apart,
  I call to drink this Soma juice.

12 That vigorous band of Maruts that abideth
  in the mountains, I
  Invoke to drink this Soma juice.

HYMN LXXXIV. *Indra.*

1. SONG-LOVER ! like a charioteer come songs
  to thee when Soma flows.
  O Indra, they have called to thee as
  mother-kine unto their calves.

1 *The Cow* : Pṛśni.

2 *In whose bosom* : 'in whose presence.'—Wilson.

3 *The Maruts* : are to be invoked, understood.

5 *Set in three places* : first, in a trough ; then in a
straining cloth ; then in a third trough or vessel
called *Pūtabhṛt. Procreant* : granting progeny to the
worshipper.

6 *The Herald Priest* : Agni.

---

1 *Like a charioteer* : straight and swift to their object.

2 Bright juices hitherward have sped thee,
Indra, Lover of the Song.
Drink, Indra, of this flowing sap : in every
house 'tis set for thee.

3 Drink Soma to inspirit thee, juice, Indra,
which the Falcon brought :
For thou art King and Sovran Lord of all
the families of men.

4 O Indra, hear Tiraści's call, the call of
him who serveth thee.
Satisfy him with wealth of kine and
valiant offspring : Great art thou.

5 For he, O Indra, hath produced for thee
the newest gladdening song,
A hymn that springs from careful thought,
ancient, and full of sacred truth.

6 That Indra will we laud whom songs and
hymns of praise have magnified.
Striving to win, we celebrate his many
deeds of hero might.

7 Come now and let us glorify pure Indra
with pure Sāma hymns.
Let the pure milky draught delight him
strengthened by pure songs of praise.

8 O Indra, come thou pure to us, with pure
assistance, pure thyself.
Pure, send thou riches down to us, and,
meet for Soma, pure, be glad.

9 O Indra, pure, vouchsafe us wealth, and,
pure, enrich the worshipper.
Pure, thou dost strike the Vṛtras dead, and
strivest, pure, to win the spoil.

HYMN LXXXV.   *Indra.*

1. For him the Mornings made their courses
longer, and Nights with pleasant voices
spake to Indra.
For him the Floods stood still, the Seven
Mothers, Streams easy for the heroes to
pass over.

2 The Darter penetrated, though in trouble,
thrice-seven close-pressed ridges of the
mountains.

Neither might God nor mortal man
accomplish what the Strong Hero wrought
in full-grown vigour.

3 The mightiest force is Indra's bolt of iron
when firmly grasped in both the arms
of Indra.
His head and mouth have powers that
pass all others, and all his people hasten
near to listen.

4 I count thee as the Holiest of the Holy,
the caster-down of what hath ne'er been
shaken.
I count thee as the Banner of the heroes,
I count thee as the Chief of all men
living.

5 What time, O Indra, in thine arms thou
tookest thy wildly rushing bolt to slay
the Dragon,
The mountains roared, the cattle loudly
bellowed, the Brāhmans with their
hymns drew nigh to Indra.

6 Let us praise him who made these worlds
and creatures, all things that after him
sprang into being.
May we win Mitra with our songs, and
Indra, and · wait upon our Lord with
adoration.

7 Flying in terror from the snort of Vṛtra,
all Deities who were thy friends forsook
thee.
So, Indra, be thy friendship with the
Maruts : in all these battles thou shalt
be the vietor.

8 Thrice-sixty Maruts, waxing strong, were
with thee, like piles of beaming light,
worthy of worship.
We come to thee : grant us a happy
portion. Let us adore thy might with
this oblation.

9 A sharpened weapon is the host of Maruts.
Who, Indra, dares withstand thy bolt
of thunder ?

3 *Which the Falcon brought* : See I. 80. 2, and 93. 6.

5 *Newest......ancient* : recent in form and expression,
but ancient in substance. See Muir, *O. S. Texts*, III.
238, 239.

7. *Pure Indra with pure Sāma hymns* : according to
Sāyaṇa, 'Indra, purified with pure Sāma-hymns,' from
the pollution he had incurred by killing the Brāhman
Vṛtra. See Wilson's Translation, note.

1 *The heroes* : perhaps Turvaśa and Yadu.—Ludwig.
2 *The Darter* : of the thunderbolt ; Indra. *Though
in trouble* : because he had none to aid him. What the
thrice-seven close-pressed ridges of the mountains are, is uncertain. See Wilson's Translation, note. Ludwig thinks

that the battle of the Sun with the demons of winter
may be meant.

3 *To listen* : to the commands which issue from his
mouth.

5 *Wildly rushing* : this is M. Müller's translation of
madacyutam. It might be rendered also 'sped in thy
rapturous joy.' 'Rauschbeschleunigten.'—Ludwig. *The
Dragon* : Ahi.

7 *With the Maruts* : as they alone stood by him in
the conflict.

8 *Thrice-sixty* : or sixty-three, according to Sāyaṇa,
nine companies consisting of seven each. See Cowell's
note in Wilson's Translation. *Like piles of beaming
light* : 'like cows gathered together.'—Wilson; 'like
morning stars.'—Grassmann. I have followed Ludwig.

Weaponless are the Asuras, the godless :
scatter them with thy wheel, Impetuous
Hero.

10 To him the Strong and Mighty, most
auspicious, send up the beauteous hymn
for sake of cattle.
Lay on his body many songs for Indra
invoked with song, for will not he regard
them ?

11 To him, the Mighty, who accepts laudation, send forth thy thought as by a
boat o'er rivers,
Stir with thy hymn the body of the Famous
and Dearest One, for will not he regard
it ?

12 Serve him with gifts of thine which Indra
welcomes : praise with fair praise, invite him with thine homage.
Draw near, O singer, and refrain from
outcry. Make thy voice heard, for will
not he regard it ?

13 The Black Drop sank in Aṁśumatī's
bosom, advancing with ten thousand
round about it.
Indra with might longed for it as it
panted : the hero-hearted laid aside
his weapons.

14 I saw the Drop in the far distance moving,
on the slope bank of Aṁśumatī's river,
Like a black cloud that sank into the
water. Heroes, I send you forth. Go,
fight in battle.

15 And then the Drop in Aṁśumatī's bosom,
splendid with light, assumed its proper
body ;
And Indra, with Bṛhaspati to aid him,
conquered the godless tribes that came
against him.

9 *With thy wheel :* or discus, a sharp-edged quoit
used as a weapon of war.

12 *Draw near, O singer, and refrain from outcry :* 'O
priest, adorn thyself grieve not (for poverty).'—Wilson.

13 *The Black Drop :* the darkened Moon. *Aṁśumatī :*
a mystical river of the air into which the Moon dips to
recover its vanished light. *Ten thousand :* probably,
demons of darkness ; the numerals are without a substantive. *As it panted :* while striving against its
assailants. *Laid aside his weapons :* after conquering the
demons and restoring the darkened Moon.

14 Indra addresses the Maruts.

Sāyaṇa explains stanzas 13—15 differently, in accordance with a legend which was probably suggested by
this passage. He takes *drapsáḥ kṛṣṇáḥ*, black drop, to
mean 'the swift moving Kṛṣṇaḥ,' an Asura or demon
who with ten thousand of his kind had occupied the
banks of the river Aṁśumatī, which, he says, is the
Yamunā or Jumna, and was there defeated by Indra,
Bṛhaspati, and the Maruts. See Cowell's note in Wilson's
Translation.

16 Then, at thy birth, thou wast the foeman,
Indra, of those the seven who ne'er
had met a rival.
The hidden Pair, the Heaven and Earth,
thou foundest, and to the mighty worlds
thou gavest pleasure.

17 So, Thunder-armed ! thou with thy bolt
of thunder didst boldly smite that power
which none might equal ;
With weapons broughtest low the might
of Śuṣṇa, and, Indra, foundest by thy
strength the cattle.

18 Then wast thou, Chieftain of all living
mortals, the very mighty slayer of the
Vṛtras.
Then didst thou set the obstructed rivers
flowing, and win the floods that were
enthralled by Dāsas.

19 Most wise is he, rejoicing in libations,
splendid as day, resistless in his anger.
He only doth great deeds, the only Hero,
sole Vṛtra-slayer he, with none beside
him.

20 Indra is Vṛtra's slayer, man's sustainer :
he must be called ; with fair praise let
us call him.
Maghavan is our Helper, our Protector,
giver of spoil and wealth to make us
famous.

21 This Indra, Vṛtra-slayer, this Ṛbhukṣan,
even at his birth, was meet for invocation.
Doer of many deeds for man's advantage,
like Soma quaffed, for friends we must
invoke him.

HYMN LXXXVI.   *Indra.*

1. O INDRA, Lord of Light, what joys thou
broughtest from the Asuras,
Prosper therewith, O Maghavan, him who
lauds that deed, and those whose grass
is trimmed for thee.

2 The unwasting share of steeds and kine
which, Indra, thou hast fast secured,
Grant to the worshipper who presses Soma
and gives guerdon, not unto the churl.

16 *The seven :* Kṛṣṇa, Vṛtra, Namuci, Śambara,
and others.'—Sāyaṇa.

21 *Ṛbhukṣan :* or, Lord of Ṛbhus.

1 *Joys :* riches.—Sāyaṇa. *From the Asuras :* from
the powerful Rākṣasas.—Sāyaṇa.

2 *Gives guerdon :* liberally rewards the priests.

3 The riteless, godless man who sleeps, O
Indra, his unbroken sleep,—
May he by following his own devices die.
Hide from him wealth that nourishes.

4 Whether, O Śakra, thou be far, or, Vṛtra-
slayer, near at hand,
Thence by heaven-reaching songs he who
hath pressed the juice invites thee with
thy long-maned Steeds.

5 Whether thou art in heaven's bright sphere,
or in the basin of the sea ;
Whether, chief Vṛtra-slayer, in some place
on earth, or in the firmament, approach.

6 Thou Soma-drinker, Lord of Strength,
beside our flowing Soma juice
Delight us with thy bounty rich in pleasantness, O Indra, with abundant wealth.

7 O Indra, turn us not away : be the companion of our feast.
For thou art our protection, yea, thou art
our kin : O Indra, turn us not away.

8 Sit down with us, O Indra, sit beside the
juice to drink the meath.
Show forth great favour to the singer,
Maghavan ; Indra, with us, beside the
juice.

9 O Caster of the Stone, nor Gods nor
mortals have attained to thee.
Thou in thy might surpassest all that hath
been made : the Gods have not attained
to thee.

10 Of one accord they made and formed for
kingship Indra, the Hero who in all
encounters overcometh,
Most eminent for power, destroyer in the
conflict, fierce and exceeding strong,
stalwart and full of vigour.

11 Bards joined in song to Indra so that he
might drink the Soma juice,
The Lord of Light, that he whose laws
stand fast might aid with power and
with the help he gives.

12 The holy sages form a ring, looking and
singing to the Ram.
Inciters, full of vigour, not to be deceived,
are with the chanters, nigh to hear.

13 Loudly I call that Indra, Maghavan the
Mighty, who evermore possesses power,
ever resistless.
Holy, most liberal, may he lead us on to
riches, and, Thunder-armed, make all
our pathways pleasant for us.

14 Thou knowest well, O Śakra, thou Most
Potent, with thy strength, Indra, to
destroy these castles.
Before thee, Thunder-armed ! all beings
tremble : the heavens and earth before
thee shake with terror.

15 May thy truth, Indra, Wondrous Hero !
be my guard : bear me o'er much woe,
Thunderer ! as over floods.
When, Indra, wilt thou honour us with
opulence, all-nourishing and much-to-be-
desired, O King ?

HYMN LXXXVII.   *Indra.*

1. To Indra sing a Sāma hymn, a lofty song
to Lofty Sage,
To him who guards the Law, inspired,
and fain for praise.

2 Thou, Indra, art the Conqueror : thou
gavest splendour to the Sun.
Maker of all things, thou art Mighty and
All-God.

3 Radiant with light thou wentest to the
sky, the luminous realm of heaven.
The Deities, Indra strove to win thee for
their Friend.

4 Come unto us, O Indra, dear, still con-
quering, unconcealable,
Vast as a mountain spread on all sides,
Lord of Heaven.

5 O truthful Soma-drinker, thou art mightier
than both the worlds.
Thou strengthenest him who pours libation, Lord of Heaven.

6 For thou art he, O Indra, who stormeth
all castles of the foe,
Slayer of Dasyus, man's Supporter, Lord
of Heaven.

7 Now have we, Indra, Friend of Song, sent
our great wishes forth to thee,
Coming like floods that follow floods.

8 As rivers swell the ocean, so, Hero, our
prayers increase thy might,
Though of thyself, O Thunderer, waxing
day by day.

9 With holy song they bind to the broad
wide-yoked car the Bay Steeds of the
rapid God,
Bearers of Indra, yoked by word.

12 *The Ram* : Indra See I. 51. 1. and VIII 2. 40.
Inciters : apparently, the Gods themselves.

———

2 *All-God* : viśvádevaḥ : 'the lord of all the gods.'—
Wilson.

4 *Unconcealable* : as the Sun-God.

7 *Coming like floods* : in crowds. But the half-line is
very obscure. 'As men going by water (splash their
friends) with handfuls.'—Wilson.

10 O Indra, bring great strength to us, bring
   valour, Śatakratu, thou most active, bring
   A hero conquering in war.

11 For, gracious Śatakratu, thou hast ever
   been a Mother and a Sire to us,
   So now for bliss we pray to thee.

12 To thee, Strong, Much-invoked, who
   showest forth thy strength, O Śatakratu,
   do I speak :
   So grant thou us heroic strength.

HYMN LXXXVIII.   *Indra.*

1. O THUNDERER, zealous worshippers gave
   thee drink this time yesterday.
   So, Indra, listen here to those who bring
   the laud : come near unto our dwelling-
   place.

2 Lord of Bay Steeds, fair-helmed, rejoice
   thee : this we crave. Here the disposers
   wait on thee.
   Thy loftiest glories claim our lauds beside
   the juice, O Indra, Lover of the Song.

3 Turning, as 'twere, to meet the Sun, enjoy,
   from Indra all good things.
   When he who will be born is born with
   power we look to treasures as our heritage.

4 Praise him who sends us wealth, whose
   bounties injure none : good are the
   gifts which Indra grants.
   He is not worth with one who satisfies his
   wish : he turns his mind to giving boons.

5 Thou in thy battles, Indra, art subduer
   of all hostile bands.
   Father art thou, all-conquering, cancelling
   the curse, thou victor of the vanquisher.

6 The Earth and Heaven clung close to thy
   victorious might, as to their calf two
   mother-cows.
   When thou attackest Vṛtra all the hostile
   bands shrink and faint, Indra, at thy
   wrath.

7 Bring to your aid the Eternal One, who
   shoots and none may shoot at him,

Inciter, swift, victorious, best of Charioteers.
Tugrya's unvanquished Strengthener ;

8 Arranger of things unarranged, e'en
   Śatakratu, source of might,
   Indra, the Friend of all, for succour we
   invoke, Guardian of treasure, sending
   wealth.

HYMN LXXXIX   *Indra. Vāk.*

1. I MOVE before thee here present in person,
   and all the Deities follow behind me.
   When, Indra, thou securest me my portion,
   with me thou shalt perform heroic
   actions.

2 The food of meath in foremost place I give
   thee, thy Soma shall be pressed, thy
   share appointed.
   Thou on my right shalt be my friend and
   comrade : then shall we two smite dead
   full many a foeman.

3 Striving for strength bring forth a laud to
   Indra, a truthful hymn if he in truth
   existeth.
   One and another say, There is no Indra.
   Who hath beheld him ? Whom then
   shall we honour ?

4 Here am I, look upon me here, O singer.
   All that existeth I surpass in greatness.
   The Holy Law's commandments make me
   mighty. Rending with strength I rend
   the worlds asunder.

5 When the Law's lovers mounted and approached me as I sate lone upon the dear
   sky's summit.
   Then spake my spirit to the heart within
   me, My friends have cried unto me with
   their children.

6 All these thy deeds must be declared at
   Soma-feasts, wrought, Indra, Bounteous
   Lord, for him who sheds the juice,

---

7 *Tugrya* is Bhujyu, the son of Tugra. See Vol. I.,
Index.

8 *Arranger of things unarranged* : 'the consecrator of
others but himself consecrated by none.'—Wilson.

---

10 *A hero* : a heroic son.

---

2 *Disposers* : the priests who order religious ceremonies.

3 This stanza is difficult and obscure. Mahīdhara's
explanation is : 'The gathering (rays) proceeding to
the sun distribute all Indra's treasures (to living beings,
sc. as rain, corn, etc.) ; may we too by our power
leave those treasures as an inheritance to him who has
been or will be born.' See Cowell's note in Wilson's
Translation.

6 *As to their calf* : or the translation may be, as
sire and mother to their child.

1 This stanza is spoken by Agni.

2 Indra answers

3 Addressed to the priests. *One and another* : néma :
but according to Sāyaṇa, Nema is the name of the
Ṛṣi. Nema says, "verily there is no Indra."—Wilson.

4 Indra speaks this and the following stanza.

5 *The Law's lovers* : the priests who in sacrifice
ascend to Indra. According to Hillebrandt (*V. Mythologie*, I. 354), the Maruts ; *śiśumantaḥ* meaning not
'with their children,' but 'with the Infant (Soma).'

When thou didst open wealth heaped up
by many, brought from far away to
Śarabha, the Ṛṣi's kin.

7 Now run ye forth your several ways : he
is not here who kept you back.
For hath not Indra sunk his bolt deep
down in Vṛtra's vital part ?

8 On-rushing with the speed of thought
within the iron fort he pressed :
The Falcon went to heaven and brought
the Soma to the Thunderer.

9 Deep in the ocean lies the bolt with
waters compassed round about,
And in continuous onward flow the floods
their tribute bring to it.

10 When, uttering words which no one comprehended, Vāk, Queen of Gods, the
Gladdener, was seated,
The heaven's four regions drew forth drink
and vigour : now whither hath her
noblest portion vanished ?

11 The Deities generated Vāk the Goddess,
and animals of every figure speak her.
May she, the Gladdener, yielding food and
vigour, the Milch-cow Vāk, approach us
meetly lauded.

12 Step forth with wider stride, my comrade
Viṣṇu ; make room, Dyaus, for the
leaping of the lightning.
Let us slay Vṛtra, let us free the rivers :
let them flow loosed at the command
of Indra.

HYMN XC.   *Various.*

1. YEA, specially that mortal man hath toiled
for service of the Gods,

6 The priest addresses Indra. *Śarabha* : a Ṛṣi of
that name.—Sāyaṇa. The original hymn appears to
end with this stanza.

7 Addressed to the waters of heaven after Indra's
battle with Vṛtra.

8 *He* : the Falcon. *The iron fort* : the stronghold
or cloud in which the Soma or ambrosial rain was
imprisoned. Cf. IV. 27. 2.

9 *In the ocean* : as produced naturally in the sea of
air.

10 This and the following stanza have no apparent
connexion with what precedes. *Vāk* : or Vāc, vox,
voice, or Speech personified. Her unintelligible words
are the thunder. *Her noblest portion* : according to
Sāyaṇa, the rain which follows thunder. Or the thunder
itself may be intended. See Cowell's note in Wilson's
Translation. *Was seated* : at the sacrifice offered to her.

11 *Speak her* : articulately-speaking men and lower
animals all derive their voices from her.

12 This stanza, which is out of place here, is spoken
by Indra when he is about to attack Vṛtra. See IV.
18. 11.

Who quickly hath brought near Mitra
and Varuṇa to share his sacrificial gifts.

2 Supreme in sovran power, far-sighted,
Chiefs and Kings, most swift to hear
from far away,
Both, wondrously, set them in motion as
with arms, in company with Sūrya's
beams.

3 The rapid messenger who runs before you,
Mitra-Varuṇa, with iron head, swift to
the draught,

4 He whom no man may question, none
may summon back, who stands not still
for colloquy,—
From hostile clash with him keep ye us
safe this day : keep us in safety with
your arms.

5 To Aryaman and Mitra sing a reverent
song, O pious one,
A pleasant hymn that shall protect to
Varuṇa : sing forth a laud unto the
Kings.

6 The true, Red Treasure they have sent,
one only Son born of the Three.
They, the Immortal Ones, never deceived,
survey the families of mortal men.

7 My songs are lifted up, and acts most
splendid are to be performed.
Come hither, ye Nāsatyas, with accordant
mind, to meet and to enjoy my gifts.

8 Lords of great wealth, when we invoke
your bounty which no demon checks,
Both of you, furthering our eastward-offered
praise, come, Chiefs whom Jamadagni
lauds !

9 Come, Vāyu, drawn by fair hymns, to our
sacrifice that reaches heaven.
Poured on the middle of the straining-
cloth, and cooked, this bright drink
hath been offered thee.

10 He comes by straightest paths, as ministering Priest, to taste the sacrificial
gifts.
Then, Lord of harnessed teams ! drink of
the twofold draught, bright Soma mingled
with the milk.

11 Verily, Sūrya, thou art great ; truly,
Āditya, thou art great.
As thou art great indeed, thy greatness is
admired : yea, verily, thou, God, art
great.

3 *The rapid messenger* : the lightning, as one of the
forms of Agni.

6 *The true, Red Treasure* : the Sun. *The Three* :
heaven, mid-air, and earth.

12 Yea, Sūrya, thou art great in fame :
thou evermore, O God, art great.
Thou by thy greatness art the Gods' High
Priest, divine, far-spread unconquerable
light.

13 She yonder, bending lowly down, clothed
in red hues and rich in rays,
Is seen, advancing as it were with various
tints, amid the ten surrounding arms.

14 Past and gone are three mortal generations : the fourth and last into the Sun
hath entered.
He mid the worlds his lofty place hath
taken. Into green plants is gone the
Purifying.

15 The Rudras' Mother, Daughter of the
Vasus, centre of nectar, the Ādityas'
Sister—
To folk who understand will I proclaim
it—injure not Aditi, the Cow, the sinless.

16 Weak-minded men have as a cow adopted
me who came hither from the Gods, a
Goddess,
Who, skilled in eloquence, her voice uplif-
teth, who standeth near at hand with
all devotions.

HYMN XCI.   *Agni.*

1. LORD of the house, Sage, ever young,
high power of life, O Agni, God,
Thou givest to thy worshipper.

2 So with our song that prays and serves,
attentive, Lord of spreading light,
Agni, bring hitherward the Gods.

3 For, Ever-Youthful One, with thee, best
Furtherer, as our ally,
We overcome, to win the spoil.

4 As Aurva Bhṛgu used, as Apnavāna used,
I call the pure
Agni who clothes him with the sea.

5 I call the Sage who sounds like wind, the
Might that like Parjanya roars,
Agni who clothes him with the sea.

6 As Savitar's productive Power, as him who
sends down bliss, I call
Agni who clothes him with the sea.

7 Hither, for powerful kinship, I call Agni,
him who prospers you,
Most frequent at our solemn rites ;

8 That through this famed One's power, he
may stand by us even as Tvaṣṭar comes
Unto the forms that must be shaped.

9 This Agni is the Lord supreme above all
glories mid the Gods :
May he come nigh to us with strength.

10 Here praise ye him the most renowned of
all the ministering Priests,
Agni, the Chief at sacrifice ;

11 Piercing, with purifying flame, enkindled
in our homes, most high,
Swiftest to hear from far away.

12 Sage, laud the Mighty One who wins the
spoil of victory like a steed,
And, Mitra like, unites the folk.

13 Still turning to their aim in thee, the oblation-bearer's sister hymns
Have come to thee before the wind.

14 The waters find their place in him, for
whom the threefold sacred grass
Is spread unbound, unlimited.

15 The station of the Bounteous God hath,
through his aid which none impair,
A pleasant aspect like the Sun.

13 *She yonder* : Uṣas or Dawn. *The ten surrounding arms* : the ten regions of the world.

14 *Three mortal generations* : according to the legend, Prajāpati produced in succession three kinds of creatures who all died. The fourth generation lived and enjoyed the light and warmth of the Sun. See Cowell's note in Wilson's Translation, or *Śatapatha-Brāhmaṇa*, II. 5. 1. *Into green plants* : Sāyaṇa explains *haritaḥ* as the quarters of the sky, and *pávamānaḥ* (the Purifying) as Vāyu or the Wind. Grassmann takes *pávamānaḥ* to be the Soma, and *haritaḥ* to be the horses of the Sun. I have followed Ludwig's interpretation ; but I find the stanza almost unintelligible.

15 *Centre of nectar* : or, of amṛta, or immortality, or the world of the immortal Gods. *The cow* ; the earthly cow, as the type of Aditi or universal Nature, must not be offended. The stanza is spoken by the priest who has received the cow as his reward.

16 *Weak-minded men* : 'Men are too feeble in their intellect to comprehend me in my true form and my real nature : they can only understand my worth in the shape of a cow.'—See Ludwig, *R. V.*, IV. 245, 246.
The concluding stanza is spoken by Aditi as a cow.

4 *Aurva Bhṛgu* : or, perhaps, Aurva, and Bhṛgu. The ancient Ṛṣi Aurva is said to have been the grand-son of Bhṛgu. *Apnavāna* : another ancient Ṛṣi, mention-ed in connexion with the Bhṛgus and the earliest wor-shipper of Agni, in Book IV. 7. 1.

12 *Sage* : the priest is addressed.

13 *Before the wind* : or, in front of the wind, with which the flame is fanned.

14 'The waters rest in Agni, who abides as lightning in the firmament.'—Note in Wilson's Translation which I have followed closely in this stanza.

15 Or, a comma being substituted for the full stop at the end of the preceding stanza, and *padám* (station) taken as in apposition to *padám* (place) in 14 : 'The station of the bounteous : he hath, through his aid which none impair, A pleasant aspect like the Sun.'

16 Blazing with splendour, Agni, God, through
   pious gifts of sacred oil,
   Bring thou the Gods and worship them.

17 The Gods as mothers brought thee forth, the
   Immortal Sage, O Aṅgiras,
   The bearer of our gifts to heaven.

18 Wise Agni, Gods established thee, the
   Seer, noblest messenger,
   As bearer of our sacred gifts.

19 No cow have I to call mine own, no axe
   at hand wherewith to work,
   Yet what is here I bring to thee.

20 O Agni, whatsoever be the fuel that we
   lay for thee,
   Be pleased therewith, Most Youthful God.

21 That which the white-ant eats away, that
   over which the emmet crawls—
   May all of this be oil to thee.

22 When he enkindles Agni, man should with
   his heart attend the song :
   I with the priests have kindled him.

HYMN XCII.   *Agni*

1. THAT noblest Furtherer hath appeared, to
   whom men bring their holy works.
   Our songs of praise have risen aloft to
   Agni who was born to give the Ārya
   strength.

2 Agni of Divodāsa turned, as 'twere in
   majesty, to the Gods.
   Onward he sped along the mother earth,
   and took his station in the height of
   heaven.

3 Him before whom the people shrink when
   he performs his glorious deeds,
   Him who wins thousands at the worship
   of the Gods, himself, that Agni, serve
   with songs.

4 The mortal man whom thou wouldst lead
   to opulence, O Vasu, he who brings thee
   gifts.

He, Agni, wins himself a hero singing
lauds, yea, one who feeds a thousand
men.

5 He with the steed wins spoil even in the
   fenced fort, and gains imperishable fame.
   In thee, O Lord of wealth, continually
   we lay all precious offerings to the
   Gods.

6 To him who dealeth out all wealth, who
   is the cheerful Priest of men,
   To him, like the first vessels filled with
   savoury juice, to Agni go the songs of
   praise.

7 Votaries, richly-gifted, deck him with
   their songs, even as the steed who draws
   the car.
   On both, Strong Lord of men ! on child
   and grandson pour the bounties which
   our nobles give.

8 Sing forth to him, the Holy, most munificent, sublime with his refulgent
   glow,
   To Agni, ye Upastutas.

9 Worshipped with gifts, enkindled, splendid,
   Maghavan shall win himself heroic
   fame.
   And will not his most newly shown benevolence come to us with abundant
   strength ?

10 Priest, presser of the juice ! praise now
   the dearest Guest of all our friends,
   Agni, the driver of the cars.

11 Who, finder-out of treasures open and
   concealed, bringeth them hither, Holy
   One ;
   Whose waves, as in a cataract, are hard
   to pass, when he, through song, would
   win him strength.

12 Let not the noble Guest, Agni, be wroth
   with us : by many a man his praise is
   sung,
   Good Herald, skilled in sacrifice.

---

19 As Prayoga, the Ṛṣi of the hymn, has no cow
and no axe to cut wood, Agni is asked in this and the
two following stanzas to dispense with the customary
offerings of milk, and to accept such wood as the
worshipper can pick up.

22 *With his heart* : a devout spirit will compensate
the want of milk and properly prepared fuel.

---

2 *Of Divodāsa* : whom Divodāsa especially worshipped and claimed as his tutelary God. The stanza
is obscure, and my translation founded on von Roth's
interpretation of *prá vi vāvṛte*, which has been accepted
by Cowell, must be regarded as conjectural. See
Wilson's Translation and note.

4 *A hero* : a brave son.

7 The second line is obscure. 'Graceful lord of men,
grant wealth to us rich in children and grandchildren.'
—Wilson.

8 *Upastutas* : singers so named after the Ṛṣi Upastuta. See I. 36. 10.

10 *Priest, presser of the juice* : *āsāva* : *stotaḥ*—Sāyaṇa.
'Singer of hymns.'—Wilson.

11 *Whose waves* : billowy floods of flame rushing on
like waters falling down a precipice. 'Whose (flames),
as he hastens to wage the battle by means of our
sacred rite, are hard to be passed through as waves
rushing down a declivity.'—Wilson. See also Pischel,
Vedische Studien, I. p. 184. *Through song* : inspirited
and strengthened by our hymns.

13 O Vasu, Agni, let not them be harmed
    who come in any way with lauds to
    thee.
   Even the lowly, skilled in rites, with offered
    gifts, seeketh thee for the envoy's task.

14 Friend of the Maruts, Agni, come with
    Rudras to the Soma-draught,
   To Sobhari's fair song of praise, and be
    thou joyful in the light.

13 *For the envoy's task* : to bear his oblations to the
Gods.

VĀLAKHILYA

(BOOK VIII. HYMNS 49—59. *M. Müller.*)

HYMN I. *Indra.*

1. To you will I sing Indra's praise who
gives good gifts as well we know ;
The praise of Maghavan who, rich in
treasure, aids his singers with wealth
thousandfold.

2 As with a hundred hosts, he rushes boldly
on, and for the offerer slays his foes.
As from a mountain flow the water-brooks,
thus flow his gifts who feedeth many
a one.

3 The drops effused, the gladdening draughts, O Indra, Lover of the Song,
As waters seek the lake where they are
wont to rest, fill thee, for bounty,
Thunderer.

4 The matchless draught that strengthens
and gives eloquence, the sweetest of the
meath drink thou,
That in thy joy thou mayst scatter thy
gifts o'er us, plenteously, even as the
dust.

5 Come quickly to our laud, urged on by
Soma-pressers like a horse—
Laud, Godlike Indra, which milch-kine
make sweet for thee : with Kaṇva's sons
are gifts for thee.

6 With homage have we sought thee as a
Hero, strong, preëminent, with unfail-
ing wealth.
O Thunderer, as a plenteous spring pours
forth its stream, so,
Indra, flow our songs to thee.

7 If now thou art at sacrifice, or if thou art
upon the earth,
Come thence, high-thoughted ! to our
sacrifice with the Swift, come, Mighty
with the Mighty Ones.

See Book VIII., Hymn XLIX., note. Professor
Cowell's version of these eleven hymns will be found
in Appendix I. of Wilson's Translation, Vol. V. I am
indebted to him for some improvements on the version
which I had previously prepared.

8 The active, fleet-foot, tawny Coursers that
are thine are swift to victory, like the
Wind,
Wherewith thou goest round to visit
Manus' seed, wherewith all heaven is
visible.

9 Indra, from thee so great we crave prosperity in wealth of kine,
As, Maghavan, thou favouredst Medhyātithi, and, in the fight, Nīpātithi.

10 As, Maghavan, to Kaṇva, Trasadasyu, and
to Paktha and Daśavraja ;
As, Indra, to Gośarya and Rjiśvan, thou
vouchsafedst wealth in kine and gold.

HYMN II. *Indra.*

1. ŚAKRA I praise, to win his aid, far-famed,
exceeding bountiful,
Who gives, as 'twere in thousands, precious
wealth to him who sheds the juice and
worships him.

2 Arrows with hundred points, unconquerable, are this Indra's mighty arms in
war.
He streams on liberal worshippers like a
hill with springs, when juices poured
have gladdened him.

3 What time the flowing Soma-drops have
gladdened with their taste the Friend,
Like water, gracious Lord ! were my
libations made, like milch-kine to the
worshipper.

4 To him the peerless, who is calling you
to give you aid, forth flow the drops of
pleasant meath.
The Soma-drops which call on thee, O
gracious Lord, have brought thee to
our hymn of praise.

5 He rushes hurrying like a steed to Soma
that adorns our rite,

2 *As with a hundred hosts* : 'like a weapon with a
hundred edges.'—Cowell.
4 *That...gives eloquence* : vivākṣaṇam from vac ; 'swelling,' from vakṣ=ukṣ.—von Roth, and Cowell. *Plenteously. even as the dust* : the meaning of the text is obscure.
The St. Petersburg Lexicon takes dhṛṣād=dṛṣad, the
nether millstone : 'just as the mill-stone pours out meal.
—Cowell.
7 *The Swift* and *the Mighty Ones*, are Indra's horses.

9 *Medhyātithi* : a Ṛṣi whose name has frequently
occurred. *Nīpātithi* : mentioned only here and Vālakhilya Hymn III.

10 *Trasadasyu* : See. Vol. I., Index. *Paktha* : a
favourite of the Aśvins. See VIII. 22. 10. *Daśavraja* :
See VIII. 8. 20. *Gośarya* : See VIII. 8. 20. *Rjiśvan* :
See Vol. I., Index.

Which hymns make sweet to thee, lover
of pleasant food. The call to Paura
thou dost love.

6 Praise the strong, grasping Hero, winner
of the spoil, ruling supreme o'er mighty
wealth.
Like a full spring, O Thunderer, from
thy store hast thou poured on the worshipper evermore.

7 Now whether thou be far away, or in the
heavens, or on the earth,
O Indra, mighty-thoughted, harnessing
thy Bays, come Lofty with the Lofty
Ones.

8 The Bays who draw thy chariot, Steeds
who injure none, surpass the wind's
impetuous strength—
With whom thou silencest the enemy of
man, with whom thou goest round the
sky.

9 O gracious Hero, may we learn anew to
know thee as thou art :
As in decisive fight thou holpest Etaśa, or
Vaśa 'gainst Daśavraja,

10 As, Maghavan, to Kaṇva at the sacred
feast, to Dīrghanītha thine home-friend,
As to Gośarya thou, Stone-darter, gavest
wealth, give me a gold-bright stall of
kine.

HYMN III.   *Indra.*

1. As with Manu Sāmvaraṇi, Indra, thou
drankest Soma juice,
And, Maghavan, with Nīpātithi, Medhyātithi, with Puṣṭigu and Śruṣṭigu,—

2 The son of Pṛsadvāna was Praskaṇva's
host, who lay decrepit and forlorn.

5 *The Call to Paura* : the invitation to Paura's house.
According to von Roth *paurá* means the filler,
the satisfier ; 'thou approvest the summons to the
satisfying beverage.'—Cowell. See V. 74. 4.

7 This stanza is almost a repetition of stanza 7 of
Hymn I.

9 *Etaśa* : See I. 61. 15. *Vaśa* : mentioned as a
favourite of the Aśvins in X. 40. 7. *Daśavraja* : said
in stanza 10 of Hymn I, to have been helped by Indra.

10 *Dīrghanītha* : Ludwig takes this word to be an
adjective qualifying *medhe adhvaré*, 'at the sacrificial feast
of long duration.' *A gold-bright stall of kine* : according
to Ludwig, a stall graced with bay steeds, would be a
better translation.

1 *Sāmvaraṇi* : son of the Vedic Ṛṣi Savaraṇa.
See V. 33. 10. At the end of the stanza, 'so drink with
us,' is to be understood.

2 *Forlorn* : rejected and cast out by his kindred.
Dasyave-vṛka : literally, the Wolf-to-the-Dasyu, that is,
Destroyer of fiends or barbarians.

Aided by thee the Ṛṣi Dasyave-vṛka strove
to obtain thousands of kine.

3 Call hither with thy newest song Indra
who lacks not hymns of praise,
Him who observes and knows, inspirer of
the sage, him who seems eager to enjoy.

4 He unto whom they sang the seven-headed hymn, three-parted, in the loftiest
place,
He sent his thunder down on all these
living things, and so displayed heroic
might.

5 We invocate that Indra who bestoweth
precious things on us.
Now do we know his newest favour ; may
we gain a stable that is full of kine.

6 He whom thou aidest, gracious Lord, to
give again, obtains great wealth to nourish him.
We with our Soma ready, Lover of the
Song ! call, Indra Maghavan, on thee.

7 Ne'er art thou fruitless, Indra ; ne'er dost
thou desert the worshipper :
But now, O Maghavan, thy bounty as a
God is poured forth ever more and
more.

8 He who hath overtaken Kṛvi with his
might, and silenced Śuṣṇa with death-
bolts,—
When he supported yonder heaven and
spread it out, then first the son of earth
was born.

9 Good Lord of wealth is he to whom all
Āryas, Dāsas here belong.
Directly unto thee, the pious Ruśama
Pavīru, is that wealth brought nigh.

10 In zealous haste the singers have sung
forth a song distilling oil and rich in
sweets.
Riches have spread among us and heroic
strength, with us are flowing Soma-drops.

HYMN IV.   *Indra.*

1. As, Śakra, thou with Manu called Vivasvān
drankest Soma juice,
As, Indra, thou didst love the hymn by

4 *The seven-headed* : sung by seven heavenly singers.

8 *The son of earth* : man.

9 *Ruśama Pavīru* : the Ruśamas are mentioned in V.
30. 13–15. The name of Pavīru does not occur
again.

1 *Vivasvān* : or Vivasvat, was the father of Manu
who is generally called Vaivasvata. *Āyu* : the Ṛṣi of
the hymn, or the sacrificer.

Trita's side, so dost thou joy with Āyu now.

2 As thou with Mātariśvan, Medhya, Pṛṣadhra, hast cheered thee Indra, with
pressed juice,
Drunk Soma with Rjūnas, Syūmaraśmi,
by Daśoṇya's Daśaśipra's side.

3 'Tis he who made the lauds his own and
boldly drank the Soma juice,
He to whom Viṣṇu came striding his
three wide steps, as Mitra's statutes
ordered it.

4 In whose laud thou didst joy, Indra, at
the great deed, O Śatakratu, Mighty
One !
Seeking renown we call thee as the milkers
call the cow who yields abundant milk.

5 He is our Sire who gives to us, Great,
Mighty, ruling as he wills.
Unsought, may he the Strong, Rich, Lord
of ample wealth, give us of horses and
of kine.

6 He to whom thou, Good Lord, givest
that he may give increases wealth that
nourishes.
Eager for wealth we call on Indra, Lord
of wealth, on Śatakratu with our
lauds.

7 Never art thou neglectful : thou guardest
both races with thy care.
The call on Indra, fourth Āditya ! is thine
own. Amṛta is stablished in the heavens.

8 The offerer whom thou, Indra, Lover of
the Song, liberal Maghavan, favourest,—
As at the call of Kaṇva so, O gracious
Lord, hear, thou our songs and eulogy.

9 Sung is the song of ancient time : to Indra
have ye said the prayer.
They have sung many a Bṛhatī of sacrifice,
poured forth the worshipper's many
thoughts.

10 Indra hath tossed together mighty stores
of wealth, and both the worlds, yea,
and the Sun.
Pure, brightly-shining, mingled with the
milk, the draughts of Soma have made
Indra glad.

HYMN V.   *Indra.*

1. As highest of the Maghavans, preëminent
among the Bulls,
Best breaker-down of forts, kine-winner,
Lord of wealth, we seek thee, Indra
Maghavan.

2 Thou who subduedst Āyu, Kutsa, Atithigva, waxing daily in thy might,
As such, rousing thy power, we invocate
thee now, thee Śatakratu, Lord of Bays.

3 The pressing-stones shall pour for us the
essence of the meath of all,
Drops that have been pressed out afar
among the folk, and those that have
been pressed near us.

4 Repel all enmities and keep them far
away : let all win treasure for their
own.
Even among Śiṣṭas are the stalks that make
thee glad, where thou with Soma satest
thee.

5 Come, Indra, very near to us with aids of
firmly-based resolve ;
Come, most auspicious, with thy most
auspicious help, good Kinsman, with
good kinsmen, come !

6 Bless thou with progeny the chief of men,
the lord of heroes, victor in the fray.
Aid with thy powers the men who sing
thee lauds and keep their spirits ever
pure and bright.

7 May we be such in battle as are surest
to obtain thy grace :
With holy offerings and invocations of the
Gods, we mean, that we may win the
spoil.

8 Thine, Lord of Bays, am I. Prayer longeth
for the spoil. Still with thy help I seek
the fight.
So, at the raiders' head, I, craving steeds

---

2 *Mātariśvan* : the Ṛṣi of Hymn VI, of the Vālakhilya. *Medhya* : the Ṛṣi of Hymns V, IX, and X.
Pṛṣadhra : the Ṛṣi of Hymn VIII. *Syūmaraśmi* : mentioned, as a favourite of the Aśvins, in I. 112. 16. The
names of Rjūnas, Daśoṇya, and Daśaśipra do not occur
again in the Ṛgveda.

5 *Ruling as he wills* : 'he who acts as the sovereign.'
—Cowell.

7 *Both races* : Gods and men. *Fourth Āditya* :
Varuṇa, Mitra, and Aryaman being the other three.
Amṛta : 'ambrosia.'— Cowell.

8 As thou hearest, must be supplied at the beginning of the stanza.

9 *Bṛhatī* : verse in the Bṛhatī metre.

---

1 *Highest* : or, nearest. *The Bulls* : strong heroes.

2 *Āyu, Kutsa, Atithigva* : See I. 53. 10.

4 *Śiṣṭas* : apparently a tribe of no great importance.
Stalks : of the Soma-plant.

8 *At the raiders' head* : at the head of the band who
are going forth to seize the cattle of their enemies.
Von Roth thinks that *matīnām* should be read in stead

and kine, unite myself with thee alone.

HYMN VI.   *Indra.*

1. INDRA, the poets with their hymns extol
   this hero might of thine :
   They strengthened, loud in song, thy power
   that droppeth oil. With hymns the
   Pauras came to thee.

2 Through piety they came to Indra for his
   aid, they whose libations give thee joy.
   As thou with Kṛśa and Saṁvarta hast
   rejoiced, so, Indra, be thou glad with
   us.

3 Agreeing in your spirit, all ye Deities,
   come nigh to us.
   Vasus and Rudras shall come near to give
   us aid, and Maruts listen to our call.

4 May Pūṣan, Viṣṇu, and Sarasvatī befriend, and the Seven Streams, this call
   of mine :
   May Waters, Wind, the Mountains, and
   the Forest-Lord, and Earth give ear
   unto my cry.

5 Indra, with thine own bounteous gift,
   most liberal of the Mighty Ones,
   Be our boon benefactor, Vṛtra-slayer, be
   our feast-companion for our weal.

6 Leader of heroes, Lord of battle, lead
   thou us to combat, thou Most Sapient
   One.
   High fame is theirs who win by invocations,
   feasts and entertainment of the Gods.

7 Our hopes rest on the Faithful One : in
   Indra is the people's life.
   O Maghavan, come nigh that thou mayst
   give us aid : make plenteous food stream
   forth for us.

8 Thee would we worship, Indra, with our
   songs of praise : O Śatakratu, be thou
   ours.
   Pour down upon Praskaṇva bounty vast
   and firm, exuberant, that shall never
   fail.

HYMN VII.   *Praskaṇva's Gift.*

1. GREAT, verily, is Indra's might. I have
   beheld, and hither comes
   Thy bounty, Dasyave-vṛka !

2 A hundred oxen white of hue are shining
   like the stars in heaven,
   So tall, they seem to prop the sky.

3 Bamboos a hundred, hundred dogs, a
   hundred skins of beasts well-tanned,
   A hundred tufts of Balbaja, four hundred
   red-hued mares are mine.

4 Blest by the Gods, Kāṇvāyanas ! be ye
   who spread through life on life:
   Like horses have ye stridden forth.

5 Then men extolled the team of seven :
   not yet full-grown, its fame is great.
   The dark mares rushed along the paths,
   so that no eye could follow them.

HYMN VIII.   *Praskaṇva's Gift.*

1. THY bounty, Dasyave-vṛka, exhaustless
   hath displayed itself :
   Its fulness is as broad as heaven.

2 Ten thousand Dasyave-vṛka, the son of
   Pūtakratā, hath
   From his own wealth bestowed on me.

3 A hundred asses hath he given, a hundred
   head of fleecy sheep,

---

1 'Great is Indra's power, and the gifts which I
have received from thee, O destroyer of the Dasyus,
can be compared only to his bounty.' Dasyavevṛka,
here, is the name, not of the Ṛṣi, but of a hero who
in alliance with the Kaṇvas has been victorious in his
attack on the hostile barbarians. See Ludwig, Vol. III.
p. 164.

3 *Balbaja*: a kind of coarse grass (Eleusine Indica),
used in religious ceremonies, and for other purposes
when plaited.

4 *Kāṇvāyanas* : descendants of Kaṇva.

5 *The team of seven* : 'siebengespannes.'—Grassmann;
'seven-yoked team.'—Cowell. But the exact meaning
here of *sáptásya* is uncertain. Von Roth thinks that it
is probably a proper name. Ludwig takes it in the
sense of a bond of friendship or alliance. *The dark
mares* : there is no substantive, and 'mares' is conjecturally supplied. According to Ludwig, the dark hosts of
the Dasyus conquered by Dasyave-vṛka are intended,
and the whole stanza would be more correctly translated :

'Then no more thought they of the great renown of
the collective bond.
The dark tribes rushed along the paths so that no
eye could reach to them.' See Ludwig's Commentary,.
Vol. V. p. 552.

---

2 *The son of Pūtakratā* : or, more probably, called
Pautakrata after his father Pūtakratu—Ludwig.

3 *Slaves* : *dāsān* : conquered barbarians.

---

of *mathinām*, and Grassmann translates accordingly, 'in
Anfang meiner Bitten,' 'at the beginning of my prayers.'

---

1 *Pauras* : 'the offerers.'—Cowell. See Vālakhilya,
II. 5.

2 *Kṛśa* : the Ṛṣi of Hymn VII. of the Vālakhilya.
[*Saṁvarta* : not mentioned elsewhere.

4 *The Forest Lord* : *vanaspati* : the tall timber tree,
frequently meaning the Sacrificial Post.

5 *Benefactor* : or Bhaga, the God who distributes
wealth.

A hundred slaves, and wreaths besides.

4 There also was a mare led forth, picked
out for Pūtakratā's sake,
Not of the horses of the herd.

5 Observant Agni hath appeared, oblation-
bearer with his car.
Agni with his resplendent flame hath shone
on high as shines the Sun, hath shone
like Sūrya in the heavens.

HYMN IX.   *Aśvins.*

1. ENDOWED, O Gods, with your primeval
wisdom, come quickly with your chariot,
O ye Holy.
Come with your mighty powers, O ye
Nāsatyas; come hither, drink ye this
the third libation.

2 The truthful Deities, the Three-and-Thirty,
saw you approach before the Ever-
Truthful.
Accepting this our worship and libation,
O Aśvins bright with fire, drink ye the
Soma.

3 Aśvins, that work of yours deserves our
wonder,—the Bull of heaven and earth
and air's mid region;
Yea, and your thousand promises in battle,
—to all of these come near and drink
beside us.

4 Here is your portion laid for you, ye
Holy : come to these songs of ours, O
ye Nāsatyas.
Drink among us the Soma full of sweetness, and with your powers assist the
man who worships.

HYMN X.   *Viśvedevas.*

1. HE whom the priests in sundry ways
arranging the sacrifice, of one accord,
bring hither,

Who was appointed as a learned Brāhman,
—what is the sacrificer's knowledge of
him?

2 Kindled in many a spot, still One is Agni;
Sūrya is One though high o'er all he
shineth.
Illumining this All, still One is Uṣas.
That which is One hath into All
developed.

3 The chariot bright and radiant, treasure-
laden, three-wheeled, with easy seat, and
lightly rolling,
Which She of Wondrous Wealth was born
to harness,—this car of yours I call.
Drink what remaineth.

HYMN XI.   *Indra-Varuṇa.*

1. IN offerings poured to you, O Indra-
Varuṇa, these shares of yours stream
forth to glorify your state.
Ye haste to the libations at each sacrifice
when ye assist the worshipper who sheds
the juice.

2 The waters and the plants, O Indra-
Varuṇa, had efficacious vigour, and
attained to might :
Ye who have gone beyond the path of
middle air,—no godless man is worthy to
be called your foe.

3 True is your Kṛṣa's word, Indra and
Varuṇa : The seven holy voices pour a
wave of meath.
For their sake, Lords of splendour ! aid
the pious man who, unbewildered, keeps
you ever in his thoughts.

4 Dropping oil, sweet with Soma, pouring
forth their stream, are the Seven Sisters
in the seat of sacrifice.
These, dropping oil, are yours, O Indra-
Varuṇa : with these enrich with gifts
and help the worshipper.

---

4 *Picked out* or, adorned. *Pūtakratā* : the wife of
Pūtakratu.

---

1 *Nāsatyas*; 'truthful ones.'—Cowell. See Vol I., Index.
2 *The Three-and-Thirty* : or, Thrice-Eleven. See I.
34. 11. *The Ever-Truthful* : the Sun, whose approach is
heralded by the Aśvins.
3 *The Bull* : the Sun, whom, as his heralds and
revealers, they may be said to have created. *Thousand
promises* : 'a characteristic periphrasis for the Maghavans,
or wealthy nobles.'—Ludwig.

---

1 The hymn appears to consist of unconnected
fragments, and the purport of this stanza is not obvious.

---

3 *She of Wondrous Wealth* : Uṣas or Dawn. *Was
born to harness* : or, as Prof. Cowell translates : 'At
whose yoking the Dawn was born.' The chariot of the
Aśvins precedes that of the Dawn.

---

2 *The waters and the plants* : used in sacrifice ; the
Soma-plants and the water employed in preparing the
juice for libation. The meaning of the stanza seems to
be: although you are far away in the most distant firmament, our libations have had power to attract you.
Regard us only : the godless man is unworthy of your
consideration even as an enemy.
3 *The seven holy voices* : the voices of the seven priests
or sacred bards. See IX. 103. 3. *A wave of meath* : 'a
stream of honey.'—Cowell.
4 *The Seven Sisters* : 'sister-streams of the Soma.'—
Cowell.

5 To our great happiness have we ascribed
   to these Two Bright Ones truthfulness,
   great strength, and majesty.
  O Lords of splendour, aid us through the
    Three-times-Seven, as we pour holy oil,
    O Indra-Varuna.
6 What ye in time of old, Indra and Varuna,
   gave Ṛṣis—revelation, thought, and
   power of song,

And places which the wise made, weaving
   sacrifice,—these through my spirit's
   fervid glow have I beheld.
7 O Indra-Varuna, grant to the worshippers
   cheerfulness void of pride, and wealth
   to nourish them.
  Vouchsafe us food, prosperity, and progeny,
   and lengthen out our days that we may
   see long life.

---

5 *The Three-times-Seven* : perhaps the Maruts, thrice-
seven being used indefinitely for a larger number
consisting of troops of seven. See I. 133. 6.

6 *Revelation* : *śrutám* : that which was heard (from
the beginning); sacred knowledge. 'Fame.'—Cowell.
Places : perhaps, as Ludwig suggests, homes in the world
to come, which the wise Ṛṣis have prepared for themselves by performing sacrifice here below. *Through my
spirit's fervid glow* : *tápasā* : according to Grassmann and
Cowell, this *tápas* means 'the holy austerities' of the
Ṛṣis, and not the sacred fervour of the seer of the hymn.
I have followed Ludwig.

BOOK THE NINTH

HYMN I. *Soma Pavamāna.*

1. In sweetest and most gladdening stream
flow pure, O Soma, on thy way,
Pressed out for Indra, for his drink.

2 Fiend-queller, Friend of all men, he hath
with the wood attained unto
His place, his iron-fashioned home.

3 Be thou best Vṛtra-slayer, best granter of
bliss, most liberal :
Promote our wealthy princes' gifts.

4 Flow onward with thy juice unto the
banquet of the Mighty Gods :
Flow hither for our strength and fame.

5 O Indu, we draw nigh to thee, with this
one object day by day :
To thee alone our prayers are said.

6 By means of this eternal fleece may Sūrya's
Daughter purify
Thy Soma that is foaming forth.

7 Ten sister maids of slender form seize him
within the press and hold
Him firmly on the final day.

8 The virgins send him forth : they blow
the skin musician-like and fuse
The triple foe-repelling meath.

9 Inviolable milch-kine round about him
blend for Indra's drink,
The fresh young Soma with their milk.

10 In the wild raptures of this draught, Indra
slays all the Vṛtras : he,
The Hero, pours his wealth on us.

HYMN II. *Soma Pavamāna.*

1. SOMA, flow on, inviting Gods, speed to
the purifying cloth :
Pass into Indra, as a Bull.

2 As mighty food speed hitherward, Indu,
as a most splendid Steer :
Sit in thy place as one with strength.

3 The well-loved meath was made to flow,
the stream of the creative juice :
The Sage drew waters to himself.

4 The mighty waters, yea, the floods accompany thee Mighty One,
When thou wilt clothe thee with the milk.

5 The lake is brightened in the floods. Soma,
our Friend, heaven's prop and stay,
Falls on the purifying cloth.

6 The tawny Bull hath bellowed, fair as
mighty Mitra to behold:
He shines together with the Sun.

7 Songs, Indu, active in their might are
beautified for thee, wherewith
Thou deckest thee for our delight.

8 To thee who givest ample room we pray,
to win the joyous draught :
Great are the praises due to thee.

9 Indu as, Indra's Friend, on us pour with
a stream of sweetness, like
Parjanya sender of the rain.

10 Winner of kine, Indu, art thou, winner
of heroes, steeds, and strength :
Primeval Soul of sacrifice.

Nearly all the hymns of this Book are addressed to
the deified Soma juice, or to Soma, or Indu, the
Moon, who as containing the celestial nectar, the drink
of the Gods, is identified with the Soma-plant and its
exhilarating juice. As the Moon-God pours down his
ambrosial rain through the sieve of heaven, he is
addressed and worshipped as Pavamāna (Self-Purifying),
represented by the Soma juice as it undergoes purification by flowing through the wool which is used as a
filter or strainer. See Muir, *O. S. Texts*, V. 258 sqq.,
Hillebrandt, *Vedische Mythologie*, I. 385 sqq., and Max
Müller, *Chips*, IV. 353—367. But cf. Oldenberg,
Religion des Veda, 599—612.

1 *Flow pure* : *pávasva* : 'purify thyself.'—Ludwig.

2 *With the wood* : some wooden vessel or implement,
perhaps the *sruva* or dipping-spoon. *Iron-fashioned home*:
receptacle that has been hammered or formed with a
tool of *āyas*, iron or other metal. It is not clear what
vessel is intended.

6 *Sūrya's Daughter* : Śraddhā or Faith. See
Śatapatha-Brāhmaṇa, XII. 7. 3. 11.

7 *Ten sister maids* : the priest's fingers. *The final
day* : on which the Soma is effused.

8 *Virgins* : the unwedded ones : the fingers. *Musician-like* : or, as men blow a bagpipe ; but the meaning of *bākuram* and the second half-line is not clear.
'They seize it glittering like a water skin.'—Wilson.

3 *The Sage* : the Soma. *Waters* : with which the
stalks or the plant are sprinkled.

5 *The lake* : the Soma juice.

6 *The tawny Bull* : 'the golden-hued showerer of
blessings.'—Wilson. The strong greenish-yellow Soma
juice. *Hath bellowed* : an exaggerated expression for the
sound made by the juice as it drops, but in keeping
with its representation as a bull.

9 *Like Parjanya* : enriching and blessing us as the
rain-cloud fertilizes the ground.

HYMN III.   *Soma Pavamāna.*

1. HERE present this Immortal God flies,
   like a bird upon her wings,
   To settle in the vats of wood.

2. This God, made ready with the hymn,
   runs swiftly through the winding ways,
   Inviolable as he flows.

3. This God while flowing is adorned, like a
   bay steed for war, by men
   Devout and skilled in holy songs.

4. He, like a warrior going forth with heroes,
   as he flows along
   Is fain to win all precious boons.

5. This God, as he is flowing on, speeds
   like a car and gives his gifts :
   He lets his voice be heard of all

6. Praised by the sacred bards, this God dives
   into waters, and bestows
   Rich gifts upon the worshipper.

7. Away he rushes with his stream, across
   the regions, into heaven,
   And roars as he is flowing on.

8. While flowing, meet for sacrifice, he hath
   gone up to heaven across
   The regions, irresistible.

9. After the way of ancient time, this God,
   pressed out for Deities,
   Flows tawny to the straining-cloth.

10. This Lord of many Holy Laws, even at
    his birth engendering strength,
    Effused, flows onward in a stream.

HYMN IV.   *Soma Pavamāna.*

1. O SOMA flowing on thy way, win thou
   and conquer high renown;
   And make us better than we are.

2. Win thou the light, win heavenly light,
   and, Soma, all felicities;
   And make us better than we are.

3. Win skilful strength and mental power.
   O Soma, drive away our foes;
   And make us better than we are.

4. Ye purifiers, purify Soma for Indra, for
   his drink :
   Make thou us better than we are.

5. Give us our portion in the Sun through
   thine own mental power and aids;
   And make us better than we are.

6. Through thine own mental power and aid
   long may we look upon the Sun;
   Make thou us better than we are.

7. Well-weaponed Soma, pour to us a stream
   of riches doubly great;
   And make us better than we are.

8. As one victorious unsubdued in battle
   pour forth wealth to us;
   And make us better than we are.

9. By worship, Pavamāna ! men have strengthened thee to prop the Law :
   Make thou us better than we are.

10. O Indu, bring us wealth in steeds, mani-
    fold, quickening all life;
    And make us better than we are.

HYMN V   *Ápris.*

1. ENKINDLED, Pavamāna, Lord, sends forth
   his light on every side
   In friendly show, the bellowing Bull.

2. He, Pavamāna, Self-produced, speeds onward sharpening his horns :
   He glitters through the firmament.

3. Brilliant like wealth, adorable, with
   splendour Pavamāna shines,
   Mightily with the streams of meath.

4. The tawny Pavamāna, who strews from
   of old the grass with might,
   Is worshipped, God amid the Gods.

5. The golden, the Celestial Doors are
   lifted with their frames on high,
   By Pavamāna glorified.

---

4 *Purifiers* : priests whose business is to purify the juice. *Make thou* : O Soma.

9 *To prop the Law* : *vidharmani* : 'for their own up-holding.'—Wilson.

10 *Quickening all life* : *viśvdyum* : explained by Sāyaṇa as = *sarvagāminam* : 'all-reaching.'—Wilson.

In this Āprī hymn attributes of Agni are transferred to Soma Pavamāna.

1 *Enkindled* : *sdmiddhaḥ* : properly applicable to Agni. *The bellowing Bull* : 'the showerer of blessings, uttering a loud sound.'—Wilson.

2 *Self-produced* : *Tanūndpāt* ; properly a name of Agni; here, the Moon.

5 *The Celestial Doors* : the doors of the hall of sacrifice are here identified with the portals of the east through which light comes into the world. See II. 3. 5.

---

1 *The vats of wood* : *drốṇāni* : large wooden vessels, tubs or troughs which receive the Soma juice.

2 *The winding ways* : of the wool which forms the strainer.—Ludwig. 'Rushes against the enemies.'—Wilson.

6 *Dives into waters* : called *vasativaryaḥ*, with which the stalks of the Soma-plant are sprinkled.

9 *Pressed out for Deities* : the Soma juice being identified with the Amṛta or nectar, the drink of the Gods, contained in the Moon.

---

1 *Better than we are* : or, happier than we are.

6 With passion Pavamāna longs for the great
    lofty Pair, well-formed,
  Like beauteous maidens, Night and Dawn.

7 Both Gods who look on men I call, Celestial
    Heralds : Indra's Self
  Is Pavamāna, yea, the Bull.

8 This, Pavamāna's sacrifice, shall the three
    beauteous Goddesses,
  Sarasvatī and Bhāratī and Ilā, Mighty
    One, attend.

9 I summon Tvaṣṭar hither, our protector,
    champion, earliest-born,
  Indu is Indra, tawny Steer; Pavamāna
    is Prajāpati.

10 O Pavamāna, with the meath in streams
     anoint Vanaspati,
   The ever-green, the golden-hued, reful-
     gent, with a thousand boughs.

11 Come to the consecrating rite of Pavamāna,
     all ye Gods,—
   Vāyu, Sūrya, Bṛhaspati, Indra, and Agni,
     in accord.

HYMN VI.   *Soma Pavamāna.*

1. SOMA, flow on with pleasant stream, a Bull
     devoted to the Gods,
   Our Friend, unto the woollen sieve.

2 Pour hitherward, as Indra's Self, Indu,
    that gladdening stream of thine,
  And send us coursers full of strength.

3 Flow to the filter hitherward, pouring that
    ancient gladdening juice,
  Streaming forth power and high renown.

4 Hither the sparkling drops have flowed,
    like waters down a steep descent :
  They have reached Indra purified.

5 Whom, having passed the filter, ten dames
    cleanse, as 'twere a vigorous steed,
  While he disports him in the wood,—

6 The steer-strong juice with milk pour
    forth, for feast and service of the Gods,
  To him who bears away the draught.

7 Effused, the God flows onward with his
    stream to Indra, to the God,
  So that his milk may strengthen him.

8 Soul of the sacrifice, the juice effused
    flows quickly on : he keeps
  His ancient wisdom of a Sage.

9 So pouring forth, as Indra's Friend, strong
    drink, best Gladdener ! for the feast,
  Thou, even in secret, storest hymns.

HYMN VII.   *Soma Pavamāna.*

1. FORTH on their way the glorious drops
     have flowed for maintenance of Law,
   Knowing this sacrifice's course.

2 Down in the mighty waters sinks the stream
    of meath, most excellent,
  Oblation best of all in worth.

3 About the holy place, the Steer true,
    guileless, noblest, hath sent forth
  Continuous voices in the wood.

4 When, clothed in manly strength, the
    Sage flows in celestial wisdom round,
  The Strong would win the light of heaven.

5 When purified, he sits as King above the
    hosts, among his folk,
  What time the sages bring him nigh.

6 Dear, golden-coloured, in the fleece he
    sinks and settles in the wood :
  The Singer shows his zeal in hymns.

7 He goes to Indra, Vāyu, to the Aśvins,
    as his custom is,
  With gladdening juice which gives them
    joy.

8 The streams of pleasant Soma flow to
    Bhaga, Mitra-Varuṇa,—
  Well-knowing through his mighty powers.

---

7 *Celestial Heralds* : See I. 13. 8. *Indra's Self* : *indraḥ*
here is explained by Sāyaṇa as=*dīptaḥ* ; 'radiant.'—
Wilson.

10 *Vanaspati* : the sacrificial stake.

11 *The consecrating rite* : *svāhākṛtim* : oblation accompanied with the utterance of the sacred formula Svāhā.

5 *Whom* : relative to juice in the following stanza.
Ten dames : the fingers. *The wood* : the vat or trough.

6 *To him who bears away the draught* : to Indra. Others
take *bhdrāya* to mean 'for strength or prowess in battle.'

9 *Even in secret* : wisdom lies hidden in the Soma,
and cannot be recognized until one drinks the juice.
—Ludwig.

---

2 *The mighty waters* : the holy waters called *vasativaryaḥ.*

3 *In the wood* : according to Sāyaṇa, *vāne* here=*udake*,
in the water. The stanza is very difficult, and I am
unable to offer a satisfactory translation.

4 *The Strong* : Indra. 'Then the mighty (Indra) in
heaven is eager to repair to the oblation.'—Wilson.

5 *Above the hosts, among his folk* : or, as preferred by
Prof. Ludwig in his Commentary, above the contending
tribes or people (*viśaḥ*)

8 *Well-knowing, through his mighty powers* : that is, the
streams that, through the power of Soma, know the
way they should go. 'The worshippers knowing its
(virtues are rewarded) with happiness.'—Wilson.

---

9 Gain for us, O ye Heaven and Earth,
   riches of meath to win us wealth:
Gain for us treasures and renown.

HYMN VIII.   *Soma Pavamāna.*

1. OBEYING Indra's dear desire these Soma
   juices have flowed forth,
Increasing his heroic might.

2 Laid in the bowl, pure-flowing on to
   Vāyu and the Aśvins, may
These give us great heroic strength.

3 Soma, as thou art purified, incite to bounty
   Indra's heart,
To sit in place of sacrifice.

4 The ten swift fingers deck thee forth, seven
   ministers impel thee on :
The sages have rejoiced in thee.

5 When through the filter thou art poured,
   we clothe thee with a robe of milk
To be a gladdening draught for Gods.

6 When purified within the jars, Soma, bright-
   red and golden-hued,
Hath clothed him with a robe of milk.

7 Flow on to us and make us rich. Drive
   all our enemies away.
O Indu, flow into thy Friend.

8 Send down the rain from heaven, a stream
   of opulence from earth. Give us,
O Soma, victory in war.

9 May we obtain thee, Indra's drink, who
   viewest men and findest light,
Gain thee, and progeny and food.

HYMN IX.   *Soma Pavamāna.*

1. THE Sage of Heaven whose heart is wise,
   when laid between both hands and
   pressed,
Sends us delightful powers of life.

2 On, onward to a glorious home; dear to
   the people void of guile,
With excellent enjoyment, flow.

3 He, the bright Son, when born illumed
   his Parents who had sprung to life,
Great Son great Strengtheners of Law.

4 Urged by the seven devotions he hath
   stirred the guileless rivers which
Have magnified the Single Eye.

5 These helped to might the Youthful One,
   high over all, invincible,
Even Indu, Indra ! in thy law.

6 The Immortal Courser, good to draw,
   looks down upon the Seven : the fount
Hath satisfied the Goddesses

7 Aid us in holy rites, O Man : O Pavamāna,
   drive away
Dark shades that must be met in fight.

8 Make the paths ready for a hymn newer
   and newer evermore :
Make the lights shine as erst they shone.

9 Give, Pavamāna, high renown, give kine
   and steeds and hero sons :
Win for us wisdom, win the light.

HYMN X.   *Soma Pavamāna.*

1. LIKE cars that thunder on their way, like
   coursers eager for renown,
Have Soma-drops flowed forth for wealth.

2 Forth have they rushed from holding hands,
   like chariots that are urged to speed,
Like joyful songs of singing-men.

3 The Somas deck themselves with milk, as
   Kings are graced with eulogies,
And, with seven priests, the sacrifice.

4 Pressed for the gladdening draught, the
   drops flow forth abundantly with song,
The Soma juices in a stream.

5 Winning Vivasvān's glory and producing
   Morning's light, the Suns
Pass through the openings of the cloth.

6 The singing-men of ancient time open the
   doors of sacred songs,—
Men, for the mighty to accept.

---

7 *Flow on to us and make us rich* : or, 'Flow to us
wealthy worshippers.' *Thy Friend* : Indra. Cf. IX. 2. 1.

---

1 *The Sage of Heaven* : the Soma. *Both hands* :
naptyoḥ : literally, two granddaughters. According to
Sāyaṇa, two boards used in pressing the Soma are intended. See Cowell's note in Wilson's Translation.

3 *His Parents* : *mātarā* : literally, his two mothers;
Heaven and Earth.

4 *Seven devotions* : practised in the preparation of
the Soma. Sāyaṇa takes *saptá* with *nadyáḥ* : 'gladdens
the seven guileless rivers.'—Wilson. *Single Eye* : Soma,
the Moon.

6 *Courser* : the flowing Soma. *The Seven* : rivers.
The fount : 'Full, as a well, he has satisfied the divine
streams.'—Wilson.

7 *O Man* : manly Soma.

---

5 *The Suns* : so called as being creators of the light:
'the sun-bright juices.'—Wilson. *Vivasvān* : the morning Sun.

6 *Men, for the mighty to accept* : 'men, offerers of
Soma,' according to Sāyaṇa.

7 Combined in close society sit the seven
   priests, the brother-hood,
   Filling the station of the One.

8 He gives us kinship with the Gods, and
   with the Sun unites our eye :
   The Sage's offspring hath appeared.

9 The Sun with his dear eye beholds that
   quarter of the heavens which priests
   Have placed within the sacred cell.

HYMN XI.   *Soma Pavamāna.*

1. SING forth to Indu, O ye men, to him
   who is purified,
   Fain to pay worship to the Gods.

2 Together with thy pleasant juice the
   Atharvans have commingled milk,
   Divine, devoted to the God.

3 Bring, by thy flowing, weal to kine, weal
   to the people, weal to steeds.
   Weal, O thou King, to growing plants

4 Sing a praise-song to Soma brown of hue,
   of independent might.
   The Red, who reaches up to heaven.

5 Purify Soma when effused with stones which
   hands move rapidly,
   And pour the sweet milk in the meath.

6 With humble homage draw ye nigh; blend
   the libation with the curds :

7 *The seven priests* : the *adhvaryus* who bring the
water with which the stalks of the Soma-plants are
sprinkled. *The One* : Soma.—Sāyaṇa.

8 *He gives us kinship with the Gods* : I follow Prof.
Pischel's interpretation of this difficult passage. 'Soma
unites our navel with the navel of the Gods, our eye
with the Sun, that is, he brings us into union with the
Gods in heaven.'—*Vedische Studien*, I., p. 6 . 'I take
into my navel the navel of the sacrifice (the Soma).'—
Wilson. 'He (Soma) as kinsman has brought us a
kinsman (Sūrya).'—Ludwig. *The Sage's offspring* : a
periphrasis for the Sage himself, that is, Soma.—Ludwig.

9 This stanza is very obscure. I have adopted
Benfey's explanation who 'here follows an occasional
interpretation of *div* or *dyuloka*, given by the Scholiast,
which identifies it with the *droṇakalaśa* or large Soma-
trough. He takes it as meaning that the Sun looks
towards the place where the Soma lies while it is
pressed...Sāyaṇa seems to interpret this verse as meaning that Indra views the Soma with affection even
after it has been drunk by the priests (fixed in the heart).'
—Cowell, in Wilson's Translation.

2 *The Atharvans* : the priests, who perform the duties
of the Adhvaryus.

3 *King* : the usual designation of Soma in the
Brāhmaṇa.

4 *The Red* : kadācidaruṇavarṇāya : 'sometimes red-
coloured.'—Sāyaṇa.

To Indra offer Indu up.

7 Soma, foe-queller, chief o'er men, doing
   the will of Gods, pour forth
   Prosperity upon our kine.

8 Heart-knower, Sovran of the heart, thou
   art effused, O Soma, that Indra may
   drink thee and rejoice.

9 O Soma Pavamāna, give us riches and
   heroic strength,—
   Indu ! with Indra for ally.

HYMN XII.   *Soma Pavamāna.*

1. To Indra have the Soma drops, exceeding
   rich in sweets, been poured,
   Shed in the seat of sacrifice.

2 As mother kine low to their calves, to
   Indra have the sages called,
   Called him to drink the Soma juice.

3 In the stream's wave wise Soma dwells,
   distilling rapture, in his seat,
   Resting upon a wild-cow's hide.

4 Far-sighted Soma, Sage and Seer, is worshipped in the central point
   Of heaven, the straining-cloth of wool.

5 In close embraces Indu holds Soma when
   poured within the jars.
   And on the purifying sieve.

6 Indu sends forth a voice on high to
   regions of the sea of air,
   Shaking the vase that drops with meath.

7 The Tree whose praises never fail yields
   heavenly milk among our hymns,
   Urging men's generations on.

3 *In the stream's wave* : in the water with which the
stalks are sprinkled. *Upon a wild-cow's hide* : this, which
is Benfey's explanation of *gaurī*, seems to be borne out
by *gor ádhi tvací*, upon the ox-hide, of IX. 101. 11.
Sāyaṇa's interpretation is different : 'to a chant in the
middle tone.'—Wilson.

4 *Of heaven* : *divaḥ* : See IX. 10. 9, and note.

5 *Indu holds Soma* : 'the deity seems to be thus
opposed to the mere plant.'—Cowell's note. Ludwig
suggests that Indu here may be the Moon, as the time
of important liturgical ceremonies depends upon the
Moon's phases. So also Hillebrandt, *V. M.*, I., p. 316.

6 *To regions of the sea of air* : or *samudrásya* here may
mean, of the sea or water into which the Soma juice
falls. *Shaking* : or, perhaps, stirring (with joy . *The
vase* : *kośam* : the *droṇakalaśa*, the large wooden vessel for
holding the juice. According to Sāyaṇa, whose interpretation I have followed in the first line, *kośam* here
means the cloud.

7 *The Tree* : Soma. *Men's generations* : sacrificial
seasons, according to Sāyaṇa.

8 The Wise One, with the Sage's stream,
   the Soma urged to speed, flows on
To the dear places of the sky.

9 O Pavamāna, bring us wealth bright with
   a thousand splendours. Yea.
O Indu, give us ready help.

HYMN XIII.   *Soma Pavamāna.*

1. PASSED through, the fleece in thousand
   streams the Soma, purified, flows on
To Indra's, Vāyu's special place.

2 Sing forth, ye men who long for help, to
   Pavamāna, to the Sage,
Effused to entertain the Gods.

3 The Soma-drops with thousand powers
   are purified for victory,
Hymned to become the feast of Gods.

4 Yea, as thou flowest bring great store of
   food that we may win the spoil :
Indu, bring splendid manly might.

5 May they in flowing give us wealth in
   thousands, and heroic power,—
These Godlike Soma-drops effused.

6 Like coursers by their drivers urged, they
   were poured forth, for victory,
Swift through the woollen straining-cloth.

7 Noisily flow the Soma-drops, like milch-
   kine lowing to their calves :
They have run forth from both the hands.

8 As Gladdener whom Indra loves, O
   Pavamāna, with a roar
Drive all our enemies away.

9 O Pavamānas, driving off the godless, looking on the light,
Sit in the place of sacrifice.

HYMN XIV.   *Soma Pavamāna.*

1. REPOSING on the river's wave the Sage
   hath widely flowed around,
Bearing the hymn which many love.

2 When the Five kindred Companies, active
   in duty, with the song
Establish him, the Powerful,

3 Then in his juice whose strength is great,
   have all the Gods rejoiced themselves,
When he hath clothed him in the milk.

4 Freeing himself he flows away, leaving
   his body's severed limbs,
And meets his own Companion here.

5 He by the daughters of the priest, like a
   fair youth, hath been adorned,
Making the milk, as 'twere, his robe.

6 O'er the fine fingers, through desire of
   milk, in winding course he goes,
And utters voice which he hath found.

7 The nimble fingers have approached,
   adorning him the Lord of Strength :
They grasp the vigorous Courser's back.

8 Comprising all the treasures that are in
   the heavens and on the earth,
Come, Soma, as our faithful Friend.

HYMN XV.   *Soma Pavamāna.*

1. THROUGH the fine fingers, with the song,
   this Hero comes with rapid ears,
Going to Indra's special place.

2 In holy thought he ponders much for the
   great worship of the Gods.
Where the Immortals have their seat.

3 Like a good horse is he led out, when on
   the path that shines with light
The mettled steeds exert their strength.

4 He brandishes his horns on high, and
   whets them, Bull who leads the herd,
Doing with might heroic deeds.

5 He moves, a vigorous Steed, adorned with
   beauteous rays of shining gold,

---

1 *Indra's, Vāyu's special place* : the vessels especially
prepared to hold libations intended for Indra and
Vāyu.

3 *For victory* : *vājasātaye.* : 'for the attainment of food '
—Wilson. So explains Sāyaṇa in stanzas 3 and 4; but in
6 the word is explained by *saṁgrāmāya* to battle, in the
first clause where he inserts it after *hiyānāḥ*, urged,
and by *annalābhāya*, for the attainment of food, in the
second clause.

8 *With a roar* : making a loud noise in dropping.

———

1 *On the river's wave* : in the *vasatīvarī* waters, which
are used to sprinkle the stalks. *Bearing the hymn* : Prof.
Geldner explains this as meaning, 'Bearing away the
much coveted prize,' Soma being regarded as a courser or race-horse. See *Vedische Studien*, I., p. 120.

2 *Five kindred Companies* : referring, probably, to
some sacrifice instituted in common by representatives of
the five Āryan tribes.

4 *His own Companion* : Indra. *He meets* : this (*saṅgato
bhavati*) is Sāyaṇa's explanation of *samjighnate*; but it
is not easy to see how the word can bear this signification.

5 *Daughters* : or granddaughters; the fingers.

6 *Which he hath found* : 'which the worshipper reco-
gnizes.'—Wilson.

———

1 *Indra's special place* : 'Indra's abode'.—Wilson. In
Hymn XIII. 1, *niṣkṛtām* is explained by Sāyaṇa as the
vessel prepared and set apart.

3 *Like a good horse* : the text has only *hitáḥ* which
may mean either good or placed. 'Placed (in the cart)
he is brought.'—Wilson.

4 *Horns* : cf. IX. 5. 2.

5 *Rays of shining gold* : as the Moon.

Becoming Sovran of the streams.

6 He, over places rough to pass, bringing
    rich treasures closely packed.
Descends into the reservoirs.

7 Men beautify him in the vats, him worthy
    to be beautified,
Him who brings forth abundant food.

8 Him, even him, the fingers ten and the
    seven songs make beautiful,
Well-weaponed, best of gladdeners.

HYMN XVI. *Soma Pavamāna.*

1. THE pressers from the Soma-press send
    forth thy juice for rapturous joy :
The speckled sap runs like a flood.

2 With strength we follow through the sieve
    him who brings might and wins the
    kine,
Enrobed in water with his juice.

3 Pour on the sieve the Soma, ne'er subdued
    in waters, waterless,
And make it pure for Indra's drink.

4 Moved by the purifier's thought, the
    Soma flows into the sieve:
By wisdom it hath gained its home.

5 With humble homage, Indra, have the
    Soma-drops flowed forth to thee,
Contending for the glorious prize.

6 Purified in his fleecy garb, attaining every
    beauty, he
Stands, hero-like, amid the kine.

7 Swelling, as 'twere, to heights of heaven,
    the stream of the creative juice
Falls lightly on the cleansing sieve.

8 Thus, Soma, purifying him who knoweth
    song mid living men,
Thou wanderest through the cloth of wool.

---

6 *Places rough to pass* : the wool of the strainer.
Sāyaṇa gives a totally different explanation of this stanza.
See Wilson's Translation. I have followed Prof.
Ludwig.

8 *Seven songs* : the songs of the seven priests.

---

1. *From the Soma-press* : *oṇyoḥ*, ablative dual of *oṇi*,
signifying apparently an implement or a vessel, consisting of two pieces, used in the preparation of the Soma
juice. The word is said to be employed to denote,
metaphorically, heaven and earth. 'They who express
thee, the juice of heaven and earth '—Wilson.

3 *Waterless* : *ánaptam*, which Sāyaṇa explains by
anāptam, not reached, or overtaken, by enemies. The
meaning is not clear.

4 *Its home* : in the large wooden vessel called
droṇakalaśa.

5 *Contending for the glorious prize* : like race-horses.
'Giving thee vigour for the great conflict.'—Wilson.

HYMN XVII. *Soma Pavamāna.*

1. LIKE rivers down a steep descent, slaying
    the Vṛtras, full of zeal,
The rapid Soma-streams have flowed.

2 The drops of Soma juice effused fall like
    the rain upon the earth :
To Indra flow the Soma-streams.

3 With swelling wave the gladdening drink,
    the Soma, flows into the sieve,
Loving the Gods and slaying fiends.

4 It hastens to the pitchers, poured upon
    the sieve it waxes strong
At sacrifices through the lauds.

5 Soma, thou shinest mounting heaven as
    'twere above light's triple realm,
And moving seem'st to speed the Sun.

6 To him, the head of sacrifice, singers and
    bards have sung their songs,
Offering what he loves to see.

7 The men, the sages with their hymns,
    eager for help, deck thee strong steed,
Deck thee for service of the Gods.

8 Flow onward to the stream of meath :
    rest efficacious in thy home,
Fair, to be drunk at sacrifice.

HYMN XVIII. *Soma Pavamāna.*

1. THOU, Soma, dweller on the hills, effused,
    hast flowed into the sieve :
All-bounteous art thou in carouse.

2 Thou art a sacred Bard, a Sage; the meath
    is offspring of thy sap :
All-bounteous art thou in carouse.

3 All Deities of one accord have come that
    they may drink of thee :
All-bounteous art thou in carouse.

4 He who containeth in his hands all treasures
    much to be desired :
All-bounteous art thou in carouse.

5 Who milketh out this mighty Pair, the
    Earth and Heaven, like mother kine :
All-bounteous art thou in carouse.

---

5 Addressed to Soma as the Moon.

6 *The head of sacrifice* : the most important element
of the ceremony. According to Sāyaṇa, at the head,
that is, on the last and most important day of the
effusion of the Soma juice. *Offering what he loves to see*:
'entertaining affection for him the all-beholding.'—
Wilson.

8 *Meath* : or honey. *In thy home* : in the *droṇakalaśa*.

---

1 *Dweller on the hills* : 'pressed between the stones.'—
Wilson.

6 Who in a moment mightily floweth around
these two world-halves :
All-bounteous art thou in carouse.

7 The Strong One, being purified, hath in
the pitchers cried aloud :
All-bounteous art thou in carouse.

HYMN XIX. *Soma Pavamāna.*

1. O SOMA, being purified bring us the
wondrous treasure, meet
For lauds, that is in earth and heaven.

2 For ye Twain, Indra, Soma, are Lords
of the light, Lords of the kine :
Great Rulers, prosper ye our songs.

3 The tawny Steer, while cleansed among
the living, bellowing on the grass,
Hath sunk and settled in his home.

4 Over the Steer's productive flow the sacred
songs were resonant,
The mothers of the darling Son.

5 Hath he not, purified, impregned the kine
who long to meet their Lord,
The kine who yield the shining milk?

6 Bring near us those who stand aloof :
strike fear into our enemies:
O Pavamāna, find us wealth.

7 Soma, bring down the foeman's might, his
vigorous strength and vital power,
Whether he be afar or near.

HYMN XX. *Soma Pavamāna.*

1. FORTH through the straining-cloth the
Sage flows to the banquet of the Gods,
Subduing all our enemies.

2 For he, as Pavamāna, sends thousandfold
treasure in the shape
Of cattle to the singing-men.

3 Thou graspest all things with thy mind,
and purifiest thee with thoughts :
As such, O Soma, find us fame.

4 Pour lofty glory on us, send sure riches
to our liberal lords,
Bring food to those who sing thy praise.

5 As thou art cleansed, O Wondrous Steed,
O Soma, thou hast entered, like
A pious King, into the songs.

6 He, Soma, like a courser in the floods
invincible, made clean
With hands, is resting in the jars.

7 Disporting, like a liberal chief, thou goest,
Soma, to the sieve,
Lending the laud a Hero's strength.

HYMN XXI. *Soma Pavamāna.*

1. To Indra flow these running drops, these
Somas frolicsome in mood.
Exhilarating, finding light;

2 Driving off foes, bestowing room upon the
presser, willingly
Bringing their praiser vital force.

3 Lightly disporting them, the drops flow
to one common reservoir,
And fall into the river's wave.

4 These Pavamānas have obtained all blessings much to be desired,
Like coursers harnessed to a car.

5 With view to us, O Soma-drops, bestow
his manifold desire
On him who yet hath given us naught.

6 Bring us our wish with this design, as a
wright brings his new-wrought wheel:
Flow pure and shining with the stream.

7 These drops have cried with resonant voice:
like swift steeds they have run the course,
And roused the good man's hymn to life.

HYMN XXII. *Soma Pavamāna.*

1. THESE rapid Soma-streams have stirred
themselves to motion like strong steeds,
Like cars, like armies hurried forth.

2 Swift as wide winds they lightly move,
like rain-storms of Parjanya, like
The flickering flames of burning fire.

3 These Soma juices, blent with curds,
purified, skilled in sacred hymns,
Have gained by song their hearts' desire.

---

6 *Like a courser* : 'the bearer (of oblations).'—
Wilson.

7 *Chief* : Sāyaṇa explains *makhâḥ* by *dânam, gift.*

---

5 This stanza is obscure, and Sāyaṇa's commentary
is imperfect. It seems that the Soma-drops are prayed
to enrich the institutor of the sacrifice who has not as
yet rewarded the priests.

7 *Run the course* : reached the *droṇakalaśa.*

---

3 *By song* : *vipâ* : by knowledge, according to
Sāyaṇa. 'The St. Petersb. Dict. explains *vip* as the
twigs (cf. *vepres*) which form the bottom of the funnel
and support the filtering-cloth.'—Cowell, in Wilson's
Translation.

---

4 Hymns are sung over the Soma-stream, and are
called mothers of the precious juice because it is prepared while they are sung.

5 *The kine* : the vasatīvarī waters which long to
mingle with the Soma.

---

5 *Steed* : *vahne* : 'bearer (of our offerings).'—Wilson.

4 Immortal, cleansed, these drops, since
   first they flowed, have never wearied,
   fain
  To reach the regions and their paths.

5 Advancing they have travelled o'er the
   ridges of the earth and heaven,
  And this the highest realm of all.

6 Over the heights have they attained the
   highest thread that is spun out,
  And this which must be deemed most
   high.

7 Thou, Soma, holdest wealth in kine which
   thou hast seized from niggard churls:
  Thou calledst forth the outspun thread.

HYMN XXIII. *Soma Pavamāna.*

1. SWIFT Soma drops have been effused in
   streams of meath, the gladdening drink,
  For sacred lore of every kind.

2 Hither to newer resting-place the ancient
   Living Ones are come.
  They made the Sun that he might shine.

3 O Pavamāna, bring to us the unsacrificing
   foeman's wealth,
  And give us food with progeny.

4 The living Somas being cleansed diffuse
   exhilarating drink,
  Turned to the vat which drips with
   meath.

5 Soma flows on intelligent, possessing sap
   and mighty strength,
  Brave Hero who repels the curse.

6 For Indra, Soma ! thou art cleansed, a
   feast-companion for the Gods :
  Indu, thou fain wilt win us strength

7 When he had drunken draughts of this,
   Indra smote down resistless foes :
  Yea, smote them, and shall smite them
   still.

HYMN XXIV. *Soma Pavamāna.*

1. HITHERWARD have the Soma streamed,
   the drops while they are purified :
  When blent, in waters they are rinsed.

2 The mild hath run to meet them like
   floods rushing down a precipice :
  They come to Indra, being cleansed.

3 O Soma Pavamāna, thou art flowing to
   be Indra's drink :
  The men have seized and lead thee forth.

4 Victorious, to be hailed with joy, O Soma,
   flow, delighting men,
  To him who ruleth o'er mankind.

5 Thou, Indu, when, effused by stones, thou
   runnest to the filter, art,
  Ready for Indra's high decree.

6 Flow on, best Vṛtra-slayer; flow meet to
   be hailed with joyful lauds.
  Pure, purifying, wonderful.

7 Pure, purifying is he called the Soma of
   the meath effused,
  Slayer of sinners, dear to Gods.

HYMN XXV. *Soma Pavamāna.*

1. GREEN-HUED ! as one who giveth strength
   flow on for Gods to drink, a draught
  For Vāyu and the Marut host.

2 O Pavamāna, sent by song, roaring about
   thy dwelling-place,
  Pass into Vāyu as Law bids.

3 The Steer shines with the Deities, dear
   Sage in his appointed home,
  Foe-Slayer, most beloved by Gods.

4 Taking each beauteous form, he goes,
   desirable, while purified,
  Thither where the Immortals sit.

5 To Indra Soma flows, the Red, engendering song, exceeding wise,
  The visitor of living men.

---

6 Or, 'Streams rushing down have filled the threads,
most excellent, spread out beneath'; that is, the threads
of the straining-cloth. See note in Wilson. According
to Sāyaṇa 'the thread' is sacrifice ; and 'this which
must be deemed most high' may be, as Ludwig suggests,
the place of sacrifice which is also to be held holy.
Wilson translates the second line :—'this rite is glorified
thereby.'

7 *From niggard churls* : or from the Paṇis. *Thou
calledst out the outspun thread* : 'thou hast called aloud at
the outspread sacrifice.'—Wilson.

2 *Newer resting-place* : a newly-prepared place of
sacrifice. *The ancient Living Ones* : the Soma-drops.

4 *To him who ruleth o'er mankind* : to Indra.

5 *Ready for Indra's high decree* : Wilson, following
Sāyaṇa, translates : 'an ample portion for Indra's belly.'
See Bergaigne, *La Religion Védique*, III. 210 ff., for the
meaning of *dhāman* in the Ṛgveda.

2 *Into Vāyu*: into the vessel appropriated to Vāyu—
Sāyaṇa.

5 *The Red* : *aruṣáḥ* : here explained by Sāyaṇa as=
ārocamānaḥ, shining or radiant. *The visitor of living men* :
āyuṣák : the meaning of this word is uncertain. The
St. Petersburg Lexicon explains it as conjointly
with men ; with human co-operation. Ludwig in his
translation renders it by 'der den lebenden besucht,'
who visits the living man ; but in his Commentary
suggests that it may mean, during the whole of life.
'Constantly.'—Wilson.

The visitor of living men.

6 Flow, best exhilarator, Sage, flow to the
filter in a stream
To seat thee in the place of song.

HYMN XXVI.   *Soma Pavamāna.*

1. THE sages with the fingers' art have
dressed and decked that vigorous Steed
Upon the lap of Aditi.

2 The kine have called aloud to him exhaustless with a thousand streams,
To Indu who supporteth heaven.

3 Him, nourisher of many, Sage, creative
Pavamāna, they
Have sent, by wisdom, to the sky.

4 Him, dweller with Vivasvān, they with
use of both arms have sent forth,
The Lord of Speech infallible.

5 Him, green, beloved, many eyed, the
Sisters with pressing stones
Send down to ridges of the sieve.

6 O Pavamāna, Indu, priests hurry thee on
to Indra, thee
Who aidest song and cheerest him.

HYMN XXVII.   *Soma Pavamāna.*

1. THIS Sage, exalted by our lauds, flows to
the purifying cloth,
Scattering foes as he is cleansed.

2 As giving power and winning light, for
Indra and for Vāyu he
Is poured upon the filtering-cloth.

3 The men conduct him, Soma, Steer,
Omniscient, and the Head of Heaven,
Effused into the vats of wood.

---

6 *Of song* : *arkásya* : *arcanīyasyendrasya*, of the adorable Indra, according so Sāyaṇa. *Arka* has two meanings in the Ṛgveda (1) song or hymn of praise and (2)
light or splendour. See Pischel, *Vedische Studien*, I. pp.
23—26.

---

1 *Aditi* : the earth.

2 *The kine* : who supply the milk that is mixed
with the Soma juice.

4 *Vivasvān* : meaning here the sacrificer. *Of both
arms* : *bhuríjoḥ* : according to Sāyana=*bāhvoḥ* the arms
of the body. The St. Petersburg Lexicon explains the
word as meaning a sort of vice or im lement for holding wood while it is being cut. *Lord of speech* : making
men eloquent.

5 *Many-eyed* : 'far beholding.'—Wilson. *The Sisters* :
the fingers of the officiating priest.

---

3 *Omniscient* : or, all-possessing. *Vats of wood* :
vánesu : according to Benfey, into the streams of water.

4 Longing for kine, longing for gold hath
Indu Pavamāna lowed,
Still Conqueror, never overcome.

5 This Pavamāna, gladdening draught, drops
on the filtering cloth, and then
Mounts up with Sūrya to the sky.

6 To Indra in the firmament this mighty tawny
Steer hath flowed,
This Indu, being purified.

HYMN XXVIII.   *Soma Pavamāna.*

1. URGED by the men, this vigorous Steed,
Lord of the mind, Omniscient,
Runs to the woollen straining-cloth.

2 Within the filter hath he flowed, this Soma
for the Gods effused,
Entering all their essences.

3 He shines in beauty there, this God Immortal in his dwelling-place,
Foe-slayer, dearest to the Gods.

4 Directed by the Sisters ten, bellowing on
his way this Steer
Runs onward to the wooden vats.

5 This Pavamāna, swift and strong, Omniscient, gave splendour to
The Sun and all his forms of light.

6 This Soma, being purified, flows mighty
and infallible,
Slayer of sinners, dear to Gods.

HYMN XXIX.   *Soma Pavamāna.*

1. FORWARD with mighty force have flowed
the currents of this Steer effused,
Of him who sets him by the Gods.

2 The singers praise him with their song,
and learned priests adorn the Steed,
Brought forth as light that merits laud.

3 These things thou winnest lightly while
purified, Soma, Lord of wealth :
Fill full the sea that claims our praise.

4 Winning all precious things at once, flow
on, O Soma, with thy stream :
Drive to one place our enemies.

---

4 *Longing for kine* : who supply milk to mix with
the Soma juice. *Gold* : worn on the finger of the priest
who presses out the juice. *Lowed* : made a noise in
dropping.

5 *Mounts up* : as the Moon.

---

1 *Who sets him by the Gods* : or, who decorates the
Gods. 'Who seeks to surpass the gods.' —Wilson.

3 *These things* : for which we pray. *The sea* : the
Soma-vat or reservoir.

5 Preserve us from the godless, from ill-
omened voice of one and all,
That so we may be freed from blame.

6 O Indu, as thou flowest on bring us the
wealth of earth and heaven,
And splendid vigour, in thy stream.

HYMN XXX.   Soma Pavamāna.

1. STREAMS of this Potent One have flowed
easily to the straining-cloth :
While he is cleansed he lifts his voice.

2 Indu, by pressers urged to speed, bellowing
out while beautified.
Sends forth a very mighty sound.

3 Pour on us, Soma, with thy stream man-
conquering might which many crave,
Accompanied with hero sons.

4 Hither hath Pavamāna flowed, Soma
flowed hither in a stream,
To settle in the vats of wood.

5 To waters with the stones they drive thee
tawny-hued, most rich in sweets,
O Indu, to be Indra's drink.

6 For Indra, for the Thunderer press the
Soma very rich in sweets,
Lovely, inspiriting, for strength.

HYMN XXXI.   Soma Pavamāna.

1. THE Soma-drops, benevolent, come forth
as they are purified,
Bestowing wealth which all may see.

2 O Indu, high o'er heaven and earth be
thou, increaser of our might :
The Master of all strength be thou.

3 The winds are gracious in their love to
thee, the rivers flow to thee :
Soma, they multiply thy power.

4 Soma, wax great. From every side may
vigorous powers unite in thee :
Be in the gathering-place of strength.

5 For thee, brown-hued ! the kine have
poured imperishable oil and milk.
Aloft on the sublimest height.

6 Friendship, O Indu, we desire with thee
who bearest noble arms,
With thee, O Lord of all that is.

HYMN XXXII.   Soma Pavamāna.

1. THE rapture-shedding Soma-drops, effused
in our assembly, have
Flowed forth to glorify our prince.

2 Then Trita's Maidens onward urge the
Tawny-coloured with the stones,
Indu for Indra, for his drink.

3 Now like a swan he maketh all the company sing each his hymn :
He, like a steed, is bathed in milk.

4 O Soma, viewing heaven and earth, thou
runnest like a darting deer :
Set in the place of sacrifice.

5 The cows have sung with joy to him,
even as a woman to her love :
He came as to a settled race.

6 Bestow illustrious fame on us, both on our
liberal lords and me,
Glory, intelligence, and wealth.

HYMN XXXIII.   Soma Pavamāna.

1. LIKE waves of waters, skilled in song the
juices of the Soma speed
Onward, as buffaloes to woods.

2 With stream of sacrifice the brown bright
drops have flowed with strength in store
Of kine into the wooden vats.

3 To Indra, Vāyu, Varuṇa, to Viṣṇu, and
the Maruts, flow
The drops of Soma juice effused.

---

5 Ill-omened voice : svandt, explained by Sāyaṇa as =
śabdânnindārūpât, sound or word in the form of blame;
the raging fury of the demon or the godless man,
according to Grassmann.

---

2 A very mighty sound: or, a sound which Indra loves.

---

1 Wealth which all may see : 'intellectual wealth.'—
Wilson.

3 The winds; cf. 'Vāyu is Soma's guardian God' (X.
85. 5).

4 This stanza has occurred before. See I. 91. 16.
Be in the gathering place of strength : be the central point
and source of all power.

5 The kine : of the clouds, the waters. Oil and milk:
sweet and fertilizing rain. Or the cows who supply
for the libation may be intended, in which case 'the
sublimest' would be the place of sacrifice.

---

1 Our prince : the noble who institutes the sacrifice.

2 Trita's Maidens : the fingers of the priest. See
IX 38. 2.

3 Like a swan: as a sentinel haṁsa (swan, wild-goose,
or flamingo) at the approach of danger sounds a note of
alarm which is answered by all the rest.—Ludwig.

4 Darting ; Sāyaṇa takes taktâḥ with 'thou,' Soma
and explains it by gavyaiḥ payaâdibhirmiśritaḥ san, being
mixed with milk, curds, etc. Elsewhere Sāyaṇa explains
it by 'swift.'

5 Cows : praises, according to Sāyaṇa. As to a
settled race : as a horse is brought to run a race that has
been arranged. 'As a hero hastens to the welcome contest.'—Wilson.

4 Three several words are uttered : kine are lowing, cows who give their milk :
The Tawny-hued goes bellowing on.

5 The young and sacred mothers of the holy rite have uttered praise :
They decorate the Child of Heaven.

6 From every side, O Soma, for our profit, pour thou forth four seas
Filled full of riches thousandfold.

HYMN XXXIV. *Soma Pavamāna.*

1. THE drop of Soma juice effused flows onward with this stream impelled.
Rending strong places, with its might.

2 Poured forth to Indra, Varuṇa, to Vāyu and the Marut host,
To Viṣṇu, flows the Soma juice.

3 With stones they press the Soma forth, the Strong conducted by the strong :
They milk the liquor out with skill.

4 'Tis he whom Trita must refine, 'tis he who shall make Indra glad :
The Tawny One is decked with tints.

5 Him do the Sons of Pṛśni milk, the dwelling-place of sacrifice,
Oblation lovely and most dear.

6 To him in one united stream these songs flow' on straight forward : he,
Loud voiced, hath made the milch-kine low.

HYMN XXXV. *Soma Pavamāna.*

1. POUR forth on us abundant wealth, O Pavamāna, with thy stream.
Wherewith thou mayest find us light.

2 O Indu, swayer of the sea, shaker of all things, flow thou on,
Bearer of wealth to us with might.

3 With thee for Hero, Valiant One ! may we subdue our enemies :
Let what is precious flow to us.

4 Indu arouses strength, the Sage who strives for victory, winning power,
Discovering holy works and means.

5 Mover of speech, we robe him with our songs as he is purified
Soma, the Guardian of the folk;

6 On whose way, Lord of Holy Law, most rich, as he is purified.
The people all have set their hearts.

HYMN XXXVI. *Soma Pavamāna.*

1. FORTH from the mortar is the juice sent, like a car-horse, to the sieve :
The Steed steps forward to the goal.

2 Thus, Soma, watchful, bearing well, cheering the Gods, flow past the sieve,
Turned to the vat that drops with meath.

3 Excellent Pavamāna, make the lights shine brightly out for us :
Speed us to mental power and skill.

4 He, beautified by pious men, and coming from their hands adorned,
Flows through the fleecy straining-cloth.

5 May Soma pour all treasures of the heavens, the earth, the firmament
Upon the liberal worshipper.

6 Thou mountest to the height of heaven, O Soma, seeking steeds and kine,
And seeking heroes, Lord of Strength !

HYMN XXXVII. *Soma Pavamāna.*

1. SOMA, the Steer, effused for draught, flows to the purifying sieve,
Slaying the fiends, loving the Gods.

---

4 *Three several words* : according to Sāyaṇa, *trividhā stutiḥ*, praise of three kinds, from the three Vedas. 'The priests utter the three sacred texts.'—Wilson. Probably three triplets chanted during the ceremony. See Bergaigne, I. 288.

5 *Mothers of the holy rite* : apparently, the cows who supply milk for libations. *The Child of Heaven* : the Soma, which, according to a text quoted by Sāyaṇa, 'was in the third heaven from hence.'

6 *Four seas* : imaginary seas, to correspond with the four quarters of heaven.

———

1 *Strong places* : the strongholds of enemies, the fiends who withhold the rain.

4 *Trita* : the preparer of the Celestial Soma.

5 *The dwelling-place of sacrifice* : the Soma-plant contains within itself the chief element of sacrifice, and the preparation of the juice is only the development of its nature.—Ludwig.

———

2 *The sea* : The reservoir of Soma juice.

4 *Discovering holy works and means* : acquainted with sacred rites and arms.— Wilson.

6 *On whose way* : on whose statutes or decrees.

———

1 *To the goal: kárṣman* : apparently, a line or furrow drawn across the end of the race-course. In I. 116. 17, Sāyaṇa explains *kárṣman* as a piece of wood serving as a goal, but in this place he takes it to mean, 'the God-attracting battle-field called a sacrifice,' *devānāmākarṣaṇavati yajñākhye sangrāme.* See Cowell's note in Wilson's Translation.

———

2 *The vat* : the *droṇakalaśa.*

———

1 *For draught* : *pītáye* : 'for the drinking (of the gods).'—Wilson.

2 Far-sighted, tawny-coloured, he flows to
the sieve, intelligent,
Bellowing, to his place of rest.

3 This vigorous Pavamāna runs forth to the
luminous realm of heaven,
Fiend-slayer, through the fleecy sieve.

4 This Pavamāna up above Trita's high ridge
hath made the Sun,
Together with the Sisters, shine.

5 This Vṛtra-slaying Steer, effused, Soma
room-giver, ne'er deceived,
Hath gone, as 'twere, to win the spoil.

6 Urged onward by the sage, the God
speeds forward to the casks of wood,
Indu to Indra willingly.

HYMN XXXVIII. *Soma Pavamāna.*

1. THIS Steer, this Chariot, rushes through
the woollen filter, as he goes
To war that wins a thousand spoils.

2 The Dames of Trita with the stones onward impel this Tawny One,
Indu to Indra for his drink.

3 Ten active fingers carefully adorn him
here; they make him bright
And beauteous for the gladdening draught.

4 He like a falcon settles down amid the
families of men.
Speeding like lover to his love.

5 This young exhilarating juice looks downward from its place in heaven,
This Soma-drop that pierced the sieve.

6 Poured for the draught, this tawny juice
flows forth, intelligent, crying out,
Unto the well-beloved place.

HYMN XXXIX. *Soma Pavamāna.*

1. FLOW on, O thou of lofty thought, flow
swift in thy beloved form,
Saying, I go where dwell the Gods.

2 Preparing what is unprepared, and bringing store of food to man,
Make thou the rain descend from heaven.

3 With might, bestowing power, the juice
enters the purifying sieve,
Far-seeing, sending forth its light.

4 This is it which in rapid course hath with
the river's wave flowed down
From heaven upon the straining cloth.

5 Inviting him from far away, and even from
near at hand, the juice
For Indra is poured forth as meath.

6 In union they have sung the hymn : with
stones they urge the Tawny One.
Sit in the place of sacrifice.

HYMN XL. *Soma Pavamāna.*

1. THE Very Active hath assailed, while
purified, all enemies :
They deck the Sage with holy songs.

2 The Red hath mounted to his place; to
Indra goes the mighty juice:
He settles in his firm abode.

3 O Indu, Soma, send us now great opulence
from every side, Pour on us treasures
thousandfold.

4 O Soma Pavamāna, bring, Indu, all
splendours hitherward :
Find for us food in boundless store.

5 As thou art cleansed, bring hero strength
and riches to thy worshipper,
And prosper thou the singer's hymns.

6 O Indu, Soma, being cleansed, bring
hither riches doublypiled,
Wealth, mighty Indu, meet for lauds.

HYMN XLI. *Soma Pavamāna.*

1. ACTIVE and bright have they come forth,
impetuous in speed like bulls,
Driving the black skin far away.

2 *Intelligent* : or, endowed with strength.

4 *Trita's high ridge* : according to Sāyaṇa, 'the high
place (of the sacrifice) of Trita' the Ṛṣi. But the
heavenly home of Trita, the celestial preparer of the
Soma for Indra, is intended. *The Sisters* : the Dawns.

6 *Willingly* : *maṁhānā* : 'plenteously.'—Ludwig. 'In
his might.'—Cowell.

1 *To war that wins a thousand spoils* : more literally,
to thousandfold booty, or deed of might.

2 *The Dames of Trita* : as Trita is the celestial
purifier of the Soma, the fingers of the earthly purifiers
are called his dames, or his maidens as in IX. 32. 2.

5 *From its place in heaven* : or *diváḥ* may be the
genitive case, taken with *śiśuḥ*, the Child of Heaven, as
in IX. 33. 5.

6 *The well beloved place* : the droṇakalaśa or vat in
which it rests.

2 *Preparing what is unprepared* : 'consecrating the
unconsecrated worshipper or place' is Sāyaṇa's explanation.
6 *Sit* : O Gods.—Sāyaṇa.

2 *The Red* : Soma. *His place* : the droṇakalaśd, or
reservoir. *His firm abode* : heaven.
6 *Doubly-piled* : *dvibárhasam* : according to Sāyaṇa,
'from both worlds, heaven and earth.'

1 *They* : the Soma juices. *The black skin* : meaning,
apparently, both the black pall or covering of night
and the Rākṣasas or dark-skinned Dasyus or hostile
aborigines.

2 Quelling the riteless Dasyu, may we think
   upon the bridge of bliss,
   Leaving the bridge of woe behind.

3 The mighty Pavamāna's roar is heard as
   'twere the rush of rain
   Lightnings are flashing to the sky.

4 Pour out on us abundant food, when thou
   art pressed, O Indu wealth
   In kine and gold and steeds and spoil.

5 Flow on thy way, Most Active, thou: fill
   full the mighty heavens and earth,
   As Dawn, as Sūrya with his beams.

6 On every side, O Soma, flow round us
   with thy protecting stream,
   As Rasā flows around the world.

HYMN XLII.   *Soma Pavamāna.*

1. ENGENDERING the Sun in floods, engendering heaven's lights, green-hued,
   Robed in the waters and the milk,

2 According to primeval plan this Soma,
   with his stream, effused
   Flows purely on, a God for Gods.

3 For him victorious, waxen great, the juices
   with a thousand powers
   Are purified for winning spoil.

4 Shedding the ancient fluid he is poured
   into the cleansing sieve:
   He, thundering, hath produced the Gods.

5 Soma, while purifying, sends hither all
   things to be desired,
   He sends the Gods who strengthen Law.

6 Soma, effused, pour on us wealth in kine,
   in heroes, steeds, and spoil,
   Send us abundant store of food.

HYMN XLIII.   *Soma Pavamāna.*

1. WE will enrobe with sacred song the
   Lovely One who, as a Steed,
   Is decked with milk for rapturous joy.

2 All songs of ours desiring grace adorn him
   in the ancient way,
   Indu for Indra, for his drink.

3 Soma flows on when purified, beloved and
   adorned with songs,
   Songs of the sage Medhyātithi.

4 O Soma Pavamāna, find exceeding glorious
   wealth for us,
   Wealth, Indu, fraught with boundless
   might.

5 Like courser racing to the prize Indu, the
   lover of the Gods,
   Roars, as he passes, in the sieve.

6 Flow on thy way to win us strength, to
   speed the sage who praises thee:
   Soma, bestow heroic power.

HYMN XLIV.   *Soma Pavamāna.*

1. INDU, to us for this great rite, bearing as
   'twere thy wave to Gods,
   Unwearied, thou art flowing forth.

2 Pleased with the hymn, impelled by prayer,
   Soma is hurried far away,
   The Wise One in the Singer's stream.

3 Watchful among the gods, this juice
   advances to the cleansing sieve :
   Soma, most active, travels on.

4 Flow onward, seeking strength for us,
   embellishing the sacrifice :
   The priest with trimmed grass calleth thee.

5 May Soma, ever bringing power to Bhaga
   and to Vāyu, Sage
   And Hero, lead us to the Gods.

6 So, to increase our wealth to-day, Inspirer,
   best of Furtherers,
   Win for us strength and high renown.

HYMN XLV.   *Soma Pavamāna.*

1. FLOW, thou who viewest men, to give
   delight, to entertain the Gods,
   Indu, to Indra for his drink.

---

3 The cleansing of the terrestrial Soma is identified
with the purification of the celestial nectar accompanied
by rain and lightning. See Hillebrandt, *V. M.* 343, 362.

6 *Rasā* : a mythical stream that flows round the
atmosphere and the earth. See V. 41. 15, and X. 108. 1.

1 *In floods* : in the waters on high; in the firmament.

4 *Hath produced the Gods* : *yatra somo 'bhiṣūyate tatra
devā niyatam prādurbhavanti* ; where Soma is effused, there
the gods constantly appear.—Sāyaṇa.

---

1 *As a steed* : is bathed in water. *For rapturous joy* :
'for the exhilaration (of the gods).'—Wilson.

---

3 *Medhyātithi* : the Ṛṣi of the hymn.

5 *Racing to the prize* : *vājasṛt* : 'rushing into battle.'—
Wilson.

6 *Heroic power* : 'excellent male offspring.'—Wilson.

---

1 *For this great rite* : 'to give us abundant wealth.'
—Wilson. *Unwearied* : *aydsyaḥ* : according to Sāyaṇa,
this is the name of the Ṛṣi : 'Ayāsya (goeth) towards
the gods (in sacrifice).'—Wilson.

2 Stream to thine embassy for us : thou
hastenest, for Indra, to
The Gods, O better than our friends.

3 We balm thee, red of hue, with milk to
fit thee for the rapturous joy :
Unbar for us the doors of wealth.

4 He through the sieve hath passed, as comes
a courser to the pole, to run :
Indu belongs unto the Gods.

5 All friends have lauded him as he sports
in the wood, beyond the fleece :
Singers have chanted Indu's praise.

6 Flow, Indu, with that stream wherein
steeped thou announcest to the man
Who worships thee heroic strength.

HYMN XLVI.   *Soma Pavamāna.*

1. LIKE able coursers they have been sent
forth to be the feast of Gods,
Joying in mountains, flowing on.

2 To Vāyu flow the Soma-streams, the drops
of juice made beautiful
Like a bride dowered by her sire.

3 Pressed in the mortar, these, the drops of
juice, the Somas rich in food,
Give strength to Indra with their work.

4 Deft-handed men, run hither, seize the
brilliant juices blent with meal,
And cook with milk the gladdening draught.

5 Thus, Soma, Conqueror of wealth ! flow,
finding furtherance for us,
Giver of ample opulence.

6 This Pavamāna, meet to be adorned, the
fingers ten adorn,
The draught that shall make Indra glad.

HYMN XLVII.   *Soma Pavamāna.*

1. GREAT as he was, Soma hath gained
strength by this high solemnity :
Joyous he riseth like a bull.

2 His task is done : his crushings of the
Dasyus are made manifest :
He sternly reckoneth their debts.

3 Soon as his song of praise is born, the
Soma, Indra's juice, becomes
A thousand-winning thunderbolt.

4 Seer and Sustainer, he himself desireth
riches for the sage
When he embellisheth his songs.

5 Fain would they both win riches as in
races of the steeds. In war
Thou art upon the conquerors' side.

HYMN XLVIII.   *Soma Pavamāna.*

1. WITH sacrifice we seek to thee kind
Cherisher of manly might
In mansions of the lofty heavens;

2 Gladdening crusher of the bold, ruling with
very mighty sway,
Destroyer of a hundred forts.

3 Hence, Sapient One ! the Falcon, strong
of wing, unwearied, brought thee down,
Lord over riches, from the sky.

---

2 *Thou hastenest*: Sāyaṇa gives a different explanation
of this part of the stanza : 'thou (who) art drunk for
Indra, (pour) on the gods wealth for (us) their friends.'
—Wilson. I have adopted Ludwig's interpretation.

3 *We balm thee, red of hue* : or, 'Yea, we adorn thee,
red.' *For the rapturous joy* : *mādāya* : 'for the purpose of
exhilaration.'—Wilson.

4 *To the pole* : the meaning of *dhúram* here is not
clear, and the comparison is not obvious. 'As a horse
in going passes the shaft (of the chariot).'—Wilson.
'As a horse (presses) through the yoke,' Grassmann.
Ludwig suggests 'hedge' or 'barrier' as the probable
meaning of the word in this place.

5 *In the wood, beyond the fleece* : when he has passed
through the woollen strainer and fallen into the wooden
trough or vat. *Singers* : *nāvdḥ* : shouts of joy, according to the St. Petersburg Lexicon.

---

1 *They have been sent forth* : *ásṛgran* (effusi sunt) is
applicable both to the effused Soma-drops and to horses
loosed or started for a race. *Joying in mountains* :
coming from plants grown on hills.

2 *Dowered by her sire* : meaning, perhaps, possessed
of property inherited from her father.

4 *Deft-handed* : *suhastyaḥ* cannot be satisfactorily
accounted for. *Suhastyā*, a dual, may have been the
original reading. See Ludwig's Commentary, Vol. V.,
pp. 347, 348.

---

1 *Riseth* : or, roareth *Śabdam karoti.*—Sāyaṇa.

2 *He sternly reckoneth their debts* : 'resolute he acquits
the debts (of the worshipper).'—Wilson.

3 *A thousand-winning thunderbolt* : all powerful to slay
the wicked and to reward worshippers.

4 *Sustainer* : I follow Ludwig in taking *vidhartári* as
a nominative singular. But see Cowell's note in Wilson's
Translation.

5 *They both* : Soma and the sage of singer.—Ludwig.
Sāyaṇa interprets the stanza differently : 'Thou desirest
to give wealth to those who conquer in combat as (men
often fodder) to horses in battle.' Wilson.

---

1 *Kind Cherisher of manly might* : 'auspicious bearing
wealth.'—Wilson.

2 *Hundred forts* : cf. IV. 26. 3.

3 *The Falcon* : See IV. 26 and 27.

4 That each may see the light, the Bird
  brought us the guard of Law, the Friend
Of all, the speeder through the air.

5 And now, sent forth, it hath attained to
  mighty power and majesty,
Most active, ready to assist.

HYMN XLIX.   *Soma Pavamāna.*

1. POUR down the rain upon us, pour a
   wave of waters from the sky,
And plenteous store of wholesome food.

2 Flow onward with that stream of thine,
  whereby the cows have come to us,
The kine of strangers to our home.

3 Chief Friend of Gods in sacred rites, pour
  on us fatness with thy stream,
Pour down on us a flood of rain.

4 To give us vigour, with thy stream run
  through the fleecy straining-cloth :
For verily the Gods will hear.

5 Onward hath Pavamāna flowed and beaten
  off the Rākṣasas,
Flashing out splendour as of old.

HYMN L.   *Soma Pavamāna.*

1. LOUD as a river's roaring wave thy powers
   have lifted up themselves :
Urge on thine arrow's sharpened point.

2 At thine effusion upward rise three voices
  full of joy, when thou
Flowest upon the fleecy ridge.

3 On to the fleece they urge with stone the
  tawny well-beloved One,
Even Pavamāna, dropping meath.

---

4 *The Friend of all* : or, the common possession.
The speeder through the air : rajasturam : 'the showerer of
water.'—Wilson.

---

4 *The Gods will hear* : the sound that thou makest
in flowing.—Sāyaṇa.

5 *Flashing out splendour as of old* : or, 'Making lights
shine as erst they shone.'

---

1 *Urge on thine arrow's sharpened point* : vāṇḍsya codayā
pavim : apparently a bold metaphorical expression for
'make a noise like that of a discharged arrow.' 'Emit
thy sound like that of a (rushing) arrow.'—Wilson. Or
vāṇḍsya may mean of (thy) reed, pipe, flute, or other
musical instrument, and Sāyaṇa explains pavim by
śabdam. Benfey accordingly (Sāmaveda, II. 5. 1. 5. 1.)
renders the passage : 'Erhebe deiner Flote Schall.' 'Lift
up the music of thy flute.' According to Hillebrandt,
V. M., I. p. 43, the reed or arrow means the sharp-
pointed stalk of the Soma-plant.

2 *Three voices full of joy* : or, three several joyful words.
See IX. 33. 4. *The fleecy ridge* : 'the summit of the
fleece.'—Wilson.

---

4 Flow with thy current to the sieve, O Sage
  most powerful to cheer,
To seat thee in the place of song.

5 Flow, Most Exhilarating ! flow anointed
  with the milk for balm,
Indu, for Indra, for his drink.

HYMN LI.   *Soma Pavamāna.*

1. ADHVARYU, on the filter pour the Soma
   juice expressed with stones,
And make it pure for Indra's drink.

2 Pour out for Indra, Thunder-armed, the
  milk of heaven, the Soma's juice,
Most excellent, most rich in sweets.

3 These Gods and all the Marut host, Indu !
  enjoy this juice of thine,
This Pavamāna's flowing meath.

4 For, Soma, thou hast been effused,
  strengthening for the wild carouse,
O Steer, the singer, for our help.

5 Flow with thy stream, Far-sighted One,
  effused, into the cleansing sieve :
Flow on to give us strength and fame.

HYMN LII.   *Soma Pavamāna.*

1. WEALTH-WINNER, dwelling in the sky, bringing us vigour with the juice,
Flow to the filter when effused.

2 So, in thine ancient ways, may he, beloved,
  with a thousand streams
Run o'er the fleecy straining-cloth.

3 Him who is like a caldron shake : O Indu,
  shake thy gift to us
Shake it, armed Warrior ! with thine
arms.

4 Indu, invoked with many a prayer, bring
  down the vigour of these men,
Of him who threatens us with war.

---

4 *In the place of song* : See IX. 25. 6. 'On Indra's
lap.'—Wilson.

---

4 *For the wild carouse* : 'for speedy exhilaration.'—
Wilson.

---

2 *May he* : the juice, regarded as distinct from
Soma who is addressed.

3 *Him who is like a caldron* : beat or bruise the Soma
that is full of juice as a caldron is of water. *With
thine arms* : or, with the blows (of the pressing-stones).
The meaning of the second and third 'shake' seems to
be 'send rapidly.' '(Soma), send (us) him who is like
a pot; Indu, send us now wealth ; swift-flowing (Soma)
send it with blows (of the stones).'—Wilson. Professor
Grassmann says that by 'him who is like a caldron'
the wealthy-enemy is intended, whose possessions are
to be poured out upon the pious worshippers.

5 Indu, Wealth-giver, with thine help pour
out for us a hundred, yea,
A thousand of thy pure bright streams.

HYMN LIII.　　　*Soma Pavamāna.*

1. O THOU with stones for arms, thy powers,
crushing the fiends, have raised themselves :
Chase thou the foes who compass us.

2 Thou conquerest thus with might when
car meets car, and when the prize is
staked:
With fearless heart will I sing praise.

3 No one with evil thought assails this
Pavamāna's holy laws :
Crush him who fain would fight with thee.

4 For Indra to the streams they drive the
tawny rapture-dropping Steed,
Indu the bringer of delight.

HYMN LIV.　　　*Soma Pavamāna.*

1. AFTER his ancient splendour, they, the
bold, have drawn the bright milk from
The Sage who wins a thousand gifts.

2 In aspect he is like the Sun; he runneth
forward to the lakes,
Seven currents flowing through the sky.

3 He, shining in his splendour, stands high
over all things that exist—
Soma, a God as Sūrya is.

4 Thou, Indu, in thy brilliancy, pourest on
us, as Indra's Friend,
Wealth from the kine to feast the Gods.

HYMN LV.　　　*Soma Pavamāna.*

1. POUR on us with thy juice all kinds of
corn, each sort of nourishment,
And, Soma, all felicities.

2 As thine, O Indu, is the praise, and thine
what springeth from the juice,
Seat thee on the dear sacred grass.

3 And, finding for us kine and steeds, O
Soma, with thy juice flow on
Through days that fly most rapidly.

4 As one who conquers, ne'er subdued,
attacks and slays the enemy,
Thus, Vanquisher of thousands ! flow.

HYMN LVI.　　　*Soma Pavamāna.*

1. SWIFT to the purifying sieve flows Soma
as exalted Law,
Slaying the fiends, loving the Gods.

2 When Soma pours the strengthening food
a hundred ever-active streams
To Indra's friendship win their way.

3 Ten Dames have sung to welcome thee,
even as a maiden greets her love:
O Soma, thou art decked to win.

4 Flow hitherward, O Indu, sweet to Indra
and to Viṣṇu : guard
The men, the singers, from distress.

HYMN LVII.　　　*Soma Pavamāna.*

1. THY streams that never fail or waste flow
forth like showers of rain from heaven,
To bring a thousand stores of strength.

2 He flows beholding on his way all well-
beloved sacred lore,
Green-tinted, brandishing his arms.

3 He, when the people deck him like a docile
king of elephants.
Sits as a falcon in the wood.

4 So bring thou hitherward to us, Indu,
while thou art purified,
All treasures both of heaven and earth.

---

1 *With stones for arms* : *adrivaḥ* : generally an appellative of Indra, the slinger or caster of the stone or
thunderbolt ; here, according to Sāyaṇa,=*grāvavan
soma,* O Soma, possessor of, that is expressed by, the
stones.

2 *When car meets car* : in battle. *When the prize is
staked* : in the chariot-race ; or the reference may be
also to battle.

4 *To the streams* : the *vasatīvarī* waters.

---

1 *They, the bold* : the Soma-pressers. *The Sage* or
Ṛṣi ; Soma.

2 *The lakes* : of air. *Seven currents* : corresponding
to the seven earthly rivers. 'He unites with the seven
down-descending rivers of heaven.'—Wilson.

4 *From the kine* : consisting of milk, curds, etc.

---

4 *Vanquisher of thousands* : or, thou who winnest
thousands, *i.e.* countless spoils or treasures.

---

3 *Ten Dames* : the fingers, whose sound is heard in
the operation of pressing the Soma juice.

---

3 *Like a docile king of elephants* : von Roth, in the
St. Petersburg Lexicon, suggests *ibhe* for *ibhah,* 'like a
pious king among his retinue;' but no alteration is
necessary, *ibhah* and *rājā* being taken together in the
sense of elephant king or stately and noble elephant.
See *Vedische Studien,* I. p. XV. *Sit as a falcon in the wood*:
in the wood, as referring to the Soma, meaning the
wooden trough or vat. 'Sits on the waters like a hawk.'
—Wilson.

HYMN LVIII.   *Soma Pavamāna.*

1. Swift runs this giver of delight, even the
   stream of flowing juice:
   Swift runs this giver of delight.

2 The Morning knows all precious things,
   the Goddess knows her grace to man:
   Swift runs this giver of delight.

3 We have accepted thousands from Dhvasra's
   and Puruṣanti's hands :
   Swift runs this giver of delight.

4 From whom we have accepted thus
   thousands and three times ten besides:
   Swift runs this giver of delight.

HYMN LIX.   *Soma Pavamāna.*

1. Flow onward, Soma, winning kine, and
   steeds, and all that gives delight:
   Bring hither wealth with progeny.

2 Flow onward from the waters, flow, inviolable, from the plants:
   Flow onward from the pressing-boards.

3 Soma, as Pavamāna, pass over all trouble
   and distress :
   Sit on the sacred grass, a Sage.

4 Thou, Pavamāna, foundest light; thou at
   thy birth becamest great:
   O Indu, thou art over all.

HYMN LX.   *Soma Pavamāna.*

1. Sing forth and laud with sacred song
   most active Pavamāna, laud
   Indu who sees with thousand eyes.

2 Thee who hast thousand eyes to see, bearer
   of thousand burthens, they
   Have filtered through the fleecy cloth.

3 He, Pavamāna, hath streamed through
   the fleece then: he runs into the jars,
   Finding his way to Indra's heart.

4 That Indra may be bounteous, flow, most
   active Soma, for our weal :
   Bring genial seed with progeny.

HYMN LXI.   *Soma Pavamāna.*

1. Flow onward, Indu, with this food for him
   who in thy wild delight
   Battered the nine-and-ninety down,

2 Smote swiftly forts, and Śambara, then
   Yadu and that Turvaśa,
   For pious Divodāsa's sake.

3 Finder of horses, pour on us horses and
   wealth in kine and gold,
   And, Indu, food in boundless store.

4 We seek to win thy friendly love, even
   Pavamāna's flowing o'er
   The limit of the cleansing sieve.

5 With those same waves which in their
   stream o'erflow the purifying sieve,
   Soma, be gracious unto us.

6 O Soma, being purified, bring us from
   all sides,—for thou canst,—
   Riches and food with hero sons.

7 Him here, the Child whom streams have
   borne, the ten swift fingers beautify :
   With the Ādityas is he seen.

8 With Indra and with Vāyu he, effused,
   flows onward with the beams
   Of Sūrya to the cleansing sieve.

9 Flow rich in sweets and lovely for our
   Bhaga, Vāyu, Pūṣan flow
   For Mitra and for Varuṇa.

10 High is thy juice's birth : though set in
   heaven, on earth it hath obtained
   Strong sheltering power and great renown.

11 Striving to win, with him we gain all
   wealth from the ungodly man,
   Yea, all the glories of mankind.

1 *Swift* : *tárat* : 'rescuing (his worshippers from sin).'
—Wilson.
3 *Dhvasra* and *Puruṣanti* were 'two kings who conferred
great wealth on *Taranta* and *Purumīḷha*, two ṛṣis of the
family of *Vidadaśva.* See p. XXXIII. of Max-Müller's
Ṛgveda, Vol. V.' Cowell's note in Wilson's Translation.
4 *Thus thousands and three times ten* : Sāyaṇa, taking
tánā (thus, in this manner) to mean 'garments,'
mistaking *triṁśátam*, thirty, for *triśatam*, three hundred,
and neglecting the *cd* (and), interprets 'three hundred
thousand garments.' 'Thirty robes and thousands.'—
E. B. Cowell. Grassmann places this hymn in his
Appendix as a composition of fragments and out of place
where it stands in the text.

2 *The waters*: the *vasatīvarī* waters. *The pressing-boards* :
dhiṣáṇābhyaḥ : according to Sāyaṇa, *grā́vābhyaḥ*, the
pressing-stones.

1 *With sacred song* : *gāyatréṇa* : 'with a *Gāyatrī* hymn.'
—Wilson.

2 *Bearer of thousand burthens* : or, bringer of thousand
bounties.

1 *The niue-and-ninety* : 'ninety-nine (cities of the
foe).'—Wilson.
3 *In boundless store* : literally, in thousands.
7 *Whom streams have borne* : *sindhumātaram* : 'whose
parents are the rivers.' Wilson. Born as the Moon in
the ocean of air. *With the Ādityas is he seen* : that is, he
is counted as one of the Ādityas.

12 Finder of room and freedom, flow for
Indra whom we must adore,
For Varuṇa and the Marut host.

13 The Gods have come to Indu well-descended, beautified with milk,
The active crusher of the foe.

14 Even as mother cows their calf, so let our
praise-songs strengthen him,
Yea, him who winneth Indra's heart.

15 Soma, pour blessings on our kine, pour
forth the food that streams with milk :
Increase the sea that merits laud.

16 From heaven hath Pavamāna made, as
'twere, the marvellous thunder, and
The lofty light of all mankind.

17 The gladdening and auspicious juice of
thee, of Pavamāna, King !
Flows o'er the woollen straining-cloth.

18 Thy juice, O Pavamāna, sends its rays
abroad like splendid skill,
Like lustre, all heaven's light, to see.

19 Flow onward with that juice of thine
most excellent, that brings delight,
Slaying the wicked, dear to Gods.

20 Killing the foeman and his hate, and
winning booty every day,
Gainer art thou of steeds and kine.

21 Red-hued, be blended with the milk that
seems to yield its lovely breast,
Falcon-like resting in thine home.

22 Flow onward thou who strengthenedst
Indra to slaughter Vṛtra who
Compassed and stayed the mighty floods.

23 Soma who rainest gifts, may we win riches
with our hero sons :
Strengthen, as thou art cleansed, our
hymns.

24 Aided by thee, and through thy grace,
may we be slayers when we war :
Watch, Soma, at our solemn rites.

25 Chasing our foemen, driving off the godless, Soma floweth on,

Going to Indra's special place.

26 O Pavamāna, hither bring great riches,
and destroy our foes :
O Indu, grant heroic fame.

27 A hundred obstacles have ne'er checked
thee when fain to give thy boons,
When, being cleansed, thou combatest.

28 Indu, flow on, a mighty juice; glorify us
among the folk :
Drive all our enemies away.

29 Indu, in this thy friendship most lofty
and glorious may we
Subdue all those who war with us.

30 Those awful weapons that thou hast,
sharpened at point to strike men down—
Guard us therewith from every foe.

HYMN LXII. *Soma Pavamāna.*

1. THESE rapid Soma-drops have been
poured through the purifying sieve
To bring us all felicities.

2 Dispelling manifold mishap, giving the
courser's progeny,
Yea, and the warrior steed, success.

3 Bringing prosperity to kine, they make
perpetual Iḷā flow
To us for noble eulogy.

4 Strong, mountain-born, the stalk hath been
pressed in the streams for rapturous
joy :
Hawk-like he settles in his home.

5 Fair is the God-loved juice; the plant is
washed in waters, pressed by men :
The milch-kine sweeten it with milk.

6 As drivers deck a courser, so have they
adorned the meath's juice for
Ambrosia, for the festival.

---

13 *Well-descended* : literally, well-born or well-produ-
ced; '(who is) completely generated.'—Wilson.

15 *The sea* : samudrám : according to Sāyaṇa, water
generally.

16 'The purified (Soma) has generated the great light
which is common to all mankind, like the wonderful
thundering of the sky.' Muir, *O.S. Texts*, IV. 112. The
great light common to all men, or vaiśvānaràm or *the
lofty light of all mankind*, is Agni Vaiśvānara.

20 *The foeman and his hate* : 'the hostile Vṛtra.'—
Wilson.

25 *The godless* : drávṇah : those who present no
sacrificial offerings; 'the withholders (of wealth).'—
Wilson. *Special place* : that is, the vessel set apart for
his libations.

26 *Heroic fame* : or, fame with brave sons.

27 *Obstacles* : or, enemies, according to Sāyaṇa. *Thou
combatest* : makhasyáse : according to Sāyaṇa, 'when
thou wishest to give us wealth.' 'The meanings "fight,"
"strive," etc., are foreign to Sāyaṇa, being derived from
a comparison of macto, etc.'—Editor's note in Wilson's
Translation.

30 *Weapons* : the Moon being the warrior who
overcomes the darkness of night. See Hillebrandt,
V.M., I 340. Cf 'The moon...advances like an indig-
nant warrior through a fleeing army.'—S.T. Coleridge.

———

3 *Iḷā* ; here, according to Sāyaṇa, meaning 'food.'
'Labetrank,' refreshing draught.—Grassmann.

4 *The stalk* : the Soma-plant, which is said to have
grown on the mountains.

5 *In waters* : the vasatívarī waters.

6 *For ambrosia* : amṛtáya : 'for the sake of immortality.'—Wilson.

7 Thou, Indu, with thy streams that drop
sweet juices, which were poured for
help,
Hast settled in the cleansing sieve.

8 So flow thou onward through the fleece,
for Indra flow, to be his drink,
Finding thine home in vats of wood.

9 As giving room and freedom, as most
sweet, pour butter forth and milk,
O Indu, for the Angirases.

10 Most active and benevolent, this Pavamāna,
sent to us
For lofty friendship, meditates.

11 Queller of curses, mighty, with strong
sway, this Pavamāna shall
Bring treasures to the worshipper.

12 Pour thou upon us thousandfold possessions,
both of kine and steeds,
Exceeding glorious, much-desired.

13 Wandering far, with wise designs, the
juice here present is effused,
Made beautiful by living men.

14 For Indra flows the gladdening drink, the
measurer of the region, Sage,
With countless wealth and endless help.

15 Born on the mountain, lauded here, Indu
for Indra is set down,
As in her sheltering nest a bird.

16 Pressed by the men, as 'twere to war hath
Soma Pavamāna sped,
To test with might within the vats.

17 That he may move, they yoke him to the
three-backed triple-seated car
By the Seven Ṛṣis' holy songs.

18 Drive ye that Tawny Courser, O ye
pressers, on his way to war,
Swift Steed who carries off the spoil.

19 Pouring all glories hither, he, effused and
entering the jar,
Stands like a hero mid the kine.

20 Indu, the living men milk out the juice to
make the rapturous draught :
Gods for the Gods milk out the meath.

21 Pour for the Gods into the sieve our
Soma very rich in sweets,
Him whom the Gods most gladly hear.

22 Into his stream who gladdens best these
Soma juices have been poured,
Lauded with songs for lofty fame.

23 Thou flowest to enjoy the milk, and
bringest valour, being cleansed :
Winning the spoil flow hitherward.

24 And, hymned by Jamadagnis, let all
nourishment that kine supply,
And general praises, flow to us.

25 Soma, as leader of the song flow onward
with thy wondrous aids,
For holy lore of every kind.

26 Do thou as leader of the song, stirring
the waters of the sea,
Flow onward, thou who movest all.

27 O Soma, O thou Sage, these worlds stand
ready to attest thy might :
For thy behoof the rivers flow.

28 Like showers of rain that fall from heaven
thy streams perpetually flow
To the bright fleece spread under them.

29 For potent Indra purify Indu effectual
and strong,
Enjoyment-giver, Mighty Lord.

30 Soma, true, Pavamāna, Sage, is seated
in the cleansing sieve,
Giving his praiser hero strength.

HYMN LXIII. *Soma Pavamāna.*

1. POUR hitherward, O Soma, wealth in
thousands and heroic strength,
And keep renown secure for us.

2 Thou makest food and vigour swell for
Indra, best of gladdeners !
Within the cups thou seatest thee.

3 For Indra and for Viṣṇu poured, Soma
hath flowed into the jar :
May Vāyu find it rich in sweets.

4 These Somas swift and brown of hue, in
stream of solemn sacrifice

---

9 *For the Angirases* : or, from the Angirases. The Jamadagnis were not members of that family.—Ludwig.

10 *Meditates* : 'is known (to all).' Wilson.

13 *Wandering far* : urugāyáḥ : according to Sāyaṇa, much-lauded, or praised by many.

14 *The measurer of the region* : who measured out and made the firmament.

15 *Born on the mountain* : or, perhaps, as Sāyaṇa takes it, 'made manifest by song.'

17 *By the Seven Ṛṣis' holy songs* : or 'Of Ṛṣis, with seven holy songs'; the *car* being the sacrifice, the three backs or ridges being the three daily libations, the three seats being the three Vedas.

19 *Mid the kine* : among the enemy's cattle, for whose possession he is fighting. So, says Sāyaṇa, Soma stands among the sacrifices.

20 *The living men* : the worshippers, according to Sāyaṇa; but perhaps, as Ludwig suggests, his *stotāraḥ* should be *sotāraḥ*, pressers. *Gods* : *devāḥ* : the priests.

26 *Waters of the sea* : of the sea of air, the firmament.

Have flowed through twisted obstacles,

5 Performing every noble work, active,
augmenting Indra's strength,
Driving away the godless ones.

6 Brown Soma-drops, effused that seek
Indra, to their appropriate place
Flow through the region hitherward.

7 Flow onward with that stream of thine
wherewith thou gavest Sūrya light,
Urging on waters good to men.

8 He, Pavamāna, high o'er man yoked the
Sun's courser Etaśa
To travel through the realm of air.

9 And those ten Coursers, tawny-hued, he
harnessed that the Sun might come :
Indu, he said, is Indra's self.

10 Hence, singers, pour the gladdening juice
to Vāyu and to Indra, pour
The drops upon the fleecy cloth.

11 O Soma Pavamāna, find wealth for us
not to be assailed,
Wealth which the foeman may not win.

12 Send riches hither with thy stream in
thousands, both of steeds and kine,
Send spoil of war and high renown.

13 Soma the God, expressed with stones,
like Sūrya, floweth on his way,
Pouring the juice within the jar.

14 These brilliant drops have poured for us,
in stream of solemn sacrifice,
Worshipful laws and strength in kine.

15 Over the cleansing sieve have flowed the
Somas, blent with curdled milk,
Effused for Indra Thunder-armed.

16 Soma, do thou most rich in sweets, a
gladdening drink most dear to Gods,
Flow to the sieve to bring us wealth.

17 For Indra, living men adorn the Tawny
Courser in the streams, Indu, the giver
of delight.

18 Pour for us, Soma, wealth in gold, in
horses and heroic sons,
Bring hither strength in herds of kine.

19 For Indra pour ye on the fleece him very
sweet to taste, who longs.
For battle as it were in war.

20 The singers, seeking help, adorn the Sage
who must be decked with songs :
Loud bellowing the Steer comes on.

21 The singers with their thoughts and hymns
have, in the stream of sacrifice,
Caused Soma, active Steer, to roar.

22 God, working with mankind, flow on; to
Indra go thy gladdening juice :
To Vāyu mount as Law commands

23 O Soma, Pavamāna, thou pourest out
wealth that brings renown :
Enter the lake, as one we love.

24 Soma thou flowest chasing foes and bringing wisdom and delight :
Drive off the folk who love not Gods.

25 The Pavamānas have been poured, the
brilliant drops of Soma juice,
For holy lore of every kind.

26 The Pavamānas have been shed, the
beautiful swift Soma-drops,
Driving all enemies afar.

27 From heaven, from out the firmament,
hath Pavamāna been effused
Upon the summit of the earth.

28 O Soma, Indu, very wise, drive, being
purified, with thy stream
All foes, all Rākṣasas away.

29 Driving the Rākṣasas afar, O Soma,
bellowing, pour for us
Most excellent and splendid strength.

30 Soma, do thou secure for us the treasures
of the earth and heaven,
Indu, all boons to be desired.

HYMN LXIV.   Soma Pavamāna.

1. SOMA, thou art a splendid Steer, a Steer,
O God, with steerlike sway :
Thou as a Steer ordainest laws.

2 Steer-strong thy might is as a steer's, steer-
strong thy wood, steer-like thy drink :
A Steer indeed, O Steer, art thou.

3 Thou, Indu, as a vigorous horse, hast
neighed together steeds and kine :

---

4 *Twisted obstacles* : either the twigs of which the frame of the filter was made, or the rough surface of the wool of the strainer. 'Are let loose upon the *Rākṣasas.*'—Wilson.

8 In this and the following stanza Soma is identified with the Sun.

9 *Coursers* : or Harits. Cf. IV. 6. 9 and 13. 3.

10 *Hence* : from this vessel.

14 *Worshipful laws* : the meaning of *dhāmānyāryā* is not clear. '(Flowing) towards the dwellings of respectable (worshippers).'—Wilson. 'Venerable might.'—Ludwig.

---

23 *The lake* : the *droṇakalaśa,* vat or reservoir.
27 *The summit of the earth* : the raised altar.

---

1 *Steer* : Sāyaṇa, as usual, explains *vṛṣā* by *varṣakaḥ* 'Sprinkler.'—Wilson.

3 *Neighed together* : collected, through the efficacy of the sound thou makest in dropping through the filter, and enriched us with steeds and kine.

Unbar for us the doors to wealth.

4 Out of desire of cows and steeds and
   horses potent Soma-drops,
   Brilliant and swift, have been effused.

5 They purified in both the hands, made
   beautiful by holy men,
   Flow onward to the fleecy cloth.

6 These Soma juices shall pour forth all
   treasures for the worshipper
   From heaven and earth and firmament.

7 The streams of Pavamāna, thine, Finder
   of all, have been effused,
   Even as Sūrya's rays of light.

8 Making the light that shines from heaven
   thou flowest on to every form :
   Soma, thou swellest like a sea.

9 Urged on thou sendest out thy voice,
   O Pavamāna; thou hast moved,
   Like the God Sūrya, to the sieve.

10 Indu, Enlightener, Friend, hath been
   purified by the sages' hymns :
   So starts the charioteer his steed—

11 Thy God-delighting wave which hath
   flowed to purifying seive,
   Alighting 'in the home of Law.

12 Flow to our sieve, a gladdening draught
   that hath most intercourse with Gods,
   Indu, to Indra for his drink.

13 Flow onward with a stream for food,
   made beautiful by sapient men :
   Indu with sheen approach the milk.

14 While thou art cleansed, Song-Lover,
   bring comfort and vigour to the folk,
   Poured, Tawny One ! on milk and curds.

15 Purified for the feast of Gods, go thou to
   Indra's special place,
   Resplendent, guided by the strong.

16 Accelerated by the hymn, the rapid
   drops of Soma juice
   Have flowed, urged onward, to the lake.

17 Easily have the living drops, made
   beautiful, approached the lake,
   Yea, to the place of sacrifice.

18 Compass about, our faithful Friend, all
   our possessions with thy might :
   Guard, hero like, our sheltering home.

19 Loud neighs the Courser Etaśa, with
   singers, harnessed for the place,
   Guided for travel to the lake.

20 What time the Swift One resteth in the
   golden place of sacrifice,
   He leaves the foolish far away.

21 The friends have sung in unison, the
   prudent wish to sacrifice :
   Down sink the unintelligent.

22 For Indra girt by Maruts, flow, thou
   Indu, very rich in sweets,
   To sit in place of sacrifice.

23 Controlling priests and sages skilled in
   holy song adorn thee well :
   The living make thee beautiful.

24 Aryaman, Mitra, Varuṇa drink Pavamāna's juice, yea, thine :
   O Sage, the Maruts drink thereof.

25 O Soma, Indu, thou while thou art
   purified urgest onward speech.
   Thousandfold, with the lore of hymns.

26 Yea, Soma, Indu, while thou art purified
   do thou bring to us
   Speech thousandfold that longs for war.

27 O Indu, Much-invoked, while thou art
   purifying, as the Friend.
   Of these men enter thou the lake.

28 Bright are these Somas blent with milk,
   with light that flashes brilliantly.
   And form that utters loud acclaim.

29 Led by his drivers, and sent forth, the
   Strong Steed hath come nigh for spoil,
   Like warriors when they stand arrayed.

30 Specially, Soma, coming as a Sage from
   heaven to prosper us,
   Flow like the Sun for us to see.

HYMN LXV.   *Soma Pavamāna.*

1. THE glittering maids send Sūra forth,
   the glorious sisters, close-allied,
   Send Indu forth, their mighty Lord.

19 *The Courser Etaśa* : here meaning Soma. *Vāhniḥ*
(from *vah*, Lat. veh-o) is properly a horse of burden,
or draught-horse.

21 *The friends* : the priests ; or perhaps the Maruts.
Down sink : *narake*, into hell, says Sāyaṇa.

26 *That longs for war* : *makhasyúvam* 'desiring wealth.'
—Wilson. See IX. 6ˑ. 27, note.

28 *Form* : *kṛpā* : stream, according to Sāyaṇa.

30 *Specially* : *ṛdhák* : said by Yāska to be the Vedic
form of *pṛthak*, and to be used in the sense of prospering.
See Wilson's Translation, Editor's note. Or *ṛdhák* may
mean, lightly, easily, without effort.

———

1 *The glittering maids* : the fingers, perhaps with
reference to the gold rings worn by the priests when
they press the Soma. *Sūra* : here said to mean Soma;
'the invigorating.'—Wilson. *The glorious sisters* : the
fingers.

8 *To every form* : to bring us blessings in every shape.

9 *To the sieve*: *vidharmaṇi* : 'in observance of the law,'
according to M. Bergaigne. See *La Religion Védique*,
III. 218, note.

16 *The Lake* : *samudrám* : acccording to Sāyaṇa, the
sea of air, the firmament. The *droṇakalaśa*, vat or reservoir, is probably intended.

2 Pervade, O Pavamāna, all our treasures
with repeated light,
God, coming hither from the Gods.

3 Pour on us, Pavamāna, rain, as service
and rain praise for Gods :
Pour all to be our nourishment.

4 Thou art a Steer by lustre : we, O
Pavamāna, faithfully
Call upon thee the Splendid One.

5 Do thou, rejoicing, nobly-armed ! pour
upon us heroic strength :
O Indu, come thou hitherward.

6 When thou art cleansed with both the
hands and dipped in waters, with the
wood.
Thou comest to the gathering-place.

7 Sing forth your songs, as Vyaśva sang, to
Soma Pavamāna, to,
The Mighty One with thousand eyes;

8 Whose coloured sap they drive with stones,
the yellow meath-distilling juice,
Indu for Indra, for his drink.

9 We seek to gain the friendly love of thee
that Strong and Mighty One,
Of thee the winner of all wealth.

10 Flow onward with thy stream, a Steer,
inspiriting the Maruts' Lord,
Winning all riches by thy might.

11 I send thee forth to battle from the press,
O Pavamāna, Strong,
Sustainer, looker on the light.

12 Acknowledged by this song of mine, flow,
tawny-coloured, with thy stream :
Incite to battle thine ally.

13 O Indu, visible to all pour out for us
abundant food:
Soma, be thou our prosperer.

14 The pitchers, Indu, with thy streams
have sung aloud in vigorous might :
Enter them, and let Indra drink.

15 O thou whose potent gladdening juice
they milk out with the stones, flow on,
Destroyer of our enemies.

16 King Pavamāna is implored with holy
songs, on man's behalf,
To travel through the firmament.

17 Bring us, O Indu, hundredfold increase
of kine, and noble steeds,
The gift of fortune for our help.

18 Pressed for the banquet of the Gods, O
Soma, bring us might, and speed,
Like beauty for a brilliant show.

19 Soma, flow on exceeding bright with loud
roar to the wooden vats,
Falcon-like resting in thine home.

20 Soma, the Water-winner flows to Indra,
Vāyu, Varuṇa,
To Viṣṇu and the Marut host.

21 Soma, bestowing food upon our progeny,
from every sides,
Pour on us riches thousandfold !

22 The Soma juices which have been
expressed afar or near at hand,
Or there on Śaryanāvān's bank,

23 Those pressed among Ārjīkas, pressed
among the active, in men's homes,
Or pressed among the Races Five—

24 May these celestial drops, expressed, pour
forth upon us, as they flow,
Rain from the heavens and hero strength.

25 Urged forward o'er the ox-hide flows the
Lovely One of tawny hue,
Lauded by Jamadagni's song.

26 Like horses urged to speed, the drops,
bright, stirring vital power, when blent
With milk, are beautified in streams.

27 So they who toil with juices send thee
forward for the Gods' repast :
So with this splendour flow thou on.

28 We choose to-day that chariot-steed of
thine, the Strong, that brings us bliss,
The Guardian, the desire of all,

29 The Excellent, the Gladdener, the Sage
with heart that understands,
The Guardian, the desire of all;

30 Who for ourselves, O thou Most Wise, is
wealth and fair intelligence,
The Guardian, the desire of all.

HYMN LXVI. *Soma Pavamāna.*

1. FOR holy lore of every sort, flow onward
thou whom all men love.
A Friend to be besought by friends.

22 *Śaryaṇāvān's bank* : this lake is said to be on the
borders of the Kurukṣetra country.

23 *Ārjīkas* : apparently a non-Āryan people in the
North-West, See VIII. 53. 11.

25 *O'er the ox-hide* : the leather sheet that received the
droppings of the Soma.

28 *The guardian* : *pāntam* : according to Pischel, 'den
schwellenden,' 'the swelling one.' See his exhaustive
excursus on the word in *Vedische Studien*, I. pp. 191—
194.

The Ṛṣis are the hundred Vaikhānasas, said to have
been a race of saintly hermits sprung from the nails
of Prajāpati.

3 *As service* : as the cause of worship.
6 *With the wood* : '(taken up) with the wooden
vessel.'—Wilson. Cf. IX. 1. 2.

7 *Vyaśva* : a Ṛṣi frequently mentioned in Book VIII.
12 *Thine ally* : Indra.

2 O'er all thou rulest with these Two
which, Soma Pavamāna, stand,
Turned, as thy stations, hitherward.

3 Wise Soma Pavamāna, thou encompassest on every side
Thy stations as the seasons come.

4 Flow onward, generating food, for precious
boons of every kind,
A Friend for friends, to be our help.

5 Upon the lofty ridge of heaven thy bright
rays with their essences,
Soma, spread purifying power.

6 O Soma, these Seven Rivers flow, as being
thine, to give command:
The Streams of milk run forth to thee.

7 Flow onward, Soma in a stream, effused
to gladden Indra's heart,
Bringing imperishable fame.

8 Driving thee in Vivasvān's course, the
Seven Sisters with their hymns
Made melody round thee the Sage.

9 The virgins deck thee o'er fresh streams to
drive thee to the sieve when thou,
A singer, bathest in the wood.

10 The streams of Pavamāna, thine, Sage,
Mighty One, have poured them forth.
Like coursers eager for renown.

11 They have been poured upon the fleece
towards the meath-distilling vat :
The holy songs have sounded forth.

12 Like milch-kine coming home, the drops
of Soma juice have reached the lake,
Have reached the place of sacrifice.

13 O Indu, to our great delight the running
waters flow to us,
When thou wilt robe thyself in milk.

14 In this thy friendship, and with thee to
help us, fain to sacrifice,
Indu, we crave thy friendly love.

15 Flow on, O Soma, for the great Viewer of
men, for gain of kine
Enter thou into Indra's throat.

16 Best art thou, Soma, of the great, Strongest
of strong ones, Indu : thou
As Warrior ever hast prevailed.

17 Mightier even than the strong, more
valiant even than the brave,
More liberal than the bountiful,

18 Soma, as Sūra, bring us food, win offspring of our bodies : we
Elect thee for our friendship, we elect
thee for companionship.

19 Agni, thou pourest life; send down upon
us food and vigorous strength ;
Drive thou misfortune far away,

20 Agni is Pavamāna, Sage, Chief Priest of
all the Races Five :
To him whose wealth is great we pray.

21 Skilled in thy task, O Agni, pour splendour
with hero strength on us,
Granting me wealth that nourishes.

22 Beyond his enemies away to sweet praise
Pavamāna flows,
Like Sūrya visible to all.

23 Adorned by living men, set forth for
entertainment, rich in food,
Far-sighted Indu is a Steed.

24 He, Pavamāna, hath produced the lofty
Law, the brilliant light,
Destroying darkness black of hue.

25 From tawny Pavamāna, the Destroyer,
radiant streams have sprung,
Quick streams from him whose gleams
are swift.

26 Best rider of the chariot, praised with
fairest praise mid beauteous ones,
Gold-gleaming with the Marut host,

27 May Pavamāna, best to win the booty,
penetrate with rays,
Giving the singer hero strength.

28 Over the fleecy sieve hath flowed the
drop effused : to Indra comes
Indu while he is purified

29 This Soma, through the pressing-stones,
is sporting on the oxhide, and
Summoning Indra to the draught.

---

2 *With these Two* : probably a double asterism. See
Hillebrandt, *V. M.* p. 446 ; and Gaidicke, *Der Accusativ
im Veda*, p. 199.

8 The stream of Soma is likened to the course of
Vivasvān or the Sun.

The Seven Sisters are probably the *Seven Rivers* of
stanza 6. According to Sāyaṇa 'the seven kindred
(priests)' are intended

9 *The virgins* : the fingers.

12 *The lake* : the *droṇakalaśā* or reservoir.

15 *For gain of kine* : *gdviṣṭaye* : according to Sāyaṇa,
'for the seeker of the kine of the Aṅgirases.'

18 *As Sūra*: See IX. 65. 1. 'Who art a hero.'—Wilson.
'From the Sun.' —Ludwig.

19. *Misfortune* : *ducchunām* : frequently personified as
an evil power; 'the *Rākṣasas*.'—Wilson.

23 *Is a Steed* : 'one who continually goes to the Gods,'
is Sāyaṇa's explanation of *ātyaḥ*, horse or courser.

25 *The Destroyer* : of darkness. Cf. IX. 61. 30.

27 *Penetrate* : the whole world.—Sāyaṇa.

29 *On the ox-hide* : See IX. 65. 25.

30 O Pavamāna, bless us, so that we may
    live, with that bright milk
    Of thine which hath been brought from
    heaven.

HYMN LXVII. *Soma and Others.*

1. THOU, Soma, hast a running stream, joyous,
    most strong at sacrifice :
    Flow bounteously bestowing wealth.

2 Effused as cheerer of the men, flowing
    best gladdener, thou art
    A Prince to Indra with thy juice.

3 Poured forth by pressing-stones, do thou
    with loud roar send us in a stream
    Most excellent illustrious might.

4 Indu, urged forward, floweth through the
    fleecy cloth : the Tawny One
    With his loud roar hath brought as
    strength.

5 Indu, thou flowest through the fleece,
    bringing felicities and fame,
    And, Soma, spoil and wealth in kine.

6 Hither, O Indu, bring us wealth in steeds
    and cattle hundredfold :
    Bring wealth, O Soma, thousandfold.

7 In purifying, through the sieve the rapid
    drops of Soma juice
    Come nigh to Indra in their course.

8 For Indra floweth excellent Indu, the
    noblest Soma juice
    The Living for the Living One.

9 The glittering maids send Sūra forth :
    they with their song have sung aloud
    To Pavamāna dropping meath.

10 May Pūsan, drawn by goats, be our
    protector, and on all his paths
    Bestow on us our share of maids.

11 This Soma flows like gladdening oil for
    him who wears the braided locks :
    He shall give us our share of maids.

12 This Soma juice, O glowing God, flows
    like pure oil, effused for thee :
    He shall give us our share of maids.

13 Flow onward, Soma, in thy stream, be-
    getter of the sages' speech :
    Wealth-giver among Gods art thou.

14 The Falcon dips within the jars : he wraps
    him in his robe and goes
    Loud roaring to the vats of wood.

15 Soma, thy juice hath been effused and
    poured into the pitcher : like
    A rapid hawk it rushes on.

16 For Indra flow most rich in sweets, O
    Soma, bringing him delight.

17 They were sent forth to feast the Gods,
    like chariots that display their strength.

18 Brilliant, best givers of delight, these juices
    have sent Vāyu forth.

19 Bruised by the press-stones and extolled,
    Soma, thou goest to the sieve,
    Giving the worshipper hero strength.

20 This juice bruised by the pressing-stones
    and lauded passes through the sieve,
    Slayer of demons, through the fleece.

21 O Pavamāna, drive away the danger,
    whether near at hand
    Or far remote, that finds me here.

22 This day may Pavamāna cleanse us with
    his purifying power,
    Most active purifying Priest.

23 O Agni, with the cleansing light diffused
    through all thy fiery glow,
    Purify thou this prayer of ours.

24 Cleanse us with thine own cleansing
    power, O Agni, that is bright with
    flame,
    And by libations poured to thee.

25 Savitar, God, by both of these, libation,
    purifying power,
    Purify me on every side.

26 Cleanse us, God Savitar, with Three, O
    Soma, with sublimest forms,
    Agni, with forms of power and might.

27 May the Gods' company make me clean,
    and Vasus make me pure by song.
    Purify me, ye General Gods; O Jātavedas,
    make me pure.

28 Fill thyself full of juice, flow forth, O
    Soma, thou with all thy stalks,
    The best oblation to the Gods.

29 We with our homage have approached
    the Friend who seeks our wondering
    praise,
    Young, strengthener of the solemn rite.

---

2 *A Prince*: *sūriḥ* : a rich and liberal patron.

9 *The glittering maids send Sūra forth* : repeated from
IX. 65. 1.

10 *Our share of maids* : desirable and approved wives.—
Sāyaṇa.

11 *For him who wears the braided locks* : *kapardine* See I.
114. 1. and VII. 83. 8. Here Pūṣan is intended.

12 *O glowing God.* Pūṣan.

14 *The Falcon* : the falcon-like Soma.

18 *Have sent Vāyu forth* : have drawn him down from
heaven 'Are let forth for Vāyu.'—Wilson.

26 The *Three sublimest forms* are said to be Agni, Vāyu,
and Sūrya, or Fire, Wind, and Sun.

27 *The Gods' company* : the *yajamānas* or sacrificers, or
the troop of Gods, Indra and others.—Sāyaṇa, *General
Gods* : *viśve devāḥ* : or, all ye Gods.

30 Lost is Alāyya's axe. O Soma, God :
   do thou send it back hither in thy flow
Even, Soma, God, if 'twere a mole.

31 The man who reads the essence stored by
   saints, the Pāvamānī hymns,
Tastes food completely purified, made sweet
   by Mātariśvan's touch.

32 Whoever reads the essence stored by saints,
   the Pāvamānī hymns,
Sarasvatī draws forth for him water and
   butter, milk and meath.

HYMN LXVIII. *Soma Pavamāna.*

1. THE drops of Soma juice like cows who
   yield their milk have flowed forth, rich
   in meath, unto the Shining One,
And, seated on the grass, raising their
   voice, assumed the milk, the covering
   robe wherewith the udders stream.

2 He bellows with a roar around the highest
   twigs : the Tawny One is sweetened as
   he breaks them up.
Then, passing through the sieve into the
   ample room, the God throws off the
   dregs according to his wish.

3 The gladdening drink that measured out
   the meeting Twins fills full with milk
   the Eternal Ever-waxing Pair.
Bringing to light the Two great Regions
   limitless, moving above them he gained
   sheen that never fades.

4 Wandering through the Parents, strengthening the floods, the Sage makes his
   place swell with his own native might.
The stalk is mixed with grain : he comes
   led by the men together with the sisters,
   and preserves the Head.

5 With energetic intellect the Sage is born,
   deposited as germ of Law, far from the
   Twins.
They being young at first showed visibly
   distinct the Creature that is half-concealed and half-exposed.

6 The sages knew the form of him the
   Gladdener, what time the Falcon brought
   the plant from far away.
Him who assures success they beautified
   in streams, the stalk who yearned therefor, mighty and meet for praise.

7 Together with the Ṛṣis, with their prayers
   and hymns ten women deck thee, Soma,
   friendly when effused.
Led by the men, with invocations of the
   Gods, through the fleece, thou hast given
   us strength to win the spoil.

8 Songs resonant with praise have celebrated him. Soma, Friend, springing forth
   with his fair company.
Even him who rich in meath, with undulating stream, Winnner of Wealth,
   Immortal, sends his voice from heaven.

9 He sends it into all the region forth from
   heaven. Soma, while he is filtered,
   settles in the jars.
With milk and waters is he decked when
   pressed with stones : Indu, when purified,
   shall find sweet rest and room.

10 Even thus poured forth flow on thy way,
   O Soma, vouchsafing us most manifold
   lively vigour.
We will invoke benevolent Earth and
   Heaven. Give us, ye Gods, riches with
   noble heroes.

---

30 This stanza is well-nigh unintelligible. Alāyya
may, as is suggested in the St. Petersburg Lexicon, be a
name of Indra, and the lost axe may be the thunderbolt
which the poet thinks has long lain idle, and which
Soma is prayed to replace in the hands of the Thunderer,
even though it were worthless and mischievous like a mole.
Sāyaṇa's interpretation is different.—'May the battle-axe
of the foe destroy the foe alone: flow to us, bright Soma;
(slay) the villain only, bright Soma.'—Wilson.

31 *By saints* : by the Ṛṣis to whom they were revealed.
Pāvamānī hymns : the hymns in this Book dedicated to the
purification of the Soma juice. *By Mātariśvan's touch* :
Sāyaṇa says *Mātariśvan* means *Vāyu* because it breathes
in the atmosphere *antarikṣe svasiti*: the food is sweetened
and purified by the purifying wind and the man eats
it.'—Wilson. Mātariśvan probably represents Agni.

1 *The Shining One devám* : the radiant Indra. The
second line is obscure. According to Sāyaṇa, *usriyāḥ*
here means 'cows' and not milk :— 'the lowing kine
sitting on the *barhis* grass hold in their udders the pure
(juice) welling up.'—Wilson.

2 *The highest twigs*: of the Soma-plant, which as being
the tenderest and juiciest are crushed first.—Ludwig.
'He with a noise reëchoes the principal (praises): separating the growing herbs, the green tinted (Soma) sweetens
them.'—Wilson.

3 *The meeting Twins* : Soma is called the Creator and
Preserver of heaven and earth.

4 *The Parents* : heaven and earth. *The floods* : the
waters of the firmament. *Grain* : especially barley. *Makes
his place swell* ; enriches his own station, the *uttaravedi*
or northward altar. *The sisters* : the fingers. *The
Head* : apparently Sūrya. 'Sāyaṇa's explanation of *śiraḥ*,
viz., *śirṇam bhūtajātam* (the withered world?), needs
explaining more than the original itself.'—Wilson.

5 *The Sage* : the Sun. *Far from the Twins* : rising
in a distant region beyond heaven and earth. *The Creature
that is half-concealed and half exposed* : the meaning appears to be, as Ludwig says, that heaven and earth
while they were yet unseparated, produced the Moon :
the Sun came into being only when they had been
separated through Soma's energetic agency.

7 *Ten women* : the fingers.

HYMN LXIX. *Soma Pavamāna.*

1. LAID like an arrow on the bow the hymn hath been loosed like a young calf to the udder of its dam.
As one who cometh first with full stream she is milked the Soma is impelled to this man's holy rites.

2 The thought is deeply fixed; the savoury juice is shed; the tongue with joyous sound is stirring in the mouth;
And Pavamāna, like the shout of combatants, the drop rising in sweet juice, is flowing through the fleece.

3 He flows about the sheep-skin, longing for a bride : he looses Aditi's Daughters for the worshipper.
The sacred drink hath come, gold-tinted, well-restrained : like a strong Bull he shines, whetting his manly might.

4 The Bull is bellowing; the Cows are coming nigh : the Goddesses approach the God's own resting-place.
Onward hath Soma passed through the sheep's fair bright fleece, and hath, as 'twere, endued a garment newly washed.

5 The golden-hued, Immortal, newly bathed, puts on a brightly shining vesture that is never harmed.

He made the ridge of heaven to be his radiant robe, by sprinkling of the bowls from moisture of the sky.

6 Even as the beams of Sūrya, urging men to speed, that cheer and send to sleep, together rush they forth,
These swift outpourings in long course of holy rites : no form save only Indra shows itself so pure.

7 As down the steep slope of a river to the vale, drawn from the Steer the swift strong draughts have found a way.
Well be it with the men and cattle in our home. May powers, O Soma, may the people stay with us.

8 Pour out upon us wealth in goods, in gold, in steeds, in cattle and in corn, and great heroic strength.
Ye, Soma, are my Fathers, lifted up on high as heads of heaven and makers of the strength of life.

9 These Pavamānas here, these drops of Soma, to Indra have sped forth like cars to booty.
Effused, they pass the cleansing fleece, while, gold-hued, they cast their covering off to pour the rain down.

10 O Indu, flow thou on for lofty Indra, flow blameless, very gracious, foe-destroyer.
Bring splendid treasures to the man who lauds thee. O Heaven and Earth, with all the Gods protect us.

HYMN LXX. *Soma Pavamāna.*

1. THE three times seven Milch-kine in the eastern heaven have for this Soma poured the genuine milky draught.
Four other beauteous Creatures hath he made for his adornment, when he waxed in strength through holy rites.

---

1 *Hath been loosed, &c.* : is let loose to (Indra) the fosterer as a calf to the udder of its mother, 'Sāyaṇa takes *ūdhani* [to the udder] twice over : he says it is used of *Indra* because he is the nourisher of everything.' —Wilson. *As one who cometh first* : according to Sāyaṇa, as a cow coming before her calf yields her milk, (so Indra coming before his worshippers pours vast blessings upon them). *First : ágre* : at the head; at the beginning of religious ceremony.

2 *The tongue with joyous sound is stirring in the mouth* : probably priest's tongue influenced by the exhilarating Soma juice. 'The *Soma* stream emitting pleasant juice is driven into (Indra's) mouth.'—Wilson.

3 *Longing for a bride* : seeking the waters with which he is to be united. *Aditi's Daughters*: probably, the plants, whose buds Soma as the Moon opens and fertilizes with his nectareous beams. 'The daughters of Infinity (Aditi (are probably the quarters of the sky.'—Ludwig.

4 *The Bull* : Soma. According to Sāyaṇa, *the Cows* are the propitiatory hymns of praise, which are called also *Goddesses* or divine.

5 *Brightly-shining vesture*: the milk with which the Soma juice is mixed. Sāyaṇa explains the second half of the stanza differently, taking *chamvah* bowls or beakers into which the Soma juice is poured, as meaning metaphorically the two great receptacles of all living beings, or heaven and earth, and introducing Āditya what is not mentioned in the text :—'he has created Āditya who stands on the back of the sky for the destruction (of sin) and purification (and has created) Āditya's brilliance, the cover of the two worlds.'—Wilson.

7 *Vājāḥ* and *kṛṣṭáyaḥ, powers* and *people*, are explained by Sāyaṇa as 'food' and 'offspring.'

8 *Ye, Soma* : 'Soma is treated as plural by attraction; or, as Sāyaṇa puts it, the plurality of the *pitṛs* is applied to Soma.'—Wilson. Probably Moon and Stars are intended. See Hillebrandt, *V. M.* I. p 398.

10 *With all the Gods* : *devaiḥ* : 'subhagairdhanaiḥ with auspicious riches.'—Sāyaṇa.

---

1 *The three times seven Milch-kine* are, according to Sāyaṇa, the twelve months, the five seasons, the three worlds, and Āditya or the Sun. Probably, as Ludwig says, the seven celestial rivers, multiplied by three to correspond with the threefold division of the heavens, are intended. These supply the genuine draught, in contrast to the *four other beauteous creatures*, the Vasatīvari and the three Ekadhanā waters, which are terrestrial and factitious, made to adorn or purify Soma.

2 Longing for lovely Amṛta, by his wisdom
he divided, each apart from other, earth
and heaven.
He gladly wrapped himself in the most
lucid floods, when through their glory
they found the God's resting-place.

3 May those his brilliant rays be ever free
from death, inviolate, for both classes of
created things,—
Rays wherewith powers of men and Gods
are purified. Yea, even for this have
sages welcomed him as King.

4 He, while he is adorned by the ten skilful
ones, that he too in the Midmost Mothers
may create,
While he is watching o'er the lovely
Amṛta's ways, looks on both races as
Beholder of mankind.

5 He, while he is adorned to stream forth
mighty strength, rejoices in his place
between the earth and heaven.
The Steer dispels the evil-hearted with
his might, aiming at offerings as an
archer at the game.

6 Beholding, as it were, Two Mother Cows,
the Steer goes roaring on his way even
as the Maruts roar.
Knowing Eternal Law, the earliest light
of heaven, he, passing wise, was chosen
out to tell it forth.

7 The fearful Bull is bellowing with violent
might, far-sighted, sharpening his yellow-
coloured horns.
Soma assumes his seat in the well-fashioned
place : the cowhide and the sheepskin
are his ornament.

8 Bright, making pure his body free from
spot and stain, on the sheep's back the
Golden-coloured hath flowed down.
Acceptable to Mitra, Vāyu, Varuṇa, he
is prepared as threefold meath by
skilful men.

9 Flow on for the God's banquet, Soma, as
a Steer, and enter Indra's heart, the
Soma's reservoir.
Bear us beyond misfortune ere we be oppressed : the man who knows the land
directs the man who asks.

10 Urged like a car-steed, flow to strength,
O Soma : Indu, flow onward to the
throat of Indra.
Skilled, bear us past, as in a boat o'er
water : as battling Hero save us from
the foeman.

HYMN LXXI. *Soma Pavamāna.*

1. THE guerdon is bestowed : the Mighty
takes his seat, and, ever-watchful, guards
from fiend and evil sprite.
Gold-hued, he makes the cloud his diadem,
the milk his carpet in both worlds, and
prayer his robe of state.

2 Strong, bellowing, he goes, like one who
slays the folk; he lets this hue of Asuras
flow off from him,
Throws off his covering, seeks his father's
meeting-place, and thus makes for himself the bright robe he assumes.

3 Onward he flows, from both the hands,
pressed out with stones : excited by the
prayer, the water makes him wild.

---

9 *The man who knows the Land* : who is acquainted
with the roads or ways. 'Sāyaṇa completes the simile :
"as by telling him he protects (helps) him, so do thou
who knowest the roads of the sacrifice protect us by
telling us the sacrificial paths." '—Wilson. But, of
course, the application is intended to be general.

10 *Bear us past* : carry us over all difficulties and
dangers. *From the foeman : nidáḥ* : from the reviling
(of the foe).'—Wilson.

1 *The guerdon* : the honorarium given to the priests,
consisting originally of a cow. *The Mighty* : Soma.
His carpet : upastire : that which is spread, scattered, or
sprinkled. Cp. IX. 69. 5, where *upastāraṇam* is translated
by 'sprinkling.'

2 *Hue of Asuras* : or, celestial brightness; 'Himmels-
glanz.'—Grassmann. 'He puts forth that *Asura*-slaying
tint of his'.—Wilson. *Seeks his father's meeting-place* :
goes to meet the *yajamāna* or sacrificer. According
to Sāyaṇa : 'the food (*pituḥ*), that is, the Soma, goes
to the prepared reservoir.'

3 *The water makes him wild* : *vṛṣāyáte nábhasā* : *nábhas*
in the Soma-hymns is used to signify either the rain-
water in which, or the cloud from which, the Soma
flows to the earth. Here it means the water with
which the Soma-plant is sprinkled. See *Vedische Studien*,
1. p 135. According to Ludwig : 'he acts like a bull in
the sea of cloud.' *To satisfy the worshipper* : I adopt
Ludwig's suggestion and take *ydjate* as a dative of the
participle. Wilson translates, after Sāyaṇa :—'he is
honoured at the (god—)protected (sacrifice).'

---

3 *Both classes* : animate and inanimate. Or Gods
and men.

4 *The ten skilful ones* : the fingers. *The Midmost
Mothers* : the clouds that hang between heaven and
earth, in which, perhaps, Soma aids in producing the
rain. But the meaning is uncertain. Sāyaṇa explains
pramé by *lokân pramātum*, 'to measure out, or create,
the worlds.' *Both races* : Gods and men.

6 *As it were, Two Mother Cows* : Heaven and Earth.
Sāyaṇa explains the second Pāda of the second line
differently :—'the intelligent (*Pavamāna*) chose man to
be the offerer of his praise.'—Wilson.

8 *Threefold* : according to Sāyaṇa, mixed with the
Vasativarī water, curds, and milk. Probably, poured
into three separate vessels, one for each of the three
deities mentioned.

He frolics and draws near, completes his
work with song, and bathes in streams
to satisfy the worshipper.

4 They pour out meath around the Master
of the house, Celestial Strengthener of
the mountain that gives might;
In whom, through his great powers, oblation-
eating cows in their uplifted udder mix
their choicest milk.

5 They, the ten sisters, on the lap of Aditi,
have sent him forward like a car from
both the arms.
He wanders and comes near the Cow's
mysterious place, even the place which
his inventions have produced.

6 Like as a falcon to his home, so speeds the
God to his own golden wisely-fashioned
place to rest.
With song they urge the darling to the
sacred grass : the Holy One goes like
a courser to the Gods.

7 From far away, from heaven, the red-
hued noted Sage, Steer of the triple
height, hath sung unto the kine.
With thousand guidings he, leading this
way and that, shines, as a singer, splendidly through many a morn.

8 His covering assumes a radiant hue;
where'er he comes into the fight he drives
the foe afar.
The Winner of the Floods, with food he
seeks the host of heaven, he comes to
praises glorified with milk.

9 Like a bull roaming round the herds he
bellows : he hath assumed the brilliancy
of Sūrya.
Down to the earth hath looked the heavenly
Falcon : Soma with wisdom views all
living creatures.

HYMN LXXII. *Soma Pavamāna.*

1. THEY cleanse the Gold-hued : like a red
Steed is he yoked, and Soma in the jar
is mingled with the milk.
He sendeth out his voice, and many
loving friends of him the highly-lauded
hasten with their songs.

2 The many sages utter words in unison,
while into Indra's throat they pour the
Soma juice,
When, with the ten that dwell together
closely joined, the men whose hands
are skilful cleanse the lovely meath.

3 He goes upon his way, unresting, to the
cows, over the roaring sound which
Sūrya's Daughter loves.
The Falcon brought it to him for his own
delight : now with the twofold kindred
sisters is his home.

4 Washed by the men, stone-pressed, dear
on the holy grass, faithful to seasons,
Lord of cattle from of old,
Most liberal, completing sacrifice for men,
O Indra, pure bright Soma, Indu, flows
for thee.

5 O Indra, urged by arms of men and poured
in streams, Soma flows on for thee after
his Godlike kind.
Plans thou fulfillest, gatherest thoughts for
sacrifice : in the bowls sits the Gold-
hued like a roosting bird.

6 Sages well-skilled in work, intelligent,
drain out the stalk that roars, the Sage,
the Everlasting One.
The milk, the hymns unite them with
him in the place of sacrifice, his seat
who is produced anew.

7 Earth's central point, sustainer of the
mighty heavens, distilled into the streams,
into the waters' wave,
As Indra's thunderbolt, Steer with far-
spreading wealth, Soma is flowing on
to make the heart rejoice.

---

4 *The Master of the house* : according to Sāyaṇa, the
conqueror of the fort of the enemy. See IX. 78. 3.
The mountain that gives might : the cloud. In the second
half of this stanza I adopt Sāyaṇa's interpretation as a
makeshift, although it seems impossible that *mūrdhán*,
'head,' should here mean 'uplifted.' Ludwig takes
údhani, 'udder,' in the sense of 'behälter,' or receptacle
into which the Soma flows.

5 *On the lap of Aditi* : on the earth. 'near to the
ground.'—Wilson. *The Cow's mysterious place* : or, distant
place, is the udder of heaven, the cloud.

7 *Of the triple height* : working in heaven, firmament
and earth.—Ludwig. See IX. 75. 3.

9 *The heavenly Falcon* : *divyáḥ suparṇáḥ* : 'celestial,
flying gracefully.'—Wilson. Soma, says Sāyaṇa, is said
to go gracefully, 'because it is carried off by *Gāyatrī* in
the shape of a hawk.'

---

2 *Indra's throat* : literally, belly ; the *droṇakalaśá* or
reservoir. *The ten* : the fingers.

3 *The cows* : the milk and curds. *The roaring sound*
of the effused Soma is said to be dear to Sūrya's Daughter, Uṣas or Dawn, because it is chiefly heard in the
early morning. *The Falcon* : I adopt Ludwig's interpretation of the strange word *vinaṁgṛsáḥ* as no other
meaning seems suitable here. According to Sāyaṇa,
the word means praiser, or worshipper. *The twofold
kindred sisters* : the fingers of both hands.

7 *The heart* : of Indra. *As Indra's thunderbolt* : cp.
IX. 77. 1.

8 Over the earthly region flow thou on thy
way, helping the praiser and the pourer,
thou Most Wise.
Let us not lack rich treasure reaching to
our home, and may we clothe ourselves
in manifold bright wealth.

9 Hither, O Indu, unto us a hundred gifts of
steeds, a thousand gifts of cattle and
of gold,
Measure thou forth, yea, splendid ample
strengthening food do thou, O Pavamāna,
heed this laud of ours.

HYMN LXXIII. *Soma Pavamāna.*

1. THEY from the spouting drop have sounded at the rim : naves speed together
to the place of sacrifice.
That Asura hath formed, to seize, three
lofty heights. The ships of truth have
borne the pious man across.

2 The strong Steers, gathering, have duly
stirred themselves, and over the stream's
wave the friends sent forth the song.
Engendering the hymn, with flowing
streams of meath, Indra's dear body
have they caused to wax in strength.

3 With sanctifying gear they sit around the
song : their ancient Father guards their
holy work from harm.
Varuṇa hath o'erspread the mighty sea of
air. Sages had power to hold him in
sustaining floods.

4 Sweet-tongued, exhaustless, they have sent
their voices down together, in heaven's
vault that pours a thousand streams.
His wildly-restless warders never close an
eye : in every place are found the bonds
that bind man fast.

5 O'er Sire and Mother they have roared
in unison, bright with the verse of praise,
burning up riteless men,
Blowing away with supernatural might
from earth and from the heavens the
swarthy skin which Indra hates.

6 Those which, as guides of song and coun-
sellors of speed, were manifested from
their ancient dwelling place,—
From these the eyeless and the deaf have
turned aside : the wicked travel not
the pathway of the Law.

7 What time the filter with a thousand
streams is stretched, the thoughtful sages
purify their song therein.
Bright-coloured are their spies, vigorous,
void of guile, excellent, fair to see,
beholders of mankind.

8 Guardian of Law, most wise, he may not
be deceived : three Purifiers hath he
set within his heart.
With wisdom he beholds all creatures that
exist : he drives into the pit the hated
riteless ones.

9 The thread of sacrifice spun in the cleansing sieve, on Varuṇa's tongue-tip, by
supernatural might,—
This, by their striving, have the prudent
ones attained : he who hath not this
power shall sink into the pit.

HYMN LXXIV. *Soma Pavamāna*

1. BORN like a youngling he hath clamoured
in the wood, when he, the Red, the
Strong, would win the light of heaven.
He comes with heavenly seed that makes

---

1 *They* : the pressing-stones, from whose rim or edge
the Soma-drops fall noisily. *Naves*: by synecdoche wheels,
again by the same figure, chariots, and then by metaphor the swiftly-running Soma-drops. *That Asura* : the
divine Soma. *To seize* : to be held and used. *Three
lofty heights* : the three elevated worlds. *The ships of truth*
or, of the truthful (Soma). According to Sāyaṇa, the
four vessels which hold the Āditya, Āgrayaṇa, Ukthya,
and Dhruva libations.

2 *The strong Steers* : the priests.

3 *Their ancient Father* : Soma ; or, perhaps, Agni.
Varuṇa : 'Soma the all-enveloper.'—Wilson. *Him* :
Soma. *In sustaining floods* : in the Vasatīvarī waters.—
Sāyaṇa.

4 *They* : the beams that radiate from Soma :
somaraśmayaḥ : Soma-rays.—Sāyaṇa.

5 *Sire and Mother* : the general parents, Heaven and
Earth. *The swarthy skin* : 'the black skinned (Rākṣasas).'
—Wilson.

6. *Those* : rays. I follow Sāyaṇa's interpretation.
The first line is very obscure.

7 *The filter* : the tip of their tongue. Cf. stanza 9,
and hymn 75. 2. See Bergaigne, *La Religion Védique*, I.
283. *Bright coloured* : *rudrāsaḥ* : sons of Rudra, according
to Sāyaṇa. But see *Vedische Studien*, I. pp. 55, 56.

8 *Of Law* : of law-ordained sacrifice. The *three Purifiers* whom Soma sets within his heart and combines in
his own being are Agni, Vāyu, Sūrya, the purifying
powers of fire, wind, and sun.

9 *On Varuṇa's tongue-tip* : the Vasatīvarī waters in
which Soma dwells (vasati) stand on the tip of Varuṇa's
tongue—Sāyaṇa. *He who hath not this power* : 'he who
is incompetent for the rite.'—Wilson.

———

1 *In the wood* : in the wooden vat. According to
Sāyaṇa, 'in the water.'

the water swell : him for wide-spreading shelter we implore with prayer.

2 A far-extended pillar that supports the sky, the Soma-stalk, filled full, moves itself every way.
He shall bring both these great worlds while the rite proceeds : the Sage holds these who move together and all food.

3 Wide space hath he who follows Aditi's right path, and mighty, well-made food, meath blent with Soma juice;
He who from hence commands the rain, Steer of the kine, Leader of floods, who helps us hence, who claims our laud.

4 Butter and milk are drawn from animated cloud; thence Amṛta is produced, centre of sacrifice.
Him the Most Bounteous Ones, ever united, love; him as our Friend the Men who make all swell rain down.

5 The Soma-stalk hath roared, following with the wave : he swells with sap for man the skin which Gods enjoy.
Upon the lap of Aditi he lays the germ, by means whereof we gain children and progeny.

6 In the third region which distils a thousand streams, may the Exhaustless Ones descend with procreant power.
The kindred Four have been sent downward from the heavens : dropping with oil they bring Amṛta and sacred gifts.

7 Soma assumes white colour when he strives to gain : the bounteous Asura knows full many a precious boon.

Down the steep slope, through song, he comes to sacrifice, and he will burst the water-holding cask of heaven,

8 Yea, to the shining milk-anointed beaker, as to his goal, hath stepped the conquering Courser.
Pious-souled men have sent their gifts of cattle unto Kakṣīvān of the hundred winters.

9 Soma, thy juice when thou art blended with the streams, flows, Pavamāna, through the long wool of the sheep.
So, cleansed by sages, O best giver of delight, grow sweet for Indra, Pavamāna ! for his drink.

HYMN LXXV.   Soma Pavamāna.

1. GRACIOUSLY-MINDED he is flowing on his way to win dear names o'er which the Youthful One grows great.
The Mighty and Far-seeing One hath mounted now the mighty Sūrya's car which moves to every side.

2 The Speaker, unassailable Master of this hymn, the Tongue of sacrifice pours forth the pleasant meath.
Within the lustrous region of the heavens the Son makes the third secret name of Mother and of Sire.

3 Sending forth flashes he hath bellowed to the jars, led by the men into the golden reservoir.
The milky streams of sacrifice have sung to him : he of the triple height shines brightly through the morns.

4 Pressed by the stones, with hymns, and

---

2 *He shall bring both these great worlds* : shall bring Heaven and Earth to the sacrifice.

3 *He who follows Aditi's right path* : the regularly moving moon. Sāyaṇa takes *āditeḥ* with *gávyūtiḥ* : the way to earth is broad.'—Wilson Somewhat similarly Hillebrandt, V.M., I. 360.

4 *The Most Bounteous Ones, the Men who make all swell,* are, probably, the Maruts who fertilize the earth, and send Soma down in the rain. Sāyaṇa's explanation is different :—'the assembled liberal givers [the *yajamānas* or sacrificers] delight him : (the Soma juices) the leaders, the protectors shower down the accumulated (water),'— Wilson. For the meaning of *pèravaḥ* those who swell, or cause to swell, 'protectors' according to Sāyaṇa, see *Vedische Studien, I.* p. 85

5 *For man* : for the sacrificer. *The skin* : his own body.—Sāyaṇa. *Upon the lap of Aditi* : of the earth, according to Sāyaṇa. The meaning is that Soma is the source of all Nature's productive power.

6 *In the third region*; dwelling in heaven. *The Exhaustless Ones* ; these are *the kindred Four* of the following line, meaning according to Sāyaṇa, four rays or digits of Soma. It is most probable that the four Goddesses Sinivālī, Kuhū or Gungū, Rākā, and Anumati are meant. Cp. II. 32. 6.'—Ludwig.

7 *Strives to gain* : seeks to enjoy heaven.—Sāyaṇa. *The water-holding cask* : the water-laden cloud.

---

8 *The conquering Courser* : the swiftly-flowing Soma. *Kakṣīvān* : the Ṛṣi of the hymn.

---

1 *O'er which* : that is the Youthful One, the fresh and strong Soma, exceeds in greatness even the high titles which he wins by his gracious deeds.

2 *Speaker* ; *Master* ; *Tongue of sacrifice* : Soma, the giver of eloquence. *The Son* : Soma. *Of Mother and of Sire* : of his parents, Heaven and Earth. What *the third secret name*, that is, probably, a name in addition to those of Heaven and Earth, and comprising both deities, may be, does not appear. Sāyaṇa's explanation is different : 'the son (the sacrificer) assumes a third name unknown to his parents ;' that is, Wilson adds, 'a name not given at birth...He (Sāyaṇa) cites Baudhā-yana, who gives *Somayājin* [Somayāga sacrificer] as an instance of a third name.

3 *The milky streams* : cf. I. 144. 2. *Of the triple height* : dwelling in three high places, heaven, the firmament or the mountain-top, and the place of sacrifice. Cf. IX. 71. 7.

graciously inclined, illuminating both
the Parents, Heaven and Earth,
He flows in ordered season onward through
the fleece, a current of sweet juice still
swelling day by day.

5 Flow onward, Soma, flow to bring prosperity : cleansed by the men, invest
thee with the milky draught.
What gladdening drinks thou hast, foaming,
exceeding strong, even with these incite
Indra to give us wealth.

HYMN LXXVI. *Soma Pavamāna.*

1. ON flows the potent juice, sustainer of
the heavens, the strength of Gods, whom
men must hail with shouts of joy.
The Gold-hued, started like a courser by
brave men, impetuously winneth splendour in the streams.

2 He takes his weapons, like a hero, in his
hands, fain to win light, car-borne, in
forays for the kine.
Indu, while stimulating Indra's might, is
urged forward and balmed by sages
skilful in their task.

3 Soma, as thou art purified with flowing
wave, exhibiting thy strength enter
thou Indra's throat.
Make both worlds stream for us, as
lightning doth the clouds : mete out
exhaustless powers for us, as 'twere
through song.

4 Onward he flows, the King of all that
sees the light : the Ṛṣis' Lord hath
raised the song of sacrifice;
Even he who is adorned with Sūrya's
arrowy beam, Father of hymns, whose
wisdom is beyond our reach.

5 Like as a bull to herds, thou flowest to the
pail, bellowing as a steer upon the water's
lap.
So, best of Cheerers, thou for Indra flowest
on that we, with thy protection, may
o'ercome in fight.

HYMN LXXVII. *Soma Pavamāna.*

1. MORE beauteous than the beautiful, as
Indra's bolt, this Soma, rich in sweets,
hath clamoured in the vat.
Dropping with oil, abundant, streams of
sacrifice flow unto him like milch-kine,
lowing, with their milk.

2 On flows that Ancient One whom, hitherward, from heaven, sped through the
region of the air, the Falcon snatched.
He, quivering with alarm and terrified in
heart before bow-armed Kṛśānu, holdeth
fast the sweet.

3 May those first freshest drops of Soma
juice effused flow on their way to bring
us mighty strength in kine.
Beauteous as serpents, worthy to be looked
upon, they whom each sacred gift and
all our prayers have pleased.

4 May that much-lauded Indu, with a heart
inclined to us, well-knowing, fight against
our enemies.
He who hath brought the germ beside the
Strong One's seat moves onward to the
widely-opened stall of kine.

5 The active potent juice of heaven is flowing on, great Varuṇa whom the forward
man can ne'er deceive.
Mitra, the Holy, hath been pressed for
troubled times, neighing like an impatient horse amid the herd.

HYMN LXXVIII. *Soma Pavamāna.*

1. RAISING his voice the King hath flowed
upon his way : invested with the waters
he would win the kine.
The fleece retains his solid parts as though
impure, and bright and cleansed he seeks
the special place of Gods.

2 Thou, Soma, art effused for Indra by the
men, balmed in the wood as wave, Sage,
Viewer of mankind.

2 *The Falcon*: See I. 93. 5. *He*: Soma, according to
Sāyaṇa, but more probably the falcon. *Kṛśānu* : the
archer who guards the celestial Soma. See I. 112. 21.

3 *Serpents* : the meaning of *ahyāḥ* is uncertain here.
Sāyaṇa explains it by *striyaḥ,* women :—'pleasing to
look upon like beautiful well-adorned (.women).'—
Wilson.

4. *He who hath brought the germ* : here the sacrificer
and not Soma is meant.—Ludwig. *The Strong One* :
Agni.

5 In this stanza Soma is compared to, or mystically
identified with, Varuṇa and Mitra. Sāyaṇa leaves
Varuṇa unexplained, but interprets *Mitra* by *sarveṣām
mitrabhūtaḥ,* '(Soma) the friend of all.'

1 *The fleece* : literally, the sheep; the filter made
of wool. *Solid parts* : *tánvā* : the fragments of stalk which
will not pass through the strainer. According to Sāyaṇa,
'with its own covering,'— the sheep with its fleece.'—
Wilson. *The special place of Gods* : the vessels which
hold the libations assigned to various Gods.

2 *Balmed in the wood* : according to Sāyaṇa, 'art
driven into the water.' *Bay steeds*: swiftly-running tawny
drops.

3 *As 'twere through song* : 'now with the rite, *i.e.* at
the very time the rite is being performed.'—Wilson.

Full many are the paths whereon thou
mayest go : a thousand bay steeds hast
thou resting in the bowls.

3 Apsarases who dwell in waters of the sea,
sitting within, have flowed to Soma wise
of heart.
They urge the Master of the house upon
his way, and to the Eternal Pavamāna
pray for bliss.

4 Soma flows on for us as winner of the kine,
winner of thousands, cars, water, and
light, and gold;
He whom the Gods have made a gladdening
draught to drink, the drop most sweet
to taste, weal-bringing, red of hue.

5 Soma, as Pavamāna thou, our faithful
Friend, making for us these real treasures,
flowest on.
Slay thou the enemy both near and far
away : grant us security and ample
pasturage.

HYMN LXXIX.   *Soma Pavamāna.*

1. SPONTANEOUS let our drops of Soma juice
flow on, pressed, golden-hued, among
the Gods of lofty heaven.
Perish among us they who give no gifts
of food ! perish the godless ! May our
prayers obtain success.

2 Forward to us the drops, distilling meath,
shall flow, like riches for whose sake
we urge the horses on.
Beyond the crafty hindering of all mortal
men may we continually bear precious
wealth away.

3 Yea, yerily, foe of hate shown to himself
is he, yea, verily, destroyer too of other
hate.

3 *Apsarases who dwell in waters of the sea* : 'nymphs of
the firmament.—Wilson. The nymphs are identified
with their element, and represent the water with which
the Soma juice is mixed. *The Master of the house* : *har-*
myḍsya sakṣḍṇim : Soma. In IX. 71. 4, Sāyaṇa explains
these words as 'overpowerer, or stormer of the fort of
the enemy,' and in this place as the sprinkler of the
hall of sacrifice.' *Sakṣḍṇi,* from the root *sah,* means
overpowerer, and from the root *sac,* connected with,
especially as master and possessor.

1 *They who give no gifts of food* : I can find no satisfactory explanation of *iṣḍḥ dṛātiyah,* so I give Sāyaṇa's
interpretation as a makeshift. 'May they be destroyed
who are the withholders of food from us.'—Wilson.

2 *Urge the horses on* : Sāyaṇa explains *dṛvataḥ,* horses,
by, 'strong enemy.' 'By whose aid we encounter the
powerful (enemy).'—Wilson.

3 'Soma knows how to defend not only himself, but
us also.'—Ludwig. *Destroyer* : literally, the wolf.

As thirst subdueth in the desert, conquer
thou, O Soma Pavamāna, men of evil
thoughts.

4 Near kin to thee is he, raised loftiest in
the heavens : upon the earth's high
ridge thy scions have grown forth.
The press-stones chew and crunch thee
on the ox's hide : sages have milked
thee with their hands into the streams.

5 So do they hurry on thy strong and beauteous juice, O Indu, as the first ingredient
of the draught.
Bring low, thou Pavamāna, every single
foe, and be thy might shown forth as
sweet and gladdening drink.

HYMN LXXX.   *Soma Pavamāna.*

1. ON flows the stream of Soma who beholds
mankind : by everlasting Law he calls
the Gods from heaven.
He lightens with the roaring of Bṛhaspati:
the lakes have not contained the pourings
of juice.

2 Thou, powerful Soma, thou to whom the
cows have lowed, ascendest bright with
sheen, thine iron-fashioned home.
Thou, lengthening our princes' life and
high renown, flowest for Indra as his
might to gladdening drink.

3 Best giver of delight, he flows to Indra's
throat, robing himself in might, Auspicious One, for fame.
He spreads himself abroad to meet all
things that be : the vigorous Tawny
Steed flows sporting on his way.

4 The men, the ten swift fingers, milk thee
out for Gods, even thee most rich in
meath, with thousand flowing streams.
Soma who winnest thousands, driven by
the men, expressed with stones, bring,
as thou flowest, all the Gods.

4 *He* : 'the Moon.'—Ludwig. 'Thy best juice
dwells in the navel of heaven, that which receives (the
oblation).' Wilson. *On the ox's hide* : Although men
of the present time pour out the Soma upon the skin
of a black antelope and not on a cowhide or oxhide,
still it is measured out for sale on an oxhide.'—Sāyaṇa.

1 *The roaring of Bṛhaspati* : that is, says Sāyaṇa,
the voice or praise of the worshipper. Agni may be
intended, as Ludwig suggests. *The lakes* : or seas
(*samudrḍsaḥ*), probably the Soma-reservoirs. Sāyaṇa
takes *nd* as a particle of comparison : 'the libations
cover (the earth) like rivers.' Wilson.

2 *Iron-fashioned home* : See IX. 1. 2.

5 Deft-handed men with stones, the ten
   swift fingers, drain thee into waters, thee,
   the Steer enriched with sweets.
   Thou, Soma, gladdening Indra and the
   Heavenly Host, flowest as ˑPavamāna
   like a river's wave.

HYMN LXXXI. *Soma Pavamāna.*

1. ONWARD to Indra's throat move, beauteously
   adorned, the waves of Soma as he
   purifies himself,
   When they, brought forward with the
   lovely curd of kine, effused, have cheered
   the Hero to bestow his gifts.
2 Hither hath Soma flowed unto the beakers,
   like a chariot-horse, a stallion swift upon
   his way.
   Thus, knowing both the generations, he
   obtains the rights and dues of Gods
   from yonder and from hence.
3 While thou art cleansed, O Soma, scatter
   wealth on us; Indu, bestow great bounty
   as a liberal Prince.
   Giver of life, with wisdom help to
   opulence; strew not our home possessions far away from us.
4 Hither let Pūṣan Pavamāna come to us,
   Varuṇa, Mitra, bountiful, of one accord,
   The Maruts, Aśvins, Vāyu, and Bṛhaspati,
   Savitar, Tvaṣṭar, tractable Sarasvatī.
5 Both Heaven and Earth, the all-invigorating Pair, Vidhātar, Aditi, and
   Aryaman the God,
   Bhaga who blesses men, the spacious
   Firmament,—let all the Gods in Pavamāna
   take delight.

HYMN LXXXII. *Soma Pavamāna.*

1. EVEN as a King hath Soma, red and tawny
   Bull, been pressed : the Wondrous One
   hath bellowed to the kine.

While purified he passes through the
filtering fleece to seat him hawk-like on
the place that drops with oil.
2. To glory goest thou, Sage with disposing
   skill, like a groomed steed thou rushest
   forward to the prize.
   O Soma, be thou gracious, driving off
   distress : thou goest, clothed in butter,
   to a robe of state.
3 Parjanya is the Father of the Mighty
   Bird : on mountains, in earth's centre
   hath he made his home.
   The waters too have flowed, the Sisters, to
   the kine : he meets the pressing-stones
   at the beloved rite.
4 Thou givest pleasure as a wife delights
   her lord. Listen, O Child of Pajrā,
   for to thee I speak.
   Amid the holy songs go on that we may
   live : in time of trouble, Soma, watch
   thou free from blame.
5 As to the men of old thou camest, Indu
   unharmed, to strengthen, winning
   hundreds, thousands,
   So now for new felicity flow onward : the
   waters follow as thy law ordaineth.

HYMN LXXXIII. *Soma Pavamāna.*

1. SPREAD is thy cleansing filter, Brahmaṇaspati : as Prince, thou enterest its limbs
   from every side.
   The raw, whose mass hath not been heated
   gains not this : they only which are
   dressed, which bear, attain to it.
2 High in the seat of heaven is spread the
   Scorcher's sieve : its threads are standing
   separate, glittering with light.
   The Swift Ones favour him who purifieth
   this : with consciousness they stand
   upon the height of heaven.

---

2 *Both the generations* : of Gods and men. Sāyaṇa takes
ubháyasya jánmanaḥ with *devǎnām* :—'and knowing both
races of gods—those who come to (the sacrifice) from the
other world and those who (come) from this world.'
—Wilson.

3 *Help to opulence* : according to Sāyaṇa, 'help Vasu
(the Ṛṣi of the hymn) to prosperity.'

4 *Tractable* : *suyāmā* : easily led by prayer). According to Sāyaṇa=*suvigrahā*, beautiful in form.

5 *All-invigorating* : *viśvaminvé* : 'all-pervading.'—Sāyaṇa.
Vidhātar : the Disposer, regarded as a separate deity, as
Dhātar is the Maker, Ordainer, or Establisher.

---

1 *As a King* : 'magnificent as a king.'—Wilson. *That
drops with oil* : Sāyaṇa here explains *ghṛtdvantam* by *udaka-
vantam*, watery.

---

2 *To a robe of state*: *nirṇijam* : 'to the cleansing (vessel).'
—Wilson.

3 *Parjanya* : the God of the rain-cloud and waters of
the air in which the mighty Bird, the Moon, is born. *In
earth's centre* : at the altar, in the oblation.

4 *Pajrā* : according to Sāyaṇa, the earth. The St.
Petersburg Lexicon explains the word as meaning the
moist fresh Soma-plant of which Soma, the juice, is the
child. Perhaps, as Ludwig suggests, Pajrā may be the
name of the sacrificer's wife.

1 Brahmaṇaspati's filter appears to be the heavenly filter
through which the rain descends to earth. See Bergaigne,
La Religion Védique, I. 79, 201. *The raw* : uncooked oblation. *Which bear* : 'bearing (the sacrifice.)'—Wilson.
This : according to Sāyaṇa, to this filter. Ludwig thinks
that Agni or Sūrya is meant by '*tat*.'

2 *The Scorcher's sieve*: 'The filter of the foe-scorching
(Soma).'—Wilson. *The Swift Ones* : 'his swift-flowing
(juices) protect the purifier (the worshipper).'—Wilson

3 The foremost spotted Steer hath made the
   Mornings   shine, and yearning after
   strength sustains all things that be.
   By his high wisdom have the mighty
   Sages wrought : the Fathers who behold
   mankind laid down the germ,
4 Gandharva verily protects his dwelling-
   place; Wondrous, he guards the generations of the Gods.
   Lord of the snare, he takes the foeman
   with the snare : those who are most
   devout have gained a share of meath.
5 Rich in oblations ! robed in cloud, thou
   compassest oblation, sacrifice, the mighty
   seat of Gods.
   King, on thy chariot-sieve thou goest up
   to war, and with a thousand weapons
   winnest lofty fame.

HYMN LXXXIV.   *Soma Pavamāna.*

1. Flow, cheering Gods, most active, winner of
   the flood, for Indra, and for Vāyu, and
   for Varuṇa.
   Bestow on us to-day wide room with
   happiness, and in thine ample dwelling
   laud the Host of Heaven.
2 He who hath come anear to creatures that
   have life, Immortal Soma flows onward
   to all of them.
   Effecting, for our aid, both union and
   release, Indu, like Sūrya, follows closely
   after Dawn.
3 He who is poured with milk, he who
   within the plants hastes bringing treasure
   for the happiness of Gods,
   He, poured forth in a stream flows with
   the lightning's flash, Soma who gladdens
   Indra and the Host of Heaven.

3 *The Mighty Sages* : those who possess supernatural
wisdom; the Gods. *The Fathers*: 'The fruitfulness of heaven
and earth, which give birth to gods and men, is described
as produced by the fathers.'—Walli s, *Cosmology of the
RV.*, p. 72. See X. 64. 14.

4 *Gandharva* : here, the Sun. *His* : Soma's.

5 *Robed in cloud* : *nábhaḥ* : meaning, water from the
clouds. *With a thousand weapons* : more literally, having
a thousand, that is, countless sharp points 'Thousand-
raved.'—Ludwig.

———

1 *In thine ample dwelling* : 'on the spacious sacrificial
ground.'—Sāyaṇa.

2 The second line is obscure. Wilson translates,
after Sāyaṇa :—'Indu, binding and loosing, accompanies
the sacrifice (for its protection) as the Sun the Dawn ;'
that is, binding or connecting the sacrifice with the gods
and loosing or separating it from the Asuras or evil spirits.
But this explanation is unsatisfactory. Ludwig suggests
that 'union' refers to Soma's binding together heaven
and earth, Gods and men, and for the meaning of 'release'
he refers to IX. 68. 5.

4 Winner of thousands, he, this Soma, flows
   along, raising a vigorous voice that
   wakens with the dawn.
   Indu with winds drives on the ocean of
   the air, he sinks within the jars, he
   rests in Indra's heart.
5 The kine with milk dress him who makes
   the milk increase, Soma, amid the songs,
   who finds the light of heaven.
   Winner of wealth, the effectual juice is
   flowing on, Singer and Sage by wisdom,
   dear as heaven itself.

HYMN LXXXV.   *Soma Pavamāna.*

1. Flow on to Indra, Soma, carefully effused:
   let sickness stay afar together with the
   fiends.
   Let not the double-tongued delight them
   with thy juice : here be thy flowing
   drops laden with opulence.
2 O Pavamāna, urge us forward in the fight :
   thou art the vigour of the Gods, the
   well-loved drink.
   Smite thou our enemies who raise the
   shout of joy : Indra, drink Soma juice,
   and drive away our foes.
3 Unharmed, best Cheerer, thou, O Indu,
   flowest on : thou, even thou thyself,
   art Indra's noblest food.
   Full many a wise man lifts to thee the
   song of praise, and hails thee with a
   kiss as Sovran of this world.
4 Wondrous, with hundred streams, hymned
   in a thousand songs, Indu pours out
   for Indra his delightful meath.
   Winning us land and waters, flow thou
   hitherward : Rainer of bounties, Soma,
   make broad way for us.
5 Roaring within the beaker thou art balmed
   with milk : thou passest through the
   fleecy filter all at once.
   Carefully cleansed and decked like a prize-
   winning steed, O Soma, thou hast
   flowed down within Indra's throat.
6 Flow onward sweet of flavour for the
   Heavenly Race, for Indra sweet, whose
   name is easily invoked :
   Flow sweet for Mitra, Varuṇa, and Vāyu,
   rich in meath, inviolable for Bṛhaspati.
7 Ten rapid fingers deck the Courser in the
   jar : with hymns the holy singers send
   their voices forth.
   The filtering juices hasten to their eulogy,
   the drops that gladden find their way
   to Indra's heart.

8 While thou art purified pour on us hero
strength, great, far-extended shelter,
spacious pasturage.
Let no oppression master this our holy
work : may we, O Indu, gain all
opulence through thee.

9 The Steer who sees afar hath risen above
the sky : the Sage hath caused the lights
of heaven to give their shine.
The King is passing through the filter
with a roar : they drain the milk of
heaven from him who looks on men.

10 High in the vault of heaven, unceasing,
honey-tongued, the Loving Ones drain
out the mountain-haunting Steer,—
The drop that hath grown great in waters,
in the lake, meath-rich, in the stream's
wave and in the cleansing sieve.

11 The Loving Ones besought with many
voices the Eagle who had flown away
to heaven.
Hymns kiss the Youngling worthy of
laudation, resting on earth, the Bird of
golden colour.

12 High to heaven's vault hath the Gandharva
risen, beholding all his varied forms
and figures.
His ray hath shone abroad with gleaming
splendour : pure, he hath lighted both
the worlds, the Parents.

HYMN LXXXVI. *Soma Pavamāna.*

1. THY gladdening draughts, O Pavamāna,
urged by song flow swiftly of themselves
like sons of fleet-foot mares.
The drops of Soma juice, those eagles of
the heavens, most cheering, rich in
meath, rest in the reservoir.

2 As rapid chariot-steeds, so turned in several
ways have thine exhilarating juices darted
forth,
Soma-drops rich in meath, waves, to the
Thunder-armed, to Indra, like milch-
kine who seek their calf with milk.

3 Like a steed urged to battle, finder of the
light, speed onward to the cloud-born
reservoir of heaven,
A Steer that o'er the woolly surface seeks
the sieve, Soma while purified for Indra's
nourishment.

4 Fleet as swift steeds, thy drops, divine,
thought-swift, have been, O Pavamāna,
poured with milk into the vat.
The Rṣis have poured in continuous Soma
drops, ordainers who adorn thee, Friend
whom Rṣis love.

5 O thou who seest all things, Sovran as
thou art and passing strong, thy rays
encompass all abodes.
Pervading with thy natural powers thou
flowest on, and as the whole world's
Lord, O Soma, thou art King.

6 The beams of Pavamāna, sent from earth
and heaven, his ensigns who is ever
steadfast, travel round.
When on the sieve the Golden-hued is
cleansed, he rests within the vats as one
who seats him in his place.

7 Served with fair rites he flows, ensign of
sacrifice : Soma advances to the special
place of Gods.
He speeds with thousand currents to the
reservoir, and passes through the filter
bellowing as a bull.

8 The Sovran dips him in the seain and the
streams, and set in rivers with the waters'
wave moves on.
High heaven's Sustainer at the central
point of earth, raised on the fleecy
surface Pavamāna stands.

9 He on whose high decree the heavens and
earth depend hath roared and thundered
like the summit of the sky.
Soma flows on obtaining Indra's friendly
love, and, as they purify him, settles
in the jars.

10 He, light of sacrifice distils delicious meath,
most wealthy, Father and begetter of
the Gods.

---

9 *The Steer who sees afar* : wise Soma, the Moon.

10 *The Loving Ones* : *vendh* : the Gods or, specially,
the Maruts. According to Sāyaṇa, great Rṣis, called
Venas. *The mountain-haunting Steer* : Soma, first seen
over the mountain heights. See Hillebrandt, *V. M.*, I. 389.

11 Soma in this stanza is *the Eagle, the Youngling* or
infant, and *the Bird of golden colour*.

12 *The Gandharva* : here Soma, the Moon. See
Hillebrandt, *V. M.*, I. 429.

3 *Speed onward* : hasten to pour down the rain from
the cloud.

4 *Friend whom Rṣis love* : *ṛṣiṣāṇa* : the word does not
occur elsewhere, and its precise meaning is uncertain.
'O ṛṣi-enjoyed.'—Wilson. 'Thou who playest the part
of a Rṣi.'—Ludwig.

8 *The sea and the streams* are the firmament and its
waters. Soma, who is at the same time the God in heaven
and the earthly beverage, is said to combine with the
solar rays in the clouds, and thus to cause the rain to
descend. See Hillebrandt, *V. M.*, I. 215. *Central point of
earth* : the place of sacrifice.

He, gladdening, best of Cheerers, juice that Indra loves, enriches with mysterious treasure earth and heaven.

11 The vigorous and far-seeing one, the Lord of heaven, flows, shouting to the beaker, with his thousand streams.
Coloured like gold he rests in seats where Mitra dwells, the Steer made beautiful by rivers and by sheep.

12 In forefront of the rivers Pavamāna speeds, in forefront of the hymn, foremost among the kine.
He shares the mighty booty in the van of war : the well-armed Steer is purified by worshippers.

13 This heedful Pavamāna, like a bird sent forth, hath with his wave flowed onward to the fleecy sieve.
O Indra, through thy wisdom, by thy thought, O Sage, Soma flows bright and pure between the earth and heaven.

14 He, clad in mail that reaches heaven, the Holy One, filling the firmament, stationed amid the worlds,
Knowing the realm of light, hath come to us in rain : he summons to himself his own primeval Sire.

15 He who was first of all to penetrate his form bestowed upon his race wide shelter and defence.
From that high station which he hath in loftiest heaven he comes victorious to all encounters here.

16 Indu hath started for Indra's special place and slights not as a Friend the promise of his Friend.
Soma speeds onward like a youth to youthful maids, and gains the beaker by a course of hundred paths.

17 Your songs, exhilarating, tuneful, uttering praise, are come into the places where the people meet.
Worshippers have exalted Soma with their hymns, and milch kine have come near to meet him with their milk.

18 O Soma, Indu, while they cleanse thee, pour on us accumulated, plentiful, nutritious food,
Which, ceaseless, thrice a day shall yield us hero power enriched with store of nourishment, and strength, and meath.

19 Far-seeing Soma flows, the Steer, the Lord of hymns, the Furtherer of day, of morning, and of heaven.
Mixt with the streams he caused the beakers to resound, and with the singers' aid they entered Indra's heart.

20 On, with the prudent singers, flows the ancient Sage and guided by the men hath roared about the vats.
Producing Trita's name, may he pour forth the meath, that Vāyu and that Indra may become his Friends.

21 He, being purified, hath made the Mornings shine : this, even this is he who gave the rivers room.
He made the Three Times Seven pour out the milky flow : Soma, the Cheerer, yields whate'er the heart finds sweet.

22 Flow onward, Soma, in thine own celestial forms, flow, Indu, poured within the beaker and the sieve.
Sinking into the throat of Indra with a roar, led by the men thou madest Sūrya mount to heaven.

23 Pressed out with stones thou flowest onward to the sieve, O Indu, entering the depths of Indra's throat.
Far-sighted Soma, now thou lookest on mankind : thou didst unbar the cow-stall for the Angirases.

24 In thee, O Soma, while thou purifiedst thee, high-thoughted sages, seeking favour, have rejoiced.
Down from the heavens the Falcon brought thee hitherward, even thee, O Indu, thee whom all our hymns adorn.

18 *Thrice a day* : at the three appointed sacrifices.

20 *Producing Trita's name* : literally, begetting, that is, making (*janáyan*) the name of Trita; meaning probably, as Prof. Ludwig suggests, reminding us of Trita, with whom he is closely connected. 'Generating the water of the threefold (Indra).'—Wilson.

21 *The Three Times Seven* : the seven celestial rivers, corresponding to the rivers of earth, multiplied by three to accord with the threefold division of the heavens. According to Sāyaṇa, cows are meant.

23 *Thou didst unbar the cow-stall* : didst recover the cattle stolen by the Paṇis, that is the rays of light that the fiends of darkness had carried off; the great deed of Indra being ascribed to Soma his inspirer.

11 *By rivers and by sheep* : by the purifying waters and the woollen strainer.

14 *His own primeval Sire* : or, the ancient Father of this (All). Indra is meant.

15 *He* : Soma. *His form* : Indra's. *His race* : Indra and the Gods.

16 *Slights not as a Friend the promise of his Friend* : 'the friend leaves not the stomach of his friend.'—Wilson. Sāyaṇa derives *saṁgiram* from *saṁgṛ*, to swallow, instead of from *saṁgṛ*, to assent. *Hundred paths* : through the interstices of the wool.

25 Seven Milch-kine glorify the Tawny-coloured One while with his wave in wool he purifies himself.
The living men, the mighty, have impelled the Sage into the waters' lap, the place of sacrifice.

26 Indu, attaining purity, plunges through the foe, making his ways all easy for the pious man.
Making the kine his mantle, he, the lovely Sage, runs like a sporting courser onward through the fleece.

27 The ceaseless watery fountains with their hundred streams sing, as they hasten near, to him the Golden-hued
Him, clad in robes of milk, swift fingers beautify on the third height and in the luminous realm of heaven.

28 These are thy generations of celestial seed : thou art the Sovran Lord of all the world of life.
This universe, O Pavamāna, owns thy sway; thou, Indu, art the first establisher of Law.

29 Thou art the sea, O Sage who bringest all to light : under thy Law are these five regions of the world.
Thou reachest out beyond the earth, beyond the heavens : thine are the lights, O Pavamāna, thine the Sun.

30 Thou in the filter, Soma Pavamāna, art purified to support the region for the Gods.
The chief, the longing ones have sought to hold thee fast, and all these living creatures have been turned to thee.

31 Onward the Singer travels o'er the fleecy sieve : the Tawny Steer hath bellowed in the wooden vats.
Hymns have been sung aloud in resonant harmony, and holy songs kiss him, the Child who claims our praise.

32 He hath assumed the rays of Sūrya for his robe, spinning, as he knows how, the triply-twisted thread.

He, guiding to the newest rules of Holy Law, comes as the Women's Consort to the special place.

33 On flows the King of rivers and the Lord of heaven : he follows with a shout the paths of Holy Law.
The Golden-hued is poured forth with his hundred streams, Wealth-bringer, lifting up his voice while purified.

34 Fain to be cleansed, thou, Pavamāna, pourest out, like wondrous Sūra, through the fleece, an ample sea.
Purified with the hands, pressed by the men with stones, thou speedest on to mighty booty-bringing war.

35 Thou, Pavamāna, sendest food and power in streams : thou sittest in the beakers as a hawk on trees,
For Indra poured as cheering juice to make him glad, as nearest and far-seeing bearer-up of heaven.

36 The Sisters Seven, the Mothers, stand around the Babe, the noble, new-born Infant, skilled in holy song,
Gandharva of the floods, divine, beholding men, Soma, that he may reign as King of all the world.

37 As Sovran Lord thereof thou passest through these worlds, O Indu, harnessing thy tawny well-winged Mares.
May they pour forth for thee milk and oil rich in sweets : O Soma, let the folk abide in thy decree.

38 O Soma, thou beholdest men from every side : O Pavamāna, Steer, thou wanderest through these.
Pour out upon us wealth in treasure and in gold : may we have strength to live among the things that be.

39 Winner of gold and goods and cattle flow thou on, set as impregner, Indu, mid the worlds of life.
Rich in brave men art thou, Soma, who winnest all : these holy singers wait upon thee with the song.

---

25 *Seven Milch-kine* : the celestial rivers.

26 *Making the kine his mantle*: he who is afterwards covered or mingled with milk.

29 *Thou art the sea* : Soma and the sea being alike producers of rain. *Lights* : stars.

30 *The region* : mid-air; the firmament. *The chief, the longing ones* : the Venas; the Maruts.

32 *Spinning...the triply-twisted thread* : bearing his part in morning, noon-day and evening sacrifice. *The Women's Consort* : Lord and husband of the Waters of heaven. *The special place* : 'the consecrated (vessel).'—Wilson.

34 *Like wondrous Sūra* : adorable like the Sun.

36 *The Sisters Seven* : the great rivers which may provide water for Soma-sacrifices. *Gandharva* : frequently identified with the Sun, here means Soma, the Moon.

37 *Tawny...Mares* : haritaḥ; Harits. Cf. IV. 6. 9; 13. 3; VII. 66. 15; IX. 63. 9.

38 *Through these* : there is no substantive. Sāyaṇa supplies apaḥ, waters.

40 The wave of flowing meath hath wakened up desires : the Steer enrobed in milk plunges into the streams.
Borne on his chariot-sieve the King hath risen to war, and with a thousand rays hath won him high renown.

41 Dear to all life, he sends triumphant praises forth, abundant, bringing off-spring, each succeeding day.
From Indra crave for us, Indu, when thou art quaffed, the blessing that gives children, wealth that harbours steeds.

42 When days begin, the strong juice, lovely, golden-hued, is recognized by wisdom more and more each day,
He, stirring both the Races, goes between the two, the bearer of the word of men and word of Gods.

43 They balm him, balm him over, balm him thoroughly, caress the mighty strength and balm it with the meath.
They seize the flying Steer at the stream's breathing-place : cleansing with gold they grasp the Animal herein.

44 Sing forth to Pavamāna skilled in holy song : the juice is flowing onward like a mighty stream.
He glideth like a serpent from his ancient skin, and like a playful horse the Tawny Steer hath run.

45 Dweller in floods, King, foremost, he displays his might, set among living things as measurer of days.
Distilling oil he flows, fair, billowy, golden-

hued, borne on a car of light, sharing one home with wealth.

46 Loosed is the heavens' support, the up-lifted cheering juice : the triply-mingled draught flows round into the worlds.
The holy hymns caress the stalk that claims our praise, when singers have approached his beauteous robe with song.

47 Thy streams that flow forth rapidly collected run over the fine fleece of the sheep as thou art cleansed.
When, Indu, thou art balmed with milk within the bowl, thou sinkest in the jars, O Soma, when expressed.

48 Winner of power, flow, Soma, worthy of our laud : run onward to the fleece as well-beloved meath.
Destroy, O Indu, all voracious Rākṣasas. With brave sons in the assembly let our speech be bold.

HYMN LXXXVII. Soma Pavamāna.

1. RUN onward to the reservoir and seat thee : cleansed by the men speed forward to the battle.
Making thee beauteous like an able courser, forth to the sacred grass with reins they lead thee.

2 Indu, the well-armed God, is flowing onward, who quells the curse and guards from treacherous onslaught,
Father, begetter of the Gods, most skil-ful, the buttress of the heavens and earth's supporter.

3. Ṛsi and Sage, the Champion of the people, deft and sagacious, Uśanā in wisdom,
He hath discovered even their hidden nature, the Cows' concealed and most mysterious title.

40 Desires : the meaning of vanánāḥ : is not certain ; 'voices (of praise).'—Wilson. With a thousand rays : sahásrabhṛṣṭiḥ : literally, having a thousand edges or sharp points. Cp. IX. 83. 5.

41 The blessing : this seems to be very nearly the meaning of bráhma here, But the word may as usual be rendered by prayer, or devotion. 'Solicit Indra (to give) us food productive of progeny.'—Wilson.

42 When days begin : according to Sāyaṇa, ealry in the morning. The commencement of the year is more probably intended. The second half of the stanza is obscurely expressed. It appears to mean that Soma acts as a mediator between heaven and earth, urging men to offer, and the Gods to receive, worship, bearing up to heaven the hymns and praises of human worshippers and bringing back to them the assurance that their petitions will be granted. Sāyaṇa's explanation is different : 'approaching the two men (the praiser and the worshipper or secular and sacred people) he passes n the midst (of heaven and earth, bestowing), upon the upholder (of the rite) both human and divine (riches).'—Wilson. I follow Ludwig who takes dhaitdri as nominative singular.

43 At the stream's breathing-place : where the stream seems to stay still for a moment to recover breath. Cleansing with gola : with gold-ringed fingers. The Animal : Soma.

45 As measurer of days : Soma being identified with the Moon.

46 Triply-mingled : or, poured into three vessels, the droṇakalaśa, adhavanīya, and pūtabhṛt. Robe : the integu-ments which cover the juice : that is the exterior of the stalk and shoots.

———

3 Uśanā in wisdom : as wise as the celebrated Uśanā. Sāyaṇa explains differently, regarding Uśanā as the dis-coverer : 'Uśanas—he verily by his poetic gift discovered the secret milk of those cows which was hidden and con-cealed.'—Wilson. By title or name of the Cows, water appears to be intended.

4 This thine own Soma rich in meath, O
Indra, Steer for the Steer, hath flowed
into the filter.
The strong Free-giver, winning hundreds,
thousands, hath reached the holy grass
that never fails him.

5 These Somas are for wealth of countless
cattle, renown therefor, and mighty
strength immortal.
These have been sent forth, purified by
strainers, like steeds who rush to battle
fain for glory.

6 He, while he cleanses him, invoked of
many, hath flowed to give the people
all enjoyment.
Thou whom the Falcon brought, bring
dainty viands, bestir thyself and send
us wealth and booty.

7 This Soma, pressed into the cleansing
filter, hath run as 'twere a host let
loose, the Courser;
Like a strong bull who whets his horns
keen-pointed, like a brave warrior in
the fray for cattle.

8 He issued forth from out the loftiest
mountain, and found kine hidden
somewhere in a stable.
Soma's stream clears itself for thee, O
Indra, like lightning thundering through
the clouds of heaven,

9 Cleansing thyself, and borne along with
Indra, Soma, thou goest round the herd
of cattle.
May thy praise help us, Mighty One,
prompt Giver, to the full ample food
which thou bestowest.

HYMN LXXXVIII. *Soma Pavamāna.*

1. FOR thee this Soma is effused, O Indra :
drink of this juice; for thee the stream
is flowing—

Soma, which thou thyself hast made and
chosen, even Indu, for thy special drink
to cheer thee.

2 Like a capacious car hath it been harnessed, the Mighty; to acquire abundant treasures.
Then in the sacrifice they celebrated all
triumphs won by Nahus in the battle.

3 Like Vāyu with his team, moving at
pleasure, most gracious when invoked
like both Nāsatyas,
Thou art thyself like the Wealth-Giver,
Soma ! who grants all boons, like song-
inspiring Pūṣan.

4 Like Indra who hath done great deeds,
thou, Soma, art slayer of the Vṛtras,
Fort-destroyer.
Like Pedu's horse who killed the brood
of serpents, thus thou, O Soma, slayest
every Dasyu.

5 Like Agni loosed amid the forest, fiercely
he winneth splendour in the running
waters.
Like one who fights, the roaring of the
mighty, thus Soma Pavamāna sends his
current.

6 These Somas passing through the fleecy
filter, like rain descending from the
clouds of heaven,
Have been effused and poured into the
beakers, swiftly like rivers running lowly
seaward.

7 Flow onward like the potent band of
Maruts, like that Celestial Host whom
none revileth.
Quickly be gracious unto us like waters, like
sacrifice victorious, thousand-fashioned.

8 Thine are King Varuṇa's eternal statutes,
lofty and deep, O Soma, is thy glory.
All-pure art thou like Mitra the beloved,
adorable, like Aryaman, O Soma.

---

4 *Steer for the Steer* : or, Strong for the Strong.

5 *Mighty strength immortal* : 'ample food and ambrosia.'
—Wilson.

8 *From out the loftiest mountain* : Sāyaṇa makes *antdrd-
draḥ* depend upon *kúcit,* somewhere : 'This Soma stream
has come from on high and has detected the cattle which
were in a stall (hidden) somewhere within the mountain.'—Wilson. Grassmann translates : 'Er ist entsprun-
gen aus dem höchsten Pressstein' 'He hath sprung forth
from the most lofty press-stone.'

9 *The herd of cattle* : Soma accompanies Indra in his
expedition to recover the stolen cattle.—Sāyaṇa. *Or* the
cattle or cows may be the milk with which Soma is mixed.

2 I can make nothing out of the second line of this
stanza. The version which I give as a temporary makeshift is founded on Ludwig's remarks in his Commentary
on the passage. Vol. V. p. 308, of the *Ṛgveda.* Wilson,
following Sāyaṇa, translates :—'After this (*i. e.* after the
harnessing of the waggon—Note.) may all the races of
men expecting our (attack) go to the desirable battle.'
'Now let the races of all men, rising up like trees, come
near to him in order to obtain success,' would, according
to Grassmann, be nearer the meaning.

4 *Pedu's horse* : given to him by the Aśvins. See I.
116. 6; 117. 9; 118. 9; 119. 10.

7 *Like sacrifice* : according to Sāyaṇa, *yajñáḥ,* sacrifice,
means here, worthy of sacrifice :—'(thou art) of a
thousand shapes, adorable like (Indra) the victor in
battle.'—Wilson.

8 This stanza is found also in Book I.91. 3.

HYMN LXXXIX. *Soma Pavamāna.*

1. THIS Chariot-horse hath moved along the pathways, and Pavamāna flowed like rain from heaven.
   With us hath Soma with a thousand currents sunk in the wood, upon his Mother's bosom.

2. King, he hath clothed him in the robe of rivers, mounted the straightest-going ship of Order.
   Sped by the Hawk the drop hath waxed in waters : the father drains it, drains the Father's offspring.

3. They come to him, red, tawny, Lord of Heaven, the watchful Guardian of the meath, the Lion.
   First, Hero in the fight, he seeks the cattle, and with his eye the Steer is our protector.

4. They harness to the broad-wheeled car the mighty Courser whose back bears meath, unwearied, awful.
   The twins, the sisters brighten him, and strengthen—these children of one dame— the vigorous Racer.

5. Four pouring out the holy oil attend him, sitting together in the same container.
   To him they flow, when purified, with homage, and still, from every side, are first about him.

6. He is the buttress of the heavens, supporter of earth, and in his hand are all the people.
   Be the team's Lord a well to thee the singer : cleansed is the sweet plant's stalk for deed of glory.

7. Fighting, uninjured come where Gods are feasted ; Soma, as Vṛtra-slayer flow for Indra.
   Vouchsafe us ample riches very splendid : may we be masters of heroic vigour.

HYMN XC. *Soma Pavamāna,*

1. URGED on, the Father of the Earth and Heaven hath gone forth like a car to gather booty,
   Going to Indra, sharpening his weapons, and in his hand containing every treasure.

2. To him the tones of sacred song have sounded, Steer of the triple height, the Life-bestower.
   Dwelling in wood as Varuṇa in rivers, lavishing treasure he distributes blessings

3. Great Conqueror, warrior-girt, Lord of all heroes, flow on thy way as he who winneth riches ;
   With sharpened arms, with swift bow, never vanquished in battle, vanquishing in fight the foemen.

4. Giving security, Lord of wide dominion, send us both earth and heaven with all their fulness.
   Striving to win the Dawns, the light, the waters, and cattle, call to us abundant vigour.

5. O Soma, gladden Varuṇa and Mitra ; cheer, Indu Pavamāna ! Indra, Viṣṇu.
   Cheer thou the Gods, the Company of Maruts : Indu, cheer mighty Indra to rejoicing.

6. Thus like a wise and potent King flow onward, destroying with thy vigour all misfortunes.
   For our well-spoken hymn give life, O Indu. Do ye preserve us evermore with blessings.

HYMN XCI. *Soma Pavamāna.*

1. As for a chariot-race, the skilful Speaker, Chief, Sage, Inventor, hath, with song, been started.
   The sisters ten upon the fleecy summit drive on the Car-horse to the resting-places.

---

2 *The father drains it* : 'The scholiast finds it difficult to make sense of this : *pitā* (*pālako lokaḥ*) he supposes to mean the *Adhvaryu*, who extracts the juice of the *Soma* which is born from the heaven as from a father; or the first milker may be the *yajamāna* and the second the *Adhvaryu* ; or *duhe* may be repeated out of respect.' Wilson.

4 *Sisters......children of one dame* : the priest's fingers.

5 *Four* : the quarters of the sky. *Container* : the firmament.

6 *The team's Lord* : Soma as resembling Vāyu. Cp. IX. 88. 3. Sāyaṇa explains differently : may (*Soma*) the fountain (of desires) be possessed of horses for thee (his) adorer.'—Wilson.

---

1 *Father* : *janitā* : generator, of earth by sending rain; and of heaven by obtaining oblations for the gods.— —Sāyaṇa.

2 *Of the triple height* : See IX. 71. 7.

4 *Call to us* : send us with thy shout or roar.

6 The hymn ends with the usual concluding half-line of the hymns ascribed to the Vasiṣṭhas.

---

1 *The skilful Speaker* : Soma who makes us eloquent. *The resting-places* : *sádanāni*: the seats, the reservoirs in which he settles,

2 The drop of Soma, pressed by wise Nahuṣyas, becomes the banquet of the Heavenly People—
Indu, by hands of mortal men made beauteous, immortal, with the sheep and cows and waters.

3 Steer roaring unto Steer, this Pavamāna, this juice runs to the white milk of the milch-cow.
Through thousand fine hairs goes the tuneful Singer, like Sūra by his fair and open pathways.

4 Break down the strong seats even of the demons : cleansing thee, Indu, robe thyself in vigour.
Rend with thy swift bolt, coming from above them, those who are near and those who yet are distant.

5 Prepare the forward paths in ancient manner for the new hymn, thou Giver of all bounties.
Those which are high and hard for foes to conquer may we gain from thee, Active ! Food-bestower !

6 So purifying thee vouchsafe us waters, heaven's light, and cows, offspring and many children.
Give us health, ample land, and lights, O Soma, and grant us long to look upon the sunshine.

HYMN XCII. *Soma Pavamāna.*

1. THE gold-hued juice, poured out upon the filter, is started like a car sent forth to conquer.
He hath gained song and vigour while they cleansed him, and hath rejoiced the Gods with entertainments.

2 He who beholdeth man hath reached the filter : bearing his name, the Sage hath sought his dwelling.
The Ṛṣis came to him, seven holy singers, when in the bowls he settled as Invoker.

3 Shared by all Gods, most wise, propitious, Soma goes, while they cleanse him, to his constant station.
Let him rejoice in all his lofty wisdom : to the Five Tribes the Sage attains with labour.

4 In thy mysterious place, O Pavamāna Soma, are all the Gods, the Thrice-Eleven.
Ten on the fleecy height, themselves, self-prompted, and seven fresh rivers, brighten and adorn thee.

5 Now let this be the truth of Pavamāna, there where all singers gather them together,
That he hath given us room and made the daylight, hath holpen Manu and repelled the Dasyu.

6 As the priest seeks the station rich in cattle, like a true King who goes to great assemblies,
Soma hath sought the beakers while they cleansed him, and like a wild bull, in the wood hath settled.

HYMN XCIII. *Soma Pavamāna.*

1. TEN sisters, pouring out the rain together, swift-moving thinkers of the sage, adorn him.
Hither hath run the gold-hued Child of Sūrya and reached the vat like a fleet vigorous courser.

2 Even as a youngling crying to his mothers, the bounteous Steer hath flowed along to waters.
As youth to damsel, so with milk he hastens on to the chose meeting-place, the beaker.

3 Yea, swollen is the udder of the milch-cow : thither in streams goes very sapient Indu.

---

2 *Nahuṣyas* : probably a neighbouring people. See VI. 46. 7, and note on *Nahuṣas* which has the same meaning.

3 *Sūra* : Sūrya, the Sun. *Fair and open: adhvasmábhiḥ* : 'imperishable.'—Wilson.

5 *Those* : portions of thee, according to Sāyaṇa.

6 In the second half of the stanza, instead of taking *urú*, wide, ample, with *kṣetram*, field, land. Sāyaṇa joins it, as=*ur úṇi*, with *jyotíṁṣi*, lights :—'make our land prosper, diffuse the luminaries widely (in the firmament).'—Wilson.

---

2 *The Ṛṣis*: according to Sāyaṇa, Bharadvāja, Kaśyapa, Gotama, Atri, Viśvāmitra, Jamadagni, Vasiṣṭha.

---

3 *The Five Tribes* : the five Āryan tribes. According to Sāyaṇa, 'the five classes of beings.' *i. e.*, four castes and the Niṣādas.
4 *The Thrice-Eleven* : See I. 139. 11. *Ten* : the fingers.
5 *Manu* : as the representative of the Āryan race.
6 *The station rich in cattle* : 'the hall where the victim is stationed.'—Wilson. *To great assemblies* : or, to war and battle. *The wood* : the wooden vat or reservoir.

---

1 *Ten sisters* : the fingers which press out the juice of the Soma-plant. *Thinkers* : or thoughts, devotions. According to Sāyaṇa, fingers. *Child of Sūrya* : Sāyaṇa explains *jáḥ*, offspring, by *jáyáḥ* wives, *i.e.*, the quarters of the heaven, called Sūrya's wives because they are made manifest by his rays.

The kine make ready, as with new-washed treasures, the Head and Chief with milk within the vessels.

4 With all the Gods, O Indu Pavamāna, while thou art roaring send us wealth in horses.
Hither upon her car come willing Plenty, inclined to us, to give us of her treasures.

5 Now unto us mete riches, while they cleanse thee, all-glorious, swelling wealth, with store of heroes.
Long be his life who worships thee, O Indu. May he, enriched with prayer, come soon and early.

HYMN XCIV.   *Soma Pavamāna.*

1. WHEN beauties strive for him as for a charger, then strive the songs like soldiers for the sunlight.
Acting the Sage, he flows enrobed in waters and song as 'twere a stall that kine may prosper.

2 The worlds expand to him who from aforetime found light to spread the law of life eternal.
The swelling songs, like kine within the stable, in deep devotion call aloud on Indu.

3 When the sage bears his holy wisdom round him, like a car visiting all worlds, the Hero,
Becoming fame, mid Gods, unto the mortal, wealth to the skilled, worth praise mid the Ever-present.

4 For glory born he hath come forth to glory : he giveth life and glory to the singers.

3 *The Head and Chief* : 'the elevated *Soma.*'—Wilson.
4 *Send us*: more literally, open or disclose to us.
5 The hymn ends with the half-line which is the special conclusion of the hymns ascribed to Nodhas. See Book I. 58, 60—64.

1 The meaning is apparently : when the beautifying 'waters hasten emulously to cleanse Soma as though he were a horse, the voices of singing worshippers vie with each other like the shouts of men who are fighting for light and life. Soma flows on in his wisdom, blent with the waters, and surrounded with hymns into the midst of which he enters as into a stable full of kine in order to make them increase and multiply.

3 The stanza is somewhat obscure. *Worth praise* : or, adorable. *The Ever-present* : the Gods who come to help men. Wilson, following Sāyaṇa, translates the second line : 'then desirous of bestowing upon mortals the wealth that abides with the gods, he (is) to be glorified in the many places of sacrifice for the preservation of the riches he has given.'

They, clothed in glory, have become immortal. He, measured in his course, makes frays successful.

5 Stream to us food and vigour, kine and horses : give us broad lights and fill the Gods with rapture.
All these are easy things for thee to master : thou, Pavamāna Soma, quellest foemen.

HYMN XCV   *Soma Pavamāna.*

1. LOUD neighs the Tawny Steed when started, settling deep in the wooden vessel while they cleanse him.
Led by the men he takes the milk for raiment : then shall he, through his powers, engender praise-songs.

2 As one who rows drives on his boat, he, Gold-hued, sends forth his voice, loosed on the path of Order.
As God, the secret names of Gods he utters, to be declared on sacred grass more widely.

3 Hastening onward like the waves of waters, our holy hymns are pressing nigh to Soma.
To him they come with lowly adoration, and, longing, enter him who longs to meet them.

4 They drain the stalk, the Steer who dwells on mountains, even as a Bull who decks him on the upland.
Hymns follow and attend him as he bellows : Trita bears Varuna aloft in ocean.

5 Sending thy voice out as Director, loosen the Invoker's thought, O Indu, as they cleanse thee.
While thou and Indra rule for our advantage, may we be masters of heroic vigour.

5 *All these* : all the Rākṣasas, according to Sāyaṇa.

1 *Deep in the wooden vessel* : literally 'in the belly of the wood.'

2 *He utters* : reveals to the priest who is to declare them at sacrifice.

4 *Trita* : The preparer of the celestial Soma. *Varuṇa* : here meaning Soma; 'the defeater of enemies.'—Wilson *In ocean* : in the firmament.

5 *As Director* : *upavaktéva* : *upavaktá* here appears to mean Adhvaryu : *yathādhvaryuḥ*—Sāyaṇa. *Loosen the Invoker's thought* : aid the Hotar or invoking priest to give free utterance to his thought or hymn.

HYMN XCVI. *Soma Pavamāna*

1. IN forefront of the cars forth goes the Hero, the Leader, winning spoil : his host rejoices.
Soma endues his robes of lasting colours, and blesses, for his friends, their calls on Indra.

2 Men decked with gold adorn his golden tendril, incessantly with steed-impelling homage.
The Friend of Indra mounts his car : well-knowing, he comes thereon to meet the prayer we offer.

3 O God, for service of the Gods flow onward, for food sublime, as Indra's drink, O Soma.
Making the floods, bedewing earth and heaven, come from the vast, comfort us while we cleanse thee

4 Flow for prosperity and constant vigour, flow on for happiness and high perfection.
This is the wish of these friends assembled : this is my wish, O Soma Pavamāna.

5 Father of holy hymns, Soma flows onward, the Father of the earth, Father of heaven :
Father of Agni, Sūrya's generator, the Father who begat Indra and Viṣṇu.

6 Brahman of Gods, the Leader of the poets, Ṛṣi of sages, Bull of savage creatures,
Falcon amid the vultures, Axe of forests, over the cleansing sieve goes Soma singing.

7 He, Soma Pavamāna, like a river, hath stirred the wave of voice, our songs and praises.
Beholding these inferior powers in cattle, he rests among them as a Steer well-knowing.

8 As Gladdener, Warrior never harmed in battle, with thousand genial streams, pour strength and vigour.
As thoughtful Pavamāna, urge O Indu, speeding the kine, the plant's wave on to Indra.

9 Dear, grateful to the Gods, on to the beaker moves Soma, sweet to Indra, to delight him.
With hundred powers, with thousand currents, Indu, like a strong car-horse, goes to the assembly.

10 Born in old time as finder-out of treasures, drained with the stone, decking himself in waters,
Warding off curses, King of all existence, he shall find way for prayer the while they cleanse him.

11 For our sage fathers, Soma Pavamāna, of old performed, by thee, their sacred duties.
Fighting unvanquished, open the enclosures : enrich us with large gifts of steeds and heroes.

12 As thou didst flow for Manu Life-bestowing, Foe-queller, Comforter, rich in oblations,
Even thus flow onward now conferring riches : combine with Indra, and bring forth thy weapons.

13 Flow onward, Soma, rich in sweets and holy, enrobed in waters on the fleecy summit.
Settle in vessels that are full of fatness, as cheering and most gladdening drink for Indra.

14 Pour, hundred-streamed, winner of thousands, mighty at the Gods' banquet, pour the rain of heaven,
While thou with rivers roarest in the beaker, and blent with milk prolongest our existence.

15 Purified with our holy hymns, this Soma o'ertakes malignities like some strong charger,
Like fresh milk poured by Aditi, like

---

1 *Of lasting colours* : *rabhasāni* : 'hastily made.'—Wilson. 'Brilliant.'—Grassmann.

2 *Steed-impelling*: urging him on, as a whip urges on a horse.

3 *From the vast* : from the wide firmament. There is no substantive in the text.

6 *Brahman of Gods* : thou art Bṛhaspati, the Lord of Prayer, among the Gods, or, chief among the priests. *Axe* : the handle of the axe being naturally made of the strongest wood.—M. Müller, Ludwig thinks that lightning may be intended. According to the St. Petersburg Lexicon, *svadhitiḥ* here means a tree with very hard wood. See V. 32. 10.

7 The second line is obscure. Wilson translates : 'the showerer (of benefits) beholding the hidden (treasure) presides over these irresistible powers, knowing about the cattle.'

9 *Goes to the assembly* : 'proceeds like a strong horse to battle.'—Wilson.

11 *The enclosures* : the obstructions which keep the rain from falling.

13 *Full of fatness* : *ghṛtāvānti* according to Sāyaṇa, 'water-holding .

15 *By Aditi* : regarding as the Cosmic Cow.

passage in ample room, or like a docile car-horse.

16 Cleansed by the pressers, armed with noble weapons, stream to us the fair secret name thou bearest.

Pour booty, like a horse, for love of glory : God, Soma, send us kine, and send us Vāyu.

17 They deck him at his birth, the lovely Infant, the Maruts with their troop adorn the Car-horse.

By songs a Poet and a Sage by wisdom, Soma goes singing through the cleansing filter.

18 Light-winner, Ṛṣi-minded, Ṛṣi-maker, hymned in a thousand hymns, Leader of sages,

A Steer who strives to gain his third form, Soma is, like Virāj, resplendent as a Singer.

19 Hawk seated in the bowls, Bird wide-extended, the Banner seeking kine and wielding weapons,

Following close the sea, the wave of waters, the great Bull tells his fourth form and declares it.

20 Like a fair youth who decorates his body, a courser rushing to the gain of riches,

A steer to herds, so, flowing to the pitcher, he with a roar hath passed into the beakers.

21 Flow on with might as Pavamāna, Indu : flow loudly roaring through the fleecy filter.

Enter the beakers sporting, as they cleanse thee, and let thy gladdening juice make Indra joyful.

22 His streams have been effused in all their fulness, and he hath entered, balmed with milk, the goblets.

Singing his psalm, well-skilled in song, a Chanter, he comes as 'twere to his friend's sister roaring.

16 *Vāyu* : the breath of life, life.—Sāyaṇa.

18 *His third form* : the form that he wears in heaven; 'the third region (heaven).'—Wilson . *Virāj* : splendid or most illustrious Indra.—Sāyaṇa.

19 *The banner* : *drapsáḥ* : usually meaning, a drop, or a spark. See IV. 13. 2. *His fourth form* : the Moon. According to Sāyaṇa, the region of the Moon which is said to be above that of the Sun.

22 *As 'twere to his friend's sister* : Sāyaṇa explains *jāmím*, sister, by *jāyām*, wife : 'like (a libertine) to the wife of a friend.'—Wilson. The meaning is probably no more than 'as lover to his darling' in the following stanza.

23 Chasing our foes thou comest, Pavamāna ! Indu, besung, as lover to his darling.

As a bird flies and settles in the forest, thus Soma settles, purified, in goblets.

24 With full stream and abundant milk, O Soma, thy beams come, like a woman, as they cleanse thee.

He, gold-hued, rich in boons, brought to the waters, hath roared within the goblet of the pious.

HYMN XCVII.   *Soma Pavamāna*

1. MADE pure by this man's urgent zeal and impulse the God hath to the Gods his juice imparted.

He goes, effused and singing, to the filter, like priest to measured seats supplied with cattle.

2 Robed in fair raiment meet to wear in battle, a mighty Sage pronouncing invocations.

Roll onward to the beakers as they cleanse thee, far-seeing at the feast of Gods, and watchful.

3 Dear, he is brightened on the fleecy summit, a Prince among us, nobler than the noble.

Roar out as thou art purified, run forward. Do ye preserve us evermore with blessings.

4 Let us sing praises to the Gods : sing loudly, send ye the Soma forth for mighty riches:

Let him flow, sweetly-flavoured, through the filter, and let our pious one rest in the pitcher.

5 Winning the friendship of the Deities, Indu flows in a thousand streams to make them joyful.

Praised by the men after the ancient statute, he hath come nigh, for our great bliss, to Indra.

6 Flow, Gold-hued, cleansing thee, to enrich the singer : let thy juice go to Indra to support him.

Come nigh, together with the Gods, for bounty. Do ye preserve us evermore with blessings.

1 *Urgent zeal and impulse* : *hemánā*, by impulse (from the root *hi*) is said by Sāyaṇa to mean 'by gold,' that is, by the gold-adorned hand of the priest. *Measured seats supplied with cattle* : 'the halls prepared (for sacrifice) containing victims.'—Wilson.   *Singing* : the sound of the flowing juice is compared to the priest's recitation of sacred texts.

7 The God declares the Deities' generations,
　　like Uṣaṇā, proclaiming lofty wisdom.
　With brilliant kin, far-ruling, sanctifying,
　　the Boar advances, singing, to the places.

8 The Swans, the Vṛṣagaṇas from anear us
　　have brought their restless spirit to our
　　dwelling.
　Friends come to Pavamāna meet for
　　praises, and sound in concert their
　　resistless music.

9 He follows the Wide-strider's rapid move-
　　ment : cows low, as 'twere, to him who
　　sports at pleasure.
　He with the sharpened horns brings forth
　　abundance : the Silvery shines by night,
　　by day the Golden.

10 Strong Indu, bathed in milk, flows on for
　　Indra, Soma exciting strength, to make
　　him joyful.
　He quells malignities and slays the demons,
　　the King of mighty power who brings
　　us comfort.

11 Then in a stream he flows, milked out
　　with press-stones, mingled with sweetness,
　　through the fleecy filter—
　Indu rejoicing in the love of Indra, the
　　God who gladdens, for the God's enjoy-
　　ment.

12 As he is purified he pours out treasures,
　　a God bedewing Gods with his own
　　juices.
　Indu hath, wearing qualities by seasons,
　　on the raised fleece engaged the ten
　　swift fingers.

13 The Red Bull bellowing to the kine ad-
　　vances, causing the heavens and earth
　　to roar and thunder.
　Well is he heard like Indra's shout in

battle : letting this voice be known he
　hastens hither.

14 Swelling with milk, abounding in sweet
　　flavours, urging the meath-rich plant
　　thou goest onward.
　Raising a shout thou flowest as they
　　cleanse thee, when thou, O Soma, art
　　effused for Indra.

15 So flow thou on inspiriting, for rapture,
　　aiming death-shafts at him who stays
　　the waters,
　Flow to us wearing thy resplendent colour,
　　effused and eager for the kine, O Soma.

16 Pleased with us, Indu, send us as thou
　　flowest good easy paths in ample space
　　and comforts.
　Dispelling, as 'twere with a club, misfor-
　　tunes, run o'er the height, run o'er the
　　fleecy summit.

17 Pour on us rain celestial, quickly stream-
　　ing, refreshing, fraught with health and
　　ready bounty.
　Flow, Indu, send these Winds thy lower
　　kinsmen, setting them free like locks of
　　hair unbraided.

18 Part, like a knotted tangle, while they
　　cleanse thee, O Soma, righteous and
　　unrighteous conduct.
　Neigh like a tawny courser who is loosen-
　　ed, come like a youth, O God, a house-
　　possessor.

19 For the God's service, for delight, O Indu,
　　run o'er the height, run o'ver the fleecy
　　summit.
　With thousand streams, inviolate, sweet-
　　scented, flow on for gain of strength
　　that conquers heroes.

20 Without a car, without a rein to guide
　　them, unyoked, like coursers started in
　　the contest,
　These brilliant drops of Soma juice run
　　forward. Do ye, O Deities, come nigh
　　to drink them.

21 So for our banquet of the Gods, O Indu,
　　pour down the rain of heaven into the
　　vessels.
　May Soma grant us riches sought with
　　longing, mighty, exceeding strong, with
　　store of heroes.

22 What time the loving spirit's word had
　　formed him Chief of all food, by statute
　　of the Highest,

---

7 *The God* : Soma, who has been called the Father of
Gods. *Like Uṣaṇā* : the sound of the flowing and dropping Soma juice is likened to the song of the famous sage
and sacred poet. *The Boar* : strong, swift Soma.
Singing : making a sound with the descending drops of
juice. Sāyaṇa explains differently :—'making a noise
(as) a wild boar (makes a noise) with its foot.' Wilson.
The places : the filters.

8 *The Swans* : the singers, descendants of the Ṛṣi
Vṛṣagaṇa.

9 *The Wide-strider's rapid movement* : the swift course
of the Sun. *Cows low as 'twere* : Sāyaṇa explains *gāvaḥ,*
cows, by *anye gantāraḥ.* other goers, takes *nd* as negative, and derives *mimate* from *mā,* to measure, instead of
from *mā,* to bleat or low :—'other goers cannot overtake
him (though he is) moving easily.'—Wilson. *He with
the sharpened horns* : Soma as the Moon : the silvery light
by night and the golden-coloured juice by day.

12 *Wearing qualities by seasons* : 'clothed in pleasant
radiance according to the season.'—Wilson.

15 *Him who stays the waters* : Vṛtra.
17 *Winds* : cf. 'Vāyu is Soma's guardian God' (X.
85. 5).
22 Sāyaṇa's explanation of the first line is extremely
laboured :—'When the praise of the zealous worshipper

Then loudly lowing came the cows to Indu, the chosen, well-loved Master in the beaker.

23 The Sage, Celestial, liberal, raining bounties, pours as he flows the Genuine for the Truthful.
The King shall be effectual strength's upholder : he by the ten bright reins is mostly guided.

24 He who beholds mankind, made pure with filters, the King supreme of Deities and mortals,
From days of old is Treasure-Lord of riches : he, Indu, cherishes fair well-kept Order.

25 Haste, like a steed, to victory for glory, to Indra's and to Vāyu's entertainment.
Give us food ample, thousandfold : be, Soma, the finder-out of riches when they cleanse thee.

26 Effused by us let God-delighting Somas bring as they flow a home with noble heroes.
Rich in all boons like priests acquiring favour, the worshippers of heaven, the best of Cheerers.

27 So, God, for service of the Gods flow onward, flow, drink of Gods, for ample food, O Soma.
For we go forth to war against the mighty : make heaven and earth well stablished by thy cleansing.

28 Thou, yoked by strong men, neighest like a courser, swifter than thought is, like an awful lion.
By paths directed hitherward, the straightest, send thou us happiness, Indu, while they cleanse thee.

29 Sprung from the Gods, a hundred streams, a thousand, have been effused : sages prepare and purge them.
Bring us from heaven the means of winnning, Indu; thou art forerunnner of abundant riches.

30 The streams of days were poured as'twere from heaven : the wise King doth not treat his friend unkindly.

Like a son following his father's wishes, grant to this family success and safety.

31 Now are thy streams poured forth with all their sweetness, when, purified. thou goest through the filter.
The race of kine is thy gift, Pavamāna: when born thou madest Sūrya rich with brightness.

32 Bright, bellowing along the path of Order, thou shinest as the form of life eternal.
Thou flowest on as gladdening drink for Indra, sending thy voice out with the hymns of sages.

33 Pouring out streams at the Gods' feast with service, thou, Soma, lookest down, a heavenly Eagle.
Enter the Soma-holding beaker, Indu, and with a roar approach the ray of Sūrya.

34 Three are the voices that the Courser utters : he speaks the thought of prayer, the law of Order.
To the Cow's Master come the Cows inquiring : the hymns with eager longing come to Soma.

35 To Soma come the Cows, the Milch-kine longing, to Soma sages with their hymns inquiring.
Soma, effused, is purified and blended : our hymns and Tṛṣṭup songs unite in Soma.

36 Thus, Soma, as we pour thee into vessels, while thou art purified flow for our welfare.
Pass into Indra with a mighty roaring make the voice swell, and generate abundance.

37 Singer of true songs, ever-watchful, Soma hath settled in the ladles when they cleanse him.
Him the Adhvaryus, paired and eager, follow, leaders of sacrifice and skilful-handed.

38 Cleansed near the Sun as 'twere, he as Creator hath filled full heaven and earth, and hath disclosed them.
He by whose dear help men gain all their wishes shall yield the precious meed as to a victor.

sanctifies him as that of a noisy (crowd) in front (praises) a distinguished (prince) for the support (he affords).'—Wilson.

23 *The Genuine for the Truthful* : ṛtám ṛtáya : the Soma juice for Indra. *The ten bright reins* : or rays, i.e., the fingers. The half-line is difficult.

30 *The streams of days* : the libations of Soma juice which we offered every day. *Like a son* : the Soma juice is regarded as the son of the yajamāna or sacrificer who causes it to be prepared.

34 *The Courser*: is Soma, and the three voices (vācaḥ), or words which he utters are according to Sāyaṇa praises or sacred texts in the form of the three Vedas. The three tones, low, middle, and high, are probably intended. Or váhniḥ (the courser) may mean the bearer of the oblation, yajamāna, as Sāyaṇa explains.

39 He, being cleansed, the Strengthener and
Increaser, Soma the Bounteous, helped
us with his lustre,
Wherewith our sires of old who knew the
footsteps found light and stole the cattle
from the mountain.

40 In the first vault of heaven loud roared
the Ocean, King of all being, generating creatures.
Steer, in the filter, on the fleecy summit,
Soma, the Drop effused, hath waxen
mighty.

41 Soma the Steer, in that as Child of Waters
he chose the Gods, performed that great
achievement.
He, Pavamāna, granted strength to Indra;
he, Indu, generated light in Sūrya.

42 Make Vāyu glad, for furtherance and
bounty : cheer Varuṇa and Mitra, as
they cleanse thee.
Gladden the Gods, gladden the host of
Maruts : make Heaven and Earth rejoice,
O God, O Soma.

43 Flow onward righteous slayer of the wicked,
driving away our enemies and sickness,
Blending thy milk with milk which cows
afford us. We are thy friends, thou art
the Friend of Indra.

44 Pour us a fount of meath, a spring of
treasure ; send us a hero son and happy
fortune.
Be sweet to Indra when they cleanse thee,
Indu, and pour down riches on us from
the ocean.

45 Strong Soma, pressed, like an impetuous
courser, hath flowed in stream as a
flood speeding downward.
Cleansed, he hath settled in his wooden
dwelling : Indu hath flowed with milk
and with the waters.

46 Strong, wise, for thee who longest for his
coming this Soma here flows to the
bowls, O Indra.
He, chariot-borne, sun-bright, and truly
potent, was poured forth like the longing
of the pious.

47 He, purified with ancient vital vigour,
pervading all his Daughter's forms and
figures,

Finding his threefold refuge in the waters,
goes singing, as a priest, to the assemblies.

48 Now, chariot-borne, flow unto us, God
Soma, as thou art purified flow to the
saucers,
Sweetest in waters, rich in meath, and
holy, as Savitar the God is, truthful-
minded.

49 To feast him, flow mid song and hymn,
to Vāyu, flow purified to Varuṇa and
Mitra.
Flow to the song-inspiring car-borne Hero,
to mighty Indra, him who wields the
thunder.

50 Pour on us garments that shall clothe us
meetly, send, purified, milch-kine, abundant yielders.
God Soma, send us chariot-drawing horses
that they may bring us treasures bright
and golden.

51 Send to us in a stream celestial riches,
send us, when thou art cleansed, what
earth containeth,
So that thereby we may acquire possessions
and Ṛṣihood in Jamadagni's manner.

52 Pour forth this wealth with this purification : flow onward to the yellow lake,
O Indu.
Here, too, the Ruddy, wind-swift, full of
wisdom, shall give a son to him who
cometh quickly.

53 Flow on for us with this purification to
the famed ford of thee whose due is
glory.
May the Foe-queller shake us down, for
triumph, like a tree's ripe fruit, sixty
thousand treasures.

54 Eagerly do we pray for those two exploits,
at the blue lake and Pṛṣana, wrought
in battle.

51 *Ṛṣihood in Jamadagni's manner* : 'make our sacred
prayer (sweet) as Jamadagni.'—Wilson.

52 *Yellow*: the meaning of *māṁścatvé* is uncertain. See
VII. 44. 3, note.

53 *To the famed ford* : possibly, as Ludwig suggests,
the aid of Soma is craved at some ford of a neighbouring
river, famous on account of a battle that has been fought
there, and destined to be the scene of an approaching
conflict.

54 The first line is conjecturally translated after
Ludwig, who takes *Pṛṣana* to be the name of a place.
Sāyaṇa's elaborate explanation is different :—'These
two great acts, the raining (of arrows) and the humilia-
tion (of foes) are the givers of happiness ; they are deadly
either in a fight on horseback or in a hand-to-hand fight.'
—Wilson. Here Sāyaṇa explains *māṁścatvé* (at the blue or

40 *In the first vault* : that is in the highest firmament.
The Ocean : Soma.

47 *His Daughter's forms and figures* : Soma pervades,
and imparts a share of his nutritious power to, the grass,
herbs, and shrubs which are the varied forms assumed
by Earth his daughter.

He sent our enemies to sleep and slew them, and turned away the foolish and unfriendly.

55 Thou comest unto three extended filters, and hastenest through each one as they cleanse thee.
Thou art the giver of the gift, a Bhaga, a Maghavan for liberal lords, O Indu.

56 This Soma here, the Wise, the All-obtainer, flows on his way as King of all existence.
Driving the drops at our assemblies, Indu completely traverses the fleecy filter.

57 The Great Inviolate are kissing Indu, and singing in his place like eager sages.
The wise men send him forth with ten swift fingers, and balm his form with essence of the waters.

58 Soma, may we, with thee as Pavamāna, pile up together all our spoil in battle.
This boon vouchsafe us Varuṇa and Mitra, and Aditi and Sindhu, Earth and Heaven.

HYMN XCVIII. *Soma Pavamāna*

1. STREAM on us riches that are sought by many, best at winning strength,
Riches, O Indu, thousandfold, glorious, conquering the great.

2 Effused, he hath, as on a car, invested him in fleecy mail :
Onward hath Indu flowed in streams, impelled, surrounded by the wood.

3 Effused, this Indu hath flowed on, distilling rapture, to the fleece :
He goes erect, as seeking kine in stream, with light, to sacrifice.

4 For thou thyself, O Indu, God, to every mortal worshipper
Attractest riches thousandfold, made manifest in hundred forms.

5 Good Vṛtra-slayer, may we be still nearest to this wealth of thine

Which many crave, nearest to food and happiness, Resistless One !

6 Whom, bright with native splendour, crushed between the pair of pressing-stones—
The wavy Friend whom Indra loves—the twice-five sisters dip and bathe,

7 Him with the fleece they purify, brown, golden-hued, beloved of all,
Who with exhilarating juice goes forth to all the Deities.

8 Through longing for this sap of yours ye drink what brings ability,
Even him who, dear as heaven's own light, gives to our princes high renown.

9 Indu at holy rites produced you, Heaven and Earth, the Friends of men,
Hill-haunting God the Goddesses. They bruised him where the roar was loud.

10 For Vṛtra-slaying Indra, thou, Soma, art poured that he may drink,
Poured for the guerdon-giving man, poured for the God who sitteth there.

11 These ancient Somas, at the break of day, have flowed into the sieve,
Snorting away at early morn these foolish evil-hearted ones.

12 Friends, may the princes, ye and we, obtain this Most Resplendent One.
Gain him who hath the smell of strength, win him whose home is very strength.

HYMN XCIX. *Soma Pavamāna.*

1. THEY for the Bold and Lovely One ply manly vigour like a bow :

---

9 This stanza is difficult. Sāyaṇa explains it differently :—'Divine heaven and earth the progeny of Manu, the *Soma* juice is generated at your sacrifices, radiant, abiding in the grinding stones ; (the priests) bruise him at the loud-sounding ceremony.'— Wilson. *Hill-haunting*: cf. IX. 85. 10.

10 *For the guerdon-giving man* : for the good of the institutor of the sacrifice.

11 *Snorting away* : driving away with the bubbling sound they make

12 *Who hath the smell of strength* : *vājagandhyam* : 'fragrant and invigorating.'—Wilson. 'Forming or having a wagon-load of goods or spoil.'—S. P. Lexicon. *Him whose home is strength* : *vājapastyam* : 'food and dwellings.' —Wilson. 'Him who has a house full of goods.'—S. P. Lexicon.

---

yellow lake ?) by 'in battle with horses,' and *pṛsane* (at Pṛṣana !) by 'in close, or hand-to-hand encounter.' Two victories appear to be referred to, and that is about all that can be said.

55 The *three extended filters* are said to be fire, wind, and sun, in addition to the one artificial filter of wool.

57 *The Great Inviolate* : the Gods. *Kissing* : or sipping.

58 *All our spoil in battle* : yet to be won in the approaching fight wherein we look to Soma for help and victory.

---

2 *By the wood* : the wooden vat or trough.

3 *Seeking kine* : desirous of the milk which is to be ixed with his juice.

1 *They* : the priests. *Ply manly vigour like a bow* : 'stretch the bow of manhood.'—Wilson.They exert all their manly strength, or as Benfey suggests, attack and storm the God with prayer and sacrifice, 'beseeching and besieging' as Milton says. *The Lord Divine* : the Asura (Zend, Ahura), here meaning Soma.

Joyous, in front of songs they weave bright
raiment for the Lord Divine.

2 And he, made beautiful by night, dips
forward into strengthening food,
What time the sacrificer's thoughts speed
on his way the Golden-hued.

3 We cleanse this gladdening drink of his,
the juice which Indra chiefly drinks,—
That which kine took into their mouths,
of old, and princes take it now.

4 To him, while purifying, they have raised
the ancient psalm of praise:
And sacred songs which bear the names of
Gods have supplicated him.

5 They purify him as he drops, courageous,
in the fleecy sieve.
Him they instruct as messenger to bear
the sage's morning prayer.

6 Soma, best Cheerer, takes his seat, the
while they cleanse him in the bowls.
He as it were impregns the cow, and
babbles on, the Lord of Song.

7 He is effused and beautified, a God for
Gods, by skilful men.
He penetrates the mighty floods collecting
all he knows therein.

8 Pressed, Indu, guided by the men, thou
art led to the cleaning sieve.
Thou, yielding Indra highest joy, takest
thy seat within the bowls.

HYMN C.   *Soma Pavamāna.*

1. THE Guileless Ones are singing praise to
Indra's well beloved Friend,
As, in the morning of its life, the mothers
lick the new-born calf.

2 O Indu, while they cleanse thee, bring,
O Soma, doubly-waxing wealth:
Thou in the worshipper's abode causest all
treasures to increase.

3 Set free the song which mind hath yoked,
even as thunder frees the rain:
All treasures of the earth and heaven, O
Soma, thou dost multiply.

4 Thy stream when thou art pressed runs
on like some victorious warrior's steed,
Hastening onward through the fleece like
a swift horse who wins the prize.

5 Flow on, Sage Soma, with thy stream to
give us mental power and strength,
Effused for Indra, for his drink, for Mitra
and for Varuṇa.

6 Flow to the filter with thy stream, effused,
best winner, thou, of spoil,
O Soma, as most rich in sweets for Indra,
Viṣṇu, and the Gods.

7 The mothers, void of guiles, caress thee
Golden-coloured, in the sieve,
As cows, O Pavamāna, lick the new-born
calf, as Law commands.

8 Thou, Pavamāna, movest on with wondrous rays to great renown.
Striving within the votary's house thou
drivest all the glooms away.

9 Lord of great sway, thou liftest thee above
the heavens, above the earth.
Thou, Pavamāna hast assumed thy coat
of mail in majesty.

HYMN CI.   *Soma Pavamāna*

1. FOR first possession of your juice, for the
exhilarating drink,
Drive ye away the dog, my friends, drive
ye the long-tongued dog away.

2 He who with purifying stream, effused,
comes flowing hitherward,
Indu, is like an able steed.

3 The men with all-pervading song send
unassailable Soma forth,
By pressing-stones, to sacrifice.

4 The Somas, very rich in sweets, for which
the sieve is destined, flow,
Effused, the source of Indra's joy: may
your strong juices reach the Gods.

5 Indu flows on for Indra's sake: thus
have the Deities declared.
The Lord of Speech exerts himself, Ruler
of all, because of might.

---

2 *By night* : *kṣapā* : 'at the end of the night.'—Wilson.
Ludwig translates *kṣapā* by 'der fürst,' 'the prince.'

3 *Which kine took into their mouths* : in the form of the
juices of grass from which the milky portion of the libation
is evolved.

4 Sāyaṇa's explanation of the second line of this stanza,
is different : —'and the fingers exercising their pressure
are able (to prepare the oblation) for the gods.'—Wilson.

6 *He as it were impregns the cow* : meaning, perhaps, as
Ludwig suggests, that the milk becomes efficacious as
a libation only when it is mixed with Soma-juice.

7 *Collecting all he knows therein* : the meaning of this
half-line is not clear : —'when he is recognized amongst
these (people) as the giver (of riches).'—Wilson.

1 *The Guileless Ones* : the *vasatīvarī* waters.

7 *As Law commands* : *vídharmaṇi* : see Bergaigne, *La
Religion Védique*, 111. 218. note 2. 'At the sacrifice.'—
—Wilson. 'In the realm of heaven.'—Grassmann.

9 *Thy coat of mail* : *drāpím* : See IX. 86. 14.

1 *Drive ye away* : prevent dogs or Rākṣasas from drinking the Soma juice.

6 Inciter of the voice of song, with thousand streams the ocean flows,
Even Soma, Lord of opulence, the Friend of Indra, day by day.

7 As Pūṣan, Fortune, Bhaga, comes this Soma while they make him pure.
He, Lord of the multitude, hath looked upon the earth and heaven.

8 The dear cows lowed in joyful mood together to the gladdening drink.
The drops as they were purified, the Soma juices, made then paths.

9 O Pavamāna, bring the juice, the mightiest, worthy to be famed,
Which the Five Tribes have over them, whereby we may win opulence.

10 For us the Soma juices flow, the drops best furtherers of our weal,
Effused as friends without a spot, benevolent, finders of the light.

11 Effused by means of pressing-stones, upon the ox-hide visible,
They, treasure-finders, have announced food unto us from every side. •

12 These Soma juices, skilled in song, purified, blent with milk and curd,
When moving and when firmly laid in oil, resemble lovely Suns.

13 Let not the power of men restrain the voice of the outpouring Juice :
As Bhṛgu's sons chased Makha, so drive ye the greedy hound away.

14 The Friend hath wrapped him in his robe, as in his parents arms, a son.
He went, as lover to a dame, to take his station suitor-like.

15 That Hero who produces strength, he who hath propped both worlds apart,
Gold-hued, hath wrapped him in the sieve, to settle, priest-like, in his place.

16 Soma upon the ox's skin through the sheep's wool flows purified.
Bellowing out, the Tawny Steer goes on to Indra's special place.

HYMN CII.   Soma Pavamāna.

1. THE Child, when blended with the streams, speeding the plan of sacrifice,
Surpasses all things that are dear, yea, from of old.

1'3 *Makha* : apparently, a demon whose name does not occur again in the Ṛgveda.

16 *Special place* : 'prepared station.'—Wilson. The vessel containing the libation appropriated to Indra.

---

1 *The streams* : literally 'the great,' 'waters' being understood.

2 The place, near the two pressing-stones of Trita, hath he occupied,
Secret and dear through seven lights of sacrifice.

3 Urge to three courses, on the heights of Trita, riches in a stream .
He who is passing wise measures his courses out.

4 Even at his birth the Mothers Seven taught him, for glory, like a sage,
So that he, firm and sure, hath set his mind on wealth.

5 Under his sway, of one accord, are all the guileless Deities :
Warriors to be envied, they, when they are pleased.

6 The Babe whom they who strengthen Law have generated fair to see,
Much longed for at the sacrifice, most liberal Sage,—

7 To him, united, of themselves, come the young Parents of the rite,
When they adorn him, duly weaving sacrifice.

8 With wisdom and with radiant eyes unbar to us the stall of heaven,
Speeding at solemn rite the plan of Holy Law.

HYMN CIII.   Soma Pavamāna.

1. To Soma who is purified as ordering Priest the song is raised :
Bring meed, as 'twere, to one who makes thee glad with hymns.

2 I am indebted to Prof. Macdonell (Journal of the R. A. S., July, 1893, pp. 457-8) for the translation and explanation of this and the following very difficult stanzas. *The place* : far away in heaven where Trita presses and prepares the celestial Soma for Indra. *He* : Soma. *Dear* : to Soma. *Seven lights of sacrifice* : probably the seven rays or tongues of the sacrificial fire with which Soma is closely connected. 'Through the seven ordinances of sacrifices.'—Macdonell.

3 'The main justification of my interpretation,' says Prof. Macdonell, 'is that I supply no extraneous word with 'trīṇi', but explain it by the third line. The meaning of my translation is : 'Do thou, Soma, on the heights of Trita, direct the fertilizing streams which produce wealth into the channels of Trita, for thou knowest these channels, having measured them out with thy streams.' *Three courses* : or channels, of Trita. *He who is passing wise* : Soma. *His* : Trita's.

4 *The Mothers Seven* : the Seven Rivers.

5 *Warriors to be envied* : the meaning of the line is uncertain.

6 *They who strengthen Law* : according to Sāyaṇa, the *vasatīvarī* waters.

7 *The young Parents of the rite* : ever-young, fresh and strong Heaven and Earth.

2 Blended with milk and curds he flows on through the long wool of the sheep.
The Gold-hued, purified, makes him three seats for rest.

3 On through the long wool of the sheep to the meath-dropping vat he flows :
The Ṛṣis' sevenfold quire hath sung aloud to him.

4 Shared by all Gods, Infallible, the Leader of our holy hymns,
Golden-hued Soma, being cleansed, hath reached the bowls.

5 After thy Godlike qualities, associate with Indra, go,
As a Priest purified by priests, Immortal One.

6 Like a car-horse who shows his strength, a God effused for Deities.
The penetrating Pavamāna flows along.

HYMN CIV.   Soma Pavamāna.

1. SIT down, O friends, and sing aloud to him who purifies himself :
Deck him for glory, like a child, with holy rites.

2 Unite him bringing household wealth, even as a calf, with mother kine,
Him who hath double strength, the God, delighting juice.

3 Purify him who gives us power, that he, most Blessed One, may be
A banquet for the Troop, Mitra, and Varuṇa.

4 Voices have sung aloud to thee as finder-out of wealth for us :
We clothe the hue thou wearest with a robe of milk.

5 Thou, Indu, art the food of Gods, O Sovran of all gladdening drinks :
As Friend for friend, be thou best finder of success.

6 Drive utterly away from us each demon, each voracious fiend,

2 *Three seats for rest* : three reservoirs in which he may settle. The *droṇakalaśa*,-the *ādhavanīya*, and the *pūtabhṛt*.

3 *The Ṛṣis' sevenfold quire* : 'the seven metres of the Ṛṣis.'—Wilson.

5 *After thy Godlike qualities* : according to Sāyaṇa, 'to the hosts of the gods.'

6 *Penetrating* : *vyānaśiḥ* : 'spreading widely into the vessels.'—Wilson.

2 *Unite him* : 'Associate him the support of the mansion with the maternal (waters) as the calf (with the mother).'—Wilson.

3 *The Troop* : the banded Maruts.

The godless and the false : keep sorrow far away.

HYMN CV.   Soma Pavamāna

1. SING ye aloud, O friends, to him who makes him pure for gladdening drink :
They shall make sweet the Child with sacrifice and laud.

2 Like as a calf with mother cows, so Indu is urged forth and sent,
Glorified by our hymns, the God-delighting juice.

3 Effectual means of power is he, he is a banquet for the Troop,
He who hath been effused, most rich in meath, for Gods.

4 Flow to us, Indu, passing, strong, effused, with wealth of kine and steeds :
I will spread forth above the milk thy radiant hue.

5 Lord of the tawny, Indu thou who art the God's most special food,
As Friend to friend, for splendour be thou good to men.

6 Drive utterly, far away from us each godless, each voracious foe.
O Indu, overcome and drive the false afar.

HYMN CVI.   Soma Pavamāna.

1. To Indra, to the Mighty Steer, may these gold-coloured juices go,
Drops rapidly produced, that find the light of heaven.

2 Effused, this juice victorious flows for Indra, for his maintenance.
Soma bethinks him of the Conqueror, as he knows.

3 May Indra in his raptures gain from him the grasp that gathers spoil,
And, winning waters, wield the steer-strong thunderbolt.

4 Flow vigilant for Indra, thou Soma, yea, Indu, run thou on :
Bring hither splendid strength that finds the light of heaven.

5 Do thou, all-beautiful, purify for Indra's sake the mighty juice,
Path-maker thou, far seeing, with a thousand ways.

5 *Lord of the tawny* : *hariṇām* : Sāyaṇa supplies *paśū-nām*, cattle.

The hymn is a sort of *rifaccimento of* Hymn 104.
2 *For his maintenance* : *bhárāya* : or, for battle. *The Conqueror* : Indra.

6 Best finder of prosperity for us, most rich
in sweets for Gods,
Proceed thou loudly roaring on a thousand
paths.

7 O Indu, with thy streams, in might, flow
for the banquet of the Gods :
Rich in meath, Soma, in our beaker take
thy place.

8 Thy drops that swim in water have
exalted Indra to delight :
The Gods have drunk thee up for immortality.

9 Stream opulence to us, ye drops of Soma,
pressed and purified,
Pouring down rain from heaven in floods,
and finding light.

10 Soma, while filtered, with his wave flows
through the long wool of the sheep,
Shouting while purified before the voice
of song.

11 With songs they send the Mighty forth,
sporting in wood, above the fleece :
Our psalms have glorified him of the triple
height.

12 Into the jars hath he been loosed, like an
impetuous steed for war,
And lifting up his voice, while filtered,
glided on.

13 Gold-hued and lovely in his course, through tangles of the wool he flows,
And pours heroic fame upon the worshippers.

14 Flow thus, a faithful votary : the streams
of meath have been effused.
Thou comest to the filter, singing, from
each side.

HYMN CVII. Soma Pavamāna.

1. HENCE sprinkle forth the juice effused,
Soma, the best of sacred gifts,
Who, friend of man, hath run amid the
water-streams. He hath pressed Soma
out with stones.

2 Now, being purified, flow hither through
the fleece inviolate and most odorous.
We gladden thee in waters when thou art
effused, blending thee still with juice
and milk.

3 Pressed out for all to see, delighting Gods,
Indu, Far-sighted One, is mental power.

4 Cleansing thee, Soma, in thy stream, thou
flowest in a watery robe :
Giver of wealth, thou sittest in the place
of Law, O God, a fountain made of
gold.

5 Milking the heavenly udder for dear meath,
he hath sat in the ancient gathering-
place.
Washed by the men, the Strong, Far-
seeing One streams forth nutritious food
that all desire.

6 O Soma, while they cleanse thee, dear
and watchful in the sheep's long wool,
Thou hast become a Singer most like
Aṅgiras : thou madest Sūrya mount to
heaven.

7 Bountiful, best of furtherers, Soma floweth
on, Ṛṣi and Singer, keen of sight.
Thou hast become a Sage most welcome
to the Gods : thou madest Sūrya mount
to heaven.

8 Pressed out by pressers, Soma goes over
the fleecy backs of sheep,
Goes, even as with a mare, in tawny-
coloured stream, goes in exhilarating
stream.

9 Down to the water-Soma, rich in kine,
hath flowed with cows, with cows that
have been milked.
They have approached the mixing-vessels
as a sea : the cheerer streams for the
carouse.

10 Effused by stones, O Soma, and urged
through the long wool of the sheep,
Thou, entering the saucers as a man the
fort, gold-hued hast settled in the wood.

11 He beautifies himself through the sheep's
long fine wool, like an impetuous steed
in war,
Even Soma Pavamāna who shall be the
joy of sages and of holy bards.

12 O Soma,—for the feast of Gods, river-like
he hath swelled with surge,

---

11 Him of the triple height : tripṛṣṭhám : the three heights
are probably the firmament, the mountain and the altar.
'Abiding in three receptacles.'—Wilson.

1 He : the priest.

---

4 In the place of Law : in the place of Law-ordained
sacrifice.

5 Milking the heavenly uaaer for dear meath : extracting
the sweet and precious juice from the stalk and tendrils
of the Soma plant.

9 They have approached the mixing-vessels as a sea : saṃ-
vāraṇāni, from saṃvṛ, to cover, enclose, surround, must,
apparently, mean the vessels that contain the juices
and not the juices themselves as Sāyaṇa explains :—'his
enjoyable juices go (to the pitcher as waters) to the
ocean.'—Wilson.

12 O Soma......he, is a sort of periphrasis for Soma in
the nominative case.

With the stalk's juice, exhilarating, resting not, into the vat that drops with meath.

13 Like a dear son who must be decked, the Lovely One hath clad him in a shining robe.

Men skilful at their work drive him forth, like a car, into the rivers from their hands.

14 The living drops of Soma juice pour, as they flow, the gladdening drink,

Intelligent drops above the basin of the sea, exhilarating, finding light.

15 May Pavamāna, King and God, speed with his wave over the sea the lofty rite :

May he by Mitra's and by Varuṇa's decree flow furthering the lofty rite.

16 Far-seeing, lovely, guided by the men, the God whose home is in the sea—

17 Soma, the gladdening juice, flows pressed for Indra with his Marut host :

He hastens o'er the fleece with all his thousand streams : men make him bright and beautiful.

18 Purified in the bowl and gendering the hymn, wise Soma joys among the Gods.

Robed in the flood, the Mighty One hath clad himself with milk and settled in the vats.

19 O Soma, Indu, every day thy friendship hath been my delight.

Many fiends follow me; help me, thou Tawny-hued; pass on beyond these barriers.

20 Close to thy bosom am I, Soma, day and night. O Tawny-hued, for friendship sake.

Sūrya himself refulgent with his glow have we o'ertaken in his course like birds.

21 Deft-handed ! thou when purified liftest thy voice amid the sea.

Thou, Pavamāna, makest riches flow to us, yellow, abundant, much-desired.

22 Making thee pure and bright in the sheep's long wool, thou hast bellowed, steer-like, in the wood.

Thou flowest, Soma Pavamāna, balmed with milk unto the special place of Gods.

23 Flow on to win us strength, flow on to lofty lore of every kind.

Thou, Soma, as Exhilarator wast the first to spread the sea abroad for Gods.

24 Flow to the realm of earth, flow to the realm of heaven, O Soma, in thy righteous ways.

Fair art thou whom the sages, O Far-seeing One, urge onward with their songs and hymns.

25 Over the cleansing sieve have flowed the Pavamānas in a stream,

Girt by the Maruts, gladdening, Steeds with Indra's strength, for wisdom and for dainty food.

26 Urged onward by the pressers, clad in watery robes, Indu is speeding to the vat.

He gendering light, hath made the glad Cows low, while he takes them as his garb of state.

HYMN CVIII. *Soma Pavamāna.*

1. For Indra, flow thou Soma on, as gladdening juice most sweet, intelligent,

Great, cheering, dwelling most in heaven.

2 Thou, of whom having drunk the Steer acts like a steer : drinking of this that finds the light,

He, Excellently Wise, is come to strengthening food, to spoil and wealth like Etaśa.

3 For, verily, Pavamāna, thou hast, splendidest, called all the generations of The Gods to immortality.

4 By whom Dadhyac Navagva opens fastened doors, by whom the sages gained their wish,

By whom they won the fame of lovely Amṛta in the felicity of Gods.

5 Effused, he floweth in a stream, best rapture-giver, in the long wool of the sheep,

Sporting, as 'twere the waters' wave.

---

14 *Of the sea* : of the firmament, or sea of air.

19 *Many fiends* : the text has only *puruṇi*, many, in the neuter plural. Sāyaṇa supplies *rakṣaṃsi* Rākṣasas or *fiends. Pass on beyond these barriers* : 'overcome those who surround me.' —Wilson.

20 *Close to thy bosom am I* : 'I (delight) in thy presence.' —Wilson.

21 *Amid the sea* : *antarikṣe kalaśe vā*, in the firmament or in the beaker, says Sāyaṇa.

---

2 *The Steer acts like a steer* : *vṛṣabho vṛṣāyáte* : 'the showerer Indra is invigorated.'—Wilson. *Etaśa* : one of the horses of the Sun; or a horse in general);—'as a horse comes to the battle.—Sāyaṇa.

4 *Dadhyac Navagva* : Dadhyac was the son of Atharvan the priest who first obtained fire and offered Soma and prayer to the Gods. Here he is called a Navagva and consequently one of the Aṅgirases. See both names in Vol. I., Index. *Won the fame of lovely Amṛta* : 'obtained the sustenance of the delicious (ambrosial) water.' —Wilson.

6 He who from out the rocky cavern took
with might the red-refulgent watery Cows,
Thou masterest the stable full of kine and
steeds : burst it, brave Lord, like one
in mail.

7 Press ye and pour him, like a steed, laud-
worthy, speeding through the region and
the flood,
Who swims in water, roars in wood;

8 Increaser of the water, Steer with thousand
streams, dear to the race of Deities;
Who born in Law hath waxen mighty by
the Law, King, God, and lofty Ordinance.

9 Make splendid glory shine on us, thou
Lord of strengthening food, God, as the
Friend of Gods :
Unclose the fount of middle air.

10 Roll onward to the bowls, O Mighty One,
effused, as Prince supporter of the tribes.
Pour on us rain from heaven, send us the
waters' flow : incite our thoughts to win
the spoil.

11 They have drained him the Steer of heaven,
him with a thousand streams, distilling
rapturous joy,
Him who brings all things excellent.

12 The Mighty One was born Immortal, giving
life, lightening darkness with his shine.
Well-praised by sages he hath by his
wondrous power assumed the Threefold
as his robe.

13 Effused is he who brings good things, who
brings us bounteous gifts and sweet
refreshing food,
Soma who brings us quiet homes:

14 He whom our Indra and the Marut host
shall drink, Bhaga shall drink with
Aryaman,
By whom we bring to us Mitra and Varuṇa
and Indra for our great defence.

15 Soma, for Indra's drink do thou, led by
the men, well-weaponed and most gladdening,
Flow on with greatest store of sweets.

16 Enter the Soma-holder, even Indra's heart,
as rivers pass into the sea,
Acceptable to Mitra, Vāyu, Varuṇa, the
noblest Pillar of the heavens.

HYMN CIX.   *Soma Pavamāna.*

1. PLEASANT to Indra's, Mitra's, Pūṣan's
Bhaga's taste, sped onward, Soma, with
thy flowing stream.

2 Let Indra drink, O Soma, of thy juice for
wisdom, and all Deities for strength.

3 So flow thou on as bright celestial juice,
flow to the vast, immortal dwelling-place.

4 Flow onward, Soma, as a mighty sea, as
Father of the Gods to every form.

5 Flow on, O Soma, radiant for the Gods
and Heaven and Earth and bless our
progeny.

6 Thou, bright Juice, art Sustainer of the
sky : flow, mighty, in accordance with
true Law.

7 Soma, flow splendid with thy copious
stream through the great fleece as in
the olden time.

8 Born, led by men, joyous, and purified,
let the Light-finder make all blessings
flow:

9 Indu, while cleansed, keeping the people
safe, shall give us all possessions for our
own.

10 Flow on for wisdom, Soma, and for power,
as a strong courser bathed, to win the
prize.

11 The pressers purify this juice of thine, the
Soma, for delight, and lofty fame

12 They deck the Gold-hued Infant, newly-
born, even Soma, Indu, in the sieve for
Gods.

13 Fair Indu hath flowed on for rapturous
joy, Sage for good fortune in the waters'
lap.

14 He bears the beauteous name of Indra,
that wherewith he overcame all demon
foes.

15 All Deities are wont to drink of him,
pressed by the men and blent with milk
and curds.

The Ṛṣis are the Agnayo Dhiṣṇyāḥ, sacrificial Agnis
or Fires, said to be sons of Íśvara the Supreme Deity of
post-Vedic times.

3 *Flow to the vast, immortal dwelling-place* : 'flow for
immortality and spacious abode '—Wilon.

4 *To every form* : to all the forms or essences of the
Gods into which he enters. Or to every power, to aid
us in every way.

14 *He bears* : according to Sāyana, the translation
of the first half-line would be : Indra's fair body he
supports, wherewith, etc.

12. *The Threefold* : the morning, noon, and evening
libation.

13 The metre of this stanza is Gāyatrī Yavamadhyā,
that is Gāyatrī having the middle like a barley-corn
thick in the middle and tapering at both ends. : first a
Pāda of eight syllables, then one of twelve, and lastly
another of eight.

16 He hath flowed forth with thousand streams effused, flowed through the filter and the sheep's long wool.

17 With endless genial flow the Strong hath run, purified by the waters, blent with milk.

18 Pressed out with stones, directed by the men, go forth, O Soma, into Indra's throat.

19 The mighty Soma with a thousand streams is poured to Indra through the cleansing sieve.

20 Indu they balm with pleasant milky juice for Indra, for the Steer, for his delight.

21 Lightly, for sheen, they cleanse thee for the Gods, gold-coloured, wearing water as thy robe.

22 Indu to Indra streams, yea, downward streams, Strong, flowing to the floods, and mingling there.

HYMN CX. *Soma Pavamāna.*

1. O'ERPOWERING Vṛtras, forward run to win great strength :
Thou speedest to subdue like one exacting debts.

2 In thee, effused, O Soma, we rejoice ourselves for great supremacy in fight.
Thou, Pavamāna, enterest into mighty deeds,

3 O Pavamāna, thou didst generate the Sun, and spread the moisture out with power,
Hasting to us with plenty vivified with milk.

4 Thou didst produce him, Deathless God ! mid mortal men for maintenance of Law and lovely Amṛta :
Thou evermore hast moved making strength flow to us.

5 All round about hast thou with glory pierced for us as 'twere a never-failing well for men to drink,
Borne on thy way in fragments from the presser's arms.

6 Then, beautifully radiant, certain Heavenly Ones, have sung to him their kinship as they looked thereon,

And Savitar the God opens as 'twere a stall.

7 Soma, the men of old whose grass was trimmed addressed the hymn to thee for mighty strength and for renown :
So, Hero, urge us onward to heroic power.

8 They have drained forth from out the great depth of the sky the old primeval milk of heaven that claims the laud:
They lifted up their voice to Indra at his birth.

9 As long as thou, O Pavamāna, art above this earth and heaven and all existence in thy might,
Thou standest like a Bull the chief amid the herd.

10 In the sheep's wool hath Soma Pavamāna flowed, while they cleanse him, like a playful infant,
Indu with hundred powers and hundred currents.

11 Holy and sweet, while purified, this Indu flows on, a wave of pleasant taste, to Indra,—
Strength-winner, Treasure-finder, Life-bestower.

12 So flow thou on, subduing our assailants, chasing the demons hard to be encountered,
Well-armed and conquering our foes, O Soma.

HYMN CXI. *Soma Pavamāna.*

1. WITH this his golden splendour purifying him, he with his own allies subdues all enemies, as Sūra with his own allies.
Cleansing himself with stream of juice he shines forth yellow-hued and red, when with the praisers he encompasses all forms, with praisers having seven mouths.

2 That treasure of the Paṇis thou discoveredst; thou with thy mothers deckest thee in thine abode, with songs of worship in thine home.

---

3 *With plenty vivified with milk* : 'with abundant wisdom that procures   cattle (for thy worshippers).'—Wilson.

5 *In fragments*: in pieces of the crushed stalk and shoots of the Soma plant

6 *Beautifully radiant : vasurucaḥ :* according to Sāyaṇa, a proper name, Vasurucas, plural of Vasuruc. *Opens as 'twere a stall* : 'drives away the obstructing (darkness).'—Wilson.

---

1 *He* : Soma. *All enemies* : the fiends of darkness. *As Sūra with his own allies* : as Sūrya or the Sun with his attendant beams of light. *All forms* : *viśvā rūpā* : all the lunar mansions, according to Sāyaṇa. According to Hillebrandt, (assumest) all beauty. *With the praisers* : *ṛkvabhiḥ* : perhaps the Aṅgirases are intended. *Having seven mouths* : that is, one mouth each, the mouth being mentioned in reference to their love of Soma juice.

2 *Treasure of the Paṇis* : the rays of light carried off and concealed by the demons of darkness. *Thy Mothers* : apparently the Dawns. According to Sāyaṇa the *vasativarī* waters. *Threefold* : there is no substantive in the text, and it is uncertain what *tridhātubhiḥ* refers to.

As 'twere from far, the hymn is heard,
where holy songs resound in joy. He
with the ruddy-hued, threefold hath won
life-power, he, glittering, hath won life-
power.

3 He moves intelligent, directed to the East.
The very beauteous car rivals the beams
of light, the beautiful celestial car.
Hymns, lauding manly valour, came, inciting Indra to success, that ye may be
unconquered, both thy bolt and thou,
both be unconquered in the war.

HYMN CXII. *Soma Pavamāna.*

1. We all have various thoughts and plans,
and diverse are the ways of men.
The Brahman seeks the worshipper, wright
seeks the cracked, and leech the maimed.
Flow, Indu, flow for Indra's sake.

2 The smith with ripe and seasoned plants,
with feathers of the birds of air,
With stones, and with enkindled flames,
seeks him who hath a store of gold.
Flow, Indu, flow for Indra's sake.

3 A bard am I, my dad's a leech, mammy
lays corn upon the stones.
Striving for wealth, with varied plans, we
follow our desires like kine. Flow, Indu,
flow for Indra's sake.

4 The horse would draw an easy car, gay
hosts attract the laugh and jest.
The male desires his mate's approach, the
frog is eager for the flood, Flow, Indu,
flow for Indra's sake.

Sāyaṇa refers it to the *vasativarī* waters, and explains it
by 'the supporters of the three worlds.' Grassmann thinks
that the beverages, consisting of three ingredients, mixed
with the Soma juice are intended. Probably the Dawns
sometimes spoken of as three (cf. VIII. 41.3), are meant.

3 *The very beauteous car* : of Soma. *Beams of light* :
sunbeams.

The hymn appears to be an old popular song transformed into an address to Soma by attaching to each
stanza a refrain which has no connexion with the subject
of the song. But see *Vedische Studien* I. p. 107. The hymn
is translated in Muir's *O S. Texts*, V. 424.

1 *The Brahman* : 'This verse distinctly proves that
the priesthood already formed a profession.'—Muir, *O.
S. Texts*, I. 252.

2 *Plants* : meaning here reeds which were made into
arrows. *With stones, and with enkindled flames* : according
to Sāyaṇa, with glistening stones to form the heads of
the arrows. *Who hath a store of gold* : and will be able
to pay well for the arrows which the artisan makes for
him.

3 *My dad* : *tatáḥ* : a familiar expression, corresponding to *naná*, mammy.

HYMN CXIII. *Soma Pavamāna.*

1. Let Vṛtra-slaying Indra drink Soma by
Śaryaṇāvān's side,
Storing up vigour in his heart, prepared
to do heroic deeds. Flow, Indu, flow for
Indra's sake.

2 Lord of the Quarters, flow thou on, boon
Soma, from Ārjika land,
Effused with ardour and with faith, and
the true hymn of sacrifice. Flow, Indu,
flow for Indra's sake.

3 Hither hath Sūrya's Daughter brought
the wild Steer whom Parjanya nursed.
Gandharvas have seized hold of him, and
in the Soma laid the juice. Flow, Indu,
flow for Indra's sake.

4 Splendid by Law ! declaring Law, truth-
speaking, truthful in thy works,
Enouncing faith, King Soma ! thou, O
Soma, whom thy maker decks. Flow,
Indu, flow for Indra's sake.

5 Together flow the meeting streams of him
the Great and truly Strong.
The juices of the juicy meet. Made pure
by prayer, O Golden-hued, flow, Indu,
flow for Indra's sake.

6 O Pavamāna, where the priest, as he recites
the rhythmic prayer,
Lords it o'er Soma with the stone, with
Soma bringing forth delight, flow, Indu,
flow for Indra's sake.

7 O Pavamāna, place me in that deathless,
undecaying world
Wherein the light of heaven is set, and
everlasting lustre shines. Flow, Indu,
flow for Indra's sake.

8 Make me immortal in that realm where
dwells the King, Vivasvān's Son,
Where is the secret shrine of heaven,
where are those waters young and fresh.
Flow, Indu, flow for Indra's sake.

---

1 *Śaryaṇāvān* : a lake in the Kurukṣetra district.

2 *Of the Quarters* : of the four regions of the sky. *Ārjika-
land* : according to Sāyaṇa, the country of the Ṛjikas.
Cf. VIII. 7 29.

3 *The wild Steer whom Parjanya nursed* : the mighty
Soma-plant whose growth has been fostered by the God
of the rainy cloud. *Sūrya's Daughter* : Śraddhā or Faith.
Cf. IX. 1. 6. *Gandharvas* : guardians of the heavenly
Soma. See Vol. I., Index.

4 *Thy maker* : the Soma-presser, or the institutor of
the sacrifice :—'the upholder (of the rite).'—Wilson.

8 *The King* : Yama, the ruler of departed spirits, son of
Vivasvān. See Vol. I., Index.

9 Make me immortal in that realm where
  they move even as they list,
  In the third sphere of inmost heaven where
  lucid worlds are full of light. Flow, Indu,
  flow for Indra's sake.

10 Make me immortal in that realm of eager
  wish and strong desire,
  The region of the radiant Moon, where food
  and full delight are found. Flow, Indu,
  flow for Indra's sake

11 Make me immortal in that realm where
  happiness and transports, where
  Joys and felicities combine, and longing
  wishes are fulfilled. Flow, Indu, flow
  for Indra's sake.

HYMN CXIV. *Soma Pavamāna.*

1. THE man who walketh as the Laws of
  Indu Pavamāna bid,—
  Men call him rich in children, him, O
  Soma, who hath met thy thought. Flow,
  Indu, flow for Indra's sake.

2 Kaśyapa, Ṛṣi, lifting up thy voice with
  hymn-composers' lauds,
  Pav reverence to King Soma born the
  Sovran Ruler of the plants. Flow, Indu,
  flow for Indra's sake.

3 Seven regions have their several Suns;
  the ministering priests are seven;
  Seven are the Āditya Deities,—with these,
  O Soma, guard thou us. Flow, Indu,
  flow for Indra's sake.

4 Guard us with this oblation which, King
  Soma, hath been dressed for thee.
  Let not malignity conquer us, let nothing
  evil do us harm. Flow, Indu, flow for
  Indra's sake.

---

9 *Where they move even as they list* : 'where action is
unrestrained.'—Muir. 'Where the sun wanders at will.'
—Wilson.

10 *Of the radiant Moon* : the adjective *bradhnasya*, of
the ruddy or brilliant, stands without a substantive.
'Sun' is supplied by Sāyaṇa. 'Des rotstralenden.'
—Ludwig. See Hillebrandt, *Vedische Mythologie*, I.,
396.

As regards the joys of the departed, referred to in
stanzas 7—12, Professor von Roth observes (Journ. Amer.
Orient. Soc. iii. 343, quoted by Dr. Muir, *O. S. Texts*,
V. 307) 'The place where these glorified ones are to
live is heaven. In order to show that not ·merely an
outer court of the divine dwellings is set apart for them,
the highest heaven, the midst or innermost parts of
heaven, is expressly spoken of as their seat. This is
their place of rest ; and its divine splendour is not dis-
figured by any specification of particular beauties or
enjoyments, such as those with which other religions have
been wont to adorn the mansions of the blest......There
they are happy : the language used to describe their
condition is the same with which is denoted the most
exalted felicity.'

2 *Kaśyapa* : the seer of the hymn addresses himself.
3 *Seven regions* : the regions of the sky, the four quarters with intermediate points. They are sometimes said
to be five, six, or seven in number, but more frequently
eight. *Āditya Deities* : Varuṇa, Mitra, Aryaman, Bhaga,
Dakṣa, Aṁśa, and perhaps Dhātar. Other enumera-
tions also are given. and their number is sometimes said
to be eight. See M. Müller, *Vedic Hymns*, I. p. 232
(Sacred Books of the East, XXXII).

BOOK THE TENTH

HYMN I. *Agni.*

1. HIGH hath the Mighty risen before the
dawning, and come to us with light
from out the darkness.
Fair-shapen Agni with white-shining splendour hath filled at birth all human
habitations.

2 Thou, being born, art Child of Earth and
Heaven, parted among the plants in
beauty, Agni !
The glooms of night thou, Brilliant Babe,
subduest, and art come forth, loud
roaring, from thy Mothers.

3 Here, being manifested, lofty Viṣṇu, full
wise, protects his own supremest station.
When they have offered in his mouth their
sweet milk, to him with one accord
they sing forth praises.

4 Thence bearing food the Mothers come to
meet thee, with food, for thee who givest
food its increase.
These in their altered form again thou
meetest. Thou art Invoking Priest in
homes of mortals.

5 Priest of the holy rite, with car that glitters,
refulgent Banner of each act of worship,
Sharing in every God through might and
glory, even Agni Guest of men I summon
hither.

6 So Agni stands on earth's most central
station, invested in well-decorated
garments.
Born, red of hue, where men pour out
libations, O King, as great High Priest
bring the Gods hither.

7 Over the earth and over heaven, O Agni,
thou, Son, hast ever spread above thy
Parents.
Come, Youthfullest ! to those who long to
meet thee, and hither bring the Gods,
O Mighty Victor.

1 *The Mighty* : Agni.
2 *Among the plants* : according to Sāyaṇa, in the fire-
sticks.
3 *Viṣṇu* : in the form of Agni who is his manifestation
on earth. *They* : worshippers.
4 *The Mothers* : the plants which nourish life. *In
their altered form* : as dry wood which Agni, as fire, consumes.
5 *Sharing in* : because Agni as the bearer of men's
oblations supports all other Gods.

HYMN II. *Agni.*

1. GLADDEN the yearning Gods, O thou
Most Youthful : bring them, O Lord
of Seasons, knowing seasons,
With all the Priests Celestial, O Agni.
Best worshipper art thou of all Invokers.

2 Thine is the Herald's, thine the Cleanser's
office, thinker art thou, wealth-giver,
true to Order.
Let us with Svāhā offer up oblations,
and Agni, worthy God, pay the Gods
worship.

3 To the Gods' pathway have we travelled,
ready to execute what work we may
accomplish.
Let Agni, for he knows, complete the
worship. He is the Priest : let him fix
rites and seasons.

4 When we most ignorant neglect the statutes
of you, O Deities with whom is knowledge,
Wise Agni shall correct our faults and
failings, skilled to assign each God his
fitting season.

5 When, weak in mind, of feeble understanding, mortals bethink them not of sacrificing,
Then shall the prudent and discerning
Agni worship the Gods, best worshipper,
in season.

6 Because the Father hath produced thee,
Leader of all our solemn rites, their
brilliant Banner :
So win by worship pleasant homes abounding in heroes, and rich food to nourish
all men.

7 Thou whom the Heaven and Earth, thou
whom the Waters, and Tvaṣṭar, maker
of fair things, created,
Well knowing, all along the Fathers' path-

1 *Seasons* : the proper times of worship. *Priests
Celestial* : Agni being the Hotar, the Aśvins, the
Adhvaryus, Tvaṣṭar the Agnīdh, and Mitra the Upa-
vaktar. Aśvalāyana, as cited by Sāyaṇa, gives a different
enumeration. See Wilson, note.
2 *The Herald* is the Hotar or invoking priest : *the
Cleanser* is the Potar or Purifier, the assistant of the Brahman. *Svāhā* : an exclamation=Ave ! or Hail !
3 *The Gods' pathway* : 'the way that leads to the gods'
—Wilson.
6 *The father* : Prajāpati; or the institutor of the sacrifice
—Sāyaṇa.
7 *The Fathers' pathway* : the way that leads to the
home of the Manes or Ancestral Spirits.

way, shine with resplendent light,
enkindled, Agni

HYMN III.   *Agni.*

1. O KING, the potent and terrific envoy,
kindled for strength, is manifest in beauty.
He shines, all-knowing, with his lofty
splendour : chasing black Night he comes
with white-rayed Morning.

2 Having o'ercome the glimmering Black
with beauty, and bringing forth the
dame the Great Sire's Daughter,
Holding aloft the radiant light of Sūrya,
as messenger of heaven he shines with
treasures.

3 Attendant on the Blessed Dame the Blessed
hath come : the Lover followeth his
Sister.
Agni, far-spreading with conspicuous lustre,
hath compassed Night with whitely-
shining garments.

4 His goings-forth kindle as 'twere high
voices the goings of the auspicious
Friend of Agni.
The rays, the bright beams of the strong-
jawed, mighty, adorable Steer are visible
as he cometh.

5 Whose radiant splendours flow, like sounds,
about us, his who is lofty, brilliant,
and effulgent,
Who reaches heaven with best and brightest lustres, sportive and piercing even to
the summit.

6 His powers, whose chariot fellies gleam and
glitter have loudly roared while, as
with teams, he hasted.
He, the most Godlike, far-extending envoy,
shines with flames ancient, resonant,
whitely-shining.

7 So bring us ample wealth : seat thee as
envoy of the two - youthful Matrons,
Earth and Heaven.
Let Agni rapid with his rapid horses,
impetuous with impetuous Steeds, come
hither.

---

1 *O King* : Ludwig takes *rājan* here as the nominative
case. *With white-rayed Morning* : I follow Ludwig in
taking *ruṣatīm* as instrumental for *ruṣutyām*.

2 *Glimmering Black* : dark night, faintly lighted by
stars. *The Great Sire's Daughter* : Uṣas or Dawn, daughter
of Dyaus or Heaven.

3 *The lover* : Agni who appears together with Dawn.

4 The first line is almost unintelligible. 'The blazing
flames of that mighty Agni do not (deter) his adorers.'
—Wilson.

HYMN IV.   *Agni.*

1. To thee will I send praise and bring oblation, as thou hast merited lauds when
we invoked thee.
A fountain in the desert art thou, Agni, O
Ancient King, to man who fain would
worship,

2 Thou unto whom resort the gathered people, as the kine seek the warm stall,
O Most Youthful.
Thou art the messenger of Gods and
mortals, and goest glorious with thy
light between them.

3 Making thee grow as 'twere some noble
infant, thy Mother nurtures thee with
sweet affection.
Over the desert slopes thou passest longing,
and seekest, like some beast set free,
thy fodder.

4 Foolish are we, O Wise and free from
error : verily, Agni, thou dost know
thy grandeur.
There lies the form : he moves and licks,
and swallows, and, as House-Lord,
kisses the Youthful Maiden.

5 He rises ever fresh in ancient fuel : smoke-
bannered, gray, he makes the wood his
dwelling.
No swimmer, Steer, he presses through the
waters, and to his place accordant mortals bear him.

6 Like thieves who risk their lives and haunt
the forest, the twain with their ten
girdles have secured him.
This is a new hymn meant for thee, O
Agni : yoke as it were thy car with
parts that glitter.

7 Homage and prayer are thine, O Jātavedas,
and this my song shall evermore exalt
thee.
Agni, protect our children and descendants,
and guard with ever-watchful care our
bodies.

HYMN V.   *Agni.*

1. HE only is the Sea, holder of treasures :
born many a time he views the hearts
within us.

---

1 *To man* : or, to Pūru.

3 *Thy Mother* : Earth.

4 *The form* : the *Āhavanīya* fire. *The Youthful Maiden* :
according to Sāyaṇa, either the mixed oblation, or
the young earth as compared with her withered plants.

6. *The twain* : the two arms, with their grasping
fingers which produce fire by agitation of the fire-stick.

---

1 *He* : Agni as the Sun. *The secret couple's bosom* : the
meaning is uncertain. The fire-sticks in which Agni is

He hides him in the secret couple's bosom.
The Bird dwells in the middle of the
fountain.

2 Inhabiting one dwelling-place in common,
strong Stallions and the Mares have
come together.
The sages guard the seat of Holy Order,
and keep the highest names concealed
within them.

3 The Holy Pair, of wondrous power, have
coupled : they formed the Infant, they
who bred produced him.
The central point of all that moves and
moves not, the while they wove the
Sage's thread with insight

4 For tracks of Order and refreshing viands
attend from ancient times the goodly
Infant.
Wearing him as a mantle, Earth and
Heaven grow strong by food of pleasant
drink and fatness.

5 He, calling loudly to the Seven red Sisters,
hath, skilled in sweet drink, brought
them to be looked on.
He, born of old, in middle air hath halted,
and sought and found the covering robe
of Pūṣan.

6 Seven are the pathways which the wise
have fashioned ; to one of these may
come the troubled mortal.
He standeth in the dwelling of the Highest,

a Pillar, on sure ground where paths
are parted.

7 Not Being, Being in the highest heaven,
in Aditi's bosom and in Dakṣa's birth-
place,
Is Agni, our first-born of Holy Order,
the Milch-cow and the Bull in life's
beginning.

HYMN VI.   Agni

1. THIS is that Agni, he by whose protection, favour, and help the singer is
successful ;
Who with the noblest flames of glowing
fuel comes forth encompassed with far-
spreading lustre.

2 Agni, the Holy One, the everlasting,
who shines far beaming with celestial
splendours ;
He who hath come unto his friends with
friendship, like a fleet steed who never
trips or stumbles.

3 He who is Lord of all divine oblation,
shared by all living men at break of
morning,
Agni to whom our offerings are devoted,
in whom rests he whose car, through
might, is scatheless.

4 Increasing by his strength. while lauds
content him, with easy flight unto the
Gods he travels.
Agni the cheerful Priest, best Sacrificer,
balms with his tongue the Gods with
whom he mingles.

5 With songs and adorations bring ye hither
Agni who stirs himself at dawn like
Indra,

---

latent may be intended. 'He waits on the cloud in the
neighbourhood of the hidden (firmament).'—Wilson.
The Bird : the Sun. *The fountain* : the source of light in
the east.

2 *Strong Stallions* : perhaps the flames of the Sun.
Mares : waters of the firmament. *The highest names* : of
Agni, such as Jātavedas and Vaiśvānara. *Concealed within
them* : in their secret hearts, for worship.

3 *The Holy Pair* : Heaven and Earth. *The Infant* : Agni.
The while they wove : *viyántaḥ* in the text is unintelligible,
and I follow Wallis in reading *vayantī* in its stead. *The
Sage's thread* : the series of sacrifices to which Agni is
entitled.

5 *The Seven red Sisters* : the seven tongues or flames of
Agni, called *kālī, karālī,* etc.—Sāyaṇa. *And found the
covering robe of Pūṣan* : and hath reappeared in the form
of Pūṣan or the Sun.

6 *Pathways* : long lines of light. *The Wise* : the Fathers.
The troubled mortal : the man who is longing for daybreak
may approach the pathway of light. Wallis, translates
the second line differently :—'The support of life in
the home of the highest, at the divergence of the ways,
standeth on sure ground.' *He* : apparently Agni as the
Sun, to whom the troubled or sinful man comes for
light or forgiveness. *Pillar* : support and stay of the universe, like the Skambha of Atharva-veda, X. 7. *Where
paths are parted* : where ends the dark road which the Sun
travels by night, and the bright path of his daily course
begins.

7 *Not Being, Being* : non-existent, existent. *asacca
sacca* 'both unevolved and evolved,' identifying Agni
with the first cause and first effect, with a reference to
such texts as *Asad eva idam agra āsit* 'the non existent
existent (or unevolved) was verily before this (creation).'—
Wilson, from Sāyaṇa. Here Agni is represented as
Prajāpati who as a yet undeveloped embryo is at the
same time both male and female.—Ludwig. Or Dakṣa
may be the Sun and Aditi the Earth. 'In fact Agni
is identified with all things. These latter hymns to
Agni are very obscure : the notions are mystical; many
of the terms are unusual, or are unusually applied;
and the construction is singularly elliptical and loose.'—
Wilson.
This Hymn has been wholly translated, with comments
by Wallis. See *The Cosmology of the Rgveda,* pp. 48-50.

———

3 The exact meaning of the second line is uncertain :—
'and in whom (the sacrificer), whose sacrifice is undisturbed by his foes, throws his choice oblation.'—Wilson.

5 *At dawn* : with Grassmann I take *usrám* here to be
a locative. Sāyaṇa explains it as *bhogānām utsrāviṇam,*
the bestower of enjoyments. According to Ludwig's

Whom sages laud with hymns as Jātavedas of those who wield the sacrificial ladle.

6 In whom all goodly treasures meet together, even as steeds and riders for the booty.
Inclining hither bring us help, O Agni, even assistance most desired by Indra.

7 Yea, at thy birth, when thou hadst sat in glory, thou, Agni, wast the aim of invocations.
The Gods came near, obedient to thy summons, and thus attained their rank as chief Protectors.

HYMN VII. *Agni.*

1. O AGNI, shared by all men living bring us good luck for sacrifice from earth and heaven.
With us be thine intelligence, Wonder-Worker ! Protect us, God, with thy far-reaching blessings.

2 These hymns brought forth for thee, O Agni, laud thee for bounteous gifts, with cattle and with horses.
Good Lord, when man from thee hath gained enjoyment, by hymns, O nobly-born, hath he obtained it.

3 Agni I deem my Kinsman and my Father, count him my Brother and my Friend for ever.
I honour as the face of lofty Agni in heaven the bright and holy light of Sūrya.

4 Effectual, Agni, are our prayers for profit. He whom, at home thou, Priest for ever, guardest
Is rich in food, drawn by red steeds, and holy : by day and night to him shall all be pleasant.

5 Men with their arms have generated Agni, helpful as some kind friend, adorned with splendours,
And stablished as Invoker mid the people the ancient Priest the sacrifice's lover.

6 Worship, thyself, O God, the Gods in heaven : what, void of knowledge, shall the fool avail thee ?
As thou, O God, hast worshipped Gods by seasons, so, nobly-born ! to thine own self pay worship.

7 Agni, be thou our Guardian and Protector : bestow upon us life and vital vigour.
Accept, O Mighty One, the gifts we offer, and with unceasing care protect our bodies.

HYMN VIII. *Agni.*

1. AGNI advances with his lofty banner : the Bull is bellowing to the earth and heavens.
He hath attained the sky's supremest limits : the Steer hath waxen in the lap of waters.

2 The Bull, the youngling with the hump, hath frolicked, the strong and never-ceasing Calf hath bellowed.
Bringing our offerings to the God's assembly, he moves as Chief in his own dwelling-places.

3 Him who hath grasped his Parents' head, they stablished at sacrifice a wave of heavenly lustre.
In his swift flight the red Dawns borne by horses refresh their bodies in the home of Order.

4 For, Vasu thou precedest every Morning, and still hast been the Twins' illuminator.
For sacrifice, seven places thou retainest while for thine own self thou engenderest Mitra.

5 Thou art the Eye and Guard of mighty Order, and Varuna when to sacrifice thou comest.

---

7 *Be thou our Guardian and Protector:* avitā, says Sāyaṇa, is a protector from obvious dangers and gopā a preserver from perils that are unseen.

1 *Advances* through the firmament. *His lofty banner :* the lightning. *Waters :* of the firmament.

2 *Never-ceasing :* asremá : according to Sāyaṇa, 'undecaying.' 'Glorious.'—Wilson.

3 *His Parents' head :* the head or forehead of Heaven and Earth, or of the two fire-sticks. *The red Dawns :* or the flames, according to Sāyaṇa. There is no substantive in the text. *The home of Order :* probably the Sun, if the Dawns are spoken of; and the place of law-ordained sacrifice according to Sāyaṇa's explanation.

4 *The Twins' illuminator :* lighter-up of day and night, that is, of the end of night, or very early morning. But see Hillebrandt, *Varuṇa and Mitra*, p. 116. *Seven places :* seven altars for the sacrificial fire. *Mitra :* the Sun.

5 *Varuṇa :* King and Governor.

---

interpretation, the translation for the first line would be : 'With songs and adorations bring ye hither the Lord *of morning's kine,* the quivering Agni.'

6 *Riders :* saptivantaḥ : the word properly means 'possessed of horses, and is applicable to drivers as well as riders. *For the booty :* to win the spoil, or to guard it from others.

---

1 *Thine intelligence :* the meaning of praketaiḥ here is not *clear.* Wilson translates it by 'indications (of favour)': Ludwig by 'wishes'; and Grassmann by 'light.'

3 The second line is remarkable as a direct declaration of the relationship of Agni and Sūrya—Ludwig.

Thou art the Waters' Child O Jātavedas,
envoy of him whose offering thou acceptest.

6 Thou art the Leader of the rite and
region, to which with thine auspicious
teams thou tendest,
Thy light-bestowing head to heaven thou
liftest, making thy tongue the oblation-
bearer, Agni.

7 Through his wise insight Trita in the
cavern, seeking as ever the Chief Sire's
intention,
Carefully tended in his Parents' bosom,
calling the weapons kin, goes forth to
combat.

8 Well-skilled to use the weapons of his
Father, Āptya, urged on by Indra,
fought the battle.
Then Trita slew the foe seven-rayed,
three-headed, and freed the cattle of
the Son of Tvaṣṭar.

9 Lord of the brave, Indra cleft him in
pieces who sought to gain much strength
and deemed him mighty.
He smote his three heads from his body,
seizing the cattle of the omniform Son
of Tvaṣṭar.

HYMN IX.   *Waters.*

1. YE, Waters, are beneficent : so help ye
us to energy
That we may look on great delight.

2 Give us a portion of the sap, the most
auspicious that ye have,
Like mothers in their longing love.

3 To you we gladly come for him to whose
abode ye send us on ;
And, Waters, give us procreant strength.

4 The Waters be to us for drink, Goddesses
for our aid and bliss :
Let them stream to us health and strength.

5 I beg the Floods to give us balm, these
Queens who rule o'er precious things,
And have supreme control of men.

6 Within the Waters—Soma thus hath told
me—dwell all balms that heal,
And Agni, he who blesseth all.

7 O Waters, teem with medicine to keep my
body safe from harm,
So that I long may see the Sun.

8 Whatever sin is found in me, whatever
evil I have wrought,
If I have lied or falsely sworn, Waters,
remove it far from me.

9 The Waters I this day have sought, and
to their moisture have we come :
O Agni, rich in milk, come thou, and
with thy splendour cover me.

HYMN X.   *Yama Yami.*

1. FAIN would I win my friend to kindly
friendship. So may the Sage, come
through the air's wide ocean,
Remembering the earth and days to follow,
obtain a son, the issue of his father.

---

6 *And region* : thou knowest, and canst show the way
through the firmament.

7 *In the cavern* : in the secret depth of the firmament.
Seeking.........the Chief Sire's intention : wishing to carry
out the design of Indra or perhaps of Dyaus or Dyu
His Parents : 'the parental heaven and earth.'—Wilson.
Calling the weapons kin : calling the weapons, *i. e.* the bolts
which are produced from the sky, akin, simply means
claiming them as belonging to his father Dyu as they are
in the next stanza spoken of as paternal (pitryāṇi).—
Macdonell, J. R. A. S., July, 1893, p. 428.

8 *Of his Father* : belonging to the *Chief Sire* of stanza 7.
The foe : the special enemy of Tṛta is Triśiras, the son
of Tvaṣṭar, called Viśvarūpa or the Multiform. *The
cattle of the Son of Tvaṣṭar* : the cows imprisoned by him,
the showers obstructed by the fiend.

For the legends founded on the last three stanzas of
this hymn, see Muir, *O. S. Texts*, V. pp. 229—233. See
also Bergaigne, *La Religion Védique*, II. 329, 330.

---

1 *Great delight* : according to the scholiast, meaning
perfect knowledge of Brahma. See Wilson's note.

---

3 The meaning of the stanza is obscure. It appears
to have been recited by the priest at the consecration
of a new house.

The first three stanzas are to be repeated by Brāhmans
at their morning ablutions. See Colebrooke's Essays,
Essay I. *On the Religious Ceremonies of the Hindus*. See also
Lanman, *Sanskrit Reader*, p. 376.

6 Stanzas 6—9 are repeated from Book I. 23. 20-23.

Yama and Yamī, son and daughter of Vivasvān, are
the Ṛṣis as well as the deities of the hymn which is a dialogue between them.

Yama and Yamī are, says von Roth, 'as their names
denote, twin brother and sister, and are the first human
pair, the originators of the race. As the Hebrew conception closely connected the parents of mankind by making
the woman formed from a portion of the body of the man,
so by the Indian tradition they are placed in the relationship of twins. This thought is laid by the hymn in
question in the mouth of Yamī herself, when she is made
to say : 'Even in the womb the Creator made us for
husband and wife. ' Professor Müller, on the other
hand, says (Lectures on the Science of Language, second
series p. 510) : 'There is a curious dialogue between
her (Yamī) and her brother, where she (the night)
implores her brother (the day) to make her his wife,
and where he declines her offer, 'because', as he says,
'they have called it a sin that a brother should marry his
sister.'' Again, p. 521, 'There is not a single word in
the Veda pointing to Yama and Yami as the first couple

2 Thy friend loves not the friendship which
  considers her who is near in kindred as
  a stranger.
  Sons of the mighty Asura, the Heroes,
  supporters of the heavens, see far around
  them.

3 Yea, this the Immortals seek of thee with
  longing, progeny of the sole existing
  mortal.
  Then let thy soul and mine be knit together, and as a loving husband take thy
  consort.

4 Shall we do now what we ne'er did aforetime ? we who spake righteously now
  talk impurely ?
  Gandharva in the floods, the Dame of
  Waters—such is our bond, such our
  most lofty kinship.

5 Even in the womb God Tvaṣṭar, Vivifier,
  shaping all forms, Creator, made us
  consorts.
  None violates his holy ordinances : that
  we are his the heavens and earth
  acknowledge.

6 Who knows that earliest day whereof thou
  speakest ? Who hath beheld it ? Who
  can here declare it ?
  Great is the Law of Varuna and Mitra.
  What, wanton ! wilt thou say to men
  to tempt them ?

7 I, Yamī, am possessed by love of Yama,
  that I may rest on the same couch
  beside him.
  I as a wife would yield me to my husband.
  Like car-wheels let us speed to meet
  each other.

8 They stand not still, they never close their
  eyelids, those sentinels of Gods who
  wander round us.
  Not me—go quickly, wanton, with another,
  and hasten like a chariot wheel to meet
  him.

9 May Sūrya's eye with days and nights
  endow him, and ever may his light
  spread out before him.
  In heaven and earth the kindred Pair
  commingle. On Yamī be the unbro-
  therly act of Yama.

10 Sure there will come succeeding times
  when brothers and sisters will do acts
  unmeet for kinsfolk.
  Not me, O fair one,—seek another husband, and make thine arm a pillow
  for thy consort.

11 Is he a brother when no lord is left her ?
  Is she a sister when Destruction cometh ?
  Forced by my love these many words I
  utter. Come near, and hold me in thy
  close embraces.

12 I will not fold mine arms about thy
  body : they call it sin when one comes
  near his sister.
  Not me,—prepare thy pleasures with
  another : thy brother seeks not this
  from thee, O fair one.

13 Alas ! thou art indeed a weakling, Yama ;
  we find in thee no trace of heart or
  spirit.
  As round the tree the woodbine clings,
  another will cling about thee girt as
  with a girdle.

of mortals, the Indian Adam and Eve......If Yama had
been the first created of men, surely the Vedic poets, in
speaking of him, could not have passed this over in
silence.' See, however, the passage from the Atharva-
veda, XVIII. 3, 13, to be quoted further on, 'Reverence ye with an oblation Yama, the son of Vivasvat,
the assembler of men, who was the first of men that died,
and the first that departed to this (celestial) world).'
Muir, O. S. Texts, V. p. 288. Yama as the first man may
perhaps be, as Prof. Max Müller holds, 'a later phase of
religious thought.'

1 Yamī speaks The Sage : vedhāḥ : Yama, whom she
wishes to give her a son: Come : Sāyaṇa explains the
masculine participle jaganvān by the feminine gatavatī,
that is, I, Yamī, who have come. The earth : which,
otherwise, will remain without human inhabitants.

2 Yama replies . A stranger : of a different family,
and so a lawful wife. Sons of the mighty Asura : the spies
or sentinels spoken of in stanza 8.

3 Yamī speaks.

4 Yama replies. Gandharva : Vivasvān or the Sun.
In the floods : in the waters of the firmament. The Dame
of Waters : Saraṇyū. 'His aqueous wife.' —Muir.
Such is our bond : these are our parents. But see Ludwig,
Ueber die neuesten Arbeiten, u. s. w; p. 107.

5 Yamī speaks.

6 Yama replies. To tempt them : the meaning of vicyā
is uncertain. The S. P. Lexicon explains it by 'deceit-
fully'. 'Falsely.'—Grassmann. 'What sayest thou,
who punishest men with hell ?'—Wilson.

7 Same couch : see Benfey, Vedica und Verwandtes, pp.
39—42, for a different explanation of samāne yonau.

8 Yama replies. Sentinels of Gods : recording angels
who watch men's actions.

9 Yamī speaks. The meaning seems to be : if there
be any guilt let me take it upon myself, and let not
Yama's life be shortened by way of punishment. The
kindred Pair : Day and Night.

10 Yama replies. 'Make thine arm a pillow.'— Wilson.

11 Yamī speaks. Destruction : Nirṛti; the utter extinction of the human race. 'The meaning is, a true
brother will not let his sister lack a husband, and a true
sister will not let her brother lack a wife.'—Wilson's
Translation, Editor's note.

12 Yama replies.

13 Yamī speaks.
Sāyaṇa's interpretation of this difficult hymn differs

14 Embrace another, Yamī ; let another, even
as the woodbine rings the tree, enfold
thee.
Win thou his heart and let him win thy
fancy, and he shall form with thee a
blest alliance.

HYMN XI.   *Agni*

1. THE Bull hath yielded for the Bull the
milk of heaven : the Son of Aditi can
never be deceived.
According to his wisdom Varuṇa knoweth
all : may he, the Holy, hallow times
for sacrifice.

2 Gandharvī spake : may she, the Lady of
the flood, amid the river's roaring leave
my heart untouched.
May Aditi accomplish all that we desire,
and may our eldest Brother tell us this
as Chief.

3 Yea, even this blessed Morning, rich in
store of food, splendid, with heavenly
lustre, hath shone out for man,
Since they, as was the wish of yearning
Gods, brought forth that yearning Agni
for the assembly as the Priest.

4 And the fleet Falcon brought for sacrifice

in many places from that which I have adopted, and
Wilson's Translation should be consulted for the views
of the great Indian Commentator and the Pandits of his
time. The hymn has been transliterated, translated,
and annotated by Dr. Muir, *O. S. Texts*, V. 288—291.
It has also been translated by the authors of the *Siebenzig
Lieder*, and fully discussed by Dr. J. Ehni in Der *Vedische
Mythus des Yama*. See also Hillebrandt, *Vedische Mythologie*, I. p. 495.

The subject of the hymn is the origin and institution
of sacrifice, first established by Agni under the authority
of Varuṇa, who must be regarded as the deity of the first
stanza.

1 *The Bull* : the mighty Soma. *For the Bull* : for
mighty Varuṇa. *The milk of heaven* : the divine Soma
juice, to be used at sacrifice. *The Son of Aditi* : Varuṇa.

According to his wisdom : *yáthā dhiyā́* : the two words taken
together as an adverbial phrase. According to Sāyaṇa,
it is Agni who milks the streams of prosperity from heaven
for the worshipper. I have generally followed Pischel's
interpretation of the first five stanzas (*Vedische Studien*, I.
pp. 188, 189).

2 *Gandharvī* : said to be the daughter of Surabhi (one
of the daughters of Dakṣa), and the mother of the race
of horses. Here she appears to be an Apsaras or water-
nymph, haunting the banks of rivers and practising the
seductive arts of a siren. The meaning seems to be, let
no disturbing influence unsettle my devout thoughts.
Our eldest Brother : Varuṇa, regarded as the founder of
society united by common religious observances.

3 The poet regards the coming of the dawn as a proof
that the sacrifice is successful. *Since they* : the priests.

from afar this flowing Drop most excellent and keen of sight,
Then when the Āryan tribes chose as Invoking Priest Agni the Wonder-Worker,
and the hymn rose up.

5 Still art thou kind to him who feeds thee
as with grass, and, skilled in sacrifice,
offers thee holy gifts.
When thou, having received the sage's
strengthening food with lauds, after long
toil, comest with many more.

6 Urge thou thy Parents, as a lover, to
delight : the Lovely One desires and
craves it from his heart.
The priest calls out, the sacrificer shows
his skill, the Asura tries his strength,
and with the hymn is stirred.

7 Far-famed is he, the mortal man, O Agni,
thou Son of Strength, who hath obtained thy favour.
He, gathering power, borne onward by
his horses, makes his days lovely in his
might and splendour.

8 When, Holy Agni, the divine assembly,
the sacred synod mid the Gods, is gathered,
And when thou, Godlike One, dealest
forth treasures, vouchsafe us, too, our
portion of the riches.

9 Hear us, O Agni, in your common dwelling : harness thy rapid car of Amṛta.
Bring Heaven and Earth, the Deities'
Parents, hither : stay with us here, nor
from the Gods be distant.

HYMN XII.   *Agni*

1. HEAVEN and Earth, first by everlasting
Order, speakers of truth, are near enough to hear us,
When the God, urging men to worship,
sitteth as Priest, assuming all his vital
vigour.

4 *This flowing Drop* : the Soma, brought from heaven
by the Falcon. See IV. 26 and 27.

5 *Thou* : Agni. *As with grass* : 'as pasture satisfies (the
herds).'—Wilson. *With many more* : bringing many other
Gods to the sacrifice.

6 *As a lover* : woos his mistress. Agni is called upon
to entreat his parents, Heaven and Earth, to reproduce
him perpetually. *The Lovely One* : Agni. *Sacrificer* :
makhaḥ; see *Vedic Hymns*, I. p. 47. The original hymn
appears to end with this difficult stanza.

9 *Rapid* : *dravitnúm* : taken by Sāyana with *amṛtasya*
and explained by 'distilling the drink of Gods.' *Nor from
the Gods be distant* : 'let none of the gods be absent.'—Wilson.

1 *First* : most exalted as well as most ancient. *The
God* : Agni. *As Priest* : as Hotar, invoker, or herald.

2 As God comprising Gods by Law Eternal,
bear, as the Chief who knoweth, our
oblation,
Smoke-bannered with the fuel, radiant,
joyous, better to praise and worship,
Priest for ever.

3 When the cow's nectar wins the God completely, men here below are heaven's
sustainers.
All the Gods came to this thy heavenly
Yajus, which from the motley Pair
milked oil and water.

4 I praise your work that ye may make me
prosper : hear, Heaven and Earth,
Twain Worlds that drop with fatness.
While days and nights go to the world
of spirits, here let the Parents with
sweet meath refresh us.

5 Hath the King seized us ? How have we
offended against his holy ordinance ?
Who knoweth ?
For even Mitra mid the Gods is angry :
there are both song and strength for
those who come not.

6 'Tis hard to understand the Immortal's
nature, where she who is akin becomes
a stranger.
Guard ceaselessly, great Agni, him who
ponders Yama's name, easy to be comprehended.

7 They in the synod where the Gods rejoice
them, where they are seated in Vivasvān's dwelling,
Have given the Moon his beams, the Sun
his splendour—the Two unweariedly
maintain their brightness.

8 The counsel which the Gods meet to
consider, their secret plan,—of that we
have no knowledge.
There let God Savitar, Aditi, and Mitra
proclaim to Varuṇa that we are sinless.

9 Hear us, O Agni, in your common dwelling:
harness thy rapid car, the car of Amṛta.
Bring Heaven and Earth, the Deities'
Parents, hither : stay with us here, nor
from the Gods be distant.

HYMN XIII.   *Havirdhānas.*

1. I YOKE with prayer your ancient inspiration : may the laud rise as on the
prince's pathway.
All Sons of Immortality shall hear it, all
the possessors of celestial natures.

2 When speeding ye came nigh us like twin
sisters, religious-hearted votaries brought
you forward.
Take your place, ye who know your proper
station : be near, be very near unto our
Soma.

3 Five paces have I risen from Earth : I
follow her who hath four feet with devout
observance.
This by the Sacred Syllable have I measured:
I purify in the central place of Order.

4 He, for God's sake, chose death to be his
portion. He chose not, for men's good,
a life eternal

2 *Better to praise* : more skilled than men in praising the
Gods.

3 This stanza is very obscure. The meaning seems
to be that, by possessing the amṛta, ambrosia, or nectar
contained in the milk of the sacrificial cow and in the
Soma juice which wins and captivates Agni, men are
enabled to offer acceptable sacrifices to the Gods, and
thus to support the heavens and earth. *Heavenly Yajus* :
divine sacrificial prayer or formula. But *divyám* by its
position in the verse seems rather to belong to *ghṛtám*, butter
or sacrificial oil. *The motley Pair* : *enī* : many-coloured
heaven and earth.

'When the self-aggregated ambrosia of the divine Agni
is generated from his radiance, then the products from it
sustain both heaven and earth, all the worshippers glorify
this thy oblation, the celestial nutritious water which thy
white radiance milks forth.'—Wilson. According to
Sāyaṇa, *the products from it* are the plants and trees which
spring from the *amṛta* or rain which rewards the oblations
of men, and the *vi ve devāḥ* of the text are *sarve stotāraḥ*,
all the worshippers. Some meaning is apparent in this
paraphrase, but it cannot be extracted from the words of
the text.

5 *The King* : Varuṇa. *For even Mitra* : we must have
committed some sin, for even Mitra, the Friend, the
gracious God, is wroth with us. *Strength* : strengthening
sacrificial viands. *For those who come not* : for the Gods who
will not yet come to receive our worship and oblations.

6 This stanza is apparently a later addition. The
latter half of the first line is taken from X. 10. 2, but its
application here is not obvious.

7 *In Vivasvān's dwelling* : 'on the altar of the sacrificer.'
—Wilson. Heaven or the realm of the Sun is intended.

——

'The deities are the two *Śakaṭas*, small carts or barrows
used at sacrifices to carry the materials, especially the
Soma-plant, hence called *Havirdhānas*, oblation-bearers.'
—Wilson.

1 *The prince* is the noble who institutes the sacrifice.
'Like the path of the worshipper.'—Wilson.

3 This stanza is most obscure. Wilson, following
Sāyaṇa, translates : 'I make the five stages of the sacrifice
ascend ; I take four steps by pious observances; with the
sacred syllable I perfect this (adoration); I purify (the
Soma) on the navel of the sacrifice.' The *five stages* are,
according to Sāyaṇa, the five elements of the sacrifice,
grain, Soma, the kine, the Puroḍāśa cake, and the clarified butter. The *four steps* are the metres most commonly
used.

The words as they stand in the text do not appear to
be susceptible of any satisfactory explanation.

4 *He* : Yama. See X. 14. 1. *For Gods' sake* : his
death being the type of the sacrifices which support

They sacrificed Bṛhaspati the Ṛṣi. Yama delivered up his own dear body.

5 The Seven flow to the Youth on whom the Maruts wait : the Sons unto the Father brought the sacrifice.

Both these are his, as his they are the Lords of both : both toil; belonging unto both they prosper well.

HYMN XIV.   *Yama.*

1. HONOUR the King with thine oblations, Yama, Vivasvān's Son, who gathers men together,

Who travelled to the lofty heights above us, who searches out and shows the path to many.

2 Yama first found for us a place to dwell in : this pasture never can be taken from us.

Men born on earth tread their own paths that lead them whither our ancient Fathers have departed.

3 Mātali prospers there with Kavyas, Yama with Aṅgiras' sons, Bṛhaspati with Ṛkvans :

Exalters of the Gods, by Gods exalted, some joy in praise and some in our oblation.

4 Come, seat thee on this bed of grass, O Yama, in company with Aṅgirases and Fathers.

Let texts recited by the sages bring thee : O King, let this oblation make thee joyful.

5 Come, Yama, with the Aṅgirases the Holy, rejoice thee here with children of Virūpa.

To sit on sacred grass at this our worship, I call Vivasvān, too, thy Father hither.

6 Our Fathers are Aṅgirases, Navagvas, Atharvans, Bhṛgus who deserve the Soma.

May these, the Holy, look on us with favour, may we enjoy their gracious loving-kindness.

7 Go forth, go forth upon the ancient pathways whereon our sires of old have gone before us.

There shalt thou look on both the Kings enjoying their sacred food, God Varuṇa and Yama.

8 Meet Yama, meet the Fathers, meet the merit of free or ordered acts, in highest heaven.

Leave sin and evil, seek anew thy dwelling, and bright with glory wear another body.

9 Go hence, depart ye, fly in all directions: this place for him the Fathers have provided.

Yama bestows on him a place to rest in adorned with days and beams of light and waters.

10 Run and outspeed the two dogs, Saramā's offspring, brindled, four-eyed, upon thy happy pathway.

---

delight the Gods. *For men's good* : See X. 90. 8—14 for the results of the sacrifice of Puruṣa, with whom Yama may be identified. *They* : the Gods. This Pāda is unintelligible as it stands. Instead of *bṛhaspátim yajñám akṛṇvato ṛṣim*, Prof. Ludwig would read *Vaivasvatam yajñam atanuta ṛṣiḥ*, the Ṛṣi performed the Vaivasvata, or funeral, sacrifice (*Ueber die neuesten, u. s. w.,* p. 110). I have mainly followed Ehni, *Der Vedische Mythus des Yama,* pp. 160—162, but the exact meaning of the stanza is still doubtful to me.

5 *The Seven* : rivers. According to Sāyaṇa, metres. *The Youth* : Indra. *The Sons* : the Maruts. *The Father* : Indra. *Both these* : havirdhānas. *Of both* : Gods and men. *Unto both* : to Gods and men, or to Heaven and Earth.

The hymn is a funeral address, partly to Yama the God of the Dead and partly to the soul of the departed whose body is being consumed on the pile.

1 *Yama* : the deified Lord of the Dead : originally the first who died and so showed the souls of his successors the way to the home of the departed. See X. 12. *Lofty heights* : of heaven, the abode of the Blest.

3 *Mātali* : a divine being, identified by the Commentators with Indra whose charioteer was Mātali. *Kavyas* : a class of Manes, the spirits of a pious race of ancient time. *Aṅgiras' sons* : the Aṅgirases, the typical first sacrificers. See Vol. I., Index. *Ṛkvans* : or singers, a class of spirits or deities who attend and sing the praises of Bṛhaspati. See VII. 10. 4. *Some joy in praise* : the Gods delight in Svāhā, the sacrificial exclamation, worship or praise. *Some in our oblation* : the Manes delight in Svadhā, the sweet food or oblation which is presented to them.

4 *Aṅgirases and Fathers* : or, perhaps, Aṅgirases our Fathers.

5 *Children of Virūpa* : Vairūpas, a sub-division of the Aṅgirases.

6 *Navagvas, Atharvans, Bhṛgus* : priestly families of ancient times.

7 This and the following stanza are addressed to the spirit of the dead man whose funeral rites are being celebrated.

8 *Free or ordered acts* : voluntary good works and prescribed sacrifices, whose merit is stored up in heaven to be enjoyed on arrival by the spirits of the pious who have performed them.

9 According to Sāyaṇa, this stanza is addressed to the Piśācas and other evil spirits that haunt the place of cremation.

10 The spirit of the departed is addressed. *The two dogs* : offspring of Saramā, the hound of Indra. See Index.

Draw nigh then to the gracious-minded Fathers where they rejoice in company with Yama.

11 And those two dogs of thine, Yama, the watchers, four-eyed, who look on men and guard the pathway,—
Entrust this man, O King, to their protection, and with prosperity and health endow him.

12 Dark-hued, insatiate, with distended nostrils, Yama's two envoys roam among the people;
May they restore to us a fair existence here and to-day, that we may see the sunlight.

13 To Yama pour the Soma, bring to Yama consecrated gifts :
To Yama sacrifice prepared and heralded by Agni goes.

14 Offer to Yama holy gifts enriched with butter, and draw near :
So may he grant that we may live long days of life among the Gods.

15 Offer to Yama, to the King, oblation very rich in meath :
Bow down before the Ṛṣis of the ancient times, who made this path in days of old.

16 Into the six Expanses flies the Great One in Tṛkadrukas.
The Gāyatrī, the Tṛṣṭup, all metres in Yama are contained.

HYMN XV.   *Fathers.*

1. MAY they ascend, the lowest, highest, midmost, the Fathers who deserve a share of Soma.
May they who have attained the life of spirits, gentle and righteous, aid us when we call them.

2 Now let us pay this homage to the Fathers, to those who passed of old and those who followed,
Those who have rested in the earthly region, and those who dwell among the Mighty Races.

3 I have attained the gracious-minded Fathers, I have gained son and progeny from Viṣṇu.
They who enjoy pressed juices with oblation seated on sacred grass, come oftenest hither.

4 Fathers who sit on sacred grass, come, help us : these offerings have we made for you; accept them.
So come to us with most auspicious favour, and give us health and strength without a trouble.

5 May they, the Fathers, worthy of the Soma, invited to their favourite oblations.
Laid on the sacred grass, come nigh and listen : may they be gracious unto us and bless us.

6 Bowing your bended knees and seated southward, accept this sacrifice of ours with favour.
Punish us not for any sin, O Fathers, which we through human frailty have committed.

7 Lapped in the bosom of the purple Mornings, give riches to the man who brings oblations.
Grant to your sons a portion of that treasure, and, present, give them energy, ye Fathers.

8 Our ancient Fathers who deserve the Soma, who came, most noble, to our Soma banquet,—
With these let Yama, yearning with the yearning, rejoicing eat our offerings at his pleasure.

9 Come to us, Agni, with the gracious Fathers who dwell in glowing light, the very Kavyas,
Who thirsted mid the Gods, who hasten hither, oblation winners, theme of singers' praises.

13 The three following stanzas are addressed to the priests.

16 The meaning appears to be that the Great Unit, Yama as All-God, broadens and fills the universe after plentiful libations of Soma juice in the Three Kadruka days, or first three days of the Abhiplava festival. See Ehni, *Yama*, pp. 154—157. For different explanations, see Bergaigne, I. 178; II 122, 127.

This hymn, with the exception of the last stanza, has been translated and annotated by Muir, *O. S. Texts.* V. pp. 291—295, by the authors of the *Siebenzig Lieder*, and by Prof. Peterson, *Hymns from the Ṛgveda.*

1 *Ascend* : rise to higher rank; obtain the best oblation, according to Sāyaṇa. *Lowest, highest, midmost* : the Fathers are classified according to their degrees of merit acquired on earth.

2 *The earthly region* : the firmament nearest to the earth. See VIII. 77. 5. *The Mighty Races* : of the Gods.

3 *Son and progeny* : *ndpātam ca vikrámaṇam ca* : the meaning appears to be, as suggested by Ludwig, that the speaker has discharged his obligation to the Fathers by begetting a son through the favour of Viṣṇu. Still *vikrámaṇam* is an unintelligible expression in this connexion. See *The Hymns of the Atharva-veda,* XVIII. 1. 45, note.

7 *Lapped in the bosom of the purple Mornings* : 'Seated in the proximity of the radiant flames (of the altar).'—Wilson
9 *Kavyas* : See X. 14. 3.

10 Come, Agni, come with countless ancient
Fathers, dwellers in light, primeval,
God-adorers,
Eaters and drinkers of oblations, truthful,
who travel with the Deities and Indra.

11 Fathers whom Agni's flames have tasted,
come ye nigh : ye kindly leaders, take
ye each your proper place.
Eat sacrificial food presented on the grass:
grant riches with a multitude of hero
sons.

12 Thou, Agni Jātavedas, when entreated,
didst bear the offerings which thou
madest fragrant,
And give them to the Fathers who did
eat them with Svadhā. Eat, thou God,
the gifts we bring thee.

13 Thou, Jātavedas, knowest well the number
of Fathers who are here and who are
absent,
Of Fathers whom we know and whom
we know not : accept the sacrifice well-
prepared with portions.

14 They who, consumed by fire or not crema-
ted, joy in their offering in the midst
of heaven,
Grant them, O Sovran Lord, the world
of spirits and their own body, as thy
pleasure wills it.

HYMN XVI.   *Agni.*

1. BURN him not up, nor quite consume him,
Agni : let not his body or his skin be
scattered.
O Jātavedas, when thou hast matured him,
then send him on his way unto the
Fathers.

2 When thou hast made him ready, Jātavedas,
then do thou give him over to the
Fathers.
When he attains unto the life that waits

him, he shall become the Deities' controller.

3 The Sun receive thine eye, tne Wind thy
spirit; go, as thy merit is, to earth or
heaven.
Go, if it be thy lot, unto the waters; go,
make thine home in plants with all thy
members.

4 Thy portion is the goat : with heat
consume him: let thy fierce flame, thy
glowing splendour, burn him
With thine auspicious forms, O Jātavedas,
bear this man to the region of the pious.

5 Again, O Agni, to the Fathers send him
who, offered in thee, goes with our
oblations.
Wearing new life let him increase his
offspring : let him rejoin a body,
Jātavedas.

6 What wound soe'er the dark bird hath
inflicted, the emmet, or the serpent,
or the jackal,
May Agni who devoureth all things heal
it and Soma who hath passed into the
Brāhmans.

7 Shield thee with flesh against the flames
of Agni, encompass thee about with
fat and marrow,
So will the Bold One, eager to attack thee
with fierce glow fail to girdle and consume thee.

8 Forbear, O Agni, to upset this ladle : the
Gods and they who merit Soma love it.
This ladle, this which serves the Gods to
drink from, in this the Immortal Deities
rejoice them.

9 I send afar flesh eating Agni, bearing off
stains may he depart to Yama's subjects.
But let this other Jātavedas carry oblation
to the Gods, for he is skilful.

---

11 *Whom Agni's flames have tasted* : whose bodies have
been burnt. A class of Manes called Agnisvāttas,
according to Sāyaṇa.
12 *With Svadhā* : with the sacrificial exclamation
Svadhā, or, with their allotted portion.
13 *With portions* : or, with Svadhās.
14 *The world of spirits : ásunītim* : a difficult word whose
meaning is somewhat uncertain. Sāyaṇa joins it with
tanvàm, and explains the two words by 'the body that
leads to life,' 'that body that is endowed with breath.'—
Wilson. See X. 12. 4
This hymn has been partially transliterated and
annotated by Muir, *O. S. Texts*, V. pp. 295—297.

Stanzas 1—6 are to be repeated while the body of the
departed is being partially consumed on the funeral pile.
2 *The life that waits him : ásunītim :* See X. 15. 14. Con-
troller : by winning their favour.

3 *The Sun receive thine eye, the Wind thy spirit* : let like
return to like. See Muir's note, *O. S. Texts*, V. 298.
4 *Agni is addressed. The goat* : that was slaughtered
and laid limb by limb on the corpse.
5 *Let him increase his offspring* : when he becomes one
of the Fathers to whom is ascribed the fruitfulness of heaven
and earth, the parents of Gods and men. See X. 64. 14.
Let him rejoin : or, let life rejoin his body : the nominative
is not expressed.
7 *The corpse is addressed. Flesh* : the caul and
other parts of a slaughtered animal which covered the
corpse to prevent too quick and complete cremation.
9 *Stains* : of sin or impurity which may have attached
to the departed. Cp. stanza 6.

10 I choose as God for Father-worship Agni,
flesh-eater, who hath past within your
dwelling,
While looking on this other Jātavedas.
Let him light flames in the supreme
assembly.

11 With offerings meet let Agni bring the
Fathers who support the Law.
Let him announce oblations paid to Fathers
and to Deities.

12 Right gladly would we set thee down,
right gladly make thee burn and glow.
Gladly bring yearning Fathers nigh to eat
the food of sacrifice.

13 Cool, Agni, and again refresh the spot
which thou hast scorched and burnt.
Here let the water-lily grow, and tender
grass and leafy herb.

14 O full of coolness, thou cool Plant, full
of fresh moisture, freshening Herb,
Come hither with the female frog : fill
with delight this Agni here.

HYMN XVII.   *Various Deities.*

1. TVAṢṬAR prepares the bridal of his
Daughter : all the world hears the
tidings and assembles.
But Yama's Mother, Spouse of great
Vivasvān, vanished as she was carried
to her dwelling.

10 *Light flames* : typically offer sacrifice in the assembly
of the Gods.

11 *With offerings* meet : literally, bearing Kavyas or
Kavya-worship, that is, offerings to the *kavis*, sages, or
Fathers.

12 *Thee* : Agni; the fire.

13 *Water-lily* : *kiyâmbu* : some kind of acquatic plant.
Tender grass : *pâkadûrvâ* : a variety of *dûrvâ* grass (Panicum Dactylon).

14 *Fill* with *delight* : meaning, euphemistically, extinguish. 'After the fire has consumed the corpse, water
is poured upon it to extinguish it. Then furthermore
certain water plants are put there. In addition to these
a frog—here a female, elsewhere a male—is put upon the
place where the fire has burned. These, as representatives of life in the waters, are symbolically supposed
both to prevent and extinguish fire.' (M. Bloomfield,
Contributions to the Interpretation of the Veda. Second Series,
Baltimore : 1890).

Dr. Muir's *Original Sanskrit Texts*, V. pp. 297—299,
should be consulted with regard to this funeral hymn
addressed to Agni, and much additional information on
the subject may be obtained from the essays, there referred
to, by von Roth and Max Müller.

1 The first two stanzas are difficult, and appear to
have no connexion with the rest of the hymn. *Tvaṣṭar* :
a God often regarded, as here, as an agent in natural
phenomena. *His Daughter* : Saraṇyū, the stormy cloud:
or, perhaps, the dawn. *Vivasvân*: representing the bright

2 From mortal men they hid the Immortal
Lady, made one like her and gave her
to Vivasvān.
Saraṇyū brought to him the Aśvin brothers,
and then deserted both twinned pairs
of children.

3 Guard of the world, whose cattle ne'er
are injured, may Pūṣan bear thee hence,
for he hath knowledge.
May he consign thee to these Fathers' keeping, and to the gracious Gods let Agni
give thee.

4 May Āyu, giver of all life, protect thee,
and bear thee forward on the distant
pathway.
Thither let Savitar the God transport
thee, where dwell the pious who have
passed before thee.

5 Pūṣan knows all these realms : may he
conduct us by ways that are most free
from fear and danger.
Giver of blessings, glowing, all-heroic,
may he, the wise and watchful, go before
us.

6 Pūṣan was born to move on distant pathways, on the road far from earth and
far from heaven.
To both most wonted places of assembly he
travels and returns with perfect knowledge.

7 The pious call Sarasvatī, they worship
Sarasvatī while sacrifice proceedeth.
The pious called Sarasvatī aforetime.
Sarasvatī send bliss to him who giveth.

8 Sarasvatī, who camest with the Fathers,
with them rejoicing thee in our oblations,
Seated upon this sacred grass be joyful,
and give us strengthening food that
brings no sickness.

heavens, or the Sun, *Yama's Mother* : Saraṇyū, who afterwards gave birth to Yama and Yamī. See X. 10, note.
Vanished : or was stolen away. *Carried* : as a bride, in
procession.

2 *They* : the Gods. *The Immortal Lady* : Saraṇyū.
Brought to him : under another form bore to Vivasvān.
Both twinned pairs : Yama and Yamī and the Aśvins. For
the legend which has been formed out of these obscure
hints, see Wilson's Translation, and Muir, *O. S. Texts*,
V. 228.

3 Here the funeral hymn begins, with an address to
the spirit of the departed. *Pūṣan* : as a Sun-God and
the heavenly Herdsman who knows the path through the
heavens and is therefore a good conductor of the spirit of
the departed.

4 *Āyu* : according to Sāyaṇa, Vāyu is intended, the
letter 'v' being elided. Or the meaning may be, life of
full vitality.

7 *Sarasvatī* : See I. 3. 10.

9 Thou, called on as Sarasvatī by Fathers
who come right forward to our solemn
service,
Give food and wealth to present sacrificers,
a portion, worth a thousand, of refreshment.

10 The Mother Floods shall make us bright
and shining, cleansers of holy oil, with
oil shall cleanse us :
For, Goddesses, they bear off all defilement:
I rise up from them purified and
brightened.

11 Through days of earliest date the Drop
descended on this place and on that
which was before it.
I offer up, throughout the seven oblations,
the Drop which still to one same place
is moving.

12 The Drop that falls, thy stalk which arms
have shaken, which from the bosom of
the press hath fallen,
Or from the Adhvaryu's purifying filter,
I offer thee with heart and cry of
Vaṣaṭ !

13 That fallen Drop of thine, the stalk which
from the ladle fell away,
This present God Brhaspati shall pour it
forth to make us rich.

14 The plants of earth are rich in milk, and
rich in milk is this my speech;
And rich in milk the essence of the
Waters : make me pure therewith.

HYMN XVIII.   *Various Deities.*

1. Go hence, O Death, pursue thy special
pathway apart from that which Gods
are wont to travel.
To thee I say it who hast eyes and hearest:
Touch not our offspring, injure not our
heroes.

2 As ye have come effacing Mṛtyu's footstep,
to further times prolonging your existence,

11 This stanza is not very intelligible. *The Drop* is
apparently the Soma; but Sāyaṇa explains it, alternatively, by Āditya or the Sun. See *Satapatha-Brāhmaṇa*, VII.
4. 1. 20 (Sacred Books of the East, XLI. 368).

14 *Rich in milk* : full of sap, vigour, vital and vivifying
power.

————

1 *Death* : Mṛtyu, the God of Death ; distinct from
Yama, the judge and ruler of the departed. *Our offspring
prajām* : meaning here, says Sāyaṇa, female offspring,
duhitṛdauhitrātmikām, in the form of daughters and their
daughters. *Our heroes* : sons and their sons.—Sāyaṇa.

2 Addressed to the kinsmen of the deceased. *Effacing
Mṛtyu's footstep* : a wisp or clog was fastened to the foot
of the corpse which represented Mṛtyu or Death, in order
to prevent the premature return of Death to carry off

May ye be rich in children and possessions.
cleansed, purified, and meet for sacrificing.

3 Divided from the dead are these, the
living : now be our calling on the Gods
successful.
We have gone forth for dancing and for
laughter, to further times prolonging our
existence.

4 Here I erect this rampart for the living;
let none of these, none other, reach this
limit.
May they survive a hundred lengthened
autumns, and may they bury Death
beneath this mountain.

5 As the days follow days in close succession,
as with the seasons duly come the
seasons,
As each successor fails not his foregoer,
so form the lives of these, O great
Ordainer.

6 Live your full lives and find old age delightful, all of you striving one behind the
other.
May Tvaṣṭar, maker of fair things, be
gracious and lengthen out the days of
your existence.

7 Let these unwidowed dames with noble
husbands adorn themselves with fragrant
balm and unguent.
Decked with fair jewels, tearless, free from
sorrow, first let the dames go up to
where he lieth.

8 Rise, come unto the world of life, O
woman : come, he is lifeless by whose
side thou liest.
Wifehood with this thy husband was thy

the living. See *A. V.*, 19. 12. *Cleansed* : from sins of a
former life. *Purified* : from sins of the present life.

3 *Dancing and laughter* : the enjoyments of ordinary
life after the fulfilment of our duties to the dead.

4 *This rampart* : of stone, or earth, raised by the
Adhvaryu as a line of demarcation between the dead and
the living, and limiting as it were, the jurisdiction of
Death until the natural time for his approach. *This
mountain* : the mound or bank.

5 *So form the lives* : let them pass away in due order of
seniority. *Ordainer* : Dhātar : the name of a divine being
who is the creator, arranger, maintainer. and manager
of all things.

6 *One behind the other* : the oldest reaching the end of
their journey first.

7 *First* : *ágre* : to begin with; *i. e.*, before the ceremonies
begin. See M. Müller, *Chips*, IV. 35—39 (edition of
1895). On the whole stanza, see Dr. F. Hall, Journal of
R. A. S., Vol. III. Part I., p. 185f.

8 'This verse is to be spoken by the husband's brother,
etc., to the wife of the dead man, and he is to make her
leave her husband's body. See the *Āśvalāyana Gṛhya
Sūtras*, IV. 2'—Editor's note, in Wilson's Translation.

portion, who took thy hand and wooed thee as a lover.

9 From his dead hand I take the bow he carried, that it may be our power and might and glory.

There art thou, there; and here with noble heroes may we o'ercome all hosts that fight against us.

10 Betake thee to the lap of Earth the Mother, of Earth far-spreading, very kind and gracious.

Young Dame, wool-soft unto the guerdon-giver, may she preserve thee from Destruction's bosom.

11 Heave thyself, Earth, nor press thee downward heavily: afford him easy access, gently tending him.

Cover him, as a mother wraps her skirt about her child, O Earth.

12 Now let the heaving earth be free from motion : yea, let a thousand clods remain above him.

Be they to him a home distilling fatness, here let them ever be his place of refuge.

13 I stay the earth from thee, while over thee I place this piece of earth. May I be free from injury.

Here let the Fathers keep this pillar firm for thee, and there let Yama make thee an abiding-place.

14 Even as an arrow's feathers, they have set me on a fitting day.

The fit word have I caught and held as 'twere a courser with the rein.

---

9 This stanza is applicable only when the deceased was a Kṣatriya or man of the princely and military order.

10 Addressed to the body. *Guerdon-giver* : the liberal rewarder of the priests. *Destruction's bosom* : or the lap of Nirṛti.

13 *I stay the earth* : 'I keep off the earth above thee with thy lid.' 'This is addressed to the urn containing the bones and ashes, which is buried after the corpse has been burnt.'—Wilson. *Pillar* : perhaps a beam laid over the remains.

14 This stanza, which seems to be a later addition, is not noticed in Sāyaṇa's Commentary, and the meaning of the second line is not very clear. I have followed Prof. Whitney's rendering (Lanman, p. 386). The verse, says Lanman, 'seems to express the poet's satisfaction at having made a good hymn at the right time and place, and with as good skill as a skilful horse-man has.'

The hymn has been translated by the authors of the *Siebenzig Lieder.* See Zimmer's *Altindisches Leben,* pp. 400—407, Mr. Romesh Chunder Dutt's *Civilization in Ancient India,* pp. 108, and 278, 279. Lanman's *Sanskrit Reader,* pp. 382—386, and Zenaide Ragozin's *Vedic India,* pp. 351—353. The essays of von Roth and Max Müller have already been referred to.

HYMN XIX.   *Waters or Cows.*

1. TURN, go not farther on your way: visit us, O ye Wealthy Ones.

Agni and Soma, ye who bring riches again, secure us wealth.

2 Make these return to us again, bring them beside us once again.

May Indra give them back to us, and Agni drive them hither-ward.

3 Let them return to us again : under this herdsman let them feed.

Do thou, O Agni, keep them here, and let the wealth we have remain.

4 I call upon their herdsman, him who knoweth well their coming nigh,

Their parting and their home-return, and watcheth their approach and rest.

5 Yea, let the herdsman, too, return, who marketh well their driving-forth;

Marketh their wandering away, their turning back and coming home.

6 Home-leader, lead them home to us; Indra, restore to us our kine:

We will rejoice in them alive.

7 I offer you on every side butter and milk and strengthening food.

May all the Holy Deities pour down on us a flood of wealth.

8 O thou Home-leader, lead them home, restore them thou who bringest home.

Four are the quarters of the earth ; from these bring back to us our kine.

HYMN XX.   *Agni.*

1. SEND unto us a good and happy mind.

2 I worship Agni, Youthfullest of Gods, resistless, Friend of laws ;

Under whose guard and heavenly light the Spotted seek the Mother's breast :

The hymn is a prayer for the return of strayed cows, to whom the first line is addressed.

1 *Ye who bring riches again* : *punarvasū* : 'ye who clothe (your worshippers) again.'—Wilson. See Hillebrandt, *V. M.,* I. 460.

2 *These* : cows, or waters.—Sāyaṇa. *Make return* is the imperative singular, and Sāyaṇa says that the seer of the hymn addresses himself. The address is to Indra.

4 Sāyaṇa explains this stanza somewhat differently : —'I invoke the knowledge of the place, of their going, of their coming, of their departure, of their wandering, of their returning : (I invoke) him who is their keeper. —Wilson. This is a more strictly literal rendering of the abstract nouns in the text.

———

2 *The Spotted* : there is no noun. The variegated oblations, as Sāyaṇa says, appear to be intended; and *the Mother's breast* may be the clouds of the firmament. The stanza is difficult, and translation must be tentative,

3 Whom with their mouth they magnify,
   bannered with flame and homed in
   light.
   He glitters with his row of teeth.

4 Kind, Furtherer of men, he comes, when
   he hath reached the ends of heaven,
   Sage, giving splendour to the clouds.

5 To taste man's offerings, he, the Strong,
   hath risen erect at sacrifice :
   Fixing his dwelling he proceeds.

6 Here are oblation, worship, rest : rapidly
   comes his furtherance.
   To sword-armed Agni come the Gods.

7 With service for chief bliss I seek the Lord
   of Sacrifice, Agni, whom
   They call the Living, Son of Cloud.

8 Blest evermore be all the men who come
   from us, who magnify
   Agni with sacrificial gifts.

9 The path he treads is black and white
   and red, and striped, and brown,
   crimson, and glorious.
   His sire begat him bright with hues of
   gold.

10 Thus with his thoughts, O Son of Strength,
   O Agni, hath Vimada, accordant with
   the Immortals,
   Offered thee hymns, soliciting thy favour.
   Thou hast brought all food, strength,
   a prosperous dwelling.

HYMN XXI.   *Agni.*

1. WITH offerings of our own we choose thee,
   Agni, as Invoking Priest,
   For sacrifice with trimmed grass,—at your
   glad carouse—piercing and brightly
   shining. Thou art waxing great.

2 The wealthy ones adorn thee, they who
   bring us horses as their gift :

3 *Homed in light*: the meaning of *kṛpaṇilam* is uncertain .'Pitying prayer.' according to Ludwig. 'Sustainer of pious works'.—Wilson.

5 *He proceeds* : is carried from one fire receptacle or altar to another.

6 *Sword-armed* : armed with his sword or knife of piercing flames.

8 *The men who come from us* : sons and grandsons of the worshippers.

9 *The path he treads* : according to Sāyaṇa, his chariot.
10 *Vimada* : the Ṛṣi of the hymn.

1 *At your glad carouse* : apparently a Soma-drinking refrain, addressed to the Viśvedevas or All-Gods. *Thou art waxing great* ; a similar refrain or burden addressed to Agni. See Wilson's Translation, note. Grassmann omits both refrains, which he considers to be later interpolations.

2 *Taste thee* ; feel the power of the fire.

The sprinkling ladle, Agni,—at your glad
carouse—and glowing offering taste thee.
Thou art waxing great.

3 The holy statutes rest by thee, as 'twere
   with ladles that o'erflow.
   Black and white-gleaming colours,—at
   your glad carouse—all glories thou
   assumest. Thou art waxing great.

4 O Agni, what thou deemest wealth, Victorious and Immortal One !
   Bring thou to give us vigour,—at your
   glad carouse—splendid at sacrifices.
   Thou art waxing great.

5 Skilled in all lore is Agni, he whom erst
   Atharvan brought to life.
   He was Vivasvān's envoy, at your glad
   carouse—the well-loved friend of Yama,
   Thou art waxing great.

6 At sacrifices they adore thee, Agni, when
   the rite proceeds.
   All fair and lovely treasures—at your
   glad carouse—thou givest him who
   offers. Thou art waxing great.

7 Men, Agni, have established thee as welcome Priest at holy rites,
   Thee whose face shines with butter,—at
   your glad carouse—bright, with eyes
   most observant. Thou art waxing great.

8 Wide and aloft thou spreadest thee, O
   Agni, with thy brilliant flame.
   A Bull art thou when bellowing,—at your
   glad carouse—thou dost impregn the
   Sisters. Thou art waxing great.

HYMN XXII.   *Indra.*

1. WHERE is famed Indra heard of ? With
   what folk is he renowned to-day as
   Mitra is,—
   Who in the home of Ṛṣis and in secret is
   extolled with song ?

2 Even here is Indra famed, and among us
   this day the glorious Thunderer is
   praised,

3 The first line is difficult :—'The establishers (of the rite) worship thee with their ladles (filled with the oblation), like (earth—) sprinkling (showers). —Wilson. I follow Ludwig's interpretation. Those who worship Agni according to his Law are regarded as his own statutes incarnate.

5 *Atharvan* : the priest who is said to have been the first to obtain fire and offer Soma and prayers. *Vivasvān*: the Soma-priest, or the sacrificer.

8 *The Sisters* : the plants, which Agni, descending in rain, makes fruitful.

1 *In secret* : in the forest, according to Sāyaṇa.

He who like Mitra mid the folk hath won
complete and full renown.

3 He who is Sovran Lord of great and perfect strength, exerter of heroic might,
Who bears the fearless thunder as a father
bears his darling son.

4 Harnessing to thy car, as God, two
blustering Steeds of the Wind-God, O
Thunderer,
That speed along the shining path, thou
making ways art glorified.

5 Even to these dark Steeds of Wind thou
of thyself hast come to ride,
Of which no driver may be found, none,
be he God or mortal man.

6 When ye approach, men ask you, thee
and Uśanā : Why come ye to our
dwelling-place ?
Why are ye come to mortal man from distant realms of earth and heaven ?

7 O Indra, thou shalt speak us fair : our
holy prayer is offered up.
We pray to thee for help as thou didst
strike the monster Śuṣṇa dead.

8 Around us is the Dasyu, riteless, void of
sense, inhuman, keeping alien laws.
Baffle, thou Slayer of the foe, the weapon
which this Dāsa wields.

9 Hero with Heroes, thou art ours : yea,
strong are they whom thou dost help.
In many a place are thy full gifts, and
men, like vassals, sing thy praise.

10 Urge thou these heroes on to slay the
enemy, brave Thunderer ! in the fight
with swords,
Even when hid among the tribes of Sages
numerous as stars.

11 Swift come those gifts of thine whose hand
is prompt to rend and burn, O Hero
Thunder-armed :
As thou with thy Companions didst destroy
the whole of Śuṣṇa's brood.

12 Let not thine excellent assistance come to
us, O Hero Indra, profitless.
May we, may we enjoy the bliss of these
thy favours, Thunderer !

13 May those soft impulses of thine, O Indra,
be fruitful and innocent to us.
May we know these whose treasures are
like those of milch-kine, Thunderer !

14 That Earth, through power of knowing
things that may be known, handless
and footless yet might thrive,
Thou slewest, turning to the right, Śuṣṇa
for every living man.

15 Drink, drink the Soma, Hero Indra ; be
not withheld as thou art good, O Trea-
sure-giver.
Preserve the singers and our liberal princes,
and make us wealthy with abundant
riches.

HYMN XXIII.   *Indra.*

1. INDRA, whose right hand wields the bolt,
we worship, driver of Bay Steeds seeking sundered courses.
Shaking his beard with might he hath
arisen, casting his weapons forth and
dealing bounties.

2 The treasure which his Bay Steeds found
at sacrifice,—this wealth made opulent
Indra slayer of the foe.
Ṛbhu, Ṛbhukṣan, Vāja—he is Lord of
Might. The Dāsa's very name I utterly
destroy.

3 When, with the Princes, Maghavan, famed
of old, comes nigh the thunderbolt of
gold, and the Controller's car
Which his two Tawny Coursers draw,
then Indra is the Sovran Lord of power
whose glory spreads afar.

13 *Soft impulses of thine* : 'our (praises) reaching
thee.'—Wilson.
14 *For every living man* : *viśvāyave* : according to Sāyaṇa
for the sake of Viśvāyu, a king, the son of Urvaśī, the
Apsaras or nymph of heaven who became the wife of
Purūravas. *Turning to the right* : circumambulating
Śuṣṇa with the right hand towards him for good luck;
performing the Gaelic deasil.

1 *Seeking sundered courses* : *vivratānām* : unruly, and
pulling away from each other, or wandering. According
to Sāyaṇa, having many functions.
2 *At sacrifice* : Sāyaṇa explains *vāne* by 'at sacrifice,
or, in the forest.' The exact meaning of the word here
is not certain. *Of the foe* : or, of Vṛtra.
Ṛbhu, Ṛbhukṣan, Vāja : Indra combining the three
Ṛbhus in his own person.
3 *With the Princes* : with the Maruts.

4 *Making ways* : as a God of light, making paths
through the pathless darkness.

6 *Uśanā*: Uśanā or Uśanas Kāvya, who has been frequently mentioned as a favoured friend and companion
of Indra.

9 *With Heroes* : the attendant Maruts.

10 *The enemy* : or Vṛtra. *Hid among the tribes of Sages*:
dwelling among the wise Gods and invisible to me.
Numerous as stars : the meaning of *nākṣatra avasām* is uncertain.

11 *Whose hand is prompt to rend and burn* : I follow
Ludwig's interpretation, but the meaning which he
gives to *ākṣaṇe* is doubtful.

4 With him too is this rain of his that comes like herds : Indra throws drops of moisture on his yellow beard.
  When the sweet juice is shed he seeks the pleasant place, and stirs the worshipper as wind disturbs the wood.

5 We laud and praise his several deeds of valour who, fatherlike, with power hath made us stronger ;
  Who with his voice slew many thousand wicked ones who spake in varied manners with contemptuous cries.

6 Indra, the Vimadas have formed for thee a laud, copious, unparalleled, for thee Most Bountiful.
  We know the good we gain from him the Mighty One when we attract him as a herdsman calls the kine.

7 Ne'er may this bond of friendship be dissevered, the Ṛṣi Vimada's and thine, O Indra.
  We know thou carest for us as a brother : with us, O God, be thine auspicious friendship.

HYMN XXIV.   *Indra. Aśvins.*

1. O INDRA, drink this Soma, pressed out in the mortar, full of sweets.
  Send down to us great riches,—at your glad carouse—in thousands, O Most Wealthy. Thou art waxing great.

2 To thee with sacrifices, with oblations, and with lauds we come.
  Lord of all strength and power, grant—at your glad carouse—the best choice-worthy treasure. Thou art waxing great.

3 Thou who art Lord of precious boons, inciter even of the churl.
  Guardian of singers, Indra,—at your glad carouse—save us from woe and hatred. Thou art waxing great.

4 Strong, Lords of Magic power, ye Twain churned the united worlds apart,
  When ye, implored by Vimada, Nāsatyas, forced apart the pair.

4 *Drops of moisture* : perhaps the rain which he pours upon the lightning which may be regarded as his beard. —Ludwig. *The pleasant place*: the chamber of sacrifice. *The worshipper*: or, according to Sāyaṇa, his own body. The text has no word to express the object here.

The double burden or refrain of Hymn XXI, is employed in the first three stanzas.
3 *Of singers* : worshippers; 'eulogists.'—Wilson.
4 *Churned......apart* : or perhaps , produced by churning or violent agitation. Sāyaṇa explains differently :— 'you have churned forth (the fire).'—Wilson.

5 When the united pair were rent asunder all the Gods complained.
  The Gods to the Nāsatyas cried, Bring these together once again.

6 Sweet be my going forth, and rich in sweets be my approach to home.
  So, through your Deity, both Gods, enrich us with all pleasantness.

HYMN XXV.   *Soma.*

1. SEND us a good and happy mind, send energy and mental power.
  Then—at your glad carouse—let men joy in thy love, Sweet Juice ! as kine in pasture. Thou art waxing great.

2 In all thy forms, O Soma, rest thy powers that influence the heart.
  So also these my longings—at your glad carouse—spread themselves seeking riches. Thou art waxing great.

3 Even if, O Soma, I neglect thy laws through my simplicity,
  Be gracious—at your glad carouse—as sire to son. Preserve us even from slaughter. Thou art waxing great.

4 Our songs in concert go to thee as streams of water to the wells.
  Soma, that we may live, grant—at your glad carouse—full powers of mind, like beakers. Thou art waxing great.

5 O Soma, through thy might who art skilful and strong, these longing men,
  These sages, have thrown open—at your glad carouse—the stall of kine and horses. Thou art waxing great.

6 Our herds thou guardest, Soma, and the moving world spread far and wide.
  Thou fittest them for living,—at your glad carouse—looking upon all beings. Thou art waxing great.

7 On all sides, Soma, be to us a Guardian ne'er to be deceived.
  King, drive away our foemen—at your glad carouse :—let not the wicked rule us. Thou art waxing great.

1 The first half line of this stanza has occurred before as the first line of X. 20. The double burden or refrain is again employed, with little or no connexion with the rest of the stanza.

4 *Like beakers* : filled full, like chalices of Soma juice.
5 *The longing men* : the priests. *Have thrown open, etc.* : have, by their sacrifices, opened the way to wealth.

8 Be watchful, Soma, passing wise, to give
us store of vital strength.
More skilled than man to guide us,—at
your glad carouse—save us from harm
and sorrow. Thou art waxing great.

9 Chief slayer of our foemen, thou, Indu,
art Indra's gracious Friend,
When warriors invoke him—at your glad
carouse—in fight, to win them offspring.
Thou art waxing great.

10 Victorious is this gladdening drink : to
Indra dear it grows in strength.
This—at your glad carouse—enhanced the
mighty hymn of the great sage Kakṣīvān.
Thou art waxing great.

11 This to the sage who offers gifts brings
power that comes from wealth in kine.
This, better than the seven, hath—at your
glad carouse—furthered the blind, the
cripple. Thou art waxing great.

HYMN XXVI. *Pūṣan.*

1. FORWARD upon their way proceed the
ready teams, the lovely songs.
Further them glorious Pūṣan with yoked
chariot, and the Mighty Twain !

2 With sacred hymns let this man here, this
singer, win the God to whom
Belong this majesty and might. He hath
observed our eulogies.

3 Pusan the Strong hath knowledge of sweet
praises even as Indu hath.
He dews our corn with moisture, he
bedews the pasture of our kine.

4 We will bethink ourselves of thee, O
Pūṣan, O thou God, as One.
Who brings fulfilment of our hymns, and
stirs the singer and the sage.

5 Joint-sharer of each sacrifice, the driver
of the chariot steeds ;
The Ṛṣi who is good to man, the singer's
Friend and faithful Guard.

6 One who is Lord of Śuca, Lord of Sucā
caring for herself :
Weaving the raiment of the sheep and
making raiment beautiful.

7 The mighty Lord of spoil and wealth,
Strong Friend of all prosperity ;
He with light movement shakes his beard,
lovely and ne'er to be deceived.

8 O Pūṣan, may those goats of thine turn
hitherward thy chariot-pole.
Friend of all suppliants art thou, born in
old time, and firm and sure.

9 May the majestic Pūṣan speed our chariot
with his power and might.
May he increase our store of wealth and
listen to this call of ours.

HYMN XXVII. *Indra.*

1. THIS, singer, is my firm determination, to
aid the worshipper who pours the Soma.
I slay the man who brings no milk-
oblation, unrighteous, powerful, the
truth's perverter.

2 Then will I, when I lead my friends to
battle against the radiant persons of the
godless,
Prepare for thee at home a vigorous
bullock, and pour for thee the fifteenfold strong juices.

3 I know not him who sayeth and declareth
that he hath slain the godless in the
battle.
Soon as they see the furious combat raging,
men speak forth praises of my vigorous
horses.

---

10 *Kakṣīvān* : a famous Ṛṣi, the seer of some hymns of
Book I. See Index, Vol. I.

11 *Better than the seven* : more effectually than the seven
priests. Sāyaṇa explains differently :—'it gives wealth
to the seven (priests).—Wilson. *The blind* : the Ṛṣi
Dīrghatamas, according to Sāyaṇa. *The cripple* : Parāvṛj. See both names in Vol. I., Index.

1 *Ready teams* ; ordered series of our words. *The Mighty
Twain* : the Aśvins. According to Sāyaṇa, *dasrā=
darśanīyaḥ*, of goodly aspect, applied to Pūṣan; or, the
two performers of the rite, the *Yajamāna* and his wife.

---

6 *Śuca* and *Sucā* : names of a man and women.—
—Ludwig. According to Sāyaṇa and Wilson, 'the pure
(he-goat) and the pure (she-goat).' *Weaving the raiment* :
'making woollen cloths such as the woollen filter, etc.'—
Wilson. *And making raiment beautiful* : or, he hath made
vesture pure and bright ; that is, says Sāyaṇa, he hath
purified all around with his heat and light.

7 *Friend* : the augmenter. *Shakes his beard* : when he
drinks the Soma juice.

8 *Those goats* : Pūṣan's chariot is said to be drawn by
a team of goats. Cf. I. 38. 4.

---

1 Indra addresses the Ṛṣi. *Powerful : ābhum* : perhaps,
possessed of the means that would enable him to offer
sacrifices.

2 The Ṛṣi replies. *Fifteenfold strong juices* : according
to Sāyaṇa, the juices of the Soma-plant whose leaves
grow during the light half of the month and die away
during the dark-half.

3 Indra speaks, rebuking the Ṛṣi and ascribing all
victories to himself.

4 While yet my deeds of might were unre-
corded, all passed for Maghavans
though I existed.
The potent one who dwelt in peace I
conquered, grasped by the foot and
slew him on the mountain.

5 None hinder me in mine heroic exploits,
no, not the mountains when I will and
purpose.
Even the deaf will tremble at my roaring,
and every day will dust be agitated.

6 To see the Indraless oblation-drinkers,
mean offerers, o'ertaken by destruction !
Then shall the fellies of my car pass over
those who have blamed my joyous
Friend and scorned him.

7 Thou wast, thou grewest to full vital
vigour : an earlier saw, a later one
shall see thee.
Two canopies, as 'twere, are round about
him who reacheth to the limit of this
region.

8 The freed kine eat the barley of the pious.
I saw them as they wandered with the
herdsman.
The calling of the pious rang around them.
What portion will these kine afford
their owner ?

9 When we who eat the grass of men are
gathered I am with barley-eaters in the
corn-land.

There shall the captor yoke the yokeless
bullock, and he who hath been yoked
seek one to loose him.

10 There wilt thou hold as true my spoken
purpose, to bring together quadrupeds.
and bipeds.
I will divide, without a fight, his riches
who warreth here, against the Bull,
with women.

11 When a man's daughter hath been ever
eyeless, who, knowing, will be wroth
with her for blindness ?
Which of the two will loose on him his
anger—the man who leads her home or
he who woos her ?

12 How many a maid is pleasing to the suitor
who fain would marry for her splendid
riches ?
If the girl be both good and fair of fea-
ture, she finds, herself, a friend among
the people.

13 His feet have grasped : he eats the man
who meets him. Around his head he sets
the head for shelter.
Sitting anear and right above he smites
us, and follows earth that lies spread
out beneath him.

14 High, leafless, shadowless, and swift is
Heaven : the Mother stands, the Youngling, loosed, is feeding.

4 *The potent one* : the powerful fiend Śambara, for
instance.

5 *Dust* : of battle, stirred up by Indra.

6 *To see* : *dárśan* : according to Sāyaṇa, I, Indra, see.
Oblation-drinkers : who themselves consume the offerings
that should be presented to Indra. *Mean offerers, bāhu-
kṣadaḥ* : literally, arm-cutters. According to Von Roth,
parsimonious worshippers who offer the forelegs, or
inferior parts of the sacrificial animal. 'Who cut (the
worshippers) to pieces with their hands.'—Wilson.
Joyous Friend : Viṣṇu.—Ludwig. Or the meaning may
be, your joyous friend; Indra himself, the friend of his
worshippers.

7 The Ṛṣi speaks. *An earlier saw* : the meaning of the
half-line is not clear. Perhaps, foes have already felt
thy power, and others yet shall feel it. 'The ancient
Indra verily destroys (his foe), the other does not destroy Indra.'—Wilson. *Two canopies* : heaven and earth.
Him : Indra.

8 Indra speaks, fearing, apparently, that the worshipper will have no milk to offer him.

9 'There is no comment on this obscure verse, and
Wilson leaves a blank in his MS.'—Editor of Wilson's
Translation, Vol. VI. Ludwig says that Indra declares
that he has brought men and cattle together and made the
latter subject to the former, to be yoked and to remain
yoked when and as long as their masters please. According to this interpretation, the first half of the stanza might
be rendered: 'Grass-eating beasts with men have I connected, and those who eat grain in the widespread corn-
a nd.'

10 *Against the Bull* : against me, the mighty Indra.
With women : with weak allies.

11 'Hitherto,' says Prof. Ludwig, 'it is possible to
establish a connexion and interdependence of the separate
strophes ; with strophe 11 the difficulty begins.' *On
him* : on the father. *Who woos her* : seeks her in marriage
for his friend or employer.

12 *Herself* : *svayám cit* : by her own worth, indepen-
dently of her dowry.

13 *His feet have grasped* : Indra, as the Sun, has seized
and drawn up the water of the rivers with the rays which
are his feet. *Eats the man who meets him* : perhaps merely,
scorches the man who exposes himself to his burning
rays. According to Sāyaṇa, 'feeds upon, *i. e.* takes into
his orb, the water that approaches him.' Another explanation is, that the pious after death go to the Sun and
become sunbeams.—Ludwig. *He sets the head for shelter* :
he takes the height of heaven as a covering. *Anear and
right above* : in his meridian height. *Follows earth* :
descends to the horizon and sets beyond it.

14 *Leafless, shadowless* : heaven being compared to a
tree that overshadows the earth. According to Sāyaṇa,
árvā here is the ever-moving Sun. *The Mother* : Uṣas or
Dawn. According to Sāyaṇa, *mātā* here means 'the
builder (of the world.)' *The Youngling* : or Calf ; Agni
who feeds on the oblations. *She* : Heaven , or the atmospheric Pṛthivi, roaring as the rain comes down.
Another's offspring : Indra as Āditya or the Sun, the offspring of Aditi. *In what world, etc.* : that is, who knows
where the rain comes from ? *The Cow* : the Sky.
The second half-stanza has occurred before. See III.
55. 13.

Loud hath she lowed, licking Another's offspring. In what world hath the Cow laid down her udder ?

15 Seven heroes from the nether part ascended, and from the upper part came eight together.
Nine from behind came armed with winnowing-baskets : ten from the front pressed o'er the rock's high ridges.

16 One of the ten, the tawny, shared in common, they send to execute their final purpose.
The Mother carries on her breast the Infant of noble form and soothes it while it knows not.

17 The Heroes dressed with fire the fatted wether : the dice were thrown by way of sport and gaming.
Two reach the plain amid the heavenly waters, hallowing and with means of purifying.

18 Crying aloud they ran in all directions : One half of them will cook, and not the other.
To me hath Savitar, this God, declared it : He will perform, whose food is wood and butter.

19 I saw a troop advancing from the distance, moved, not by wheels but their own God-like nature.
The Friendly One seeks human generations, destroying, still new bands of evil beings.

20 These my two Bulls, even Pramara's, are harnessed : drive them not far ; here let them often linger.
The waters even shall aid him to his object, and the all-cleansing Sun who is above us.

21 This is the thunderbolt which often whirleth down from the lofty misty realm of Sūrya.
Beyond this realm there is another glory : so through old age they pass and feel no sorrow.

22 Bound fast to every tree the cow is lowing, and thence the man-consuming birds are flying,
Then all this world, though pressing juice for Indra and strengthening the Ṛṣi, is affrighted.

23 In the Gods' mansion stood the first-created, and from their separation came the later.
Three warm the Earth while holding stores of water, and Two of these convey the murmuring moisture.

24 This is thy life : and do thou mark and know it. As such, hide not thyself in time of battle.

20 *Bulls* : steeds according to Sāyaṇa. *Pramara's* : belonging to me, the Destroyer or Death. But the whole stanza is obscure. *All-cleansing* : so Sāyaṇa explains *markā*, which Von Roth interprets by 'obscuration.' Ludwig thinks that the Moon, 'the obscurer of the Sun' is meant.
21 *This is the thunderbolt* : the meaning, probably, is 'this *dakṣiṇā* or honorarium given to the priests is a veritable thunderbolt. '—Ludwig. But as Wilson observes, the stanza may be 'intended to express the usual theory of rain ; the moisture of the earth being drawn up into the solar region as vapour, and thence descending as rain by the action of the thunderbolt and the wind.'
22 According to Sāyaṇa, *tree* here means 'bow', *cow* means 'bowstring', and *man-consuming birds* 'deadly arrows.' The general meaning is that sacrifices to Indra and liberal gifts to priests will not free men from the fear of death.
23 *The first-created* : the clouds. *The later* : the waters of the rain. *Three* : Parjanya, Vāyu, and Āditya or the Sun. *Holding stores of water* : *anūpāḥ* : 'Sowing in succession.'—Wilson. 'Following the water.'—Ludwig. 'Rich in water.'—Grassmann. *Two* : Vāyu and Āditya.
24 According to Sāyaṇa, Indra is addressed. The following is Wilson's translation of Sāyaṇa's paraphrase of the stanza :—'That thy (divine nature identified with the sun) is the cause of life : and know such (solar form) of his (to be worthy of adoration) as the sacrifice; conceal nothing : that motion of him the all-cleansing (sun) makes manifest the universe; it absorbs the moisture; it is never discontinued.' The *robes that veil* the foot, or rays, of the Sun are the waters into which they are supposed to vanish.
The hymn is enigmatical and difficult in the highest degree, and neither Sāyaṇa nor later scholars have succeeded in making it intelligible throughout.

15 *Seven heroes* : according to Sāyaṇa, Viśvāmitra and other Ṛṣis, sons of Prajāpati. *Eight* : the Vālakhilyas, a numerous race of divine pygmies. *Nine* : the Bhṛgus. *Ten* : Aṅgirases. Or, alternatively, seven Maruts, on Indra's right, eight on his left, nine behind him, and ten in front. These explanations by Sāyaṇa cannot be accepted ; but it is hard to say what is meant. Ludwig thinks that the various classes of letters of the alphabet are intended. His ingenious explanation will be found in the Preface to his fourth volume of the Ṛgveda, pp. XXXIII—XXXV.
16 *The tawny* : *kapilám* : according to Sāyaṇa, the famous Ṛṣi Kapila. 'The Sun ?'—Grassmann. *The Mother* : Night ?—Grassmann. *The Infant* : the young Sun, if *the Mother* is Night.
17 *The fatted wether* : perhaps, the swollen rain-cloud. *The dice* : the stars. *Two* : the Sun and Moon. These are Ludwig's suggestions.
18 *They* : according to Sāyaṇa, the Aṅgirases. Perhaps the contentious priests with whom Agni the veritable priest is contrasted.—Ludwig. *He* : Agni.
19 *A troop* : the stars. *The Friendly One* : Indra as the Sun. *Evil beings* : *śiśnā* : Rākṣasas and spirits of darkness that vanish at the coming of the Sun.

He manifests the light and hides the vapour : his foot is never free from robes that veil it.

HYMN XXVIII. *Indra. Vasukra.*

1. Now all my other friends are here assembled : my Sire-in-law alone hath not come hither.
So might he eat the grain and drink the Soma, and, satisfied, return unto his dwelling.

2 Loud belloweth the Bull whose horns are sharpened : upon the height above earth's breadth he standeth.
That man I guard and save in all his troubles who fills my flanks when he hath shed the Soma.

3 Men with the stone press out for thee, O Indra, strong, gladdening Soma, and thereof thou drinkest.
Bulls they dress for thee, and of these thou eatest when, Maghavan, with food thou art invited.

4 Resolve for me, O singer, this my riddle : The rivers send their swelling water backward :
The fox steals up to the approaching lion : the jackal drives the wild-boar from the brushwood.

5 How shall I solve this riddle, I, the simple, declare the thought of thee the Wise and Mighty ?
Tell us, well knowing, as befits the season : Whitherward is thy prosperous car advancing ?

6 Thus do they magnify me, me the mighty : higher than even high heaven is my car-pole.
I all at once demolish many thousands : my Sire begot me with no foe to match me.

7 Yea, and the Gods have known me also, Indra, as mighty, fierce and strong in every exploit.
Exulting with the bolt I slaughtered Vrtra, and for the offerer oped with might the cow-stall.

8 The Deities approached, they carried axes ; splitting the wood they came with their attendants.
They laid good timber in the fire-receivers, and burnt the grass up where they found it growing.

9 The hare hath swallowed up the opposing razor : I sundered with a clod the distant mountain.
The great will I make subject to the little : the calf shall wax in strength and eat the bullock.

10 There hath the strong-winged eagle left his talon, as a snared lion leaves the trap that caught him.
Even the wild steer in his thirst is captured : the leather strap still holds his foot entangled.

11 So may the leather strap their foot entangle who fatten on the viands of the Brahman.
They all devour the bulls set free to wander, while they themselves destroy their bodies' vigour.

12 They were well occupied with holy duties who sped in person with their lauds to Soma.
Speaking like man, mete to us wealth and booty : in heaven thou hast the name and fame of Hero.

The Rṣi is Vasukra son of Indra, and the hymn is mainly a dialogue between the Father and the son. Vasukra's wife is the seer as well as the speaker of stanza 1.

1 This stanza is spoken by Vasukra's wife in ignorance, says the legend, that her Father-in-law Indra is present in disguise.

2 Indra speaks. *The Bull* : the mighty Indra.

3 Vasukra speaks.

4 Indra must be the speaker, although Sāyaṇa gives the stanza to Vasukra. Indra declares his power to alter the course of nature. See Wilson's Translation, note by the Editor.

5 Vasukra speaks.

6 Indra speaks. *My Sire* : or, the general Father Prajāpati.—Sāyaṇa.

7 Vasukra speaks, and tells what he has done with Indra's help.

8 This obscure stanza is probably an account of the Gods' first sacrifice. See Pischel, *Vedische Studien*, I. pp. 178—180. According to Sāyaṇa it refers to the cleaving of the clouds, and the filling of the rivers. Ludwig sees in it a reference to the beginning of agriculture. *Their attendants* : the Maruts.

9 Cf. with stanza 4.

10 The application of this stanza is not apparent. Sāyaṇa's explanation of this and the following verse is entirely different from that of most recent scholars.

HYMN XXIX.   *Indra.*

1. As sits the young bird on the tree rejoicing, ye, swift Pair, have been roused
by clear laudation,
Whose Herald-Priest through many days
is Indra, earth's Guardian, Friend of
men, the best of Heroes.

2 May we, when this Dawn and the next
dance hither, be thy best servants, most
heroic Hero !
Let the victorious car with triple splendour
bring hitherward the hundred chiefs
with Kutsa.

3 What was the gladdening draught that
pleased thee, Indra ? Speed through our
doors to songs, for thou art mighty.
Why comest thou to me, what gift
attracts thee ? Fain would I bring thee
food most meet to offer.

4 Indra, what fame hath one like thee mid
heroes ? With what plan wilt thou act ?
Why hast thou sought us ?
As a true Friend, Wide-Strider ! to sustain
us, since food absorbs the thought of
each among us.

5 Speed happily those, as Sūrya ends his
journey, who meet his wish as bridegrooms meet their spouses ,
Men who present, O Indra strong by
nature, with food the many songs that
tell thy praises.

6 Thine are two measures, Indra, wide-well-
meted, heaven for thy majesty, earth for
thy wisdom.
Here for thy choice are Somas mixed with
butter : may the sweet meath be pleasant for thy drinking.

7 They have poured out a bowl to him, to
Indra, full of sweet juice, for faithful
is his bounty.
O'er earth's expanse hath he grown great
by wisdom, the Friend of man, and by
heroic exploits.

8 Indra hath conquered in his wars, the
Mighty : men strive in multitudes to
win his friendship.
Ascend thy chariot as it were in battle,
which thou shalt drive to us with gracious favour.

HYMN XXX.   *Waters.*

1. As 'twere with swift exertion of the spirit,
let the priest speed to the celestial
Waters,
The glorious food of Varuṇa and Mitra.
To him who spreadeth far this laud I
offer.

2 Adhvaryus, be ye ready with oblations,
and come with longing to the longing
Waters,
Down on which looks the purple-tinted
Eagle. Pour ye that flowing wave this
day, deft-handed.

3 Go to the reservoir, O ye Adhvaryus :
worship the Waters' Child with your
oblations.
A consecrated wave he now will give you,
so press for him the Soma rich in sweetness.

4 He who shines bright in floods, unfed with
fuel, whom sages worship at their
sacrifices :
Give waters rich in sweets, Child of the
Waters, even those which gave heroic
might to Indra :

5 Those in which Soma joys and is delighted,
as a young man with fair and pleasant
damsels.
Go thou unto those Waters, O Adhvaryu,
and purify with herbs what thou infusest.

---

1 The meaning of the stanza is obscure, and the
text of the first half-line is unintelligible. I follow the
reading which Sāyaṇa gives in his Commentary,
vāyo instead *vā yó.* 'As (the bird) who deposits its young
(in its nest) in the tree (is) eagerly looking around.'—
Wilson. *Swift Pair* : Aśvins.

2 *Dance hither* or, come dancing. Cp. Milton's 'Now
the bright morning-star, day's harbinger, Comes dancing
from the east.' *Triple splendour* : perhaps with reference
to Agni, Vāyu, and Sūrya.—Ludwig. *Hundred chiefs* :
the Maruts may be intended, 'hundred' being used
indefinitely. *Kutsa* : Indra's favourite companion.

4 Indra is reminded that the protection of his worshippers is his special glory. *Wide-Strider* ! : as identified
with the Sun; 'widely renowned,' according to Sāyaṇa.
Food : the hymn appears to have been 'seen' or revealed
in a time of dearth or famine.'—Ludwig.

5 *Meet his wish* : satisfy his, Indra's, longing for Soma-
libations.

6 *Thine are two measures* : Thy majesty or greatness is
vast and lofty as heaven, and thy wisdom is wide as earth;
or, 'with confusion of the measure and the thing measured,'
thou hast measured out the heaven by thy greatness and
the earth by thy wisdom. See Wallis, *Cosmology of the
Ṛgveda*, p. 18. ———

The subject is the ceremony of fetching the sacred
waters required for the preparation of the Soma juice.

1 *To him who spreadeth far* : Indra, according to
Sāyaṇa.

2 *The purple-tinted Eagle* : Soma, the Moon.

3 *To the reservoir* : to fetch the holy Waters. *The
Waters' Child* usually Agni, as the lightning that springs
from the clouds or waters of the firmament, but here the
Deity who produces the rain, the Moon. See Hillebrandt,
V. M., I. 374.

4 *In floods* : of the aerial ocean. Cp. II. 35. 4.

5 *With herbs* : probably Darbha or Kuśa grass.

6 So maidens bow before the youthful gallant
who comes with love to them who yearn
to meet him.
In heart accordant and in wish one-minded are the Adhvaryus and the heavenly
Waters.
7 He who made room for you when fast
imprisoned, who freed you from the
mighty imprecation,—
Even to that Indra send the meath-rich
current, the wave that gratifies the Gods,
O Waters.
8 Send forth to him the meath-rich wave,
O Rivers, which is your offspring and
a well of sweetness,
Oil-balmed, to be implored at sacrifices.
Ye wealthy Waters, hear mine invocation.
9 Send forth the rapture-giving wave, O
Rivers, which Indra drinks, which sets
the Twain in motion ;
The well that springeth from the clouds,
desirous, that wandereth triple-formed,
distilling transport.
10 These winding Streams which with their
double current, like cattle-raiders, seek
the lower pastures,—
Waters which dwell together, thrive together, Queens, Mothers of the world,
these, Ṛsi, honour.
11 Send forth our sacrifice with holy worship
send forth the hymn and prayer for gain
of riches.
For need of sacrifice disclose the udder.
Give gracious hearing to our call, O
Waters.
12 For, wealthy Waters, ye control all treasures : ye bring auspicious intellect and
Amṛta.
Ye are the Queens of independent riches
Sarasvatī give full life to the singer !
13 When I behold the Waters coming hither,
carrying with them milk and meath and
butter,
Bearing the well-pressed Soma juice to
Indra, they harmonize in spirit with
Adhvaryus.

14 Rich, they are come with wealth for
living beings, O friends, Adhvaryus,
seat them in their places.
Seat them on holy grass, ye Soma-bringers,
in harmony with the Offspring of the
Waters.
15 Now to this grass are come the longing
Waters : the Pious Ones are seated at
our worship.
Adhvaryus, press the Soma juice for Indra :
so will the service of the Gods be easy.

HYMN XXXI. *Viśvedevas.*

1. MAY benediction of the Gods approach
us, holy, to aid us with all rapid succours.
Therewith may we be happily befriended,
and pass triumphant over all our troubles.
2 A man should think on wealth and strive
to win it by adoration on the path of
Order,
Counsel himself with his own mental insight, and grasp still nobler vigour with
his spirit.
3 The hymn is formed, poured are the
allotted portions : as to a ford friends
come unto the Wondrous.
We have obtained the power of ease and
comfort, we have become acquainted,
with Immortals.
4 Pleased be the Eternal Lord who loves
the household with this man whom
God Savitar created.
May Bhaga Aryaman grace him with
cattle : may he appear to him, and be,
delightful.
5 Like the Dawns' dwelling-place be this
assembly, where in their might men rich
in food have gathered.
Striving to share the praises of this singer.
To us come strengthening and effectual
riches !
6 This Bull's most gracious far-extended
favour existed first of all in full abundance.
By his support they are maintained in
common who in the Asura's mansion
dwell together.

6 The Waters bow to Soma as maidens to their lovers.
9 *The Twain* : *ubhe* : probably, Heaven and Earth.
Sāyaṇa explains differently :—'which sends us both (kinds
of fruit)'; that is, 'the fruit, whether reward or punishment, of the present life, and of a former life.'—Wilson,
and Editor's note. *Desirous* : eager to mix with the
Soma, according to Sāyaṇa; but the meaning of *auśānám*
is uncertain. Ludwig and Hillebrandt translate it by
'des Uśanas,' belonging to Uśanas or Uśanā *Triple-
formed* : Soma with two admixtures.—Grassmann.
10 *Double current* : meaning probably, the two kinds
of waters called respectively Ekadhanā and Vasativarī.
11 *Disclose the udder* : let your streams flow.
12 *Sarasvatī* : as chief and wisest of the Water-Goddesses.

1 *Benediction* : or, the laudation ; that is, Ludwig suggests, 'May the power of praising the Gods, and at the
same time the Gods themselves come to us.'
3 *The Wondrous* : meaning, perhaps, Soma.
4 *The Eternal Lord* : Agni. According to Sāyaṇa,
Prajāpati. *This man* : the institutor of the sacrifice. Savitar
has given him life and now let Agni bless him. *Bhaga
Aryaman* : Aryaman as Bhaga who distributes wealth.
6 *This Bull* : Agni as the Sun. *The Asura* is Dyaus.

7 What was the tree, what wood, in sooth,
produced it, from which they fashioned
forth the Earth and Heaven ?
These Twain stand fast and wax not old
for ever : these have sung praise to many
a day and morning.

8 Not only here is this : more is beyond us.
He is the Bull, the Heaven's and Earth's
supporter.
With power divine he makes his skin a
filter, when the Bay Coursers bear him
on as Sūrya.

9 He passes o'er the broad earth like a
Stega : he penetrates the world as Wind
the mist-cloud.
He, balmed with oil, near Varuṇa and
Mitra, like Agni in the wood, hath shot
forth splendour.

10 When suddenly called the cow that erst
was barren, she, self-protected, ended
all her troubles.
Earth, when the first son sprang from
sire and mother, cast up the Śamī, that
which men were seeking.

11 To Nṛṣad's son they gave the name of
Kaṇva, and he the brown-hued courser
won the treasure.
For him dark-coloured streamed the shin-
ing udder : none made it swell for him.
Thus Order willed it.

8 *Not only here* : the first half-line is obscure. 'Not such
(is their power); there is another greater than they.'
—Wilson. 'There is no other thing besides like unto
him.'—Wallis. *A filter* : *pavítram* : which purifies the
rays of light which stream through it.

9 *A Stega* : said to be a certain biting or stinging
insect. According to Sāyaṇa, 'the aggregation of rays,
the Sun.' Ludwig conjectures that 'plough-share' may
be the meaning.

10 This stanza is very obscure. 'The cow which was
barren is the *Śamī* tree, which brings forth the *Aśvattha*,
and from the wood of these two trees are made the
araṇi, the two pieces of wood which are rubbed together
to produce the sacred fire—the upper and harder piece is
the *Śamī* (the Acacia Suma), and the lower and soft
is the *Aśvattha* (the Ficus religiosa).'—Wilson.

'The verses (7—10) deal with the formation of the
three main components of the universe, heaven, earth,
and the sun. Of the first two the poet has little to tell
us and passes on at once to the third. The sun is identified with the bull, Agni of the sacrifice, and the earth
with the lower rubbing-stick anointed with ghee, which
is licked up ('devours' instead of 'cast up') as soon as
fire is struck.'—Wallis, *Cosmology of the Rgveda*, pp. 47,
48.

11 This stanza appears to have no connexion with
the hymn, and is inexplicable as it stands here. See I.
117. 8, where the son of Nṛṣad is mentioned as a favourite
of the Aśvins.

HYMN XXXII.　　　　*Indra.*

1. FORTH speed the Pair to bring the meditating God, benevolent with boons sent
in return for boons.
May Indra graciously accept both gifts
from us, when he hath knowledge of the
flowing Soma juice.

2 Thou wanderest far, O Indra, through the
spheres of light and realms of earth, the
region, thou whom many praise !
Let those who often bring their solemn
rites conquer the noisy babblers who
present no gifts.

3 More beautiful than beauty must this seem
to me, when the son duly careth for his
parents' line.
The wife attracts the husband : with a
shout of joy the man's auspicious marriage is performed aright.

4 This beauteous place of meeting have I
looked upon, where, like milch-cows, the
kine order the marriage train;
Where the Herd's Mother counts as first
and best of all, and round her are the
seven-toned people of the choir.

5 The Pious One hath reached your place
before the rest : One only moves victorious with the Rudras' band.
To these your helpers pour our meath,
Immortal Gods, with whom your song
of praise hath power to win their gifts.

6 He who maintains the Laws of God inform-
ed me that thou wast lying hidden in
the waters.

1 *The meditating God* : Indra. My version of the first
line follows the explanation given by Ludwig in his Commentary. Sāyaṇa's interpretation is different :—'Indra
sends his quick-going horses to the service of the (worshipper) expectant (of his arrival).'—Wilson. *Both gifts* :
oblation and praise.

3 *Careth for his parents' line*: by marrying and becoming
a father; or as Sāyaṇa explains, by having his birth proclaimed according to custom in sacrifices instituted by
him.

4 *Order the marriage train* : the meaning of this half-
line is uncertain. According to Sāyaṇa, *the herd* is the
company of sacrificers and priests, its *mother* is Stuti or
Praise, the *seven-toned*, or sevenfold, are the metres, or the
seasons, or the Hotar priests. *The Herd's Mother* is more
probably Pṛśni, the mother of the Maruts. The whole
stanza is translated by Wilson:—'Shine, Indra, upon this
elegant chamber of sacrifice, when our praises desire (thy
approach) as milch-kine (desire) their stalls; since the
praise of me the worshipper precedes (the adoration) of
the company, and this person accompanied by the seven
officiating priests is the offerer of praise.'

5 *The Pious One* : Agni, the special worshipper of Gods.
One only : Indra.

6 *He* : perhaps Soma. *Thou* : Agni, Cp. I. 23, 20.

Indra, who knoweth well, beheld and showed thee. By him instructed am I come, O Agni.

7 The stranger asks the way of him who knows it : taught by the skilful guide he travels onward.
This is, in truth, the blessing of instruction : he finds the path that leads directly forward.

8 Even now he breathed : these days hath he remembered. Concealed, he sucked the bosom of his Mother.
Yet in his youth old age hath come upon him : he hath grown gracious, good, and free from anger.

9 O Kalaśa, all these blessings will we bring them, O Kuruśravaṇa, who give rich presents.
May he, O wealthy princes, and this Soma which I am bearing in my heart, reward you.

HYMN XXXIII.   *Various Deities.*

1. THE urgings of the people have impelled me, and by the nearest way I bring you Pūṣan.
The Universal Gods have brought me safely. The cry was heard, Behold, Duḥśāsu cometh !

2 The ribs that compass me give pain and trouble me like rival wives.
Indigence, nakedness, exhaustion press me sore : my mind is fluttering like a bird's.

3 As rats eat weavers' threads, cares are consuming me, thy singer, Śatakratu, me.
Have mercy on us once, O Indra, Bounteous Lord : be thou a Father unto us.

4 I the priests' Ṛṣi chose as prince most liberal Kuruśravaṇa,
The son of Trasadasyu's son,

5 Whose three bays harnessed to the car bear me straight onward : I will laud
The giver of a thousand meeds,

6 The sire of Upamaśravas, even him whose words were passing sweet,
As a fair field is to its lord.

7 Mark, Upamaśravas, his son, mark, grandson of Mitrātithi :
I am thy father's eulogist.

8 If I controlled Immortal Gods, yea, even were I Lord of men,
My liberal prince were living still.

9 None lives, even had he hundred lives, beyond the statute of the Gods :
So am I parted from my friend.

HYMN XXXIV.   *Dice, Etc.*

1. SPRUNG from tall trees on windy heights, these rollers transport me as they turn upon the table.
Dearer to me the die that never slumbers than the deep draught of Mūjavān's own Soma.

2 She never vexed me nor was angry with me, but to my friends and me was ever gracious.
For the die's sake, whose single point is final, mine own devoted wife I alienated.

3 My wife holds me aloof, her mother hates me : the wretched man finds none to give him comfort.

8 *Even now he breathed* : began to show signs of life. The connexion between stanzas 1—4 and 5—8 is not apparent. *Sucked the bosom of his Mother* : enjoyed oblations, in the shape of Soma juice, etc., produced by the earth.

9 The meaning of *Kalaśa*, literally 'pitcher' or 'beaker,' here is uncertain. '(Indra), the possessor of the pitchers.'—Wilson. Ludwig suggests *kalāśaḥ* as the right reading : 'We will perform these holy ceremonies in their minutest details.' *Kuruśravaṇa* : according to Sāyaṇa, 'hearer of the praise of priests,' but probably the name of a prince, as in the following hymn.

1 *Duḥśāsu* : literally, 'the malevolent.' Perhaps, as Ludwig suggests, a hostile prince whose victory over Kuruśravaṇa has caused the distress mentioned in the following stanza.
2 The first line is taken from I. 105. 8.
3 This first line is taken from I. 105. 5. *Weavers' threads* : threads steeped in water, according to Sāyaṇa. *Once*; 'after having so often given us up to misery.' —Ludwig.

4 *The Priests' Ṛṣi* : higher in rank than the other priests. *Chose* : i. e. I chose to keep him as my master in order to go out to battle with him.'—Lanman, *Sanskrit Reader*, p. 386.

6 This and the three following stanzas are said to be consolatory verses addressed by the Ṛṣi Kavaṣa to Upamaśravas on the death of his father Mitrātithi.

8 *Were I Lord of men* : as one of the Gods. *My liberal prince* : Mitrātithi.

9 *Beyond the statute of the Gods* : beyond the time fixed for the duration of his life.
This hymn has been placed by Grassmann in his Appendix as a composite production consisting of incoherent fragments. See Lanman, *Sanskrit Reader*, pp. 386, 389.

1 *Sprung from tall trees* : the nuts of the Vibhīdaka, or, later, Vibhītaka, tree (Terminalia Bellerica) were used as dice in early times. *Rollers* : swiftly rolling dice. *Mūjavān* : said to be a mountain on which the finest Soma plants grew.

2 *Whose single point is final* : the speaker has apparently lost all by throwing aces.

As of a costly horse grown old and feeble,
I find not any profit of the gamester.

4 Others caress the wife of him whose riches
the die hath coveted, that rapid courser :
Of him speak father, mother, brothers
saying, We know him not : bind him
and take him with you.

5 When I resolve to play with these no longer,
my friends depart from me and leave
me lonely.
When the brown dice, thrown on the
board, have rattled, like a fond girl I
seek the place of meeting.

6 The gamester seeks the gambling-house,
and wonders, his body all afire, Shall
I be lucky ?
Still do the dice extend his eager longing,
staking his gains against his adversary.

7 Dice, verily, are armed with goads and
driving-hooks, deceiving and tormenting,
causing grievous woe.
They give frail gifts and then destroy the
man who wins, thickly anointed with the
player's fairest good.

8 Merrily sports their troop, the three-and-
fifty, like Savitar the God whose ways
are faithful.
They bend not even to the mighty's
anger : the King himself pays homage
and reveres them.

9 Downward they roll, and then spring
quickly upward, and, handless, force the
man with hands to serve them.
Cast on the board, like lumps of magic
charcoal, though cold themselves they
burn the heart to ashes.

10 The gambler's wife is left forlorn and
wretched : the mother mourns the son
who wanders homeless.
In constant fear, in debt, and seeking
riches, he goes by night unto the home
of others.

11 Sad is the gambler when he sees a matron,
another's wife, and his well-ordered
dwelling.
He yokes the brown steeds in the early
morning, and when the fire is cold sinks
down an outcast.

12 To the great captain of your mighty army,
who hath become the host's imperial
leader,
To him I show my ten extended fingers :
I speak the truth. No wealth am I
withholding.

13 Play not with dice : no, cultivate thy
corn-land. Enjoy the gain, and deem that
wealth sufficient.
There are thy cattle, there thy wife, O
gambler. So this good Savitar himself
hath told me.

14 Make me your friend : show us some little
mercy. Assail us not with your terrific
fierceness.
Appeased be your malignity and anger,
and let the brown dice snare some
other captive.

HYMN XXXV.   *Viśvedevas.*

1. THESE fires associate with Indra are
awake, bringing their light when first
the Dawn begins to shine.
May Heaven and Earth, great Pair, observe
our holy work. We claim for us this
day the favour of the Gods.

2 Yea, for ourselves we claim the grace of
Heaven and Earth, of Śaryaṇāvān, of
the Hills and Mother Streams.
For innocence we pray to Sūrya and to
Dawn. So may the flowing Soma bring
us bliss to-day.

3 May the great Twain, the Mothers, Heaven
and Earth, this day preserve us free
from sin for peace and happiness.

---

4 *Bind him* : he has staked his personal freedom, and
lost; and his people renounce him.

7 *Driving-hooks* : used by mahouts or elephant-drivers.
The last half-line of the stanza is difficult :—'they appear
to the gambler covered with honey.'—Muir.

8 *Three-and-fifty* : or, perhaps, thrice five in number.
It would appear from Sāyaṇa's Commentary that fifty-
three was the usual number of dice employed; and yet
this seems hardly probable. Ludwig suggests 'three times
five' as the meaning here of *tripañcaśáḥ*, and Prof. Weber
would read *tripañcaśáḥ* instead of *tripañcāśáḥ* (*Ueber den
Rājasūya*, p. 72). Like *Saritar* : '(disposing men's destinies) like the god S.'—Muir.

10 *Riches* : wealth gained by robbery, according to
Sāyaṇa.

11 *Yokes the brown steeds* : begins throwing the nut-dice.
When the fire is cold : 'by the time when the fire goes out
he has sunk into a degraded wretch.'—Muir.

12 *The great captain*: the highest numbered of all
the dice. *Ten fingers*: to show that I have nothing left.

14 This stanza is a farewell address to the Dice.
Some other: our enemy.— Sāyaṇa.

The hymn or lay has been transliterated, translated in prose, and freely reproduced in rhymed
octosyllabic verse, by Dr. J. Muir, *O.S. Texts*, V.
425—429. It has also been translated by the authors
of the *Siebenzig Lieder*.

1 *With Indra* : as a God of the morning light.

2 *Of Śaryaṇāvān, of the Hills*: according to Sāyaṇa,
'of the mountains of Śaryaṇāvān,' a lake in the
district of Kurukṣetra. I follow Ludwig in
taking both *párvatān* and *śaryaṇávataḥ* as genitives.

May Morning sending forth her light drive sin afar. We pray to kindled Agni for felicity.

4 May this first Dawn bring us the host of gracious Gods : rich, may it richly shine for us who strive for wealth.
The wrath of the malignant may we keep afar. We pray to kindled Agni for felicity.

5 Dawns, who come forward with the bright beams of the Sun, and at your earliest flushing bring to us the light,
Shine ye on us to-day auspicious, for renown. We pray to kindled Agni for felicity.

6 Free from all sickness may the Mornings come to us, and let our fires mount upward with a lofty blaze.
The Aśvin Pair have harnessed their swift-moving car. We pray to kindled Agni for felicity.

7 Send us to-day a portion choice and excellent, O Savitar, for thou art he who dealeth wealth.
I cry to Dhiṣaṇā, Mother of opulence. We pray to kindled Agni for felicity.

8 Further me this declaring of Eternal Law, the Law of Gods, as we mortals acknowledge it !
The Sun goes up beholding all the rays of morn. We pray to kindled Agni for felicity.

9 This day we pray with innocence in strewing grass, adjusting pressing-stones, and perfecting the hymn.
Thou in the Ādityas' keeping movest restlessly. We pray to kindled Agni for felicity.

10 To our great holy grass I bid the Gods at morn to banquet, and will seat them as the seven priests,—
Varuṇa, Indra, Mitra, Bhaga for our gain. We pray to kindled Agni for felicity.

11 Come hither, O Ādityas, for our perfect weal : accordant help our sacrifice that we may thrive.

Pūṣan, Bṛhaspati, Bhaga, both Aśvins, and enkindled Agni we implore for happiness.

12 Ādityas, Gods, vouchsafe that this our home may be praise-worthy, prosperous, our heroes' sure defence,
For cattle, for our sons, for progeny, for life. We pray to kindled Agni for felicity.

13 This day may all the Maruts, all be near us with aid : may all our fires be well enkindled.
May all Gods come to us with gracious favour. May spoil and wealth be ours, and all possessions.

14 He whom ye aid, O Deities, in battle, whom ye protect and rescue from affliction,
Who fears no danger at your milk-libation, —such may we be to feast the Gods, ye Mighty.

HYMN XXXVI.   *Viśvedevas.*

1. THERE are the Dawn and Night, the grand and beauteous Pair, Earth, Heaven, and Varuṇa, Mitra, and Aryaman.
Indra I call, the Maruts, Mountains, and the Floods, Ādityas, Heaven and Earth, the Waters, and the Sky.

2 May Dyaus and Pṛthivi, wise, true to Holy Law, keep us in safety from distress and injury.
Let not malignant Nirṛti rule over us. We crave to-day this gracious favour of the Gods.

3 Mother of Mitra and of opulent Varuṇa, may Aditi preserve us safe from all distress.
May we obtain the light of heaven without a foe. We crave this gracious favour of the Gods to-day.

4 May ringing press-stones keep the Rākṣasas afar, ill dream, and Nirṛti, and each voracious fiend.
May the Ādityas and the Maruts shelter us. We crave this gracious favour of the Gods to-day.

---

5 *Your*: according to the text 'their,' the verb in the first line being in the third person.

7 *Dhiṣaṇā*: a Goddess who presides over Prosperity, according to Hillebrandt, the Earth

8 *Further me*: 'May that glorification of the gods which men repeat in connexion with the rite preserve me.'—Wilson.

9 *Movest restlessly*: performest thy duties, according to Sāyaṇa. Agni rapidly burning the fuel appears to be intended.

14 *Who fears no danger*: who feels assured that his worship of the Gods will protect him.

---

1 *The Waters*: of the firmament.

2 *Dyaus and Pṛthivi*: Heaven and Earth. *Nirṛti* Death or Destruction.

5 Full flow libations; on our grass let Indra
sit; Bṛhaspati the singer laud with Sāma
hymns !
Wise be our hearts' imaginings that we
may live. We crave this gracious favour
of the Gods to-day.

6 Ye Aśvins, make our sacrifice ascend to
heaven, and animate the rite that it
may send us bliss,
Offered with holy oil, with forward-speed-
ing rein. We crave the gracious favour
of the Gods to-day.

7 Hither I call the band of Maruts, swift to
hear, great, purifying, bringing bliss, to
be our Friends.
May we increase our wealth to glorify our
name. We crave this gracious favour of
the Gods to-day.

8 We bring the Stay of Life, who makes the
waters swell, swift-hearing, Friend of Gods,
who waits on sacrifice.
May we control that Power, Soma whose
rays are bright. We crave this gracious
favour of the Gods to-day.

9 Alive ourselves, with living sons, devoid of
guilt, may we win this with winners by
fair means to win.
Let the prayer-haters bear our sin to every
side. We crave this gracious favour of
the Gods to-day.

10 Hear us, O ye who claim the worship of
mankind, and give us, O ye Gods, the
gift for which we pray,
Victorious wisdom, fame with heroes and
with wealth. We crave to-day this gracious favour of the Gods.

11 We crave the gracious favour of the Gods
to-day, great favour of great Gods,
sublime and free from foes,
That we may gain rich treasure sprung
from hero sons. We crave this gracious
favour of the Gods to-day.

12 In great enkindled Agni's keeping, and, for
bliss, free from all sin before Mitra and
Varuṇa.
May we share Savitar's best animating
help. We crave this gracious favour of
the Gods to-day.

13 All ye, the Gods whom Savitar the Father
of truth, and Varuṇa and Mitra govern,

Give us prosperity with hero children, and
opulence in kine and various treasure.

14 Savitar, Savitar from east and westward,
Savitar, Savitar from north and south-
ward,
Savitar send us perfect health and comfort,
Savitar let our days of life be leng-
thened !

HYMN XXXVII.   *Sūrya.*

1. Do homage unto Varuṇa's and Mitra's
Eye : offer this solemn worship to the
Mighty God,
Who seeth far away, the Ensign, born of
Gods. Sing praises unto Sūrya, to the
Son of Dyaus.

2 May this my truthful speech guard me on
every side, wherever heaven and earth
and days are spread abroad.
All else that is in motion finds a place of
rest : the waters ever flow and ever
mounts the Sun.

3 No godless man from time remotest draws
thee down when thou art driving forth
with winged dappled Steeds.
One lustre waits upon thee moving to the
east, and, Sūrya, thou arisest with a
different light.

4 O Sūrya, with the light whereby thou
scatterest gloom, and with thy ray im-
pellest every moving thing,
Keep far from us all feeble, worthless sacrifice, and drive away disease and every
evil dream.

5 Sent forth thou guardest well the Universe's law, and in thy wonted way
arisest free from wrath.
When Sūrya, we address our prayers to
thee to-day, may the Gods favour this
our purpose and desire.

6 This invocation, these our words may
Heaven and Earth, and Indra and the
Waters and the Maruts hear.
Ne'er may we suffer want in presence of
the Sun, and, living happy lives, may
we attain old age.

---

8 *Who makes the waters swell*: apām perum: 'protector
of the waters.'—Sāyaṇa. 'Drinker of the waters'.—
Ludwig. Soma is meant. See IX, 76, 4.

---

1 *Varuṇa's and Mitra's Eye*: Sūrya or the Sun. 'The
eye of Mitra, Varuṇa and Agni.'—I. 115. I.
3 *Dappled Steeds*: 'with Etaśas.'—Ludwig. *One lustre*:
by night. Cf. I. 115. 5; and *Aitareya-Brāhmaṇa*, III,
4.44. 'One ancient radiance follows* (thee) whilst thou
risest with another.'—Wilson. See Wallis, *Cosmology of the
Rgveda*, p. 117.
5 *In thy wonted way* : svadhā dnu: 'after the svadhā
offerings.'—Wilson.

7 Cheerful in spirit, evermore, and keen
of sight, with store of children, free
from sickness and from sin,
Long-living, may we look, O Sūrya, upon
thee uprising day by day, thou great as
Mitra is !

8 Sūrya, may we live long and look upon
thee still, thee, O Far-seeing One, bringing the glorious light,
The radiant God, the spring of joy to
every eye, as thou art mounting up o'er
the high shining flood.

9 Thou by whose lustre all the world of life
comes forth, and by thy beams again
returns unto its rest,
O Sūrya with the golden hair, ascend for
us day after day, still bringing purer
innocence.

10 Bless us with shine, bless us with perfect
daylight, bless us with cold, with fervent
heat and lustre.
Bestow on us, O Sūrya, varied riches, to
bless us in our home and when we
travel.

11 Gods, to our living creatures of both kinds
vouchsafe protection, both to bipeds
and to quadrupeds,
That they may drink and eat invigorating
food. So grant us health and strength
and perfect innocence.

12 If by some grievous sin we have provoked
the Gods, O Deities, with the tongue or
thoughtlessness of heart,
That guilt, O Vasus, lay upon the Evil
One, on him who ever leads us into
deep distress.

HYMN XXXVIII. *Indra.*

1. O INDRA, in this battle great and glorious, in this loud din of war help us
to victory,
Where in the strife for kine among bold
ring-decked men arrows fly all around
and heroes are subdued.

2 At home disclose to us opulence rich in
food, streaming with milk, O Indra,
meet to be renowned.

8 *Flood*: or floor of heaven.

12 *The Evil One*: *drāvā*: here probably a kind of
Diabolus or Devil.—Ludwig.

———

1 *Ring-decked*: adorned with armlets, or quoits as
weapons.

Śakra, may we be thine, the friendly
Conqueror's : even as we desire, O Vasu,
so do thou.

3 The godless man, much-lauded Indra,
whether he be Dāsa or be Ārya, who
would war with us,—
Easy to conquer be for thee, with us, these
foes : with thee may we subdue them
in the clash of fight.

4 Him who must be invoked by many and
by few, who standeth nigh with comfort
in the war of men,
Indra, famed Hero, winner in the deadly
strife, let us bring hitherward to-day to
favour us.

5 For, Indra, I have heard thee called Self-
capturer, One, Steer ! who never yields,
who urges even the churl.
Release thyself from Kutsa and come
hither. How shall one like thee sit still
bound that he may not move ?

HYMN XXXIX. *Aśvins.*

1. As 'twere the name of father, easy to
invoke, we all assembled here invoke
this Car of yours,
Aśvins, your swiftly-rolling circumambient
Car which he who worships must invoke
at eve and dawn.

2 Awake all pleasant strains and let the
hymns flow forth : raise up abundant
fulness : this is our desire.
Aśvins, bestow on us a glorious heritage,
and give our princes treasure fair as
Soma is.

3 Ye are the bliss of her who groweth old
at home, and helpers of the slow although he linger last.

5 *Self-capturer*; it is difficult to assign a reasonable
and appropriate meaning to *svavrjam*. Sāyaṇa explains
it by *svayam eva cchettāram*, 'one who cuts himself:' 'self
mutilator'.—Wilson. According to the St. Petersburg
Lexicon, the meaning is 'one who appropriates or takes
to himself;' according to Ludwig 'the self-rescuer,' and
according to Geldner 'one who suffers himself to be
captured.' The poet calls on Indra to tear himself
away from his favourite Kutsa in order to aid his
worshippers in the coming fight. 'A legend is here
somewhat obscurely related, that *Kutsa* and *Luśa* having
summoned Indra at the same time to their respective
sacrifices, he went first to *Kutsa* who then detained him,
having fastened him...with a hundred leather thongs.
This verse is addressed to *Indra* and *Luśa* exhorting him
to free himself.—Wilson.

———

The Ṛṣi is Ghoṣā, daughter of Kakṣivān.

3 *Of her who groweth old at home*: referring to
Ghoṣā herself. See I. 17. 7. *Healers of the blind*: See I.
112. 8.

Men call you too, Nāsatyas, healers of the
blind, the thin and feeble, and the man
with broken bones.

4 Ye made Cyavāna, weak and worn with
length of days, young again, like a car,
that he had power to move.
Ye lifted up the son of Tugra from the
floods. At our libations must all these
your acts be praised.

5 We will declare among the folk your
ancient deeds heroic ; yea, ye were
Physicians bringing health.
You, you who must be lauded, will we
bring for aid, so that this foe of ours,
O Aśvins, may believe.

6 Listen to me, O Aśvins ; I have cried to
you. Give me your aid as sire and
mother aid their son.
Poor, without kin or friend or ties of
blood am I. Save me before it be too
late, from this my curse.

7 Ye, mounted on your chariot brought to
Vimada the comely maid of Purumitra
as a bride.
Ye, came unto the calling of the weakling's dame, and granted noble offspring
to the happy wife.

8 Ye gave again the vigour of his youthful
life to the sage Kali when old age was
coming nigh.
Ye rescued Vandana and raised him from
the pit, and in a moment gave Viśpalā
power to move.

9 Ye Aśvins Twain, endowed with manly
strength, brought forth Rebha when
hidden in the cave and well-nigh dead,
Freed Saptavadhri, and for Atri caused
the pit heated with fire to be a pleasant resting-place.

10 On Pedu ye bestowed, Aśvins, a courser
white, mighty with nine-and-ninety
varied gifts of strength,
A horse to be renowned, who bore his
friend at speed, joy-giving, Bhaga-like to
be invoked of men.

11 From no side, ye Two Kings whom none
may check or stay, doth grief, distress,
or danger come upon the man
Whom, Aśvins swift to hear, borne on
your glowing path, ye with your Consort
make the foremost in the race.

12 Come on that Chariot which the Ṛbhus
wrought for you, the Chariot, Aśvins,
that is speedier than thought,
At harnessing whereof Heaven's Daughter
springs to birth, and from Vivasvān
come auspicious Night and Day.

13 Come, Conquerors of the sundered mountain, to our home, Aśvins who made
the cow stream milk for Śayu's sake,
Ye who delivered even from the wolf's deep
throat and set again at liberty the swallowed quail.

14 We have prepared this laud for you, O
Aśvins, and, like the Bhṛgus, as a car
have framed it,
Have decked it as a maid to meet the
bridegroom, and brought it as a son,
our stay for ever.

HYMN XL.   Aśvins.

1. YOUR radiant Chariot—whither goes it on
its way ?—who decks it for you, Heroes,
for its happy course,
Starting at daybreak, visiting each morning
every house, borne hitherward through
prayer unto the sacrifice ?

2 Where are ye, Aśvins, in the evening,
where at morn ? Where is your halting-
place, where rest ye for the night ?
Who brings you homeward, as the widow
bedward draws her husband's brother,
as the bride attracts the groom ?

---

11 *Whom none may check or stay: adite—adīnau.—*
Sāyaṇa. *Your Consort*: Sūryā. *The foremost in the race*:
that is, generally, preëminent.

12 *Heaven's Daughter*: Uṣas or Dawn. *Vivasvān*: the
morning Sun.

13 *Conquerors of the sundered mountain*: probably with
reference to the deliverance of Jāhuṣa—Ludwig. See
I. 116. 20. *The swallowed quail*: see I. 112.8. The quail
is probably Dawn delivered from the jaws of the wolf
Night by the twin Light-Gods.

14 *Our stay for ever* : who will perpetuate our family;
'the eternal performer of rites.'—Wilson.

---

4 *Cyavāna*: See I. 116. 10, and 117. 13. *Son of
Tugra*: Bhujyu. See Vol. I., Index.

6 *My curse*: leprosy, which prevented her
marriage.

7 *Vimada*: See I. 117. 20. *The weakling's dame*: See
I. 117. 24.

8 For *Kali, Vandana,* and *Viśpalā* in this stanza,
and *Rebha, Atri,* and *Pedu* in 9 and 10, See Vol. I.,
Index. For *Saptavadhri* (stanza 9) See V. 78, 6.

---

2 *As the widow*: in certain circumstances a widow
was bound to marry her deceased husband's brother. See
Manu (*Mānavadharmaśāstra*), IX 69. 70. The law of the
Jews was the same. See Deuteronomy, xxv. 5.

3 Early ye sing forth praise as with a herald's
voice, and, meet for worship, go each
morning to the house.
Whom do ye ever bring to ruin ? Unto
whose libations come ye, Heroes, like
two Sons of Kings ?

4 Even as hunters follow two wild elephants,
we with oblations call you down at
morn and eve.
To folk who pay you offerings at appointed times, Chiefs, Lords of splendour, ye
bring food to strengthen them.

5 To you, O Aśvins, came the daughter of
a King, Ghoṣā, and said, O Heroes,
this I beg of you :
Be near me in the day, be near me in the
night : help me to gain a car-borne
chieftain rich in steeds.

6 O Aśvins, ye are wise : as Kutsa comes to
men, bring your car nigh the folk of
him who sings your praise.
The bee, O Aśvins, bears your honey in
her mouth, as the maid carries it purified in her hand.

7 To Bhujyu and to Vaśa ye come near
with help, O Aśvins, to Śiñjāra and to
Uśanā.
Your worshipper secures your friendship
for himself. Through your protection I
desire felicity.

8 Kṛśa and Śayu ye protect, ye Aśvins
Twain : ye Two assist the widow and
the worshipper ;
And ye throw open, Aśvins, unto those
who win the cattle-stall that thunders
with its sevenfold mouth.

9 The Woman hath brought forth, the Infant
hath appeared, the plants of wondrous
beauty straightway have sprung up.

To him the rivers run as down a deep
descent, and he this day becomes their
master and their lord.

10 They mourn the living, cry aloud, at
sacrifice : the men have set their thoughts upon a distant cast.
A lovely thing for fathers who have gathered here,—a joy to husbands,—are the
wives their arms shall clasp

11 Of this we have no knowledge. Tell it
forth to us, now the youth rests within
the chambers of the bride.
Fain would we reach the dwelling of the
vigorous Steer who loves the kine, O
Aśvins : this is our desire.

12 Your favouring grace hath come, ye
Lords of ample wealth : Aśvins, our
longings are stored up within your hearts.
Ye, Lords of splendour, have become our
twofold guard : may we as welcome
friends reach Aryaman's abode.

13 Even so, rejoicing in the dwelling-place
of man, give hero sons and riches to
the eloquent.
Make a ford, Lords of splendour, where
men well may drink : remove the spiteful tree-stump standing in the path.

14 O Aśvins, Wonder-Workers, Lords of lustre,
where and with what folk do ye delight
yourselves to-day ?
Who hath detained them with him ? Whither are they gone ? Unto what sage's
or what worshipper's abode ?

HYMN XLI. Aśvins.

1. THAT general Car of yours, invoked by
many a man, that comes to our libations,
three-wheeled, meet for lauds,

3 *As with a herald's voice*: *kāpayā* is thus explained
by Sāyaṇa. *The house*: of the sacrificer.

5 The second half of the second line is difficult:
'be able (to grant favour) to the son of my brother,
who has horses and a chariot.'—Wilson.

6 *As Kutsa comes to men*: borne on Indra's chariot.
Bears your honey: sips honey when the Aśvins have
ushered in the day. *As the maid*: Dr. Muir and Prof.
Grassmann explain this half-line differently. 'as a maid,
or a woman, resorts to her rendezvous (with her
lover).'

7 *Vaśa*: See I. 112, 10 *Śiñjāra*: See VIII. 5.25. *Uśanā*:
see Vol. I., Index.

8 *Kṛśa*: a Ṛṣi favoured by Indra; or, as Sāyaṇa
explains the word here, the feeble man in general. *Śayu*:
has been mentioned frequently. *The cattle-stall*: the rain-
cloud whose waters are the cows.

9 *The Woman*: perhaps the water of the cloud. *The
Infant*: the lightning. *To him*: the sacrificer may perhaps
be intended.

10 *They mourn the living*: perhaps, show their sorrow
for the widower at the funeral of his wife. See Lanman
(*Sanskrit Reader*. p. 387) from whom I have borrowed.
Set their thoughts upon a distant cast: of the noose or
snaring-net: apparently a periphrasis for, have taken
thought for the distant future and children to live after
them.

11 Ghoṣā appears to speak of herself in the
plural number. She plainly expresses her wishes for
marriage.

12 *Aryaman's abode*: Aryaman is here used in the
original sense of the word, bosom-friend and companion,
especially the friend who asks a woman in marriage for
another.

Prof. Grassmann places stanzas 10—14 in his
Appendix as being obscure and in his opinion forming
no part of the original hymn.

1 *Three-wheeled*: See I, 34.9.

That circumambient Car, worthy of sacrifice, we call with our pure hymns at earliest flush of dawn.

2 Ye, O Nāsatyas, mount that early-harnessed Car, that travels early, laden with its freight of balm,

Wherewith ye, Heroes, visit clans who sacrifice, even the poor man's worship where the priest attends.

3 If to the deft Adhvaryu with the meath in hand, or to the Kindler firm in strength, the household friend,

Or to the sage's poured libations ye approach, come thence, O Aśvins, now to drink the offered meath.

HYMN XLII.   *Indra.*

1. EVEN as an archer shoots afar his arrow, offer the laud to him with meet adornment.

Quell with your voice the wicked's voice, O sages. Singer, make Indra rest beside the Soma.

2 Draw thy Friend to thee like a cow at milking : O Singer, wake up Indra as a lover.

Make thou the Hero haste to give us riches even as a vessel filled brimful with treasure.

3 Why, Maghavan, do they call thee Bounteous Giver ? Quicken me : thou, I hear, art he who quickens.

Śakra, let my intelligence be active, and bring us luck that finds great wealth, O Indra.

4 Standing, in battle for their rights, together, the people, Indra, in the fray invoke thee.

Him who brings gifts the Hero makes his comrade : with him who pours no juice he seeks not friendship.

5 Whoso with plenteous food for him expresses strong Somas as much quickly-coming treasure,

For him he overthrows in early morning his swift well-weaponed foes, and slays the tyrant.

---

3 *The Kindler*: the Agnidh, the priest who kindles the sacrificial fire.

---

1 *The wicked's voice*: 'the praises of your adversaries.' —Wilson.

4 *The Hero*: Indra.

5 *As much quickly-coming treasure*: representing the wealth which the offering of the libations is expected to produce.

6 He unto whom we offer praises, Indra, Maghavan, who hath joined to ours his wishes,—

Before him even afar the foe must tremble : low before him must bow all human glories.

7 With thy fierce bolt, O God invoked of many, drive to a distance from afar the foeman.

O Indra, give us wealth in corn and cattle, and make thy singer's prayer gain strength and riches.

8 Indra, the swallower of strong libations rich in the boons they bring, the potent Somas,

He, Maghavan, will not restrict his bounty : he brings much wealth unto the Soma-presser.

9 Yea, by superior play he wins advantage, when he, a gambler, piles his gains in season.

Celestial-natured, he o'erwhelms with riches the devotee who keeps not back his treasure.

10 O Much-invoked, may we subdue all famine and evil want with store of grain and cattle.

May we allied, as first in rank, with princes obtain possessions by our own exertion.

11 Bṛhaspati protect us from the rearward, and from above, and from below, from sinners !

May Indra from the front, and from the centre, as Friend to friends, vouchsafe us room and freedom.

HYMN XLIII.   *Indra.*

1. IN perfect unison all yearning hymns of mine that find the light of heaven have sung forth Indra's praise.

As wives embrace their lord, the comely bridegroom, so they compass Maghavan about that he may help.

2 Directed unto thee my spirit never strays, for I have set my hopes on thee, O Much-invoked !

Sit, Wonderful ! as King upon the sacred grass, and let thy drinking-place be by the Soma juice.

---

6 *Unto whom we offer praises*; or, in whom we have placed our hope.

9 *When he, a gambler*: cp. X 43, 5.

10 *With princes*: with men eminent for their wealth: *rājabhir-dhanānāmīśvarai ḥ*—Sāyaṇa.

3 From indigence and hunger Indra turns
away : Maghavan hath dominion over
precious wealth.
These the Seven Rivers flowing on their
downward path increase the vital vigour
of the potent Steer.

4 As on the fair-leafed tree rest birds, to
Indra flow the gladdening Soma juices
that the bowls contain.
Their face that glows with splendour
through their mighty power hath found
the shine of heaven for man, the Āryas'
light.

5 As in the game a gambler piles his winnings, so Maghavan, sweeping all together,
gained the Sun
This mighty deed of thine none other
could achieve, none, Maghavan, before
thee, none in recent time.

6 Maghavan came by turns to all the tribes
of men : the Steer took notice of the
people's songs of praise.
The man in whose libations Sakra hath
delight by means of potent Somas
vanquisheth his foes.

7 When Soma streams together unto Indra
flow like waters to the river, rivulets to
the lake,
In place of sacrifice sages exalt his might,
as the rain swells the corn by moisture
sent from heaven.

8 He rushes through the region like a furious
Bull, he who hath made these floods
the dames of worthy lords.
This Maghavan hath found light for the
man who brings oblation, sheds the
juice, and promptly pours his gifts.

9 Let the keen axe come forth together with
the light : here be, as erst, the teeming
cow of sacrifice.
Let the Red God shine bright with his
refulgent ray, and let the Lord of heroes
glow like heaven's clear sheen.

10 O Much-invoked, may we subdue all
famine and evil want with store of
grain and cattle.
May we allied, as first in rank, with princes obtain possessions by our own
exertion.

11 Brhaspati protect us from the rearward, and
from above, and from below, from
sinners.
May Indra from the front, and from the
centre, as Friend to friends, vouchsafe
us room and freedom.

HYMN XLIV.   Indra.

1. MAY Sovran Indra come to the carousal,
he who by Holy Law is strong and
active,
The overcomer of all conquering forces
with his great steer-like power that hath
no limit.

2 Firm-seated is thy car, thy Steeds are
docile ; thy hand, O King, holds, firmly
grasped, the thunder.
On thy fair path, O Lord of men, come
quickly : we will increase thy powers
when thou hast drunken.

3 Let strong and mighty Steeds who bear
this Mighty Indra, the Lord of men,
whose arm wields thunder,
Bring unto us, as sharers of our banquet,
the Steer of conquering might, of real
vigour.

4 So like a Bull thou rushest to the Lord
who loves the trough, the Sage, the
prop of vigour, in the vat,
Prepare thine energies, collect them in
thyself : be for our profit as the Master
of the wise.

5 May precious treasures come to us—so
will I pray. Come to the votary's
gift offered with beauteous laud.
Thou art the Lord, as such sit on this
holy grass : thy vessels are inviolate as
Law commands.

6 Far went our earliest invocation of the Gods,
and won us glories that can never be
surpassed.

---

3 *Turns away*: Sâyana makes *viṣuvṛ*' transitive:—
'May Indra be the remover of thirst and hunger.'—
Wilson.

5 *Gained the Sun*: conquers him by taking away
his moisture, that is, the water that he has absorbed.—
Sâyana.

8 *The dames of worthy lords*: that is, subjected them
to the Āryans, whereas they had been the thralls of
Dāsas. See I 32. 11.

9 *The keen axe*: Agni, who is frequently likened
to an axe. See I, 127. 3, and VI. 3. 4. *The Red God*:
aruṣaḥ: according to Sâyana, 'the radiant Indra'; but
Agni is probably intended, or perhaps 'the red bolt' as
M. Müller prefers.

10 The two concluding stanzas are identical in
Hymns 52, 53, 54.   ——

4 *The Lord*: *patim*: the Soma. *Collect them in
thyself*: take us into thyself.—Wilson. *Of the wise*:
kenipānām is thus explained by the Commentators, but
the meaning seems doubtful. Ludwig thinks that
'the master *of the oars*' that is, the steersman, is
intended.

6 *In desolation* : *irmā*—Ludwig. *Trembling
in alarm*: or, doers of ill deeds according to Yāska's
interpretation of *kepayaḥ*.

They who could not ascend the ship of
sacrifice, sink down in desolation, trembling with alarm.

7 So be the others, evil-hearted, far away,
whose horses, difficult to harness, have
been yoked.
Here in advance men stand anear to offer
gifts, by whom full many a work that
brings reward is done.

8 He firmly fixed the plains and mountains
as they shook. Dyaus thundered forth
and made the air's mid-region quake.
He stays apart the two confronting bowls;
he sings lauds in the potent Soma's joy
when he hath drunk.

9 I bear this deftly-fashioned goad of thine,
wherewith thou, Maghavan, shalt break
the strikers with the hoof.
At this libation mayst thou be well satisfied. Partake the juice, partake the
worship, Maghavan.

10 O Much-invoked, may we subdue all
famine and evil want with store of grain
and cattle.
May we allied, as first in rank, with
princes obtain possessions by our own
exertion.

11 Bṛhaspati protect us from the rearward,
and from above, and from below, from
sinners.
May Indra from the front and from the
centre, as Friend to friends, vouchsafe
us room and freedom.

HYMN XLV.   *Agni.*

1. FIRST Agni sprang to life from out of
Heaven : the second time from us came
Jātavedas.
Thirdly the Manly-souled was in the waters.
The pious lauds and kindles him the
Eternal.

2 Agni, we know thy three powers in three
stations, we know thy forms in many a
place divided.
We know what name supreme thou hast in
secret : we know the source from which
thou hast proceeded.

3 The Manly-souled lit thee in sea and waters,
man's Viewer lit thee in the breast of
heaven,
There as thou stoodest in the third high
region the Steers increased thee in the
water's bosom.

4 Agni roared out, like Dyaus what time
he thunders : he licked the ground,
about the plants he flickered.
At once, when born, he looked around
enkindled, and lightened heaven and
earth within with splendour.

5 The spring of glories and support of riches,
rouser of thoughts and guardian of the
Soma,
Good Son of Strength, a King amid the
waters, in forefront of the Dawns he
shines enkindled.

6 Germ of the world, ensign of all creation,
be sprang to life and filled the earth
and heavens.
Even the firm rock he cleft when passing
over, when the Five Tribes brought
sacrifice to Agni.

7 So among mortals was Immortal Agni
stablished as holy wise and willing envoy.
He waves the red smoke that he lifts above
him, striving to reach the heavens with
radiant lustre.

8 Like gold to look on, far he shone refulgent, beaming imperishable life for glory,
Agni by vital powers became immortal
when his prolific Father Dyaus begat
him.

9 Whoso this day, O God whose flames are
lovely, prepares a cake, O Agni, mixt
with butter,

---

7 *Whose horses, difficult to harness, have been yoked*:
whose ill-managed attempts to perform acceptable sacrifice have failed. *In advance*: before death according to
Sāyaṇa.

8 *He* Indra. *As they shook*: cp. II. 12. 2. *Two
confronting bowls*: heaven and earth.

9 *Goad*: the hymn of praise which urges Indra
to action. *The strikers with the hoof*: a class of Yātudhānas
or demons. See X. 87. 12.   ——

1 *From out of heaven*: or, from Dyaus or Heaven
his father; in the shape of the Sun. *From us*: produced
by men in the shape of sacrificial and domestic fire. *In
the waters*: of the firmament, in the shape of lightning,
the third form of Agni.

2 *In secret*: unknown to those who know not the
Veda.—Sāyaṇa.

3 *The Manly souled*: or, the Friend of men:
Varuṇa, according to Sāyaṇa, and Prajāpati, according
to Mahīdhara. Perhaps Dyaus (cp. stanza 8) may be
intended—Ludwig. Grassmann thinks that Indra, the
kindler of the lightning, is meant. *The Steers*: or, the
Mighty Ones ; the Maruts.

6 *The firm rock*: 'the solid cloud.'—Wilson. Some
extraordinary conflagration of jungle may perhaps be
referred to. *The Five Tribes*: pañca janāh: literally, the
five men, meaning, according to Sāyaṇa, men
in general, and, according to Mahīdhara,
the institutor of the sacrifice and the four chief
priests.

Lead thou and further him to higher fortune, to bliss bestowed by Gods, O thou
Most Youthful.

10 Endow him, Agni, with a share of glory,
at every song of praise sung forth enrich
him.
Dear let him be to Sūrya, dear to Agni,
preëminent with son and children's
children.

11 While, Agni, day by day men pay thee
worship they win themselves all treasures
worth the wishing.
Allied with thee, eager and craving riches,
they have disclosed the stable filled
with cattle.

12 Agni, the Friend of men, the Soma's
keeper, Vaiśvānara, hath been lauded
by the Ṛṣis.
We will invoke benignant Earth and
Heaven : ye Deities, give us wealth with
hero children.

HYMN XLVI.   *Agni.*

1. STABLISHED for thee, to lend thee vital
forces, Giver of wealth, Guard of his
servant's body.
The Great Priest, born, who knows the
clouds, Abider with men, is seated in
the lap of waters.

2 Worshipping, seeking him with adoration
like some lost creature followed by its
footprints,
Wise Bhṛgus, yearning in their hearts,
pursued him, and found him lurking
where the floods are gathered.

3 On the Cow's forehead, with laborious
searching, Trita, the offspring of
Vibhūvas, found him.
Born in our houses, Youthful, joy-bestower,
he now becomes the central point of
brightness.

4 Yearning, with homage, they have set and
made him blithe Priest among mankind,
oblation-bearer,
Leader of rites and Purifier, envoy of men,
as sacrifice that still advances.

5 The foolish brought the ne'er-bewildered
forward, great, Victor, Song-inspirer,
Fort-destroyer.
Leading the Youth gold-bearded, like a
courser gleaming with wealth, they
turned their hymn to profit.

6 Holding his station firmly in the houses,
Trita sat down within his home surroun-
ded
Thence, as Law bids, departs the Tribes'
Companion having collected men with
no compulsion.

7 His are the fires, eternal, purifying, that
make the houses move, whose smoke is
shining,
White, waxing in their strength, for ever
stirring, and sitting in the wood ; like
winds are Somas.

8 The tongue of Agni bears away the praise-
song, and, through his care for Earth,
her operations.
Him, bright and radiant, living men have
stablished as their blithe Priest, the
Chief of Sacrificers.

9 That Agni, him whom Heaven and Earth
engendered, the Waters, Tvaṣṭar, and
with might, the Bhṛgus,

---

12 *Soma's keeper*: as identified with the Moon, the
great receptacle of the celestial Soma, the nectar or
ambrosia of the Gods. See Hillebrandt, *V. M.*, I.
330—336.

---

1 *For thee*: the Ṛṣi addresses himself *Who knows
the clouds*: from which he (Agni) comes in the form of
Lightning. *Of waters*: of the firmament.

2 *Wise Bhṛgus*: frequently mentioned as specially
connected with the worship of Agni. Cf II 4. 2. *Pursued
him*: see I. 65. 1.

3 *On the Cow's forehead*: 'on the head of the
cloud.' *Trita*: Agni in his third form as lightning.
The abstract personified form of the celestial Agni
is here represented as endeavouring to find the lurking
fire in the sky.—Macdonell. *Offspring of Vibhūvas* : or,
connected with Vibhūvasu, the very wealthy, Soma.

4 *As sacrifice that still advances* : 'als das sich vorwärts
bewegende opfer.' —Ludwig. According to Sāyaṇa, 'the
object of sacrifice, him who goes forward (from one fire
receptacle to another).'

5 *The foolish* : human priests, weak and foolish in
comparison with the wise Agni. *Gleaming with wealth* :
the meaning of *dhánarcam* is uncertain. The St. Petersburg Lexicon offers *dhanarjam*, 'striving to win the prize'
as probably the right reading.

6 On stanzas 3 and 6 see Macdonell (J. R. A. S., July,
1893, pp. 450—452), who translates the second half of
6 as follows : From hence the house-friend of settlers
collecting (them) goes among men by distribution, not
by (means of) bonds; *i. e.* carried from place, not freshly
produced by cord and drill.

7 *That make the houses move* : this seems to be what the
words *damām arítrā* should mean, though how flames can
be thus qualified is not clear. 'The rescuers from the
humiliated (spirits of ill).'—Wilson. 'Protectors of the
houses.'—Mahidhara. *Like winds are Somas* : as winds
fan flame, so Soma libations increase the might of Agni.
According to Sāyaṇa, the flames are 'like the fast-flowing
juices of the *Soma*.'—Wilson. I follow Ludwig's explanation, but the meaning of the passage is doubtful.

8 *Her operations* : holy works performed by men.

Him Mātariśvan and the Gods have fashioned holy for man and first to be entreated.

10 Agni, whom Gods have made oblation-bearer, and much-desiring men regard as holy,
Give life to him who lauds thee when he worships, and then shall glorious men in troops adore thee.

HYMN XLVII. *Indra Vaikuṇṭha.*

1. Thy right hand have we grasped in ours, O Indra, longing for treasure, Treasure-Lord of treasures !
Because we know thee, Hero, Lord of cattle : vouchsafe us mighty and resplendent riches.

2 Wealth, fully armed, good guard and kind protector, sprung from four seas, the prop and stay of treasures,
Fraught with great bounties, meet for praise and glory ; vouchsafe us mighty and resplendent riches.

3 Wealth, with good Brahmans, Indra ! God-attended, high, wide, and deep, and based on broad foundations,
Strong, with famed Ṛṣis, conquering our foemen : vouchsafe us mighty and resplendent riches.

4 Victorious, winning strength, with hero sages, confirmed in power, most useful, wealth-attracting,
True, Indra ! crushing forts and slaying Dasyus : vouchsafe us mighty and resplendent riches.

5 Wealthy in heroes and in cars and horses, strength hundredfold and thousandfold, O Indra,
With manly sages, happy troops, light-winning : vouchsafe us mighty and resplendent riches.

6 To Saptagu the sage, the holy-minded, to him, Bṛhaspati, the song approaches,

Aṅgiras' Son who must be met with homage : vouchsafe us mighty and resplendent riches.

7 My lauds, like envoys, craving loving-kindness, go forth to Indra with their strong entreaty,
Moving his heart and uttered by my spirit : vouchsafe us mighty and resplendent riches.

8 Grant us the boon for which I pray, O Indra, a spacious home unmatched among the people.
To this may Heaven and Earth accord approval : vouchsafe us mighty and resplendent riches.

HYMN XLVIII. *Indra Vaikuṇṭha.*

1. I was the first possessor of all precious gear : the wealth of every man I win and gather up.
On me as on a Father living creatures call ; I deal enjoyment to the man who offers gifts.

2 I, Indra, am Atharvan's stay and firm support : I brought forth kine to Trita from the Dragon's grasp.
I stripped the Dasyus of their manly might, and gave the cattle-stalls to Mātariśvan and Dadhyac.

3 For me hath Tvaṣṭar forged the iron thunderbolt : in me the Gods have centred intellectual power.
My sheen is like the Sun's insufferably bright : men honour me as Lord for past and future deeds.

4 I won myself these herds of cattle, steeds and kine, and gold in ample store, with my destructive bolt.
I give full many a thousand to the worshipper, what time the Somas and the lauds have made me glad.

5 Indra am I ; none ever wins my wealth from me : never at any time am I a thrall to death.
Pressing the Soma, ask riches from me alone : ye, Pūrus, in my friendship shall not suffer harm.

---

9 *Mātariśvan* : a divine or semi-divine being who brought Agni from heaven. See I. 31. 3, and 60. 1.

Vaikuṇṭha is said to mean son of Vikuṇṭhā, an Asurī or female demon who was allowed by Indra to become his second mother.

2 *Wealth* : Sāyaṇa gives another interpretation :— '(We know thee to be) well armed ' etc.—Wilson. *Sprung from four seas* : regarded as the store-houses of jewels. '(Renowned throughout) the four oceans.'—(applied to Indra) Wilson.

6 *Bṛhaspati* : according to the Scholiast meaning Saptagu. 'the lord of much (praise)'.—Wilson. According to others, the God Bṛhaspati called Saptagu as being drawn by seven oxen : 'der fährt mit sieben Rindern'—Grassmann. *Aṅgiras' Son* : meaning apparently Bṛhaspati as especially loved and honoured by Aṅgiras and his descendants. See VI. 73. 1.

---

8 *Unmatched* : *ásamam* : 'not held in common.'—Wilson.

Indra Vaikuṇṭha is the Ṛṣi of this hymn, which is a self-laudatory reply to Saptagu in Hymn XLVII.

2 *Atharvan* is the name of the priest who first obtained fire and offered Soma and prayers to the Gods. See I. 80. 16, and 85. 5. *The Dragon* is apparently Ahi or Vṛtra. 'I generated the waters above the cloud for the sake of Trita.'—Wilson. *Mātariśvan and Dadhyac* : or, according to Sāyaṇa, 'Mātariśvan's son Dadhyac.'

5 *Ye, Pūrus* : 'O men.'—Wilson.

6 These, breathing loud in fury, two and two,
who caused Indra to bring his bolt of
thunder to the fray,
The challengers, I struck with deadly
weapon down : firm stand what words
the God speaks to his worshippers.

This One by stronger might I conquered
singly ; yea, also two : shall three prevail against me ?
Like many sheaves upon the floor I thrash
them. How can my foes, the Indraless,
revile me ?

8 Against the Gungus I made Atithigva
strong, and kept him mid the folk like
Vṛtra-conquering strength,
When I won glory in the great foe-slaying
fight, in battle where Karañja fell, and
Parṇaya.

9 With food for mine enjoyment Sāpya Namī
came : he joined me as a friend of old
in search of kine.
As I bestowed on him an arrow for the
fight I made him worthy of the song
and hymn of praise.

10 One of the two hath Soma, seen within
it ; the Herdsman with the bone shows
forth the other.
He, fain to fight the Bull whose horns were
sharpened, stood fettered in the demon's
ample region.

11 I, as a God, ne'er violate the statutes of
Gods, of Vasus, Rudriyas, Ādityas.
These Gods have formed me for auspicious
vigour, unconquered and invincible for
ever.

HYMN XLIX.   *Indra Vaikuṇṭha.*

1. I HAVE enriched the singer with surpassing wealth ; I have allowed the holy
hymn to strengthen me.
I, furtherer of him who offers sacrifice, have
conquered in each fight the men who
worship not.

2 The People of the heavens, the waters, and
the earth have stablished me among
the Gods with Indra's name.
I took unto myself the two swift vigorous
Bays that speed on divers paths, and
the fierce bolt for strength.

3 With deadly blows I smote Atka for Kavi's
sake ; I guarded Kutsa well with these
my saving helps.
As Śuṣṇa's slayer I brandished the dart
of death : I gave not up the Āryan
name to Dasyu foes.

4 Smadibha, Tugra, and the Vetasus I gave
as prey to Kutsa, father-like, to succour
him.
I was a worthy King to rule the worshipper, when I gave Tuji dear inviolable
gifts.

5 I gave up Mṛgaya to Śrutarvan as his
prey because he ever followed me and
kept my laws.
For Āyu's sake I caused Veśa to bend and
bow, and into Savya's hand delivered
Paḍgṛbhi.

6 I, I crushed Navavāstva of the lofty car,
the Dāsa, as the Vṛtra-slayer kills the
fiends ;
When straightway on the region's farthest
edge I brought the God who makes the
lights to broaden and increase.

---

6 *These* : who these were is uncertain. *Two and two* :
probably the warrior who fights on the chariot and the
charioteer.—Ludwig. The literal translation of the last
half-line of the stanza appears to be:—'the non-worshipper
speaking firm words to worshippers ; *ánamasyuḥ*, he who
has no other to reverence, being Indra, whose promise
of victory to his worshippers is never broken.'—Ludwig.

7 *This One* : or, this one thing, that is, 'the primordial
substance or unit out of which the universe was developed.'
—Wallis, *Cosmology of the Ṛgveda*, p. 58.

8 *Against the Gungus* : or, to aid the Gungus, as
Sāyaṇa explains. Who these people were is uncertain.
Atithigva : Divodāsa, son of Atithigu, according to Sāyaṇa.
See Vol. I., Index. *Karañja...and Parṇaya* : apparently
tree-demons. See I. 53. 8.

9 *Sāpya* : a famous name of Indra's friend Nami, who
in VI. 20. 6 is called Sayya's son.

10 *One of the two* : i. e. Moon. *The Herdsman* : Indra.
With the bone : of Dadhyac. See I. 84. 13. *The other* :
Vṛtra. *He* : Vṛtra. *The Bull* : Indra. *The demon's
ample region* : mid-air, which was then dominated by the
Druh or malignant spirit of drought. I follow Prof.
Ludwig's interpretation of this obscure stanza which is
evidently an interpolation motivated by the mention of
Dadhyac in stanza 2. For a somewhat different inter-
pretation, see Hillebrandt, *V. M.*, I. 337.

11 *Rudriyas* : the Maruts, sons of Rudra.

Indra Vaikuṇṭha is the Ṛṣi also.

3 *Atka* : mentioned again in Hymn 99 of this Book.
Kavi : the father of Indra's friend Uśanā.

4 *Smadibha* : or, as an adjective joined with Tugra,
'with all his followers.' See VI. 20. 8, where *Vetasu* and
Tugra are mentioned as having been conquered by Indra,
and VI. 26. 4, where their names occur again together
with that of Tuji.

5 *Mṛgaya* : a demon of the air. See IV. 16. 13, and
VIII. 3. 19. *Śrutarvan* : a prince whose liberality is
lauded in VIII. 63. *Āyu* : sometimes spoken of as a King
favoured by Indra and at other times as conquered by
him. See Index. The name of *Veśa* does not occur again.
Savya : the Ṛṣi of Hymns 51—57 of Book I. *Paḍgṛbhi*:
some demon or savage enemy who is not mentioned again.

6 *Navavāstva* : see I. 36. 18, and VI. 20. 11. *Of the
lofty car* : or Bṛhadratha, as a name of Navavāstva. *The
lights* : the stars or perhaps light in general. In the
former case *the God* would be Dyaus or Varuṇa, and in
the latter case Sūrya or the Sun.—Ludwig.

7 I travel round about borne onward in my might by the fleet-footed dappled Horses of the Sun.
When man's libation calls me to the robe of state I soon repel the powerful Dasyu with my blows.

8 Stronger am I than Nahus, I who slew the seven : I glorified with might Yadu and Turvaśa.
I brought another low, with strength I bent his strength : I let the mighty nine-and-ninety wax in power.

9 Bull over all the streams that flow along the earth, I took the Seven Rivers as mine own domain.
I, gifted with great wisdom, spread the floods abroad : by war I found for man the way to high success.

10 I set within these cows the white milk which no God, not even Tvaṣṭar's self, had there deposited,—
Much-longed-for, in the breasts, the udders of the kine, the savoury sweets of meath, the milk and Soma juice.

11 Even thus hath Indra Maghavan, truly bounteous, sped Gods and men with mighty operation.
The pious glorify all these thine exploits, Lord of Bay Coursers, Strong, and Self-resplendent.

HYMN L.   *Indra Vaikuṇṭha.*

1. I LAUD your Mighty One who joyeth in the juice, him who is shared by all men, who created all ;
Indra, whose conquering strength is powerful in war, whose fame and manly vigour Heaven and Earth revere.

2 He with his friend is active, lauded, good to man, Indra who must be glorified by one like me.
Hero, Lord of the brave, all cars are thy delight, warring with Vṛtra, or for waters, or for spoil.

3 Who are the men whom thou wilt further, Indra, who strive to win thy bliss allied with riches?
Who urged thee forward to exert thy power divine, to valour, in the war for waters on their fields ?

4 Thou, Indra, through the holy prayer art mighty, worthy of sacrifice at all libations.
In every fight thou castest heroes on the ground : thou art the noblest song, O Lord of all the folk.

5 Help now, as Highest, those who toil at sacrifice: well do the people know thy great protecting might.
Thou shalt be Everlasing, Giver of success : yea, on all these libations thou bestowest strength.

6 All these libations thou makest effectual, of which thou art thyself supporter, Son of Power.
Therefore thy vessel is to be esteemed the best, sacrifice, holy text, prayer, and exalted speech.

7 They who with flowing Soma pray to thee, O Sage, to pour on them thy gifts of opulence and wealth,
May they come forward, through their spirit, on the path of bliss, in the wild joy of Soma juice effused.

HYMN LI.   *Agni. Gods.*

1. LARGE was that covering, and firm of texture, folded wherein thou enteredst the waters.
One Deity alone, O Jātavedas Agni, saw all thy forms in sundry places.

---

7 *The robe of state*: apparently the milk which is the royal mantle wherewith Soma is invested.

8 *Stronger am I than Nahus* : *náhuṣo náhuṣṭaraḥ* ; literally, more Nahus than Nahus; I out-Nahus Nahus, a King who contended with Indra : 'I am nearer than the neighbour,' according to Roth whom Grassmann follows. 'I am the especial bond of bonds.'—Wilson. I follow Ludwig's interpretation. *I who slew the seven* : the seven, perhaps, are the chief of the demons destroyed by Indra. Ludwig takes *saptahā* to mean 'seven times' :— 'I am seven times stronger than Nahus.' *Another* : whom, is uncertain. *Wax in power* : until they became worthy antagonists. ' I have demolished ninety and nine powerful (foes).'—Wilson.

10 *Milk and Soma juice*: sweet ambrosial rain; *the kine* being the teeming clouds.

11 In this stanza Indra—Ṛṣi addresses himself as the deity of the hymn.

---

2 *His friend* : his constant companion. the thunderbolt.
3 *Allied with riches* : the happiness which Indra sends being given in return for costly sacrificial offerings.
4 *Song* : *mántraḥ* : subject of thy worshippers' songs of praise.
6 *Vessel* : *pātram* : 'protection.'—Wilson.

The legend says that Agni, fearing to share the fate of his three elder brothers who had perished in the service of the Gods, fled away and hid himself in the waters. The Gods discovered him and persuaded him to return to his sacred duties. Stanzas 1, 3, 5, 7, 9 are spoken by the Gods, and 2, 4, 6, 8 by Agni.
1 He must have been very well wrapped up, the Gods ironically say, or the water would have extinguished him.—Ludwig. *Forms* : literally, 'bodies.'

2 What God hath seen me? Who of all their
number clearly beheld my forms in
many places?
Where lie, then, all the sacred logs of
Agni that lead him God-ward, Varuṇa
and Mitra?

3 In many places, Agni Jātavedas, we sought
thee hidden in the plants and waters.
Then Yama marked thee, God of wondrous
splendour! effulgent from thy tenfold
secret dwelling.

4 I fled in fear from sacrificial worship,
Varuṇa, lest the Gods should thus engage
me.
Thus were my forms laid down in many
places. This, as my goal, I Agni saw
before me.

5 Come; man is pious and would fain do
worship; he waits prepared: in gloom
thou, Agni, dwellest.
Make pathways leading God-ward clear
and easy, and bear oblations with a
kindly spirit.

6 This goal mine elder brothers erst selected,
as he who drives a car the way to travel.
So, Varuṇa, I fled afar through terror, as
flies the wild-bull from an archer's bowstring.

7 We give thee life unwasting, Jātavedas, so
that, employed, thou never shalt be
injured.
So, nobly born! shalt thou with kindly
spirit bear to the Gods their share of men's
oblations.

8 Grant me the first oblations and the latter,
entire, my forceful shares of holy
presents,
The soul of plants, the fatness of the
waters, and let there be long life, ye
Gods, to Agni.

9 Thine be the first oblations and the latter,
entire, thy forceful shares of holy
presents.
Let all this sacrifice be thine, O Agni, and
let the world's four regions bow before
thee.

HYMN LII. *Gods.*

1. INSTRUCT me, all ye Gods, how I, elected
your Priest, must seat me here, and how
address you.
Instruct me how to deal to each his portion, and by what path to bring you
man's oblation.

2 I sit as Priest most skilled in sacrificing:
the Maruts and all Deities impel me.
Aśvins, each day yours is the Adhvaryu's
duty: Brahman and wood are here : 'tis
yours to offer.

3 Who is the Priest ? Is he the Priest of
Yama? On whom is thrust this God-
appointed honour?
He springs to life each month, each day
that passes; so Gods have made him
their oblation-bearer.

4 The Gods have made me bearer of oblations, who slipped away and passed
through many troubles.
Wise Agni shall ordain for us the worship,
whether five-wayed, threefold, or seven-
threaded.

---

2 *Sacred logs* : pieces of Śamī and Aśvattha wood,
from which alone the sacrificial fire is produced. Others
explain *samidhaḥ* by 'flames.'

3 *Thy tenfold secret dwelling* : according to Sāyaṇa,
'the three worlds,—heaven, mid-air, earth ; three divinities, Agni, Vāyu, Āditya; the waters, the shrubs, the
trees, and the bodies of living beings.'—Wilson. The
meaning appears to be, as Ludwig conjectures that
Yama knew that Agni would appear again from the fire-
sticks worked by the fingers of both hands.

8 *The first oblations and the latter* : or the Prayājas and
the Anuyājas, the former being texts and oblations
forming part of the introductory ceremony at a Soma
sacrifice, and the latter the secondary or final offerings.
Forceful share : the potent concentrated portion. *The
fatness* : *ghṛtám : ghī*, clarified butter.

1 Agni, having been elected Oblation-bearer, asks
the Gods to instruct him in his duties.

3 The first line is spoken by some God who doubts
Agni's competence. *Is he the Priest of Yama ?* : can he
convey offerings to the Blest in the realms of the God of
the departed ? In the second half of the first line I follow
Ludwig, but the meaning is uncertain. The second line
is the answer of another God. *Each month, each day;*
the *Pitṛyajña*, or sacrifice to the Fathers, is offered
monthly, and the *Agnihotra*, or oblation to Agni and the
Gods, daily. These comprehend all other periodical
rites.

4 The first line is spoken by Agni. *Slipped away* : see
the preceding hymn. The second line is what the Gods
said. *Five-wayed* : consisting of five courses or parts,
see X. 124. 1. *Threefold* : consisting of the three daily
Soma-libations, see X. 124. 1. *Seven-threaded* : performed
by seven priests. See X. 124. 1.

Stanza 5 is spoken by Agni. Stanza 6 is the poet's
conclusion.

For an explanation of the number of the Gods (33—
305—3003) see *The Hymns of the Atharva-veda*, X. 7. 13,
note.

On Hymns 51—53 see Macdonell, J. R. A. S.,
January, 1894, pp 11-22.

5 So will I win you strength and life for
ever, O Gods, that I may give you room
and freedom.
To Indra's arms would I consign the
thunder; in all these battles shall he then
be victor.
6 The Deities three hundred and thirty-nine,
have served and honoured Agni,
Strewn sacred grass, anointed him with
butter, and seated him as Priest, the
Gods' Invoker.

HYMN LIII. *Agni Saucīka Gods.*

1. HE hath arrived, he whom we sought with
longing, who skilled in sacrifice well
knows its courses.
Let him discharge his sacrificial duties: let
him sit down as Friend who was before
us.
2 Best Priest, he hath been won by being
seated, for he hath looked on the well-
ordered viands.
Come, let us worship Gods who must be
worshipped, and pouring oil, laud those
who should be lauded.
3 Now hath he made the feast of Gods effective : now have we found the secret
tongue of worship.
Now hath he come, sweet, robed in vital
vigour, and made our calling on the
Gods effective.
4 This prelude of my speech I now will
utter, whereby we Gods may quell our
Asura foemen.
Eaters of strengthening food who merit
worship, O ye Five Tribes, be pleased
with mine oblation.
5 May the Five Tribes be pleased with mine
oblation, and the Cow's Sons and all
who merit worship.
From earthly trouble may the earth protect us, and air's mid realm from woe
that comes from heaven.

1 The Gods speak. *Courses* : or portions.
2 *By being seated* : 'by his seat (at the altar).'—Wilson.
3 *Tongue of worship* : Agni, by whose fiery tongues the
Gods drink libations.
4 Agni speaks. *Asura foemen* : the Asuras in the later
hymns of the Veda are evil spirits in perpetual hostility
with the Gods, not to be confounded with the great
celestial Asuras, the chiefs of the Gods, nor with the
Rākṣasas, demons or ogres, who disturb the sacrifices
of men.
5 *The Five Tribes* : according to some, says Yāska
'the Gandharvas, gods, Fathers, Asuras, and Rākṣasas.'
See Muir, *O. S. Texts*, I. 177. But the five Āryan tribes
may be intended. *The Cow's Sons* : the Maruts, children
of Pṛśni. Von Roth explains *gojātāḥ* as 'born in the starry
heaven.' See VII. 35. 14.

6 Spinning the thread, follow the region's
splendid light : guard thou the path
ways well which wisdom hath prepared.
Weave ye the knotless labour of the bards
who sing : be Manu thou, and bring
the Heavenly People forth.
7 Lovers of Soma, bind the chariot traces
fast : set ye the reins in order and
embellish them.
Bring hitherward the car with seats where
eight may sit, whereon the Gods have
brought the treasure that we love.
8 Here flows Aśmanvatī : hold fast each other,
keep yourselves up, and pass, my friends,
the river.
There let us leave the Powers that brought
no profit, and cross the flood to Powers
that are auspicious.
9 Tvaṣṭar, most deft of workmen, knew each
magic art, bringing most blessed bowls
that hold the drink of Gods.
His axe, wrought of good metal, he is
sharpening now, wherewith the radiant
Brahmaṇaspati will cut.
10 Now, O ye Sapient Ones, make ye the
axes sharp wherewith ye fashion bowls
to hold the Amṛta.
Knowing the secret places make ye ready
that whereby the Gods have gotten
immortality.
11 Ye with a secret tongue and dark intention
laid the maiden deep within, the calf
within the mouth.

6 The Gods speak. *The region's splendid light* : the
Sun. *Weave ye* : flames of Agni. Assist the singer in his
holy task and let there be no difficulties in his way.
7 This stanza appears to begin a new hymn, made
up of fragments. According to Sāyaṇa it is spoken by
the Gods to one another.
8 *Aśmanvatī* : or, the stony stream. See *The Hymns
of the Atharva-veda*, XII. 2. 26.
9 *Will cut* : perhaps, will cut and destroy demons;
but the meaning is uncertain.
10 *O ye Sapient Ones* ye Ṛbhus. *That* : perhaps
Amṛta or celestial Soma juice. Cf. I. 20. 6; 110. 3.
11 The first line is obscure. '(The Maruts) placed
a female in the enveloping hide (of a dead cow), and a
calf in the mouth (of a dead cow).'—Wilson. According
to this interpretation the miracle ascribed to them would
somewhat resemble that mentioned in I. 110. 8. See
Bergaigne, *La Religion Védique*, II. 27. The first line
of the second line is hard to construe. Wilson paraphrases the line :—'daily the generous (fraternity of
the Ṛbhus) offers suitable praise (to the gods), granting
victory over our foes.' Prof. Geldner takes *kārá*, against
the Pada text, as a locative, and renders the last half-
line to the following effect :—"May he (the sacrificer),
when he wishes to win, gain the victory in the race.'

They evermore are near us with their gracious help : successful is the song that strives for victory.

HYMN LIV. *Indra.*

1. I SING thy fame that, Maghavan, through thy Greatness the heavens and earth invoked thee in their terror,
Thou, aiding Gods, didst quell the power of Dāsas, what time thou holpest many a race, O Indra.

2 When thou wast roaming, waxen strong in body, telling thy might, Indra, among the people,
All that men called thy battles was illusion : no foe hast thou to-day, nor erst hast found one.

3 Who are the Ṛṣis, then, who comprehended before our time the bounds of all thy greatness ?
For from thy body thou hast generated at the same time the Mother and the Father.

4 Thou, Mighty Steer, hast four supremest natures, Asura natures that may ne'er be injured.
All these, O Maghavan, thou surely knowest, wherewith thou hast performed thy great achievements.

5 Thou hast all treasures in thy sole possession, treasures made manifest and treasures hidden.
Defer not thou, O Maghavan, my longing : thou. art Director, Indra, thou art Giver.

6 To him who set the light in things of splendour, and with all sweetness blent essential sweetness,
To Indra hath this welcome hymn that strengthens been uttered by the votary Bṛhaduktha.

HYMN LV. *Indra.*

1. FAR is that secret name by which, in terror, the worlds invoked thee and thou gavest vigour

3 The question is rhetorical. The great Ṛṣis of the olden time could not comprehend thy greatness, much less can we comprehend it.

The Mother and the Father : Earth and Heaven, parents of all. See M. Müller, *India, What can it Teach Us ?*, p. 161.

4 *Asura* : divine, with a vague sense of supreme grandeur.

6 *Who set the light* : the first essential light.

1 *Far is that secret name* : thou art not present with us now. *In terror* : terrified by Vṛtra. *Thy Brother's*

The earth and heaven thou settest near each other, and Maghavan, madest bright thy Brother's Children.

2 Great is that secret name and far-extending, whereby thou madest all that is and shall be.
The Five Tribes whom he loveth well have entered the light he loveth that was made aforetime.

3 He filled the heaven and earth and all between them, Gods five times sevenfold in their proper seasons.
With four-and-thirty lights he looks around him, lights of one colour though their ways are divers.

4 As first among the lights, O Dawn, thou shonest, whereby thou broughtest forth the Stay of Increase,
Great art thou, matchless is thine Asura nature, who, high above, art kin to those beneath thee.

5 The old hath waked the young Moon from his slumber who runs his circling course with many round him.
Behold the Gods' high wisdom in its greatness : he who died yesterday to-day is living.

6 Strong is the Red Bird in his strength, great Hero, who from of old hath had no nest to dwell in.
That which he knows is truth and never idle : he wins and gives the wealth desired of many.

Children : according to Sāyaṇa, Indra's brother is Parjanya, the God of the rain-cloud, and his children are the gathered waters. Varuṇa and his stars are probably intended.—Ludwig.

3 *Gods five times sevenfold* : 'It cannot be doubted that the original Gods were the constellations.'—Ludwig. According to Sāyaṇa, the five orders of beings and the classes of seven; that is, Gods, men, Fathers and Rākṣasas, and the seven troops of Maruts, the seven rays of the Sun, the seven senses, etc. The *four-and-thirty lights* : are probably the sun, moon, and five planets, and the twenty seven lunar asterisms or mansions of the moon. According to Sāyaṇa, the *four-and-thirty* are eight Vasus, eleven Rudras, twelve Ādityas, Prajāpati, Vaṣaṭkāra, and Virāj.

4 *The Stay of Increase* : that which is the foundation and support of all subsistence; according to Sāyaṇa, the Sun. *Art kin to those beneath thee* : art allied and connected with men as provider of their food. The second line is difficult, and is differently interpreted by others.

5 Sāyaṇa explains this stanza differently, making Indra, identified with Time, the subject. I follow Ludwig's interpretation (Commentary, II. p. 203) which seems to be nearer to the sense of the words, and is simpler and more rational. *With many round him* : stars of the asterisms through which he passes.

6 *The Red Bird* : the Sun, with whom Indra is identified.

7 Through these the Thunderer gained strong manly vigour, through whom he waxed in power to smite down Vṛtra,—
Who through the might of Indra's operation came forth as Gods in course of Law and Order.

8 All-strong, performing works with his companion, All-marking, rapid Victor, Curse-averter,
The Hero, waxing, after draughts of Soma, blew far from heaven the Dasyus with his weapon.

HYMN LVI. *Viśvedevas.*

1. HERE is one light for thee, another yonder : enter the third and be therewith united.
Uniting with a body be thou welcome, dear to the Gods in their sublimest birth-place.

2 Bearing thy body, Vājin, may thy body afford us blessing and thyself protection.
Unswerving, stablish as it were in heaven thine own light as the mighty God's supporter.

3 Strong Steed art thou : go to the yearning Maidens with vigour, happily go to heaven and praises :
Fly happily to the Gods with easy passage, according to the first and faithful statutes.

4 Part of their grandeur have the Fathers also gained : the Gods have seated mental power in them as Gods.
They have embraced within themselves all energies, which, issuing forth, again into their bodies pass.

5 They strode through all the region with victorious might, establishing the old immeasurable laws.
They compassed in their bodies all existing things, and streamed forth offspring in many successive forms.

6 In two ways have the sons established in his place the Asura who finds the light, by the third act,
As fathers, they have set their heritage on earth, their offspring, as a thread continuously spun out.

7 As in a ship through billows, so through regions of air, with blessings, through toils and troubles
Hath Bṛhaduktha brought his seed with glory, and placed it here and in the realms beyond us.

HYMN LVII. *Viśvedevas.*

1. LET us not, Indra, leave the path, the Soma-presser's sacrifice :
Let no malignity dwell with us.

2 May we obtain, completely wrought, the thread spun out to reach the Gods,
That perfecteth the sacrifice.

3 We call the spirit hither with the Soma of our parted sires,
Yea, with the Fathers' holy hymns.

---

7 *Through these* : probably the stars are intended. '(Accompanied) by these Maruts.'—Wilson.
8 *His companion* : the thunderbolt.

'The mystical union of the Fathers with the rays of light is the fundamental idea underlying the abstruse allusions' of this funeral hymn. 'The poet bids the deceased man unite himself with the beams of the heavenly light; he takes occasion to celebrate the power and greatness of the Fathers, to whom the spirit of the departed is journeying ; and ends with a statement of the success of the journey for which he has prayed.' See Wallis, *Cosmology of the Rgveda*, pp. 72, 73.

1 *One light* : the earthly fire of the funeral pile. *Another* : in the firmament. *The third* : the light in the highest region above the firmament. *A body* : a new body after cremation. *Their sublimest birth-place* : the Sun.

2 *Vājin* : apparently the name of the deceased, the son of Bṛhaduktha the Ṛṣi of the hymn. The word means originally 'strong' strong steed' as in stanza 3.

3 *The yearning Maidens* : perhaps the Dawns; but the meaning of *suveniḥ* is uncertain. *To heaven and praises*: 'to the (land of) praise, and to the sky.'—Wallis.

4 *Of their grandeur* : of the greatness of the Gods.

5 *Establishing the old immeasurable laws* : or, in accordance with the more generally received interpretation of *dhāmāni* here, 'measuring ancient stations never measured out.'

6 *In two ways* : in heaven and on earth. *The sons* : explained by Sāyaṇa as the Aṅgirases, sons of Āditya. The Fathers in general appear to be intended. *The Asura* : Agni. *The third act* : or third sacred duty, that of continuing their family ; religious study and sacrifice being the first and second.—Sāyaṇa.

7 *Placed it here and in the realm beyond us* : established his offspring in heavenly regions as well as here upon earth.

Mr Wallis, from whose translation I have borrowed, remarks :—'The interpretation of one or two expressions is uncertain ; the general sense is clear. The rays of light are here the bodies of the fathers, which emanate from the sun, assume the forms of all things on the earth and of the later sacrificers, the descendants of the fathers, and again return to their birth-place in the sky from which they had extended themselves.'—*Cosmology of the Rgveda*, pp. 74, 75.

For Prof. Max Müller's translation of Hymns 57—60, with the legend founded upon them and ample elucidative matter, see Journal R. A. S., Vol. II. Part II., 1866, p. 426—465.

3 *The spirit* : of the deceased whose obsequies are performed. *Of our sires* : *nārāśaṁsena* : explained as meaning, suited to man; that is to deified men, the Fathers or Spirits of the Blest.

4 Thy spirit come to thee again for wisdom,
    energy, and life,
That thou mayst long behold the sun!

5 O Fathers, may the Heavenly Folk give us
    our spirit once again,
That we may be with those who live.

6 O Soma with the spirit still within us,
    blest with progeny,
May we be busied in the law.

HYMN LVIII.   *Manas or Spirit.*

1. THY spirit, that went far away to Yama
    to Vivasvān's Son,
We cause to come to thee again that thou
    mayst live and sojourn here.

2 Thy spirit, that went far away, that passed
    away to earth and heaven,
We cause to come to thee again that thou
    mayst live and sojourn here.

3 Thy spirit, that went far away, away to
    the four-cornered earth,
We cause to come to thee again that thou
    mayst live and sojourn here.

4 Thy spirit, that went far away to the four
    quarters of the world,
We cause to come to thee again that thou
    mayst live and sojourn here.

5 Thy spirit, that went far away, away unto
    the billowy sea,
We cause to come to thee again that thou
    mayst live and sojourn here.

6 Thy spirit, that went far away to beams of
    light that flash and flow,
We cause to come to thee again that thou
    mayst live and sojourn here.

7 Thy spirit, that went far away, went to the
    waters and the plants,
We cause to come to thee again that thou
    mayst live and sojourn here.

8 Thy spirit, that went far away, that visited
    the Sun and Dawn,
We cause to come to thee again that thou
    mayst live and sojourn here.

9 Thy spirit, that went far away, away to
    lofty mountain heights,
We cause to come to thee again that thou
    mayst live and sojourn here.

10 Thy spirit, that went far away into this
    All that lives and moves,
We cause to come to thee again that
    thou mayst live and sojourn here.

The hymn is an address to recall the fleeting spirit of
a man at the point of death.

7 *Waters......plants* : cf. X. 16. 3.

— — —

11 Thy spirit, that went far away to distant
    realms beyond our ken,
We cause to come to thee again that thou
    mayst live and sojourn here.

12 Thy spirit, that went far away to all that
    is and is to be,
We cause to come to thee again that thou
    mayst live and sojourn here.

HYMN LIX.   *Nirṛti and Others.*

1. His life hath been renewed and carried
    forward as two men, car-borne, by the
    skilful driver.
One falls, then seeks the goal with quicke-
    ned vigour. Let Nirṛti depart to distant
    places.

2 Here is the psalm for wealth, and food, in
    plenty : let us do many deeds to bring
    us glory.
All these our doings shall delight the singer.
    Let Nirṛti depart to distant places.

3 May we o'ercome our foes with acts of
    valour, as heaven is over earth, hills
    over lowlands.
All these our deeds the singer hath consi-
    dered. Let Nirṛti depart to distant
    places.

4 Give us not up as prey to death, O Soma :
    still let us look upon the Sun arising.
Let our old age with passing days be
    kindly. Let Nirṛti depart to distant
    places.

5 O Asunīti, keep the soul within us, and
    make the days we have to live yet
    longer.
Grant that we still may look upon the
    sunlight : strengthen thy body with the
    oil we bring thee.

6 Give us our sight again, O Asunīti, give
    us again our breath and our enjoyment.
Long may we look upon the Sun uprising ;
    O Anumati, favour thou and bless us.

1 *His life* : the life of Subandhu one of the R̥ṣis of the
hymn. According to Sāyaṇa the first line is a prayer :—
'May the life of Subandhu be augmented so as to be more
lasting and newer.'—Wilson. Subandhu is not mentioned in the text. *Two men* : the warrior and the
charioteer. *One falls* : Sāyaṇa explains diffe ontly:—
'he who falls (from life) increases (his) desire to
live.'—Wilson. *Nirṛti* : the Goddess of death and
destruction.

5 *Asunīti* : apparently the personification of a deity
presiding over funerals. It may be a name for Yama,
or it may mean 'guide to life' or 'way to life.' See Muir,
O. S. Texts, V. 297, and Bergaigne, *La Religion Vedique* I.
96.

6 *Anumati* : a personification of the favour with which
the Gods regard the sacrifices and prayers of the pious.
'Gracious (goddess).'—Wilson.

7 May Earth restore to us our vital spirit,
  may Heaven the Goddess and mid-air
  restore it.
  May Soma give us once again our body,
  and Pūṣan show the Path of peace and
  comfort.

8 May both Worlds bless Subandhu, young
  Mothers of everlasting Law.
  May Heaven and Earth uproot and sweep
  iniquity and shame away : nor sin nor
  sorrow trouble thee.

9 Health-giving medicines descend sent down
  from heaven in twos and threes,
  Or wandering singly on the earth. May
  Heaven and Earth uproot and sweep
  iniquity and shame away : nor sin
  nor sorrow trouble thee.

10 Drive forward thou the wagon-ox, O Indra,
  which brought Uśīnarāṇī's wagon hither.
  May Heaven and Earth uproot and sweep
  iniquity and shame away : nor sin nor
  sorrow trouble thee.

HYMN LX.   *Asamāti and Others.'*

1. BRINGING our homage we have come to
  one magnificent in look.
  Glorified of the mighty Gods ;

2 To Asamāti, spring of gifts, lord of the
  brave, a radiant car,
  The conqueror of Bhajeratha ;

3 Who, when the spear hath armed his
  hand, or even weaponless o'erthrows
  Men strong as buffaloes in fight ;

4 Him in whose service flourishes Ikṣvāku,
  rich and dazzling-bright.
  As the Five Tribes that are in heaven.

5 Indra, support the princely power of
  Rathaproṣṭhas matched by none,
  Even as the Sun for all to see.

6 Thou for Agastya's sister's sons yokest thy
  pair of ruddy steeds.
  Thou troddest niggards under foot, all
  those, O King, who brought no gifts.

7 This is the mother, this the sire, this one
  hath come to be thy life.
  What brings thee forth is even this. Now
  come, Subandhu, get thee forth.

8 As with the leather thong they bind the
  chariot yoke to hold it fast,
  So have I held thy spirit fast, held it for
  life and not for death, held it for thy
  security.

9 Even as this earth, the mighty earth, holds
  fast the monarchs of the wood.
  So have I held thy spirit fast, held it
  for life and not for death, held it for
  thy security.

10 Subandhu's spirit I have brought from
  Yama, from Vivasvān's Son,
  Brought it for life and not for death, yea,
  brought it for security.

11 The wind blows downward from on high,
  downward the Sun-God sends his heat,
  Downward the milch-cow pours her milk :
  so downward go thy pain and grief.

---

8 *Iniquity and shame* : *rápas*, according to William's Dictionary means, defect, fault, sin, hurt, injury. In his Commentary on I. 69. 4. Sāyaṇa paraphrases *rapāṁsi*, the plural of the word, by *bādhakāni rākṣasādīni*, disturbing Rākṣasas, etc.

9 *In twos and threes* : according to Sāyaṇa, in the persons of the two Aśvins and of the three Goddesses Ilā, Sarasvatī, and Bhāratī.

10 *Uśīnarāṇī* must mean the wife of Uśīnara, chief of the Uśīnaras who are mentioned in later times as living in Madhyadeśa or the Midland country. The meaning of the line is not obvious.

Stanzas 8, 9, 10, which Prof. Grassmann places in his Appendix, are of a different character from that of the preceding part of the hymn, and seem to be a separate song or fragment of a song.

---

2 *Asamāti* : according to Sāyaṇa, the name of a King. But the word is more probably an adjective, as in stanza 5. qualifying *rátham*, car, and signifying unequalled. *Bhajeratha* : it is uncertain whether this is the name of a prince or of a country.

3 *Who* : Asamāti, according to Sāyaṇa.

4 *Ikṣvāku* : a prince or a people; the name does not occur again in the Ṛgveda. *The Five Tribes* : the deities regarded as forming five tribes corresponding to the five tribes on earth, in the same manner as the seven rivers of the land of the Āryans have their counterparts in heaven. See Muir, *O. S. Texts*, I. p. 177. Sāyaṇa explains differently :—'(so that) the five orders of men (are as happy) as if they were in heaven.'—Wilson.

5 *Rathaproṣṭhas* : the family of the prince. Asamāti or another, whose praises the poet celebrates.

6 *Agastya's sister's sons* : Bandhu and his brothers, the Ṛṣis of the hymn. Stanzas I—6 have no apparent connexion with the six stanzas that follow.

7 *This* : Agni, according to Sāyaṇa. The speaker probably means himself.—Ludwig. Subandhu seems to have been in a trance and apparently dead. 'It is supposed that the brothers of Subandhu have addressed their supplication to Agni, to restore him to life, and that he has come accordingly, being, as it were, his parent and begetter. Another interpretation explains the terms literally as, Subandhu, your father, mother, and son, have come to mourn your decease.'—Wilson.

8 *So have I held* : 'so has Agni placed,' according to Sāyaṇa.

11 *Thy pain and grief* : 'thy sin.'—Sāyaṇa.

12 Felicitous is this mine hand, yet more felicitous is this.
This hand contains all healing balms, and this makes whole with gentle touch.

HYMN LXI. *Viśvedevas.*

1. THE welcome speaker in the storm of battle uttered with might this prayer to win the Aśvins,
When the most liberal God, for Paktha, rescued his parents, and assailed the seven Hotras.

2 Cyavāna, purposing deceptive presents, with all ingredients, made the altar ready.
Most sweet-voiced Tūrvayāṇa poured oblations like floods of widely fertilizing water.

3 To his oblations, swift as thought, ye hurried, and welcomed eagerly the prayers he offered.
With arrows in his hand the Very Mighty forced from him all obedience of a servant.

4 I call on you the Sons of Dyaus, the Aśvins, that a dark cow to my red kine be added.
Enjoy my sacrifice, come to my viands, contented, not deceiving expectation.

10 Uttering praise to suit the rite Navagvas came speedily to win the damsel's friendship.
They who approached the twice-strong stable's keeper, meedless would milk the rocks that naught had shaken.

11 Swift was new friendship with the maid : they quickly accepted it as genuine seed and bounty.
Milk which the cow Sabardughā had yielded was the bright heritage which to thee they offered.

12 When afterwards they woke and missed the cattle, the speaker thus in joyful mood addressed them :
Matchless are singers through the Vasu's nature; he bringeth them all food and all possessions.

13 his followers then who dwelt in sundry places came and desired to slay the son of Nṛṣad.
Resistless foe, he found the hidden treasure of Śuṣṇa multiplied in numerous offspring.

14 Thou, called Effulgence, in whose threefold

---

12 *More felicitous is this* : my other hand, probably the right. *With gentle touch* : with light friction, laying on of hands, or hypnotizing passes.

This Hymn, as Ludwig observes, belongs to the most difficult, one might almost say most hopeless, portions of the Ṛgveda. It is made up of several parts which are in no intelligible connexion with one another.

1 According to the view taken by Pischel who has most carefully studied and elaborately discussed the first three stanzas (*Vedische Studien I.* pp. 71—77), they contain in brief their ancient story of Tūrvayāṇa, the young King of the Pakthas, and Cyavāna. Cyavāna, a favourite of the Aśvins who had restored him to youth (I. 116. 10, and 117. 13), intended to sacrifice to them, hoping with their aid to conquer Tūrvayāṇa and his parents. But Indra stays the sacrifice, drives the priests away, and enables Tūrvayāṇa who had poured rich libations to him to gain the victory over his opponent.

The welcome speaker : Tūrvayāṇa, whose words were welcome to the Gods. *To win the Aśvins* : *raudram* : not addressed to Rudra,' but to the Aśvins who are called *raudrau* in stanza 15, and, elsewhere, *rudrā* and *rudrāvartanī*. *The most liberal God* ; Indra. *Paktha* : King of the Pakthas (see VII. 18.7), that is, apparently, Tūrvayāṇa, who has been mentioned in I. 53. 10, and VI. 18. 13, as especially aided by Indra. *Seven Hotras* : the usual number of Hotar priests employed at important sacrifices.

2 *Deceptive presents* : his intended sacri ce was displeasing to Indra, whom, possibly, Cyavāna falsely pretended that he was about to worship. *With all ingredients* : required for the preparation of the Soma juice. *Poured oblations* : to Indra.

3 *To his oblations* : to the offerings of Cyavāna. *Ye*: Aśvins. *The Very Mighty* : Indra, who threatened Cyavāna, and made him his obedient servant.

4 The Ṛṣi now prays to the Aśvins on his own account, and asks for a dark-coloured cow as a reward. Sāyaṇa, whom Professors Ludwig and Grassmann follow, explains the second half of the first line more poetically : 'When the dark night retires before the purple oxen (of the chariot of the dawn).'—Wilson. 'When the black sits among the red cows; that is, while it is still dark, but the grey of morning is beginning to appear.'—Ludwig.

5 I pass over stanzas 5—9, which contain an ancient legend, probably the germ of the later story of Brahmā or Prajāpati and his daughter, concerning two deities or powers of nature, male and female. See Appendix.

10 *Navagvas* : 'the Aṅgirasas.'—Wilson. *The damsel's* : Sāyaṇa says that Pṛśni may be meant. Perhaps Saramā is intended. *The twice-strong stable's keeper* : the Paṇi or Paṇis who kept the stolen cows or vanished rays of light concealed. *Meedless* : as the Paṇis refused to give up the cows. *Would milk the rocks* : would force from the rocky prison the meed or honorarium which they deserved in the shape of the cows.

11 *Sabardughā* : 'nectar-yielding;' the general name or cows milked at sacrifices. *Which to thee they offered* : which the Aṅgirases offered to Indra.

12 The *Vasu* is Indra.

13 *The son of Nṛṣad* : Nārṣada, usually a patronymic of Kaṇva, but said to be in this place the name of a certain demon. *Resistless foe* : Indra.

14 Here begins another part of the hymn. Agni is addressed. *Effulgence* : identified with the Sun. *Three-fold dwelling* : earth, firmament, and heaven.

dwelling, as in the light of heaven, the Gods are sitting,

Thou who art called Agni or Jātavedas, Priest, hear us, guileless Priest of holy worship.

15 And, Indra, bring, that I may laud and serve them, those Two resplendent glorious Nāsatyas,

Blithe, bounteous, man-like, to the sacrificer, honoured among our men with offered viands.

16 This King is praised and honoured as Ordainer : himself the bridge, the Sage speeds o'er the waters.

He hath stirred up Kakṣīvān, stirred up Agni, as the steed's swift wheel drives the felly onward.

17 Vaitarana, doubly kinsman, sacrificer, shall milk the cow who ne'er hath calved, Sabardhu,

When I encompass Varuṇa and Mitra with lauds, and Aryaman in safest shelter.

18 Their kin, the Prince in heaven, thy nearest kinsman, turning his thought to thee thus speaks in kindness :

This is our highest bond : I am his offspring. How many others came ere I succeeded ?

19 Here is my kinship, here the place I dwell in : these are my Gods; I in full strength am present.

Twice-born am I, the first-born Son of Order : the Cow milked this when first she had her being.

20 So mid these tribes he rests, the friendly envoy, borne on two paths, refulgent Lord of fuel.

When, like a line, the Babe springs up erectly, his Mother straight hath borne him strong to bless us.

21 Then went the milch-kine forth to please the damsel, and for the good of every man that liveth.

Hear us, O wealthy Lord; begin our worship. Thou hast grown mighty through Aśvaghna's virtues.

22 And take thou notice of us also, Indra, for ample riches, King whose arm wields thunder !

Protect our wealthy nobles, guard our princes unmenaced near thee, Lord of Tawny Coursers.

23 When he goes forth, ye Pair of Kings, for booty, speeding to war and praise to please the singer,—

I was the dearest sage of those about him,—let him lead these away and bring them safely.

24 Now for this noble man's support and comfort, singing with easy voice we thus implore thee :

Impetuous be his son and fleet his courser : and may I be his priest to win him glory.

25 If, for our strength, the priest with adoration to win your friendship made the laud accepted,

That laud shall be a branching road to virtue for every one to whom the songs are suited.

26 Glorified thus, with holy hymns and homage :—Of noble race, with Waters, God-attended—

---

15 *Man-like* : as men reward one who institutes a sacrifice for their benefit.

16 *This King* : Sūrya, the Sun-God. 'This royal Soma.'—Wilson. *Himself the bridge* : the long beams of light from the bridge by which Sūrya passes over the waters of the firmament or sea of air. *Kakṣīvān* : the celebrated Ṛṣi. See Vol. I., Index.

17 *Vaitarana* : '(Agni), the conveyer (of all).'—Wilson. Agni is so called, probably as sacrificer for a prince Vitarana. *Doubly kinsman* : closely allied to heaven and earth. *Sabardhu* : the Cow whose milk is used in sacrifice; also called Sabardughā, as in stanza 11. According to Ludwig, the New Year which has not yet distributed its treasures is meant.

18 *Their kin* : akin to Mitra, Varuṇa, and Aryaman. *The Prince* : *sūri* : Sūrya, the Sun-God. *Thy nearest kinsman* : Sūrya. I adopt Ludwig's interpretation of *nābhānédiṣṭhah*, which appears unintelligible as the name of the son of Manu who was deprived of his inheritance by his father according to the *Yajur-veda*, and by his brothers according to the *Aitareya-Brāhmaṇa*. But see Weber, *Episches im V. Ritual*, pp. 40f. *This* : Dyaus. *How many others*: many Savitars (suns that introduce the new year) have been before me.—Ludwig.

19 *These are my Gods* : 'these are my resplendent (rays).'—Wilson. Probably the priests are intended.—Ludwig. *The Cow* : Aditi. *Milked this* : milked forth this universe.'—Wilson. Agni is the speaker of this stanza.

20 *He* : Agni. *Two paths* : from earth to heaven and from heaven to earth.

21 The reference in the first line is, apparently, to the imprisoned cows and Saramā (see stanza 10); but all explanations of the allusions in this hymn are more or less conjectural. Ludwig thinks that the reference may be to the actual milking of the sacrificial cows at the ceremony which this hymn accompanied. Wilson translates :—'The words of a desirable praise, of a certain tranquil person (Nābhānediṣṭha), attain the prototype (Indra). *Aśvaghna* : probably the patronymic of Vitarana.—Ludwig. See note on Vaitaraṇa in stanza 17.

23 *He* : Aśvaghna Vitarana. *Ye Pair of Kings* : Mitra and Varuṇa.

26 *Glorified thus* : that is, May Varuṇa glorified with song beginning, 'Of noble race, etc.,' enrich us. *Now*

May he enrich us for our prayers and praises : now can the cow be milked; the path is open.

27 Be to us, then, ye Gods who merit worship, be ye of one accord our strong protection, Who went on various ways and brought us vigour, ye who are undeceivable explorers.

HYMN LXII. *Viśvedevas, Etc.*

1. YE who, adorned with guerdon through the sacrifice, have won you Indra's friendship and eternal life, Even to you be happiness, Aṅgirases. Welcome the son of Manu, ye who are most wise.

2 The Fathers, who drave forth the wealth in cattle, have in the year's courses cleft Vala by Eternal Law: A lengthened life be yours, O ye Aṅgirases. Welcome the son of Manu, ye who are most wise.

3 Ye raised the Sun to heaven by everlasting Law, and spread broad earth, the Mother, out on every side. Fair wealth of progeny be yours, Aṅgirases. Welcome the son of Manu, ye who are most wise.

4 This kinsman in your dwellingplace speaks pleasant words: give ear to this, ye Ṛṣis, children of the Gods. High Brahman dignity be yours, Aṅgirases. Welcome the son of Manu, ye who are most wise.

5 Distinguished by their varied form, these Ṛṣis have been deeply moved. These are the sons of Aṅgiras : from Agni have they sprung to life.

6 Distinguished by their varied form, they sprang from Agni, from the sky. Navagva and Daśagva, noblest Aṅgiras, he giveth bounty with the Gods.

7 With Indra for associate the priests have cleared the stable full of steeds and kine, Giving to me a thousand with their eight-marked ears, they gained renown among the Gods.

8 May this man's sons be multiplied ; like springing corn may Manu grow, Who gives at once in bounteous gift a thousand kine, a hundred steeds.

9 No one attains to him, as though a man would grasp the heights of heaven. Sāvarṇya's sacrificial meed hath broadened like an ample flood.

10 Yadu and Turva, too, have given two Dāsas, well-disposed, to serve, Together with great store of kine.

11 Blest be the hamlet's chief, most liberal Manu, and may his bounty rival that of Sūrya. May the God let Sāvarṇi's life be lengthened, with whom, unwearied, we have lived and prospered.

HYMN LXIII. *Viśvedevas.*

1. MAY they who would assume kinship from far away, Vivasvān's generations, dearly loved of men, Even the Gods who sit upon the sacred grass of Nahuṣa's son Yayāti, bless and comfort us.

2 For worthy of obeisance, Gods, are all your names, worthy of adoration and of sacrifice. Ye who were born from waters, and from Aditi, and from the earth, do ye here listen to my call.

---

7 *With their eight-marked ears* : having marks branded on their ears; or perhaps, with slit ears. Cf. *Hymns of the Atharva-veda*, VI. 141. 2.

8 *Manu* : here apparently the name of Sāvarṇi the prince whose munificence is the subject of stanzas 8—11. *A thousand kine, a hundred steeds* : 'kine' is conjecturally supplied. 'A thousand and a hundred horses.'—Wilson. 'A thousand times a hundred horses.'—Ludwig.

9 *Sāvarṇya* here means Sāvarṇi.

10 *Turva* : equivalent to Turvaśa; a prince of the clan called after the eponymus Turva. *Dāsas* : enslaved natives.

---

1 *Kinship* ; relationship with us, and the duties of protection and aid which relationship implies. Cf. I. 109. 7, note. *Vivasvān's generations* : Sāyaṇa supplies a verb, and explains differently :—(support) the generations of (Manu the son of) Vivasvat.'—Wilson. *Yayāti* : see I. 31. 17, and 108. 8, note.

2 *From waters* : the aerial waters, or intermediate region of air. *Aditi* : von Roth understands Aditi here to mean 'infinity', the boundlessness of heaven as opposed to the limitation of earth. See Muir, *O. S. Texts*, V. 39. Sāyaṇa's explanation is similar.

---

can the cow be milked : it is now time for the morning Agnihotram.—Ludwig.

Prof. Grassmann has banished this almost unintelligible hymn to his Appendix.

---

1 *The son of Manu* : Nābhānediṣṭha Mānava. See X. 61. 18 note.

2 *The Fathers* : the Aṅgirases: *Vala* : the demon who stole the cows of the Gods.

3 *By everlasting Law* : 'by means of your sacrifice.' —Wilson.

4. *This kinsman* : or, this Nābhā, that is Nābhānediṣṭha.

5 *Distinguished by their varied form* : or, Virūpas. See III. 53. 7.

6 *From the sky* : or, from Dyaus. *Noblest Aṅgiras* : Agni himself, according to Sāyaṇa. He is also called Navagva and Daśagva as these priestly names or titles belong to or are closely connected with the Aṅgirases.

3 I will rejoice in these Ādityas for my weal,
for whom the Mother pours forth water
rich in balm,
And Dyaus the Infinite, firm as a rock,
sweet milk,—Gods active, strong through
lauds, whose might the Bull upholds.

4 Looking on men, ne'er slumbering, they
by their deserts attained as Gods to lofty
immortality.
Borne on refulgent cars, sinless, with serpents' powers, they robe them, for our
welfare, in the height of heaven.

5 Great Kings who bless us, who have come
to sacrifice, who, ne'er assailed, have set
their mansion in the sky,—
These I invite with adoration and with
hymns, mighty Ādityas, Aditi, for happiness.

6 Who offereth to you the laud that ye accept,
O ye All-Gods of Manu, many as ye
are?
Who, Mighty Ones, will prepare for you
the sacrifice to bear us over trouble to
felicity?

7 Ye to whom Manu, by seven priests, with
kindled fire, offered the first oblation
with his heart and soul,
Vouchsafe us, ye Ādityas, shelter free from
fear, and make us good and easy paths
to happiness.

8 Wise Deities, who have dominion o'er the
world, ye thinkers over all that moves
not and that moves,
Save us from uncommitted and committed
sin, preserve us from all sin to-day for
happiness.

9 In battles we invoke Indra still swift to
hear, and all the holy Host of Heaven
who banish grief,
Agni, Mitra, and Varuṇa that we may
gain, Dyaus, Bhaga, Maruts, Pṛthivi for
happiness :

10 Mightily-saving Earth, incomparable
Heaven the good guide Aditi who gives
secure defence
The well-oared heavenly Ship that lets no
waters in, free from defect, will we ascend
for happiness.

11 Bless us, all Holy Ones, that we may have
your help, guard and protect us from
malignant injury.
With fruitful invocation may we call on
you, Gods, who give ear to us for grace,
for happiness.

12 Keep all disease afar and sordid sacrifice,
keep off the wicked man's malicious
enmity.
Keep far away from us all hatred, O
ye Gods, and give us ample shelter for
our happiness.

13 Untouched by any evil, every mortal
thrives, and, following the Law, spreads
in his progeny.
Whom ye with your good guidance, O
Ādityas, lead safely through all his pain
and grief to happiness.

14 That which ye guard and grace in battle,
O ye Gods, ye Maruts, where the prize
is wealth, where heroes win,
That conquering Car, O Indra, that sets
forth at dawn, that never breaks, may
we ascend for happiness.

15 Vouchsafe us blessing in our paths and
desert tracts, blessing in waters and in
battle for the light ;
Blessing upon the wombs that bring male
children forth, and blessing, O ye
Maruts, for the gain of wealth.

16 The noblest Svasti with abundant riches,
who comes to what is good by distant
pathway,—
May she at home and far away preserve
us, and dwell with us under the Gods'
protection

17 Thus hath the thoughtful sage, the son of
Plati, praised you, O Aditi and all
Ādityas,
Men are made rich by those who are
Immortal : the Heavenly Folk have been
extolled by Gaya.

HYMN LXIV.   *Viśvedevas.*

1. WHAT God, of those who hear, is he whose
well-praised name we may record in this
our sacrifice ; and how ?
Who will be gracious ? Who of many give
us bliss ? Who out of all the Host will
come to lend us aid ?

---

3 *The Mother* : Earth. *Dyaus* : Heaven. *The Bull* :
the Sun. Sāyaṇa explains *vṛṣabharān* as 'bringers of rain.'

4 *With serpents' powers* : 'of unsurpassable wisdom'.
—Wilson.

10 *The heavenly Ship* : according to Sāyaṇa, a metaphorical expression for sacrifice.

14 *For happiness* : *svastáye*, for happiness or welfare,
recurs at the end of all the stanzas from 3 to 14 inclusive.

16 *Svasti* : Pathyā Svasti, according to the Index;
the Goddess of prosperity and happiness.

17 *The son of Plati* : Gaya, the Ṛṣi of the hymn.

2 The will and thoughts within my breast
exert their power : they yearn with love,
and fly to all the regions round.
None other comforter is found save only
these : my longings and my hopes are
fixt upon the Gods.

3 To Narāśaṁsa and to Pūṣan I sing forth,
unconcealable Agni kindled by the Gods.
To Sun and Moon, two Moons, to Yama
in the heaven, to Trita, Vāta, Dawn,
Night, and the Aśvins Twain.

4 How is the Sage extolled whom the loud
singers praise ? What voice, what hymn
is used to laud Bṛhaspati ?
May Aja-Ekapād with Ṛkvans swift to hear,
and Ahi of the Deep listen unto our
call.

5 Aditi, to the birth of Dakṣa and the vow
thou summonest the Kings Mitra and
Varuṇa.
With course unchecked, with many chariots
Aryaman comes with the seven priests
to tribes of varied sort.

6 May all those vigorous Coursers listen to
our cry, hearers of invocation, speeding
on their way ;
Winners of thousands where the priestly
meed is won, who gather of themselves
great wealth in every race.

7 Bring ye Purandhi, bring Vāyu who yokes
his steeds, for friendship bring ye Pūṣan
with your songs of praise :
They with one mind, one thought attend
the sacrifice, urged by the favouring
aid of Savitar the God.

8 The thrice-seven wandering Rivers, yea,
the mighty floods, the forest trees, the
mountains, Agni to our aid,
Kṛśānu, Tiṣya, archers to our gathering-
place, and Rudra strong amid the Rudras
we invoke.

9 Let the great Streams come hither with
their mighty help, Sindhu, Sarasvatī, and
Sarayu with waves.
Ye Goddess Floods, ye Mothers, animating
all, promise us water rich in fatness and
in balm.

10 And let Bṛhaddivā, the Mother, hear our
call, and Tvaṣṭar, Father, with the
Goddesses and Dames.
Ṛbhukṣan, Vāja, Bhaga, and Rathaspati,
and the sweet speech of him who labours
guard us well !

11 Pleasant to look on as a dwelling rich in
food is the blest favour of the Maruts,
Rudra's Sons.
May we be famed among the folk for
wealth in kine, and ever come to you, ye
Gods, with sacred food.

12 The thought which ye, O Maruts, Indra
and ye Gods have given to me, and ye,
Mitra and Varuṇa,—
Cause this to grow and swell like a milch-
cow with milk. Will ye not bear away
my songs upon your car ?

13 O Maruts, do ye never, never recollect and
call again to mind this our relationship ?
When next we meet together at the central
point, even there shall Aditi confirm
our brotherhood.

14 The Mothers, Heaven and Earth, those
mighty Goddesses, worthy of sacrifice,
come with the race of Gods.
These Two with their support uphold both
Gods and men, and with the Fathers
pour the copious genial stream.

---

3 *Unconcealable Agni* : or, to the unconcealable (Savitar).
and Agni. *Two Moons* : New Moon and Full Moon

4 *Aja-Ekapād* : see VI. 50. 14. *Ṛkvans* : singers ;
minor deities who attend and sing the praises of some
superior God. *Ahi of the Deep* : the great Dragon of the
depths of the aerial ocean; Ahibudhnya. See Vol. I.,
Index.

5 *Dakṣa* : meaning here the Sun, according to Sāyaṇa.
Ludwig thinks that the sacrificer, regarded as Dakṣa or
Prajāpati, and said to be born again through completion
of his vow, is intended. In the second line also *Aryaman*
is considered by Sāyaṇa to be the Sun :—'Aryaman,
whose course is not hurried, the giver of delight to many,
having seven ministering (rays) proceeds in his multiform births.'—Wilson.

6 *Coursers* : the horses which bring the Gods to men's
sacrifices.

7 *Purandhi* : Plenty personified as a deity. Or
pu andhim may be an adjective 'the spirited, or liberal.
Pūṣan.'

8 *Thrice-seven* : the seven rivers of the Āryans
having their counterparts in heaven and in the firmament. *Kṛśānu* : the archer who guards the heavenly
Soma. *Tiṣya* : an asterism regarded as being in the form
of an arrow, and so here identified with Kṛśānu.

10 *Bṛhaddivā* : a Goddess associated with Iḷā, Sarasvatī,
and others. *Dames* : the consorts of the Gods. *Rathapati* :
the God who presides over chariots of war. *Speech*: or
prayer. *Who labours* : at the sacrifice.

13 *At the central point* : the place of sacrifice.

14 *With the Fathers* : 'The fruitfulness of heaven and
earth, which give birth to gods and men, is described as
produced by the fathers.' See Wallis, *Cosmology of the
Ṛgveda*, p. 72.

15 This invocation wins all good that we desire
Bṛhaspati, highly-praised Aramati, are
here,
Even where the stone that presses meath
rings loudly out, and where the sages
make their voices heard with hymns.

16 Thus hath the sage, skilled in loud singers'
duties, desiring riches, yearning after
treasure,
Gaya, the priestly singer, with his praises
and hymns contented the Celestial people.

17 Thus hath the thoughtful sage, the son of
Plati, praised you, O Aditi and all
Ādityas.
Men are made rich by those who are
Immortal : the Heavenly Folk have
been extolled by Gaya.

HYMN LXV.   *Viśvedevas.*

1. MAY Agni, Indra, Mitra, Varuṇa consent,
Aryaman, Vāyu, Pūṣan, and Sarasvatī,
Ādityas, Maruts, Viṣṇu, Soma, lofty Sky,
Rudra and Aditi, and Brahmaṇaspati.

2 Indra and Agni, Hero-lords when Vṛtra
fell, dwelling together, speeding emulously on,
And Soma blent with oil, putting his greatness forth, have with their power filled
full the mighty firmament.

3 Skilled in the Law I lift the hymn of praise
to these, Law-strengtheners, unassailed,
and great in majesty.
These in their wondrous bounty send the
watery sea : may they as kindly Friends
send gifts to make us great.

4 They with their might have stayed Heaven,
Earth, and Pṛthivī, the Lord of Light,
the firmament, the lustrous spheres.
Even as fleet-foot steeds who make their
masters glad, the princely Gods are
praised, most bountiful to man.

5 Bring gifts to Mitra and to Varuṇa who,
Lords of all, in spirit never fail the
worshipper,
Whose statute shines on high through everlasting Law, whose places of sure refuge
are the heavens and earth.

6 The cow who yielding milk goes her
appointed way hither to us as leader
of holy rites,
Speaking aloud to Varuṇa and the worshipper, shall with oblation serve Vivasvān
and the Gods.

7 The Gods whose tongue is Agni dwell in
heaven, and sit, aiders of Law, reflec-
ting, in the seat of Law.
They propped up heaven and then brought waters with their might, got sacrifice
and in a body made it fair.

8 Born in the oldest time, the Parents dwelling
round are sharers of one mansion in
the home of Law.
Bound by their common vow Dyaus, Pṛthivī
stream forth the moisture rich in oil to
Varuṇa the Steer.

9 Parjanya, Vāta, mighty, senders of the rain,
Indra and Vāyu, Varuṇa, Mitra, Aryaman :
We call on Aditi, Ādityas, and the Gods,
those who are on the earth, in waters,
and in heaven.

10 Tvaṣṭar and Vāyu, those who count as
Ṛbhus, both celestial Hotar-priests, and
Dawn for happiness,
Winners of wealth, we call, and wise
Bṛhaspati, destroyer of our foes, and
Soma Indra's Friend.

11 They generated prayer, the cow, the horse,
the plants, the forest trees, the earth, the
waters, and the hills.
These very bounteous Gods made the Sun
mount to heaven, and spread the
righteous laws of Āryas o'er the land.

12 O Aśvins, ye delivered Bhujyu from
distress, ye animated Śyāva, Vadhṛmatī's
son.
To Vimada ye brought his consort
Kamadyū, and gave his lost Viṣṇāpū
back to Viśvaka.

13 Thunder, the lightning's daughter, Aja-
Ekapād, heaven's bearer, Sindhu, and
the waters of the sea :
Hear all the Gods my words, Sarasvatī
give ear together with Purandhi and
with Holy Thoughts.

15 *Aramati* : the Genius of Devotion.
17 The concluding stanza of Hymn 63 is repeated here.

———

3 *The watery sea* : the clouds and rain.

4 *Pṛthivī* : meaning here the region of mid-air.

5 *Places of sure refuge* : Sāyaṇa explains *nādhasī* differently :—'upon whom the two *solicitous* worlds remain dependent.'

6 *The cow* : who is milked at sacrifice. According
to Sāyaṇa, thunder may be meant, and by 'milk'
strength may be intended.

7 *In a body* : that is, personified. Cf. X. 66. 9, note.

8 *The Parents* : Heaven and Earth.

10 *Celestial Hotar-priests* : See I. 13. 8.

12 These deeds of the Aśvins are told in I. 16 and 17.

13 *Aja-Ekapād* : see VI. 50. 14. *Holy Thoughts* : Devotions personified.

14 With Holy Thoughts and with Purandhi
may all Gods, knowing the Law immortal, Manu's Holy Ones,
Boon-givers, favourers, finders of light,
and Heaven, with gracious love accept
my songs, my prayer, my hymn.

15 Immortal Gods have I, Vasiṣṭha, lauded,
Gods set on high above all other beings.
May they this day grant us wide space
and freedom : ye Gods, preserve us
evermore with blessings.

HYMN LXVI.   *Viśvedevas.*

1. I CALL the Gods of lofty glory for our
weal, the makers of the light, well-
skilled in sacrifice ;
Those who have waxen mightily, Masters
of all wealth, Immortal, strengthening
Law, the Gods whom Indra leads.

2 For the strong band of Maruts will we
frame a hymn : the chiefs shall bring
forth sacrifice for Indra's troop,
Who, sent by Indra and advised by
Varuna, have gotten for themselves a
share of Sūrya's light

3 May Indra with the Vasus keep our
dwelling safe, and Aditi with Ādityas
lend us sure defence.
May the God Rudra with the Rudras
favour us, and Tvaṣṭar with the Dames
further us to success.

4 Aditi, Heaven and Earth, the great eternal
Law, Indra, Viṣṇu, the Maruts, and
the lofty Sky.
We call upon Ādityas, on the Gods, for
help, on Vasus, Rudras, Savitar of
wondrous deeds.

5 With Holy Thoughts Sarasvān, firm-lawed
Varuṇa, great Vāyu, Pūṣan, Viṣṇu, and
the Aśvins Twain,
Lords of all wealth, Immortal, furtherers
of prayer, grant us a triply-guarding
refuge from distress.

6 Strong be the sacrifice, strong be the
Holy Ones, strong the preparers of
oblation, strong the Gods.

Mighty be Heaven and Earth, true to
eternal Law, strong be Parjanya, strong
be they who laud the Strong.

7 To win us strength I glorify the Mighty
Twain, Agni and Soma, Mighty Ones
whom many laud.
May these vouchsafe us shelter with a
triple guard, these whom the strong
have served in worship of the Gods.

8 Potent, with firm-fixt laws, arranging
sacrifice, visiting solemn rites in splendour of the day,
Obeying Order, these whose priest is
Agni, free from falsehood, poured the
waters out when Vṛtra died.

9 The Holy Ones engendered, for their
several laws, the heavens and earth, the
waters, and the plants and trees.
They filled the firmament with heavenly
light for help : the Gods embodied
Wish and made it beautiful.

10 May they who bear up heaven, the Ṛbhus
deft of hand, and Vāta and Parjanya
of the thundering Bull,
The waters and the plants, promote the
songs we sing : come Bhaga, Rāti, and
the Vājins to my call.

11 Sindhu, the sea, the region, and the
firmament, the thunder, and the ocean,
Aja-Ekapād,
The Dragon of the Deep, shall listen to
my words, and all the Deities and
Princes shall give ear.

12 May we be yours, we men, to entertain
the Gods : further our sacrifice and give
it full success.
Ādityas, Rudras, Vasus, givers of good
gifts, quicken the holy hymns which we
are singing now

13 I follow with success upon the path of
Law the two celestial Hotars, Priests of
oldest time.
We pray to him who dwelleth near, Guard
of the Field, to all Immortal Gods who
never are remiss.

---

14 *Manu's Holy Ones* : deities whom Manu worshipped.

15 *Vasiṣṭha* : that is, a descendant of the great Ṛṣi Vasiṣṭha.

---

4 The names in the first line are in the nominative
case and without a verb : 'are invoked', may be understood.

6 *Strong* : vṛṣan repeated in the way loved by some
of the Vedic poets ; 'showerer of benefits,' according to
Sāyaṇa. *The Gods* : meaning, says Sāyaṇa, the priests.

9 *Laws* : courses of action. *Embodied Wish* : gave
a body to the wishes and hopes of worshippers, and personified them in the same manner as sacrifice is said to
have been embodied and beautified in X. 65. 7.

10 *Vāta and Parjanya of the thundering Bull* : meaning
the wind and storm that attend the thunderous rain-cloud.
Rāti : divine Favour or Bounty. *Vājins* : a class of divinities according to Sāyaṇa. See VII. 38. 7.

11 *Aja-Ekapād* : See VI. 50. 14. *Dragon of the Deep* :
Ahibudhnya. See VI. 49. 14.

13 *Two celestial Hotars* : Agni and Āditya, according
to Sāyaṇa. *Guard of the Field* : probably Indra.

14 Vasiṣṭha's sons have raised their voices,
like their sire. Ṛṣi-like praying to the
Gods for happiness.
Like friendly-minded kinsmen, come at
our desire, O Gods, and shake down
treasures on us from above.

15 Immortal Gods have I, Vasiṣṭha, lauded,
Gods set on high above all other beings.
May they this day grant us wide space
and freedom : ye Gods, preserve us
evermore with blessings.

HYMN LXVII.   *Bṛhaspati.*

1. THIS holy hymn, sublime and seven-
headed, sprung from eternal Law, our
sire discovered.
Ayāsya, friend of all men, hath engendered the fourth hymn as he sang his laud
to Indra.

2 Thinking aright, praising eternal Order,
the sons of Dyaus the Asura, those
heroes,
Aṅgirases, holding the rank of sages, first
honoured sacrifice's holy statute.

3 Girt by his friends who cried with swan-
like voices, bursting the stony barriers
of the prison,
Bṛhaspati spake in thunder to the cattle,
and uttered praise and song when he
had found them.

4 Apart from one, away from two above
him, he drave the kine that stood in
bonds of falsehood.
Bṛhaspati, seeking light amid the darkness,
drave forth the bright cows : three he
made apparent.

5 When he had cleft the lairs and western
castle, he cut off three from him who
held the waters.

15 Repeated from the preceding hymn.

---

1 *Seven-headed* : having seven divisions. Accompanied
by seven bands of the Maruts, or having seven metres,
according to Sāyaṇa. *Our sire* : Aṅgiras. *Fourth* : or,
extending to all four sides, mighty.

3 *The cattle* : the lost cows of the Aṅgirases, representing metaphorically the rays of light which had been
stolen by the fiends of darkness. See I. 62. 3.

4 *Apart from one, away from two* : the meaning is uncertain. Perhaps at a distance from the earth, down
from heaven and the firmament. *Falsehood* : the wickedness of the treacherous Paṇis. *Three* : heaven, firmament, and earth.

5 *Western castle* : this is obscure. Ludwig suggests that
ápācim may mean 'hostile' or 'detested.' *Three* : heaven,
firmament, and earth. *Him who held the waters* : the
demon Vala, who kept the rain, as well as the cows or
rays of light, imprisoned. *The cow* : the cattle; the
beams of light.

Bṛhaspati discovered, while he thundered
like Dyaus, the dawn, the Sun, the cow,
the lightning.

6 As with a hand, so with his roaring Indra
cleft Vala through, the guardian of the
cattle.
Seeking the milk-draught with sweat-
shining comrades he stole the Paṇi's
kine and left him weeping.

7 He with bright faithful Friends, winners
of booty, hath rent the milker of the
cows asunder.
Bṛhaspati with wild boars strong and
mighty, sweating with heat, hath gained
a rich possession.

8 They, longing for the kine, with faithful
spirit incited with their hymns the Lord
of cattle.
Bṛhaspati freed the radiant cows with
comrades self-yoked, averting shame
from one another.

9 In our assembly with auspicious praises
exalting him who roareth like a lion,
May we, in every fight where heroes
conquer, rejoice in strong Bṛhaspati
the Victor.

10 When he had won him every sort of booty
and gone to heaven and its most
lofty mansions,
Men praised Bṛhaspati the Mighty, bringing
the light within their mouths from sundry
places.

11 Fulfil the prayer that begs for vital vigour :
aid in your wonted manner even the
humble.
Let all our foes be turned and driven
backward. Hear this, O Heaven and
Earth, ye All-producers.

12 Indra with mighty strength cleft asunder
the head of Arbuda the watery monster,
Slain Ahi, and set free the Seven Rivers.
O Heaven and Earth, with all the Gods
protect us.

HYMN LXVIII.   *Bṛhaspati.*

1. LIKE birds who keep their watch, plashing
in water, like the loud voices of the
thundering rain-cloud,

---

6 *Comrades* : his faithful friends the Maruts.

7 *Wild boars* : the strong fierce Maruts ; according
to Sāyaṇa, 'bearers of excellent water.'

8 *The Lord of cattle* : Bṛhaspati, so called because he
had released them.

10 *The light* : that is, the hymns of praise which will
bring them the light of help. The stanza is difficult.

12 *The watery monster* : the fiend who dominated the
ocean of air. *Ahi* : or, the Dragon, Vṛtra or his brother.

Like merry streamlets bursting from the
mountain, thus to Bṛhaspati our hymns
have sounded.

2 The Son of Aṅgiras, meeting the cattle,
as Bhaga, brought in Aryaman among
us.
As Friend of men he decks the wife and
husband : as for the race, Bṛhaspati,
nerve our coursers.

3 Bṛhaspati, having won them from the
mountains, strewed down, like barley
out of winnowing-baskets,
The vigorous, wandering cows who aid
the pious, desired of all, of blameless
form, well-coloured.

4 As the Sun dews with meath the seat
of Order, and casts a flaming meteor
down from heaven.
So from the rock Bṛhaspati forced the
cattle, and cleft the earth's skin as it
were with water.

5 Forth from mid air with light he drave
the darkness, as the gale blows a lily
from the river.
Like the wind grasping at the cloud of
Vala, Bṛhaspati gathered to himself
the cattle.

6 Bṛhaspati, when he with fiery lightnings
cleft through the weapon of reviling
Vala,
Consumed him as tongues eat what teeth
have compassed : he threw the prisons
of the red cows open.

7 That secret name borne by the lowing
cattle within the cave Bṛhaspati
discovered,
And drave, himself, the bright kine from
the mountain, like a bird's young after
the egg's disclosure.

8 He looked around on rock-imprisoned
sweetness as one who eyes a fish in
scanty water.
Bṛhaspati, cleaving through with varied
clamour, brought it forth like a bowl
from out the timber.

9 He found the light of heaven, and fire,
and Morning : with lucid rays he
forced apart the darkness.
As from a joint, Bṛhaspati took the
marrow of Vala as he gloried in his
cattle.

10 As trees for foliage robbed by winter,
Vala mourned for the cows Bṛhaspati
had taken.
He did a deed ne'er done, ne'er to be
equalled, whereby the Sun and Moon
ascend alternate.

11 Like a dark steed adorned with pearl,
the Fathers have decorated heaven with
constellations.
They set the light in day, in night the
darkness. Bṛhaspati cleft the rock and
found the cattle.

12 This homage have we offered to the Cloud
God who thunders out to many in
succession.
May this Bṛhaspati vouchsafe us fulness
of life with kine and horses, men, and
heroes.

HYMN LXIX.   Agni.

1. AUSPICIOUS is the aspect of Vadhryaśva's
fire good is its guidance, pleasant are
its visitings.

2 *The Son of Aṅgiras* : Bṛhaspati, especially, worshipped and cherished by Aṅgiras. *Aryaman* : the institution
of marriage, represented by Aryaman ; one meaning
of the name being groomsman or matchmaker.

3 *Out of winnowing baskets* : *sthivíbhyaḥ* : the exact
meaning of the word is somewhat uncertain, but it is
evidently a measure, basket, or instrument connected
with corn. *Sthivímántaḥ,* 'armed with *sthivis,*' occurs
in X. 27. 15. and is said by Sāyaṇa to mean 'occupants
of stations.' Wilson renders *sthivíbhyaḥ* in
this place by 'from the granaries'. The cows bestowed
by Bṛhaspati are countless as grains of barley on the
threshing floor or winnowing-place.

4 *Cleft the earth's skin* : or surface, with the hoofs of
many cattle.

5 *A lily* : *śápāla* : according to Sāyaṇa the same as
Śaivala, the Vallisneria Octandra, a common aquatic
plant.

6 *Weapon* : I adopt Sāyaṇa's explanation of *jásum,*
although in X. 33. 2, the same word means 'exhaustion.

8 *Sweetness* : the sweet milk; that is, the cows who
produced it.
Like a bowl : which already exists potentially in the
wood from which it is produced by cutting.

9 Wilson, following Sāyaṇa, paraphrases the second
line :—'he seized (the cattle from the rock) of Vala
surrounded by the kine as (one extracts) marrow from
a bone.'

11 *The Fathers* : 'The connection of the fathers with
the light, of which they are both the embodiments and
the guardians, is alone sufficient to explain their action
in placing the stars in the sky.'—Wallis, *Cosmology of the
Ṛgveda,* p. 68 Or, as Ludwig remarks, the Fathers themselves may be the stars.

12 *To many* : 'cows' is, apparently, understood.
Sāyaṇa supplies *ṛcas* :—'who recites in order many
(sacred stanzas).'—Wilson.

1 *Vadhryaśva* has been mentioned, in VI. 61. 1, as a
worshipper of Sarasvatī : here he appears as a special
worshipper of Agni.

When first the people of Sumitra kindle it, with butter poured thereon it crackles and shines bright.

2 Butter is that which makes Vadhryaśva's fire grow strong : the butter is its food, the butter makes it fat.

It spreads abroad when butter hath been offered it, and balmed with streams of butter shines forth like the Sun.

3 Still newest is this face of thine, O Agni, which Manu and Sumitra have enkindled.

So richly shine, accept our songs with favour, so give us strengthening food, so send us glory.

4 Accept this offering, Agni, whom aforetime Vadhryaśva hath entreated and enkindled.

Guard well our homes and people, guard our bodies, protect thy gift to us which thou hast granted.

5 Be splendid, guard us Kinsman of Vadhryaśva : let not the enmity of men o'ercome thee.

Like the bold hero Cyavana, I Sumitra tell forth the title of Vadhryaśva's Kinsman.

6 All treasures hast thou won, of plains and mountains, and quelled the Dāsas' and Āryas' hatred.

Like the bold hero Cyavana, O Agni, mayst thou subdue the men who long for battle.

7 Deft Agni hath a lengthened thread, tall oxen, a thousand heifers, numberless devices.

Decked by the men, splendid among the splendid, shine brightly forth amid devout Sumitras.

8 Thine is the teeming cow, O Jātavedas, who pours at once her ceaseless flow, Sabardhuk.

Thou art lit up by men enriched with guerdon, O Agni, by the pious-souled Sumitras.

9 Even Immortal Gods, O Jātavedas, Vadhryaśva's Kinsman, have declared thy grandeur.

When human tribes drew near with supplication thou conqueredst with men whom thou hadst strengthened.

10 Like as a father bears his son, O Agni, Vadhryaśva bare thee in his lap and served thee.

Thou, Youngest God, having enjoyed his fuel, didst vanquish those of old though they were mighty.

11 Vadhryaśva's Agni evermore hath vanquished his foes with heroes who had pressed the Soma.

Lord of bright rays, thou burntest up the battle, subduing, as our help, e'en mighty foemen.

12 This Agni of Vadhryaśva, Vrtra-slayer, lit from of old, must be invoked with homage.

As such assail our enemies, Vadhryaśva, whether the foes be strangers or be kinsmen.

HYMN LXX.   Āprīs.

1. ENJOY, O Agni, this my Fuel, welcome the oil-filled ladle where we pour libation.

Rise up for worship of the Gods, wise Agni, on the earth's height, while days are bright with beauty.

2 May he who goes before the Gods come hither with steeds whose shapes are varied, Narāśaṁsa.

May he, most Godlike, speed our offered viands with homage God-ward on the path of Order.

3 Men with oblations laud most constant Agni, and pray him to perform an envoy's duty.

With lightly-rolling car and best draught-horses, bring the Gods hither and sit down as Hotar.

4 May the delight of Gods spread out transversely : may it be with us long in length and fragrant.

O Holy Grass divine, with friendly spirit bring thou the willing Gods whose Chief is Indra.

---

3 *Sumitra* : son of Vadhryaśva and Ṛṣi of the hymn.

5 *Cyavana* : a son of Bhṛgu. Or the word may mean conquering, as Sāyaṇa interprets it. *Vadhryaśva's Kinsman* : as having been especially worshipped and cherished by that Ṛṣi. See stanza 10.

7 A *lengthened thread* : continual sacrifices, from ancient to present times. *Devices* : ways of attaining his object. Or *śataniīha* may mean, 'having a hundred or many musical modes or sacred songs ;' or 'praised by many, 'the leader of hundreds (of) burnt offerings). —Wilson.

Other Āprī hymns may be compared ; I. 13, 142, and 188; II. 3; III. 4. V. 5; VII. 2, and IX. 5. The usual deities and deified objects with the exception of Tanūnapāt, are invoked.

3 *As Hotar* : 'as ministrant priest'.—Wilson.

4 *The delight of Gods* : the sacred grass.

5 Touch ye the far-extending height of heaven
or spring apart to suit the wide earth's
measure.
Yearning, ye Doors, with those sublime in
greatness, seize eagerly the heavenly Car
that cometh.

6 Here in this shrine may Dawn and Night,
the Daughters of Heaven, the skilful
Goddesses, be seated.
In your wide lap, auspicious, willing Ladies
may the Gods seat them with a willing
spirit.

7 Up stands the stone, high burns the fire
enkindled : Aditi's lap contains the
Friendly Natures
Ye Two Chief Priests who serve at this
our worship, may ye, more skilled, win
for us rich possessions.

8 On our wide grass, Three Goddesses be
seated : for you have we prepared and
made it pleasant.
May Ilà, she whose foot drops oil, the
Goddess, taste, man-like, sacrifice and
well-set presents.

9 Since thou, God Tvaṣṭar, hast made
beauty perfect, since thou hast been the
Aṅgirases' Companion,
Willing, most wealthy, Giver of possessions, grant us the Gods' assembly, thou
who knowest.

10 Well-knowing, binding with thy cord, bring
hither, Lord of the Wood, the Deities'
assembly.
The God prepare and season our oblations :
may Heaven and Earth be gracious to
my calling.

11 Agni, bring hither Varuṇa to help us,
Indra from heaven, from air's mid-realm
the Maruts.

On sacred grass all Holy ones be seated,
and let the Immortal Gods rejoice in
Svāhā.

HYMN LXXI. *Jñānam*

1. WHEN-men, Bṛhaspati, giving names to
objects, sent out Vāk's first and earliest
utterances,
All that was excellent and spotless, treasured within them, was disclosed through
their affection.

2 Where, like men cleansing corn-flour in a
cribble, the wise in spirit have created
language,
Friends see and recognize the marks of
friendship : their speech retains the
blessed sign imprinted.

3 With sacrifice the trace of Vāk they followed, and found her harbouring within
the Ṛṣis.
They brought her, dealt her forth in many
places : seven singers make her tones
resound in concert.

4 One man hath ne'er seen Vāk, and yet
he seeth : one man hath hearing but
hath never heard her.
But to another hath she shown her beauty
as a fond well-dressed woman to her
husband.

5 One man they call a laggard, dull in
friendship : they never urge him on to
deeds of valour.
He wanders on in profitless illusion : the
Voice he heard yields neither fruit nor
blossom.

6 No part in Vāk hath he who hath abandoned his own dear friend who knows the
truth of friendship.
Even if he hears her still in vain he listens:
naught knows he of the path of righteous
action.

---

5 *The neavenly Car* : which brings the Gods.

7. *The stone* : with which the Soma juice is expressed.
Aditi's lap : the surface of the earth. *The Friendly Natures*:
the Gods. According to Sāyaṇa, 'the acceptable sacrificial vessels.' *Two Chief Priests* : *purohitau* : perhaps
Agni and Āditya. *More skilled* : than human priests.

8 *Three Goddesses* : Iḷā, Sarasvatī, and Bhāratī. *Taste*:
the verb is plural, meaning may Iḷā and the others
taste. *Man-like* : as at the sacrifice of Manu, according
to Sāyaṇa.

9 *Grant us the Gods' assembly* : the Commentators
explain *pāthas* some times as 'place', sometimes as 'food'
or 'air' or 'water'. Here Wilson, following Sāyaṇa,
translates :—'offer the food of the gods (to them).'

10 *Binding with thy cord* : it is not clear what is to be
bound, or ranged in order. According to Sāyaṇa the
pāthas, which he explains as *annaṁ devānām*, food of the
Gods, is to be fastened with a rope. *Lord of the Wood* :
vánaspati : the *yūpa* or Sacrificial Post.

11 *Svāhā* : that is, in the sacrificial offerings presented with the exclamation Svāhā, Ave, or Hail.

Jñānam or Knowledge, the subject of this very difficult
hymn, is said by Sāyaṇa to mean Parama brahmajñānam,
knowledge of the higher truths of Religion, which teaches
man his own nature and how he may be reunited to the
Supreme Spirit.

1 *Vāk* : Voice or Speech, the Sacred Word. Here
specially the voice of the hymn regarded as the means
of communication between men and Gods. See *Vedic
India* (Story of the Nations Series), pp. 269—271).

3 *Harbouring within the Ṛṣis* : they discovered, in the
course of sacrifice, that the inspired Ṛṣis alone understood Speech as required for religious purposes. *In many
places* : among the Hotar-priests. *Seven singers* : 'the
seven noisy (birds) meet together.'—Wilson : referring,
says Sāyana, to the seven metres, the Gāyatrī, etc.

7 Unequal in the quickness of their spirit
are friends endowed alike with eyes and
hearing.
Some look like tanks that reach the mouth
or shoulder, others like pools of water
fit to bathe in.

8 When friendly Brāhmans sacrifice together
with mental impulse which the heart
hath fashioned,
They leave one far behind through their
attainments, and some who count as
Brāhmans wander elsewhere.

9 Those men who step not back and move
not forward, nor Brāhmans nor preparers
of libations,
Having attained to Vāk in sinful fashion
spin out their thread in ignorance like
spinsters.

10 All friends are joyful in the friend who
cometh in triumph, having conquered
in assembly.
He is their blame-averter, food-provider :
prepared is he and fit for deed of vigour.

11 One plies his constant task reciting verses :
one sings the holy psalm in Śakvarī
measures.
One more, the Brāhman, tells the lore of
being, and one lays down the rules of
sacrificing.

HYMN LXXII.   *The Gods.*

1. LET us with tuneful skill proclaim these
generations of the Gods,
That one may see them when these hymns
are chanted in a future age.

2 These Brahmaṇaspati produced with blast
and smelting, like a smith,
Existence, in an earlier age of Gods, from
Non-existence sprang.

3 Existence, in the earliest age of Gods, from
Non-existence sprang.
Thereafter were the regions born. This
sprang from the Productive Power.

4 Earth sprang from the Productive Power ;
the regions from the earth were born.
Dakṣa was born of Aditi, and Aditi was
Dakṣa's Child.

5 For Aditi, O Dakṣa, she who is thy
Daughter, was brought forth.
After her were the blessed Gods born
sharers of immortal life.

6 When ye, O Gods, in yonder deep close-
clasping one another stood,
Thence, as of dancers, from your feet a
thickening cloud of dust arose.

7 When, O ye Gods, like Yatis, ye caused
all existing things to grow,
Then ye brought Sūrya forward who was
lying hidden in the sea.

8 Eight are the Sons of Aditi who from her
body sprang to life.
With seven she went to meet the Gods :
she cast Mārtāṇḍa far away.

9 So with her Seven Sons Aditi went forth
to meet the earlier age.
She brought Mārtāṇḍa thitherward to
spring to life and die again.

8 *Some who count as Brāhmans wander elsewhere* : 'others
walk about boasting to be *Brāhmans*.'—Muir.

9 *Step not back and move not forward* : take no active
part in religious ceremonies. 'Those who do not walk
(with the Brāhmans) in this lower world, nor (with
the gods) in the upper world, ' is Wilson's paraphrase
of the text which I have rendered literally. *Like spinsters* :
'(like) female weavers. Such is the sense which Prof.
Aufrecht thinks may, with probability, be assigned to
siris, a word which occurs only here.'—Muir.

11 *Reciting verses* : repeating *ṛcas* or verses of the Ṛgveda. This is the duty of the Hotar. *The holy psalm* :
the Gāyatra or Sāman. The Udgātar or Chanter,
one of the four chief priests is intended. *The
lore of being* : the knowledge of all that exists. *Lays down
the rules* : 'prescribes the order.'—Muir. 'Measures
the materials.'—Wilson. This is the duty of the Adhvaryu, another of the chief priests. The hymn has been
transliterated and translated by Dr. J. Muir, *O. S. Texts*,
I, pp. 254—256. It has also been metrically rendered by the
authors of the *Siebenzig Lieder des Ṛgveda*, who have en-
deavoured, by transposing some of the stanzas, to bring
them into closer connexion. According to Sāyaṇa, the
subject of the whole hymn is 'the eulogy of the understanding of the Veda as essential to divine knowledge.'

2 *These* : all beings. *Like a smith* : as a blacksmith
blows up his fire and melts metal.

3 *The regions*: 'the quarters (of the horizon).'—Wilson.
This : meaning earth. *Productive Power* : the meaning
of *uttānpadaḥ* is uncertain. Wallis renders it by 'the
begetter (the sky); Wilson by 'the upward-growing
(tree).'

4 *And Aditi was Dakṣa's Child* : 'Yāska remarks......
How can this be possible ? They may have had the same
origin ; or, according to the nature of the gods, they
may have been born from each other,—have derived
their substance from one another.'—*O. S. Texts*. IV. 13
Aditi is Infinity or the Infinite, and Dakṣa is Force or.
Power personified. See *Vedic Hymns*, I. p. 245.

6 'The two verses 6 and 7 are interesting as containing an independent story of the origin of the world : the
gods are said to have kicked up in dancing the atoms
which formed the earth.—Wallis, *Cosmology of the Ṛgveda*
p. 43.

7 *Yatis* : devotees.

8 *Eight are the Sons* : according to the Commentator,
Mitra, Varuṇa, Dhātar, Aryaman, Aṁśa, Bhaga, Vivasvān, and Āditya (the Sun). *Mārtāṇḍa* : Sūrya, the
Sun. His exposure probably refers to his sweeping
through the sky.—Ludwig. But see Bergaigne, *La Religion Védique*, III. 107.

HYMN LXXIII. *Indra.*

1. THOU wast born mighty for victorious valour, exulting, strongest, full of pride and courage.
There, even there, the Maruts strengthened Indra when his most rapid Mother stirred the Hero.

2 There with fiend's ways e'en Pṛśanī was seated : with much laudation they exalted Indra.
As if encompassed by the Mighty-footed, from darkness, near at hand, forth came the Children.

3 High are thy feet when on thy way thou goest : the strength thou foundest here hath lent thee vigour.
Thousand hyenas in thy mouth thou holdest. O Indra, mayst thou turn the Aśvins hither.

4 Speeding at once to sacrifice thou comest : for friendship thou art bringing both Nāsatyas.
Thou hadst a thousand treasures in possession. The Aśvins, O thou Hero, gave thee riches.

5 Glad, for the race that rests on holy Order, with friends who hasten to their goal, hath Indra
With these his magic powers assailed the Dasyu : he cast away the gloomy mists, the darkness.

6 Two of like name for him didst thou demolish, as Indra striking down the car of Uṣas.
With thy beloved lofty Friends thou camest, and with the assurance of thine heart thou slewest.

7 War-loving Namuci thou smotest, robbing the Dāsa of his magic for the Ṛṣi.

For man thou madest ready pleasant pathways, paths leading as it were directly God-ward.

8 These names of thine thou hast fulfilled completely : as Lord, thou holdest in thine arm, O Indra.
In thee, through thy great might, the Gods are joyful : the roots of trees hast thou directed upward.

9 May the sweet Soma juices make him happy to cast his quoit that lies in depth of waters.
Thou from the udder which o'er earth is fastened hast poured the milk into the kine and herbage.

10 When others call him offspring of the Courser, my meaning is that Mighty Power produced him.
He came from Manyu and remained in houses : whence he hath sprung is known to Indra only.

11 Like birds of beauteous wing the Priyamedhas, Ṛṣis, imploring, have come nigh to Indra :
Dispel the darkness and fill full our vision : deliver us as men whom snares entangle.

HYMN LXXIV. *Indra.*

1. I AM prepared to laud with song or worship the Noble Ones who are in earth and heaven,
Or Coursers who have triumphed in the contest, or those who famed, have won the prize with glory.

1 *Mother* : Aditi. *Stirred the Hero* : gave him free motion as soon as he was born, or incited him to action by telling him of his future opponent. See VIII. 45. 5, and 66. 2.

2 This stanza is unintelligible to me *Pṛśanī* : meaning perhaps Pṛśnī, as Ludwig conjectures. *The Mighty-footed* : Indra. *The Children* : the new-born Maruts Wilson translates, after Sāyaṇa :—'The martial troop of (Indra) the injurer encamped around Indra (accompanied) by the swift-moving (Maruts) : they animated him with abundant praise; like (cattle) penned up within a great stall, the embryonic (waters) issued from the (Vṛtra) who had arrived in the form of darkness.'

3 *High are thy feet* : as travelling through the heavens. *Hyenas sālāvṛkān* jackals.'—Wilson.

6 *Two of like name* : or, of similar nature; gloomy mists and darkness. *The car of Uṣas* : See IV. 30. 8—11. *The assurance of thine heart* : thy trusted thunderbolt.

8 *Thou hast fulfilled* : hast acted in full accordance with the names thou bearest, such as Vṛtra-slayer, Śakra, etc. *Thou holdest* : the thunderbolt. *The roots of trees* : the clouds are often compared to trees. The rain is their fruit, and when they pour it down their roots are supposed to be turned upward.

9 *Quoit* : *cakrám* : meaning the thunderbolt. *The udder* : the firmament.

10 *The Courser* : meaning Heaven. *Manyu* : wrath, passion or ardour, personified. *My meaning is* : the speaker declares that he is raised above the common mythological explanations. He considers the God to have sprung from a transcendental Power.—Ludwig.

Grassmann banishes this hymn to his Appendix as being generally obscure and in parts absolutely unintelligible. I have, for the most part, followed Ludwig's interpretation.

The subject of the hymn is a coming horse-race, and the Ṛṣi invokes in favour of the Yajamāna, the Vasus, racers who have won the prize in former times and the men who owned them. Indra also is appealed to for help. See *Vedische Studien*, I. p. 129.

2 Their call, the call of Gods, went up to
heaven : they kissed the ground with
glory-seeking spirit,
There where the Gods look on for happy
fortune, and like the kindly heavens
bestow their bounties.

3 This is the song of those Immortal Beings
who long for treasures in their full
perfection.
May these, completing prayers and sacrifices, bestow upon us wealth where
naught is wanting.

4 Those living men extolled thy deed, O
Indra, those who would fain burst
through the stall of cattle,
Fain to milk her who bare but once, great,
lofty, whose Sons are many and her
streams past number.

5 Śacīvan, win to your assistance Indra
who never bends, who overcomes his
foemen.
Ṛbhukṣan, Maghavan, the hymn's upholder, who, rich in food, bears man's
kind friend, the thunder.

6 Since he who won of old anew hath
triumphed, Indra hath earned his name
of Vṛtra-slayer.
He hath appeared, the mighty Lord of
Conquest. What we would have him
do let him accomplish.

HYMN LXXV.   The Rivers.

1. THE singer, O ye Waters in Vivasvān's
place, shall tell your grandeur forth
that is beyond compare.
The Rivers have come forward triply, seven
and seven. Sindhu in might surpasses all
the streams that flow.

2 Varuṇa cut the channels for thy forward
course, O Sindhu, when thou rannest on
to win the race.
Thou speedest o'er precipitous ridges of
the earth, when thou art Lord and
Leader of these moving floods.

3 His roar is lifted up to heaven above the
earth : he puts forth endless vigour with
a flash of light.
Like floods of rain that fall in thunder
from the cloud, so Sindhu rushes on
bellowing like a bull.

4 Like mothers to their calves, like milch
kine with their milk, so, Sindhu, unto
thee the roaring rivers run.
Thou leadest as a warrior king thine
army's wings what time thou comest in
the van of these swift streams.

5 Favour ye this my laud, O Gaṅgā, Yamunā,
O Śutudrī, Paruṣṇī and Sarasvatī :
With Asiknī, Vitastā, O Marudvṛdhā, O
Ārjīkīyā with Suṣomā hear my call.

6 First with Tṛṣṭāmā thou art eager to flow
forth, with Rasā, and Susartu, and with
Śvetyā here,
With Kubhā ; and with these, Sindhu !
and Mehatnu, thou seekest in thy course
Krumu and Gomatī.

7 Flashing and whitely-gleaming in her
mightiness, she moves along her ample
volumes through the realms,
Most active of the active, Sindhu unrestrained, like to a dappled mare, beautiful,
fair to see.

---

2 *The call of Gods* : the Gods are imagined as present
and interested in the race. *They kissed the ground* : the
horses lightly touched the earth as they ran.

4 *Those living men* : the Aṅgirases. *Her who bare but
once* : Heaven, according to Sāyaṇa ; Earth, according
to Grassmann. Pṛśni, the mother of the Maruts, must
be meant.—Ludwig. See VI. 48. 22.

5 *Śacīvan* : apparently a man's name. 'Celebrator
of holy rites.'—Wilson.

6 *He who won of old* : the Yajamāna. *He hath appeared* :
the poet imagines Indra himself to be present.

---

1 *O ye Waters* : apparently the Rivers are addressed
as representing all the divine Waters. *Vivasvān's place* :
where the singers stand when they sing hymns. *Triply,
seven and seven* : twenty-one rivers ; two other sets of seven
each being added to the seven chief rivers of the Panjāb.
Sāyaṇa explains differently :—'they flowed by
sevens through the three (worlds).'—Wilson. 'Each set
of seven (streams) has followed a threefold course.'—
Muir. 'By seven and seven......in three courses.'—M.
Müller.

5 The poet addresses first the most distant rivers.
Gaṅgā : the Ganges is mentioned, indirectly, in only one
other verse of the *Ṛgveda*, and even there, the word is
said by some to be the name of a woman. See VI. 45.31.
Yamunā : the Jumna. *Śutudrī* : the Sutlej or Satlaj. *Paruṣṇī*:
the Rāvī : *Sarasvatī* : see VI. 61. 2. *Asiknī* : the ancient
Acesines : the Vedic name of the Candrabhāgā, the
present Cenāb. *Vitastā* : probably the Jhelum, the
Hydaspes of the Greeks. *Marudvṛdhā* : meaning, increased
by the Maruts : not identified. *Ārjīkīyā* and *Suṣomā*
are said by Yāska to be the Vipās and the Sindhu ;
but this is not possible, and it is uncertain what rivers
are meant.

6 *Kubhā, Krumu,* and *Gomatī* have been mentioned in
previous Books. The other streams whose names occur
in this stanza are probably unimportant affluents of the
Indus. All that is known regarding the rivers mentioned
in stanzas 5 and 6 may be found in Zimmer's *Altindisches Leben*, pp. 4ff.

7 *In her mightiness* : in the preceding stanzas Sindhu
appears to be a River-God, but in this and following
verses the epithets are feminine.

8 Rich in good steeds is Sindhu, rich in cars
and robes, rich in gold, nobly-fashioned,
rich in ample wealth.
Blest Sīlamāvatī and young Ūrṇāvatī invest
themselves with raiment rich in store of
sweets.

9 Sindhu hath yoked her car, light-rolling,
drawn by steeds, and with that car
shall she win booty in this fight.
So have I praised its power, mighty and
unrestrained, of independent glory,
roaring as it runs.

HYMN LXXVI. *Press-stones.*

1. I GRASP at you when power and strength
begin to dawn : bedew ye, Indra and
the Maruts, Heaven and Earth,
That Day and Night, in every hall of
sacrifice, may wait on us and bless us
when they first spring forth.

2 Press the libation out, most excellent of
all : the Pressing-stone is grasped like a
hand-guided steed.
So let it win the valour that subdues the
foe, and the fleet courser's might that
speeds to ample wealth.

3 Juice that this Stone pours out removes
defect of ours, as in old time it brought
prosperity to man.
At sacrifices they established holy rites on
Tvaṣṭar's milk-blent juice bright with
the hue of steeds.

8 *Sīlamāvatī* and *Ūrṇāvatī* appear to be names of rivers.
According to Sāyaṇa, the words are epithets of Sindhu
and mean respectively 'abounding in *Sīlamā* plants,' said
to be used for cordage, and 'rich in wool'. The meaning of the second half of the second line is uncertain :—
'wears (as only one river is supposed to be the subject)
honey-growing (flowers).'—Wilson.

9 *In this fight* : the hymn may, as Prof. Ludwig suggests, be a prayer for aid in a battle that is to be fought
on the banks of the Sindhu or Indus. The hymn has
been transliterated and translated by Dr. J. Muir, *O. S.
Texts*, V. 343—345, and a version of stanzas 1—8 is
given by Prof. Zimmer, *Altindisches Leben*, p. 4. A complete translation, with full explanatory notes, is given
in Max Müller's *India, What can it Teach Us ?*, pp. 164—
168.

1 *I grasp at you* : 'I propitiate you.'—Wilson. *Power
and strength* : the morning beams which bring new vigour.
Day and Night : or, 'both day-halves.'

3 *To man* : or, to Manu. *Tvaṣṭar's milk-blent juice* :
the Soma juice brewed by Tvaṣṭar for the year, which
represents the life sustaining power of Nature.—Ludwig.
Bright with the hue of steeds : tawny-coloured. Sāyaṇa interprets differently :—'when the son of Tvaṣṭṛ, hidden by
the (stolen) cows, and assuming the form of a horse,
(was to be slain).—Wilson. Triśiras the son of Tvaṣṭar
was regarded as an enemy of the Gods. Indra slew him
and took possession of the Soma.

4 Drive ye the treacherous demons far away
from us: keep Nirṛti afar and banish
penury.
Pour riches forth for us with troops of
hero sons, and bear ye up, O Stones,
the song that visits Gods.

5 To you who are more mighty than the
heavens themselves, who, finishing
your task with more than Vibhvan's
speed,
More rapidly than Vāyu seize the Soma
juice, better than Agni give us food,
to you I sing.

6 Stirred be the glorious Stones: let it press
out the juice, the Stone with heavenly
song that reaches up to heaven,
There where the men draw forth the
meath for which they long,
sending their voice around in rivalry
of speed.

7 The Stones press out the Soma, swift as
car-borne men, and, eager for the spoil,
drain forth the sap thereof.
To fill the beaker, they exhaust the udder's
store, as the men purify oblations with
their lips.

8 Ye, present men, have been most skilful
in your work, even ye, O Stones
who pressed Soma for Indra's
drink.
May all ye have of fair go to the Heavenly
Race, and all your treasure to the
earthly worshipper.

HYMN LXXVII. *Maruts.*

1. As with their voice from cloud they sprinkle
treasure so are the wise man's liberal
sacrifices.

4 *Nirṛti* : the Goddess of Death and Destruction.

5 *Vibhvan* : one of the three Ṛbhus. *Vāyu* : or, the
wind.

6 *The men* : meaning the press-stones. Cf. stanza 8.

7 *The udder's store* : the juice contained in the milky
Soma-plant. *With their lips* : with the praises that they
utter.

8 *Worshipper* : Sāyaṇa explains *sunvaté* by *yajamānāya*,
to the Yajamāna or sacrificer. The more literal translation would be 'to the presser,' the man who presses
out or effuses the Soma juice.

1 This stanza is obscure. According to Sāyaṇa,
vijānuṣaḥ (the wise man's) is formed from *jan*, to generate, and not from *jñā*, to know :—'they are the generators (of the world) like sacrifices abounding in libations.'—Wilson. *The good Maruts' priest* : either the band
of the Maruts themselves regarded as a Brahman, or a
human priest specially skilled in propitiating them.
Prof. M. Müller translates differently. See *Vedic Hymns*,
I p. 412.

I praise their Company that merits worship
as the good Maruts' priest to pay them
honour.

2 The youths have wrought their ornaments
for glory through many nights,—this
noble band of Maruts.
Like stags the Sons of Dyaus have striven
onward, the Sons of Aditi grown strong
like pillars.

3 They who extend beyond the earth and
heaven, by their own mass, as from the
cloud spreads Sūrya;
Like mighty Heroes covetous of glory,
like heavenly gallants who destroy the
wicked.

4 When ye come nigh, as in the depth of
waters, the earth is loosened, as it were,
and shaken.
This your all-feeding sacrifice approaches:
come all united, fraught, as 'twere, with
viands.

5 Ye are like horses fastened to the chariot
poles, luminous with your beams, with
splendour as at dawn;
Like self-bright falcons, punishers of wicked
men, like hovering birds urged forward,
scattering rain around.

6 When ye come forth, O Maruts, from the
distance, from the great treasury of rich
possessions,
Knowing, O Vasus, boons that should be
granted, even from afar drive back the
men who hate us.

7 He who, engaged in the rite's final duty
brings, as a man, oblation to the
Maruts,
Wins him life's wealthy fulness, blest with
heroes: he shall be present, too, where
Gods drink Soma.

8 For these are helps adored at sacrifices,
bringing good fortune by their name
Ādityas.
Speeding on cars let them protect our
praises, delighting in our sacrifice and
worship.

HYMN LXXVIII.   Maruts.

1. YE by your hymns are like high-thoughted
singers, skilful, inviting Gods with sacrifices;
Fair to behold, like Kings, with bright
adornment, like spotless gallants, leaders
of the people :

2 Like fire with flashing flame, breast-bound
with chains of gold, like tempest-blasts,
self-moving, swift to lend your aid;
As best of all foreknowers, excellent to
guide, like Somas, good to guard the
man who follows Law.

3 Shakers of all, like gales of wind they
travel, like tongues of burning fires in
their effulgence.
Mighty are they as warriors clad in
armour, and, like the Fathers' prayers,
Most Bounteous Givers.

4 Like spokes of car-wheels in one nave
united, ever victorious like heavenly
Heroes,
Shedding their precious balm like youthful
suitors, they raise their voice and chant
their psalm as singers.

5 They who are fleet to travel like the
noblest steeds, long to obtain the prize
like bounteous charioteers,
Like waters speeding on with their precipitous floods, like omniform Aṅgirases
with Sāma-hymns.

6 Born from the stream, like press-stones
are the Princes, for ever like the stones
that crush in pieces;
Sons of a beauteous Dame, like playful
children, like a great host upon the
march with splendour.

7 Like rays of Dawn, the visitors of sacrifice,
they shine with ornaments as eager to be
bright.

2 *This noble band of Maruts* : Prof. Ludwig suggests that
sumārutam means here a festival held in honour of the
Maruts at the end of the periodical rains, and that, after
many nights, the Maruts adorn themselves for this.
Pillars : I follow Ludwig ; but the meaning of *akṛāḥ* is
uncertain. Geldner takes it to mean 'horses, a parallel-
ism to stags or antelopes. Sāyaṇa makes *nā*, like,
negative, and explains *akṛāḥ* by *ākramaṇaśīlāḥ* :—'the
swift-going sons of Aditi do not increase in glory.'—Wilson.

4 *This your all-feeding sacrifice approaches* : 'this manifold sacrifice comes towards you.'—Wilson.

7 *In the rite's final duty* : Sāyaṇa explains *udṛici yajñe*
by *yajñe samāptastutike sampūrṇe sati*, when the sacrifice
has its praise perfected, when the sacrifice is complete.
As a man : according to Ludwig, 'no longer a man, that
is, not in his human character but having become divine
by worship. *Where the Gods drink Soma* : he, a God himself, shall be admitted to the Gods' society.

4 *Shedding their precious balm* : pouring out the fertilizing
rain as liberally as young wooers give presents.

6 *Born from the stream* : from the sea of air, or from
Sindhu, the Indus.

7 *They measure out the distance* : 'have traversed leagues.'
—Wilson. 'They measure many miles.'—M. Müller.

Like rivers hasting on, glittering with their
spears, from far away they measure out
the distances.

8 Gods, send us happiness and make us
wealthy, letting us singers prosper, O
ye Maruts.
Bethink you of our praise and of our
friendship : ye from of old have riches
to vouchsafe us.

HYMN LXXIX.   *Agni.*

1. I HAVE beheld the might of this Great
Being. Immortal in the midst of tribes
of mortals.
His jaws now open and now shut together:
much   they   devour,   insatiately
chewing.

2 His eyes are turned away, his head is
hidden : unsated with his tongue he
eats the fuel.
With hands upraised, with reverence in
the houses, for him they quickly bring
his food together.

3 Seeking, as 'twere, his Mother's secret
bosom, he, like a child, creeps on
through wide-spread bushes.
One he finds glowing like hot food made
ready, and kissing deep within the
earth's recesses.

4 This holy Law I tell you, Earth and
Heaven : the   Infant at   his birth
devours his Parents.
No knowledge of the God have I, a
mortal. Yea, Agni knoweth best, for
he hath wisdom.

5 This man who quickly gives him food, who
offers his gifts of oil and butter and
supports him,—
Him with his thousand eyes he closely
looks on : thou showest him thy face
from all sides, Agni.

6 Agni, hast thou committed sin or treason
among the Gods ? In ignorance I ask
thee.
Playing, not playing, he gold-hued and
toothless, hath cut his food up as the
knife a victim.

7 He born in wood hath yoked his horses
rushing in all   directions, held with
reins that glitter.
The well-born friend hath carved his food
with Vasus : in all his limbs he hath
increased and prospered.

HYMN LXXX.   *Agni.*

1. AGNI bestows the fleet prize-winning
courser : Agni, the hero famed and
firm in duty.
Agni pervades and decks the earth and
heaven, and fills the fruitful dame who
teems with heroes.

2 Blest be the wood that feeds the active
Agni : within the two great worlds hath
Agni entered.
Agni impels a single man to battle, and
with him rends in pieces many a
foeman.

3 Agni rejoiced the ear of him who praised
him, and from the waters burnt away
Jarūtha.
Agni saved Atri in the fiery cavern, and
made Nṛmedha rich with troops of
children.

4 Agni hath granted wealth that decks the
hero, and sent the sage who wins a
thousand cattle.
Agni hath made oblations rise to heaven :
to every   place   are   Agni's   laws
extended.

5 With songs of praise the Ṛṣis call on
Agni; on Agni, heroes worsted in the
foray.
Birds flying in the region call on Agni :
around a thousand cattle Agni wanders.

---

2 *His eyes* : according to Sāyaṇa, the eyes of Agni
are the distant Sun and Moon, and *his head* is hidden in
mens' stomachs, in the shape of the heat which enables
them to digest their food. *His food* : the sticks for fuel,
which are bound up into fagots.

3 This stanza is very obscure. Agni, born from the
wood of the fire-sticks, seems, as he creeps through the
brushwood that he is burning, to seek entrance again
into his mother's side. He then finds an old dry tree or
log, which had been deeply rooted in the earth, and
feeds on it as on food that has been specially prepared
for him.

4 *His Parents* : the two fire-sticks from which he has
been produced.

6 *Hast thou committed sin ?* : Art thou as voracious and
destructive in heaven as thou art on earth ? *Playing,
not playing* : playing about the fuel, and yet earnestly
intent on devouring his food. 'Sporting (here), not
sporting (there).—Wilson. *A victim* : *gām* : ox or cow.

7 *The well-born Friend* : Agni. *In all his limbs* : *párva-
bhiḥ* : 'with logs of wood.'—Wilson.

---

3 *Jarūtha* : See VII. 1. 7, and 9. 6. *Atri* : his deliverance is ascribed to the Aśvins in I. 112. 7, 116. 8, 117. 3.
and 118. 7.

5 *Around a thousand cattle* : in the fires lighted to keep
off wild beasts and demons of darkness.

6 Races of human birth pay Agni worship,
men who have sprung from Nahus'
line adore him.
Stablished in holy oil is Agni's pasture,
on the Gandharva path of Law and
Order.

7 The Ṛbhus fabricated prayer for Agni,
and we with mighty hymns have called
on Agni.
Agni, Most Youthful God, protect the
singer : win us by worship, Agni,
great possessions.

HYMN LXXXI.   *Viśvakarman.*

1. HE who sate down as Hotar-priest, the
Ṛṣi, our Father, offering up all
things existing,—
He, seeking through his wish a great
possession, came among men on earth
as archetypal.

2 What was the place whereon he took his
station ? What was it that supported
him ? How was it ?
Whence Viśvakarman, seeing all, producing the earth, with mighty power
disclosed the heavens.

3 He who hath eyes on all sides round
about him, a mouth on all sides, arms
and feet on all sides,
He, the Sole God, producing earth and
heaven, weldeth them, with his arms as
wings, together.

4 What was the tree, what wood in sooth
produced it, from which they fashioned
out the earth and heaven ?
Ye thoughtful men inquire within your
spirit whereon he stood when he
established all things.

5 Thine highest, lowest, sacrificial natures,
and these thy mid-most here, O Viśvakarman,
Teach thou thy friends at sacrifice, O
Blessed, and come thyself, exalted, to
our worship.

6 Bring thou thyself, exalted with oblation,
O Viśvakarman, Earth and Heaven to
worship.
Let other men around us live in folly :
here let us have a rich and liberal
patron.

7 Let us invoke to-day, to aid our labour,
the Lord of Speech, the thought-swift
Viśvakarman.
May he hear kindly all our invocations
who gives all bliss for aid, whose
works are righteous.

HYMN LXXXII.   *Viśvakarman.*

1. THE Father of the eye, the Wise in spirit,
created both these worlds submerged in
fatness.
Then when the eastern ends were firmly
fastened, the heavens and the earth
were far extended.

2 Mighty in mind and power is Viśva-
karman, Maker, Disposer, and most lofty
Presence.
Their offerings joy in rich juice where they
value One, only One, beyond the Seven
Ṛṣis.

---

6 *Gandharva path*: sublime ; that which the Gandharvas
in heaven use to travel.

7 *The Ṛbhus* : or Ṛṣis skilful as the Ṛbhus.
Viśvakarman, the Omnific, is represented in this
hymn as the universal Father and Generator, the Creator
of all things and Architect of the worlds.

1 *All things existing* : regarded as being contained
in the offerings presented by Viśvakarman.
Through his wish : through his desire to create. *Archetypal* : the meaning of *prathamachhád* is uncertain. In
Wilson's Translation 'inventor' is a misprint for 'investor',
that is, 'first investing Agni with the worlds,' according
to Sāyaṇa's explanation. 'First appeatring '—Ludwig.
The first worshipper.'—Wallis.

3 *Weldeth them* : cp. IV. 2. 17, and X. 72. 2. *With his
arms as wings* : fanning the flame in which the matter is
smelted. Ludwig thinks that whirlwinds, produced by
the action of hands, feet, and wings, are intended.

4 The first half-line occurs also in X. 31. 7. *They* :
the makers of the world directed by Parameśvara.—Sāyaṇa.

5 Or the first half-line may be rendered :—'Thy
sacrificial forms, the highest, lowest.' *Come thyself, exalted,
to our worship* : 'exhilarated, thyself offer up thyself.'
— Muir. 'Do thou sacrifice to thyself delighting thyself.'—
Wallis. 'According to Mahīdhara the meaning is that
man is incompetent to worship the creator, that is, in
his forms, and it must be done by himself.'—Wilson. I
have adopted Prof. Ludwig's explanation of the last clause.

6 *Bring.........to worship* : or, sacrifice to Heaven and
Earth.

7 *Our labour* : the arduous work of sacrificing. 'In
our conflict.'—Muir. The hymn has been translated by
Dr. J. Muir, *O. S. Texts*, IV. pp. 6, 7, by Mr. Wallis,
Cosmology of the Ṛgveda, pp. 81—83, and, partly, by Prof.
F. Max Müller in his *Hibbert Lectures*, p. 293f.

See also Mme. Zénaide Ragozin, *Vedic India*, pp. 263,
416.

---

1 *The Father of the eye* : Viśvakarman, who made the
light which enables the eye to see. *Submerged in fatness* :
Sāyaṇa explains *ghṛtám* here by 'water :'—'engendered
the water, (and then) these two (heaven and earth)
floating (on the waters).'—Wilson.

2 *Most lofty Presence* : literally, the highest apparition;
the highest image or object of spiritual contemplation.
Their offerings : the offerings, or perhaps the wishes, of
the Fathers, semi-personified. *The Seven Ṛṣis* : the
constellation Ursa Major, the seven stars of which are

3 Father who made us, he who, as Disposer, knoweth all races and all things existing, Even he alone, the Deities' name-giver,— him other beings seek for information.

4 To him in sacrifice they offered treasures,—Ṛṣis of old, in numerous troops, as singers, Who, in the distant, near, and lower region, made ready all these things that have existence.

5 That which is earlier than this earth and heaven, before the Asuras and Gods had being,— What was the germ primeval which the waters received where all the Gods were seen together ?

6 The waters, they received that germ primeval wherein the Gods were gathered all together. It rested set upon the Unborn's navel, that One wherein abide all things existing.

7 Ye will not find him who produced these creatures : another thing hath risen up among you. Enwrapt in misty cloud, with lips that stammer, hymn-chanters wander and are discontented.

the great Ṛṣis Marīci, Atri, Aṅgiras, Pulastya, Pulaha, Kratu, and Vasiṣṭha. The meaning is that the spirits of the blest enjoy the fulfilment of all their desires beyond the starry heavens where the One Being, the great Creator, dwells.

3 *For information* : to learn who is the Supreme God; or what their several functions are.

4 *Distant, near, and lower region* : meaning, apparently, the heavenly, the earthly, and the intermediate atmosphere.

6 *The Unborn*, Aja, seems here to be identified with Viśvakarman. See *Vedic India*, pp. 423, 424.

7 *Another thing* : meaning according to the Commentator, 'Viśvakarman is a different entity from you who are sentient beings, who have individual consciousness, and so forth.'—See Editor's note in Wilson's translation. Sāyaṇa 'gives the general sense of the last clause (of the stanza) as "You are merely anxious for enjoyment in this world and in the next, therefore you know nothing of *Viśvakarman*," taking *ukthaśāsaḥ* as implying singing hymns with a view to gaining felicity in a future state. Mahīdhara has a similar explanation : "you who are engaged in the enjoyments of this world or the next, being subject to false knowledge or ignorance, have no knowledge of the Truth."'—Wilson.

With regard to this and the preceding hymn Mr. Wallis observes that they make no attempt to explain in what way the process of sacrifice could be regarded as an act of creation. We are told little more than that Viśvakarman was a primeval sacrificer and also a creator; we have no hint how to combine the two ideas into a harmonious unity. See *Cosmology of the Ṛgveda*, pp. 83, 84, and Muir, *O. S. Texts*, IV. 7, 8, where the hymn is translated and some of its difficulties are discussed. Prof. Ludwig's Commentary is especially full and valuable, and should be consulted by all students of the Veda.

HYMN LXXXIII. *Manyu.*

1. HE who hath reverenced thee, Manyu, destructive bolt, breeds for himself forthwith all conquering energy. Ārya and Dāsa will we conquer with thine aid, with thee the Conqueror, with conquest conquest-sped.

2 Manyu was Indra, yea, the God was Manyu, Manyu was Hotar, Varuna, Jātavedas. The tribes of human lineage worship Manyu. Accordant with thy fervour, Manyu, guard us.

3 Come hither, Manyu, mightier than the mighty ; chase, with thy fervour for ally, our foemen. Slayer of foes, of Vṛtra, and of Dasyu, bring thou to us all kinds of wealth and treasure.

4 For thou art, Manyu, of surpassing vigour, fierce, queller of the foe, and self-existent, Shared by all men, victorious, subduer : vouchsafe to us superior strength in battles.

5 I have departed, still without a portion, wise God ! according to thy will, the Mighty. I, feeble man, was wroth thee, O Manyu ! I am myself ; come thou to give me vigour.

6 Come hither, I am all thine own ; advancing turn thou to me, Victorious, All-supporter ! Come to me, Manyu, Wielder of the Thunder : bethink thee of thy friend, and slay the Dasyus.

7 Approach, and on my right hand hold thy station : so shall we slay a multitude of foemen. The best of meath I offer to support thee: may we be first to drink thereof in quiet.

1 *Manyu* : Anger, Passion, personified.

3 *With thy fervour* : tápasā : tápas means 'heat', 'burning,' and, secondly, penance, rigorous abstraction.

5 *Without a portion* : without a share in thy favours. *I am myself* : I am just what I am; a weak mortal, for whose infirmity allowance should be made. 'Being (incorporated with) my body, approach me.'—Wilson

HYMN LXXXIV.   *Manyu.*

1. BORNE on with thee, O Manyu girt by
   Maruts, let our brave men, impetuous,
   bursting forward,
   March on, like flames of fire in form,
   exulting, with pointed arrows, sharpening their weapons.

2 Flashing like fire, be thou, O conquering
   Manyu, invoked, O Victor, as our
   army's leader.
   Slay thou our foes, distribute their possessions : show forth thy vigour, scatter
   those who hate us.

3 O Manyu, overcome thou our assailant :
   on ! breaking, slaying, crushing down
   the foemen.
   They have not hindered thine impetuous
   vigour : Mighty, Sole born ! thou
   makest them thy subjects.

4 Alone of many thou art worshipped,
   Manyu : sharpen the spirit of each clan
   for battle.
   With thee to aid, O thou of perfect splendour, we will uplift the glorious shout
   for conquest.

5 Unyielding bringing victory like Indra, O
   Manyu, be thou here our Sovran Ruler.
   To thy dear name, O Victor, we sing
   praises : we know the spring from which
   thou art come hither.

6 Twin-born with power, destructive bolt
   of thunder, the highest conquering
   might is thine, Subduer !
   Be friendly to us in thy spirit, Manyu, O
   Much-invoked, in shock of mighty battle.

7 For spoil let Varuṇa and Manyu give us
   the wealth of both sides gathered and
   collected ;
   And let our enemies with stricken spirits,
   o'erwhelmed with terror, slink away
   defeated.

1 *Like flames of fire in form : agnirūpāḥ.*

3 *Sole born :* 'O thou who art without companion.—
—Wilson.

5 *The spring :* the source.

7 *For spoil :* the preservation of their own property
and the seizure of their enemies' goods being regarded
as a double conquest. Or *dhánam ubháyam* may mean
wealth of both kinds, horses and cows.
   This hymn and the preceding are to be repeated, Sāyaṇa
says, at sacrifices to ensure the destruction of enemies.

———

HYMN LXXXV.   *Sūryā's Bridal.*

1. TRUTH is the base that bears the earth ;
   by Sūrya are the heavens sustained.
   By Law the Ādityas stand secure, and
   Soma holds his place in heaven.

2 By Soma are the Ādityas strong, by Soma
   mighty is the earth.
   Thus Soma in the midst of all these
   constellations hath his place.

3 One thinks, when they have brayed the
   plant, that he hath drunk the Soma's
   juice ;
   Of him whom Brahmans truly know as
   Soma no one ever tastes.

4 Soma, secured by sheltering rules, guarded
   by hymns in Bṛhatī,
   Thou standest listening to the stones :
   none tastes of thee who dwells on earth.

5 When they begin to drink thee then, O
   God, thou swellest out again.
   Vāyu is Soma's guardian God. The Moon
   is that which shapes the years.

6 Raibhī was her dear bridal friend, and
   Nārāśaṁsī led her home.
   Lovely was Sūryā's robe : she came to
   that which Gāthā had adorned.

7 Thought was the pillow of her couch,
   sight was the unguent for her eyes :
   Her treasury was earth and heaven ..when
   Sūryā went unto her Lord.

The main subject of this composite hymn, which is
one of the latest in the Ṛgveda, is the ceremony of marriage in general and more especially the wedding of Sūryā,
the Daughter of the Sun, another form of Dawn, who
is regarded as the typical bride.

1 *Truth* ; or reality; *sátyam,* used interchangeably
with *ṛtam,* the Law and Order of the universe.

2 *By Soma :* by the power of the deified Soma whose
influence pervades, quickens, and supports all existence.
In the second line *Soma* is the Moon, but perhaps there
is an allusion to the other sense also of the word. *These
constellations :* the *nakṣatras* or lunar mansions. 'In the
centre of these stars.'—Muir.

3 *Know as Soma :* know to be the Moon, regarded
as the food of Gods only.

4 *By hymns in Bṛhatī :* that is by hymns in that metre.
But the meaning of *bārhataiḥ* is uncertain. According to
Sāyaṇa, the Bārhatas are the seven guardians of the Soma,
Svāna, Bhrāja, Aṅghāri, and others.

5 *They :* the Gods. *Thee :* the ambrosia contained in
thee, which the Gods drink during the waning of the
Moon. *O Soma :* Soma, the Moon.

6 Soma is the deity of the preceding five stanzas.
Sūryā's Bridal is the subject of 6—17. *Raibhī, Nārāśaṁsī,*
and *Gāthā* are ritual verse, eulogistic hymn, and non-
Vedic song personified.

7 *Treasury : kośaḥ :* meaning probably, trousseau or
bridal outfit. According to some the box or body of the
chariot is intended.

8 Hymns were the cross-bars of the pole,
Kurīra-metre decked the car :
The bridesmen were the Aśvin Pair :
Agni was leader of the train.

9 Soma was he who wooed the maid : the
groomsmen were both Aśvins, when
The Sun-God Savitar bestowed his willing
Sūryā on her Lord.

10 Her spirit was the bridal car ; the covering thereof was heaven :
Bright were both Steers that drew it,
when Sūryā approached her husband's
home.

11 Thy Steers were steady, kept in place by
holy verse and Sāma-hymn :
All ear were thy two chariot wheels : thy
path was tremulous in the sky,

12 Clean, as thou wentest, were thy wheels :
wind was the axle fastened there.
Sūryā, proceeding to her Lord, mounted
a spirit-fashioned car.

13 The bridal pomp of Sūryā, which Savitar
started, moved along.
In Maghā days are oxen slain, in Arjunīs
they wed the bride.

14 When on your three-wheeled chariot, O
Aśvins, ye came as wooers unto Sūryā's
bridal,
Then all the Gods agreed to your proposal :
Pūṣan as Son elected you as Fathers.

15 O ye Two Lords of lustre, then when ye
to Sūryā's wooing came,
Where was one chariot wheel of yours ?
Where stood ye for the Sire's command ?

16 The Brahmans, by their seasons, know, O
Sūryā, those two wheels of thine :
One kept concealed, those only who are
skilled in highest truths have learned.

17 To Sūryā and the Deities, to Mitra and
to Varuṇa.
Who know aright the thing that is, this
adoration have I paid.

18 By their own power these Twain in close
succession move ;
They go as playing children round the
sacrifice.
One of the Pair beholdeth all existing
things ; the other ordereth seasons and
is born again.

19 He, born afresh, is new and new for ever :
ensign of days he goes before the Mornings.
Coming, he orders for the Gods their
portion. The Moon prolongs the days
of our existence.

20 Mount this, all-shaped, gold-hued, with
strong wheels, fashioned of Kiṁśuka
and Śalmali, light-rolling,
Bound for the world of life immortal,
Sūryā : make for thy lord a happy
bridal journey.

21 Rise up from hence : this maiden hath a
husband. I laud Viśvāvasu with hymns
and homage.
Seek in her father's home another fair
one, and find the portion from of old
assigned thee.

22 Rise up from hence, Viśvāvasu : with
reverence we worship thee.
Seek thou another willing maid, and with
her husband leave the bride.

8 *Decked the car* : formed its canopy. But the meaning
of *opaśāḥ* here is uncertain. 'Kurīra metre was the thong
of the whip.'—Wilson. *The bridesmen* : in I. 119. 7 and
elsewhere the Aśvins are said to be the husbands of Sūryā.
Here they are represented as the friends who had asked
her in marriage for Soma.

11 *All ear* : the text has *śrotram*, an ear, which Sāyaṇa
says, means *śrotre*, two ears. 'The two wheels were
thy ears,'—Wilson.

13 *In Maghā days* : or in stricter accordance with the
text, 'In Aghā days, when the Moon is in the lunar
mansion Maghā. See Jacobi, *Festgruss an R. von Roth*
p. 69, and Weber, *Vedische Beiträge*, p. 32f. *Slain* : only
on especially festive occasions, weddings for instance.
'Are whipped along.'—Wilson. *In Arjunīs* : two asterisms
or lunar mansions, more commonly called Phālgunīs.
They wed the bride : she is escorted to her husband's home.

14 *As wooers* : on behalf of Soma. *Pūṣan* : here
meaning Savitar. *Son* and *Fathers* : intended to express
close relationship and Savitar's obligation to the Aśvins
who had arranged the marriage.

15 *For the Sire's command* : to receive Savitar's invitation to take part in the bridal procession. According
to Sāyaṇa, 'to offer your gift.'

16 The *two wheels* are probably heaven and earth,
and the third, *one kept concealed*, is the mysterious invisible
world beyond them.

18 In this stanza and the following one, which are but
loosely connected with the rest of the hymn, Sūryā represents the Sun, and Soma is the Moon.

20 Stanzas 20—33 contain a collection of formulae
repeated when the bride mounts her chariot, while she
is travelling to her husband's house, when she arrives
there, and on the following morning. *This* : chariot.
Kiṁśuka : the wood of the Butea frondosa. *Śalmali* :
the silk-cotton tree; Salmalia malabarica. *Sūryā* : the
girl is addressed by the name of Sūryā, the typical bride.

21 *Viśvāvasu* : one of the Gandharvas, the protector
of virgins. He is told to leave the bride who no longer
needs his care, and to transfer his guardianship to some
marriageable maiden who has not yet found a husband.
Fair one : *vyāktām* : 'decorated with ornaments.'—Wilson.

23 Straight in direction be the paths, and thornless, whereon our fellows travel to the wooing.
Let Aryaman and Bhaga lead us : perfect, O Gods, the union of the wife and husband.

24 Now from the noose of Varuṇa I free thee, wherewith Most Blessed Savitar hath bound thee.
In Law's seat, to the world of virtuous action, I give thee up uninjured with thy consort.

25 Hence, and not thence, I send thee free. I make thee softly fettered there.
That, Bounteous Indra, she may live blest in her fortune and her sons.

26 Let Pūsan take thy hand and hence conduct thee ; may the two Aśvins on their car transport thee.
Go to the house to be the household's mistress and speak as lady to thy gathered people.

27 Happy be thou and prosper with thy children here : be vigilant to rule thy household in this home.
Closely unite thy body with this man, thy lord. So shall ye, full of years, address your company.

28 Her hue is blue and red : the fiend who clingeth close is driven off.
Well thrive the kinsmen of this bride : the husband is bound fast in bonds.

29 Give thou the woollen robe away : deal treasure to the Brahman priests.

This female fiend hath got her feet, and as a wife attends her lord.

30 Unlovely is his body when it glistens with this wicked fiend,
What time the husband wraps about his limbs the garment of his wife.

31 Consumptions, from her people, which follow the bride's resplendent train,—
These let the Holy Gods again bear to the place from which they came.

32 Let not the highway thieves who lie in ambush find the wedded pair.
By pleasant ways let them escape the danger, and let foes depart.

33 Signs of good fortune mark the bride : come all of you and look at her.
Wish her prosperity, and then return unto your homes again.

34 Pungent is this, and bitter this, filled, as it were, with arrow-barbs, Empoisoned and not fit for use.
The Brahman who knows Sūryā well deserves the garment of the bride.

35 The fringe, the cloth that decks her head, and then the triply parted robe,—
Behold the hues which Sūryā wears : these doth the Brahman purify.

36 I take thy hand in mine for happy fortune that thou mayst reach old age with me thy husband.
Gods, Aryaman, Bhaga, Savitar, Purandhi, have given thee to be my household's mistress.

37 O Puṣan, send her on as most auspicious, her who shall be the sharer of my pleasures ;
Her who shall twine her loving arms about me, and welcome all my love and mine embraces.

23 *To the wooing* : to the father, to whom the interceders are to apply for his daughter's hand on behalf of their friend, according to Sāyaṇa.

24 *The noose of Varuṇa* : the girdle with which the bride is girded after she has been bathed, combed, and dressed for the marriage ceremony. See Prof. Max Müller's *Rgveda-Samhitā*, Vol. VI., Preface, p. 14. Or, as Lanman suggests, the noose may mean the tie by which a girl is bound to her father till marriage. *Law's seat* : the place of sacrifice, the altar.
Stanzas 24—26 and 32, 33 are spoken just before the bride's departure from her father's house.

25 *Hence, and not thence* : from thy father's house and not from thy husband's.

27 *Be vigilant to rule thy household* : this is Sāyaṇa's explanation. 'Be watchful over the domestic fire.'—Wilson. The verse is addressed to the bride, and to the newly-wedded pair on arrival at the bridegroom's house.

28 *Her hue* : the colour of Kṛtyā, Magic personified, a female deity or fiend.

29 *The woollen robe* : 'the garment soiled by the body.'—Wilson. *Attends her lord* : the magic, or evil spell, returns to its originator.—Ludwig.

31 *From her people* : 'a most remarkable and direct assumption of "heredity" as a lurking danger.'—Mme. Zenaïde. Ragozin, *Vedic India*, p. 371.

33 Perhaps spoken, on the way, to the spectators of the procession.

34 *This* : the bride's garment. *Sūryā* : meaning here the song of Sūryā's Bridal.

35 The meaning of *āśāsanam, viśasanam,* and *adhivikártanam* is uncertain. Prof. Wilson renders these words by border-cloth,' 'head-cloth,' and 'divided skirt.' Prof. Weber and the St. Petersburg Lexicon explain the passage as referring to the preparation of the carcass of the animal that has been slaughtered for the festivity. According to this view the first line might be rendered :—'The butchering, the cutting up, the severing of limb and joint'; and for 'hues' 'forms' might be substituted.

36 The bridegroom addresses the bride.

38 For thee, with bridal train, they, first,
   escorted Sūryā to her home.
   Give to the husband in return, Agni, the
   wife with progeny.

39 Agni hath given the bride again with
   splendour and with ample life.
   Long lived be he who is her lord; a
   hundred autumns let him live.

40 Soma obtained her first of all; next
   the Gandharva was her lord.
   Agni was thy third husband: now one
   born of woman is thy fourth.

41 Soma to the Gandharva, and to Agni the
   Gandharva gave:
   And Agni hath bestowed on me riches
   and sons and this my spouse.

42 Be ye not parted; dwell ye here;
   reach the full time of human life.
   With sons and grandsons sport and play,
   rejoicing in your own abode.

43 So may Prajāpati bring children forth to
   us; may Aryaman adorn us till old
   age come nigh.
   Not inauspicious enter thou thy husband's
   house: bring blessing to our bipeds
   and our quadrupeds.

44 Not evil-eyed, no slayer of thy husband,
   bring weal to cattle, radiant, gentle-
   hearted;
   Loving the Gods, delightful, bearing
   heroes, bring blessing to our quadrupeds and bipeds.

45 O Bounteous Indra, make this bride
   blest in her sons and fortunate.
   Vouchsafe to her ten sons, and make
   her husband the eleventh man.

46 Over thy husband's father and thy
   husband's mother bear full sway.
   Over the sister of thy lord, over his
   brothers rule supreme.

47 So may the Universal Gods, so may the
   Waters join our hearts.

   38 *Thee*: Agni. *They*: the Gandharvas, according
to Sāyaṇa.

   40 As the typical bride Sūryā was first married to
Soma, so the young maid originally belongs to him, then
to the Gandharva, as the guardian of virginity, then, to
Agni as the sacred fire round which she walks in the
marriage ceremony, and fourthly to her human husband.
—Grassmann.

   42 The formulae contained in stanzas 42—47 are
repeated when the bridegroom has returned with his
bride to his home, and offers sacrifice with fire. The
wedded pair are addressed first, and then the bride is
exhorted and blessed. Stanza 47 is spoken by the
bridegroom for his wife and himself.

   47 *Deṣṭrī*: Instructress, a female deity, not mentioned
elsewhere in the Ṛgveda. According to Sāyaṇa, *dātrī
phalānām sarasvatī* is meant: 'the bountiful (Sarasvatī).'
—Wilson.

May Mātariśvan, Dhātar, and Deṣṭrī
together bind us close.

HYMN LXXXVI.   *Indra.*

1. MEN have abstained from pouring juice:
   they count not Indra as a God.
   Where at the votary's store my friend
   Vṛṣākapi hath drunk his fill. Supreme
   is Indra over all.

2 Thou, Indra, heedless passest by the ill
   Vṛṣākapi hath wrought;
   Yet nowhere else thou findest place wherein
   to drink the Soma juice. Supreme is
   Indra over all.

3 What hath he done to injure thee, this
   tawny beast Vṛṣākapi,
   With whom thou art so angry now? What
   is the votary's foodful store? Supreme
   is Indra over all.

4 Soon may the hound who hunts the boar
   seize him and bite him in the ear,
   O Indra, that Vṛṣākapi whom thou protectest as a friend, Supreme is Indra
   over all.

5 Kapi hath marred the beauteous things,
   all deftly wrought, that were my joy.
   In pieces will I rend his head; the sinner's
   portion shall be woe. Supreme is Indra
   over all.

   For a full account of the marriage ceremonies of the
Hindus, derived from the ritual of Brāhmans who use
the Sāma-veda, see Colebrooke's *Miscellaneous Essays*,
No. III., and Weber and Hass, *Indische Studien*, V. pp.
177 ff. See also *Hymns of the Atharva-veda* Book XIV.,
and Dr. J. Ehni's paper. *Zeitschrift der Deutschen Mor-
genländischen Gesellschaft*, XXXIII. pp. 166 ff. I have
relied mainly on Ludwig's Commentary. Prof. Grassmann
has banished the hymn to his Appendix.

   1 Sāyaṇa ascribes this stanza to Indra; others make
Indrāṇī the speaker. Vṛṣākapi is said to have mono-
polized the offerings that should have been presented to
Indra. *Vṛṣākapi*—literally 'the strong ape.' or 'the male
ape' —appears to be a sort of intermediate being between a demigod and a demon; but it is not easy to
determine his nature. Sāyaṇa calls him the son of Indra.
   He is also said to be the setting sun, and the sun who
draws up vapour and irrigates with mist. According
to M. Bergaigne, *La Religion Védique*, II. 270, he was a
mythical sacrificer.
   2 Indrāṇī blames Indra for his apathy.
   3 Indra speaks. *What is the votary's foodful store?*
why should his appropriation of the worshipper's offerings
make thee so angry?
   4 Indrāṇī is the speaker of this stanza and of the two,
or three, that follow.
   5 *Kapi*: the ape; an abbreviation of Vṛṣākapi. *Hath
marred the beauteous things*: according to Sāyaṇa, hath
spoiled the oblations prepared for me by my worshippers. But it seems more probable that Vṛṣākapi has assaulted Indrāṇī and inflicted injuries on her person.

6 No Dame hath ampler charms than I, or greater wealth of love's delights.
   None with more ardour offers all her beauty to her lord's embrace. Supreme is Indra over all.

7 Mother whose love is quickly won, I say what verily will be.
   My breast, O Mother, and my head and both my hips seem quivering. Supreme is Indra over all.

8 Dame with the lovely hands and arms, with broad hair-plaits add ample hips,
   Why, O thou Hero's wife, art thou angry with our Vṛṣākapi? Supreme is Indra over all.

9 This noxious creature looks on me as one bereft of hero's love,
   Yet Heroes for my sons have I, the Maruts' Friend and Indra's Queen. Supreme is Indra over all.

10 From olden time the matron goes to feast and general sacrifice.
   Mother of Heroes, Indra's Queen, the rite's ordainer is extolled. Supreme is Indra over all.

11 So have I heard Indrāṇī called most fortunate among these Dames,
   For never shall her Consort die in future time through length of days. Supreme is Indra over all.

12 Never, Indrāṇī, have I joyed without my friend Vṛṣākapi,
   Whose welcome offering here, made pure with water, goeth to the Gods. Supreme is Indra over all.

13 Wealthy Vṛṣākapāyī, blest with sons and consorts of thy sons,
   Indra will eat thy bulls, thy dear oblation that effecteth much. Supreme is Indra over all.

14 Fifteen in number, then, for me a score of bullocks they prepare,
   And I devour the fat thereof: they fill my belly full with food. Supreme is Indra over all.

15 Like as a bull with pointed horn, loud bellowing amid the herds,
   Sweet to thine heart, O Indra, is the brew which she who tends thee pours. Supreme is Indra over all.

18 O Indra this Vṛṣākapi hath found a slain wild animal,
   Dresser, and new-made pan, and knife, and wagon with a load of wood. Supreme is Indra over all.

19 Distinguishing the Dāsa and the Ārya, viewing all, I go.
   I look upon the wise, and drink the simple votary's Soma juice. Supreme is Indra over all.

20 The desert plains and steep descents, how many leagues in length they spread!
   Go to the nearest houses, go unto thine home, Vṛṣākapi. Supreme is Indra over all.

21 Turn thee again Vṛṣākapi: we twain will bring thee happiness.
   Thou goest homeward on thy way along this path which leads to sleep. Supreme is Indra over all.

22 When, Indra and Vṛṣākapi, ye travelled upward to your home,
   Where was that noisome beast, to whom went it, the beast that troubles man? Supreme is Indra over all.

---

6 Indrāṇī speaks with pride of her voluptuous charms which incited Vṛṣākapi to his amorous assault.

7 This stanza is ascribed by Sāyaṇa to Vṛṣākapi. It is hardly intelligible; but, as Ludwig says, it seems to be spoken by Indrāṇī, expressing her indignation at Vṛṣākapi's audacity which makes all her body quiver with rage.

8 Indra speaks.

9 Indrāṇī speaks this and the following stanza. *Bereft of hero's love*: who has no brave husband to protect her.

10 *The matron goes to feast*: Indrāṇī means that Vṛṣākapi assaulted her when she was on her way to a festival, which women were accustomed to attend; and that her rank as Indra's consort did not preserve her from insult.

11 Indra speaks this and the following stanza.

13 Spoken by Vṛṣākapi to his wife Vṛṣākapāyī who is said to represent the dawn, or, by others, the gloaming which follows the setting sun Vṛṣākapi.

14 Indra speaks. *Fifteen*: sacrificers; probably Vṛṣākapi and his wife, and their sons and daughters-in-law. Sāyaṇa explains differently:—'The worshippers dress for me fifteen (and) twenty bulls.'—Wilson.

15 Indrāṇī speaks, endeavouring to attract him to her own libation instead of the offerings of Vṛṣākapi.

I pass over stanzas 16 and 17, which I cannot translate into decent English.

18 Indrāṇī speaks, but her speech is difficult to understand. *Wild animal*: von Roth conjectures 'wild ass' as the meaning of *párasvantam* here. *Dresser*: or slaughter-bench. 'A fire-place (to cook it).'—Wilson. Indrāṇī seems to speak depreciatingly of a sacrifice offered by Vṛṣākapi as consisting of an unsuitable victim, prepared with instruments and means which chance has thrown in his way. Ludwig thinks that Vṛṣākapi may represent the Moon whose spots are fancifully considered to be the objects mentioned by Indrāṇī.

19 *I look*: with favour. *The simple votary* is the worshipper who offers his libation in a sincere spirit of devotion. The stanza and the two following are spoken by Indra.

20 Vṛṣākapi appears to meditate flight into distant deserts to escape from the wrathful Indrāṇī. Indra dissuades him, and promises to reconcile Indrāṇī to him.

23 Daughter of Manu, Parśu bare a score of
children at a birth.
Her portion verily was bliss although her
burthen caused her grief.

HYMN LXXXVII.   *Agni.*

1. I BALM with oil the mighty Rakṣas-
slayer ; to the most famous Friend I
come for shelter
Enkindled, sharpened by our rites, may
Agni protect us in the day and night
from evil.

2 O Jātavedas with the teeth of iron, enkindled with thy flame attack the demons.
Seize with thy tongue the foolish gods'
adorers : rend, put within thy mouth
the raw-flesh eaters.

3 Apply thy teeth, the upper and the lower,
thou who hast both, enkindled and
destroying.
Roam also in the air, O King, around
us, and with thy jaws assail the wicked
spirits.

4 Bending thy shafts through sacrifices, Agni,
whetting their points with song as if
with whetstones,
Pierce to the heart therewith the Yātudhānas, and break their arms uplifed to
attack thee.

5 Pierce through the Yātudhāna's skin, O
Agni ; let the destroying dart with fire
consume him.

22 The two concluding stanzas to be spoken by
Indrāṇī. Stanza 22 is obscure, and stanza 23 has no
discoverable connexion with the rest of the hymn.

23 *Daughter of Manu :* that is, of the progenitor of men.
Nothing more is known of *Parśu,* which means a rib. Much
of this hymn appears to be inexplicable. M. Bergaigne
thinks that Vṛṣākapi, Indra's friend, represents Soma,
and Indrāṇī the wife of Indra represents Prayer. 'This
bizarre myth would symbolize the frequently expressed
idea that Indra loves neither the sacred beverage without
prayer nor prayer without the sacred beverage. He
wishes therefore his union with Prayer to be accompanied
by the union of Prayer with Soma, and he neglects sacrifice as long as this union of the two essential elements of
worship remains unaccomplished.'—See *La Religion Védique,* II. 270, 271.

Prof. Geldner gives a different interpretation of the
hymn, which he has translated and exhaustively discussed
in *Vedische Studien,* II. pp. 22-42. See also Oldenberg,
Religion des Veda, 172-174.

2 *The demons :* Yātudhānas, explained by Sāyaṇa
as=Rākṣasas. See VII. 104. 15. *Foolish gods' adorers:*
mūradevān : according to Sāyaṇa, a special class of evil
spirits called Mūradevas because they make destruction
their sport.

5 *The eater of flesh :* the wolf or other carnivorous animal.

Rend his joints, Jātavedas, let the eater
of flesh, flesh-seeking, track his mangled
body.

6 Where now thou seest Agni Jātavedas,
one of these demons standing still or
roaming,
Or flying on those paths in air's mid-
region, sharpen the shaft and as an
archer pierce him.

7 Tear from the evil spirit, Jātavedas, what
he hath seized and with his spears hath
captured.
Blazing before him strike him down, O
Agni ; let spotted carrion-eating kites
devour him.

8 Here tell this forth, O Agni : whosoever
is, he himself, or acteth as, a demon,
Him grasp, O thou Most Youthful, with thy
fuel : to the Man-seer's eye give him as
booty.

9 With keen glance guard the sacrifice, O
Agni : thou Sage, conduct it onward to
the Vasus.
Let not the fiends, O Man-beholder,
harm thee burning against the Rākṣasas
to slay them.

10 Look on the fiend mid men, as Man-
beholder: rend thou his three extremities
in pieces.
Demolish with thy flame his ribs, O Agni,
the Yātudhāna's root destroy thou
triply.

11 Thrice, Agni, let thy noose surround the
demon who with his falsehood injures
Holy Order.
Loud roaring with thy flame, O Jātavedas,
crush him and cast him down before
the singer.

12 Lend thou the worshipper that eye, O
Agni, wherewith thou lookest on the
hoof-armed demon.
With light celestial in Atharvan's manner
burn up the fool who ruins truth with
falsehood.

8 *The Man-seer* here is either Agni himself or Sūrya
the Sun.

9 *To the Vas̄s :* to the Gods to whom the oblations
are made. Sāyaṇa explains *vásubhyih* here by *vasūnām-
arthāya :*—'to (the acquisition of) riches.'—Wilson.

10 *His three extremities :* his three heads, according to
Sāyaṇa. "Kopf und Schultern," head and shoulders.—
Grassmann. *Root :* meaning his feet. *Triply:* used
vaguely, to correspond with the three upper extremities.
'Cut off the triple foot of the *Yātudhāna.'*—Wilson.

12 *Hoof-armed :* striking with the hoof. According
to Sāyaṇa 'having nails like hoofs.' *In Atharvan's manner :*
like Atharvan, the ancient priest who is said to have
been the first who obtained fire.

13 Agni, what curse the pair this day have
   uttered, what heated word the worshippers have spoken,
   Each arrowy taunt sped from the angry
   spirit,—pierce to the heart therewith
   the Yātudhānas.

14 With fervent heat exterminate the demons;
   destroy the fiends with burning flame,
   O Agni.
   Destroy with fire the foolish gods' adorers ;
   blaze and destroy the insatiable mons-
   ters.

15 May Gods destroy this day the evil-doer :
   may each hot curse of his return and
   blast him.
   Let arrows pierce the liar in his vitals,
   and Viśva's net enclose the Yātudhāna.

16 The fiend who ·smears himself with flesh
   of cattle, with flesh of horses and of
   human bodies,
   Who steals the milch-cow's milk away,
   O Agni,—tear off the heads of such
   with fiery fury.

17 The cow gives milk each year, O Man-
   regarder : let not the Yātudhāna ever
   taste it.
   If one would glut him with the biesting,
   Agni, pierce with thy flame his vitals
   as he meets thee.

18 Let the fiends drink the poison of the
   cattle ; may Aditi cast off the evil-
   doers.
   May the God Savitar give them up to
   ruin, and be their share of plants and
   herbs denied them.

19 Agni, from days of old thou slayest
   demons : never shall Rākṣasas in fight
   o'ercome thee.
   Burn up the foolish ones, the flesh-devo-
   urers : let none of them escape thine
   heavenly arrow.

20 Guard us, O Agni, from above and under,
   protect us from behind us and before
   us ;
   And may thy flames, most fierce and
   never wasting, glowing with fervent heat,
   consume the sinner.

21 From rear, from front, from under, from
   above us, O King, protect us as a Sage
   with wisdom.
   Guard to old age thy friend, O Friend,
   Eternal : O Agni, as Immortal, guard
   us mortals.

22 We set thee round us as a fort, victorious
   Agni, thee a Sage,
   Of hero lineage, day by day, destroyer
   of our treacherous foes.

23 Burn with thy poison turned against the
   treacherous brood of Rākṣasas,
   O Agni, with thy sharpened glow, with
   lances armed with points of flame.

24 Burn thou the paired Kimīdins, burn, Agni,
   the Yātudhāna pairs.
   I sharpen thee, Infallible, with hymns. O
   Sage, be vigilant.

25 Shoot forth, O Agni, with thy flame :
   demolish them on every side.
   Break thou the Yātudhāna's strength, the
   vigour of the Rākṣasa.

HYMN LXXXVIII.   *Agni.*

1. DEAR, ageless sacrificial drink is offered
   in light-discovering, heaven-pervading
   Agni.
   The Gods spread forth through his Celestial Nature, that he might bear the
   world up and sustain it.

2 The world was swallowed and concealed
   in darkness : Agni was born, and light
   became apparent.
   The Deities, the broad earth, and the
   heavens, and plants, and waters gloried
   in his friendship.

3 Inspired by Gods who claim our adoration,
   I now will laud Eternal Lofty Agni,
   Him who hath spread abroad the earth
   with lustre, this heaven, and both the
   worlds, and air's mid-region.

4 Earliest Priest whom all the Gods accepted,
   and chose him, and anointed him with
   butter,
   He swiftly made all things that fly, stand,
   travel, all that hath motion, Agni
   Jātavedas.

5 Because thou, Agni, Jātavedas, stoodest at
   the world's head with thy refulgent
   splendour,

---

13 *The pair* . the married pair : perhaps the sacrificer and his wife. The Ṛṣi prays that every hasty word
that may have been uttered by pious people in their
anger may be used as a weapon to wound the Yātudhāna.

15 *Viśva's net* : the noose of the all-pervading Agni.

18 *The poison of the cattle* : if they drink milk, let it
poison them. According to Sāyaṇa, let them drink the
poison of the cattle (which is kept in the house), meaning
perhaps some poisonous ointment used for external application only.

24 *Kimīdins* : treacherous and malevolent spirits.
See VII. 104. 2, note.

———

1 *Sacrificial drink* : 'swelling oblation,' according to
Prof. Pischel.
5 *We sent thee forth* : the Ṛṣi glorifies the power of the
priests who made Agni their messenger to the Gods.

We sent thee forth with hymns and songs and praises : thou filledst heaven and earth, God meet for worship.

6 Head of the world is Agni in the night-time ; then, as the Sun, at morn springs up and rises.
Then to his task goes the prompt Priest foreknowing the wondrous power of Gods who must be honoured.

7 Lovely is he who, kindled in his greatness, hath shone forth, seated in the heavens, refulgent.
With resonant hymns all Gods who guard our bodies have offered up oblation in this Agni.

8 First the Gods brought the hymnal into being ; then they engendered Agni, then oblation.
He was their sacrifice that guards our bodies : him the heavens know, the earth, the waters know him.

9 He, Agni, whom the Gods have generated, in whom they offered up all worlds and creatures,
He with his bright glow heated earth and heaven, urging himself right onward in his grandeur.

10 Then by the laud the Gods engendered Agni in heaven, who fills both worlds through strength and vigour.
They made him to appear in threefold essence : he ripens plants of every form and nature.

11 What time the Gods, whose due is worship, set him as Sūrya, Son of Aditi, in heaven,
When the Pair, ever wandering, sprang to being, all creatures that existed looked upon them.

12 For all the world of life the Gods made Agni Vaiśvānara to be the days' bright Banner,—
Him who hath spread abroad the radiant Mornings, and, coming with his light, unveils the darkness.

13 The wise and holy Deities engendered Agni Vaiśvānara whom age ne'er touches.
The Ancient Star that wanders on for ever, lofty and strong, Lord of the Living Being.

14 We call upon the Sage with holy verses, Agni Vaiśvānara the ever-beaming,
Who hath surpassed both heaven and earth in greatness : he is a God below, a God above us.

15 I have heard mention of two several pathways, ways of the Fathers and of Gods and mortals.
On these two paths each moving creature travels, each thing between the Father and the Mother.

16 These two united paths bear him who journeys born from the head and pondered with the spirit
He stands directed to all things existing, hasting, unresting in his fiery splendour.

17 Which of us twain knows where they speak together, upper and lower of the two rite-leaders ?
Our friends have helped to gather our assembly. They came to sacrifice ; who will announce it ?

18 How many are the Fires and Suns in number ? What is the number of the Dawns and Waters ?
Not jestingly I speak to you, O Fathers. Sages, I ask you this for information.

19 As great as is the fair-winged Morning's presence to him who dwells beside us, Mātariśvan !

13 *Lord of the Living Being* : the meaning of *yakṣásya* is uncertain. Sāyaṇa explains it by *pūjyasya devasya*, of the adorable God. 'The observer of what is firm.'—Ludwig. 'The lord of meteors.'—Grassmann. 'Surveillant du Yakṣa.'—Bergaigne.

14 *Below* : on earth.

15 *Two several pathways* : the way to the other world and the way back to the earth. *The Father and the Mother* : heaven and earth.

16 *Him who journeys* : Agni. *From the head* : of the world. From Āditya, the head or chief of all existence, according to Sāyaṇa.

17 *Us twain* : Agni and the Ṛṣi. *Upper and lower* : according to Sāyaṇa, the upper fire is Vāyu and the lower is terrestrial Agni. *Who will announce it ?* : Agni alone will make the sacrifice known to the Gods.

19 *Morning's presence* : the light of Dawn which spreads over heaven and earth. *Him who dwells beside us* : the Yajamāna, or institutor of the sacrifice.—Ludwig. *Below the Hotar* : below the regular Hotar-priest. Sāyaṇa explains this stanza differently :—'As long, Mātariśvan, as the swiftly-moving (nights) cover the face of the dawn, (so long) the *Brāhman*, the inferior sitting down (to perform the work) of the *Hotṛ*, approaching the sacrifice supports (the ceremony).'—Wilson.

6 Agni, who is the Moon by night, at dawn becomes Sūrya or the Sun-God who when he sets again becomes Agni.

9 *All worlds and creatures* : proleptically : meaning that the oblation offered by the gods was destined to produce the universe.—Ludwig. According to Sāyaṇa :—'in whom all beings have offered oblations; ' but it is clear that the oblations of the Gods are intended.

10 *Through strength and vigour* : *śáktibhiḥ* : 'by his functions :'—Wilson. *In threefold essence* : or in three conditions, or places, as the Sun, lightning, and terrestrial fire.

11 *The Pair* : the Sun and Moon. According to Sāyaṇa, Uṣas and Sūrya.

Is what the Brāhman does when he approaches to sacrifice and sits below the Hotar.

HYMN LXXXIX.   *Indra.*

1. I WILL extol the most heroic Indra who with his might forced earth and sky asunder;
Who hath filled all with width as man's Upholder, surpassing floods and rivers in his greatness.

2 Sūrya is he : throughout the wide expanses shall Indra turn him, swift as car-wheels, hither,
Like a stream resting not but ever active : he hath destroyed, with light, the black-hued darkness.

3 To him I sing a holy prayer, incessant, new, matchless, common to the earth and heaven,
Who marks, as they were backs, all living creatures : ne'er doth he fail a friend, the noble Indra.

4 I will send forth my songs in flow unceasing, like water from the ocean's depth, to Indra,
Who to his car on both its sides securely hath fixed the earth and heaven as with an axle.

5 Rousing with draughts, the Shaker, rushing onward, impetuous, very strong, armed as with arrows
Is Soma ; forest trees and all the bushes deceive not Indra with their offered likeness.

6 Soma hath flowed to him whom naught can equal, the earth, the heavens, the firmament, the mountains,—
When heightened in his ire his indignation shatters the firm and breaks the strong in pieces.

7 As an axe fells the tree so he slew Vṛtra, brake down the strongholds and dug out the rivers.
He cleft the mountain like a new-made pitcher. Indra brought forth the kine with his Companions.

8 Wise art thou, Punisher of guilt, O Indra. The sword lops limbs, thou smitest down the sinner,
The men who injure, as it were a comrade, the lofty Law of Varuṇa and Mitra.

9 Men who lead evil lives, who break agreements, and injure Varuṇa, Aryaman and Mitra,—
Against these foes, O Mighty Indra, sharpen, as furious death, thy Bull of fiery colour.

10 Indra is Sovran Lord of Earth and Heaven, Indra is Lord of waters and of mountains.
Indra is Lord of prosperers and sages : Indra must be invoked in rest and effort.

11 Vaster than days and nights, Giver of increase, vaster than firmament and flood of ocean,
Vaster than bounds of earth and wind's extension, vaster than rivers and our lands is Indra.

12 Forward, as herald of refulgent Morning, let thine insatiate arrow fly, O Indra.
And pierce, as 'twere a stone launched forth from heaven, with hottest blaze the men who love deception.

13 Him, verily, the moons, the mountains followed, the tall trees followed and the plants and herbage.
Yearning with love both Worlds approached, the Waters waited on Indra when he first had being.

14 Where was the vengeful dart when thou, O Indra, clavest the demon ever bent on outrage ?

---

1 *With width* : with his own extended magnitude. 'With radiance.'—Wilson.

2 *Sūrya is he* : Indra is identified with the Sun whose course he directs. According to Sāyaṇa, *sūryaḥ* here = *suvīryaḥ,* heroic.

3 *Incessant* : or unerring that is, in strict accordance with the rules of the ritual. *As they were backs* : as if they were horses or oxen, the length and shape of whose backs must be carefully considered in forming a judgment of their worth.

5 Prof. Wilson observes:—'This verse is obscure, partly because the words are unusual, partly because there is a confusion between *Indra* and *Soma.*' *Deceive not Indra* : he will not accept any substitutes : he will have nothing but the genuine Soma-plant and its juice.

7 *His Companions* : the Maruts, who assisted him in performing his exploit.

8 *Punisher of guilt* : here Indra is said to discharge the duties which in more ancient hymns are ascribed to Agni and to Mitra and Varuṇa.

9 *Thy Bull* : thy thunderbolt. 'The heavy strong red weapon.'—M. Müller.

10 *In rest and effort* : 'for the acquirement and preservation of wealth.'—Wilson.

13 *The moons* : or, the months. *Waited on Indra* : as the representative of the Sun, the originator of all life. —Ludwig.

14 *Fiends* : *mitrakrúvaḥ* : the exact meaning of the word is uncertain. Prof. Ludwig takes it as a genitive case : 'What time they lay there on the earth extended like oxen in a demon's place of slaughter.'

When fiends lay there upon the ground
extended like cattle in the place of
immolation ?

15 Those who are set in enmity against us, the
Oganas, O Indra, waxen mighty,—
Let blinding darkness follow those our
foemen, while these shall have bright
shining nights to light them.

16 May plentiful libations of the people, and
singing Ṛṣis' holy prayers rejoice thee.
Hearing with love this common invocation,
come unto us, pass by all those who
praise thee.

17 O Indra, thus may we be made partakers
of thy new favours that shall bring us
profit.
Singing with love, may we the Viśvāmitras win daylight even now through
thee, O Indra.

18 Call we on Maghavan, auspicious Indra,
best hero in the fight where spoil is
gathered,
The Strong who listens, who gives aid in
battles, who slays the Vṛtras, wins and
gathers riches.

HYMN XC. *Puruṣa.*

1. A THOUSAND heads hath Puruṣa, a thousand
eyes, a thousand feet.
On every side pervading earth he fills a
space ten fingers wide.

2 This Puruṣa is all that yet hath been and
all that is to be ;
The Lord of Immortality which waxes
greater still by food.

3 So mighty is his greatness ; yea, greater
than this is Puruṣa.
All creatures are one-fourth of him, three-
fourths eternal life in heaven.

4 With three-fourths Puruṣa went up : one-
fourth of him again was here.
Thence he strode out to every side over
what eats not and what eats.

5 From him Virāj was born ; again Puruṣa
from Virāj was born.
As soon as he was born he spread eastward
and westward o'er the earth.

6 When Gods prepared the sacrifice with
Puruṣa as their offering,
Its oil was spring, the holy gift was autumn;
summer was the wood.

7 They balmed as victim on the grass Puruṣa
born in earliest time.

that living beings may obtain the fruits of their actions
and gain *mokṣa* or final liberation from their bonds, 'he
is also the lord of immortality ; for he mounts beyond
(his own condition) for the food (of living beings).'—
Wilson. Colebrooke translates the line :—'he is that
which grows by nourishment, and he is the distributor of
immortality .' Dr. Muir renders it by :—'He is also the
lord of immortality, since by food he expands.' According to the paraphrase in the *Bhāgavata-Purāṇa*, the meaning of the last clause is: 'since he hath transcended mortal
nutriment.' Prof. Ludwig's version is : 'auch über die
unsterblichkeit gebietend, (da er,) was durch speise
(ist,) weit überragt,' ruling also over immortality, (since
he) far transcends what (exists) through food; but in
his Commentary a somewhat different explanation is
given. 'Ruling over immortality, he was all that grows
by food'.—Peterson.

3 *Eternal life* : *amṛtam* : immortality, or the immortal
Gods.

4 *Over what eats not and what eats* : over animate and
inanimate creation. According to Sāyaṇa and Mahīdhara, over both classes of created things, those capable
of enjoyment, that is, who can taste the reward and punishment of good and evil actions, such as Gods, men, and
lower animals, and those who are incapable thereof, such
as mountains and rivers—*cetanam*, or conscious, *aceta-
nam*, or unconscious, creation.

5 *From him* : or, from that, the 'one-fourth' mentioned
in stanzas 3 and 4. *Virāj*, or, in the nominative form,
Virāṭ, is said to have come, in the form of the mundane
egg, from Ādi-Puruṣa, the primeval Puruṣa, or presiding
Male or Spirit, 'who then entered into this egg, which
he animates as its vital soul or divine principle.' Or Virāj
may 'be the female counterpart of Puruṣa as Aditi of
Dakṣa in X.72. 4, 5.' See Dr. Muir's exhaustive Note
on this passage, *O. S. Texts*, V. pp. 369, 370; and Wallis,
Cosmology of the Ṛgveda, p. 87. *Eastward and westward* : or,
before and behind.

6 *The sacrifice* : *mānasam yajñam*, a mental or imaginary
sacrifice, according to Sāyaṇa. *Summer* : *grīṣmá* does
not occur in any other ṚV. hymn. *Spring* : *vasantá* occurs
in only one other ṚV. hymn.

7 *On the grass* : on the sacred grass used in sacrifices.
Sādhyas : a class of celestial beings, probably ancient
divine sacrificers.

---

15 *Oganas* : probably the name of some hostile clan.
According to Sāyaṇa, enemies assembled in numbers.
These : us and our friends here.

16 *All those who praise thee* : all other worshippers.

18 This is the concluding stanza of several hymns of
the Viśvāmitras. See III. 30. 22; 31.22; 32. 17; 34. 11;
35. 11; 36. 11.

---

1 *Puruṣa*, embodied spirit, or Man personified and
regarded as the soul and original source of the universe,
the personal and life-giving principle in all animated
beings, is said to have a *thousand*, that is, innumerable,
heads, eyes, and *feet*, as being one with all created life. A
space ten fingers wide : the region of the heart of man,
wherein the soul was supposed to reside. Although as the
Universal Soul he pervades the universe, as the Individual
Soul he is enclosed in a space of narrow dimensions. See
Hymns of the Atharva-veda, XIX. 6. 1, note.

2 The second line is explained in various ways. The
meaning of the words seems to be : he is lord of immortality or the immortal world of the Gods, which grows
greater by food, that is, by the sacrificial offerings of men.
According to Sāyaṇa : he is the lord or distributor of immortality because he becomes the visible world in order

With him the Deities and all Sādhyas and
Ṛṣis sacrificed.

8 From that great general sacrifice the dripping fat was gathered up.
He formed the creatures of the air, and
animals both wild and tame.

9 From that great general sacrifice Ṛcas
and Sāma-hymns were born :
Therefrom were spells and charms produced;
the Yajus had its birth from it.

10 From it were horses born, from it all
cattle with two rows of teeth :
From it were generated kine, from it the
goats and sheep were born.

11 When they divided Puruṣa how many por-
tions did they make?
What do they call his mouth, his arms ?
What do they call his thighs and feet ?

12 The Brāhman was his mouth, of both his
arms was the Rājanya made.
His thighs became the Vaiśya, from his
feet the Śūdra was produced.

13 The Moon was gendered from his mind,
and from his eye the Sun had birth;
Indra and Agni from his mouth were
born, and Vāyu from his breath.

14 Forth from his navel came mid-air ; the
sky was fashioned from his head ;
Earth from his feet, and from his ear the
regions. Thus they formed the worlds.

15 Seven fencing-sticks had he, thrice seven
layers of fuel were prepared,
When the Gods, offering sacrifice, bound,
as their victim, Puruṣa.

16 Gods, sacrificing, sacrificed the victim :
these were the earliest holy ordinances.
The Mighty Ones attained the height of
heaven, there where the Sādhyas, Gods
of old, are dwelling.

HYMN XCI.   *Agni.*

1. BRISK, at the place of Ilā, hymned by
men who wake, our own familiar Friend
is kindled in the house ;
Hotar of all oblation, worthy of our choice,
Lord, beaming, trusty friend to one who
loveth him.

2 He, excellent in glory, guest in every house,
finds like a swift-winged bird a home in
every tree.
Benevolent to men, he scorns no living
man : Friend to the tribes of men he
dwells with every tribe.

3 Most sage with insight, passing skilful
with thy powers art thou, O Agni, wise
with wisdom, knowing all.
As Vasu, thou alone art Lord of all good
things, of all the treasures that the heavens and earth produce.

4 Foreknowing well, O Agni, thou in Ilā's
place hast occupied thy regular station
balmed with oil.
Marked are thy comings like the comings
of the Dawns, the rays of him who
shineth spotless as the Sun.

5 Thy glories are, as lightnings from the
rainy cloud, marked, many-hued, like
heralds of the Dawns' approach,

---

8 *The dripping fat* : 'the mixture of curds and butter.'
—Wilson. *He* : or, it; the sacrificed victim Puruṣa, or
the sacred clarified butter. *The creatures of the air* : 'those
animals over whom Vāyu presides.'—Wilson.

9 *Spells and charms*: probably those of the later collection of the Atharvaveda. *The Yajus* : the Yajur-veda.

12 *Rājanya* : the second or Kṣatriya caste, the regal
and military class. *Vaiśya* : the husbandman; he whose
business is agriculture and trade. *Śūdra* : the labourer.
The Brāhman is called the mouth of Puruṣa, as having
the special privilege, as a priest, of addressing the Gods
in prayer. The arms of Puruṣa became the Rājanya
the prince and soldier who wields the sword and spear.
His thighs, the strongest parts of his body, became the
agriculturist and tradesman, the chief support of society;
and his feet, the emblems of vigour and activity, became
the Śūdra or labouring man on whose toil and industry
all ultimately rests. This is the only passage in the
Ṛgveda which enumerates the four castes.

14 Cf. the creation myth of the world-giant Ymir
or Hymir in old Northern poetry. The hills are his bones,
the vault of the sky his skull, the sea his blood, and the
clouds his brains.—*Corpus Poeticum Boreale*, Vol. II. p. 468.

15 *Fencing-sticks* : guards, or pieces of wood laid round
the sacrificial fire to enclose it. Sāyaṇa explains *pari-
dhyaḥ* as the seven metres, or as six shallow trenches dug

round the fire, and an imaginary one round the Sun.
Mahīdhara says that the seven oceans may be intended.

This pantheistic hymn, which is generally called the
Puruṣasūkta, is of comparatively recent origin, and
appears to be an attempt to harmonise the two ideas of
sacrifice and creation. For further information regarding it, see Muir, *O. S. Texts*, I. pp. 6—11, and V. 368—
377, Prof. Max Müller, *Ancient Sanskrit Literature*, pp.
570f, and Dr. Scherman, *Philosophische Hymnen aus der
Ṛg-und Atharva-veda-Saṁhitā*, pp. 11—23. The hymn has
also been translated by Colebrooke, *Miscellaneous Essays*,
pp. 167, 168 ; by Wallis, *Cosmology of the Rgveda*, pp. 87,
88; and by Peterson, *Hymns from the Rgveda*, pp. 289,
290; also by Burnouf, *Bhāgavata Purāṇa*, Preface to
Vol. I., and by Weber, *Indische Studien*, IX. p. 5.
Grassmann's Translation in his Appendix to Vol. II,
and Ludwig's Translation and Commentary should be
consulted. See also *Hymns of the Atharva-veda*, XIX. 6,
which is a reproduction of this hymn with transpositions
and variations.

1 *The place of Ilā* : the shrine where clarified butter is
poured upon the fire. *Our own familiar Friend* : Agni, the
Friend of the house.

2 *Swift-winged bird* : or, bird of prey. 'Hunter,'
according to Ludwig.

3 *Vasu* : the word meaning also *good* and *treasure*.

When, loosed to wander over plants and
forest trees, thou crammest by thyself
thy food into thy mouth.

6 Him, duly coming as their germ, have
plants received : this Agni have maternal
Waters brought to life.
So in like manner do the forest trees and
plants bear him within them and produce
him evermore.

7 When, sped and urged by wind, thou
spreadest thee abroad, swift piercing
through thy food according to thy will,
Thy never-ceasing blazes, longing to consume, like men on chariots, Agni, strive
on every side.

8 Agni, the Hotar-priest who fills the assembly full, Waker of knowledge, chief
Controller of the thought,—
Him, yea, none other than thyself, doth
man elect at sacrificial offerings great
and small alike.

9 Here, Agni, the arrangers, those attached
to thee, elect thee as their Priest in
sacred gatherings,
When men with strewn clipt grass and
sacrificial gifts offer thee entertainment,
piously inclined.

10 Thine is the Herald's task and Cleanser's
duly timed; Leader art thou, and Kindler
for the pious man.
Thou art Director, thou the ministering
Priest : thou art the Brahman, Lord and
Master in our home.

11 When mortal man presents to thee Immortal God, Agni, his fuel or his sacrificial
gift,
Then thou art his Adhvaryu, Hotar,
messenger, callest the Gods and orderest
the sacrifice.

12 From us these hymns in concert have gone
forth to him, these holy words, these
Ṛcas, songs and eulogies,

Eager for wealth, to Jātavedas fain for
wealth : when they have waxen strong
they please their Strengthener.

13 This newest eulogy will I speak forth to
him, the Ancient One who loves it. May
he hear our voice.
May it come near his heart and make it
stir with love, as a fond well-dressed
matron clings about her lord.

14 He in whom horses, bulls, oxen, and barren
cows, and rams, when duly set apart,
are offered up,—
To Agni, Soma-sprinkled, drinker of sweet
juice, Disposer, with my heart I bring a
fair hymn forth.

15 Into thy mouth is poured the offering,
Agni, as Soma into cup, oil into ladle.
Vouchsafe us wealth, strength-winning,
blest with heroes, wealth lofty, praised
by men, and full of splendour.

HYMN XCII.   Viśvedevas.

1. I PRAISE your Charioteer of sacrifice, the
Lord of men, Priest of the tribes, refulgent, Guest of night.
Blazing amid dry plants, snatching amid
the green, the Strong, the Holy Herald
hath attained to heaven.

2 Him, Agni, Gods and men have made
their chief support, who drinks the
fatness and completes the sacrifice.
With kisses they caress the Grandson of the
Red, like the swift ray of light, the
Household Priest of Dawn.

3 Yea, we discriminate his and the niggard's
ways : his branches evermore are sent
forth to consume.
When his terrific flames have reached the
Immortal's world, then men remember
and extol the Heavenly Folk.

4 For then the net of Law, Dyaus, and the
wide expanse, Earth, Worship, and
Devotion meet for highest praise,
Varuṇa, Indra, Mitra were of one accord,
and Savitar and Bhaga, Lords of holy
might.

---

6 Agni is produced in the form of lightning by the
waters of the firmament, or the clouds, and descends with
the rain into plants and trees, from the wood of which he
is brought forth by attrition.

8 *Great and small* : with Soma or without it.

9 *The arrangers* : priests who order and conduct the
sacrificial ceremonies.

10 Agni discharges the duties of the seven chief priests,
officiating as Hotar, Potar, Neṣṭar, Agnīdh, Praśāstar,
Adhvaryu, and Brahman. See II. I. 2, where this stanza
originally occurs.

11 *Callest the Gods* : 'sayest the formulae.'—Ludwig.

12 *Ṛcas* : verses of praise.   ——

2 *Completes the sacrifice* : or, fills the assembly full.
Grandson of the Red : son of the brilliant Vāyu.'—Wilson.
Sprung from his own red glow, one fire being kindled
from another.

3 *Men remember* : because then their prayers are granted.

5 Onward, with ever-roaming Rudra, speed
the floods : over Aramati the Mighty
have they run.
With them Parijman, moving round his
vast domain, loud bellowing, bedews all
things that are within.

6 Straightway the Rudras, Maruts visiting
all men, Falcons of Dyaus, home-
dwellers with the Asura,—
Varuna, Mitra, Aryaman look on with
these, and the swift-moving Indra with
swift-moving Gods.

7 With Indra have they found enjoyment,
they who toil, in the light's beauty, in
the very Strong One's strength;
The singers who in men's assemblies
forged for him, according to his due,
his friend the thunderbolt.

8 Even the Sun's Bay Coursers hath he held
in check : each one fears Indra as the
mightiest of all.
Unhindered, from the air's vault thunders
day by day the loud triumphant breathing of the fearful Bull.

9 With humble adoration show this day
your song of praise to mighty Rudra,
Ruler of the brave :
With whom, the Eager Ones, going their
ordered course, he comes from heaven
Self-bright, auspicious, strong to guard.

10 For these have spread abroad the fame of
human kind, the Bull Brhaspati and
Soma's brotherhood.
Atharvan first by sacrifices made men
sure : through skill the Bhrgus were
esteemed of all as Gods.

11 For these, the Earth and Heaven with
their abundant seed, four-bodied
Narāśaṁsa, Yama, Aditi,
God Tvaṣṭar Wealth-bestower, the
Rbhukṣaṇas, Rodasī Maruts, Viṣṇu,
claim and merit praise.

12 And may he too give ear, the Sage, from
far away, the Dragon of the Deep, to
this our yearning call.
Ye Sun and Moon who dwell in heaven
and move in turn, and with your
thought, O Earth and Sky, observe this
well.

13 Dear to all Gods, may Pūṣan guard the
ways we go, the Waters' Child and Vāyu
help us to success.
Sing lauds for your great bliss to Wind,
the breath of all : ye Aśvins prompt to
hear, hear this upon your way.

14 With hymns of praise we sing him who is
throned as Lord over these fearless
tribes, the Self-resplendent One.
We praise Night's youthful Lord benevolent to men, the foeless One, the free,
with all celestial Dames.

15 By reason of his birth here Aṅgiras first
sang: the pressing-stones upraised beheld
the sacrifice—
The stones through which the Sage became exceeding vast, and the sharp axe
obtains in fight the beauteous place.

HYMN XCIII.   Viśvedevas.

1. MIGHTY are ye, and far-extended, Heaven
and Earth: both Worlds are evermore
to us like two young Dames.
Guard us thereby from stronger foe;
guard us hereby to give us strength.

2 In each succeeding sacrifice that mortal
honoureth the Gods,
He who, most widely known and famed
for happiness, inviteth them.

3 Ye who are Rulers over all, great is your
sovran power as Gods.
Ye all possess all majesty: all must be
served in sacrifice.

---

5 *Aramati*: the earth.—Sāyaṇa. Armaiti, of the Avestā,
also means Earth personified as well as Devotion or Piety.
Parijman : 'the circumambient (Indra).'—Wilson.

6 *The Asura* : Dyaus himself.

7 Worshippers are rewarded in heaven for the hymns
and prayers with which they have strengthened and armed
Indra for his great deeds.

9 *With whom* : the Maruts.

10 *Soma's brotherhood* : all Gods who are entitled to
drink Soma juice. *Made men sure* : gave them assurance
of obtaining what they asked.

11 *Four-bodied Narāśaṁsa* : Agni provided with four
fires, or complete in all his parts. *Rbhukṣaṇas* : Rbhus.
Rodasī : consort of the Maruts.

12 *The Dragon of the Deep* : Ahibudhnya; regent of
the sea or air.

13 *The Waters' Child* : Agni, born as lightning from
the clouds.

14 *The Self-resplendent One* : Agni. *Night's youthful Lord*:
the Moon. *Celestial Dames* : the lunar asterisms.

15 *The Sage* : Indra, according to Sāyaṇa. *Sharp axe* :
the thunderbolt. The meaning of this stanza is obscure.

---

1 *Thereby......hereby* : literally 'by those'......'by these.'
Sāyaṇa supplies *pālanaiḥ*, protections, in both cases. The
former may refer to the Maghavans, and the latter to
the people in general.

4 These are the joyous Kings of Immor-
tality, Parijman, Mitra, Aryaman, and
Varuṇa.
What else is Rudra, praised of men ? the
Maruts, Bhaga, Pūṣaṇa ?

5 Come also to our dwelling, Lords of
ample wealth, common partakers of our
waters, Sun and Moon,
When the great Dragon of the Deep hath
settled down upon their floors.

6 And let the Aśvins, Lords of splendour,
set us free,— both Gods, and, with their
Laws, Mitra and Varuṇa.
Through woes, as over desert lands, he
speeds to ample opulence.

7 Yea, let the Aśvins Twain be gracious
unto us, even Rudras, and all Gods,
Bhaga, Rathaspati;
Parijman, Ṛbhu, Vāja, O Lords of all
wealth Ṛbhukṣaṇas.

8 Prompt is Ṛbhukṣan, prompt the worshipper's strong drink : may thy fleet
Bay Steeds, thine who speedest on,
approach.
Not man s but God's is sacrifice whose
psalm is unassailable.

9 O God Savitar, harmed by none, lauded,
give us a place among wealthy princes.
With his Car-steeds at once hath our
Indra guided the reins and the car of
these men.

10 To these men present here, O Heaven and
Earth, to us grant lofty fame extending
over all mankind.
Give us a steed to win us strength, a
steed with wealth for victory.

11 This speaker, Indra—for thou art our
Friend—wherever he may be, guard
thou, Victor ! for help, ever for help :
Thy wisdom, Vasu ! prosper him.

12 So have they strengthened this mine hymu
which seems to take its bright path to
the Sun, and reconciles the men :
Thus forms a carpenter the yoke of
horses, not to be displaced.

13 Whose chariot-seat hath come again laden
with wealth and bright with gold,
Lightly, with piercing ends, as 'twere two
ranks of heroes ranged for fight.

14 This to Duḥśīma Pṛthavāna have I sung,
to Vena, Rāma, to the nobles, and the
King.
They yoked five hundred, and their love
of us was famed upon their way.

15 Besides, they showed us seven-and-seventy
horses here.
Tānva at once displayed his gift, Pārthya
at once displayed his gift; and straightway Māyava showed his.

HYMN XCIV.   *Press-stones.*

1. LET these speak loudly forth; let us speak
out aloud: to the loud speaking Pressing-
stones address the speech;
When, rich with Soma juice, Stones
of the mountain, ye, united, swift to
Indra bring the sound of praise.

2 They speak out like a hundred, like a
thousand men : they cry aloud to us
with their green-tinted mouths,

---

4 *Immortality* : or, the immortal world. *Parijman* :
Roamer round ; Vāyu. *What else* : that is, Rudra is
also one of these Kings. *Pūṣaṇa* : a lengthened form of
the usual Pūṣan.

5 *Waters* : libations of Soma juice, Sāyaṇa explains
nāktam by *rātrau* 'by night.' It is, as Prof. Ludwig has
pointed out, a shortened form of *nakṣtam*, 'come ye.'
Upon their floors : 'in their company in the firmamental
(clouds).'—Wilson. The meaning is obscure.

6 *He* : the sacrificer whom these Gods protect.

7 *Rathaspati* : the guardian of war-chariots. Cf. X. 64.
10. *Ṛbhukṣaṇas* : Ṛbhus.

8 *Ṛbhukṣan* : 'the mighty (Indra).'—Wilson.

9 *With his Car-steeds* : with us priests, who draw the
chariot of sacrifice.

12 *So have they strengthened* : 'May (the priests) strengthen.'—Wilson. *The yoke* : as the yoke keeps a pair of
horses together so the hymn addressed to the Gods reconciles worshippers and fills them with the like feelings
of devotion.

13 *Piercing ends* : of the axle, which pass through the
naves.

14 *Duḥśīma Pṛthavāna*, *Vena*, and *Rāma* were Maghavans or wealthy institutors of sacrifices. *To the King* :
āsure : to the Asura, lord or chief. *Five hundred* : horses
or chariots.

15 *Horses* : there is no substantive in the text.
Sāyaṇa supplies *gavām*, cows. These horses or cows,
were presented to the priests. *Tānva*, *Pārthya*, and
Māyava are patronymics which do not occur again in
the Ṛgveda.

Ludwig thinks that a quarrel had arisen between the
Maghavans or nobles (stanza 14) and the Viśas or
people (stanza 9), and that the priests, who had reconciled the two parties, were presented with the chariots
which had been prepared for battle. See stanza 13, in
which, according to this explanation, *nā* should be
rendered by 'and not' instead of 'as 'twere.' The hymn,
which is difficult and in parts almost unintelligible, is
placed by Grassmann in his Appendix.

Hotar : '(Agni) the invoker (of the gods),'—Wilson.
Or the human Hotar-priest may be intended.

While, pious Stones, they ply their task with piety, and, even before the Hotar, taste the offered food.

3 Loudly they speak, for they have found the savoury meath: they make a humming sound over the meat prepared.
As they devour the branch of the Red-coloured Tree, these, the well-pastured Bulls, have uttered bellowings.

4 They cry aloud, with strong exhilarating drink, calling on Indra now, for they have found the meath.
Bold, with the sisters they have danced, embraced by them, making the earth reecho with their ringing sound.

5 The Eagles have sent forth their cry aloft in heaven; in the sky's vault the dark impetuous ones have danced.
Then downward to the nether stone's fixt place they sink, and, splendid as the Sun, effuse their copious stream.

6 Like strong ones drawing, they have put forth all their strength: the Bulls, harnessed together, bear the chariot-poles.
When they have bellowed, panting, swallowing their food, the sound of their loud snorting is like that of steeds.

7 To these who have ten workers and a tenfold girth, to these who have ten yoke-straps and ten binding thongs,
To these who bear ten reins, the eternal, sing ye praise, to these who bear ten car-poles, ten when they are yoked.

8 These Stones with ten conductors, rapid in their course, with lovely revolution travel round and round.
They have been first to drink the flowing Soma juice, first to enjoy the milky fluid of the stalk.

9 These Soma-eaters kiss Indra's Bay-coloured Steeds: draining the stalk they sit upon the ox's hide.
Indra, when he hath drunk Soma-meath drawn by them, waxes in strength, is famed, is mighty as a Bull.

10. Strong is your stalk; ye, verily, never shall be harmed; ye have refreshment, ye are ever satisfied.
Fair are ye, as it were, through splendour of his wealth, his in whose sacrifice, O Stones, ye find delight.

11 Bored deep, but not pierced through with holes, are ye, O Stones, not loosened, never weary, and exempt from death,
Eternal, undiseased, moving in sundry ways, unthirsting, full of fatness, void of all desire.

12 Your fathers, verily, stand firm from age to age: they, loving rest, are not dissevered from their seat.
Untouched by time, ne'er lacking green plants and green trees, they with their voice have caused the heavens and earth to hear.

13 This, this the Stones proclaim, what time they are disjoined, and when with ringing sounds they move and drink the balm.
Like tillers of the ground when they are sowing seed, they mix the Soma, nor, devouring, minish it.

14 They have raised high their voice for juice, for sacrifice, striking the Mother earth as though they danced thereon.
So loose thou too his thought who hath effused the sap, and let the Stones which we are honouring be disjoined

HYMN XCV. *Urvaśī. Purūravas.*

1. Ho there, my consort ! Stay, thou fierce-souled lady, and let us reason for a while together.
Such thoughts as these of ours, while yet unspoken in days gone by have never brought us comfort.

---

3 *Red-coloured Tree* : the Soma-plant. *Well-pastured* : the meaning of *sūbharvā* is obscure. See Hillebrandt, *V. M.*, I. 18.

4 *The sisters* : the fingers.

5 *The Eagles* : the rapidly moving celestial press-stones.

7 *Ten workers* : the fingers of both hands.

9 *The ox's hide* : spread underneath to catch and hold the droppings.

12 *Your fathers* : the mountains from which you came.

14 *Striking the Mother Earth* : 'Earth' is not in the text :—'they made a noise like (children) at play, striking their mother.'—Wilson. I have followed Prof. Ludwig's explanation.

The hymn is a dialogue between Purūravas and Urvaśī, and they are severally the Ṛṣis of the stanzas which they speak. The dialogue, which is sometimes almost unintelligible, contains the germs of a legend which is related in the *Śatapatha-Brāhmaṇa*, reappears in the *Mahābhārata* and *Purāṇas*, and forms the plot of the well-known drama, *Vikramorvaśī*, or *The Hero and the Nymph*. According to this legend, Urvaśī, an Apsaras or Nymph

2 What am I now to do with this thy saying? I have gone from thee like the first of Mornings.
Purūravas, return thou to thy dwelling: I, like the wind, am difficult to capture.

3 Like a shaft sent for glory from the quiver, or swift-steed winning cattle winning hundreds.
The lightning seemed to flash, as cowards planned it. The minstrels bleated like a lamb in trouble.

4 Giving her husband's father life and riches, from the near dwelling, when her lover craved her,
She sought the home wherein she found her pleasure, accepting day and night her lord's embraces.

5 Thrice in the day didst thou embrace thy consort, though coldly she received thy fond caresses.
To thy desires, Purūravas, I yielded: so wast thou king, O hero, of my body.

6 The maids Sujūrṇi, Śreṇi, Sumne-āpi, Charaṇyu, Granthinī, and Hradecakṣus,—

These like red kine have hastened forth, the bright ones, and like milch-cows have lowed in emulation.

7 While he was born the Dames sate down together, the Rivers with free kindness gave him nurture;
And then, Purūravas, the Gods increased thee for mighty battle, to destroy the Dasyus.

8 When I, a mortal, wooed to mine embraces these heavenly nymphs who laid aside their raiment,
Like a scared snake they fled from me in terror, like chariot horses when the car has touched them.

9 When, loving these Immortal Ones, the mortal hath converse with the nymphs as they allow him.
Like swans they show the beauty of their bodies, like horses in their play they bite and nibble.

10 She who flashed brilliant as the falling lightning brought me delicious presents from the waters.
Now from the flood be born a strong young hero! May Urvaśī prolong her life for ever!

11 Thy birth hath made me drink from earthly milch-kine: this power, Purūravas, hast thou vouchsafed me.

of heaven, has been banished to earth where she consents to live with King Purūravas on condition that he takes care of her two pet rams, and that she never sees him unclothed. She lives with Purūravas for four years, when the Gandharvas, heavenly minstrels, resolve to bring her back. They steal one of the rams by night. Purūravas springs from his bed; the Gandharvas send on him a flash of magic lightning, and Urvaśī sees her husband naked. One of the conditions of the continuance of their union is broken, and the nymph instantly vanishes. Purūravas meets her afterwards and in vain implores her to return. At last she relents, and in due time a son is born to them. These are the main outlines of a somewhat variously told story.

1 Purūravas speaks, when he has met Urvaśī again after her sudden departure.

2 Urvaśī replies.

3 Purūravas speaks, reminding her of the circumstances in which she vanished. 'Yea,' he says, 'thou wentest from me with the speed of an arrow or a racer. The cowardly Gandharvas deluded us. They bleated like a lamb to make us think that one of thy pets was in pain or danger, and then, by a flash of factitious lightning, made me visible to thee in my nakedness.'

4 Life and riches: meaning, perhaps, as Prof. Ludwig suggests, the future grandson. The near dwelling: her father-in-law's house, where she spent much of her time. Her lover: her husband Purūravas.
This stanza and the next are spoken by Urvaśī.

6 This stanza is ascribed by Sāyaṇa to Purūravas, who mentions the names of the Apsarases who were the companions of Urvaśī after her flight. They are compared to red kine, meaning, perhaps, bright flashes of lightning followed by the lowing or bellowing of the thunder.

7 Urvaśī speaks, reminding Purūravas of the favour shown him at his birth, by the celestial Dames who were present, the Rivers who nursed him, and the Gods who gave him strength. Another explanation is that in the first half of the stanza Urvaśī speaks, by anticipation, of the son whom she will bear to Purūravas.

8 Purūravas complains of the shyness of the nymphs mentioned in stanza 6, with whose society he had sought to console himself. A mortal: meaning that if he had been a God their behaviour would have been different. Raiment: dtkam: explained by Sāyaṇa as svakīyam rūpam, their own proper form.

9 Urvaśī replies. The Apsarases, she says, as a rule only coquet with mortal men. As they allow him: krdtubhir nd; see Geldner, V. S., I. 276. Like swans: Sāyaṇa explains nd here differently:—'they (becoming) ducks do not show their bodies.'—Wilson.

10 Purūravas speaks. Urvaśī, he says, did not treat him so coldly. From the waters: of the firmament. From the flood: from Urvaśī who comes from the watery regions above. Sāyaṇa explains apdḥ differently:—'a son able in act and friendly to man has been born.' —Wilson.

11 Urvaśī speaks. According to Sāyaṇa, whom Wilson, Grassmann, and Geldner follow, the translation of the first half-line would be:— 'Thou hast been born to give the earth protection.' Warned thee on that day: told thee, when I agreed to live with thee what would happen if the conditions of the agreement were not strictly observed.

12 I knew, and, warned thee, on that
　　day. Thou wouldst not hear me.
　　What sayest thou, when naught avails
　　thee ?

12 When will the son be born and seek his
　　father ? Mourner-like, will he weep
　　when first he knows him ?
　　Who shall divide the accordant wife and
　　husband, while fire is shining with thy
　　consort's parents ?

13 I will console him when his tears are
　　falling: he shall not weep and cry for
　　care that blesses.
　　That which is thine, between us, will I
　　send thee. Go home again, thou fool;
　　.thou hast not won me.

14 Thy lover shall flee forth this day for ever,
　　to seek, without return, the farthest
　　distance.
　　Then let his bed be in Destruction's
　　bosom, and there let fierce rapacious
　　wolves devour him.

15 Nay, do not die, Purūravas, nor vanish:
　　let not the evil-omened wolves devour
　　thee.
　　With women there can be no lasting
　　friendship: hearts of hyenas are the
　　hearts of women.

16 When amid men in altered shape I
　　sojourned, and through four autumns
　　spent the nights among them,
　　I tasted once a day a drop of butter; and
　　even now with that am I contented.

17 I, her best love, call Urvaśī to meet me,
　　her who fills air and measures out the
　　region.
　　Let the gift brought by piety approach
　　thee. Turn thou to me again: my heart
　　is troubled.

18 Thus speak these Gods to thee, O son of
　　Iḷā: As death hath verily got thee for
　　his subject,
　　Thy sons shall serve the Gods with their
　　oblation, and thou, moreover, shalt
　　rejoice in Svarga.

HYMN XCVI.　　　　　　*Indra.*

1 In the great synod will I laud thy two
　　Bay Steeds : I prize the sweet strong
　　drink of thee the Warrior-God,
　　His who pours lovely oil as 'twere with
　　yellow drops. Let my songs enter thee
　　whose form hath golden tints.

2 Ye who in concert sing unto the gold-
　　hued place, like Bay Steeds driving
　　onward to the heavenly seat,
　　For Indra laud ye strength allied with
　　Tawny Steeds, laud him whom cows
　　content as 'twere with yellow drops.

3 His is that thunderbolt, of iron, golden-
　　hued, gold-coloured, very dear, and
　　yellow in his arms;
　　Bright with strong teeth, destroying with
　　its tawny rage. In Indra are set fast
　　all forms of golden hue.

18 There is an hiatus between this stanza and 17,
an entire break of continuity. The fragment is ascribed
to Urvaśī, who consoles Purūravas by telling him of
the promise of the deities that after his death his sons shall
offer sacrifice to the Gods and he himself shall be blest
in heaven . *Son of Iḷā* : Purūravas, called Aiḷa or son
of Iḷā who was the daughter of Manu.
　　Some of the stanzas should be transposed, and their
order should be, 1, 2, 3, 4, 5, 16, 6, 7, 8, 9, 11, 12, 13,
14, 15, 10.—Ludwig.
　　Of this very difficult hymn there is a complete translation, with a very full and generally convincing commentary (to both of which I am indebted for much assistance), by Prof. Geldner, *Vedische Studien*, I. pp. 243—
295. The myth has been discussed by von Roth, *Illustrations of the Nirukta*, and *Indische Studien*, I. 196; by Prof.
Max Müller, *Oxford Essays* (*Chips*, IV. 109f); by Prof.
Adalbert Kuhn, *Die Herabkunft des Feuers*, pp. 85 ff; and
by Professors Holtzmann and Oldenberg in more recent
days. Professor Max Müller considers the story to be
'one of the myths of the Vedas which expresses the corre-
lation of the dawn and the sun.' According to Dr. Gold-
stucker, Urvaśī is the morning mist which vanishes away
as soon as Purūravas the Sun displays himself. See
Chamber's Encyclopaedia, *1st edition*, under Purūravas.

Throughout the hymn the poet rings the changes on
words said to be derivatives of the root *hṛ*, to take, as
haryatá, delightsome, *haryán*, loving, *hári*, bay or tawny,
hárit, green, yellow, or gold-coloured Cp. III. 44. These
words are conjecturally explained by the Commentator,
and are susceptible of various renderings.
　　1 *Oil* : or fatness, fertilizing rain.
　　2 *Cows* : milked for sacrificial purposes.
　　3 *Tawny rage* : perhaps with reference to the effect of
anger on the face.—Ludwig.

12 Purūravas speaks. *Knows him* : 'on recognizing
(me).'—Wilson Or, when he knows my story, knows
how his father has been .deserted. *While fire is shining* :
so long as the father-in-law and mother-in-law who sanc-
tioned the union live and maintain their household fire.

13 Urvaśī answers. *That which is thine, between us* :
our child, our common treasure.

14 Purūravas threatens to destroy himself.

15 Urvaśī speaks this and the next stanza.

16 *A drop of butter* : one of the conditions on which the
continuance of their union depended was that she should
eat nothing but a small quantity of *ghṛtá or* clarified
butter daily. See stanza 11.

17 Purūravas speaks. *Her best love* : *vasiṣṭhaḥ* here
is evidently, as the Scholiast says, an epithet and not
a name, meaning 'most excellent.' 'most. precious.'
Fills air : representing the morning mist, or the first
flush of light, that spreads over the heavens before the
rising of the sun.

4 As if a lovely ray were laid upon the
sky, the golden thunderbolt spread out
as in a race.
That iron bolt with yellow jaw smote
Ahi down. A thousand flames had he
who bore the tawny-hued.

5 Thou, thou, when praised by men who
sacrificed of old, hadst pleasure in
their lauds, O Indra golden-haired.
All that befits thy song of praise thou
welcomest, the perfect pleasant gift,
O Golden-hued from birth.

6 These two dear Bays bring hither Indra
on his car, Thunder-armed, joyous,
meet for laud, to drink his fill.
Many libations flow for him who loveth
them : to Indra have the gold-hued
Soma juices run.

7 The gold-hued drops have flowed to
gratify his wish : the yellow drops
have urged the swift Bays to the
Strong.
He who speeds on with Bay Steeds even
as he lists hath satisfied his longing for
the golden drops.

8 At the swift draught the Soma-drinker
waxed in might, the Iron One with
yellow beard and yellow hair.
He, Lord of Tawny Coursers, Lord of
fleet-foot Mares, will bear his Bay
Steeds safely over all distress.

9 His yellow-coloured jaws, like ladles,
move apart, what time, for strength,
he makes the yellow-tinted stir,
When, while the bowl stands there, he
grooms his Tawny Steeds, when he
hath drunk strong drink, the sweet
juice that he loves.

10 Yea, to the Dear One's seat in homes of
heaven and earth the Bay Steeds' Lord
hath whinnied like a horse for food.
Then the great wish hath seized upon him
mightily, and the Beloved One hath
gained high power of life.

11 Thou, comprehending with thy might the
earth and heaven, acceptest the dear
hymn for ever new and new.
O Asura, disclose thou and make visible
the Cow's beloved home to the bright
golden Sun.

12 O Indra, let the eager wishes of the folk
bring thee, delightful, golden-visored,
on thy car,
That, pleased with sacrifice wherein ten
fingers toil, thou mayest, at the feast,
drink of our offered meath.

13 Juices aforetime, Lord of Bays, thou
drankest ; and thine especially is this
libation.
Gladden thee, Indra, with the meath-rich
Soma : pour it down ever, Mighty
One ! within thee.

HYMN XCVII.   *Praise of Herbs.*

1. HERBS that sprang up in time of old, three
ages earlier than the Gods,—
Of these, whose hue is brown, will I
declare the hundred powers and
seven.

2 Ye, Mothers, have a hundred homes, yea,
and a thousand are your growths.
Do ye who have a thousand powers free
this my patient from disease.

3 Be glad and joyful in the Plants, both
blossoming and bearing fruit,
Plants that will lead us to success like
mares who conquer in the race.

4 Plants, by this name I speak to you,
Mothers, to you the Goddesses :
Steed, cow, and garment may I win, win
back thy very self, O man.

5 The Holy Fig tree is your home, your
mansion is the Parṇa tree :
Winners of cattle shall ye be if ye regain
for me this man.

---

4 *The tawny-hued* : the thunderbolt wielded by Indra.

7 *To the Strong* : to Indra; that they may be harnessed
and come to the sacrifice.

8 *The Iron One* : 'iron-hearted Indra.'—Wilson.

9 *For strength* : for strengthening food. *The yellow-
tinted* : his yellow jaws.

10 *The Dear One* must be the Soma, found both in
heaven and earth, the homes of Gods and men. According to Sāyaṇa, Indra himself is meant. *The Beloved One* :
Indra, whose vital vigour is increased by Soma-draughts.

11 *The Cow's beloved home* : the Cow may be the Sun
whose home is the universe which Indra will allow Sūrya
to illumine.

12 *Sacrifice* : according to Sāyaṇa, the sacrificial
Soma juice which is pressed and prepared by the fingers
of the priest.

1 *Three ages earlier than the Gods* : 'for the gods before
the three ages.'—Wilson. See *Śatapatha-Brāhmaṇa*, VII.
2. 4. 26 (*S. B. E.*, XLI. p. 389.)

4 *Steed, cow, and garment* : as my fee for curing you.

5 *Holy Fig-tree* : the Aśvattha, or Ficus Religiosa.
Parṇa tree : the Palāśa Butea Frondosa. Sacrificial vessels
are made of the wood of these trees which are therefore
said to be the home of plants used in religious ceremonies.

6 He who hath store of Herbs at hand like
    Kings amid a crowd of men,—
  Physician is that sage's name, fiend-slayer,
    chaser of disease.

7 Herbs rich in Soma, rich in steeds, in
    nourishments, in strengthening power,—
  All these have I provided here, that this
    man may be whole again.

8 The healing virtues of the Plants stream
    forth like cattle from the stall,—
  Plants that shall win me store of wealth,
    and save thy vital breath, O man.

9 Reliever is your mother's name, and
    hence Restorers are ye called.
  Rivers are ye with wings that fly : keep
    far whatever brings disease.

10 Over all fences have they passed, as steals
    a thief into the fold.
   The Plants have driven from the frame
    whatever malady was there.

11 When, bringing back the vanished strength,
    I hold these herbs within my hand,
   The spirit of disease departs ere he can
    seize upon the life.

12 He through whose frame, O Plants, ye
    creep member by member, joint by
    joint,—
   From him ye drive away disease like
    some strong arbiter of strife.

13 Fly, Spirit of Disease, begone, with the
    blue jay and kingfisher.
   Fly with the wind's impetuous speed, vanish
    together with the storm.

14 Help every one the other, lend assistance
    each of you to each,
   All of you be accordant, give furtherance
    to this speech of mine.

15 Let fruitful Plants, and fruitless, those
    that blossom, and the blossomless,
   Urged onward by Bṛhaspati, release us
    from our pain and grief ;

16 Release me from the curse's plague and
    woe that comes from Varuṇa;
   Free me from Yama's fetter, from sin and
    offence against the Gods.

17 What time, descending from the sky, the

Plants flew earthward, thus they
  spake :
No evil shall befall the man whom while
  he liveth we pervade.

18 Of all the many Plants whose King is
    Soma, Plants of hundred forms,
   Thou art the Plant most excellent, prompt
    to the wish, sweet to the heart.

19 O all ye various Herbs whose King is
    Soma, that o'erspread the earth,
   Urged onward by Bṛhaspati, combine
    your virtue in this Plant.

20 Unharmed be he who digs you up,
    unharmed the man for whom I dig:
   And let no malady attack biped or
    quadruped of ours.

21 All Plants that hear this speech, and
    those that have departed far away,
   Come all assembled and confer your
    healing power upon this Herb.

22 With Soma as their Sovran Lord the
    Plants hold colloquy and say :
   O King, we save from death the man
    whose cure a Brāhman undertakes.

23 Most excellent of all art thou, O Plant :
    thy vassals are the trees.
   Let him be subject to our power, the man
    who seeks to injure us.

HYMN XCVIII.   *The Gods.*

1. Come, be thou Mitra, Varuṇa, or Pūṣan,
     come, O Bṛhaspati, to mine oblation :
   With Maruts, Vasus, or Ādityas, make
     thou Parjanya pour for Śantanu his
     rain-drops.

2 The God, intelligent, the speedy envoy
    whom thou hast sent hath come to me,
    Devāpi :
  Address thyself to me and turn thee hither :

---

19 *This Plant* : the medicinal herb which I, the physician, am about to make use of.

---

12 *Like some strong arbiter of strife* : 'like a mighty
(prince) stationed in the midst of his host.'—Wilson.

13 *With the blue jay and kingfisher* : with the speed of
the swiftest birds. *Together with the storm* : according to
Sāyaṇa, 'perish along with the iguana.'

15 *Urged onward* : Bṛhaspati, says Sāyaṇa, is the deity
who presides over *mantras* or spells and charms.

·This Sūkta is remarkable as representing one of two
brothers, both of the Kṣatriya caste, becoming the
Purohita, or family priest, and *Hotṛ* or sacrificing priest, of
the other who is the *Rājā*.'—Wilson.

1 Devāpi addresses Bṛhaspati, who is identifiable with
Mitra, Varuṇa, Pūṣan and others in his special character,
of Purohita, or family Priest, of the Gods, and as the prototype of all human Purohitas. *With Maruts* : whether
thou be attended by Maruts, Vasus, or Ādityas. *For
Śantanu* : the brother of Devāpi.

within thy lips will I put brilliant language.

3 Within my mouth, Bṛhaspati, deposit speech lucid, vigorous, and free from weakness,
Thereby to win for Śantanu the rain-fall.
The meath-rich drop from heaven hath passed within it.

4 Let the sweet drops descend on us, O Indra : give us enough to lade a thousand wagons.
Sit to thy Hotar task ; pay worship duly, and serve the Gods, Devāpi, with oblation.

5 Knowing the God's good-will, Devāpi, Ṛṣi, the son of Ṛṣṭiṣeṇa, sate as Hotar.
He hath brought down from heaven's most lofty summit the ocean of the rain, celestial waters.

6 Gathered together in that highest ocean, the waters stood, by deities obstructed.
They hurried down set free by Ārṣṭiṣeṇa, in gaping .clefts, urged onward by Devāpi.

7 When as chief priest for Śantanu, Devāpi, chosen for Hotar's duty, prayed beseeching,
Graciously pleased Bṛhaspati vouchsafed him a voice that reached the Gods and won the waters.

8 O Agni whom Devāpi Ārṣṭiṣeṇa, the mortal man, hath kindled in his glory,
Joying in him with all the Gods together, urge on the sender of the rain, Parjanya.

9 All ancient Ṛṣis with their songs approached thee, even thee, O Much-invoked, at sacrifices.
We have provided wagon-loads in thousands : come to the solemn rite, Lord of Red Horses.

10 The wagon-loads, the nine-and-ninety thousand, these have been offered up to thee, O Agni.
Hero, with these increase thy many bodies,

and, stimulated, send us rain from heaven.

11 Give thou these ninety thousand loads, O Agni, to Indra, to the Bull, to be his portion.
Knowing the paths which Deities duly travel, set mid the Gods in heaven Aulāna also.

12 O Agni, drive afar our foes, our troubles ; chase malady away and wicked demons.
From this air-ocean, from the lofty heavens, send down on us a mighty flood of waters.

HYMN XCIX. *Indra.*

1. WHAT Splendid One, Loud-voiced, Far-striding, dost thou, well knowing, urge us to exalt with praises?
What give we him ? When his might dawned, he fashioned the Vṛtra-slaying bolt, and sent us waters.

2 He goes to end his work with lightning flashes : wide is the seat his Asura glory gives him.
With his Companions, not without his Brother, he quells Saptatha's magic devices.

3 On most auspicious path he goes to battle : he toiled to win heaven's light, full fain to gain it ;
He seized the hundred-gated castle's trea-

2 Bṛhaspati replies. *Brilliant language* : a 'brilliant hymn.'—Muir.

3 Devāpi speaks, praying Bṛhaspati, as Lord of Speech (cp. X. 71. 1), to inspire him with eloquence that he may address the Gods effectually. *The meath-rich drop* : the sweet eloquence for which he has prayed.

4 *The sweet drops* : of rain. This stanza is spoken by Śantanu.

5 *Knowing* : how to win.

6 *Ārṣṭiṣeṇa* : patronymic, son of Ṛṣṭiṣeṇa; Devāpi.

7 *Chief priest* : or family or household priest ; Purohita.

9 *Wagon-loads* : an extraordinary quantity of fuel for the sacrifice, as the occasion was one of the greatest importance.

11 *Aulāna* : Śantanu, as a descendant of Ula, appears to be meant. According to some scholars, *aulānám* means oblation or sacrificial offering. 'The fact of Devāpi being reputed as the author of this hymn, and as the purohita and hotṛ of his brother seems to have led the legendary writers to invent the story of his becoming a Brāhman, which (as mentioned by Professor Weber, *Indische Studien,* i. p. 203) is recorded in the Śalya-parvan of the Mahābhārata, verses 2281 ff, where he is said to have attained this distinction at a certain place of pilgrimage called Pṛthūdaka, where Sindhudvīpa and Viśvāmitra also were received into the higher caste.'—Muir, *O. S. Texts,* I. 270 ff. For the legend on which the hymn is said to be based, quoted by Sāyaṇa from the *Nirukta,* see Wilson's Translation.

1 The question in the first line is a rhetorical figure, the meaning being, How splendid is he (Indra) whom thou (the Yajamāna ?) urgest us to exalt ! *What give we him ?* what can we give him in return for what he has done for us ?

2 *His Companions* : the Maruts. *His Brother* : Viṣṇu, Who *Saptatha* was is uncertain. The word means Septimus, the seventh, and probably some Rākṣasa or demon is intended.

3 *The lustful demons* : the exact meaning of *śiśnádevān* is uncertain. See VII. 21. 5 and note.

sure by craft, unchecked, and slew the lustful demons.

4 Fighting for kine, the prize of war, and roaming among the herd he brings the young streams hither,
Where, footless, joined, without a car to bear them, with jars for steeds, they pour their flood like butter.

5 Bold, unsolicited for wealth, with Rudras he came, the Blameless, having left his dwelling,
Came, seized the food of Vamra and his consort, and left the couple weeping and unsheltered.

6 Lord of the dwelling, he subdued the demon who roared aloud, six-eyed and triple-headed.
Trta, made stronger by the might he lent him, struck down the boar with shaft whose point was iron.

7 He raised himself on high and shot his arrow against the guileful and oppressive foeman.
Strong, glorious, manliest, for us he shattered the forts of Nahus when he slew the Dasyus.

8 He, like a cloud that rains upon the pasture, hath found for us the way to dwell in safety.
When the Hawk comes in body to the Soma, armed with his iron claws he slays the Dasyus.

9 He with his potent Friends gave up the mighty, gave Śuṣṇa up to Kutsa for affliction.
He led the lauded Kavi, he delivered Atka as prey to him and to his heroes.

10 He, with his Gods who love mankind, the Wondrous, giving like Varuṇa who works with magic,
Was known, yet young, as guardian of

the seasons ; and he quelled Araru, four-footed demon.

11 Through lauds of him hath Auśija Ṛjiśvan burst, with the Mighty's aid, the stall of Pipru.
When the saint pressed the juice and shone as singer, he seized the forts and with his craft subdued them.

12 So, swiftly Asura, for exaltation, hath the great Vamraka come nigh to Indra.
He will, when supplicated, bring him blessing : he hath brought all, food, strength, a happy dwelling.

HYMN C.   *Viśvedevas.*

1. BE, like thyself, O Indra, strong for our delight : here lauded, aid us, Maghavan, drinker of the juice.
Savitar with the Gods protect us : hear ye Twain. We ask for freedom and complete felicity.

2 Bring swift, for offering, the snare that suits the time, to the pure-drinker Vāyu, roaring as he goes,
To him who hath approached the draught of shining milk. We ask for freedom and complete felicity.

3 May Savitar the God send us full life, to each who sacrifices, lives aright and pours the juice ;
That we with simple hearts may wait upon the Gods. We ask for freedom and complete felicity.

4 May Indra evermore be gracious unto us, and may King Soma meditate our happiness,
Even as men secure the comfort of a friend. We ask for freedom and complete felicity.

---

5 I can make nothing intelligible of the second line. 'I think of the two (parents) of Vamra, who are free from fever. Having obtained (the enemy's) food, he called aloud whilst stealing it.'—Wilson. Vamra is mentioned in I. 51. 9; 112. 15.

6 *Lord of the dwelling* : or, with Ludwig, The Lord and Giver. *The demon* : or Dāsa Viśvarūpa, son of Tvaṣṭar. See X. 8. 8. *The boar* : Vṛtra Cf. I. 61. 7.

8 *The Hawk* : the fierce and swift Indra.

9 *Kavi* : according to Sāyaṇa, Uśanā Kāvya or son of Kavi is intended. *Atka* : See X. 49. 3.

10 *His Gods* : the Maruts. *Araru* : I follow Sāyaṇa. Cf. *Śatapatha-Brāhmaṇa*, I. 2 4.17 (S.B.E. XII.57) According to Prof. Ludwig's conjectural explanation the translation would be :—'he measured out the year in four divisions.'

11 *Auśija* : son of Uśij. But as this patronymic does not properly belong to Ṛjiśvan, the word here may perhaps mean, 'vehement,' 'eagerly desirous.' *Pipru* : one of the demons of drought.

12 *Asura* : O divine and mighty Indra. *For exaltation*: of Indra. *Vamraka* : a lengthened form of Vamra, the Ṛṣi of the hymn. The last clause of the stanza is borrowed from X. 20. 10.

This hymn, which is obscure and in some places unintelligible, is placed by Prof. Grassmann in his Appendix. Dr. Muir has translated stanzas 1—7 in *O. S. Texts*, IV. pp. 408, 409 (2nd edition).

1 *Ye Twain* : Indra and Savitar. *Freedom* : *áditim*. Prof. M. Müller translates differently : 'We implore Aditi for health and wealth.'

2 *Pure-drinker* : drinker of pure Soma juice.

5 Indra hath given the body with its song and strength : Bṛhaspati, thou art the lengthener of life.
The sacrifice is Manu, Providence, our Sire. We ask for freedom and complete felicity.

6 Indra possesseth might celestial nobly formed : the singer in the house is Agni, prudent Sage.
He is the sacrifice in synod, fair, most near. We ask for freedom and complete felicity.

7 Not often have we sinned against you secretly, nor, Vasus, have we openly provoked the Gods.
Not one of us, ye Gods, hath worn an alien shape. We ask for freedom and complete felicity.

8 May Savitar remove from us our malady, and may the Mountains keep it far away from where
The press-stone as it sheds the meath rings loudly forth. We ask for freedom and complete felicity.

9 Ye Vasus, let the stone, the presser, stand erect : avert all enmities and keep them far remote.
Our guard to be adored is Savitar this God. We ask for freedom and complete felicity.

10 Eat strength and fatness in the pasture, kine, who are balmed at the reservoir and at the seat of Law.
So let your body be our body's medicine. We ask for freedom and complete felicity.

11 The singer fills the spirit : all mens' love hath he. Indra takes kindly care of those who pour the juice.
For his libation is the heavenly udder full. We ask for freedom and complete felicity.

12 Wondrous thy spirit-filling light, triumphant ; thy hosts save from decay and are resistless.
The pious votary by straightest pathway speeds to possess the best of all the cattle.

HYMN CI. Viśvedevas.

1. WAKE with one mind, my friends, and kindle Agni, ye who are many and who dwell together.
Agni and Dadhikrās and Dawn the Goddess, you, Gods with Indra, I call down to help us.

2 Make pleasant hymns, spin out your songs and praises : build ye a ship equipped with oars for transport.
Prepare the implements, make all things ready, and let the sacrifice, my friends, go forward.

3 Lay on the yokes, and fasten well the traces : formed is the furrow, sow the seed within it.
Through song may we find hearing fraught with plenty : near to the ripened grain approach the sickle.

4 Wise, through desire of bliss from Gods, the skilful bind the traces fast,
And lay the yokes on either side.

5 Arrange the buckets in their place : securely fasten on the straps.
We will pour forth the well that hath a copious stream, fair-flowing well that never fails.

6 I pour the water from the well with pails prepared and goodly straps,
Unfailing, full, with plenteous stream.

7 Refresh the horses, win the prize before you : equip a chariot fraught with happy fortune.
Pour forth the well with stone wheel,

5 *The sacrifice is Manu* : we owe our existence and preservation to sacrifice, which is to us another Manu, the father of Āryan men.

6 *The sacrifice in synod* : "worthy of sacrifice at the altar."—Wilson.

7 *An alien shape* : as sorcerers are accustomed to do.

10 *Balmed at the reservoir* : anointed before being milked. Sāyaṇa explains *kośe* by *goṣṭhe*, 'in the cowstall.' *Let your body* : may the milk, the produce of your bodies, offered in libation, keep our bodies in health. Or 'may the body of the cow offered in sacrifice be the expiation for the body of the sacrificer, enabling him to attain *svarga*. Or may the milk be the corrective of the Soma.'—Wilson.

11 *The heavenly udder* : the clouds of the firmament.

12 *Save from decay* : this is Prof. Ludwig's interpretation of the obscure word *jaraṇiprāh*, which means, according to Sāyaṇa, replenishing the wealth of thy worshippers. The last line is explained differently by Sāyaṇa. —'(therefore) Duvasyu hastens in front of the victim cow, (leading it) with a straight cord.'—Wilson. According to the same authority the meaning of the refrain of stanzas 1—11 is :—'We long for the universal Aditi.'

1 *Dadhikrās* : probably a personification of the Morning Sun. See III. 20. 1; IV. 38. 2; 40. 5 note.

2 *Ship* : sacrifice, represented under this figure.

3 In this and the following stanzas sacrifice is figuratively spoken of as ploughing, sowing and reaping. See *Śatapatha-Brāhmaṇa*, VII. 2. 2. 4. (S. B. E. XLI. 320).

5 The flowing Soma is an inexhaustible well.

7 The sacrifice is a chariot; and the ritual is a race. *The well* : the stream of Soma juice. *Stone wheel* : with allusion to the press-stones.

wooden buckets, the drink of heroes, with the trough for armour.

8 Prepare the cow-stall, for there drink your heroes : stitch ye the coats of armour, wide and many.

Make iron forts, secure from all assailants : let not your pitcher leak : stay it securely.

9 Hither, for help, I turn the holy heavenly mind of you the Holy Gods, that longs for sacrifice.

May it pour milk for us, even as a stately cow who, having sought the pasture, yields a thousand streams.

10 Pour golden juice within the wooden vessel : with stone-made axes fashion ye and form it.

Embrace and compass it with tenfold girdle, and to both chariot-poles attach the car-horse.

11 Between both poles the car-horse goes pressed closely, as in his dwelling moves the doubly-wedded.

Lay in the wood the Sovran of the Forest, and sink the well although ye do not dig it.

12 Indra is he, O men, who gives us happiness : sport, urge the giver of delight to win us strength

Bring quickly down, O priests, hither to give us aid, to drink the Soma, Indra Son of Niṣṭigrī.

HYMN CII.   *Indra.*

1. For thee may Indra boldly speed the car that works on either side.

8 *The cow-stall* : figuratively, for the place where the Soma is pressed. *Coats of armour* : the filters for straining the juice. *Iron forts* : the safeguards obtained by sacrificing.

9 *Milk* : abundant blessing.

10 *Stone-made* : with allusion to the press-stones. *Tenfold girdle* : the fingers of both hands. *Both chariot-poles* : the arms. *The car-horse* : the upper press-stone ; or the pestle.

11 *The doubly-wedded* : the man who has two wives. The comparison is not clear. *The Sovran of the Forest* : the Soma plant. *Sink the well* : 'store up the juice.' —Wilson.

12 I follow Sāyaṇa in his interpretation of the first line. Von Roth, Ludwig, and Grassmann explain it differently. *Niṣṭigrī* : meaning according to Sāyaṇa, 'she who swallows up her rival wife *Niṣṭi, i. e.* Diti,' is said to be Aditi, the mother of Indra.

The deified subject of the hymn is said to be, alternatively, Drughaṇa (Mace, Club or Hammer. See stanza 9). The Ṛṣi is Mudgala.

According to the legend quoted by Sāyaṇa, all Mudgala's cattle had been stolen except an old ox which he harnessed to his wagon and went in pursuit of the robbers. He threw his club or mace before him, which

Favour us, Much-invoked ! in this most glorious fight against the raiders of our wealth.

2 Loose in the wind the woman's robe was streaming what time she won a car-load worth a thousand.

The charioteer in fight was Mudgalānī : she Indra's dart, heaped up the prize of battle.

3 O Indra, cast thy bolt among assailants who would slaughter us :

The weapon both of Dāsa and of Ārya foe keep far away, O Maghavan.

4 The bull in joy had drunk a lake of water. His shattering horn encountered an opponent.

Swiftly, in vigorous strength, eager for glory, he stretched his forefeet, fain to win and triumph.

5 They came anear the bull ; they made him thunder, made him pour rain down ere the fight was ended.

And Mudgala thereby won in the contest well-pastured kine in hundreds and in thousands.

6 In hope of victory that bull was harnessed : Keśī the driver urged him on with shouting.

As he ran swiftly with the car behind him his lifted heels pressed close on Mudgalānī.

7 Deftly for him he stretched the car-pole

showed him the way to the thieves, and thus recovered his property.

1 *For thee* : O Mudgala. *That works on either side* : mithūkṛtam : according to Sāyaṇa = asahāyam, 'that has no companion.' The meaning is uncertain.

2 *Mudgalānī* : Mudgala's wife. *Indra's dart* : sped swiftly on her way by Indra.

3 This stanza seems to be an interpolation.

4 *The bull* : apparently one of the buffaloes which drew the chariot of Mudgala's chief opponent. *Had drunk* : just before the fight began. *Encountered an opponent* : meaning perhaps, that feeling uneasy he hung his head and struck the ground with his horns. 'He cleft the mountain peak, he went against the enemy.' —Wilson.

6 *In hope of victory* : kakárdave : the meaning is uncertain ; according to Sāyaṇa, 'for the destruction of the enemy.' Ludwig thinks that the farther end of the chariot-pole is intended.

7 Mudgala's better fortune is now related. *For him* : for his own buffalo. *He* : Mudgala. *Car-pole* : I follow Ludwig's conjecture ; but it is uncertain what part of the chariot the *pradhi* was ; the periphery of the wheel,' according to the St. Petersburg Lexicon ; 'the frame of the waggon.'—Wilson. Sāyaṇa's explanation is not very clear, but he seems to think that the linchpin is intended. None of these three explanations seems suitable here. *The lord of cows* : the bull buffalo.

forward, guided the bull thereto and firmly yoked him.

Indra vouchsafed the lord of cows his favour : with mighty steps the buffalo ran onward.

8 Touched by the goad the shaggy beast went nobly, bound to the pole by the yoke's thong of leather.

Performing deeds of might for many people, he, looking on the cows, gained strength and vigour.

9 Here look upon this mace, this bull's companion, now lying midway on the field of battle.

Therewith hath Mudgala in ordered contest won for cattle for himself, a hundred thousand.

10 Far is the evil : who hath here beheld it? Hither they bring the bull whom they are yoking. .

To this they give not either food or water. Reaching beyond the pole it gives directions.

11 Like one forsaken, she hath found a husband, and teemed as if her breast were full and flowing.

With swiftly-racing chariot may we conquer, and rich and blessed be our gains in battle.

12 Thou, Indra, art the mark whereon the eyes of all life rest, when thou,

---

9 *Mace* : *drughanám* : according to Sāyaṇa, the club which Mudgala had carried with him on his expedition, and which, together with the ox that drew his car had enabled him to recover his cattle. *Lying midway* : after the victory, the King had thrown down his mace upon the field of battle.—Ludwig.

10 I find this stanza unintelligible. Perhaps the second line contains the germ of that part of the legend which mentions the club thrown in front of the chariot to point out the way that the robbers had taken.

11 *Like one forsaken* : *parivṛktéva* : 'Apparently Mudgalāni was a *parivṛktā* (a wife lightly esteemed in comparison with the favourite wife) who made amends for her sterility by driving her husband's chariot to battle and bringing him back victorious, with the booty which she had helped him to gain instead of the children that she had not borne him.'—Ludwig.

12 *With thy bull* : thy fierce and strong thunderbolt. *With thy weakling friend* : with the mortal man whom thou protectest, and who is weak and effiminate in comparison with thee.

The hymn is fragmentary, and it seems impossible to interpret it fully and satisfactorily. I have followed in some stanzas the interpretations of the authors of *Vedische Studien*, I. pp. 124 and 138. But see the later translation and exhaustive discussion by Prof. Geldner in Part II. pp. 1—22, and Prof. Ludwig's remarks thereon in *Ueber die neuesten Arbeiten auf dem Gebiete der Ṛgveda-forschung*.

A Bull who drivest with thy bull, wilt win the race together with thy weakling friend.

HYMN CIII. *Indra.*

1. Swift, rapidly striking, like a bull who sharpens his horns, terrific, stirring up the people,

With eyes that close not, bellowing, Sole Hero, Indra subdued at once a hundred armies.

2 With him loud-roaring, ever watchful, Victor, bold, hard to overthrow, Rouser of battle,

Indra the Strong, whose hand bears arrows, conquer, ye warriors, now, now vanquish in the combat.

3 He rules with those who carry shafts and quivers, Indra who with his band brings hosts together,

Foe-conquering, strong of arm, the Somadrinker, with mighty bow, shooting with well-laid arrows.

4 Bṛhaspati, fly with thy chariot hither, slayer of demons, driving off our foemen.

Be thou protector of our cars, destroyer, victor in battle, breaker-up of armies.

5 Conspicuous by thy strength, firm, foremost fighter, mighty and fierce, victorious, all-subduing,

The Son of Conquest, passing men and heroes, kine-winner, mount thy conquering car, O Indra.

6 Cleaver of stalls, kine-winner, armed with thunder, who quells an army and with might destroys it.—

Follow him, brothers ! quit yourselves like heroes, and like this Indra show your zeal and courage.

7 Piercing the cow-stalls with surpassing vigour, Indra, the pitiless Hero, wild with anger,

Victor in fight, unshaken and resistless,— may he protect our armies in our battles.

8 Indra guide these : Bṛhaspati precede them, the guerdon, and the sacrifice, and Soma;

The hymn is a prayer for aid and victory in battle.

8 *Guide these* : be the leader of our troops. *The guerdon* : *dákṣiṇā* : the reward of the priests who perform the sacrifice offered before battle.

And let the banded Maruts march in forefront of heavenly hosts that conquer and demolish.

9 Ours be the potent host of mighty Indra, King Varuṇa, and Maruts, and Ādityas. Uplifted is the shout of Gods who conquer high-minded Gods who cause the worlds to tremble.

10 Bristle thou up, O Maghavan, our weapons : excite the spirits of my warring heroes. Urge on the strong steeds' might, O Vṛtra-slayer, and let the din of conquering cars go upward.

11 May Indra aid us when our flags are gathered : victorious be the arrows of our army. May our brave men of war prevail in battle. Ye Gods, protect us in the shout of onset.

12 Bewildering the senses of our foemen, seize thou their bodies and depart, O Apvā. Attack them, set their hearts on fire and burn them : so let our foes abide in utter darkness.

13 Advance, O heroes, win the day. May Indra be your sure defence. Exceeding mighty be your arms, that none may wound or injure you.

HYMN CIV.   *Indra.*

1. SOMA hath flowed for thee, Invoked of many ! Speed to our sacrifice with both thy Coursers. To thee have streamed the songs of mighty singers, imploring, Indra, drink of our libation.

2 Drink of the juice which men have washed in waters, and fill thee full, O Lord of Tawny Horses. O Indra, hearer of the laud, with Soma which stones have mixed for thee enhance thy rapture.

3 To make thee start, a strong true draught

I offer to thee, the Bull, O thou whom Bay Steeds carry. Here take delight, O Indra, in our voices while thou art hymned with power and all our spirit.

4 O Mighty Indra, through thine aid, thy prowess, obtaining life, zealous, and skilled in Order, Men in the house who share the sacred banquet stand singing praise that brings them store of children.

5 Through thy directions, Lord of Tawny Coursers, thine who art firm, splendid, and blest, the people Obtain most liberal aid for their salvation, and praise thee, Indra, through thine excellencies.

6 Lord of the Bays, come with thy two Bay Horses, come to our prayers, to drink the juice of Soma. To thee comes sacrifice which thou acceptest : thou, skilled in holy rites, art he who giveth.

7 Him of a thousand powers, subduing foemen, Maghavan praised with hymns and pleased with Soma,— Even him our songs approach, resistless Indra : the adorations of the singer laud him.

8 The way to bliss for Gods and man thou foundest, Indra, seven lovely floods, divine, untroubled, Wherewith thou, rending forts, didst move the ocean, and nine-and-ninety flowing streams of water.

9 Thou from the curse didst free the mighty Waters, and as their only God didst watch and guard them. O Indra, cherish evermore thy body with those which thou hast won in quelling Vṛtra.

10 Heroic power and noble praise is Indra : yea, the song worships him invoked of many. Vṛtra he quelled, and gave men room and freedom : Śakra, victorious, hath conquered armies.

11 Call we on Maghavan, auspicious Indra,

---

11 *When our flags are gathered* : 'apparently comparable with the signis collatis of the Romans.'—Ludwig.

12 *Apvā* : according to Sāyaṇa, a female deity who presides over sin according to Mahīdhara, sickness, or fear. Apparently Apvā was a sort of colic, or dysentery, likely to attack soldiers in the field. *And depart* : or, pass us by ; do not attack us.

3 *True* : which produces the results expected in the shape of favour.

---

8 *Didst move the ocean* : didst bring the sea of rain from heaven.

9 *Those* : waters.

11 This is the concluding verse of several hymns of the Viśvāmitras in Book III.

best Hero in this fight where spoil is gathered,
The Strong, who listens, who gives aid in battles, who slays the Vṛtras, wins and gathers riches.

HYMN CV. *Indra.*

1. WHEN, Vasu, wilt thou love the laud? Now let the channel bring the stream. The juice is ready to ferment.

2 He whose two Bay Steeds harnessed well, swerving, pursue the Bird's tail-plumes, With flowing manes, like heaven and earth, he is the Lord with power to give.

3 Bereft of skill is Indra, if, like some out-wearied man he fears The sinner, when the Mighty hath prepared himself for victory.

4 Indra with these drives round, until he meets with one to worship him : Indra is Master of the pair who snort and swerve upon their way.

5 Borne onward by the long-maned Steeds who stretch themselves as 'twere for food, The God who wears the helm defends them with his jaws.

6 The Mighty sang with Lofty Ones : the Hero fashioned with his strength,

Like skilful Mātariśvan with his power and might,

7 The bolt, which pierced at once the vitals of the Dasyu easy to be slain, With jaw uninjured like the wondrous firmament.

8 Grind off our sins: with sòng will we conquer the men who sing no hymns : Not easily art thou pleased with prayerless sacrifice.

9 When threefold flame burns high for thee, to rest on poles of sacrifice, Thou with the living joyest in the self-bright Ship.

10 Thy glory was the speckled cup, thy glory was the flawless scoop. Wherewith thou pourest into thy receptacle.

11 As hundreds, O Immortal God, have sung to thee, so hath Sumitra, yea, Durmitra praised thee here, What time thou holpest Kutsa's son, when Dasyus fell, yea, holpest Kutsa's darling when the Dasyus died.

HYMN CVI. *Aśvins.*

1. THIS very thing ye Twain hold as your object : ye weave your songs as skilful men weave garments. That ye may come united have I waked you : ye spread out food like days of lovely weather.

2 Like two plough-bulls ye move along in traces, and seek like eager guests your bidder's banquet. Ye are like glorious envoys mid the people: like bulls, approach the place where ye are watered.

1 *Vasu* : Indra. *Let the channel bring the stream* : to the Soma juice which has stood long enough for fermentation.—Ludwig. The phraseology is very obscure, and Sāyaṇa gives a totally different explanation.—'When will he, (like) a dam, obstruct and let loose the long-protracted libation for the sake of wind-driven (rain) ?'—Wilson.

2 *The Bird* : the allusion seems to be a race between the horses of Indra and those of Sūrya or the Sun who is the Bird of the heavens.—Ludwig. *Like heaven and earth* : the meaning of *raji* is unknown. Sāyaṇa explains the word by 'heaven and earth,' or 'sun and moon;' but these are mere guesses. Prof. Ludwig thinks that two animals of some kind ('rajitiere', 'raji-beasts') are meant. In VI. 26. 6, Raji is said by Sāyana to be the name of a maiden.

3 *The sinner* : Vṛtra, the chief of sinners, according to Sāyaṇa. Or *pāpaje* may be a verb, and the stanza may be rendered :—'Without them Indra holds him still, like a man weary and alarmed. When he hath made himself ready for noble deed.'—See Pischel, *Vedische Studien*, I. p. 198.

4 *Is Master* : literally 'hero'. The meaning apparently is that when Indra meets with a worshipper he stops his horses and attends the sacrifice.

5 *Who wears the helm* : śipriṇīnān ; 'possessing mighty jaws.'—Wilson. *With his jaws* : with his roar, the thunder.

6 *Lofty Ones* : the Maruts.

7 The stanza is obscure. I follow Prof. Ludwig's interpretation of *hirimaśo hirimān*, which mean, according to Sāyana, 'gold-bearded' and 'lord of bay horses.'

8 *Grind off* : remove them by whetting. 'Comminute.'—Wilson.

9 *Threefold flame* : of the three sacred fires. *The living* : the sacrificer. *The self-bright Ship* : the sacrifice; 'the vessel of thy glory.'—Wilson.

10 *Cup* : upasécani : a ladle or cup used for sprinkling. *Thy receptacle*, drinking-vessel, or perhaps Agni, that is, the fire, may be intended.

11 *Sumitra* and *Durmitra* are alternative names of the Ṛṣi of the hymn. *Kutsa's son* : Durmitra himself, according to Sāyana.

The metres in some places are somewhat irregular, the meanings of some words are uncertain, and the hymn generally is obscure. Prof. Grassmann has placed the hymn in his Appendix.

3 Like the two pinions of a bird, connected,
like two choice animals, ye have sought
our worship.
Bright as the fire the votary hath kindled,
ye sacrifice in many a spot as roamers.

4 Ye are our kinsmen, like two sons, two
fathers, strong in your splendour and like
kings for conquest ;
Like rays for our enjoyment, Lords to feed
us, ye, like quick hearers, have obeyed
our calling.

9 Like giants, ye will find firm ground to
stand on in depths, like feet for one who
fords a shallow.
Like ears ye will attend to him who orders:
ye Two enjoy our wondrous work as
sharers.

10 Like toiling bees ye bring to us your honey,
as bees into the hide that opens downward.

11 May we increase the laud and gain us
vigour : come to our song, ye whom
one chariot carries.
Filled be our kine with ripened meath
like glory : Bhūtāṁśa hath fulfilled the
Aśvins' longing.

HYMN CVII.   *Dakṣiṇā.*

1. THESE men's great bounty hath been
manifested, and the whole world of life
set free from darkness.
Great light hath come, vouchsafed us by
the Fathers : apparent is the spacious
path of Guerdon.

2 High up in heaven abide the Guerdon-
givers : they who give steeds dwell with
the Sun for ever.
They who give gold are blest with life
eternal : they who give robes prolong
their lives, O Soma.

4 *Like rays for our enjoyment* : 'like brooms to sweep
with,' according to Prof. Ludwig.
I do not attempt the hopeless task of translating
stanzas 5, 6, 7, 8, in which nearly every word is a difficult
riddle. See Appendix.

10 *The hide that opens downward* : the honey-comb is
compared to a water-skin inverted. I cannot translate
intelligibly the second line :—'like two labourers you are
dripping with perspiration, like a tired cow eating sweet
herbage, you attend (the sacrifice).'—Wilson.

The hymn eulogizes Dakṣiṇā, the largess, guerdon,
or honorarium presented by the institutors of the sacrifices
to the priests who perform the ceremonies. The *yajamānas* who give this guerdon liberally are alternatively
the deified subjects of the hymn.

1 *These men* : the wealthy institutors of the sacrifice.
Fathers : who are the embodiments and guardians of
the light.

3 Not from the niggards—for they give not
freely—comes Meed at sacrifice, Gods'
satisfaction :
Yea, many men with hands stretched out
with Guerdon present their gifts because
they dread dishonour.

4 These who observe mankind regard obla-
tion as streamy Vāyu and light-finding
Arka.
They satisfy and give their gifts in synod,
and pour in streams the seven-mothered
Guerdon.

5 He who brings Guerdon comes as first
invited : chief of the hamlet comes the
Guerdon-bearer.
Him I account the ruler of the people
who was the first to introduce the
Guerdon.

6 They call him Ṛṣi, Brahman, Sāma-chanter,
reciter of the laud, leader of worship.
The brightly-shining God's three forms he
knoweth who first bestowed the sacrificial Guerdon.

7 Guerdon bestows the horse, bestows the
bullock, Guerdon bestows, moreover,
gold that glisters.
Guerdon gives food which is our life and
spirit. He who is wise takes Guerdon
for his armour.

8 The liberal die not, never are they ruined:
the liberal suffer neither harm nor
trouble.
The light of heaven, the universe about
us,—all this doth sacrificial Guerdon give
them.

9 First have the liberal gained a fragrant
dwelling, and got themselves a bride in
fair apparel.
The liberal have obtained their draught
of liquor, and conquered those who,
unprovoked, assailed them.

10 They deck the fleet steed for the bounteous giver : the maid adorns herself
and waits to meet him.

4 *These who observe mankind* : the Maghavans or wealthy
nobles, who do not consider the cost of sacrifice, but
regard it as an occasion that enables them to show their
liberality, and to gain the favour of Vāyu, the Wind-God
who brings countless showers of rain, and Arka or the
Sun who brings the light. *Seven-mothered* : originating in,
and accompanying, seven forms of sacrifice; or, regulated
by the seven priests.

6 *Three forms* : Agni as the Sun, lightning, and fire.

9 *Draught of liquor* : *antaḥpeyam surāyāḥ* : 'deep potations
of wine.'—Wilson.

10 *The maid adorns herself* ; 'he obtains a brilliant
damsel for his portion.'—Muir.

His home is like a lake with lotus blossoms, like the Gods' palaces adorned and splendid.

11 Steeds good at draught convey the liberal giver, and lightly rolling moves the car of Guerdon.

Assist, ye Gods, the liberal man in battles: the liberal giver conquers foes in combat.

HYMN CVIII.   Saramā. Paṇis.

1. WHAT wish of Saramā hath brought her hither? The path leads far away to distant places.

What charge hast thou for us? Where turns thy journey? How hast thou made thy way o'er Rasā's waters.

2 I come appointed messenger of Indra, seeking your ample stores of wealth, O Paṇis.

This hath preserved me from the fear of crossing: thus have I made my way o'er Rasā's waters.

3 What is that Indra like, what is his aspect whose envoy, Saramā, from afar thou comest?

Let him approach, and we will show him friendship: he shall be made the herdsman of our cattle.

4 I know him safe from harm: but he can punish who sent me hither from afar as envoy.

Him rivers flowing with deep waters hide not. Low will ye be, O Paṇis, slain by Indra.

5 These are the kine which, Saramā, thou seekest, flying, O Blest One, to the ends of heaven.

Who will loose these for thee without a battle? Yea, and sharp-pointed are our warlike weapons.

6 Even if your wicked bodies, O ye Paṇis, were arrow-proof, your words are weak for wounding;

And were the path to you as yet unmastered, Bṛhaspati in neither case will spare you.

7 Paved with the rock is this our treasure-chamber; filled full of precious things, of kine, and horses.

These Paṇis who are watchful keepers guard it. In vain hast thou approached this lonely station.

8 Ṛṣis will come inspirited with Soma, Aṅgirases unwearied, and Navagvas.

This stall of cattle will they part among them: then will the Paṇis wish these words unspoken.

9 Even thus, O Saramā, hast thou come hither, forced by celestial might to make the journey.

Turn thee not back, for thou shalt be our sister: O Blest One, we will give thee of the cattle.

10 Brotherhood, sisterhood, I know not either: the dread Aṅgirases and Indra know them.

They seemed to long for kine when I departed. Hence, into distance, be ye gone, O Paṇis.

11 Hence, far away, ye Paṇis! Let the cattle lowing come forth as holy Law commandeth,

Kine which Bṛhaspati, and Soma, Ṛṣis, sages, and pressing-stones have found when hidden.

HYMN CIX.   Viśvedevas.

I. THESE first, the boundless Sea, and Māta-riśvan, fierce-glowing Fire, the Strong, the Bliss-bestower.

---

11 *Car of Guerdon* : cf. I. 123. 1.

The hymn is a colloquy between Saramā, the messenger of the Gods or of Indra (see I. 62. 3, note; 72. 8; III. 31. 6; V. 45. 8), and the Paṇis or envious demons who have carried off the cows or rays of light which Indra wishes to recover. Saramā and the Paṇis are alternately subject and Ṛṣi.

1 The Paṇis address Saramā who has found her way to the rocky stronghold in which the stolen cows are imprisoned. The Paṇis speak the uneven stanzas, with the exception of stanza 11, and Saramā the even. *Rasā* is in this place a mythical stream that flows round the atmosphere and the earth. See V. 41. 15. In I. 112, 12, and V. 53. 9, Rasā appears to be a river of the Panjāb, probably an affluent of the Indus. See Zimmer, *Altindisches Leben* pp. 15, 16.

6 *Weak for wounding* : 'not in the place of armies.' —Wilson. *Bṛhaspati* : as Indra's companion and ally in battle.

8 *Navagvas* : members of a mythological family, forming a division of the Aṅgirases or closely connected with them. *Wish these words unspoken* : more literally, reject them from their mouths ; retract their threads.

10 *Know them* : are allied by such ties of kinship.

11 It is uncertain to whom this stanza is to be ascribed. Sāyaṇa assigns it to Saramā. Prof. Ludwig thinks that Bṛhaspati may be the speaker. *Pressing-stones* : which prepare the Soma juice that inspirits Indra.

The hymn has been translated by the authors of *Siebenzig Lieder des Rigveda*. See also Mme. Zénaïde Ragozin, *Vedic India*, p. 256.

And heavenly Floods, first-born by holy Order, exclaimed against the outrage on a Brahman.

2 King Soma first of all, without reluctance, made restitution of the Brahman's consort.
Mitra and Varuṇa were the inviters: Agni as Hotar took her hand and led her.

3 The man, her pledge, must by her hand be taken when they have cried, She is a Brahman's consort.
She stayed not for a herald to conduct her: thus is the kingdom of a ruler guarded.

4 Thus spake of her those Gods of old, Seven Ṛṣis who sate them down to their austere devotion:
Dire is a Brahman's wife led home by others: in the supremest heaven she plants confusion.

5 The Brahmacārī goes engaged in duty: he is a member of the Gods' own body.
Through him Bṛhaspati obtained his consort, as the Gods gained the ladle brought by Soma.

6 So then the Gods restored her, so men gave the woman back again.
The Kings who kept their promises restored the Brahman's wedded wife.

7 Having restored the Brahman's wife, and freed them, with Gods' aid, from sin,
They shared the fulness of the earth, and won themselves extended sway.

HYMN CX.   *Āpris.*

1. THOU in the house of man this day enkindled worshippest Gods as God, O Jātavedas.

1 *Outrage on a Brahman* : 'Brahmā's sin,' according to Sāyaṇa.
5 *Brahmacārī* : a religious student. For his glorification, see *Hymns of the Atharva-veda*, XI. 5. *The ladle* : *juhvam*: Prof. Ludwig takes it to be a proper name :—'Juhū, O Gods, conducted home by Soma.'
The wife of a Brahman appears to have been taken to his home by a Kṣatriya, and then restored. A legend quoted by Sāyaṇa says that Juhū or Vāk, the wife of Bṛhaspati who is identified with Brahmā, had been deserted by her husband. The Gods then consulted together as to the means of expiating his sin and restored heₜ to him. See Wilson's Translation.

The hymn is an almost unintelligible fragment and of comparatively late origin.

See preceding hymns addressed to the same deities and deified objects : I. 13; 142, 188; II. 3; III. 4; V. 5. VII. 2; and IX. 5.

1 *Jātavedas* and *Tanūnapāt* are names of Agni. The

Observant, bright as Mitra, bring them hither : thou art a sapient and foreknowing envoy.

2 Tanūnapāt, fair-tongued, with sweet meath balming the paths and ways of Order, make them pleasant.
Convey our sacrifice to heaven, exalting with holy thoughts our hymns of praise and worship.

3 Invoked, deserving prayer and adoration, O Agni, come accordant with the Vasus.
Thou art, O Youthful Lord, the Gods' Invoker, so, best of Sacrificers, bring them quickly.

4 By rule the Sacred Grass is scattered east-ward, a robe to clothe this earth when dawns are breaking:
Widely it spreads around and far-extended, fair for the Gods and bringing peace and freedom.

5 Let the expansive Doors be widely opened, like wives who deck their beauty for their husbands.
Lofty, celestial, all-impelling Portals, admit the Gods and give them easy entrance.

6 Pouring sweet dews let holy Night and Morning, each close to each, be seated at their station,—
Lofty, celestial Dames with gold to deck them, assuming all their fair and radiant beauty.

7 Come the two first celestial sweet-voiced Hotars, arranging sacrifice for man to worship
As singers who inspire us in assemblies, showing the eastward light with their direction.

8 Let Bhāratī come quickly to our worship, and Ilā showing like a human being.
So let Sarasvatī and both her fellows, deft Goddesses, on this fair grass be seated.

9 Hotar more skilled in sacrifice, bring hither with speed to-day God Tvaṣṭar, thou who knowest.
Even him who formed these two, the Earth and Heaven the Parents, with their forms, and every creature.

Doors of the sacrificial chamber represent the portals of the eastern heaven. *Vanaspati* is the sacrificial post to which the victim is tied.

10 Send to our offerings which thyself thou balmest the Companies of Gods in ordered season.

Agni, Vanaspati the Immolator sweeten our offered gift with meath and butter.

11 Agni, as soon as he was born, made ready the sacrifice, and was the Gods' preceder.

May the Gods eat our offering consecrated according to this true Priest's voice and guidance.

HYMN CXI.   *Indra.*

1. BRING forth your sacred song ye prudent singers, even as are the thoughts of human beings.

Let us draw Indra with true deeds anear us : he loves our songs, the Hero, and is potent.

2 The hymn shone brightly from the seat of worship: to the kine came the Bull, the Heifer's Offspring

With mighty bellowing hath he arisen, and hath pervaded even the spacious regions.

3 Indra knows, verily, how to hear our singing, for he, victorious, made a path for Sūrya.

He made the Cow, and he became the Sovran of Heaven, primeval, matchless, and unshaken.

4 Praised by Aṅgirases, Indra demolished with might the works of the great watery monster

Full many regions, too, hath he pervaded, and by his truth supported earth's foundation.

5 The counterpart of heaven and earth is Indra: he knoweth all libations, slayeth Śuṣṇa.

The vast sky with the Sun hath he extended, and, best of pillars, stayed it with a pillar.

6 The Vṛtra-slayer with his bolt felled Vṛtra: the magic of the godless, waxen mighty,

Here hast thou, Bold Assailant, boldly conquered. Yea, then thine arms, O Maghavan, were potent.

7 When the Dawns come attendant upon Sūrya their rays discover wealth of divers colours.

The Star of heaven is seen as 'twere approaching : none knoweth aught of it as it departeth.

8 Far have they gone, the first of all these waters, the waters that flowed forth when Indra sent them.

Where is their spring, and where is their foundation ? Where now, ye Waters, is your inmost centre ?

9 Thou didst free rivers swallowed by the Dragon ; and rapidly they set themselves in motion,

Those that were loosed and those that longed for freedom. Excited now to speed they run unresting.

10 Yearning together they have sped to Sindhu : the Fort-destroyer, praised, of old, hath loved them.

Indra, may thy terrestrial treasures reach us, and our full songs of joy approach thy dwelling.

HYMN CXII.   *Indra.*

1. DRINK of the juice, O Indra, at thy pleasure, for thy first draught is early morn's libation.

Rejoice, that thou mayst slay our foes, O Hero, and we with lauds will tell thy mighty exploits.

2 Thou hast a car more swift than thought, O Indra ; thereon come hither, come to drink the Soma.

Let thy Bay Steeds, thy Stallions, hasten hither, with whom thou comest nigh and art delighted.

3 Deck out thy body with the fairest colours, with golden splendour of the Sun adorn it.

O Indra, turn thee hitherward invited by us thy friends; be seated and be joyful.

---

2 *The kine* : who are milked for sacrificial purposes. *The Bull* : Indra. *The Heifer's Offspring* : cp. IV.18. 10: 'The Heifer hath brought forth the strong, the mighty, the unconquerable Bull, the furious Indra   The Heifer is Aditi.

3 *He made the Cow* : the words *ménām...góḥ* the cow, 'the female of the bull.'—Muir; 'Des Stieres Weib,' —Grassmann,—are difficult. Prof. Ludwig suggests that the earth may be intended.

4 *Watery monster* : Arbuda, a demon of the clouds. See X. 67, 12.

7 *The Star of heaven* : the Sun.   *Departeth* : on its nightly journey from west to east.

9 *The Dragon* : Ahi; Vṛtra or his brother-fiend.

10 *The Fort-destroyer* : Indra.

4 O thou whose grandeur in thy festive transports not even these two great worlds have comprehended.
Come, Indra, with thy dear Bay Horses harnessed, come to our dwelling and the food thou lovest.

5 Pressed for thy joyous banquet is the Soma, Soma whereof thou, Indra, ever drinking,
Hast waged unequalled battles with thy foemen, which prompts the mighty flow of thine abundance.

6 Found from of old is this thy cup, O Indra : Śatakratu, drink therefrom the Soma.
Filled is the beaker with the meath that gladdens, the beaker which all Deities delight in.

7 From many a side with proffered entertainment the folk are calling thee, O Mighty Indra.
These our libations shall for thee be richest in sweet meath : drink thereof and find them pleasant.

8 I will declare thy deeds of old, O Indra, the mighty acts which thou hast first accomplished.
In genuine wrath thou loosenedst the mountain so that the Brahman easily found the cattle.

9 Lord of the hosts, amid our bands be seated : they call thee greatest Sage among the sages.
Nothing is done, even far away, without thee : great, wondrous, Maghavan, is the hymn I sing thee.

10 Aim of our eyes be thou, for we implore thee, O Maghavan, Friend of friends and Lord of treasures.
Fight, Warrior strong in truth, fight thou the battle : give us our share of undivided riches.

HYMN CXIII.   *Indra.*

1. THE Heavens and the Earth accordant with all Gods encouraged graciously that vigorous might of his.
When he came showing forth his majesty and power, he drank of Soma juice and waxed exceeding strong.

8 *The Brahman* : according to Sāyaṇa, Brahmā who is identified with Bṛhaspati, the owner of the cows which the Paṇis had stolen.

2 This majesty of his Viṣṇu extols and lauds, making the stalk that gives the meath flow forth with might.
When Indra Maghavan with those who followed him had smitten Vṛtra he deserved the choice of Gods.

3 When, bearing warlike weapons, fain to win thee praise, thou mettest Vṛtra, yea, the Dragon, for the fight,
Then all the Maruts who were gathered with thee there extolled, O Mighty One, thy powerful majesty.

4 Soon as he sprang to life he forced asunder hosts : forward the Hero looked to manly deed and war.
He cleft the rock, he let concurrent streams flow forth, and with his skilful art stablished the heavens' wide vault.

5 Indra hath evermore possessed surpassing power : he forced, far from each other, heaven and earth apart.
He hurled impetuous down his iron thunderbolt, a joy to Varuṇa's and Mitra's worshipper.

6 Then to the mighty powers of Indra, to his wrath, his the fierce Stormer, loud of voice, they came with speed;
What time the Potent One rent Vṛtra with his strength, who held the waters back, whom darkness compassed round.

7 Even in the first of those heroic acts which they who strove together came with might to execute,
Deep darkness fell upon the slain, and Indra won by victory the right of being first invoked.

8 Then all the Gods extolled, with eloquence inspired by draughts of Soma juice, thy deeds of manly might.
As Agni eats the dry food with his teeth, he ate Vṛtra, the Dragon, maimed by Indra's deadly dart.

9 Proclaim his many friendships, met with friendship, made with singers, with the skilful and the eloquent.
Indra, when he subdues Dhuni and

6 *They came* : it is uncertain whether the Gods, or the Maruts, or the waters are the understood subject.

7 *Deep darkness fell upon the slain* : 'Vṛtra being slain, the thick darkness was destroyed,'—Wilson.

8 *He ate* : Indra utterly destroyed him. Sāyaṇa explains in a more matter-of-fact way : people devoured Vṛtra, that is, the food produced by the waters which were no longer obstructed by him.

9 *Dhuni* and *Cumuri* were demons and enemies of Indra's friend Dabhīti. See Vol. I., Index.

Cumuri, lists to Dabhīti for his faithful spirit's sake.

10 Give riches manifold with noble horses,
to be remembered while my songs
address thee.
May we by easy paths pass all our troubles : find us this day a ford wide and
extensive.

HYMN CXIV.   *Viśvedevas.*

1. Two perfect springs of heat pervade the
Threefold, and come for their delight
is Mātariśvan.

Craving the milk of heaven the Gods are
present : well do they know the praise-
song and the Sāman.

2 The priests heard far away, as they are
ordered, serve the three Nirṛtis, for well
they know them.
Sages have traced the cause that first
produced them, dwelling in distant and
mysterious chambers.

3 The Youthful One, well-shaped, with four
locks braided, brightened with oil, puts
on the ordinances.
Two Birds of mighty power are seated
near her, there where the Deities receive
their portion.

4 One of these Birds hath passed into the
sea of air : thence he looks round and
views this universal world.
With simple heart I have beheld him
from anear : his Mother kisses him and
he returns her kiss.

5 Him with fair wings though only One in
nature, wise singers shape, with songs,
in many figures.
While they at sacrifices fix the metres, they
measure out twelve chalices of Soma.

6 While they arrange the four and six-and-
thirty, and duly order, up to twelve,
the measures,
Having disposed the sacrifice thoughtful
sages send the Car forward with the
Ṛc and Sāman.

7 The Chariot's majesties are fourteen others :
seven sages lead it onward with their
voices.
Who will declare to us the ford Āpnāna,
the path whereby they drink first draughts of Soma ?

8 The fifteen lauds are in a thousand places :
that is as vast as heaven and earth in
measure.
A thousand spots contain the mighty
thousand. Vāk spreadeth forth as far
as Prayer extendeth.

9 What sage hath learned the metres' appli-
cation ? Who hath gained Vāk, the
spirit's aim and object ?
Which ministering priest is called eighth
Hero ? Who then hath tracked the two
Bay Steeds of Indra ?

10 Yoked to his chariot-pole there stood the
Coursers : they only travel round earth's
farthest limits.
These, when their driver in his home is
settled, receive the allotted meed of
their exertion.

HYMN CXV.   *Agni.*

1. VERILY wondrous is the tender Youngling's
growth who never draweth nigh to drink
his Mothers' milk.

1 *Springs of heat* : *gharmā* : Agni and Sūrya. *The
Threefold* : the universe, sky, firmament, and earth.
Mātariśvan : Vāyu, according to Sāyaṇa. 'Thus we have
here the well-known triad, Agni, Vāyu, Sūrya.'—Ludwig.

2 *Three Nirṛtis* : according to Sāyaṇa, heaven, mid-
air, and earth, or the deities that control them. Prof.
Ludwig thinks that the Dawns are meant, which by
their regular appearance bring men nearer to death.
The plural appears in one other place, VIII. 24. 24.

3 *TheYouthful One* : the altar, represented as a woman.
With four locks braided : quadrangular, according to
Sāyaṇa. *Puts on the ordinances* : is dressed or arranged in
the manner prescribed for sacrifice. *Two Birds* : probably Agni and Soma. According to Sāyaṇa, the husband
and his wife, or the Yajamāna and the Brahman.

4 *One* : Agni as the Sun. *His mother* : perhaps, as Prof.
Ludwig says, Dawn.

6 Thirty-six *grahas*, chalices, or saucers for Soma juice
or other libations, are to be used at the Agniṣṭoma, and
four in addition at the Atyagniṣṭoma sacrifice. *The
measures* : the proper metres for particular rites or parts of
the service. *The Car* : the sacrifice. *Ṛc* : the holy verse
that is recited. *Sāman* : the psalm that is sung or chanted.

7 *Majesties* : the abstract used for the concrete, the
mighty ones, probably the priests. *The ford Āpnāna* : the
passage leading to the place of sacrifice. *They* : the
Gods.

8 *That* : meaning the fifteen lauds regarded as a whole.
The mighty thousand : the meaning is uncertain : 'the
thousand great (functions) are in a thousand places.'—
Wilson. This means, according to Sāyaṇa, that every
function of the body has its appropriate object. Dr. Muir
translates :—'There are a thousand times fifteen *ukthas
.........*A thousand times a thousand are their glorious
manifestations.' *Vāk* : or Speech. See X. 71 and 125.

9 *Eighth Hero* : Agni is meant, as presiding over the
seven *ṛtvijas* or ministering priests.

1 *His Mothers* are the two fire-sticks, the lower of
which, in which the spark is produced, being *she who
hath no udder.*

As soon as she who hath no udder bore
him, he, faring on his great errand,
suddenly grew strong.

2 Then Agni was his name, most active to
bestow, gathering up the trees with his
consuming tooth ;
Skilled in fair sacrifice, armed with
destroying tongue, impetuous as a bull
that snorteth in the mead.

3 Praise him, your God who, bird-like, rests
upon a tree, scattering drops of juice
and pouring forth his flood,
Speaking aloud with flame as with his lips
a priest, and broadening his paths like
one of high command.

4 Thou Everlasting, whom, far-striding fain
to burn, the winds, uninterrupted, never
overcome,
They have approached, as warriors eager
for the fight, heroic Trita, guiding him
to gain his wish.

5 This Agni is the best of Kaṇvas, Kaṇvas'
Friend, Conqueror of the foe whether
afar or near.
May Agni guard the singers, guard the
princes well : may Agni grant to us our
princes' gracious help.

6 Do thou, Supitrya, swiftly following, make
thyself the lord of Jātavedas, mightiest
of all,
Who surely gives a boon even in thirsty
land, most powerful, prepared to aid
us in the wilds.

7 Thus noble Agni with princes and mortal
men is lauded, excellent for conquering
strength with chiefs,
Men who are well-disposed as friends and
true to Law, even as the heavens in
majesty surpass mankind.

8 O Son of Strength, Victorious, with this
title Upastuta's most potent voice reveres
thee.

4 *Trita* : according to Sāyaṇa, him who is stationed
in the three fire-receptacles, that is, Agni.

5 *Kaṇvas* : a well-known family with which Upastuta
was connected. According to Sāyaṇa, worshippers in
general are meant :—'the most earnest of eulogists, the
friend of those who praise him.'—Wilson.

6 *Supitrya* ('who hast fair ancestors.'—Wilson) seems
to be an epithet of the Ṛṣi as addressed by himself.
Sāyaṇa applies it to Agni. The construction of the
stanza is difficult, and the translation of the first half,
which follows Prof. Ludwig, is somewhat conjectural.
Thirsty land : Agni by his intercession causes rain to fall.

Prof. Grassmann observes : 'Das Lied enthält, nament-
lich in Verses 3—6, manches Dunkle, sodass hier die
Auslegung zweifelhaft bleibt.'

Blest with brave sons by thee we will extol
thee, and lengthen out the days of our
existence.

9 Thus, Agni, have the sons of Vṛṣṭihavya,
the Ṛṣis, the Upastutas invoked thee.
Protect them, guard the singers and the
princes. With Vaṣaṭ ! have they come,
with hands uplifted, with their uplifted
hands and cries of Glory !

HYMN CXVI.   *Indra.*

1. DRINK Soma juice for mighty power and
vigour, drink, Strongest One, that thou
mayst smite down Vṛtra.
Drink thou, invoked, for strength, and
riches : drink thou thy fill of meath and
pour it down, O Indra.

2 Drink of the foodful juice stirred into
motion, drink what thou choosest of
the flowing Soma.
Giver of weal, be joyful in thy spirit, and
turn thee hitherward to bless and prosper.

3 Let heavenly Soma gladden thee, O Indra,
let that effused among mankind delight
thee.
Rejoice in that whereby thou gavest
freedom, and that whereby thou conquerest thy foemen.

4 Let Indra come, impetuous, doubly mighty,
to the poured juice, the Bull, with two
Bay Coursers.
With juices pressed in milk, with meath
presented, glut evermore thy bolt, O
Foe-destroyer.

5 Dash down, outflaming their sharp flaming
weapons, the strong-holds of the men
urged on by demons.
I give thee, Mighty One, great strength
and conquest : go, meet thy foes and
rend them in the battle.

6 Extend afar the votary's fame and glory,
as the firm archer's strength drives off
the foeman.
Ranged on our side, grown strong in

1 *Pour it down* : 'shower down (blessings).'—Wilson.

3 *Gavest freedom* : by slaying Vṛtra : or, riches, according to Sāyaṇa.

4 *Foe-destroyer* : *aruśahā* : according to the St. Petersburg Lexicon, 'striker of the red clouds' (*aruśa*=*aruṣa* ?).
I adopt Sāyaṇa's explanation.

6 *As the firm archer's strength* : the construction is obscure :—'(stretch out) thy strength like strong bows against
our enemies.'—Wilson.

might that conquers, never defeated, still increase thy body.

7 To thee have we presented this oblation : accept it, Sovran Ruler, free from anger.
Juice, Maghavan, for thee is pressed and ripened : eat, Indra, drink of that which stirs to meet thee.

8 Eat, Indra, these oblations which approach thee : be pleased with food made ready and with Soma.
With entertainment we receive thee friendly : effectual be the sacrificer's wishes.

9 I send sweet speech to Indra and to Agni : with hymns I speed it like a boat through waters.
Even thus, the Gods seem moving round about me, the fountains and bestowers of our riches.

HYMN CXVII. *Liberality.*

1. THE Gods have 'not ordained hunger to be our death : even to the well-fed man comes death in varied shape.
The riches of the liberal never waste away, while he who will not give finds none to comfort him.

2 The man with food in store who, when the needy comes in miserable case begging for bread to eat,
Hardens his heart against him—even when of old he did him service—finds not one to comfort him.

3 Bounteous is he who gives unto the beggar who comes to him in want of food and feeble.
Success attends him in the shout of battle. He makes a friend of him in future troubles.

4 No friend is he who to his friend and comrade who comes imploring food, will offer nothing.
Let him depart—no home is that to rest in—, and rather seek a stranger to support him.

5 Let the rich satisfy the poor implorer, and bend his eye upon a longer pathway.
Riches come now to one, now to another,

and like the wheels of cars are ever rolling.

6 The foolish man wins food with fruitless labour : that food—I speak the truth—shall be his ruin.
He feeds no trusty friend, no man to love him. All guilt is he who eats with no partaker.

7 The ploughshare ploughing makes the food that feeds us, and with its feet cuts through the path it follows.
Better the speaking than the silent Brahman : the liberal friend outvalues him who gives not.

8 He with one foot hath far outrun the biped, and the two-footed catches the three-footed.
Four-footed creatures come when bipeds call them, and stand and look where five are met together.

9 The hands are both alike : their labour differs. The yield of sister milch-kine is unequal.
Twins even differ in their strength and vigour : two, even kinsmen, differ in their bounty.

HYMN CXVIII. *Agni.*

1. AGNI, refulgent among men thou slayest the devouring fiend,
Bright Ruler in thine own abode.

2 Thou springest up when worshipped well : the drops of butter are thy joy
When ladles are brought near to thee.

The hymn eulogises Liberality or Bounty in the shape of gifts of wealth and food.

1 *To be our death* : men must not attempt to justify their refusal of food to the hungry by saying that the Gods send hunger as a punishment for sin.

5 *Bend his eye upon a longer pathway* : carefully consider the future and not the present only. He himself may need the same assistance hereafter.

6 *Shall be his ruin* : with reference to stanza I.

7 Active exertion is necessary for success. *The speaking Brahman* : the priest who duly discharges the task of recitation for which he is engaged. 'A Brahman expounding (the Veda).'—Wilson.

8 The victory is not always theirs who appear to be more richly endowed than others. *He with one foot* : *êkapâd* : the Sun appears to be meant, elsewhere called Aja-Ekapâd. See VI. 50. 14. *The biped* is man. *The three-footed* is the old man who walks with a staff and is overtaken by one who does not require such assistance. *Four-footed creatures* : dogs. *Five* : several men together ; the dogs being at first uncertain whether their masters are among them or not. *Panktih*, sets of five, is apparently used with reference to the one, two, three, and four in the preceding compound words. Others explain *panktih* by 'steps' or 'traces'.

I have adopted the explanation given by the authors of the *Siebenzig Lieder*.

9 All men should be liberal; but we must not expect all to be equally generous.

The hymn has been translated by Dr. Muir, *O. S. Texts*, V. pp. 431—433.

3 Honoured with gifts he shines afar, Agni
  adorable with song :
  The dripping ladle balms his face.

4 Agni with honey in his mouth, honoured
  with gifts, is balmed with oil,
  Refulgent in his wealth of light.

5 Praised by our hymns thou kindlest thee,
  Oblation-bearer, for the Gods :
  As such do mortals call on thee.

6 To that Immortal Agni pay worship with
  oil, ye mortal men,—
  Lord of the house, whom none deceives.

7 O Agni, burn the Rākṣasas with thine
  unconquerable flame :
  Shine guardian of Eternal Law.

8 So, Agni, with thy glowing face burn
  fierce against the female fiends,
  Shining among Urukṣayas.

9 Urukṣayas have kindled thee, Oblation-
  bearer, thee, with hymns.
  Best Worshipper among mankind.

HYMN CXIX.   *Indra.*

1. THIS, even this was my resolve, to win a
   cow, to win a steed :
   Have I not drunk of Soma juice?

2 Like violent gusts of wind the draughts
  that I have drunk have lifted me :
  Have I not drunk of Soma juice ?

3 The draughts I drank have borne me up,
  as fleet-foot horses draw a car :
  Have I not drunk of Soma juice ?

4 The hymn hath reached me, like a cow
  who lows to meet her darling calf:
  Have I not drunk of Soma juice ?

5 As a wright bends a chariot-seat so round
  my heart I bend the hymn :
  Have I not drunk of Soma juice ?

6 Not as a mote within the eye count the
  Five Tribes of men with me :
  Have I not drunk of Soma juice ?

7 The heavens and earth themselves have
  not grown equal to one half of me :
  Have I not drunk of Soma juice ?

8 *Urukṣayas* : members of the Ṛṣi's family.

———

The Ṛṣi is Indra himself in the form of Lava. He
describes his sensations after drinking Soma juice. But
see Bergaigne, I. 151, who considers it to be the utterance of an exhilarated mortal.

1 *To win a cow* : to strengthen and inspirit himself for
battle, and so to win kine and horses for his worshippers.

6 Sāyaṇa explains differently :—'The five castes have
not eluded the glance of my eye'.—Wilson.

8 I in my grandeur have surpassed the
  heavens and all this spacious earth :
  Have I not drunk of Soma juice ?

9 Aha ! this spacious earth will I deposit
  either here or there
  Have I not drunk of Soma juice ?

10 In one short moment will I smite the earth
   in fury here or there :
   Have I not drunk of Soma juice ?

11 One of my flanks is in the sky; I let the
   other trail below :
   Have I not drunk of Soma juice ?

12 I, greatest of the Mighty Ones, am lifted
   to the firmament :
   Have I not drunk of Soma juice ?

13 I seek the worshipper's abode ; oblation-
   bearer to the Gods :
   Have I not drunk of Soma juice ?

HYMN CXX.   *Indra.*

1. IN all the worlds That was the Best and
   Highest whence sprang the Mighty Gods,
   of splendid valour.
   As soon as born he overcomes his foemen,
   he in whom all who lend him aid are
   joyful.

2 Grown mighty in his strength, with ample
  vigour, he as a foe strikes fear into the
  Dāsa,
  Eager to win the breathing and the
  breathless. All sang thy praise at banquet and oblation.

3 All concentrate on thee their mental
  vigour, what time these, twice or thrice,
  are thine assistants.

11 Cp. III. 32. 11.

13 This stanza is difficult. The word *gṛho* is unintelligible, and *gṛham*, as Prof. Ludwig suggests, should perhaps, be read instead. *Oblation-bearer* : Indra, in his
excitement, fancies that he is Agni. Prof. Grassmann,
who with Dr. Muir, considers *gṛho* to mean servant or
minister, places the stanza in his Appendix as a fragment
from a hymn to Agni.
  The hymn has been translated by Dr. Muir, *O. S.
Texts* V. p. 91, by the authors of the *Siebenzig Lieder*, and
by Prof. Peterson,*Hymns from the Ṛgveda* (Bombay Sanskrit
Series).

1 *That* : meaning, according to Sāyaṇa, Brahmā the
original cause of the universe.

2 *Eager to win* : Prof. Ludwig makes *sḍsni* an infinitive.
Sḍsniḥ may be the correct reading. See Grassmann,
Wörterbuch zum Ṛgveda. *The breathing and the breathless* :
the animate and the inanimate world.

3 *Mental vigour* : *krátum* : 'adoration.'—Wilson. *These* :
Soma juices. *Twice or thrice* : with reference, perhaps,
to the three daily libations. *What is sweeter than the
sweet* : thine own celestial Soma. Sāyaṇa explains the
stanza differently :—'To thee all (worshippers) offer

Blend what is sweeter than the sweet with sweetness : win quickly with our meath that meath in battle.

4 Therefore in thee too, thou who winnest riches, at every banquet are the sages joyful.
With mightier power, Bold God, extend thy firmness : let not malignant Yātu-dhānas harm thee.

5 Proudly we put our trust in thee in battles, when we behold great wealth the prize of combat.
I with my words impel thy weapons onward, and sharpen with my prayer thy vital vigour.

6 Worthy of praises, many-shaped, most skilful, most energetic, Āptya of the Āptyas :
He with his might destroys the seven Dānus, subduing many who were deemed his equals.

7 Thou in that house which thy protection guardeth bestowest wealth, the higher and the lower.
Thou stablishest the two much-wandering Mothers, and bringest many deeds to their completion.

8 Brhaddiva, the foremost of light-winners, repeats these holy prayers, this strength of Indra.
He rules the great self-luminous fold of cattle, and all the doors of light hath he thrown open.

9 Thus hath Brhaddiva, the great Atharvan, spoken to Indra as himself in person.
The spotless Sisters, they who are his Mothers, with power exalt him and impel him onward.

HYMN CXXI.   Ka.

1. In the beginning rose Hiranyagarbha, born Only Lord of all created beings.
He fixed and holdeth up this earth and heaven. What God shall we adore with our oblation ?

2 Giver of vital breath, of power and vigour, he whose commandments all the Gods acknowledge :
The Lord of death, whose shade is life immortal. What God shall we adore with our oblation ?

3 Who by his grandeur hath become Sole Ruler of all the moving world that breathes and slumbers;
He who is Lord of men and Lord of cattle. What God shall we adore with our oblation ?

4 His, through his might, are these snow-covered mountains, and men call sea and Rasā his possession :
His arms are these, his are these heavenly regions. What God shall we adore with our oblation ?

5 By him the heavens are strong and earth is stedfast, by him light's realm and sky-vault are supported :
By him the regions in mid-air were measured. What God shall we adore with our oblation ?

6 To him, supported by his help, two armies embattled look while trembling in their spirit,
When over them the risen Sun is shining. What God shall we adore with our oblation ?

7 What time the mighty waters came, containing the universal germ, producing Agni,
Thence sprang the   Gods' one spirit into

adoration, whether these propitiators be two or three. Combine that which is sweeter than the sweet with sweetness, unite that honey with honey.'—Wilson. The 'two or three,' according to Sāyana, are the sacrificer and his wife and child, and the second half of the stanza contains a reference to the propagation of children.

6 Āptya : the name of a class of deities, of which Trita Āptya is the chief. 'Most accessible of the accessible.'—Wilson. The first line is without a verb : I praise him, may be understood. Dānus : a class of demons.

7 The higher and the lower : heavenly and earthly, Mothers : Heaven and Earth.

8 Foremost of light-winners : according to Sāyana, 'chief of Rsis and enjoyer of heaven, or servant of Āditya, the Sun, Indra.' Fold of cattle : the region of light.

9 The great Atharvan : 'the great priest.'—Grassmann. As himself : he identifies himself with the God whom he worships. The spotless Sisters, they who are his Mothers : according to Sāyana, the sister rivers which abide in the mother earth. Von Roth adopts the reading of Atharva-veda V. 2. 9. mātarišvarī, instead of the mātaribhvarīh of the text. Heaven and Earth appear to be intended.

Ka, kah, (quis) meaning Who ? that is, the Unknown God, has been applied as a name to Prajāpati, and to other Gods, from a forced interpretation of the interrogative pronoun which occurs in the refrain of each verse of the hymn. ———
1 Hiranyagarbha : literally 'the gold-germ; ' 'source of golden light; the Sun-god 'as the great power of the universe, from which all other powers and existences, divine and earthly, are derived, a conception which is the nearest approach to the later mystical conception of Brahmā, the creator of the world.'—Wallis. Which God : kásmai deváya : cui deo ? According to others: 'Worship we Ka the God with our oblation.' According to Ludwig, the meaning is 'What other God than Prajāpati shall we worship ?'
3 Breathes and slumbers : that is of Gods and men. Of men and......cattle : literally, 'of quadruped and biped.'
4 Sea : air. Rasā : the mythical river of the firmament. Cf. X. 108. 1.
7 Thence : from the coming of the waters. One spirit :

being. What God shall we adore with our oblation ?

8 He in his might surveyed the floods containing productive force and generating Worship.
He is the God of gods, and none beside him. What God shall we adore with our oblation ?

9 Ne'er may he harm us who is earth's Begetter, nor he whose laws are sure, the heavens' Creator,
He who brought forth the great and lucid waters. What God shall we adore with our oblation ?

10 Prajāpati ! thou only comprehendest all these created things, and none beside thee.
Grant us our hearts' desire when we invoke thee : may we have store of riches in possession.

HYMN CXXII. *Agni.*

1. I PRAISE the God of wondrous might like Indra, the lovely pleasant Guest whom all must welcome.
May Agni, Priest and Master of the household, give hero strength and all-sustaining riches.

2 O Agni, graciously accept this song of mine, thou passing wise who knowest every ordinance.
Enwrapped in holy oil further the course of prayer : the Gods bestow according to thy holy law.

3 Immortal, wandering round the seven stations, give, a liberal Giver, to the pious worshipper,

Wealth, Agni, with brave sons and ready for his use : welcome the man who comes with fuel unto thee.

4 The seven who bring oblations worship thee, the Strong, the first, the Great Chief Priest, Ensign of sacrifice,
The oil-anointed Bull, Agni who hears, who sends as God full hero strength to him who freely gives.

5 First messenger art thou, meet for election: drink thou thy fill invited to the Amṛta,
The Maruts in the votary's house adorned thee; with lauds the Bhṛgus gave thee light and glory.

6 Milking the teeming Cow for all-sustaining food. O Wise One, for the worship-loving worshipper,
Thou, Agni, dropping oil, thrice lighting works of Law, showest thy wisdom circling home and sacrifice.

7 They who at flushing of this dawn appointed thee their messenger, these men have paid thee reverence.
Gods strengthened thee for work that must be glorified, Agni, while they made butter pure for sacrifice.

8 Arrangers in our synods, Agni, while they sang, Vasiṣṭha's sons have called thee down, the Potent One.
Maintain the growth of wealth with men who sacrifice. Ye Gods, preserve us with your blessings evermore.

HYMN CXXIII. *Vena.*

1. SEE, Vena, born in light, hath driven hither, on chariot of the air, the Calves of Pṛśni.
Singers with hymns caress him as an infant there where the waters and the sunlight mingle.

2 Vena draws up his wave from out the ocean : mist-born, the fair one's back is

ékaḥ, one, in the text gives two superfluous syllables, and is suspicious.

8 *Generating Worship* : 'giving birth to sacrifice.' —Wilson.

10 *Prajāpati* : Lord of life, creatures or creation. Savitar the Sun-God is so called in IV. 53, 2, and Soma Pavamāna in IX. 5. 9. Prajāpati was afterwards the name of a separate God, the bestower of progeny and cattle, and sometimes invoked as the Creator.

The hymn has been translated by Dr. Muir, *O. S. Texts*, IV., pp. 16, 17; by Prof. Max Müller, *A. S. Lit.*, p. 569, and *Vedic Hymns, Part* I. (Sacred Books of the East, XXXII) p. 1. ; by Mr. Wallis, *Cosmology of the Ṛgveda*, p. 50f.; by Prof. Peterson, *Hymns from the Ṛgveda*; and by Dr. L. Scherman, *Philosophische Hymnen Aus der Ṛg-veda und-Atharva-veda-Saṁhitā*, p. 24.

1 *Like Indra* : *vásum ná* : like the Vasu, or chief Vasu. 'Like the sun'.—Wilson. *Riches* : or viands.

3 *Seven stations* : regions of the universe, according to Sāyaṇa.

4 *The seven* : the priests.

7 *Gods* : here meaning priests. 'Verily there are two kinds of gods ; for, indeed, the gods are the gods, and the Brāhmans who have studied and teach holy lore are the human gods'. (*Śatapatha-Brāhmaṇa*, II. 2. 2. 6; S. B. E. XII. 309).

Vena, 'the loving Sun' of I. 83, 5, *Kānta* or 'the beloved' is said by the Scholiast in this place to be *madhyasthāno devaḥ* 'the God of the middle region'. He is, apparently, the Sun as he rises in the mist and dew of the morning.

1 *Pṛśni*, the Speckled Cow, is the variegated cloud, and her *Calves* are the masses of mist which the Sun dispels.

2 *Ocean* : the sea of air. *On Order's summit* : 'on the summit of nature's course.'—Wallis. *Order*, here and in the following stanza, is Kosmos, the ordered or law-regulated universe. *Common birthplace* : the sky.

made apparent,
Brightly he shone aloft on Order's summit:
the hosts sang glory to their common
birthplace.

3 Full many, lowing to their joint-possession, dwelling together stood the Darling's Mothers.
Ascending to the lofty height of Order,
the bands of singers sip the sweets of
Amṛta.

4 Knowing his form, the sages yearned to
meet him: they have come nigh to hear
the wild Bull's bellow.
Performing sacrifice they reached the river:
for the Gandharva found the immortal
waters.

5 The Apsaras, the Lady, sweetly smiling,
supports her Lover in sublimest
heaven.
In his Friend's dwelling as a Friend he
wanders: he, Vena, rests him on his
golden pinion.

6 They gaze on thee with longing in their
spirit, as on a strong-winged bird that
mounteth sky-ward;
On thee with wings of gold, Varuṇa's
envoy, the Bird that hasteneth to the
home of Yama.

7 Erect, to heaven hath the Gandharva
mounted, pointing at us his many-coloured weapons;
Clad in sweet raiment beautiful to look on,
for he, as light, produceth forms that
please us.

8 When as a spark he cometh near the
ocean, still looking with a vulture's eye
to heaven,
His lustre, joying in its own bright splendour, maketh dear glories in the lowest
region.

HYMN CXXIV.   *Agni, Etc.*

1. COME to this sacrifice of ours, O Agni,
threefold, with seven threads and five
divisions.
Be our oblation-bearer and preceder: thou
hast lain long enough in during
darkness.

2 I come a God foreseeing from the godless
to immortality by secret pathways,
While I, ungracious one, desert the
gracious, leave mine own friends and
seek the kin of strangers.

3 I, looking to the guest of other lineage,
have founded many a rule of Law and
Order.
I bid farewell to the Great God, the Father,
and, for neglect, obtain my share of
worship.

4 I tarried many a year within this altar:
I leave the Father, for my choice is
Indra.
Away pass Agni, Varuṇa and Soma.
Rule ever changes: this I come to
favour.

3 *Joint-possession* : the child which they have produced
in common. *The Darling's Mothers* : the Dawns, or the
Waters, or the songs.

4 *The wild Bull's bellow* : the sound made by the dropping of Soma juice. *The Gandharva* : Vena, the rising Sun.

5 *The Apsaras* : the celestial nymph who symbolizes
the waters of heaven. *Her Lover* : Vena, the Gandharva,
Sūrya. 'Our hymn illustrates the two senses in which
the sun is brought into connection with the waters; first,
as penetrating with his beams the watery masses of the
sky, and secondly in the assimilation of his light to the
waters, as soma or ambrosia, whence the depths of light
become the aerial ocean. This association is stereotyped
in the union of the Gandharvas and the Apsarasas.'
—Wallis. *His Friend's dwelling* : the mansion of his
father Heaven.

6 *Varuṇa's envoy* : the setting sun. Cf. VII. 87. 6.
Yama : Cf. X. 14. 7.

7 *Clad in sweet raiment* : surabhi, sweet, may, as Mr.
Wallis conjectures, be a play on the word *gandhá*, occurring in the name Gandharva. Stanzas 7 and 8 merely
recapitulate, as Ludwig observes, the deeds of Sūrya, first
as the light of living men and then as the illuminator of
the regions below the earth.
The hymn is one of the obscurest in the whole Ṛgveda. Mahīdhara interprets Vena by *candra*, the Moon.
Wilson says : 'The general purport of the *Sūkta* makes it

(Vena) equivalent to the thunder-cloud'. Von Roth,
whom Grassmann follows, identifies Vena Gandharva
with the Rainbow. According to Ludwig Vena is the
Moon and the Gandharva is the Sun. Mr. Wallis has
translated and explained the hymn in his *Cosmology of
the Ṛgveda*, pp. 34 ff. For a different interpretation
see Hillebrandt, *V. M.*, I. 430ff. and Ludwig's criticisms
thereon (*Ueber die neuesten Arbeiten, u. s. w.*, p. 109f). See
also Bergaigne, II. 38—40

1 Indra speaks. *Threefold* : performed with three
daily libations; or comprising the *pākayajña*, the *haviryajña*,
and the *somayajña*, the simple domestic oblation, the
oblation of clarified butter, etc., and the offering of
Soma juice. *With seven threads* : conducted by the seven
chief priests. *With five divisions* : with five oblations,
or regulated by the Yajamāna and four of the chief priests,
according to Sāyaṇa. The exact meaning is uncertain.

2 Agni speaks. He has left Varuṇa, originally the
Supreme Deity, whose power was waning, and associated
himself with Indra who has superseded that God. *From
the godless* : from Varuṇa who in the decline of his supremacy has neglected Agni and sacrifice. Sāyaṇa interprets the first line differently :—'From being no divinity
I issue a divinity from the cave at the solicitation (of the
gods), and being manifest I attain immortality.'—
Wilson. *Seek the kin of strangers* : come to be born and
domesticated in a new place, with Indra.

3 *Of other lineage* : of the other branch : terrestrial
fire. *Father* : Varuṇa.

4 *Within this altar* : or, close to this Varuṇa. *This* :
the supremacy of Indra.

5 These Asuras have lost their powers of
  magic. But thou, O Varuṇa, if thou
  dost love me,
  O King, discerning truth and right from
  falsehood, come and be Lord and Ruler
  of my kingdom.

6 Here is the light of heaven, here all is
  lovely; here there is radiance, here is air's
  wide region.
  Let us two · slaughter Vṛtra. Forth, O
  Soma! Thou art oblation: we therewith
  will serve thee.

7 The Sage hath fixed his form by wisdom
  in the heavens: Varuṇa with no violence
  let the waters flow.
  Like women-folk, the floods that bring
  prosperity have caught his hue and
  colour as they gleamed and shone.

8 These wait upon his loftiest power and
  vigour: he dwells in these who triumph in
  their Godhead;
  And they, like people who elect their ruler,
  have in abhorrence turned away from
  Vṛtra.

9 They call him Swan, the abhorrent floods'
  Companion, moving in friendship with
  celestial Waters.
  The poets in their thought have looked on
  Indra swiftly approaching when Anuṣṭup
  calls him.

HYMN CXXV.   *Vāk.*

1. I TRAVEL with the Rudras and the Vasus,
  with the Ādityas and All-Gods I
  wander.

I hold aloft both Varuṇa and Mitra,
Indra and Agni, and the Pair of
Aśvins.

2 I cherish and sustain high-swelling Soma,
  and Tvaṣṭar I support, Pūṣan, and
  Bhaga.
  I load with wealth the zealous sacrificer
  who pours the juice and offers his
  oblation

3 I am the Queen, the gatherer-up of
  treasures, most thoughtful, first of those
  who merit worship.
  Thus Gods have stablished me in many
  places with many homes to enter and
  abide in.

4 Through me alone all eat the food that
  feeds them,—each man who sees,
  breathes, hears the word outspoken
  They know it not, but yet they dwell beside
  me. Hear, one and all, the truth as I
  declare it.

5 I, verily, myself announce and utter the
  word that Gods and men alike shall
  welcome.
  I make the man I love exceeding mighty,
  make him a sage, a Ṛṣi, and a
  Brahman.

6 I bend the bow for Rudra that his arrow
  may strike and slay the hater of
  devotion.
  I rouse and order battle for the people,
  and I have penetrated Earth and
  Heaven.

7 On the world's summit I bring forth the
  Father: my home is in the waters, in
  the ocean.

---

5 *Indra speaks. These Asuras :* Agni, Varuṇa, and
Soma. *Come and be Lord :* Indra offers Varuṇa spiritual
and moral sovereignty as compensation for his loss of
general supremacy.

6 *Let us two :* the exhortation is addresssed by Indra
to Soma. *Vṛtra:* regarded as in league with Varuṇa, the
fiendish enemy in the shape of Varuṇa.

7 *The Sage :* perhaps Soma, in answer to Indra's appeal;
Mitra, according to Sāyaṇa.

8 *His loftiest power :* the supreme might of Indra.

9 This stanza appears to have been added on account
of the occurrence of the word *bibhatsūnām* (abhorrentium)
which seems to connect it with the preceding stanza
where *bibhatsuvaḥ* (abhorrentes) occurs. *Swan : haṁsa :*
Sūrya the Sun-God is sometimes so called. Cf. IV. 40. 5.
Swiftly approaching when Anuṣṭup calls him : 'or the ceaselessly moving Indra, who is worthy to be praised with
an *Anuṣṭubh.*'—Wilson. Or, 'dancing the Anuṣṭup,'
according to Prof. Max Müller's interpretation.

M. Bergaigne has translated and explained this hymn.

See *La Religion Védique,* III. pp. 145—149. See also
Book IV. 42, for hints of the rivalry between Varuṇa and
Indra.

———

Vāk is Speech personified, the Word, the first creation
and representative of Spirit, and the means of communication between men and Gods. Here she is said to be
the daughter of the Ṛṣi Ambhṛṇa.

7 *The Father :* Heaven or Sky, produced from Vāk
identified with Paramātmā, the supreme and universal
Soul.

The hymn has been translated by Colebrooke, *Miscellaneous Essays,* I. 32; by the authors of the *Siebenzig
Lieder ;* by Prof. Peterson, *Hymns from the Ṛgveda* (Bombay
Sanskrit Series); and by Prof. Whitney, Notes to Colebrooke's *Essay on the Vedas,* p. 113.

Mr. Wallis observes : 'Vāc, 'Speech' is celebrated
alone in two whole hymns, X. 71 and X. 125, of which
the former shows that the primary application of the
name was to the voice of the hymn, the means of communication between heaven and earth at the sacrifice.
The other hymn illustrates the constant assimilation of
the varied phenomena of nature to the sacrifice; all
that has a voice in nature, the thunder of the storm, the
reawaking of life at dawn, with songs of rejoicing over
the new birth of the world, are embodied in this Vāc in
the same way as it is said of Bṛhaspati, that he embraces
all things that are. It is thus another expression for
that idea of the unity of the world, which we have seen
crowning the mystical speculations of all the more abstract
hymns of the collection.'—*Cosmology of the Ṛgveda,* p. 85.

Thence I extend o'er all existing creatures,
and touch even yonder heaven with my
forehead.

8 I breathe a strong breath like the wind
and tempest, the while I hold together
all existence.

Beyond this wide earth and beyond the
heavens I have become so mighty in my
grandeur.

HYMN CXXVI. *Viśvedevas.*

1. No peril, no severe distress, ye Gods,
affects the mortal man,

Whom Aryaman and Mitra lead, and
Varuṇa, of one accord, beyond his foes.

2 This very thing do we desire, Varuṇa,
Mitra, Aryaman,

Whereby ye guard the mortal man from
sore distress, and lead him safe beyond
his foes.

3 These are, each one, our present helps,
Varuṇa, Mitra, Aryaman.

Best leaders, best deliverers to lead
us on and bear as safe beyond our
foes.

4 Ye compass round and guard each man,
Varuṇa, Mitra, Aryaman:

In your dear keeping may we be, ye who
are excellent as guides beyond our
foes.

5 Ādityas are beyond all foes,—Varuna,
Mitra, Aryaman:

Strong Rudra with the Marut host,
Indra, Agni let us call for weal beyond
our foes.

6 These lead us safely over all, Varuṇa,
Mitra, Aryaman,

These who are Kings of living men, over
all troubles far away beyond our foes.

7 May they give bliss to aid us well, Varuṇa,
Mitra, Aryaman:

May the Ādityas, when we pray, grant us
wide shelter and defence beyond our
foes.

8 As in this place, O Holy Ones, ye Vasus
freed even the Gaurī when her feet were
fettered.

So free us now from trouble and affliction:
and let our life be lengthened still,
O Agni.

See also Weber, Vāc *Indische Studien,* IX. 473—480;
and Max Müller, *The Vedānta Philosophy,* 144—147.

---

8 *Gauri :* the wild-cow, the female of the Gaura or
Bos Gaurus. The Vasus are said to have delivered her
from Viśvāvasu the Gandharva.

HYMN CXXVII. *Night.*

1. WITH all her eyes the Goddess Night looks
forth approaching many a spot:
She hath put all her glories on.

2 Immortal. she hath filled the waste,
the Goddess hath filled height and
depth:
She conquers darkness with her light.

3 The Goddess as she comes hath set the
Dawn her Sister in her place:
And then the darkness vanishes.

4 So favour us this night, O thou whose
pathways we have visited
As birds their nest upon the tree.

5 The villagers have sought their homes,
and all that walks and all that flies,
Even the falcons fain for prey.

6 Keep off the she-wolf and the wolf; O
Ūrmyā, keep the thief away;
Easy be thou for us to pass.

7 Clearly hath she come nigh to me who
decks the dark with richest hues:
O Morning, cancel it like debts.

8 These have I brought to thee like
kine. O Night, thou Child of Heaven,
accept
This laud as for a conqueror.

HYMN CXXVIII. *Viśvedevas.*

1. LET me win glory, Agni, in our battles:
enkindling thee, may we support our
bodies.

May the four regions bend and bow before
me: with thee for guardian may we win
in combat.

2 May all the Gods be on my side in
battle, the Maruts led by Indra,
Viṣṇu, Agni.

Mine be the middle air's extended
region, and may the wind blow favouring
these my wishes.

3 May the Gods grant me riches; may the
blessing and invocation of the Gods
assist me.

Foremost in fight be the divine Invokers:

---

2 *The waste :* the expanded (firmament).'—Wilson.
6 *Ūrmyā :* 'undulating'; Night.
8 *These :* verses.

---

1 *The four regions :* the King who is praying for assistance is about to undertake a *Digvijaya,* the subjugation
of all neighbouring countries in all directions.
3 *Divine Invokers :* the Hotar-priests of the Gods.
Sāyaṇa explains differently :—'may my invokers of the
gods be the first to propitiate them.'—Wilson.

may we, unwounded, have brave heroes round us.

4 For me let them present all mine oblations, and let my mind's intention be accomplished.

May I be guiltless of the least transgression : and, all ye Gods, do ye combine to bless us.

5 Ye six divine Expanses, grant us freedom: here, all ye Gods, acquit yourselves like heroes.

Let us not lose our children or our bodies: let us not benefit the foe, King Soma !

6 Baffling the wrath of our opponents, Agni, guard us as our infallible Protector.

Let these thy foes turn back and seek their houses, and let their thought who watch at home be ruined.

7 Lord of the world, Creator of creators : the saviour God who overcomes the foeman.

May Gods, Bṛhaspati, both Aśvins shelter from ill this sacrifice and sacrificer.

8 Foodful, and much-invoked, at this our calling may the great Bull vouchsafe us wide protection.

Lord of Bay Coursers, Indra, bless our children : harm us not, give us not as prey to others.

9 Let those who are our foemen stay afar from us : with Indra and with Agni we will drive them off.

Vasus, Ādityas, Rudras have exalted me, made me far-reaching, mighty, thinker, sovran lord.

HYMN CXXIX. *Creation.*

1. THEN was not non-existent nor existent : there was no realm of air, no sky beyond it.

5 *Six divine Expanses* : the four cardinal points and upper and lower spaces; or, according to Sāyaṇa, Heaven, Earth, Day, Night, Water, and Plants.

7 After *Creator of creators* Sāyaṇa supplies *taṁ devaṁ staumi*, 'that God I praise'. Indra or Savitar is intended.

8 *The great Bull* : Indra.

1 *Then* : in the beginning. *Non-existent* : *ásat* : that does not yet actually exist, but which has in itself the latent potentiality of existence. 'There was a certain unapparent condition,' says an Indian Commentator, which, from the absence of distinctness, was not an 'entity,' while from its being the instrument of the world's production, it was not a 'non-entity.'

What covered in, and where ? and what gave shelter ? Was water there, unfathomed depth of water ?

2 Death was not then, nor was there aught immortal : no sign was there, the day's and night's divider.

That One Thing, breathless, breathed by its own nature : apart from it was nothing whatsoever.

3 Darkness there was : at first concealed in darkness this All was indiscriminated chaos.

All that existed then was void and formless : by the great power of Warmth was born that Unit.

4 Thereafter rose Desire in the beginning, Desire, the primal seed and germ of Spirit.

Sages who searched with their heart's thought discovered the existent's kinship in the non-existent.

5 Transversely was their severing line extended : what was above it then, and what below it ?

There were begetters, there were mighty forces, free action here and energy up yonder

6 Who verily knows and who can here declare it, whence it was born and whence comes this creation ?

The Gods are later than this world's pro-

2 *That One Thing* : the single primordial substance, the unit out of which the universe was developed. Cp. I. 164. 6 and 46.

3 *Warmth* : Prof. Wilson, following Sāyaṇa, translates *tápasaḥ* by 'austerity,' meaning the contemplation of the things that were to be created. M. Burnouf, in *La Science des Religions*, pp. 207ff., has shown how *warmth* was regarded by the Āryas as the principle explaining movement, life, and thought.

4 *Desire* : Kāma, Eros, or Love. *Sages* : ancient Ṛṣis.

5 *Line* : a line drawn by the ancient Ṛṣis to make a division between the upper world and the lower, and to bring duality out of unity. *Begetters* : the Fathers may be meant. *Free action* : the happiness of the Fathers. The stanza is obscure, and its connection with stanza 4 is not obvious. An intervening stanza may, perhaps, have been lost.

The hymn has been translated by Colebrooke, *Miscellaneous Essays*, I. pp. 33, 34; by Dr. Muir, *O. S. Texts*, V. 356, 357; by the authors of the *Siebenzig Lieder*, and by Mr. Wallis, *Cosmology of the Ṛgveda*, pp. 59 ff. 'The latest of the many Commentators on this hymn are Professor Whitney in the Journal of the American Oriental Society, vol. xi. p. cix, and Dr. Scherman, Philosophische Hymnen aus der Ṛg-und-Atharva-veda Saṁhitā 1887.'—Wallis. See Prof. Max Müller, *History of Ancient Literature*, pp. 559—563.

duction. Who knows then whence it first came into being ?

7 He, the first origin of this creation, whether he formed it all or did not form it,
Whose eye controls this world in highest heaven, he verily knows it, or perhaps he knows not.

HYMN CXXX. *Creation.*

1. THE sacrifice drawn out with threads on every side, stretched by a hundred sacred ministers and one,—
This do these Fathers weave who hitherward are come : they sit beside the warp and cry, Weave forth, weave back.

2 The Man extends it and the Man unbinds it : even to this vault of heaven hath he outspun it.
These pegs are fastened to the seat of worship : they made the Sāma-hymns their weaving shuttles.

3 What were the rule, the order and the model ? What were the wooden fender and the butter ?
What were the hymn, the chant, the recitation, when to the God all Deities paid worship ?

4 Closely was Gāyatrī conjoined with Agni, and closely Savitar combined with Uṣṇih.
Brilliant with Ukthas, Soma joined Anuṣṭup : Bṛhaspati's voice by Bṛhatī was aided.

5 Virāj adhered to Varuṇa and Mitra : here Triṣṭup day by day was Indra's portion.
Jagatī entered all the Gods together : so by this knowledge men were raised to Ṛṣis.

6 So by this knowledge men were raised to Ṛṣis, when ancient sacrifice sprang up, our Fathers.
With the mind's eye I think that I behold them who first performed this sacrificial worship.

7 They who were versed in ritual and metre, in hymns and rules, were the Seven Godlike Ṛṣis.
Viewing the path of those of old, the sages have taken up the reins like chariot-drivers.

HYMN CXXXI. *Indra.*

1. DRIVE all our enemies away, O Indra, the western, mighty Conqueror, and the eastern.
Hero, drive off our northern foes and southern, that we in thy wide shelter may be joyful.

2 Wnat then ? As men whose fields are full of barley reap the ripe corn removing it in order,
So bring the food of those men, bring it hither, who went not to prepare the grass for worship.

3 Men come not with one horse at sacred seasons ; thus they obtain no honour in assemblies.
Sages desiring herds of kine and horses strengthen the mighty Indra for his friendship.

4 Ye, Aśvins, Lords of Splendour, drank full draughts of grateful Soma juice,
And aided Indra in his work with Namuci of Asura birth.

As the subject of the hymn is creation typified and originated by the mysterious primeval sacrifice (cp. X. 90), Prajāpati the Creator is said by Sāyaṇa to be the deity. The Ṛṣi is Yajña (Sacrifice) Prajāpati's son.

1 *The sacrifice* : *sargātmako yajñaḥ* : the sacrifice which constitutes creation.—Sāyaṇa. *A hundred and one* : meaning an indefinitely large number. *Fathers* : Sāyaṇa explains *pitáraḥ* here by *pālakāḥ*, protectors, the Gods.

2 *The Man* : the first Man or Male ; Puruṣa, Ādipuruṣa, Prajāpati, according to Sāyaṇa.

3 *Wooden fender* : the enclosing sticks placed round the sacrificial fire.

4 *Brilliant with Ukthas* : 'gladdening (us) through hymns (*ukthas*).'—Muir. *Bṛhaspati's voice* : because his duty was to speak as Priest. According to the *Aitareya Brāhmaṇa*, III. 13, Prajāpati 'alloted to the deities their (different) parts in the sacrifice and metres.'.

5 *Day by day* : was Indra's portion of the mid-day (oblation).'—Wilson.

6 *I behold them* : or, according to Prof. Ludwig's interpretation :—'These with the eyes of mind, I think, beheld them.'

7 'The seven Ṛṣis here are not the Aṅgirases, but Bharadvāja, Kaśyapa, Gotama, Atri, Vasiṣṭha, Viśvāmitra, and Jamadagni. The knowledge of the ritual is derived from the divine priests ; the sages or Ṛṣis have followed them in sacrificing, and modern priests are only imitators of those who preceded them.'—Ludwig.
The hymn has been translated by Dr. Muir, *O. S. Texts*, III. pp. 278, 279 and by Prof. Whitney, Notes to Colebrooke's *Essay on the Vedas*, p. 114.

3 *With one horse* : it seems to have been considered undignified and disreputable for a wealthy man to come to the sacrifice in a one-horse car ; but the precise meaning of the first line is somewhat uncertain.

4 Hillebrandt, *V. M.*, I. 146, and Eggeling, *Sacred Books of the East*, XLI. 135, interpret differently. The myth referred to in the following stanza has not been preserved. See Weber, *Ueber den Rājasūya*, pp. 95, 101.

5 As parents aid a son, both Aśvins, Indra,
    aided thee with their wondrous powers
    and wisdom.
  When thou, with might, hadst drunk the
    draught that gladdens, Sarasvatī, O
    Maghavan, refreshed thee.

6 Indra is strong to save, rich in assistance :
    may he, possessing all, be kind and
    gracious.
  May he disperse our foes and give us
    safety, and may we be the lords of hero
    vigour.

7 May we enjoy his favour, his the Holy :
    may we enjoy his blessed loving kindness.
  May this rich Indra, as our good Protector,
    drive off and keep afar all those who
    hate us.

HYMN CXXXII.   *Mitra. Varuṇa.*

1. MAY Dyaus the Lord of lauded wealth,
    and Earth stand by the man who offers
    sacrifice,
  And may the Aśvins, both the Gods, stren-
    gthen the worshipper with bliss.

2 As such we honour you, Mitra and Varuna,
    with hasty zeal, most blest, you who
    sustain the folk.
  So may we, through your friendship for
    the worshipper, subdue the fiends.

3 And when we seek to win your love and
    friendship, we who have precious wealth
    in our possession,
  Or when the worshipper augments his riches,
    let not his treasures be shut up

4 That other, Asura ! too was born of
    Heaven : thou art, O Varuna, the King
    of all men.
  The chariot's Lord was well content,
    forbearing to anger Death by sin so
    great.
  This sin hath Śakapūta here committed.
    Heroes who fled to their dear friend he
    slayeth,
  When the Steed bringeth down your grace
    and favour in bodies dear and worship-
    ful.

6 Your Mother Aditi, ye wise, was purified
    with water even as earth is purified from
    heaven.
  Show love and kindness here below : wash
    her in rays of heavenly light.

7 Ye Twain have seated you as Lords of
    Wealth, as one who mounts a car to
    him who sits upon the pole, upon the
    wood.
  These our disheartened tribes Nṛmedhas
    saved from woe, Sumedhas saved from
    woe.

HYMN CXXXIII.   *Indra.*

1. SING strength to Indra that shall set his
    chariot in the foremost place.
  Giver of room in closest fight, slayer of
    foes in shock of war, be thou our great
    encourager. Let the weak bowstrings
    break upon the bows of feeble enemies.

2 Thou didst destroy the Dragon : thou
    sentest the rivers down to earth.
  Foeless, O Indra, wast thou born. Thou
    tendest well each choicest thing. There-
    fore we draw us close to thee. Let the
    weak bowstrings, etc.

3 Destroyed be all malignities and all our
    enemy's designs.
  Thy bolt thou castest at the foe, O Indra,
    who would smite us dead : thy liberal
    bounty gives us wealth.

4 The robber people round about, Indra,
    who watch and aim at us,—
  Trample them down beneath thy foot ; a
    conquering scatterer art thou.

5 Whoso assails us, Indra, be the man a
    stranger or akin,
  Bring down, thyself, his strength although
    it be as vast as are the heavens.

6 Close to thy friendship do we cling, O
    Indra, and depend on thee.
  Lead us beyond all pain and grief along
    the path of holy Law.

7 Do thou bestow upon us her, O Indra,
    who yields according to the singer's
    longing,
  That the great Cow may, with exhaustless
    udder, pouring a thousand streams, give
    milk to feed us.

---

4 *That other* : Mitra. *The chariot's Lord* : literally,
'head of the chariot.' The meaning is uncertain. I find
the rest of the hymn unintelligible. Prof. Ludwig conjectures that two brothers, Nṛmedhas and Sumedhas,
had contended for sovereignty, and that the adherents
of one had wished to put the other brother to death,
but had not carried out their purpose. Śakapūta absolves
and purifies the former, and the brothers are reconciled.

5 *The Steed* : the Sun.—Ludwig. *Your grace* : Mitra's
and Varuṇa's.

---

6 *Your Mother Aditi* : perhaps the mother of the two
brothers is intended.—Ludwig.

---

2 *Let the weak bowstrings, etc.*: the refrain is repeated
in all the stanzas except the last.

7 *The great Cow* : probably the Earth.

HYMN CXXXIV. *Indra.*

1. As, like the Morning, thou hast filled, O
Indra, both the earth and heaven.
So as the Mighty One, great King of all
the mighty world of men, the Goddess
Mother brought thee forth, the Blessed
Mother gave thee life.

2 Relax that mortal's stubborn strength
whose heart is bent on wickedness.
Trample him down beneath thy feet who
watches for and aims at us. The Goddess
Mother brought thee forth, etc.

3 Shake down, O Slayer of the foe, those
great all splendid energies.
With all thy powers, O Śakra, all thine
helps, O Indra, shake them down :

4 As thou, O Śatakratu, thou, O Indra,
shakest all things down
As wealth for him who sheds the juice,
with thine assistance thousandfold.

5 Around, on every side like drops of sweat
let lightning-flashes fall.
Let all malevolence pass away from us like
threads of Dūrvā grass.

6 Thou bearest in thine hand a lance like a
long hook, great Counsellor !
As with his foremost foot a goat, draw
down the branch, O Maghavan.

7 Never, O Gods, do we offend, nor are
we ever obstinate : we walk as holy
texts command.
Closely we clasp and cling to you, cling to
your sides, beneath your arms.

HYMN CXXXV. *Yama.*

1. In the Tree clothed with goodly leaves
where Yama drinketh with the Gods,
The Father, Master of the house, tendeth
with love our ancient Sires.

2 I looked reluctantly on him who cherishes
those men of old,
On him who treads that evil path, and
then I yearned for this again.

1 *The Goddess Mother* : Aditi. The refrain is repeated
in all the stanzas except the last.

3 *Energies* : influences in the shape of rain and sunlight.

4 *Śatakratu* : or, Lord of Hundred Powers.

5 *Dūrvā grass* : Panicum Dactylon; a species of bent
grass whose filaments stretch horizontally away from the
stem.

6 *The branch* : that is loaded with fruit for us.

1 *The Tree* : where the spirits of the pious dead rest
after their labours. *The Father* : Yama.

2 The spirit of the dead child speaks. *I yearned for this* :
to return to the world of life.

3 Thou mountest, though thou dost not see,
O Child, the new and wheel-less car
Which thou hast fashioned mentally, one-
poled but turning every way.

4 The car which thou hast made to roll
hitherward from the Sages, Child !
This hath the Sāman followed close, hence,
laid together on a ship.

5 Who was the father of the child ? Who
made the chariot roll away ?
Who will this day declare to us how the
funeral gift was made ?

6 When the funeral gift was placed, straightway the point of flame appeared.
A depth extended in the front : a passage
out was made behind.

7 Here is the seat where Yama dwells, that
which is called the Home of Gods :
Here minstrels blow the flute for him :
here he is glorified with songs.

HYMN CXXXVI. *Keśins.*

1. He with the long loose locks supports
Agni, and moisture, heaven, and earth :
He is all sky to look upon : he with long
hair is called this light.

2 The Munis, girdled with the wind, wear
garments soiled of yellow hue.
They, following the wind's swift course
go where the Gods have gone before.

3 Yama speaks. *Fashioned mentally* : figuratively prepared by being burnt on the funeral pile.

4 *Ship* : meaning, apparently, the funeral pile. *The
funeral gift* : the meaning of *anudeyī* is uncertain. 'Restitution.'—Wilson. 'Surrender' or 'delivery,' according
to Prof. Zimmer. Stanzas 5—7 are spoken by the poet.

6 *A depth* : the meaning is obscure. *Passage out* :
probably for the removal of the ashes.

The subject of the hymn appears to be the funeral
ceremony of a boy (*kumāra*, said by some to be the name
of a man). According to the legend cited by Sāyaṇa
a youth named Naciketas was sent by his father to the
kingdom of Yama who treated him kindly and allowed
him to return to this world. 'The hymn is made throughout applicable to *Āditya* as well as to Yama, with, if
possible, a still greater degree of obscurity. It seems to
have been the basis of the discussion in the Taittirīya
Brāhmaṇa (III. 11. 8) and in the Katha Upaniṣad,
respecting what becomes of the soul after death, in
dialogues between *Naciketas* and Yama.'—Wilson.

The Keśins, *keśinaḥ*, wearers of long loose hair, are
Agni, Vāyu, and Sūrya. Each stanza has for its Ṛṣi one
of the seven sons of Vātaraśana. See Index of Hymns.

1 *He with the long loose locks* : probably the ascetic, the
Muni or Yogī. According to Sāyaṇa, the radiant Sun.
Moisture : *viṣām*, usually meaning 'poison' is so explained
in this place.

2 *Munis* : ascetics inspired or in a state of ecstasy.
Girdled with the wind : exposed without girdles to the wind.
According to Sāyaṇa, sons of Vātaraśana, or Wind-Girdled.

3 Transported with our Munihood we have
pressed on into the winds :
You therefore, mortal men, behold our
natural bodies and no more.

4 The Muni, made associate in the holy
work of every God,
Looking upon all varied forms flies through
the region of the air.

5 The Steed of Vāta, Vāyu's friend, the
Muni, by the Gods impelled,
In both the oceans hath his home, in
eastern and in western sea.

6 Treading the path of sylvan beasts,
Gandharvas, and Apsarases,
He with long locks, who knows the wish,
is a sweet most delightful friend

7 Vāyu hath churned for him : for him he
poundeth things most hard to bend,
When he with long loose locks hath drunk,
with Rudra, water from the cup.

HYMN CXXXVII.   *Viśvedevas.*

1. YE Gods, raise up once more the man
whom ye have humbled and brought
low.
O Gods, restore to life again the man who
hath committed sin.

2 Two several winds are blowing here, from
Sindhu, from a distant land.
May one breathe energy to thee, the other
blow disease away.

3 Hither, O Wind, blow healing balm, blow
all disease away, thou Wind ;
For thou who hast all medicine comest
as envoy of the Gods.

5 *In both the oceans* : everywhere in the firmament
from its eastern to its western extremity.

'The hymn shows the conception that by a life of
sanctity the Muni can attain to the fellowship of the
deities of the air, the Vāyus, the Rudras, the Apsarasas,
and the Gandharvas; and, furnished like them with
wonderful powers, can travel along with them on their
course......The beautiful-haired, the long-haired, that
is to say, the Muni, who during the time of his austerities does not shave his hair, upholds fire, moisture, heaven,
and earth, and resembles the world of light, ideas which
the later literature so largely contains.'—Von Roth, quoted
by Dr. Muir, *O. S. Texts*, IV. 319, the hymn being transliterated and translated on page 318.

Each stanza is ascribed to one of the seven great
Ṛṣis. See Index of Hymns. The hymn is a charm to
restore a sick man to health. Cf. *Hymns of the Atharva-veda*,
IV. 13.

1 *Who hath committed sin* : sickness and death being
regarded as the consequence of sin.

2 *Sindhu* : or, ocean.

4 I am come nigh to thee with balms to
give thee rest and keep thee safe.
I bring thee blessed strength, I drive thy
weakening malady away.

5 Here let the Gods deliver him, the Maruts'
band deliver him :
All things that be deliver him that he be
freed from his disease.

6 The Waters have their healing power, the
Waters drive disease away.
The Waters have a balm for all : let
them make medicine for thee.

7 The tongue that leads the voice precedes.
Then with our ten-fold branching hands,
With these two chasers of disease we
stroke thee with a gentle touch.

HYMN CXXXVIII.   *Indra.*

1. ALLIED with thee in friendship, Indra,
these thy priests, remembering Holy
Law, rent Vṛtra limb from limb,
When they bestowed the Dawns and let
the waters flow, and when thou didst
chastise dragons at Kutsa's call.

2 Thou sentest forth productive powers,
clavest the hills, thou dravest forth the
kine, thou drankest pleasant meath.
Thou gavest increase through this Tree's
surpassing might.
The Sun shone by the hymn that sprang
from Holy Law.

3 In the mid-way of heaven the Sun unyoked his car : the Ārya found a
match to meet his Dāsa foe.
Associate with Ṛjiśvan Indra overthrew
the solid forts of Pipru, conjuring
Asura.

4 He boldly cast down forts which none
had e'er assailed: unwearied he destroyed the godless treasure-stores.

4 *The Wind speaks. Weakening malady : yákṣma* may
be sickness in general, or the name of a large class of
diseases, probably of a consumptive nature.

7 The stanza is important as showing that the Indians
employed touches or laying-on of hands to relieve suffering or to restore health. Cp. X. 60. 12.

1 *Thy priests* : the Aṅgirases. But see *Vedic Hymns*, I.
p. 44. *Didst chastise* : this clause is very difficult. I adopt
Prof. Grassmann's interpretation.

2 *This Tree's surpassing might* : the power of the juice
of the Soma plant.

3 *Unyoked his car* : the allusion is, perhaps, to an eclipse,
or a detention of the Sun to enable the Āryans to complete the overthrow of their enemies. *Ṛjiśvan* : a pious
worshipper befriended by Indra. *Pipru* : a demon of
drought. See Vol. I., Index.

Like Sun and Moon he took the stronghold's wealth away, and, praised in
song, demolished foes with flashing
dart.

5 Armed with resistless weapons, with vast
power to cleave, the Vṛtra-slayer whets
his darts and deals forth wounds.
Bright Uṣas was afraid of Indra's
slaughtering bolt : she went upon her
way and left her chariot there.

6 These are thy famous exploits, only thine,
when thou alone hast left the other reft
of sacrifice.
Thou in the heavens hast set the ordering
of the Moons : the Father bears the
felly portioned out by thee.

HYMN CXXXIX. Savitar.

1. SAVITAR, golden-haired, hath lifted eastward, bright with the sunbeams, his
eternal lustre;
He in whose energy wise Pūṣan marches,
surveying all existence like a herdsman.

2 Beholding men he sits amid the heavens,
filling the two world-halves and air's
wide region.
He looks upon the rich far-spreading
pastures between the eastern and the
western limit.

3 He, root of wealth, the gatherer-up of
treasures, looks with his might on every
form and figure.
Savitar, like a God whose Law is constant,
stands in the battle for the spoil like
Indra.

4 Waters from sacrifice came to the Gandharva Viśvāvasu, O Soma, when they
saw him.
Indra, approaching quickly, marked their
going, and looked around upon the
Sun's enclosures.

5 This song Viśvāvasu shall sing us, meter
of air's mid-realm celestial Gandharva,
That we may know aright both truth and
falsehood: may he inspire our thoughts
and help our praises.

6 In the floods' track he found the booty-
seeker : the rocky cow-pen's doors he
threw wide open.
These, the Gandharva told him, flowed
with Amṛta. Indra knew well the puissance of the dragons.

HYMN CXL. Agni.

1. AGNI, life-power and fame are thine :
thy fires blaze mightily, thou rich in
wealth of beams !
Sage, passing bright, thou givest to the
worshipper, with strength, the food that
merits laud.

2 With brilliant, purifying sheen, with
perfect sheen thou liftest up thyself in
light.
Thou, visiting both thy Mothers, aidest
them as Son : thou joinest close the
earth and heaven.

3 O Jātavedas, Son of Strength, rejoice
thyself, gracious, in our fair hymns and
songs.
In thee are treasured various forms of
strengthening food, born nobly and of
wondrous help.

4 Agni, spread forth, as Ruler, over living
things : give wealth to us, Immortal
God.
Thou shinest out from beauty fair to look
upon : thou leadest us to conquering
power.

5 To him, the wise, who orders sacrifice,
who hath great riches under his control,
Thou givest blest award of good, and
plenteous food, givest him wealth that
conquers all.

---

5 *Bright Uṣas was afraid* : see II. 15. 6, IV. 30. 8—11,
and X. 73. 6.

6 *The other* : thy foe, the demon or Rākṣasa. *The
Father* : Dyaus or Heaven. *The felly portioned out by thee* :
the course of the Moon through the asterisms, which
thou hast arranged.

2 *Pastures* : there is no substantive in the text. Sāyaṇa
supplies 'quarters of space;' Ludwig 'ladles;' and
Grassmann 'pastures.'

4 *Waters* : used in the preparation of the Soma juice.
The Gandharva : regarded as the custodian of the celestial
Soma. *The Sun's enclosures* : 'the rims of the sun.'—Wilson.

5 *Viśvāvasu* : the celestial Gandharva, here the Sun-
God. *He* : Viśvāvasu.

6 *The booty-seeker* : Indra who sought to win the
waters. *Of the dragons* : the serpentdemons who obstructed the floods of heaven. The last three stanzas
are very difficult and obscure. See Hillebrandt,
V. M., I. pp. 436, 437, and Ludwig, *Ueber die neuesten
A. u. s. w.*, p. 101.

2 *Thy Mothers* : Heaven and Earth. *Joinest close* : or,
fillest full.

5 *To him* : to the institutor of the sacrifice.
See the exposition of the hymn in *Śatapatha Brāhmaṇa*, VII. 3. 1. 29—34 (*Sacred Books of the East*, XLI.
349—351).

6 The men have set before them for their
welfare Agni, strong, visible to all, the
Holy.
Thee, Godlike One, with ears to hear,
most famous, men's generations magnify
with praise-songs.

HYMN CXLI.   *Viśvedevas.*

1. TURN hither, Agni, speak to us : come
to us with a gracious mind.
Enrich us, Master of the house : thou art
the Giver of our wealth.

2 Let Aryaman vouchsafe us wealth, and
Bhaga, and Bṛhaspati.
Let the Gods give their gifts, and let
Sūnṛtā, Goddess, grant us wealth.

3 We call King Soma to our aid, and Agni
with our songs and hymns,
Ādityas, Viṣṇu, Sūrya, and the Brahman
Priest Bṛhaspati.

4 Indra, Vāyu, Bṛhaspati, Gods swift to
listen, we invoke,
That in the synod all the folk may be
benevolent to us.

5 Urge Aryaman to send us gifts, and Indra,
and Bṛhaspati,
Vāta, Viṣṇu, Sarasvatī and the Strong
Courser Savitar.

6 Do thou, O Agni, with thy fires strengthen
our prayer and sacrifice :
Urge givers to bestow their wealth to aid
our service of the Gods.

HYMN CXLII.   *Agni.*

1. WITH thee, O Agni, was this singer of the
laud : he hath no other kinship, O
thou Son of Strength.
Thou givest blessed shelter with a triple
guard. Keep the destructive lightning
far away from us.

2 Thy birth who seekest food is in the falling
flood, Agni : as Comrade thou winnest
all living things.
Our coursers and our songs shall be victorious : they of themselves advance like
one who guards the herd.

3 And thou, O Agni, thou of Godlike
nature, sparest the stones, while earing
up the brushwood.

Then are thy tracks like deserts in the
corn-lands. Let us not stir to wrath thy
mighty arrow.

4 O'er hills through vales devouring as thou
goest, thou partest like an army fain for
booty
As when a barber shaves a beard, thou
shavest earth when the wind blows on
thy flame and fans it.

5 Apparent are his lines as he approaches :
the course is single, but the cars are
many,
When, Agni, thou, making thine arms
resplendent, advancest o'er the land
spread out beneath thee.

6 Now let thy strength, thy burning flames
fly upward, thine energies, O Agni, as
thou toilest.
Gape widely, bend thee, waxing in thy
vigour : let all the Vasus sit this day
beside thee.

7 This is the waters' reservoir, the great
abode of gathered streams.
Take thou another path than this, and as
thou listest walk thereon.

8 On thy way hitherward and hence let
flowery Dūrvā grass spring up
Let there be lakes with lotus blooms.
These are the mansions of the flood.

HYMN CXLIII.   *Aśvins.*

1. YE made that Atri, worn with eld, free
as a horse to win the goal.
When ye restored to youth and strength
Kakṣīvān like a car renewed,

2 Ye freed that Atri like a horse, and brought
him newly-born to earth.
Ye loosed him like a firm-tied knot which
Gods unsoiled by dust had bound.

3 Heroes who showed most wondrous
power to Atri, strive to win fair songs ;
For then, O Heroes of the sky, your hymn
of praise shall cease no more.

---

6 Stanzas 7 and 8 seem to belong to some other hymn ,
being a prayer to Agni that he may spare the speaker's
house where, he says, there is nothing to invite the devouring God. See *Hymns of the Atharva-veda*, VI. 106.

1 *Atri* : see I. 112. 7. *Kakṣīvān* : the Scholiast says that
this Ṛṣi was originally dull of understanding and that
the Aśvins endowed him with knowledge. Prof. Ludwig
takes *kakṣīvantam* to be an adjective agreeing with
rátham : 'Again ye made him youthful like a chariot that
is braced with bands.'

---

2 *Sūnṛtā* : Pleasantness; Gladness, personified. Cf.
I. 40. 3.

---

3 *Sparest the stones* : see Pischel, *Vedische Studien*, I. p.
180. Cp. III. 29. 6.

4 This claims your notice, Bounteous Gods !—
oblation, Aśvins ! and our love,
That ye, O Heroes, in the fight may
bring us safe to ample room.

5 Ye Twain to Bhujyu tossed about in ocean
at the region's end,
Nāsatyas, with your winged steeds came
nigh, and gave him strength to win.

6 Come with your joys, most liberal Gods,
Lords of all treasures, bringing weal.
Like fresh full waters to a well, so, Heroes,
come and be with us.

HYMN CXLIV. *Indra.*

1. THIS deathless Indu, like a steed, strong
and of full vitality,
Belongs to thee, the Orderer.

2 Here, by us, for the worshipper, is the
wise bolt that works with skill.
It brings the bubbling beverage as a
dexterous man brings the effectual strong
drink.

3 Impetuous Ahīśuva, a bull among these
cows of his,
looked down upon the restless Hawk.

4 That the strong-pinioned Bird hath
brought, Child of the Falcon, from afar,
What moves upon a hundred wheels along
the female Dragon's path.

5 Which, fair, unrobbed, the Falcon brought
thee in his foot, the red-hued dwelling
of the juice ;
Through this came vital power which lengthens out our days, and kinship through
its help awoke.

6 So Indra is by Indu's power ; e'en among
Gods will it repel great treachery.

5 *Bhujyu* : see Vol. I., Index.

1 *Indu* : Soma. *The Orderer* : disposer and arranger
of the universe.

2 *Bolt* : the Vaṣaṭkāra, or sacrificial exclamation, is
to the priests what the thunderbolt is to Indra.

3 I find this and the following stanza unintelligible.
Ahīśuva in other places is the name of a demon; but the
meaning here is uncertain. *Cows* : there is no substantive to *āsú svāsu*, 'these his own,' in the feminine gender.

4 *What moves upon a hundred wheels* : *śatācakram* : 'the
bestower of many boons.'—Wilson.

5 *Dwelling of the juice* : the Soma-plant, which the
Falcon brought from heaven. See IV. 26 and 27.

6 *It* : or he; Indu or the Soma juice.
Prof. Grassmann places this hymn in his Appendix
as being in his opinion made up of fragments. He considers Ahīśuva (stanza 3) to be 'the archer Kṛśānu', of
IV. 27. 3 and other places, who guards the celestial Soma,
and instead of 'cows' he understands 'wives.'

Wisdom, Most Sapient One, brings force
that lengthens life. May wisdom bring
the juice to us.

HYMN CXLV. *Sapatnībādhanam.*

1. FROM out the earth I dig this plant, a
herb of most effectual power,
Wherewith one quells the rival wife and
gains the husband for oneself.

2 Auspicious, with expanded leaves, sent by
the Gods, victorious plant,
Blow thou the rival wife away, and make
my husband only mine.

3 Stronger am I, O Stronger One, yea, mightier than the mightier ;
And she who is my rival wife is lower
than the lowest dames.

4 Her very name I utter not : she takes no
pleasure in this man.
Far into distance most remote drive we
the rival wife away.

5 I am the conqueror, and thou, thou also
act victorious :
As victory attends us both we will subdue
my fellow-wife.

6 I have gained thee for vanquisher, have
grasped thee with a stronger spell.
As a cow hastens to her calf, so let thy
spirit speed to me, hasten like water on
its way.

HYMN CXLVI. *Araṇyānī.*

1. GODDESS of wild and forest who seemest to
vanish from the sight.
How is it that thou seekest not the
village ? Art thou not afraid ?

2 What time the grasshopper replies and
swells the shrill cicala's voice,
Seeming to sound with tinkling bells, the
Lady of the Wood exults.

The hymn is a spell to rid a jealous wife of a more
favoured rival. The Ṛṣi is Indrāṇī, the Consort of Indra.

1 *This plant* : said to be the Pāṭā, probably identical
with Pāṭhā (Clypea Hernandifolia), a climbing plant
possessing various medicinal properties.

6 *Thy spirit* : the husband's.

The deity, Araṇyānī, is the tutelary Goddess of the
forest and wilderness.

2 *Grasshopper......cicala* : the *ciccikā* is said to be a
little creature that cries *cici* : and the *vṛṣāravd* is said to
be a sort of cricket. Others take them to be birds of
some unascertained kind.

3 And, yonder, cattle seem to graze, what
   seems a dwelling-place appears :
   Or else at eve the Lady of the Forest
   seems to free the wains.

4 Here one is calling to his cow, another
   there hath felled a tree :
   At eve the dweller in the wood fancies
   that somebody hath screamed.

5 The Goddess never slays, unless some
   murderous enemy approach.
   Man eats of savoury fruit and then takes,
   even as he wills, his rest.

6 Now have I praised the Forest Queen,
   sweet-scented, redolent of balm,
   The Mother of all sylvan things, who tills
   not but hath stores of food.

HYMN CXLVII.   *Indra.*

1. I TRUST in thy first wrathful deed, O
   Indra, when thou slewest Vṛtra and didst
   work to profit man ;
   What time the two world-halves fell short
   of thee in might, and the earth trembled at thy force, O Thunder-armed.

2 Thou with thy magic powers didst rend
   the conjurer Vṛtra, O Blameless One,
   with heart that longed for fame.
   Heroes elect thee when they battle for the
   prey, thee in all sacrifices worthy of
   renown.

3 God Much-invoked, take pleasure in
   these princes here, who, thine
   exalters, Maghavan, have come to
   wealth.
   In synods, when the rite succeeds, they
   hymn the Strong for sons and progeny
   and riches undisturbed.

4 That man shall find delight in well-pro-

tected wealth whose care provides for
him the quick-sought joyous draught.
Bringing oblations, strengthened, Maghavan, by thee, he swiftly wins the spoil
with heroes in the fight.

5 Now for our band, O Maghavan, when
   lauded, make ample room with might,
   and grant us riches.
   Magician thou, our Varuṇa and Mitra,
   deal food to us, O Wondrous, as
   Dispenser.

HYMN CXLVIII.   *Indra.*

1. WHEN we have pressed the juice we laud
   thee, Indra, and when, Most Valorous !
   we have won the booty.
   Bring us prosperity, as each desires it :
   under thine own protection may we
   conquer.

2 Sublime from birth, mayst thou O Indra,
   Hero, with Sūrya overcome the Dāsa
   races.
   As by a fountain's side, we bring the Soma
   that lay concealed, close-hidden in the
   waters.

3 Answer the votary's hymns, for these thou
   knowest, craving the Ṛṣis' prayer, thy-
   self a Singer,
   May we be they who take delight in
   Somas : these with sweet food for thee,
   O Chariot-rider.

4 These holy prayers, O Indra, have I sung
   thee : grant to the men the strength of
   men, thou Hero.
   Be of one mind with those in whom thou
   joyest : keep thou the singers safe and
   their companions.

5 Listen to Pṛthī's call, heroic Indra, and
   be thou lauded by the hymns of Venya,
   Him who hath sung thee to thine oil-rich
   dwelling, whose rolling songs have sped
   thee like a torrent.

HYMN CXLIX.   *Savitar.*

1. SAVITAR fixed the earth with bands to
   bind it, and made heaven stedfast
   where no prop supported.

---

3 *Cattle seem to graze* : deer feeding in the glades.
What seems a dwelling-place : a natural bower of branches
and creepers.

4 Sounds are heard as of a cowman calling his cattle,
or of a woodman at work. 'We must imagine the thousand
strange sounds and delusions which seem to encompass
the solitary listener of an evening in the darkening forest.'
—Mme. Zénaïde Ragozin, *Vedic India* (Story of the
Nations), p. 272.

5 *Murderous enemy* : the text has only *anyáḥ*, 'another,'
by which, according to Sāyaṇa, a tiger or robber is meant.
Prof. Ludwig suggests that the reading should be *hanyáḥ*,
'one who is destined to be killed.' The hymn has been
translated by Dr. Muir, *O. S. Texts*, V. p. 423; and by
the authors of the *Siebenzig Lieder des Ṛgveda.*

3 *Princes* : the Sūris, the wealthy institutors of the
sacrifice. *The Strong* : thee, the mighty Indra.

3 *These with sweet food* : 'these (praises are offered)
with sacrificial viands.—Wilson.

4 *Companions* : or, dependents.

5 *Pṛthī's call*: the invocation of Pṛthu, the Ṛṣi of the
hymn, according to Sāyaṇa Prof. Ludwig suggests that
Pṛthu's wife is intended. *Venya* : Pṛthī, son of Vena.

Savitar milked, as 'twere a restless courser,
air, sea bound fast to what no foot had
trodden.

2 Well knoweth Savitar, O Child of Waters,
where ocean, firmly fixt, o'erflowed its
limit.
Thence sprang the world, from that up-
rose the region : thence heaven spread
out and the wide earth expanded.

3 Then, with a full crowd of Immortal
Beings, this other realm came later,
high and holy.
First, verily, Savitar's strong-pinioned Eagle
was born : and he obeys his law for
ever.

4 As warriors to their steeds, kine to their
village, as fond milk giving cows
approach their youngling,
As man to wife, let Savitar come downward to us, heaven's bearer, Lord of
every blessing.

5 Like the Āṅgirasa Hiraṇyastūpa, I call
thee, Savitar, to this achievement :
So worshipping and lauding thee for
favour I watch for thee as for the stalk
of Soma.

HYMN CL.   *Agni.*

1. THOU, bearer of oblations, though kindled,
art kindled for the Gods.
With the Ādityas, Rudras, Vasus, come to
us : to show us favour come to us.

2 Come hither and accept with joy this
sacrifice and hymn of ours.
O kindled God, we mortals are invoking
thee, calling on thee to show us grace.

3 I laud thee Jātavedas, thee Lord of all
blessings, with my song.
Agni, bring hitherward the Gods whose
Laws we love, whose laws we love, to
show us grace.

4 Agni the God was made the great High-

Priest of Gods, Ṛṣis have kindled Agni,
men of mortal mould.
Agni I invoke for winning ample wealth,
kindly disposed for winning wealth.

5 Atri and Bharadvāja and Gaviṣṭhira,
Kaṇva and Trasadasyu, in our fight he
helped.
On Agni calls Vasiṣṭha, even the household
priest, the household priest to win his
grace.

HYMN CLI.   *Faith.*

1. By Faith is Agni kindled, through Faith
is oblation offered up.
We celebrate with praises Faith upon the
height of happiness.

2 Bless thou the man who gives, O Faith ;
Faith, bless the man who fain would
give.
Bless thou the liberal worshippers : bless
thou the word that I have said.

3 Even as the Deities maintained Faith in
the mighty Asuras,
So make this uttered wish of mine true
for the liberal worshippers.

4 Guarded by Vāyu, Gods and men who
sacrifice draw near to Faith.
Man winneth Faith by yearnings of the
heart, and opulence by Faith.

5 Faith in the early morning, Faith at noonday will we invocate,
Faith at the setting of the Sun. O Faith,
endow us with belief.

HYMN CLII.   *Indra.*

1. A MIGHTY Governor art thou, Wondrous,
Destroyer of the foe,
Whose friend is never done to death, and
never, never overcome.

2 Lord of the clan, who brings us bliss,
Strong, Warrior, Slayer of the fiend,
May Indra, Soma-drinker, go before us,
Bull who gives us peace.

3 Drive Rākṣasas and foes away, break thou
in pieces Vṛtra's jaws :
O Vṛtra-slaying Indra, quell the foeman's
wrath who threatens us.

---

1 *To what no foot had trodden* : *atūrte* : 'to the indestructible (ether).'—Wilson.

3 *Eagle* : identified by Sāyaṇa with Tārkṣya,
brother of Garuḍa, who brought the Soma from the Moon
at Savitar's command.

5 *Āṅgirasa* : a descendant of the Aṅgirases. *Achievement* : *vāje* : food; according to Sāyaṇa, *i. e.* oblation.
Lauding : *árcan* : or, I, Arcan, honouring thee to
win thy favour.

---

1 *Though kindled* : although thou art already burning,
fresh fire is added to thee. *To show us favour* : *mṛlīkāya* :
this play upon the Ṛṣi's name Mṛlīka is repeated in each
stanza.

The Ṛṣi is Śraddhā (Faith) of the family of Kāma
(Love).

1 *Upon the height of happiness* : '(who is seated)
on Bhaga's head'.—Wilson.

3 *Asuras* : the primeval Āryan Gods, Dyaus, Varuṇa,
and some others, who were venerated by Indra and other
Indo-Āryan deities of a later creation.

4 *Guarded by Vāyu* : the meaning is not clear.

4 O Indra, beat our foes away, humble the men who challenge us :
Send down to nether darkness him who seeks to do us injury.

5 Baffle the foeman's plan, ward off his weapon who would conquer us.
Give shelter from his furious wrath, and keep his murdering dart afar.

HYMN CLIII.   *Indra.*

1. SWAYING about, the Active Ones came nigh to Indra at his birth,
And shared his great heroic might.

2 Based upon strength and victory and power, O Indra is thy birth :
Thou, Mighty One, art strong indeed.

3 Thou art the Vṛtra-slayer, thou, Indra, hast spread the firmament :
Thou hast with might upheld the heavens.

4 Thou, Indra, bearest in thine arms the lightning that accords with thee,
Whetting thy thunderbolt with might.

5 Thou, Indra, art preëminent over all creatures in thy might :
Thou hast pervaded every place.

HYMN CLIV.   *New Life.*

1. FOR some is Soma purified, some sit by sacrificial oil :
To those for whom the meath flows forth, even to those let him depart.

2 Invincible through Fervour, those whom Fervour hath advanced to heaven,
Who showed great Fervour in their lives, — even to those let him depart.

3 The heroes who contend in war and boldly cast their lives away,
Or who give guerdon thousandfold,—even to those let him depart.

4 Yea, the first followers of Law, Law's pure and holy strengtheners,
The Fathers, Yama ! Fervour-moved,— even to those let him depart.

5 Skilled in a thousand ways and means, the sages who protect the Sun,
The Ṛṣis, Yama ! Fervour-moved,—even to those let him depart.

HYMN CLV.   *Various.*

1. ARĀYĪ, one-eyed limping hag, fly, ever-screeching, to the hill.
We frighten thee away with these, the heroes of Śirimbiṭha.

2 Scared from this place and that is she, destroyer of each germ unborn.
Go, sharp-horned Brahmaṇaspti and drive Arāyī far away.

3 Yon log that floats without a man to guide it on the river's edge,—
Seize it, thou thing with hideous jaws, and go thou far away thereon.

4 When, foul with secret stain and spot, ye hastened onward to the breast,
All Indra's enemies were slain and passed away like froth and foam.

5 These men have led about the cow, have duly carried Agni round,
And raised their glory to the Gods. Who will attack them with success ?

---

4 *Fervour-moved* : or, Penance-rich ; filled with or full of religious austerity.

5 *Who protect the Sun* : see Muir *O. S. T.,* V. 319.

The hymn has been translated by Dr. J. Muir, *O. S. Texts,* V. p. 310, and by Prof. Zimmer, *Altindisches Leben,* p. 416.

The subject or object of the hymn is the averting or removal of misfortune.

1 *Arāyī*: 'the stingy,' one of a class of malevolent she-fiends. *Ever-screeching* : according to Sāyaṇa's explanation of *sadānve* : according to others 'allied with Dānus, Dānavas, or demons.' *Śirimbiṭha* : the Ṛṣi of the hymn.

2 *Sharp-horned* : armed with piercing rays of light.

4 The meaning of this stanza is not clear. *Maṇḍūra-dhāṇikīḥ* and *budbudayāśavaḥ* are difficult words that do not occur again.

5 *These men* : the text has only *imé,* 'these'. According to Sāyaṇa, the Viśvedevas are meant, who have brought back the stolen cattle. But the reference is probably to the sacrifice which the priests are performing.

---

1 *The Active Ones* : the Water-Goddesses may be meant. The Consorts of the Gods, according to Sāyaṇa.

2 *Thou, Mighty One* : or, 'O Bull, thou art a Bull indeed.' 'Thou O hero, art indeed a hero'.—Max Müller.

4 *Lightning* : or, praise-song, hymn. Sāyaṇa explains *arkám* here by *stutyam* : thy laudable or adorable thunderbolt.

The Ṛṣi of this funeral hymn is Yamī, sister of Yama.

1 *To those let him depart* : let the spirit of the dead go to the realm of the blessed, to the Fathers who receive offerings of Soma juice and clarified butter. *Meath* : according to Sāyaṇa, honey, which is offered to the spirits of their ancestors by students of the Atharva-veda, Soma juice and *ghṛtám* or clarified butter (sacrificial oil) being offered, respectively, by students of the Sāmaveda and Yajurveda.

2 *Fervour* : *tápas* : literally, warmth, heat; religious fervour, asceticism, austerity, self-denial and abstracted meditation.

HYMN CLVI. *Agni.*

1. LET songs of ours speed Agni forth like a fleet courser in the race,
And we will win each prize through him.

2 Agni, the dart whereby we gain kine for ourselves with help from thee,—
That send us for the gain of wealth.

3 O Agni, bring us wealth secure, vast wealth in horses and in kine :
Oil thou the socket, turn the wheel.

4 O Agni, thou hast made the Sun, Eternal Star, to mount the sky,
Bestowing light on living men.

5 Thou, Agni, art the people's light, best, dearest, seated in thy shrine :
Watch for the singer, give him life.

HYMN CLVII. *Viśvedevas.*

1. WE will, with Indra and all Gods to aid us, bring these existing worlds into subjection.

2 Our sacrifice, our bodies, and our offspring, let Indra form together with Ādityas.

3 With the Ādityas, with the band of Maruts, may Indra be Protector of our bodies.

4 As when the Gods came, after they had slaughtered the Asuras, keeping safe their Godlike nature,

5 Brought the Sun hitherward with mighty powers, and looked about them on their vigorous Godhead.

HYMN CLVIII. *Sūrya.*

1. MAY Sūrya guard us out of heaven, and Vāta from the firmament,
And Agni from terrestrial spots.

2 Thou Savitar whose flame deserves hundred libations, be thou pleased:
From falling lightning keep us safe.

2 *The dart* : 'that army'—Wilson.

3 *Turn the wheel* : I adopt the reading of the Sāmaveda, *pavim*, instead of *paṇim*. According to the text, the rendering would be : 'Balm heaven and drive the Paṇi hence.'

The first three verses of this hymn were recited at the Aśvamedha or Horse-Sacrifice.

5 Sāyaṇa explains the second half of the stanza differently :—'then (men) beheld around them the swift descending rain.'—Wilson.

1 *Out of heaven* : 'from (foes dwelling in) heaven.'—Wilson.

3 May Savitar the God, and may Parvata also give us sight;
May the Creator give us sight.

4 Give sight unto our eye, give thou our bodies sight that they may see:
May we survey, discern this world.

5 Thus, Sūrya, may we look on thee, on thee most lovely to behold,
See clearly with the eyes of men.

HYMN CLIX. *Śacī Paulomī.*

1. YON Sun hath mounted up, and this my happy fate hate mounted high.
I knowing this, as conqueror have won my husband for mine own.

2 I am the banner and the head, a mighty arbitress am I:
I am victorious, and my Lord shall be submissive to my will.

3 My Sons are slayers of the foe, my Daughter is a ruling Queen:
I am victorious: o'er my Lord my song of triumph is supreme.

4 Oblation, that which Indra gave and thus grew glorious and most high,—
This have I offered, O ye Gods, and rid me of each rival wife.

5 Destroyer of the rival wife, Sole Spouse, victorious, conqueror,
The others' glory have I seized as 'twere the wealth of weaker Dames.

6 I have subdued as conqueror these rivals, these my fellow-wives,
That I may hold imperial sway over this Hero and the folk.

HYMN CLX. *Indra.*

1. TASTE this strong draught enriched with offered viands: with all thy chariot here unyoke thy Coursers.
Let not those other sacrificers stay thee, Indra: these juices shed for thee are ready.

2 Thine is the juice effused, thine are the juices yet to be pressed : our resonant songs invite thee.

3 *The Creator* : Dhātar.

Śacī Paulomī, called also Indrāṇī, the Consort of Indra, is also the Ṛṣi of the hymn. 'Literally, this is a song of exultation by *Śacī* over her rival wives : but *śacī* means also an "act", "exploit," and this hymn is metaphorically the praise of *Indra's* glorious acts.'—Wilson.

O Indra, pleased to-day with this libation, come, thou who knowest all and drink the Soma.

3 Whoso, devoted to the God, effuses Soma for him with yearning heart and spirit,—

Never doth Indra give away his cattle : for him he makes the lovely Soma famous.

4 He looks with loving favour on the mortal who, like a rich man, pours for him the Soma.

Maghavan in his bended arm supports him : he slays, unasked, the men who hate devotion.

5 We call on thee to come to us, desirous of goods and spoil, of cattle, and of horses.

For thy new love and favour are we present : let us invoke thee, Indra, as our welfare.

HYMN CLXI.   Indra.

1. For life I set thee free by this oblation from the unknown decline and from Consumption ;

Or, if the grasping demon have possessed him, free him from her, O Indra, thou and Agni.

2 Be his days ended, be he now departed, be he brought very near to death already,

Out of Destruction's lap again I bring him, save him for life to last a hundred autumns.

3 With hundred-eyed oblation, hundred-autumned, bringing a hundred lives, have I restored him,

That Indra for a hundred years may lead him safe to the farther shore of all misfortune.

4 Live, waxing in thy strength, a hundred autumns, live through a hundred springs, a hundred winters.

Through hundred-lived oblation Indra, Agni, Bṛhaspati, Savitar yield him for a hundred !

5 So have I found and rescued thee : thou hast returned with youth renewed.

Whole in thy members ! I have found thy sight and all thy life for thee.

HYMN CLXIV.   Dream-charm.

1. Avaunt, thou Master of the mind ! Depart, and vanish far away.

Look on Destruction far from hence. The live man's mind is manifold.

2 A happy boon do men elect, a mighty blessing they obtain.

Bliss with Vaivasvata they see. The live man's mind seeks many a place.

3 If by address, by blame, by imprecation we have committed sin, awake or sleeping,

All hateful acts of ours, all evil doings may Agni bear away to distant places.

4 When, Indra, Brahmaṇaspati, our deeds are wrongful and unjust,

May provident Āṅgirasa prevent our foes from troubling us.

5 We have prevailed this day and won : we are made free from sin and guilt.

Ill thoughts, that visit us awake or sleeping, seize the man we hate, yea, seize the man who hateth us.

HYMN CLXV.   Viśvedevas.

1. Gods, whatsoe'er the Dove came hither seeking, sent to us as the envoy of Destruction,

For that let us sing hymns and make atonement. Well be it with our quadrupeds and bipeds.

4 *For a hundred* : years, understood.

For Hymns CLXII, CLXIII, and CLXXXIV see Appendix.

----

4 Dr. Gaedicke (*Accusativ im Veda*, p. 127) translates Pādas 1—3 of the stanza differently : der wird von ihm erspäht, der, obwohl reich, ihm keinen Soma presst, den holt der mächtige heraus aus dem Winkel (Versteck).

According to the Index the subject of the hymn is the cure of the disease called Rājayakṣma (Consumption or Atrophy).

1 *Unknown decline* : some insidious disease, differing from Rājayakṣma. Perhaps, as Prof. Zimmer suggests, hypertrophy and atrophy are the two diseases intended. See *Altindisches Leben*, p. 377. *The grasping demon* : grāhi : from *grah*, to seize; a female spirit who seizes men and kills them.

1 *Master of the mind* the spirit of evil dreams is addressed. *Destruction* : the Goddess Nirṛti. *Manifold* : 'attentive to various objects, and soon diverted from any regard to evil dreams.—Wilson.

2 *Vaivasvata* : Yama, the son of Vivasvān, who presides over evil dreams.—Sāyaṇa.

4 *Āṅgirasa* according to Sāyaṇa, Varuṇa, the wise God who is especially connected with his worshippers the Aṅgirases, may be intended. Cf. *Hymns of the Atharva-veda*, VI. 45. 3.

----

1 A dove, regarded as an ill-omened bird and the messenger of Death, has flown into the house. Similarly'

2 Auspicious be the Dove that hath been
sent us, a harmless bird, ye Gods,
within our dwelling.

May Agni, Sage, be pleased with our
oblation, and may the Missile borne
on wings avoid us.

3 Let not the Arrow that hath wings distract
us : beside the fire-place, on the hearth
it settles.

May' it bring welfare to our men and
cattle : here let the Dove, ye Gods,
forbear to harm us.

4 The screeching of the owl is ineffective ;
and when beside the fire the Dove hath
settled,

To him who sent it hither as an envoy,
to him be reverence paid, to Death, to
Yama.

5 Drive forth the Dove, chase it with holy
verses : rejoicing, bring ye hither food
and cattle,

Barring the way against all grief and
trouble. Let the swift bird fly forth
and leave us vigour.

HYMN CLXVI. *Sapatnanāśanam.*

1. MAKE me a bull among my peers, make
me my rivals' conqueror :

Make me the slayer of my foes, a sovran
ruler, lord of kine

2 I am my rivals' slayer, like Indra unwounded and unhurt,

And all these enemies of mine are vanquished and beneath my feet.

3 Here, verily, I bind you fast, as the two
bow-ends with the string.

Press down these men, O Lord of Speech,
that they may humbly speak to me.

4 Hither I came as conqueror with mighty
all-effecting power,

And I have mastered all your thought,
your synod, and your holy work.

5 May I be highest, having gained your
strength in war, your skill in peace :
my feet have trodden on your heads.

Speak to me from beneath my feet, as
frogs from out the water croak, as frogs
from out the water croak.

HYMN CLXVII. *Indra.*

1. THIS pleasant meath, O Indra, is effused
for thee : thou art the ruling Lord of
beaker and of juice.

Bestow upon us wealth with many hero
sons : thou, having glowed with Fervour,
wonnest heavenly light.

2 Let us call Śakra to libations here effused,
winner of light who joyeth in the potent
juice.

Mark well this sacrifice of ours and come
to us : we pray to Maghavan the
Vanquisher of hosts.

3 By royal Soma's and by Varuṇa's decree,
under Bṛhaspati's and Anumati's guard,

This day by thine authority, O Maghavan,
Maker, Disposer thou ! have I enjoyed
the jars.

4 I, too, urged on, have had my portion,
in the bowl, and as first Prince I drew
forth this my hymn of praise,

When with the prize I came unto the
flowing juice, O Viśvāmitra, Jamadagni,
to your home.

HYMN CLXVIII. *Vāyu.*

1. O THE Wind's chariot, O its power and
glory! Crashing it goes and hath a voice
of thunder.

It makes the regions red and touches
heaven, and as it moves the dust of
earth is scattered.

2 Along the traces of the Wind they hurry,
they come to him as dames to an
assembly.

Borne on his car with these for his attendants, the God speeds forth, the universe's
Monarch.

3 Travelling on the paths of air's mid-
region, no single day doth he take
rest or slumber.

---

in North-Lincolnshire, 'If a pigeon is seen sitting on a
tree, or comes into the house, or from being wild suddenly becomes tame, it is a sign of death.'—*Notes and
Queries*, viii. p. 382.

2 *Missile borne on wings* : the ill-omened bird.

5 *With holy verses* : Sāyaṇa takes *ṛcā* with *stūyamānāḥ*,
understood :—(Praised) by our hymn (O Gods).

The subject is the Destruction of Rivals.

The Ṛṣis are Viśvāmitra and Jamadagni. Stanzas
1—3 are spoken by the Ṛṣis and 4 by Indra.

1 *Having glowed with Fervour* : 'performing arduous
penance,'—Wilson.

3 *Anumati* : Divine Favour personified.

4 *The prize* : the wealth won for you.

---

2 *They* : the Waters. Prof. Max Müller interprets
differently. See his translation, *Vedic Hymns*, I. 449.

Holy and earliest-born, Friend of the waters, where did he spring and from what region came he ?

4 Germ of the world, the Deities' vital spirit, this God moves ever as his will inclines him.

His voice is heard, his shape is ever viewless. Let us adore this Wind with our oblation.

HYMN CLXIX.   *Cows.*

1. MAY the wind blow upon our Cows with healing : may they eat herbage full of vigorous juices.

May they drink waters rich in life and fatness : to food that moves on feet be gracious, Rudra.

2 Like-coloured, various-hued, or single-coloured, whose names through sacrifice are known to Agni,

Whom the Aṅgirases produced by Fervour,— vouchsafe to these, Parjanya, great protection.

3 Those who have offered to the Gods their bodies, whose varied forms are all well known to Soma,—

Those grant us in our cattle-pen, O Indra, with their full streams of milk and plenteous offspring.

4 Prajāpati, bestowing these upon me, one-minded with all Gods and with the Fathers,

Hath to our cow-pen brought auspicious cattle : so may we own the offspring they will bear us.

HYMN CLXX.   *Sūrya.*

1. MAY the Bright God drink glorious Soma-mingled meath, giving the sacrifice's lord uninjured life;

He who, wind-urged, in person guards our offspring well, hath nourished them with food and shines o'er many a land.

2 Radiant, as high Truth, cherished, best at winning strength, Truth based upon the statute that supports the heavens,

He rose, a light, that kills Vṛtras and enemies, best slayer of the Dasyus, Asuras, and foes.

1 *Food that moves on feet* : the wandering milch-cows. But see Bergaigne, III. 159.

4 *Prajāpati......hath brought* : 'may Prajāpati bring,' according to Sāyaṇa

3 This light, the best of lights, supreme, all-conquering, winner of riches, is exalted with high laud.

All-lighting, radiant, mighty as the Sun to see, he spreadeth wide unfailing victory and strength.

4 Beaming forth splendour with thy light, thou hast attained heaven's lustrous realm.

By thee were brought together all existing things, possessor of all Godhead, All-effecting God.

HYMN CLXXI.   *Indra.*

1. FOR Iṭa's sake who pressed the juice, thou, Indra, didst protect his car, And hear the Soma-giver's call.

2 Thou from his skin hast borne the head of the swift-moving combatant, And sought the Soma-pourer's home.

3 Venya, that mortal man, hast thou, for Āstrabudhna the devout, O Indra, many a time set free.

4 Bring, Indra, to the east again that Sun who now is in the west, Even against the will of Gods.

HYMN CLXXII.   *Dawn.*

1. WITH all thy beauty come : the kine approaching with full udders follow on thy path.

2 Come with kind thoughts, most liberal, rousing the warrior's hymn of praise, with bounteuos ones,

3 As nourishers we tie the thread, and, liberal with our bounty, offer sacrifice.

4 Dawn drives away her Sister's gloom, and, through her excellence, makes her retrace her path.

2 *Skin* : here meaning 'body.' *Combatant* : *makhásya* : according to the legend cited by Sāyaṇa Sacrifice personified, whose head, as he attempted to escape in human form from the Gods, was cut off by Indra. See Wilson.

3 *Venya* : said to be Pṛthu, the son of Vena. See X. 148.5. *Astrabudhna* : the name of a man not mentioned elsewhere, the son of Astrabudhna. *Set free* : Cp.I. 24. 15.

2 *Most liberal* : Sūrya appears to be meant. *Rousing the warrior's hymn of praise* : *jārayánmakhaḥ* : the meaning is uncertain :—'bringing the sacrifice to completion', according to Sāyaṇa.

3 *As nourishers* : because sacrifice brings the food that nourishes life. *The thread* : of sacrifice.

4 *Her Sister's gloom* : the darkness of Night.

HYMN CLXXIII. *The King.*

1. BE with us; I have chosen thee : stand
stedfast and immovable.
Let all the people wish for thee : let not
thy kingship fall away.

2 Be even here ; fall not away ; be like
a mountain unremoved.
Stand stedfast here like Indra's self, and
hold the kingship in the grasp.

3 This man hath Indra stablished, made
secure by strong oblation's power.
May Soma speak a benison, and Brahmaṇaspati, on him.

4 Firm is the sky and firm the earth, and
stedfast also are these hills.
Stedfast is all this living world, and stedfast
is this King of men.

5 Stedfast, may Varuṇa the King, stedfast,
the God Bṛhaspati,
Stedfast, may Indra, stedfast too, may
Agni keep thy stedfast reign.

6 On constant Soma let us think with constant sacrificial gift
And then may Indra make the clans bring
tribute unto thee alone.

HYMN CLXXIV. *The King.*

1. WITH offering for success in fight whence
Indra was victorious.
With this, O Brahmaṇaspati, let us attain
to royal sway.

2 Subduing those who rival us, subduing all
malignities,
Withstand the man who menaces, withstand the man who angers us.

3 Soma and Savitar the God have made
thee a victorious King
All elements have aided thee, to make
thee general conqueror.

4 Oblation, that which Indra gave and thus
grew glorious and most high,—
This have I offered, Gods ! and hence
now, verily, am rivalless.

5 Slayer of rivals, rivalless, victorious, with
royal sway,
Over these beings may I rule, may I be
Sovran of the folk.

The subject is the benediction of a newly-elected king.

---

1 *With offering for success* : 'By the *abhivarta* oblation.'
—Wilson.

4 Cp. X. 159. 4.

HYMN CLXXV. *Press-stones.*

1. MAY Savitar the God, O Stones, stir you
according to the Law :
Be harnessed to the shafts, and press.

2 Stones, drive calamity away, drive ye
away malevolence :
Make ye the Cows our medicine.

3 Of one accord the upper Stones, giving
the Bull his bull-like strength,
Look down with pride on those below.

4 May Savitar the God, O Stones, stir you
as Law commands for him
Who sacrifices, pouring juice.

HYMN CLXXVI. *Agnī.*

1. WITH hymns of praise their sons have
told aloud the Ṛbhus' mighty deeds.
Who, all-supporting, have enjoyed the earth
as 'twere a mother cow.

2 Bring forth the God with song divine,
being Jātavedas hitherward,
To bear our gifts at once to heaven.

3 He here, a God-devoted Priest, led forward
comes to sacrifice.
Like a car covered for the road, he, glowing, knows, himself, the way.

4 This Agni rescues from distress, as 'twere
from the Immortal Race,
A God yet mightier than strength, a God
who hath been made for life.

HYMN CLXXVII. *Māyābheda.*

1. THE sapient with their spirit and their
mind behold the Bird adorned with all
an Asura's magic might.
Sages observe him in the ocean's inmost
depth : the wise disposers seek the
station of his rays.

1 *The shafts* : or chariot-poles ; here meaning the
guiding arms of the Soma-press.
2 *The Cows* : or, the rays of morning, at whose
approach robbers and demons fly.
3 *The Bull* : Soma.

---

3 *Like a car* : perhaps, as Prof. Ludwig suggests, like
a chariot which, as the driver is concealed from sight by
he canopy, seems to find its way without a guide.
4 *As 'twere from the Immortal Race* : 'as (well as) from
peril caused by the immortals.'—Wilson. Stanzas 2—4
are recited at the Agni-praṇayana, the ceremony of
carrying the sacrificial fire to the altar used for animal
and Soma sacrifices. See Haug's *Aitareya Brāhmaṇam*, II.
60, 61.

The subject is Māyābheda, 'the discernment of *Māyā*,
or illusion (the cause of material creation).'—Wilson.
1 *The Bird* : the Sun. *In the ocean's inmost depth* : ir
the solar orb, according to Sāyaṇa. *Wise disposers* :
'ordainers (of solar worship).'—Wilson.

2 The flying Bird bears Speech within his spirit : erst the Gandharva in the womb pronounced it :
And at the seat of sacrifice the sages cherish this radiant, heavenly-bright invention.

3 I saw the Herdsman, him who never resteth, approaching and departing on his pathways.
He, clothed in gathered and diffusive splendour, within the worlds continually travels.

HYMN CLXXVIII. *Tārkṣya.*

1. THIS very mighty one whom Gods commission, the Conqueror of cars, ever triumphant,
Swift, fleet to battle, with uninjured fellies, even Tārkṣya for our weal will we call hither.

2 As though we offered up our gifts to Indra, may we ascend. him as a ship. for safety.
Like the two wide worlds, broad, deep, far-extended, may we be safe both when he comes and leaves you.

3 He who with might the Five Lands hath pervaded, like Sūrya with his lustre, and the waters—
His strength wins hundreds, thousands : none avert it, as the young maid repelleth not her lover.

HYMN CLXXIX. *Indra.*

1. Now lift ye up yourselves and look on Indra's seasonable share.
If it be ready, offer it ; unready, ye have been remiss

2 Oblation is prepared : come to us, Indra; the Sun hath travelled over half his journey.
Friends with their stores are sitting round thee waiting like lords of clans for the tribe's wandering chieftain.

3 Dressed in the udder and on fire, I fancy ; well-dressed, I fancy, is this recent present.
Drink, Indra, of the curd of noon's libation with favour, Thunderer, thou whose deeds are mighty.

HYMN CLXXX. *Indra.*

1. O MUCH-INVOKED, thou hast subdued thy foemen : thy might is loftiest ; here display thy bounty.
In thy right hand, O Indra, bring us treasures : thou art the Lord of rivers filled with riches.

2 Like a dread wild beast roaming on the mountain thou hast approached us from the farthest distance.
Whetting thy bold and thy sharp blade, O Indra, crush thou the foe and scatter those who hate us.

3 Thou, mighty Indra, sprangest into being as strength for lovely lordship o'er the people.
Thou drovest off the folk who were unfriendly, and to the Gods thou gavest room and freedom.

HYMN CLXXXI. *Viśvedevas:*

1. VASIṢṬHA mastered the Rathantara, took it from radiant Dhātar, Savitar, and Viṣṇu,
Oblation, portion of fourfold oblation, known by the names of Saprathas and Prathas.

2. These sages found what lay remote and hidden, the sacrifice's loftiest secret essence.
From radiant Dhātar, Savitar, and Viṣṇu, from Agni, Bharadvāja brought the Brhat.

3 They found with mental eyes the earliest

---

2 *Speech* : or song; the morning song of the Sun-Bird. *The Gandharva* : the breath of life, according to Sāyaṇa. The ray of the Sun is probably meant.
3 This stanza has occurred before. See I. 164. 31. *The Herdsman* : the Sun. *Resteth* : or, stumbleth; literally, sinks or falls down.

---

1 *Tārkṣya* : a personification of the Sun, usually described as a divine horse. Cp. I. 89. 6.

3 *Her lover* : I adopt, with a modification, Professor Pischel's interpretation of the difficult words *yuvatím na śáryām*. See *Vedische Studien*, I. p. 106.

---

3 The milk is twice cooked; first matured in the cow's udder and then heated on the fire. *Curd* : the hymn was employed in the Dadhigharma ceremony when Soma juice was offered mixed with curd or sour inspissated milk. Cf. VIII. 2. 9, and IX. 11. 6. See Hillebrandt, *V.M.*, I. 221.

---

1 *Rathantara* : one of the most important Sāma-hymns, consisting of verses 22 and 23 of Ṛgveda VII. 32=Sāmaveda II. i. 11. The meaning here is uncertain, and the whole stanza is obscure. *Saprathas and Prathas* : meaning, apparently, 'far-extending' and 'extending', the former referring to the Rathantara and the latter to the Brhat, which is also one of the most important Sāmans (Ṛgveda VI. 46. 1, 2=Sāmaveda II. ii. 1. 12).

Yajus, a pathway to the Gods, that
had descended.
From radiant Dhātar, Savitar, and Viṣṇu,
from Sūrya did these sages bring the
Gharma.

HYMN CLXXXII. *Bṛhaspati.*

1. BṚHASPATI lead us safely over troubles,
and turn his evil thought against the
sinner ;
Repel the curse, and drive away ill-feeling,
and give the sacrificer peace and comfort !

2 May Narāśaṁsa aid us at Prayāja : blest
be our Anuyāja at invokings.
May he repel the curse, and chase ill-
feeling, and give the sacrificer peace
and comfort.

3 May he whose head is flaming burn the
demons, haters of prayer, so that the
arrow slay them.
May he repel the curse and chase ill-feeling,
and give the sacrificer peace and comfort.

HYMN CLXXXIII. *The Sacrificer, Etc.*

1. I SAW thee meditating in thy spirit what
sprang from Fervour and hath thence
developed.
Bestowing offspring here, bestowing riches,
spread in thine offspring, thou who
cravest children.

2 I saw thee pondering in thine heart, and
praying that in due time thy body might
be fruitful.
Come as a youthful woman, rise to meet

me : spread in thine offspring, thou
who cravest children.

3 In plants and herbs, in all existent beings
I have deposited the germ of increase.
All progeny on earth have I engendered,
and sons in women who will be hereafter.

HYMN CLXXXV. *Aditi.*

1. GREAT, unassailable must be the heavenly
favour of Three Gods,
Varuṇa, Mitra, Aryaman.

2 O'er these, neither at home nor yet abroad
or pathways that are strange,
The evil-minded foe hath power :

3 Nor over him,. the man on whom the
Sons of Aditi bestow Eternal light that
he may live.

HYMN CLXXXVI. *Vāyu.*

1. FILLING our hearts with health and joy,
may Vāta breathe his balm on us :
May he prolong our days of life.

2 Thou art our Father, Vāta, yea, thou art
a Brother and a friend,
So give us strength that we may live.

3 The store of Amṛta laid away yonder, O
Vāta, in thine home,—
Give us thereof that we may live.

HYMN CLXXXVII. *Agni.*

1. To Agni send I forth my song, to him
the Bull of all the folk :
So may he bear us past our foes.

2 Who from the distance far away shines
brilliantly across the wastes :
So may he bear us past our foes.

3 The Bull with brightly-gleaming flame
who utterly consumes the fiends :
So may he bear us past our foes.

4 Who looks on all existing things and comprehends them with his view :
So may he bear us past our foes.

---

3 *Yajus* : sacrificial prayers and formulas of the Yajur-
veda. *Gharma* : warm libation of milk or other beverage.
'The Sūkta refers evidently to technical ritual to
which no key is given by the commentary.'—Wilson.
See Mme. Zenaïde Ragozin's *Vedic India,* p. 398.

---

2 *Narāśaṁsa* : Agni. *Prayāja* : part of the introductory
ceremony at a Soma sacrifice. *Anuyāja* : a secondary or
final sacrifice.

3 *He whose head is flaming* : *tápurmūrdhan* : Bṛhaspati
or Agni as Lightning.

The deities are the Sacrificer, his Wife, and the Hotar-
priest.

1 According to Sāyaṇa, the wife is the speaker of the
first stanza, the Yajamāna or sacrificer of the second, and
the Hotar-priest of the third. Ludwig considers Agni
to be the speaker of the whole hymn. *What sprang from
Fervour* : the results of ardent devotion or *tápas*.

---

3 The Hotar-priest regards himself as the procreator
of all living beings through the efficacy of the sacrifices
which he performs : *matsādhyena yāgena sarvasyotpattera-
ham sarvajanaheturbhavāmi.*—Sāyaṇa.

---

1 *Bull* : chief and lord, as the indispensable household
fire.

2 *Across the wastes* : as the fire that burns the jungle
and prepares the ground for cultivation.

5 Resplendent Agni, who was born in farthest region of the air :
So may he bear us past our foes.

HYMN CLXXXVIII. *Agni.*

1. Now send ye Jātavedas forth, send hitherward the vigorous Steed
To seat him on our sacred grass.

2 I raise the lofty eulogy of Jātavedas, raining boons,
With sages for his hero band.

3 With flames of Jātavedas which carry
oblation to the Gods,
May he promote our sacrifice.

HYMN CLXXXIX. *Sūrya.*

1. THIS spotted Bull hath come, and sat
before the Mother in the east,
Advancing to his Father heaven.

2 Expiring when he draws his breath, she
moves along the lucid spheres :
The Bull shines out through all the sky.

3 Song is bestowed upon the Bird : it rules
supreme through thirty realms
Throughout the days at break of morn.

HYMN CXC. *Creation.*

1. FROM Fervour kindled to its height
Eternal Law and Truth were born :
Thence was the Night produced, and
thence the billowy flood of sea arose.

2 From that same billowy flood of sea the
Year was afterwards produced,
Ordainer of the days nights, Lord over
all who close the eye.

3 Dhātar, the great Creator, then formed
in due order Sun and Moon.
He formed in order Heaven and Earth,
the regions of the air, and light.

HYMN CXCI. *Agni.*

1. THOU, mighty Agni, gatherest up all
that is precious for thy friend.
Bring us all treasures as thou art enkindled
in libation's place

2 Assemble, speak together : let your minds
be all of one accord,
As ancient Gods unanimous sit down to
their appointed share.

3 The place is common, common the assembly, common the mind, so be their
thought united.
A common purpose do I lay before you,
and worship with your general oblation.

4 One and the same be your resolve, and
be your minds of one accord.
United be the thoughts of all that all may
happily agree.

---

5 *In farthest region of the air :* or beyond the firmament,
as the Sun.

The deity is alternatively Sārparājñī, the Serpent-
Queen, Kadru, who is also the Ṛṣi of the hymn.
1 *This spotted Bull :* the Sun. *The Mother :* Dawn.
3 *The Bird :* the Sun. His morning song, representing
prayer, is supreme through all the divisions of the world,
the number thirty being used indefinitely. Cf. I. 123.8.

---

1 *From Fervour :* from the *tápas,* devotional ardour
or asceticism of Brahmā, according to Sāyaṇa. But
the meaning here may be from warmth. See X. 129. 3
and note. *Thence :* from that fervour, or warmth.

The deity or subject of stanzas 2—4 is Saṁjñānam,
Agreement or unanimity in assembly.

3 *Common the assembly :* this *samiti* appears to have
been a general assembly of the people on some important
occasion, such as the election of a King. Cf. *Hymns of
the Atharvaveda,* VI. 64.

PAGE 87, HYMN CXXVI.

I subjoin a Latin version of the two stanzas omitted in my translation. They are in a different metre from the rest of the hymn, have no apparent connexion with what precedes, and look like a fragment of a liberal shepherd's love-song. The seventh stanza should, it seems, precede the sixth :

6 [Ille loquitur]. Adhaerens, arcte adhaerens, illa quae mustelae similis se abdidit, multum humorem effundens, dat mihi complexuum centum gaudia.

7 [Illa loquitur]. Prope, prope accede ; molliter me tange. Ne putes pilos corporis mei-paucos esse : tota sum villosa sicut Gandharidum ovis.

Professor Ludwig thinks that *Yāduri* (multum humorem, *i.e.*, semen genitale, effundens) may be the name of a slave-girl. *Gandharidun ovis* : a ewe of the Gandhāris. The country of Gandhāra is placed by Lassen to the west of the Indus and to the south of the Kophen or Kābul river. King Darius in a rock-inscription mentions the *Ga(n) dāra* together with the *Hi(n) du* as people subject to him, and the Gandarii, together with the Parthians, Khorasmians, Sogdians, and Dadikae, are said by Herodotus to have formed part of the army of Xerxes. The name of the country is preserved in the modern Kandahār. See Muir, *O.S. Texts*, ii. 342, and Zimmer, *Altindisches Leben*, p. 30.

PAGE 221, HYMN CLXXIX.

The deified object of this omitted hymn is said to be Rati or Love, and its Ṛṣis or authors are Lopāmudrā, Agastya, and a disciple. Lopāmudrā is represented as inviting the caresses of her aged husband Agastya, and complaining of his coldness and neglect. Agastya responds in stanza 3, and in the second half of stanza 4 the disciple or the poet briefly tells the result of the dialogue. Stanza 5 is supposed to be spoken by the disciple who has overheard the conversation, but its connexion with the rest of the hymn is not very apparent. In stanza 6 'toiling with strong endeavour' is a paraphrase and not a translation of the original *khanamānaḥ*

khanītraiḥ (ligonibus fodiens) which Sāyaṇa explains by 'obtaining the desired result by means of lauds and sacrifices.'

M. Bergaigne is of opinion that the hymn has a mystical meaning, Agastya being identifiable with the celestial Soma whom Lopāmudrā, representing fervent Prayer, succeeds after long labour in drawing down from his secret dwelling place. See *La Religion Vedique*, ii. 394 f.

1 'Through many autumns have I toiled and laboured, at night and morn, through age-inducing dawnings.
  Old age impairs the beauty of our bodies. Let husbands still come near unto their spouses.

2 For even the men aforetime, law-fulfillers, who with the Gods declared eternal statutes,--
  They have decided, but have not accomplished : so now let wives come near unto their husbands.

3 Non inutilis est labor cui Dii favent : nos omnes aemulos et aemulas vincamus.
  Superemus in hac centum artium pugna in qua duas partes convenientes utrinque commovemus.

4 Cupido me cepit illius tauri [viri] qui me despicit, utrum hinc utrum illinc ab aliqua parte nata sit.
  Lopamudra taurum [maritum suum] ad se detrahit : insipiens illa sapientem anhelantem absorbet.

5 This Soma I address that is most near us, that which hath been imbibed within the spirit,
  To pardon any sins we have committed. Verily mortal man is full of longings.

6 Agastya thus, toiling with strong endeavour, wishing for children, progeny and power,
  Cherished—a sage of mighty strength— both classes, and with the Gods obtained his prayer's fulfilment.

By 'both classes' probably priests and princes, or institutors of sacrifices, are meant. M. Bergaigne understands the expression to mean the two forms or essences of Soma, the celestial and the terrestrial.

Page 574 Hymn LXI

5 Membrum suum virile, quod vrotentum fuerat, mas ille retraxit. Rursus illud quod in juvenem filiam sublatum fuerat, non aggressurus, ad se rerahit.

6 Quum jam in medio connessu, semiperfecto opere, amorem in puellam pater impleverat, ambo discedentes seminis paulum in terrae superficiem sacrorum sede effusum emiserunt.

7 Quum pater suam nliam adiverat, cum eā congressus suum semen supra wrram effudit. Tum Dii benigni precem (brahma) prgenuerunt, et Vastoshpatim, legum sacrarum custodem, formaverunt.

8 Ille tauro similis spumam in certamine jactavit ; tunc discedens pusillaximis huc profectus est. Quasi dextro pede claudus processit, "inutiles fuerunt illi mei complexus," ita locutus.

9 'The fire, burning the people, does not approach quickly (by day): the naked (Rakṣasas approach) not Agni by night; the giver of fuel, and the giver of food, he, the upholder (of the rite), is born, overcoming enemies by his might.'

Page 619, Hymn CVI

I borrow Wilson's translation of the omitted stanzas.

5 'You are like two pleasantly moving well-fed (hills) like Mitra and Varuṇa, the two bestowers of felicity, veracious, possessors of infinite wealth, happy, like two horses plump with fodder, abiding in the firmament, like two rams (are you) to be nourished with sacrificial food, to be cherished (with oblations).

6 'You are like two mad elephants bending their forequarters and smiting the foe, like the two sons of Nitoṣa destroying (foes), and cherishing (friends); you are bright as two water-born (jewels), do you, who are victorious, (render) my decaying mortal body free from decay.

7 'Fierce (Aśvins), like two powerful (heroes), you enable this moving, perishable mortal (frame) to cross over to the objects (of its destination) as over water; extremely strong, like the Ṛbhus, your chariot attained its destination swift as the wind, it pervaded (everywhere), it dispensed riches.

8 'With your bellies full of the Soma, like two saucepans, preservers of wealth, destroyers of enemies. (you are) armed with hatchets, moving like two flying (birds) with forms like the moon, attaining success through the mind, like two laudable beings, (you are) approaching (the sacrifice).'

Page 645, Hymn CLXII.

1 May Agni, yielding to our prayer, the Rakṣas-slayer, drive away
The malady of evil name that hath beset thy labouring womb.

2 Agni, concurring in the prayer, drive off the eater of thy flesh,
The malady of evil name that hath attacked thy babe and womb.

3 That which destroys the sinking germ, the settled, moving embryo,
That which will kill the babe at birth,— even this will we drive far away.

4 That which divides thy legs that it may lie between the married pair,
That penetrates and licks thy side,— even this will we exterminate.

The whole passage is difficult and obscure, and stanza 9 is unintelligible. With regard to the myth of Prajāpati and his daughter, Prof. Max Müller says:—'When Kumārila is hard pressed by his opponents about the immoralities of his gods, he answers with all the freedom of a comparative mythologist : "It is fabled that Prajāpati, the Lord of Creation, did violence to his daughter. But what does it mean ? Prajāpati, the Lord of Creation, is a name of the sun, and he is called so, because he protects all creatures. His daughter Uṣas is the dawn. And when it is said that he was in love with her, this only means that, at sunrise, the sun runs after the dawn, the dawn being at the same time called the daughter of the sun, because she rises when he approaches".'—History of Anc. Sans. Literature, pp. 529, 530. See Muir, O.S. Te ts. IV. pp. 46, 47, where stanzas 4—7 are translated.

Vāstoṣpatim : Vāstoṣpati, the guardian of the house ; 'the lord of the hearth (of sacrifice).'— Wilson. The word may be in apposition with brāhma prayer.

9 The fire : according to Sāyaṇa, Rākṣasas who consume like fire.

The subject is Prevention of Abortion. The Ṛṣi is Rakṣohā (Slayer of Rākṣasas) son of Brahmā.

Stanzas 1, 2 are directed against diseases, and 3—6 against evil-spirits which attack women who are about to become mothers.

5. What rests by thee in borrowed form of
    brother, lover, or of lord,
And would destroy thy progeny,—even
    this will we exterminate.
6 That which through sleep or darkness hath
    deceived thee and lies down by thee,
And will destroy thy progeny,—even this
    will we exterminate.

PAGE 645, HYMN CLXIII

1. FROM both thy nostrils, from thine eyes,
    from both thine ears and from thy chin,
Forth from thy head and brain and tongue
    I drive thy malady away.
2 From the neck-tendons and the neck, from
    the breast-bones and from the spine,
From shoulders, upper, lower arms, I
    drive thy malady away.
3 From viscera and all within, forth from
    the rectum, from the heart,
From kidneys, liver, and from spleen, I
    drive thy malady away.
4 From thighs, from knee-caps, and from
    heels, and from the forepart of the
    feet,
From hips, from stomach, and from groin
    I drive thy malady away.

5 From what is voided from within, and
    from thy hair, and from they nails,
From all thyself from top to toe, I drive
    thy malady away.
6 From every member, every hair, disease
    that comes in every joint,
From all thyself, from top to toe, I drive
    thy malady away.

PAGE 650, HYMN CLXXXIV.

1. MAY Viṣṇu form and mould the womb,
    may Tvaṣṭar duly shape the forms,
Prajāpati infuse the stream, and Dhātar
    lay the germ for thee.
2 O Sinīvālī, set the germ, set thou the
    germ, Sarasvatī :
May the Twain Gods bestow the germ,
    the Aśvins crowned with lotuses.
3 That which the Aśvins Twain rub forth
    with the attrition-sticks of gold,—
That germ of thine we invocate, that in
    the tenth month thou mayst bear.

---

2 *Sinīvālī* : a lunar Goddess, who aids the birth of
children. Cp. II. 32. 6.
Verses 1 and 2 are incorporated in Atharva-veda,
V. 25 which is a charm to accompany the Garbh-
ādhāna ceremony to ensure or facilitate and bless
conception.

The deity or subject is the cure of Yakṣman or
phthisis or consumption.

METRE.

Rhyme is not used in the Ṛgveda. The metres are regulated by the number of syllables in the stanza, which consists generally of three or four Pādas, measures, divisions, or quarter verses, with a distinctly marked interval at the end of the second Pāda, and so forming two hemistichs or semi-stanzas of equal or unequal length. These Pādas most usually contain eight or eleven or twelve syllables each; but occasionally they consist of fewer and sometimes of more than these numbers. The Pādas of a stanza are generally of equal length and of more or less corresponding prosodial quantities: but sometimes two or more kinds of metre are employed in one stanza, and then the Pādas vary in quantity and length. As regards quantity, the first syllables of the Pāda are not subject to very strict laws, but the last four are more regular, their measure being generally iambic in Pādas of eight and of twelve syllables and trochaic in those of eleven. In the printed text the first and second Pādas form one line, and the third, or third and fourth, or third, fourth, and fifth, complete the distich or stanza. This arrangement I have followed in my translation.

Subjoined, in alphabetical arrangement, are the names, with brief descriptions, of the metres used in the Hymns of the Ṛgveda. The Index of Hymns will show the metre or metres employed in each Hymn.

Abhisāriṇī : a species of Tṛṣṭup, in which two Pādas contain twelve instead of eleven syllables.

Anuṣṭup or *Anuṣṭubh* : consisting of four Pādas of eight syllables each, two Pādas forming a line. This is the prevailing form of metre in the Mānava-dharma-śāstra, the Mahābhārata, the Rāmāyaṇa, and the Purāṇas.

Anuṣṭubgarbhā : a metre of the Uṣṇih class: the first Pāda containing five syllables, and the three following Pādas of eight syllables each.

Anuṣṭup Pipīlikamadhyā : a species of Anuṣṭup having the second Pāda shorter than the first and third (8 syllables + 4 + 8 + 8).

Aṣṭi : consisting of four Pādas of sixteen syllables each, or sixty-four syllables in the stanza.

Āstārapaṅkti : consisting of two Pādas of eight syllables each, followed by two Pādas of twelve syllables each.

Atidhṛti : four Pādas of nineteen syllables each, = 76 syllables.

Atijagatī : four Pādas of thirteen syllables each.

Atinicṛti : consisting of three Pādas containing respectively seven, six, and seven syllables.

Atiśakvarī : four Pādas of fifteen syllables each.

Atyaṣṭi : four Pādas of seventeen syllables each.

Bṛhatī : four Pādas (8 + 8 + 12 + 8) containing 36 syllables in the stanza.

Caturviṁśatikā Dvipadā : a Dvipadā containing 24 syllables instead of 20.

Dhṛti : consisting of seventy-two syllables in a stanza.

Dvipadā Virāj : a species of Gāyatrī consisting of two Pādas only (12 + 8 or 10 + 10 syllables) ; inadequately represented in the translation by two decasyllabic iambic lines.

Ekapadā Triṣṭup : a Tṛṣṭup consisting of a single Pāda or quarter stanza.

Ekapadā Virāj : a Virāj consisting of a single Pāda.

Gāyatrī : the stanza usually consists of twenty-four syllables, variously arranged, but generally as a triplet of three Pādas of eight syllables each, or in one line of sixteen syllables and a second line of eight. There are eleven varieties of this metre, and the number of syllables in the stanza varies accordingly from nineteen to thirty-three.

Jagatī : a metre consisting of forty-eight syllables arranged in four Pādas of twelve syllables each, two Pādas forming a line or hemistich which in the translation is represented by a double Alexandrine.

Kakup or *Kakubh* : a metre of three Pādas consisting of eight, twelve, and eight syllables respectively.

Kakubh Nyaṅkuśirā ; consisting of three Pādas of 9 + 12 + 4 syllables.

Kṛti : a metre of four Pādas of twenty syllables each.

Madhyejyotis : a metre in which a Pāda of eight syllables stands between two Pādas of twelve.

Mahābṛhatī : four Pādas of eight syllables each, followed by one of twelve.

Mahāpadapaṅkti : a two-lined metre of thirty-one syllables, the first line consisting of four Pādas of five syllables each, and the second being a Triṣṭup of the usual eleven syllables. See Vedic Hymns, part I. (S. Books of the East, XXXII), p. xcviii.

Mahāpaṅkti : a metre of forty-eight syllables 8×6 or 12×4).

Mahāsatobṛhatī : a lengthened form of Satobṛhatī.

Naṣṭarūpī : a variety of Anuṣṭup.

Nyaṅkusāriṇī : a metre of four Pādas of 8 + 12 + 8 + 8 syllables.

Pādanicṛt : a variety of Gāyatrī in which one syllable is wanting in each Pāda : 7 + 3 = 21 syllables.

Pādapaṅkti : a metre consisting of five Pādas of five syllables each.

Paṅkti : a metre of five octosyllabic Pādas, like Anuṣṭup with an additional Pāda.

Paṅktyuttarā : a metre which ends with a Paṅkti of 5 + 5 syllables.

Pipīlikāmadhyā : any metre the middle Pāda of which is shorter than the preceding and the following.

Pragātha : a metre in Book VIII, consisting of strophes combining two verses, viz. a Bṛhatī or Kakup followed by a Satobṛhatī.

Prastārapaṅkti : a metre of forty syllables : 12 + 12 + 8 + 8

Pratiṣṭhā : a metre of four Pādas of four syllables each ; also a variety of the Gāyatrī consisting of three Pādas of eight, seven, and six syllables respectively.

Purastādbṛhatī : a variety of Bṛhatī with twelve syllables in the first Pāda.

Pura-uṣṇih : a metre of three Pādas, containing 12 + 8 + 8 syllables.

Śakvarī : a metre of four Pādas of fourteen syllables each.

Satobṛhatī : a metre whose even Pādas contain eight syllables each, and the uneven twelve : 12 + 8 + 12 + 8 = 40.

Skandhogrīva : consisting of Pādas of 8 + 12 + 8 + 8 syllables.

Tanuśirā : consisting of three Pādas of 11 + 11 + 6 syllables.

Triṣṭup or Triṣṭubh : a metre of four Pādas of eleven syllables each.

Upariṣṭādbṛhatī : consisting of four Pādas of 12 + 8 + 8 + 8 syllables.

Upariṣṭājjyotis : a Triṣṭup stanza the last Pāda of which contains only eight syllables.

Ūrdhvabṛhatī : a variety of Bṛhatī.

Urobṛhatī : a variety of Bṛhatī : 8 + 12 8 + 8 syllables.

Uṣṇiggarbhā : Gāyatrī of three Pādas of six, seven, and eleven syllables respectively.

Uṣṇih: consisting of three Pādas of 8 + 8 + 12 syllables.

Vardhamānā: a species of Gāyatrī; 6 + 7 + 8 = 21 syllables.

Viparītā: a metre of four Pādas resembling Viṣṭārapaṅkti.

Virāḍrūpā: a Triṣṭup metre of four Pādas, 11 + 11 + 11 + 7 or 8 syllables.

Virāj: a metre of four Pādas of ten syllables each.

Virāṭpūrvā: a variety of Triṣṭup.

Virāṭsthānā: a variety of Triṣṭup.

Viṣamapadā: metre of uneven stanzas.

Viṣṭārabṛhatī : a form of Bṛhatī of four Pādas containing 8 + 10 + 10 + 8 = 36 syllables.

Viṣṭārapaṅkti: a form of Paṅkti consisting of four Pādas of 8 + 12 + 12 + 8 = 40 syllables.

Yavamadhyā: a metre having a longer Pāda between two shorter ones.